Pocket
Spanish
Dictionary

Spanish ⟩English English ⟩Spanish

Collins
An Imprint of HarperCollinsPublishers

fifth printing/quinto impresión
second edition/segundo edición 2004

© HarperCollins Publishers 1995, 1999, 2002
© William Collins Sons & Co. Ltd. 1990

latest reprint 2004

HarperCollins Publishers
Westerhill Road, Bishopbriggs, Glasgow G64 2QT
Great Britain

www.collinsdictionaries.com

Collins® and Bank of English® are registered trademarks
of HarperCollins Publishers Limited

Collins is an imprint of HarperCollins Publishers

ISBN 0-00-712291-8

HarperCollins Publishers, Inc.
10 East 53rd Street, New York, NY 10022

ISBN 0-06-008451-0

Library of Congress Cataloging-in-Publication Data
has been applied for

www.harpercollins.com

A catalogue record for this book is available from the British Library

Typeset by Morton Word Processing Ltd, Scarborough

Printed and bound in the United States of America

editors/redactores
Mike Gonzalez • Alicia de Benito de Harland
Soledad Pérez-López • José Ramón Parrondo

contributors/colaboradores
Bob Grossmith • Teresa Álvarez García
Sharon Hunter • Claire Evans

editorial staff/redacción
Joyce Littlejohn • Val McNulty

series editor/colección dirigida por
Lorna Sinclair Knight

INTRODUCTION

We are delighted that you have decided to buy the Collins Pocket Spanish Dictionary, and hope you will enjoy and benefit from using it at home, at school, on holiday or at work.

The innovative use of colour guides you quickly and efficiently to the word you want, and the comprehensive wordlist provides a wealth of modern and idiomatic phrases not normally found in a dictionary this size.

In addition, the supplement provides you with guidance on using the dictionary, along with entertaining ways of improving your dictionary skills.

We hope that you will enjoy using it and that it will significantly enhance your language studies.

Note on trademarks

ABREVIATURAS

ABBREVIATIONS

adjetivo, locución adjetiva	adj	adjective, adjectival phrase
abreviatura	ab(b)r	abbreviation
adverbio, locución adverbial	adv	adverb, adverbial phrase
administración, lengua administrativa	ADMIN	administration
agricultura	AGR	agriculture
América Latina	AM	Latin America
anatomía	ANAT	anatomy
arquitectura	ARQ, ARCH	architecture
artículo	art	article
el automóvil	AUT(O)	the motor car and motoring
aviación, viajes aéreos	AVIAT	flying, air travel
biología	BIO(L)	biology
botánica, flores	BOT	botany
inglés británico	BRIT	British English
química	CHEM	chemistry
comercio, finanzas, banca	COM(M)	commerce, finance, banking
comparativo	compar	comparative
informática	COMPUT	computers
conjunción	conj	conjunction
construcción	CONSTR	building
compuesto	cpd	compound element
cocina	CULIN	cookery
definido	def	definite
demostrativo	demos	demonstrative
economía	ECON	economics
electricidad, electrónica	ELEC	electricity, electronics
enseñanza, sistema escolar y universitario	ESCOL	schooling, schools and universities
España	ESP	Spain
especialmente	esp	especially
exclamación, interjección	excl	exclamation, interjection
femenino	f	feminine
lengua familiar (! vulgar)	fam(!)	informal usage (! particularly offensive)
ferrocarril	FERRO	railways
uso figurado	fig	figurative use
fotografía	FOTO	photography
(verbo inglés) del cual la partícula es inseparable	fus	(phrasal verb) where the particle is inseparable
generalmente	gen	generally
geografía, geología	GEO	geography, geology
geometría	GEOM	geometry
indefinido	indef	indefinite
lengua familiar (! vulgar)	inf(!)	informal usage
infinitivo	infin	infinitive
informática	INFORM	computers
interrogativo	interr	interrogative
invariable	inv	invariable
irregular	irreg	irregular
lo jurídico	JUR	law

ABREVIATURAS

ABBREVIATIONS

América Latina	LAM	Latin America
gramática, lingüística	LING	grammar, linguistics
masculino	m	masculine
matemáticas	MAT(H)	mathematics
medicina	MED	medical term, medicine
masculino/femenino	m/f	masculine/feminine
lo militar, ejército	MIL	military matters
música	MUS	music
sustantivo, nombre	n	noun
navegación, náutica	NAUT	sailing, navigation
sustantivo numérico	num	numeral noun
complemento	obj	(grammatical) object
	o.s.	oneself
peyorativo	pey, pej	derogatory, pejorative
fotografía	PHOT	photography
fisiología	PHYSIOL	physiology
plural	pl	plural
política	POL	politics
participio de pasado	pp	past participle
preposición	prep	preposition
pronombre	pron	pronoun
psicología, psiquiatría	PSICO, PSYCH	psychology, psychiatry
tiempo pasado	pt	past tense
química	QUIM	chemistry
ferrocarril	RAIL	railways
religión, lo eclesiástico	REL	religion, church service
	sb	somebody
enseñanza, sistema escolar y universitario	SCH	schooling, schools and universities
singular	sg	singular
España	SP	Spain
	sth	something
sujeto	su(b)j	(grammatical) subject
subjuntivo	subjun	subjunctive
superlativo	superl	superlative
tauromaquia	TAUR	bullfighting
también	tb	also
técnica, tecnología	TEC(H)	technical term, technology
telecomunicaciones	TELEC, TEL	telecommunications
televisión	TV	television
imprenta, tipografía	TIP, TYP	typography, printing
inglés norteamericano	US	American English
verbo	vb	verb
verbo intransitivo	vi	intransitive verb
verbo pronominal	vr	reflexive verb
verbo transitivo	vt	transitive verb
zoología, animales	ZOOL	zoology
marca registrada	®	registered trademark
indica un equivalente cultural	≈	introduces a cultural equivalent

SPANISH PRONUNCIATION

Consonants

b	[b, ß]	**b**oda **b**om**b**a la**b**or	see notes on **v** below
c	[k]	**c**aja	**c** before **a, o** or **u** is pronounced as in **c**at
ce, ci	[θe, θi]	**ce**ro **ci**elo	**c** before **e** or **i** is pronounced as in **th**in
ch	[tʃ]	**ch**iste	**ch** is pronounced as **ch** in **ch**air
d	[d, ð]	**d**anés ciu**d**a**d**	at the beginning of a phrase or after **l** or **n**, **d** is pronounced as in English. In any other position it is pronounced like **th** in **th**e
g	[g, ɣ]	**g**afas pa**g**a	**g** before **a, o** or **u** is pronounced as in **g**ap, if at the beginning of a phrase or after **n**. In other positions the sound is softened
ge, gi	[xe, xi]	**ge**nte **gi**rar	**g** before **e** or **i** is pronounced similar to **ch** in Scottish lo**ch**
h		**h**aber	**h** is always silent in Spanish
j	[x]	**j**ugar	**j** is pronounced similar to **ch** in Scottish lo**ch**
ll	[ʎ]	ta**ll**e	**ll** is pronounced like the **lli** in mi**lli**on
ñ	[ɲ]	ni**ñ**o	**ñ** is pronounced like the **ni** in o**ni**on
q	[k]	**q**ue	**q** is pronounced as **k** in **k**ing
r, rr	[r, rr]	quita**r** ga**rr**a	**r** is always pronounced in Spanish, unlike the silent **r** in dance**r**. **rr** is trilled, like a Scottish **r**
s	[s]	qui**z**ás i**s**la	**s** is usually pronounced as in pa**ss**, but before **b, d, g, l, m** or **n** it is pronounced as in ro**s**e
v	[b, ß]	**v**ía di**v**idir	**v** is pronounced something like **b**. At the beginning of a phrase or after **m** or **n** it is pronounced as **b** in **b**oy. In any other position the sound is softened
z	[θ]	tena**z**	**z** is pronounced as **th** in **th**in

f, k, l, m, n, p, t and **x** are pronounced as in English.

Vowels

a	[a]	p**a**ta	not as long as **a** in f**a**r. When followed by a consonant in the same syllable (i.e. in a closed syllable), as in am**a**nte, the **a** is short, as in b**a**t
e	[e]	m**e**	like **e** in th**e**y. In a closed syllable, as in g**e**nte, the **e** is short as in p**e**t
i	[i]	p**i**no	as in m**ea**n or mach**i**ne
o	[o]	l**o**	as in l**o**cal. In a closed syllable, as in c**o**ntrol, the **o** is short as in c**o**t
u	[u]	l**u**nes	as in r**u**le. It is silent after **q**, and in **gue, gui**, unless marked **güe, güi** e.g. antig**ü**edad, when it is pronounced like **w** in **w**olf

Semivowels

i, y	[j]	b**i**en h**i**elo **y**unta	pronounced like **y** in **y**es
u	[w]	h**u**evo f**u**ento antig**ü**edad	unstressed **u** between consonant and vowel is pronounced like **w** in **w**ell. See also notes on **u** above

Diphthongs

ai, ay	[ai]	b**ai**le	as **i** in r**i**de
au	[au]	**au**to	as **ou** in sh**ou**t
ei, ey	[ei]	bu**ey**	as **ey** in gr**ey**
eu	[eu]	d**eu**da	both elements pronounced independently [e] + [u]
oi, oy	[oi]	h**oy**	as **oy** in t**oy**

Stress

The rules of stress in Spanish are as follows:

(a) when a word ends in a vowel or in **n** or **s**, the second last syllable is stressed: pa**ta**ta, pa**ta**tas, **co**me, **co**men

(b) when a word ends in a consonant other than **n** or **s**, the stress falls on the last syllable: pa**red**, ha**blar**

(c) when the rules set out in (a) and (b) are not applied, an acute accent appears over the stressed vowel: co**mún**, geogra**fía**, in**glés**

In the phonetic transcription, the symbol ['] precedes the syllable on which the stress falls.

PRONUNCIACIÓN INGLESA

Vocales y diptongos

	Ejemplo inglés	*Ejemplo español/explicación*
ɑː	father	Entre *a* de p**a**dre y *o* de n**o**che
ʌ	b**u**t, c**o**me	*a* muy breve
æ	m**a**n, c**a**t	Con los labios en la posición de *e* en p**e**na se pronuncia el sonido *a* parecido a la *a* de c**a**rro
ə	fath**er**, **a**go	Vocal neutra parecida a una *e* u *o* casi mudas
əː	b**ir**d, h**ear**d	Entre *e* abierta, y *o* cerrada, sonido alargado
ɛ	g**e**t, b**e**d	Como en p**e**rro
ɪ	**i**t, b**i**g	Más breve que en s**i**
iː	t**ea**, s**ee**	Como en f**i**no
ɔ	h**o**t, w**a**sh	Como en t**o**rre
ɔː	s**aw**, **a**ll	Como en p**o**r
u	p**u**t, b**oo**k	Sonido breve, más cerrado que b**u**rro
uː	t**oo**, y**ou**	Sonido largo, como en **u**no
aɪ	fl**y**, h**igh**	Como en fr**ai**le
au	h**ow**, h**ou**se	Como en p**au**sa
ɛə	th**ere**, b**ear**	Casi como en v**ea**, pero el segundo elemento es la vocal neutra [ə]
eɪ	d**ay**, ob**ey**	*e* cerrada seguida por una *i* débil
ɪə	h**ere**, h**ear**	Como en man**ía**, mezclándose el sonido *a* con la vocal neutra [ə]
əu	g**o**, n**o**te	[ə] seguido por una breve *u*
ɔɪ	b**oy**, **oi**l	Como en v**oy**
uə	p**oor**, s**ure**	*u* bastante larga más la vocal neutra [ə]

Consonantes

	Ejemplo inglés	*Ejemplo español/explicación*
b	**b**ig, lo**bb**y	Como en tum**b**a
d	men**ded**	Como en con**d**e, an**d**ar
g	**g**o, **g**et, bi**g**	Como en **g**rande, **g**ol
dʒ	**g**in, **j**u**dge**	Como en la **ll** andaluza y en **G**eneralitat (catalán)
ŋ	si**ng**	Como en ví**n**culo
h	**h**ouse, **h**e	Como la jota hispanoamericana
j	**y**oung, **y**es	Como en **y**a
k	**c**ome, mo**ck**	Como en **c**aña, Es**c**ocia
r	**r**ed, t**r**ead	Se pronuncia con la punta de la lengua hacia atrás y sin hacerla vibrar
s	**s**and, ye**s**	Como en ca**s**a, **s**e**s**ión
z	ro**s**e, **z**ebra	Como en de**s**de, mi**s**mo
ʃ	**sh**e, ma**ch**ine	Como en **ch**ambre (francés), ro**x**o (portugués)
tʃ	**ch**in, ri**ch**	Como en **ch**ocolate
v	**v**alley	Como en f, pero se retiran los dientes superiores vibrándolos contra el labio inferior
w	**w**ater, **wh**ich	Como en la **u** de h**u**evo, p**u**ede
ʒ	vi**s**ion	Como en **j**ournal (francés)
θ	**th**ink, my**th**	Como en re**c**eta, **z**apato
ð	**th**is, **th**e	Como en la **d** de habla**d**o, verda**d**

p, f, m, n, l, t iguales que en español
El signo * indica que la r final escrita apenas se pronuncia en inglés británico cuando la palabra siguiente empieza con vocal. El signo ['] indica la sílaba acentuada.

SPANISH VERB TABLES

1 Gerund *2* Imperative *3* Present *4* Preterite *5* Future *6* Present subjunctive *7* Imperfect subjunctive *8* Past participle *9* Imperfect. *Etc* indicates that the irregular root is used for all persons of the tense, e.g. oír: *6* oiga *etc* = oigas, oigamos, oigáis, oigan. Forms which consist of the unmodified verb root + verb ending are not shown, e.g. acertamos, acertáis.

acertar *2* acierta *3* acierto, aciertas, acierta, aciertan *6* acierte, aciertes, acierte, acierten

acordar *2* acuerda *3* acuerdo, acuerdas, acuerda, acuerdan *6* acuerde, acuerdes, acuerde, acuerden

advertir *1* advirtiendo *2* advierte *3* advierto, adviertes, advierte, advierten *4* advirtió, advirtieron *6* advierta, adviertas, advierta, advirtamos, advirtáis, adviertan *7* advirtiera *etc*

agradecer *3* agradezco *6* agradezca *etc*

aparecer *3* aparezco *6* aparezca *etc*

aprobar *2* aprueba *3* apruebo, apruebas, aprueba, aprueban *6* apruebe, apruebes, apruebe, aprueben

atravesar *2* atraviesa *3* atravieso, atraviesas, atraviesa, atraviesan *6* atraviese, atravieses, atraviese, atraviesen

caber *3* quepo *4* cupe, cupiste, cupo, cupimos, cupisteis, cupieron *5* cabré *etc* *6* quepa *etc* *7* cupiera *etc*

caer *1* cayendo *3* caigo *4* cayó, cayeron *6* caiga *etc* *7* cayera *etc*

calentar *2* calienta *3* caliento, calientas, calienta, calientan *6* caliente, calientes, caliente, calienten

cerrar *2* cierra *3* cierro, cierras, cierra, cierran *6* cierre, cierres, cierre, cierren

COMER *1* comiendo *2* come, comed *3* como, comes, come, comemos, coméis, comen *4* comí, comiste, comió, comimos, comisteis, comieron *5* comeré, comerás, comerá, comeremos, comeréis, comerán *6* coma, comas, coma, comamos, comáis, coman *7* comiera, comieras, comiera, comiéramos, comierais, comieran *8* comido *9* comía, comías, comía, comíamos, comíais, comían

conocer *3* conozco *6* conozca *etc*

contar *2* cuenta *3* cuento, cuentas, cuenta, cuentan *6* cuente, cuentes, cuente, cuenten

costar *2* cuesta *3* cuesto, cuestas, cuesta, cuestan *6* cueste, cuestes, cueste, cuesten

dar *3* doy *4* di, diste, dio, dimos, disteis, dieron *7* diera *etc*

decir *2* di *3* digo *4* dije, dijiste, dijo, dijimos, dijisteis, dijeron *5* diré *etc* *6* diga *etc* *7* dijera

etc *8* dicho

despertar *2* despierta *3* despierto, despiertas, despierta, despiertan *6* despierte, despiertes, despierte, despierten

divertir *1* divirtiendo *2* divierte *3* divierto, diviertes, divierte, divierten *4* divirtió, divirtieron *6* divierta, diviertas, divierta, divirtamos, divirtáis, diviertan *7* divirtiera *etc*

dormir *1* durmiendo *2* duerme *3* duermo, duermes, duerme, duermen *4* durmió, durmieron *6* duerma, duermas, duerma, durmamos, durmáis, duerman *7* durmiera *etc*

empezar *2* empieza *3* empiezo, empiezas, empieza, empiezan *4* empecé *6* empiece, empieces, empiece, empecemos, empecéis, empiecen

entender *2* entiende *3* entiendo, entiendes, entiende, entienden *6* entienda, entiendas, entienda, entiendan

ESTAR *2* está *3* estoy, estás, está, están *4* estuve, estuviste, estuvo, estuvimos, estuvisteis, estuvieron *6* esté, estés, esté, estén *7* estuviera *etc*

HABER *3* he, ha, ha, hemos, han *4* hube, hubiste, hubo, hubimos, hubisteis, hubieron *5* habré *etc* *6* haya *etc* *7* hubiera *etc*

HABLAR *1* hablando *2* habla, hablad *3* hablo, hablas, habla, hablamos, habláis, hablan *4* hablé, hablaste, habló, hablamos, hablasteis, hablaron *5* hablaré, hablarás, hablará, hablaremos, hablaréis, hablarán *6* hable, hables, hable, hablemos, habléis, hablen *7* hablara, hablaras, hablara, habláramos, hablarais, hablaran *8* hablado *9* hablaba, hablabas, hablaba, hablábamos, hablabais, hablaban

hacer *2* haz *3* hago *4* hice, hiciste, hizo, hicimos, hicisteis, hicieron *5* haré *etc* *6* haga *etc* *7* hiciera *etc* *8* hecho

instruir *1* instruyendo *2* instruye *3* instruyo, instruyes, instruye, instruyen *4* instruyó, instruyeron *6* instruya *etc* *7* instruyera *etc*

ir *1* yendo *2* ve *3* voy, vas, va, vamos, vais, van *4* fui, fuiste, fue, fuimos, fuisteis, fueron *6* vaya, vayas, vaya, vayamos, vayáis, vayan

7 fuera *etc* **9** iba, ibas, iba, íbamos, ibais, iban

jugar 2 juega **3** juego, juegas, juega, juegan **4** jugué **6** juegue *etc*

leer 1 leyendo **4** leyó, leyeron **7** leyera *etc*

morir 1 muriendo **2** muere **3** muero, mueres, muere, mueren **4** murió, murieron **6** muera, mueras, muera, muramos, muráis, mueran **7** muriera *etc* **8** muerto

mostrar 2 muestra **3** muestro, muestras, muestra, muestran **6** muestre, muestres, muestre, muestren

mover 2 mueve **3** muevo, mueves, mueve, mueven **6** mueva, muevas, mueva, muevan

negar 2 niega **3** niego, niegas, niega, niegan **4** negué **6** niegue, niegues, niegue, neguemos, neguéis, nieguen

ofrecer 3 ofrezco **6** ofrezca *etc*

oír 1 oyendo **2** oye **3** oigo, oyes, oye, oyen **4** oyó, oyeron **6** oiga *etc* **7** oyera *etc*

oler 2 huele **3** huelo, hueles, huele, huelen **6** huela, huelas, huela, huelan

parecer 3 parezco **6** parezca *etc*

pedir 1 pidiendo **2** pide **3** pido, pides, pide, piden **4** pidió, pidieron **6** pida *etc* **7** pidiera *etc*

pensar 2 piensa **3** pienso, piensas, piensa, piensan **6** piense, pienses, piense, piensen

perder 2 pierde **3** pierdo, pierdes, pierde, pierden **6** pierda, pierdas, pierda, pierdan

poder 1 pudiendo **2** puede **3** puedo, puedes, puede, pueden **4** pude, pudiste, pudo, pudimos, pudisteis, pudieron **5** podré *etc* **6** pueda, puedas, pueda, puedan **7** pudiera *etc*

poner 2 pon **3** pongo **4** puse, pusiste, puso, pusimos, pusisteis, pusieron **5** pondré *etc* **6** ponga *etc* **7** pusiera *etc* **8** puesto

preferir 1 prefiriendo **2** prefiere **3** prefiero, prefieres, prefiere, prefieren **4** prefirió, prefirieron **6** prefiera, prefieras, prefiera, prefiramos, prefiráis, prefieran **7** prefiriera *etc*

querer 2 quiere **3** quiero, quieres, quiere, quieren **4** quise, quisiste, quiso, quisimos, quisisteis, quisieron **5** querré *etc* **6** quiera, quieras, quiera, quieran **7** quisiera *etc*

reir 2 rie **3** río, ríes, ríe, ríen **4** rio, rieron **6** ría, rías, ría, riamos, riáis, rían **7** riera *etc*

repetir 1 repitiendo **2** repite **3** repito, repites, repite, repiten **4** repitió, repitieron **6** repita *etc* **7** repitiera *etc*

rogar 2 ruega **3** ruego, ruegas, ruega, ruegan **4** rogué **6** ruegue, ruegues, ruegue, roguemos, roguéis, rueguen

saber 3 sé **4** supe, supiste, supo, supimos, supisteis, supieron **5** sabré *etc* **6** sepa *etc* **7** supiera *etc*

salir 2 sal **3** salgo **5** saldré *etc* **6** salga *etc*

seguir 1 siguiendo **2** sigue **3** sigo, sigues, sigue, siguen **4** siguió, siguieron **6** siga *etc* **7** siguiera *etc*

sentar 2 sienta **3** siento, sientas, sienta, sientan **6** siente, sientes, siente, sienten

sentir 1 sintiendo **2** siente **3** siento, sientes, siente, sienten **4** sintió, sintieron **6** sienta, sientas, sienta, sintamos, sintáis, sientan **7** sintiera *etc*

SER 2 sé **3** soy, eres, es, somos, sois, son **4** fui, fuiste, fue, fuimos, fuisteis, fueron **6** sea *etc* **7** fuera *etc* **9** era, eras, era, éramos, erais, eran

servir 1 sirviendo **2** sirve **3** sirvo, sirves, sirve, sirven **4** sirvió, sirvieron **6** sirva *etc* **7** sirviera *etc*

soñar 2 sueña **3** sueño, sueñas, sueña, sueñan **6** sueñe, sueñes, sueñe, sueñen

tener 2 ten **3** tengo, tienes, tiene, tienen **4** tuve, tuviste, tuvo, tuvimos, tuvisteis, tuvieron **5** tendré *etc* **6** tenga *etc* **7** tuviera *etc*

traer 1 trayendo **3** traigo **4** traje, trajiste, trajo, trajimos, trajisteis, trajeron **6** traiga *etc* **7** trajera *etc*

valer 2 val **3** valgo **5** valdré *etc* **6** valga *etc*

venir 2 ven **3** vengo, vienes, viene, vienen **4** vine, viniste, vino, vinimos, vinisteis, vinieron **5** vendré *etc* **6** venga *etc* **7** viniera *etc*

ver 3 veo **6** vea **8** veía **9** veía *etc*

vestir 1 vistiendo **2** viste **3** visto, vistes, viste, visten **4** vistió, vistieron **6** vista *etc* **7** vistiera *etc*

VIVIR 1 viviendo **2** vive, vivid **3** vivo, vives, vive, vivimos, vivís, viven **4** viví, viviste, vivió, vivimos, vivisteis, vivieron **5** viviré, vivirás, vivirá, viviremos, viviréis, vivirán **6** viva, vivas, viva, vivamos, viváis, vivan **7** viviera, vivieras, viviera, viviéramos, vivierais, vivieran **8** vivía **9** vivía, vivías, vivía, vivíamos, vivíais, vivían

volver 2 vuelve **3** vuelvo, vuelves, vuelve, vuelven **6** vuelva, vuelvas, vuelva, vuelvan **8** vuelto

VERBOS IRREGULARES EN INGLÉS

present	pt	pp	present	pt	pp
arise	arose	arisen	feed	fed	fed
awake	awoke	awoken	feel	felt	felt
be (am, is, are; being)	was, were	been	fight	fought	fought
			find	found	found
bear	bore	born(e)	flee	fled	fled
beat	beat	beaten	fling	flung	flung
become	became	become	fly (flies)	flew	flown
begin	began	begun	forbid	forbade	forbidden
behold	beheld	beheld	forecast	forecast	forecast
bend	bent	bent	forego	forewent	foregone
beseech	besought	besought	foresee	foresaw	foreseen
beset	beset	beset	foretell	foretold	foretold
bet	bet, betted	bet, betted	forget	forgot	forgotten
bid	bid, bade	bid, bidden	forgive	forgave	forgiven
bind	bound	bound	forsake	forsook	forsaken
bite	bit	bitten	freeze	froze	frozen
bleed	bled	bled	get	got	got, (US) gotten
blow	blew	blown			
break	broke	broken	give	gave	given
breed	bred	bred	go (goes)	went	gone
bring	brought	brought	grind	ground	ground
build	built	built	grow	grew	grown
burn	burnt, burned	burnt, burned	hang	hung, hanged	hung, hanged
burst	burst	burst	have (has; having)	had	had
buy	bought	bought			
can	could	(been able)	hear	heard	heard
cast	cast	cast	hide	hid	hidden
catch	caught	caught	hit	hit	hit
choose	chose	chosen	hold	held	held
cling	clung	clung	hurt	hurt	hurt
come	came	come	keep	kept	kept
cost	cost	cost	kneel	knelt, kneeled	knelt, kneeled
creep	crept	crept			
cut	cut	cut	know	knew	known
deal	dealt	dealt	lay	laid	laid
dig	dug	dug	lead	led	led
do (3rd person: he/she/it does)	did	done	lean	leant, leaned	leant, leaned
			leap	leapt, leaped	leapt, leaped
draw	drew	drawn			
dream	dreamed, dreamt	dreamed, dreamt	learn	learnt, learned	learnt, learned
drink	drank	drunk	leave	left	left
drive	drove	driven	lend	lent	lent
dwell	dwelt	dwelt	let	let	let
eat	ate	eaten	lie (lying)	lay	lain
fall	fell	fallen	light	lit, lighted	lit, lighted

present	pt	pp	present	pt	pp
lose	lost	lost	spell	spelt, spelled	spelt, spelled
make	made	made			
may	might	—	spend	spent	spent
mean	meant	meant	spill	spilt, spilled	spilt, spilled
meet	met	met			
mistake	mistook	mistaken	spin	spun	spun
mow	mowed	mown, mowed	spit	spat	spat
must	(had to)	(had to)	split	split	split
pay	paid	paid	spoil	spoiled, spoilt	spoiled, spoilt
put	put	put			
quit	quit, quitted	quit, quitted	spread	spread	spread
			spring	sprang	sprung
read	read	read	stand	stood	stood
rid	rid	rid	steal	stole	stolen
ride	rode	ridden	stick	stuck	stuck
ring	rang	rung	sting	stung	stung
rise	rose	risen	stink	stank	stunk
run	ran	run	stride	strode	stridden
saw	sawed	sawn	strike	struck	struck, stricken
say	said	said			
see	saw	seen	strive	strove	striven
seek	sought	sought	swear	swore	sworn
sell	sold	sold	sweep	swept	swept
send	sent	sent	swell	swelled	swollen, swelled
set	set	set			
shake	shook	shaken	swim	swam	swum
shall	should	—	swing	swung	swung
shear	sheared	shorn, sheared	take	took	taken
shed	shed	shed	teach	taught	taught
shine	shone	shone	tear	tore	torn
shoot	shot	shot	tell	told	told
show	showed	shown	think	thought	thought
shrink	shrank	shrunk	throw	threw	thrown
shut	shut	shut	thrust	thrust	thrust
sing	sang	sung	tread	trod	trodden
sink	sank	sunk	wake	woke	woken
sit	sat	sat	waylay	waylaid	waylaid
slay	slew	slain	wear	wore	worn
sleep	slept	slept	weave	wove, weaved	woven, weaved
slide	slid	slid			
sling	slung	slung	wed	wedded, wed	wedded, wed
slit	slit	slit			
smell	smelt, smelled	smelt, smelled	weep	wept	wept
			win	won	won
sow	sowed	sown, sowed	wind	wound	wound
speak	spoke	spoken	wring	wrung	wrung
speed	sped, speeded	sped, speeded	write	wrote	written

LOS NÚMEROS

NUMBERS

un, uno(a)	**1**	one
dos	**2**	two
tres	**3**	three
cuatro	**4**	four
cinco	**5**	five
seis	**6**	six
siete	**7**	seven
ocho	**8**	eight
nueve	**9**	nine
diez	**10**	ten
once	**11**	eleven
doce	**12**	twelve
trece	**13**	thirteen
catorce	**14**	fourteen
quince	**15**	fifteen
dieciséis	**16**	sixteen
diecisiete	**17**	seventeen
dieciocho	**18**	eighteen
diecinueve	**19**	nineteen
veinte	**20**	twenty
veintiuno	**21**	twenty-one
veintidós	**22**	twenty-two
treinta	**30**	thirty
treinta y uno(a)	**31**	thirty-one
treinta y dos	**32**	thirty-two
cuarenta	**40**	forty
cuarenta y uno(a)	**41**	forty-one
cincuenta	**50**	fifty
sesenta	**60**	sixty
setenta	**70**	seventy
ochenta	**80**	eighty
noventa	**90**	ninety
cien, ciento	**100**	a hundred, one hundred
ciento uno(a)	**101**	a hundred and one
doscientos(as)	**200**	two hundred
doscientos(as) uno(a)	**201**	two hundred and one
trescientos(as)	**300**	three hundred
trescientos(as) uno(a)	**301**	three hundred and one
cuatrocientos(as)	**400**	four hundred
quinientos(as)	**500**	five hundred
seiscientos(as)	**600**	six hundred
setecientos(as)	**700**	seven hundred
ochocientos(as)	**800**	eight hundred
novecientos(as)	**900**	nine hundred
mil	**1000**	a thousand
mil dos	**1002**	a thousand and two
cinco mil	**5000**	five thousand
un millón	**1000000**	a million

LOS NÚMEROS

NUMBERS

primer, primero(a), 1º, 1er (1ª, 1era) — first, 1st
segundo(a), 2º (2ª) — second, 2nd
tercer, tercero(a), 3º (3ª) — third, 3rd
cuarto(a), 4º (4ª) — fourth, 4th
quinto(a), 5º (5ª) — fifth, 5th
sexto(a), 6º (6ª) — sixth, 6th
séptimo(a) — seventh
octavo(a) — eighth
noveno(a) — ninth
décimo(a) — tenth
undécimo(a) — eleventh
duodécimo(a) — twelfth
decimotercio(a) — thirteenth
decimocuarto(a) — fourteenth
decimoquinto(a) — fifteenth
decimosexto(a) — sixteenth
decimoséptimo(a) — seventeenth
decimoctavo(a) — eighteenth
decimonoveno(a) — nineteenth
vigésimo(a) — twentieth
vigésimo(a) primero(a) — twenty-first
vigésimo(a) segundo(a) — twenty-second
trigésimo(a) — thirtieth
centésimo(a) — hundredth
centésimo(a) primero(a) — hundred-and-first
milésimo(a) — thousandth

Números Quebrados etc

Fractions etc

un medio — a half
un tercio — a third
dos tercios — two thirds
un cuarto — a quarter
un quinto — a fifth
cero coma cinco, 0,5 — (nought) point five, 0.5
tres coma cuatro, 3,4 — three point four, 3.4
diez por cien(to) — ten per cent
cien por cien — a hundred per cent

Ejemplos

Examples

va a llegar el 7 (de mayo) — he's arriving on the 7th (of May)
vive en el número 7 — he lives at number 7
el capítulo/la página 7 — chapter/page 7
llegó séptimo — he came in 7th

N.B. In Spanish the ordinal numbers from 1 to 10 are commonly used; from 11 to 20 rather less; above 21 they are rarely written and almost never heard in speech. The custom is to replace the forms for 21 and above by the cardinal number.

LA HORA

THE TIME

¿qué hora es?

what time is it?

es/son

it's o it is

medianoche, las doce (de la noche)	midnight, twelve p.m.
la una (de la madrugada)	one o'clock (in the morning), one (a.m.)
la una y cinco	five past one
la una y diez	ten past one
la una y cuarto *or* quince	a quarter past one, one fifteen
la una y veinticinco	twenty-five past one, one twenty-five
la una y media *or* treinta	half-past one, one thirty
las dos menos veinticinco, la una treinta y cinco	twenty-five to two, one thirty-five
las dos menos veinte, la una cuarenta	twenty to two, one forty
las dos menos cuarto, la una cuarenta y cinco	a quarter to two, one forty-five
las dos menos diez, la una cincuenta	ten to two, one fifty
mediodía, las doce (de la tarde)	twelve o'clock, midday, noon
la una (de la tarde)	one o'clock (in the afternoon), one (p.m.)
las siete (de la tarde)	seven o'clock (in the evening), seven (p.m.)

¿a qué hora?

(at) what time?

a medianoche	at midnight
a las siete	at seven o'clock
en veinte minutos	in twenty minutes
hace quince minutos	fifteen minutes ago

ESPAÑOL – INGLÉS
SPANISH – ENGLISH

A, a

a [a] (*a+el = al*) *prep* **1** (*dirección*) to;
fueron ~ Madrid/Grecia they went to
Madrid/Greece; **me voy ~ casa** I'm going
home
2 (*distancia*): **está ~ 15 km de aquí** it's
15 kms from here
3 (*posición*): **estar ~ la mesa** to be at
table; **al lado de** next to, beside; *ver tb*
puerta
4 (*tiempo*): **~ las 10/~ medianoche** at
10/midnight; **~ la mañana siguiente** the
following morning; **~ los pocos días**
after a few days; **estamos ~ 9 de julio**
it's the ninth of July; **~ los 24 años** at the
age of 24; **al año/~ la semana** (*AM*) a
year/week later
5 (*manera*): **~ la francesa** the French
way; **~ caballo** on horseback; **~ oscuras**
in the dark
6 (*medio, instrumento*): **~ lápiz** in pencil;
~ mano by hand; **cocina ~ gas** gas stove
7 (*razón*): **~ 30 ptas el kilo** at 30 pesetas
a kilo; **~ más de 50 km/h** at more than
50 kms per hour
8 (*dativo*): **se lo di ~ él** I gave it to him;
vi al policía I saw the policeman; **se lo
compré ~ él** I bought it from him
9 (*tras ciertos verbos*): **voy ~ verle** I'm
going to see him; **empezó ~ trabajar** he
started working *o* to work
10 (*+infin*): **al verle, le reconocí
inmediatamente** when I saw him I
recognized him at once; **el camino ~
recorrer** the distance we (*etc*) have to
travel; **¡~ callar!** keep quiet!; **¡~ comer!**
let's eat!

abad, esa [a'βað, 'ðesa] *nm/f* abbot/

abbess; **~ía** *nf* abbey
abajo [a'βaxo] *adv* (*situación*) (down)
below, underneath; (*en edificio*)
downstairs; (*dirección*) down, downwards;
el piso de ~ the downstairs flat; **la parte
de ~** the lower part; **¡~ el gobierno!**
down with the government!; **cuesta/río
~** downhill/downstream; **de arriba ~** from
top to bottom; **el ~ firmante** the
undersigned; **más ~** lower *o* further down
abalanzarse [aβalan'θarse] *vr*: **~ sobre *o*
contra** to throw o.s. at
abandonado, a [aβando'naðo, a] *adj*
derelict; (*desatendido*) abandoned;
(*desierto*) deserted; (*descuidado*) neglected
abandonar [aβando'nar] *vt* to leave;
(*persona*) to abandon, desert; (*cosa*) to
abandon, leave behind; (*descuidar*) to
neglect; (*renunciar a*) to give up; (*INFORM*)
to quit; **~se** *vr*: **~se a** to abandon o.s. to;
abandono *nm* (*acto*) desertion,
abandonment; (*estado*) abandon, neglect;
(*renuncia*) withdrawal, retirement; **ganar
por abandono** to win by default
abanicar [aβani'kar] *vt* to fan; **abanico**
nm fan; (*NAUT*) derrick
abaratar [aβara'tar] *vt* to lower the price
of; **~se** *vr* to go *o* come down in price
abarcar [aβar'kar] *vt* to include, embrace;
(*AM*) to monopolize
abarrotado, a [aβarro'taðo, a] *adj* packed
abarrotar [aβarro'tar] *vt* (*local, estadio,
teatro*) to fill, pack
abarrotero, a [aβarro'tero, a] (*AM*) *nm/f*
grocer; **abarrotes** *nmpl* (*AM*) groceries,
provisions
abastecer [aβaste'θer] *vt*: **~ (de)** to supply
(with); **abastecimiento** *nm* supply
abasto [a'βasto] *nm* supply; **no dar ~ a** to
be unable to cope with

abatido, a [aβa'tiðo, a] *adj* dejected, downcast

abatimiento [aβati'mjento] *nm* (*depresión*) dejection, depression

abatir [aβa'tir] *vt* (*muro*) to demolish; (*pájaro*) to shoot *o* bring down; (*fig*) to depress; **~se** *vr* to get depressed; **~se sobre** to swoop *o* pounce on

abdicación [aβðika'θjon] *nf* abdication

abdicar [aβði'kar] *vi* to abdicate

abdomen [aβ'ðomen] *nm* abdomen; **abdominales** *nmpl* (*tb: ejercicios abdominales*) sit-ups

abecedario [aβeθe'ðarjo] *nm* alphabet

abedul [aβe'ðul] *nm* birch

abeja [a'βexa] *nf* bee

abejorro [aβe'xorro] *nm* bumblebee

abertura [aβer'tura] *nf* = **apertura**

abeto [a'βeto] *nm* fir

abierto, a [a'βjerto, a] *pp de* **abrir** ♦ *adj* open; (*AM*) generous

abigarrado, a [aβixa'rraðo, a] *adj* multi-coloured

abismal [aβis'mal] *adj* (*fig*) vast, enormous

abismar [aβis'mar] *vt* to humble, cast down; **~se** *vr* to sink; **~se en** (*fig*) to be plunged into

abismo [a'βismo] *nm* abyss

abjurar [aβxu'rar] *vi*: **~ de** to abjure, forswear

ablandar [aβlan'dar] *vt* to soften; **~se** *vr* to get softer

abnegación [aβneɣa'θjon] *nf* self-denial

abnegado, a [aβne'ɣaðo, a] *adj* self-sacrificing

abocado, a [aβo'kaðo, a] *adj*: **verse ~ al desastre** to be heading for disaster

abochornar [aβotʃor'nar] *vt* to embarrass

abofetear [aβofete'ar] *vt* to slap (in the face)

abogado, a [aβo'ɣaðo, a] *nm/f* lawyer; (*notario*) solicitor; (*en tribunal*) barrister (*BRIT*), attorney (*US*); **~ defensor** defence lawyer *o* attorney (*US*)

abogar [aβo'ɣar] *vi*: **~ por** to plead for; (*fig*) to advocate

abolengo [aβo'lengo] *nm* ancestry, lineage

abolición [aβoli'θjon] *nf* abolition

abolir [aβo'lir] *vt* to abolish; (*cancelar*) to cancel

abolladura [aβoʎa'ðura] *nf* dent

abollar [aβo'ʎar] *vt* to dent

abominable [aβomi'naβle] *adj* abominable

abonado, a [aβo'naðo, a] *adj* (*deuda*) paid(-up) ♦ *nm/f* subscriber

abonar [aβo'nar] *vt* (*deuda*) to settle; (*terreno*) to fertilize; (*idea*) to endorse; **~se** *vr* to subscribe; **abono** *nm* payment; fertilizer; subscription

abordar [aβor'ðar] *vt* (*barco*) to board; (*asunto*) to broach

aborigen [aβo'rixen] *nm/f* aborigine

aborrecer [aβorre'θer] *vt* to hate, loathe

abortar [aβor'tar] *vi* (*malparir*) to have a miscarriage; (*deliberadamente*) to have an abortion; **aborto** *nm* miscarriage; abortion

abotonar [aβoto'nar] *vt* to button (up), do up

abovedado, a [aβoβe'ðaðo, a] *adj* vaulted, domed

abrasar [aβra'sar] *vt* to burn (up); (*AGR*) to dry up, parch

abrazar [aβra'θar] *vt* to embrace, hug

abrazo [a'βraθo] *nm* embrace, hug; **un ~** (*en carta*) with best wishes

abrebotellas [aβreβo'teʎas] *nm inv* bottle opener

abrecartas [aβre'kartas] *nm inv* letter opener

abrelatas [aβre'latas] *nm inv* tin (*BRIT*) *o* can opener

abreviar [aβre'βjar] *vt* to abbreviate; (*texto*) to abridge; (*plazo*) to reduce; **abreviatura** *nf* abbreviation

abridor [aβri'ðor] *nm* bottle opener; (*de latas*) tin (*BRIT*) *o* can opener

abrigar [aβri'ɣar] *vt* (*proteger*) to shelter; (*suj: ropa*) to keep warm; (*fig*) to cherish

abrigo [a'βriɣo] *nm* (*prenda*) coat, overcoat; (*lugar protegido*) shelter

abril [a'βril] *nm* April

abrillantar [aßriʎan'tar] vt to polish

abrir [a'ßrir] vt to open (up) ♦ vi to open; ~se vr to open (up); (extenderse) to open out; (cielo) to clear; ~se paso to find o force a way through

abrochar [aßro'tʃar] vt (con botones) to button (up); (zapato, con broche) to do up

abrumar [aßru'mar] vt to overwhelm; (sobrecargar) to weigh down

abrupto, a [a'ßrupto, a] adj abrupt; (empinado) steep

absceso [aßs'θeso] nm abscess

absentismo [aßsen'tismo] nm absenteeism

absolución [aßsolu'θjon] nf (REL) absolution; (JUR) acquittal

absoluto, a [aßso'luto, a] adj absolute; en ~ adv not at all

absolver [aßsol'ßer] vt to absolve; (JUR) to pardon; (: acusado) to acquit

absorbente [aßsor'ßente] adj absorbent; (interesante) absorbing

absorber [aßsor'ßer] vt to absorb; (embeber) to soak up

absorción [aßsor'θjon] nf absorption; (COM) takeover

absorto, a [aß'sorto, a] pp de absorber ♦ adj absorbed, engrossed

abstemio, a [aßs'temjo, a] adj teetotal

abstención [aßsten'θjon] nf abstention

abstenerse [aßste'nerse] vr: ~ (de) to abstain o refrain (from)

abstinencia [aßsti'nenθja] nf abstinence; (ayuno) fasting

abstracción [aßstrak'θjon] nf abstraction

abstracto, a [aß'strakto, a] adj abstract

abstraer [aßstra'er] vt to abstract; ~se vr to be o become absorbed

abstraído, a [aßstra'iðo, a] adj absent-minded

absuelto [aß'swelto] pp de absolver

absurdo, a [aß'surðo, a] adj absurd

abuchear [aßutʃe'ar] vt to boo

abuelo, a [a'ßwelo, a] nm/f grandfather/mother; ~s nmpl grandparents

abulia [a'ßulja] nf apathy

abultado, a [aßul'taðo, a] adj bulky

abultar [aßul'tar] vi to be bulky

abundancia [aßun'danθja] nf: una ~ de plenty of; abundante adj abundant, plentiful

abundar [aßun'dar] vi to abound, be plentiful

aburguesarse [aßurɣe'sarse] vr to become middle-class

aburrido, a [aßu'rriðo, a] adj (hastiado) bored; (que aburre) boring; aburrimiento nm boredom, tedium

aburrir [aßu'rrir] vt to bore; ~se vr to be bored, get bored

abusar [aßu'sar] vi to go too far; ~ de to abuse

abusivo, a [aßu'sißo, a] adj (precio) exorbitant

abuso [a'ßuso] nm abuse

abyecto, a [aß'jekto, a] adj wretched, abject

acá [a'ka] adv (lugar) here; ¿de cuándo ~? since when?

acabado, a [aka'ßaðo, a] adj finished, complete; (perfecto) perfect; (agotado) worn out; (fig) masterly ♦ nm finish

acabar [aka'ßar] vt (llevar a su fin) to finish, complete; (consumir) to use up; (rematar) to finish off ♦ vi to finish, end; ~se vr to finish, stop; (terminarse) to be over; (agotarse) to run out; ~ con to put an end to; ~ de llegar to have just arrived; ~ por hacer to end (up) by doing; ¡se acabó! it's all over!; (¡basta!) that's enough!

acabóse [aka'ßose] nm: esto es el ~ this is the last straw

academia [aka'ðemja] nf academy; académico, a adj academic

acaecer [akae'θer] vi to happen, occur

acallar [aka'ʎar] vt (persona) to silence; (protestas, rumores) to suppress

acalorado, a [akalo'raðo, a] adj (discusión) heated

acalorarse [akalo'rarse] vr (fig) to get heated

acampar [akam'par] vi to camp

acantilado [akanti'laðo] nm cliff

acaparar [akapa'rar] vt to monopolize; (acumular) to hoard

acariciar [akari'θjar] vt to caress; (esperanza) to cherish

acarrear [akarre'ar] vt to transport; (fig) to cause, result in

acaso [a'kaso] adv perhaps, maybe; **(por) si ~** (just) in case

acatamiento [akata'mjento] nm respect; (ley) observance

acatar [aka'tar] vt to respect; (ley) obey

acatarrarse [akata'rrarse] vr to catch a cold

acaudalado, a [akauða'laðo, a] adj well-off

acaudillar [akauði'ʎar] vt to lead, command

acceder [akθe'ðer] vi: ~ **a** (petición etc) to agree to; (tener acceso a) to have access to; (INFORM) to access

accesible [akθe'siβle] adj accessible

acceso [ak'θeso] nm access, entry; (camino) access, approach; (MED) attack, fit

accesorio, a [akθe'sorjo, a] adj, nm accessory

accidentado, a [akθiðen'taðo, a] adj uneven; (montañoso) hilly; (azaroso) eventful ♦ nm/f accident victim

accidental [akθiðen'tal] adj accidental; **accidentarse** vr to have an accident

accidente [akθi'ðente] nm accident; **~s** nmpl (de terreno) unevenness sg

acción [ak'θjon] nf action; (acto) action, act; (COM) share; (JUR) action, lawsuit; **accionar** vt to work, operate; (INFORM) to drive

accionista [akθjo'nista] nm/f shareholder, stockholder

acebo [a'θeβo] nm holly; (árbol) holly tree

acechar [aθe'tʃar] vt to spy on; (aguardar) to lie in wait for; **acecho** nm: **estar al acecho (de)** to lie in wait (for)

aceitar [aθei'tar] vt to oil, lubricate

aceite [a'θeite] nm oil; (de oliva) olive oil; **~ra** nf oilcan; **aceitoso, a** adj oily

aceituna [aθei'tuna] nf olive

acelerador [aθelera'ðor] nm accelerator

acelerar [aθele'rar] vt to accelerate

acelga [a'θelɣa] nf chard, beet

acento [a'θento] nm accent; (acentuación) stress

acentuar [aθen'twar] vt to accent; to stress; (fig) to accentuate

acepción [aθep'θjon] nf meaning

aceptable [aθep'taβle] adj acceptable

aceptación [aθepta'θjon] nf acceptance; (aprobación) approval

aceptar [aθep'tar] vt to accept; (aprobar) to approve

acequia [a'θekja] nf irrigation ditch

acera [a'θera] nf pavement (BRIT), sidewalk (US)

acerca [a'θerka]: ~ **de** prep about, concerning

acercar [aθer'kar] vt to bring o move nearer; **~se** vr to approach, come near

acerico [aθe'riko] nm pincushion

acero [a'θero] nm steel

acérrimo, a [a'θerrimo, a] adj (partidario) staunch; (enemigo) bitter

acertado, a [aθer'taðo, a] adj correct; (apropiado) apt; (sensato) sensible

acertar [aθer'tar] vt (blanco) to hit; (solución) to get right; (adivinar) to guess ♦ vi to get it right, be right; ~ **a** to manage to; ~ **con** to happen o hit on

acertijo [aθer'tixo] nm riddle, puzzle

achacar [atʃa'kar] vt to attribute

achacoso, a [atʃa'koso, a] adj sickly

achantar [atʃan'tar] (fam) vt to scare, frighten; **~se** vr to back down

achaque etc [a'tʃake] vb ver **achacar** ♦ nm ailment

achicar [atʃi'kar] vt to reduce; (NAUT) to bale out

achicharrar [atʃitʃa'rrar] vt to scorch, burn

achicoria [atʃi'korja] nf chicory

aciago, a [a'θjaɣo, a] adj ill-fated, fateful

acicalar [aθika'lar] vt to polish; (persona) to dress up; **~se** vr to get dressed up

acicate [aθi'kate] nm spur

acidez [aθi'ðeθ] *nf* acidity
ácido, a ['aθiðo, a] *adj* sour, acid ♦ *nm* acid
acierto *etc* [a'θjerto] *vb ver* **acertar** ♦ *nm* success; (*buen paso*) wise move; (*solución*) solution; (*habilidad*) skill, ability
aclamación [aklama'θjon] *nf* acclamation; (*aplausos*) applause
aclamar [akla'mar] *vt* to acclaim; (*aplaudir*) to applaud
aclaración [aklara'θjon] *nf* clarification, explanation
aclarar [akla'rar] *vt* to clarify, explain; (*ropa*) to rinse ♦ *vi* to clear up; **~se** *vr* (*explicarse*) to understand; **~se la garganta** to clear one's throat
aclaratorio, a [aklara'torjo, a] *adj* explanatory
aclimatación [aklimata'θjon] *nf* acclimatization
aclimatar [aklima'tar] *vt* to acclimatize; **~se** *vr* to become acclimatized
acné [ak'ne] *nm* acne
acobardar [akoβar'ðar] *vt* to intimidate
acodarse [ako'ðarse] *vr:* **~ en** to lean on
acogedor, a [akoxe'ðor, a] *adj* welcoming; (*hospitalario*) hospitable
acoger [ako'xer] *vt* to welcome; (*abrigar*) to shelter; **~se** *vr* to take refuge
acogida [ako'xiða] *nf* reception; refuge
acometer [akome'ter] *vt* to attack; (*emprender*) to undertake; **acometida** *nf* attack, assault
acomodado, a [akomo'ðaðo, a] *adj* (*persona*) well-to-do
acomodador, a [akomoða'ðor, a] *nm/f* usher(ette)
acomodar [akomo'ðar] *vt* to adjust; (*alojar*) to accommodate; **~se** *vr* to conform; (*instalarse*) to install o.s.; (*adaptarse*): **~se (a)** to adapt (to)
acompañar [akompa'ɲar] *vt* to accompany; (*documentos*) to enclose
acondicionar [akondiθjo'nar] *vt* to arrange, prepare; (*pelo*) to condition
acongojar [akongo'xar] *vt* to distress, grieve

aconsejar [akonse'xar] *vt* to advise, counsel; **~se** *vr:* **~se con** to consult
acontecer [akonte'θer] *vi* to happen, occur; **acontecimiento** *nm* event
acopio [a'kopjo] *nm* store, stock
acoplamiento [akopla'mjento] *nm* coupling, joint; **acoplar** *vt* to fit; (*ELEC*) to connect; (*vagones*) to couple
acorazado, a [akora'θaðo, a] *adj* armour-plated, armoured ♦ *nm* battleship
acordar [akor'ðar] *vt* (*resolver*) to agree, resolve; (*recordar*) to remind; **~se** *vr* to agree; **~se (de algo)** to remember (sth); **acorde** *adj* (*MUS*) harmonious ♦ *nm* chord; **acorde con** (*medidas etc*) in keeping with
acordeón [akorðe'on] *nm* accordion
acordonado, a [akorðo'naðo, a] *adj* (*calle*) cordoned-off
acorralar [akorra'lar] *vt* to round up, corral
acortar [akor'tar] *vt* to shorten; (*duración*) to cut short; (*cantidad*) to reduce; **~se** *vr* to become shorter
acosar [ako'sar] *vt* to pursue relentlessly; (*fig*) to hound, pester; **acoso** *nm* harassment; **acoso sexual** sexual harassment
acostar [akos'tar] *vt* (*en cama*) to put to bed; (*en suelo*) to lay down; **~se** *vr* to go to bed; to lie down; **~se con uno** to sleep with sb
acostumbrado, a [akostum'braðo, a] *adj* usual; **~ a** used to
acostumbrar [akostum'brar] *vt:* **~ a uno a algo** to get sb used to sth ♦ *vi:* **~ (a) hacer** to be in the habit of doing; **~se** *vr:* **~se a** to get used to
acotación [akota'θjon] *nf* marginal note; (*GEO*) elevation mark; (*de límite*) boundary mark; (*TEATRO*) stage direction
ácrata ['akrata] *adj, nm/f* anarchist
acre ['akre] *adj* (*olor*) acrid; (*fig*) biting ♦ *nm* acre
acrecentar [akreθen'tar] *vt* to increase, augment
acreditar [akreði'tar] *vt* (*garantizar*) to

vouch for, guarantee; (*autorizar*) to authorize; (*dar prueba de*) to prove; (COM: *abonar*) to credit; (*embajador*) to accredit; **~se** *vr* to become famous

acreedor, a [akree'ðor, a] *adj*: **~ de** worthy of ♦ *nm/f* creditor

acribillar [akriβi'ʎar] *vt*: **~ a balazos** to riddle with bullets

acróbata [a'kroβata] *nm/f* acrobat

acta ['akta] *nf* certificate; (*de comisión*) minutes *pl*, record; **~ de nacimiento/de matrimonio** birth/marriage certificate; **~ notarial** affidavit

actitud [akti'tuð] *nf* attitude; (*postura*) posture

activar [akti'ßar] *vt* to activate; (*acelerar*) to speed up

actividad [aktißi'ðað] *nf* activity

activo, a [ak'tißo, a] *adj* active; (*vivo*) lively ♦ *nm* (COM) assets *pl*

acto ['akto] *nm* act, action; (*ceremonia*) ceremony; (TEATRO) act; **en el ~** immediately

actor [ak'tor] *nm* actor; (JUR) plaintiff ♦ *adj*: **parte ~a** prosecution

actriz [ak'triθ] *nf* actress

actuación [aktwa'θjon] *nf* action; (*comportamiento*) conduct, behaviour; (JUR) proceedings *pl*; (*desempeño*) performance

actual [ak'twal] *adj* present(-day), current; **~idad** *nf* present; **~idades** *nfpl* (*noticias*) news *sg*; **en la ~idad** at present; (*hoy día*) nowadays

actualizar [aktwali'θar] *vt* to update, modernize

actualmente [aktwal'mente] *adv* at present; (*hoy día*) nowadays

actuar [ak'twar] *vi* (*obrar*) to work, operate; (*actor*) to act, perform ♦ *vt* to work, operate; **~ de** to act as

acuarela [akwa'rela] *nf* watercolour

acuario [a'kwarjo] *nm* aquarium; (ASTROLOGÍA): **A~** Aquarius

acuartelar [akwarte'lar] *vt* (MIL) to confine to barracks

acuático, a [a'kwatiko, a] *adj* aquatic

acuchillar [akutʃi'ʎar] *vt* (TEC) to plane (down), smooth

acuciante [aku'θjante] *adj* urgent

acuciar [aku'θjar] *vt* to urge on

acudir [aku'ðir] *vi* (*asistir*) to attend; (*ir*) to go; **~ a** (*fig*) to turn to; **~ en ayuda de** to go to the aid of

acuerdo *etc* [a'kwerðo] *vb ver* **acordar** ♦ *nm* agreement; **¡de ~!** agreed!; **de ~ con** (*persona*) in agreement with; (*acción, documento*) in accordance with; **estar de ~** to be agreed, agree

acumular [akumu'lar] *vt* to accumulate, collect

acuñar [aku'ɲar] *vt* (*moneda*) to mint; (*frase*) to coin

acupuntura [akupun'tura] *nf* acupuncture

acurrucarse [akurru'karse] *vr* to crouch; (*ovillarse*) to curl up

acusación [akusa'θjon] *nf* accusation

acusar [aku'sar] *vt* to accuse; (*revelar*) to reveal; (*denunciar*) to denounce

acuse [a'kuse] *nm*: **~ de recibo** acknowledgement of receipt

acústica [a'kustika] *nf* acoustics *pl*

acústico, a [a'kustiko, a] *adj* acoustic

adaptación [aðapta'θjon] *nf* adaptation

adaptador [aðapta'ðor] *nm* (ELEC) adapter

adaptar [aðap'tar] *vt* to adapt; (*acomodar*) to fit

adecuado, a [aðe'kwaðo, a] *adj* (*apto*) suitable; (*oportuno*) appropriate

adecuar [aðe'kwar] *vt* to adapt; to make suitable

a. de J.C. *abr* (= *antes de Jesucristo*) B.C.

adelantado, a [aðelan'taðo, a] *adj* advanced; (*reloj*) fast; **pagar por ~** to pay in advance

adelantamiento [aðelanta'mjento] *nm* (AUTO) overtaking

adelantar [aðelan'tar] *vt* to move forward; (*avanzar*) to advance; (*acelerar*) to speed up; (AUTO) to overtake ♦ *vi* to go forward, advance; **~se** *vr* to go forward, advance

adelante [aðe'lante] *adv* forward(s), ahead ♦ *excl* come in!; **de hoy en ~** from now on; **más ~** later on; (*más allá*) further on

adelanto [aðe'lanto] *nm* advance; (*mejora*) improvement; (*progreso*) progress

adelgazar [aðelɣa'θar] *vt* to thin (down) ♦ *vi* to get thin; (*con régimen*) to slim down, lose weight

ademán [aðe'man] *nm* gesture; **ademanes** *nmpl* manners; **en ~ de** as if to

además [aðe'mas] *adv* besides; (*por otra parte*) moreover; (*también*) also; **~ de** besides, in addition to

adentrarse [aðen'trarse] *vr*: **~ en** to go into, get inside; (*penetrar*) to penetrate (into)

adentro [a'ðentro] *adv* inside, in; **mar ~** out at sea; **tierra ~** inland

adepto, a [a'ðepto, a] *nm/f* supporter

aderezar [aðere'θar] *vt* (*ensalada*) to dress; (*comida*) to season; **aderezo** *nm* dressing; seasoning

adeudar [aðeu'ðar] *vt* to owe; **~se** *vr* to run into debt

adherirse [aðe'rirse] *vr*: **~ a** to adhere to; (*partido*) to join

adhesión [aðe'sjon] *nf* adhesion; (*fig*) adherence

adicción [aðik'θjon] *nf* addiction

adición [aði'θjon] *nf* addition

adicto, a [a'ðikto, a] *adj*: **~ a** addicted to; (*dedicado*) devoted to ♦ *nm/f* supporter, follower; (*toxicómano etc*) addict

adiestrar [aðjes'trar] *vt* to train, teach; (*conducir*) to guide, lead; **~se** *vr* to practise; (*enseñarse*) to train o.s.

adinerado, a [aðine'raðo, a] *adj* wealthy

adiós [a'ðjos] *excl* (*para despedirse*) goodbye!, cheerio!; (*al pasar*) hello!

aditivo [aði'tiβo] *nm* additive

adivinanza [aðiβi'nanθa] *nf* riddle

adivinar [aðiβi'nar] *vt* to prophesy; (*conjeturar*) to guess; **adivino, a** *nm/f* fortune-teller

adj *abr* (= *adjunto*) encl.

adjetivo [aðxe'tiβo] *nm* adjective

adjudicación [aðxuðika'θjon] *nf* award; adjudication

adjudicar [aðxuði'kar] *vt* to award; **~se** *vr*: **~se algo** to appropriate sth

adjuntar [aðxun'tar] *vt* to attach, enclose; **adjunto, a** *adj* attached, enclosed ♦ *nm/f* assistant

administración [aðministra'θjon] *nf* administration; (*dirección*) management; **administrador, a** *nm/f* administrator; manager(ess)

administrar [aðminis'trar] *vt* to administer; **administrativo, a** *adj* administrative

admirable [aðmi'raβle] *adj* admirable

admiración [aðmira'θjon] *nf* admiration; (*asombro*) wonder; (*LING*) exclamation mark

admirar [aðmi'rar] *vt* to admire; (*extrañar*) to surprise; **~se** *vr* to be surprised

admisible [aðmi'siβle] *adj* admissible

admisión [aðmi'sjon] *nf* admission; (*reconocimiento*) acceptance

admitir [aðmi'tir] *vt* to admit; (*aceptar*) to accept

admonición [aðmoni'θjon] *nf* warning

adobar [aðo'βar] *vt* (*CULIN*) to season

adobe [a'ðoβe] *nm* adobe, sun-dried brick

adoctrinar [aðoktri'nar] *vt*: **~ en** to indoctrinate with

adolecer [aðole'θer] *vi*: **~ de** to suffer from

adolescente [aðoles'θente] *nm/f* adolescent, teenager

adonde [a'ðonde] *conj* (to) where

adónde [a'ðonde] *adv* = **dónde**

adopción [aðop'θjon] *nf* adoption

adoptar [aðop'tar] *vt* to adopt

adoptivo, a [aðop'tiβo, a] *adj* (*padres*) adoptive; (*hijo*) adopted

adoquín [aðo'kin] *nm* paving stone

adorar [aðo'rar] *vt* to adore

adormecer [aðorme'θer] *vt* to put to sleep; **~se** *vr* to become sleepy; (*dormirse*) to fall asleep

adornar [aðor'nar] *vt* to adorn

adorno [a'ðorno] *nm* ornament; (*decoración*) decoration

adosado, a [aðo'saðo, a] *adj*: **casa**

adosada semi-detached house

adquiero *etc vb ver* **adquirir**

adquirir [aðkiˈrir] *vt* to acquire, obtain

adquisición [aðkisiˈθjon] *nf* acquisition

adrede [aˈðreðe] *adv* on purpose

adscribir [aðskriˈβir] *vt* to appoint

adscrito *pp de* **adscribir**

aduana [aˈðwana] *nf* customs *pl*

aduanero, a [aðwaˈnero, a] *adj* customs *cpd* ♦ *nm/f* customs officer

aducir [aðuˈθir] *vt* to adduce; (*dar como prueba*) to offer as proof

adueñarse [aðweˈɲarse] *vr*: ~ **de** to take possession of

adulación [aðulaˈθjon] *nf* flattery

adular [aðuˈlar] *vt* to flatter

adulterar [aðulteˈrar] *vt* to adulterate

adulterio [aðulˈterjo] *nm* adultery

adúltero, a [aˈðultero, a] *adj* adulterous ♦ *nm/f* adulterer/adulteress

adulto, a [aˈðulto, a] *adj, nm/f* adult

adusto, a [aˈðusto, a] *adj* stern; (*austero*) austere

advenedizo, a [aðβeneˈðiθo, a] *nm/f* upstart

advenimiento [aðβeniˈmjento] *nm* arrival; (*al trono*) accession

adverbio [aðˈβerβjo] *nm* adverb

adversario, a [aðβerˈsarjo, a] *nm/f* adversary

adversidad [aðβersiˈðað] *nf* adversity; (*contratiempo*) setback

adverso, a [aðˈβerso, a] *adj* adverse

advertencia [aðβerˈtenθja] *nf* warning; (*prefacio*) preface, foreword

advertir [aðβerˈtir] *vt* to notice; (*avisar*): ~ **a uno de** to warn sb about *o* of

Adviento [aðˈβjento] *nm* Advent

advierto *etc vb ver* **advertir**

adyacente [aðjaˈθente] *adj* adjacent

aéreo, a [aˈereo, a] *adj* aerial

aerobic [aeˈroβik] *nm* aerobics *sg*

aerodeslizador [aeroðesliθaˈðor] *nm* hovercraft

aeromozo, a [aeroˈmoθo, a] (*AM*) *nm/f* air steward(ess)

aeronáutica [aeroˈnautika] *nf* aeronautics

sg

aeronave [aeroˈnaβe] *nm* spaceship

aeroplano [aeroˈplano] *nm* aeroplane

aeropuerto [aeroˈpwerto] *nm* airport

aerosol [aeroˈsol] *nm* aerosol

afabilidad [afaβiliˈðað] *nf* friendliness; afable *adj* affable

afamado, a [afaˈmaðo, a] *adj* famous

afán [aˈfan] *nm* hard work; (*deseo*) desire

afanar [afaˈnar] *vt* to harass; (*fam*) to pinch; ~**se** *vr*: ~**se por hacer** to strive to do

afear [afeˈar] *vt* to disfigure

afección [afekˈθjon] *nf* (*MED*) disease

afectación [afektaˈθjon] *nf* affectation; **afectado, a** *adj* affected

afectar [afekˈtar] *vt* to affect

afectísimo, a [afekˈtisimo, a] *adj* affectionate; **suyo** ~ yours truly

afectivo, a [afekˈtiβo, a] *adj* (*problema etc*) emotional

afecto [aˈfekto] *nm* affection; **tenerle** ~ **a uno** to be fond of sb

afectuoso, a [afekˈtwoso, a] *adj* affectionate

afeitar [afeiˈtar] *vt* to shave; ~**se** *vr* to shave

afeminado, a [afemiˈnaðo, a] *adj* effeminate

Afganistán [afvanisˈtan] *nm* Afghanistan

afianzamiento [afjanθaˈmjento] *nm* strengthening; security

afianzar [afjanˈθar] *vt* to strengthen; to secure; ~**se** *vr* to become established

afiche [aˈfitʃe] (*AM*) *nf* poster

afición [afiˈθjon] *nf* fondness, liking; **la** ~ the fans *pl*; **pinto por** ~ I paint as a hobby; **aficionado, a** *adj* keen, enthusiastic; (*no profesional*) amateur ♦ *nm/f* enthusiast, fan; amateur; **ser aficionado a algo** to be very keen on *o* fond of sth

aficionar [afiθjoˈnar] *vt*: ~ **a uno a algo** to make sb like sth; ~**se** *vr*: ~**se a algo** to grow fond of sth

afilado, a [afiˈlaðo, a] *adj* sharp

afilar [afiˈlar] *vt* to sharpen

afiliarse [afiˈljarse] *vr* to affiliate

afín [aˈfin] *adj* (*parecido*) similar; (*conexo*) related

afinar [afiˈnar] *vt* (*TEC*) to refine; (*MUS*) to tune ♦ *vi* (*tocar*) to play in tune; (*cantar*) to sing in tune

afincarse [afinˈkarse] *vr* to settle

afinidad [afiniˈðað] *nf* affinity; (*parentesco*) relationship; **por ~** by marriage

afirmación [afirmaˈθjon] *nf* affirmation

afirmar [afirˈmar] *vt* to affirm, state; **afirmativo, a** *adj* affirmative

aflicción [aflikˈθjon] *nf* affliction; (*dolor*) grief

afligir [afliˈxir] *vt* to afflict; (*apenar*) to distress; **~se** *vr* to grieve

aflojar [afloˈxar] *vt* to slacken; (*desatar*) to loosen, undo; (*relajar*) to relax ♦ *vi* to drop; (*bajar*) to go down; **~se** *vr* to relax

aflorar [afloˈrar] *vi* to come to the surface, emerge

afluente [afluˈente] *adj* flowing ♦ *nm* tributary

afluir [afluˈir] *vi* to flow

afmo, a *abr* (= *afectísimo(a) suyo(a)*) Yours

afónico, a [aˈfoniko, a] *adj*: **estar ~** to have a sore throat; to have lost one's voice

aforo [aˈforo] *nm* (*de teatro etc*) capacity

afortunado, a [afortuˈnaðo, a] *adj* fortunate, lucky

afrancesado, a [afranθeˈsaðo, a] *adj* francophile; (*pey*) Frenchified

afrenta [aˈfrenta] *nf* affront, insult; (*deshonra*) dishonour, shame

África [ˈafrika] *nf* Africa; **africano, a** *adj*, *nm/f* African

afrontar [afronˈtar] *vt* to confront; (*poner cara a cara*) to bring face to face

afuera [aˈfwera] *adv* out, outside; **~s** *nfpl* outskirts

agachar [aɣaˈtʃar] *vt* to bend, bow; **~se** *vr* to stoop, bend

agalla [aˈɣaʎa] *nf* (*ZOOL*) gill; **tener ~s** (*fam*) to have guts

agarradera [aɣarraˈðera] (*esp AM*) *nf* handle

agarrado, a [aɣaˈrraðo, a] *adj* mean, stingy

agarrar [aɣaˈrrar] *vt* to grasp, grab; (*AM*) to take, catch; (*recoger*) to pick up ♦ *vi* (*planta*) to take root; **~se** *vr* to hold on (tightly)

agarrotar [aɣarroˈtar] *vt* (*persona*) to squeeze tightly; (*reo*) to garrotte; **~se** *vr* (*motor*) to seize up; (*MED*) to stiffen

agasajar [aɣasaˈxar] *vt* to treat well, fête

agazaparse [aɣaθaˈparse] *vr* to crouch down

agencia [aˈxenθja] *nf* agency; **~ inmobiliaria** estate (*BRIT*) o real estate (*US*) agent's (office); **~ de viajes** travel agency

agenciarse [axenˈθjarse] *vr* to obtain, procure

agenda [aˈxenda] *nf* diary

agente [aˈxente] *nm/f* agent; (*de policía*) policeman/policewoman; **~ inmobiliario** estate agent (*BRIT*), realtor (*US*); **~ de seguros** insurance agent

ágil [ˈaxil] *adj* agile, nimble; **agilidad** *nf* agility, nimbleness

agilizar [axiliˈθar] *vt* (*trámites*) to speed up

agitación [axitaˈθjon] *nf* (*de mano etc*) shaking, waving; (*de líquido etc*) stirring; (*fig*) agitation

agitado, a [axiˈaðo, a] *adj* hectic; (*viaje*) bumpy

agitar [axiˈtar] *vt* to wave, shake; (*líquido*) to stir; (*fig*) to stir up, excite; **~se** *vr* to get excited; (*inquietarse*) to get worried o upset

aglomeración [aɣlomeraˈθjon] *nf*: **~ de tráfico/gente** traffic jam/mass of people

aglomerar [aɣlomeˈrar] *vt* to crowd together; **~se** *vr* to crowd together

agnóstico, a [aɣˈnostiko, a] *adj*, *nm/f* agnostic

agobiar [aɣoˈβjar] *vt* to weigh down; (*oprimir*) to oppress; (*cargar*) to burden

agolparse [aɣolˈparse] *vr* to crowd together

agonía [aɣoˈnia] *nf* death throes *pl*; (*fig*)

agony, anguish

agonizante [aɣoni'θante] *adj* dying

agonizar [aɣoni'θar] *vi* to be dying

agosto [a'ɣosto] *nm* August

agotado, a [aɣo'taðo, a] *adj (persona)* exhausted; *(libros)* out of print; *(acabado)* finished; *(COM)* sold out

agotador, a [aɣota'ðor, a] *adj* exhausting

agotamiento [aɣota'mjento] *nm* exhaustion

agotar [aɣo'tar] *vt* to exhaust; *(consumir)* to drain; *(recursos)* to use up, deplete; **~se** *vr* to be exhausted; *(acabarse)* to run out; *(libro)* to go out of print

agraciado, a [aɣra'θjaðo, a] *adj (atractivo)* attractive; *(en sorteo etc)* lucky

agradable [aɣra'ðaβle] *adj* pleasant, nice

agradar [aɣra'ðar] *vt*: **él me agrada** I like him

agradecer [aɣraðe'θer] *vt* to thank; *(favor etc)* to be grateful for; **agradecido, a** *adj* grateful; **¡muy agradecido!** thanks a lot!; **agradecimiento** *nm* thanks *pl*; gratitude

agradezco *etc vb ver* **agradecer**

agrado [a'ɣraðo] *nm*: **ser de tu** *etc* **~** to be to your *etc* liking

agrandar [aɣran'dar] *vt* to enlarge; *(fig)* to exaggerate; **~se** *vr* to get bigger

agrario, a [a'ɣrarjo, a] *adj* agrarian, land *cpd*; *(política)* agricultural, farming

agravante [aɣra'ßante] *adj* aggravating ♦ *nm*: **con el ~ de que ...** with the further difficulty that ....

agravar [aɣra'ßar] *vt (pesar sobre)* to make heavier; *(irritar)* to aggravate; **~se** *vr* to worsen, get worse

agraviar [aɣra'ßjar] *vt* to offend; *(ser injusto con)* to wrong; **~se** *vr* to take offence; **agravio** *nm* offence; wrong; *(JUR)* grievance

agredir [aɣre'ðir] *vt* to attack

agregado, a [aɣre'ɣaðo, a] *nm/f*: **A~** ≈ teacher *(who is not head of department)* ♦ *nm* aggregate; *(persona)* attaché

agregar [aɣre'ɣar] *vt* to gather; *(añadir)* to add; *(persona)* to appoint

agresión [aɣre'sjon] *nf* aggression

agresivo, a [aɣre'sißo, a] *adj* aggressive

agriar [a'ɣrjar] *vt* to (turn) sour; **~se** *vr* to turn sour

agrícola [a'ɣrikola] *adj* farming *cpd*, agricultural

agricultor, a [aɣrikul'tor, a] *nm/f* farmer

agricultura [aɣrikul'tura] *nf* agriculture, farming

agridulce [aɣri'ðulθe] *adj* bittersweet; *(CULIN)* sweet and sour

agrietarse [aɣrje'tarse] *vr* to crack; *(piel)* to chap

agrimensor, a [aɣrimen'sor, a] *nm/f* surveyor

agrio, a [a'ɣrjo, a] *adj* bitter

agrupación [aɣrupa'θjon] *nf* group; *(acto)* grouping

agrupar [aɣru'par] *vt* to group

agua ['aɣwa] *nf* water; *(NAUT)* wake; *(ARQ)* slope of a roof; **~s** *nfpl (de piedra)* water *sg*, sparkle *sg*; *(MED)* water *sg*, urine *sg*; *(NAUT)* waters; **~s abajo/arriba** downstream/upstream; **~s bendita/ destilada/potable** holy/distilled/drinking water; **~ caliente** hot water; **~ corriente** running water; **~ de colonia** eau de cologne; **~ mineral (con/sin gas)** (carbonated/uncarbonated) mineral water; **~ oxigenada** hydrogen peroxide; **~s jurisdiccionales** territorial waters

aguacate [aɣwa'kate] *nm* avocado (pear)

aguacero [aɣwa'θero] *nm* (heavy) shower, downpour

aguado, a [a'ɣwaðo, a] *adj* watery, watered down

aguafiestas [aɣwa'fjestas] *nm/f inv* spoilsport, killjoy

aguanieve [aɣwa'njeße] *nf* sleet

aguantar [aɣwan'tar] *vt* to bear, put up with; *(sostener)* to hold up ♦ *vi* to last; **~se** *vr* to restrain o.s.; **aguante** *nm (paciencia)* patience; *(resistencia)* endurance

aguar [a'ɣwar] *vt* to water down

aguardar [aɣwar'ðar] *vt* to wait for

aguardiente [aɣwar'ðjente] *nm* brandy,

liquor

aguarrás [aɣwaˈrras] *nm* turpentine

agudeza [aɣuˈðeθa] *nf* sharpness; (*ingenio*) wit

agudizar [aɣuðiˈθar] *vt* (*crisis*) to make worse; **~se** *vr* to get worse

agudo, a [aˈɣuðo, a] *adj* sharp; (*voz*) high-pitched, piercing; (*dolor, enfermedad*) acute

agüero [aˈɣwero] *nm*: **buen/mal ~** good/bad omen

aguijón [aɣiˈxon] *nm* sting; (*fig*) spur

águila [ˈaɣila] *nf* eagle; (*fig*) genius

aguileño, a [aɣiˈleɲo, a] *adj* (*nariz*) aquiline; (*rostro*) sharp-featured

aguinaldo [aɣiˈnaldo] *nm* Christmas box

aguja [aˈɣuxa] *nf* needle; (*de reloj*) hand; (*ARQ*) spire; (*TEC*) firing-pin; **~s** *nfpl* (*ZOOL*) ribs; (*FERRO*) points

agujerear [aɣuxereˈar] *vt* to make holes in

agujero [aɣuˈxero] *nm* hole

agujetas [aɣuˈxetas] *nfpl* stitch *sg*; (*rigidez*) stiffness *sg*

aguzar [aɣuˈθar] *vt* to sharpen; (*fig*) to incite

ahí [aˈi] *adv* there; **de ~ que** so that, with the result that; **~ llega** here he comes; **por ~** that way; (*allá*) over there; **200 o por ~** 200 or so

ahijado, a [aiˈxaðo, a] *nm/f* godson/daughter

ahínco [aˈinko] *nm* earnestness

ahogar [aoˈɣar] *vt* to drown; (*asfixiar*) to suffocate, smother; (*fuego*) to put out; **~se** *vr* (*en el agua*) to drown; (*por asfixia*) to suffocate

ahogo [aˈoɣo] *nm* breathlessness; (*fig*) financial difficulty

ahondar [aonˈdar] *vt* to deepen, make deeper; (*fig*) to study thoroughly ♦ *vi*: **~ en** to study thoroughly

ahora [aˈora] *adv* now; (*hace poco*) a moment ago, just now; (*dentro de poco*) in a moment; **~ voy** I'm coming; **~ mismo** right now; **~ bien** now then; **por ~** for the present

ahorcar [aorˈkar] *vt* to hang

ahorita [aoˈrita] (*fam: esp AM*) *adv* right now

ahorrar [aoˈrrar] *vt* (*dinero*) to save; (*esfuerzos*) to save, avoid; **ahorro** *nm* (*acto*) saving; **ahorros** *nmpl* (*dinero*) savings

ahuecar [aweˈkar] *vt* to hollow (out); (*voz*) to deepen; **~se** *vr* to give o.s. airs

ahumar [auˈmar] *vt* to smoke, cure; (*llenar de humo*) to fill with smoke ♦ *vi* to smoke; **~se** *vr* to fill with smoke

ahuyentar [aujenˈtar] *vt* to drive off, frighten off; (*fig*) to dispel

airado, a [aiˈraðo, a] *adj* angry

airar [aiˈrar] *vt* to anger; **~se** *vr* to get angry

aire [ˈaire] *nm* air; (*viento*) wind; (*corriente*) draught; (*MUS*) tune; **~s** *nmpl*: **darse ~s** to give o.s. airs; **al ~ libre** in the open air; **~ acondicionado** air conditioning; **airearse** *vr* (*persona*) to go out for a breath of fresh air; **airoso, a** *adj* windy; draughty; (*fig*) graceful

aislado, a [aisˈlaðo, a] *adj* isolated; (*incomunicado*) cut-off; (*ELEC*) insulated

aislar [aisˈlar] *vt* to isolate; (*ELEC*) to insulate

ajardinado, a [axarðiˈnaðo, a] *adj* landscaped

ajedrez [axeˈðreθ] *nm* chess

ajeno, a [aˈxeno, a] *adj* (*que pertenece a otro*) somebody else's; **~ a** foreign to

ajetreado, a [axetreˈaðo, a] *adj* busy

ajetreo [axeˈtreo] *nm* bustle

ají [aˈxi] (*AM*) *nm* chil(l)i, red pepper; (*salsa*) chil(l)i sauce

ajillo [aˈxiʎo] *nm*: **gambas al ~** garlic prawns

ajo [ˈaxo] *nm* garlic

ajuar [aˈxwar] *nm* household furnishings *pl*; (*de novia*) trousseau; (*de niño*) layette

ajustado, a [axusˈtaðo, a] *adj* (*tornillo*) tight; (*cálculo*) right; (*ropa*) tight(-fitting); (*resultado*) close

ajustar [axusˈtar] *vt* (*adaptar*) to adjust; (*encajar*) to fit; (*TEC*) to engage; (*IMPRENTA*) to make up; (*apretar*) to tighten; (*concertar*) to agree (on); (*reconciliar*) to reconcile; (*cuentas, deudas*) to settle ♦ *vi* to fit; **~se** *vr*: **~se a** (*precio etc*) to be in keeping with, fit in with; **~ las cuentas a uno** to get even with sb

ajuste [a'xuste] *nm* adjustment; (*COSTURA*) fitting; (*acuerdo*) compromise; (*de cuenta*) settlement

al [al] (= **a** +**el**) *ver* **a**

ala ['ala] *nf* wing; (*de sombrero*) brim; (*futbolista*) winger; **~ delta** *nf* hang-glider

alabanza [ala'ßanθa] *nf* praise

alabar [ala'ßar] *vt* to praise

alacena [ala'θena] *nf* kitchen cupboard (*BRIT*), kitchen closet (*US*)

alacrán [ala'kran] *nm* scorpion

alambique [alam'bike] *nm* still

alambrada [alam'braða] *nf* wire fence; (*red*) wire netting

alambrado [alam'braðo] *nm* = **alambrada**

alambre [a'lambre] *nm* wire; **~ de púas** barbed wire

alameda [ala'meða] *nf* (*plantío*) poplar grove; (*lugar de paseo*) avenue, boulevard

álamo ['alamo] *nm* poplar; **~ temblón** aspen

alarde [a'larðe] *nm* show, display; **hacer ~ de** to boast of

alargador [alarɣa'ðor] *nm* (*ELEC*) extension lead

alargar [alar'ɣar] *vt* to lengthen, extend; (*paso*) to hasten; (*brazo*) to stretch out; (*cuerda*) to pay out; (*conversación*) to spin out; **~se** *vr* to get longer

alarido [ala'riðo] *nm* shriek

alarma [a'larma] *nf* alarm

alarmar *vt* to alarm; **~se** to get alarmed; **alarmante** [alar'mante] *adj* alarming

alba ['alßa] *nf* dawn

albacea [alßa'θea] *nm/f* executor/executrix

albahaca [al'ßaka] *nf* basil

Albania [al'ßanja] *nf* Albania

albañil [alßa'ɲil] *nm* bricklayer; (*cantero*) mason

albarán [alßa'ran] *nm* (*COM*) delivery note,

invoice

albaricoque [alßari'koke] *nm* apricot

albedrío [alße'ðrio] *nm*: **libre ~** free will

alberca [al'ßerka] *nf* reservoir; (*AM*) swimming pool

albergar [alßer'ɣar] *vt* to shelter

albergue *etc* [al'ßerɣe] *vb ver* **albergar** ♦ *nm* shelter, refuge; **~ juvenil** youth hostel

albóndiga [al'ßondiɣa] *nf* meatball

albornoz [alßor'noθ] *nm* (*de los árabes*) burnous; (*para el baño*) bathrobe

alborotar [alßoro'tar] *vi* to make a row ♦ *vt* to agitate, stir up; **~se** *vr* to get excited; (*mar*) to get rough; **alboroto** *nm* row, uproar

alborozar [alßoro'θar] *vt* to gladden; **~se** *vr* to rejoice

alborozo [alßo'roθo] *nm* joy

álbum ['alßum] (*pl* **~s**, **~es**) *nm* album; **~ de recortes** scrapbook

alcachofa [alka'tʃofa] *nf* artichoke

alcalde, esa [al'kalde, esa] *nm/f* mayor(ess)

alcaldía [alkal'dia] *nf* mayoralty; (*lugar*) mayor's office

alcance *etc* [al'kanθe] *vb ver* **alcanzar** ♦ *nm* reach; (*COM*) adverse balance

alcantarilla [alkanta'riʎa] *nf* (*de aguas cloacales*) sewer; (*en la calle*) gutter

alcanzar [alkan'θar] *vt* (*algo: con la mano, el pie*) to reach; (*alguien: en el camino etc*) to catch up (with); (*autobús*) to catch; (*suj: bala*) to hit, strike ♦ *vi* (*ser suficiente*) to be enough; **~ a hacer** to manage to do

alcaparra [alka'parra] *nf* caper

alcayata [alka'jata] *nf* hook

alcázar [al'kaθar] *nm* fortress; (*NAUT*) quarter-deck

alcoba [al'koßa] *nf* bedroom

alcohol [al'kol] *nm* alcohol; **~ metílico** methylated spirits *pl* (*BRIT*), wood alcohol (*US*); **alcohólico, a** *adj*, *nm/f* alcoholic

alcoholímetro [alko'limetro] *nm* Breathalyser ® (*BRIT*), drunkometer (*US*)

alcoholismo [alko'lismo] *nm* alcoholism

lcornoque [alkor'noke] *nm* cork tree; (*fam*) idiot

lcurnia [al'kurnja] *nf* lineage

ldaba [al'daßa] *nf* (door) knocker

ldea [al'dea] *nf* village; ~**no, a** *adj* village *cpd* ♦ *nm/f* villager

leación [alea'θjon] *nf* alloy

leatorio, a [alea'torjo, a] *adj* random

leccionar [alekθejo'nar] *vt* to instruct; (*adiestrar*) to train

legación [aleɣa'θjon] *nf* allegation

legar [ale'ɣar] *vt* to claim; (*JUR*) to plead ♦ *vi* (*AM*) to argue

legato [ale'ɣato] *nm* (*JUR*) allegation; (*AM*) argument

legoría [aleɣo'ria] *nf* allegory

legrar [ale'ɣrar] *vt* (*causar alegría*) to cheer (up); (*fuego*) to poke; (*fiesta*) to liven up; ~**se** *vr* (*fam*) to get merry *o* tight; ~**se de** to be glad about

legre [a'leɣre] *adj* happy, cheerful; (*fam*) merry, tight; (*chiste*) risqué, blue; **alegría** *nf* happiness; merriment

lejamiento [alexa'mjento] *nm* removal; (*distancia*) remoteness

lejar [ale'xar] *vt* to remove; (*fig*) to estrange; ~**se** *vr* to move away

lemán, ana [ale'man, ana] *adj, nm/f* German ♦ *nm* (*LING*) German

lemania [ale'manja] *nf*: ~ **Occidental/Oriental** West/East Germany

lentador, a [alenta'ðor, a] *adj* encouraging

lentar [alen'tar] *vt* to encourage

lergia [a'lerxja] *nf* allergy

lero [a'lero] *nm* (*de tejado*) eaves *pl*; (*de carruaje*) mudguard

lerta [a'lerta] *adj, nm* alert

leta [a'leta] *nf* (*de pez*) fin; (*de ave*) wing; (*de foca, DEPORTE*) flipper; (*AUTO*) mudguard

letargar [aletar'ɣar] *vt* to make drowsy; (*entumecer*) to make numb; ~**se** *vr* to grow drowsy; to become numb

letear [alete'ar] *vi* to flutter

levín [ale'ßin] *nm* fry, young fish

levosía [aleßo'sia] *nf* treachery

alfabeto [alfa'ßeto] *nm* alphabet

alfalfa [al'falfa] *nf* alfalfa, lucerne

alfarería [alfare'ria] *nf* pottery; (*tienda*) pottery shop; **alfarero, a** *nm/f* potter

alféizar [al'feiθar] *nm* window-sill

alférez [al'fereθ] *nm* (*MIL*) second lieutenant; (*NAUT*) ensign

alfil [al'fil] *nm* (*AJEDREZ*) bishop

alfiler [alfi'ler] *nm* pin; (*broche*) clip

alfiletero [alfile'tero] *nm* needlecase

alfombra [al'fombra] *nf* carpet; (*más pequeña*) rug; **alfombrar** *vt* to carpet; **alfombrilla** *nf* rug, mat; (*INFORM*) mouse mat *o* pad

alforja [al'forxa] *nf* saddlebag

algarabía [alɣara'ßia] (*fam*) *nf* gibberish; (*griterío*) hullabaloo

algas ['alɣas] *nfpl* seaweed

álgebra ['alxeßra] *nf* algebra

álgido, a ['alxiðo, a] *adj* (*momento etc*) crucial, decisive

algo ['alɣo] *pron* something; anything ♦ *adv* somewhat, rather; **¿~ más?** anything else?; (*en tienda*) is that all?; **por ~ será** there must be some reason for it

algodón [alɣo'ðon] *nm* cotton; (*planta*) cotton plant; ~ **de azúcar** candy floss (*BRIT*), cotton candy (*US*); ~ **hidrófilo** cotton wool (*BRIT*), absorbent cotton (*US*)

algodonero, a [alɣoðo'nero, a] *adj* cotton *cpd* ♦ *nm/f* cotton grower ♦ *nm* cotton plant

alguacil [alɣwa'θil] *nm* bailiff; (*TAUR*) mounted official

alguien ['alɣjen] *pron* someone, somebody; (*en frases interrogativas*) anyone, anybody

alguno, a [al'ɣuno, a] *adj* (*delante de nm*: **algún**) some; (*después de n*): **no tiene talento** ~ he has no talent, he doesn't have any talent ♦ *pron* (*alguien*) someone, somebody; **algún que otro libro** some book or other; **algún día iré** I'll go one *o* some day; **sin interés** ~ without the slightest interest; ~ **que otro** an occasional one; ~**s piensan** some (people) think

alhaja [a'laxa] *nf* jewel; (*tesoro*) precious

object, treasure
alhelí [ale'li] *nm* wallflower, stock
aliado, a [a'ljaðo, a] *adj* allied
alianza [a'ljanθa] *nf* alliance; (*anillo*) wedding ring
aliar [a'ljar] *vt* to ally; **~se** *vr* to form an alliance
alias ['aljas] *adv* alias
alicates [ali'kates] *nmpl* pliers; **~ de uñas** nail clippers
aliciente [ali'θjente] *nm* incentive; (*atracción*) attraction
alienación [aljena'θjon] *nf* alienation
aliento [a'ljento] *nm* breath; (*respiración*) breathing; **sin ~** breathless
aligerar [alixe'rar] *vt* to lighten; (*reducir*) to shorten; (*aliviar*) to alleviate; (*mitigar*) to ease; (*paso*) to quicken
alijo [a'lixo] *nm* consignment
alimaña [ali'maɲa] *nf* pest
alimentación [alimenta'θjon] *nf* (*comida*) food; (*acción*) feeding; (*tienda*) grocer's (shop); **alimentador** *nm*: **alimentador de papel** sheet-feeder
alimentar [alimen'tar] *vt* to feed; (*nutrir*) to nourish; **~se** *vr* to feed
alimenticio, a [alimen'tiθjo, a] *adj* food *cpd*; (*nutritivo*) nourishing, nutritious
alimento [ali'mento] *nm* food; (*nutrición*) nourishment
alineación [alinea'θjon] *nf* alignment; (*DEPORTE*) line-up
alinear [aline'ar] *vt* to align; **~se** *vr* (*DEPORTE*) to line up; **~se en** to fall in with
aliñar [ali'ɲar] *vt* (*CULIN*) to season; **aliño** *nm* (*CULIN*) dressing
alioli [ali'oli] *nm* garlic mayonnaise
alisar [ali'sar] *vt* to smooth
aliso [a'liso] *nm* alder
alistarse [alis'tarse] *vr* to enlist; (*inscribirse*) to enrol
aliviar [ali'ßjar] *vt* (*carga*) to lighten; (*persona*) to relieve; (*dolor*) to relieve, alleviate
alivio [a'lißjo] *nm* alleviation, relief
aljibe [al'xiße] *nm* cistern

allá [a'ʎa] *adv* (*lugar*) there; (*por ahí*) over there; (*tiempo*) then; **~ abajo** down there; **más ~** further on; **más ~ de** beyond; **¡~ tú!** that's your problem!
allanamiento [aʎana'mjento] *nm*: **~ de morada** burglary
allanar [aʎa'nar] *vt* to flatten, level (out); (*igualar*) to smooth (out); (*fig*) to subdue; (*JUR*) to burgle, break into
allegado, a [aʎe'ɣaðo, a] *adj* near, close ♦ *nm/f* relation
allí [a'ʎi] *adv* there; **~ mismo** right there; **por ~** over there; (*por ese camino*) that way
alma ['alma] *nf* soul; (*persona*) person
almacén [alma'θen] *nm* (*depósito*) warehouse, store; (*MIL*) magazine; (*AM*) shop; **(grandes) almacenes** *nmpl* department store *sg*; **almacenaje** *nm* storage
almacenar [almaθe'nar] *vt* to store, put in storage; (*proveerse*) to stock up with; **almacenero** *nm* (*AM*) shopkeeper
almanaque [alma'nake] *nm* almanac
almeja [al'mexa] *nf* clam
almendra [al'mendra] *nf* almond; **almendro** *nm* almond tree
almíbar [al'mißar] *nm* syrup
almidón [almi'ðon] *nm* starch; **almidonar** *vt* to starch
almirante [almi'rante] *nm* admiral
almirez [almi'reθ] *nm* mortar
almizcle [al'miθkle] *nm* musk
almohada [almo'aða] *nf* pillow; (*funda*) pillowcase; **almohadilla** *nf* cushion; (*TEC*) pad; (*AM*) pincushion
almohadón [almoa'ðon] *nm* large pillow; bolster
almorranas [almo'rranas] *nfpl* piles, haemorrhoids
almorzar [almor'θar] *vt*: **~ una tortilla** to have an omelette for lunch ♦ *vi* to (have) lunch
almuerzo *etc* [al'mwerθo] *vb ver* **almorzar** ♦ *nm* lunch
alocado, a [alo'kaðo, a] *adj* crazy
alojamiento [aloxa'mjento] *nm* lodging(s)

(pl); *(viviendas)* housing

alojar [alo'xar] *vt* to lodge; **~se** *vr* to lodge, stay

alondra [a'londra] *nf* lark, skylark

alpargata [alpar'ɣata] *nf* rope-soled sandal, espadrille

Alpes ['alpes] *nmpl*: **los ~** the Alps

alpinismo [alpi'nismo] *nm* mountaineering, climbing; **alpinista** *nm/f* mountaineer, climber

alpiste [al'piste] *nm* birdseed

alquilar [alki'lar] *vt* (*suj: propietario*: *inmuebles*) to let, rent (out) (: *coche*) to hire out; (: *TV*) to rent (out); (*suj: alquilador: inmuebles, TV*) to rent; (: *coche*) to hire; **"se alquila casa"** "house to let (*BRIT*) o for rent (*US*)"

alquiler [alki'ler] *nm* renting; letting; hiring; *(arriendo)* rent; hire charge; **~ de automóviles** car hire; **de ~** for hire

alquimia [al'kimja] *nf* alchemy

alquitrán [alki'tran] *nm* tar

alrededor [alreðe'ðor] *adv* around, about; **~ de** around, about; **mirar a su ~** to look (round) about one; **~es** *nmpl* surroundings

alta ['alta] *nf* (certificate of) discharge; **dar de ~** to discharge

altanería [altane'ria] *nf* haughtiness, arrogance; **altanero, a** *adj* arrogant, haughty

altar [al'tar] *nm* altar

altavoz [alta'ßoθ] *nm* loudspeaker; *(amplificador)* amplifier

alteración [altera'θjon] *nf* alteration; *(alboroto)* disturbance

alterar [alte'rar] *vt* to alter; to disturb; **~se** *vr* (*persona*) to get upset

altercado [alter'kaðo] *nm* argument

alternar [alter'nar] *vt* to alternate ♦ *vi* to alternate; *(turnar)* to take turns; **~se** *vr* to alternate; to take turns; **~ con** to mix with; **alternativa** *nf* alternative; *(elección)* choice; **alternativo, a** *adj* alternative; *(alterno)* alternating; **alterno, a** *adj* alternate; *(ELEC)* alternating

Alteza [al'teθa] *nf* *(tratamiento)* Highness

altibajos [alti'ßaxos] *nmpl* ups and downs

altiplanicie [altipla'niθje] *nf* high plateau

altiplano [alti'plano] *nm* = **altiplanicie**

altisonante [altiso'nante] *adj* high-flown, high-sounding

altitud [alti'tuð] *nf* height; *(AVIAT, GEO)* altitude

altivez [alti'ßeθ] *nf* haughtiness, arrogance; **altivo, a** *adj* haughty, arrogant

alto, a ['alto, a] *adj* high; *(persona)* tall; *(sonido)* high, sharp; *(noble)* high, lofty ♦ *nm* halt; *(MUS)* alto; *(GEO)* hill; *(AM)* pile ♦ *adv* *(de sitio)* high; *(de sonido)* loud, loudly ♦ *excl* halt!; **la pared tiene 2 metros de ~** the wall is 2 metres high; **en alta mar** on the high seas; **en voz alta** in a loud voice; **las altas horas de la noche** the small o wee hours; **en lo ~ de** at the top of; **pasar por ~** to overlook

altoparlante [altopar'lante] *(AM)* *nm* loudspeaker

altruismo [altru'ismo] *nm* altruism

altura [al'tura] *nf* height; *(NAUT)* depth; *(GEO)* latitude; **la pared tiene 1.80 de ~** the wall is 1 metre 80cm high; **a estas ~s** at this stage; **a estas ~s del año** at this time of the year

alubia [a'lußja] *nf* bean

alucinación [aluθina'θjon] *nf* hallucination

alucinar [aluθi'nar] *vi* to hallucinate ♦ *vt* to deceive; *(fascinar)* to fascinate

alud [a'luð] *nm* avalanche; *(fig)* flood

aludir [alu'ðir] *vi*: **~ a** to allude to; **darse por aludido** to take the hint

alumbrado [alum'braðo] *nm* lighting; **alumbramiento** *nm* lighting; *(MED)* childbirth, delivery

alumbrar [alum'brar] *vt* to light (up) ♦ *vi* *(MED)* to give birth

aluminio [alu'minjo] *nm* aluminium (*BRIT*), aluminum (*US*)

alumno, a [a'lumno, a] *nm/f* pupil, student

alunizar [aluni'θar] *vi* to land on the moon

alusión [alu'sjon] *nf* allusion

alusivo, a [alu'siβo, a] *adj* allusive

aluvión [alu'βjon] *nm* alluvium; *(fig)* flood

alverja [al'βerxa] *(AM) nf* pea

alza ['alθa] *nf* rise; *(MIL)* sight

alzada [al'θaða] *nf (de caballos)* height; *(JUR)* appeal

alzamiento [alθa'mjento] *nm (rebelión)* rising

alzar [al'θar] *vt* to lift (up); *(precio, muro)* to raise; *(cuello de abrigo)* to turn up; *(AGR)* to gather in; *(IMPRENTA)* to gather; **~se** *vr* to get up, rise; *(rebelarse)* to revolt; *(COM)* to go fraudulently bankrupt; *(JUR)* to appeal

ama ['ama] *nf* lady of the house; *(dueña)* owner; *(institutriz)* governess; *(madre adoptiva)* foster mother; **~ de casa** housewife; **~ de llaves** housekeeper

amabilidad [amaβili'ðað] *nf* kindness; *(simpatía)* niceness; **amable** *adj* kind; nice; **es usted muy amable** that's very kind of you

amaestrado, a [amaes'traðo, a] *adj (animal: en circo etc)* performing

amaestrar [amaes'trar] *vt* to train

amago [a'maɣo] *nm* threat; *(gesto)* threatening gesture; *(MED)* symptom

amainar [amai'nar] *vi (viento)* to die down

amalgama [amal'ɣama] *nf* amalgam; **amalgamar** *vt* to amalgamate; *(combinar)* to combine, mix

amamantar [amaman'tar] *vt* to suckle, nurse

amanecer [amane'θer] *vi* to dawn ♦ *nm* dawn; **~ afiebrado** to wake up with a fever

amanerado, a [amane'raðo, a] *adj* affected

amansar [aman'sar] *vt* to tame; *(persona)* to subdue; **~se** *vr (persona)* to calm down

amante [a'mante] *adj:* **~ de** fond of ♦ *nm/f* lover

amapola [ama'pola] *nf* poppy

amar [a'mar] *vt* to love

amargado, a [amar'ɣaðo, a] *adj* bitter

amargar [amar'ɣar] *vt* to make bitter; *(fig)* to embitter; **~se** *vr* to become embittered

amargo, a [a'marɣo, a] *adj* bitter; **amargura** *nf* bitterness

amarillento, a [amari'ʎento, a] *adj* yellowish; *(tez)* sallow; **amarillo, a** *adj*, *nm* yellow

amarrar [ama'rrar] *vt* to moor; *(sujetar)* to tie up

amarras [a'marras] *nfpl:* **soltar ~** to set sail

amasar [ama'sar] *vt (masa)* to knead; *(mezclar)* to mix, prepare; *(confeccionar)* to concoct; **amasijo** *nm* kneading; mixing; *(fig)* hotchpotch

amateur ['amatur] *nm/f* amateur

amazona [ama'θona] *nf* horsewoman; **A~s** *nm:* **el A~s** the Amazon

ambages [am'baxes] *nmpl:* **sin ~** in plain language

ámbar ['ambar] *nm* amber

ambición [ambi'θjon] *nf* ambition; **ambicionar** *vt* to aspire to; **ambicioso, a** *adj* ambitious

ambidextro, a [ambi'ðekstro, a] *adj* ambidextrous

ambientación [ambjenta'θjon] *nf (CINE, TEATRO etc)* setting; *(RADIO)* sound effects

ambiente [am'bjente] *nm (tb fig)* atmosphere; *(medio)* environment

ambigüedad [ambiɣwe'ðað] *nf* ambiguity; **ambiguo, a** *adj* ambiguous

ámbito ['ambito] *nm (campo)* field; *(fig)* scope

ambos, as ['ambos, as] *adj pl, pron pl* both

ambulancia [ambu'lanθja] *nf* ambulance

ambulante [ambu'lante] *adj* travelling *cpd*, itinerant

ambulatorio [ambula'torio] *nm* state health-service clinic

amedrentar [ameðren'tar] *vt* to scare

amén [a'men] *excl* amen; **~ de** besides

amenaza [ame'naθa] *nf* threat

amenazar [amena'θar] *vt* to threaten ♦ *vi:* **~ con hacer** to threaten to do

amenidad [ameni'ðað] *nf* pleasantness

ameno, a [a'meno, a] *adj* pleasant
América [a'merika] *nf* America; ~ **del Norte/del Sur** North/South America; ~ **Central/Latina** Central/Latin America; **americana** *nf* coat, jacket; *ver tb* **americano; americano, a** *adj, nm/f* American
amerizar [ameri'θar] *vi* (*avión*) to land (on the sea)
ametralladora [ametraʎa'ðora] *nf* machine gun
amianto [a'mjanto] *nm* asbestos
amigable [ami'ɣaßle] *adj* friendly
amígdala [a'miɣðala] *nf* tonsil; **amigdalitis** *nf* tonsillitis
amigo, a [a'miɣo, a] *adj* friendly ♦ *nm/f* friend; (*amante*) lover; **ser** ~ **de algo** to be fond of sth; **ser muy ~s** to be close friends
amilanar [amila'nar] *vt* to scare; ~**se** *vr* to get scared
aminorar [amino'rar] *vt* to diminish; (*reducir*) to reduce; ~ **la marcha** to slow down
amistad [amis'tað] *nf* friendship; ~**es** *nfpl* (*amigos*) friends; **amistoso, a** *adj* friendly
amnesia [am'nesja] *nf* amnesia
amnistía [amnis'tia] *nf* amnesty
amo ['amo] *nm* owner; (*jefe*) boss
amodorrarse [amoðo'rrarse] *vr* to get sleepy
amoldar [amol'dar] *vt* to mould; (*adaptar*) to adapt
amonestación [amonesta'θjon] *nf* warning; **amonestaciones** *nfpl* (*REL*) marriage banns
amonestar [amones'tar] *vt* to warn; (*REL*) to publish the banns of
amontonar [amonto'nar] *vt* to collect, pile up; ~**se** *vr* to crowd together; (*acumularse*) to pile up
amor [a'mor] *nm* love; (*amante*) lover; **hacer el** ~ to make love; ~ **propio** self-respect
amoratado, a [amora'taðo, a] *adj* purple
amordazar [amorða'θar] *vt* to muzzle;

(*fig*) to gag
amorfo, a [a'morfo, a] *adj* amorphous, shapeless
amoroso, a [amo'roso, a] *adj* affectionate, loving
amortajar [amorta'xar] *vt* to shroud
amortiguador [amortiɣwa'ðor] *nm* shock absorber; (*parachoques*) bumper; ~**es** *nmpl* (*AUTO*) suspension *sg*
amortiguar [amorti'ɣwar] *vt* to deaden; (*ruido*) to muffle; (*color*) to soften
amortización [amortiθa'θjon] *nf* (*de deuda*) repayment; (*de bono*) redemption
amotinar [amoti'nar] *vt* to stir up, incite (to riot); ~**se** *vr* to mutiny
amparar [ampa'rar] *vt* to protect; ~**se** *vr* to seek protection; (*de la lluvia etc*) to shelter; **amparo** *nm* help, protection; **al amparo de** under the protection of
amperio [am'perjo] *nm* ampère, amp
ampliación [amplja'θjon] *nf* enlargement; (*extensión*) extension
ampliar [am'pljar] *vt* to enlarge; to extend
amplificación [amplifika'θjon] *nf* enlargement; **amplificador** *nm* amplifier
amplificar [amplifi'kar] *vt* to amplify
amplio, a ['ampljo, a] *adj* spacious; (*de falda etc*) full; (*extenso*) extensive; (*ancho*) wide; **amplitud** *nf* spaciousness; extent; (*fig*) amplitude
ampolla [am'poʎa] *nf* blister; (*MED*) ampoule
ampuloso, a [ampu'loso, a] *adj* bombastic, pompous
amputar [ampu'tar] *vt* to cut off, amputate
amueblar [amwe'ßlar] *vt* to furnish
amurallar [amura'ʎar] *vt* to wall up o in
anacronismo [anakro'nismo] *nm* anachronism
anales [a'nales] *nmpl* annals
analfabetismo [analfaße'tismo] *nm* illiteracy; **analfabeto, a** *adj, nm/f* illiterate
analgésico [anal'xesiko] *nm* painkiller, analgesic

análisis [a'nalisis] *nm inv* analysis
analista [ana'lista] *nm/f* (*gen*) analyst
analizar [anali'θar] *vt* to analyse
analogía [analo'xia] *nf* analogy
analógico, a [ana'loxiko, a] *adj* (*INFORM*) analog; (*reloj*) analogue (*BRIT*), analog (*US*)
análogo, a [a'naloxo, a] *adj* analogous, similar
ananá(s) [ana'na(s)] (*AM*) *nm* pineapple
anaquel [ana'kel] *nm* shelf
anarquía [anar'kia] *nf* anarchy; **anarquismo** *nm* anarchism; **anarquista** *nm/f* anarchist
anatomía [anato'mia] *nf* anatomy
anca ['anka] *nf* rump, haunch; **~s** *nfpl* (*fam*) behind *sg*
ancho, a ['antʃo, a] *adj* wide; (*falda*) full; (*fig*) liberal ♦ *nm* width; (*FERRO*) gauge; **ponerse ~** to get conceited; **estar a sus anchas** to be at one's ease
anchoa [an'tʃoa] *nf* anchovy
anchura [an'tʃura] *nf* width; (*extensión*) wideness
anciano, a [an'θjano, a] *adj* old, aged ♦ *nm/f* old man/woman; elder
ancla ['ankla] *nf* anchor; **~dero** *nm* anchorage; **anclar** *vi* to (drop) anchor
andadura [anda'ðura] *nf* gait; (*de caballo*) pace
Andalucía [andalu'θia] *nf* Andalusia; **andaluz, a** *adj, nm/f* Andalusian
andamiaje [anda'mjaxe] *nm* = **andamio**
andamio [an'damjo] *nm* scaffold(ing)
andar [an'dar] *vt* to go, cover, travel ♦ *vi* to go, walk, travel; (*funcionar*) to go, work; (*estar*) to be ♦ *nm* walk, gait, pace; **~se** *vr* to go away; **~ a pie/a caballo/en bicicleta** to go on foot/on horseback/by bicycle; **~ haciendo algo** to be doing sth; **¡anda!** (*sorpresa*) go on!; **anda por** *o* **en los 40** he's about 40
andén [an'den] *nm* (*FERRO*) platform; (*NAUT*) quayside; (*AM: de la calle*) pavement (*BRIT*), sidewalk (*US*)
Andes ['andes] *nmpl*: **los ~** the Andes
Andorra [an'dorra] *nf* Andorra
andrajo [an'draxo] *nm* rag; **~so, a** *adj*
ragged
anduve *etc* [an'duβe] *vb ver* **andar**
anécdota [a'nekðota] *nf* anecdote, story
anegar [ane'xar] *vt* to flood; (*ahogar*) to drown; **~se** *vr* to drown; (*hundirse*) to sink
anejo, a [a'nexo, a] *adj, nm* = **anexo**
anemia [a'nemja] *nf* anaemia
anestesia [anes'tesja] *nf* (*sustancia*) anaesthetic; (*proceso*) anaesthesia
anexar [anek'sar] *vt* to annex; (*documento*) to attach; **anexión** *nf* annexation; **anexionamiento** *nm* annexation; **anexo, a** *adj* attached ♦ *nm* annexe
anfibio, a [an'fiβjo, a] *adj* amphibious ♦ *nm* amphibian
anfiteatro [anfite'atro] *nm* amphitheatre; (*TEATRO*) dress circle
anfitrión, ona [anfi'trjon, ona] *nm/f* host(ess)
ángel ['anxel] *nm* angel; **~ de la guarda** guardian angel; **tener ~** to be charming; **angelical** *adj*, **angélico, a** *adj* angelic(al)
angina [an'xina] *nf* (*MED*) inflammation of the throat; **~ de pecho** angina; **tener ~s** to have tonsillitis
anglicano, a [angli'kano, a] *adj, nm/f* Anglican
anglosajón, ona [anglosa'xon, ona] *adj* Anglo-Saxon
angosto, a [an'gosto, a] *adj* narrow
anguila [an'gila] *nf* eel
angula [an'gula] *nf* elver, baby eel
ángulo ['angulo] *nm* angle; (*esquina*) corner; (*curva*) bend
angustia [an'gustja] *nf* anguish; **angustiar** *vt* to distress, grieve
anhelar [ane'lar] *vt* to be eager for; (*desear*) to long for, desire ♦ *vi* to pant, gasp; **anhelo** *nm* eagerness; desire
anidar [ani'ðar] *vi* to nest
anillo [a'niʎo] *nm* ring; **~ de boda** wedding ring
animación [anima'θjon] *nf* liveliness; (*vitalidad*) life; (*actividad*) activity; bustle
animado, a [ani'maðo, a] *adj* lively;

(*vivaz*) animated; **animador, a** *nm/f*
(*TV*) host(ess), compère; (*DEPORTE*)
cheerleader

animadversión [animaðßer'sjon] *nf* ill-
will, antagonism

animal [ani'mal] *adj* animal; (*fig*) stupid
♦ *nm* animal; (*fig*) fool; (*bestia*) brute

animar [ani'mar] *vt* (*BIO*) to animate, give
life to; (*fig*) to liven up, brighten up,
cheer up; (*estimular*) to stimulate; **~se** *vr*
to cheer up; to feel encouraged;
(*decidirse*) to make up one's mind

ánimo ['animo] *nm* (*alma*) soul; (*mente*)
mind; (*valentía*) courage ♦ *excl* cheer up!

animoso, a [ani'moso, a] *adj* brave; (*vivo*)
lively

aniquilar [aniki'lar] *vt* to annihilate,
destroy

anís [a'nis] *nm* aniseed; (*licor*) anisette

aniversario [anißer'sarjo] *nm* anniversary

anoche [a'notʃe] *adv* last night; **antes de**
~ the night before last

anochecer [anotʃe'θer] *vi* to get dark
♦ *nm* nightfall, dark; **al ~** at nightfall

anodino, a [ano'ðino, a] *adj* dull,
anodyne

anomalía [anoma'lia] *nf* anomaly

anonadado, a [anona'ðaðo, a] *adj*:
estar/quedar/sentirse ~ to be
overwhelmed *o* amazed

anonimato [anoni'mato] *nm* anonymity

anónimo, a [a'nonimo, a] *adj*
anonymous; (*COM*) limited ♦ *nm* (*carta*)
anonymous letter; (: *maliciosa*) poison-
pen letter

anormal [anor'mal] *adj* abnormal

anotación [anota'θjon] *nf* note;
annotation

anotar [ano'tar] *vt* to note down;
(*comentar*) to annotate

anquilosamiento [ankilosa'mjento] *nm*
(*fig*) paralysis; stagnation

anquilosarse [ankilo'sarse] *vr* (*fig:
persona*) to get out of touch; (*método,
costumbres*) to go out of date

ansia ['ansja] *nf* anxiety; (*añoranza*)
yearning; **ansiar** *vt* to long for

ansiedad [ansje'ðað] *nf* anxiety

ansioso, a [an'sjoso, a] *adj* anxious;
(*anhelante*) eager; **~ de** *o* **por algo**
greedy for sth

antagónico, a [anta'γoniko, a] *adj*
antagonistic; (*opuesto*) contrasting;
antagonista *nm/f* antagonist

antaño [an'taɲo] *adv* long ago, formerly

Antártico [an'tartiko] *nm*: **el ~** the
Antarctic

ante ['ante] *prep* before, in the presence
of; (*problema etc*) faced with ♦ *nm* (*piel*)
suede; **~ todo** above all

anteanoche [antea'notʃe] *adv* the night
before last

anteayer [antea'jer] *adv* the day before
yesterday

antebrazo [ante'ßraθo] *nm* forearm

antecedente [anteθe'ðente] *adj* previous
♦ *nm* antecedent; **~s** *nmpl* (*JUR*): **~s**
penales criminal record; (*procedencia*)
background

anteceder [anteθe'ðer] *vt* to precede, go
before

antecesor, a [anteθe'sor, a] *nm/f*
predecessor

antedicho, a [ante'ðitʃo, a] *adj*
aforementioned

antelación [antela'θjon] *nf*: **con ~** in
advance

antemano [ante'mano]: **de ~** *adv*
beforehand, in advance

antena [an'tena] *nf* antenna; (*de televisión
etc*) aerial; **~ parabólica** satellite dish

anteojo [ante'oxo] *nm* eyeglass; **~s** *nmpl*
(*AM*) glasses, spectacles

antepasados [antepa'saðos] *nmpl*
ancestors

anteponer [antepo'ner] *vt* to place in
front; (*fig*) to prefer

anteproyecto [antepro'jekto] *nm*
preliminary sketch; (*fig*) blueprint

anterior [ante'rjor] *adj* preceding,
previous; **~idad** *nf*: **con ~idad a** prior to,
before

antes ['antes] *adv* (*con prioridad*) before
♦ *prep*: **~ de** before ♦ *conj*: **~ de ir/de**

que te vayas before going/before you go; **~ bien** (but) rather; **dos días ~** two days before o previously; **no quiso venir ~** she didn't want to come any earlier; **tomo el avión ~ que el barco** I take the plane rather than the boat; **~ que yo** before me; **lo ~ posible** as soon as possible; **cuanto ~ mejor** the sooner the better

antiaéreo, a [antia'ereo, a] *adj* anti-aircraft

antibalas [anti'ßalas] *adj inv*: **chaleco ~** bullet-proof jacket

antibiótico [anti'ßjotiko] *nm* antibiotic

anticipación [antiθipa'θjon] *nf* anticipation; **con 10 minutos de ~** 10 minutes early

anticipado, a [antiθi'paðo, a] *adj* (*pago*) advance; **por ~** in advance

anticipar [antiθi'par] *vt* to anticipate; (*adelantar*) to bring forward; (COM) to advance; **~se** *vr*: **~se a su época** to be ahead of one's time

anticipo [anti'θipo] *nm* (COM) advance

anticonceptivo, a [antikonθep'tißo, a] *adj, nm* contraceptive

anticongelante [antikonxe'lante] *nm* antifreeze

anticuado, a [anti'kwaðo, a] *adj* out-of-date, old-fashioned; (*desusado*) obsolete

anticuario [anti'kwarjo] *nm* antique dealer

anticuerpo [anti'kwerpo] *nm* (MED) antibody

antidepresivo [antiðepre'sißo] *nm* antidepressant

antídoto [an'tiðoto] *nm* antidote

antiestético, a [anties'tetiko, a] *adj* unsightly

antifaz [anti'faθ] *nm* mask; (*velo*) veil

antigualla [anti'ɣwaʎa] *nf* antique; (*reliquia*) relic

antiguamente [antiɣwa'mente] *adv* formerly; (*hace mucho tiempo*) long ago

antigüedad [antiɣwe'ðað] *nf* antiquity; (*artículo*) antique; (*rango*) seniority

antiguo, a [an'tiɣwo, a] *adj* old, ancient; (*que fue*) former

Antillas [an'tiʎas] *nfpl*: **las ~** the West Indies

antílope [an'tilope] *nm* antelope

antinatural [antinatu'ral] *adj* unnatural

antipatía [antipa'tia] *nf* antipathy, dislike; **antipático, a** *adj* disagreeable, unpleasant

antirrobo [anti'rroßo] *adj inv* (*alarma etc*) anti-theft

antisemita [antise'mita] *adj* anti-Semitic ♦ *nm/f* anti-Semite

antiséptico, a [anti'septiko, a] *adj* antiseptic ♦ *nm* antiseptic

antítesis [an'titesis] *nf inv* antithesis

antojadizo, a [antoxa'ðiθo, a] *adj* capricious

antojarse [anto'xarse] *vr* (*desear*): **se me antoja comprarlo** I have a mind to buy it; (*pensar*): **se me antoja que** I have a feeling that

antojo [an'toxo] *nm* caprice, whim; (*rosa*) birthmark; (*lunar*) mole

antología [antolo'xia] *nf* anthology

antorcha [an'tortʃa] *nf* torch

antro ['antro] *nm* cavern

antropófago, a [antro'pofaɣo, a] *adj, nm/f* cannibal

antropología [antropolo'xia] *nf* anthropology

anual [a'nwal] *adj* annual

anuario [a'nwarjo] *nm* yearbook

anudar [anu'ðar] *vt* to knot, tie; (*unir*) to join; **~se** *vr* to get tied up

anulación [anula'θjon] *nf* annulment; (*cancelación*) cancellation

anular [anu'lar] *vt* (*contrato*) to annul, cancel; (*ley*) to revoke, repeal; (*suscripción*) to cancel ♦ *nm* ring finger

Anunciación [anunθja'θjon] *nf* (REL) Annunciation

anunciante [anun'θjante] *nm/f* (COM) advertiser

anunciar [anun'θjar] *vt* to announce; (*proclamar*) to proclaim; (COM) to advertise

anuncio [a'nunθjo] *nm* announcement; (*señal*) sign; (COM) advertisement; (*cartel*) poster

anzuelo [an'θwelo] *nm* hook; *(para pescar)* fish hook

añadidura [aɲaðiˈðura] *nf* addition, extra; **por ~** besides, in addition

añadir [aɲaˈðir] *vt* to add

añejo, a [aˈɲexo, a] *adj* old; *(vino)* mellow

añicos [aˈɲikos] *nmpl:* **hacer ~** to smash, shatter

añil [aˈɲil] *nm* (BOT, color) indigo

año [ˈaɲo] *nm* year; **¡Feliz A~ Nuevo!** Happy New Year!; **tener 15 ~s** to be 15 (years old); **los ~s 90** the nineties; **~ bisiesto/escolar** leap/school year; **el ~ que viene** next year

añoranza [aɲoˈranθa] *nf* nostalgia; *(anhelo)* longing

apabullar [apaβuˈʎar] *vt* (tb fig) to crush, squash

apacentar [apaθenˈtar] *vt* to pasture, graze

apacible [apaˈθiβle] *adj* gentle, mild

apaciguar [apaθiˈɣwar] *vt* to pacify, calm (down)

apadrinar [apaðriˈnar] *vt* to sponsor, support; (REL) to be godfather to

apagado, a [apaˈɣaðo, a] *adj (volcán)* extinct; *(color)* dull; *(voz)* quiet; *(sonido)* muted, muffled; *(persona: apático)* listless; **estar ~** *(fuego, luz)* to be out; (RADIO, TV etc) to be off

apagar [apaˈɣar] *vt* to put out; (ELEC, RADIO, TV) to turn off; *(sonido)* to silence, muffle; *(sed)* to quench

apagón [apaˈɣon] *nm* blackout; power cut

apalabrar [apalaˈβrar] *vt* to agree to; *(contratar)* to engage

apalear [apaleˈar] *vt* to beat, thrash

apañar [apaˈɲar] *vt* to pick up; *(asir)* to take hold of, grasp; *(reparar)* to mend, patch up; **~se** *vr* to manage, get along

aparador [aparaˈðor] *nm* sideboard; (AM: escaparate) shop window

aparato [apaˈrato] *nm* apparatus; *(máquina)* machine; *(doméstico)* appliance; *(boato)* ostentation; **~ de facsímil** facsimile (machine), fax; **~ digestivo** (ANAT) digestive system; **~so,**

a *adj* showy, ostentatious

aparcamiento [aparkaˈmjento] *nm* car park (BRIT), parking lot (US)

aparcar [aparˈkar] *vt, vi* to park

aparear [apareˈar] *vt (objetos)* to pair, match; *(animales)* to mate; **~se** *vr* to make a pair; to mate

aparecer [apareˈθer] *vi* to appear; **~se** *vr* to appear

aparejado, a [apareˈxaðo, a] *adj* fit, suitable; **llevar** *o* **traer ~** to involve; **aparejador, a** *nm/f* (ARQ) master builder

aparejo [apaˈrexo] *nm* harness; rigging; *(de poleas)* block and tackle

aparentar [aparenˈtar] *vt (edad)* to look; *(fingir):* **~ tristeza** to pretend to be sad

aparente [apaˈrente] *adj* apparent; *(adecuado)* suitable

aparezco etc vb ver **aparecer**

aparición [apariˈθjon] *nf* appearance; *(de libro)* publication; *(espectro)* apparition

apariencia [apaˈrjenθja] *nf* (outward) appearance; **en ~** outwardly, seemingly

apartado, a [aparˈtaðo, a] *adj* separate; *(lejano)* remote ♦ *nm (tipográfico)* paragraph; **~ (de correos)** post office box

apartamento [apartaˈmento] *nm* apartment, flat (BRIT)

apartamiento [apartaˈmjento] *nm* separation; *(aislamiento)* remoteness, isolation; (AM) apartment, flat (BRIT)

apartar [aparˈtar] *vt* to separate; *(quitar)* to remove; **~se** *vr* to separate, part; *(irse)* to move away; to keep away

aparte [aˈparte] *adv (separadamente)* separately; *(además)* besides ♦ *nm* aside; *(tipográfico)* new paragraph

aparthotel [apartoˈtel] *nm* serviced apartments

apasionado, a [apasjoˈnaðo, a] *adj* passionate

apasionar [apasjoˈnar] *vt* to excite; **le apasiona el fútbol** she's crazy about football; **~se** *vr* to get excited

apatía [apaˈtia] *nf* apathy

apático, a [aˈpatiko, a] *adj* apathetic

Apdo *abr* (= *Apartado (de Correos)*) PO Box

apeadero [apea'ðero] *nm* halt, stop, stopping place

apearse [ape'arse] *vr* (*jinete*) to dismount; (*bajarse*) to get down *o* out; (*AUTO, FERRO*) to get off *o* out

apechugar [apetʃu'var] *vr*: **~ con algo** to face up to sth

apedrear [apeðre'ar] *vt* to stone

apegarse [ape'varse] *vr*: **~ a** to become attached to; **apego** *nm* attachment, devotion

apelación [apela'θjon] *nf* appeal

apelar [ape'lar] *vi* to appeal; **~ a** (*fig*) to resort to

apellidar [apeʎi'ðar] *vt* to call, name; **~se** *vr*: **se apellida Pérez** her (sur)name's Pérez

apellido [ape'ʎiðo] *nm* surname

apelmazarse [apelma'θarse] *vr* (*masa, arroz*) to go hard; (*prenda de lana*) to shrink

apenar [ape'nar] *vt* to grieve, trouble; (*AM: avergonzar*) to embarrass; **~se** *vr* to grieve, sadden; (*AM*) to be embarrassed

apenas [a'penas] *adv* scarcely, hardly ♦ *conj* as soon as, no sooner

apéndice [a'pendiθe] *nm* appendix; **apendicitis** *nf* appendicitis

aperitivo [aperi'tiβo] *nm* (*bebida*) aperitif; (*comida*) appetizer

apero [a'pero] *nm* (*AGR*) implement; **~s** *nmpl* farm equipment *sg*

apertura [aper'tura] *nf* opening; (*POL*) liberalization

apesadumbrar [apesaðum'brar] *vt* to grieve, sadden; **~se** *vr* to distress o.s.

apestar [apes'tar] *vt* to infect ♦ *vi*: **~ (a)** to stink (of)

apetecer [apete'θer] *vt*: **¿te apetece un café?** do you fancy a (cup of) coffee?; **apetecible** *adj* desirable; (*comida*) appetizing

apetito [ape'tito] *nm* appetite; **~so, a** *adj* appetizing; (*fig*) tempting

apiadarse [apja'ðarse] *vr*: **~ de** to take

pity on

ápice ['apiθe] *nm* whit, iota

apilar [api'lar] *vt* to pile *o* heap up; **~se** *vr* to pile up

apiñarse [api'ɲarse] *vr* to crowd *o* press together

apio ['apjo] *nm* celery

apisonadora [apisona'ðora] *nf* steamroller

aplacar [apla'kar] *vt* to placate; **~se** *vr* to calm down

aplanar [apla'nar] *vt* to smooth, level; (*allanar*) to roll flat, flatten

aplastante [aplas'tante] *adj* overwhelming; (*lógica*) compelling

aplastar [aplas'tar] *vt* to squash (flat); (*fig*) to crush

aplatanarse [aplata'narse] *vr* to get lethargic

aplaudir [aplau'ðir] *vt* to applaud

aplauso [a'plauso] *nm* applause; (*fig*) approval, acclaim

aplazamiento [aplaθa'mjento] *nm* postponement

aplazar [apla'θar] *vt* to postpone, defer

aplicación [aplika'θjon] *nf* application; (*esfuerzo*) effort

aplicado, a [apli'kaðo, a] *adj* diligent, hard-working

aplicar [apli'kar] *vt* (*ejecutar*) to apply; **~se** *vr* to apply o.s.

aplique *etc* [a'plike] *vb ver* **aplicar** ♦ *nm* wall light

aplomo [a'plomo] *nm* aplomb, self-assurance

apocado, a [apo'kaðo, a] *adj* timid

apodar [apo'ðar] *vt* to nickname

apoderado [apoðe'raðo] *nm* agent, representative

apoderarse [apoðe'rarse] *vr*: **~ de** to take possession of

apodo [a'poðo] *nm* nickname

apogeo [apo'xeo] *nm* peak, summit

apolillarse [apoli'ʎarse] *vr* to get moth-eaten

apología [apolo'xia] *nf* eulogy; (*defensa*) defence

apoltronarse [apoltro'narse] *vr* to get

lazy

apoplejía [apople'xia] *nf* apoplexy, stroke

apoquinar [apoki'nar] *(fam) vt* to fork out, cough up

aporrear [aporre'ar] *vt* to beat (up)

aportar [apor'tar] *vt* to contribute ♦ *vi* to reach port; **~se** *vr (AM: llegar)* to arrive, come

aposento [apo'sento] *nm* lodging; *(habitación)* room

aposta [a'posta] *adv* deliberately, on purpose

apostar [apos'tar] *vt* to bet, stake; *(tropas etc)* to station, post ♦ *vi* to bet

apóstol [a'postol] *nm* apostle

apóstrofo [a'postrofo] *nm* apostrophe

apoyar [apo'jar] *vt* to lean, rest; *(fig)* to support, back; **~se** *vr:* **~se en** to lean on; **apoyo** *nm (gen)* support; backing, help

apreciable [apre'θjaßle] *adj* considerable; *(fig)* esteemed

apreciar [apre'θjar] *vt* to evaluate, assess; *(COM)* to appreciate, value; *(persona)* to respect; *(tamaño)* to gauge, assess; *(detalles)* to notice

aprecio [a'preθjo] *nm* valuation, estimate; *(fig)* appreciation

aprehender [apreen'der] *vt* to apprehend, detain

apremiante [apre'mjante] *adj* urgent, pressing

apremiar [apre'mjar] *vt* to compel, force ♦ *vi* to be urgent, press; **apremio** *nm* urgency

aprender [apren'der] *vt, vi* to learn

aprendiz, a [apren'diθ, a] *nm/f* apprentice; *(principiante)* learner; **~ de conductor** learner driver; **~aje** *nm* apprenticeship

aprensión [apren'sjon] *nm* apprehension, fear; **aprensivo, a** *adj* apprehensive

apresar [apre'sar] *vt* to seize; *(capturar)* to capture

aprestar [apres'tar] *vt* to prepare, get ready; *(TEC)* to prime, size; **~se** *vr* to get ready

apresurado, a [apresu'raðo, a] *adj*

hurried, hasty; **apresuramiento** *nm* hurry, haste

apresurar [apresu'rar] *vt* to hurry, accelerate; **~se** *vr* to hurry, make haste

apretado, a [apre'taðo, a] *adj* tight; *(escritura)* cramped

apretar [apre'tar] *vt* to squeeze; *(TEC)* to tighten; *(presionar)* to press together, pack ♦ *vi* to be too tight

apretón [apre'ton] *nm* squeeze; **~ de manos** handshake

aprieto [a'prjeto] *nm* squeeze; *(dificultad)* difficulty; **estar en un ~** to be in a fix

aprisa [a'prisa] *adv* quickly, hurriedly

aprisionar [aprisjo'nar] *vt* to imprison

aprobación [aproßa'θjon] *nf* approval

aprobar [apro'ßar] *vt* to approve (of); *(examen, materia)* to pass ♦ *vi* to pass

apropiación [apropja'θjon] *nf* appropriation

apropiado, a [apro'pjaðo, a] *adj* suitable

apropiarse [apro'pjarse] *vr:* **~ de** to appropriate

aprovechado, a [aproße'tʃaðo, a] *adj* industrious, hard-working; *(económico)* thrifty; *(pey)* unscrupulous; **aprovechamiento** *nm* use; exploitation

aprovechar [aproße'tʃar] *vt* to use; *(explotar)* to exploit; *(experiencia)* to profit from; *(oferta, oportunidad)* to take advantage of ♦ *vi* to progress, improve; **~se** *vr:* **~se de** to make use of; to take advantage of; **¡que aproveche!** enjoy your meal!

aproximación [aproksima'θjon] *nf* approximation; *(de lotería)* consolation prize; **aproximado, a** *adj* approximate

aproximar [aproksi'mar] *vt* to bring nearer; **~se** *vr* to come near, approach

apruebo *etc vb ver* **aprobar**

aptitud [apti'tuθ] *nf* aptitude

apto, a ['apto, a] *adj* suitable

apuesta [a'pwesta] *nf* bet, wager

apuesto, a [a'pwesto, a] *adj* neat, elegant

apuntador [apunta'ðor] *nm* prompter

apuntalar [apunta'lar] *vt* to prop up

apuntar [apun'tar] *vt* (*con arma*) to aim at; (*con dedo*) to point at *o* to; (*anotar*) to note (down); (*TEATRO*) to prompt; **~se** *vr* (*DEPORTE: tanto, victoria*) to score; (*ESCOL*) to enrol

apunte [a'punte] *nm* note

apuñalar [apuɲa'lar] *vt* to stab

apurado, a [apu'raðo, a] *adj* needy; (*difícil*) difficult; (*peligroso*) dangerous; (*AM*) hurried, rushed

apurar [apu'rar] *vt* (*agotar*) to drain; (*recursos*) to use up; (*molestar*) to annoy; **~se** *vr* (*preocuparse*) to worry; (*darse prisa*) to hurry

apuro [a'puro] *nm* (*aprieto*) fix, jam; (*escasez*) want, hardship; (*vergüenza*) embarrassment; (*AM*) haste, urgency

aquejado, a [ake'xaðo, a] *adj*: **~ de** (*MED*) afflicted by

aquél, aquélla [a'kel, a'keʎa] (*pl* **aquéllos, as**) *pron* that (one); (*pl*) those (ones)

aquel, aquella [a'kel, a'keʎa] (*pl* **aquellos, as**) *adj* that; (*pl*) those

aquello [a'keʎo] *pron* that, that business

aquí [a'ki] *adv* (*lugar*) here; (*tiempo*) now; **~ arriba** up here; **~ mismo** right here; **~ yace** here lies; **de ~ a siete días** a week from now

aquietar [akje'tar] *vt* to quieten (down), calm (down)

ara ['ara] *nf*: **en ~s de** for the sake of

árabe ['araβe] *adj, nm/f* Arab ♦ *nm* (*LING*) Arabic

Arabia [a'raβja] *nf*: **~ Saudí** *o* **Saudita** Saudi Arabia

arado [a'raðo] *nm* plough

Aragón [ara'ɣon] *nm* Aragon; **aragonés, esa** *adj, nm/f* Aragonese

arancel [aran'θel] *nm* tariff, duty; **~ de aduanas** customs (duty)

arandela [aran'dela] *nf* (*TEC*) washer

araña [a'raɲa] *nf* (*ZOOL*) spider; (*lámpara*) chandelier

arañar [ara'ɲar] *vt* to scratch

arañazo [ara'ɲaθo] *nm* scratch

arar [a'rar] *vt* to plough, till

arbitraje [arβi'traxe] *nm* arbitration

arbitrar [arβi'trar] *vt* to arbitrate in; (*DEPORTE*) to referee ♦ *vi* to arbitrate

arbitrariedad [arβitrarje'ðað] *nf* arbitrariness; (*acto*) arbitrary act; **arbitrario, a** *adj* arbitrary

arbitrio [ar'βitrjo] *nm* free will; (*JUR*) adjudication, decision

árbitro ['arβitro] *nm* arbitrator; (*DEPORTE*) referee; (*TENIS*) umpire

árbol ['arβol] *nm* (*BOT*) tree; (*NAUT*) mast; (*TEC*) axle, shaft; **arbolado, a** *adj* wooded; (*camino etc*) tree-lined ♦ *nm* woodland

arboleda [arβo'leða] *nf* grove, plantation

arbusto [ar'βusto] *nm* bush, shrub

arca ['arka] *nf* chest, box

arcada [ar'kaða] *nf* arcade; (*de puente*) arch, span; **~s** *nfpl* (*náuseas*) retching *sg*

arcaico, a [ar'kaiko, a] *adj* archaic

arce ['arθe] *nm* maple tree

arcén [ar'θen] *nm* (*de autopista*) hard shoulder; (*de carretera*) verge

archipiélago [artʃi'pjelaɣo] *nm* archipelago

archivador [artʃiβa'ðor] *nm* filing cabinet

archivar [artʃi'βar] *vt* to file (away); **archivo** *nm* file, archive(s) (*pl*)

arcilla [ar'θiʎa] *nf* clay

arco ['arko] *nm* arch; (*MAT*) arc; (*MIL, MUS*) bow; **~ iris** rainbow

arder [ar'ðer] *vi* to burn; **estar que arde** (*persona*) to fume

ardid [ar'ðið] *nm* ploy, trick

ardiente [ar'ðjente] *adj* burning, ardent

ardilla [ar'ðiʎa] *nf* squirrel

ardor [ar'ðor] *nm* (*calor*) heat; (*fig*) ardour; **~ de estómago** heartburn

arduo, a ['arðwo, a] *adj* arduous

área ['area] *nf* area; (*DEPORTE*) penalty area

arena [a'rena] *nf* sand; (*de una lucha*) arena; **~s movedizas** quicksand *sg*

arenal [are'nal] *nm* (*arena movediza*) quicksand

arengar [aren'gar] *vt* to harangue

arenisca [are'niska] *nf* sandstone; (*cascajo*) grit

arenoso, a [are'noso, a] *adj* sandy

arenque [a'renke] *nm* herring

argamasa [arɣa'masa] *nf* mortar, plaster

Argel [ar'xel] *n* Algiers; **Argelia** *nf* Algeria; **argelino, a** *adj, nm/f* Algerian

Argentina [arxen'tina] *nf*: **(la)** ~ Argentina

argentino, a [arxen'tino, a] *adj* Argentinian; *(de plata)* silvery ♦ *nm/f* Argentinian

argolla [ar'voʎa] *nf* (large) ring

argot [ar'vo] *(pl* ~**s)** *nm* slang

argucia [ar'vuθja] *nf* subtlety, sophistry

argüir [ar'vwir] *vt* to deduce; *(discutir)* to argue; *(indicar)* to indicate, imply; *(censurar)* to reproach ♦ *vi* to argue

argumentación [arvumenta'θjon] *nf* (line of) argument

argumentar [arvumen'tar] *vt, vi* to argue

argumento [arvu'mento] *nm* argument; *(razonamiento)* reasoning; *(de novela etc)* plot; *(CINE, TV)* storyline

aria ['arja] *nf* aria

aridez [ari'ðeθ] *nf* aridity, dryness

árido, a ['ariðo, a] *adj* arid, dry; ~**s** *nmpl* *(COM)* dry goods

Aries ['arjes] *nm* Aries

ario, a ['arjo, a] *adj* Aryan

arisco, a [a'risko, a] *adj* surly; *(insociable)* unsociable

aristócrata [aris'tokrata] *nm/f* aristocrat

aritmética [arit'metika] *nf* arithmetic

arma ['arma] *nf* arm; ~**s** *nfpl* arms; ~ **blanca** blade, knife; *(espada)* sword; ~ **de fuego** firearm; ~**s cortas** small arms

armada [ar'maða] *nf* armada; *(flota)* fleet

armadillo [arma'ðiʎo] *nm* armadillo

armado, a [ar'maðo, a] *adj* armed; *(TEC)* reinforced

armador [arma'ðor] *nm* *(NAUT)* shipowner

armadura [arma'ðura] *nf* *(MIL)* armour; *(TEC)* framework; *(ZOOL)* skeleton; *(FÍSICA)* armature

armamento [arma'mento] *nm* armament; *(NAUT)* fitting-out

armar [ar'mar] *vt* *(soldado)* to arm; *(máquina)* to assemble; *(navío)* to fit out; ~**la**, ~ **un lío** to start a row, kick up a fuss

armario [ar'marjo] *nm* wardrobe; *(de cocina, baño)* cupboard

armatoste [arma'toste] *nm* *(mueble)* monstrosity; *(máquina)* contraption

armazón [arma'θon] *nf o m* body, chassis; *(de mueble etc)* frame; *(ARQ)* skeleton

armería [arme'ria] *nf* gunsmith's

armiño [ar'miɲo] *nm* stoat; *(piel)* ermine

armisticio [armis'tiθjo] *nm* armistice

armonía [armo'nia] *nf* harmony

armónica [ar'monika] *nf* harmonica

armonioso, a [armo'njoso, a] *adj* harmonious

armonizar [armoni'θar] *vt* to harmonize; *(diferencias)* to reconcile ♦ *vi*: ~ **con** *(fig)* to be in keeping with; *(colores)* to tone in with, blend

arnés [ar'nes] *nm* armour; **arneses** *nmpl* *(de caballo etc)* harness *sg*

aro ['aro] *nm* ring; *(tejo)* quoit; *(AM: pendiente)* earring

aroma [a'roma] *nm* aroma, scent

aromático, a [aro'matiko, a] *adj* aromatic

arpa ['arpa] *nf* harp

arpía [ar'pia] *nf* shrew

arpillera [arpi'ʎera] *nf* sacking, sackcloth

arpón [ar'pon] *nm* harpoon

arquear [arke'ar] *vt* to arch, bend; ~**se** *vr* to arch, bend

arqueología [arkeolo'xia] *nf* archaeology; **arqueólogo, a** *nm/f* archaeologist

arquero [ar'kero] *nm* archer, bowman

arquetipo [arke'tipo] *nm* archetype

arquitecto [arki'tekto] *nm* architect; **arquitectura** *nf* architecture

arrabal [arra'ßal] *nm* suburb; *(AM)* slum; ~**es** *nmpl* *(afueras)* outskirts

arraigado, a [arrai'vaðo, a] *adj* deep-rooted; *(fig)* established

arraigar [arrai'var] *vt* to establish ♦ *vi* to take root; ~**se** *vr* to take root; *(persona)* to settle

arrancar [arran'kar] *vt* *(sacar)* to extract, pull out; *(arrebatar)* to snatch (away); *(INFORM)* to boot; *(fig)* to extract ♦ *vi* *(AUTO, máquina)* to start; *(ponerse en marcha)* to get going; ~ **de** to stem from

arranque *etc* [a'rranke] *vb ver* **arrancar**
♦ *nm* sudden start; (*AUTO*) start; (*fig*) fit, outburst
arrasar [arra'sar] *vt* (*aplanar*) to level, flatten; (*destruir*) to demolish
arrastrado, a [arras'traðo, a] *adj* poor, wretched; (*AM*) servile
arrastrar [arras'trar] *vt* to drag (along); (*fig*) to drag down, degrade; (*suj: agua, viento*) to carry away ♦ *vi* to drag, trail on the ground; **~se** *vr* to crawl; (*fig*) to grovel; **llevar algo arrastrado** to drag sth along
arrastre [a'rrastre] *nm* drag, dragging
arre ['arre] *excl* gee up!
arrear [arre'ar] *vt* to drive on, urge on ♦ *vi* to hurry along
arrebatado, a [arreβa'taðo, a] *adj* rash, impetuous; (*repentino*) sudden, hasty
arrebatar [arreβa'tar] *vt* to snatch (away), seize; (*fig*) to captivate; **~se** *vr* to get carried away, get excited
arrebato [arre'βato] *nm* fit of rage, fury; (*éxtasis*) rapture
arrecife [arre'θife] *nm* (*tb: ~ de coral*) reef
arredrarse [arre'ðrarse] *vr:* **~ (ante algo)** to be intimidated (by sth)
arreglado, a [arre'ɣlaðo, a] *adj* (*ordenado*) neat, orderly; (*moderado*) moderate, reasonable
arreglar [arre'ɣlar] *vt* (*poner orden*) to tidy up; (*algo roto*) to fix, repair; (*problema*) to solve; **~se** *vr* to reach an understanding; **arreglárselas** (*fam*) to get by, manage
arreglo [a'rreɣlo] *nm* settlement; (*orden*) order; (*acuerdo*) agreement; (*MUS*) arrangement, setting
arrellanarse [arreʎa'narse] *vr:* **~ en** to sit back in/on
arremangar [arreman'gar] *vt* to roll up, turn up; **~se** *vr* to roll up one's sleeves
arremeter [arreme'ter] *vi:* **~ contra** to attack, rush at
arrendamiento [arrenda'mjento] *nm* letting; (*alquilar*) hiring; (*contrato*) lease; (*alquiler*) rent; **arrendar** *vt* to let, lease; to rent; **arrendatario, a** *nm/f* tenant

arreos [a'rreos] *nmpl* (*de caballo*) harness *sg*, trappings
arrepentimiento [arrepenti'mjento] *nm* regret, repentance
arrepentirse [arrepen'tirse] *vr* to repent; **~ de** to regret
arrestar [arres'tar] *vt* to arrest; (*encarcelar*) to imprison; **arresto** *nm* arrest; (*MIL*) detention; (*audacia*) boldness, daring; **arresto domiciliario** house arrest
arriar [a'rrjar] *vt* (*velas*) to haul down; (*bandera*) to lower, strike; (*cable*) to pay out

┌─────────────────────────┐
│ *PALABRA CLAVE* │
└─────────────────────────┘

arriba [a'rriβa] *adv* **1** (*posición*) above; **desde ~** from above; **~ de todo** at the very top, right on top; **Juan está ~** Juan is upstairs; **lo ~ mencionado** the aforementioned
2 (*dirección*): **calle ~** up the street
3: **de ~ abajo** from top to bottom; **mirar a uno de ~ abajo** to look sb up and down
4: **para ~: de 5000 pesetas para ~** from 5000 pesetas up(wards)
♦ *adj*: **de ~: el piso de ~** the upstairs flat (*BRIT*) *o* apartment; **la parte de ~** the top *o* upper part
♦ *prep*: **~ de** (*AM*) above; **~ de 200 dólares** more than 200 dollars
♦ *excl*: **¡~!** up!; **¡manos ~!** hands up!; **¡~ España!** long live Spain!

arribar [arri'βar] *vi* to put into port; (*llegar*) to arrive
arribista [arri'βista] *nm/f* parvenu(e), upstart
arriendo *etc* [a'rrjendo] *vb ver* **arrendar**
♦ *nm* = **arrendamiento**
arriero [a'rrjero] *nm* muleteer
arriesgado, a [arrjes'ɣaðo, a] *adj* (*peligroso*) risky; (*audaz*) bold, daring
arriesgar [arrjes'ɣar] *vt* to risk; (*poner en peligro*) to endanger; **~se** *vr* to take a risk
arrimar [arri'mar] *vt* (*acercar*) to bring close; (*poner de lado*) to set aside; **~se** *vr*

to come close o closer; **~se a** to lean on

arrinconar [arrinko'nar] vt (colocar) to put in a corner; (enemigo) to corner; (fig) to put on one side; (abandonar) to push aside

arrodillarse [arroði'ʎarse] vr to kneel (down)

arrogancia [arro'ɣanθja] nf arrogance; **arrogante** adj arrogant

arrojar [arro'xar] vt to throw, hurl; (humo) to emit, give out; (COM) to yield, produce; **~se** vr to throw o hurl o.s.

arrojo [a'rroxo] nm daring

arrollador, a [arroʎa'ðor, a] adj overwhelming

arrollar [arro'ʎar] vt (AUTO etc) to run over, knock down; (DEPORTE) to crush

arropar [arro'par] vt to cover, wrap up; **~se** vr to wrap o.s. up

arroyo [a'rrojo] nm stream; (de la calle) gutter

arroz [a'rroθ] nm rice; **~ con leche** rice pudding

arruga [a'rruɣa] nf (de cara) wrinkle; (de vestido) crease

arrugar [arru'ɣar] vt to wrinkle; to crease; **~se** vr to get creased

arruinar [arrwi'nar] vt to ruin, wreck; **~se** vr to be ruined, go bankrupt

arrullar [arru'ʎar] vi to coo ♦ vt to lull to sleep

arsenal [arse'nal] nm naval dockyard; (MIL) arsenal

arsénico [ar'seniko] nm arsenic

arte ['arte] (gen m en sg y siempre f en pl) nm art; (maña) skill, guile; **~s** nfpl (bellas ~s) arts

artefacto [arte'fakto] nm appliance

arteria [ar'terja] nf artery

artesanía [artesa'nia] nf craftsmanship; (artículos) handicrafts pl; **artesano, a** nm/f artisan, craftsman/woman

ártico, a ['artiko, a] adj Arctic ♦ nm: **el Á~** the Arctic

articulación [artikula'θjon] nf articulation; (MED, TEC) joint; **articulado, a** adj articulated; jointed

articular [artiku'lar] vt to articulate; to join together

artículo [ar'tikulo] nm article; (cosa) thing, article; **~s** nmpl (COM) goods

artífice [ar'tifiθe] nm/f (fig) architect

artificial [artifi'θjal] adj artificial

artificio [arti'fiθjo] nm art, skill; (astucia) cunning

artillería [artiʎe'ria] nf artillery

artillero [arti'ʎero] nm artilleryman, gunner

artilugio [arti'luxjo] nm gadget

artimaña [arti'maɲa] nf trap, snare; (astucia) cunning

artista [ar'tista] nm/f (pintor) artist, painter; (TEATRO) artist, artiste; **~ de cine** film actor/actress; **artístico, a** adj artistic

artritis [ar'tritis] nf arthritis

arveja [ar'βexa] (AM) nf pea

arzobispo [arθo'βispo] nm archbishop

as [as] nm ace

asa ['asa] nf handle; (fig) lever

asado [a'saðo] nm roast (meat); (AM: barbacoa) barbecue

asador [asa'ðor] nm spit

asadura [asa'ðura] nf entrails pl, offal

asalariado, a [asala'rjaðo, a] adj paid, salaried ♦ nm/f wage earner

asaltante [asal'tante] nm/f attacker

asaltar [asal'tar] vt to attack, assault; (fig) to assail; **asalto** nm attack, assault; (DEPORTE) round

asamblea [asam'blea] nf assembly; (reunión) meeting

asar [a'sar] vt to roast

asbesto [as'βesto] nm asbestos

ascendencia [asθen'denθja] nf ancestry; (AM) ascendancy; **de ~ francesa** of French origin

ascender [asθen'der] vi (subir) to ascend, rise; (ser promovido) to gain promotion ♦ vt to promote; **~ a** to amount to; **ascendiente** nm influence ♦ nm/f ancestor

ascensión [asθen'sjon] nf ascent; (REL): **la A~** the Ascension

ascenso [as'θenso] *nm* ascent; (*promoción*) promotion

ascensor [asθen'sor] *nm* lift (*BRIT*), elevator (*US*)

ascético, a [as'θetiko, a] *adj* ascetic

asco ['asko] *nm*: **¡qué ~!** how revolting *o* disgusting; **el ajo me da ~** I hate *o* loathe garlic; **estar hecho un ~** to be filthy

ascua ['askwa] *nf* ember; **estar en ~s** to be on tenterhooks

aseado, a [ase'aðo, a] *adj* clean; (*arreglado*) tidy; (*pulcro*) smart

asear [ase'ar] *vt* to clean, wash; to tidy (up)

asediar [ase'ðjar] *vt* (*MIL*) to besiege, lay siege to; (*fig*) to chase, pester; **asedio** *nm* siege; (*COM*) run

asegurado, a [aseɣu'raðo, a] *adj* insured

asegurador, a [aseɣura'ðor, a] *nm/f* insurer

asegurar [aseɣu'rar] *vt* (*consolidar*) to secure, fasten; (*dar garantía de*) to guarantee; (*preservar*) to safeguard; (*afirmar, dar por cierto*) to assure, affirm; (*tranquilizar*) to reassure; (*tomar un seguro*) to insure; **~se** *vr* to assure o.s., make sure

asemejarse [aseme'xarse] *vr* to be alike; **~ a** to be like, resemble

asentado, a [asen'taðo, a] *adj* established, settled

asentar [asen'tar] *vt* (*sentar*) to seat, sit down; (*poner*) to place, establish; (*alisar*) to level, smooth down *o* out; (*anotar*) to note down ♦ *vi* to be suitable, suit

asentir [asen'tir] *vi* to assent, agree; **~ con la cabeza** to nod (one's head)

aseo [a'seo] *nm* cleanliness; **~s** *nmpl* (*servicios*) toilet *sg* (*BRIT*), cloakroom *sg* (*BRIT*), restroom *sg* (*US*)

aséptico, a [a'septiko, a] *adj* germ-free, free from infection

asequible [ase'kiβle] *adj* (*precio*) reasonable; (*meta*) attainable; (*persona*) approachable

aserradero [aserra'ðero] *nm* sawmill; **aserrar** *vt* to saw

asesinar [asesi'nar] *vt* to murder; (*POL*) to

assassinate; **asesinato** *nm* murder; assassination

asesino, a [ase'sino, a] *nm/f* murderer, killer; (*POL*) assassin

asesor, a [ase'sor, a] *nm/f* adviser, consultant

asesorar [aseso'rar] *vt* (*JUR*) to advise, give legal advice to; (*COM*) to act as consultant to; **~se** *vr*: **~se con** *o* **de** to take advice from, consult; **asesoría** *nf* (*cargo*) consultancy; (*oficina*) consultant's office

asestar [ases'tar] *vt* (*golpe*) to deal, strike

asfalto [as'falto] *nm* asphalt

asfixia [as'fiksja] *nf* asphyxia, suffocation

asfixiar [asfik'sjar] *vt* to asphyxiate, suffocate; **~se** *vr* to be asphyxiated, suffocate

asgo *etc vb ver* **asir**

así [a'si] *adv* (*de esta manera*) in this way, like this, thus; (*aunque*) although; (*tan pronto como*) as soon as; **~ que** so; **~ como** as well as; **~ y todo** even so; **¿no es ~?** isn't it?, didn't you? *etc*; **~ de grande** this big

Asia ['asja] *nf* Asia; **asiático, a** *adj, nm/f* Asian, Asiatic

asidero [asi'ðero] *nm* handle

asiduidad [asiðwi'ðað] *nf* assiduousness; **asiduo, a** *adj* assiduous; (*frecuente*) frequent ♦ *nm/f* regular (customer)

asiento [a'sjento] *nm* (*mueble*) seat, chair; (*de coche, en tribunal etc*) seat; (*localidad*) seat, place; (*fundamento*) site; **~ delantero/trasero** front/back seat

asignación [asiɣna'θjon] *nf* (*atribución*) assignment; (*reparto*) allocation; (*sueldo*) salary; **~ (semanal)** pocket money

asignar [asiɣ'nar] *vt* to assign, allocate

asignatura [asiɣna'tura] *nf* subject; course

asilado, a [asi'laðo, a] *nm/f* inmate; (*POL*) refugee

asilo [a'silo] *nm* (*refugio*) asylum, refuge; (*establecimiento*) home, institution; **~ político** political asylum

asimilación [asimila'θjon] *nf* assimilation

asimilar [asimi'lar] *vt* to assimilate

asimismo [asi'mismo] *adv* in the same

way, likewise

asir [a'sir] *vt* to seize, grasp

asistencia [asis'tenθja] *nf* audience; (*MED*) attendance; (*ayuda*) assistance; **asistente** *nm/f* assistant; **los asistentes** those present; **asistente social** social worker

asistido, a [asis'tiðo, a] *adj*: **~ por ordenador** computer-assisted

asistir [asis'tir] *vt* to assist, help ♦ *vi*: **~ a** to attend, be present at

asma ['asma] *nf* asthma

asno ['asno] *nm* donkey; (*fig*) ass

asociación [asoθja'θjon] *nf* association; (*COM*) partnership; **asociado, a** *adj* associate ♦ *nm/f* associate; (*COM*) partner

asociar [aso'θjar] *vt* to associate

asolar [aso'lar] *vt* to destroy

asomar [aso'mar] *vt* to show, stick out ♦ *vi* to appear; **~se** *vr* to appear, show up; **~ la cabeza por la ventana** to put one's head out of the window

asombrar [asom'brar] *vt* to amaze, astonish; **~se** *vr* (*sorprenderse*) to be amazed; (*asustarse*) to get a fright; **asombro** *nm* amazement, astonishment; (*susto*) fright; **asombroso, a** *adj* astonishing, amazing

asomo [a'somo] *nm* hint, sign

aspa ['aspa] *nf* (*cruz*) cross; (*de molino*) sail; **en ~** X-shaped

aspaviento [aspa'ßjento] *nm* exaggerated display of feeling; (*fam*) fuss

aspecto [as'pekto] *nm* (*apariencia*) look, appearance; (*fig*) aspect

aspereza [aspe'reθa] *nf* roughness; (*agrura*) sourness; (*de carácter*) surliness; **áspero, a** *adj* rough; bitter, sour; harsh

aspersión [asper'sjon] *nf* sprinkling

aspiración [aspira'θjon] *nf* breath, inhalation; (*MUS*) short pause; **aspiraciones** *nfpl* (*ambiciones*) aspirations

aspirador [aspira'ðor] *nm* = **aspiradora**

aspiradora [aspira'ðora] *nf* vacuum cleaner, Hoover ®

aspirante [aspi'rante] *nm/f* (*candidato*) candidate; (*DEPORTE*) contender

aspirar [aspi'rar] *vt* to breathe in ♦ *vi*: **~ a** to aspire to

aspirina [aspi'rina] *nf* aspirin

asquear [aske'ar] *vt* to sicken ♦ *vi* to be sickening; **~se** *vr* to feel disgusted; **asqueroso, a** *adj* disgusting, sickening

asta ['asta] *nf* lance; (*arpón*) spear; (*mango*) shaft, handle; (*ZOOL*) horn; **a media ~** at half mast

asterisco [aste'risko] *nm* asterisk

astilla [as'tiʎa] *nf* splinter; (*pedacito*) chip; **~s** *nfpl* (*leña*) firewood *sg*

astillero [asti'ʎero] *nm* shipyard

astringente [astrin'xente] *adj, nm* astringent

astro ['astro] *nm* star

astrología [astrolo'xia] *nf* astrology; **astrólogo, a** *nm/f* astrologer

astronauta [astro'nauta] *nm/f* astronaut

astronave [astro'naße] *nm* spaceship

astronomía [astrono'mia] *nf* astronomy; **astrónomo, a** *nm/f* astronomer

astucia [as'tuθja] *nf* astuteness; (*ardid*) clever trick

asturiano, a [astu'rjano, a] *adj, nm/f* Asturian

astuto, a [as'tuto, a] *adj* astute; (*taimado*) cunning

asumir [asu'mir] *vt* to assume

asunción [asun'θjon] *nf* assumption; (*REL*): **A~** Assumption

asunto [a'sunto] *nm* (*tema*) matter, subject; (*negocio*) business

asustar [asus'tar] *vt* to frighten; **~se** *vr* to be (o become) frightened

atacar [ata'kar] *vt* to attack

atadura [ata'ðura] *nf* bond, tie

atajar [ata'xar] *vt* (*enfermedad, mal*) to stop ♦ *vi* (*persona*) to take a short cut

atajo [a'taxo] *nm* short cut

atañer [ata'ɲer] *vi*: **~ a** to concern

ataque *etc* [a'take] *vb ver* **atacar** ♦ *nm* attack; **~ cardíaco** heart attack

atar [a'tar] *vt* to tie, tie up

atardecer [atarðe'θer] *vi* to get dark ♦ *nm* evening; (*crepúsculo*) dusk

atareado, a [atare'aðo, a] *adj* busy

atascar [atas'kar] *vt* to clog up; (*obstruir*) to jam; (*fig*) to hinder; **~se** *vr* to stall; (*cañería*) to get blocked up; **atasco** *nm* obstruction; (*AUTO*) traffic jam

ataúd [ata'uð] *nm* coffin

ataviar [ata'βjar] *vt* to deck, array; **~se** *vr* to dress up

atavío [ata'βio] *nm* attire, dress; **~s** *nmpl* finery *sg*

atemorizar [atemori'θar] *vt* to frighten, scare; **~se** *vr* to get scared

Atenas [a'tenas] *n* Athens

atención [aten'θjon] *nf* attention; (*bondad*) kindness ♦ *excl* (be) careful!, look out!

atender [aten'der] *vt* to attend to, look after ♦ *vi* to pay attention

atenerse [ate'nerse] *vr*: **~ a** to abide by, adhere to

atentado [aten'taðo] *nm* crime, illegal act; (*asalto*) assault; **~ contra la vida de uno** attempt on sb's life

atentamente [atenta'mente] *adv*: **Le saluda ~** Yours faithfully

atentar [aten'tar] *vi*: **~ a** *o* **contra** to commit an outrage against

atento, a [a'tento, a] *adj* attentive, observant; (*cortés*) polite, thoughtful

atenuante [ate'nwante] *adj* extenuating

atenuar [ate'nwar] *vt* (*disminuir*) to lessen, minimize

ateo, a [a'teo, a] *adj* atheistic ♦ *nm/f* atheist

aterciopelado, a [aterθjope'laðo, a] *adj* velvety

aterido, a [ate'riðo, a] *adj*: **~ de frío** frozen stiff

aterrador, a [aterra'ðor, a] *adj* frightening

aterrar [ate'rrar] *vt* to frighten; to terrify

aterrizaje [aterri'θaxe] *nm* landing

aterrizar [aterri'θar] *vi* to land

aterrorizar [aterrori'θar] *vt* to terrify

atesorar [ateso'rar] *vt* to hoard

atestado, a [ates'taðo, a] *adj* packed ♦ *nm* (*JUR*) affidavit

atestar [ates'tar] *vt* to pack, stuff; (*JUR*) to attest, testify to

atestiguar [atesti'ɣwar] *vt* to testify to, bear witness to

atiborrar [atiβo'rrar] *vt* to fill, stuff; **~se** *vr* to stuff o.s.

ático ['atiko] *nm* attic; **~ de lujo** penthouse (flat (*BRIT*) *o* apartment)

atinado, a [ati'naðo, a] *adj* (*sensato*) wise; (*correcto*) right, correct

atinar [ati'nar] *vi* (*al disparar*): **~ al blanco** to hit the target; (*fig*) to be right

atisbar [atis'βar] *vt* to spy on; (*echar una ojeada*) to peep at

atizar [ati'θar] *vt* to poke; (*horno etc*) to stoke; (*fig*) to stir up, rouse

atlántico, a [at'lantiko, a] *adj* Atlantic ♦ *nm*: **el (océano) A~** the Atlantic (Ocean)

atlas ['atlas] *nm inv* atlas

atleta [at'leta] *nm* athlete; **atlético, a** *adj* athletic; **atletismo** *nm* athletics *sg*

atmósfera [at'mosfera] *nf* atmosphere

atolladero [atoʎa'ðero] *nm* (*fig*) jam, fix

atolondramiento [atolondra'mjento] *nm* bewilderment; (*insensatez*) silliness

atómico, a [a'tomiko, a] *adj* atomic

atomizador [atomiθa'ðor] *nm* atomizer; (*de perfume*) spray

átomo ['atomo] *nm* atom

atónito, a [a'tonito, a] *adj* astonished, amazed

atontado, a [aton'taðo, a] *adj* stunned; (*bobo*) silly, daft

atontar [aton'tar] *vt* to stun; **~se** *vr* to become confused

atormentar [atormen'tar] *vt* to torture; (*molestar*) to torment; (*acosar*) to plague, harass

atornillar [atorni'ʎar] *vt* to screw on *o* down

atosigar [atosi'ɣar] *vt* to harass, pester

atracador, a [atraka'ðor, a] *nm/f* robber

atracar [atra'kar] *vt* (*NAUT*) to moor; (*robar*) to hold up, rob ♦ *vi* to moor; **~se** *vr*: **~se (de)** to stuff o.s. (with)

atracción [atrak'θjon] *nf* attraction

atraco [a'trako] *nm* holdup, robbery

atracón [atra'kon] *nm*: **darse** *o* **pegarse**

un ~ (de) (*fam*) to stuff o.s. (with)
atractivo, a [atrak'tiβo, a] *adj* attractive
♦ *nm* appeal
atraer [atra'er] *vt* to attract
atragantarse [atrayan'tarse] *vr*: **~ (con)** to
choke (on); **se me ha atragantado el
chico** I can't stand the boy
atrancar [atran'kar] *vt* (*puerta*) to bar, bolt
atrapar [atra'par] *vt* to trap; (*resfriado etc*)
to catch
atrás [a'tras] *adv* (*movimiento*) back
(-wards); (*lugar*) behind; (*tiempo*)
previously; **ir hacia ~** to go back(wards);
to go to the rear; **estar ~** to be behind *o*
at the back
atrasado, a [atra'saðo, a] *adj* slow; (*pago*)
overdue, late; (*país*) backward
atrasar [atra'sar] *vi* to be slow; **~se** *vr* to
remain behind; (*tren*) to be *o* run late;
atraso *nm* slowness; lateness, delay; (*de
país*) backwardness; **atrasos** *nmpl* (*COM*)
arrears
atravesar [atraße'sar] *vt* (*cruzar*) to cross
(over); (*traspasar*) to pierce; to go
through; (*poner al través*) to lay *o* put
across; **~se** *vr* to come in between;
(*intervenir*) to interfere
atravieso *etc vb ver* **atravesar**
atrayente [atra'jente] *adj* attractive
atreverse [atre'ßerse] *vr* to dare;
(*insolentarse*) to be insolent; **atrevido, a**
adj daring; insolent; **atrevimiento** *nm*
daring; insolence
atribución [atriβu'θjon] *nf*: **atribuciones**
(*POL*) powers; (*ADMIN*) responsibilities
atribuir [atriβu'ir] *vt* to attribute;
(*funciones*) to confer
atribular [atriβu'lar] *vt* to afflict, distress
atributo [atri'ßuto] *nm* attribute
atril [a'tril] *nm* (*para libro*) lectern; (*MUS*)
music stand
atrocidad [atroθi'ðað] *nf* atrocity, outrage
atropellar [atrope'ʎar] *vt* (*derribar*) to
knock over *o* down; (*empujar*) to push
(aside); (*AUTO*) to run over, run down;
(*agraviar*) to insult; **~se** *vr* to act hastily;
atropello *nm* (*AUTO*) accident; (*empujón*)

push; (*agravio*) wrong; (*atrocidad*) outrage
atroz [a'troθ] *adj* atrocious, awful
ATS *nm/f abr* (= *Ayudante Técnico
Sanitario*) nurse
atto, a *abr* = **atento**
atuendo [a'twendo] *nm* attire
atún [a'tun] *nm* tuna
aturdir [atur'ðir] *vt* to stun; (*de ruido*) to
deafen; (*fig*) to dumbfound, bewilder
atusar [atu'sar] *vt* to smooth (down)
audacia [au'ðaθja] *nf* boldness, audacity;
audaz *adj* bold, audacious
audible [au'ðißle] *adj* audible
audición [auði'θjon] *nf* hearing; (*TEATRO*)
audition
audiencia [au'ðjenθja] *nf* audience; **A~**
(*JUR*) High Court
audífono [au'ðifono] *nm* (*para sordos*)
hearing aid
auditor [auði'tor] *nm* (*JUR*) judge advocate;
(*COM*) auditor
auditorio [auði'torjo] *nm* audience; (*sala*)
auditorium
auge ['auxe] *nm* boom; (*clímax*) climax
augurar [auɣu'rar] *vt* to predict;
(*presagiar*) to portend
augurio [au'ɣurjo] *nm* omen
aula ['aula] *nf* classroom; (*en universidad
etc*) lecture room
aullar [au'ʎar] *vi* to howl, yell
aullido [au'ʎiðo] *nm* howl, yell
aumentar [aumen'tar] *vt* to increase;
(*precios*) to put up; (*producción*) to step
up; (*con microscopio, anteojos*) to magnify
♦ *vi* to increase, be on the increase; **~se**
vr to increase, be on the increase;
aumento *nm* increase; rise
aun [a'un] *adv* even; **~ así** even so; **~ más**
even *o* yet more
aún [a'un] *adv*: **~ está aquí** he's still here;
~ no lo sabemos we don't know yet;
¿no ha venido ~? hasn't she come yet?
aunque [a'unke] *conj* though, although,
even though
aúpa [a'upa] *excl* come on!
aureola [aure'ola] *nf* halo
auricular [auriku'lar] *nm* (*TEL*) earpiece,

receiver; **~es** *nmpl* (*para escuchar música etc*) headphones

aurora [au'rora] *nf* dawn

auscultar [auskul'tar] *vt* (*MED: pecho*) to listen to, sound

ausencia [au'senθja] *nf* absence

ausentarse [ausen'tarse] *vr* to go away; (*por poco tiempo*) to go out

ausente [au'sente] *adj* absent

auspicios [aus'piθjos] *nmpl* auspices

austero, a [aus'tero, a] *adj* austere

austral [aus'tral] *adj* southern ♦ *nm* monetary unit of Argentina

Australia [aus'tralja] *nf* Australia; **australiano, a** *adj, nm/f* Australian

Austria ['austrja] *nf* Austria; **austríaco, a** *adj, nm/f* Austrian

auténtico, a [au'tentiko, a] *adj* authentic

auto ['auto] *nm* (*JUR*) edict, decree; (: *orden*) writ; (*AUTO*) car; **~s** *nmpl* (*JUR*) proceedings; (: *acta*) court record *sg*

autoadhesivo [autoaðe'siβo] *adj* self-adhesive; (*sobre*) self-sealing

autobiografía [autoβjoɣra'fia] *nf* autobiography

autobronceador [autoβronθea'ðor] *adj* self-tanning

autobús [auto'βus] *nm* bus

autocar [auto'kar] *nm* coach (*BRIT*), (passenger) bus (*US*)

autóctono, a [au'toktono, a] *adj* native

autodefensa [autoðe'fensa] *nf* self-defence

autodeterminación [autoðetermina'θjon] *nf* self-determination

autodidacta [autoði'ðakta] *adj* self-taught

autoescuela [autoes'kwela] *nf* driving school

autógrafo [au'toɣrafo] *nm* autograph

autómata [au'tomata] *nm* automaton

automático, a [auto'matiko, a] *adj* automatic ♦ *nm* press stud

automotor, triz [automo'tor, 'triθ] *adj* self-propelled ♦ *nm* diesel train

automóvil [auto'moβil] *nm* (motor) car (*BRIT*), automobile (*US*); **automovilismo** *nm* (*actividad*) motoring; (*DEPORTE*) motor

racing; **automovilista** *nm/f* motorist, driver; **automovilístico, a** *adj* (*industria*) motor *cpd*

autonomía [autono'mia] *nf* autonomy; **autónomo, a** (*ESP*), **autonómico, a** (*ESP*) *adj* (*POL*) autonomous

autopista [auto'pista] *nf* motorway (*BRIT*), freeway (*US*); **~ de peaje** toll road (*BRIT*), turnpike road (*US*)

autopsia [au'topsja] *nf* autopsy, postmortem

autor, a [au'tor, a] *nm/f* author

autoridad [autori'ðað] *nf* authority; **autoritario, a** *adj* authoritarian

autorización [autoriθa'θjon] *nf* authorization; **autorizado, a** *adj* authorized; (*aprobado*) approved

autorizar [autori'θar] *vt* to authorize; (*aprobar*) to approve

autorretrato [autorre'trato] *nm* self-portrait

autoservicio [autoser'βiθjo] *nm* (*tienda*) self-service shop (*BRIT*) o store (*US*); (*restaurante*) self-service restaurant

autostop [auto'stop] *nm* hitch-hiking; **hacer ~** to hitch-hike; **~ista** *nm/f* hitch-hiker

autosuficiencia [autosufi'θjenθja] *nf* self-sufficiency

autovía [auto'βia] *nf* ≈ A-road (*BRIT*), dual carriageway (*BRIT*), ≈ state highway (*US*)

auxiliar [auksi'ljar] *vt* to help ♦ *nm/f* assistant; **auxilio** *nm* assistance, help; **primeros auxilios** first aid *sg*

Av *abr* (= *Avenida*) Av(e).

aval [a'βal] *nm* guarantee; (*persona*) guarantor

avalancha [aβa'lantʃa] *nf* avalanche

avance [a'βanθe] *nm* advance; (*pago*) advance payment; (*CINE*) trailer

avanzar [aβan'θar] *vt, vi* to advance

avaricia [aβa'riθja] *nf* avarice, greed; **avaricioso, a** *adj* avaricious, greedy

avaro, a [a'βaro, a] *adj* miserly, mean ♦ *nm/f* miser

avasallar [aβasa'ʎar] *vt* to subdue, subjugate

Avda *abr* (= *Avenida*) Av(e).
AVE ['aβe] *nm abr* (= *Alta Velocidad Española*) ≈ bullet train
ave ['aβe] *nf* bird; **~ de rapiña** bird of prey
avecinarse [aβeθi'narse] *vr* (*tormenta, fig*) to be on the way
avellana [aβe'ʎana] *nf* hazelnut; **avellano** *nm* hazel tree
avemaría [aβema'ria] *nm* Hail Mary, Ave Maria
avena [a'βena] *nf* oats *pl*
avenida [aβe'niða] *nf* (*calle*) avenue
avenir [aβe'nir] *vt* to reconcile; **~se** *vr* to come to an agreement, reach a compromise
aventajado, a [aβenta'xaðo, a] *adj* outstanding
aventajar [aβenta'xar] *vt* (*sobrepasar*) to surpass, outstrip
aventura [aβen'tura] *nf* adventure; **aventurado, a** *adj* risky; **aventurero, a** *adj* adventurous
avergonzar [aβerɣon'θar] *vt* to shame; (*desconcertar*) to embarrass; **~se** *vr* to be ashamed; to be embarrassed
avería [aβe'ria] *nf* (*TEC*) breakdown, fault
averiado, a [aβe'rjaðo, a] *adj* broken down; **"~"** "out of order"
averiguación [aβeriɣwa'θjon] *nf* investigation; (*descubrimiento*) ascertainment
averiguar [aβeri'ɣwar] *vt* to investigate; (*descubrir*) to find out, ascertain
aversión [aβer'sjon] *nf* aversion, dislike
avestruz [aβes'truθ] *nm* ostrich
aviación [aβja'θjon] *nf* aviation; (*fuerzas aéreas*) air force
aviador, a [aβja'ðor, a] *nm/f* aviator, airman/woman
avicultura [aβikul'tura] *nf* poultry farming
avidez [aβi'ðeθ] *nf* avidity, eagerness; **ávido, a** *adj* avid, eager
avinagrado, a [aβina'ɣraðo, a] *adj* sour, acid
avión [a'βjon] *nm* aeroplane; (*ave*) martin; **~ de reacción** jet (plane)
avioneta [aβjo'neta] *nf* light aircraft

avisar [aβi'sar] *vt* (*advertir*) to warn, notify; (*informar*) to tell; (*aconsejar*) to advise, counsel; **aviso** *nm* warning; (*noticia*) notice
avispa [a'βispa] *nf* wasp
avispado, a [aβis'paðo, a] *adj* sharp, clever
avispero [aβis'pero] *nm* wasp's nest
avispón [aβis'pon] *nm* hornet
avistar [aβis'tar] *vt* to sight, spot
avituallar [aβitwa'ʎar] *vt* to supply with food
avivar [aβi'βar] *vt* to strengthen, intensify; **~se** *vr* to revive, acquire new life
axila [ak'sila] *nf* armpit
axioma [ak'sjoma] *nm* axiom
ay [ai] *excl* (*dolor*) owl!, ouch!; (*aflicción*) oh!, oh dear!; **¡~ de mi!** poor me!
aya ['aja] *nf* governess; (*niñera*) nanny
ayer [a'jer] *adv, nm* yesterday; **antes de ~** the day before yesterday
ayote [a'jote] (*AM*) *nm* pumpkin
ayuda [a'juða] *nf* help, assistance ♦ *nm* page; **ayudante, a** *nm/f* assistant, helper; (*ESCOL*) assistant; (*MIL*) adjutant
ayudar [aju'ðar] *vt* to help, assist
ayunar [aju'nar] *vi* to fast; **ayunas** *nfpl*: **estar en ayunas** to be fasting; **ayuno** *nm* fast; fasting
ayuntamiento [ajunta'mjento] *nm* (*consejo*) town (*o* city) council; (*edificio*) town (*o* city) hall
azabache [aθa'βatʃe] *nm* jet
azada [a'θaða] *nf* hoe
azafata [aθa'fata] *nf* air stewardess
azafrán [aθa'fran] *nm* saffron
azahar [aθa'ar] *nm* orange/lemon blossom
azar [a'θar] *nm* (*casualidad*) chance, fate; (*desgracia*) misfortune, accident; **por ~** by chance; **al ~** at random
azoramiento [aθora'mjento] *nm* alarm; (*confusión*) confusion
azorar [aθo'rar] *vt* to alarm; **~se** *vr* to get alarmed
Azores [a'θores] *nfpl*: **las ~** the Azores
azotar [aθo'tar] *vt* to whip, beat; (*pegar*) to spank; **azote** *nm* (*látigo*) whip;

(latigazo) lash, stroke; *(en las nalgas)* spank; *(calamidad)* calamity

azotea [aθoˈtea] *nf* (flat) roof

azteca [aθˈteka] *adj, nm/f* Aztec

azúcar [aˈθukar] *nm* sugar; **azucarado, a** *adj* sugary, sweet

azucarero, a [aθukaˈrero, a] *adj* sugar *cpd* ♦ *nm* sugar bowl

azucena [aθuˈθena] *nf* white lily

azufre [aˈθufre] *nm* sulphur

azul [aˈθul] *adj, nm* blue; ~ **marino** navy blue

azulejo [aθuˈlexo] *nm* tile

azuzar [aθuˈθar] *vt* to incite, egg on

B, b

baba [ˈbaβa] *nf* spittle, saliva; **babear** *vi* to drool, slaver

babero [baˈβero] *nm* bib

babor [baˈβor] *nm* port (side)

baboso, a [baˈβoso, a] *(AM: fam) adj* silly

baca [ˈbaka] *nf (AUTO)* luggage *o* roof rack

bacalao [bakaˈlao] *nm* cod(fish)

bache [ˈbatʃe] *nm* pothole, rut; *(fig)* bad patch

bachillerato [batʃiʎeˈrato] *nm* higher *secondary school course*

bacteria [bakˈterja] *nf* bacterium, germ

báculo [ˈbakulo] *nm* stick, staff

bagaje [baˈvaxe] *nm* baggage, luggage

Bahama [baˈama]: **las (Islas)** ~ *nfpl* the Bahamas

bahía [baˈia] *nf* bay

bailar [baiˈlar] *vt, vi* to dance; ~**ín, ina** *nm/f* (ballet) dancer; **baile** *nm* dance; *(formal)* ball

baja [ˈbaxa] *nf* drop, fall; *(MIL)* casualty; **dar de** ~ *(soldado)* to discharge; *(empleado)* to dismiss

bajada [baˈxaða] *nf* descent; *(camino)* slope; *(de aguas)* ebb

bajar [baˈxar] *vi* to go down, come down; *(temperatura, precios)* to drop, fall ♦ *vt* *(cabeza)* to bow; *(escalera)* to go down,

come down; *(precio, voz)* to lower; *(llevar abajo)* to take down; ~**se** *vr (de coche)* to get out; *(de autobús, tren)* to get off; ~ **de** *(coche)* to get out of; *(autobús, tren)* to get off

bajeza [baˈxeθa] *nf* baseness *no pl*; *(una ~)* vile deed

bajío [baˈxio] *nm (AM)* lowlands *pl*

bajo, a [ˈbaxo, a] *adj (mueble, número, precio)* low; *(piso)* ground; *(de estatura)* small; short; *(color)* pale; *(sonido)* faint, soft, low; *(voz: en tono)* deep; *(metal)* base; *(humilde)* low, humble ♦ *adv (hablar)* softly, quietly; *(volar)* low ♦ *prep* under, below, underneath ♦ *nm (MUS)* bass; ~ **la lluvia** in the rain

bajón [baˈxon] *nm* fall, drop

bakalao [bakaˈlao] *(fam) nm* rave (music)

bala [ˈbala] *nf* bullet

balance [baˈlanθe] *nm (COM)* balance; *(: libro)* balance sheet; *(: cuenta general)* stocktaking

balancear [balanθeˈar] *vt* to balance ♦ *vi* to swing (to and fro); *(vacilar)* to hesitate; ~**se** *vr* to swing (to and fro); to hesitate; **balanceo** *nm* swinging

balanza [baˈlanθa] *nf* scales *pl*, balance; *(ASTROLOGÍA)* B~ Libra; ~ **comercial** balance of trade; ~ **de pagos** balance of payments

balar [baˈlar] *vi* to bleat

balaustrada [balausˈtraða] *nf* balustrade; *(pasamanos)* banisters *pl*

balazo [baˈlaθo] *nm (golpe)* shot; *(herida)* bullet wound

balbucear [balβuθeˈar] *vi, vt* to stammer, stutter; **balbuceo** *nm* stammering, stuttering

balbucir [balβuˈθir] *vi, vt* to stammer, stutter

balcón [balˈkon] *nm* balcony

balde [ˈbalde] *nm* bucket, pail; **de** ~ (for) free, for nothing; **en** ~ in vain

baldío, a [balˈdio, a] *adj* uncultivated; *(terreno)* waste ♦ *nm* waste land

baldosa [balˈdosa] *nf (azulejo)* floor tile; *(grande)* flagstone; **baldosín** *nm* (small) tile

Baleares [bale'ares] *nfpl*: **las (Islas) ~** the Balearic Islands

balido [ba'liðo] *nm* bleat, bleating

baliza [ba'liθa] *nf* (AVIAT) beacon; (NAUT) buoy

ballena [ba'ʎena] *nf* whale

ballesta [ba'ʎesta] *nf* crossbow; (AUTO) spring

ballet [ba'le] (*pl* **~s**) *nm* ballet

balneario, a [balne'arjo, a] *adj*: **estación balnearia** (AM) (bathing) resort ♦ *nm* spa, health resort

balón [ba'lon] *nm* ball

baloncesto [balon'θesto] *nm* basketball

balonmano [balon'mano] *nm* handball

balonvolea [balombo'lea] *nm* volleyball

balsa ['balsa] *nf* raft; (BOT) balsa wood

bálsamo ['balsamo] *nm* balsam, balm

baluarte [ba'lwarte] *nm* bastion, bulwark

bambolear [bambole'ar] *vi* to swing, sway; (silla) to wobble; **~se** *vr* to swing, sway; to wobble; **bamboleo** *nm* swinging, swaying; wobbling

bambú [bam'bu] *nm* bamboo

banana [ba'nana] (AM) *nf* banana; **banano** (AM) *nm* banana tree

banca ['banka] *nf* (COM) banking

bancario, a [ban'karjo, a] *adj* banking *cpd*, bank *cpd*

bancarrota [banka'rrota] *nf* bankruptcy; **hacer ~** to go bankrupt

banco ['banko] *nm* bench; (ESCOL) desk; (COM) bank; (GEO) stratum; **~ de crédito/de ahorros** credit/savings bank; **~ de arena** sandbank; **~ de datos** databank

banda ['banda] *nf* band; (pandilla) gang; (NAUT) side, edge; **la B~ Oriental** Uruguay; **~ sonora** soundtrack

bandada [ban'daða] *nf* (de pájaros) flock; (de peces) shoal

bandazo [ban'daθo] *nm*: **dar ~s** to sway from side to side

bandeja [ban'dexa] *nf* tray

bandera [ban'dera] *nf* flag

banderilla [bande'riʎa] *nf* banderilla

banderín [bande'rin] *nm* pennant, small flag

bandido [ban'diðo] *nm* bandit

bando ['bando] *nm* (edicto) edict, proclamation; (facción) faction; **los ~s** (REL) the banns

bandolera [bando'lera] *nf*: **llevar en ~** to wear across one's chest

bandolero [bando'lero] *nm* bandit, brigand

banquero [ban'kero] *nm* banker

banqueta [ban'keta] *nf* stool; (AM: en la calle) pavement (BRIT), sidewalk (US)

banquete [ban'kete] *nm* banquet; (para convidados) formal dinner

banquillo [ban'kiʎo] *nm* (JUR) dock, prisoner's bench; (banco) bench; (para los pies) footstool

bañador [baɲa'ðor] *nm* swimming costume (BRIT), bathing suit (US)

bañar [ba'ɲar] *vt* to bath, bathe; (objeto) to dip; (de barniz) to coat; **~se** *vr* (en el mar) to bathe, swim; (en la bañera) to have a bath

bañera [ba'ɲera] *nf* bath(tub)

bañero, a [ba'ɲero, a] (AM) *nm/f* lifeguard

bañista [ba'ɲista] *nm/f* bather

baño ['baɲo] *nm* (en bañera) bath; (en río) dip, swim; (cuarto) bathroom; (bañera) bath(tub); (capa) coating

baqueta [ba'keta] *nf* (MUS) drumstick

bar [bar] *nm* bar

barahúnda [bara'unda] *nf* uproar, hubbub

baraja [ba'raxa] *nf* pack (of cards); **barajar** *vt* (naipes) to shuffle; (fig) to jumble up

baranda [ba'randa] *nf* = **barandilla**

barandilla [baran'diʎa] *nf* rail, railing

baratija [bara'tixa] *nf* trinket

baratillo [bara'tiʎo] *nm* (tienda) junkshop; (subasta) bargain sale; (conjunto de cosas) secondhand goods *pl*

barato, a [ba'rato, a] *adj* cheap ♦ *adv* cheap, cheaply

baraúnda [bara'unda] *nf* = **barahúnda**

barba ['barßa] *nf* (mentón) chin; (pelo) beard

barbacoa [barˈβaˈkoa] *nf* (*parrilla*) barbecue; (*carne*) barbecued meat

barbaridad [barβariˈðað] *nf* barbarity; (*acto*) barbarism; (*atrocidad*) outrage; **una ~** (*fam*) loads; **¡qué ~!** (*fam*) how awful!

barbarie [barˈβarje] *nf* barbarism, savagery; (*crueldad*) barbarity

barbarismo [barβaˈrismo] *nm* = **barbarie**

bárbaro, a [ˈbarβaro, a] *adj* barbarous, cruel; (*grosero*) rough, uncouth ♦ *nm/f* barbarian ♦ *adv*: **lo pasamos ~** (*fam*) we had a great time; **¡qué ~!** (*fam*) how marvellous!; **un éxito ~** (*fam*) a terrific success; **es un tipo ~** (*fam*) he's a great bloke

barbecho [barˈβetʃo] *nm* fallow land

barbero [barˈβero] *nm* barber, hairdresser

barbilla [barˈβiʎa] *nf* chin, tip of the chin

barbo [ˈbarβo] *nm* barbel; **~ de mar** red mullet

barbotear [barβoteˈar] *vt, vi* to mutter, mumble

barbudo, a [barˈβuðo, a] *adj* bearded

barca [ˈbarka] *nf* (small) boat; **~ pesquera** fishing boat; **~ de pasaje** ferry; **~za** *nf* barge; **~za de desembarco** landing craft

Barcelona [barθeˈlona] *n* Barcelona

barcelonés, esa [barθeloˈnes, esa] *adj* of *o* from Barcelona

barco [ˈbarko] *nm* boat; (*grande*) ship; **~ de carga** cargo boat; **~ de vela** sailing ship

baremo [baˈremo] *nm* (*MAT, fig*) scale

barítono [baˈritono] *nm* baritone

barman [ˈbarman] *nm* barman

Barna *n* = **Barcelona**

barniz [barˈniθ] *nm* varnish; (*en la loza*) glaze; (*fig*) veneer; **~ar** *vt* to varnish; (*loza*) to glaze

barómetro [baˈrometro] *nm* barometer

barquero [barˈkero] *nm* boatman

barquillo [barˈkiʎo] *nm* cone, cornet

barra [ˈbarra] *nf* bar, rod; (*de un bar, café*) bar; (*de pan*) French stick; (*palanca*) lever; **~ de carmín** *o* **de labios** lipstick; **~ libre** free bar

barraca [baˈrraka] *nf* hut, cabin

barranco [baˈrranko] *nm* ravine; (*fig*) difficulty

barrena [baˈrrena] *nf* drill; **barrenar** *vt* to drill (through), bore; **barreno** *nm* large drill

barrer [baˈrrer] *vt* to sweep; (*quitar*) to sweep away

barrera [baˈrrera] *nf* barrier

barriada [baˈrrjaða] *nf* quarter, district

barricada [barriˈkaða] *nf* barricade

barrida [baˈrriða] *nf* sweep, sweeping

barrido [baˈrriðo] *nm* = **barrida**

barriga [baˈrriɣa] *nf* belly; (*panza*) paunch; **barrigón, ona** *adj* potbellied; **barrigudo, a** *adj* potbellied

barril [baˈrril] *nm* barrel, cask

barrio [ˈbarrjo] *nm* (*vecindad*) area, neighborhood (*US*); (*en las afueras*) suburb; **~ chino** red-light district

barro [ˈbarro] *nm* (*lodo*) mud; (*objetos*) earthenware; (*MED*) pimple

barroco, a [baˈrroko, a] *adj, nm* baroque

barrote [baˈrrote] *nm* (*de ventana*) bar

barruntar [barrunˈtar] *vt* (*conjeturar*) to guess; (*presentir*) to suspect; **barrunto** *nm* guess; suspicion

bartola [barˈtola]: **a la ~** *adv*: **tirarse a la ~** to take it easy, be lazy

bártulos [ˈbartulos] *nmpl* things, belongings

barullo [baˈruʎo] *nm* row, uproar

basar [baˈsar] *vt* to base; **~se** *vr*: **~se en** to be based on

báscula [ˈbaskula] *nf* (*platform*) scales

base [ˈbase] *nf* base; **a ~ de** on the basis of; (*mediante*) by means of; **~ de datos** (*INFORM*) database

básico, a [ˈbasiko, a] *adj* basic

basílica [baˈsilika] *nf* basilica

PALABRA CLAVE

bastante [basˈtante] *adj* **1** (*suficiente*) enough; **~ dinero** enough *o* sufficient money; **~s libros** enough books
2 (*valor intensivo*): **~ gente** quite a lot of people; **tener ~ calor** to be rather hot
♦ *adv*: **~ bueno/malo** quite good/rather

bad; **~ rico** pretty rich; **(lo) ~ inteligente (como) para hacer algo** clever enough *o* sufficiently clever to do sth

bastar [bas'tar] *vi* to be enough *o* sufficient; **~se** *vr* to be self-sufficient; **~ para** to be enough to; **¡basta!** (that's) enough!

bastardilla [bastar'ðiʎa] *nf* italics

bastardo, a [bas'tarðo, a] *adj, nm/f* bastard

bastidor [basti'ðor] *nm* frame; (*de coche*) chassis; (*TEATRO*) wing; **entre ~es** (*fig*) behind the scenes

basto, a ['basto, a] *adj* coarse, rough; **~s** *nmpl* (*NAIPES*) ≈ clubs

bastón [bas'ton] *nm* stick, staff; (*para pasear*) walking stick

bastoncillo [baston'θiʎo] *nm* cotton bud

basura [ba'sura] *nf* rubbish (*BRIT*), garbage (*US*)

basurero [basu'rero] *nm* (*hombre*) dustman (*BRIT*), garbage man (*US*); (*lugar*) dump; (*cubo*) (rubbish) bin (*BRIT*), trash can (*US*)

bata ['bata] *nf* (*gen*) dressing gown; (*cubretodo*) smock, overall; (*MED, TEC etc*) lab(oratory) coat

batalla [ba'taʎa] *nf* battle; **de ~** (*fig*) for everyday use

batallar [bata'ʎar] *vi* to fight

batallón [bata'ʎon] *nm* battalion

batata [ba'tata] *nf* sweet potato

batería [bate'ria] *nf* battery; (*MUS*) drums; **~ de cocina** kitchen utensils

batido, a [ba'tiðo, a] *adj* (*camino*) beaten, well-trodden ♦ *nm* (*CULIN*): **~ (de leche)** milk shake

batidora [bati'ðora] *nf* beater, mixer; **~ eléctrica** food mixer, blender

batir [ba'tir] *vt* to beat, strike; (*vencer*) to beat, defeat; (*revolver*) to beat, mix; **~se** *vr* to fight; **~ palmas** to clap, applaud

batuta [ba'tuta] *nf* baton; **llevar la ~** (*fig*) to be the boss, be in charge

baúl [ba'ul] *nm* trunk; (*AUTO*) boot (*BRIT*), trunk (*US*)

bautismo [bau'tismo] *nm* baptism, christening

bautizar [bauti'θar] *vt* to baptize, christen; (*fam: diluir*) to water down; **bautizo** *nm* baptism, christening

baya ['baja] *nf* berry

bayeta [ba'jeta] *nf* floorcloth

baza ['baθa] *nf* trick; **meter ~** to butt in

bazar [ba'θar] *nm* bazaar

bazofia [ba'θofja] *nf* trash

BCE *nm abr* (= *Banco Central Europeo*) ECB

beato, a [be'ato, a] *adj* blessed; (*piadoso*) pious

bebé [be'ße] (*pl* **~s**) *nm* baby

bebedor, a [beße'ðor, a] *adj* hard-drinking

beber [be'ßer] *vt, vi* to drink

bebida [be'ßiða] *nf* drink; **bebido, a** *adj* drunk

beca ['beka] *nf* grant, scholarship

becario, a [be'karjo, a] *nm/f* scholarship holder, grant holder

bedel [be'ðel] *nm* (*ESCOL*) janitor; (*UNIV*) porter

béisbol ['beisßol] *nm* (*DEPORTE*) baseball

belén [be'len] *nm* (*de navidad*) nativity scene, crib; **B~** Bethlehem

belga ['belɣa] *adj, nm/f* Belgian

Bélgica ['belxika] *nf* Belgium

bélico, a ['beliko, a] *adj* (*actitud*) warlike; **belicoso, a** *adj* (*guerrero*) warlike; (*agresivo*) aggressive, bellicose

beligerante [belixe'rante] *adj* belligerent

belleza [be'ʎeθa] *nf* beauty

bello, a ['beʎo, a] *adj* beautiful, lovely; **Bellas Artes** Fine Art

bellota [be'ʎota] *nf* acorn

bemol [be'mol] *nm* (*MUS*) flat; **esto tiene ~es** (*fam*) this is a tough one

bencina [ben'θina] (*AM*) *nf* (*gasolina*) petrol (*BRIT*), gasoline (*US*)

bendecir [bende'θir] *vt* to bless

bendición [bendi'θjon] *nf* blessing

bendito, a [ben'dito, a] *pp de* **bendecir** ♦ *adj* holy; (*afortunado*) lucky; (*feliz*) happy; (*sencillo*) simple ♦ *nm/f* simple soul

beneficencia [benefi'θenθja] *nf* charity
beneficiar [benefi'θjar] *vt* to benefit, be of benefit to; **~se** *vr* to benefit, profit; **~io, a** *nm/f* beneficiary
beneficio [bene'fiθjo] *nm* (*bien*) benefit, advantage; (*ganancia*) profit, gain; **~so, a** *adj* beneficial
benéfico, a [be'nefiko, a] *adj* charitable
beneplácito [bene'plaθito] *nm* approval, consent
benevolencia [beneβo'lenθja] *nf* benevolence, kindness; **benévolo, a** *adj* benevolent, kind
benigno, a [be'nivno, a] *adj* kind; (*suave*) mild; (*MED: tumor*) benign, non-malignant
berberecho [berβe'retʃo] *nm* (*ZOOL, CULIN*) cockle
berenjena [beren'xena] *nf* aubergine (*BRIT*), eggplant (*US*)
Berlín [ber'lin] *n* Berlin; **berlinés, esa** *adj* of o from Berlin ♦ *nm/f* Berliner
bermudas [ber'muðas] *nfpl* Bermuda shorts
berrear [berre'ar] *vi* to bellow, low
berrido [be'rriðo] *nm* bellow(ing)
berrinche [be'rrintʃe] (*fam*) *nm* temper, tantrum
berro ['berro] *nm* watercress
berza ['berθa] *nf* cabbage
besamel [besa'mel] *nf* (*CULIN*) white sauce, bechamel sauce
besar [be'sar] *vt* to kiss; (*fig: tocar*) to graze; **~se** *vr* to kiss (one another); **beso** *nm* kiss
bestia ['bestja] *nf* beast, animal; (*fig*) idiot; **~ de carga** beast of burden
bestial [bes'tjal] *adj* bestial; (*fam*) terrific; **~idad** *nf* bestiality; (*fam*) stupidity
besugo [be'suɣo] *nm* sea bream; (*fam*) idiot
besuquear [besuke'ar] *vt* to cover with kisses; **~se** *vr* to kiss and cuddle
betún [be'tun] *nm* shoe polish; (*QUÍM*) bitumen
biberón [biβe'ron] *nm* feeding bottle
Biblia ['biβlja] *nf* Bible

bibliografía [biβljoɣra'fia] *nf* bibliography
biblioteca [biβljo'teka] *nf* library; (*mueble*) bookshelves; **~ de consulta** reference library; **~rio, a** *nm/f* librarian
bicarbonato [bikarβo'nato] *nm* bicarbonate
bicho ['bitʃo] *nm* (*animal*) small animal; (*sabandija*) bug, insect; (*TAUR*) bull
bici ['biθi] (*fam*) *nf* bike
bicicleta [biθi'kleta] *nf* bicycle, cycle; **ir en ~** to cycle
bidé [bi'ðe] (*pl* **~s**) *nm* bidet
bidón [bi'ðon] *nm* (*de aceite*) drum; (*de gasolina*) can

┌─────────────────────┐
│ **PALABRA CLAVE**   │
└─────────────────────┘

bien [bjen] *nm* **1** (*bienestar*) good; **te lo digo por tu ~** I'm telling you for your own good; **el ~ y el mal** good and evil
2 (*posesión*): **~es** goods; **~es de consumo** consumer goods; **~es inmuebles** *o* **raíces/~es muebles** real estate *sg*/personal property *sg*
♦ *adv* **1** (*de manera satisfactoria, correcta etc*) well; **trabaja/come ~** she works/eats well; **contestó ~** he answered correctly; **me siento ~** I feel fine; **no me siento ~** I don't feel very well; **se está ~ aquí** it's nice here
2 (*frases*): **hiciste ~ en llamarme** you were right to call me
3 (*valor intensivo*) very; **un cuarto ~ caliente** a nice warm room; **~ se ve que ...** it's quite clear that ...
4: **estar ~**: **estoy muy ~ aquí** I feel very happy here; **está ~ que vengan** it's all right for them to come; **¡está ~!** lo haré oh all right, I'll do it
5 (*de buena gana*): **yo ~ que iría pero ...** I'd gladly go but ...
♦ *excl*: **¡~!** (*aprobación*) O.K.!; **¡muy ~!** well done!
♦ *adj inv* (*matiz despectivo*): **niño ~** rich kid; **gente ~** posh people
♦ *conj* **1**: **~ ... ~**: **~ en coche ~ en tren** either by car or by train
2: **no ~** (*esp AM*): **no ~ llegue te llamaré**

as soon as I arrive I'll call you
3: **si** ~ even though; *ver tb* **más**

---

bienal [bje'nal] *adj* biennial

bienaventurado, a [bjenaßentu'raðo, a] *adj (feliz)* happy, fortunate

bienestar [bjenes'tar] *nm* well-being, welfare

bienhechor, a [bjene'tʃor, a] *adj* beneficent ♦ *nm/f* benefactor/benefactress

bienvenida [bjembe'niða] *nf* welcome; **dar la ~ a uno** to welcome sb

bienvenido [bjembe'niðo] *excl* welcome!

bife ['bife] *(AM) nm* steak

bifurcación [bifurka'θjon] *nf* fork

bifurcarse [bifur'karse] *vr (camino, carretera, río)* to fork

bigamia [bi'xamja] *nf* bigamy; **bígamo, a** *adj* bigamous ♦ *nm/f* bigamist

bigote [bi'xote] *nm* moustache; **bigotudo, a** *adj* with a big moustache

bikini [bi'kini] *nm* bikini; *(CULIN)* toasted ham and cheese sandwich

bilbaíno, a [bilßa'ino, a] *adj* from *o* of Bilbao

bilingüe [bi'lingwe] *adj* bilingual

billar [bi'ʎar] *nm* billiards *sg; (lugar)* billiard hall; *(mini-casino)* amusement arcade; ~ **americano** pool

billete [bi'ʎete] *nm* ticket; *(de banco)* (bank)note, bill *(US); (carta)* note; ~ **sencillo, ~ de ida solamente** single *(BRIT) o* one-way *(US)* ticket; ~ **de ida y vuelta** return *(BRIT) o* round-trip *(US)* ticket; ~ **de 20 libras** £20 note

billetera [biʎe'tera] *nf* wallet

billetero [biʎe'tero] *nm* = **billetera**

billón [bi'ʎon] *nm* billion

bimensual [bimen'swal] *adj* twice monthly

bimotor [bimo'tor] *adj* twin-engined ♦ *nm* twin-engined plane

biodegradable [bioðeɣra'ðaßle] *adj* biodegradable

biografía [bjoɣra'fia] *nf* biography; **biógrafo, a** *nm/f* biographer

biología [bjolo'xia] *nf* biology; **biológico, a** *adj* biological; *(cultivo, producto)* organic; **biólogo, a** *nm/f* biologist

biombo ['bjombo] *nm* (folding) screen

biopsia [bi'opsja] *nf* biopsy

biquini [bi'kini] *nm* bikini

birlar [bir'lar] *(fam) vt* to pinch

Birmania [bir'manja] *nf* Burma

birria ['birrja] *nf*: **ser una ~** *(película, libro)* to be rubbish

bis [bis] *excl* encore! ♦ *adv*: **viven en el 27** ~ they live at 27

bisabuelo, a [bisa'ßwelo, a] *nm/f* great-grandfather/mother

bisagra [bi'saɣra] *nf* hinge

bisiesto [bi'sjesto] *adj*: **año** ~ leap year

bisnieto, a [bis'njeto, a] *nm/f* great-grandson/daughter

bisonte [bi'sonte] *nm* bison

bisté [bis'te] *nm* = **bistec**

bistec [bis'tek] *nm* steak

bisturí [bistu'ri] *nm* scalpel

bisutería [bisute'ria] *nf* imitation *o* costume jewellery

bit [bit] *nm (INFORM)* bit

bizco, a ['biθko, a] *adj* cross-eyed

bizcocho [biθ'kotʃo] *nm (CULIN)* sponge cake

bizquear [biθke'ar] *vi* to squint

blanca ['blanka] *nf (MUS)* minim; **estar sin** ~ to be broke; *ver tb* **blanco**

blanco, a ['blanko, a] *adj* white ♦ *nm/f* white man/woman, white ♦ *nm (color)* white; *(en texto)* blank; *(MIL, fig)* target; **en** ~ blank; **noche en** ~ sleepless night

blancura [blan'kura] *nf* whiteness

blandir [blan'dir] *vt* to brandish

blando, a ['blando, a] *adj* soft; *(tierno)* tender, gentle; *(carácter)* mild; *(fam)* cowardly; **blandura** *nf* softness; tenderness; mildness

blanquear [blanke'ar] *vt* to whiten; *(fachada)* to whitewash; *(paño)* to bleach ♦ *vi* to turn white; **blanquecino, a** *adj* whitish

blasfemar [blasfe'mar] *vi* to blaspheme, curse; **blasfemia** *nf* blasphemy

blasón [bla'son] *nm* coat of arms

bledo ['bleðo] *nm*: **me importa un ~** I couldn't care less

blindado, a [blin'daðo, a] *adj* (MIL) armour-plated; (*antibala*) bullet-proof; **coche** (ESP) o **carro** (AM) ~ armoured car

blindaje [blin'daxe] *nm* armour, armour-plating

bloc [blok] (*pl* ~**s**) *nm* writing pad

bloque ['bloke] *nm* block; (POL) bloc; ~ **de cilindros** cylinder block

bloquear [bloke'ar] *vt* to blockade; **bloqueo** *nm* blockade; (COM) freezing, blocking

blusa ['blusa] *nf* blouse

boato [bo'ato] *nm* show, ostentation

bobada [bo'ßaða] *nf* foolish action; foolish statement; **decir ~s** to talk nonsense

bobería [boße'ria] *nf* = **bobada**

bobina [bo'ßina] *nf* (TEC) bobbin; (FOTO) spool; (ELEC) coil

bobo, a ['boßo, a] *adj* (*tonto*) daft, silly; (*cándido*) naïve ♦ *nm/f* fool, idiot ♦ *nm* (TEATRO) clown, funny man

boca ['boka] *nf* mouth; (*de crustáceo*) pincer; (*de cañón*) muzzle; (*entrada*) mouth, entrance; ~**s** *nfpl* (*de río*) mouth *sg*; ~ **abajo/arriba** face down/up; **se me hace agua la** ~ my mouth is watering

bocacalle [boka'kaʎe] *nf* (entrance to a) street; **la primera** ~ the first turning *o* street

bocadillo [boka'ðiʎo] *nm* sandwich

bocado [bo'kaðo] *nm* mouthful, bite; (*de caballo*) bridle; ~ **de Adán** Adam's apple

bocajarro [boka'xarro]: **a** ~ *adv* (*disparar*, *preguntar*) point-blank

bocanada [boka'naða] *nf* (*de vino*) mouthful, swallow; (*de aire*) gust, puff

bocata [bo'kata] (*fam*) *nm* sandwich

bocazas [bo'kaθas] (*fam*) *nm inv* bigmouth

boceto [bo'θeto] *nm* sketch, outline

bochorno [bo'tʃorno] *nm* (*vergüenza*) embarrassment; (*calor*): **hace** ~ it's very muggy; ~**so, a** *adj* muggy; embarrassing

bocina [bo'θina] *nf* (MUS) trumpet; (AUTO)

horn; (*para hablar*) megaphone

boda ['boða] *nf* (*tb*: ~**s**) wedding, marriage; (*fiesta*) wedding reception; ~**s de plata/de oro** silver/golden wedding

bodega [bo'ðexa] *nf* (*de vino*) (wine) cellar; (*depósito*) storeroom; (*de barco*) hold

bodegón [boðe'ɣon] *nm* (ARTE) still life

bofe ['bofe] *nm* (*tb*: ~**s**: *de res*) lights

bofetada [bofe'taða] *nf* slap (in the face)

bofetón [bofe'ton] *nm* = **bofetada**

boga ['boxa] *nf*: **en** ~ (*fig*) in vogue

bogar [bo'xar] *vi* (*remar*) to row; (*navegar*) to sail

bogavante [boxa'ßante] *nm* lobster

Bogotá [boxo'ta] *n* Bogotá

bohemio, a [bo'emjo, a] *adj*, *nm/f* Bohemian

boicot [boi'kot] (*pl* ~**s**) *nm* boycott; ~**ear** *vt* to boycott; ~**eo** *nm* boycott

boina ['boina] *nf* beret

bola ['bola] *nf* ball; (*canica*) marble; (NAIPES) (grand) slam; (*betún*) shoe polish; (*mentira*) tale, story; ~**s** (AM) *nfpl* bolas *sg*; ~ **de billar** billiard ball; ~ **de nieve** snowball

bolchevique [boltʃe'ßike] *adj*, *nm/f* Bolshevik

boleadoras [bolea'ðoras] (AM) *nfpl* bolas *sg*

bolera [bo'lera] *nf* skittle *o* bowling alley

boleta [bo'leta] (AM) *nf* (*billete*) ticket; (*permiso*) pass, permit

boletería [bolete'ria] (AM) *nf* ticket office

boletín [bole'tin] *nm* bulletin; (*periódico*) journal, review; ~ **de noticias** news bulletin

boleto [bo'leto] *nm* ticket

boli ['boli] (*fam*) *nm* Biro ®, pen

bolígrafo [bo'liɣrafo] *nm* ball-point pen, Biro ®

bolívar [bo'lißar] *nm monetary unit of Venezuela*

Bolivia [bo'lißja] *nf* Bolivia; **boliviano, a** *adj*, *nm/f* Bolivian

bollería [boʎe'ria] *nf* cakes *pl* and pastries *pl*

bollo ['boʎo] nm (pan) roll; (bulto) bump, lump; (abolladura) dent

bolo ['bolo] nm skittle; (píldora) (large) pill; **(juego de) ~s** nmpl skittles sg

bolsa ['bolsa] nf bag; (AM) pocket; (ANAT) cavity, sac; (COM) stock exchange; (MINERÍA) pocket; **de ~** pocket cpd; **~ de agua caliente** hot water bottle; **~ de aire** air pocket; **~ de papel** paper bag; **~ de plástico** plastic bag

bolsillo [bol'siʎo] nm pocket; (cartera) purse; **de ~** pocket(-size)

bolsista [bol'sista] nm/f stockbroker

bolso ['bolso] nm (bolsa) bag; (de mujer) handbag

bomba ['bomba] nf (MIL) bomb; (TEC) pump ♦ (fam) adj: **noticia ~** bombshell ♦ (fam) adv: **pasarlo ~** to have a great time; **~ atómica/de humo/de efecto retardado** atomic/smoke/time bomb

bombardear [bombarðe'ar] vt to bombard; (MIL) to bomb; **bombardeo** nm bombardment; bombing

bombardero [bombar'ðero] nm bomber

bombear [bombe'ar] vt (agua) to pump (out o up); **~se** vr to warp

bombero [bom'bero] nm fireman

bombilla [bom'biʎa] (ESP) nf (light) bulb

bombín [bom'bin] nm bowler hat

bombo ['bombo] nm (MUS) bass drum; (TEC) drum

bombón [bom'bon] nm chocolate

bombona [bom'bona] nf (de butano, oxígeno) cylinder

bonachón, ona [bona'tʃon, ona] adj good-natured, easy-going

bonanza [bo'nanθa] nf (NAUT) fair weather; (fig) bonanza; (MINERÍA) rich pocket o vein

bondad [bon'dað] nf goodness, kindness; **tenga la ~ de** (please) be good enough to; **~oso, a** adj good, kind

bonificación [bonifika'θjon] nf bonus

bonito, a [bo'nito, a] adj pretty; (agradable) nice ♦ nm (atún) tuna (fish)

bono ['bono] nm voucher; (FIN) bond

bonobús [bono'βus] (ESP) nm bus pass

bonoloto [bono'loto] nf state-run weekly lottery

boquerón [boke'ron] nm (pez) (kind of) anchovy; (agujero) large hole

boquete [bo'kete] nm gap, hole

boquiabierto, a [bokia'βjerto, a] adj: **quedar ~** to be amazed o flabbergasted

boquilla [bo'kiʎa] nf (para riego) nozzle; (para cigarro) cigarette holder; (MUS) mouthpiece

borbotón [borβo'ton] nm: **salir a borbotones** to gush out

borda ['borða] nf (NAUT) (ship's) rail; **tirar algo/caerse por la ~** to throw sth/fall overboard

bordado [bor'ðaðo] nm embroidery

bordar [bor'ðar] vt to embroider

borde ['borðe] nm edge, border; (de camino etc) side; (en la costura) hem; **al ~ de** (fig) on the verge o brink of; **ser ~** (ESP: fam) to be rude; **~ar** vt to border

bordillo [bor'ðiʎo] nm kerb (BRIT), curb (US)

bordo ['borðo] nm (NAUT) side; **a ~** on board

borinqueño, a [borin'keɲo, a] adj, nm/f Puerto Rican

borla ['borla] nf (adorno) tassel

borrachera [borra'tʃera] nf (ebriedad) drunkenness; (orgía) spree, binge

borracho, a [bo'rratʃo, a] adj drunk ♦ nm/f (habitual) drunkard, drunk; (temporal) drunk, drunk man/woman

borrador [borra'ðor] nm (escritura) first draft, rough sketch; (goma) rubber (BRIT), eraser

borrar [bo'rrar] vt to erase, rub out

borrasca [bo'rraska] nf storm

borrico, a [bo'rriko, a] nm/f donkey/she-donkey; (fig) stupid man/woman

borrón [bo'rron] nm (mancha) stain

borroso, a [bo'rroso, a] adj vague, unclear; (escritura) illegible

bosque ['boske] nm wood; (grande) forest

bosquejar [boske'xar] vt to sketch; **bosquejo** nm sketch

bostezar [boste'θar] vi to yawn; **bostezo**

nm yawn

bota ['bota] *nf* (*calzado*) boot; (*para vino*) leather wine bottle; **~s de agua, ~s de goma** Wellingtons

botánica [bo'tanika] *nf* (*ciencia*) botany; *ver tb* **botánico**

botánico, a [bo'taniko, a] *adj* botanical ♦ *nm/f* botanist

botar [bo'tar] *vt* to throw, hurl; (*NAUT*) to launch; (*AM*) to throw out ♦ *vi* to bounce

bote ['bote] *nm* (*salto*) bounce; (*golpe*) thrust; (*vasija*) tin, can; (*embarcación*) boat; **de ~ en ~** packed, jammed full; **~ de la basura** (*AM*) dustbin (*BRIT*), trashcan (*US*); **~ salvavidas** lifeboat

botella [bo'teʎa] *nf* bottle; **botellín** *nm* small bottle

botica [bo'tika] *nf* chemist's (shop) (*BRIT*), pharmacy; **~rio, a** *nm/f* chemist (*BRIT*), pharmacist

botijo [bo'tixo] *nm* (earthenware) jug

botín [bo'tin] *nm* (*calzado*) half boot; (*polaina*) spat; (*MIL*) booty

botiquín [boti'kin] *nm* (*armario*) medicine cabinet; (*portátil*) first-aid kit

botón [bo'ton] *nm* button; (*BOT*) bud; **~ de oro** buttercup

botones [bo'tones] *nm inv* bellboy (*BRIT*), bellhop (*US*)

bóveda ['boβeða] *nf* (*ARQ*) vault

boxeador [boksea'ðor] *nm* boxer

boxear [bokse'ar] *vi* to box

boxeo [bok'seo] *nm* boxing

boya ['boja] *nf* (*NAUT*) buoy; (*de caña*) float

boyante [bo'jante] *adj* prosperous

bozal [bo'θal] *nm* (*de caballo*) halter; (*de perro*) muzzle

bracear [braθe'ar] *vi* (*agitar los brazos*) to wave one's arms

bracero [bra'θero] *nm* labourer; (*en el campo*) farmhand

bragas ['braɣas] *nfpl* (*de mujer*) panties, knickers (*BRIT*)

bragueta [bra'ɣeta] *nf* fly, flies *pl*

braille [breil] *nm* braille

bramar [bra'mar] *vi* to bellow, roar;

bramido *nm* bellow, roar

brasa ['brasa] *nf* live *o* hot coal

brasero [bra'sero] *nm* brazier

Brasil [bra'sil] *nm*: **(el) ~** Brazil; **brasileño, a** *adj, nm/f* Brazilian

bravata [bra'βata] *nf* boast

braveza [bra'βeθa] *nf* (*valor*) bravery; (*ferocidad*) ferocity

bravío, a [bra'βio, a] *adj* wild; (*feroz*) fierce

bravo, a ['braβo, a] *adj* (*valiente*) brave; (*feroz*) ferocious; (*salvaje*) wild; (*mar etc*) rough, stormy ♦ *excl* bravo!; **bravura** *nf* bravery; ferocity

braza ['braθa] *nf* fathom; **nadar a la ~** to swim (the) breast-stroke

brazada [bra'θaða] *nf* stroke

brazado [bra'θaðo] *nm* armful

brazalete [braθa'lete] *nm* (*pulsera*) bracelet; (*banda*) armband

brazo ['braθo] *nm* arm; (*ZOOL*) foreleg; (*BOT*) limb, branch; **luchar a ~ partido** to fight hand-to-hand; **ir cogidos del ~** to walk arm in arm

brea ['brea] *nf* pitch, tar

brebaje [bre'βaxe] *nm* potion

brecha ['bretʃa] *nf* (*hoyo, vacío*) gap, opening; (*MIL, fig*) breach

brega ['breɣa] *nf* (*lucha*) struggle; (*trabajo*) hard work

breva ['breβa] *nf* early fig

breve ['breβe] *adj* short, brief ♦ *nf* (*MUS*) breve; **~dad** *nf* brevity, shortness

brezo ['breθo] *nm* heather

bribón, ona [bri'βon, ona] *adj* idle, lazy ♦ *nm/f* (*pícaro*) rascal, rogue

bricolaje [briko'laxe] *nm* do-it-yourself, DIY

brida ['briða] *nf* bridle, rein; (*TEC*) clamp; **a toda ~** at top speed

bridge [britʃ] *nm* bridge

brigada [bri'ɣaða] *nf* (*unidad*) brigade; (*trabajadores*) squad, gang ♦ *nm* ≈ staff-sergeant, sergeant-major

brillante [bri'ʎante] *adj* brilliant ♦ *nm* diamond

brillar [bri'ʎar] *vi* (*tb fig*) to shine; (*joyas*)

to sparkle

brillo [ˈbriʎo] *nm* shine; (*brillantez*) brilliance; (*fig*) splendour; **sacar ~ a** to polish

brincar [brinˈkar] *vi* to skip about, hop about, jump about; **está que brinca** he's hopping mad

brinco [ˈbrinko] *nm* jump, leap

brindar [brinˈdar] *vi*: **~ a** *o* **por** to drink (a toast) to ♦ *vt* to offer, present

brindis [ˈbrindis] *nm inv* toast

brío [ˈbrio] *nm* spirit, dash; **brioso, a** *adj* spirited, dashing

brisa [ˈbrisa] *nf* breeze

británico, a [briˈtaniko, a] *adj* British ♦ *nm/f* Briton, British person

brizna [ˈbriθna] *nf* (*de hierba, paja*) blade; (*de tabaco*) leaf

broca [ˈbroka] *nf* (*TEC*) drill, bit

brocal [broˈkal] *nm* rim

brocha [ˈbrotʃa] *nf* (large) paintbrush; **~ de afeitar** shaving brush

broche [ˈbrotʃe] *nm* brooch

broma [ˈbroma] *nf* joke; **en ~** in fun, as a joke; **~ pesada** practical joke; **bromear** *vi* to joke

bromista [broˈmista] *adj* fond of joking ♦ *nm/f* joker, wag

bronca [ˈbronka] *nf* row; **echar una ~ a uno** to tick sb off

bronce [ˈbronθe] *nm* bronze; **~ado, a** *adj* bronze; (*por el sol*) tanned ♦ *nm* (sun)tan; (*TEC*) bronzing

bronceador [bronθeaˈðor] *nm* suntan lotion

broncearse [bronθeˈarse] *vr* to get a suntan

bronco, a [ˈbronko, a] *adj* (*manera*) rude, surly; (*voz*) harsh

bronquio [ˈbronkjo] *nm* (*ANAT*) bronchial tube

bronquitis [bronˈkitis] *nf inv* bronchitis

brotar [broˈtar] *vi* (*BOT*) to sprout; (*aguas*) to gush (forth); (*MED*) to break out

brote [ˈbrote] *nm* (*BOT*) shoot; (*MED, fig*) outbreak

bruces [ˈbruθes]: **de ~** *adv*: **caer** *o* **dar de**

~ to fall headlong, fall flat

bruja [ˈbruxa] *nf* witch; **brujería** *nf* witchcraft

brujo [ˈbruxo] *nm* wizard, magician

brújula [ˈbruxula] *nf* compass

bruma [ˈbruma] *nf* mist; **brumoso, a** *adj* misty

bruñir [bruˈɲir] *vt* to polish

brusco, a [ˈbrusko, a] *adj* (*súbito*) sudden; (*áspero*) brusque

Bruselas [bruˈselas] *n* Brussels

brutal [bruˈtal] *adj* brutal

brutalidad [brutaliˈðað] *nf* brutality

bruto, a [ˈbruto, a] *adj* (*idiota*) stupid; (*bestial*) brutish; (*peso*) gross; **en ~** raw, unworked

Bs.As. *abr* (= *Buenos Aires*) B.A.

bucal [buˈkal] *adj* oral; **por vía ~** orally

bucear [buθeˈar] *vi* to dive ♦ *vt* to explore; **buceo** *nm* diving

bucle [ˈbukle] *nm* curl

budismo [buˈðismo] *nm* Buddhism

buen [bwen] *adj m ver* **bueno**

buenamente [bwenaˈmente] *adv* (*fácilmente*) easily; (*voluntariamente*) willingly

buenaventura [bwenaβenˈtura] *nf* (*suerte*) good luck; (*adivinación*) fortune

┌─────────────────┐
│ *PALABRA CLAVE* │
└─────────────────┘

bueno, a [ˈbweno, a] *adj* (*antes de nmsg:* **buen**) **1** (*excelente etc*) good; **es un libro ~, es un buen libro** it's a good book; **hace ~, hace buen tiempo** the weather is fine, it is fine; **el ~ de Paco** good old Paco; **fue muy ~ conmigo** he was very nice *o* kind to me

2 (*apropiado*): **ser ~ para** to be good for; **creo que vamos por buen camino** I think we're on the right track

3 (*irónico*): **le di un buen rapapolvo** I gave him a good *o* real ticking off; **¡buen conductor estás hecho!** some *o* a fine driver you are!; **¡estaría ~ que ...!** a fine thing it would be if ...!

4 (*atractivo, sabroso*): **está ~ este bizcocho** this sponge is delicious;

Carmen está muy buena Carmen is gorgeous
5 (*saludos*): **¡buen día!, ¡~s días!** (good) morning!; **¡buenas (tardes)!** (good) afternoon!; (*más tarde*) (good) evening!; **¡buenas noches!** good night!
6 (*otras locuciones*): **estar de buenas** to be in a good mood; **por las buenas o por las malas** by hook or by crook; **de buenas a primeras** all of a sudden
♦ *excl*: **¡~!** all right!; **~, ¿y qué?** well, so what?

Buenos Aires *nm* Buenos Aires
buey [bwei] *nm* ox
búfalo ['bufalo] *nm* buffalo
bufanda [bu'fanda] *nf* scarf
bufar [bu'far] *vi* to snort
bufete [bu'fete] *nm* (*despacho de abogado*) lawyer's office
buffer ['bufer] *nm* (*INFORM*) buffer
bufón [bu'fon] *nm* clown
buhardilla [buar'ðiʎa] *nf* attic
búho ['buo] *nm* owl; (*fig*) hermit, recluse
buhonero [buo'nero] *nm* pedlar
buitre ['bwitre] *nm* vulture
bujía [bu'xia] *nf* (*vela*) candle; (*ELEC*) candle (power); (*AUTO*) spark plug
bula ['bula] *nf* (*papal*) bull
bulbo ['bulβo] *nm* bulb
bulevar [bule'βar] *nm* boulevard
Bulgaria [bul'xarja] *nf* Bulgaria; **búlgaro, a** *adj, nm/f* Bulgarian
bulla ['buʎa] *nf* (*ruido*) uproar; (*de gente*) crowd
bullicio [bu'ʎiθjo] *nm* (*ruido*) uproar; (*movimiento*) bustle
bullir [bu'ʎir] *vi* (*hervir*) to boil; (*burbujear*) to bubble
bulto ['bulto] *nm* (*paquete*) package; (*fardo*) bundle; (*tamaño*) size, bulkiness; (*MED*) swelling, lump; (*silueta*) vague shape
buñuelo [bu'ɲwelo] *nm* ≈ doughnut (*BRIT*), ≈ donut (*US*); (*fruta de sartén*) fritter
BUP [bup] *nm abr* (*ESP:* = *Bachillerato Unificado Polivalente*) *secondary education and leaving certificate for 14–17 age group*
buque ['buke] *nm* ship, vessel
burbuja [bur'ßuxa] *nf* bubble; **burbujear** *vi* to bubble
burdel [bur'ðel] *nm* brothel
burdo, a ['burðo, a] *adj* coarse, rough
burgués, esa [bur'ɣes, esa] *adj* middle-class, bourgeois; **burguesía** *nf* middle class, bourgeoisie
burla ['burla] *nf* (*mofa*) gibe; (*broma*) joke; (*engaño*) trick
burladero [burla'ðero] *nm* (*bullfighter's*) refuge
burlar [bur'lar] *vt* (*engañar*) to deceive ♦ *vi* to joke; **~se** *vr* to joke; **~se de** to make fun of
burlesco, a [bur'lesko, a] *adj* burlesque
burlón, ona [bur'lon, ona] *adj* mocking
burocracia [buro'kraθja] *nf* civil service
burócrata [bu'rokrata] *nm/f* civil servant
burrada [bu'rraða] *nf*: **decir/soltar ~s** to talk nonsense; **hacer ~s** to act stupid; **una ~** (*mucho*) a (hell of a) lot
burro, a ['burro, a] *nm/f* donkey/she-donkey; (*fig*) ass, idiot
bursátil [bur'satil] *adj* stock-exchange *cpd*
bus [bus] *nm* bus
busca ['buska] *nf* search, hunt ♦ *nm* (*TEL*) bleeper; **en ~ de** in search of
buscar [bus'kar] *vt* to look for, search for, seek ♦ *vi* to look, search, seek; **se busca secretaria** secretary wanted
busque *etc vb ver* **buscar**
búsqueda ['buskeða] *nf* = **busca** *nf*
busto ['busto] *nm* (*ANAT, ARTE*) bust
butaca [bu'taka] *nf* armchair; (*de cine, teatro*) stall, seat
butano [bu'tano] *nm* butane (gas)
buzo ['buθo] *nm* diver
buzón [bu'θon] *nm* (*en puerta*) letter box; (*en la calle*) pillar box

C, c

C. *abr* (= *centígrado*) C; (= *compañía*) Co.
c. *abr* (= *capítulo*) ch.
C/ *abr* (= *calle*) St
c.a. *abr* (= *corriente alterna*) AC
cabal [ka'ßal] *adj* (*exacto*) exact; (*correcto*) right, proper; (*acabado*) finished, complete; ~**es** *nmpl*: **estar en sus ~es** to be in one's right mind
cábalas ['kaßalas] *nfpl*: **hacer ~** to guess
cabalgar [kaßal'ɣar] *vt*, *vi* to ride
cabalgata [kaßal'ɣata] *nf* procession
caballa [ka'ßaʎa] *nf* mackerel
caballeresco, a [kaßaʎe'resko, a] *adj* noble, chivalrous
caballería [kaßaʎe'ria] *nf* mount; (*MIL*) cavalry
caballeriza [kaßaʎe'riθa] *nf* stable; **caballerizo** *nm* groom, stableman
caballero [kaßa'ʎero] *nm* gentleman; (*de la orden de caballería*) knight; (*trato directo*) sir
caballerosidad [kaßaʎerosi'ðað] *nf* chivalry
caballete [kaßa'ʎete] *nm* (*ARTE*) easel; (*TEC*) trestle
caballito [kaßa'ʎito] *nm* (*caballo pequeño*) small horse, pony; ~**s** *nmpl* (*en verbena*) roundabout, merry-go-round
caballo [ka'ßaʎo] *nm* horse; (*AJEDREZ*) knight; (*NAIPES*) queen; **ir en ~** to ride; ~ **de vapor** *o* **de fuerza** horsepower; ~ **de carreras** racehorse
cabaña [ka'ßaɲa] *nf* (*casita*) hut, cabin
cabaré [kaßa're] (*pl* ~**s**) *nm* cabaret
cabaret [kaßa're] (*pl* ~**s**) *nm* cabaret
cabecear [kaßeθe'ar] *vt*, *vi* to nod
cabecera [kaße'θera] *nf* head; (*IMPRENTA*) headline
cabecilla [kaße'θiʎa] *nm* ringleader
cabellera [kaße'ʎera] *nf* (head of) hair; (*de cometa*) tail
cabello [ka'ßeʎo] *nm* (*tb*: ~**s**) hair
caber [ka'ßer] *vi* (*entrar*) to fit, go; **caben**

3 más there's room for 3 more
cabestrillo [kaßes'triʎo] *nm* sling
cabestro [ka'ßestro] *nm* halter
cabeza [ka'ßeθa] *nf* head; (*POL*) chief, leader; ~ **rapada** skinhead; ~**da** *nf* (*golpe*) butt; **dar ~das** to nod off; **cabezón, ona** *adj* (*vino*) heady; (*fam: persona*) pig-headed
cabida [ka'ßiða] *nf* space
cabildo [ka'ßildo] *nm* (*de iglesia*) chapter; (*POL*) town council
cabina [ka'ßina] *nf* cabin; (*de camión*) cab; ~ **telefónica** telephone box (*BRIT*) *o* booth
cabizbajo, a [kaßiθ'ßaxo, a] *adj* crestfallen, dejected
cable ['kaßle] *nm* cable
cabo ['kaßo] *nm* (*de objeto*) end, extremity; (*MIL*) corporal; (*NAUT*) rope, cable; (*GEO*) cape; **al ~ de 3 días** after 3 days
cabra ['kaßra] *nf* goat
cabré *etc vb ver* **caber**
cabrear [kaßre'ar] (*fam*) *vt* to bug; ~**se** *vr* (*enfadarse*) to fly off the handle
cabrío, a [ka'ßrio, a] *adj* goatish; **macho ~** (he-)goat, billy goat
cabriola [ka'ßrjola] *nf* caper
cabritilla [kaßri'tiʎa] *nf* kid, kidskin
cabrito [ka'ßrito] *nm* kid
cabrón [ka'ßron] *nm* cuckold; (*fam!*) bastard (!)
caca ['kaka] (*fam*) *nf* pooh
cacahuete [kaka'wete] (*ESP*) *nm* peanut
cacao [ka'kao] *nm* cocoa; (*BOT*) cacao
cacarear [kakare'ar] *vi* (*persona*) to boast; (*gallina*) to crow
cacería [kaθe'ria] *nf* hunt
cacerola [kaθe'rola] *nf* pan, saucepan
cachalote [katʃa'lote] *nm* (*ZOOL*) sperm whale
cacharro [ka'tʃarro] *nm* earthenware pot; ~**s** *nmpl* pots and pans
cachear [katʃe'ar] *vt* to search, frisk
cachemir [katʃe'mir] *nm* cashmere
cacheo [ka'tʃeo] *nm* searching, frisking
cachete [ka'tʃete] *nm* (*ANAT*) cheek; (*bofetada*) slap (in the face)

cachiporra [katʃiˈporra] *nf* truncheon

cachivache [katʃiˈβatʃe] *nm* (*trasto*) piece of junk; **~s** *nmpl* junk *sg*

cacho [ˈkatʃo] *nm* (small) bit; (*AM: cuerno*) horn

cachondeo [katʃonˈdeo] (*fam*) *nm* farce, joke

cachondo, a [kaˈtʃondo, a] *adj* (*ZOOL*) on heat; (*fam: sexualmente*) randy; (: *gracioso*) funny

cachorro, a [kaˈtʃorro, a] *nm/f* (*perro*) pup, puppy; (*león*) cub

cacique [kaˈθike] *nm* chief, local ruler; (*POL*) local party boss; **caciquismo** *nm* system of control by the local boss

caco [ˈkako] *nm* pickpocket

cacto [ˈkakto] *nm* cactus

cactus [ˈkaktus] *nm inv* cactus

cada [ˈkaða] *adj inv* each; (*antes de número*) every; **~ día** each day, every day; **~ dos días** every other day; **~ uno/a** each one, every one; **~ vez más/menos** more and more/less and less; **uno de ~ diez** one out of every ten

cadalso [kaˈðalso] *nm* scaffold

cadáver [kaˈðaβer] *nm* (dead) body, corpse

cadena [kaˈðena] *nf* chain; (*TV*) channel; **trabajo en ~** assembly line work; **~ perpetua** (*JUR*) life imprisonment

cadencia [kaˈðenθja] *nf* rhythm

cadera [kaˈðera] *nf* hip

cadete [kaˈðete] *nm* cadet

caducar [kaðuˈkar] *vi* to expire; **caduco, a** *adj* expired; (*persona*) very old

caer [kaˈer] *vi* to fall (down); **~se** *vr* to fall (down); **me cae bien/mal** I get on well with him/I can't stand him; **~ en la cuenta** to realize; **su cumpleaños cae en viernes** her birthday falls on a Friday

café [kaˈfe] (*pl* **~s**) *nm* (*bebida, planta*) coffee; (*lugar*) café ♦ *adj* (*color*) brown; **~ con leche** white coffee; **~ solo** black coffee

cafetera [kafeˈtera] *nf* coffee pot

cafetería [kafeteˈria] *nf* (*gen*) café

cafetero, a [kafeˈtero, a] *adj* coffee *cpd*;

ser muy ~ to be a coffee addict

cagar [kaˈɣar] (*fam!*) *vt* to bungle, mess up ♦ *vi* to have a shit (!)

caída [kaˈiða] *nf* fall; (*declive*) slope; (*disminución*) fall, drop

caído, a [kaˈiðo, a] *adj* drooping

caiga *etc vb ver* **caer**

caimán [kaiˈman] *nm* alligator

caja [ˈkaxa] *nf* box; (*para reloj*) case; (*de ascensor*) shaft; (*COM*) cashbox; (*donde se hacen los pagos*) cashdesk; (: *en supermercado*) checkout, till; **~ de ahorros** savings bank; **~ de cambios** gearbox; **~ fuerte, ~ de caudales** safe, strongbox

cajero, a [kaˈxero, a] *nm/f* cashier; **~ automático** cash dispenser

cajetilla [kaxeˈtiʎa] *nf* (*de cigarrillos*) packet

cajón [kaˈxon] *nm* big box; (*de mueble*) drawer

cal [kal] *nf* lime

cala [ˈkala] *nf* (*GEO*) cove, inlet; (*de barco*) hold

calabacín [kalaβaˈθin] *nm* (*BOT*) baby marrow; (: *más pequeño*) courgette (*BRIT*), zucchini (*US*)

calabaza [kalaˈβaθa] *nf* (*BOT*) pumpkin

calabozo [kalaˈβoθo] *nm* (*cárcel*) prison; (*celda*) cell

calada [kaˈlaða] *nf* (*de cigarrillo*) puff

calado, a [kaˈlaðo, a] *adj* (*prenda*) lace *cpd* ♦ *nm* (*NAUT*) draught

calamar [kalaˈmar] *nm* squid *no pl*

calambre [kaˈlambre] *nm* (*tb:* **~s**) cramp

calamidad [kalamiˈðað] *nf* calamity, disaster

calar [kaˈlar] *vt* to soak, drench; (*penetrar*) to pierce, penetrate; (*comprender*) to see through; (*vela*) to lower; **~se** *vr* (*AUTO*) to stall; **~se las gafas** to stick one's glasses on

calavera [kalaˈβera] *nf* skull

calcar [kalˈkar] *vt* (*reproducir*) to trace; (*imitar*) to copy

calcetín [kalθeˈtin] *nm* sock

calcinar [kalθiˈnar] *vt* to burn, blacken

calcio [ˈkalθjo] *nm* calcium
calcomanía [kalkomaˈnia] *nf* transfer
calculador, a [kalkulaˈðor, a] *adj*
(*persona*) calculating
calculadora [kalkulaˈðora] *nf* calculator
calcular [kalkuˈlar] *vt* (*MAT*) to calculate,
compute; ~ **que ...** to reckon that ...;
cálculo *nm* calculation
caldear [kaldeˈar] *vt* to warm (up), heat
(up)
caldera [kalˈdera] *nf* boiler
calderilla [kaldeˈriʎa] *nf* (*moneda*) small
change
caldero [kalˈdero] *nm* small boiler
caldo [ˈkaldo] *nm* stock; (*consomé*)
consommé
calefacción [kalefakˈθjon] *nf* heating; ~
central central heating
calendario [kalenˈdarjo] *nm* calendar
calentador [kalentaˈðor] *nm* heater
calentamiento [kalentaˈmjento] *nm*
(*DEPORTE*) warm-up
calentar [kalenˈtar] *vt* to heat (up); **~se** *vr*
to heat up, warm up; (*fig: discusión etc*)
to get heated
calentura [kalenˈtura] *nf* (*MED*) fever,
(high) temperature
calibrar [kaliˈβrar] *vt* to gauge, measure;
calibre *nm* (*de cañón*) calibre, bore;
(*diámetro*) diameter; (*fig*) calibre
calidad [kaliˈðað] *nf* quality; **de ~** quality
cpd; **en ~ de** in the capacity of, as
cálido, a [ˈkaliðo, a] *adj* hot; (*fig*) warm
caliente *etc* [kaˈljente] *vb ver* **calentar**
♦ *adj* hot; (*fig*) fiery; (*disputa*) heated;
(*fam: cachondo*) randy
calificación [kalifikaˈθjon] *nf* qualification;
(*de alumno*) grade, mark
calificar [kalifiˈkar] *vt* to qualify; (*alumno*)
to grade, mark; ~ **de** to describe as
calima [kaˈlima] *nf* (*cerca del mar*) mist
cáliz [ˈkaliθ] *nm* chalice
caliza [kaˈliθa] *nf* limestone
calizo, a [kaˈliθo, a] *adj* lime *cpd*
callado, a [kaˈʎaðo, a] *adj* quiet
callar [kaˈʎar] *vt* (*asunto delicado*) to keep
quiet about, say nothing about; (*persona,
opinión*) to silence ♦ *vi* to keep quiet, be
silent; **~se** *vr* to keep quiet, be silent;
¡cállate! be quiet!, shut up!
calle [ˈkaʎe] *nf* street; (*DEPORTE*) lane; ~
arriba/abajo up/down the street; ~ **de
un solo sentido** one-way street
calleja [kaˈʎexa] *nf* alley, narrow street;
callejear *vi* to wander (about) the
streets; **callejero, a** *adj* street *cpd* ♦ *nm*
street map; **callejón** *nm* alley, passage;
callejón sin salida cul-de-sac;
callejuela *nf* side-street, alley
callista [kaˈʎista] *nm/f* chiropodist
callo [ˈkaʎo] *nm* callus; (*en el pie*) corn; **~s**
nmpl (*CULIN*) tripe *sg*
calma [ˈkalma] *nf* calm
calmante [kalˈmante] *nm* sedative,
tranquillizer
calmar [kalˈmar] *vt* to calm, calm down
♦ *vi* (*tempestad*) to abate; (*mente etc*) to
become calm
calmoso, a [kalˈmoso, a] *adj* calm, quiet
calor [kaˈlor] *nm* heat; (*agradable*) warmth;
hace ~ it's hot; **tener ~** to be hot
caloría [kaloˈria] *nf* calorie
calumnia [kaˈlumnja] *nf* calumny, slander;
calumnioso, a *adj* slanderous
caluroso, a [kaluˈroso, a] *adj* hot; (*sin
exceso*) warm; (*fig*) enthusiastic
calva [ˈkalβa] *nf* bald patch; (*en bosque*)
clearing
calvario [kalˈβarjo] *nm* stations *pl* of the
cross
calvicie [kalˈβiθje] *nf* baldness
calvo, a [ˈkalβo, a] *adj* bald; (*terreno*)
bare, barren; (*tejido*) threadbare
calza [ˈkalθa] *nf* wedge, chock
calzada [kalˈθaða] *nf* roadway, highway
calzado, a [kalˈθaðo, a] *adj* shod ♦ *nm*
footwear
calzador [kalθaˈðor] *nm* shoehorn
calzar [kalˈθar] *vt* (*zapatos etc*) to wear;
(*un mueble*) to put a wedge under; **~se**
vr: **~se los zapatos** to put on one's
shoes; **¿qué (número) calza?** what size
do you take?
calzón [kalˈθon] *nm* (*tb*: **calzones** *nmpl*)

shorts; (AM: de hombre) (under)pants; (: de mujer) panties

calzoncillos [kalθon'θiʎos] nmpl underpants

cama ['kama] nf bed; ~ **individual/de matrimonio** single/double bed

camafeo [kama'feo] nm cameo

camaleón [kamale'on] nm chameleon

cámara ['kamara] nf chamber; (habitación) room; (sala) hall; (CINE) cine camera; (fotográfica) camera; ~ **de aire** inner tube; ~ **de comercio** chamber of commerce; ~ **frigorífica** cold-storage room

camarada [kama'raða] nm comrade, companion

camarera [kama'rera] nf (en restaurante) waitress; (en casa, hotel) maid

camarero [kama'rero] nm waiter

camarilla [kama'riʎa] nf clique

camarón [kama'ron] nm shrimp

camarote [kama'rote] nm cabin

cambiable [kam'bjaßle] adj (variable) changeable, variable; (intercambiable) interchangeable

cambiante [kam'bjante] adj variable

cambiar [kam'bjar] vt to change; (dinero) to exchange ♦ vi to change; ~**se** vr (mudarse) to move; (de ropa) to change; ~ **de idea** to change one's mind; ~ **de ropa** to change (one's clothes)

cambio ['kambjo] nm change; (trueque) exchange; (COM) rate of exchange; (oficina) bureau de change; (dinero menudo) small change; **en** ~ on the other hand; (en lugar de) instead; ~ **de divisas** foreign exchange; ~ **de velocidades** gear lever

camelar [kame'lar] vt to sweet-talk

camello [ka'meʎo] nm camel; (fam: traficante) pusher

camerino [kame'rino] nm dressing room

camilla [ka'miʎa] nf (MED) stretcher

caminante [kami'nante] nm/f traveller

caminar [kami'nar] vi (marchar) to walk, go ♦ vt (recorrer) to cover, travel

caminata [kami'nata] nf long walk; (por el campo) hike

camino [ka'mino] nm way, road; (sendero) track; **a medio** ~ halfway (there); **en el** ~ on the way, en route; ~ **de** on the way to; ~ **particular** private road

---

Camino de Santiago

ℹ️ The **Camino de Santiago** is a medieval pilgrim route stretching from the Pyrenees to Santiago de Compostela in north-west Spain, where tradition has it the body of the Apostle James is buried. Nowadays it is a popular tourist route as well as a religious one.

---

camión [ka'mjon] nm lorry (BRIT), truck (US); ~ **cisterna** tanker; **camionero, a** nm/f lorry o truck driver

camioneta [kamjo'neta] nf van, light truck

camisa [ka'misa] nf shirt; (BOT) skin; ~ **de fuerza** straitjacket; **camisería** nf outfitter's (shop)

camiseta [kami'seta] nf (prenda) tee-shirt; (: ropa interior) vest; (de deportista) top

camisón [kami'son] nm nightdress, nightgown

camorra [ka'morra] nf: **buscar** ~ to look for trouble

campamento [kampa'mento] nm camp

campana [kam'pana] nf bell; ~ **de cristal** bell jar; ~**da** nf peal; ~**rio** nm belfry

campanilla [kampa'niʎa] nf small bell

campaña [kam'paɲa] nf (MIL, POL) campaign

campechano, a [kampe'tʃano, a] adj (franco) open

campeón, ona [kampe'on, ona] nm/f champion; **campeonato** nm championship

campesino, a [kampe'sino, a] adj country cpd, rural; (gente) peasant cpd ♦ nm/f countryman/woman; (agricultor) farmer

campestre [kam'pestre] adj country cpd, rural

camping ['kampin] (pl ~**s**) nm camping; (lugar) campsite; **ir de** o **hacer** ~ to go

camping
campo ['kampo] *nm (fuera de la ciudad)* country, countryside; *(AGR, ELEC)* field; *(de fútbol)* pitch; *(de golf)* course; *(MIL)* camp; **~ de batalla** battlefield; **~ de deportes** sports ground, playing field
camposanto [kampo'santo] *nm* cemetery
camuflaje [kamu'flaxe] *nm* camouflage
cana ['kana] *nf* white *o* grey hair; **tener ~s** to be going grey
Canadá [kana'ða] *nm* Canada; **canadiense** *adj, nm/f* Canadian ♦ *nf* fur-lined jacket
canal [ka'nal] *nm* canal; *(GEO)* channel, strait; *(de televisión)* channel; *(de tejado)* gutter; **~ de Panamá** Panama Canal; **~izar** *vt* to channel
canalla [ka'naʎa] *nf* rabble, mob ♦ *nm* swine
canalón [kana'lon] *nm (conducto vertical)* drainpipe; *(del tejado)* gutter
canapé [kana'pe] *(pl* **~s)** *nm* sofa, settee; *(CULIN)* canapé
Canarias [ka'narjas] *nfpl:* **(las Islas) ~** the Canary Islands, the Canaries
canario, a [ka'narjo, a] *adj, nm/f* (native) of the Canary Isles ♦ *nm (ZOOL)* canary
canasta [ka'nasta] *nf (round)* basket; **canastilla** *nf* small basket; *(de niño)* layette
canasto [ka'nasto] *nm* large basket
cancela [kan'θela] *nf* gate
cancelación [kanθela'θjon] *nf* cancellation
cancelar [kanθe'lar] *vt* to cancel; *(una deuda)* to write off
cáncer ['kanθer] *nm (MED)* cancer; *(ASTROLOGÍA):* **C~** Cancer
cancha ['kantʃa] *nf (de baloncesto, tenis etc)* court; *(AM: de fútbol)* pitch
canciller [kanθi'ʎer] *nm* chancellor
canción [kan'θjon] *nf* song; **~ de cuna** lullaby; **cancionero** *nm* song book
candado [kan'daðo] *nm* padlock
candente [kan'dente] *adj* red-hot; *(fig: tema)* burning
candidato, a [kandi'ðato, a] *nm/f* candidate
candidez [kandi'ðeθ] *nf (sencillez)* simplicity; *(simpleza)* naiveté; **cándido, a** *adj* simple; naive
candil [kan'dil] *nm* oil lamp; **~ejas** *nfpl (TEATRO)* footlights
candor [kan'dor] *nm (sinceridad)* frankness; *(inocencia)* innocence
canela [ka'nela] *nf* cinnamon
canelones [kane'lones] *nmpl* cannelloni
cangrejo [kan'grexo] *nm* crab
canguro [kan'guro] *nm* kangaroo; **hacer de ~** to babysit
caníbal [ka'nißal] *adj, nm/f* cannibal
canica [ka'nika] *nf* marble
canijo, a [ka'nixo, a] *adj* frail, sickly
canino, a [ka'nino, a] *adj* canine ♦ *nm* canine (tooth)
canjear [kanxe'ar] *vt* to exchange
cano, a ['kano, a] *adj* grey-haired, white-haired
canoa [ka'noa] *nf* canoe
canon ['kanon] *nm* canon; *(pensión)* rent; *(COM)* tax
canónigo [ka'noniɣo] *nm* canon
canonizar [kanoni'θar] *vt* to canonize
canoso, a [ka'noso, a] *adj* grey-haired
cansado, a [kan'saðo, a] *adj* tired, weary; *(tedioso)* tedious, boring
cansancio [kan'sanθjo] *nm* tiredness, fatigue
cansar [kan'sar] *vt (fatigar)* to tire, tire out; *(aburrir)* to bore; *(fastidiar)* to bother; **~se** *vr* to tire, get tired; *(aburrirse)* to get bored
cantábrico, a [kan'taßriko, a] *adj* Cantabrian; **mar C~** Bay of Biscay
cantante [kan'tante] *adj* singing ♦ *nm/f* singer
cantar [kan'tar] *vt* to sing ♦ *vi* to sing; *(insecto)* to chirp ♦ *nm (acción)* singing; *(canción)* song; *(poema)* poem
cántara ['kantara] *nf* large pitcher
cántaro ['kantaro] *nm* pitcher, jug; **llover a ~s** to rain cats and dogs
cante ['kante] *nm:* **~ jondo** flamenco singing

cantera [kanˈtera] *nf* quarry

cantidad [kantiˈðað] *nf* quantity, amount

cantimplora [kantimˈplora] *nf* (*frasco*) water bottle, canteen

cantina [kanˈtina] *nf* canteen; (*de estación*) buffet

canto [ˈkanto] *nm* singing; (*canción*) song; (*borde*) edge, rim; (*de un cuchillo*) back; ~ **rodado** boulder

cantor, a [kanˈtor, a] *nm/f* singer

canturrear [kanturreˈar] *vi* to sing softly

canuto [kaˈnuto] *nm* (*tubo*) small tube; (*fam: droga*) joint

caña [ˈkaɲa] *nf* (BOT: *tallo*) stem, stalk; (*carrizo*) reed; (*vaso*) tumbler; (*de cerveza*) glass of beer; (ANAT) shinbone; ~ **de azúcar** sugar cane; ~ **de pescar** fishing rod

cañada [kaˈɲaða] *nf* (*entre dos montañas*) gully, ravine; (*camino*) cattle track

cáñamo [ˈkaɲamo] *nm* hemp

cañería [kaɲeˈria] *nf* (*tubo*) pipe

caño [ˈkaɲo] *nm* (*tubo*) tube, pipe; (*de albañal*) sewer; (MUS) pipe; (*de fuente*) jet

cañón [kaˈɲon] *nm* (MIL) cannon; (*de fusil*) barrel; (GEO) canyon, gorge

caoba [kaˈoßa] *nf* mahogany

caos [ˈkaos] *nm* chaos

cap. *abr* (= *capítulo*) ch.

capa [ˈkapa] *nf* cloak, cape; (GEO) layer, stratum; **so ~ de** under the pretext of; ~ **de ozono** ozone layer

capacidad [kapaθiˈðað] *nf* (*medida*) capacity; (*aptitud*) capacity, ability

capacitar [kapaθiˈtar] *vt*: ~ **a algn para (hacer)** to enable sb to (do)

capar [kaˈpar] *vt* to castrate, geld

caparazón [kaparaˈθon] *nm* shell

capataz [kapaˈtaθ] *nm* foreman

capaz [kaˈpaθ] *adj* able, capable; (*amplio*) capacious, roomy

capcioso, a [kapˈθjoso, a] *adj* wily, deceitful

capellán [kapeˈʎan] *nm* chaplain; (*sacerdote*) priest

caperuza [kapeˈruθa] *nf* hood

capicúa [kapiˈkua] *adj inv* (*número, fecha*) reversible

capilla [kaˈpiʎa] *nf* chapel

capital [kapiˈtal] *adj* capital ♦ *nm* (COM) capital ♦ *nf* (*ciudad*) capital; ~ **social** share o authorized capital

capitalismo [kapitaˈlismo] *nm* capitalism; **capitalista** *adj, nm/f* capitalist

capitán [kapiˈtan] *nm* captain

capitanear [kapitaneˈar] *vt* to captain

capitulación [kapitulaˈθjon] *nf* (*rendición*) capitulation, surrender; (*acuerdo*) agreement, pact; **capitulaciones (matrimoniales)** *nfpl* marriage contract *sg*

capitular [kapituˈlar] *vi* to make an agreement

capítulo [kaˈpitulo] *nm* chapter

capó [kaˈpo] *nm* (AUTO) bonnet

capón [kaˈpon] *nm* (*gallo*) capon

capota [kaˈpota] *nf* (*de mujer*) bonnet; (AUTO) hood (BRIT), top (US)

capote [kaˈpote] *nm* (*abrigo: de militar*) greatcoat; (: *de torero*) cloak

capricho [kaˈpritʃo] *nm* whim, caprice; **~so, a** *adj* capricious

Capricornio [kapriˈkornjo] *nm* Capricorn

cápsula [ˈkapsula] *nf* capsule

captar [kapˈtar] *vt* (*comprender*) to understand; (RADIO) to pick up; (*atención, apoyo*) to attract

captura [kapˈtura] *nf* capture; (JUR) arrest; **capturar** *vt* to capture; to arrest

capucha [kaˈputʃa] *nf* hood, cowl

capullo [kaˈpuʎo] *nm* (BOT) bud; (ZOOL) cocoon; (*fam*) idiot

caqui [ˈkaki] *nm* khaki

cara [ˈkara] *nf* (ANAT, *de moneda*) face; (*de disco*) side; (*descaro*) boldness; ~ **a** facing; **de ~** opposite, facing; **dar la ~** to face the consequences; **¿~ o cruz?** heads or tails?; **¡qué ~ (más dura)!** what a nerve!

carabina [karaˈßina] *nf* carbine, rifle; (*persona*) chaperone

Caracas [kaˈrakas] *n* Caracas

caracol [karaˈkol] *nm* (ZOOL) snail; (*concha*) (sea) shell

carácter [kaˈrakter] (*pl* **caracteres**) *nm*

character; **tener buen/mal ~** to be good natured/bad tempered

característica [karakte'ristika] *nf* characteristic

característico, a [karakte'ristiko, a] *adj* characteristic

caracterizar [karakteri'θar] *vt* to characterize, typify

caradura [kara'ðura] *nm/f*: **es un ~** he's got a nerve

carajillo [kara'xiʎo] *nm* coffee with a dash of brandy

carajo [ka'raxo] (*fam!*) *nm*: **¡~!** shit! (*!*)

caramba [ka'ramba] *excl* good gracious!

carámbano [ka'rambano] *nm* icicle

caramelo [kara'melo] *nm* (*dulce*) sweet; (*azúcar fundida*) caramel

caravana [kara'ßana] *nf* caravan; (*fig*) group; (*AUTO*) tailback

carbón [kar'ßon] *nm* coal; **papel ~** carbon paper; **carboncillo** *nm* (*ARTE*) charcoal; **carbonero, a** *nm/f* coal merchant; **carbonilla** [-'niʎa] *nf* coal dust

carbonizar [karßoni'θar] *vt* to carbonize; (*quemar*) to char

carbono [kar'ßono] *nm* carbon

carburador [karßura'ðor] *nm* carburettor

carburante [karßu'rante] *nm* (*para motor*) fuel

carcajada [karka'xaða] *nf* (loud) laugh, guffaw

cárcel ['karθel] *nf* prison, jail; (*TEC*) clamp; **carcelero, a** *adj* prison *cpd* ♦ *nm/f* warder

carcoma [kar'koma] *nf* woodworm

carcomer [karko'mer] *vt* to bore into, eat into; (*fig*) to undermine; **~se** *vr* to become worm-eaten; (*fig*) to decay

cardar [kar'ðar] *vt* (*pelo*) to backcomb

cardenal [karðe'nal] *nm* (*REL*) cardinal; (*MED*) bruise

cardíaco, a [kar'ðiako, a] *adj* cardiac, heart *cpd*

cardinal [karði'nal] *adj* cardinal

cardo ['karðo] *nm* thistle

carearse [kare'arse] *vr* to come face to face

carecer [kare'θer] *vi*: **~ de** to lack, be in need of

carencia [ka'renθja] *nf* lack; (*escasez*) shortage; (*MED*) deficiency

carente [ka'rente] *adj*: **~ de** lacking in, devoid of

carestía [kares'tia] *nf* (*escasez*) scarcity, shortage; (*COM*) high cost

careta [ka'reta] *nf* mask

carga ['karßa] *nf* (*peso, ELEC*) load; (*de barco*) cargo, freight; (*MIL*) charge; (*responsabilidad*) duty, obligation

cargado, a [kar'ßaðo, a] *adj* loaded; (*ELEC*) live; (*café, té*) strong; (*cielo*) overcast

cargamento [karßa'mento] *nm* (*acción*) loading; (*mercancías*) load, cargo

cargar [kar'ßar] *vt* (*barco, arma*) to load; (*ELEC*) to charge; (*COM: algo en cuenta*) to charge; (*INFORM*) to load ♦ *vi* (*MIL*) to charge; (*AUTO*) to load (up); **~ con** to pick up, carry away; (*peso, fig*) to shoulder, bear; **~se** (*fam*) *vr* (*estropear*) to break; (*matar*) to bump off

cargo ['karßo] *nm* (*puesto*) post, office; (*responsabilidad*) duty, obligation; (*JUR*) charge; **hacerse ~ de** to take charge of *o* responsibility for

carguero [kar'ßero] *nm* freighter, cargo boat; (*avión*) freight plane

Caribe [ka'rißе] *nm*: **el ~** the Caribbean; **del ~** Caribbean

caribeño, a [kari'ßeɲo, a] *adj* Caribbean

caricatura [karika'tura] *nf* caricature

caricia [ka'riθja] *nf* caress

caridad [kari'ðað] *nf* charity

caries ['karjes] *nf inv* tooth decay

cariño [ka'riɲo] *nm* affection, love; (*caricia*) caress; (*en carta*) love ...; **tener ~ a** to be fond of; **~so, a** *adj* affectionate

carisma [ka'risma] *nm* charisma

caritativo, a [karita'tißo, a] *adj* charitable

cariz [ka'riθ] *nm*: **tener *o* tomar buen/ mal ~** to look good/bad

carmesí [karme'si] *adj, nm* crimson

carmín [kar'min] *nm* lipstick

carnal [kar'nal] *adj* carnal; **primo ~** first cousin

carnaval [karna'βal] *nm* carnival

---
carnaval
---

i **Carnaval** *is the traditional period of fun, feasting and partying which takes place in the three days before the start of Lent ("Cuaresma"). Although in decline during the Franco years the carnival has grown in popularity recently in Spain. Cádiz and Tenerife are particularly well-known for their flamboyant celebrations with fancy-dress parties, parades and firework displays being the order of the day.*

---

carne ['karne] *nf* flesh; (*CULIN*) meat; **~ de cerdo/cordero/ternera/vaca** pork/lamb/veal/beef; **~ de gallina** (*fig*): **se me pone la ~ de gallina sólo verlo** I get the creeps just seeing it

carné [kar'ne] (*pl* **~s**) *nm*: **~ de conducir** driving licence (*BRIT*), driver's license (*US*); **~ de identidad** identity card

carnero [kar'nero] *nm* sheep, ram; (*carne*) mutton

carnet [kar'ne] (*pl* **~s**) *nm* = **carné**

carnicería [karniθe'ria] *nf* butcher's (shop); (*fig: matanza*) carnage, slaughter

carnicero, a [karni'θero, a] *adj* carnivorous ♦ *nm/f* (*tb fig*) butcher; (*carnívoro*) carnivore

carnívoro, a [kar'niβoro, a] *adj* carnivorous

carnoso, a [kar'noso, a] *adj* beefy, fat

caro, a ['karo, a] *adj* dear; (*COM*) dear, expensive ♦ *adv* dear, dearly

carpa ['karpa] *nf* (*pez*) carp; (*de circo*) big top; (*AM: de camping*) tent

carpeta [kar'peta] *nf* folder, file

carpintería [karpinte'ria] *nf* carpentry, joinery; **carpintero** *nm* carpenter

carraspear [karraspe'ar] *vi* to clear one's throat

carraspera [karras'pera] *nf* hoarseness

carrera [ka'rrera] *nf* (*acción*) run(ning); (*espacio recorrido*) run; (*competición*) race; (*trayecto*) course; (*profesión*) career;

(*ESCOL*) course

carreta [ka'rreta] *nf* wagon, cart

carrete [ka'rrete] *nm* reel, spool; (*TEC*) coil

carretera [karre'tera] *nf* (main) road, highway; **~ de circunvalación** ring road; **~ nacional** ≈ A road (*BRIT*), ≈ state highway (*US*)

carretilla [karre'tiʎa] *nf* trolley; (*AGR*) (wheel)barrow

carril [ka'rril] *nm* furrow; (*de autopista*) lane; (*FERRO*) rail

carrillo [ka'rriʎo] *nm* (*ANAT*) cheek; (*TEC*) pulley

carrito [ka'rrito] *nm* trolley

carro ['karro] *nm* cart, wagon; (*MIL*) tank; (*AM: coche*) car

carrocería [karroθe'ria] *nf* bodywork, coachwork

carroña [ka'rroɲa] *nf* carrion *no pl*

carroza [ka'rroθa] *nf* (*carruaje*) coach

carrusel [karru'sel] *nm* merry-go-round, roundabout

carta ['karta] *nf* letter; (*CULIN*) menu; (*naipe*) card; (*mapa*) map; (*JUR*) document; **~ de ajuste** (*TV*) test card; **~ de crédito** credit card; **~ certificada** registered letter; **~ marítima** chart; **~ verde** (*AUTO*) green card

cartabón [karta'βon] *nm* set square

cartel [kar'tel] *nm* (*anuncio*) poster, placard; (*ESCOL*) wall chart; (*COM*) cartel; **~era** *nf* hoarding, billboard; (*en periódico etc*) entertainments guide; **"en ~era"** "showing"

cartera [kar'tera] *nf* (*de bolsillo*) wallet; (*de colegial, cobrador*) satchel; (*de señora*) handbag; (*para documentos*) briefcase; (*COM*) portfolio; **ocupa la ~ de Agricultura** she is Minister of Agriculture

carterista [karte'rista] *nm/f* pickpocket

cartero [kar'tero] *nm* postman

cartilla [kar'tiʎa] *nf* primer, first reading book; **~ de ahorros** savings book

cartón [kar'ton] *nm* cardboard; **~ piedra** papier-mâché

cartucho [kar'tutʃo] *nm* (*MIL*) cartridge

cartulina [kartu'lina] *nf* card

casa ['kasa] *nf* house; (*hogar*) home; (*COM*) firm, company; **en ~** at home; **~ consistorial** town hall; **~ de huéspedes** boarding house; **~ de socorro** first aid post

casado, a [ka'saðo, a] *adj* married ♦ *nm/f* married man/woman

casamiento [kasa'mjento] *nm* marriage, wedding

casar [ka'sar] *vt* to marry; (*JUR*) to quash, annul; **~se** *vr* to marry, get married

cascabel [kaska'ßel] *nm* (small) bell

cascada [kas'kaða] *nf* waterfall

cascanueces [kaska'nweθes] *nm inv* nutcrackers *pl*

cascar [kas'kar] *vt* to crack, split, break (open); **~se** *vr* to crack, split, break (open)

cáscara ['kaskara] *nf* (*de huevo, fruta seca*) shell; (*de fruta*) skin; (*de limón*) peel

casco ['kasko] *nm* (*de bombero, soldado*) helmet; (*NAUT: de barco*) hull; (*ZOOL: de caballo*) hoof; (*botella*) empty bottle; (*de ciudad*): **el ~ antiguo** the old part; **el ~ urbano** the town centre; **los ~s azules** the UN peace-keeping force, the blue berets

cascote [kas'kote] *nm* rubble

caserío [kase'rio] *nm* hamlet; (*casa*) country house

casero, a [ka'sero, a] *adj* (*pan etc*) home-made ♦ *nm/f* (*propietario*) landlord/lady; **ser muy ~** to be home-loving; **"comida casera"** "home cooking"

caseta [ka'seta] *nf* hut; (*para bañista*) cubicle; (*de feria*) stall

casete [ka'sete] *nm o f* cassette

casi ['kasi] *adv* almost, nearly; **~ nada** hardly anything; **~ nunca** hardly ever, almost never; **~ te caes** you almost fell

casilla [ka'siʎa] *nf* (*casita*) hut, cabin; (*AJEDREZ*) square; (*para cartas*) pigeonhole; **casillero** *nm* (*para cartas*) pigeonholes *pl*

casino [ka'sino] *nm* club; (*de juego*) casino

caso ['kaso] *nm* case; **en ~ de ...** in case of ...; **en ~ de que ...** in case ...; **el ~ es**

que the fact is that; **en ese ~** in that case; **hacer ~ a** to pay attention to; **hacer o venir al ~** to be relevant

caspa ['kaspa] *nf* dandruff

cassette [ka'sete] *nm o f =* **casete**

casta ['kasta] *nf* caste; (*raza*) breed; (*linaje*) lineage

castaña [kas'taɲa] *nf* chestnut

castañetear [kastaɲete'ar] *vi* (*dientes*) to chatter

castaño, a [kas'taɲo, a] *adj* chestnut (-coloured), brown ♦ *nm* chestnut tree

castañuelas [kasta'ɲwelas] *nfpl* castanets

castellano, a [kaste'ʎano, a] *adj, nm/f* Castilian ♦ *nm* (*LING*) Castilian, Spanish

castidad [kasti'ðað] *nf* chastity, purity

castigar [kasti'var] *vt* to punish; (*DEPORTE*) to penalize; **castigo** *nm* punishment; (*DEPORTE*) penalty

Castilla [kas'tiʎa] *nf* Castile

castillo [kas'tiʎo] *nm* castle

castizo, a [kas'tiθo, a] *adj* (*LING*) pure

casto, a ['kasto, a] *adj* chaste, pure

castor [kas'tor] *nm* beaver

castrar [kas'trar] *vt* to castrate

castrense [kas'trense] *adj* (*disciplina, vida*) military

casual [ka'swal] *adj* chance, accidental; **~idad** *nf* chance, accident; (*combinación de circunstancias*) coincidence; **¡qué ~idad!** what a coincidence!

cataclismo [kata'klismo] *nm* cataclysm

catador, a [kata'ðor, a] *nm/f* wine taster

catalán, ana [kata'lan, ana] *adj, nm/f* Catalan ♦ *nm* (*LING*) Catalan

catalizador [kataliθa'ðor] *nm* catalyst; (*AUT*) catalytic convertor

catalogar [katalo'var] *vt* to catalogue; **~ a algn (de)** (*fig*) to categorize sb (as)

catálogo [ka'talovo] *nm* catalogue

Cataluña [kata'luɲa] *nf* Catalonia

catar [ka'tar] *vt* to taste, sample

catarata [kata'rata] *nf* (*GEO*) waterfall; (*MED*) cataract

catarro [ka'tarro] *nm* catarrh; (*constipado*) cold

catástrofe [ka'tastrofe] *nf* catastrophe

catear [kate'ar] (*fam*) *vt* (*examen, alumno*) to fail

cátedra ['kateðra] *nf* (*UNIV*) chair, professorship

catedral [kate'ðral] *nf* cathedral

catedrático, a [kate'ðratiko, a] *nm/f* professor

categoría [kateɣo'ria] *nf* category; (*rango*) rank, standing; (*calidad*) quality; **de ~** (*hotel*) top-class

categórico, a [kate'ɣoriko, a] *adj* categorical

cateto, a ['kateto, a] (*pey*) *nm/f* peasant

catolicismo [katoli'θismo] *nm* Catholicism

católico, a [ka'toliko, a] *adj, nm/f* Catholic

catorce [ka'torθe] *num* fourteen

cauce ['kauθe] *nm* (*de río*) riverbed; (*fig*) channel

caucho ['kautʃo] *nm* rubber; (*AM: llanta*) tyre

caución [kau'θjon] *nf* bail; **caucionar** *vt* (*JUR*) to bail, go bail for

caudal [kau'ðal] *nm* (*de río*) volume, flow; (*fortuna*) wealth; (*abundancia*) abundance; **~oso, a** *adj* (*río*) large

caudillo [kau'ðiʎo] *nm* leader, chief

causa ['kausa] *nf* cause; (*razón*) reason; (*JUR*) lawsuit, case; **a ~ de** because of

causar [kau'sar] *vt* to cause

cautela [kau'tela] *nf* caution, cautiousness; **cauteloso, a** *adj* cautious, wary

cautivar [kauti'ßar] *vt* to capture; (*atraer*) to captivate

cautiverio [kauti'ßerjo] *nm* captivity

cautividad [kautißi'ðað] *nf* = **cautiverio**

cautivo, a [kau'tißo, a] *adj, nm/f* captive

cauto, a ['kauto, a] *adj* cautious, careful

cava ['kaßa] *nm* champagne-type wine

cavar [ka'ßar] *vt* to dig

caverna [ka'ßerna] *nf* cave, cavern

cavidad [kaßi'ðað] *nf* cavity

cavilar [kaßi'lar] *vt* to ponder

cayado [ka'jaðo] *nm* (*de pastor*) crook; (*de obispo*) crozier

cayendo *etc vb ver* **caer**

caza ['kaθa] *nf* (*acción: gen*) hunting;

(*: con fusil*) shooting; (*una ~*) hunt, chase; (*animales*) game ♦ *nm* (*AVIAT*) fighter

cazador, a [kaθa'ðor, a] *nm/f* hunter; **cazadora** *nf* jacket

cazar [ka'θar] *vt* to hunt; (*perseguir*) to chase; (*prender*) to catch

cazo ['kaθo] *nm* saucepan

cazuela [ka'θwela] *nf* (*vasija*) pan; (*guisado*) casserole

CD *abbr* (= *compact disc*) CD

CD-ROM *abbr m* CD-ROM

CE *nf abr* (= *Comunidad Europea*) EC

cebada [θe'ßaða] *nf* barley

cebar [θe'ßar] *vt* (*animal*) to fatten (up); (*anzuelo*) to bait; (*MIL, TEC*) to prime

cebo ['θeßo] *nm* (*para animales*) feed, food; (*para peces, fig*) bait; (*de arma*) charge

cebolla [θe'ßoʎa] *nf* onion; **cebolleta** *nf* spring onion; **cebollín** *nm* spring onion

cebra ['θeßra] *nf* zebra

cecear [θeθe'ar] *vi* to lisp; **ceceo** *nm* lisp

ceder [θe'ðer] *vt* to hand over, give up, part with ♦ *vi* (*renunciar*) to give in, yield; (*disminuir*) to diminish, decline; (*romperse*) to give way

cedro ['θeðro] *nm* cedar

cédula ['θeðula] *nf* certificate, document

cegar [θe'ɣar] *vt* to blind; (*tubería etc*) to block up, stop up ♦ *vi* to go blind; **~se** *vr*: **~se (de)** to be blinded (by)

ceguera [θe'ɣera] *nf* blindness

CEI *abbr* (= *Confederación de Estados Independientes*) CIS

ceja ['θexa] *nf* eyebrow

cejar [θe'xar] *vi* (*fig*) to back down

celador, a [θela'ðor, a] *nm/f* (*de edificio*) watchman; (*de museo etc*) attendant

celda ['θelda] *nf* cell

celebración [θeleßra'θjon] *nf* celebration

celebrar [θele'ßrar] *vt* to celebrate; (*alabar*) to praise ♦ *vi* to be glad; **~se** *vr* to occur, take place

célebre ['θelebre] *adj* famous

celebridad [θeleßri'ðað] *nf* fame; (*persona*) celebrity

celeste [θe'leste] *adj* (*azul*) sky-blue

celestial [θeles'tjal] *adj* celestial, heavenly

celibato [θeli'ßato] *nm* celibacy

célibe ['θeliße] *adj, nm/f* celibate

celo[1] ['θelo] *nm* zeal; (REL) fervour; (ZOOL): **en ~** on heat; **~s** *nmpl* jealousy *sg*; **tener ~s** to be jealous

celo[2] ® ['θelo] *nm* Sellotape ®

celofán [θelo'fan] *nm* cellophane

celoso, a [θe'loso, a] *adj* jealous; (*trabajador*) zealous

celta ['θelta] *adj* Celtic ♦ *nm/f* Celt

célula ['θelula] *nf* cell; **~ solar** solar cell

celulitis [θelu'litis] *nf* cellulite

cementerio [θemen'terjo] *nm* cemetery, graveyard

cemento [θe'mento] *nm* cement; (*hormigón*) concrete; (AM: *cola*) glue

cena ['θena] *nf* evening meal, dinner

cenagal [θena'yal] *nm* bog, quagmire

cenar [θe'nar] *vt* to have for dinner ♦ *vi* to have dinner

cenicero [θeni'θero] *nm* ashtray

cenit [θe'nit] *nm* zenith

ceniza [θe'niθa] *nf* ash, ashes *pl*

censo ['θenso] *nm* census; **~ electoral** electoral roll

censura [θen'sura] *nf* (POL) censorship

censurar [θensu'rar] *vt* (*idea*) to censure; (*cortar: película*) to censor

centella [θen'teʎa] *nf* spark

centellear [θenteʎe'ar] *vi* (*metal*) to gleam; (*estrella*) to twinkle; (*fig*) to sparkle

centenar [θente'nar] *nm* hundred

centenario, a [θente'narjo, a] *adj* centenary; hundred-year-old ♦ *nm* centenary

centeno [θen'teno] *nm* (BOT) rye

centésimo, a [θen'tesimo, a] *adj* hundredth

centígrado [θen'tixraðo] *adj* centigrade

centímetro [θen'timetro] *nm* centimetre (BRIT), centimeter (US)

céntimo [θentimo] *nm* cent

centinela [θenti'nela] *nm* sentry, guard

centollo [θen'toʎo] *nm* spider crab

central [θen'tral] *adj* central ♦ *nf* head office; (TEC) plant; (TEL) exchange; **~ eléctrica** power station; **~ nuclear** nuclear power station; **~ telefónica** telephone exchange

centralita [θentra'lita] *nf* switchboard

centralizar [θentrali'θar] *vt* to centralize

centrar [θen'trar] *vt* to centre

céntrico, a ['θentriko, a] *adj* central

centrifugar [θentrifu'yar] *vt* to spin-dry

centrista [θen'trista] *adj* centre *cpd*

centro ['θentro] *nm* centre; **~ comercial** shopping centre; **~ juvenil** youth club; **~ de atención al cliente** call centre

centroamericano, a [θentroameri'kano, a] *adj, nm/f* Central American

ceñido, a [θe'ɲiðo, a] *adj* (*chaqueta, pantalón*) tight(-fitting)

ceñir [θe'ɲir] *vt* (*rodear*) to encircle, surround; (*ajustar*) to fit (tightly)

ceño ['θeɲo] *nm* frown, scowl; **fruncir el ~** to frown, knit one's brow

CEOE *nf abr* (ESP: = *Confederación Española de Organizaciones Empresariales*) ≈ CBI (BRIT), employers' organization

cepillar [θepi'ʎar] *vt* to brush; (*madera*) to plane (down)

cepillo [θe'piʎo] *nm* brush; (*para madera*) plane; **~ de dientes** toothbrush

cera ['θera] *nf* wax

cerámica [θe'ramika] *nf* pottery; (*arte*) ceramics

cerca ['θerka] *nf* fence ♦ *adv* near, nearby, close; **~ de** near, close to

cercanías [θerka'nias] *nfpl* (*afueras*) outskirts, suburbs

cercano, a [θer'kano, a] *adj* close, near

cercar [θer'kar] *vt* to fence in; (*rodear*) to surround

cerciorar [θerθjo'rar] *vt* (*asegurar*) to assure; **~se** *vr* (*asegurarse*) to make sure

cerco ['θerko] *nm* (AGR) enclosure; (AM) fence; (MIL) siege

cerdo, a ['θerðo, a] *nm/f* pig/sow

cereal [θere'al] *nm* cereal; **~es** *nmpl* cereals, grain *sg*

cerebro [θe'reßro] *nm* brain; (*fig*) brains *pl*

ceremonia [θere'monja] *nf* ceremony; **ceremonial** *adj, nm* ceremonial;

ceremonioso, a adj ceremonious
cereza [θe'reθa] nf cherry
cerilla [θe'riʎa] nf (fósforo) match
cernerse [θer'nerse] vr to hover
cero ['θero] nm nothing, zero
cerrado, a [θe'rraðo, a] adj closed, shut; (con llave) locked; (tiempo) cloudy, overcast; (curva) sharp; (acento) thick, broad
cerradura [θerra'ðura] nf (acción) closing; (mecanismo) lock
cerrajero [θerra'xero] nm locksmith
cerrar [θe'rrar] vt to close, shut; (paso, carretera) to close; (grifo) to turn off; (cuenta, negocio) to close ♦ vi to close, shut; (la noche) to come down; **~se** vr to close, shut; **~ con llave** to lock; **~ un trato** to strike a bargain
cerro ['θerro] nm hill
cerrojo [θe'rroxo] nm (herramienta) bolt; (de puerta) latch
certamen [θer'tamen] nm competition, contest
certero, a [θer'tero, a] adj (gen) accurate
certeza [θer'teθa] nf certainty
certidumbre [θerti'ðumbre] nf = **certeza**
certificado [θertifi'kaðo] nm certificate
certificar [θertifi'kar] vt (asegurar, atestar) to certify
cervatillo [θerßa'tiʎo] nm fawn
cervecería [θerßeθe'ria] nf (fábrica) brewery; (bar) public house, pub
cerveza [θer'ßeθa] nf beer
cesante [θe'sante] adj redundant
cesar [θe'sar] vi to cease, stop ♦ vt (funcionario) to remove from office
cesárea [θe'sarea] nf (MED) Caesarean operation o section
cese ['θese] nm (de trabajo) dismissal; (de pago) suspension
césped ['θespeð] nm grass, lawn
cesta ['θesta] nf basket
cesto ['θesto] nm (large) basket, hamper
cetro ['θetro] nm sceptre
cfr abr (= confróntese) cf.
chabacano, a [tʃaßa'kano, a] adj vulgar, coarse

chabola [tʃa'ßola] nf shack; **barrio de ~s** shanty town sg
chacal [tʃa'kal] nm jackal
chacha ['tʃatʃa] (fam) nf maid
cháchara ['tʃatʃara] nf chatter; **estar de ~** to chatter away
chacra ['tʃakra] (AM) nf smallholding
chafar [tʃa'far] vt (aplastar) to crush; (plan etc) to ruin
chal [tʃal] nm shawl
chalado, a [tʃa'lado, a] (fam) adj crazy
chalé [tʃa'le] (pl ~s) nm villa; ≈ detached house
chaleco [tʃa'leko] nm waistcoat, vest (US); **~ salvavidas** life jacket
chalet [tʃa'le] (pl ~s) nm = **chalé**
champán [tʃam'pan] nm champagne
champaña [tʃam'paɲa] nm = **champán**
champiñón [tʃampi'ɲon] nm mushroom
champú [tʃam'pu] (pl **champúes, champús**) nm shampoo
chamuscar [tʃamus'kar] vt to scorch, sear, singe
chance ['tʃanθe] (AM) nm chance
chancho, a ['tʃantʃo, a] (AM) nm/f pig
chanchullo [tʃan'tʃuʎo] (fam) nm fiddle
chandal [tʃan'dal] nm tracksuit
chantaje [tʃan'taxe] nm blackmail
chapa ['tʃapa] nf (de metal) plate, sheet; (de madera) board, panel; (AM: AUTO) number (BRIT) o license (US) plate; **~do, a** adj: **~do en oro** gold-plated
chaparrón [tʃapa'rron] nm downpour, cloudburst
chapotear [tʃapote'ar] vi to splash about
chapurrear [tʃapurre'ar] vt (idioma) to speak badly
chapuza [tʃa'puθa] nf botched job
chapuzón [tʃapu'θon] nm: **darse un ~** to go for a dip
chaqueta [tʃa'keta] nf jacket
chaquetón [tʃake'ton] nm long jacket
charca ['tʃarka] nf pond, pool
charco ['tʃarko] nm pool, puddle
charcutería [tʃarkute'ria] nf (tienda) shop selling chiefly pork meat products; (productos) cooked pork meats pl

charla ['tʃarla] *nf* talk, chat; (*conferencia*) lecture

charlar [tʃar'lar] *vi* to talk, chat

charlatán, ana [tʃarla'tan, ana] *nm/f* (*hablador*) chatterbox; (*estafador*) trickster

charol [tʃa'rol] *nm* varnish; (*cuero*) patent leather

chascarrillo [tʃaska'rriʎo] (*fam*) *nm* funny story

chasco ['tʃasko] *nm* (*desengaño*) disappointment

chasis ['tʃasis] *nm inv* chassis

chasquear [tʃaske'ar] *vt* (*látigo*) to crack; (*lengua*) to click; **chasquido** *nm* crack; click

chatarra [tʃa'tarra] *nf* scrap (metal)

chato, a ['tʃato, a] *adj* flat; (*nariz*) snub

chaval, a [tʃa'βal, a] *nm/f* kid, lad/lass

checo, a ['tʃeko, a] *adj*, *nm/f* Czech ♦ *nm* (*LING*) Czech

checo(e)slovaco, a [tʃeko(e)slo'βako, a] *adj*, *nm/f* Czech, Czechoslovak

Checo(e)slovaquia [tʃeko(e)slo'βakja] *nf* Czechoslovakia

cheque ['tʃeke] *nm* cheque (*BRIT*), check (*US*); **~ de viajero** traveller's cheque (*BRIT*), traveler's check (*US*)

chequeo [tʃe'keo] *nm* (*MED*) check-up; (*AUTO*) service

chequera [tʃe'kera] (*AM*) *nf* chequebook (*BRIT*), checkbook (*US*)

chicano, a [tʃi'kano, a] *adj*, *nm/f* chicano

chícharo ['tʃitʃaro] (*AM*) *nm* pea

chichón [tʃi'tʃon] *nm* bump, lump

chicle ['tʃikle] *nm* chewing gum

chico, a ['tʃiko, a] *adj* small, little ♦ *nm/f* (*niño*) child; (*muchacho*) boy/girl

chiflado, a [tʃi'flaðo, a] *adj* crazy

chiflar [tʃi'flar] *vt* to hiss, boo

Chile ['tʃile] *nm* Chile; **chileno, a** *adj*, *nm/f* Chilean

chile ['tʃile] *nm* chilli pepper

chillar [tʃi'ʎar] *vi* (*persona*) to yell, scream; (*animal salvaje*) to howl; (*cerdo*) to squeal

chillido [tʃi'ʎiðo] *nm* (*de persona*) yell, scream; (*de animal*) howl

chillón, ona [tʃi'ʎon, ona] *adj* (*niño*) noisy; (*color*) loud, gaudy

chimenea [tʃime'nea] *nf* chimney; (*hogar*) fireplace

China ['tʃina] *nf*: **(la) ~** China

chinche ['tʃintʃe] *nf* (*insecto*) (bed)bug; (*TEC*) drawing pin (*BRIT*), thumbtack (*US*) ♦ *nm/f* nuisance, pest

chincheta [tʃin'tʃeta] *nf* drawing pin (*BRIT*), thumbtack (*US*)

chino, a ['tʃino, a] *adj*, *nm/f* Chinese ♦ *nm* (*LING*) Chinese

chipirón [tʃipi'ron] *nm* (*ZOOL, CULIN*) squid

Chipre ['tʃipre] *nf* Cyprus; **chipriota** *adj*, *nm/f* Cypriot

chiquillo, a [tʃi'kiʎo, a] *nm/f* (*fam*) kid

chirimoya [tʃiri'moja] *nf* custard apple

chiringuito [tʃirin'ɣito] *nm* small open-air bar

chiripa [tʃi'ripa] *nf* fluke

chirriar [tʃi'rrjar] *vi* to creak, squeak

chirrido [tʃi'rriðo] *nm* creak(ing), squeak(ing)

chis [tʃis] *excl* sh!

chisme ['tʃisme] *nm* (*habladurías*) piece of gossip; (*fam: objeto*) thingummyjig

chismoso, a [tʃis'moso, a] *adj* gossiping ♦ *nm/f* gossip

chispa ['tʃispa] *nf* spark; (*fig*) sparkle; (*ingenio*) wit; (*fam*) drunkenness

chispear [tʃispe'ar] *vi* (*lloviznar*) to drizzle

chisporrotear [tʃisporrote'ar] *vi* (*fuego*) to throw out sparks; (*leña*) to crackle; (*aceite*) to hiss, splutter

chiste ['tʃiste] *nm* joke, funny story

chistoso, a [tʃis'toso, a] *adj* funny, amusing

chivo, a ['tʃiβo, a] *nm/f* (billy-/nanny-)goat; **~ expiatorio** scapegoat

chocante [tʃo'kante] *adj* startling; (*extraño*) odd; (*ofensivo*) shocking

chocar [tʃo'kar] *vi* (*coches etc*) to collide, crash ♦ *vt* to shock; (*sorprender*) to startle; **~ con** to collide with; (*fig*) to run into, run up against; **¡chócala!** (*fam*) put it there!

chochear [tʃotʃe'ar] *vi* to dodder, be senile

chocho, a ['tʃotʃo, a] *adj* doddering, senile; (*fig*) soft, doting

chocolate [tʃoko'late] *adj, nm* chocolate; **chocolatina** *nf* chocolate

chofer [tʃo'fer] *nm* = **chófer**

chófer ['tʃofer] *nm* driver

chollo ['tʃoʎo] (*fam*) *nm* bargain, snip

choque *etc* ['tʃoke] *vb ver* **chocar** ♦ *nm* (*impacto*) impact; (*golpe*) jolt; (*AUTO*) crash; (*fig*) conflict; ~ **frontal** head-on collision

chorizo [tʃo'riθo] *nm* hard pork sausage

chorrada [tʃo'rraða] (*fam*) *nf*: **¡es una ~!** that's crap! (*!*); **decir ~s** to talk crap (*!*)

chorrear [tʃorre'ar] *vi* to gush (out), spout (out); (*gotear*) to drip, trickle

chorro ['tʃorro] *nm* jet; (*fig*) stream

choza ['tʃoθa] *nf* hut, shack

chubasco [tʃu'ßasko] *nm* squall

chubasquero [tʃußas'kero] *nm* lightweight raincoat

chuchería [tʃutʃe'ria] *nf* trinket

chuleta [tʃu'leta] *nf* chop, cutlet

chulo ['tʃulo] *nm* (*de prostituta*) pimp

chupar [tʃu'par] *vt* to suck; (*absorber*) to absorb; **~se** *vr* to grow thin

chupete [tʃu'pete] *nm* dummy (*BRIT*), pacifier (*US*)

chupito [tʃu'pito] (*fam*) *nm* shot

churro ['tʃurro] *nm* (type of) fritter

chusma ['tʃusma] *nf* rabble, mob

chutar [tʃu'tar] *vi* to shoot (at goal)

Cía *abr* (= *compañía*) Co.

cianuro [θja'nuro] *nm* cyanide

cibercafé [θißerka'fe] *nm* cybercafé

cicatriz [θika'triθ] *nf* scar; **~arse** *vr* to heal (up), form a scar

ciclismo [θi'klismo] *nm* cycling

ciclista [θi'klista] *adj* cycle *cpd* ♦ *nm/f* cyclist

ciclo ['θiklo] *nm* cycle

ciclón [θi'klon] *nm* cyclone

cicloturismo [θiklotu'rismo] *nm*: **hacer ~** to go on a cycling holiday

ciego, a ['θjeɣo, a] *adj* blind ♦ *nm/f* blind man/woman

cielo ['θjelo] *nm* sky; (*REL*) heaven; **¡~s!** good heavens!

ciempiés [θjem'pjes] *nm inv* centipede

cien [θjen] *num ver* **ciento**

ciénaga ['θjenaɣa] *nf* marsh, swamp

ciencia ['θjenθja] *nf* science; **~s** *nfpl* (*ESCOL*) science *sg*; **~-ficción** *nf* science fiction

cieno ['θjeno] *nm* mud, mire

científico, a [θjen'tifiko, a] *adj* scientific ♦ *nm/f* scientist

ciento ['θjento] (*tb*: **cien**) *num* hundred; **pagar al 10 por ~** to pay at 10 per cent

cierre *etc* ['θjerre] *vb ver* **cerrar** ♦ *nm* closing, shutting; (*con llave*) locking; ~ **de cremallera** zip (fastener)

cierro *etc* *vb ver* **cerrar**

cierto, a ['θjerto, a] *adj* sure, certain; (*un tal*) a certain; (*correcto*) right, correct; ~ **hombre** a certain man; **ciertas personas** certain *o* some people; **sí, es ~** yes, that's correct

ciervo ['θjerßo] *nm* deer; (*macho*) stag

cierzo ['θjerθo] *nm* north wind

cifra ['θifra] *nf* number; (*secreta*) code

cifrar [θi'frar] *vt* to code, write in code

cigala [θi'ɣala] *nf* Norway lobster

cigarra [θi'ɣarra] *nf* cicada

cigarrillo [θiɣa'rriʎo] *nm* cigarette

cigarro [θi'ɣarro] *nm* cigarette; (*puro*) cigar

cigüeña [θi'ɣweɲa] *nf* stork

cilíndrico, a [θi'lindriko, a] *adj* cylindrical

cilindro [θi'lindro] *nm* cylinder

cima ['θima] *nf* (*de montaña*) top, peak; (*de árbol*) top; (*fig*) height

cimbrearse [θimbre'arse] *vr* to sway

cimentar [θimen'tar] *vt* to lay the foundations of; (*fig: fundar*) to found

cimiento [θi'mjento] *nm* foundation

cinc [θink] *nm* zinc

cincel [θin'θel] *nm* chisel; **~ar** *vt* to chisel

cinco ['θinko] *num* five

cincuenta [θin'kwenta] *num* fifty

cine ['θine] *nm* cinema

cineasta [θine'asta] *nm/f* film director

cinematográfico, a [θinemato'ɣrafiko, a] *adj* cine-, film *cpd*

cínico, a ['θiniko, a] *adj* cynical ♦ *nm/f* cynic

cinismo [θi'nismo] *nm* cynicism

cinta ['θinta] *nf* band, strip; (*de tela*) ribbon; (*película*) reel; (*de máquina de escribir*) ribbon; ~ **adhesiva** sticky tape; ~ **de vídeo** videotape; ~ **magnetofónica** tape; ~ **métrica** tape measure

cintura [θin'tura] *nf* waist

cinturón [θintu'ron] *nm* belt; ~ **de seguridad** safety belt

ciprés [θi'pres] *nm* cypress (tree)

circo ['θirko] *nm* circus

circuito [θir'kwito] *nm* circuit

circulación [θirkula'θjon] *nf* circulation; (*AUTO*) traffic

circular [θirku'lar] *adj, nf* circular ♦ *vi, vt* to circulate ♦ *vi* (*AUTO*) to drive; **"circule por la derecha"** "keep (to the) right"

círculo ['θirkulo] *nm* circle; ~ **vicioso** vicious circle

circuncidar [θirkunθi'dar] *vt* to circumcise

circundar [θirkun'dar] *vt* to surround

circunferencia [θirkunfe'renθja] *nf* circumference

circunscribir [θirkunskri'ßir] *vt* to circumscribe; ~**se** *vr* to be limited

circunscripción [θirkunskrip'θjon] *nf* (*POL*) constituency

circunspecto, a [θirkuns'pekto, a] *adj* circumspect, cautious

circunstancia [θirkuns'tanθja] *nf* circumstance

cirio ['θirjo] *nm* (wax) candle

ciruela [θi'rwela] *nf* plum; ~ **pasa** prune

cirugía [θiru'xia] *nf* surgery; ~ **estética** *o* **plástica** plastic surgery

cirujano [θiru'xano] *nm* surgeon

cisne ['θisne] *nm* swan

cisterna [θis'terna] *nf* cistern, tank

cita ['θita] *nf* appointment, meeting; (*de novios*) date; (*referencia*) quotation

citación [θita'θjon] *nf* (*JUR*) summons *sg*

citar [θi'tar] *vt* (*gen*) to make an appointment with; (*JUR*) to summons; (*un autor, texto*) to quote; ~**se** *vr*: **se citaron en el cine** they arranged to meet at the

cinema

cítricos ['θitrikos] *nmpl* citrus fruit(s)

ciudad [θju'ðað] *nf* town; (*más grande*) city; ~**anía** *nf* citizenship; ~**ano, a** *nm/f* citizen

cívico, a ['θißiko, a] *adj* civic

civil [θi'ßil] *adj* civil ♦ *nm* (*guardia*) policeman

civilización [θißiliθa'θjon] *nf* civilization

civilizar [θißili'θar] *vt* to civilize

civismo [θi'ßismo] *nm* public spirit

cizaña [θi'θaɲa] *nf* (*fig*) discord

cl. *abr* (= *centilitro*) cl.

clamar [kla'mar] *vt* to clamour for, cry out for ♦ *vi* to cry out, clamour

clamor [kla'mor] *nm* clamour, protest

clandestino, a [klandes'tino, a] *adj* clandestine; (*POL*) underground

clara ['klara] *nf* (*de huevo*) egg white

claraboya [klara'ßoja] *nf* skylight

clarear [klare'ar] *vi* (*el día*) to dawn; (*el cielo*) to clear up, brighten up; ~**se** *vr* to be transparent

clarete [kla'rete] *nm* rosé (wine)

claridad [klari'ðað] *nf* (*del día*) brightness; (*de estilo*) clarity

clarificar [klarifi'kar] *vt* to clarify

clarinete [klari'nete] *nm* clarinet

clarividencia [klarißi'ðenθja] *nf* clairvoyance; (*fig*) far-sightedness

claro, a ['klaro, a] *adj* clear; (*luminoso*) bright; (*color*) light; (*evidente*) clear, evident; (*poco espeso*) thin ♦ *nm* (*en bosque*) clearing ♦ *adv* clearly ♦ *excl* (*tb*: ~ **que sí**) of course!

clase ['klase] *nf* class; ~ **alta/media/obrera** upper/middle/working class; ~**s particulares** private lessons, private tuition *sg*

clásico, a ['klasiko, a] *adj* classical

clasificación [klasifika'θjon] *nf* classification; (*DEPORTE*) league (table)

clasificar [klasifi'kar] *vt* to classify

claudicar [klauði'kar] *vi* to give in

claustro ['klaustro] *nm* cloister

cláusula ['klausula] *nf* clause

clausura [klau'sura] *nf* closing, closure;

clausurar vt (congreso etc) to bring to a close

clavar [kla'ßar] vt (clavo) to hammer in; (cuchillo) to stick, thrust

clave ['klaße] nf key; (MUS) clef

clavel [kla'ßel] nm carnation

clavícula [kla'ßikula] nf collar bone

clavija [kla'ßixa] nf peg, dowel, pin; (ELEC) plug

clavo ['klaßo] nm (de metal) nail; (BOT) clove

claxon ['klakson] (pl ~s) nm horn

clemencia [kle'menθja] nf mercy, clemency

cleptómano, a [klep'tomano, a] nm/f kleptomaniac

clérigo ['kleriɣo] nm priest

clero ['klero] nm clergy

cliché [kli'tʃe] nm cliché; (FOTO) negative

cliente, a ['kljente, a] nm/f client, customer

clientela [kljen'tela] nf clientele, customers pl

clima ['klima] nm climate

climatizado, a [klimati'θaðo, a] adj air-conditioned

clímax ['klimaks] nm inv climax

clínica ['klinika] nf clinic; (particular) private hospital

clip [klip] (pl ~s) nm paper clip

clítoris ['klitoris] nm inv (ANAT) clitoris

cloaca [klo'aka] nf sewer

cloro ['kloro] nm chlorine

club [klub] (pl ~s o ~es) nm club; ~ de jóvenes youth club

cm abr (= centímetro, centímetros) cm

C.N.T. (ESP) abr = Confederación Nacional de Trabajo

coacción [koak'θjon] nf coercion, compulsion; **coaccionar** vt to coerce

coagular [koaɣu'lar] vt (leche, sangre) to clot; ~**se** vr to clot; **coágulo** nm clot

coalición [koali'θjon] nf coalition

coartada [koar'taða] nf alibi

coartar [koar'tar] vt to limit, restrict

coba ['koßa] nf: **dar ~ a uno** to soft-soap sb

cobarde [ko'ßarðe] adj cowardly ♦ nm coward; **cobardía** nf cowardice

cobaya [ko'ßaja] nf guinea pig

cobertizo [koßer'tiθo] nm shelter

cobertura [koßer'tura] nf cover

cobija [ko'ßixa] (AM) nf blanket

cobijar [koßi'xar] vt (cubrir) to cover; (proteger) to shelter; **cobijo** nm shelter

cobra ['koßra] nf cobra

cobrador, a [koßra'ðor, a] nm/f (de autobús) conductor/conductress; (de impuestos, gas) collector

cobrar [ko'ßrar] vt (cheque) to cash; (sueldo) to collect, draw; (objeto) to recover; (precio) to charge; (deuda) to collect ♦ vi to be paid; **cóbrese al entregar** cash on delivery

cobre ['koßre] nm copper; ~s nmpl (MUS) brass instruments

cobro ['koßro] nm (de cheque) cashing; **presentar al ~** to cash

cocaína [koka'ina] nf cocaine

cocción [kok'θjon] nf (CULIN) cooking; (en agua) boiling

cocear [koθe'ar] vi to kick

cocer [ko'θer] vt, vi to cook; (en agua) to boil; (en horno) to bake

coche ['kotʃe] nm (AUTO) car (BRIT), automobile (US); (de tren, de caballos) coach, carriage; (para niños) pram (BRIT), baby carriage (US); **ir en ~** to drive; ~ **celular** Black Maria, prison van; ~ **de bomberos** fire engine; ~ **fúnebre** hearse; **coche-cama** (pl **coches-cama**) nm (FERRO) sleeping car, sleeper

cochera [ko'tʃera] nf garage; (de autobuses, trenes) depot

coche restaurante (pl **coches restaurante**) nm (FERRO) dining car, diner

cochinillo [kotʃi'niʎo] nm (CULIN) suckling pig, sucking pig

cochino, a [ko'tʃino, a] adj filthy, dirty ♦ nm/f pig

cocido [ko'θiðo] nm stew

cocina [ko'θina] nf kitchen; (aparato) cooker, stove; (acto) cookery; ~ **eléctrica / de gas** electric/gas cooker; ~

francesa French cuisine; **cocinar** *vt, vi* to cook

cocinero, a [koθi'nero, a] *nm/f* cook

coco ['koko] *nm* coconut

cocodrilo [koko'ðrilo] *nm* crocodile

cocotero [koko'tero] *nm* coconut palm

cóctel ['koktel] *nm* cocktail

codazo [ko'ðaθo] *nm*: **dar un ~ a uno** to nudge sb

codicia [ko'ðiθja] *nf* greed; **codiciar** *vt* to covet; **codicioso, a** *adj* covetous

código ['koðiɣo] *nm* code; **~ de barras** bar code; **~ civil** common law; **~ de (la) circulación** highway code; **~ postal** postcode

codillo [ko'ðiʎo] *nm* (*ZOOL*) knee; (*TEC*) elbow (joint)

codo ['koðo] *nm* (*ANAT, de tubo*) elbow; (*ZOOL*) knee

codorniz [koðor'niθ] *nf* quail

coerción [koer'θjon] *nf* coercion

coetáneo, a [koe'taneo, a] *adj, nm/f* contemporary

coexistir [koe(k)sis'tir] *vi* to coexist

cofradía [kofra'ðia] *nf* brotherhood, fraternity

cofre ['kofre] *nm* (*de joyas*) case; (*de dinero*) chest

coger [ko'xer] (*ESP*) *vt* to take (hold of); (*objeto caído*) to pick up; (*frutas*) to pick, harvest; (*resfriado, ladrón, pelota*) to catch ♦ *vi*: **~ por el buen camino** to take the right road; **~se** *vr* (*el dedo*) to catch; **~se a algo** to get hold of sth

cogollo [ko'ɣoʎo] *nm* (*de lechuga*) heart

cogote [ko'ɣote] *nm* back *o* nape of the neck

cohabitar [koaβi'tar] *vi* to live together, cohabit

cohecho [ko'etʃo] *nm* (*acción*) bribery; (*soborno*) bribe

coherente [koe'rente] *adj* coherent

cohesión [koe'sjon] *nm* cohesion

cohete [ko'ete] *nm* rocket

cohibido, a [koi'βiðo, a] *adj* (*PSICO*) inhibited; (*tímido*) shy

cohibir [koi'βir] *vt* to restrain, restrict

coincidencia [koinθi'ðenθja] *nf* coincidence

coincidir [koinθi'ðir] *vi* (*en idea*) to coincide, agree; (*en lugar*) to coincide

coito ['koito] *nm* intercourse, coitus

coja *etc vb ver* **coger**

cojear [koxe'ar] *vi* (*persona*) to limp, hobble; (*mueble*) to wobble, rock

cojera [ko'xera] *nf* limp

cojín [ko'xin] *nm* cushion; **cojinete** *nm* (*TEC*) ball bearing

cojo, a *etc* ['koxo, a] *vb ver* **coger** ♦ *adj* (*que no puede andar*) lame, crippled; (*mueble*) wobbly ♦ *nm/f* lame person, cripple

cojón [ko'xon] (*fam*) *nm*: **¡cojones!** shit! (*!*); **cojonudo, a** (*fam*) *adj* great, fantastic

col [kol] *nf* cabbage; **~es de Bruselas** Brussels sprouts

cola ['kola] *nf* tail; (*de gente*) queue; (*lugar*) end, last place; (*para pegar*) glue, gum; **hacer ~** to queue (up)

colaborador, a [kolaβora'ðor, a] *nm/f* collaborator

colaborar [kolaβo'rar] *vi* to collaborate

colada [ko'laða] *nf*: **hacer la ~** to do the washing

colador [kola'ðor] *nm* (*de líquidos*) strainer; (*para verduras etc*) colander

colapso [ko'lapso] *nm* collapse; **~ nervioso** nervous breakdown

colar [ko'lar] *vt* (*líquido*) to strain off; (*metal*) to cast ♦ *vi* to ooze, seep (through); **~se** *vr* to jump the queue; **~se en** to get into without paying; (*fiesta*) to gatecrash

colcha ['koltʃa] *nf* bedspread

colchón [kol'tʃon] *nm* mattress; **~ inflable** *o* **neumático** air bed, air mattress

colchoneta [koltʃo'neta] *nf* (*en gimnasio*) mat; (*de playa*) air bed

colección [kolek'θjon] *nf* collection; **coleccionar** *vt* to collect; **coleccionista** *nm/f* collector

colecta [ko'lekta] *nf* collection

colectivo, a [kolek'tiβo, a] *adj* collective,

joint ♦ *nm (AM)* (small) bus
colega [ko'leɣa] *nm/f* colleague
colegial, a [kole'xjal, a] *nm/f* schoolboy/girl
colegio [ko'lexjo] *nm* college; (*escuela*) school; (*de abogados etc*) association; ~ **electoral** polling station; ~ **mayor** hall of residence

---

colegio

A **colegio** *is normally a private primary or secondary school. In the state system it means a primary school although these are also called* **escuelas**. *State secondary schools are called* **institutos**.

---

colegir [kole'xir] *vt* to infer, conclude
cólera ['kolera] *nf* (*ira*) anger ♦ *nm (MED)* cholera; **colérico, a** [ko'leriko, a] *adj* irascible, bad-tempered
colesterol [koleste'rol] *nm* cholesterol
coleta [ko'leta] *nf* pigtail
colgante [kol'ɣante] *adj* hanging ♦ *nm* (*joya*) pendant
colgar [kol'ɣar] *vt* to hang (up); (*ropa*) to hang out ♦ *vi* to hang; (*TELEC*) to hang up
cólico ['koliko] *nm* colic
coliflor [koli'flor] *nf* cauliflower
colilla [ko'liʎa] *nf* cigarette end, butt
colina [ko'lina] *nf* hill
colisión [koli'sjon] *nf* collision; ~ **de frente** head-on crash
collar [ko'ʎar] *nm* necklace; (*de perro*) collar
colmar [kol'mar] *vt* to fill to the brim; (*fig*) to fulfil, realize
colmena [kol'mena] *nf* beehive
colmillo [kol'miʎo] *nm* (*diente*) eye tooth; (*de elefante*) tusk; (*de perro*) fang
colmo ['kolmo] *nm*: **¡es el ~!** it's the limit!
colocación [koloka'θjon] *nf* (*acto*) placing; (*empleo*) job, position
colocar [kolo'kar] *vt* to place, put, position; (*dinero*) to invest; (*poner en empleo*) to find a job for; **~se** *vr* to get a

job
Colombia [ko'lombja] *nf* Colombia; **colombiano, a** *adj, nm/f* Colombian
colonia [ko'lonja] *nf* colony; (*de casas*) housing estate; (*agua de ~*) cologne
colonización [koloniθa'θjon] *nf* colonization; **colonizador, a** [koloniθa'ðor, a] *adj* colonizing ♦ *nm/f* colonist, settler
colonizar [koloni'θar] *vt* to colonize
coloquio [ko'lokjo] *nm* conversation; (*congreso*) conference
color [ko'lor] *nm* colour
colorado, a [kolo'raðo, a] *adj* (*rojo*) red; (*LAM: chiste*) rude
colorante [kolo'rante] *nm* colouring
colorear [kolore'ar] *vt* to colour
colorete [kolo'rete] *nm* blusher
colorido [kolo'riðo] *nm* colouring
columna [ko'lumna] *nf* column; (*pilar*) pillar; (*apoyo*) support
columpiar [kolum'pjar] *vt* to swing; **~se** *vr* to swing; **columpio** *nm* swing
coma ['koma] *nf* comma ♦ *nm (MED)* coma
comadre [ko'maðre] *nf* (*madrina*) godmother; (*chismosa*) gossip; **comadrona** *nf* midwife
comandancia [koman'danθja] *nf* command
comandante [koman'dante] *nm* commandant
comarca [ko'marka] *nf* region
comba ['komba] *nf* (*curva*) curve; (*cuerda*) skipping rope; **saltar a la ~** to skip
combar [kom'bar] *vt* to bend, curve
combate [kom'bate] *nm* fight; **combatiente** *nm* combatant
combatir [komba'tir] *vt* to fight, combat
combinación [kombina'θjon] *nf* combination; (*QUÍM*) compound; (*prenda*) slip
combinar [kombi'nar] *vt* to combine
combustible [kombus'tiβle] *nm* fuel
combustión [kombus'tjon] *nf* combustion
comedia [ko'meðja] *nf* comedy; (*TEATRO*) play, drama

comediante [kome'ðjante] *nm/f* (comic) actor/actress

comedido, a [kome'ðiðo, a] *adj* moderate

comedor, a [kome'ðor, a] *nm* (*habitación*) dining room; (*cantina*) canteen

comensal [komen'sal] *nm/f* fellow guest (*o diner*)

comentar [komen'tar] *vt* to comment on

comentario [komen'tarjo] *nm* comment, remark; (*literario*) commentary; **~s** *nmpl* (*chismes*) gossip *sg*

comentarista [komenta'rista] *nm/f* commentator

comenzar [komen'θar] *vt, vi* to begin, start; **~ a hacer algo** to begin *o* start doing sth

comer [ko'mer] *vt* to eat; (*DAMAS, AJEDREZ*) to take, capture ♦ *vi* to eat; (*almorzar*) to have lunch; **~se** *vr* to eat up

comercial [komer'θjal] *adj* commercial; (*relativo al negocio*) business *cpd*; **comercializar** *vt* (*producto*) to market; (*pey*) to commercialize

comerciante [komer'θjante] *nm/f* trader, merchant

comerciar [komer'θjar] *vi* to trade, do business

comercio [ko'merθjo] *nm* commerce, trade; (*negocio*) business; (*fig*) dealings *pl*; **~ electrónico** e-commerce

comestible [komes'tiβle] *adj* eatable, edible; **~s** *nmpl* food *sg*, foodstuffs

cometa [ko'meta] *nm* comet ♦ *nf* kite

cometer [kome'ter] *vt* to commit

cometido [kome'tiðo] *nm* task, assignment

comezón [kome'θon] *nf* itch, itching

cómic ['komik] *nm* comic

comicios [ko'miθjos] *nmpl* elections

cómico, a ['komiko, a] *adj* comic(al) ♦ *nm/f* comedian

comida [ko'miða] *nf* (*alimento*) food; (*cena*) meal; (*de mediodía*) lunch

comidilla [komi'ðiʎa] *nf*: **ser la ~ de la ciudad** to be the talk of the town

comienzo *etc* [ko'mjenθo] *vb ver* **comenzar** ♦ *nm* beginning, start

comillas [ko'miʎas] *nfpl* quotation marks

comilona [komi'lona] (*fam*) *nf* blow-out

comino [ko'mino] *nm*: **(no) me importa un ~** I don't give a damn

comisaría [komisa'ria] *nf* (*de policía*) police station; (*MIL*) commissariat

comisario [komi'sarjo] *nm* (*MIL etc*) commissary; (*POL*) commissar

comisión [komi'sjon] *nf* commission

comité [komi'te] (*pl* **~s**) *nm* committee

comitiva [komi'tiβa] *nf* retinue

como ['komo] *adv* as; (*tal ~*) like; (*aproximadamente*) about, approximately ♦ *conj* (*ya que, puesto que*) as, since; **¡~ no!** of course!; **~ no lo haga hoy** unless he does it today; **~ si** as if; **es tan alto ~ ancho** it is as high as it is wide

cómo ['komo] *adv* how?, why? ♦ *excl* what?, I beg your pardon? ♦ *nm*: **el ~ y el porqué** the whys and wherefores

cómoda ['komoða] *nf* chest of drawers

comodidad [komoði'ðað] *nf* comfort; **venga a su ~** come at your convenience

comodín [komo'ðin] *nm* joker

cómodo, a ['komoðo, a] *adj* comfortable; (*práctico, de fácil uso*) convenient

compact disc *nm* compact disk player

compacto, a [kom'pakto, a] *adj* compact

compadecer [kompaðe'θer] *vt* to pity, be sorry for; **~se** *vr*: **~se de** to pity, be *o* feel sorry for

compadre [kom'paðre] *nm* (*padrino*) godfather; (*amigo*) friend, pal

compañero, a [kompa'ɲero, a] *nm/f* companion; (*novio*) boy/girlfriend; **~ de clase** classmate

compañía [kompa'ɲia] *nf* company

comparación [kompara'θjon] *nf* comparison; **en ~ con** in comparison with

comparar [kompa'rar] *vt* to compare

comparecer [kompare'θer] *vi* to appear (in court)

comparsa [kom'parsa] *nm/f* (*TEATRO*) extra

compartimiento [komparti'mjento] *nm* (*FERRO*) compartment

compartir [kompar'tir] *vt* to share; (*dinero,*

comida etc) to divide (up), share (out)

compás [kom'pas] *nm* (*MUS*) beat, rhythm; (*MAT*) compasses *pl*; (*NAUT etc*) compass

compasión [kompa'sjon] *nf* compassion, pity

compasivo, a [kompa'sißo, a] *adj* compassionate

compatibilidad [kompatißili'ðað] *nf* compatibility

compatible [kompa'tißle] *adj* compatible

compatriota [kompa'trjota] *nm/f* compatriot, fellow countryman/woman

compendiar [kompen'djar] *vt* to summarize; **compendio** *nm* summary

compenetrarse [kompene'trarse] *vr* to be in tune

compensación [kompensa'θjon] *nf* compensation

compensar [kompen'sar] *vt* to compensate

competencia [kompe'tenθja] *nf* (*incumbencia*) domain, field; (*JUR, habilidad*) competence; (*rivalidad*) competition

competente [kompe'tente] *adj* competent

competición [kompeti'θjon] *nf* competition

competir [kompe'tir] *vi* to compete

compilar [kompi'lar] *vt* to compile

complacencia [kompla'θenθja] *nf* (*placer*) pleasure; (*tolerancia excesiva*) complacency

complacer [kompla'θer] *vt* to please; **~se** *vr* to be pleased

complaciente [kompla'θjente] *adj* kind, obliging, helpful

complejo, a [kom'plexo, a] *adj, nm* complex

complementario, a [komplemen'tarjo, a] *adj* complementary

completar [komple'tar] *vt* to complete

completo, a [kom'pleto, a] *adj* complete; (*perfecto*) perfect; (*lleno*) full ♦ *nm* full complement

complicado, a [kompli'kaðo, a] *adj* complicated; **estar ~ en** to be mixed up

in

cómplice ['kompliθe] *nm/f* accomplice

complot [kom'plo(t)] (*pl* **~s**) *nm* plot

componer [kompo'ner] *vt* (*MUS, LITERATURA, IMPRENTA*) to compose; (*algo roto*) to mend, repair; (*arreglar*) to arrange; **~se** *vr*: **~se de** to consist of; **componérselas para hacer algo** to manage to do sth

comportamiento [komporta'mjento] *nm* behaviour, conduct

comportarse [kompor'tarse] *vr* to behave

composición [komposi'θjon] *nf* composition

compositor, a [komposi'tor, a] *nm/f* composer

compostura [kompos'tura] *nf* (*actitud*) composure

compra ['kompra] *nf* purchase; **ir de ~s** to go shopping; **comprador, a** *nm/f* buyer, purchaser

comprar [kom'prar] *vt* to buy, purchase

comprender [kompren'der] *vt* to understand; (*incluir*) to comprise, include

comprensión [kompren'sjon] *nf* understanding; **comprensivo, a** *adj* (*actitud*) understanding

compresa [kom'presa] *nf*: **~ higiénica** sanitary towel (*BRIT*) o napkin (*US*)

comprimido, a [kompri'miðo, a] *adj* compressed ♦ *nm* (*MED*) pill, tablet

comprimir [kompri'mir] *vt* to compress

comprobante [kompro'ßante] *nm* proof; (*COM*) voucher; **~ de recibo** receipt

comprobar [kompro'ßar] *vt* to check; (*probar*) to prove; (*TEC*) to check, test

comprometer [komprome'ter] *vt* to compromise; (*poner en peligro*) to endanger; **~se** *vr* (*involucrarse*) to get involved

compromiso [kompro'miso] *nm* (*obligación*) obligation; (*cometido*) commitment; (*convenio*) agreement; (*apuro*) awkward situation

compuesto, a [kom'pwesto, a] *adj*: **~ de** composed of, made up of ♦ *nm* compound

computador [komputa'ðor] *nm*
computer; **~ central** mainframe
computer; **~ personal** personal computer
computadora [komputa'ðora] *nf* =
computador
cómputo ['komputo] *nm* calculation
comulgar [komul'var] *vi* to receive
communion
común [ko'mun] *adj* common ♦ *nm*: **el ~**
the community
comunicación [komunika'θjon] *nf*
communication; (*informe*) report
comunicado [komuni'kaðo] *nm*
announcement; **~ de prensa** press release
comunicar [komuni'kar] *vt, vi* to
communicate; **~se** *vr* to communicate;
está comunicando (*TEL*) the line's
engaged (*BRIT*) o busy (*US*);
comunicativo, a *adj* communicative
comunidad [komuni'ðað] *nf* community;
~ autónoma (*POL*) autonomous region;
C~ Económica Europea European
Economic Community
comunión [komu'njon] *nf* communion
comunismo [komu'nismo] *nm*
communism; **comunista** *adj, nm/f*
communist

PALABRA CLAVE
---

con [kon] *prep* **1** (*medio, compañía*) with;
comer ~ cuchara to eat with a spoon;
pasear ~ uno (*a pesar de*): **~ todo, merece nuestros**
2 (*a pesar de*): **~ todo, merece nuestros**
respetos all the same, he deserves our
respect
3 (*para ~*): **es muy bueno para ~ los**
niños he's very good with (the) children
4 (+*infin*): **~ llegar tan tarde se quedó**
sin comer by arriving so late he missed
out on eating
♦ *conj*: **~ que: será suficiente ~ que le**
escribas it will be sufficient if you write
to her

---

conato [ko'nato] *nm* attempt; **~ de robo**
attempted robbery
concebir [konθe'ßir] *vt, vi* to conceive

conceder [konθe'ðer] *vt* to concede
concejal, a [konθe'xal, a] *nm/f* town
councillor
concentración [konθentra'θjon] *nf*
concentration
concentrar [konθen'trar] *vt* to
concentrate; **~se** *vr* to concentrate
concepción [konθep'θjon] *nf* conception
concepto [kon'θepto] *nm* concept
concernir [konθer'nir] *vi* to concern; **en**
lo que concierne a ... as far as ... is
concerned; **en lo que a mí concierne** as
far as I'm concerned
concertar [konθer'tar] *vt* (*MUS*) to
harmonize; (*acordar: precio*) to agree;
(: *tratado*) to conclude; (*trato*) to arrange,
fix up; (*combinar: esfuerzos*) to coordinate
♦ *vi* to harmonize, be in tune
concesión [konθe'sjon] *nf* concession
concesionario [konθesjo'narjo] *nm*
(licensed) dealer, agent
concha ['kontʃa] *nf* shell
conciencia [kon'θjenθja] *nf* conscience;
tener/tomar ~ de to be/become aware
of; **tener la ~ limpia/tranquila** to have a
clear conscience
concienciar [konθjen'θjar] *vt* to make
aware; **~se** *vr* to become aware
concienzudo, a [konθjen'θuðo, a] *adj*
conscientious
concierto *etc* [kon'θjerto] *vb ver*
concertar ♦ *nm* concert; (*obra*) concerto
conciliar [konθi'ljar] *vt* to reconcile
concilio [kon'θiljo] *nm* council
conciso, a [kon'θiso, a] *adj* concise
concluir [konklu'ir] *vt, vi* to conclude;
~se *vr* to conclude
conclusión [konklu'sjon] *nf* conclusion
concluyente [konklu'jente] *adj* (*prueba,*
información) conclusive
concordar [konkor'ðar] *vt* to reconcile
♦ *vi* to agree, tally
concordia [kon'korðja] *nf* harmony
concretar [konkre'tar] *vt* to make
concrete, make more specific; **~se** *vr* to
become more definite
concreto, a [kon'kreto, a] *adj, nm* (*AM*)

concrete; **en ~** (*en resumen*) to sum up; (*específicamente*) specifically; **no hay nada en ~** there's nothing definite

concurrencia [konku'rrenθja] *nf* turnout

concurrido, a [konku'rriðo, a] *adj* (*calle*) busy; (*local, reunión*) crowded

concurrir [konku'rrir] *vi* (*juntarse: ríos*) to meet, come together; (: *personas*) to gather, meet

concursante [konkur'sante] *nm/f* competitor

concurso [kon'kurso] *nm* (*de público*) crowd; (*ESCOL, DEPORTE, competencia*) competition; (*ayuda*) help, cooperation

condal [kon'dal] *adj*: **la Ciudad C~** Barcelona

conde ['konde] *nm* count

condecoración [kondekora'θjon] *nf* (*MIL*) medal

condecorar [kondeko'rar] *vt* (*MIL*) to decorate

condena [kon'dena] *nf* sentence

condenación [kondena'θjon] *nf* condemnation; (*REL*) damnation

condenar [konde'nar] *vt* to condemn; (*JUR*) to convict; **~se** *vr* (*REL*) to be damned

condensar [konden'sar] *vt* to condense

condesa [kon'desa] *nf* countess

condición [kondi'θjon] *nf* condition; **condicional** *adj* conditional

condicionar [kondiθjo'nar] *vt* (*acondicionar*) to condition; **~ algo a** to make sth conditional on

condimento [kondi'mento] *nm* seasoning

condolerse [kondo'lerse] *vr* to sympathize

condón [kon'don] *nm* condom

conducir [kondu'θir] *vt* to take, convey; (*AUTO*) to drive ♦ *vi* to drive; (*fig*) to lead; **~se** *vr* to behave

conducta [kon'dukta] *nf* conduct, behaviour

conducto [kon'dukto] *nm* pipe, tube; (*fig*) channel

conductor, a [konduk'tor, a] *adj* leading, guiding ♦ *nm* (*FÍSICA*) conductor; (*de*

vehículo) driver

conduje *etc vb ver* **conducir**

conduzco *etc vb ver* **conducir**

conectado, a [konek'taðo, a] *adj* (*INFORM*) on-line

conectar [konek'tar] *vt* to connect (up); (*enchufar*) plug in

conejillo [kone'xiʎo] *nm*: **~ de Indias** (*ZOOL*) guinea pig

conejo [ko'nexo] *nm* rabbit

conexión [konek'sjon] *nf* connection

confección [confe(k)'θjon] *nf* preparation; (*industria*) clothing industry

confeccionar [konfekθjo'nar] *vt* to make (up)

confederación [konfeðera'θjon] *nf* confederation

conferencia [konfe'renθja] *nf* conference; (*lección*) lecture; (*TEL*) call

conferir [konfe'rir] *vt* to award

confesar [konfe'sar] *vt* to confess, admit

confesión [konfe'sjon] *nf* confession

confesionario [konfesjo'narjo] *nm* confessional

confeti [kon'feti] *nm* confetti

confiado, a [kon'fjaðo, a] *adj* (*crédulo*) trusting; (*seguro*) confident

confianza [kon'fjanθa] *nf* trust; (*seguridad*) confidence; (*familiaridad*) intimacy, familiarity

confiar [kon'fjar] *vt* to entrust ♦ *vi* to trust

confidencia [konfi'ðenθja] *nf* confidence

confidencial [konfiðen'θjal] *adj* confidential

confidente [konfi'ðente] *nm/f* confidant/ e; (*policial*) informer

configurar [konfiɣu'rar] *vt* to shape, form

confín [kon'fin] *nm* limit; **confines** *nmpl* confines, limits

confinar [konfi'nar] *vi* to confine; (*desterrar*) to banish

confirmar [konfir'mar] *vt* to confirm

confiscar [konfis'kar] *vt* to confiscate

confite [kon'fite] *nm* sweet (*BRIT*), candy (*US*)

confitería [konfite'ria] *nf* (*tienda*) confectioner's (shop)

confitura [konfi'tura] *nf* jam

conflictivo, a [konflik'tiβo, a] *adj* (*asunto, propuesta*) controversial; (*país, situación*) troubled

conflicto [kon'flikto] *nm* conflict; (*fig*) clash

confluir [kon'flwir] *vi* (*ríos*) to meet; (*gente*) to gather

conformar [konfor'mar] *vt* to shape, fashion ♦ *vi* to agree; **~se** *vr* to conform; (*resignarse*) to resign o.s.

conforme [kon'forme] *adj* (*correspondiente*): **~ con** in line with; (*de acuerdo*): **estar ~s (con algo)** to be in agreement (with sth) ♦ *adv* as ♦ *excl* agreed! ♦ *prep*: **~ a** in accordance with; **quedarse ~ (con algo)** to be satisfied (with sth)

conformidad [konformi'ðað] *nf* (*semejanza*) similarity; (*acuerdo*) agreement; **conformista** *adj, nm/f* conformist

confortable [konfor'taβle] *adj* comfortable

confortar [konfor'tar] *vt* to comfort

confrontar [konfron'tar] *vt* to confront; (*dos personas*) to bring face to face; (*cotejar*) to compare

confundir [konfun'dir] *vt* (*equivocar*) to mistake, confuse; (*turbar*) to confuse; **~se** *vr* (*turbarse*) to get confused; (*equivocarse*) to make a mistake; (*mezclarse*) to mix

confusión [konfu'sjon] *nf* confusion

confuso, a [kon'fuso, a] *adj* confused

congelado, a [konxe'laðo, a] *adj* frozen; **~s** *nmpl* frozen food(s); **congelador** *nm* (*aparato*) freezer, deep freeze

congelar [konxe'lar] *vt* to freeze; **~se** *vr* (*sangre, grasa*) to congeal

congeniar [konxe'njar] *vi* to get on (*BRIT*) *o* along (*US*) well

congestión [konxes'tjon] *nf* congestion

congestionar [konxestjo'nar] *vt* to congest

congoja [kon'goxa] *nf* distress, grief

congraciarse [kongra'θjarse] *vr* to ingratiate o.s.

congratular [kongratu'lar] *vt* to congratulate

congregación [kongreɣa'θjon] *nf* congregation

congregar [kongre'ɣar] *vt* to gather together; **~se** *vr* to gather together

congresista [kongre'sista] *nm/f* delegate, congressman/woman

congreso [kon'greso] *nm* congress

congrio ['kongrjo] *nm* conger eel

conjetura [konxe'tura] *nf* guess; **conjeturar** *vt* to guess

conjugar [konxu'ɣar] *vt* to combine, fit together; (*LING*) to conjugate

conjunción [konxun'θjon] *nf* conjunction

conjunto, a [kon'xunto, a] *adj* joint, united ♦ *nm* whole; (*MUS*) band; **en ~** as a whole

conjurar [konxu'rar] *vt* (*REL*) to exorcise; (*fig*) to ward off ♦ *vi* to plot

conmemoración [konmemora'θjon] *nf* commemoration

conmemorar [konmemo'rar] *vt* to commemorate

conmigo [kon'miɣo] *pron* with me

conmoción [konmo'θjon] *nf* shock; (*fig*) upheaval; **~ cerebral** (*MED*) concussion

conmovedor, a [konmoβe'ðor, a] *adj* touching, moving; (*emocionante*) exciting

conmover [konmo'βer] *vt* to shake, disturb; (*fig*) to move

conmutador [konmuta'ðor] *nm* switch; (*AM: TEL: centralita*) switchboard; (*: central*) telephone exchange

cono ['kono] *nm* cone

conocedor, a [konoθe'ðor, a] *adj* expert, knowledgeable ♦ *nm/f* expert

conocer [kono'θer] *vt* to know; (*por primera vez*) to meet, get to know; (*entender*) to know about; (*reconocer*) to recognize; **~se** *vr* (*una persona*) to know o.s.; (*dos personas*) to (get to) know each other

conocido, a [kono'θiðo, a] *adj* (well-)known ♦ *nm/f* acquaintance

conocimiento [konoθi'mjento] *nm*

knowledge; (MED) consciousness; ~s nmpl
(saber) knowledge sg

conozco etc vb ver **conocer**

conque ['konke] conj and so, so then

conquista [kon'kista] nf conquest;
conquistador, a adj conquering ♦ nm
conqueror

conquistar [konkis'tar] vt to conquer

consagrar [konsa'vrar] vt (REL) to
consecrate; (fig) to devote

consciente [kons'θjente] adj conscious

consecución [konseku'θjon] nf
acquisition; (de fin) attainment

consecuencia [konse'kwenθja] nf
consequence, outcome; (coherencia)
consistency

consecuente [konse'kwente] adj
consistent

consecutivo, a [konseku'tiβo, a] adj
consecutive

conseguir [konse'vir] vt to get, obtain;
(objetivo) to attain

consejero, a [konse'xero, a] nm/f adviser,
consultant; (POL) councillor

consejo [kon'sexo] nm advice; (POL)
council; ~ **de administración** (COM)
board of directors; ~ **de guerra** court
martial; ~ **de ministros** cabinet meeting

consenso [kon'senso] nm consensus

consentimiento [konsenti'mjento] nm
consent

consentir [konsen'tir] vt (permitir, tolerar)
to consent to; (mimar) to pamper, spoil;
(aguantar) to put up with ♦ vi to agree,
consent; ~ **que uno haga algo** to allow
sb to do sth

conserje [kon'serxe] nm caretaker;
(portero) porter

conservación [konserβa'θjon] nf
conservation; (de alimentos, vida)
preservation

conservador, a [konserβa'ðor, a] adj
(POL) conservative ♦ nm/f conservative

conservante [konser'ßante] nm
preservative

conservar [konser'ßar] vt to conserve,
keep; (alimentos, vida) to preserve; ~**se** vr

to survive

conservas [kon'serßas] nfpl canned
food(s) (pl)

conservatorio [konserßa'torjo] nm (MUS)
conservatoire, conservatory

considerable [konsiðe'raßle] adj
considerable

consideración [konsiðera'θjon] nf
consideration; (estimación) respect

considerado, a [konsiðe'raðo, a] adj
(atento) considerate; (respetado) respected

considerar [konsiðe'rar] vt to consider

consigna [kon'sivna] nf (orden) order,
instruction; (para equipajes) left-luggage
office

consigo etc [kon'sivo] vb ver **conseguir**
♦ pron (m) with him; (f) with her; (Vd)
with you; (reflexivo) with o.s.

consiguiendo etc vb ver **conseguir**

consiguiente [konsi'vjente] adj
consequent; **por** ~ and so, therefore,
consequently

consistente [konsis'tente] adj consistent;
(sólido) solid, firm; (válido) sound

consistir [konsis'tir] vi: ~ **en** (componerse
de) to consist of

consola [kon'sola] nf (mueble) console
table; (de videojuegos) console

consolación [konsola'θjon] nf consolation

consolar [konso'lar] vt to console

consolidar [konsoli'ðar] vt to consolidate

consomé [konso'me] (pl ~s) nm
consommé, clear soup

consonante [konso'nante] adj consonant,
harmonious ♦ nf consonant

consorcio [kon'sorθjo] nm consortium

conspiración [konspira'θjon] nf
conspiracy

conspirador, a [konspira'ðor, a] nm/f
conspirator

conspirar [konspi'rar] vi to conspire

constancia [kons'tanθja] nf constancy;
dejar ~ **de** to put on record

constante [kons'tante] adj, nf constant

constar [kons'tar] vi (evidenciarse) to be
clear o evident; ~ **de** to consist of

constatar [konsta'tar] vt to verify

consternación [konsterna'θjon] *nf*
consternation

constipado, a [konsti'paðo, a] *adj*: **estar
~** to have a cold ♦ *nm* cold

constitución [konstitu'θjon] *nf*
constitution; **constitucional** *adj*
constitutional

constituir [konstitu'ir] *vt* (*formar,
componer*) to constitute, make up;
(*fundar, erigir, ordenar*) to constitute,
establish

constituyente [konstitu'jente] *adj*
constituent

constreñir [konstre'pir] *vt* (*restringir*) to
restrict

construcción [konstruk'θjon] *nf*
construction, building

constructor, a [konstruk'tor, a] *nm/f*
builder

construir [konstru'ir] *vt* to build, construct

construyendo *etc vb ver* **construir**

consuelo [kon'swelo] *nm* consolation,
solace

cónsul ['konsul] *nm* consul; **consulado**
nm consulate

consulta [kon'sulta] *nf* consultation;
(*MED*): **horas de ~** surgery hours

consultar [konsul'tar] *vt* to consult

consultorio [konsul'torjo] *nm* (*MED*)
surgery

consumar [konsu'mar] *vt* to complete,
carry out; (*crimen*) to commit; (*sentencia*)
to carry out

consumición [konsumi'θjon] *nf*
consumption; (*bebida*) drink; (*comida*)
food; **~ mínima** cover charge

consumidor, a [konsumi'ðor, a] *nm/f*
consumer

consumir [konsu'mir] *vt* to consume; **~se**
vr to be consumed; (*persona*) to waste
away

consumismo [konsu'mismo] *nm*
consumerism

consumo [kon'sumo] *nm* consumption

contabilidad [kontaβili'ðað] *nf*
accounting, book-keeping; (*profesión*)
accountancy; **contable** *nm/f* accountant

contacto [kon'takto] *nm* contact; (*AUTO*)
ignition

contado, a [kon'taðo, a] *adj*: **~s** (*escasos*)
numbered, scarce, few ♦ *nm*: **pagar al ~**
to pay (in) cash

contador [konta'ðor] *nm* (*aparato*) meter;
(*AM*: *contante*) accountant

contagiar [konta'xjar] *vt* (*enfermedad*) to
pass on, transmit; (*persona*) to infect; **~se**
vr to become infected

contagio [kon'taxjo] *nm* infection;
contagioso, a *adj* infectious; (*fig*)
catching

contaminación [kontamina'θjon] *nf*
contamination; (*polución*) pollution

contaminar [kontami'nar] *vt* to
contaminate; (*aire, agua*) to pollute

contante [kon'tante] *adj*: **dinero ~ (y
sonante)** cash

contar [kon'tar] *vt* (*páginas, dinero*) to
count; (*anécdota, chiste etc*) to tell ♦ *vi* to
count; **~ con** to rely on, count on

contemplación [kontempla'θjon] *nf*
contemplation

contemplar [kontem'plar] *vt* to
contemplate; (*mirar*) to look at

contemporáneo, a [kontempo'raneo, a]
adj, nm/f contemporary

contendiente [konten'djente] *nm/f*
contestant

contenedor [kontene'ðor] *nm* container

contener [konte'ner] *vt* to contain, hold;
(*retener*) to hold back, contain; **~se** *vr* to
control *o* restrain o.s.

contenido, a [konte'niðo, a] *adj*
(*moderado*) restrained; (*risa etc*)
suppressed ♦ *nm* contents *pl*, content

contentar [konten'tar] *vt* (*satisfacer*) to
satisfy; (*complacer*) to please; **~se** *vr* to be
satisfied

contento, a [kon'tento, a] *adj* (*alegre*)
pleased; (*feliz*) happy

contestación [kontesta'θjon] *nf* answer,
reply

contestador [kontesta'ðor] *nm*: **~
automático** answering machine

contestar [kontes'tar] *vt* to answer, reply;

(JUR) to corroborate, confirm
contexto [kon'te(k)sto] *nm* context
contienda [kon'tjenda] *nf* contest
contigo [kon'tivo] *pron* with you
contiguo, a [kon'tivwo, a] *adj* adjacent, adjoining
continente [konti'nente] *adj, nm* continent
contingencia [kontin'xenθja] *nf* contingency; *(riesgo)* risk; **contingente** *adj, nm* contingent
continuación [kontinwa'θjon] *nf* continuation; **a ~** then, next
continuar [konti'nwar] *vt* to continue, go on with ♦ *vi* to continue, go on; **~ hablando** to continue talking *o* to talk
continuidad [kontinwi'ðað] *nf* continuity
continuo, a [kon'tinwo, a] *adj (sin interrupción)* continuous; *(acción perseverante)* continual
contorno [kon'torno] *nm* outline; *(GEO)* contour; **~s** *nmpl* neighbourhood *sg*, surrounding area *sg*
contorsión [kontor'sjon] *nf* contortion
contra ['kontra] *prep, adv* against ♦ *nm inv* con ♦ *nf*: **la C~** *(de Nicaragua)* the Contras *pl*
contraataque [kontraa'take] *nm* counter-attack
contrabajo [kontra'ßaxo] *nm* double bass
contrabandista [kontraßan'dista] *nm/f* smuggler
contrabando [kontra'ßando] *nm (acción)* smuggling; *(mercancías)* contraband
contracción [kontrak'θjon] *nf* contraction
contracorriente [kontrako'rrjente]: **(a) ~** *adv* against the current
contradecir [kontraðe'θir] *vt* to contradict
contradicción [kontraðik'θjon] *nf* contradiction
contradictorio, a [kontraðik'torjo, a] *adj* contradictory
contraer [kontra'er] *vt* to contract; *(limitar)* to restrict; **~se** *vr* to contract; *(limitarse)* to limit o.s.
contraluz [kontra'luθ] *nf*: **a ~** against the light

contrapartida [kontrapar'tiða] *nf*: **como ~ (de)** in return (for)
contrapelo [kontra'pelo]: **a ~** *adv* the wrong way
contrapesar [kontrape'sar] *vt* to counterbalance; *(fig)* to offset; **contrapeso** *nm* counterweight
contraportada [kontrapor'taða] *nf (de revista)* back cover
contraproducente [kontraproðu'θente] *adj* counterproductive
contrariar [kontra'rjar] *vt (oponerse)* to oppose; *(poner obstáculo)* to impede; *(enfadar)* to vex
contrariedad [kontrarje'ðað] *nf (obstáculo)* obstacle, setback; *(disgusto)* vexation, annoyance
contrario, a [kon'trarjo, a] *adj* contrary; *(persona)* opposed; *(sentido, lado)* opposite ♦ *nm/f* enemy, adversary; *(DEPORTE)* opponent; **al/por el ~** on the contrary; **de lo ~** otherwise
contrarreloj [kontrarre'lo] *nf (tb:* **prueba ~)** time trial
contrarrestar [kontrarres'tar] *vt* to counteract
contrasentido [kontrasen'tiðo] *nm*: **es un ~ que él ...** it doesn't make sense for him to ...
contraseña [kontra'sena] *nf (INFORM)* password
contrastar [kontras'tar] *vt, vi* to contrast
contraste [kon'traste] *nm* contrast
contratar [kontra'tar] *vt (firmar un acuerdo para)* to contract for; *(empleados, obreros)* to hire, engage; **~se** *vr* to sign on
contratiempo [kontra'tjempo] *nm* setback
contratista [kontra'tista] *nm/f* contractor
contrato [kon'trato] *nm* contract
contravenir [kontraße'nir] *vi*: **~ a** to contravene, violate
contraventana [kontraßen'tana] *nf* shutter
contribución [kontrißu'θjon] *nf (municipal etc)* tax; *(ayuda)* contribution
contribuir [kontrißu'ir] *vt, vi* to

contribute; (*COM*) to pay (in taxes)

contribuyente [kontriβu'jente] *nm/f* (*COM*) taxpayer; (*que ayuda*) contributor

contrincante [kontrin'kante] *nm* opponent

control [kon'trol] *nm* control; (*inspección*) inspection, check; **~ador, a** *nm/f* controller; **~ador aéreo** air-traffic controller

controlar [kontro'lar] *vt* to control; (*inspeccionar*) to inspect, check

controversia [kontro'βersja] *nf* controversy

contundente [kontun'dente] *adj* (*instrumento*) blunt; (*argumento, derrota*) overwhelming

contusión [kontu'sjon] *nf* bruise

convalecencia [kombale'θenθja] *nf* convalescence

convalecer [kombale'θer] *vi* to convalesce, get better

convaleciente [kombale'θjente] *adj, nm/f* convalescent

convalidar [kombali'ðar] *vt* (*título*) to recognize

convencer [komben'θer] *vt* to convince

convencimiento [kombenθi'mjento] *nm* (*certidumbre*) conviction

convención [komben'θjon] *nf* convention

conveniencia [kombe'njenθja] *nf* suitability; (*conformidad*) agreement; (*utilidad, provecho*) usefulness; **~s** *nfpl* (*convenciones*) conventions; (*COM*) property *sg*

conveniente [kombe'njente] *adj* suitable; (*útil*) useful

convenio [kom'benjo] *nm* agreement, treaty

convenir [kombe'nir] *vi* (*estar de acuerdo*) to agree; (*venir bien*) to suit, be suitable

convento [kom'bento] *nm* convent

convenza *etc vb ver* **convencer**

converger [komber'xer] *vi* to converge

convergir [komber'xir] *vi* = **converger**

conversación [kombersa'θjon] *nf* conversation

conversar [komber'sar] *vi* to talk, converse

conversión [komber'sjon] *nf* conversion

convertir [komber'tir] *vt* to convert

convicción [kombik'θjon] *nf* conviction

convicto, a [kom'bikto, a] *adj* convicted

convidado, a [kombi'ðaðo, a] *nm/f* guest

convidar [kombi'ðar] *vt* to invite

convincente [kombin'θente] *adj* convincing

convite [kom'bite] *nm* invitation; (*banquete*) banquet

convivencia [kombi'βenθja] *nf* coexistence, living together

convivir [kombi'βir] *vi* to live together

convocar [kombo'kar] *vt* to summon, call (together)

convocatoria [komboka'torja] *nf* (*de oposiciones, elecciones*) notice; (*de huelga*) call

convulsión [kombul'sjon] *nf* convulsion

conyugal [konju'ɣal] *adj* conjugal; **cónyuge** ['konjuxe] *nm/f* spouse

coñac [ko'ɲa(k)] (*pl* **~s**) *nm* cognac, brandy

coño ['koɲo] (*fam!*) *excl* (*enfado*) shit! (*!*); (*sorpresa*) bloody hell! (*!*)

cooperación [koopera'θjon] *nf* cooperation

cooperar [koope'rar] *vi* to cooperate

cooperativa [koopera'tiβa] *nf* cooperative

coordinadora [koorðina'ðora] *nf* (*comité*) coordinating committee

coordinar [koorði'nar] *vt* to coordinate

copa ['kopa] *nf* cup; (*vaso*) glass; (*bebida*): (**tomar una**) **~** (to have a) drink; (*de árbol*) top; (*de sombrero*) crown; **~s** *nfpl* (*NAIPES*) ≈ hearts

copia ['kopja] *nf* copy; **~ de respaldo** *o* **seguridad** (*INFORM*) back-up copy; **copiar** *vt* to copy

copioso, a [ko'pjoso, a] *adj* copious, plentiful

copla ['kopla] *nf* verse; (*canción*) (popular) song

copo ['kopo] *nm*: **~ de nieve** snowflake; **~s de maíz** cornflakes

coqueta [ko'keta] *adj* flirtatious,

coquettish; **coquetear** *vi* to flirt

coraje [ko'raxe] *nm* courage; (*ánimo*) spirit; (*ira*) anger

coral [ko'ral] *adj* choral ♦ *nf* (*MUS*) choir ♦ *nm* (*ZOOL*) coral

coraza [ko'raθa] *nf* (*armadura*) armour; (*blindaje*) armour-plating

corazón [kora'θon] *nm* heart

corazonada [koraθo'naða] *nf* impulse; (*presentimiento*) hunch

corbata [kor'ßata] *nf* tie

corchete [kor'tʃete] *nm* catch, clasp

corcho ['kortʃo] *nm* cork; (*PESCA*) float

cordel [kor'ðel] *nm* cord, line

cordero [kor'ðero] *nm* lamb

cordial [kor'ðjal] *adj* cordial; **~idad** *nf* warmth, cordiality

cordillera [korði'ʎera] *nf* range (of mountains)

Córdoba ['korðoßa] *n* Cordova

cordón [kor'ðon] *nm* (*cuerda*) cord, string; (*de zapatos*) lace; (*MIL etc*) cordon

cordura [kor'ðura] *nf*: **con ~** (*obrar, hablar*) sensibly

corneta [kor'neta] *nf* bugle

cornisa [kor'nisa] *nf* (*ARQ*) cornice

coro ['koro] *nm* chorus; (*conjunto de cantores*) choir

corona [ko'rona] *nf* crown; (*de flores*) garland; **coronación** *nf* coronation; **coronar** *vt* to crown

coronel [koro'nel] *nm* colonel

coronilla [koro'niʎa] *nf* (*ANAT*) crown (of the head)

corporación [korpora'θjon] *nf* corporation

corporal [korpo'ral] *adj* corporal, bodily

corpulento, a [korpu'lento a] *adj* (*persona*) heavily-built

corral [ko'rral] *nm* farmyard

correa [ko'rrea] *nf* strap; (*cinturón*) belt; (*de perro*) lead, leash

corrección [korrek'θjon] *nf* correction; (*reprensión*) rebuke; **correccional** *nm* reformatory

correcto, a [ko'rrekto, a] *adj* correct; (*persona*) well-mannered

corredizo, a [korre'ðiθo, a] *adj* (*puerta etc*) sliding

corredor, a [korre'ðor, a] *nm* (*pasillo*) corridor; (*balcón corrido*) gallery; (*COM*) agent, broker ♦ *nm/f* (*DEPORTE*) runner

corregir [korre'xir] *vt* (*error*) to correct; **~se** *vr* to reform

correo [ko'rreo] *nm* post, mail; (*persona*) courier; **C~s** *nmpl* Post Office *sg*; **~ aéreo** airmail; **~ electrónico** electronic mail, e-mail

correr [ko'rrer] *vt* to run; (*cortinas*) to draw; (*cerrojo*) to shoot ♦ *vi* to run; (*líquido*) to run, flow; **~se** *vr* to slide, move; (*colores*) to run

correspondencia [korrespon'denθja] *nf* correspondence; (*FERRO*) connection

corresponder [korrespon'der] *vi* to correspond; (*convenir*) to be suitable; (*pertenecer*) to belong; (*concernir*) to concern; **~se** *vr* (*por escrito*) to correspond; (*amarse*) to love one another

correspondiente [korrespon'djente] *adj* corresponding

corresponsal [korrespon'sal] *nm/f* correspondent

corrida [ko'rriða] *nf* (*de toros*) bullfight

corrido, a [ko'rriðo, a] *adj* (*avergonzado*) abashed; **3 noches corridas** 3 nights running; **un kilo ~** a good kilo

corriente [ko'rrjente] *adj* (*agua*) running; (*dinero etc*) current; (*común*) ordinary, normal ♦ *nf* current ♦ *nm* current month; **~ eléctrica** electric current

corrija *etc vb ver* **corregir**

corrillo [ko'rriʎo] *nm* ring, circle (of people); (*fig*) clique

corro ['korro] *nm* ring, circle (of people)

corroborar [korroßo'rar] *vt* to corroborate

corroer [korro'er] *vt* to corrode; (*GEO*) to erode

corromper [korrom'per] *vt* (*madera*) to rot; (*fig*) to corrupt

corrosivo, a [korro'sißo, a] *adj* corrosive

corrupción [korrup'θjon] *nf* rot, decay; (*fig*) corruption

corsé [kor'se] *nm* corset

cortacésped [korta'θespeð] *nm* lawn mower

cortado, a [kor'taðo, a] *adj* (*gen*) cut; (*leche*) sour; (*tímido*) shy; (*avergonzado*) embarrassed ♦ *nm* coffee (with a little milk)

cortar [kor'tar] *vt* to cut; (*suministro*) to cut off; (*un pasaje*) to cut out ♦ *vi* to cut; **~se** *vr* (*avergonzarse*) to become embarrassed; (*leche*) to turn, curdle; **~se el pelo** to have one's hair cut

cortauñas [korta'uɲas] *nm inv* nail clippers *pl*

corte ['korte] *nm* cut, cutting; (*de tela*) piece, length ♦ *nf*: **las C~s** the Spanish Parliament; **~ y confección** dressmaking; **~ de luz** power cut

cortejar [korte'xar] *vt* to court

cortejo [kor'texo] *nm* entourage; **~ fúnebre** funeral procession

cortés [kor'tes] *adj* courteous, polite

cortesía [korte'sia] *nf* courtesy

corteza [kor'teθa] *nf* (*de árbol*) bark; (*de pan*) crust

cortijo [kor'tixo] *nm* farm, farmhouse

cortina [kor'tina] *nf* curtain

corto, a ['korto, a] *adj* (*breve*) short; (*tímido*) bashful; **~ de luces** not very bright; **~ de vista** short-sighted; **estar ~ de fondos** to be short of funds; **~circuito** *nm* short circuit; **~metraje** *nm* (*CINE*) short

cosa ['kosa] *nf* thing; **~ de** about; **eso es ~ mía** that's my business

coscorrón [kosko'rron] *nm* bump on the head

cosecha [ko'setʃa] *nf* (*AGR*) harvest; (*de vino*) vintage

cosechar [kose'tʃar] *vt* to harvest, gather (in)

coser [ko'ser] *vt* to sew

cosmético, a [kos'metiko, a] *adj, nm* cosmetic

cosquillas [kos'kiʎas] *nfpl*: **hacer ~** to tickle; **tener ~** to be ticklish

costa ['kosta] *nf* (*GEO*) coast; **C~ Brava** Costa Brava; **C~ Cantábrica** Cantabrian

Coast; **C~ del Sol** Costa del Sol; **a toda ~** at all costs

costado [kos'taðo] *nm* side

costar [kos'tar] *vt* (*valer*) to cost; **me cuesta hablarle** I find it hard to talk to him

Costa Rica *nf* Costa Rica; **costarricense** *adj, nm/f* Costa Rican; **costarriqueño, a** *adj, nm/f* Costa Rican

coste ['koste] *nm* = **costo**

costear [koste'ar] *vt* to pay for

costero, a [kos'tero, a] *adj* (*pueblecito, camino*) coastal

costilla [kos'tiʎa] *nf* rib; (*CULIN*) cutlet

costo ['kosto] *nm* cost, price; **~ de la vida** cost of living; **~so, a** *adj* costly, expensive

costra ['kostra] *nf* (*corteza*) crust; (*MED*) scab

costumbre [kos'tumbre] *nf* custom, habit

costura [kos'tura] *nf* sewing, needlework; (*zurcido*) seam

costurera [kostu'rera] *nf* dressmaker

costurero [kostu'rero] *nm* sewing box *o* case

cotejar [kote'xar] *vt* to compare

cotidiano, a [koti'ðjano, a] *adj* daily, day to day

cotilla [ko'tiʎa] *nm/f* (*fam*) gossip; **cotillear** *vi* to gossip; **cotilleo** *nm* gossip(ing)

cotización [kotiθa'θjon] *nf* (*COM*) quotation, price; (*de club*) dues *pl*

cotizar [koti'θar] *vt* (*COM*) to quote, price; **~se** *vr*: **~se a** to sell at, fetch; (*BOLSA*) to stand at, be quoted at

coto ['koto] *nm* (*terreno cercado*) enclosure; (*de caza*) reserve

cotorra [ko'torra] *nf* parrot

COU [kou] (*ESP*) *nm abr* (= *Curso de Orientación Universitaria*) *1 year course leading to final school-leaving certificate and university entrance examinations*

coyote [ko'jote] *nm* coyote, prairie wolf

coyuntura [kojun'tura] *nf* juncture, occasion

coz [koθ] *nf* kick

crack [krak] *nm* (*droga*) crack

cráneo ['kraneo] *nm* skull, cranium

cráter ['krater] *nm* crater

creación [krea'θjon] *nf* creation

creador, a [krea'ðor, a] *adj* creative ♦ *nm/f* creator

crear [kre'ar] *vt* to create, make

crecer [kre'θer] *vi* to grow; (*precio*) to rise

creces ['kreθes]: **con ~** *adv* amply, fully

crecido, a [kre'θiðo, a] *adj* (*persona, planta*) full-grown; (*cantidad*) large

creciente [kre'θjente] *adj* growing; (*cantidad*) increasing; (*luna*) crescent ♦ *nm* crescent

crecimiento [kreθi'mjento] *nm* growth; (*aumento*) increase

credenciales [kreðen'θjales] *nfpl* credentials

crédito ['kreðito] *nm* credit

credo ['kreðo] *nm* creed

crédulo, a ['kreðulo, a] *adj* credulous

creencia [kre'enθja] *nf* belief

creer [kre'er] *vt, vi* to think, believe; **~se** *vr* to believe o.s. (to be); **~ en** to believe in; **¡ya lo creo!** I should think so!

creíble [kre'iβle] *adj* credible, believable

creído, a [kre'iðo, a] *adj* (*engreído*) conceited

crema ['krema] *nf* cream; **~ pastelera** (confectioner's) custard

cremallera [krema'ʎera] *nf* zip (fastener)

crematorio [krema'torjo] *nm* (*tb*: **horno ~**) crematorium

crepitar [krepi'tar] *vi* to crackle

crepúsculo [kre'puskulo] *nm* twilight, dusk

cresta ['kresta] *nf* (GEO, ZOOL) crest

creyendo *vb ver* **creer**

creyente [kre'jente] *nm/f* believer

creyó *etc vb ver* **creer**

crezco *etc vb ver* **crecer**

cría *etc* ['kria] *vb ver* **criar** ♦ *nf* (*de animales*) rearing, breeding; (*animal*) young; *ver tb* **crío**

criadero [kria'ðero] *nm* (ZOOL) breeding place

criado, a [kri'aðo, a] *nm* servant ♦ *nf* servant, maid

criador [kria'ðor] *nm* breeder

crianza [kri'anθa] *nf* rearing, breeding; (*fig*) breeding

criar [kri'ar] *vt* (*educar*) to bring up; (*producir*) to grow, produce; (*animales*) to breed

criatura [kria'tura] *nf* creature; (*niño*) baby, (small) child

criba ['kriβa] *nf* sieve; **cribar** *vt* to sieve

crimen ['krimen] *nm* crime

criminal [krimi'nal] *adj*, *nm/f* criminal

crin [krin] *nf* (*tb*: **~es** *nfpl*) mane

crío, a ['krio, a] (*fam*) *nm/f* (*niño*) kid

crisis ['krisis] *nf inv* crisis; **~ nerviosa** nervous breakdown

crispar [kris'par] *vt* (*nervios*) to set on edge

cristal [kris'tal] *nm* crystal; (*de ventana*) glass, pane; (*lente*) lens; **~ino, a** *adj* crystalline; (*fig*) clear ♦ *nm* lens (of the eye); **~izar** *vt*, *vi* to crystallize

cristiandad [kristjan'daθ] *nf* Christendom

cristianismo [kristja'nismo] *nm* Christianity

cristiano, a [kris'tjano, a] *adj*, *nm/f* Christian

Cristo ['kristo] *nm* Christ; (*crucifijo*) crucifix

criterio [kri'terjo] *nm* criterion; (*juicio*) judgement

crítica ['kritika] *nf* criticism; *ver tb* **crítico**

criticar [kriti'kar] *vt* to criticize

crítico, a ['kritiko, a] *adj* critical ♦ *nm/f* critic

Croacia [kro'aθja] *nf* Croatia

croar [kro'ar] *vi* to croak

cromo ['kromo] *nm* chrome

crónica ['kronika] *nf* chronicle, account

crónico, a ['kroniko, a] *adj* chronic

cronómetro [kro'nometro] *nm* stopwatch

croqueta [kro'keta] *nf* croquette

cruce *etc* ['kruθe] *vb ver* **cruzar** ♦ *nm* crossing; (*de carreteras*) crossroads

crucificar [kruθifi'kar] *vt* to crucify

crucifijo [kruθi'fixo] *nm* crucifix

crucigrama [kruθi'γrama] *nm* crossword

(puzzle)

crudo, a ['kruðo, a] *adj* raw; *(no maduro)* unripe; *(petróleo)* crude; *(rudo, cruel)* cruel ♦ *nm* crude (oil)

cruel [krwel] *adj* cruel; **~dad** *nf* cruelty

crujido [kru'xiðo] *nm (de madera etc)* creak

crujiente [kru'xjente] *adj (galleta etc)* crunchy

crujir [kru'xir] *vi (madera etc)* to creak; *(dedos)* to crack; *(dientes)* to grind; *(nieve, arena)* to crunch

cruz [kruθ] *nf* cross; *(de moneda)* tails *sg*; **~ gamada** swastika

cruzada [kru'θaða] *nf* crusade

cruzado, a [kru'θaðo, a] *adj* crossed ♦ *nm* crusader

cruzar [kru'θar] *vt* to cross; **~se** *vr (líneas etc)* to cross; *(personas)* to pass each other

Cruz Roja *nf* Red Cross

cuaderno [kwa'ðerno] *nm* notebook; *(de escuela)* exercise book; *(NAUT)* logbook

cuadra ['kwaðra] *nf (caballeriza)* stable; *(AM)* block

cuadrado, a [kwa'ðraðo, a] *adj* square ♦ *nm (MAT)* square

cuadrar [kwa'ðrar] *vt* to square ♦ *vi*: **~ con** to square with, tally with; **~se** *vr (soldado)* to stand to attention

cuadrilátero [kwaðri'latero] *nm (DEPORTE)* boxing ring; *(GEOM)* quadrilateral

cuadrilla [kwa'ðriʎa] *nf* party, group

cuadro ['kwaðro] *nm* square; *(ARTE)* painting; *(TEATRO)* scene; *(diagrama)* chart; *(DEPORTE, MED)* team; **tela a ~s** checked *(BRIT)* o chequered *(US)* material

cuádruple ['kwaðruple] *adj* quadruple

cuajar [kwa'xar] *vt (leche)* to curdle; *(sangre)* to congeal; *(CULIN)* to set; **~se** *vr* to curdle; to congeal; to set; *(llenarse)* to fill up

cuajo ['kwaxo] *nm*: **de ~** *(arrancar)* by the roots; *(cortar)* completely

cual [kwal] *adv* like, as ♦ *pron*: **el ~** *etc* which; *(persona: sujeto)* who; *(: objeto)* whom ♦ *adj* such as; **cada ~** each one;

déjalo tal ~ leave it just as it is

cuál [kwal] *pron interr* which (one)

cualesquier(a) [kwales'kjer(a)] *pl de* **cualquier(a)**

cualidad [kwali'ðað] *nf* quality

cualquier [kwal'kjer] *adj ver* **cualquiera**

cualquiera [kwal'kjera] *(pl* **cualesquiera)** *adj (delante de nm y f:* **cualquier)** any ♦ *pron* anybody; **un coche ~ servirá** any car will do; **no es un hombre ~** he isn't just anybody; **cualquier día/libro** any day/book; **eso ~ lo sabe hacer** anybody can do that; **es un ~** he's a nobody

cuando ['kwando] *adv* when; *(aún si)* if, even if ♦ *conj (puesto que)* since ♦ *prep*: **yo, ~ niño ...** when I was a child ...; **~ no sea así** even if it is not so; **~ más** at (the) most; **~ menos** at least; **~ no** if not, otherwise; **de ~ en ~** from time to time

cuándo ['kwando] *adv* when; **¿desde ~?, ¿de ~ acá?** since when?

cuantía [kwan'tia] *nf (importe: de pérdidas, deuda, daños)* extent

cuantioso, a [kwan'tjoso, a] *adj* substantial

PALABRA CLAVE

cuanto, a ['kwanto, a] *adj* 1 *(todo)*: **tiene todo ~ desea** he's got everything he wants; **le daremos ~s ejemplares necesite** we'll give him as many copies as *o* all the copies he needs; **~s hombres la ven** all the men who see her
2: **unos ~s: había unos ~s periodistas** there were a few journalists
3 *(+más)*: **~ más vino bebes peor te sentirás** the more wine you drink the worse you'll feel

♦ *pron*: **tiene ~ desea** he has everything he wants; **tome ~/~s quiera** take as much/many as you want

♦ *adv*: **en ~:** **en ~ profesor** as a teacher; **en ~ a mí** as for me; *ver tb* **antes**

♦ *conj* 1: **~ más gana menos gasta** the more he earns the less he spends; **~ más joven más confiado** the younger you are the more trusting you are

2: en ~: en ~ llegue/llegué as soon as I arrive/arrived

cuánto, a ['kwanto, a] adj (exclamación) what a lot of; (interr: sg) how much?; (: pl) how many? ♦ pron, adv how; (interr: sg) how much?; (: pl) how many?; **¡cuánta gente!** what a lot of people!; **¿~ cuesta?** how much does it cost?; **¿a ~ estamos?** what's the date?; **Señor no sé ~s** Mr. So-and-So

cuarenta [kwa'renta] num forty

cuarentena [kwaren'tena] nf quarantine

cuaresma [kwa'resma] nf Lent

cuarta ['kwarta] nf (MAT) quarter, fourth; (palmo) span

cuartel [kwar'tel] nm (MIL) barracks pl; **~ general** headquarters pl

cuarteto [kwar'teto] nm quartet

cuarto, a ['kwarto, a] adj fourth ♦ nm (MAT) quarter, fourth; (habitación) room; **~ de baño** bathroom; **~ de estar** living room; **~ de hora** quarter (of an) hour; **~ de kilo** quarter kilo

cuatro ['kwatro] num four

Cuba ['kuβa] nf Cuba; **cubano, a** adj, nm/f Cuban

cuba ['kuβa] nf cask, barrel

cubata [ku'βata] nm (fam) large drink (of rum and coke etc)

cúbico, a ['kuβiko, a] adj cubic

cubierta [ku'βjerta] nf cover, covering; (neumático) tyre; (NAUT) deck

cubierto, a [ku'βjerto, a] pp de **cubrir** ♦ adj covered ♦ nm cover; (lugar en la mesa) place; **~s** nmpl cutlery sg; **a ~** under cover

cubil [ku'βil] nm den; **~ete** nm (en juegos) cup

cubito [ku'βito] nm: **~ de hielo** ice-cube

cubo ['kuβo] nm (MATH) cube; (balde) bucket, tub; (TEC) drum

cubrecama [kuβre'kama] nm bedspread

cubrir [ku'βrir] vt to cover; **~se** vr (cielo) to become overcast

cucaracha [kuka'ratʃa] nf cockroach

cuchara [ku'tʃara] nf spoon; (TEC) scoop;

~da nf spoonful; **~dita** nf teaspoonful

cucharilla [kutʃa'riʎa] nf teaspoon

cucharón [kutʃa'ron] nm ladle

cuchichear [kutʃitʃe'ar] vi to whisper

cuchilla [ku'tʃiʎa] nf (large) knife; (de arma blanca) blade; **~ de afeitar** razor blade

cuchillo [ku'tʃiʎo] nm knife

cuchitril [kutʃi'tril] nm hovel

cuclillas [ku'kliʎas] nfpl: **en ~** squatting

cuco, a ['kuko, a] adj pretty; (astuto) sharp ♦ nm cuckoo

cucurucho [kuku'rutʃo] nm cornet

cuello ['kweʎo] nm (ANAT) neck; (de vestido, camisa) collar

cuenca ['kwenka] nf (ANAT) eye socket; (GEO) bowl, deep valley

cuenco ['kwenko] nm bowl

cuenta etc ['kwenta] vb ver **contar** ♦ nf (cálculo) count, counting; (en café, restaurante) bill (BRIT), check (US); (COM) account; (de collar) bead; **a fin de ~s** in the end; **caer en la ~** to catch on; **darse ~ de** to realize; **tener en ~** to bear in mind; **echar ~s** to take stock; **~ corriente/de ahorros** current/savings account; **~ atrás** countdown; **~-kilómetros** nm inv ≈ milometer; (de velocidad) speedometer

cuento etc ['kwento] vb ver **contar** ♦ nm story

cuerda ['kwerða] nf rope; (fina) string; (de reloj) spring; **dar ~ a un reloj** to wind up a clock; **~ floja** tightrope

cuerdo, a ['kwerðo, a] adj sane; (prudente) wise, sensible

cuerno ['kwerno] nm horn

cuero ['kwero] nm leather; **en ~s** stark naked; **~ cabelludo** scalp

cuerpo ['kwerpo] nm body

cuervo ['kwerβo] nm crow

cuesta etc ['kwesta] vb ver **costar** ♦ nf slope; (en camino etc) hill; **~ arriba/abajo** uphill/downhill; **a ~s** on one's back

cueste etc vb ver **costar**

cuestión [kwes'tjon] nf matter, question, issue

cueva ['kweßa] nf cave
cuidado [kwi'ðaðo] nm care, carefulness; (*preocupación*) care, worry ♦ *excl* careful!, look out!
cuidadoso, a [kwiða'ðoso, a] *adj* careful; (*preocupado*) anxious
cuidar [kwi'ðar] vt (MED) to care for; (*ocuparse de*) to take care of, look after ♦ vi: ~ de to take care of, look after; ~se vr to look after o.s.; ~se de hacer algo to take care to do sth
culata [ku'lata] nf (*de fusil*) butt
culebra [ku'leßra] nf snake
culebrón [kule'ßron] (*fam*) nm (TV) soap(-opera)
culinario, a [kuli'narjo, a] *adj* culinary, cooking *cpd*
culminación [kulmina'θjon] nf culmination
culo ['kulo] nm bottom, backside; (*de vaso, botella*) bottom
culpa ['kulpa] nf fault; (JUR) guilt; por ~ de because of; tener la ~ (de) to be to blame (for); ~bilidad nf guilt; ~ble *adj* guilty ♦ nm/f culprit
culpar [kul'par] vt to blame; (*acusar*) to accuse
cultivar [kulti'ßar] vt to cultivate
cultivo [kul'tißo] nm (*acto*) cultivation; (*plantas*) crop
culto, a ['kulto, a] *adj* (*que tiene cultura*) cultured, educated ♦ nm (*homenaje*) worship; (*religión*) cult
cultura [kul'tura] nf culture
culturismo [kultu'rismo] nm body-building
cumbre ['kumbre] nf summit, top
cumpleaños [kumple'aɲos] nm *inv* birthday
cumplido, a [kum'pliðo, a] *adj* (*abundante*) plentiful; (*cortés*) courteous ♦ nm compliment; visita de ~ courtesy call
cumplidor, a [kumpli'ðor, a] *adj* reliable
cumplimentar [kumplimen'tar] vt to congratulate
cumplimiento [kumpli'mjento] nm (*de un deber*) fulfilment; (*acabamiento*) completion
cumplir [kum'plir] vt (*orden*) to carry out, obey; (*promesa*) to carry out, fulfil; (*condena*) to serve ♦ vi: ~ con (*deberes*) to carry out, fulfil; ~se vr (*plazo*) to expire; hoy cumple dieciocho años he is eighteen today
cúmulo ['kumulo] nm heap
cuna ['kuna] nf cradle, cot
cundir [kun'dir] vi (*noticia, rumor, pánico*) to spread; (*rendir*) to go a long way
cuneta [ku'neta] nf ditch
cuña ['kuɲa] nf wedge
cuñado, a [ku'ɲaðo, a] nm/f brother-/sister-in-law
cuota ['kwota] nf (*parte proporcional*) share; (*cotización*) fee, dues pl
cupe *etc vb ver* caber
cupiera *etc vb ver* caber
cupo ['kupo] vb ver caber ♦ nm quota
cupón [ku'pon] nm coupon
cúpula ['kupula] nf dome
cura ['kura] nf (*curación*) cure; (*método curativo*) treatment ♦ nm priest
curación [kura'θjon] nf cure; (*acción*) curing
curandero, a [kuran'dero, a] nm/f quack
curar [ku'rar] vt (MED: *herida*) to treat, dress; (: *enfermo*) to cure; (CULIN) to cure, salt; (*cuero*) to tan; ~se vr to get well, recover
curiosear [kurjose'ar] vt to glance at, look over ♦ vi to look round, wander round; (*explorar*) to poke about
curiosidad [kurjosi'ðað] nf curiosity
curioso, a [ku'rjoso, a] *adj* curious ♦ nm/f bystander, onlooker
currante [ku'rrante] (*fam*) nm/f worker
currar [ku'rrar] (*fam*) vi to work
currículo [ku'rrikulo] = curriculum
curriculum [ku'rrikulum] nm curriculum vitae
cursi ['kursi] (*fam*) *adj* affected
cursillo [kur'siʎo] nm short course
cursiva [kur'sißa] nf italics pl
curso ['kurso] nm course; en ~ (*año*)

current; (*proceso*) going on, under
way
cursor [kur'sor] *nm* (*INFORM*) cursor
curtido, a [kur'tiðo, a] *adj* (*cara etc*)
weather-beaten; (*fig: persona*)
experienced
curtir [kur'tir] *vt* (*cuero etc*) to tan
curva ['kurßa] *nf* curve, bend
cúspide ['kuspiðe] *nf* (*GEO*) peak; (*fig*) top
custodia [kus'toðja] *nf* safekeeping;
custody; **custodiar** *vt* (*conservar*) to take
care of; (*vigilar*) to guard
cutis ['kutis] *nm inv* skin, complexion
cutre ['kutre] (*fam*) *adj* (*lugar*) grotty
cuyo, a ['kujo, a] *pron* (*de quien*) whose;
(*de que*) whose, of which; **en ~ caso** in
which case
C.V. *abr* (= *caballos de vapor*) H.P.

D, d

D. *abr* (= *Don*) Esq.
Da. *abr* = **Doña**
dádiva ['daðißa] *nf* (*donación*) donation;
(*regalo*) gift; **dadivoso, a** *adj*
generous
dado, a ['daðo, a] *pp de* **dar** ♦ *nm* die; **~s**
nmpl dice; **~ que** given that
daltónico, a [dal'toniko, a] *adj* colour-
blind
dama ['dama] *nf* (*gen*) lady; (*AJEDREZ*)
queen; **~s** *nfpl* (*juego*) draughts *sg*
damnificar [damnifi'kar] *vt* to harm;
(*persona*) to injure
danés, esa [da'nes, esa] *adj* Danish
♦ *nm/f* Dane
danzar [dan'θar] *vt, vi* to dance
dañar [da'ɲar] *vt* (*objeto*) to damage;
(*persona*) to hurt; **~se** *vr* (*objeto*) to get
damaged
dañino, a [da'ɲino, a] *adj* harmful
daño ['daɲo] *nm* (*a un objeto*) damage; (*a
una persona*) harm, injury; **~s y
perjuicios** (*JUR*) damages; **hacer ~ a** to
damage; (*persona*) to hurt, injure;
hacerse ~ to hurt o.s.

PALABRA CLAVE

dar [dar] *vt* **1** (*gen*) to give; (*obra de
teatro*) to put on; (*film*) to show; (*fiesta*)
to hold; **~ algo a uno** to give sb sth *o* sth
to sb; **~ de beber a uno** to give sb a
drink

2 (*producir: intereses*) to yield; (*fruta*) to
produce

3 (*locuciones +n*): **da gusto escucharle**
it's a pleasure to listen to him; *ver tb*
paseo *y otros sustantivos*

4 (*+n:* = *perífrasis de verbo*): **me da asco**
it sickens me

5 (*considerar*): **~ algo por descontado/
entendido** to take sth for granted/as
read; **~ algo por concluido** to consider
sth finished

6 (*hora*): **el reloj dio las 6** the clock
struck 6 (o'clock)

7: **me da lo mismo** it's all the same to
me; *ver tb* **igual, más**

♦ *vi* **1**: **~ con: dimos con él dos horas
más tarde** we came across him two
hours later; **al final di con la solución** I
eventually came up with the answer

2: **~ en** (*blanco, suelo*) to hit; **el sol me
da en la cara** the sun is shining (right)
on my face

3: **~ de sí** (*zapatos etc*) to stretch, give

♦ **~se** *vr* **1**: **~se por vencido** to give up

2 (*ocurrir*): **se han dado muchos casos**
there have been a lot of cases

3: **~se a: se ha dado a la bebida** he's
taken to drinking

4: **se me dan bien/mal las ciencias** I'm
good/bad at science

5: **dárselas de: se las da de experto** he
fancies himself *o* poses as an expert

---

dardo ['darðo] *nm* dart
datar [da'tar] *vi*: **~ de** to date from
dátil ['datil] *nm* date
dato ['dato] *nm* fact, piece of information;
~s personales personal details
DC *abbr m* (= *disco compacto*) CD
dcha. *abr* (= *derecha*) r.h.

d. de J.C. *abr* (= *después de Jesucristo*)
A.D.

PALABRA CLAVE
---

de [de] *prep* (*de+el* = *del*) 1 (*posesión*) of;
la casa ~ Isabel/mis padres Isabel's/my
parents' house; **es ~ ellos** it's theirs
2 (*origen, distancia, con números*) from;
soy ~ Gijón I'm from Gijón; **~ 8 a 20**
from 8 to 20; **salir del cine** to go out of
o leave the cinema; **~ 2 en 2** 2 by 2, 2 at
a time
3 (*valor descriptivo*): **una copa ~ vino** a
glass of wine; **la mesa ~ la cocina** the
kitchen table; **un billete ~ 1000 pesetas**
a 1000 peseta note; **un niño ~ tres años**
a three-year-old (child); **una máquina ~
coser** a sewing machine; **ir vestido ~
gris** to be dressed in grey; **la niña del
vestido azul** the girl in the blue dress;
trabaja ~ profesora she works as a
teacher; **~ lado** sideways; **~ atrás/
delante** rear/front
4 (*hora, tiempo*): **a las 8 ~ la mañana** at
8 o'clock in the morning; **~ día/noche**
by day/night; **~ hoy en ocho días** a week
from now; **~ niño era gordo** as a child
he was fat
5 (*comparaciones*): **más/menos ~ cien
personas** more/less than a hundred
people; **el más caro ~ la tienda** the
most expensive in the shop; **menos/más
~ lo pensado** less/more than expected
6 (*causa*): **del calor** from the heat; **~
puro tonto** out of sheer stupidity
7 (*tema*) about; **clases ~ inglés** English
classes; **¿sabes algo ~ él?** do you know
anything about him?; **un libro ~ física** a
physics book
8 (*adj +de +infin*): **fácil ~ entender** easy
to understand
9 (*oraciones pasivas*): **fue respetado ~
todos** he was loved by all
10 (*condicional +infin*) if; **~ ser posible** if
possible; **~ no terminarlo hoy** if I *etc*
don't finish it today

dé *vb ver* **dar**
deambular [deambu'lar] *vi* to wander
debajo [de'βaxo] *adv* underneath; **~ de**
below, under; **por ~ de** beneath
debate [de'βate] *nm* debate; **debatir** *vt*
to debate
deber [de'βer] *nm* duty ♦ *vt* to owe ♦ *vi*:
debe (de) it must, it should; **~es** *nmpl*
(*ESCOL*) homework; **debo hacerlo** I must
do it; **debe de ir** he should go; **~se** *vr*:
~se a to be owing *o* due to
debido, a [de'βiðo, a] *adj* proper, just; **~ a**
due to, because of
débil ['deβil] *adj* (*persona, carácter*) weak;
(*luz*) dim; **debilidad** *nf* weakness;
dimness
debilitar [deβili'tar] *vt* to weaken; **~se** *vr*
to grow weak
debutar [deβu'tar] *vi* to make one's debut
década ['dekaða] *nf* decade
decadencia [deka'ðenθja] *nf* (*estado*)
decadence; (*proceso*) decline, decay
decaer [deka'er] *vi* (*declinar*) to decline;
(*debilitarse*) to weaken
decaído, a [deka'iðo, a] *adj*: **estar ~**
(*abatido*) to be down
decaimiento [dekai'mjento] *nm*
(*declinación*) decline; (*desaliento*)
discouragement; (*MED: estado débil*)
weakness
decano, a [de'kano, a] *nm/f* (*de
universidad etc*) dean
decapitar [dekapi'tar] *vt* to behead
decena [de'θena] *nf*: **una ~** ten (or so)
decencia [de'θenθja] *nf* decency
decente [de'θente] *adj* decent
decepción [deθep'θjon] *nf*
disappointment
decepcionar [deθepθjo'nar] *vt* to
disappoint
decidir [deθi'ðir] *vt, vi* to decide; **~se** *vr*:
~se a to make up one's mind to
décimo, a ['deθimo, a] *adj* tenth ♦ *nm*
tenth
decir [de'θir] *vt* to say; (*contar*) to tell;
(*hablar*) to speak ♦ *nm* saying; **~se** *vr*: **se
dice que** it is said that; **~ para** *o* **entre sí**

to say to o.s.; **querer ~** to mean;
¡dígame! (*TEL*) hello!; (*en tienda*) can I
help you?

decisión [deθi'sjon] *nf* (*resolución*)
decision; (*firmeza*) decisiveness

decisivo, a [deθi'siβo, a] *adj* decisive

declaración [deklara'θjon] *nf*
(*manifestación*) statement; (*de amor*)
declaration; **~ de ingresos** *o* **de la renta**
o **fiscal** income-tax return

declarar [dekla'rar] *vt* to declare ♦ *vi* to
declare; (*JUR*) to testify; **~se** *vr* to propose

declinar [dekli'nar] *vt* (*gen*) to decline;
(*JUR*) to reject ♦ *vi* (*el día*) to draw to a
close

declive [de'kliβe] *nm* (*cuesta*) slope; (*fig*)
decline

decodificador [dekoðifika'ðor] *nm*
decoder

decolorarse [dekolo'rarse] *vr* to become
discoloured

decoración [dekora'θjon] *nf* decoration

decorado [deko'raðo] *nm* (*CINE, TEATRO*)
scenery, set

decorar [deko'rar] *vt* to decorate;
decorativo, a *adj* ornamental,
decorative

decoro [de'koro] *nm* (*respeto*) respect;
(*dignidad*) decency; (*recato*) propriety;
~so, a *adj* (*decente*) decent; (*modesto*)
modest; (*digno*) proper

decrecer [dekre'θer] *vi* to decrease,
diminish

decrépito, a [de'krepito, a] *adj* decrepit

decretar [dekre'tar] *vt* to decree; **decreto**
nm decree

dedal [de'ðal] *nm* thimble

dedicación [deðika'θjon] *nf* dedication

dedicar [deði'kar] *vt* (*libro*) to dedicate;
(*tiempo, dinero*) to devote; (*palabras:
decir, consagrar*) to dedicate, devote;
dedicatoria *nf* (*de libro*) dedication

dedo ['deðo] *nm* finger; **~ (del pie)** toe; **~
pulgar** thumb; **~ índice** index finger; **~
corazón** middle finger; **~ anular** ring
finger; **~ meñique** little finger; **hacer ~**
(*fam*) to hitch (a lift)

deducción [deðuk'θjon] *nf* deduction

deducir [deðu'θir] *vt* (*concluir*) to deduce,
infer; (*COM*) to deduct

defecto [de'fekto] *nm* defect, flaw;
defectuoso, a *adj* defective, faulty

defender [defen'der] *vt* to defend

defensa [de'fensa] *nf* defence ♦ *nm*
(*DEPORTE*) defender, back; **defensivo, a**
adj defensive; **a la defensiva** on the
defensive

defensor, a [defen'sor, a] *adj* defending
♦ *nm/f* (*abogado ~*) defending counsel;
(*protector*) protector

deficiencia [defi'θjenθja] *nf* deficiency

deficiente [defi'θjente] *adj* (*defectuoso*)
defective; **~ en** lacking *o* deficient in; **ser
un ~ mental** to be mentally handicapped

déficit ['defiθit] (*pl* **~s**) *nm* deficit

definición [defini'θjon] *nf* definition

definir [defi'nir] *vt* (*determinar*) to
determine, establish; (*decidir*) to define;
(*aclarar*) to clarify; **definitivo, a** *adj*
definitive; back; **en definitiva** definitively; (*en
resumen*) in short

deformación [deforma'θjon] *nf*
(*alteración*) deformation; (*RADIO etc*)
distortion

deformar [defor'mar] *vt* (*gen*) to deform;
~se *vr* to become deformed; **deforme**
adj (*informe*) deformed; (*feo*) ugly;
(*malhecho*) misshapen

defraudar [defrau'ðar] *vt* (*decepcionar*) to
disappoint; (*estafar*) to defraud

defunción [defun'θjon] *nf* death, demise

degeneración [dexenera'θjon] *nf* (*de las
células*) degeneration; (*moral*) degeneracy

degenerar [dexene'rar] *vi* to degenerate

degollar [deɣo'ʎar] *vt* to behead; (*fig*) to
slaughter

degradar [deɣra'ðar] *vt* to debase,
degrade; **~se** *vr* to demean o.s.

degustación [deɣusta'θjon] *nf* sampling,
tasting

deificar [deifi'kar] *vt* to deify

dejadez [dexa'ðeθ] *nf* (*negligencia*)
neglect; (*descuido*) untidiness, carelessness

dejar [de'xar] *vt* to leave; (*permitir*) to

allow, let; (*abandonar*) to abandon, forsake; (*beneficios*) to produce, yield ♦ *vi*: ~ **de** (*parar*) to stop; (*no hacer*) to fail to; **no dejes de comprar un billete** make sure you buy a ticket; ~ **a un lado** to leave *o* set aside

dejo ['dexo] *nm* (*LING*) accent

del [del] (= **de+el**) *ver* **de**

delantal [delan'tal] *nm* apron

delante [de'lante] *adv* in front, (*enfrente*) opposite; (*adelante*) ahead; ~ **de** in front of, before

delantera [delan'tera] *nf* (*de vestido, casa etc*) front part; (*DEPORTE*) forward line; **llevar la ~ (a uno)** to be ahead (of sb)

delantero, a [delan'tero, a] *adj* front ♦ *nm* (*DEPORTE*) forward, striker

delatar [dela'tar] *vt* to inform on *o* against, betray; **delator, a** *nm/f* informer

delegación [deleva'θjon] *nf* (*acción, delegados*) delegation; (*COM: oficina*) office, branch; ~ **de policía** police station

delegado, a [dele'xaðo, a] *nm/f* delegate; (*COM*) agent

delegar [dele'xar] *vt* to delegate

deletrear [deletre'ar] *vt* to spell (out)

deleznable [deleθ'naβle] *adj* brittle; (*excusa, idea*) feeble

delfín [del'fin] *nm* dolphin

delgadez [delxa'ðeθ] *nf* thinness, slimness

delgado, a [del'xaðo, a] *adj* thin; (*persona*) slim, thin; (*tela etc*) light, delicate

deliberación [deliβera'θjon] *nf* deliberation

deliberar [deliβe'rar] *vt* to debate, discuss

delicadeza [delika'ðeθa] *nf* (*gen*) delicacy; (*refinamiento, sutileza*) refinement

delicado, a [deli'kaðo, a] *adj* (*gen*) delicate; (*sensible*) sensitive; (*quisquilloso*) touchy

delicia [de'liθja] *nf* delight

delicioso, a [deli'θjoso, a] *adj* (*gracioso*) delightful; (*exquisito*) delicious

delimitar [delimi'tar] *vt* (*funciones, responsabilidades*) to define

delincuencia [delin'kwenθja] *nf* delinquency; **delincuente** *nm/f* delinquent; (*criminal*) criminal

delineante [deline'ante] *nm/f* draughtsman/woman

delinear [deline'ar] *vt* (*dibujo*) to draw; (*fig, contornos*) to outline

delinquir [delin'kir] *vi* to commit an offence

delirante [deli'rante] *adj* delirious

delirar [deli'rar] *vi* to be delirious, rave

delirio [de'lirjo] *nm* (*MED*) delirium; (*palabras insensatas*) ravings *pl*

delito [de'lito] *nm* (*gen*) crime; (*infracción*) offence

delta ['delta] *nm* delta

demacrado, a [dema'kraðo, a] *adj*: **estar ~** to look pale and drawn, be wasted away

demagogo, a [dema'xoxo, a] *nm/f* demagogue

demanda [de'manda] *nf* (*pedido, COM*) demand; (*petición*) request; (*JUR*) action, lawsuit

demandante [deman'dante] *nm/f* claimant

demandar [deman'dar] *vt* (*gen*) to demand; (*JUR*) to sue, file a lawsuit against

demarcación [demarka'θjon] *nf* (*de terreno*) demarcation

demás [de'mas] *adj*: **los ~ niños** the other children, the remaining children ♦ *pron*: **los/las ~** the others, the rest (of them); **lo ~** the rest (of it)

demasía [dema'sia] *nf* (*exceso*) excess, surplus; **comer en ~** to eat to excess

demasiado, a [dema'sjaðo, a] *adj*: ~ **vino** too much wine ♦ *adv* (*antes de adj, adv*) too; ~**s libros** too many books; ¡**esto es ~!** that's the limit!; **hace ~ calor** it's too hot; ~ **despacio** too slowly; ~**s** too many

demencia [de'menθja] *nf* (*locura*) madness; **demente** *nm/f* lunatic ♦ *adj* mad, insane

democracia [demo'kraθja] *nf* democracy

demócrata [de'mokrata] *nm/f* democrat;

democrático, a *adj* democratic

demoler [demo'ler] *vt* to demolish; **demolición** *nf* demolition

demonio [de'monjo] *nm* devil, demon; **¡~s!** hell!, damn!; **¿cómo ~s?** how the hell?

demora [de'mora] *nf* delay; **demorar** *vt* (*retardar*) to delay, hold back; (*detener*) to hold up ♦ *vi* to linger, stay on; **~se** *vr* to be delayed

demos *vb ver* **dar**

demostración [demostra'θjon] *nf* (*MAT*) proof; (*de afecto*) show, display

demostrar [demos'trar] *vt* (*probar*) to prove; (*mostrar*) to show; (*manifestar*) to demonstrate

demudado, a [demu'ðaðo, a] *adj* (*rostro*) pale

den *vb ver* **dar**

denegar [dene'γar] *vt* (*rechazar*) to refuse; (*JUR*) to reject

denigrar [deni'γrar] *vt* (*desacreditar, infamar*) to denigrate; (*injuriar*) to insult

---
Denominación de Origen

ⓘ The **Denominación de Origen**, abbreviated to **D.O.**, is a prestigious classification awarded to food products such as wines, cheeses, sausages and hams which meet the stringent quality and production standards of the designated region. **D.O.** labels serve as a guarantee of quality.

---

denotar [deno'tar] *vt* to denote

densidad [densi'ðað] *nf* density; (*fig*) thickness

denso, a ['denso, a] *adj* dense; (*espeso, pastoso*) thick; (*fig*) heavy

dentadura [denta'ðura] *nf* (set of) teeth *pl*; **~ postiza** false teeth *pl*

dentera [den'tera] *nf* (*sensación desagradable*) the shivers *pl*

dentífrico, a [den'tifriko, a] *adj* dental ♦ *nm* toothpaste

dentista [den'tista] *nm/f* dentist

dentro ['dentro] *adv* inside ♦ *prep*: **~ de** in, inside, within; **por ~** (on the) inside; **mirar por ~** to look inside; **~ de tres meses** within three months

denuncia [de'nunθja] *nf* (*delación*) denunciation; (*acusación*) accusation; (*de accidente*) report; **denunciar** *vt* to report; (*delatar*) to inform on *o* against

departamento [departa'mento] *nm* (*sección administrativa*) department, section; (*AM: apartamento*) flat (*BRIT*), apartment

dependencia [depen'denθja] *nf* dependence; (*POL*) dependency; (*COM*) office, section

depender [depen'der] *vi*: **~ de** to depend on

dependienta [depen'djenta] *nf* saleswoman, shop assistant

dependiente [depen'djente] *adj* dependent ♦ *nm* salesman, shop assistant

depilar [depi'lar] *vt* (*con cera*) to wax; (*cejas*) to pluck; **depilatorio** *nm* hair remover

deplorable [deplo'raßle] *adj* deplorable

deplorar [deplo'rar] *vt* to deplore

deponer [depo'ner] *vt* to lay down ♦ *vi* (*JUR*) to give evidence; (*declarar*) to make a statement

deportar [depor'tar] *vt* to deport

deporte [de'porte] *nm* sport; **hacer ~** to play sports; **deportista** *adj* sports *cpd* ♦ *nm/f* sportsman/woman; **deportivo, a** *adj* (*club, periódico*) sports *cpd* ♦ *nm* sports car

depositar [deposi'tar] *vt* (*dinero*) to deposit; (*mercancías*) to put away, store; **~se** *vr* to settle; **~io, a** *nm/f* trustee

depósito [de'posito] *nm* (*gen*) deposit; (*almacén*) warehouse, store; (*de agua, gasolina etc*) tank; **~ de cadáveres** mortuary

depreciar [depre'θjar] *vt* to depreciate, reduce the value of; **~se** *vr* to depreciate, lose value

depredador, a [depreða'ðor, a] *adj* predatory ♦ *nm* predator

depresión [depre'sjon] *nf* depression

deprimido, a [depri'miðo, a] *adj* depressed

deprimir [depri'mir] *vt* to depress; **~se** *vr* (*persona*) to become depressed

deprisa [de'prisa] *adv* quickly, hurriedly

depuración [depura'θjon] *nf* purification; (*POL*) purge

depurar [depu'rar] *vt* to purify; (*purgar*) to purge

derecha [de'retʃa] *nf* right(-hand) side; (*POL*) right; **a la ~** (*estar*) on the right; (*torcer etc*) to the right

derecho, a [de'retʃo, a] *adj* right, right-hand ♦ *nm* (*privilegio*) right; (*lado*) right(-hand) side; (*leyes*) law ♦ *adv* straight, directly; **~s** *nmpl* (*de aduana*) duty *sg*; (*de autor*) royalties; **tener ~ a** to have a right to

deriva [de'riβa] *nf*: **ir** *o* **estar a la ~** to drift, be adrift

derivado [deri'βaðo] *nm* (*COM*) by-product

derivar [deri'βar] *vt* to derive; (*desviar*) to direct ♦ *vi* to derive, be derived; (*NAUT*) to drift; **~se** *vr* to derive, be derived; to drift

derramamiento [derrama'mjento] *nm* (*dispersión*) spilling; **~ de sangre** bloodshed

derramar [derra'mar] *vt* to spill; (*verter*) to pour out; (*esparcir*) to scatter; **~se** *vr* to pour out; **~ lágrimas** to weep

derrame [de'rrame] *nm* (*de líquido*) spilling; (*de sangre*) shedding; (*de tubo etc*) overflow; (*pérdida*) leakage; (*MED*) discharge

derredor [derre'ðor] *adv*: **al** *o* **en ~ de** around, about

derretido, a [derre'tiðo, a] *adj* melted; (*metal*) molten

derretir [derre'tir] *vt* (*gen*) to melt; (*nieve*) to thaw; **~se** *vr* to melt

derribar [derri'βar] *vt* to knock down; (*construcción*) to demolish; (*persona, gobierno, político*) to bring down

derrocar [derro'kar] *vt* (*gobierno*) to bring down, overthrow

derrochar [derro'tʃar] *vt* to squander; **derroche** *nm* (*despilfarro*) waste, squandering

derrota [de'rrota] *nf* (*NAUT*) course; (*MIL, DEPORTE etc*) defeat, rout; **derrotar** *vt* (*gen*) to defeat; **derrotero** *nm* (*rumbo*) course

derruir [derru'ir] *vt* (*edificio*) to demolish

derrumbar [derrum'bar] *vt* (*edificio*) to knock down; **~se** *vr* to collapse

derruyendo *etc vb ver* **derruir**

des *vb ver* **dar**

desabotonar [desaβoto'nar] *vt* to unbutton, undo; **~se** *vr* to come undone

desabrido, a [desa'βriðo, a] *adj* (*comida*) insipid, tasteless; (*persona*) rude, surly; (*respuesta*) sharp; (*tiempo*) unpleasant

desabrochar [desaβro'tʃar] *vt* (*botones, broches*) to undo, unfasten; **~se** *vr* (*ropa etc*) to come undone

desacato [desa'kato] *nm* (*falta de respeto*) disrespect; (*JUR*) contempt

desacertado, a [desaθer'taðo, a] *adj* (*equivocado*) mistaken; (*inoportuno*) unwise

desacierto [desa'θjerto] *nm* mistake, error

desaconsejado, a [desakonse'xaðo, a] *adj* ill-advised

desaconsejar [desakonse'xar] *vt* to advise against

desacreditar [desakreði'tar] *vt* (*desprestigiar*) to discredit, bring into disrepute; (*denigrar*) to run down

desacuerdo [desa'kwerðo] *nm* disagreement, discord

desafiar [desa'fjar] *vt* (*retar*) to challenge; (*enfrentarse a*) to defy

desafilado, a [desafi'laðo, a] *adj* blunt

desafinado, a [desafi'naðo, a] *adj*: **estar ~** to be out of tune

desafinar [desafi'nar] *vi* (*al cantar*) to be *o* go out of tune

desafío *etc* [desa'fio] *vb ver* **desafiar** ♦ *nm* (*reto*) challenge; (*combate*) duel; (*resistencia*) defiance

desaforado, a [desafo'raðo, a] *adj* (*grito*) ear-splitting; (*comportamiento*) outrageous

desafortunadamente
[desafortunaða'mente] *adv* unfortunately
desafortunado, a [desafortu'naðo, a] *adj*
(*desgraciado*) unfortunate, unlucky
desagradable [desaɣra'ðaβle] *adj*
(*fastidioso, enojoso*) unpleasant; (*irritante*)
disagreeable
desagradar [desaɣra'ðar] *vi* (*disgustar*) to
displease; (*molestar*) to bother
desagradecido, a [desaɣraðe'θiðo, a] *adj*
ungrateful
desagrado [desa'ɣraðo] *nm* (*disgusto*)
displeasure; (*contrariedad*) dissatisfaction
desagraviar [desaɣra'βjar] *vt* to make
amends to
desagüe [des'aɣwe] *nm* (*de un líquido*)
drainage; (*cañería*) drainpipe; (*salida*)
outlet, drain
desaguisado [desaɣi'saðo] *nm* outrage
desahogado, a [desao'ɣaðo, a] *adj*
(*holgado*) comfortable; (*espacioso*) roomy,
large
desahogar [desao'ɣar] *vt* (*aliviar*) to ease,
relieve; (*ira*) to vent; (*relajarse*) to
relax; ~**se** *vr* (*desfogarse*) to let off steam
desahogo [desa'oɣo] *nm* (*alivio*) relief;
(*comodidad*) comfort, ease
desahuciar [desau'θjar] *vt* (*enfermo*) to
give up hope for; (*inquilino*) to evict;
desahucio *nm* eviction
desairar [desai'rar] *vt* (*menospreciar*) to
slight, snub
desaire [des'aire] *nm* (*menosprecio*) slight;
(*falta de garbo*) unattractiveness
desajustar [desaxus'tar] *vt* (*desarreglar*) to
disarrange; (*desconcertar*) to throw off
balance; ~**se** *vr* to get out of order;
(*aflojarse*) to loosen
desajuste [desa'xuste] *nm* (*de máquina*)
disorder; (*situación*) imbalance
desalentador, a [desalenta'ðor, a] *adj*
discouraging
desalentar [desalen'tar] *vt* (*desanimar*) to
discourage
desaliento *etc* [desa'ljento] *vb ver*
desalentar ♦ *nm* discouragement
desaliño [desa'liɲo] *nm* slovenliness

desalmado, a [desal'maðo, a] *adj* (*cruel*)
cruel, heartless
desalojar [desalo'xar] *vt* (*expulsar, echar*)
to eject; (*abandonar*) to move out of ♦ *vi*
to move out
desamor [desa'mor] *nm* (*frialdad*)
indifference; (*odio*) dislike
desamparado, a [desampa'raðo, a] *adj*
(*persona*) helpless; (*lugar: expuesto*)
exposed; (*desierto*) deserted
desamparar [desampa'rar] *vt* (*abandonar*)
to desert, abandon; (*JUR*) to leave
defenceless; (*barco*) to abandon
desandar [desan'dar] *vt*: ~ **lo andado** *o* **el
camino** to retrace one's steps
desangrar [desaŋ'grar] *vt* to bleed; (*fig:
persona*) to bleed dry; ~**se** *vr* to lose a lot
of blood
desanimado, a [desani'maðo, a] *adj*
(*persona*) downhearted; (*espectáculo,
fiesta*) dull
desanimar [desani'mar] *vt* (*desalentar*) to
discourage; (*deprimir*) to depress; ~**se** *vr*
to lose heart
desapacible [desapa'θiβle] *adj* (*gen*)
unpleasant
desaparecer [desapare'θer] *vi* (*gen*) to
disappear; (*el sol, la luz*) to vanish;
desaparecido, a *adj* missing;
desaparición *nf* disappearance
desapasionado, a [desapasjo'naðo, a]
adj dispassionate, impartial
desapego [desa'peɣo] *nm* (*frialdad*)
coolness; (*distancia*) detachment
desapercibido, a [desaperθi'βiðo, a] *adj*
(*desprevenido*) unprepared; **pasar ~** to go
unnoticed
desaprensivo, a [desapren'siβo, a] *adj*
unscrupulous
desaprobar [desapro'βar] *vt* (*reprobar*) to
disapprove of; (*condenar*) to condemn;
(*no consentir*) to reject
desaprovechado, a [desaproβe'tʃaðo, a]
adj (*oportunidad, tiempo*) wasted;
(*estudiante*) slack
desaprovechar [desaproβe'tʃar] *vt* to
waste

desarmar [desar'mar] *vt* (*MIL*, *fig*) to disarm; (*TEC*) to take apart, dismantle; **desarme** *nm* disarmament

desarraigar [desarrai'ɣar] *vt* to uproot; **desarraigo** *nm* uprooting

desarreglar [desarre'ɣlar] *vt* (*desordenar*) to disarrange; (*trastocar*) to upset, disturb

desarreglo [desa'rreɣlo] *nm* (*de casa*, *persona*) untidiness; (*desorden*) disorder

desarrollar [desarro'ʎar] *vt* (*gen*) to develop; **~se** *vr* to develop; (*ocurrir*) to take place; (*FOTO*) to develop; **desarrollo** *nm* development

desarticular [desartiku'lar] *vt* (*hueso*) to dislocate; (*objeto*) to take apart; (*fig*) to break up

desasir [desa'sir] *vt* to loosen

desasosegar [desasose'ɣar] *vt* (*inquietar*) to disturb, make uneasy; **~se** *vr* to become uneasy

desasosiego *etc* [desaso'sjeɣo] *vb ver* **desasosegar** ♦ *nm* (*intranquilidad*) uneasiness, restlessness; (*ansiedad*) anxiety

desastrado, a [desas'traðo, a] *adj* (*desaliñado*) shabby; (*sucio*) dirty

desastre [de'sastre] *nm* disaster; **desastroso, a** *adj* disastrous

desatado, a [desa'taðo, a] *adj* (*desligado*) untied; (*violento*) violent, wild

desatar [desa'tar] *vt* (*nudo*) to untie; (*paquete*) to undo; (*separar*) to detach; **~se** *vr* (*zapatos*) to come untied; (*tormenta*) to break

desatascar [desatas'kar] *vt* (*cañería*) to unblock, clear

desatender [desaten'der] *vt* (*no prestar atención a*) to disregard; (*abandonar*) to neglect

desatento, a [desa'tento, a] *adj* (*distraído*) inattentive; (*descortés*) discourteous

desatinado, a [desati'naðo, a] *adj* foolish, silly; **desatino** *nm* (*idiotez*) foolishness, folly; (*error*) blunder

desatornillar [desatorni'ʎar] *vt* to unscrew

desatrancar [desatran'kar] *vt* (*puerta*) to unbolt; (*cañería*) to clear, unblock

desautorizado, a [desautori'θaðo, a] *adj* unauthorized

desautorizar [desautori'θar] *vt* (*oficial*) to deprive of authority; (*informe*) to deny

desavenencia [desaβe'nenθja] *nf* (*desacuerdo*) disagreement; (*discrepancia*) quarrel

desayunar [desaju'nar] *vi* to have breakfast ♦ *vt* to have for breakfast; **desayuno** *nm* breakfast

desazón [desa'θon] *nf* anxiety

desazonarse [desaθo'narse] *vr* to worry, be anxious

desbandarse [desβan'darse] *vr* (*MIL*) to disband; (*fig*) to flee in disorder

desbarajuste [desβara'xuste] *nm* confusion, disorder

desbaratar [desβara'tar] *vt* (*deshacer*, *destruir*) to ruin

desbloquear [desβloke'ar] *vt* (*negociaciones*, *tráfico*) to get going again; (*COM*: *cuenta*) to unfreeze

desbocado, a [desβo'kaðo, a] *adj* (*caballo*) runaway

desbordar [desβor'ðar] *vt* (*sobrepasar*) to go beyond; (*exceder*) to exceed; **~se** *vr* (*río*) to overflow; (*entusiasmo*) to erupt

descabalgar [deskaβal'ɣar] *vi* to dismount

descabellado, a [deskaβe'ʎaðo, a] *adj* (*disparatado*) wild, crazy

descafeinado, a [deskafei'naðo, a] *adj* decaffeinated ♦ *nm* decaffeinated coffee

descalabro [deska'laβro] *nm* blow; (*desgracia*) misfortune

descalificar [deskalifi'kar] *vt* to disqualify; (*desacreditar*) to discredit

descalzar [deskal'θar] *vt* (*zapato*) to take off; **descalzo, a** *adj* barefoot(ed)

descambiar [deskam'bjar] *vt* to exchange

descaminado, a [deskami'naðo, a] *adj* (*equivocado*) on the wrong road; (*fig*) misguided

descampado [deskam'paðo] *nm* open space

descansado, a [deskan'saðo, a] *adj* (*gen*) rested; (*que tranquiliza*) restful

descansar [deskan'sar] *vt* (*gen*) to rest
♦ *vi* to rest, have a rest; (*echarse*) to lie down

descansillo [deskan'siʎo] *nm* (*de escalera*) landing

descanso [des'kanso] *nm* (*reposo*) rest; (*alivio*) relief; (*pausa*) break; (*DEPORTE*) interval, half time

descapotable [deskapo'taβle] *nm* (*tb:* **coche ~**) convertible

descarado, a [deska'raðo, a] *adj* shameless; (*insolente*) cheeky

descarga [des'karγa] *nf* (*ARQ , ELEC, MIL*) discharge; (*NAUT*) unloading

descargar [deskar'γar] *vt* to unload; (*golpe*) to let fly; **~se** *vr* to unburden o.s.; **descargo** *nm* (*COM*) receipt; (*JUR*) evidence

descaro [des'karo] *nm* nerve

descarriar [deska'rrjar] *vt* (*descaminar*) to misdirect; (*fig*) to lead astray; **~se** *vr* (*perderse*) to lose one's way; (*separarse*) to stray; (*pervertirse*) to err, go astray

descarrilamiento [deskarrila'mjento] *nm* (*de tren*) derailment

descarrilar [deskarri'lar] *vi* to be derailed

descartar [deskar'tar] *vt* (*rechazar*) to reject; (*eliminar*) to rule out; **~se** *vr* (*NAIPES*) to discard; **~se de** to shirk

descascarillado, a [deskaskari'ʎaðo, a] *adj* (*paredes*) peeling

descendencia [desθen'denθja] *nf* (*origen*) origin, descent; (*hijos*) offspring

descender [desθen'der] *vt* (*bajar: escalera*) to go down ♦ *vi* to descend; (*temperatura, nivel*) to fall, drop; **~ de** to be descended from

descendiente [desθen'djente] *nm/f* descendant

descenso [des'θenso] *nm* descent; (*de temperatura*) drop

descifrar [desθi'frar] *vt* to decipher; (*mensaje*) to decode

descolgar [deskol'γar] *vt* (*bajar*) to take down; (*teléfono*) to pick up; **~se** *vr* to let o.s. down

descolorido, a [deskolo'riðo, a] *adj* faded; (*pálido*) pale

descompasado, a [deskompa'saðo, a] *adj* (*sin proporción*) out of all proportion; (*excesivo*) excessive

descomponer [deskompo'ner] *vt* (*desordenar*) to disarrange, disturb; (*TEC*) to put out of order; (*dividir*) to break down (into parts); (*fig*) to provoke; **~se** *vr* (*corromperse*) to rot, decompose; (*TEC*) to break down

descomposición [deskomposi'θjon] *nf* (*de un objeto*) breakdown; (*de fruta etc*) decomposition; **~ de vientre** stomach upset, diarrhoea

descompuesto, a [deskom'pwesto, a] *adj* (*corrompido*) decomposed; (*roto*) broken

descomunal [deskomu'nal] *adj* (*enorme*) huge

desconcertado, a [deskonθer'taðo, a] *adj* disconcerted, bewildered

desconcertar [deskonθer'tar] *vt* (*confundir*) to baffle; (*incomodar*) to upset, put out; **~se** *vr* (*turbarse*) to be upset

desconchado, a [deskon'tʃaðo, a] *adj* (*pintura*) peeling

desconcierto *etc* [deskon'θjerto] *vb ver* **desconcertar** ♦ *nm* (*gen*) disorder; (*desorientación*) uncertainty; (*inquietud*) uneasiness

desconectar [deskonek'tar] *vt* to disconnect

desconfianza [deskon'fjanθa] *nf* distrust

desconfiar [deskon'fjar] *vi* to be distrustful; **~ de** to distrust, suspect

descongelar [deskonxe'lar] *vt* to defrost; (*COM, POL*) to unfreeze

descongestionar [deskonxestjo'nar] *vt* (*cabeza, tráfico*) to clear

desconocer [deskono'θer] *vt* (*ignorar*) not to know, be ignorant of

desconocido, a [deskono'θiðo, a] *adj* unknown ♦ *nm/f* stranger

desconocimiento [deskonoθi'mjento] *nm* (*falta de conocimientos*) ignorance

desconsiderado, a [deskonside'raðo, a] *adj* inconsiderate; (*insensible*) thoughtless

desconsolar [deskonso'lar] *vt* to distress;
~**se** *vr* to despair

desconsuelo *etc* [deskon'swelo] *vb ver*
desconsolar ♦ *nm* (*tristeza*) distress;
(*desesperación*) despair

descontado, a [deskon'taðo, a] *adj*: **dar
por** ~ **(que)** to take (it) for granted (that)

descontar [deskon'tar] *vt* (*deducir*) to take
away, deduct; (*rebajar*) to discount

descontento, a [deskon'tento, a] *adj*
dissatisfied ♦ *nm* dissatisfaction,
discontent

descorazonar [deskoraθo'nar] *vt* to
discourage, dishearten

descorchar [deskor'tʃar] *vt* to uncork

descorrer [desko'rrer] *vt* (*cortinas, cerrojo*)
to draw back

descortés [deskor'tes] *adj* (*mal educado*)
discourteous; (*grosero*) rude

descoser [desko'ser] *vt* to unstitch; ~**se** *vr*
to come apart (at the seams)

descosido, a [desko'siðo, a] *adj*
(*COSTURA*) unstitched

descrédito [des'kreðito] *nm* discredit

descreído, a [deskre'iðo, a] *adj*
(*incrédulo*) incredulous; (*falto de fe*)
unbelieving

descremado, a [deskre'maðo, a] *adj*
skimmed

describir [deskri'ßir] *vt* to describe;
descripción [deskrip'θjon] *nf* description

descrito [des'krito] *pp de* **describir**

descuartizar [deskwarti'θar] *vt* (*animal*) to
cut up

descubierto, a [desku'ßjerto, a] *pp de*
descubrir ♦ *adj* uncovered, bare;
(*persona*) bareheaded ♦ *nm* (*bancario*)
overdraft; **al** ~ in the open

descubrimiento [deskußri'mjento] *nm*
(*hallazgo*) discovery; (*revelación*) revelation

descubrir [desku'ßrir] *vt* to discover, find;
(*inaugurar*) to unveil; (*vislumbrar*) to
detect; (*revelar*) to reveal, show;
(*destapar*) to uncover; ~**se** *vr* to reveal
o.s.; (*quitarse sombrero*) to take off one's
hat; (*confesar*) to confess

descuento *etc* [des'kwento] *vb ver*

descontar ♦ *nm* discount

descuidado, a [deskwi'ðaðo, a] *adj* (*sin
cuidado*) careless; (*desordenado*) untidy;
(*olvidadizo*) forgetful; (*dejado*) neglected;
(*desprevenido*) unprepared

descuidar [deskwi'ðar] *vt* (*dejar*) to
neglect; (*olvidar*) to overlook; ~**se** *vr*
(*distraerse*) to be careless; (*abandonarse*)
to let o.s. go; (*desprevenirse*) to drop
one's guard; **¡descuida!** don't worry!;
descuido *nm* (*dejadez*) carelessness;
(*olvido*) negligence

PALABRA CLAVE

desde ['desðe] *prep* **1** (*lugar*) from; ~
Burgos hasta mi casa hay 30 km it's 30
kms from Burgos to my house
2 (*posición*): **hablaba** ~ **el balcón** she was
speaking from the balcony
3 (*tiempo*: +*adv, n*): ~ **ahora** from now
on; ~ **la boda** since the wedding; ~ **niño**
since I *etc* was a child; ~ **3 años atrás**
since 3 years ago
4 (*tiempo*: +*vb, fecha*) since; for; **nos
conocemos** ~ **1992/** ~ **hace 20 años**
we've known each other since 1992/for
20 years; **no le veo** ~ **1997/** ~ **hace 5
años** I haven't seen him since 1997/for 5
years
5 (*gama*): ~ **los más lujosos hasta los
más económicos** from the most
luxurious to the most reasonably priced
6: ~ **luego (que no)** of course (not)
♦ *conj*: ~ **que**: ~ **que recuerdo** for as
long as I can remember; ~ **que llegó no
ha salido** he hasn't been out since he
arrived

---

desdecirse [desðe'θirse] *vr* to retract; ~
de to go back on

desdén [des'ðen] *nm* scorn

desdeñar [desðe'ɲar] *vt* (*despreciar*) to
scorn

desdicha [des'ðitʃa] *nf* (*desgracia*)
misfortune; (*infelicidad*) unhappiness;
desdichado, a *adj* (*sin suerte*) unlucky;
(*infeliz*) unhappy

desdoblar [desðo'ßlar] vt (extender) to spread out; (desplegar) to unfold
desear [dese'ar] vt to want, desire, wish for
desecar [dese'kar] vt to dry up; ~se vr to dry up
desechar [dese'tʃar] vt (basura) to throw out o away; (ideas) to reject, discard; **desechos** nmpl rubbish sg, waste sg
desembalar [desemba'lar] vt to unpack
desembarazar [desembara'θar] vt (desocupar) to clear; (desenredar) to free; ~se vr: ~se de to free o.s. of, get rid of
desembarcar [desembar'kar] vt (mercancías etc) to unload ♦ vi to disembark; ~se vr to disembark
desembocadura [desemboka'ðura] nf (de río) mouth; (de calle) opening
desembocar [desembo'kar] vi (río) to flow into; (fig) to result in
desembolso [desem'bolso] nm payment
desembragar [desembra'var] vi to declutch
desembrollar [desembro'ʎar] vt (madeja) to unravel; (asunto, malentendido) to sort out
desemejanza [deseme'xanθa] nf dissimilarity
desempaquetar [desempake'tar] vt (regalo) to unwrap; (mercancía) to unpack
desempatar [desempa'tar] vi to replay, hold a play-off; **desempate** nm (FÚTBOL) replay, play-off; (TENIS) tie-break(er)
desempeñar [desempe'ɲar] vt (cargo) to hold; (papel) to perform; (lo empeñado) to redeem; ~ **un papel** (fig) to play (a role)
desempeño [desem'peɲo] nm redeeming; (de cargo) occupation
desempleado, a [desemple'aðo, a] nm/f unemployed person; **desempleo** nm unemployment
desempolvar [desempol'ßar] vt (muebles etc) to dust; (lo olvidado) to revive
desencadenar [desenkaðe'nar] vt to unchain; (ira) to unleash; ~se vr to break loose; (tormenta) to burst; (guerra) to break out

desencajar [desenka'xar] vt (hueso) to dislocate; (mecanismo, pieza) to disconnect, disengage
desencanto [desen'kanto] nm disillusionment
desenchufar [desentʃu'far] vt to unplug
desenfadado, a [desenfa'ðaðo, a] adj (desenvuelto) uninhibited; (descarado) forward; **desenfado** nm (libertad) freedom; (comportamiento) free and easy manner; (descaro) forwardness
desenfocado, a [desenfo'kaðo, a] adj (FOTO) out of focus
desenfrenado, a [desenfre'naðo, a] adj (descontrolado) uncontrolled; (inmoderado) unbridled; **desenfreno** nm wildness; (de las pasiones) lack of self-control
desenganchar [desengan'tʃar] vt (gen) to unhook; (FERRO) to uncouple
desengañar [desenga'ɲar] vt to disillusion; ~se vr to become disillusioned; **desengaño** nm disillusionment; (decepción) disappointment
desenlace [desen'laθe] nm outcome
desenmarañar [desenmara'ɲar] vt (fig) to unravel
desenmascarar [desenmaska'rar] vt to unmask
desenredar [desenre'ðar] vt (pelo) to untangle; (problema) to sort out
desenroscar [desenros'kar] vt to unscrew
desentenderse [desenten'derse] vr: ~ **de** to pretend not to know about; (apartarse) to have nothing to do with
desenterrar [desente'rrar] vt to exhume; (tesoro, fig) to unearth, dig up
desentonar [desento'nar] vi (MUS) to sing (o play) out of tune; (color) to clash
desentrañar [desentra'ɲar] vt (misterio) to unravel
desentumecer [desentume'θer] vt (pierna etc) to stretch
desenvoltura [desenßol'tura] nf ease
desenvolver [desenßol'ßer] vt (paquete) to unwrap; (fig) to develop; ~se vr (desarrollarse) to unfold, develop;

(*arreglárselas*) to cope
deseo [de'seo] *nm* desire, wish; **~so, a**
adj: **estar ~so de** to be anxious to
desequilibrado, a [desekili'ßraðo, a] *adj*
unbalanced
desertar [deser'tar] *vi* to desert
desértico, a [de'sertiko, a] *adj* desert *cpd*
desesperación [desespera'θjon] *nf*
(*impaciencia*) desperation, despair;
(*irritación*) fury
desesperar [desespe'rar] *vt* to drive to
despair; (*exasperar*) to drive to distraction
♦ *vi:* **~ de** to despair of; **~se** *vr* to
despair, lose hope
desestabilizar [desestaßili'θar] *vt* to
destabilize
desestimar [desesti'mar] *vt* (*menospreciar*)
to have a low opinion of; (*rechazar*) to
reject
desfachatez [desfatʃa'teθ] *nf* (*insolencia*)
impudence; (*descaro*) rudeness
desfalco [des'falko] *nm* embezzlement
desfallecer [desfaʎe'θer] *vi* (*perder las
fuerzas*) to become weak; (*desvanecerse*)
to faint
desfasado, a [desfa'saðo, a] *adj*
(*anticuado*) old-fashioned; **desfase** *nm*
(*diferencia*) gap
desfavorable [desfaßo'raßle] *adj*
unfavourable
desfigurar [desfixu'rar] *vt* (*cara*) to
disfigure; (*cuerpo*) to deform
desfiladero [desfila'ðero] *nm* gorge
desfilar [desfi'lar] *vi* to parade; **desfile**
nm procession
desfogarse [desfo'varse] *vr* (*fig*) to let off
steam
desgajar [desva'xar] *vt* (*arrancar*) to tear
off; (*romper*) to break off; **~se** *vr* to come
off
desgana [des'vana] *nf* (*falta de apetito*)
loss of appetite; (*apatía*) unwillingness;
~do, a *adj:* **estar ~do** (*sin apetito*) to
have no appetite; (*sin entusiasmo*) to have
lost interest
desgarrador, a [desvarra'ðor, a] *adj* (*fig*)
heartrending

desgarrar [desva'rrar] *vt* to tear (up); (*fig*)
to shatter; **desgarro** *nm* (*en tela*) tear;
(*aflicción*) grief
desgastar [desvas'tar] *vt* (*deteriorar*) to
wear away *o* down; (*estropear*) to spoil;
~se *vr* to get worn out; **desgaste** *nm*
wear (and tear)
desglosar [desvlo'sar] *vt* (*factura*) to break
down
desgracia [des'vraθja] *nf* misfortune;
(*accidente*) accident; (*vergüenza*) disgrace;
(*contratiempo*) setback; **por ~**
unfortunately
desgraciado, a [desvra'θjaðo, a] *adj* (*sin
suerte*) unlucky, unfortunate; (*miserable*)
wretched; (*infeliz*) miserable
desgravación [desvraßa'θjon] *nf* (COM): **~
fiscal** tax relief
desgravar [desvra'ßar] *vt* (*impuestos*) to
reduce the tax *o* duty on
deshabitado, a [desaßi'taðo, a] *adj*
uninhabited
deshacer [desa'θer] *vt* (*casa*) to break up;
(*TEC*) to take apart; (*enemigo*) to defeat;
(*diluir*) to melt; (*contrato*) to break;
(*intriga*) to solve; **~se** *vr* (*disolverse*) to
melt; (*despedazarse*) to come apart *o*
undone; **~se de** to get rid of; **~se en
lágrimas** to burst into tears
desharrapado, a [desarra'paðo, a] *adj*
(*persona*) shabby
deshecho, a [des'etʃo, a] *adj* undone;
(*roto*) smashed; (*persona*): **estar ~** to be
shattered
desheredar [desere'ðar] *vt* to disinherit
deshidratar [desiðra'tar] *vt* to dehydrate
deshielo [des'jelo] *nm* thaw
deshonesto, a [deso'nesto, a] *adj*
indecent
deshonra [des'onra] *nf* (*deshonor*)
dishonour; (*vergüenza*) shame
deshora [des'ora]: **a ~** *adv* at the wrong
time
deshuesar [deswe'sar] *vt* (*carne*) to bone;
(*fruta*) to stone
desierto, a [de'sjerto, a] *adj* (*casa, calle,
negocio*) deserted ♦ *nm* desert

designar [desiɣ'nar] vt (*nombrar*) to designate; (*indicar*) to fix

designio [de'siɣnjo] nm plan

desigual [desi'ɣwal] adj (*terreno*) uneven; (*lucha etc*) unequal

desilusión [desilu'sjon] nf disillusionment; (*decepción*) disappointment; **desilusionar** vt to disillusion; to disappoint; **desilusionarse** vr to become disillusioned

desinfectar [desinfek'tar] vt to disinfect

desinflar [desin'flar] vt to deflate

desintegración [desinteɣra'θjon] nf disintegration

desinterés [desinte'res] nm (*desgana*) lack of interest; (*altruismo*) unselfishness

desintoxicarse [desintoksi'karse] vr (*drogadicto*) to undergo detoxification

desistir [desis'tir] vi (*renunciar*) to stop, desist

desleal [desle'al] adj (*infiel*) disloyal; (*COM: competencia*) unfair; **~tad** nf disloyalty

desleír [desle'ir] vt (*líquido*) to dilute; (*sólido*) to dissolve

deslenguado, a [deslen'ɡwaðo, a] adj (*grosero*) foul-mouthed

desligar [desli'ɣar] vt (*desatar*) to untie, undo; (*separar*) to separate; **~se** vr (*de un compromiso*) to extricate o.s.

desliz [des'liθ] nm (*fig*) lapse; **~ar** vt to slip, slide

deslucido, a [deslu'θiðo, a] adj dull; (*torpe*) awkward, graceless; (*deslustrado*) tarnished

deslumbrar [deslum'brar] vt to dazzle

desmadrarse [desma'ðrarse] (*fam*) vr (*descontrolarse*) to run wild; (*divertirse*) to let one's hair down; **desmadre** (*fam*) nm (*desorganización*) chaos; (*jaleo*) commotion

desmán [des'man] nm (*exceso*) outrage; (*abuso de poder*) abuse

desmandarse [desman'darse] vr (*portarse mal*) to behave badly; (*excederse*) to get out of hand; (*caballo*) to bolt

desmantelar [desmante'lar] vt (*deshacer*) to dismantle; (*casa*) to strip

desmaquillador [desmaki.ʎa'ðor] nm make-up remover

desmayar [desma'jar] vi to lose heart; **~se** vr (*MED*) to faint; **desmayo** nm (*MED: acto*) faint; (*: estado*) unconsciousness

desmedido, a [desme'ðiðo, a] adj excessive

desmejorar [desmexo'rar] vt (*dañar*) to impair, spoil; (*MED*) to weaken

desmembrar [desmem'brar] vt (*MED*) to dismember; (*fig*) to separate

desmemoriado, a [desmemo'rjaðo, a] adj forgetful

desmentir [desmen'tir] vt (*contradecir*) to contradict; (*refutar*) to deny

desmenuzar [desmenu'θar] vt (*deshacer*) to crumble; (*carne*) to chop; (*examinar*) to examine closely

desmerecer [desmere'θer] vt to be unworthy of ♦ vi (*deteriorarse*) to deteriorate

desmesurado, a [desmesu'raðo, a] adj disproportionate

desmontable [desmon'taβle] adj (*que se quita: pieza*) detachable; (*que se puede plegar etc*) collapsible, folding

desmontar [desmon'tar] vt (*deshacer*) to dismantle; (*tierra*) to level ♦ vi to dismount

desmoralizar [desmorali'θar] vt to demoralize

desmoronar [desmoro'nar] vt to wear away, erode; **~se** vr (*edificio, dique*) to collapse; (*economía*) to decline

desnatado, a [desna'taðo, a] adj skimmed

desnivel [desni'ßel] nm (*de terreno*) unevenness

desnudar [desnu'ðar] vt (*desvestir*) to undress; (*despojar*) to strip; **~se** vr (*desvestirse*) to get undressed; **desnudo, a** adj naked ♦ nm/f nude; **desnudo de** devoid o bereft of

desnutrición [desnutri'θjon] nf malnutrition; **desnutrido, a** adj undernourished

desobedecer [desoβeðe'θer] *vt, vi* to disobey; **desobediencia** *nf* disobedience

desocupado, a [desoku'paðo, a] *adj* at leisure; (*desempleado*) unemployed; (*deshabitado*) empty, vacant

desocupar [desoku'par] *vt* to vacate

desodorante [desoðo'rante] *nm* deodorant

desolación [desola'θjon] *nf* (*de lugar*) desolation; (*fig*) grief

desolar [deso'lar] *vt* to ruin, lay waste

desorbitado, a [desorβi'taðo, a] *adj* (*excesivo: ambición*) boundless; (*deseos*) excessive; (*: precio*) exorbitant

desorden [des'orðen] *nm* confusion; (*político*) disorder, unrest

desorganizar [desorvani'θar] *vt* (*desordenar*) to disorganize; **desorganización** *nf* (*de persona*) disorganization; (*en empresa, oficina*) disorder, chaos

desorientar [desorjen'tar] *vt* (*extraviar*) to mislead; (*confundir, desconcertar*) to confuse; **~se** *vr* (*perderse*) to lose one's way

despabilado, a [despaβi'laðo, a] *adj* (*despierto*) wide-awake; (*fig*) alert, sharp

despabilar [despaβi'lar] *vt* (*el ingenio*) to sharpen ♦ *vi* to wake up; (*fig*) to get a move on; **~se** *vr* to wake up; to get a move on

despachar [despa'tʃar] *vt* (*negocio*) to do, complete; (*enviar*) to send, dispatch; (*vender*) to sell, deal in; (*billete*) to issue; (*mandar ir*) to send away

despacho [des'patʃo] *nm* (*oficina*) office; (*de paquetes*) dispatch; (*venta*) sale; (*comunicación*) message

despacio [des'paθjo] *adv* slowly

desparpajo [despar'paxo] *nm* self-confidence; (*pey*) nerve

desparramar [desparra'mar] *vt* (*esparcir*) to scatter; (*líquido*) to spill

despavorido, a [despaβo'riðo, a] *adj* terrified

despecho [des'petʃo] *nm* spite; **a ~ de** in

spite of

despectivo, a [despek'tiβo, a] *adj* (*despreciativo*) derogatory; (*LING*) pejorative

despedazar [despeða'θar] *vt* to tear to pieces

despedida [despe'ðiða] *nf* (*adiós*) farewell; (*de obrero*) sacking

despedir [despe'ðir] *vt* (*visita*) to see off, show out; (*empleado*) to dismiss; (*inquilino*) to evict; (*objeto*) to hurl; (*olor etc*) to give out *o* off; **~se** *vr*: **~se de** to say goodbye to

despegar [despe'var] *vt* to unstick ♦ *vi* (*avión*) to take off; **~se** *vr* to come loose, come unstuck; **despego** *nm* detachment

despegue *etc* [des'peve] *vb ver* **despegar** ♦ *nm* takeoff

despeinado, a [despei'naðo, a] *adj* dishevelled, unkempt

despejado, a [despe'xaðo, a] *adj* (*lugar*) clear, free; (*cielo*) clear; (*persona*) wide-awake, bright

despejar [despe'xar] *vt* (*gen*) to clear; (*misterio*) to clear up ♦ *vi* (*el tiempo*) to clear; **~se** *vr* (*tiempo, cielo*) to clear (up); (*misterio*) to become clearer; (*cabeza*) to clear

despellejar [despeʎe'xar] *vt* (*animal*) to skin

despensa [des'pensa] *nf* larder

despeñadero [despeɲa'ðero] *nm* (*GEO*) cliff, precipice

despeñarse [despe'ɲarse] *vr* to hurl o.s. down; (*coche*) to tumble over

desperdicio [desper'ðiθjo] *nm* (*despilfarro*) squandering; **~s** *nmpl* (*basura*) rubbish *sg* (*BRIT*), garbage *sg* (*US*); (*residuos*) waste *sg*

desperdigarse [desperði'varse] *vr* (*rebaño, familia*) to scatter, spread out; (*granos de arroz, semillas*) to scatter

desperezarse [despere'θarse] *vr* to stretch

desperfecto [desper'fekto] *nm* (*deterioro*) slight damage; (*defecto*) flaw, imperfection

despertador [desperta'ðor] *nm* alarm clock

despertar [desper'tar] *nm* awakening ♦ *vt* (*persona*) to wake up; (*recuerdos*) to revive; (*sentimiento*) to arouse ♦ *vi* to awaken, wake up; **~se** *vr* to awaken, wake up

despiadado, a [despja'ðaðo, a] *adj* (*ataque*) merciless; (*persona*) heartless

despido *etc* [des'piðo] *vb ver* **despedir** ♦ *nm* dismissal, sacking

despierto, a *etc* [des'pjerto, a] *vb ver* **despertar** ♦ *adj* awake; (*fig*) sharp, alert

despilfarro [despil'farro] *nm* (*derroche*) squandering; (*lujo desmedido*) extravagance

despistar [despis'tar] *vt* to throw off the track *o* scent; (*confundir*) to mislead, confuse; **~se** *vr* to take the wrong road; (*confundirse*) to become confused

despiste [des'piste] *nm* absent-mindedness; **un ~** a mistake, slip

desplazamiento [desplaθa'mjento] *nm* displacement

desplazar [despla'θar] *vt* to move; (*NAUT*) to displace; (*INFORM*) to scroll; (*fig*) to oust; **~se** *vr* (*persona*) to travel

desplegar [desple'var] *vt* (*tela, papel*) to unfold, open out; (*bandera*) to unfurl; **despliegue** *etc* [des'pleɣe] *vb ver* **desplegar** ♦ *nm* display

desplomarse [desplo'marse] *vr* (*edificio, gobierno, persona*) to collapse

desplumar [desplu'mar] *vt* (*ave*) to pluck; (*fam: estafar*) to fleece

despoblado, a [despo'ßlaðo, a] *adj* (*sin habitantes*) uninhabited

despojar [despo'xar] *vt* (*alguien: de sus bienes*) to divest of, deprive of; (*casa*) to strip, leave bare; (*alguien: de su cargo*) to strip of

despojo [des'poxo] *nm* (*acto*) plundering; (*objetos*) plunder, loot; **~s** *nmpl* (*de ave, res*) offal *sg*

desposado, a [despo'saðo, a] *adj, nm/f* newly-wed

desposar [despo'sar] *vt* to marry; **~se** *vr* to get married

desposeer [despose'er] *vt*: **~ a uno de** (*puesto, autoridad*) to strip sb of

déspota ['despota] *nm/f* despot

despreciar [despre'θjar] *vt* (*desdeñar*) to despise, scorn; (*afrentar*) to slight; **desprecio** *nm* scorn, contempt; slight

desprender [despren'der] *vt* (*broche*) to unfasten; (*olor*) to give off; **~se** *vr* (*botón: caerse*) to fall off; (*broche*) to come unfastened; (*olor, perfume*) to be given off; **~se de algo que ...** to draw from sth that ...

desprendimiento [desprendi'mjento] *nm* (*gen*) loosening; (*generosidad*) disinterestedness; (*de tierra, rocas*) landslide

despreocupado, a [despreoku'paðo, a] *adj* (*sin preocupación*) unworried, nonchalant; (*negligente*) careless

despreocuparse [despreoku'parse] *vr* not to worry; **~ de** to have no interest in

desprestigiar [despresti'xjar] *vt* (*criticar*) to run down; (*desacreditar*) to discredit

desprevenido, a [despreße'niðo, a] *adj* (*no preparado*) unprepared, unready

desproporcionado, a [desproporθjo'naðo, a] *adj* disproportionate, out of proportion

desprovisto, a [despro'ßisto, a] *adj*: **~ de** devoid of

después [des'pwes] *adv* afterwards, later; (*próximo paso*) next; **~ de comer** after lunch; **un año ~** a year later; **~ se debatió el tema** next the matter was discussed; **~ de corregido el texto** after the text had been corrected; **~ de todo** after all

desquiciado, a [deski'θjaðo, a] *adj* deranged

desquite [des'kite] *nm* (*satisfacción*) satisfaction; (*venganza*) revenge

destacar [desta'kar] *vt* to emphasize, point up; (*MIL*) to detach, detail ♦ *vi* (*resaltarse*) to stand out; (*persona*) to be outstanding *o* exceptional; **~se** *vr* to stand out; to be outstanding *o* exceptional

destajo [des'taxo] *nm*: **trabajar a ~** to do piecework

destapar [desta'par] *vt* (*botella*) to open; (*cacerola*) to take the lid off; (*descubrir*) to uncover; **~se** *vr* (*revelarse*) to reveal one's true character

destartalado, a [destarta'laðo, a] *adj* (*desordenado*) untidy; (*ruinoso*) tumbledown

destello [des'teʎo] *nm* (*de estrella*) twinkle; (*de faro*) signal light

destemplado, a [destem'plaðo, a] *adj* (*MUS*) out of tune; (*voz*) harsh; (*MED*) out of sorts; (*tiempo*) unpleasant, nasty

desteñir [deste'ɲir] *vt* to fade ♦ *vi* to fade; **~se** *vr* to fade; **esta tela no destiñe** this fabric will not run

desternillarse [desterni'ʎarse] *vr*: **~ de risa** to split one's sides laughing

desterrar [deste'rrar] *vt* (*exilar*) to exile; (*fig*) to banish, dismiss

destiempo [des'tjempo]: **a ~** *adv* out of turn

destierro *etc* [des'tjerro] *vb ver* **desterrar** ♦ *nm* exile

destilar [desti'lar] *vt* to distil; **destilería** *nf* distillery

destinar [desti'nar] *vt* (*funcionario*) to appoint, assign; (*fondos*): **~ (a)** to set aside (for)

destinatario, a [destina'tarjo, a] *nm/f* addressee

destino [des'tino] *nm* (*suerte*) destiny; (*de avión, viajero*) destination

destituir [destitu'ir] *vt* to dismiss

destornillador [destorniʎa'ðor] *nm* screwdriver

destornillar [destorni'ʎar] *vt* (*tornillo*) to unscrew; **~se** *vr* to unscrew

destreza [des'treθa] *nf* (*habilidad*) skill; (*maña*) dexterity

destrozar [destro'θar] *vt* (*romper*) to smash, break (up); (*estropear*) to ruin; (*nervios*) to shatter

destrozo [des'troθo] *nm* (*acción*)

destruction; (*desastre*) smashing; **~s** *nmpl* (*pedazos*) pieces; (*daños*) havoc *sg*

destrucción [destruk'θjon] *nf* destruction

destruir [destru'ir] *vt* to destroy

desuso [des'uso] *nm* disuse; **caer en ~** to become obsolete

desvalido, a [desßa'liðo, a] *adj* (*desprotegido*) destitute; (*sin fuerzas*) helpless

desvalijar [desßali'xar] *vt* (*persona*) to rob; (*casa, tienda*) to burgle; (*coche*) to break into

desván [des'ßan] *nm* attic

desvanecer [desßane'θer] *vt* (*disipar*) to dispel; (*borrar*) to blur; **~se** *vr* (*humo etc*) to vanish, disappear; (*color*) to fade; (*recuerdo, sonido*) to fade away; (*MED*) to pass out; (*duda*) to be dispelled

desvanecimiento [desßaneθi'mjento] *nm* (*desaparición*) disappearance; (*de colores*) fading; (*evaporación*) evaporation; (*MED*) fainting fit

desvariar [desßa'rjar] *vi* (*enfermo*) to be delirious; **desvarío** *nm* delirium

desvelar [desße'lar] *vt* to keep awake; **~se** *vr* (*no poder dormir*) to stay awake; (*preocuparse*) to be vigilant *o* watchful

desvelos [des'ßelos] *nmpl* worrying *sg*

desvencijado, a [desßenθi'xaðo, a] *adj* (*silla*) rickety; (*máquina*) broken-down

desventaja [desßen'taxa] *nf* disadvantage

desventura [desßen'tura] *nf* misfortune

desvergonzado, a [desßerɣon'θaðo, a] *adj* shameless

desvergüenza [desßer'ɣwenθa] *nf* (*descaro*) shamelessness; (*insolencia*) impudence; (*mala conducta*) effrontery

desvestir [desßes'tir] *vt* to undress; **~se** *vr* to undress

desviación [desßja'θjon] *nf* deviation; (*AUTO*) diversion, detour

desviar [des'ßjar] *vt* to turn aside; (*río*) to alter the course of; (*navío*) to divert, re-route; (*conversación*) to sidetrack; **~se** *vr* (*apartarse del camino*) to turn aside; (: *barco*) to go off course

desvío *etc* [des'ßio] *vb ver* **desviar** ♦ *nm*

(desviación) detour, diversion; *(fig)* indifference

desvirtuar [desβir'twar] *vt* to distort

desvivirse [desβi'βirse] *vr*: ~ **por** *(anhelar)* to long for, crave for; *(hacer lo posible por)* to do one's utmost for

detallar [deta'ʎar] *vt* to detail

detalle [de'taʎe] *nm* detail; *(gesto)* gesture, token; **al** ~ in detail; *(COM)* retail

detallista [deta'ʎista] *nm/f (COM)* retailer

detective [detek'tiβe] *nm/f* detective

detener [dete'ner] *vt (gen)* to stop; *(JUR)* to arrest; *(objeto)* to keep; ~**se** *vr* to stop; *(demorarse)*: ~**se en** to delay over, linger over

detenidamente [deteniða'mente] *adv (minuciosamente)* carefully; *(extensamente)* at great length

detenido, a [dete'niðo, a] *adj (arrestado)* under arrest ♦ *nm/f* person under arrest, prisoner

detenimiento [deteni'mjento] *nm*: **con** ~ thoroughly; *(observar, considerar)* carefully

detergente [deter'xente] *nm* detergent

deteriorar [deterjo'rar] *vt* to spoil, damage; ~**se** *vr* to deteriorate; **deterioro** *nm* deterioration

determinación [determina'θjon] *nf (empeño)* determination; *(decisión)* decision; **determinado, a** *adj* specific

determinar [determi'nar] *vt (plazo)* to fix; *(precio)* to settle; ~**se** *vr* to decide

detestar [detes'tar] *vt* to detest

detractor, a [detrak'tor, a] *nm/f* slanderer, libeller

detrás [de'tras] *adv* behind; *(atrás)* at the back; ~ **de** behind

detrimento [detri'mento] *nm*: **en** ~ **de** to the detriment of

deuda ['deuða] *nf* debt

devaluación [deβalwa'θjon] *nf* devaluation

devastar [deβas'tar] *vt (destruir)* to devastate

devoción [deβo'θjon] *nf* devotion

devolución [deβolu'θjon] *nf (reenvío)* return, sending back; *(reembolso)* repayment; *(JUR)* devolution

devolver [deβol'βer] *vt* to return; *(lo extraviado, lo prestado)* to give back; *(carta al correo)* to send back; *(COM)* to repay, refund ♦ *vi (vomitar)* to be sick

devorar [deβo'rar] *vt* to devour

devoto, a [de'βoto, a] *adj* devout ♦ *nm/f* admirer

devuelto *pp de* **devolver**

devuelva *etc vb ver* **devolver**

di *vb ver* **dar**; **decir**

día ['dia] *nm* day; **¿qué ~ es?** what's the date?; **estar/poner al ~** to be/keep up to date; **el ~ de hoy/de mañana** today/tomorrow; **al ~ siguiente** (on) the following day; **vivir al ~** to live from hand to mouth; **de ~** by day, in daylight; **en pleno ~** in full daylight; **D~ de Reyes** Epiphany; ~ **festivo** *(ESP)* o **feriado** *(AM)* holiday; ~ **libre** day off

diabetes [dja'βetes] *nf* diabetes

diablo ['djaβlo] *nm* devil; **diablura** *nf* prank

diadema [dja'ðema] *nf* tiara

diafragma [dja'fraɣma] *nm* diaphragm

diagnosis [djaɣ'nosis] *nf inv* diagnosis

diagnóstico [djaɣ'nostiko] *nm* = **diagnosis**

diagonal [djaɣo'nal] *adj* diagonal

diagrama [dja'ɣrama] *nm* diagram; ~ **de flujo** flowchart

dial [djal] *nm* dial

dialecto [dja'lekto] *nm* dialect

dialogar [djalo'ɣar] *vi*: ~ **con** *(POL)* to hold talks with

diálogo ['djaloɣo] *nm* dialogue

diamante [dja'mante] *nm* diamond

diana ['djana] *nf (MIL)* reveille; *(de blanco)* centre, bull's-eye

diapositiva [djaposi'tiβa] *nf (FOTO)* slide, transparency

diario, a ['djarjo, a] *adj* daily ♦ *nm* newspaper; **a** ~ daily; **de** ~ everyday

diarrea [dja'rrea] *nf* diarrhoea

dibujar [diβu'xar] *vt* to draw, sketch; **dibujo** *nm* drawing; **dibujos animados** cartoons

diccionario [dikθjo'narjo] *nm* dictionary
dice *etc vb ver* **decir**
dicho, a ['ditʃo, a] *pp de* **decir** ♦ *adj*: **en ~s países** in the aforementioned countries ♦ *nm* saying
dichoso, a [di'tʃoso, a] *adj* happy
diciembre [di'θjembre] *nm* December
dictado [dik'taðo] *nm* dictation
dictador [dikta'ðor] *nm* dictator; **dictadura** *nf* dictatorship
dictamen [dik'tamen] *nm* (*opinión*) opinion; (*juicio*) judgment; (*informe*) report
dictar [dik'tar] *vt* (*carta*) to dictate; (*JUR: sentencia*) to pronounce; (*decreto*) to issue; (*AM: clase*) to give
didáctico, a [di'ðaktiko, a] *adj* educational
diecinueve [djeθi'nweβe] *num* nineteen
dieciocho [djeθi'otʃo] *num* eighteen
dieciséis [djeθi'seis] *num* sixteen
diecisiete [djeθi'sjete] *num* seventeen
diente ['djente] *nm* (*ANAT, TEC*) tooth; (*ZOOL*) fang; (: *de elefante*) tusk; (*de ajo*) clove; **hablar entre ~s** to mutter, mumble
diera *etc vb ver* **dar**
diesel ['disel] *adj*: **motor ~** diesel engine
diestro, a ['djestro, a] *adj* (*derecho*) right; (*hábil*) skilful
dieta ['djeta] *nf* diet; **dietética** *nf*: **tienda de dietética** health food shop; **dietético, a** *adj* diet (*atr*), dietary
diez [djeθ] *num* ten
diezmar [djeθ'mar] *vt* (*población*) to decimate
difamar [difa'mar] *vt* (*JUR: hablando*) to slander; (: *por escrito*) to libel
diferencia [dife'renθja] *nf* difference; **diferenciar** *vt* to differentiate between ♦ *vi* to differ; **diferenciarse** *vr* to differ, be different; (*distinguirse*) to distinguish o.s.
diferente [dife'rente] *adj* different
diferido [dife'riðo] *nm*: **en ~** (*TV etc*) recorded
difícil [di'fiθil] *adj* difficult

dificultad [difikul'taθ] *nf* difficulty; (*problema*) trouble
dificultar [difikul'tar] *vt* (*complicar*) to complicate, make difficult; (*estorbar*) to obstruct
difteria [dif'terja] *nf* diphtheria
difundir [difun'dir] *vt* (*calor, luz*) to diffuse; (*RADIO, TV*) to broadcast; **~ una noticia** to spread a piece of news; **~se** *vr* to spread (out)
difunto, a [di'funto, a] *adj* dead, deceased ♦ *nm/f* deceased (person)
difusión [difu'sjon] *nf* (*RADIO, TV*) broadcasting
diga *etc vb ver* **decir**
digerir [dixe'rir] *vt* to digest; (*fig*) to absorb; **digestión** *nf* digestion; **digestivo, a** *adj* digestive
digital [dixi'tal] *adj* digital
dignarse [div'narse] *vr* to deign to
dignatario, a [divna'tarjo, a] *nm/f* dignitary
dignidad [divni'ðað] *nf* dignity
digno, a ['divno, a] *adj* worthy
digo *etc vb ver* **decir**
dije *etc vb ver* **decir**
dilapidar [dilapi'ðar] *vt* (*dinero, herencia*) to squander, waste
dilatar [dila'tar] *vt* (*cuerpo*) to dilate; (*prolongar*) to prolong
dilema [di'lema] *nm* dilemma
diligencia [dili'xenθja] *nf* diligence; (*ocupación*) errand, job; **~s** *nfpl* (*JUR*) formalities; **diligente** *adj* diligent
diluir [dilu'ir] *vt* to dilute
diluvio [di'lußjo] *nm* deluge, flood
dimensión [dimen'sjon] *nf* dimension
diminuto, a [dimi'nuto, a] *adj* tiny, diminutive
dimitir [dimi'tir] *vi* to resign
dimos *vb ver* **dar**
Dinamarca [dina'marka] *nf* Denmark
dinámico, a [di'namiko, a] *adj* dynamic
dinamita [dina'mita] *nf* dynamite
dínamo ['dinamo] *nf* dynamo
dineral [dine'ral] *nm* large sum of money, fortune

dinero [di'nero] *nm* money; **~ contante, ~ efectivo** (ready) cash; **~ suelto** (loose) change

dio *vb ver* **dar**

dios [djos] *nm* god; **¡D~ mío!** (oh,) my God!

diosa ['djosa] *nf* goddess

diploma [di'ploma] *nm* diploma

diplomacia [diplo'maθja] *nf* diplomacy; (*fig*) tact

diplomado, a [diplo'maðo, a] *adj* qualified

diplomático, a [diplo'matiko, a] *adj* diplomatic ♦ *nm/f* diplomat

diputación [diputa'θjon] *nf* (tb: **~ provincial**) ≈ county council

diputado, a [dipu'taðo, a] *nm/f* delegate; (*POL*) ≈ member of parliament (*BRIT*), ≈ representative (*US*)

dique ['dike] *nm* dyke

diré *etc vb ver* **decir**

dirección [direk'θjon] *nf* direction; (*señas*) address; (*AUTO*) steering; (*gerencia*) management; (*POL*) leadership; **~ única/prohibida** one-way street/no entry

directa [di'rekta] *nf* (*AUT*) top gear

directiva [direk'tiβa] *nf* (*DEP*, tb: **junta ~**) board of directors

directo, a [di'rekto, a] *adj* direct; (*RADIO, TV*) live; **transmitir en ~** to broadcast live

director, a [direk'tor, a] *adj* leading ♦ *nm/f* director; (*ESCOL*) head(teacher) (*BRIT*), principal (*US*); (*gerente*) manager(ess); (*PRENSA*) editor; **~ de cine** film director; **~ general** managing director

dirigente [diri'xente] *nm/f* (*POL*) leader

dirigir [diri'xir] *vt* to direct; (*carta*) to address; (*obra de teatro, film*) to direct; (*MUS*) to conduct; (*negocio*) to manage; **~se** *vr*: **~se a** to go towards, make one's way towards; (*hablar con*) to speak to

dirija *etc vb ver* **dirigir**

discernir [disθer'nir] *vt* to discern

disciplina [disθi'plina] *nf* discipline

discípulo, a [dis'θipulo, a] *nm/f* disciple

disco ['disko] *nm* disc; (*DEPORTE*) discus;

(*TEL*) dial; (*AUTO: semáforo*) light; (*MUS*) record; (*INFORM*): **~ flexible/rígido** floppy/hard disk; **~ compacto/de larga duración** compact disc/long-playing record; **~ de freno** brake disc

disconforme [diskon'forme] *adj* differing; **estar ~ (con)** to be in disagreement (with)

discordia [dis'korðja] *nf* discord

discoteca [disko'teka] *nf* disco(theque)

discreción [diskre'θjon] *nf* discretion; (*reserva*) prudence; **comer a ~** to eat as much as one wishes; **discrecional** *adj* (*facultativo*) discretionary

discrepancia [diskre'panθja] *nf* (*diferencia*) discrepancy; (*desacuerdo*) disagreement

discreto, a [dis'kreto, a] *adj* discreet

discriminación [diskrimina'θjon] *nf* discrimination

disculpa [dis'kulpa] *nf* excuse; (*pedir perdón*) apology; **pedir ~s a/por** to apologize to/for; **disculpar** *vt* to excuse, pardon; **disculparse** *vr* to excuse o.s.; to apologize

discurrir [disku'rrir] *vi* (*pensar, reflexionar*) to think, meditate; (*el tiempo*) to pass, go by

discurso [dis'kurso] *nm* speech

discusión [disku'sjon] *nf* (*diálogo*) discussion; (*riña*) argument

discutir [disku'tir] *vt* (*debatir*) to discuss; (*pelear*) to argue about; (*contradecir*) to argue against ♦ *vi* (*debatir*) to discuss; (*pelearse*) to argue

disecar [dise'kar] *vt* (*conservar: animal*) to stuff; (: *planta*) to dry

diseminar [disemi'nar] *vt* to disseminate, spread

diseñar [dise'nar] *vt, vi* to design

diseño [di'seno] *nm* design

disfraz [dis'fraθ] *nm* (*máscara*) disguise; (*excusa*) pretext; **~ar** *vt* to disguise; **~arse** *vr*: **~arse de** to disguise o.s. as

disfrutar [disfru'tar] *vt* to enjoy ♦ *vi* to enjoy o.s.; **~ de** to enjoy, possess

disgregarse [disɣre'ɣarse] *vr*

(*muchedumbre*) to disperse

disgustar [disɣusˈtar] *vt* (*no gustar*) to displease; (*contrariar, enojar*) to annoy, upset; **~se** *vr* (*enfadarse*) to get upset; (*dos personas*) to fall out

disgusto [disˈɣusto] *nm* (*contrariedad*) annoyance; (*tristeza*) grief; (*riña*) quarrel

disidente [disiˈðente] *nm* dissident

disimular [disimuˈlar] *vt* (*ocultar*) to hide, conceal ♦ *vi* to dissemble

disipar [disiˈpar] *vt* to dispel; (*fortuna*) to squander; (*nubes*) to vanish; (*indisciplinarse*) to dissipate

dislocarse [disloˈkarse] *vr* (*articulación*) to sprain, dislocate

disminución [disminuˈθjon] *nf* decrease, reduction

disminuido, a [disminuˈiðo, a] *nm/f*: **~ mental/físico** mentally/physically handicapped person

disminuir [disminuˈir] *vt* to decrease, diminish

disociarse [disoˈθjarse] *vr*: **~ (de)** to dissociate o.s. (from)

disolver [disolˈβer] *vt* (*gen*) to dissolve; **~se** *vr* to dissolve; (*COM*) to go into liquidation

dispar [disˈpar] *adj* different

disparar [dispaˈrar] *vt, vi* to shoot, fire

disparate [dispaˈrate] *nm* (*tontería*) foolish remark; (*error*) blunder; **decir ~s** to talk nonsense

disparo [disˈparo] *nm* shot

dispensar [dispenˈsar] *vt* to dispense; (*disculpar*) to excuse

dispersar [disperˈsar] *vt* to disperse; **~se** *vr* to scatter

disponer [dispoˈner] *vt* (*arreglar*) to arrange; (*ordenar*) to put in order; (*preparar*) to prepare, get ready ♦ *vi*: **~ de** to have, own; **~se** *vr*: **~se a o para hacer** to prepare to do

disponible [dispoˈniβle] *adj* available

disposición [disposiˈθjon] *nf* arrangement, disposition; (*INFORM*) layout; **a la ~ de** at the disposal of; **~ de ánimo** state of mind

dispositivo [disposiˈtiβo] *nm* device, mechanism

dispuesto, a [disˈpwesto, a] *pp de* **disponer** ♦ *adj* (*arreglado*) arranged; (*preparado*) disposed

disputar [dispuˈtar] *vt* (*carrera*) to compete in

disquete [disˈkete] *nm* floppy disk, diskette

distancia [disˈtanθja] *nf* distance

distanciar [distanˈθjar] *vt* to space out; **~se** *vr* to become estranged

distante [disˈtante] *adj* distant

distar [disˈtar] *vi*: **dista 5km de aquí** it is 5km from here

diste *vb ver* **dar**

disteis [ˈdisteis] *vb ver* **dar**

distensión [distenˈsjon] *nf* (*en las relaciones*) relaxation; (*POL*) détente; (*muscular*) strain

distinción [distinˈθjon] *nf* distinction; (*elegancia*) elegance; (*honor*) honour

distinguido, a [distinˈɣiðo, a] *adj* distinguished

distinguir [distinˈɣir] *vt* to distinguish; (*escoger*) to single out; **~se** *vr* to be distinguished

distintivo [distinˈtiβo] *nm* badge; (*fig*) characteristic

distinto, a [disˈtinto, a] *adj* different; (*claro*) clear

distracción [distrakˈθjon] *nf* distraction; (*pasatiempo*) hobby, pastime; (*olvido*) absent-mindedness, distraction

distraer [distraˈer] *vt* (*atención*) to distract; (*divertir*) to amuse; (*fondos*) to embezzle; **~se** *vr* (*entretenerse*) to amuse o.s.; (*perder la concentración*) to allow one's attention to wander

distraído, a [distraˈiðo, a] *adj* (*gen*) absent-minded; (*entretenido*) amusing

distribuidor, a [distriβuiˈðor, a] *nm/f* distributor; **distribuidora** *nf* (*COM*) dealer, agent; (*CINE*) distributor

distribuir [distriβuˈir] *vt* to distribute

distrito [disˈtrito] *nm* (*sector, territorio*) region; (*barrio*) district

disturbio [dis'turβjo] nm disturbance; (*desorden*) riot

disuadir [diswa'ðir] vt to dissuade

disuelto [di'swelto] pp de **disolver**

disyuntiva [disjun'tiβa] nf dilemma

DIU nm abr (= *dispositivo intrauterino*) IUD

diurno, a ['djurno, a] adj day cpd

divagar [diβa'var] vi (*desviarse*) to digress

diván [di'βan] nm divan

divergencia [diβer'xenθja] nf divergence

diversidad [diβersi'ðað] nf diversity, variety

diversificar [diβersifi'kar] vt to diversify

diversión [diβer'sjon] nf (*gen*) entertainment; (*actividad*) hobby, pastime

diverso, a [di'βerso, a] adj diverse; ~**s libros** several books; diversos nmpl sundries

divertido, a [diβer'tiðo, a] adj (*chiste*) amusing; (*fiesta etc*) enjoyable

divertir [diβer'tir] vt (*entretener, recrear*) to amuse; ~**se** vr (*pasarlo bien*) to have a good time; (*distraerse*) to amuse o.s.

dividendos [diβi'ðendos] nmpl (COM) dividends

dividir [diβi'ðir] vt (*gen*) to divide; (*distribuir*) to distribute, share out

divierta etc vb ver **divertir**

divino, a [di'βino, a] adj divine

divirtiendo etc vb ver **divertir**

divisa [di'βisa] nf (*emblema*) emblem, badge; ~**s** nfpl foreign exchange sg

divisar [diβi'sar] vt to make out, distinguish

división [diβi'sjon] nf (*gen*) division; (*de partido*) split; (*de país*) partition

divorciar [diβor'θjar] vt to divorce; ~**se** vr to get divorced; **divorcio** nm divorce

divulgar [diβul'var] vt (*ideas*) to spread; (*secreto*) to divulge

DNI (ESP) nm abr (= *Documento Nacional de Identidad*) national identity card

┌─────────┐
│ **DNI** │
└─────────┘

ⓘ The **Documento Nacional de Identidad** *is a Spanish ID card which must be carried at all times and produced on request for the police. It contains the*

holder's photo, fingerprints and personal details. It is also known as the **DNI** *or "carnet de identidad".*

Dña. abr (= *doña*) Mrs

do [do] nm (MUS) do, C

dobladillo [doβla'ðiλo] nm (*de vestido*) hem; (*de pantalón: vuelta*) turn-up (BRIT), cuff (US)

doblar [do'βlar] vt to double; (*papel*) to fold; (*caño*) to bend; (*la esquina*) to turn, go round; (*film*) to dub ♦ vi to turn; (*campana*) to toll; ~**se** vr (*plegarse*) to fold (up), crease; (*encorvarse*) to bend

doble ['doβle] adj double; (*de dos aspectos*) dual; (*fig*) two-faced ♦ nm double ♦ nm/f (TEATRO) double, stand-in; ~**s** nmpl (DEPORTE) doubles sg; **con sentido** ~ with a double meaning

doblegar [doβle'var] vt to fold, crease; ~**se** vr to yield

doblez [do'βleθ] nm fold, hem ♦ nf insincerity, duplicity

doce ['doθe] num twelve; ~**na** nf dozen

docente [do'θente] adj: **centro/personal** ~ teaching establishment/staff

dócil ['doθil] adj (*pasivo*) docile; (*obediente*) obedient

docto, a ['dokto, a] adj: ~ **en** instructed in

doctor, a [dok'tor, a] nm/f doctor

doctorado [dokto'raðo] nm doctorate

doctrina [dok'trina] nf doctrine, teaching

documentación [dokumenta'θjon] nf documentation, papers pl

documental [dokumen'tal] adj, nm documentary

documento [doku'mento] nm (*certificado*) document; ~ **national de identidad** identity card

dólar ['dolar] nm dollar

doler [do'ler] vt, vi to hurt; (*fig*) to grieve; ~**se** vr (*de su situación*) to grieve, feel sorry; (*de las desgracias ajenas*) to sympathize; **me duele el brazo** my arm hurts

dolor [do'lor] nm pain; (*fig*) grief, sorrow; ~ **de cabeza** headache; ~ **de estómago**

stomachache

domar [do'mar] *vt* to tame

domesticar [domesti'kar] *vt* = **domar**

doméstico, a [do'mestiko, a] *adj* (*vida, servicio*) home; (*tareas*) household; (*animal*) tame, pet

domiciliación [domiθilia'θjon] *nf*: ~ **de pagos** (*COM*) standing order

domicilio [domi'θiljo] *nm* home; ~ **particular** private residence; ~ **social** (*COM*) head office; **sin ~ fijo** of no fixed abode

dominante [domi'nante] *adj* dominant; (*persona*) domineering

dominar [domi'nar] *vt* (*gen*) to dominate; (*idiomas*) to be fluent in ♦ *vi* to dominate, prevail; ~**se** *vr* to control o.s.

domingo [do'mingo] *nm* Sunday

dominio [do'minjo] *nm* (*tierras*) domain; (*autoridad*) power, authority; (*de las pasiones*) grip, hold; (*de idiomas*) command

don [don] *nm* (*talento*) gift; ~ **Juan Gómez** Mr Juan Gómez, Juan Gómez Esq (*BRIT*)

Don/Doña

ⓘ *The term* **don/doña** *often abbreviated to* **D./Dña** *is placed before the first name as a mark of respect to an older or more senior person - eg Don Diego, Doña Inés. Although becoming rarer in Spain it is still used with names and surnames on official documents and formal correspondence - eg "Sr. D. Pedro Rodríguez Hernández", "Sra. Dña. Inés Rodríguez Hernández".*

---

donaire [do'naire] *nm* charm

donar [do'nar] *vt* to donate

donativo [dona'tiβo] *nm* donation

doncella [don'θeʎa] *nf* (*criada*) maid

donde ['donde] *adv* where ♦ *prep*: **el coche está allí ~ el farol** the car is over there by the lamppost *o* where the lamppost is; **en ~** where, in which

dónde ['donde] *adv interrogativo* where?; **¿a ~ vas?** where are you going (to)?;

¿de ~ vienes? where have you been?; **¿por ~?** where?, whereabouts?

dondequiera [donde'kjera] *adv* anywhere; **por ~** everywhere, all over the place ♦ *conj*: **~ que** wherever

doña ['dona] *nf*: **~ Alicia** Alicia; **~ Victoria Benito** Mrs Victoria Benito

dorado, a [do'raðo, a] *adj* (*color*) golden; (*TEC*) gilt

dormir [dor'mir] *vt*: **~ la siesta** to have an afternoon nap ♦ *vi* to sleep; **~se** *vr* to fall asleep

dormitar [dormi'tar] *vi* to doze

dormitorio [dormi'torjo] *nm* bedroom; **~ común** dormitory

dorsal [dor'sal] *nm* (*DEPORTE*) number

dorso ['dorso] *nm* (*de mano*) back; (*de hoja*) other side

dos [dos] *num* two

dosis ['dosis] *nf inv* dose, dosage

dotado, a [do'taðo, a] *adj* gifted; **~ de** endowed with

dotar [do'tar] *vt* to endow; **dote** *nf* dowry; **dotes** *nfpl* (*talentos*) gifts

doy *vb ver* **dar**

dragar [dra'var] *vt* (*río*) to dredge; (*minas*) to sweep

drama ['drama] *nm* drama

dramaturgo [drama'turvo] *nm* dramatist, playwright

drástico, a ['drastiko, a] *adj* drastic

drenaje [dre'naxe] *nm* drainage

droga ['drova] *nf* drug

drogadicto, a [drova'ðikto, a] *nm/f* drug addict

droguería [drove'ria] *nf* hardware shop (*BRIT*) *o* store (*US*)

ducha ['dutʃa] *nf* (*baño*) shower; (*MED*) douche; **ducharse** *vr* to take a shower

duda ['duða] *nf* doubt; **dudar** *vt*, *vi* to doubt; **dudoso, a** [du'ðoso, a] *adj* (*incierto*) hesitant; (*sospechoso*) doubtful

duela *etc vb ver* **doler**

duelo ['dwelo] *vb ver* **doler** ♦ *nm* (*combate*) duel; (*luto*) mourning

duende ['dwende] *nm* imp, goblin

dueño, a ['dweɲo, a] *nm/f* (*propietario*)

owner; (*de pensión, taberna*) landlord/
lady; (*empresario*) employer
duermo *etc vb ver* **dormir**
dulce ['dulθe] *adj* sweet ♦ *adv* gently,
softly ♦ *nm* sweet
dulzura [dul'θura] *nf* sweetness; (*ternura*)
gentleness
duna ['duna] *nf* (*GEO*) dune
dúo ['duo] *nm* duet
duplicar [dupli'kar] *vt* (*hacer el doble de*)
to duplicate; **~se** *vr* to double
duque ['duke] *nm* duke; **~sa** *nf* duchess
duración [dura'θjon] *nf* (*de película, disco
etc*) length; (*de pila etc*) life; (*curso: de
acontecimientos etc*) duration
duradero, a [dura'ðero, a] *adj* (*tela etc*)
hard-wearing; (*fe, paz*) lasting
durante [du'rante] *prep* during
durar [du'rar] *vi* to last; (*recuerdo*) to remain
durazno [du'raθno] (*AM*) *nm* (*fruta*) peach;
(*árbol*) peach tree
durex ['dureks] (*AM*) *nm* (*tira adhesiva*)
Sellotape ® (*BRIT*), Scotch tape ® (*US*)
dureza [du'reθa] *nf* (*calidad*) hardness
duro, a ['duro, a] *adj* hard; (*carácter*)
tough ♦ *adv* hard ♦ *nm* (*moneda*) five
peseta coin *o* piece
DVD *nm abr* (= *disco de vídeo digital*)
DVD

E, e

E *abr* (= *este*) E
e [e] *conj* and
ebanista [eßa'nista] *nm/f* cabinetmaker
ébano ['eßano] *nm* ebony
ebrio, a ['eßrjo, a] *adj* drunk
ebullición [eßuʎi'θjon] *nf* boiling
eccema [ek'θema] *nf* (*MED*) eczema
echar [e'tʃar] *vt* to throw; (*agua, vino*) to
pour (out); (*empleado: despedir*) to fire,
sack; (*hojas*) to sprout; (*cartas*) to post;
(*humo*) to emit, give out ♦ *vi*: **~ a
correr/llorar** to run off/burst into tears;
~se *vr* to lie down; **~ llave a** to lock (up);
~ abajo (*gobierno*) to overthrow; (*edificio*)

to demolish; **~ mano a** to lay hands on;
~ una mano a uno (*ayudar*) to give sb a
hand; **~ de menos** to miss
eclesiástico, a [ekle'sjastiko, a] *adj*
ecclesiastical
eco ['eko] *nm* echo; **tener ~** to catch on
ecología [ekolo'xia] *nf* ecology;
ecológico, a *adj* (*producto, método*)
environmentally-friendly; (*agricultura*)
organic; **ecologista** *adj* ecological,
environmental ♦ *nm/f* environmentalist
economato [ekono'mato] *nm* cooperative
store
economía [ekono'mia] *nf* (*sistema*)
economy; (*carrera*) economics
económico, a [eko'nomiko, a] *adj*
(*barato*) cheap, economical; (*ahorrativo*)
thrifty; (*COM: año etc*) financial;
(: *situación*) economic
economista [ekono'mista] *nm/f*
economist
ECU [eku] *nm* ECU
ecuador [ekwa'ðor] *nm* equator; **(el) E~**
Ecuador
ecuánime [e'kwanime] *adj* (*carácter*)
level-headed; (*estado*) calm
ecuatoriano, a [ekwato'rjano, a] *adj,
nm/f* Ecuadorian
ecuestre [e'kwestre] *adj* equestrian
eczema [ek'θema] *nm* = **eccema**
edad [e'ðað] *nf* age; **¿qué ~ tienes?** how
old are you?; **tiene ocho años de ~** he is
eight (years old); **de ~ mediana/
avanzada** middle-aged/advanced in
years; **la E~ Media** the Middle Ages
edición [eði'θjon] *nf* (*acto*) publication;
(*ejemplar*) edition
edificar [eðifi'kar] *vt, vi* to build
edificio [eði'fiθjo] *nm* building; (*fig*)
edifice, structure
Edimburgo [eðim'burxo] *nm* Edinburgh
editar [eði'tar] *vt* (*publicar*) to publish;
(*preparar textos*) to edit
editor, a [eði'tor, a] *nm/f* (*que publica*)
publisher; (*redactor*) editor ♦ *adj*: **casa ~a**
publishing house, publisher; **~ial** *adj*
editorial ♦ *nm* leading article, editorial;

casa ~ial publishing house, publisher
edredon [eðre'ðon] *nm* duvet
educación [eðuka'θjon] *nf* education;
(*crianza*) upbringing; (*modales*) (good)
manners *pl*
educado, a [eðu'kaðo, a] *adj*: **bien/mal ~**
well/badly behaved
educar [eðu'kar] *vt* to educate; (*criar*) to
bring up; (*voz*) to train
EE. UU. *nmpl abr* (= *Estados Unidos*)
US(A)
efectista [efek'tista] *adj* sensationalist
efectivamente [efectiβa'mente] *adv*
(*como respuesta*) exactly, precisely;
(*verdaderamente*) really; (*de hecho*) in fact
efectivo, a [efek'tiβo, a] *adj* effective;
(*real*) actual, real ♦ *nm*: **pagar en ~** to
pay (in) cash; **hacer ~ un cheque** to cash
a cheque
efecto [e'fekto] *nm* effect, result; **~s** *nmpl*
(*~s personales*) effects; (*bienes*) goods,
(*COM*) assets; **en ~** in fact; (*respuesta*)
exactly, indeed; **~ 2000** millennium bug;
~ invernadero greenhouse effect
efectuar [efek'twar] *vt* to carry out; (*viaje*)
to make
eficacia [efi'kaθja] *nf* (*de persona*)
efficiency; (*de medicamento etc*)
effectiveness
eficaz [efi'kaθ] *adj* (*persona*) efficient;
(*acción*) effective
eficiente [efi'θjente] *adj* efficient
efusivo, a [efu'siβo, a] *adj* effusive; **mis
más efusivas gracias** my warmest
thanks
EGB (*ESP*) *nf abr* (*ESCOL*) = *Educación
General Básica*
egipcio, a [e'xipθjo, a] *adj, nm/f* Egyptian
Egipto [e'xipto] *nm* Egypt
egoísmo [evo'ismo] *nm* egoism
egoísta [evo'ista] *adj* egoistical, selfish
♦ *nm/f* egoist
egregio, a [e'xrexjo, a] *adj* eminent,
distinguished
Eire ['eire] *nm* Eire
ej. *abr* (= *ejemplo*) eg
eje ['exe] *nm* (*GEO, MAT*) axis; (*de rueda*)

axle; (*de máquina*) shaft, spindle
ejecución [exeku'θjon] *nf* execution;
(*cumplimiento*) fulfilment; (*MUS*)
performance; (*JUR: embargo de deudor*)
attachment
ejecutar [exeku'tar] *vt* to execute, carry
out; (*matar*) to execute; (*cumplir*) to fulfil;
(*MUS*) to perform; (*JUR: embargar*) to
attach, distrain (on)
ejecutivo, a [exeku'tiβo, a] *adj* executive;
el (poder) ~ the executive (power)
ejemplar [exem'plar] *adj* exemplary ♦ *nm*
example; (*ZOOL*) specimen; (*de libro*)
copy; (*de periódico*) number, issue
ejemplo [e'xemplo] *nm* example; **por ~**
for example
ejercer [exer'θer] *vt* to exercise;
(*influencia*) to exert; (*un oficio*) to practise
♦ *vi* (*practicar*): **~ (de)** to practise (as)
ejercicio [exer'θiθjo] *nm* exercise;
(*período*) tenure; **~ comercial** financial
year
ejército [e'xerθito] *nm* army; **entrar en el
~** to join the army, join up
ejote [e'xote] (*AM*) *nm* green bean

PALABRA CLAVE

el [el] (*f* **la**, *pl* **los, las**, *neutro* **lo**) *art def* 1
the; **el libro/la mesa/los estudiantes**
the book/table/students
2 (*con n abstracto: no se traduce*): **el
amor/la juventud** love/youth
3 (*posesión: se traduce a menudo por adj
posesivo*): **romperse el brazo** to break
one's arm; **levantó la mano** he put his
hand up; **se puso el sombrero** she put
her hat on
4 (*valor descriptivo*): **tener la boca
grande/los ojos azules** to have a big
mouth/blue eyes
5 (*con días*) on; **me iré el viernes** I'll
leave on Friday; **los domingos suelo ir a
nadar** on Sundays I generally go
swimming
6 (*lo +adj*): **lo difícil/caro** what is
difficult/expensive; (= *cuán*): **no se da
cuenta de lo pesado que es** he doesn't

realise how boring he is
♦ *pron demos* 1: **mi libro y el de usted** my book and yours; **las de Pepe son mejores** Pepe's are better; **no la(s) blanca(s) sino la(s) gris(es)** not the white one(s) but the grey one(s)
2: **lo de: lo de ayer** what happened yesterday; **lo de las facturas** that business about the invoices
♦ *pron relativo*: **el que** *etc* 1 (*indef*): **el (los) que quiera(n) que se vaya(n)** anyone who wants to can leave; **llévese el que más le guste** take the one you like best
2 (*def*): **el que compré ayer** the one I bought yesterday; **los que se van** those who leave
3: **lo que: lo que pienso yo/más me gusta** what I think/like most
♦ *conj*: **el que: el que lo diga** the fact that he says so; **el que sea tan vago me molesta** his being so lazy bothers me
♦ *excl*: **¡el susto que me diste!** what a fright you gave me!
♦ *pron personal* 1 (*persona: m*) him; (: *f*) her; (: *pl*) them; **lo/las veo** I can see him/them
2 (*animal, cosa: sg*) it; (: *pl*) them; **lo** (*o* **la**) **veo** I can see it; **los** (*o* **las**) **veo** I can see them
3: **lo** (*como sustituto de frase*): **no lo sabía** I didn't know; **ya lo entiendo** I understand now

él [el] *pron* (*persona*) he; (*cosa*) it; (*después de prep: persona*) him; (: *cosa*) it; **de ~** his
elaborar [elaβo'rar] *vt* (*producto*) to make, manufacture; (*preparar*) to prepare; (*madera, metal etc*) to work; (*proyecto etc*) to work on *o* out
elasticidad [elastiθi'ðað] *nf* elasticity
elástico, a [e'lastiko, a] *adj* elastic; (*flexible*) flexible ♦ *nm* elastic; (*un ~*) elastic band
elección [elek'θjon] *nf* election; (*selección*) choice, selection
electorado [elekto'raðo] *nm* electorate,

voters *pl*
electricidad [elektriθi'ðað] *nf* electricity
electricista [elektri'θista] *nm/f* electrician
eléctrico, a [e'lektriko, a] *adj* electric
electro... [elektro] *prefijo* electro...;
~cardiograma *nm* electrocardiogram;
~cutar *vt* to electrocute; **~do** *nm* electrode; **~domésticos** *nmpl* (electrical) household appliances;
~magnético, a *adj* electromagnetic
electrónica [elek'tronika] *nf* electronics *sg*
electrónico, a [elek'troniko, a] *adj* electronic
elefante [ele'fante] *nm* elephant
elegancia [ele'vanθja] *nf* elegance, grace; (*estilo*) stylishness
elegante [ele'vante] *adj* elegant, graceful; (*estiloso*) stylish, fashionable
elegir [ele'xir] *vt* (*escoger*) to choose, select; (*optar*) to opt for; (*presidente*) to elect
elemental [elemen'tal] *adj* (*claro, obvio*) elementary; (*fundamental*) elemental, fundamental
elemento [ele'mento] *nm* element; (*fig*) ingredient; **~s** *nmpl* elements, rudiments
elepé [ele'pe] (*pl* **~s**) *nm* L.P.
elevación [eleβa'θjon] *nf* elevation; (*acto*) raising, lifting; (*de precios*) rise; (GEO *etc*) height, altitude
elevar [ele'βar] *vt* to raise, lift (up); (*precio*) to put up; **~se** *vr* (*edificio*) to rise; (*precios*) to go up
eligiendo *etc vb ver* **elegir**
elija *etc vb ver* **elegir**
eliminar [elimi'nar] *vt* to eliminate, remove
eliminatoria [elimina'torja] *nf* heat, preliminary (round)
elite [e'lite] *nf* elite
ella ['eʎa] *pron* (*persona*) she; (*cosa*) it; (*después de prep: persona*) her; (: *cosa*) it; **de ~** hers
ellas ['eʎas] *pron* (*personas y cosas*) they; (*después de prep*) them; **de ~** theirs
ello ['eʎo] *pron* it
ellos ['eʎos] *pron* they; (*después de prep*)

them; **de ~** theirs

elocuencia [elo'kwenθja] *nf* eloquence

elogiar [elo'xjar] *vt* to praise; **elogio** *nm* praise

elote [e'lote] (*AM*) *nm* corn on the cob

eludir [elu'ðir] *vt* to avoid

emanar [ema'nar] *vi*: **~ de** to emanate from, come from; (*derivar de*) to originate in

emancipar [emanθi'par] *vt* to emancipate; **~se** *vr* to become emancipated, free o.s.

embadurnar [embaður'nar] *vt* to smear

embajada [emba'xaða] *nf* embassy

embajador, a [embaxa'ðor, a] *nm/f* ambassador/ambassadress

embalaje [emba'laxe] *nm* packing

embalar [emba'lar] *vt* to parcel, wrap (up); **~se** *vr* to go fast

embalsamar [embalsa'mar] *vt* to embalm

embalse [em'balse] *nm* (*presa*) dam; (*lago*) reservoir

embarazada [embara'θaða] *adj* pregnant ♦ *nf* pregnant woman

embarazo [emba'raθo] *nm* (*de mujer*) pregnancy; (*impedimento*) obstacle, obstruction; (*timidez*) embarrassment; **embarazoso, a** *adj* awkward, embarrassing

embarcación [embarka'θjon] *nf* (*barco*) boat, craft; (*acto*) embarkation, boarding

embarcadero [embarka'ðero] *nm* pier, landing stage

embarcar [embar'kar] *vt* (*cargamento*) to ship, stow; (*persona*) to embark, put on board; **~se** *vr* to embark, go on board

embargar [embar'var] *vt* (*JUR*) to seize, impound

embargo [em'barvo] *nm* (*JUR*) seizure; (*COM, POL*) embargo

embargue [em'barve] *etc vb ver* **embargar**

embarque *etc* [em'barke] *vb ver* **embarcar** ♦ *nm* shipment, loading

embaucar [embau'kar] *vt* to trick, fool

embeber [embe'ßer] *vt* (*absorber*) to absorb, soak up; (*empapar*) to saturate

♦ *vi* to shrink; **~se** *vr*: **~se en un libro** to be engrossed *o* absorbed in a book

embellecer [embeλe'θer] *vt* to embellish, beautify

embestida [embes'tiða] *nf* attack, onslaught; (*carga*) charge

embestir [embes'tir] *vt* to attack, assault; to charge, attack ♦ *vi* to attack

emblema [em'blema] *nm* emblem

embobado, a [embo'ßaðo, a] *adj* (*atontado*) stunned, bewildered

embolia [em'bolja] *nf* (*MED*) clot

émbolo ['embolo] *nm* (*AUTO*) piston

embolsar [embol'sar] *vt* to pocket, put in one's pocket

emborrachar [emborra'tʃar] *vt* to make drunk, intoxicate; **~se** *vr* to get drunk

emboscada [embos'kaða] *nf* ambush

embotar [embo'tar] *vt* to blunt, dull; **~se** *vr* (*adormecerse*) to go numb

embotellamiento [emboteλa'mjento] *nm* (*AUTO*) traffic jam

embotellar [embote'λar] *vt* to bottle

embrague [em'braxe] *nm* (*tb*: **pedal de ~**) clutch

embriagar [embrja'var] *vt* (*emborrachar*) to make drunk; **~se** *vr* (*emborracharse*) to get drunk

embrión [em'brjon] *nm* embryo

embrollar [embro'λar] *vt* (*el asunto*) to confuse, complicate; (*implicar*) to involve, embroil; **~se** *vr* (*confundirse*) to get into a muddle *o* mess

embrollo [em'broλo] *nm* (*enredo*) muddle, confusion; (*aprieto*) fix, jam

embrujado, a [embru'xado, a] *adj* bewitched; **casa embrujada** haunted house

embrutecer [embrute'θer] *vt* (*atontar*) to stupefy; **~se** *vr* to be stupefied

embudo [em'buðo] *nm* funnel

embuste [em'buste] *nm* (*mentira*) lie; **~ro, a** *adj* lying, deceitful ♦ *nm/f* (*mentiroso*) liar

embutido [embu'tiðo] *nm* (*CULIN*) sausage; (*TEC*) inlay

emergencia [emer'xenθja] *nf* emergency;

(*surgimiento*) emergence

emerger [emer'xer] *vi* to emerge, appear

emigración [emixra'θjon] *nf* emigration; (*de pájaros*) migration

emigrar [emi'xrar] *vi* (*personas*) to emigrate; (*pájaros*) to migrate

eminencia [emi'nenθja] *nf* eminence; **eminente** *adj* eminent, distinguished; (*elevado*) high

emisario [emi'sarjo] *nm* emissary

emisión [emi'sjon] *nf* (*acto*) emission; (*COM etc*) issue; (*RADIO, TV: acto*) broadcasting; (: *programa*) broadcast, programme (*BRIT*), program (*US*)

emisora [emi'sora] *nf* radio *o* broadcasting station

emitir [emi'tir] *vt* (*olor etc*) to emit, give off; (*moneda etc*) to issue; (*opinión*) to express; (*RADIO*) to broadcast

emoción [emo'θjon] *nf* emotion; (*excitación*) excitement; (*sentimiento*) feeling

emocionante [emoθjo'nante] *adj* (*excitante*) exciting, thrilling

emocionar [emoθjo'nar] *vt* (*excitar*) to excite, thrill; (*conmover*) to move, touch; (*impresionar*) to impress

emotivo, a [emo'tiβo, a] *adj* emotional

empacar [empa'kar] *vt* (*gen*) to pack; (*en caja*) to bale, crate

empacho [em'patʃo] *nm* (*MED*) indigestion; (*fig*) embarrassment

empadronarse [empaðro'narse] *vr* (*POL: como elector*) to register

empalagoso, a [empala'xoso, a] *adj* cloying; (*fig*) tiresome

empalmar [empal'mar] *vt* to join, connect ♦ *vi* (*dos caminos*) to meet, join; **empalme** *nm* joint, connection; junction; (*de trenes*) connection

empanada [empa'naða] *nf* pie, pasty

empantanarse [empanta'narse] *vr* to get swamped; (*fig*) to get bogged down

empañarse [empa'ɲarse] *vr* (*cristales etc*) to steam up

empapar [empa'par] *vt* (*mojar*) to soak, saturate; (*absorber*) to soak up, absorb;

~se *vr*: **~se de** to soak up

empapelar [empape'lar] *vt* (*paredes*) to paper

empaquetar [empake'tar] *vt* to pack, parcel up

empastar [empas'tar] *vt* (*embadurnar*) to paste; (*diente*) to fill

empaste [em'paste] *nm* (*de diente*) filling

empatar [empa'tar] *vi* to draw, tie; **empate** *nm* draw, tie

empecé *etc vb ver* **empezar**

empedernido, a [empeðer'niðo, a] *adj* hard, heartless; (*fumador*) inveterate

empedrado, a [empe'ðraðo, a] *adj* paved ♦ *nm* paving

empeine [em'peine] *nm* (*de pie, zapato*) instep

empellón [empe'ʎon] *nm* push, shove

empeñado, a [empe'ɲaðo, a] *adj* (*persona*) determined; (*objeto*) pawned

empeñar [empe'ɲar] *vt* (*objeto*) to pawn, pledge; (*persona*) to compel; **~se** *vr* (*endeudarse*) to get into debt; **~se en** to be set on, be determined to

empeño [em'peɲo] *nm* (*determinación, insistencia*) determination, insistence; **casa de ~s** pawnshop

empeorar [empeo'rar] *vt* to make worse, worsen ♦ *vi* to get worse, deteriorate

empequeñecer [empekeɲe'θer] *vt* to dwarf; (*minusvalorar*) to belittle

emperador [empera'ðor] *nm* emperor; **emperatriz** *nf* empress

empezar [empe'θar] *vt, vi* to begin, start

empiece *etc vb ver* **empezar**

empiezo *etc vb ver* **empezar**

empinar [empi'nar] *vt* to raise; **~se** *vr* (*persona*) to stand on tiptoe; (*animal*) to rear up; (*camino*) to climb steeply

empírico, a [em'piriko, a] *adj* empirical

emplasto [em'plasto] *nm* (*MED*) plaster

emplazamiento [emplaθa'mjento] *nm* site, location; (*JUR*) summons *sg*

emplazar [empla'θar] *vt* (*ubicar*) to site, place, locate; (*JUR*) to summons; (*convocar*) to summon

empleado, a [emple'aðo, a] *nm/f* (*gen*)

employee; (*de banco etc*) clerk

emplear [emple'ar] *vt* (*usar*) to use, employ; (*dar trabajo a*) to employ; **~se** *vr* (*conseguir trabajo*) to be employed; (*ocuparse*) to occupy o.s.

empleo [em'pleo] *nm* (*puesto*) job; (*puestos: colectivamente*) employment; (*uso*) use, employment

empobrecer [empoβre'θer] *vt* to impoverish; **~se** *vr* to become poor *o* impoverished

empollar [empo'ʎar] (*fam*) *vt*, *vi* to swot (up); **empollón, ona** (*fam*) *nm/f* swot

emporio [em'porjo] *nm* (AM: *gran almacén*) department store

empotrado, a [empo'traðo, a] *adj* (*armario etc*) built-in

emprender [empren'der] *vt* (*empezar*) to begin, embark on; (*acometer*) to tackle, take on

empresa [em'presa] *nf* (*de espíritu etc*) enterprise; (COM) company, firm; **~rio, a** *nm/f* (COM) businessman/woman

empréstito [em'prestito] *nm* (public) loan

empujar [empu'xar] *vt* to push, shove

empujón [empu'xon] *nm* push, shove

empuñar [empu'ɲar] *vt* (*asir*) to grasp, take (firm) hold of

emular [emu'lar] *vt* to emulate; (*rivalizar*) to rival

---

en [en] *prep* **1** (*posición*) in; (: *sobre*) on; **está ~ el cajón** it's in the drawer; **~ Argentina/La Paz** in Argentina/La Paz; **~ la oficina/el colegio** at the office/school; **está ~ el suelo/quinto piso** it's on the floor/the fifth floor

2 (*dirección*) into; **entró ~ el aula** she went into the classroom; **meter algo ~ el bolso** to put sth into one's bag

3 (*tiempo*) in; on; **~ 1605/3 semanas/invierno** in 1605/3 weeks/winter; **~ (el mes de) enero** in (the month of) January; **~ aquella ocasión/época** on that occasion/at that time

4 (*precio*) for; **lo vendió ~ 20 dólares** he

sold it for 20 dollars

5 (*diferencia*) by; **reducir/aumentar ~ una tercera parte/un 20 por ciento** to reduce/increase by a third/20 per cent

6 (*manera*): **~ avión/autobús** by plane/bus; **escrito ~ inglés** written in English

7 (*después de vb que indica gastar etc*) on; **han cobrado demasiado ~ dietas** they've charged too much to expenses; **se le va la mitad del sueldo ~ comida** he spends half his salary on food

8 (*tema, ocupación*): **experto ~ la materia** expert on the subject; **trabaja ~ la construcción** he works in the building industry

9 (*adj + ~ + infin*): **lento ~ reaccionar** slow to react

---

enaguas [e'naɣwas] *nfpl* petticoat *sg*, underskirt *sg*

enajenación [enaxena'θjon] *nf*: **~ mental** mental derangement

enajenar [enaxe'nar] *vt* (*volver loco*) to drive mad

enamorado, a [enamo'raðo, a] *adj* in love ♦ *nm/f* lover

enamorar [enamo'rar] *vt* to win the love of; **~se** *vr*: **~se de alguien** to fall in love with sb

enano, a [e'nano, a] *adj* tiny ♦ *nm/f* dwarf

enardecer [enarðe'θer] *vt* (*pasiones*) to fire, inflame; (*persona*) to fill with enthusiasm; **~se** *vr*: **~se por** to get excited about; (*entusiasmarse*) to get enthusiastic about

encabezamiento [enkaβeθa'mjento] *nm* (*de carta*) heading; (*de periódico*) headline

encabezar [enkaβe'θar] *vt* (*movimiento, revolución*) to lead, head; (*lista*) to head, be at the top of; (*carta*) to put a heading to

encadenar [enkaðe'nar] *vt* to chain (together); (*poner grilletes a*) to shackle

encajar [enka'xar] *vt* (*ajustar*): **~ (en)** to fit (into); (*fam: golpe*) to take ♦ *vi* to fit (well); (*fig: corresponder a*) to match; **~se**

vr: **~se en un sillón** to squeeze into a chair

encaje [en'kaxe] *nm* (*labor*) lace

encalar [enka'lar] *vt* (*pared*) to whitewash

encallar [enka'ʎar] *vi* (NAUT) to run aground

encaminar [enkami'nar] *vt* to direct, send; **~se** *vr*: **~se a** to set out for

encantado, a [enkan'taðo, a] *adj* (*hechizado*) bewitched; (*muy contento*) delighted; **¡~!** how do you do, pleased to meet you

encantador, a [enkanta'ðor, a] *adj* charming, lovely ♦ *nm/f* magician, enchanter/enchantress

encantar [enkan'tar] *vt* (*agradar*) to charm, delight; (*hechizar*) to bewitch, cast a spell on; **me encanta eso** I love that; **encanto** *nm* (*hechizo*) spell, charm; (*fig*) charm, delight

encarcelar [enkarθe'lar] *vt* to imprison, jail

encarecer [enkare'θer] *vt* to put up the price of; **~se** *vr* to get dearer

encarecimiento [enkareθi'mjento] *nm* price increase

encargado, a [enkar'ɣaðo, a] *adj* in charge ♦ *nm/f* agent, representative; (*responsable*) person in charge

encargar [enkar'ɣar] *vt* to entrust; (*recomendar*) to urge, recommend; **~se** *vr*: **~se de** to look after, take charge of

encargo [en'karɣo] *nm* (*tarea*) assignment, job; (*responsabilidad*) responsibility; (COM) order

encariñarse [enkari'ɲarse] *vr*: **~ con** to grow fond of, get attached to

encarnación [enkarna'θjon] *nf* incarnation, embodiment

encarnizado, a [enkarni'θaðo, a] *adj* (*lucha*) bloody, fierce

encarrilar [enkarri'lar] *vt* (*tren*) to put back on the rails; (*fig*) to correct, put on the right track

encasillar [enkasi'ʎar] *vt* (*tb fig*) to pigeonhole; (*actor*) to typecast

encauzar [enkau'θar] *vt* to channel

encendedor [enθende'ðor] *nm* lighter

encender [enθen'der] *vt* (*con fuego*) to light; (*luz, radio*) to put on, switch on; (*avivar: pasiones*) to inflame; **~se** *vr* to catch fire; (*excitarse*) to get excited; (*de cólera*) to flare up; (*el rostro*) to blush

encendido [enθen'diðo] *nm* (AUTO) ignition

encerado [enθe'raðo] *nm* (ESCOL) blackboard

encerar [enθe'rar] *vt* (*suelo*) to wax, polish

encerrar [enθe'rrar] *vt* (*confinar*) to shut in, shut up; (*comprender, incluir*) to include, contain

encharcado, a [entʃar'kaðo, a] *adj* (*terreno*) flooded

encharcarse [entʃar'karse] *vr* to get flooded

enchufado, a [entʃu'faðo, a] (*fam*) *nm/f* well-connected person

enchufar [entʃu'far] *vt* (ELEC) to plug in; (TEC) to connect, fit together; **enchufe** *nm* (ELEC: *clavija*) plug; (: *toma*) socket; (*de dos tubos*) joint, connection; (*fam: influencia*) contact, connection; (: *puesto*) cushy job

encía [en'θia] *nf* gum

encienda *etc vb ver* **encender**

encierro *etc* [en'θjerro] *vb ver* **encerrar** ♦ *nm* shutting in, shutting up; (*calabozo*) prison

encima [en'θima] *adv* (*sobre*) above, over; (*además*) besides; **~ de** (*en*) on, on top of; (*sobre*) above, over; (*además de*) besides, on top of; **por ~ de** over; **¿llevas dinero ~?** have you (got) any money on you?; **se me vino ~** it took me by surprise

encina [en'θina] *nf* holm oak

encinta [en'θinta] *adj* pregnant

enclenque [en'klenke] *adj* weak, sickly

encoger [enko'xer] *vt* to shrink, contract; **~se** *vr* to shrink, contract; (*fig*) to cringe; **~se de hombros** to shrug one's shoulders

encolar [enko'lar] *vt* (*engomar*) to glue, paste; (*pegar*) to stick down

encolerizar [enkoleri'θar] *vt* to anger, provoke; **~se** *vr* to get angry

encomendar [enkomen'dar] *vt* to entrust, commend; **~se** *vr*: **~se a** to put one's trust in

encomiar [enko'mjar] *vt* to praise, pay tribute to

encomienda *etc* [enko'mjenda] *vb ver* **encomendar** ♦ *nf* (*encargo*) charge, commission; (*elogio*) tribute; **~ postal** (*AM*) parcel post

encontrado, a [enkon'traðo, a] *adj* (*contrario*) contrary, conflicting

encontrar [enkon'trar] *vt* (*hallar*) to find; (*inesperadamente*) to meet, run into; **~se** *vr* to meet (each other); (*situarse*) to be (situated); **~se con** to meet; **~se bien (de salud)** to feel well

encrespar [enkres'par] *vt* (*cabellos*) to curl; (*fig*) to anger, irritate; **~se** *vr* (*el mar*) to get rough; (*fig*) to get cross, get irritated

encrucijada [enkruθi'xaða] *nf* crossroads *sg*

encuadernación [enkwaðerna'θjon] *nf* binding

encuadernador, a [enkwaðerna'ðor, a] *nm/f* bookbinder

encuadrar [enkwa'ðrar] *vt* (*retrato*) to frame; (*ajustar*) to fit, insert; (*contener*) to contain

encubrir [enku'ßrir] *vt* (*ocultar*) to hide, conceal; (*criminal*) to harbour, shelter

encuentro *etc* [en'kwentro] *vb ver* **encontrar** ♦ *nm* (*de personas*) meeting; (*AUTO etc*) collision, crash; (*DEPORTE*) match, game; (*MIL*) encounter

encuesta [en'kwesta] *nf* inquiry, investigation; (*sondeo*) (public) opinion poll; **~ judicial** post mortem

encumbrar [enkum'brar] *vt* (*persona*) to exalt

endeble [en'deßle] *adj* (*argumento, excusa, persona*) weak

endémico, a [en'demiko, a] *adj* (*MED*) endemic; (*fig*) rife, chronic

endemoniado, a [endemo'njaðo, a] *adj* possessed (of the devil); (*travieso*) devilish

enderezar [endere'θar] *vt* (*poner derecho*) to straighten (out); (: *verticalmente*) to set upright; (*situación*) to straighten *o* sort out; (*dirigir*) to direct; **~se** *vr* (*persona sentada*) to straighten up

endeudarse [endeu'ðarse] *vr* to get into debt

endiablado, a [endja'ßlaðo, a] *adj* devilish, diabolical; (*travieso*) mischievous

endilgar [endil'yar] (*fam*) *vt*: **~le algo a uno** to lumber sb with sth; **~le un sermón a uno** to lecture sb

endiñar [endi'ɲar] (*fam*) *vt* (*bofetón*) to land, belt

endosar [endo'sar] *vt* (*cheque etc*) to endorse

endulzar [endul'θar] *vt* to sweeten; (*suavizar*) to soften

endurecer [endure'θer] *vt* to harden; **~se** *vr* to harden, grow hard

enema [e'nema] *nm* (*MED*) enema

enemigo, a [ene'miʝo, a] *adj* enemy, hostile ♦ *nm/f* enemy

enemistad [enemis'tað] *nf* enmity

enemistar [enemis'tar] *vt* to make enemies of, cause a rift between; **~se** *vr* to become enemies; (*amigos*) to fall out

energía [ener'xia] *nf* (*vigor*) energy, drive; (*empuje*) push; (*TEC, ELEC*) energy, power; **~ eolica** wind power; **~ solar** solar energy/power

enérgico, a [e'nerxiko, a] *adj* (*gen*) energetic; (*voz, modales*) forceful

energúmeno, a [ener'ɣumeno, a] (*fam*) *nm/f* (*fig*) madman/woman

enero [e'nero] *nm* January

enfadado, a [enfa'ðaðo, a] *adj* angry, annoyed

enfadar [enfa'ðar] *vt* to anger, annoy; **~se** *vr* to get angry *o* annoyed

enfado [en'faðo] *nm* (*enojo*) anger, annoyance; (*disgusto*) trouble, bother

énfasis ['enfasis] *nm* emphasis, stress

enfático, a [en'fatiko, a] *adj* emphatic

enfermar [enfer'mar] *vt* to make ill ♦ *vi* to fall ill, be taken ill

enfermedad [enferme'ðað] *nf* illness; ~ **venérea** venereal disease

enfermera [enfer'mera] *nf* nurse

enfermería [enferme'ria] *nf* infirmary; (*de colegio etc*) sick bay

enfermero [enfer'mero] *nm* (male) nurse

enfermizo, a [enfer'miθo, a] *adj* (*persona*) sickly, unhealthy; (*fig*) unhealthy

enfermo, a [en'fermo, a] *adj* ill, sick ♦ *nm/f* invalid, sick person; (*en hospital*) patient

enflaquecer [enflake'θer] *vt* (*adelgazar*) to make thin; (*debilitar*) to weaken

enfocar [enfo'kar] *vt* (*foto etc*) to focus; (*problema etc*) to approach

enfoque *etc* [en'foke] *vb ver* **enfocar** ♦ *nm* focus.

enfrascarse [enfras'karse] *vr*: ~ **en algo** to bury o.s. in sth

enfrentar [enfren'tar] *vt* (*peligro*) to face (up to), confront; (*oponer*) to bring face to face; ~**se** *vr* (*dos personas*) to face o confront each other; (*DEPORTE: dos equipos*) to meet; ~**se a** o **con** to face up to, confront

enfrente [en'frente] *adv* opposite; **la casa de** ~ the house opposite, the house across the street; ~ **de** opposite, facing

enfriamiento [enfria'mjento] *nm* chilling, refrigeration; (*MED*) cold, chill

enfriar [enfri'ar] *vt* (*algo caliente*) to cool, chill; (*algo caliente*) to cool down; ~**se** *vr* to cool down; (*MED*) to catch a chill; (*amistad*) to cool

enfurecer [enfure'θer] *vt* to enrage, madden; ~**se** *vr* to become furious, fly into a rage; (*mar*) to get rough

engalanar [engala'nar] *vt* (*adornar*) to adorn; (*ciudad*) to decorate; ~**se** *vr* to get dressed up

enganchar [engan'tʃar] *vt* to hook; (*dos vagones*) to hitch up; (*TEC*) to couple, connect; (*MIL*) to recruit; ~**se** *vr* (*MIL*) to enlist, join up

enganche [en'gantʃe] *nm* hook; (*TEC*) coupling, connection; (*acto*) hooking (up); (*MIL*) recruitment, enlistment; (*AM: depósito*) deposit

engañar [enga'nar] *vt* to deceive; (*estafar*) to cheat, swindle; ~**se** *vr* (*equivocarse*) to be wrong; (*disimular la verdad*) to deceive o.s.

engaño [en'gano] *nm* deceit; (*estafa*) trick, swindle; (*error*) mistake, misunderstanding; (*ilusión*) delusion; ~**so, a** *adj* (*tramposo*) crooked; (*mentiroso*) dishonest, deceitful; (*aspecto*) deceptive; (*consejo*) misleading

engarzar [engar'θar] *vt* (*joya*) to set, mount; (*fig*) to link, connect

engatusar [engatu'sar] (*fam*) *vt* to coax

engendrar [enxen'drar] *vt* to breed; (*procrear*) to beget; (*causar*) to cause, produce; **engendro** *nm* (*BIO*) foetus; (*fig*) monstrosity

englobar [englo'βar] *vt* to include, comprise

engordar [engor'ðar] *vt* to fatten ♦ *vi* to get fat, put on weight

engorroso, a [engo'rroso, a] *adj* bothersome, trying

engranaje [engra'naxe] *nm* (*AUTO*) gear

engrandecer [engrande'θer] *vt* to enlarge, magnify; (*alabar*) to praise, speak highly of; (*exagerar*) to exaggerate

engrasar [engra'sar] *vt* (*TEC: poner grasa*) to grease; (: *lubricar*) to lubricate, oil; (*manchar*) to make greasy

engreído, a [engre'iðo, a] *adj* vain, conceited

engrosar [engro'sar] *vt* (*ensanchar*) to enlarge; (*aumentar*) to increase; (*hinchar*) to swell

enhebrar [ene'βrar] *vt* to thread

enhorabuena [enora'βwena] *excl*: ¡~! congratulations! ♦ *nf*: **dar la** ~ **a** to congratulate

enigma [e'niɣma] *nm* enigma; (*problema*) puzzle; (*misterio*) mystery

enjabonar [enxaβo'nar] *vt* to soap; (*fam: adular*) to soft-soap

enjambre [en'xambre] *nm* swarm

enjaular [enxau'lar] *vt* to (put in a) cage; (*fam*) to jail, lock up

enjuagar [enxwa'xar] vt (*ropa*) to rinse (out)

enjuague etc [en'xwaxe] vb ver **enjuagar**
♦ nm (MED) mouthwash; (*de ropa*) rinse, rinsing

enjugar [enxu'xar] vt to wipe (off); (*lágrimas*) to dry; (*déficit*) to wipe out

enjuiciar [enxwi'θjar] vt (JUR: *procesar*) to prosecute, try; (*fig*) to judge

enjuto, a [en'xuto, a] adj (*flaco*) lean, skinny

enlace [en'laθe] nm link, connection; (*relación*) relationship; (*tb*: ~ **matrimonial**) marriage; (*de carretera, vías*) connection; ~ **sindical** shop steward

enlatado, a [enla'taðo, a] adj (*comida, productos*) tinned, canned

enlazar [enla'θar] vt (*unir con lazos*) to bind together; (*atar*) to tie; (*conectar*) to link, connect; (AM) to lasso

enlodar [enlo'ðar] vt to cover in mud; (*fig: manchar*) to stain; (: *rebajar*) to debase

enloquecer [enloke'θer] vt to drive mad
♦ vi to go mad; ~**se** vr to go mad

enlutado, a [enlu'taðo, a] adj (*persona*) in mourning

enmarañar [enmara'ɲar] vt (*enredar*) to tangle (up), entangle; (*complicar*) to complicate; (*confundir*) to confuse; ~**se** vr (*enredarse*) to become entangled; (*confundirse*) to get confused

enmarcar [enmar'kar] vt (*cuadro*) to frame

enmascarar [enmaska'rar] vt to mask; ~**se** vr to put on a mask

enmendar [enmen'dar] vt to emend, correct; (*constitución etc*) to amend; (*comportamiento*) to reform; ~**se** vr to reform, mend one's ways; **enmienda** nf correction; amendment; reform

enmohecerse [enmoe'θerse] vr (*metal*) to rust, go rusty; (*muro, plantas*) to get mouldy

enmudecer [enmuðe'θer] vi (*perder el habla*) to fall silent; (*guardar silencio*) to remain silent

ennegrecer [ennexre'θer] vt (*poner negro*) to blacken; (*oscurecer*) to darken; ~**se** vr to turn black; (*oscurecerse*) to get dark, darken

ennoblecer [ennoβle'θer] vt to ennoble

enojar [eno'xar] vt (*encolerizar*) to anger; (*disgustar*) to annoy, upset; ~**se** vr to get angry; to get annoyed

enojo [e'noxo] nm (*cólera*) anger; (*irritación*) annoyance; ~**so, a** adj annoying

enorgullecerse [enorɣuʎe'θerse] vr to be proud; ~ **de** to pride o.s. on, be proud of

enorme [e'norme] adj enormous, huge; (*fig*) monstrous; **enormidad** nf hugeness, immensity

enrarecido, a [enrare'θiðo, a] adj (*atmósfera, aire*) rarefied

enredadera [enreða'ðera] nf (BOT) creeper, climbing plant

enredar [enre'ðar] vt (*cables, hilos etc*) to tangle (up), entangle; (*situación*) to complicate, confuse; (*meter cizaña*) to sow discord among o between; (*implicar*) to embroil, implicate; ~**se** vr to get entangled, get tangled (up); (*situación*) to get complicated; (*persona*) to get embroiled; (AM: *fam*) to meddle

enredo [en'reðo] nm (*maraña*) tangle; (*confusión*) mix-up, confusion; (*intriga*) intrigue

enrejado [enre'xaðo] nm fence, railings pl

enrevesado, a [enreβe'saðo, a] adj (*asunto*) complicated, involved

enriquecer [enrike'θer] vt to make rich, enrich; ~**se** vr to get rich

enrojecer [enroxe'θer] vt to redden ♦ vi (*persona*) to blush; ~**se** vr to blush

enrolar [enro'lar] vt (MIL) to enlist; (*reclutar*) to recruit; ~**se** vr (MIL) to join up; (*afiliarse*) to enrol

enrollar [enro'ʎar] vt to roll (up), wind (up)

enroscar [enros'kar] vt (*torcer, doblar*) to coil (round), wind; (*tornillo, rosca*) to screw in; ~**se** vr to coil, wind

ensalada [ensa'laða] nf salad; **ensaladilla (rusa)** nf Russian salad

ensalzar [ensal'θar] vt (*alabar*) to praise,

extol; (*exaltar*) to exalt

ensamblaje [ensam'blaxe] *nm* assembly; (*TEC*) joint

ensanchar [ensan't∫ar] *vt* (*hacer más ancho*) to widen; (*agrandar*) to enlarge, expand; (*COSTURA*) to let out; **~se** *vr* to get wider, expand; **ensanche** *nm* (*de calle*) widening

ensangrentar [ensangren'tar] *vt* to stain with blood

ensañar [ensa'ɲar] *vt* to enrage; **~se con** *vr*: to treat brutally

ensartar [ensar'tar] *vt* (*cuentas, perlas etc*) to string (together)

ensayar [ensa'jar] *vt* to test, try (out); (*TEATRO*) to rehearse

ensayo [en'sajo] *nm* test, trial; (*QUÍM*) experiment; (*TEATRO*) rehearsal; (*DEPORTE*) try; (*ESCOL, LITERATURA*) essay

enseguida [ense'ɣiða] *adv* at once, right away

ensenada [ense'naða] *nf* inlet, cove

enseñanza [ense'ɲanθa] *nf* (*educación*) education; (*acción*) teaching; (*doctrina*) teaching, doctrine

enseñar [ense'ɲar] *vt* (*educar*) to teach; (*mostrar, señalar*) to show

enseres [en'seres] *nmpl* belongings

ensillar [ensi'ʎar] *vt* to saddle (up)

ensimismarse [ensimis'marse] *vr* (*abstraerse*) to become lost in thought; (*AM*) to become conceited

ensombrecer [ensombre'θer] *vt* to darken, cast a shadow over; (*fig*) to overshadow, put in the shade

ensordecer [ensorðe'θer] *vt* to deafen ♦ *vi* to go deaf

ensortijado, a [ensorti'xaðo, a] *adj* (*pelo*) curly

ensuciar [ensu'θjar] *vt* (*manchar*) to dirty, soil; (*fig*) to defile; **~se** *vr* to get dirty; (*niño*) to wet o.s.

ensueño [en'sweɲo] *nm* (*sueño*) dream, fantasy; (*ilusión*) illusion; (*soñando despierto*) daydream

entablar [enta'blar] *vt* (*recubrir*) to board (up); (*AJEDREZ, DAMAS*) to set up;

(*conversación*) to strike up; (*JUR*) to file ♦ *vi* to draw

entablillar [entaßli'ʎar] *vt* (*MED*) to (put in a) splint

entallar [enta'ʎar] *vt* (*traje*) to tailor ♦ *vi*: **el traje entalla bien** the suit fits well

ente ['ente] *nm* (*organización*) body, organization; (*fam: persona*) odd character

entender [enten'der] *vt* (*comprender*) to understand; (*darse cuenta*) to realize ♦ *vi* to understand; (*creer*) to think, believe; **~se** *vr* (*comprenderse*) to be understood; (*2 personas*) to get on together; (*ponerse de acuerdo*) to agree, reach an agreement; **~ de** to know all about; **~ algo de** to know a little about; **~ en** to deal with, have to do with; **~se mal** (*2 personas*) to get on badly

entendido, a [enten'diðo, a] *adj* (*comprendido*) understood; (*hábil*) skilled; (*inteligente*) knowledgeable ♦ *nm/f* (*experto*) expert ♦ *excl* agreed!; **entendimiento** *nm* (*comprensión*) understanding; (*inteligencia*) mind, intellect; (*juicio*) judgement

enterado, a [ente'raðo, a] *adj* well-informed; **estar ~ de** to know about, be aware of

enteramente [entera'mente] *adv* entirely, completely

enterar [ente'rar] *vt* (*informar*) to inform, tell; **~se** *vr* to find out, get to know

entereza [ente'reθa] *nf* (*totalidad*) entirety; (*fig: carácter*) strength of mind; (*: honradez*) integrity

enternecer [enterne'θer] *vt* (*ablandar*) to soften; (*apiadar*) to touch, move; **~se** *vr* to be touched, be moved

entero, a [en'tero, a] *adj* (*total*) whole, entire; (*fig: honesto*) honest; (*: firme*) firm, resolute ♦ *nm* (*COM: punto*) point; (*AM: pago*) payment

enterrador [enterra'ðor] *nm* gravedigger

enterrar [ente'rrar] *vt* to bury

entibiar [enti'ßjar] *vt* (*enfriar*) to cool; (*calentar*) to warm; **~se** *vr* (*fig*) to cool

entidad [enti'ðað] nf (empresa) firm, company; (organismo) body; (sociedad) society; (FILOSOFÍA) entity

entiendo etc vb ver **entender**

entierro [en'tjerro] nm (acción) burial; (funeral) funeral

entonación [entona'θjon] nf (LING) intonation

entonar [ento'nar] vt (canción) to intone; (colores) to tone; (MED) to tone up ♦ vi to be in tune

entonces [en'tonθes] adv then, at that time; **desde ~** since then; **en aquel ~** at that time; **(pues) ~** and so

entornar [entor'nar] vt (puerta, ventana) to half close, leave ajar; (los ojos) to screw up

entorpecer [entorpe'θer] vt (entendimiento) to dull; (impedir) to obstruct, hinder; (: tránsito) to slow down, delay

entrada [en'traða] nf (acción) entry, access; (sitio) entrance, way in; (INFORM) input; (COM) receipts pl, takings pl; (CULIN) starter; (DEPORTE) innings sg; (TEATRO) house, audience; (billete) ticket; (COM): **~s y salidas** income and expenditure; (TEC): **~ de aire** air intake o inlet; **de ~** from the outset

entrado, a [en'traðo, a] adj: **~ en años** elderly; **una vez ~ el verano** in the summer(time), when summer comes

entramparse [entram'parse] vr to get into debt

entrante [en'trante] adj next, coming; **mes/año ~** next month/year; **~s** nmpl starters

entraña [en'traɲa] nf (fig: centro) heart, core; (raíz) root; **~s** nfpl (ANAT) entrails; (fig) heart sg; **sin ~s** (fig) heartless; **entrañable** adj close, intimate; **entrañar** vt to entail

entrar [en'trar] vt (introducir) to bring in; (INFORM) to input ♦ vi (meterse) to go in, come in, enter; (comenzar): **~ diciendo** to begin by saying; **hacer ~** to show in; **no me entra** I can't get the hang of it

entre ['entre] prep (dos) between; (más de dos) among(st)

entreabrir [entrea'ßrir] vt to half-open, open halfway

entrecejo [entre'θexo] nm: **fruncir el ~** to frown

entrecortado, a [entrekor'taðo, a] adj (respiración) difficult; (habla) faltering

entredicho [entre'ðitʃo] nm (JUR) injunction; **poner en ~** to cast doubt on; **estar en ~** to be in doubt

entrega [en'treɣa] nf (de mercancías) delivery; (de novela etc) instalment

entregar [entre'ɣar] vt (dar) to hand (over), deliver; **~se** vr (rendirse) to surrender, give in, submit; (dedicarse) to devote o.s.

entrelazar [entrela'θar] vt to entwine

entremeses [entre'meses] nmpl hors d'œuvres

entremeter [entreme'ter] vt to insert, put in; **~se** vr to meddle, interfere; **entremetido, a** adj meddling, interfering

entremezclar [entremeθ'klar] vt to intermingle; **~se** vr to intermingle

entrenador, a [entrena'ðor, a] nm/f trainer, coach

entrenarse [entre'narse] vr to train

entrepierna [entre'pjerna] nf crotch

entresacar [entresa'kar] vt to pick out, select

entresuelo [entre'swelo] nm mezzanine

entretanto [entre'tanto] adv meanwhile, meantime

entretejer [entrete'xer] vt to interweave

entretener [entrete'ner] vt (divertir) to entertain, amuse; (detener) to hold up, delay; **~se** vr (divertirse) to amuse o.s.; (retrasarse) to delay, linger; **entretenido, a** adj entertaining, amusing; **entretenimiento** nm entertainment, amusement

entrever [entre'ßer] vt to glimpse, catch a glimpse of

entrevista [entre'ßista] nf interview; **entrevistar** vt to interview;

entrevistarse *vr* to have an interview

entristecer [entriste'θer] *vt* to sadden, grieve; **~se** *vr* to grow sad

entrometerse [entrome'terse] *vr*: **~ (en)** to interfere (in *o* with)

entroncar [entron'kar] *vi* to be connected *o* related

entumecer [entume'θer] *vt* to numb, benumb; **~se** *vr* (*por el frío*) to go *o* become numb; **entumecido, a** *adj* numb, stiff

enturbiar [entur'βjar] *vt* (*el agua*) to make cloudy; (*fig*) to confuse; **~se** *vr* (*oscurecerse*) to become cloudy; (*fig*) to get confused, become obscure

entusiasmar [entusjas'mar] *vt* to excite, fill with enthusiasm; (*gustar mucho*) to delight; **~se** *vr*: **~se con** *o* **por** to get enthusiastic *o* excited about

entusiasmo [entu'sjasmo] *nm* enthusiasm; (*excitación*) excitement

entusiasta [entu'sjasta] *adj* enthusiastic ♦ *nm/f* enthusiast

enumerar [enume'rar] *vt* to enumerate

enunciación [enunθja'θjon] *nf* enunciation

enunciado [enun'θjaðo] *nm* enunciation

envainar [embai'nar] *vt* to sheathe

envalentonar [embalento'nar] *vt* to give courage to; **~se** *vr* (*pey: jactarse*) to boast, brag

envanecer [embane'θer] *vt* to make conceited; **~se** *vr* to grow conceited

envasar [emba'sar] *vt* (*empaquetar*) to pack, wrap; (*enfrascar*) to bottle; (*enlatar*) to can; (*embolsar*) to pocket

envase [em'base] *nm* (*en paquete*) packing, wrapping; (*en botella*) bottling; (*en lata*) canning; (*recipiente*) container; (*paquete*) package; (*botella*) bottle; (*lata*) tin (*BRIT*), can

envejecer [embexe'θer] *vt* to make old, age ♦ *vi* (*volverse viejo*) to grow old; (*parecer viejo*) to age; **~se** *vr* to grow old; to age

envenenar [embene'nar] *vt* to poison; (*fig*) to embitter

envergadura [emberva'ðura] *nf* (*fig*) scope, compass

envés [em'bes] *nm* (*de tela*) back, wrong side

enviar [em'bjar] *vt* to send

enviciarse [embi'θjarse] *vr*: **~ (con)** to get addicted (to)

envidia [em'biðja] *nf* envy; **tener ~ a** to envy, be jealous of; **envidiar** *vt* to envy

envío [em'bio] *nm* (*acción*) sending; (*de mercancías*) consignment; (*de dinero*) remittance

enviudar [embju'ðar] *vi* to be widowed

envoltura [embol'tura] *nf* (*cobertura*) cover; (*embalaje*) wrapper, wrapping; **envoltorio** *nm* package

envolver [embol'ßer] *vt* to wrap (up); (*cubrir*) to cover; (*enemigo*) to surround; (*implicar*) to involve, implicate

envuelto [em'bwelto] *pp de* **envolver**

enyesar [enje'sar] *vt* (*pared*) to plaster; (*MED*) to put in plaster

enzarzarse [enθar'θarse] *vr*: **~ en** (*pelea*) to get mixed up in; (*disputa*) to get involved in

épica ['epika] *nf* epic

épico, a ['epiko, a] *adj* epic

epidemia [epi'ðemja] *nf* epidemic

epilepsia [epi'lepsja] *nf* epilepsy

epílogo [e'piloxo] *nm* epilogue

episodio [epi'soðjo] *nm* episode

epístola [e'pistola] *nf* epistle

época ['epoka] *nf* period, time; (*HISTORIA*) age, epoch; **hacer ~** to be epoch-making

equilibrar [ekili'ßrar] *vt* to balance; **equilibrio** *nm* balance, equilibrium; **equilibrista** *nm/f* (*funámbulo*) tightrope walker; (*acróbata*) acrobat

equipaje [eki'paxe] *nm* luggage; (*avíos*): **~ de mano** hand luggage

equipar [eki'par] *vt* (*proveer*) to equip

equipararse [ekipa'rarse] *vr*: **~ con** to be on a level with

equipo [e'kipo] *nm* (*conjunto de cosas*) equipment; (*DEPORTE*) team; (*de obreros*) shift

equis ['ekis] *nf inv* (the letter) X

equitación [ekita'θjon] *nf* horse riding

equitativo, a [ekita'tiβo, a] *adj* equitable, fair

equivalente [ekiβa'lente] *adj, nm* equivalent

equivaler [ekiβa'ler] *vi* to be equivalent *o* equal

equivocación [ekiβoka'θjon] *nf* mistake, error

equivocado, a [ekiβo'kaðo, a] *adj* wrong, mistaken

equivocarse [ekiβo'karse] *vr* to be wrong, make a mistake; **~ de camino** to take the wrong road

equívoco, a [e'kiβoko, a] *adj* (*dudoso*) suspect; (*ambiguo*) ambiguous ♦ *nm* ambiguity; (*malentendido*) misunderstanding

era ['era] *vb ver* **ser** ♦ *nf* era, age

erais *vb ver* **ser**

éramos *vb ver* **ser**

eran *vb ver* **ser**

erario [e'rarjo] *nm* exchequer (*BRIT*), treasury

eras *vb ver* **ser**

erección [erek'θjon] *nf* erection

eres *vb ver* **ser**

erguir [er'ɣir] *vt* to raise, lift; (*poner derecho*) to straighten; **~se** *vr* to straighten up

erigir [eri'xir] *vt* to erect, build; **~se** *vr*: **~se en** to set o.s. up as

erizarse [eri'θarse] *vr* (*pelo: de perro*) to bristle; (: *de persona*) to stand on end

erizo [e'riðo] *nm* (*ZOOL*) hedgehog; **~ de mar** sea-urchin

ermita [er'mita] *nf* hermitage

ermitaño, a [ermi'tano, a] *nm/f* hermit

erosión [ero'sjon] *nf* erosion

erosionar [erosjo'nar] *vt* to erode

erótico, a [e'rotiko, a] *adj* erotic; **erotismo** *nm* eroticism

erradicar [erraði'kar] *vt* to eradicate

errante [e'rrante] *adj* wandering, errant

errar [e'rrar] *vi* (*vagar*) to wander, roam; (*equivocarse*) to be mistaken ♦ *vt*: **~ el camino** to take the wrong road; **~ el tiro** to miss

erróneo, a [e'rroneo, a] *adj* (*equivocado*) wrong, mistaken

error [e'rror] *nm* error, mistake; (*INFORM*) bug; **~ de imprenta** misprint

eructar [eruk'tar] *vt* to belch, burp

erudito, a [eru'ðito, a] *adj* erudite, learned

erupción [erup'θjon] *nf* eruption; (*MED*) rash

es *vb ver* **ser**

esa ['esa] (*pl* **esas**) *adj demos ver* **ese**

ésa ['esa] (*pl* **ésas**) *pron ver* **ése**

esbelto, a [es'βelto, a] *adj* slim, slender

esbozo [es'βoθo] *nm* sketch, outline

escabeche [eska'βetʃe] *nm* brine; (*de aceitunas etc*) pickle; **en ~** pickled

escabroso, a [eska'βroso, a] *adj* (*accidentado*) rough, uneven; (*fig*) tough, difficult; (: *atrevido*) risqué

escabullirse [eskaβu'ʎirse] *vr* to slip away, to clear out

escafandra [eska'fandra] *nf* (*buzo*) diving suit; (*~ espacial*) space suit

escala [es'kala] *nf* (*proporción, MUS*) scale; (*de mano*) ladder; (*AVIAT*) stopover; **hacer ~ en** to stop *o* call in at

escalafón [eskala'fon] *nm* (*escala de salarios*) salary scale, wage scale

escalar [eska'lar] *vt* to climb, scale

escalera [eska'lera] *nf* stairs *pl*, staircase; (*escala*) ladder; (*NAIPES*) run; **~ mecánica** escalator; **~ de caracol** spiral staircase

escalfar [eskal'far] *vt* (*huevos*) to poach

escalinata [eskali'nata] *nf* staircase

escalofriante [eskalo'frjante] *adj* chilling

escalofrío [eskalo'frio] *nm* (*MED*) chill; **~s** *nmpl* (*fig*) shivers

escalón [eska'lon] *nm* step, stair; (*de escalera*) rung

escalope [eska'lope] *nm* (*CULIN*) escalope

escama [es'kama] *nf* (*de pez, serpiente*) scale; (*de jabón*) flake; (*fig*) resentment

escamar [eska'mar] *vt* (*fig*) to make wary *o* suspicious

escamotear [eskamote'ar] *vt* (*robar*) to lift, swipe; (*hacer desaparecer*) to make disappear

escampar [eskam'par] *vb impers* to stop raining

escandalizar [eskandali'θar] *vt* to scandalize, shock; **~se** *vr* to be shocked; (*ofenderse*) to be offended

escándalo [es'kandalo] *nm* scandal; (*alboroto, tumulto*) row, uproar; **escandaloso, a** *adj* scandalous, shocking

escandinavo, a [eskandi'naβo, a] *adj*, *nm/f* Scandinavian

escaño [es'kaɲo] *nm* bench; (*POL*) seat

escapar [eska'par] *vi* (*gen*) to escape, run away; (*DEPORTE*) to break away; **~se** *vr* to escape, get away; (*agua, gas*) to leak (out)

escaparate [eskapa'rate] *nm* shop window

escape [es'kape] *nm* (*de agua, gas*) leak; (*de motor*) exhaust

escarabajo [eskara'βaxo] *nm* beetle

escaramuza [eskara'muθa] *nf* skirmish

escarbar [eskar'βar] *vt* (*tierra*) to scratch

escarceos [eskar'θeos] *nmpl* (*fig*): **en mis ~ con la política ...** in my dealings with politics ...; **~ amorosos** love affairs

escarcha [es'kartʃa] *nf* frost

escarchado, a [eskar'tʃaðo, a] *adj* (*CULIN: fruta*) crystallized

escarlata [eskar'lata] *adj inv* scarlet; **escarlatina** *nf* scarlet fever

escarmentar [eskarmen'tar] *vt* to punish severely ♦ *vi* to learn one's lesson

escarmiento *etc* [eskar'mjento] *vb ver* **escarmentar** ♦ *nm* (*ejemplo*) lesson; (*castigo*) punishment

escarnio [es'karnjo] *nm* mockery; (*injuria*) insult

escarola [eska'rola] *nf* endive

escarpado, a [eskar'paðo, a] *adj* (*pendiente*) sheer, steep; (*rocas*) craggy

escasear [eskase'ar] *vi* to be scarce

escasez [eska'seθ] *nf* (*falta*) shortage, scarcity; (*pobreza*) poverty

escaso, a [es'kaso, a] *adj* (*poco*) scarce; (*raro*) rare; (*ralo*) thin, sparse; (*limitado*) limited

escatimar [eskati'mar] *vt* to skimp (on), be sparing with

escayola [eska'jola] *nf* plaster

escena [es'θena] *nf* scene

escenario [esθe'narjo] *nm* (*TEATRO*) stage; (*CINE*) set; (*fig*) scene; **escenografía** *nf* set design

escepticismo [esθepti'θismo] *nm* scepticism; **escéptico, a** *adj* sceptical ♦ *nm/f* sceptic

escisión [esθi'sjon] *nf* (*de partido, secta*) split

esclarecer [esklare'θer] *vt* (*misterio, problema*) to shed light on

esclavitud [esklaβi'tuð] *nf* slavery

esclavizar [esklaβi'θar] *vt* to enslave

esclavo, a [es'klaβo, a] *nm/f* slave

esclusa [es'klusa] *nf* (*de canal*) lock; (*compuerta*) floodgate

escoba [es'koβa] *nf* broom; **escobilla** *nf* brush

escocer [esko'θer] *vi* to burn, sting; **~se** *vr* to chafe, get chafed

escocés, esa [esko'θes, esa] *adj* Scottish ♦ *nm/f* Scotsman/woman, Scot

Escocia [es'koθja] *nf* Scotland

escoger [esko'xer] *vt* to choose, pick, select; **escogido, a** *adj* chosen, selected

escolar [esko'lar] *adj* school *cpd* ♦ *nm/f* schoolboy/girl, pupil

escollo [es'koʎo] *nm* (*obstáculo*) pitfall

escolta [es'kolta] *nf* escort; **escoltar** *vt* to escort

escombros [es'kombros] *nmpl* (*basura*) rubbish *sg*; (*restos*) debris *sg*

esconder [eskon'der] *vt* to hide, conceal; **~se** *vr* to hide; **escondidas** (*AM*) *nfpl*: **a escondidas** secretly; **escondite** *nm* hiding place; (*juego*) hide-and-seek; **escondrijo** *nm* hiding place, hideout

escopeta [esko'peta] *nf* shotgun

escoria [es'korja] *nf* (*de alto horno*) slag; (*fig*) scum, dregs *pl*

Escorpio [es'korpjo] *nm* Scorpio

escorpión [eskor'pjon] *nm* scorpion

escotado, a [esko'taðo, a] *adj* low-cut

escote [es'kote] *nm* (*de vestido*) low neck;

pagar a ~ to share the expenses

escotilla [esko'tiʎa] *nf* (NAUT) hatch(way)

escozor [esko'θor] *nm* (*dolor*) sting(ing)

escribir [eskri'ßir] *vt, vi* to write; **~ a máquina** to type; **¿cómo se escribe?** how do you spell it?

escrito, a [es'krito, a] *pp de* **escribir** ♦ *nm* (*documento*) document; (*manuscrito*) text, manuscript; **por ~** in writing

escritor, a [eskri'tor, a] *nm/f* writer

escritorio [eskri'torjo] *nm* desk

escritura [eskri'tura] *nf* (*acción*) writing; (*caligrafía*) (hand)writing; (JUR: *documento*) deed

escrúpulo [es'krupulo] *nm* scruple; (*minuciosidad*) scrupulousness; **escrupuloso, a** *adj* scrupulous

escrutar [eskru'tar] *vt* to scrutinize, examine; (*votos*) to count

escrutinio [eskru'tinjo] *nm* (*examen atento*) scrutiny; (POL: *recuento de votos*) count(ing)

escuadra [es'kwaðra] *nf* (MIL *etc*) squad; (NAUT) squadron; (*de coches etc*) fleet; **escuadrilla** *nf* (*de aviones*) squadron; (AM: *de obreros*) gang

escuadrón [eskwa'ðron] *nm* squadron

escuálido, a [es'kwaliðo, a] *adj* skinny, scraggy; (*sucio*) squalid

escuchar [esku'tʃar] *vt* to listen to ♦ *vi* to listen

escudilla [esku'ðiʎa] *nf* bowl, basin

escudo [es'kuðo] *nm* shield

escudriñar [eskuðri'ɲar] *vt* (*examinar*) to investigate, scrutinize; (*mirar de lejos*) to scan

escuela [es'kwela] *nf* school; **~ de artes y oficios** (ESP) ≈ technical college; **~ normal** teacher training college

escueto, a [es'kweto, a] *adj* plain; (*estilo*) simple

escuincle [es'kwinkle] (AM: *fam*) *nm/f* kid

esculpir [eskul'pir] *vt* to sculpt; (*grabar*) to engrave; (*tallar*) to carve; **escultor, a** *nm/f* sculptor/tress; **escultura** *nf* sculpture

escupidera [eskupi'ðera] *nf* spittoon

escupir [esku'pir] *vt, vi* to spit (out)

escurreplatos [eskurre'platos] *nm inv* plate rack

escurridizo, a [eskurri'ðiθo, a] *adj* slippery

escurridor [eskurri'ðor] *nm* colander

escurrir [esku'rrir] *vt* (*ropa*) to wring out; (*verduras, platos*) to drain ♦ *vi* (*líquidos*) to drip; **~se** *vr* (*secarse*) to drain; (*resbalarse*) to slip, slide; (*escaparse*) to slip away

ese ['ese] (*f* **esa**, *pl* **esos, esas**) *adj demos* (*sg*) that; (*pl*) those

ése ['ese] (*f* **ésa**, *pl* **ésos, ésas**) *pron* (*sg*) that (one); (*pl*) those (ones); **~ ... éste ...** the former ... the latter ...; **no me vengas con ésas** don't give me any more of that nonsense

esencia [e'senθja] *nf* essence; **esencial** *adj* essential

esfera [es'fera] *nf* sphere; (*de reloj*) face; **esférico, a** *adj* spherical

esforzarse [esfor'θarse] *vr* to exert o.s., make an effort

esfuerzo *etc* [es'fwerθo] *vb ver* **esforzar** ♦ *nm* effort

esfumarse [esfu'marse] *vr* (*apoyo, esperanzas*) to fade away

esgrima [es'ɣrima] *nf* fencing

esgrimir [esɣri'mir] *vt* (*arma*) to brandish; (*argumento*) to use

esguince [es'ɣinθe] *nm* (MED) sprain

eslabón [esla'ßon] *nm* link

eslip [es'lip] *nm* pants *pl* (BRIT), briefs *pl*

eslovaco, a [eslo'ßako, a] *adj, nm/f* Slovak, Slovakian ♦ *nm* (LING) Slovak, Slovakian

Eslovaquia [eslo'ßakja] *nf* Slovakia

esmaltar [esmal'tar] *vt* to enamel; **esmalte** *nm* enamel; **esmalte de uñas** nail varnish *o* polish

esmerado, a [esme'raðo, a] *adj* careful, neat

esmeralda [esme'ralda] *nf* emerald

esmerarse [esme'rarse] *vr* (*aplicarse*) to take great pains, exercise great care; (*afanarse*) to work hard

esmero [es'mero] *nm* (great) care

esnob [es'nob] (*pl* **~s**) *adj* (*persona*) snobbish ♦ *nm/f* snob; **~ismo** *nm* snobbery

eso ['eso] *pron* that, that thing *o* matter; **~ de su coche** that business about his car; **~ de ir al cine** all that about going to the cinema; **a ~ de las cinco** at about five o'clock; **en ~** thereupon, at that point; **~ es** that's it; **¡~ sí que es vida!** now that is really living!; **por ~ te lo dije** that's why I told you; **y ~ que llovía** in spite of the fact it was raining

esos ['esos] *adj demos ver* **ese**

ésos ['esos] *pron ver* **ése**

espabilar *etc* [espaβi'lar] = **despabilar** *etc*

espacial [espa'θjal] *adj* (*del espacio*) space *cpd*

espaciar [espa'θjar] *vt* to space (out)

espacio [es'paθjo] *nm* space; (*MUS*) interval; (*RADIO, TV*) programme (*BRIT*), program (*US*); **el ~** space; **~so, a** *adj* spacious, roomy

espada [es'paða] *nf* sword; **~s** *nfpl* (*NAIPES*) spades

espaguetis [espa'ɣetis] *nmpl* spaghetti *sg*

espalda [es'palda] *nf* (*gen*) back; **~s** *nfpl* (*hombros*) shoulders; **a ~s de uno** behind sb's back; **tenderse de ~s** to lie (down) on one's back; **volver la ~ a alguien** to cold-shoulder sb

espantajo [espan'taxo] *nm* = **espanta-pájaros**

espantapájaros [espanta'paxaros] *nm inv* scarecrow

espantar [espan'tar] *vt* (*asustar*) to frighten, scare; (*ahuyentar*) to frighten off; (*asombrar*) to horrify, appal; **~se** *vr* to get frightened *o* scared; to be appalled

espanto [es'panto] *nm* (*susto*) fright; (*terror*) terror; (*asombro*) astonishment; **~so, a** *adj* frightening; terrifying; astonishing

España [es'paɲa] *nf* Spain; **español, a** *adj* Spanish ♦ *nm/f* Spaniard ♦ *nm* (*LING*) Spanish

esparadrapo [espara'ðrapo] *nm* (sticking) plaster (*BRIT*), adhesive tape (*US*)

esparcimiento [esparθi'mjento] *nm* (*dispersión*) spreading; (*diseminación*) scattering; (*fig*) cheerfulness

esparcir [espar'θir] *vt* to spread; (*diseminar*) to scatter; **~se** *vr* to spread (out); to scatter; (*divertirse*) to enjoy o.s.

espárrago [es'parraɣo] *nm* asparagus

esparto [es'parto] *nm* esparto (grass)

espasmo [es'pasmo] *nm* spasm

espátula [es'patula] *nf* spatula

especia [es'peθja] *nf* spice

especial [espe'θjal] *adj* special; **~idad** *nf* speciality (*BRIT*), specialty (*US*)

especie [es'peθje] *nf* (*BIO*) species; (*clase*) kind, sort; **en ~** in kind

especificar [espeθifi'kar] *vt* to specify; **específico, a** *adj* specific

espécimen [es'peθimen] (*pl* **especímenes**) *nm* specimen

espectáculo [espek'takulo] *nm* (*gen*) spectacle; (*TEATRO etc*) show

espectador, a [espekta'ðor, a] *nm/f* spectator

espectro [es'pektro] *nm* ghost; (*fig*) spectre

especular [espeku'lar] *vt, vi* to speculate

espejismo [espe'xismo] *nm* mirage

espejo [es'pexo] *nm* mirror; **~ retrovisor** rear-view mirror

espeluznante [espeluθ'nante] *adj* horrifying, hair-raising

espera [es'pera] *nf* (*pausa, intervalo*) wait; (*JUR: plazo*) respite; **en ~ de** waiting for; (*con expectativa*) expecting

esperanza [espe'ranθa] *nf* (*confianza*) hope; (*expectativa*) expectation; **hay pocas ~s de que venga** there is little prospect of his coming

esperar [espe'rar] *vt* (*aguardar*) to wait for; (*tener expectativa de*) to expect; (*desear*) to hope for ♦ *vi* to wait; to expect; to hope

esperma [es'perma] *nf* sperm

espesar [espe'sar] *vt* to thicken; **~se** *vr* to thicken, get thicker

espeso, a [es'peso, a] *adj* thick; **espesor**

nm thickness

espía [es'pia] *nm/f* spy; **espiar** *vt* (*observar*) to spy on

espiga [es'piɣa] *nf* (*BOT: de trigo etc*) ear

espigón [espi'ɣon] *nm* (*BOT*) ear; (*NAUT*) breakwater

espina [es'pina] *nf* thorn; (*de pez*) bone; ~ **dorsal** (*ANAT*) spine

espinaca [espi'naka] *nf* spinach

espinazo [espi'naθo] *nm* spine, backbone

espinilla [espi'niʎa] *nf* (*ANAT: tibia*) shin(bone); (*grano*) blackhead

espinoso, a [espi'noso, a] *adj* (*planta*) thorny, prickly; (*asunto*) difficult

espionaje [espjo'naxe] *nm* spying, espionage

espiral [espi'ral] *adj*, *nf* spiral

espirar [espi'rar] *vt* to breathe out, exhale

espiritista [espiri'tista] *adj*, *nm/f* spiritualist

espíritu [es'piritu] *nm* spirit; **espiritual** *adj* spiritual

espita [es'pita] *nf* tap

espléndido, a [es'plendiðo, a] *adj* (*magnífico*) magnificent, splendid; (*generoso*) generous

esplendor [esplen'dor] *nm* splendour

espolear [espole'ar] *vt* to spur on

espoleta [espo'leta] *nf* (*de bomba*) fuse

espolón [espo'lon] *nm* sea wall

espolvorear [espolβore'ar] *vt* to dust, sprinkle

esponja [es'ponxa] *nf* sponge; (*fig*) sponger; **esponjoso, a** *adj* spongy

espontaneidad [espontanei'ðað] *nf* spontaneity; **espontáneo, a** *adj* spontaneous

esposa [es'posa] *nf* wife; ~**s** *nfpl* handcuffs; **esposar** *vt* to handcuff

esposo [es'poso] *nm* husband

espray [es'prai] *nm* spray

espuela [es'pwela] *nf* spur

espuma [es'puma] *nf* foam; (*de cerveza*) froth, head; (*de jabón*) lather; **espumadera** *nf* (*utensilio*) skimmer; **espumoso, a** *adj* frothy, foamy; (*vino*) sparkling

esqueleto [eske'leto] *nm* skeleton

esquema [es'kema] *nm* (*diagrama*) diagram; (*dibujo*) plan; (*FILOSOFÍA*) schema

esquí [es'ki] (*pl* ~**s**) *nm* (*objeto*) ski; (*DEPORTE*) skiing; ~ **acuático** water-skiing; **esquiar** *vi* to ski

esquilar [eski'lar] *vt* to shear

esquimal [eski'mal] *adj*, *nm/f* Eskimo

esquina [es'kina] *nf* corner

esquinazo [eski'naθo] *nm*: **dar ~ a algn** to give sb the slip

esquirol [eski'rol] *nm* blackleg

esquivar [eski'βar] *vt* to avoid

esquivo, a [es'kiβo, a] *adj* evasive; (*tímido*) reserved; (*huraño*) unsociable

esta ['esta] *adj demos ver* **este²**

está *vb ver* **estar**

ésta ['esta] *pron ver* **éste**

estabilidad [estaβili'ðað] *nf* stability; **estable** *adj* stable

establecer [estaβle'θer] *vt* to establish; ~**se** *vr* to establish o.s.; (*echar raíces*) to settle (down); **establecimiento** *nm* establishment

establo [es'taβlo] *nm* (*AGR*) stable

estaca [es'taka] *nf* stake, post; (*de tienda de campaña*) peg

estacada [esta'kaða] *nf* (*cerca*) fence, fencing; (*palenque*) stockade

estación [esta'θjon] *nf* station; (*del año*) season; ~ **de autobuses** bus station; ~ **balnearia** seaside resort; ~ **de servicio** service station

estacionamiento [estaθjona'mjento] *nm* (*AUTO*) parking; (*MIL*) stationing

estacionar [estaθjo'nar] *vt* (*AUTO*) to park; (*MIL*) to station; ~**io, a** *adj* stationary; (*COM: mercado*) slack

estadio [es'taðjo] *nm* (*fase*) stage, phase; (*DEPORTE*) stadium

estadista [esta'ðista] *nm* (*POL*) statesman; (*ESTADÍSTICA*) statistician

estadística [esta'ðistika] *nf* figure, statistic; (*ciencia*) statistics *sg*

estado [es'taðo] *nm* (*POL: condición*) state; ~ **de ánimo** state of mind; ~ **de cuenta** bank statement; ~ **de sitio** state of siege;

~ **civil** marital status; ~ **mayor** staff; **estar
en ~** to be pregnant; **(los) E~s Unidos**
nmpl the United States (of America) *sg*
estadounidense [estaðouniˈðense] *adj*
United States *cpd*, American ♦ *nm/f*
American
estafa [esˈtafa] *nf* swindle, trick; **estafar**
vt to swindle, defraud
estafeta [estaˈfeta] *nf* (*oficina de correos*)
post office; ~ **diplomática** diplomatic bag
estáis *vb ver* **estar**
estallar [estaˈʎar] *vi* to burst; (*bomba*) to
explode, go off; (*epidemia, guerra,
rebelión*) to break out; ~ **en llanto** to
burst into tears; **estallido** *nm* explosion;
(*fig*) outbreak
estampa [esˈtampa] *nf* print, engraving
estampado, a [estamˈpaðo, a] *adj* printed
♦ *nm* (*impresión: acción*) printing;
(*: efecto*) print; (*marca*) stamping
estampar [estamˈpar] *vt* (*imprimir*) to
print; (*marcar*) to stamp; (*metal*) to
engrave; (*poner sello en*) to stamp; (*fig*)
stamp, imprint
estampida [estamˈpiða] *nf* stampede
estampido [estamˈpiðo] *nm* bang, report
están *vb ver* **estar**
estancado, a [estanˈkaðo, a] *adj* stagnant
estancar [estanˈkar] *vt* (*aguas*) to hold up,
hold back; (*COM*) to monopolize; (*fig*) to
block, hold up; **~se** *vr* to stagnate
estancia [esˈtanθja] *nf* (*permanencia*) stay;
(*sala*) room; (*AM*) farm, ranch;
estanciero (*AM*) *nm* farmer, rancher
estanco, a [esˈtanko, a] *adj* watertight
♦ *nm* tobacconist's (shop), cigar store
(*US*)

Estanco

ⓘ Cigarettes, tobacco, postage stamps
and official forms are all sold under
state monopoly in shops called an
estanco. Although tobacco products can
also be bought in bars and **quioscos** they
are generally more expensive.

estándar [esˈtandar] *adj, nm* standard;

estandarizar *vt* to standardize
estandarte [estanˈdarte] *nm* banner,
standard
estanque [esˈtanke] *nm* (*lago*) pool, pond;
(*AGR*) reservoir
estanquero, a [estanˈkero, a] *nm/f*
tobacconist
estante [esˈtante] *nm* (*armario*) rack,
stand; (*biblioteca*) bookcase; (*anaquel*)
shelf; (*AM*) prop; **estantería** *nf* shelving,
shelves *pl*
estaño [esˈtaɲo] *nm* tin

PALABRA CLAVE

estar [esˈtar] *vi* **1** (*posición*) to be; **está en
la plaza** it's in the square; **¿está Juan?** is
Juan in?; **estamos a 30 km de Junín**
we're 30 kms from Junín
2 (+*adj: estado*) to be; ~ **enfermo** to be
ill; **está muy elegante** he's looking very
smart; **¿cómo estás?** how are you
keeping?
3 (+*gerundio*) to be; **estoy leyendo** I'm
reading
4 (*uso pasivo*): **está condenado a
muerte** he's been condemned to death;
está envasado en ... it's packed in ...
5 (*con fechas*): **¿a cuántos estamos?**
what's the date today?; **estamos a 5 de
mayo** it's the 5th of May
6 (*locuciones*): **¿estamos?** (*¿de acuerdo?*)
okay?; (*¿listo?*) ready?; **¡ya está bien!**
that's enough!
7: ~ **de**: ~ **de vacaciones/viaje** to be on
holiday/away *o* on a trip; **está de
camarero** he's working as a waiter
8: ~ **para**: **está para salir** he's about to
leave; **no estoy para bromas** I'm not in
the mood for jokes
9: ~ **por** (*propuesta etc*) to be in favour
of; (*persona etc*) to support, side with;
está por limpiar it still has to be cleaned
10: ~ **sin**: ~ **sin dinero** to have no money; **está sin terminar** it isn't finished yet
♦ **~se** *vr*: **se estuvo en la cama toda la
tarde** he stayed in bed all afternoon

estas ['estas] adj demos ver **este²**

éstas ['estas] pron ver **éste**

estatal [esta'tal] adj state cpd

estático, a [es'tatiko, a] adj static

estatua [es'tatwa] nf statue

estatura [esta'tura] nf stature, height

estatuto [esta'tuto] nm (JUR) statute; (de ciudad) bye-law; (de comité) rule

este¹ ['este] nm east

este² ['este] (f **esta**, pl **estos**, **estas**) adj demos (sg) this; (pl) these

esté etc vb ver **estar**

éste ['este] (f **ésta**, pl **éstos**, **éstas**) pron (sg) this (one); (pl) these (ones); **ése ... ~ ...** the former ... the latter ....

estelar [este'lar] adj (ASTRO) stellar; (actuación, reparto) star (atr)

estén etc vb ver **estar**

estepa [es'tepa] nf (GEO) steppe

estera [es'tera] nf mat(ting)

estéreo [es'tereo] adj inv, nm stereo; **estereotipo** nm stereotype

estéril [es'teril] adj sterile, barren; (fig) vain, futile; **esterilizar** vt to sterilize

esterlina [ester'lina] adj: **libra ~** pound sterling

estés etc vb ver **estar**

estética [es'tetika] nf aesthetics sg

estético, a [es'tetiko, a] adj aesthetic

estibador [estiβa'ðor] nm stevedore, docker

estiércol [es'tjerkol] nm dung, manure

estigma [es'tiɣma] nm stigma

estilarse [esti'larse] vr to be in fashion

estilo [es'tilo] nm style; (TEC) stylus; (NATACIÓN) stroke; **algo por el ~** something along those lines

estima [es'tima] nf esteem, respect

estimación [estima'θjon] nf (evaluación) estimation; (aprecio, afecto) esteem, regard

estimar [esti'mar] vt (evaluar) to estimate; (valorar) to value; (apreciar) to esteem, respect; (pensar, considerar) to think, reckon

estimulante [estimu'lante] adj stimulating ♦ nm stimulant

estimular [estimu'lar] vt to stimulate; (excitar) to excite

estímulo [es'timulo] nm stimulus; (ánimo) encouragement

estipulación [estipula'θjon] nf stipulation, condition

estipular [estipu'lar] vt to stipulate

estirado, a [esti'raðo, a] adj (tenso) (stretched o drawn) tight; (fig: persona) stiff, pompous

estirar [esti'rar] vt to stretch; (dinero, suma etc) to stretch out; **~se** vr to stretch

estirón [esti'ron] nm pull, tug; (crecimiento) spurt, sudden growth; **dar un ~** (niño) to shoot up

estirpe [es'tirpe] nf stock, lineage

estival [esti'βal] adj summer cpd

esto ['esto] pron this, this thing o matter; **~ de la boda** this business about the wedding

Estocolmo [esto'kolmo] nm Stockholm

estofado [esto'faðo] nm stew

estofar [esto'far] vt to stew

estómago [es'tomaɣo] nm stomach; **tener ~** to be thick-skinned

estorbar [estor'βar] vt to hinder, obstruct; (molestar) to bother, disturb ♦ vi to be in the way; **estorbo** nm (molestia) bother, nuisance; (obstáculo) hindrance, obstacle

estornudar [estornu'ðar] vi to sneeze

estos ['estos] adj demos ver **este²**

éstos ['estos] pron ver **éste**

estoy vb ver **estar**

estrado [es'traðo] nm platform

estrafalario, a [estrafa'larjo, a] adj odd, eccentric

estrago [es'traɣo] nm ruin, destruction; **hacer ~s en** to wreak havoc among

estragón [estra'ɣon] nm tarragon

estrambótico, a [estram'botiko, a] adj (persona) eccentric; (peinado, ropa) outlandish

estrangulador, a [estrangula'ðor, a] nm/f strangler ♦ nm (TEC) throttle; (AUTO) choke

estrangular [estrangu'lar] vt (persona) to

strangle; (*MED*) to strangulate

estratagema [estrata'xema] *nf* (*MIL*) stratagem; (*astucia*) cunning

estrategia [estra'texja] *nf* strategy; **estratégico**, a *adj* strategic

estrato [es'trato] *nm* stratum, layer

estrechamente [es'tretʃamente] *adv* (*íntimamente*) closely, intimately; (*pobremente: vivir*) poorly

estrechar [estre'tʃar] *vt* (*reducir*) to narrow; (*COSTURA*) to take in; (*abrazar*) to hug, embrace; **~se** *vr* (*reducirse*) to narrow, grow narrow; (*abrazarse*) to embrace; **~ la mano** to shake hands

estrechez [estre'tʃeθ] *nf* narrowness; (*de ropa*) tightness; **estrecheces** *nfpl* (*dificultades económicas*) financial difficulties

estrecho, a [es'tretʃo, a] *adj* narrow; (*apretado*) tight; (*íntimo*) close, intimate; (*miserable*) mean ♦ *nm* strait; **~ de miras** narrow-minded

estrella [es'treʎa] *nf* star; **~ de mar** (*ZOOL*) starfish; **~ fugaz** shooting star; **estrellado**, a *adj* (*forma*) star-shaped; (*cielo*) starry

estrellar [estre'ʎar] *vt* (*hacer añicos*) to smash (to pieces); (*huevos*) to fry; **~se** *vr* to smash; (*chocarse*) to crash; (*fracasar*) to fail

estremecer [estreme'θer] *vt* to shake; **~se** *vr* to shake, tremble; **estremecimiento** *nm* (*temblor*) trembling, shaking

estrenar [estre'nar] *vt* (*vestido*) to wear for the first time; (*casa*) to move into; (*película, obra de teatro*) to première; **~se** *vr* (*persona*) to make one's début; **estreno** *nm* (*CINE etc*) première

estreñido, a [estre'ɲiðo, a] *adj* constipated

estreñimiento [estreɲi'mjento] *nm* constipation

estrépito [es'trepito] *nm* noise, racket; (*fig*) fuss; **estrepitoso**, a *adj* noisy; (*fiesta*) rowdy

estría [es'tria] *nf* groove

estribación [estriβa'θjon] *nf* (*GEO*) spur, foothill

estribar [estri'βar] *vi*: **~ en** to lie on

estribillo [estri'βiʎo] *nm* (*LITERATURA*) refrain; (*MUS*) chorus

estribo [es'triβo] *nm* (*de jinete*) stirrup; (*de coche, tren*) step; (*de puente*) support; (*GEO*) spur; **perder los ~s** to fly off the handle

estribor [estri'βor] *nm* (*NAUT*) starboard

estricto, a [es'trikto, a] *adj* (*riguroso*) strict; (*severo*) severe

estridente [estri'ðente] *adj* (*color*) loud; (*voz*) raucous

estropajo [estro'paxo] *nm* scourer

estropear [estrope'ar] *vt* to spoil; (*dañar*) to damage; **~se** *vr* (*objeto*) to get damaged; (*persona: la piel etc*) to be ruined

estructura [estruk'tura] *nf* structure

estruendo [es'trwendo] *nm* (*ruido*) racket, din; (*fig: alboroto*) uproar, turmoil

estrujar [estru'xar] *vt* (*apretar*) to squeeze; (*aplastar*) to crush; (*fig*) to drain, bleed

estuario [es'twarjo] *nm* estuary

estuche [es'tutʃe] *nm* box, case

estudiante [estu'ðjante] *nm/f* student; **estudiantil** *adj* student *cpd*

estudiar [estu'ðjar] *vt* to study

estudio [es'tuðjo] *nm* study; (*CINE, ARTE, RADIO*) studio; **~s** *nmpl* studies; (*erudición*) learning *sg*; **~so**, a *adj* studious

estufa [es'tufa] *nf* heater, fire

estupefaciente [estupefa'θjente] *nm* drug, narcotic

estupefacto, a [estupe'fakto, a] *adj* speechless, thunderstruck

estupendo, a [estu'pendo, a] *adj* wonderful, terrific; (*fam*) great; **¡~!** that's great!, fantastic!

estupidez [estupi'ðeθ] *nf* (*torpeza*) stupidity; (*acto*) stupid thing (to do)

estúpido, a [es'tupiðo, a] *adj* stupid, silly

estupor [estu'por] *nm* stupor; (*fig*) astonishment, amazement

estuve *etc vb ver* **estar**

esvástica [es'βastika] *nf* swastika

ETA ['eta] (*ESP*) *nf abr* (= *Euskadi ta*

Askatasuna) ETA

etapa [e'tapa] *nf (de viaje)* stage; *(DEPORTE)* leg; *(parada)* stopping place; *(fase)* stage, phase

etarra [e'tarra] *nm/f* member of ETA

etc. *abr (= etcétera)* etc

etcétera [et'θetera] *adv* etcetera

eternidad [eterni'ðað] *nf* eternity; **eterno, a** *adj* eternal, everlasting

ética ['etika] *nf* ethics *pl*

ético, a ['etiko, a] *adj* ethical

etiqueta [eti'keta] *nf (modales)* etiquette; *(rótulo)* label, tag

Eucaristía [eukaris'tia] *nf* Eucharist

eufemismo [eufe'mismo] *nm* euphemism

euforia [eu'forja] *nf* euphoria

euro ['euro] *nm (moneda)* euro

eurodiputado, a [euroðipu'taðo, a] *nm/f* Euro MP, MEP

Europa [eu'ropa] *nf* Europe; **europeo, a** *adj, nm/f* European

Euskadi [eus'kaði] *nm* the Basque Country *o* Provinces *pl*

euskera [eus'kera] *nm (LING)* Basque

evacuación [eßakwa'θjon] *nf* evacuation

evacuar [eßa'kwar] *vt* to evacuate

evadir [eßa'ðir] *vt* to evade, avoid; **~se** *vr* to escape

evaluar [eßa'lwar] *vt* to evaluate

evangelio [eßan'xeljo] *nm* gospel

evaporar [eßapo'rar] *vt* to evaporate; **~se** *vr* to vanish

evasión [eßa'sjon] *nf* escape, flight; *(fig)* evasion; **~ de capitales** flight of capital

evasiva [eßa'sißa] *nf (pretexto)* excuse

evasivo, a [eßa'sißo, a] *adj* evasive, non-committal

evento [e'ßento] *nm* event

eventual [eßen'twal] *adj* possible, conditional *(upon circumstances)*; *(trabajador)* casual, temporary

evidencia [eßi'ðenθja] *nf* evidence, proof; **evidenciar** *vt (hacer patente)* to make evident; *(probar)* to prove, show; **evidenciarse** *vr* to be evident

evidente [eßi'ðente] *adj* obvious, clear

evitar [eßi'tar] *vt (evadir)* to avoid;

(impedir) to prevent

evocar [eßo'kar] *vt* to evoke, call forth

evolución [eßolu'θjon] *nf (desarrollo)* evolution, development; *(cambio)* change; *(MIL)* manoeuvre; **evolucionar** *vi* to evolve; to manoeuvre

ex [eks] *adj* ex-; **el ~ ministro** the former minister, the ex-minister

exacerbar [eksaθer'ßar] *vt* to irritate, annoy

exactamente [eksakta'mente] *adv* exactly

exactitud [eksakti'tuð] *nf* exactness; *(precisión)* accuracy; *(puntualidad)* punctuality; **exacto, a** *adj* exact; accurate; punctual; **¡exacto!** exactly!

exageración [eksaxera'θjon] *nf* exaggeration

exagerar [eksaxe'rar] *vt, vi* to exaggerate

exaltado, a [eksal'taðo, a] *adj (apasionado)* over-excited, worked-up; *(POL)* extreme

exaltar [eksal'tar] *vt* to exalt, glorify; **~se** *vr (excitarse)* to get excited *o* worked-up

examen [ek'samen] *nm* examination

examinar [eksami'nar] *vt* to examine; **~se** *vr* to be examined, take an examination

exasperar [eksaspe'rar] *vt* to exasperate; **~se** *vr* to get exasperated, lose patience

Exca. *abr* = **Excelencia**

excavadora [ekskaßa'ðora] *nf* excavator

excavar [ekska'ßar] *vt* to excavate

excedencia [eksθe'ðenθja] *nf*: **estar en ~** to be on leave; **pedir** *o* **solicitar la ~** to ask for leave

excedente [eksθe'ðente] *adj, nm* excess, surplus

exceder [eksθe'ðer] *vt* to exceed, surpass; **~se** *vr (extralimitarse)* to go too far

excelencia [eksθe'lenθja] *nf* excellence; **E~** Excellency; **excelente** *adj* excellent

excentricidad [eksθentriθi'ðað] *nf* eccentricity; **excéntrico, a** *adj, nm/f* eccentric

excepción [eksθep'θjon] *nf* exception; **excepcional** *adj* exceptional

excepto [eks'θepto] *adv* excepting, except *(for)*

exceptuar [eksθep'twar] *vt* to except, exclude

excesivo, a [eksθe'siβo, a] *adj* excessive

exceso [eks'θeso] *nm* (*gen*) excess; (*COM*) surplus; **~ de equipaje/peso** excess luggage/weight

excitación [eksθita'θjon] *nf* (*sensación*) excitement; (*acción*) excitation

excitado, a [eksθi'taðo, a] *adj* excited; (*emociones*) aroused

excitar [eksθi'tar] *vt* to excite; (*incitar*) to urge; **~se** *vr* to get excited

exclamación [eksklama'θjon] *nf* exclamation

exclamar [ekskla'mar] *vi* to exclaim

excluir [eksklu'ir] *vt* to exclude; (*dejar fuera*) to shut out; (*descartar*) to reject; **exclusión** *nf* exclusion

exclusiva [eksklu'siβa] *nf* (*PRENSA*) exclusive, scoop; (*COM*) sole right

exclusivo, a [eksklu'siβo, a] *adj* exclusive; **derecho ~** sole *o* exclusive right

Excmo. *abr* = **excelentísimo**

excomulgar [ekskomul'var] *vt* (*REL*) to excommunicate

excomunión [ekskomu'njon] *nf* excommunication

excursión [ekskur'sjon] *nf* excursion, outing; **excursionista** *nm/f* (*turista*) sightseer

excusa [eks'kusa] *nf* excuse; (*disculpa*) apology

excusar [eksku'sar] *vt* to excuse; **~se** *vr* (*disculparse*) to apologize

exhalar [eksa'lar] *vt* to exhale, breathe out; (*olor etc*) to give off; (*suspiro*) to breathe, heave

exhaustivo, a [eksaus'tiβo, a] *adj* (*análisis*) thorough; (*estudio*) exhaustive

exhausto, a [ek'sausto, a] *adj* exhausted

exhibición [eksiβi'θjon] *nf* exhibition, display, show

exhibir [eksi'βir] *vt* to exhibit, display, show

exhortar [eksor'tar] *vt*: **~ a** to exhort to

exigencia [eksi'xenθja] *nf* demand, requirement; **exigente** *adj* demanding

exigir [eksi'xir] *vt* (*gen*) to demand, require; **~ el pago** to demand payment

exiliado, a [eksi'ljaðo, a] *adj* exiled
♦ *nm/f* exile

exilio [ek'siljo] *nm* exile

eximir [eksi'mir] *vt* to exempt

existencia [eksis'tenθja] *nf* existence; **~s** *nfpl* stock(s) (*pl*)

existir [eksis'tir] *vi* to exist, be

éxito ['eksito] *nm* (*triunfo*) success; (*MUS etc*) hit; **tener ~** to be successful

exonerar [eksone'rar] *vt* to exonerate; **~ de una obligación** to free from an obligation

exorbitante [eksorβi'tante] *adj* (*precio*) exorbitant; (*cantidad*) excessive

exorcizar [eksorθi'θar] *vt* to exorcize

exótico, a [ek'sotiko, a] *adj* exotic

expandir [ekspan'dir] *vt* to expand

expansión [ekspan'sjon] *nf* expansion

expansivo, a [ekspan'siβo, a] *adj*: **onda ~a** shock wave

expatriarse [ekspa'trjarse] *vr* to emigrate; (*POL*) to go into exile

expectativa [ekspekta'tiβa] *nf* (*espera*) expectation; (*perspectiva*) prospect

expedición [ekspeði'θjon] *nf* (*excursión*) expedition

expediente [ekspe'ðjente] *nm* expedient; (*JUR: procedimiento*) action, proceedings *pl*; (: *papeles*) dossier, file, record

expedir [ekspe'ðir] *vt* (*despachar*) to send, forward; (*pasaporte*) to issue

expendedor, a [ekspende'ðor, a] *nm/f* (*vendedor*) dealer

expensas [eks'pensas] *nfpl*: **a ~ de** at the expense of

experiencia [ekspe'rjenθja] *nf* experience

experimentado, a [eksperimen'taðo, a] *adj* experienced

experimentar [eksperimen'tar] *vt* (*en laboratorio*) to experiment with; (*probar*) to test, try out; (*notar, observar*) to experience; (*deterioro, pérdida*) to suffer; **experimento** *nm* experiment

experto, a [eks'perto, a] *adj* expert, skilled
♦ *nm/f* expert

expiar [ekspi'ar] vt to atone for
expirar [ekspi'rar] vi to expire
explanada [ekspla'naða] nf (llano) plain
explayarse [ekspla'jarse] vr (en discurso) to speak at length; ~ **con uno** to confide in sb
explicación [eksplika'θjon] nf explanation
explicar [ekspli'kar] vt to explain; ~**se** vr to explain (o.s.)
explícito, a [eks'pliθito, a] adj explicit
explique etc vb ver **explicar**
explorador, a [eksplora'ðor, a] nm/f (pionero) explorer; (MIL) scout ♦ nm (MED) probe; (TEC) (radar) scanner
explorar [eksplo'rar] vt to explore; (MED) to probe; (radar) to scan
explosión [eksplo'sjon] nf explosion; **explosivo, a** adj explosive
explotación [eksplota'θjon] nf exploitation; (de planta etc) running
explotar [eksplo'tar] vt to exploit; to run, operate ♦ vi to explode
exponer [ekspo'ner] vt to expose; (cuadro) to display; (vida) to risk; (idea) to explain; ~**se** vr: ~**se a (hacer) algo** to run the risk of (doing) sth
exportación [eksporta'θjon] nf (acción) export; (mercancías) exports pl
exportar [ekspor'tar] vt to export
exposición [eksposi'θjon] nf (gen) exposure; (de arte) show, exhibition; (explicación) explanation; (declaración) account, statement
expresamente [ekspresa'mente] adv (decir) clearly; (a propósito) expressly
expresar [ekspre'sar] vt to express; **expresión** nf expression
expresivo, a [ekspre'sißo, a] adj (persona, gesto, palabras) expressive; (cariñoso) affectionate
expreso, a [eks'preso, a] pp de **expresar** ♦ adj (explícito) express; (claro) specific, clear; (tren) fast ♦ adv: **mandar** ~ to send by express (delivery)
express [eks'pres] (AM) adv: **enviar algo** ~ to send sth special delivery
exprimidor [eksprimi'ðor] nm squeezer

exprimir [ekspri'mir] vt (fruta) to squeeze; (zumo) to squeeze out
expropiar [ekspro'pjar] vt to expropriate
expuesto, a [eks'pwesto, a] pp de **exponer** ♦ adj exposed; (cuadro etc) on show, on display
expulsar [ekspul'sar] vt (echar) to eject, throw out; (alumno) to expel; (despedir) to sack, fire; (DEPORTE) to send off; **expulsión** nf expulsion; sending-off
exquisito, a [ekski'sito, a] adj exquisite; (comida) delicious
éxtasis ['ekstasis] nm ecstasy
extender [eksten'der] vt to extend; (los brazos) to stretch out, hold out; (mapa, tela) to spread (out), open (out); (mantequilla) to spread; (certificado) to issue; (cheque, recibo) to make out; (documento) to draw up; ~**se** vr (gen) to extend; (persona: en el suelo) to stretch out; (epidemia) to spread; **extendido, a** adj (abierto) spread out, open; (brazos) outstretched; (costumbre) widespread
extensión [eksten'sjon] nf (de terreno, mar) expanse, stretch; (de tiempo) length, duration; (TEL) extension; **en toda la ~ de la palabra** in every sense of the word
extenso, a [eks'tenso, a] adj extensive
extenuar [ekste'nwar] vt (debilitar) to weaken
exterior [ekste'rjor] adj (de fuera) external; (afuera) outside, exterior; (apariencia) outward; (deuda, relaciones) foreign ♦ nm (gen) exterior, outside; (aspecto) outward appearance; (DEPORTE) wing(er); (países extranjeros) abroad; **en el** ~ abroad; **al** ~ outwardly, on the surface
exterminar [ekstermi'nar] vt to exterminate; **exterminio** nm extermination
externo, a [eks'terno, a] adj (exterior) external, outside; (superficial) outward ♦ nm/f day pupil
extinguir [ekstin'gir] vt (fuego) to extinguish, put out; (raza, población) to wipe out; ~**se** vr (fuego) to go out; (BIO) to die out, become extinct

extinto, a [eks'tinto, a] *adj* extinct
extintor [ekstin'tor] *nm* (fire) extinguisher
extirpar [ekstir'par] *vt* (MED) to remove (surgically)
extorsión [ekstor'sjon] *nf* extorsion
extra ['ekstra] *adj inv* (*tiempo*) extra; (*chocolate, vino*) good-quality ♦ *nm/f* extra ♦ *nm* extra; (*bono*) bonus
extracción [ekstrak'θjon] *nf* extraction; (*en lotería*) draw
extracto [eks'trakto] *nm* extract
extradición [ekstraði'θjon] *nf* extradition
extraer [ekstra'er] *vt* to extract, take out
extraescolar [ekstraesko'lar] *adj*: **actividad ~** extracurricular activity
extralimitarse [ekstralimi'tarse] *vr* to go too far
extranjero, a [ekstran'xero, a] *adj* foreign ♦ *nm/f* foreigner ♦ *nm* foreign countries *pl*; **en el ~** abroad
extrañar [ekstra'ɲar] *vt* (*sorprender*) to find strange *o* odd; (*echar de menos*) to miss; **~se** *vr* (*sorprenderse*) to be amazed, be surprised
extrañeza [ekstra'ɲeθa] *nf* (*rareza*) strangeness, oddness; (*asombro*) amazement, surprise
extraño, a [eks'traɲo, a] *adj* (*extranjero*) foreign; (*raro, sorprendente*) strange, odd
extraordinario, a [ekstraorði'narjo, a] *adj* extraordinary; (*edición, número*) special ♦ *nm* (*de periódico*) special edition; **horas extraordinarias** overtime *sg*
extrarradio [ekstra'rraðjo] *nm* suburbs
extravagancia [ekstraβa'vanθja] *nf* oddness; outlandishness; **extravagante** *adj* (*excéntrico*) eccentric; (*estrafalario*) outlandish
extraviado, a [ekstra'βjaðo, a] *adj* lost, missing
extraviar [ekstra'βjar] *vt* (*persona: desorientar*) to mislead, misdirect; (*perder*) to lose, misplace; **~se** *vr* to lose one's way, get lost; **extravío** *nm* loss; (*fig*) deviation
extremar [ekstre'mar] *vt* to carry to extremes; **~se** *vr* to do one's utmost,

make every effort
extremaunción [ekstremaun'θjon] *nf* extreme unction
extremidad [ekstremi'ðað] *nf* (*punta*) extremity; **~es** *nfpl* (ANAT) extremities
extremo, a [eks'tremo, a] *adj* extreme; (*último*) last ♦ *nm* end; (*límite, grado sumo*) extreme; **en último ~** as a last resort
extrovertido, a [ekstroβer'tiðo, a] *adj, nm/f* extrovert
exuberancia [eksuβe'ranθja] *nf* exuberance; **exuberante** *adj* exuberant; (*fig*) luxuriant, lush
eyacular [eʝaku'lar] *vt, vi* to ejaculate

F, f

f.a.b. *abr* (= *franco a bordo*) f.o.b.
fabada [fa'βaða] *nf* bean and sausage stew
fábrica ['faβrika] *nf* factory; **marca de ~** trademark; **precio de ~** factory price
fabricación [faβrika'θjon] *nf* (*manufactura*) manufacture; (*producción*) production; **de ~ casera** home-made; **~ en serie** mass production
fabricante [faβri'kante] *nm/f* manufacturer
fabricar [faβri'kar] *vt* (*manufacturar*) to manufacture, make; (*construir*) to build; (*cuento*) to fabricate, devise
fábula ['faβula] *nf* (*cuento*) fable; (*chisme*) rumour; (*mentira*) fib
fabuloso, a [faβu'loso, a] *adj* (*oportunidad, tiempo*) fabulous, great
facción [fak'θjon] *nf* (POL) faction; **facciones** *nfpl* (*del rostro*) features
faceta [fa'θeta] *nf* facet
facha ['fatʃa] (*fam*) *nf* (*aspecto*) look; (*cara*) face
fachada [fa'tʃaða] *nf* (ARQ) façade, front
fácil ['faθil] *adj* (*simple*) easy; (*probable*) likely
facilidad [faθili'ðað] *nf* (*capacidad*) ease; (*sencillez*) simplicity; (*de palabra*) fluency; **~es** *nfpl* facilities

facilitar [faθili'tar] *vt* (*hacer fácil*) to make easy; (*proporcionar*) to provide

fácilmente ['faθilmente] *adv* easily

facsímil [fak'simil] *nm* facsimile, fax

factible [fak'tiβle] *adj* feasible

factor [fak'tor] *nm* factor

factura [fak'tura] *nf* (*cuenta*) bill; **facturación** *nf* (*de equipaje*) check-in; **facturar** *vt* (*COM*) to invoice, charge for; (*equipaje*) to check in

facultad [fakul'taθ] *nf* (*aptitud, ESCOL etc*) faculty; (*poder*) power

faena [fa'ena] *nf* (*trabajo*) work; (*quehacer*) task, job

faisán [fai'san] *nm* pheasant

faja ['faxa] *nf* (*para la cintura*) sash; (*de mujer*) corset; (*de tierra*) strip

fajo ['faxo] *nm* (*de papeles*) bundle; (*de billetes*) wad

falacia [fa'laθja] *nf* fallacy

falda ['falda] *nf* (*prenda de vestir*) skirt

falla ['faʎa] *nf* (*defecto*) fault, flaw

fallar [fa'ʎar] *vt* (*JUR*) to pronounce sentence on ♦ *vi* (*memoria*) to fail; (*motor*) to miss

---
Fallas
---

i In the week of 19 March (the feast of San José), Valencia honours its patron saint with a spectacular fiesta called **Las Fallas**. The **Fallas** are huge papier-mâché, cardboard and wooden sculptures which are built by competing teams throughout the year. They depict politicians and well-known public figures and are thrown onto bonfires and set alight once a jury has judged them - only the best sculpture escapes the flames.

---

fallecer [faʎe'θer] *vi* to pass away, die; **fallecimiento** *nm* decease, demise

fallido, a [fa'ʎiðo, a] *adj* (*gen*) frustrated, unsuccessful

fallo ['faʎo] *nm* (*JUR*) verdict, ruling; (*fracaso*) failure; **~ cardíaco** heart failure

falsedad [false'ðaθ] *nf* falseness; (*hipocresía*) hypocrisy; (*mentira*) falsehood

falsificar [falsifi'kar] *vt* (*firma etc*) to forge; (*moneda*) to counterfeit

falso, a ['falso, a] *adj* false; (*documento, moneda etc*) fake; **en ~** falsely

falta ['falta] *nf* (*defecto*) fault, flaw; (*privación*) lack, want; (*ausencia*) absence; (*carencia*) shortage; (*equivocación*) mistake; (*DEPORTE*) foul; **echar en ~** to miss; **hacer ~ hacer algo** to be necessary to do sth; **me hace ~ una pluma** I need a pen; **~ de educación** bad manners *pl*

faltar [fal'tar] *vi* (*escasear*) to be lacking, be wanting; (*ausentarse*) to be absent, be missing; **faltan 2 horas para llegar** there are 2 hours to go till arrival; **~ al respeto a uno** to be disrespectful to sb; **¡no faltaba más!** (*no hay de qué*) don't mention it

fama ['fama] *nf* (*renombre*) fame; (*reputación*) reputation

famélico, a [fa'meliko, a] *adj* starving

familia [fa'milja] *nf* family; **~ política** in-laws *pl*

familiar [fami'ljar] *adj* (*relativo a la familia*) family *cpd*; (*conocido, informal*) familiar ♦ *nm* relative, relation; **~idad** *nf* (*gen*) familiarity; (*informalidad*) homeliness; **~izarse** *vr*: **~izarse con** to familiarize o.s. with

famoso, a [fa'moso, a] *adj* (*renombrado*) famous

fanático, a [fa'natiko, a] *adj* fanatical ♦ *nm/f* fanatic; (*CINE, DEPORTE*) fan; **fanatismo** *nm* fanaticism

fanfarrón, ona [fanfa'rron, ona] *adj* boastful

fango ['fango] *nm* mud; **~so, a** *adj* muddy

fantasía [fanta'sia] *nf* fantasy, imagination; **joyas de ~** imitation jewellery *sg*

fantasma [fan'tasma] *nm* (*espectro*) ghost, apparition; (*fanfarrón*) show-off

fantástico, a [fan'tastiko, a] *adj* fantastic

farmacéutico, a [farma'θeutiko, a] *adj* pharmaceutical ♦ *nm/f* chemist (*BRIT*), pharmacist

farmacia [far'maθja] *nf* chemist's (shop)

(*BRIT*), pharmacy; ~ **de turno** duty chemist; ~ **de guardia** all-night chemist

fármaco ['farmako] *nm* drug

faro ['faro] *nm* (*NAUT: torre*) lighthouse; (*AUTO*) headlamp; **~s antiniebla** fog lamps; **~s delanteros/traseros** headlights/rear lights

farol [fa'rol] *nm* lantern, lamp

farola [fa'rola] *nf* street lamp (*BRIT*) *o* light (*US*)

farsa ['farsa] *nf* (*gen*) farce

farsante [far'sante] *nm/f* fraud, fake

fascículo [fas'θikulo] *nm* (*de revista*) part, instalment

fascinar [fasθi'nar] *vt* (*gen*) to fascinate

fascismo [fas'θismo] *nm* fascism; **fascista** *adj, nm/f* fascist

fase ['fase] *nf* phase

fastidiar [fasti'ðjar] *vt* (*molestar*) to annoy, bother; (*estropear*) to spoil; **~se** *vr*: **¡que se fastidie!** (*fam*) he'll just have to put up with it!

fastidio [fas'tiðjo] *nm* (*molestia*) annoyance; **~so, a** *adj* (*molesto*) annoying

fastuoso, a [fas'twoso, a] *adj* (*banquete, boda*) lavish; (*acto*) pompous

fatal [fa'tal] *adj* (*gen*) fatal; (*desgraciado*) ill-fated; (*fam: malo, pésimo*) awful; **~idad** *nf* (*destino*) fate; (*mala suerte*) misfortune

fatiga [fa'tiɣa] *nf* (*cansancio*) fatigue, weariness

fatigar [fati'ɣar] *vt* to tire, weary; **~se** *vr* to get tired

fatigoso, a [fati'ɣoso, a] *adj* (*cansador*) tiring

fatuo, a ['fatwo, a] *adj* (*vano*) fatuous; (*presuntuoso*) conceited

favor [fa'ßor] *nm* favour; **estar a ~ de** to be in favour of; **haga el ~ de...** would you be so good as to..., kindly...; **por ~** please; **~able** *adj* favourable

favorecer [faßore'θer] *vt* to favour; (*vestido etc*) to become, flatter; **este peinado le favorece** this hairstyle suits him

favorito, a [faßo'rito, a] *adj, nm/f* favourite

fax [faks] *nm inv* fax; **mandar por ~** to fax

faz [faθ] *nf* face; **la ~ de la tierra** the face of the earth

fe [fe] *nf* (*REL*) faith; (*documento*) certificate; **prestar ~ a** to believe, credit; **actuar con buena/mala ~** to act in good/bad faith; **dar ~ de** to bear witness to

fealdad [feal'dað] *nf* ugliness

febrero [fe'ßrero] *nm* February

febril [fe'ßril] *adj* (*actividad*) hectic; (*mente, mirada*) feverish

fecha ['fetʃa] *nf* date; **~ de caducidad** (*de producto alimenticio*) sell-by date; (*de contrato etc*) expiry date; **con ~ adelantada** postdated; **en ~ próxima** soon; **hasta la ~** to date, so far; **poner ~** to date; **fechar** *vt* to date

fecundar [fekun'dar] *vt* (*generar*) to fertilize, make fertile; **fecundo, a** *adj* (*fértil*) fertile; (*fig*) prolific; (*productivo*) productive

federación [feðera'θjon] *nf* federation

felicidad [feliθi'ðað] *nf* happiness; **~es** *nfpl* (*felicitaciones*) best wishes, congratulations

felicitación [feliθita'θjon] *nf*: **¡felicitaciones!** congratulations!

felicitar [feliθi'tar] *vt* to congratulate

feligrés, esa [feli'ɣres, esa] *nm/f* parishioner

feliz [fe'liθ] *adj* happy

felpudo [fel'puðo] *nm* doormat

femenino, a [feme'nino, a] *adj, nm* feminine

feminista [femi'nista] *adj, nm/f* feminist

fenómeno [fe'nomeno] *nm* phenomenon; (*fig*) freak, accident ♦ *adj* great ♦ *excl* great!, marvellous!; **fenomenal** *adj* = **fenómeno**

feo, a ['feo, a] *adj* (*gen*) ugly; (*desagradable*) bad, nasty

féretro ['feretro] *nm* (*ataúd*) coffin; (*sarcófago*) bier

feria ['ferja] *nf* (*gen*) fair; (*descanso*) holiday, rest day; (*AM: mercado*) village market; (: *cambio*) loose *o* small change

fermentar [fermen'tar] *vi* to ferment
ferocidad [feroθi'ðað] *nf* fierceness, ferocity
feroz [fe'roθ] *adj* (*cruel*) cruel; (*salvaje*) fierce
férreo, a ['ferreo, a] *adj* iron
ferretería [ferrete'ria] *nf* (*tienda*) ironmonger's (shop) (*BRIT*), hardware store
ferrocarril [ferroka'rril] *nm* railway
ferroviario, a [ferro'βjarjo, a] *adj* rail *cpd*
fértil ['fertil] *adj* (*productivo*) fertile; (*rico*) rich; **fertilidad** *nf* (*gen*) fertility; (*productividad*) fruitfulness
ferviente [fer'βjente] *adj* fervent
fervor [fer'βor] *nm* fervour; ~oso, a *adj* fervent
festejar [feste'xar] *vt* (*celebrar*) to celebrate
festejo [fes'texo] *nm* celebration; **festejos** *nmpl* (*fiestas*) festivals
festín [fes'tin] *nm* feast, banquet
festival [festi'βal] *nm* festival
festividad [festiβi'ðað] *nf* festivity
festivo, a [fes'tiβo, a] *adj* (*de fiesta*) festive; (*CINE, LITERATURA*) humorous; **día ~** holiday
fétido, a ['fetiðo, a] *adj* foul-smelling
feto ['feto] *nm* foetus
fiable ['fjaβle] *adj* (*persona*) trustworthy; (*máquina*) reliable
fiador, a [fja'ðor, a] *nm/f* (*JUR*) surety, guarantor; (*COM*) backer; **salir ~ por uno** to stand bail for sb
fiambre ['fjambre] *nm* cold meat
fianza ['fjanθa] *nf* surety; (*JUR*): **libertad bajo ~** release on bail
fiar [fi'ar] *vt* (*salir garante de*) to guarantee; (*vender a crédito*) to sell on credit; (*secreto*): **~ a** to confide (to) ♦ *vi* to trust; **~se** *vr* to trust (in), rely on; **~se de uno** to rely on sb
fibra ['fiβra] *nf* fibre; **~ óptica** optical fibre
ficción [fik'θjon] *nf* fiction
ficha ['fitʃa] *nf* (*TEL*) token; (*en juegos*) counter, marker; (*tarjeta*) (index) card; **fichar** *vt* (*archivar*) to file, index; (*DEPORTE*) to sign; **estar fichado** to have

a record; **fichero** *nm* box file; (*INFORM*) file
ficticio, a [fik'tiθjo, a] *adj* (*imaginario*) fictitious; (*falso*) fabricated
fidelidad [fiðeli'ðað] *nf* (*lealtad*) fidelity, loyalty; **alta ~** high fidelity, hi-fi
fideos [fi'ðeos] *nmpl* noodles
fiebre ['fjeβre] *nf* (*MED*) fever; (*fig*) fever, excitement; **~ amarilla/del heno** yellow/hay fever; **~ palúdica** malaria; **tener ~** to have a temperature
fiel [fjel] *adj* (*leal*) faithful, loyal; (*fiable*) reliable; (*exacto*) accurate, faithful ♦ *nm*: **los ~es** the faithful
fieltro ['fjeltro] *nm* felt
fiera ['fjera] *nf* (*animal feroz*) wild animal *o* beast; (*fig*) dragon; *ver tb* **fiero**
fiero, a ['fjero, a] *adj* (*cruel*) cruel; (*feroz*) fierce; (*duro*) harsh
fiesta ['fjesta] *nf* party; (*de pueblo*) festival; (*vacaciones, tb*: **~s**) holiday *sg*; (*REL*): **~ de guardar** day of obligation

---

Fiestas

ℹ️ **Fiestas** *can be official public holidays or holidays set by each autonomous region, many of which coincide with religious festivals. There are also many* **fiestas** *all over Spain for a local patron saint or the Virgin Mary. These often last several days and can include religious processions, carnival parades, bullfights and dancing.*

---

figura [fi'ɣura] *nf* (*gen*) figure; (*forma, imagen*) shape, form; (*NAIPES*) face card
figurar [fiɣu'rar] *vt* (*representar*) to represent; (*fingir*) to figure ♦ *vi* to figure; **~se** *vr* (*imaginarse*) to imagine; (*suponer*) to suppose
fijador [fixa'ðor] *nm* (*FOTO etc*) fixative; (*de pelo*) gel
fijar [fi'xar] *vt* (*gen*) to fix; (*estampilla*) to affix, stick (on); **~se** *vr*: **~se en** to notice
fijo, a ['fixo, a] *adj* (*gen*) fixed; (*firme*) firm; (*permanente*) permanent ♦ *adv*: **mirar ~** to stare

fila ['fila] nf row; (MIL) rank; **ponerse en ~** to line up, get into line

filántropo, a [fi'lantropo, a] nm/f philanthropist

filatelia [fila'telja] nf philately, stamp collecting

filete [fi'lete] nm (carne) fillet steak; (pescado) fillet

filiación [filja'θjon] nf (POL) affiliation

filial [fi'ljal] adj filial ♦ nf subsidiary

Filipinas [fili'pinas] nfpl: **las ~** the Philippines; **filipino, a** adj, nm/f Philippine

filmar [fil'mar] vt to film, shoot

filo ['filo] nm (gen) edge; **sacar ~ a** to sharpen; **al ~ del mediodía** at about midday; **de doble ~** double-edged

filón [fi'lon] nm (MINERÍA) vein, lode; (fig) goldmine

filosofía [filoso'fia] nf philosophy; **filósofo, a** nm/f philosopher

filtrar [fil'trar] vt, vi to filter, strain; **~se** vr to filter; **filtro** nm (TEC, utensilio) filter

fin [fin] nm end; (objetivo) aim, purpose; **al ~ y al cabo** when all's said and done; **a ~ de** in order to; **por ~** finally; **en ~** in short; **~ de semana** weekend

final [fi'nal] adj final ♦ nm end, conclusion ♦ nf final; **~idad** nf (propósito) purpose, intention; **~ista** nm/f finalist; **~izar** vt to end, finish; (INFORM) to log out o off ♦ vi to end, come to an end

financiar [finan'θjar] vt to finance; **financiero, a** adj financial ♦ nm/f financier

finca ['finka] nf (bien inmueble) property, land; (casa de campo) country house; (AM) farm

fingir [fin'xir] vt (simular) to simulate, feign ♦ vi (aparentar) to pretend

finlandés, esa [finlan'des, esa] adj Finnish ♦ nm/f Finn ♦ nm (LING) Finnish

Finlandia [fin'landja] nf Finland

fino, a ['fino, a] adj fine; (delgado) slender; (de buenas maneras) polite, refined; (jerez) fino, dry

firma ['firma] nf signature; (COM) firm,

company

firmamento [firma'mento] nm firmament

firmar [fir'mar] vt to sign

firme ['firme] adj firm; (estable) stable; (sólido) solid; (constante) steady; (decidido) resolute ♦ nm road (surface); **~mente** adv firmly; **~za** nf firmness; (constancia) steadiness; (solidez) solidity

fiscal [fis'kal] adj fiscal ♦ nm/f public prosecutor; **año ~** tax o fiscal year

fisco ['fisko] nm (hacienda) treasury, exchequer (BRIT)

fisgar [fis'var] vt to pry into

fisgonear [fisvone'ar] vt to poke one's nose into ♦ vi to pry, spy

física [fi'sika] nf physics sg; ver tb **físico**

físico, a [fi'siko, a] adj physical ♦ nm physique ♦ nm/f physicist

fisura [fi'sura] nf crack; (MED) fracture

flác(c)ido, a ['fla(k)θiðo, a] adj flabby

flaco, a ['flako, a] adj (muy delgado) skinny, thin; (débil) weak, feeble

flagrante [fla'vrante] adj flagrant

flamante [fla'mante] (fam) adj brilliant; (nuevo) brand-new

flamenco, a [fla'menko, a] adj (de Flandes) Flemish; (baile, música) flamenco ♦ nm (baile, música) flamenco

flan [flan] nm creme caramel

flaqueza [fla'keθa] nf (delgadez) thinness, leanness; (fig) weakness

flash [flaʃ] (pl **~s** o **~es**) nm (FOTO) flash

flauta ['flauta] nf (MUS) flute

flecha ['fletʃa] nf arrow

flechazo [fle'tʃaθo] nm love at first sight

fleco ['fleko] nm fringe

flema ['flema] nm phlegm

flequillo [fle'kiʎo] nm (pelo) fringe

flexible [flek'sißle] adj flexible

flexión [flek'sjon] nf press-up

flexo ['flekso] nm adjustable table-lamp

flojera [flo'xera] (AM: fam) nf: **me da ~** I can't be bothered

flojo, a ['floxo, a] adj (gen) loose; (sin fuerzas) limp; (débil) weak

flor [flor] nf flower; **a ~ de** on the surface of; **~ecer** vi (BOT) to flower, bloom; (fig)

to flourish; **~eciente** adj (BOT) in flower,
flowering; (fig) thriving; **~ero** nm vase;
~istería nf florist's (shop)

flota ['flota] nf fleet

flotador [flota'ðor] nm (gen) float; (para
nadar) rubber ring

flotar [flo'tar] vi (gen) to float; **flote** nm: **a
flote** afloat; **salir a flote** (fig) to get back
on one's feet

fluctuar [fluk'twar] vi (oscilar) to fluctuate

fluidez [flui'ðeθ] nf fluidity; (fig) fluency

flúido, a ['fluiðo, a] adj, nm fluid

fluir [flu'ir] vi to flow

flujo ['fluxo] nm flow; **~ y reflujo** ebb and
flow

flúor ['fluor] nm fluoride

fluvial [flu'βi'al] adj (navegación, cuenca)
fluvial, river cpd

foca ['foka] nf seal

foco ['foko] nm focus; (ELEC) floodlight;
(AM) (light) bulb

fofo, a ['fofo, a] adj soft, spongy; (carnes)
flabby

fogata [fo'yata] nf bonfire

fogón [fo'yon] nm (de cocina) ring, burner

fogoso, a [fo'yoso, a] adj spirited

folio ['foljo] nm folio, page

follaje [fo'ʎaxe] nm foliage

folletín [foʎe'tin] nm newspaper serial

folleto [fo'ʎeto] nm (POL) pamphlet

follón [fo'ʎon] nm (fam) (lío) mess; (conmoción) fuss; **armar un ~** to kick up a row

fomentar [fomen'tar] vt (MED) to foment;
fomento nm (promoción) promotion

fonda ['fonda] nf inn

fondo ['fondo] nm (de mar) bottom; (de
coche, sala) back; (ARTE etc) background;
(reserva) fund; **~s** nmpl (COM) funds,
resources; **una investigación a ~** a
thorough investigation; **en el ~** at
bottom, deep down

fonobuzón [fonoβu'θon] nm voice mail

fontanería [fontane'ria] nf plumbing;
fontanero, a nm/f plumber

footing ['futin] nm jogging; **hacer ~** to
jog, go jogging

forastero, a [foras'tero, a] nm/f stranger

forcejear [forθexe'ar] vi (luchar) to
struggle

forense [fo'rense] nm/f pathologist

forjar [for'xar] vt to forge

forma ['forma] nf (figura) form, shape;
(MED) fitness; (método) way, means; **las
~s** the conventions; **estar en ~** to be fit

formación [forma'θjon] nf (gen)
formation; (educación) education; **~
profesional** vocational training

formal [for'mal] adj (gen) formal; (fig:
serio) serious; (: de fiar) reliable; **~idad** nf
formality; seriousness; **~izar** vt (JUR) to
formalize; (situación) to put in order,
regularize; **~izarse** vr (situación) to be put
in order, be regularized

formar [for'mar] vt (componer) to form,
shape; (constituir) to make up, constitute;
(ESCOL) to train, educate; **~se** vr (ESCOL)
to be trained, educated; (cobrar forma) to
form, take form; (desarrollarse) to develop

formatear [formate'ar] vt to format

formativo, a [forma'tiβo, a] adj (lecturas,
años) formative

formato [for'mato] nm format

formidable [formi'ðaβle] adj (temible)
formidable; (estupendo) tremendous

fórmula ['formula] nf formula

formular [formu'lar] vt (queja) to make,
lodge; (petición) to draw up; (pregunta) to
pose

formulario [formu'larjo] nm form

fornido, a [for'niðo, a] adj well-built

forrar [fo'rrar] vt (abrigo) to line; (libro) to
cover; **forro** nm (de cuaderno) cover;
(COSTURA) lining; (de sillón) upholstery

fortalecer [fortale'θer] vt to strengthen

fortaleza [forta'leθa] nf (MIL) fortress,
stronghold; (fuerza) strength;
(determinación) resolution

fortuito, a [for'twito, a] adj accidental

fortuna [for'tuna] nf (suerte) fortune,
(good) luck; (riqueza) fortune, wealth

forzar [for'θar] vt (puerta) to force (open);
(compeler) to compel

forzoso, a [for'θoso, a] adj necessary

fosa ['fosa] nf (sepultura) grave; (en tierra)

pit; **~s nasales** nostrils

fósforo ['fosforo] nm (QUÍM) phosphorus; (cerilla) match

foso ['foso] nm ditch; (TEATRO) pit; (AUTO): **~ de reconocimiento** inspection pit

foto ['foto] nf photo, snap(shot); **sacar una ~** to take a photo o picture

fotocopia [foto'kopja] nf photocopy; **fotocopiadora** nf photocopier; **fotocopiar** vt to photocopy

fotografía [fotoɤra'fia] nf (ARTE) photography; (una ~) photograph; **fotografiar** vt to photograph

fotógrafo, a [fo'toɤrafo, a] nm/f photographer

fracasar [fraka'sar] vi (gen) to fail

fracaso [fra'kaso] nm failure

fracción [frak'θjon] nf fraction; **fraccionamiento** (AM) nm housing estate

fractura [frak'tura] nf fracture, break

fragancia [fra'ɤanθja] nf (olor) fragrance, perfume

frágil ['fraxil] adj (débil) fragile; (COM) breakable

fragmento [fraɤ'mento] nm (pedazo) fragment

fragua ['fraɤwa] nf forge; **fraguar** vt to forge; (fig) to concoct ♦ vi to harden

fraile ['fraile] nm (REL) friar; (: monje) monk

frambuesa [fram'bwesa] nf raspberry

francamente [franka'mente] adv (hablar, decir) frankly; (realmente) really

francés, esa [fran'θes, esa] adj French ♦ nm/f Frenchman/woman ♦ nm (LING) French

Francia ['franθja] nf France

franco, a ['franko, a] adj (cándido) frank, open; (COM: exento) free ♦ nm (moneda) franc

francotirador, a [frankotira'ðor, a] nm/f sniper

franela [fra'nela] nf flannel

franja ['franxa] nf fringe

franquear [franke'ar] vt (camino) to clear; (carta, paquete postal) to frank, stamp;

(obstáculo) to overcome

franqueo [fran'keo] nm postage

franqueza [fran'keθa] nf (candor) frankness

frasco ['frasko] nm bottle, flask; **~ al vacío** (vacuum) flask

frase ['frase] nf sentence; **~ hecha** set phrase; (pey) stock phrase

fraterno, a [fra'terno, a] adj brotherly, fraternal

fraude ['frauðe] nm (cualidad) dishonesty; (acto) fraud; **fraudulento, a** adj fraudulent

frazada [fra'saða] (AM) nf blanket

frecuencia [fre'kwenθja] nf frequency; **con ~** frequently, often

frecuentar [frekwen'tar] vt to frequent

fregadero [freɤa'ðero] nm (kitchen) sink

fregar [fre'ɤar] vt (frotar) to scrub; (platos) to wash (up); (AM) to annoy

fregona [fre'ɤona] nf mop

freír [fre'ir] vt to fry

frenar [fre'nar] vt to brake; (fig) to check

frenazo [fre'naθo] nm: **dar un ~** to brake sharply

frenesí [frene'si] nm frenzy; **frenético, a** adj frantic

freno ['freno] nm (TEC, AUTO) brake; (de cabalgadura) bit; (fig) check

frente ['frente] nm (ARQ, POL) front; (de objeto) front part ♦ nf forehead, brow; **~ a** in front of; (en situación opuesta de) opposite; **al ~ de** at the head of; **chocar de ~** to crash head-on; **hacer ~ a** to face up to

fresa ['fresa] (ESP) nf strawberry

fresco, a ['fresko, a] adj (nuevo) fresh; (frío) cool; (descarado) cheeky ♦ nm (aire) fresh air; (ARTE) fresco; (AM: jugo) fruit drink ♦ nm/f (fam): **ser un ~** to have a nerve; **tomar el ~** to get some fresh air; **frescura** nf freshness; (descaro) cheek, nerve

frialdad [frial'dað] nf (gen) coldness; (indiferencia) indifference

fricción [frik'θjon] nf (gen) friction; (acto) rub(bing); (MED) massage

frigidez [frixi'ðeθ] *nf* frigidity
frigorífico [friɣo'rifiko] *nm* refrigerator
frijol [fri'xol] *nm* kidney bean
frío, a *etc* ['frio, a] *vb ver* freír ♦ *adj* cold; (*indiferente*) indifferent ♦ *nm* cold; indifference; **hace ~** it's cold; **tener ~ to** be cold
frito, a ['frito, a] *adj* fried; **me trae ~ ese hombre** I'm sick and tired of that man; **fritos** *nmpl* fried food
frívolo, a ['friβolo, a] *adj* frivolous
frontal [fron'tal] *adj* frontal; **choque ~** head-on collision
frontera [fron'tera] *nf* frontier; **fronterizo, a** *adj* frontier *cpd*; (*contiguo*) bordering
frontón [fron'ton] *nm* (*DEPORTE: cancha*) pelota court; (: *juego*) pelota
frotar [fro'tar] *vt* to rub; **~se** *vr*: **~se las manos** to rub one's hands
fructífero, a [fruk'tifero, a] *adj* fruitful
fruncir [frun'θir] *vt* to pucker; (*COSTURA*) to pleat; **~ el ceño** to knit one's brow
frustrar [frus'trar] *vt* to frustrate
fruta ['fruta] *nf* fruit; **frutería** *nf* fruit shop; **frutero, a** *adj* fruit *cpd* ♦ *nm/f* fruiterer ♦ *nm* fruit bowl
frutilla [fru'tiʎa] (*AM*) *nf* strawberry
fruto ['fruto] *nm* fruit; (*fig: resultado*) result; (: *beneficio*) benefit; **~s secos** nuts; (*pasas etc*) dried fruit *sg*
fue *vb ver* ser, ir
fuego ['fweɣo] *nm* (*gen*) fire; **a ~ lento** on a low heat; **¿tienes ~?** have you (got) a light?; **~s artificiales** *o* **de artificio** fireworks
fuente ['fwente] *nf* fountain; (*manantial, fig*) spring; (*origen*) source; (*plato*) large dish
fuera *etc* ['fwera] *vb ver* ser, ir ♦ *adv* out(side); (*en otra parte*) away; (*excepto, salvo*) except, save ♦ *prep*: **~ de** outside; (*fig*) besides; **~ de sí** beside o.s.; **por ~** (on the) outside
fuera-borda [fwera'βorða] *nm* speedboat
fuerte ['fwerte] *adj* strong; (*golpe*) hard; (*ruido*) loud; (*comida*) rich; (*lluvia*) heavy;

(*dolor*) intense ♦ *adv* strongly; hard; loud(ly)
fuerza *etc* ['fwerθa] *vb ver* forzar ♦ *nf* (*fortaleza*) strength; (*TEC, ELEC*) power; (*coacción*) force; (*MIL: tb:* **~s**) forces *pl*; **a ~ de** by dint of; **cobrar ~s** to recover one's strength; **tener ~s para** to have the strength to; **a la ~** forcibly, by force; **por ~** of necessity; **~ de voluntad** willpower
fuga ['fuɣa] *nf* (*huida*) flight, escape; (*de gas etc*) leak
fugarse [fu'ɣarse] *vr* to flee, escape
fugaz [fu'ɣaθ] *adj* fleeting
fugitivo, a [fuxi'tiβo, a] *adj, nm/f* fugitive
fui *vb ver* ser; ir
fulano, a [fu'lano, a] *nm/f* so-and-so, what's-his-name/what's-her-name
fulminante [fulmi'nante] *adj* (*fig: mirada*) fierce; (*MED: enfermedad, ataque*) sudden; (*fam: éxito, golpe*) sudden
fumador, a [fuma'ðor, a] *nm/f* smoker
fumar [fu'mar] *vt, vi* to smoke; **~ en pipa** to smoke a pipe
función [fun'θjon] *nf* function; (*en trabajo*) duties *pl*; (*espectáculo*) show; **entrar en funciones** to take up one's duties
funcionar [funθjo'nar] *vi* (*gen*) to function; (*máquina*) to work; **"no funciona"** "out of order"
funcionario, a [funθjo'narjo, a] *nm/f* civil servant
funda ['funda] *nf* (*gen*) cover; (*de almohada*) pillowcase
fundación [funda'θjon] *nf* foundation
fundamental [fundamen'tal] *adj* fundamental, basic
fundamentar [fundamen'tar] *vt* (*poner base*) to lay the foundations of; (*establecer*) to found; (*fig*) to base; **fundamento** *nm* (*base*) foundation
fundar [fun'dar] *vt* to found; **~se** *vr*: **~se en** to be founded on
fundición [fundi'θjon] *nf* fusing; (*fábrica*) foundry
fundir [fun'dir] *vt* (*gen*) to fuse; (*metal*) to smelt, melt down; (*nieve etc*) to melt; (*COM*) to merge; (*estatua*) to cast; **~se** *vr*

(*colores etc*) to merge, blend; (*unirse*) to fuse together; (*ELEC: fusible, lámpara etc*) to fuse, blow; (*nieve etc*) to melt
fúnebre ['funeβre] *adj* funeral *cpd*, funereal
funeral [fune'ral] *nm* funeral; **funeraria** *nf* undertaker's
funesto, a [fu'nesto, a] *adj* (*día*) ill-fated; (*decisión*) fatal
furgón [fur'ɣon] *nm* wagon; **furgoneta** *nf* (*AUTO, COM*) (transit) van (*BRIT*), pick-up (truck) (*US*)
furia ['furja] *nf* (*ira*) fury; (*violencia*) violence; **furibundo, a** *adj* furious; **furioso, a** *adj* (*iracundo*) furious; (*violento*) violent; **furor** *nm* (*cólera*) rage
furtivo, a [fur'tiβo, a] *adj* furtive ♦ *nm* poacher
fusible [fu'siβle] *nm* fuse
fusil [fu'sil] *nm* rifle; **~ar** *vt* to shoot
fusión [fu'sjon] *nf* (*gen*) melting; (*unión*) fusion; (*COM*) merger
fútbol ['futβol] *nm* football; **futbolín** *nm* table football; **futbolista** *nm* footballer
futuro, a [fu'turo, a] *adj, nm* future

G, g

gabardina [gaβar'ðina] *nf* raincoat, gabardine
gabinete [gaβi'nete] *nm* (*POL*) cabinet; (*estudio*) study; (*de abogados etc*) office
gaceta [ga'θeta] *nf* gazette
gachas ['gatʃas] *nfpl* porridge *sg*
gafas ['gafas] *nfpl* glasses; **~ de sol** sunglasses
gafe ['gafe] *nm* jinx
gaita ['gaita] *nf* bagpipes *pl*
gajes ['gaxes] *nmpl*: **los ~ del oficio** occupational hazards
gajo ['gaxo] *nm* (*de naranja*) segment
gala ['gala] *nf* (*traje de etiqueta*) full dress; **~s** *nfpl* (*ropa*) finery *sg*; **estar de ~** to be in one's best clothes; **hacer ~ de** to display
galante [ga'lante] *adj* gallant; **galantería**

nf (*caballerosidad*) gallantry; (*cumplido*) politeness; (*comentario*) compliment
galápago [ga'lapaɣo] *nm* (*ZOOL*) turtle
galardón [galar'ðon] *nm* award, prize
galaxia [ga'laksja] *nf* galaxy
galera [ga'lera] *nf* (*nave*) galley; (*carro*) wagon; (*IMPRENTA*) galley
galería [gale'ria] *nf* (*gen*) gallery; (*balcón*) veranda(h); (*pasillo*) corridor
Gales ['gales] *nm* (*tb*: **País de ~**) Wales; **galés, esa** *adj* Welsh ♦ *nm/f* Welshman/woman ♦ *nm* (*LING*) Welsh
galgo ['galɣo, a] *nm/f* greyhound
galimatías [galima'tias] *nmpl* (*lenguaje*) gibberish *sg*, nonsense *sg*
gallardía [gaʎar'ðia] *nf* (*valor*) bravery
gallego, a [ga'ʎeɣo, a] *adj, nm/f* Galician
galleta [ga'ʎeta] *nf* biscuit (*BRIT*), cookie (*US*)
gallina [ga'ʎina] *nf* hen ♦ *nm/f* (*fam: cobarde*) chicken; **gallinero** *nm* henhouse; (*TEATRO*) top gallery
gallo ['gaʎo] *nm* cock, rooster
galón [ga'lon] *nm* (*MIL*) stripe; (*COSTURA*) braid; (*medida*) gallon
galopar [galo'par] *vi* to gallop
gama ['gama] *nf* (*fig*) range
gamba ['gamba] *nf* prawn (*BRIT*), shrimp (*US*)
gamberro, a [gam'berro, a] *nm/f* hooligan, lout
gamuza [ga'muθa] *nf* chamois
gana ['gana] *nf* (*deseo*) desire, wish; (*apetito*) appetite; (*voluntad*) will; (*añoranza*) longing; **de buena ~** willingly; **de mala ~** reluctantly; **me da ~s de** I feel like, I want to; **no me da la ~** I don't feel like it; **tener ~s de** to feel like
ganadería [ganaðe'ria] *nf* (*ganado*) livestock; (*ganado vacuno*) cattle *pl*; (*cría, comercio*) cattle raising
ganado [ga'naðo] *nm* livestock; **~ lanar** sheep *pl*; **~ mayor** cattle *pl*; **~ porcino** pigs *pl*
ganador, a [gana'ðor, a] *adj* winning ♦ *nm/f* winner
ganancia [ga'nanθja] *nf* (*lo ganado*) gain;

(*aumento*) increase; (*beneficio*) profit; **~s**
nfpl (*ingresos*) earnings; (*beneficios*) profit
sg, winnings
ganar [ga'nar] *vt* (*obtener*) to get, obtain;
(*sacar ventaja*) to gain; (*salario etc*) to
earn; (*DEPORTE, premio*) to win; (*derrotar
a*) to beat; (*alcanzar*) to reach ♦ *vi*
(*DEPORTE*) to win; **~se** *vr*: **~se la vida** to
earn one's living
ganchillo [gan't∫iʎo] *nm* crochet
gancho ['gant∫o] *nm* (*gen*) hook;
(*colgador*) hanger
gandul, a [gan'dul, a] *adj, nm/f* good-
for-nothing, layabout
ganga ['ganga] *nf* bargain
gangrena [gan'grena] *nf* gangrene
ganso, a ['ganso, a] *nm/f* (*ZOOL*) goose;
(*fam*) idiot
ganzúa [gan'θua] *nf* skeleton key
garabatear [garaβate'ar] *vi, vt* (*al escribir*)
to scribble, scrawl
garabato [gara'βato] *nm* (*escritura*) scrawl,
scribble
garaje [ga'raxe] *nm* garage
garante [ga'rante] *adj* responsible ♦ *nm/f*
guarantor
garantía [garan'tia] *nf* guarantee
garantizar [garanti'θar] *vt* to guarantee
garbanzo [gar'βanθo] *nm* chickpea (*BRIT*),
garbanzo (*US*)
garbo ['garβo] *nm* grace, elegance
garfio ['garfjo] *nm* grappling iron
garganta [gar'vanta] *nf* (*ANAT*) throat; (*de
botella*) neck; **gargantilla** *nf* necklace
gárgaras ['garvaras] *nfpl*: **hacer ~** to
gargle
garita [ga'rita] *nf* cabin, hut; (*MIL*) sentry
box
garra ['garra] *nf* (*de gato, TEC*) claw; (*de
ave*) talon; (*fam: mano*) hand, paw
garrafa [ga'rrafa] *nf* carafe, decanter
garrapata [garra'pata] *nf* tick
garrote [ga'rrote] *nm* (*palo*) stick; (*porra*)
cudgel; (*suplicio*) garrotte
garza ['garθa] *nf* heron
gas [gas] *nm* gas
gasa ['gasa] *nf* gauze

gaseosa [gase'osa] *nf* lemonade
gaseoso, a [gase'oso, a] *adj* gassy, fizzy
gasoil [ga'soil] *nm* diesel (oil)
gasóleo [ga'soleo] *nm* = **gasoil**
gasolina [gaso'lina] *nf* petrol, gas(oline)
(*US*); **gasolinera** *nf* petrol (*BRIT*) *o* gas
(*US*) station
gastado, a [gas'taðo, a] *adj* (*dinero*) spent;
(*ropa*) worn out; (*usado: frase etc*) trite
gastar [gas'tar] *vt* (*dinero, tiempo*) to
spend; (*fuerzas*) to use up; (*desperdiciar*)
to waste; (*llevar*) to wear; **~se** *vr* to wear
out; (*estropearse*) to waste; **~ en** to spend
on; **~ bromas** to crack jokes; **¿qué
número gastas?** what size (shoe) do you
take?
gasto ['gasto] *nm* (*desembolso*)
expenditure, spending; (*consumo, uso*)
use; **~s** *nmpl* (*desembolsos*) expenses;
(*cargos*) charges, costs
gastronomía [gastrono'mia] *nf*
gastronomy
gatear [gate'ar] *vi* (*andar a gatas*) to go
on all fours
gatillo [ga'tiʎo] *nm* (*de arma de fuego*)
trigger; (*de dentista*) forceps
gato, a ['gato, a] *nm/f* cat ♦ *nm* (*TEC*) jack;
andar a gatas to go on all fours
gaviota [ga'βjota] *nf* seagull
gay [ge] *adj inv, nm* gay, homosexual
gazpacho [gaθ'pat∫o] *nm* gazpacho
gel [xel] *nm* (*tb*: **~ de baño/ducha**) gel
gelatina [xela'tina] *nf* jelly; (*polvos etc*)
gelatine
gema ['xema] *nf* gem
gemelo, a [xe'melo, a] *adj, nm/f* twin; **~s**
nmpl (*de camisa*) cufflinks; (*prismáticos*)
field glasses, binoculars
gemido [xe'miðo] *nm* (*quejido*) moan,
groan; (*aullido*) howl
Géminis ['xeminis] *nm* Gemini
gemir [xe'mir] *vi* (*quejarse*) to moan,
groan; (*aullar*) to howl
generación [xenera'θjon] *nf* generation
general [xene'ral] *adj* general ♦ *nm*
general; **por lo** *o* **en ~** in general; **G~itat**
nf Catalan parliament; **~izar** *vt* to

generalize; **~izarse** vr to become generalized, spread; **~mente** adv generally

generar [xene'rar] vt to generate

género ['xenero] nm (clase) kind, sort; (tipo) type; (BIO) genus; (LING) gender; (COM) material; **~ humano** human race

generosidad [xenerosi'ðað] nf generosity; **generoso, a** adj generous

genial [xe'njal] adj inspired; (idea) brilliant; (afable) genial

genio ['xenjo] nm (carácter) nature, disposition; (humor) temper; (facultad creadora) genius; **de mal ~** bad-tempered

genital [xeni'tal] adj genital; **genitales** nmpl genitals

gente ['xente] nf (personas) people pl; (parientes) relatives pl

gentil [xen'til] adj (elegante) graceful; (encantador) charming; **~eza** nf grace; charm; (cortesía) courtesy

gentío [xen'tio] nm crowd, throng

genuino, a [xe'nwino, a] adj genuine

geografía [xeoɣra'fia] nf geography

geología [xeolo'xia] nf geology

geometría [xeome'tria] nf geometry

gerencia [xe'renθja] nf management; **gerente** nm/f (supervisor) manager; (jefe) director

geriatría [xeria'tria] nf (MED) geriatrics sg

germen ['xermen] nm germ

germinar [xermi'nar] vi to germinate

gesticular [xestiku'lar] vi to gesticulate; (hacer muecas) to grimace; **gesticulación** nf gesticulation; (mueca) grimace

gestión [xes'tjon] nf management; (diligencia, acción) negotiation; **gestionar** vt (lograr) to try to arrange; (dirigir) to manage

gesto ['xesto] nm (mueca) grimace; (ademán) gesture

Gibraltar [xißral'tar] nm Gibraltar; **gibraltareño, a** adj, nm/f Gibraltarian

gigante [xi'vante] adj, nm/f giant; **gigantesco, a** adj gigantic

gilipollas [xili'poʎas] (fam) adj inv daft

♦ nm/f inv wally

gimnasia [xim'nasja] nf gymnastics pl; **gimnasio** nm gymnasium; **gimnasta** nm/f gymnast

gimotear [ximote'ar] vi to whine, whimper

ginebra [xi'neßra] nf gin

ginecólogo, a [xine'koloxo, a] nm/f gynaecologist

gira ['xira] nf tour, trip

girar [xi'rar] vt (dar la vuelta) to turn (around); (: rápidamente) to spin; (COM: giro postal) to draw; (: letra de cambio) to issue ♦ vi to turn (round); (rápido) to spin

girasol [xira'sol] nm sunflower

giratorio, a [xira'torjo, a] adj revolving

giro ['xiro] nm (movimiento) turn, revolution; (LING) expression; (COM) draft; **~ bancario/postal** bank giro/postal order

gis [xis] (AM) nm chalk

gitano, a [xi'tano, a] adj, nm/f gypsy

glacial [gla'θjal] adj icy, freezing

glaciar [gla'θjar] nm glacier

glándula ['glandula] nf gland

global [glo'ßal] adj global

globo ['gloßo] nm (esfera) globe, sphere; (aerostato, juguete) balloon

glóbulo ['gloßulo] nm globule; (ANAT) corpuscle

gloria ['glorja] nf glory

glorieta [glo'rjeta] nf (de jardín) bower, arbour; (plazoleta) roundabout (BRIT), traffic circle (US)

glorificar [glorifi'kar] vt (enaltecer) to glorify, praise

glorioso, a [glo'rjoso, a] adj glorious

glotón, ona [glo'ton, ona] adj gluttonous, greedy ♦ nm/f glutton

glucosa [glu'kosa] nf glucose

gobernador, a [goßerna'ðor, a] adj governing ♦ nm/f governor; **gobernante** adj governing

gobernar [goßer'nar] vt (dirigir) to guide, direct; (POL) to rule, govern ♦ vi to govern; (NAUT) to steer

gobierno etc [go'ßjerno] vb ver **gobernar** ♦ nm (POL) government; (dirección)

goce etc ['goθe] vb ver **gozar** ♦ nm enjoyment

gol [gol] nm goal

golf [golf] nm golf

golfa ['golfa] (fam!) nf (mujer) slut, whore

golfo, a ['golfo, a] nm (GEO) gulf ♦ nm/f (fam: niño) urchin; (gamberro) lout

golondrina [golon'drina] nf swallow

golosina [golo'sina] nf (dulce) sweet; **goloso, a** adj sweet-toothed

golpe ['golpe] nm blow; (de puño) punch; (de mano) smack; (de remo) stroke; (fig: choque) clash; **no dar ~** to be bone idle; **de un ~** with one blow; **de ~** suddenly; **~ (de estado)** coup (d'état); **golpear** vt, vi to strike, knock; (asestar) to beat; (de puño) to punch; (golpetear) to tap

goma ['goma] nf (caucho) rubber; (elástico) elastic; (una ~) elastic band; **~ espuma** foam rubber; **~ de pegar** gum, glue; **~ de borrar** eraser, rubber (BRIT)

gomina [go'mina] nf hair gel

gordo, a ['gorðo, a] adj (gen) fat; (fam) enormous; **el (premio) ~** (en lotería) first prize; **gordura** nf fat; (corpulencia) fatness, stoutness

gorila [go'rila] nm gorilla

gorjear [gorxe'ar] vi to twitter, chirp

gorra ['gorra] nf cap; (de niño) bonnet; (militar) bearskin; **entrar de ~** (fam) to gatecrash; **ir de ~** to sponge

gorrión [go'rrjon] nm sparrow

gorro ['gorro] nm (gen) cap; (de niño, mujer) bonnet

gorrón, ona [go'rron, ona] nm/f scrounger; **gorronear** (fam) vi to scrounge

gota ['gota] nf (gen) drop; (de sudor) bead; (MED) gout; **gotear** vi to drip; (lloviznar) to drizzle; **gotera** nf leak

gozar [go'θar] vi to enjoy o.s.; **~ de** (disfrutar) to enjoy; (poseer) to possess

gozne ['goθne] nm hinge

gozo ['goθo] nm (alegría) joy; (placer) pleasure

gr. abr (= gramo, gramos) g

grabación [graβa'θjon] nf recording

grabado [gra'βaðo] nm print, engraving

grabadora [graβa'ðora] nf tape-recorder

grabar [gra'βar] vt to engrave; (discos, cintas) to record

gracia ['graθja] nf (encanto) grace, gracefulness; (humor) humour, wit; **¡(muchas) ~s!** thanks (very much)!; **~s a** thanks to; **tener ~** (chiste etc) to be funny; **no me hace ~** I am not keen; **gracioso, a** adj (divertido) funny, amusing; (cómico) comical ♦ nm/f (TEATRO) comic character

grada ['graða] nf (de escalera) step; (de anfiteatro) tier, row; **~s** nfpl (DEPORTE: de estadio) terraces

gradería [graðe'ria] nf (gradas) (flight of) steps pl; (de anfiteatro) tiers pl, rows pl; (DEPORTE: de estadio) terraces pl; **~ cubierta** covered stand

grado ['graðo] nm degree; (de aceite, vino) grade; (grada) step; (MIL) rank; **de buen ~** willingly

graduación [graðwa'θjon] nf (del alcohol) proof, strength; (ESCOL) graduation; (MIL) rank

gradual [gra'ðwal] adj gradual

graduar [gra'ðwar] vt (gen) to graduate; (MIL) to commission; **~se** vr to graduate; **~se la vista** to have one's eyes tested

gráfica ['grafika] nf graph

gráfico, a ['grafiko, a] adj graphic ♦ nm diagram; **~s** nmpl (INFORM) graphics

grajo ['graxo] nm rook

Gral abr (= General) Gen.

gramática [gra'matika] nf grammar

gramo ['gramo] nm gramme (BRIT), gram (US)

gran [gran] adj ver **grande**

grana ['grana] nf (color, tela) scarlet

granada [gra'naða] nf pomegranate; (MIL) grenade

granate [gra'nate] adj deep red

Gran Bretaña [-bre'taɲa] nf Great Britain

grande ['grande] (antes de nmsg: **gran**) adj (de tamaño) big, large; (alto) tall; (distinguido) great; (impresionante) grand

♦ nm grandee; **grandeza** nf greatness

grandioso, a [gran'djoso, a] adj magnificent, grand

granel [gra'nel]: **a ~** adv (COM) in bulk

granero [gra'nero] nm granary, barn

granito [gra'nito] nm (AGR) small grain; (roca) granite

granizado [grani'θaðo] nm iced drink

granizar [grani'θar] vi to hail; **granizo** nm hail

granja ['granxa] nf (gen) farm; **granjear** vt to win, gain; **granjearse** vr to win, gain; **granjero, a** nm/f farmer

grano ['grano] nm grain; (semilla) seed; (de café) bean; (MED) pimple, spot

granuja [gra'nuxa] nm/f rogue; (golfillo) urchin

grapa ['grapa] nf staple; (TEC) clamp; **grapadora** nf stapler

grasa ['grasa] nf (gen) grease; (de cocinar) fat, lard; (sebo) suet; (mugre) filth; **grasiento, a** adj greasy; (de aceite) oily; **graso, a** adj (leche, queso, carne) fatty; (pelo, piel) greasy

gratificación [gratifika'θjon] nf (bono) bonus; (recompensa) reward

gratificar [gratifi'kar] vt to reward

gratinar [grati'nar] vt to cook au gratin

gratis ['gratis] adv free

gratitud [grati'tuð] nf gratitude

grato, a ['grato, a] adj (agradable) pleasant, agreeable

gratuito, a [gra'twito, a] adj (gratis) free; (sin razón) gratuitous

gravamen [gra'ßamen] nm (impuesto) tax

gravar [gra'ßar] vt to tax

grave ['graße] adj heavy; (serio) grave, serious; **~dad** nf gravity

gravilla [gra'ßiʎa] nf gravel

gravitar [graßi'tar] vi to gravitate; **~ sobre** to rest on

graznar [graθ'nar] vi (cuervo) to squawk; (pato) to quack; (hablar ronco) to croak

Grecia ['greθja] nf Greece

gremio ['gremjo] nm trade, industry

greña ['grena] nf (cabellos) shock of hair

gresca ['greska] nf uproar

griego, a ['grjeʁo, a] adj, nm/f Greek

grieta ['grjeta] nf crack

grifo ['grifo] nm tap; (AM: AUTO) petrol (BRIT) o gas (US) station

grilletes [gri'ʎetes] nmpl fetters

grillo ['griʎo] nm (ZOOL) cricket

gripe ['gripe] nf flu, influenza

gris [gris] adj (color) grey

gritar [gri'tar] vt to shout, yell; **grito** nm shout, yell; (de horror) scream

grosella [gro'seʎa] nf (red)currant; **~ negra** blackcurrant

grosería [grose'ria] nf (actitud) rudeness; (comentario) vulgar comment; **grosero, a** adj (poco cortés) rude, bad-mannered; (ordinario) vulgar, crude

grosor [gro'sor] nm thickness

grotesco, a [gro'tesko, a] adj grotesque

grúa ['grua] nf (TEC) crane; (de petróleo) derrick

grueso, a ['grweso, a] adj thick; (persona) stout ♦ nm bulk; **el ~ de** the bulk of

grulla ['gruʎa] nf crane

grumo ['grumo] nm clot, lump

gruñido [gru'niðo] nm grunt; (de persona) grumble

gruñir [gru'nir] vi (animal) to growl; (persona) to grumble

grupa ['grupa] nf (ZOOL) rump

grupo ['grupo] nm group; (TEC) unit, set

gruta ['gruta] nf grotto

guadaña [gwa'ðana] nf scythe

guagua [gwa'ʁwa] (AM) nf (niño) baby; (bus) bus

guante ['gwante] nm glove; **~ra** nf glove compartment

guapo, a ['gwapo, a] adj good-looking, attractive; (elegante) smart

guarda ['gwarða] nm/f (persona) guard, keeper ♦ nf (acto) guarding; (custodia) custody; **~bosques** nm inv gamekeeper; **~costas** nm inv coastguard vessel ♦ nm/f guardian, protector; **~espaldas** nm/f inv bodyguard; **~meta** nm/f goalkeeper; **guardar** vt (gen) to keep; (vigilar) to guard, watch over; (dinero: ahorrar) to

save; **guardarse** vr (preservarse) to
protect o.s.; (evitar) to avoid; **guardar
cama** to stay in bed; **~rropa** nm
(armario) wardrobe; (en establecimiento
público) cloakroom

guardería [gwarðe'ria] nf nursery

guardia ['gwarðja] nf (MIL) guard;
(cuidado) care, custody ♦ nm/f guard;
(policía) policeman/woman; **estar de ~** to
be on guard; **montar ~** to mount guard;
G~ Civil Civil Guard; **G~ Nacional**
National Guard

guardián, ana [gwar'ðjan, ana] nm/f
(gen) guardian, keeper

guarecer [gware'θer] vt (proteger) to
protect; (abrigar) to shelter; **~se** vr to
take shelter

guarida [gwa'riða] nf (de animal) den, lair;
(refugio) refuge

guarnecer [gwarne'θer] vt (equipar) to
provide; (adornar) to adorn; (TEC) to
reinforce; **guarnición** nf (de vestimenta)
trimming; (de piedra) mount; (CULIN)
garnish; (arneses) harness; (MIL) garrison

guarro, a ['gwarro, a] nm/f pig

guasa ['gwasa] nf joke; **guasón, ona** adj
(bromista) joking ♦ nm/f wit; joker

Guatemala [gwate'mala] nf Guatemala

guay [gwai] (fam) adj super, great

gubernativo, a [gußerna'tißo, a] adj
governmental

guerra ['gerra] nf war; **~ civil** civil war; **~
fría** cold war; **dar ~** to annoy; **guerrear**
vi to wage war; **guerrero, a** adj
fighting; (carácter) warlike ♦ nm/f warrior

guerrilla [ge'rriʎa] nf guerrilla warfare;
(tropas) guerrilla band o group

guía etc ['gia] vb ver **guiar** ♦ nm/f
(persona) guide ♦ nf (libro) guidebook; **~
de ferrocarriles** railway timetable; **~
telefónica** telephone directory

guiar [gi'ar] vt to guide, direct; (AUTO) to
steer; **~se** vr: **~se por** to be guided by

guijarro [gi'xarro] nm pebble

guillotina [giʎo'tina] nf guillotine

guinda ['ginda] nf morello cherry

guindilla [gin'diʎa] nf chilli pepper

guiñapo [gi'ɲapo] nm (harapo) rag;
(persona) reprobate, rogue

guiñar [gi'ɲar] vt to wink

guión [gi'on] nm (LING) hyphen, dash;
(CINE) script; **guionista** nm/f scriptwriter

guiri ['giri] (fam: pey) nm/f foreigner

guirnalda [gir'nalda] nf garland

guisado [gi'saðo] nm stew

guisante [gi'sante] nm pea

guisar [gi'sar] vt, vi to cook; **guiso** nm
cooked dish

guitarra [gi'tarra] nf guitar

gula ['gula] nf gluttony, greed

gusano [gu'sano] nm worm; (lombriz)
earthworm

gustar [gus'tar] vt to taste, sample ♦ vi to
please, be pleasing; **~ de algo** to like o
enjoy sth; **me gustan las uvas** I like
grapes; **le gusta nadar** she likes o enjoys
swimming

gusto ['gusto] nm (sentido, sabor) taste;
(placer) pleasure; **tiene ~ a menta** it
tastes of mint; **tener buen ~** to have
good taste; **sentirse a ~** to feel at ease;
mucho ~ (en conocerle) pleased to meet
you; **el ~ es mío** the pleasure is mine;
con ~ willingly, gladly; **~so, a** adj
(sabroso) tasty; (agradable) pleasant

H, h

ha vb ver **haber**

haba ['aßa] nf bean

Habana [a'ßana] nf: **la ~** Havana

habano [a'ßano] nm Havana cigar

habéis vb ver **haber**

PALABRA CLAVE

---

haber [a'ßer] vb aux 1 (tiempos
compuestos) to have; **había comido** I had
eaten; **antes/después de ~lo visto**
before seeing/after seeing o having seen
it

2: **¡~lo dicho antes!** you should have
said so before!

3: **~ de: he de hacerlo** I have to do it;

ha de llegar mañana it should arrive tomorrow
♦ *vb impers* **1** (*existencia: sg*) there is; (: *pl*) there are; **hay un hermano/dos hermanos** there is one brother/there are two brothers; **¿cuánto hay de aquí a Sucre?** how far is it from here to Sucre? **2** (*obligación*): **hay que hacer algo** something must be done; **hay que apuntarlo para acordarse** you have to write it down to remember **3: ¡hay que ver!** well I never! **4: ¡no hay de** *o* **por** (*AM*) **qué!** don't mention it!, not at all! **5: ¿qué hay?** (*¿qué pasa?*) what's up?, what's the matter?; (*¿qué tal?*) how's it going?
♦ **~se** *vr*: **habérselas con uno** to have it out with sb
♦ *vt*: **he aquí unas sugerencias** here are some suggestions; **no hay cintas blancas pero sí las hay rojas** there aren't any white ribbons but there are some red ones
♦ *nm* (*en cuenta*) credit side; **~es** *nmpl* assets; **¿cuánto tengo en el ~?** how much do I have in my account?; **tiene varias novelas en su ~** he has several novels to his credit

habichuela [aßi'tʃwela] *nf* kidney bean
hábil ['aßil] *adj* (*listo*) clever, smart; (*capaz*) fit, capable; (*experto*) expert; **día ~** working day; **habilidad** *nf* skill, ability
habilitar [aßili'tar] *vt* (*capacitar*) to enable; (*dar instrumentos*) to equip; (*financiar*) to finance
hábilmente [aßil'mente] *adv* skilfully, expertly
habitación [aßita'θjon] *nf* (*cuarto*) room; (*BIO: morada*) habitat; **~ sencilla** *o* **individual** single room; **~ doble** *o* **de matrimonio** double room
habitante [aßi'tante] *nm/f* inhabitant
habitar [aßi'tar] *vt* (*residir en*) to inhabit; (*ocupar*) to occupy ♦ *vi* to live
hábito ['aßito] *nm* habit

habitual [aßi'twal] *adj* usual
habituar [aßi'twar] *vt* to accustom; **~se** *vr*: **~se a** to get used to
habla ['aßla] *nf* (*capacidad de hablar*) speech; (*idioma*) language; (*dialecto*) dialect; **perder el ~** to become speechless; **de ~ francesa** French-speaking; **estar al ~** to be in contact; (*TEL*) to be on the line; **¡González al ~!** (*TEL*) González speaking!
hablador, a [aßla'ðor, a] *adj* talkative ♦ *nm/f* chatterbox
habladuría [aßlaðu'ria] *nf* rumour; **~s** *nfpl* gossip *sg*
hablante [a'ßlante] *adj* speaking ♦ *nm/f* speaker
hablar [a'ßlar] *vt* to speak, talk ♦ *vi* to speak; **~se** *vr* to speak to each other; **~ con** to speak to; **~ de** to speak of *o* about; **"se habla inglés"** "English spoken here"; **¡ni ~!** it's out of the question!
habré *etc vb ver* **haber**
hacendoso, a [aθen'doso, a] *adj* industrious

PALABRA CLAVE

hacer [a'θer] *vt* **1** (*fabricar, producir*) to make; (*construir*) to build; **~ una película/un ruido** to make a film/noise; **el guisado lo hice yo** I made *o* cooked the stew
2 (*ejecutar: trabajo etc*) to do; **~ la colada** to do the washing; **~ la comida** to do the cooking; **¿qué haces?** what are you doing?; **~ el malo** *o* **el papel del malo** (*TEATRO*) to play the villain
3 (*estudios, algunos deportes*) to do; **~ español/económicas** to do *o* study Spanish/economics; **~ yoga/gimnasia** to do yoga/go to gym
4 (*transformar, incidir en*): **esto lo hará más difícil** this will make it more difficult; **salir te hará sentir mejor** going out will make you feel better
5 (*cálculo*): **2 y 2 hacen 4** 2 and 2 make 4; **éste hace 100** this one makes 100

6 (+subjun): **esto hará que ganemos** this
will make us win; **harás que no quiera
venir** you'll stop him wanting to come
7 (como sustituto de vb): **él bebió y
yo hice lo mismo** he drank and I did
likewise
8: **no hace más que criticar** all he does
is criticize
♦ vb semi-aux: **hacer** +infin 1 (directo):
les hice venir I made o had them come;
~ trabajar a los demás to get others to
work
2 (por intermedio de otros): **~ reparar
algo** to get sth repaired
♦ vi 1: **haz como que no lo sabes** act as
if you don't know
2 (ser apropiado): **si os hace** if it's alright
with you
3: **~ de**: **~ de madre para uno** to be like
a mother to sb; (TEATRO): **~ de Otelo** to
play Othello
♦ vb impers 1: **hace calor/frío** it's hot/
cold; ver tb **bueno**; **sol**; **tiempo**
2 (tiempo): **hace 3 años** 3 years ago;
hace un mes que voy/no voy I've been
going/I haven't been for a month
3: **¿cómo has hecho para llegar tan
rápido?** how did you manage to get here
so quickly?
♦ **~se** vr 1 (volverse) to become; **se
hicieron amigos** they became friends
2 (acostumbrarse): **~se a** to get used to
3: **se hace con huevos y leche** it's
made out of eggs and milk; **eso no se
hace** that's not done
4 (obtener): **~se de** o **con algo** to get
hold of sth
5 (fingirse): **~se el sueco** to turn a deaf
ear

hacha ['atʃa] nf axe; (antorcha) torch
hachís [a'tʃis] nm hashish
hacia ['aθja] prep (en dirección de) towards;
(cerca de) near; (actitud) towards; **~
arriba/abajo** up(wards)/down(wards); **~
mediodía** about noon
hacienda [a'θjenda] nf (propiedad)

property; (finca) farm; (AM) ranch; **~
pública** public finance; **(Ministerio de)
H~** Exchequer (BRIT), Treasury
Department (US)
hada ['aða] nf fairy
hago etc vb ver **hacer**
Haití [ai'ti] nm Haiti
halagar [ala'ɣar] vt to flatter
halago [a'laɣo] nm flattery; **halagüeño,
a** adj flattering
halcón [al'kon] nm falcon, hawk
hallar [a'ʎar] vt (gen) to find; (descubrir) to
discover; (toparse con) to run into; **~se** vr
to be (situated); **hallazgo** nm discovery;
(cosa) find
halterofilia [altero'filja] nf weightlifting
hamaca [a'maka] nf hammock
hambre ['ambre] nf hunger; (plaga)
famine; (deseo) longing; **tener ~** to be
hungry; **hambriento, a** adj hungry,
starving
hamburguesa [ambur'ɣesa] nf
hamburger; **hamburguesería** nf burger
bar
han vb ver **haber**
harapiento, a [ara'pjento, a] adj tattered,
in rags
harapos [a'rapos] nmpl rags
haré etc vb ver **hacer**
harina [a'rina] nf flour
hartar [ar'tar] vt to satiate, glut; (fig) to
tire, sicken; **~se** vr (de comida) to fill o.s.,
gorge o.s.; (cansarse) to get fed up (de
with); **hartazgo** nm surfeit, glut; **harto,
a** adj (lleno) full; (cansado) fed up ♦ adv
(bastante) enough; (muy) very; **estar
harto de** to be fed up with
has vb ver **haber**
hasta ['asta] adv even ♦ prep (alcanzando
a) as far as; up to; down to; (de tiempo: a
tal hora) till, until; (antes de) before
♦ conj: **~ que** until; **~ luego/el sábado**
see you soon/on Saturday
hastiar [as'tjar] vt (gen) to weary; (aburrir)
to bore; **~se** vr: **~se de** to get fed up
with; **hastío** nm weariness; boredom
hatillo [a'tiʎo] nm belongings pl, kit;

(*montón*) bundle, heap

hay *vb ver* **haber**

Haya ['aja] *nf*: **la ~** The Hague

haya *etc* ['aja] *vb ver* **haber** ♦ *nf* beech tree

haz [aθ] *vb ver* **hacer** ♦ *nm* (*de luz*) beam

hazaña [a'θaɲa] *nf* feat, exploit

hazmerreír [aθmerre'ir] *nm inv* laughing stock

he *vb ver* **haber**

hebilla [e'βiʎa] *nf* buckle, clasp

hebra ['eβra] *nf* thread; (*BOT: fibra*) fibre, grain

hebreo, a [e'βreo, a] *adj, nm/f* Hebrew ♦ *nm* (*LING*) Hebrew

hechizar [etʃi'θar] *vt* to cast a spell on, bewitch

hechizo [e'tʃiθo] *nm* witchcraft, magic; (*acto de magía*) spell, charm

hecho, a ['etʃo, a] *pp de* **hacer** ♦ *adj* (*carne*) done; (*COSTURA*) ready-to-wear ♦ *nm* deed, act; (*dato*) fact; (*cuestión*) matter; (*suceso*) event ♦ *excl* agreed!, done!; **¡bien ~!** well done!; **de ~** in fact, as a matter of fact

hechura [e'tʃura] *nf* (*forma*) form, shape; (*de persona*) build

hectárea [ek'tarea] *nf* hectare

heder [e'ðer] *vi* to stink, smell

hediondo, a [e'ðjondo, a] *adj* stinking

hedor [e'ðor] *nm* stench

helada [e'laða] *nf* frost

heladera [ela'ðera] (*AM*) *nf* (*refrigerador*) refrigerator

helado, a [e'laðo, a] *adj* frozen; (*glacial*) icy; (*fig*) chilly, cold ♦ *nm* ice cream

helar [e'lar] *vt* to freeze, ice (up); (*dejar atónito*) to amaze; (*desalentar*) to discourage ♦ *vi* to freeze; **~se** *vr* to freeze

helecho [e'letʃo] *nm* fern

hélice ['eliθe] *nf* (*TEC*) propeller

helicóptero [eli'koptero] *nm* helicopter

hembra ['embra] *nf* (*BOT, ZOOL*) female; (*mujer*) woman; (*TEC*) nut

hemorragia [emo'rraxja] *nf* haemorrhage

hemorroides [emo'rroiðes] *nfpl* haemorrhoids, piles

hemos *vb ver* **haber**

hendidura [endi'ðura] *nf* crack, split

heno ['eno] *nm* hay

herbicida [erβi'θiða] *nm* weedkiller

heredad [ere'ðað] *nf* landed property; (*granja*) farm

heredar [ere'ðar] *vt* to inherit; **heredero, a** *nm/f* heir(ess)

hereje [e'rexe] *nm/f* heretic

herencia [e'renθja] *nf* inheritance

herida [e'riða] *nf* wound, injury; *ver tb* **herido**

herido, a [e'riðo, a] *adj* injured, wounded ♦ *nm/f* casualty

herir [e'rir] *vt* to wound, injure; (*fig*) to offend

hermanastro, a [erma'nastro, a] *nm/f* stepbrother/sister

hermandad [erman'dað] *nf* brotherhood

hermano, a [er'mano, a] *nm/f* brother/ sister; **~ gemelo** twin brother; **hermana gemela** twin sister; **~ político** brother-in-law; **hermana política** sister-in-law

hermético, a [er'metiko, a] *adj* hermetic; (*fig*) watertight

hermoso, a [er'moso, a] *adj* beautiful, lovely; (*estupendo*) splendid; (*guapo*) handsome; **hermosura** *nf* beauty

hernia ['ernja] *nf* hernia

héroe ['eroe] *nm* hero

heroína [ero'ina] *nf* (*mujer*) heroine; (*droga*) heroin

heroísmo [ero'ismo] *nm* heroism

herradura [erra'ðura] *nf* horseshoe

herramienta [erra'mjenta] *nf* tool

herrero [e'rrero] *nm* blacksmith

herrumbre [e'rrumbre] *nf* rust

hervidero [erβi'ðero] *nm* (*fig*) swarm; (*POL etc*) hotbed

hervir [er'βir] *vi* to boil; (*burbujear*) to bubble; (*fig*): **~ de** to teem with; **~ a fuego lento** to simmer; **hervor** *nm* boiling; (*fig*) ardour, fervour

heterosexual [eterosek'swal] *adj* heterosexual

hice *etc vb ver* **hacer**

hidratante [iðra'tante] *adj*: **crema ~**

moisturizing cream, moisturizer; **hidratar** vt (*piel*) to moisturize; **hidrato** nm: **hidratos de carbono** carbohydrates

hidráulica [i'ðraulika] nf hydraulics sg

hidráulico, a [i'ðrauliko, a] adj hydraulic

hidro... [iðro] prefijo hydro..., water-...; **~eléctrico, a** adj hydroelectric; **~fobia** nf hydrophobia, rabies; **hidrógeno** nm hydrogen

hiedra ['jeðra] nf ivy

hiel [jel] nf gall, bile; (*fig*) bitterness

hiela etc vb ver **helar**

hielo ['jelo] nm (*gen*) ice; (*escarcha*) frost; (*fig*) coldness, reserve

hiena ['jena] nf hyena

hierba ['jerßa] nf (*pasto*) grass; (*CULIN, MED: planta*) herb; **mala ~** weed; (*fig*) evil influence; **~buena** nf mint

hierro ['jerro] nm (*metal*) iron; (*objeto*) iron object

hígado ['iyaðo] nm liver

higiene [i'xjene] nf hygiene; **higiénico, a** adj hygienic

higo ['iyo] nm fig; **higuera** nf fig tree

hijastro, a [i'xastro, a] nm/f stepson/ daughter

hijo, a [a ['ixo, a] nm/f son/daughter, child; **~s** nmpl children, sons and daughters; **~ de papá/mamá** daddy's/mummy's boy; **~ de puta** (*fam!*) bastard (*!*), son of a bitch (*!*)

hilar [i'lar] vt to spin; **~ fino** to split hairs

hilera [i'lera] nf row, file

hilo ['ilo] nm thread; (*BOT*) fibre; (*metal*) wire; (*de agua*) trickle, thin stream

hilvanar [ilßa'nar] vt (*COSTURA*) to tack (*BRIT*), baste (*US*); (*fig*) to do hurriedly

himno ['imno] nm hymn; **~ nacional** national anthem

hincapié [inka'pje] nm: **hacer ~ en** to emphasize

hincar [in'kar] vt to drive (in), thrust (in); **~se** vr: **~se de rodillas** to kneel down

hincha ['intʃa] (*fam*) nm/f fan

hinchado, a [in'tʃaðo, a] adj (*gen*) swollen; (*persona*) pompous

hinchar [in'tʃar] vt (*gen*) to swell; (*inflar*)

to blow up, inflate; (*fig*) to exaggerate; **~se** vr (*inflarse*) to swell up; (*fam: de comer*) to stuff o.s.; **hinchazón** nf (*MED*) swelling; (*altivez*) arrogance

hinojo [i'noxo] nm fennel

hipermercado [ipermer'kaðo] nm hypermarket, superstore

hípico, a ['ipiko, a] adj horse cpd

hipnotismo [ipno'tismo] nm hypnotism; **hipnotizar** vt to hypnotize

hipo ['ipo] nm hiccups pl

hipocresía [ipokre'sia] nf hypocrisy; **hipócrita** adj hypocritical ♦ nm/f hypocrite

hipódromo [i'poðromo] nm racetrack

hipopótamo [ipo'potamo] nm hippopotamus

hipoteca [ipo'teka] nf mortgage

hipótesis [i'potesis] nf inv hypothesis

hiriente [i'rjente] adj offensive, wounding

hispánico, a [is'paniko, a] adj Hispanic

hispano, a [is'pano, a] adj Hispanic, Spanish, Hispano- ♦ nm/f Spaniard; **H~américa** nf Latin America; **~americano, a** adj, nm/f Latin American

histeria [is'terja] nf hysteria

historia [is'torja] nf history; (*cuento*) story, tale; **~s** nfpl (*chismes*) gossip sg; **dejarse de ~s** to come to the point; **pasar a la ~** to go down in history; **~dor, a** nm/f historian; **historial** nm (*profesional*) curriculum vitae, C.V.; (*MED*) case history; **histórico, a** adj historical; (*memorable*) historic

historieta [isto'rjeta] nf tale, anecdote; (*dibujos*) comic strip

hito ['ito] nm (*fig*) landmark

hizo vb ver **hacer**

Hnos abr (= *Hermanos*) Bros.

hocico [o'θiko] nm snout

hockey ['xoki] nm hockey; **~ sobre hielo** ice hockey

hogar [o'γar] nm fireplace, hearth; (*casa*) home; (*vida familiar*) home life; **~eño, a** adj home cpd; (*persona*) home-loving

hoguera [o'γera] nf (*gen*) bonfire

hoja ['oxa] *nf* (*gen*) leaf; (*de flor*) petal; (*de papel*) sheet; (*página*) page; ~ **de afeitar** razor blade

hojalata [oxa'lata] *nf* tin(plate)

hojaldre [o'xaldre] *nm* (*CULIN*) puff pastry

hojear [oxe'ar] *vt* to leaf through, turn the pages of

hola ['ola] *excl* hello!

Holanda [o'landa] *nf* Holland; **holandés, esa** *adj* Dutch ♦ *nm/f* Dutchman/woman ♦ *nm* (*LING*) Dutch

holgado, a [ol'ɣaðo, a] *adj* (*ropa*) loose, baggy; (*rico*) comfortable

holgar [ol'ɣar] *vi* (*descansar*) to rest; (*sobrar*) to be superfluous; **huelga decir que** it goes without saying that

holgazán, ana [olɣa'θan, ana] *adj* idle, lazy ♦ *nm/f* loafer

holgura [ol'ɣura] *nf* looseness, bagginess; (*TEC*) play, free movement; (*vida*) comfortable living

hollín [o'ʎin] *nm* soot

hombre ['ombre] *nm* (*gen*) man; (*raza humana*): **el ~** man(kind) ♦ *excl*: **¡sí ~!** (*claro*) of course!; (*para énfasis*) man, old boy; **~ de negocios** businessman; **~ de pro** honest man; **~-rana** frogman

hombrera [om'brera] *nf* shoulder strap

hombro ['ombro] *nm* shoulder

hombruno, a [om'bruno, a] *adj* mannish

homenaje [ome'naxe] *nm* (*gen*) homage; (*tributo*) tribute

homicida [omi'θiða] *adj* homicidal ♦ *nm/f* murderer; **homicidio** *nm* murder, homicide

homologar [omolo'ɣar] *vt* (*COM*: *productos, tamaños*) to standardize; **homólogo, a** *nm/f*: **su** *etc* **homólogo** his *etc* counterpart *o* opposite number

homosexual [omosek'swal] *adj, nm/f* homosexual

hondo, a ['ondo, a] *adj* deep; **lo ~** the depth(s) (*pl*), the bottom; **~nada** *nf* hollow, depression; (*cañón*) ravine

Honduras [on'duras] *nf* Honduras

hondureño, a [ondu'reɲo, a] *adj, nm/f* Honduran

honestidad [onesti'ðað] *nf* purity, chastity; (*decencia*) decency; **honesto, a** *adj* chaste; decent, honest; (*justo*) just

hongo ['ongo] *nm* (*BOT*: *gen*) fungus; (: *comestible*) mushroom; (: *venenoso*) toadstool

honor [o'nor] *nm* (*gen*) honour; **en ~ a la verdad** to be fair; **~able** *adj* honourable

honorario, a [ono'rarjo, a] *adj* honorary; **~s** *nmpl* fees

honra ['onra] *nf* (*gen*) honour; (*renombre*) good name; **~dez** *nf* honesty; (*de persona*) integrity; **~do, a** *adj* honest, upright

honrar [on'rar] *vt* to honour; **~se** *vr*: **~se con algo/de hacer algo** to be honoured by sth/to do sth

honroso, a [on'roso, a] *adj* (*honrado*) honourable; (*respetado*) respectable

hora ['ora] *nf* (*una ~*) hour; (*tiempo*) time; **¿qué ~ es?** what time is it?; **¿a qué ~?** at what time?; **media ~** half an hour; **a la ~ de recreo** at playtime; **a primera ~** first thing (in the morning); **a última ~** at the last moment; **a altas ~s** in the small hours; **¡a buena ~!** about time, too!; **dar la ~** to strike the hour; **~s de oficina/de trabajo** office/working hours; **~s de visita** visiting times; **~s extras** *o* **extraordinarias** overtime *sg*; **~s punta** rush hours

horadar [ora'ðar] *vt* to drill, bore

horario, a [o'rarjo, a] *adj* hourly, hour *cpd* ♦ *nm* timetable; **~ comercial** business hours *pl*

horca ['orka] *nf* gallows *sg*

horcajadas [orka'xaðas]: **a ~** *adv* astride

horchata [or'tʃata] *nf* cold drink made from tiger nuts and water, tiger nut milk

horizontal [oriθon'tal] *adj* horizontal

horizonte [ori'θonte] *nm* horizon

horma ['orma] *nf* mould

hormiga [or'miɣa] *nf* ant; **~s** *nfpl* (*MED*) pins and needles

hormigón [ormi'ɣon] *nm* concrete; **~ armado/pretensado** reinforced/prestressed concrete

hormigueo [ormi'ɣeo] *nm* (*comezón*) itch

hormona [or'mona] *nf* hormone

hornada [or'naða] *nf* batch (of loaves *etc*)

hornillo [or'niʎo] *nm* (*cocina*) portable stove

horno ['orno] *nm* (CULIN) oven; (TEC) furnace; **alto ~** blast furnace

horóscopo [o'roskopo] *nm* horoscope

horquilla [or'kiʎa] *nf* hairpin; (AGR) pitchfork

horrendo, a [o'rrendo, a] *adj* horrendous, frightful

horrible [o'rriβle] *adj* horrible, dreadful

horripilante [orripi'lante] *adj* hair-raising, horrifying

horror [o'rror] *nm* horror, dread; (*atrocidad*) atrocity; **¡qué ~!** (*fam*) how awful!; **~izar** *vt* to horrify, frighten; **~izarse** *vr* to be horrified; **~oso, a** *adj* horrifying, ghastly

hortaliza [orta'liθa] *nf* vegetable

hortelano, a [orte'lano, a] *nm/f* (market) gardener

hortera [or'tera] (*fam*) *adj* tacky

hosco, a ['osko, a] *adj* sullen, gloomy

hospedar [ospe'ðar] *vt* to put up; **~se** *vr* to stay, lodge

hospital [ospi'tal] *nm* hospital

hospitalario, a [ospita'larjo, a] *adj* (*acogedor*) hospitable; **hospitalidad** *nf* hospitality

hostal [os'tal] *nm* small hotel

hostelería [ostele'ria] *nf* hotel business *o* trade

hostia ['ostja] *nf* (REL) host, consecrated wafer; (*fam!: golpe*) whack, punch ♦ *excl* (*fam!*): **¡~(s)!** damn!

hostigar [osti'ɣar] *vt* to whip; (*fig*) to harass, pester

hostil [os'til] *adj* hostile; **~idad** *nf* hostility

hotel [o'tel] *nm* hotel; **~ero, a** *adj* hotel *cpd* ♦ *nm/f* hotelier

hotel

ⓘ *In Spain you can choose from the following categories of accommodation, in descending order of quality and price:*

hotel *(from 5 stars to 1),* **hostal, pensión, casa de huéspedes, fonda.** *The State also runs luxury hotels called* **paradores,** *which are usually sited in places of particular historical interest and are often historic buildings themselves.*

hoy [oi] *adv* (*este día*) today; (*la actualidad*) now(adays) ♦ *nm* present time; **~ (en) día** now(adays)

hoyo ['ojo] *nm* hole, pit; **hoyuelo** *nm* dimple

hoz [oθ] *nf* sickle

hube *etc vb ver* **haber**

hucha ['utʃa] *nf* money box

hueco, a ['weko, a] *adj* (*vacío*) hollow, empty; (*resonante*) booming ♦ *nm* hollow, cavity

huelga *etc* ['welɣa] *vb ver* **holgar** ♦ *nf* strike; **declararse en ~** to go on strike, come out on strike; **~ de hambre** hunger strike

huelguista [wel'ɣista] *nm/f* striker

huella ['weʎa] *nf* (*pisada*) tread; (*marca del paso*) footprint, footstep; (: *de animal, máquina*) track; **~ digital** fingerprint

huelo *etc vb ver* **oler**

huérfano, a ['werfano, a] *adj* orphan(ed) ♦ *nm/f* orphan

huerta ['werta] *nf* market garden; (*en Murcia y Valencia*) irrigated region

huerto ['werto] *nm* kitchen garden; (*de árboles frutales*) orchard

hueso ['weso] *nm* (ANAT) bone; (*de fruta*) stone

huésped, a ['wespeð, a] *nm/f* guest

huesudo, a [we'suðo, a] *adj* bony, big-boned

hueva ['weβa] *nf* roe

huevera [we'βera] *nf* eggcup

huevo ['weβo] *nm* egg; **~ duro/ escalfado/frito** (ESP) *o* **estrellado** (AM)/ **pasado por agua** hard-boiled/poached/ fried/soft-boiled egg; **~s revueltos** scrambled eggs

huida [u'iða] *nf* escape, flight

huidizo, a [ui'ðiθo, a] *adj* shy

huir [u'ir] vi (escapar) to flee, escape; (evitar) to avoid; **~se** vr (escaparse) to escape

hule ['ule] nm oilskin

humanidad [umani'ðað] nf (género humano) man(kind); (cualidad) humanity

humanitario, a [umani'tarjo, a] adj humanitarian

humano, a [u'mano, a] adj (gen) human; (humanitario) humane ♦ nm human; **ser ~** human being

humareda [uma'reða] nf cloud of smoke

humedad [ume'ðað] nf (del clima) humidity; (de pared etc) dampness; **a prueba de ~** damp-proof; **humedecer** vt to moisten, wet; **humedecerse** vr to get wet

húmedo, a ['umeðo, a] adj (mojado) damp, wet; (tiempo etc) humid

humildad [umil'dað] nf humility, humbleness; **humilde** adj humble, modest

humillación [umiʎa'θjon] nf humiliation; **humillante** adj humiliating

humillar [umi'ʎar] vt to humiliate; **~se** vr to humble o.s., grovel

humo ['umo] nm (de fuego) smoke; (gas nocivo) fumes pl; (vapor) steam, vapour; **~s** nmpl (fig) conceit sg

humor [u'mor] nm (disposición) mood, temper; (lo que divierte) humour; **de buen/mal ~** in a good/bad mood; **~ista** nm/f comic; **~ístico, a** adj funny, humorous

hundimiento [undi'mjento] nm (gen) sinking; (colapso) collapse

hundir [un'dir] vt to sink; (edificio, plan) to ruin, destroy; **~se** vr to sink, collapse

húngaro, a ['ungaro, a] adj, nm/f Hungarian

Hungría [un'gria] nf Hungary

huracán [ura'kan] nm hurricane

huraño, a [u'raɲo, a] adj (antisocial) unsociable

hurgar [ur'ɣar] vt to poke, jab; (remover) to stir (up); **~se** vr: **~se (las narices)** to pick one's nose

hurón, ona [u'ron, ona] nm (ZOOL) ferret

hurtadillas [urta'ðiʎas]: **a ~** adv stealthily, on the sly

hurtar [ur'tar] vt to steal; **hurto** nm theft, stealing

husmear [usme'ar] vt (oler) to sniff out, scent; (fam) to pry into

huyo etc vb ver **huir**

I, i

iba etc vb ver **ir**

ibérico, a [i'ßeriko, a] adj Iberian

iberoamericano, a [ißeroameri'kano, a] adj, nm/f Latin American

Ibiza [i'ßiθa] nf Ibiza

iceberg [iθe'ßer] nm iceberg

icono [i'kono] nm ikon, icon

iconoclasta [ikono'klasta] adj iconoclastic ♦ nm/f iconoclast

ictericia [ikte'riθja] nf jaundice

I + D abr (= Investigación y Desarrollo) R & D

ida ['iða] nf going, departure; **~ y vuelta** round trip, return

idea [i'ðea] nf idea; **no tengo la menor ~** I haven't a clue

ideal [iðe'al] adj, nm ideal; **~ista** nm/f idealist; **~izar** vt to idealize

idear [iðe'ar] vt to think up; (aparato) to invent; (viaje) to plan

ídem ['iðem] pron ditto

idéntico, a [i'ðentiko, a] adj identical

identidad [iðenti'ðað] nf identity

identificación [iðentifika'θjon] nf identification

identificar [iðentifi'kar] vt to identify; **~se** vr: **~se con** to identify with

ideología [iðeolo'xia] nf ideology

idilio [i'ðiljo] nm love-affair

idioma [i'ðjoma] nm (gen) language

idiota [i'ðjota] adj idiotic ♦ nm/f idiot; **idiotez** nf idiocy

ídolo ['iðolo] nm (tb fig) idol

idóneo, a [i'ðoneo, a] adj suitable

iglesia [i'xlesja] nf church

ignorancia [iɣnoˈranθja] *nf* ignorance;
  ignorante *adj* ignorant, uninformed
  ♦ *nm/f* ignoramus
ignorar [iɣnoˈrar] *vt* not to know, be
  ignorant of; (*no hacer caso a*) to ignore
igual [iˈɣwal] *adj* (*gen*) equal; (*similar*) like,
  similar; (*mismo*) (the) same; (*constante*)
  constant; (*temperatura*) even ♦ *nm/f*
  equal; **~ que** like, the same as; **me da** *o*
  es ~ I don't care; **son ~es** they're the
  same; **al ~ que** *prep, conj* like, just like
igualada [iɣwaˈlaða] *nf* equaliser
igualar [iɣwaˈlar] *vt* (*gen*) to equalize,
  make equal; (*allanar, nivelar*) to level (off),
  even (out); **~se** *vr* (*platos de balanza*) to
  balance out
igualdad [iɣwalˈdað] *nf* equality;
  (*similaridad*) sameness; (*uniformidad*)
  uniformity
igualmente [iɣwalˈmente] *adv* equally;
  (*también*) also, likewise ♦ *excl* the same
  to you!
ikurriña [ikuˈrriɲa] *nf* Basque flag
ilegal [ileˈɣal] *adj* illegal
ilegítimo, a [ileˈxitimo, a] *adj* illegitimate
ileso, a [iˈleso, a] *adj* unhurt
ilícito, a [iˈliθito, a] *adj* illicit
ilimitado, a [ilimiˈtaðo, a] *adj* unlimited
ilógico, a [iˈloxiko, a] *adj* illogical
iluminación [iluminaˈθjon] *nf*
  illumination; (*alumbrado*) lighting
iluminar [ilumiˈnar] *vt* to illuminate, light
  (up); (*fig*) to enlighten
ilusión [iluˈsjon] *nf* illusion; (*quimera*)
  delusion; (*esperanza*) hope; **hacerse**
  ilusiones to build up one's hopes;
  ilusionado, a *adj* excited; **ilusionar**
  vi: **le ilusiona ir de vacaciones** he's
  looking forward to going on holiday;
  ilusionarse *vr*: **ilusionarse (con)** to get
  excited (about)
ilusionista [ilusjoˈnista] *nm/f* conjurer
iluso, a [iˈluso, a] *adj* easily deceived
  ♦ *nm/f* dreamer
ilusorio, a [iluˈsorjo, a] *adj* (*de ilusión*)
  illusory, deceptive; (*esperanza*) vain
ilustración [ilustraˈθjon] *nf* illustration;

(*saber*) learning, erudition; **la I~** the
  Enlightenment; **ilustrado, a** *adj*
  illustrated; learned
ilustrar [ilusˈtrar] *vt* to illustrate; (*instruir*)
  to instruct; (*explicar*) to explain, make
  clear; **~se** *vr* to acquire knowledge
ilustre [iˈlustre] *adj* famous, illustrious
imagen [iˈmaxen] *nf* (*gen*) image; (*dibujo*)
  picture
imaginación [imaxinaˈθjon] *nf*
  imagination
imaginar [imaxiˈnar] *vt* (*gen*) to imagine;
  (*idear*) to think up; (*suponer*) to suppose;
  ~se *vr* to imagine; **~io, a** *adj* imaginary;
  imaginativo, a *adj* imaginative
imán [iˈman] *nm* magnet
imbécil [imˈbeθil] *nm/f* imbecile, idiot
imitación [imitaˈθjon] *nf* imitation
imitar [imiˈtar] *vt* to imitate; (*parodiar,*
  remedar) to mimic, ape
impaciencia [impaˈθjenθja] *nf*
  impatience; **impaciente** *adj* impatient;
  (*nervioso*) anxious
impacto [imˈpakto] *nm* impact
impar [imˈpar] *adj* odd
imparcial [imparˈθjal] *adj* impartial, fair
impartir [imparˈtir] *vt* to impart, give
impasible [impaˈsiβle] *adj* impassive
impecable [impeˈkaβle] *adj* impeccable
impedimento [impeðiˈmento] *nm*
  impediment, obstacle
impedir [impeˈðir] *vt* (*obstruir*) to impede,
  obstruct; (*estorbar*) to prevent
impenetrable [impeneˈtraβle] *adj*
  impenetrable; (*fig*) incomprehensible
imperar [impeˈrar] *vi* (*reinar*) to rule,
  reign; (*fig*) to prevail, reign; (*precio*) to be
  current
imperativo, a [imperaˈtiβo, a] *adj*
  (*urgente, LING*) imperative
imperceptible [imperθepˈtiβle] *adj*
  imperceptible
imperdible [imperˈðiβle] *nm* safety pin
imperdonable [imperðoˈnaβle] *adj*
  unforgivable, inexcusable
imperfección [imperfekˈθjon] *nf*
  imperfection

imperfecto, a [imper'fekto, a] *adj* imperfect

imperial [impe'rjal] *adj* imperial; **~ismo** *nm* imperialism

imperio [im'perjo] *nm* empire; *(autoridad)* rule, authority; *(fig)* pride, haughtiness; **~so, a** *adj* imperious; *(urgente)* urgent; *(imperativo)* imperative

impermeable [imperme'aβle] *adj* waterproof ♦ *nm* raincoat, mac *(BRIT)*

impersonal [imperso'nal] *adj* impersonal

impertinencia [imperti'nenθja] *nf* impertinence; **impertinente** *adj* impertinent

imperturbable [impertur'βaβle] *adj* imperturbable

ímpetu ['impetu] *nm* *(impulso)* impetus, impulse; *(impetuosidad)* impetuosity; *(violencia)* violence

impetuoso, a [impe'twoso, a] *adj* impetuous; *(río)* rushing; *(acto)* hasty

impío [im'pio, a] *adj* impious, ungodly

implacable [impla'kaβle] *adj* implacable

implantar [implan'tar] *vt* to introduce

implicar [impli'kar] *vt* to involve; *(entrañar)* to imply

implícito, a [im'pliθito, a] *adj* *(tácito)* implicit; *(sobreentendido)* implied

implorar [implo'rar] *vt* to beg, implore

imponente [impo'nente] *adj* *(impresionante)* impressive, imposing; *(solemne)* grand

imponer [impo'ner] *vt* *(gen)* to impose; *(exigir)* to exact; **~se** *vr* to assert o.s.; *(prevalecer)* to prevail; **imponible** *adj* *(COM)* taxable

impopular [impopu'lar] *adj* unpopular

importación [importa'θjon] *nf* *(acto)* importing; *(mercancías)* imports *pl*

importancia [impor'tanθja] *nf* importance; *(valor)* value, significance; *(extensión)* size, magnitude; **importante** *adj* important; valuable, significant

importar [impor'tar] *vt* *(del extranjero)* to import; *(costar)* to amount to ♦ *vi* to be important, matter; **me importa un rábano** I couldn't care less; **no importa** it doesn't matter; **¿le importa que fume?** do you mind if I smoke?

importe [im'porte] *nm* *(total)* amount; *(valor)* value

importunar [importu'nar] *vt* to bother, pester

imposibilidad [imposiβili'ðað] *nf* impossibility; **imposibilitar** *vt* to make impossible, prevent

imposible [impo'siβle] *adj* *(gen)* impossible; *(insoportable)* unbearable, intolerable

imposición [imposi'θjon] *nf* imposition; *(COM: impuesto)* tax; *(: inversión)* deposit

impostor, a [impos'tor, a] *nm/f* impostor

impotencia [impo'tenθja] *nf* impotence; **impotente** *adj* impotent

impracticable [imprakti'kaβle] *adj* *(irrealizable)* impracticable; *(intransitable)* impassable

impreciso, a [impre'θiso, a] *adj* imprecise, vague

impregnar [impreɣ'nar] *vt* to impregnate; **~se** *vr* to become impregnated

imprenta [im'prenta] *nf* *(acto)* printing; *(aparato)* press; *(casa)* printer's; *(letra)* print

imprescindible [impresθin'diβle] *adj* essential, vital

impresión [impre'sjon] *nf* *(gen)* impression; *(IMPRENTA)* printing; *(edición)* edition; *(FOTO)* print; *(marca)* imprint; **~ digital** fingerprint

impresionable [impresjo'naβle] *adj* *(sensible)* impressionable

impresionante [impresjo'nante] *adj* impressive; *(tremendo)* tremendous; *(maravilloso)* great, marvellous

impresionar [impresjo'nar] *vt* *(conmover)* to move; *(afectar)* to impress, strike; *(película fotográfica)* to expose; **~se** *vr* to be impressed; *(conmoverse)* to be moved

impreso, a [im'preso, a] *pp de* **imprimir** ♦ *adj* printed; **~s** *nmpl* printed matter; **impresora** *nf* printer

imprevisto, a [impre'βisto, a] *adj* *(gen)* unforeseen; *(inesperado)* unexpected

imprimir [impri'mir] *vt* to imprint, impress, stamp; *(textos)* to print; *(INFORM)* to output, print out

improbable [impro'ßaßle] *adj* improbable; *(inverosímil)* unlikely

improcedente [improθe'ðente] *adj* inappropriate

improductivo, a [improðuk'tißo, a] *adj* unproductive

improperio [impro'perjo] *nm* insult

impropio, a [im'propjo, a] *adj* improper

improvisado, a [improßi'saðo, a] *adj* improvised

improvisar [improßi'sar] *vt* to improvise

improviso, a [impro'ßiso, a] *adj*: **de ~** unexpectedly, suddenly

imprudencia [impru'ðenθja] *nf* imprudence; *(indiscreción)* indiscretion; *(descuido)* carelessness; **imprudente** *adj* unwise, imprudent; *(indiscreto)* indiscreet

impúdico, a [im'puðiko, a] *adj* shameless; *(lujurioso)* lecherous

impuesto, a [im'pwesto, a] *adj* imposed ♦ *nm* tax; **~ sobre el valor añadido** value added tax

impugnar [impuɣ'nar] *vt* to oppose, contest; *(refutar)* to refute, impugn

impulsar [impul'sar] *vt* to drive; *(promover)* to promote, stimulate

impulsivo, a [impul'sißo, a] *adj* impulsive; **impulso** *nm* impulse; *(fuerza, empuje)* thrust, drive; *(fig: sentimiento)* urge, impulse

impune [im'pune] *adj* unpunished

impureza [impu'reθa] *nf* impurity; **impuro, a** *adj* impure

imputar [impu'tar] *vt* to attribute

inacabable [inaka'ßaßle] *adj (infinito)* endless; *(interminable)* interminable

inaccesible [inakθe'sißle] *adj* inaccessible

inacción [inak'θjon] *nf* inactivity

inaceptable [inaθep'taßle] *adj* unacceptable

inactividad [inaktißi'ðað] *nf* inactivity; *(COM)* dullness; **inactivo, a** *adj* inactive

inadecuado, a [inaðe'kwaðo, a] *adj (insuficiente)* inadequate; *(inapto)* unsuitable

inadmisible [inaðmi'sißle] *adj* inadmissible

inadvertido, a [inaðßer'tiðo, a] *adj (no visto)* unnoticed

inagotable [inaɣo'taßle] *adj* inexhaustible

inaguantable [inaɣwan'taßle] *adj* unbearable

inalterable [inalte'raßle] *adj* immutable, unchangeable

inanición [inani'θjon] *nf* starvation

inanimado, a [inani'maðo, a] *adj* inanimate

inapreciable [inapre'θjaßle] *adj (cantidad, diferencia)* imperceptible; *(ayuda, servicio)* invaluable

inaudito, a [inau'ðito, a] *adj* unheard-of

inauguración [inauɣura'θjon] *nf* inauguration; opening

inaugurar [inauɣu'rar] *vt* to inaugurate; *(exposición)* to open

inca ['inka] *nm/f* Inca

incalculable [inkalku'laßle] *adj* incalculable

incandescente [inkandes'θente] *adj* incandescent

incansable [inkan'saßle] *adj* tireless, untiring

incapacidad [inkapaθi'ðað] *nf* incapacity; *(incompetencia)* incompetence; **~ física / mental** physical/mental disability

incapacitar [inkapaθi'tar] *vt (inhabilitar)* to incapacitate, render unfit; *(descalificar)* to disqualify

incapaz [inka'paθ] *adj* incapable

incautación [inkauta'θjon] *nf* confiscation

incautarse [inkau'tarse] *vr*: **~ de** to seize, confiscate

incauto, a [in'kauto, a] *adj (imprudente)* incautious, unwary

incendiar [inθen'djar] *vt* to set fire to; *(fig)* to inflame; **~se** *vr* to catch fire; **~io, a** *adj* incendiary

incendio [in'θendjo] *nm* fire

incentivo [inθen'tißo] *nm* incentive

incertidumbre [inθerti'ðumbre] *nf (inseguridad)* uncertainty; *(duda)* doubt

incesante [inθe'sante] *adj* incessant

incesto [in'θesto] *nm* incest

incidencia [inθi'ðenθja] *nf* (*MAT*) incidence

incidente [inθi'ðente] *nm* incident

incidir [inθi'ðir] *vi* (*influir*) to influence; (*afectar*) to affect; **~ en un error** to fall into error

incienso [in'θjenso] *nm* incense

incierto, a [in'θjerto, a] *adj* uncertain

incineración [inθinera'θjon] *nf* incineration; (*de cadáveres*) cremation

incinerar [inθine'rar] *vt* to burn; (*cadáveres*) to cremate

incipiente [inθi'pjente] *adj* incipient

incisión [inθi'sjon] *nf* incision

incisivo, a [inθi'siβo, a] *adj* sharp, cutting; (*fig*) incisive

incitar [inθi'tar] *vt* to incite, rouse

inclemencia [inkle'menθja] *nf* (*severidad*) harshness, severity; (*del tiempo*) inclemency

inclinación [inklina'θjon] *nf* (*gen*) inclination; (*de tierras*) slope, incline; (*de cabeza*) nod, bow; (*fig*) leaning, bent

inclinar [inkli'nar] *vt* to incline; (*cabeza*) to nod, bow ♦ *vi* to lean, slope; **~se** *vr* to bow; (*encorvarse*) to stoop; **~se a** (*parecerse a*) to take after, resemble; **~se ante** to bow down to; **me inclino a pensar que** I'm inclined to think that

incluir [inklu'ir] *vt* to include; (*incorporar*) to incorporate; (*meter*) to enclose

inclusive [inklu'siβe] *adv* inclusive ♦ *prep* including

incluso [in'kluso] *adv* even

incógnita [in'koɣnita] *nf* (*MAT*) unknown quantity

incógnito [in'koɣnito] *nm*: **de ~** incognito

incoherente [inkoe'rente] *adj* incoherent

incoloro, a [inko'loro, a] *adj* colourless

incólume [in'kolume] *adj* unhurt, unharmed

incomodar [inkomo'ðar] *vt* to inconvenience; (*molestar*) to bother, trouble; (*fastidiar*) to annoy; **~se** *vr* to put o.s. out; (*fastidiarse*) to get annoyed

incomodidad [inkomoði'ðað] *nf* inconvenience; (*fastidio, enojo*) annoyance; (*de vivienda*) discomfort

incómodo, a [in'komoðo, a] *adj* (*inconfortable*) uncomfortable; (*molesto*) annoying; (*inconveniente*) inconvenient

incomparable [inkompa'raβle] *adj* incomparable

incompatible [inkompa'tiβle] *adj* incompatible

incompetencia [inkompe'tenθja] *nf* incompetence; **incompetente** *adj* incompetent

incompleto, a [inkom'pleto, a] *adj* incomplete, unfinished

incomprensible [inkompren'siβle] *adj* incomprehensible

incomunicado, a [inkomuni'kaðo, a] *adj* (*aislado*) cut off, isolated; (*confinado*) in solitary confinement

inconcebible [inkonθe'βiβle] *adj* inconceivable

incondicional [inkondiθjo'nal] *adj* unconditional; (*apoyo*) wholehearted; (*partidario*) staunch

inconexo, a [inko'nekso, a] *adj* (*gen*) unconnected; (*desunido*) disconnected

inconfundible [inkonfun'diβle] *adj* unmistakable

incongruente [inkon'grwente] *adj* incongruous

inconsciencia [inkons'θjenθja] *nf* unconsciousness; (*fig*) thoughtlessness; **inconsciente** *adj* unconscious; thoughtless

inconsecuente [inkonse'kwente] *adj* inconsistent

inconsiderado, a [inkonsiðe'raðo, a] *adj* inconsiderate

inconsistente [inkonsis'tente] *adj* weak; (*tela*) flimsy

inconstancia [inkons'tanθja] *nf* inconstancy; (*inestabilidad*) unsteadiness; **inconstante** *adj* inconstant

incontable [inkon'taβle] *adj* countless, innumerable

incontestable [inkontes'taβle] *adj*

unanswerable; (*innegable*) undeniable
incontinencia [inkonti'nenθja] *nf*
incontinence
inconveniencia [inkombe'njenθja] *nf*
unsuitability, inappropriateness;
(*descortesía*) impoliteness;
inconveniente *adj* unsuitable; impolite
♦ *nm* obstacle; (*desventaja*) disadvantage;
el inconveniente es que ... the trouble
is that ...
incordiar [inkor'ðjar] (*fam*) *vt* to bug,
annoy
incorporación [inkorpora'θjon] *nf*
incorporation
incorporar [inkorpo'rar] *vt* to incorporate;
~se *vr* to sit up
incorrección [inkorrek'θjon] *nf* (*gen*)
incorrectness, inaccuracy; (*descortesía*)
bad-mannered behaviour; **incorrecto, a**
adj (*gen*) incorrect, wrong;
(*comportamiento*) bad-mannered
incorregible [inkorre'xiβle] *adj*
incorrigible
incredulidad [inkreðuli'ðað] *nf*
incredulity; (*escepticismo*) scepticism;
incrédulo, a *adj* incredulous,
unbelieving, sceptical
increíble [inkre'iβle] *adj* incredible
incremento [inkre'mento] *nm* increment;
(*aumento*) rise, increase
increpar [inkre'par] *vt* to reprimand
incruento, a [in'krwento, a] *adj* bloodless
incrustar [inkrus'tar] *vt* to incrust;
(*piedras: en joya*) to inlay
incubar [inku'βar] *vt* to incubate
inculcar [inkul'kar] *vt* to inculcate
inculpar [inkul'par] *vt* (*acusar*) to accuse;
(*achacar, atribuir*) to charge, blame
inculto, a [in'kulto, a] *adj* (*persona*)
uneducated; (*grosero*) uncouth ♦ *nm/f*
ignoramus
incumplimiento [inkumpli'mjento] *nm*
non-fulfilment; **~ de contrato** breach of
contract
incurrir [inku'rrir] *vi*: **~ en** to incur;
(*crimen*) to commit; **~ en un error** to
make a mistake

indagación [indaɣa'θjon] *nf* investigation;
(*búsqueda*) search; (*JUR*) inquest
indagar [inda'ɣar] *vt* to investigate; to
search; (*averiguar*) to ascertain
indecente [inde'θente] *adj* indecent,
improper; (*lascivo*) obscene
indecible [inde'θiβle] *adj* unspeakable;
(*indescriptible*) indescribable
indeciso, a [inde'θiso, a] *adj* (*por decidir*)
undecided; (*vacilante*) hesitant
indefenso, a [inde'fenso, a] *adj*
defenceless
indefinido, a [indefi'niðo, a] *adj*
indefinite; (*vago*) vague, undefined
indeleble [inde'leβle] *adj* indelible
indemne [in'demne] *adj* (*objeto*)
undamaged; (*persona*) unharmed, unhurt
indemnizar [indemni'θar] *vt* to indemnify;
(*compensar*) to compensate
independencia [independen'θja] *nf*
independence
independiente [independ'jente] *adj*
(*libre*) independent; (*autónomo*) self-
sufficient
indeterminado, a [indetermi'naðo, a] *adj*
indefinite; (*desconocido*) indeterminate
India ['indja] *nf*: **la ~** India
indicación [indika'θjon] *nf* indication;
(*señal*) sign; (*sugerencia*) suggestion, hint
indicado, a [indi'kaðo, a] *adj* (*momento,
método*) right; (*tratamiento*) appropriate;
(*solución*) likely
indicador [indika'ðor] *nm* indicator; (*TEC*)
gauge, meter
indicar [indi'kar] *vt* (*mostrar*) to indicate,
show; (*termómetro etc*) to read, register;
(*señalar*) to point to
índice ['indiθe] *nm* index; (*catálogo*)
catalogue; (*ANAT*) index finger, forefinger
indicio [in'diθjo] *nm* indication, sign; (*en
pesquisa etc*) clue
indiferencia [indife'renθja] *nf*
indifference; (*apatía*) apathy;
indiferente *adj* indifferent
indígena [in'dixena] *adj* indigenous,
native ♦ *nm/f* native
indigencia [indi'xenθja] *nf* poverty, need

indigestión [indixes'tjon] *nf* indigestion
indigesto, a [indi'xesto, a] *adj* (*alimento*) indigestible; (*fig*) turgid
indignación [indiɣna'θjon] *nf* indignation
indignar [indiɣ'nar] *vt* to anger, make indignant; **~se** *vr*: **~se por** to get indignant about
indigno, a [in'diɣno, a] *adj* (*despreciable*) low, contemptible; (*inmerecido*) unworthy
indio, a ['indjo, a] *adj, nm/f* Indian
indirecta [indi'rekta] *nf* insinuation, innuendo; (*sugerencia*) hint
indirecto, a [indi'rekto, a] *adj* indirect
indiscreción [indiskre'θjon] *nf* (*imprudencia*) indiscretion; (*irreflexión*) tactlessness; (*acto*) gaffe, faux pas
indiscreto, a [indis'kreto, a] *adj* indiscreet
indiscriminado, a [indiskrimi'naðo, a] *adj* indiscriminate
indiscutible [indisku'tiβle] *adj* indisputable, unquestionable
indispensable [indispen'saβle] *adj* indispensable, essential
indisponer [indispo'ner] *vt* to spoil, upset; (*salud*) to make ill; **~se** *vr* to fall ill; **~se con uno** to fall out with sb
indisposición [indisposi'θjon] *nf* indisposition
indispuesto, a [indis'pwesto, a] *adj* (*enfermo*) unwell, indisposed
indistinto, a [indis'tinto, a] *adj* indistinct; (*vago*) vague
individual [indiβi'ðwal] *adj* individual; (*habitación*) single ♦ *nm* (DEPORTE) singles *sg*
individuo, a [indi'βiðwo, a] *adj, nm* individual
índole ['indole] *nf* (*naturaleza*) nature; (*clase*) sort, kind
indómito, a [in'domito, a] *adj* indomitable
inducir [indu'θir] *vt* to induce; (*inferir*) to infer; (*persuadir*) to persuade
indudable [indu'ðaβle] *adj* undoubted; (*incuestionable*) unquestionable
indulgencia [indul'xenθja] *nf* indulgence
indultar [indul'tar] *vt* (*perdonar*) to

pardon, reprieve; (*librar de pago*) to exempt; **indulto** *nm* pardon; exemption
industria [in'dustrja] *nf* industry; (*habilidad*) skill; **industrial** *adj* industrial ♦ *nm* industrialist
inédito, a [in'eðito, a] *adj* (*texto*) unpublished; (*nuevo*) new
inefable [ine'faβle] *adj* ineffable, indescribable
ineficaz [inefi'kaθ] *adj* (*inútil*) ineffective; (*ineficiente*) inefficient
ineludible [inelu'ðiβle] *adj* inescapable, unavoidable
ineptitud [inepti'tuð] *nf* ineptitude, incompetence; **inepto, a** *adj* inept, incompetent
inequívoco, a [ine'kiβoko, a] *adj* unequivocal; (*inconfundible*) unmistakable
inercia [in'erθja] *nf* inertia; (*pasividad*) passivity
inerme [in'erme] *adj* (*sin armas*) unarmed; (*indefenso*) defenceless
inerte [in'erte] *adj* inert; (*inmóvil*) motionless
inesperado, a [inespe'raðo, a] *adj* unexpected, unforeseen
inestable [ines'taβle] *adj* unstable
inevitable [ineβi'taβle] *adj* inevitable
inexactitud [ineksakti'tuð] *nf* inaccuracy; **inexacto, a** *adj* inaccurate; (*falso*) untrue
inexperto, a [inek'sperto, a] *adj* (*novato*) inexperienced
infalible [infa'liβle] *adj* infallible; (*plan*) foolproof
infame [in'fame] *adj* infamous; (*horrible*) dreadful; **infamia** *nf* infamy; (*deshonra*) disgrace
infancia [in'fanθja] *nf* infancy, childhood
infantería [infante'ria] *nf* infantry
infantil [infan'til] *adj* (*pueril, aniñado*) infantile; (*cándido*) childlike; (*literatura, ropa etc*) children's
infarto [in'farto] *nm* (*tb*: **~ de miocardio**) heart attack
infatigable [infati'ɣaβle] *adj* tireless, untiring

infección [infek'θjon] *nf* infection; **infeccioso, a** *adj* infectious

infectar [infek'tar] *vt* to infect; **~se** *vr* to become infected

infeliz [infe'liθ] *adj* unhappy, wretched ♦ *nm/f* wretch

inferior [infe'rjor] *adj* inferior; (*situación*) lower ♦ *nm/f* inferior, subordinate

inferir [infe'rir] *vt* (*deducir*) to infer, deduce; (*causar*) to cause

infestar [infes'tar] *vt* to infest

infidelidad [infiðeli'ðað] *nf* (*gen*) infidelity, unfaithfulness

infiel [in'fjel] *adj* unfaithful, disloyal; (*erróneo*) inaccurate ♦ *nm/f* infidel, unbeliever

infierno [in'fjerno] *nm* hell

infiltrarse [infil'trarse] *vr*: **~ en** to infiltrate in(to); (*persona*) to work one's way in(to)

ínfimo, a [l'infimo, a] *adj* (*más bajo*) lowest; (*despreciable*) vile, mean

infinidad [infini'ðað] *nf* infinity; (*abundancia*) great quantity

infinito, a [infi'nito, a] *adj, nm* infinite

inflación [infla'θjon] *nf* (*hinchazón*) swelling; (*monetaria*) inflation; (*fig*) conceit; **inflacionario, a** *adj* inflationary

inflamar [infla'mar] *vt* to inflame; **~se** *vr* to catch fire; to become inflamed

inflar [in'flar] *vt* (*hinchar*) to inflate, blow up; (*fig*) to exaggerate; **~se** *vr* to swell (up); (*fig*) to get conceited

inflexible [inflek'siβle] *adj* inflexible; (*fig*) unbending

infligir [infli'xir] *vt* to inflict

influencia [influ'enθja] *nf* influence; **influenciar** *vt* to influence

influir [influ'ir] *vt* to influence

influjo [in'fluxo] *nm* influence

influya *etc vb ver* **influir**

influyente [influ'jente] *adj* influential

información [informa'θjon] *nf* information; (*noticias*) news *sg*; (*JUR*) inquiry; **I~** (*oficina*) Information Office; (*mostrador*) Information Desk; (*TEL*) Directory Enquiries

informal [infor'mal] *adj* (*gen*) informal

informar [infor'mar] *vt* (*gen*) to inform; (*revelar*) to reveal, make known ♦ *vi* (*JUR*) to plead; (*denunciar*) to inform; (*dar cuenta de*) to report on; **~se** *vr* to find out; **~se de** to inquire into

informática [infor'matika] *nf* computer science, information technology

informe [in'forme] *adj* shapeless ♦ *nm* report

infortunio [infor'tunjo] *nm* misfortune

infracción [infrak'θjon] *nf* infraction, infringement

infranqueable [infranke'aβle] *adj* impassable; (*fig*) insurmountable

infravalorar [infrabalo'rar] *vt* to undervalue, underestimate

infringir [infrin'xir] *vt* to infringe, contravene

infructuoso, a [infruk'twoso, a] *adj* fruitless, unsuccessful

infundado, a [infun'daðo, a] *adj* groundless, unfounded

infundir [infun'dir] *vt* to infuse, instil

infusión [infu'sjon] *nf* infusion; **~ de manzanilla** camomile tea

ingeniar [inxe'njar] *vt* to think up, devise; **~se** *vr*: **~se para** to manage to

ingeniería [inxenje'ria] *nf* engineering; **~ genética** genetic engineering; **ingeniero, a** *nm/f* engineer; **ingeniero de caminos/de sonido** civil engineer/sound engineer

ingenio [in'xenjo] *nm* (*talento*) talent; (*agudeza*) wit; (*habilidad*) ingenuity, inventiveness; **~ azucarero** (*AM*) sugar refinery

ingenioso, a [inxe'njoso, a] *adj* ingenious, clever; (*divertido*) witty

ingenuidad [inxenwi'ðað] *nf* ingenuousness; (*sencillez*) simplicity; **ingenuo, a** *adj* ingenuous

ingerir [inxe'rir] *vt* (*tragar*) to ingest; (*tragar*) to swallow; (*consumir*) to consume

Inglaterra [ingla'terra] *nf* England

ingle ['ingle] *nf* groin

inglés, esa [in'gles, esa] *adj* English

♦ nm/f Englishman/woman ♦ nm (LING) English

ingratitud [ingrati'tuð] nf ingratitude; **ingrato, a** adj (gen) ungrateful

ingrediente [ingre'ðjente] nm ingredient

ingresar [ingre'sar] vt (dinero) to deposit ♦ vi to come in; ~ **en un club** to join a club; ~ **en el hospital** to go into hospital

ingreso [in'greso] nm (entrada) entry; (: en hospital etc) admission; ~**s** nmpl (dinero) income sg; (: COM) takings pl

inhabitable [inaßi'taßle] adj uninhabitable

inhalar [ina'lar] vt to inhale

inherente [ine'rente] adj inherent

inhibir [ini'ßir] vt to inhibit

inhóspito, a [i'nospito, a] adj (región, paisaje) inhospitable

inhumano, a [inu'mano, a] adj inhuman

inicial [ini'θjal] adj, nf initial

iniciar [ini'θjar] vt (persona) to initiate; (empezar) to begin, commence; (conversación) to start up

iniciativa [iniθja'tißa] nf initiative; **la ~ privada** private enterprise

ininterrumpido, a [ininterrum'piðo, a] adj uninterrupted

injerencia [inxe'renθja] nf interference

injertar [inxer'tar] vt to graft; **injerto** nm graft

injuria [in'xurja] nf (agravio, ofensa) offence; (insulto) insult; **injuriar** vt to insult; **injurioso, a** adj offensive, insulting

injusticia [inxus'tiθja] nf injustice

injusto, a [in'xusto, a] adj unjust, unfair

inmadurez [inmaðu'reθ] nf immaturity

inmediaciones [inmeðja'θjones] nfpl neighbourhood sg, environs

inmediato, a [inme'ðjato, a] adj immediate; (contiguo) adjoining; (rápido) prompt; (próximo) neighbouring, next; **de ~** immediately

inmejorable [inmexo'raßle] adj unsurpassable; (precio) unbeatable

inmenso, a [in'menso, a] adj immense, huge

inmerecido, a [inmere'θiðo, a] adj undeserved

inmigración [inmiɣra'θjon] nf immigration

inmiscuirse [inmisku'irse] vr to interfere, meddle

inmobiliaria [inmoßi'ljarja] nf estate agency

inmobiliario, a [inmoßi'ljarjo, a] adj real-estate cpd, property cpd

inmolar [inmo'lar] vt to immolate, sacrifice

inmoral [inmo'ral] adj immoral

inmortal [inmor'tal] adj immortal; ~**izar** vt to immortalize

inmóvil [in'moßil] adj immobile

inmueble [in'mweßle] adj: **bienes ~s** real estate, landed property ♦ nm property

inmundicia [inmun'diθja] nf filth; **inmundo, a** adj filthy

inmune [in'mune] adj: ~ **(a)** (MED) immune (to)

inmunidad [inmuni'ðað] nf immunity

inmutarse [inmu'tarse] vr to turn pale; **no se inmutó** he didn't turn a hair

innato, a [in'nato, a] adj innate

innecesario, a [inneθe'sarjo, a] adj unnecessary

innoble [in'noßle] adj ignoble

innovación [innoßa'θjon] nf innovation

innovar [inno'ßar] vt to introduce

inocencia [ino'θenθja] nf innocence

inocentada [inoθen'taða] nf practical joke

inocente [ino'θente] adj (ingenuo) naive, innocent; (inculpable) innocent; (sin malicia) harmless ♦ nm/f simpleton

---
Día de los Santos Inocentes

i The 28th December, **el día de los (Santos) Inocentes**, is when the Church commemorates the story of Herod's slaughter of the innocent children of Judaea. On this day Spaniards play **inocentadas** (practical jokes) on each other, much like our April Fool's Day pranks.

---

inodoro [ino'ðoro] nm toilet, lavatory

(BRIT)
inofensivo, a [inofen'siβo, a] adj inoffensive, harmless

inolvidable [inolβi'ðaβle] adj unforgettable

inopinado, a [inopi'naðo, a] adj unexpected

inoportuno, a [inopor'tuno, a] adj untimely; (molesto) inconvenient

inoxidable [inoksi'ðaβle] adj: **acero ~** stainless steel

inquebrantable [inkeβran'taβle] adj unbreakable

inquietar [inkje'tar] vt to worry, trouble; **~se** vr to worry, get upset; **inquieto, a** adj anxious, worried; **inquietud** nf anxiety, worry

inquilino, a [inki'lino, a] nm/f tenant

inquirir [inki'rir] vt to enquire into, investigate

insaciable [insa'θjaβle] adj insatiable

insalubre [insa'luβre] adj unhealthy

inscribir [inskri'βir] vt to inscribe; **~ a uno en** (lista) to put sb on; (censo) to register sb on

inscripción [inskrip'θjon] nf inscription; (ESCOL etc) enrolment; (censo) registration

insecticida [insekti'θiða] nm insecticide

insecto [in'sekto] nm insect

inseguridad [insexuri'ðað] nf insecurity

inseguro, a [inse'xuro, a] adj insecure; (inconstante) unsteady; (incierto) uncertain

insensato, a [insen'sato, a] adj foolish, stupid

insensibilidad [insensiβili'ðað] nf (gen) insensitivity; (dureza de corazón) callousness

insensible [insen'siβle] adj (gen) insensitive; (movimiento) imperceptible; (sin sentido) numb

insertar [inser'tar] vt to insert

inservible [inser'βiβle] adj useless

insidioso, a [insi'ðjoso, a] adj insidious

insignia [in'siɣnja] nf (señal distintiva) badge; (estandarte) flag

insignificante [insiɣnifi'kante] adj insignificant

insinuar [insi'nwar] vt to insinuate, imply

insípido, a [in'sipiðo, a] adj insipid

insistencia [insis'tenθja] nf insistence

insistir [insis'tir] vi to insist; **~ en algo** to insist on sth; (enfatizar) to stress sth

insolación [insola'θjon] nf (MED) sunstroke

insolencia [inso'lenθja] nf insolence; **insolente** adj insolent

insólito, a [in'solito, a] adj unusual

insoluble [inso'luβle] adj insoluble

insolvencia [insol'βenθja] nf insolvency

insomnio [in'somnjo] nm insomnia

insondable [inson'daβle] adj bottomless; (fig) impenetrable

insonorizado, a [insonori'θaðo, a] adj (cuarto etc) soundproof

insoportable [insopor'taβle] adj unbearable

insospechado, a [insospe'tʃaðo, a] adj (inesperado) unexpected

inspección [inspek'θjon] nf inspection, check; **inspeccionar** vt (examinar) to inspect, examine; (controlar) to check

inspector, a [inspek'tor, a] nm/f inspector

inspiración [inspira'θjon] nf inspiration

inspirar [inspi'rar] vt to inspire; (MED) to inhale; **~se** vr: **~se en** to be inspired by

instalación [instala'θjon] nf (equipo) fittings pl, equipment; **~ eléctrica** wiring

instalar [insta'lar] vt (establecer) to instal; (erguir) to set up, erect; **~se** vr to establish o.s.; (en una vivienda) to move into

instancia [ins'tanθja] nf (JUR) petition; (ruego) request; **en última ~** as a last resort

instantánea [instan'tanea] nf snap(shot)

instantáneo, a [instan'taneo, a] adj instantaneous; **café ~** instant coffee

instante [ins'tante] nm instant, moment

instar [ins'tar] vt to press, urge

instaurar [instau'rar] vt (costumbre) to establish; (normas, sistema) to bring in, introduce; (gobierno) to instal

instigar [insti'ɣar] vt to instigate

instinto [ins'tinto] nm instinct; **por ~**

instinctively

institución [institu'θjon] nf institution, establishment

instituir [institu'ir] vt to establish; (*fundar*) to found; **instituto** nm (*gen*) institute; (*ESP: ESCOL*) ≈ comprehensive (*BRIT*) o high (*US*) school

institutriz [institu'triθ] nf governess

instrucción [instruk'θjon] nf instruction

instructivo, a [instruk'tiβo, a] adj instructive

instruir [instru'ir] vt (*gen*) to instruct; (*enseñar*) to teach, educate

instrumento [instru'mento] nm (*gen*) instrument; (*herramienta*) tool, implement

insubordinarse [insuβorði'narse] vr to rebel

insuficiencia [insufi'θjenθja] nf (*carencia*) lack; (*inadecuación*) inadequacy; **insuficiente** adj (*gen*) insufficient; (*ESCOL: calificación*) unsatisfactory

insufrible [insu'friβle] adj insufferable

insular [insu'lar] adj insular

insultar [insul'tar] vt to insult; **insulto** nm insult

insumiso, a [insu'miso, a] nm/f (*POL*) person who refuses to do military service or its substitute, community service

insuperable [insupe'raβle] adj (*excelente*) unsurpassable; (*problema etc*) insurmountable

insurgente [insur'xente] adj, nm/f insurgent

insurrección [insurrek'θjon] nf insurrection, rebellion

intachable [inta'tʃaβle] adj irreproachable

intacto, a [in'takto, a] adj intact

integral [inte'ɣral] adj integral; (*completo*) complete; **pan** ~ wholemeal (*BRIT*) o wholewheat (*US*) bread

integrar [inte'ɣrar] vt to make up, compose; (*MAT, fig*) to integrate

integridad [inteɣri'ðað] nf wholeness; (*carácter*) integrity; **íntegro, a** adj whole, entire; (*honrado*) honest

intelectual [intelek'twal] adj, nm/f intellectual

inteligencia [inteli'xenθja] nf intelligence; (*ingenio*) ability; **inteligente** adj intelligent

inteligible [inteli'xiβle] adj intelligible

intemperie [intem'perje] nf: **a la** ~ out in the open, exposed to the elements

intempestivo, a [intempes'tiβo, a] adj untimely

intención [inten'θjon] nf (*gen*) intention, purpose; **con segundas intenciones** maliciously; **con** ~ deliberately

intencionado, a [intenθjo'naðo, a] adj deliberate; **bien** ~ well-meaning; **mal** ~ ill-disposed, hostile

intensidad [intensi'ðað] nf (*gen*) intensity; (*ELEC, TEC*) strength; **llover con** ~ to rain hard

intenso, a [in'tenso, a] adj intense; (*sentimiento*) profound, deep

intentar [inten'tar] vt (*tratar*) to try, attempt; **intento** nm attempt

interactivo, a [interak'tiβo, a] adj (*INFORM*) interactive

intercalar [interka'lar] vt to insert

intercambio [inter'kambjo] nm exchange, swap

interceder [interθe'ðer] vi to intercede

interceptar [interθep'tar] vt to intercept

intercesión [interθe'sjon] nf intercession

interés [inte'res] nm (*gen*) interest; (*parte*) share, part; (*pey*) self-interest; **intereses creados** vested interests

interesado, a [intere'saðo, a] adj interested; (*prejuiciado*) prejudiced; (*pey*) mercenary, self-seeking

interesante [intere'sante] adj interesting

interesar [intere'sar] vt, vi to interest, be of interest to; **~se** vr: **~se en** o **por** to take an interest in

interferir [interfe'rir] vt to interfere with; (*TEL*) to jam ♦ vi to interfere

interfono [inter'fono] nm intercom

interino, a [inte'rino, a] adj temporary ♦ nm/f temporary holder of a post; (*MED*) locum; (*ESCOL*) supply teacher

interior [inte'rjor] adj inner, inside; (*COM*) domestic, internal ♦ nm interior, inside;

(fig) soul, mind; **Ministerio del I~**
≈ Home Office (BRIT), ≈ Department of
the Interior (US)

interjección [interxek'θjon] nf interjection

interlocutor, a [interloku'tor, a] nm/f
speaker

intermedio, a [inter'meðjo, a] adj
intermediate ♦ nm interval

interminable [intermi'naßle] adj endless

intermitente [intermi'tente] adj
intermittent ♦ nm (AUTO) indicator

internacional [internaθjo'nal] adj
international

internado [inter'naðo] nm boarding
school

internar [inter'nar] vt to intern; (en un
manicomio) to commit; **~se** vr (penetrar)
to penetrate

Internet [inter'net] nm o nf: **el** o **la ~** the
Internet

interno, a [in'terno, a] adj internal,
interior; (POL etc) domestic ♦ nm/f
(alumno) boarder

interponer [interpo'ner] vt to interpose,
put in; **~se** vr to intervene

interpretación [interpreta'θjon] nf
interpretation

interpretar [interpre'tar] vt to interpret;
(TEATRO, MUS) to perform, play;
intérprete nm/f (LING) interpreter,
translator; (MUS, TEATRO) performer,
artist(e)

interrogación [interroya'θjon] nf
interrogation; (LING: tb: **signo de ~**)
question mark

interrogar [interro'var] vt to interrogate,
question

interrumpir [interrum'pir] vt to interrupt

interrupción [interrup'θjon] nf
interruption

interruptor [interrup'tor] nm (ELEC)
switch

intersección [intersek'θjon] nf
intersection

interurbano, a [interur'ßano, a] adj:
llamada interurbana long-distance call

intervalo [inter'ßalo] nm interval;

(descanso) break; **a ~s** at intervals, every
now and then

intervenir [interße'nir] vt (controlar) to
control, supervise; (MED) to operate on
♦ vi (participar) to take part, participate;
(mediar) to intervene

interventor, a [interßen'tor, a] nm/f
inspector; (COM) auditor

intestino [intes'tino] nm intestine

intimar [inti'mar] vi to become friendly

intimidad [intimi'ðað] nf intimacy;
(familiaridad) familiarity; (vida privada)
private life; (JUR) privacy

íntimo, a ['intimo, a] adj intimate

intolerable [intole'raßle] adj intolerable,
unbearable

intoxicación [intoksika'θjon] nf poisoning

intranet [intra'net] nf intranet

intranquilizarse [intrankili'θarse] vr to
get worried o anxious; **intranquilo, a**
adj worried

intransitable [intransi'taßle] adj
impassable

intrépido, a [in'trepiðo, a] adj intrepid

intriga [in'triva] nf intrigue; (plan) plot;
intrigar vt, vi to intrigue

intrincado, a [intrin'kaðo, a] adj intricate

intrínseco, a [in'trinseko, a] adj intrinsic

introducción [introðuk'θjon] nf
introduction

introducir [introðu'θir] vt (gen) to
introduce; (moneda etc) to insert;
(INFORM) to input, enter

intromisión [intromi'sjon] nf interference,
meddling

introvertido, a [introßer'tiðo, a] adj, nm/f
introvert

intruso, a [in'truso, a] adj intrusive
♦ nm/f intruder

intuición [intwi'θjon] nf intuition

inundación [inunda'θjon] nf flood(ing);
inundar vt to flood; (fig) to swamp,
inundate

inusitado, a [inusi'taðo, a] adj unusual,
rare

inútil [in'util] adj useless; (esfuerzo) vain,
fruitless; **inutilidad** nf uselessness

inutilizar [inutili'θar] *vt* to make *o* render useless; **~se** *vr* to become useless
invadir [imba'ðir] *vt* to invade
inválido, a [im'baliðo, a] *adj* invalid
♦ *nm/f* invalid
invariable [imba'rjaβle] *adj* invariable
invasión [imba'sjon] *nf* invasion
invasor, a [imba'sor, a] *adj* invading
♦ *nm/f* invader
invención [imben'θjon] *nf* invention
inventar [imben'tar] *vt* to invent
inventario [imben'tarjo] *nm* inventory
inventiva [imben'tiβa] *nf* inventiveness
invento [im'bento] *nm* invention
inventor, a [imben'tor, a] *nm/f* inventor
invernadero [imberna'ðero] *nm* greenhouse
inverosímil [imbero'simil] *adj* implausible
inversión [imber'sjon] *nf* (*COM*) investment
inverso, a [im'berso, a] *adj* inverse, opposite; **en el orden ~** in reverse order; **a la inversa** inversely, the other way round
inversor, a [imber'sor, a] *nm/f* (*COM*) investor
invertir [imber'tir] *vt* (*COM*) to invest; (*volcar*) to turn upside down; (*tiempo etc*) to spend
investigación [imbestiɣa'θjon] *nf* investigation; (*ESCOL*) research; **~ de mercado** market research
investigar [imbesti'ɣar] *vt* to investigate; (*ESCOL*) to do research into
invierno [im'bjerno] *nm* winter
invisible [imbi'siβle] *adj* invisible
invitado, a [imbi'taðo, a] *nm/f* guest
invitar [imbi'tar] *vt* to invite; (*incitar*) to entice; (*pagar*) to buy, pay for
invocar [imbo'kar] *vt* to invoke, call on
involucrar [imbolu'krar] *vt*: **~ en** to involve in; **~se** *vr* (*persona*): **~ en** to get mixed up in
involuntario, a [imbolun'tarjo, a] *adj* (*movimiento, gesto*) involuntary; (*error*) unintentional
inyección [injek'θjon] *nf* injection

inyectar [injek'tar] *vt* to inject

PALABRA CLAVE
---

ir [ir] *vi* **1** to go; (*a pie*) to walk; (*viajar*) to travel; **~ caminando** to walk; **fui en tren** I went *o* travelled by train; **¡(ahora) voy!** (I'm just) coming!
2: ~ (a) por: ~ (a) por el médico to fetch the doctor
3 (*progresar: persona, cosa*) to go; **el trabajo va muy bien** work is going very well; **¿cómo te va?** how are things going?; **me va muy bien** I'm getting on very well; **le fue fatal** it went awfully badly for him
4 (*funcionar*): **el coche no va muy bien** the car isn't running very well
5: te va estupendamente ese color that colour suits you fantastically well
6 (*locuciones*): **¿vino? – ¡que va!** did he come? – of course not!; **vamos, no llores** come on, don't cry; **¡vaya coche!** what a car!, that's some car!
7: no vaya a ser: tienes que correr, no vaya a ser que pierdas el tren you'll have to run so as not to miss the train
8 (+*pp*): **iba vestido muy bien** he was very well dressed
9: no me *etc* **va ni me viene** I *etc* don't care
♦ *vb aux* **1: ~ a: voy/iba a hacerlo hoy** I am/was going to do it today
2 (+*gerundio*): **iba anocheciendo** it was getting dark; **todo se me iba aclarando** everything was gradually becoming clearer to me
3 (+*pp* = *pasivo*): **van vendidos 300 ejemplares** 300 copies have been sold so far
♦ **~se** *vr* **1: ¿por dónde se va al zoológico?** which is the way to the zoo?
2 (*marcharse*) to leave; **ya se habrán ido** they must already have left *o* gone

ira ['ira] *nf* anger, rage
Irak [i'rak] *nm* = **Iraq**
Irán [i'ran] *nm* Iran; **iraní** *adj, nm/f*

Iranian

Iraq [i'rak] *nm* Iraq; **iraquí** *adj, nm/f* Iraqui

iris ['iris] *nm inv* (*tb:* **arco ~**) rainbow; (*ANAT*) iris

Irlanda [ir'landa] *nf* Ireland; **irlandés, esa** *adj* Irish ♦ *nm/f* Irishman/woman; **los irlandeses** the Irish

ironía [iro'nia] *nf* irony; **irónico, a** *adj* ironic(al)

IRPF ['i 'erre 'pe 'efe] *nm abr* (= *Impuesto sobre la Renta de las Personas Físicas*) (personal) income tax

irreal [irre'al] *adj* unreal

irrecuperable [irrekupe'raßle] *adj* irrecoverable, irretrievable

irreflexión [irreflek'sjon] *nf* thoughtlessness

irregular [irreɣu'lar] *adj* (*gen*) irregular; (*situación*) abnormal

irremediable [irreme'ðjaßle] *adj* irremediable; (*vicio*) incurable

irreparable [irrepa'raßle] *adj* (*daños*) irreparable; (*pérdida*) irrecoverable

irresoluto, a [irreso'luto, a] *adj* irresolute, hesitant

irrespetuoso, a [irrespe'twoso, a] *adj* disrespectful

irresponsable [irrespon'saßle] *adj* irresponsible

irreversible [irreßer'sible] *adj* irreversible

irrigar [irri'var] *vt* to irrigate

irrisorio, a [irri'sorjo, a] *adj* derisory, ridiculous

irritar [irri'tar] *vt* to irritate, annoy

irrupción [irrup'θjon] *nf* irruption; (*invasión*) invasion

isla ['isla] *nf* island

islandés, esa [islan'des, esa] *adj* Icelandic ♦ *nm/f* Icelander

Islandia [is'landja] *nf* Iceland

isleño, a [is'leɲo, a] *adj* island *cpd* ♦ *nm/f* islander

Israel [isra'el] *nm* Israel; **israelí** *adj, nm/f* Israeli

istmo ['istmo] *nm* isthmus

Italia [i'talja] *nf* Italy; **italiano, a** *adj,* *nm/f* Italian

itinerario [itine'rarjo] *nm* itinerary, route

IVA ['ißa] *nm abr* (= *impuesto sobre el valor añadido*) VAT

izar [i'θar] *vt* to hoist

izdo, a *abr* (= *izquierdo, a*) l.

izquierda [iθ'kjerda] *nf* left; (*POL*) left (wing); **a la ~** a (= *estar*) on the left; (*torcer etc*) (to the) left

izquierdista [iθkjer'ðista] *nm/f* left-winger, leftist

izquierdo, a [iθ'kjerðo, a] *adj* left

J, j

jabalí [xaßa'li] *nm* wild boar

jabalina [xaßa'lina] *nf* javelin

jabón [xa'ßon] *nm* soap; **jabonar** *vt* to soap

jaca ['xaka] *nf* pony

jacinto [xa'θinto] *nm* hyacinth

jactarse [xak'tarse] *vr* to boast, brag

jadear [xaðe'ar] *vi* to pant, gasp for breath; **jadeo** *nm* panting, gasping

jaguar [xa'ɣwar] *nm* jaguar

jalea [xa'lea] *nf* jelly

jaleo [xa'leo] *nm* racket, uproar; **armar un ~** to kick up a racket

jalón [xa'lon] (*AM*) *nm* tug

jamás [xa'mas] *adv* never

jamón [xa'mon] *nm* ham; **~ dulce**, **~ de York** cooked ham; **~ serrano** cured ham

Japón [xa'pon] *nm*: **el ~** Japan; **japonés, esa** *adj, nm/f* Japanese ♦ *nm* (*LING*) Japanese

jaque ['xake] *nm*: **~ mate** checkmate

jaqueca [xa'keka] *nf* (very bad) headache, migraine

jarabe [xa'raße] *nm* syrup

jarcia ['xarθja] *nf* (*NAUT*) ropes *pl*, rigging

jardín [xar'ðin] *nm* garden; **~ de infancia** (*ESP*) *o* **de niños** (*AM*) nursery (school); **jardinería** *nf* gardening; **jardinero, a** *nm/f* gardener

jarra ['xarra] *nf* jar; (*jarro*) jug

jarro ['xarro] *nm* jug

jarrón [xa'rron] *nm* vase

jaula ['xaula] *nf* cage

jauría [xau'ria] *nf* pack of hounds

jazmín [xaθ'min] *nm* jasmine

J. C. *abr* (= *Jesucristo*) J.C.

jefa ['xefa] *nf ver* **jefe**

jefatura [xefa'tura] *nf*: **~ de policía** police headquarters *sg*

jefe, a ['xefe, a] *nm/f* (*gen*) chief, head; (*patrón*) boss; **~ de cocina** chef; **~ de estación** stationmaster; **~ de estado** head of state

jengibre [xen'xiβre] *nm* ginger

jeque ['xeke] *nm* sheik

jerarquía [xerar'kia] *nf* (*orden*) hierarchy; (*rango*) rank; **jerárquico, a** *adj* hierarchic(al)

jerez [xe'reθ] *nm* sherry

jerga ['xerva] *nf* jargon

jeringa [xe'ringa] *nf* syringe; (*AM*) annoyance, bother; **~ de engrase** grease gun; **jeringar** *vt* (*fam*) to annoy, bother; **jeringuilla** *nf* syringe

jeroglífico [xero'vlifiko] *nm* hieroglyphic

jersey [xer'sei] (*pl* **~s**) *nm* jersey, pullover, jumper

Jerusalén [xerusa'len] *n* Jerusalem

Jesucristo [xesu'kristo] *nm* Jesus Christ

jesuita [xe'swita] *adj, nm* Jesuit

Jesús [xe'sus] *nm* Jesus; **¡~!** good heavens!; (*al estornudar*) bless you!

jinete, a [xi'nete, a] *nm/f* horseman/woman, rider

jipijapa [xipi'xapa] (*AM*) *nm* straw hat

jirafa [xi'rafa] *nf* giraffe

jirón [xi'ron] *nm* rag, shred

jocoso, a [xo'koso, a] *adj* humorous, jocular

joder [xo'ðer] (*fam!*) *vt, vi* to fuck(!)

jofaina [xo'faina] *nf* washbasin

jornada [xor'naða] *nf* (*viaje de un día*) day's journey; (*camino o viaje entero*) journey; (*día de trabajo*) working day

jornal [xor'nal] *nm* (day's) wage; **~ero** *nm* (day) labourer

joroba [xo'roβa] *nf* hump, hunched back; **~do, a** *adj* hunchbacked ♦ *nm/f* hunchback

jota ['xota] *nf* (the letter) J; (*danza*) Aragonese dance; **no saber ni ~** to have no idea

joven ['xoβen] (*pl* **jóvenes**) *adj* young ♦ *nm* young man, youth ♦ *nf* young woman, girl

jovial [xo'βjal] *adj* cheerful, jolly

joya ['xoja] *nf* jewel, gem; (*fig: persona*) gem; **joyería** *nf* (*joyas*) jewellery; (*tienda*) jeweller's (shop); **joyero** *nm* (*persona*) jeweller; (*caja*) jewel case

juanete [xwa'nete] *nm* (*del pie*) bunion

jubilación [xuβila'θjon] *nf* (*retiro*) retirement

jubilado, a [xuβi'laðo, a] *adj* retired ♦ *nm/f* pensioner (*BRIT*), senior citizen

jubilar [xuβi'lar] *vt* to pension off, retire; (*fam*) to discard; **~se** *vr* to retire

júbilo ['xuβilo] *nm* joy, rejoicing; **jubiloso, a** *adj* jubilant

judía [xu'ðia] *nf* (*CULIN*) bean; **~ verde** French bean; *ver tb* **judío**

judicial [xuði'θjal] *adj* judicial

judío, a [xu'ðio, a] *adj* Jewish ♦ *nm/f* Jew(ess)

judo ['juðo] *nm* judo

juego *etc* ['xweyo] *vb ver* **jugar** ♦ *nm* (*gen*) play; (*pasatiempo, partido*) game; (*en casino*) gambling; (*conjunto*) set; **fuera de ~** (*DEPORTE: persona*) offside; (*: pelota*) out of play; **J~s Olímpicos** Olympic Games

juerga ['xwerva] *nf* binge; (*fiesta*) party; **ir de ~** to go out on a binge

jueves ['xweβes] *nm inv* Thursday

juez [xweθ] *nm/f* judge; **~ de línea** linesman; **~ de salida** starter

jugada [xu'vaða] *nf* play; **buena ~** good move/shot/stroke *etc*

jugador, a [xuva'ðor, a] *nm/f* player; (*en casino*) gambler

jugar [xu'var] *vt, vi* to play; (*en casino*) to gamble; (*apostar*) to bet; **~ al fútbol** to play football

juglar [xu'vlar] *nm* minstrel

jugo ['xuvo] *nm* (*BOT*) juice; (*fig*) essence, substance; **~ de fruta** (*AM*) fruit juice;

~**so, a** *adj* juicy; (*fig*) substantial, important

juguete [xu'ɣete] *nm* toy; ~**ar** *vi* to play; ~**ría** *nf* toyshop

juguetón, ona [xuɣe'ton, ona] *adj* playful

juicio ['xwiθjo] *nm* judgement; (*razón*) sanity, reason; (*opinión*) opinion; ~**so, a** *adj* wise, sensible

julio ['xuljo] *nm* July

junco ['xunko] *nm* rush, reed

jungla ['xungla] *nf* jungle

junio ['xunjo] *nm* June

junta ['xunta] *nf* (*asamblea*) meeting, assembly; (*comité, consejo*) board, council, committee; (*TEC*) joint

juntar [xun'tar] *vt* to join, unite; (*maquinaria*) to assemble, put together; (*dinero*) to collect; ~**se** *vr* to join, meet; (*reunirse: personas*) to meet, assemble; (*arrimarse*) to approach, draw closer; ~**se con uno** to join sb

junto, a ['xunto, a] *adj* joined; (*unido*) united; (*anexo*) near, close; (*contiguo, próximo*) next, adjacent ♦ *adv*: **todo ~** all at once; ~**s** together; ~ **a** near (to), next to

jurado [xu'raðo] *nm* (*JUR: individuo*) juror; (: *grupo*) jury; (*de concurso: grupo*) panel (of judges); (: *individuo*) member of a panel

juramento [xura'mento] *nm* oath; (*maldición*) oath, curse; **prestar ~** to take the oath; **tomar ~ a** to swear in, administer the oath to

jurar [xu'rar] *vt*, *vi* to swear; ~ **en falso** to commit perjury; **jurárselas a uno** to have it in for sb

jurídico, a [xu'riðiko, a] *adj* legal

jurisdicción [xurisðik'θjon] *nf* (*poder, autoridad*) jurisdiction; (*territorio*) district

jurisprudencia [xurispru'ðenθja] *nf* jurisprudence

jurista [xu'rista] *nm/f* jurist

justamente [xusta'mente] *adv* justly, fairly; (*precisamente*) just, exactly

justicia [xus'tiθja] *nf* justice; (*equidad*) fairness, justice; **justiciero, a** *adj* just

justificación [xustifika'θjon] *nf* justification; **justificar** *vt* to justify

justo, a ['xusto, a] *adj* (*equitativo*) just, fair, right; (*preciso*) exact, correct; (*ajustado*) tight ♦ *adv* (*precisamente*) exactly, precisely; (*AM: apenas a tiempo*) just in time

juvenil [xuβe'nil] *adj* youthful

juventud [xuβen'tuð] *nf* (*adolescencia*) youth; (*jóvenes*) young people *pl*

juzgado [xuθ'ɣaðo] *nm* tribunal; (*JUR*) court

juzgar [xuθ'ɣar] *vt* to judge; **a ~ por ...** to judge by ..., judging by ...

K, k

kg *abr* (= *kilogramo*) kg

kilo ['kilo] *nm* kilo ♦ *pref*: ~**gramo** *nm* kilogramme; ~**metraje** *nm* distance in kilometres, ≈ mileage; **kilómetro** *nm* kilometre; ~**vatio** *nm* kilowatt

kiosco ['kjosko] *nm* = **quiosco**

km *abr* (= *kilómetro*) km

Kosovo [ko'soßo] *nm* Kosovo

kv *abr* (= *kilovatio*) kw

L, l

l *abr* (= *litro*) l

la [la] *art def* the ♦ *pron* her; (*Ud.*) you; (*cosa*) it ♦ *nm* (*MUS*) la; ~ **del sombrero rojo** the girl in the red hat; *tb ver* **el**

laberinto [laße'rinto] *nm* labyrinth

labia ['laßja] *nf* fluency; (*pey*) glib tongue

labio ['laßjo] *nm* lip

labor [la'ßor] *nf* labour; (*AGR*) farm work; (*tarea*) job, task; (*COSTURA*) needlework; ~**able** *adj* (*AGR*) workable; **día ~able** working day; ~**al** *adj* (*accidente*) at work; (*jornada*) working

laboratorio [laßora'torjo] *nm* laboratory

laborioso, a [laßo'rjoso, a] *adj* (*persona*) hard-working; (*trabajo*) tough

laborista [laßo'rista] *adj*: **Partido L~**

Labour Party

labrado, a [la'βraðo, a] *adj* worked;
(*madera*) carved; (*metal*) wrought

labrador, a [laβra'ðor, a] *adj* farming *cpd*
♦ *nm/f* farmer

labranza [la'βranθa] *nf* (*AGR*) cultivation

labrar [la'βrar] *vt* (*gen*) to work; (*madera
etc*) to carve; (*fig*) to cause, bring about

labriego, a [la'βrjeɣo, a] *nm/f* peasant

laca ['laka] *nf* lacquer

lacayo [la'kajo] *nm* lackey

lacio, a ['laθjo, a] *adj* (*pelo*) lank, straight

lacón [la'kon] *nm* shoulder of pork

lacónico, a [la'koniko, a] *adj* laconic

lacra ['lakra] *nf* (*fig*) blot; **lacrar** *vt*
(*cerrar*) to seal (with sealing wax); **lacre**
nm sealing wax

lactancia [lak'tanθja] *nf* lactation

lactar [lak'tar] *vt, vi* to suckle

lácteo, a ['lakteo, a] *adj*: **productos ~s**
dairy products

ladear [laðe'ar] *vt* to tip, tilt ♦ *vi* to tilt;
~se *vr* to lean

ladera [la'ðera] *nf* slope

lado ['laðo] *nm* (*gen*) side; (*fig*) protection;
(*MIL*) flank; **al ~ de** beside; **poner de ~** to
put on its side; **poner a un ~** to put
aside; **por todos ~s** on all sides, all round
(*BRIT*)

ladrar [la'ðrar] *vi* to bark; **ladrido** *nm*
bark, barking

ladrillo [la'ðriʎo] *nm* (*gen*) brick; (*azulejo*)
tile

ladrón, ona [la'ðron, ona] *nm/f* thief

lagartija [laɣar'tixa] *nf* (*ZOOL*) (small)
lizard

lagarto [la'ɣarto] *nm* (*ZOOL*) lizard

lago ['laɣo] *nm* lake

lágrima ['laɣrima] *nf* tear

laguna [la'ɣuna] *nf* (*lago*) lagoon; (*hueco*)
gap

laico, a ['laiko, a] *adj* lay

lamentable [lamen'taβle] *adj* lamentable,
regrettable; (*miserable*) pitiful

lamentar [lamen'tar] *vt* (*sentir*) to regret;
(*deplorar*) to lament; **lo lamento mucho**
I'm very sorry; **~se** *vr* to lament;

lamento *nm* lament

lamer [la'mer] *vt* to lick

lámina ['lamina] *nf* (*plancha delgada*)
sheet; (*para estampar, estampa*) plate

lámpara ['lampara] *nf* lamp; **~ de
alcohol/gas** spirit/gas lamp; **~ de pie**
standard lamp

lamparón [lampa'ron] *nm* grease spot

lana ['lana] *nf* wool

lancha ['lantʃa] *nf* launch; **~ de pesca**
fishing boat; **~ salvavidas/torpedera**
lifeboat/torpedo boat

langosta [lan'gosta] *nf* (*crustáceo*) lobster;
(: *de río*) crayfish; **langostino** *nm* Dublin
Bay prawn

languidecer [langiðe'θer] *vi* to languish;
languidez *nf* languor; **lánguido, a** *adj*
(*gen*) languid; (*sin energía*) listless

lanilla [la'niʎa] *nf* nap

lanza ['lanθa] *nf* (*arma*) lance, spear

lanzamiento [lanθa'mjento] *nm* (*gen*)
throwing; (*NAUT, COM*) launch, launching;
~ de peso putting the shot

lanzar [lan'θar] *vt* (*gen*) to throw;
(*DEPORTE: pelota*) to bowl; (*NAUT, COM*) to
launch; (*JUR*) to evict; **~se** *vr* to throw o.s.

lapa ['lapa] *nf* limpet

lapicero [lapi'θero] *nm* pencil; (*AM:
bolígrafo*) Biro ®

lápida ['lapiða] *nf* stone; **~ mortuoria**
headstone; **~ conmemorativa** memorial
stone; **lapidario, a** *adj, nm* lapidary

lápiz ['lapiθ] *nm* pencil; **~ de color**
coloured pencil; **~ de labios** lipstick

lapón, ona [la'pon, ona] *nm/f* Laplander,
Lapp

lapso ['lapso] *nm* (*de tiempo*) interval;
(*error*) error

lapsus ['lapsus] *nm inv* error, mistake

largar [lar'ɣar] *vt* (*soltar*) to release;
(*aflojar*) to loosen; (*lanzar*) to launch;
(*fam*) to let fly; (*velas*) to unfurl; (*AM*) to
throw; **~se** *vr* (*fam*) to beat it; **~se a** (*AM*)
to start to

largo, a ['larɣo, a] *adj* (*longitud*) long;
(*tiempo*) lengthy; (*fig*) generous ♦ *nm*
length; (*MUS*) largo; **dos años ~s** two

long years; **tiene 9 metros de ~** it is 9 metres long; **a lo ~ de** along; (*tiempo*) all through, throughout; **~metraje** *nm* feature film

laringe [la'rinxe] *nf* larynx; **laringitis** *nf* laryngitis

larva ['larβa] *nf* larva

las [las] *art def* the ♦ *pron* them; **~ que cantan** the ones/women/girls who sing; *tb ver* **el**

lascivo, a [las'θiβo, a] *adj* lewd

láser ['laser] *nm* laser

lástima ['lastima] *nf* (*pena*) pity; **dar ~** to be pitiful; **es una ~ que** it's a pity that; **¡qué ~!** what a pity!; **ella está hecha una ~** she looks pitiful

lastimar [lasti'mar] *vt* (*herir*) to wound; (*ofender*) to offend; **~se** *vr* to hurt o.s.; **lastimero, a** *adj* pitiful, pathetic

lastre ['lastre] *nm* (*TEC, NAUT*) ballast; (*fig*) dead weight

lata ['lata] *nf* (*metal*) tin; (*caja*) tin (*BRIT*), can; (*fam*) nuisance; **en ~** tinned (*BRIT*), canned; **dar (la) ~** to be a nuisance

latente [la'tente] *adj* latent

lateral [late'ral] *adj* side *cpd*, lateral ♦ *nm* (*TEATRO*) wings

latido [la'tiðo] *nm* (*del corazón*) beat

latifundio [lati'fundjo] *nm* large estate; **latifundista** *nm/f* owner of a large estate

latigazo [lati'xaθo] *nm* (*golpe*) lash; (*sonido*) crack

látigo ['latixo] *nm* whip

latín [la'tin] *nm* Latin

latino, a [la'tino, a] *adj* Latin; **~americano, a** *adj, nm/f* Latin-American

latir [la'tir] *vi* (*corazón, pulso*) to beat

latitud [lati'tuð] *nf* (*GEO*) latitude

latón [la'ton] *nm* brass

latoso, a [la'toso, a] *adj* (*molesto*) annoying; (*aburrido*) boring

laúd [la'uð] *nm* lute

laurel [lau'rel] *nm* (*BOT*) laurel; (*CULIN*) bay

lava ['laβa] *nf* lava

lavabo [la'βaβo] *nm* (*pila*) washbasin; (*tb:*

**~s) toilet

lavado [la'βaðo] *nm* washing; (*de ropa*) laundry; (*ARTE*) wash; **~ de cerebro** brainwashing; **~ en seco** dry-cleaning

lavadora [laβa'ðora] *nf* washing machine

lavanda [la'βanda] *nf* lavender

lavandería [laβande'ria] *nf* laundry; (*automática*) launderette

lavaplatos [laβa'platos] *nm inv* dishwasher

lavar [la'βar] *vt* to wash; (*borrar*) to wipe away; **~se** *vr* to wash o.s.; **~se las manos** to wash one's hands; **~se los dientes** to brush one's teeth; **~ y marcar** (*pelo*) to shampoo and set; **~ en seco** to dry-clean; **~ los platos** to wash the dishes

lavavajillas [laβaβa'xiʎas] *nm inv* dishwasher

laxante [lak'sante] *nm* laxative

lazada [la'θaða] *nf* bow

lazarillo [laθa'riʎo] *nm:* **perro ~** guide dog

lazo ['laθo] *nm* knot; (*lazada*) bow; (*para animales*) lasso; (*trampa*) snare; (*vínculo*) tie

le [le] *pron* (*directo*) him (*o* her); (: *usted*) you; (*indirecto*) to him (*o* her *o* it); (: *usted*) to you

leal [le'al] *adj* loyal; **~tad** *nf* loyalty

lección [lek'θjon] *nf* lesson

leche ['letʃe] *nf* milk; **tiene mala ~** (*fam!*) he's a swine (!); **~ condensada / en polvo** condensed/powdered milk; **~ desnatada** skimmed milk; **~ra** *nf* (*vendedora*) milkmaid; (*recipiente*) (milk) churn; (*AM*) cow; **~ro, a** *adj* dairy

lecho ['letʃo] *nm* (*cama, de río*) bed; (*GEO*) layer

lechón [le'tʃon] *nm* sucking (*BRIT*) *o* suckling (*US*) pig

lechoso, a [le'tʃoso, a] *adj* milky

lechuga [le'tʃuxa] *nf* lettuce

lechuza [le'tʃuθa] *nf* owl

lector, a [lek'tor, a] *nm/f* reader ♦ *nm:* **~ de discos compactos** CD player

lectura [lek'tura] *nf* reading

leer [le'er] *vt* to read

legado [le'xaðo] *nm* (*don*) bequest;

(herencia) legacy; *(enviado)* legate

legajo [le'xaxo] *nm* file

legal [le'ɣal] *adj (gen)* legal; *(persona)* trustworthy; **~idad** *nf* legality

legalizar [leɣali'θar] *vt* to legalize; *(documento)* to authenticate

legaña [le'ɣaɲa] *nf* sleep *(in eyes)*

legar [le'ɣar] *vt* to bequeath, leave

legendario, a [lexen'darjo, a] *adj* legendary

legión [le'xjon] *nf* legion; **legionario, a** *adj* legionary ♦ *nm* legionnaire

legislación [lexisla'θjon] *nf* legislation

legislar [lexis'lar] *vi* to legislate

legislatura [lexisla'tura] *nf (POL)* period of office

legitimar [lexiti'mar] *vt* to legitimize; **legítimo, a** *adj (genuino)* authentic; *(legal)* legitimate

lego, a ['leɣo, a] *adj (REL)* secular; *(ignorante)* ignorant ♦ *nm* layman

legua ['leɣwa] *nf* league

legumbres [le'ɣumbres] *nfpl* pulses

leído, a [le'iðo, a] *adj* well-read

lejanía [lexa'nia] *nf* distance; **lejano, a** *adj* far-off; *(en el tiempo)* distant; *(fig)* remote

lejía [le'xia] *nf* bleach

lejos ['lexos] *adv* far, far away; **a lo ~** in the distance; **de** *o* **desde ~** from afar; **~ de** far from

lelo, a ['lelo, a] *adj* silly ♦ *nm/f* idiot

lema ['lema] *nm* motto; *(POL)* slogan

lencería [lenθe'ria] *nf* linen, drapery

lengua ['lengwa] *nf* tongue; *(LING)* language; **morderse la ~** to hold one's tongue

lenguado [len'gwaðo] *nm* sole

lenguaje [len'gwaxe] *nm* language

lengüeta [len'gweta] *nf (ANAT)* epiglottis; *(zapatos)* tongue, *(MUS)* reed

lente ['lente] *nf* lens; *(lupa)* magnifying glass; **~s** *nfpl (gafas)* glasses; **~s de contacto** contact lenses

lenteja [len'texa] *nf* lentil; **lentejuela** *nf* sequin

lentilla [len'tiʎa] *nf* contact lens

lentitud [lenti'tuð] *nf* slowness; **con ~** slowly

lento, a ['lento, a] *adj* slow

leña ['leɲa] *nf* firewood; **~dor, a** *nm/f* woodcutter

leño ['leɲo] *nm (trozo de árbol)* log; *(madera)* timber; *(fig)* blockhead

Leo ['leo] *nm* Leo

león [le'on] *nm* lion; **~ marino** sea lion

leopardo [leo'parðo] *nm* leopard

leotardos [leo'tarðos] *nmpl* tights

lepra ['lepra] *nf* leprosy; **leproso, a** *nm/f* leper

lerdo, a ['lerðo, a] *adj (lento)* slow; *(patoso)* clumsy

les [les] *pron (directo)* them; *(: ustedes)* you; *(indirecto)* to them; *(: ustedes)* to you

lesbiana [les'βjana] *adj, nf* lesbian

lesión [le'sjon] *nf* wound, lesion; *(DEPORTE)* injury; **lesionado, a** *adj* injured ♦ *nm/f* injured person

letal [le'tal] *adj* lethal

letanía [leta'nia] *nf* litany

letargo [le'tarxo] *nm* lethargy

letra ['letra] *nf* letter; *(escritura)* handwriting; *(MUS)* lyrics *pl*; **~ de cambio** bill of exchange; **~ de imprenta** print; **~do, a** *adj* learned ♦ *nm/f* lawyer; **letrero** *nm (cartel)* sign; *(etiqueta)* label

letrina [le'trina] *nf* latrine

leucemia [leu'θemja] *nf* leukaemia

levadizo [leβa'ðiθo] *adj*: **puente ~** drawbridge

levadura [leβa'ðura] *nf (para el pan)* yeast; *(de la cerveza)* brewer's yeast

levantamiento [leβanta'mjento] *nm* raising, lifting; *(rebelión)* revolt, uprising; **~ de pesos** weight-lifting

levantar [leβan'tar] *vt (gen)* to raise; *(del suelo)* to pick up; *(hacia arriba)* to lift (up); *(plan)* to make, draw up; *(mesa)* to clear; *(campamento)* to strike; *(fig)* to cheer up, hearten; **~se** *vr* to get up; *(enderezarse)* to straighten up; *(rebelarse)* to rebel; **~ el ánimo** to cheer up

levante [le'βante] *nm* east coast; **el L~** region of Spain extending from Castellón *to Murcia*

levar [le'ßar] *vt* to weigh

leve ['leße] *adj* light; *(fig)* trivial; ~**dad** *nf* lightness

levita [le'ßita] *nf* frock coat

léxico ['leksiko] *nm (vocabulario)* vocabulary

ley [lei] *nf (gen)* law; *(metal)* standard

leyenda [le'jenda] *nf* legend

leyó *etc vb ver* **leer**

liar [li'ar] *vt* to tie (up); *(unir)* to bind; *(envolver)* to wrap (up); *(enredar)* to confuse; *(cigarrillo)* to roll; ~**se** *vr (fam)* to get involved; ~**se a palos** to get involved in a fight

Líbano ['lißano] *nm*: **el ~** (the) Lebanon

libelo [li'ßelo] *nm* satire, lampoon

libélula [li'ßelula] *nf* dragonfly

liberación [lißera'θjon] *nf* liberation; *(de la cárcel)* release

liberal [liße'ral] *adj, nm/f* liberal; ~**idad** *nf* liberality, generosity

liberar [liße'rar] *vt* to liberate

libertad [lißer'tað] *nf* liberty, freedom; ~ **de culto/de prensa/de comercio** freedom of worship/of the press/of trade; ~ **condicional** probation; ~ **bajo palabra** parole; ~ **bajo fianza** bail

libertar [lißer'tar] *vt (preso)* to set free; *(de una obligación)* to release; *(eximir)* to exempt

libertino, a [lißer'tino, a] *adj* permissive ♦ *nm/f* permissive person

libra ['lißra] *nf* pound; *(ASTROLOGÍA)*: **L~** Libra; ~ **esterlina** pound sterling

librar [li'ßrar] *vt (de peligro)* to save; *(batalla)* to wage, fight; *(de impuestos)* to exempt; *(cheque)* to make out; *(JUR)* to exempt; ~**se** *vr*: ~**se de** to escape from, free o.s. from

libre ['lißre] *adj* free; *(lugar)* unoccupied; *(asiento)* vacant; *(de deudas)* free of debts; ~ **de impuestos** free of tax; **tiro ~** free kick; **los 100 metros ~** the 100 metres free-style (race); **al aire ~** in the open air

librería [lißre'ria] *nf (tienda)* bookshop; **librero, a** *nm/f* bookseller

libreta [li'ßreta] *nf* notebook; ~ **de ahorros** savings book

libro ['lißro] *nm* book; ~ **de bolsillo** paperback; ~ **de caja** cashbook; ~ **de cheques** chequebook *(BRIT)*, checkbook *(US)*; ~ **de texto** textbook

Lic. *abr* = **licenciado, a**

licencia [li'θenθja] *nf (gen)* licence; *(permiso)* permission; ~ **por enfermedad** sick leave; ~ **de caza** game licence; ~**do, a** *adj* licensed ♦ *nm/f* graduate; **licenciar** *vt (empleado)* to dismiss; *(permitir)* to permit, allow; *(soldado)* to discharge; *(estudiante)* to confer a degree upon; **licenciarse** *vr*: **licenciarse en letras** to graduate in arts

licencioso, a [liθen'θjoso, a] *adj* licentious

licitar [liθi'tar] *vt* to bid for; *(AM)* to sell by auction

lícito, a ['liθito, a] *adj (legal)* lawful; *(justo)* fair, just; *(permisible)* permissible

licor [li'kor] *nm* spirits *pl (BRIT)*, liquor *(US)*; *(de frutas etc)* liqueur

licuadora [likwa'ðora] *nf* blender

licuar [li'kwar] *vt* to liquidize

líder ['liðer] *nm/f* leader; **liderato** *nm* leadership; **liderazgo** *nm* leadership

lidia ['liðja] *nf* bullfighting; *(una ~)* bullfight; **toros de ~** fighting bulls; **lidiar** *vt, vi* to fight

liebre ['ljeßre] *nf* hare

lienzo ['ljenθo] *nm* linen; *(ARTE)* canvas; *(ARQ)* wall

liga ['liɣa] *nf (de medias)* garter, suspender; *(AM: gomita)* rubber band; *(confederación)* league

ligadura [liɣa'ðura] *nf* bond, tie; *(MED, MUS)* ligature

ligamento [liɣa'mento] *nm* ligament

ligar [li'ɣar] *vt (atar)* to tie; *(unir)* to join; *(MED)* to bind up; *(MUS)* to slur ♦ *vi* to mix, blend; *(fam)*: **(él) liga mucho** he pulls a lot of women; ~**se** *vr* to commit o.s.

ligereza [lixe'reθa] *nf* lightness; *(rapidez)* swiftness; *(agilidad)* agility; *(superficialidad)* flippancy

ligero, a [li'xero, a] *adj* (*de peso*) light; (*tela*) thin; (*rápido*) swift, quick; (*ágil*) agile, nimble; (*de importancia*) slight; (*de carácter*) flippant, superficial ♦ *adv*: **a la ligera** superficially

liguero [li'vero] *nm* suspender (*BRIT*) *o* garter (*US*) belt

lija ['lixa] *nf* (*ZOOL*) dogfish; (*tb*: **papel de** ~) sandpaper

lila ['lila] *nf* lilac

lima ['lima] *nf* file; (*BOT*) lime; ~ **de uñas** nailfile; **limar** *vt* to file

limitación [limita'θjon] *nf* limitation, limit; ~ **de velocidad** speed limit

limitar [limi'tar] *vt* to limit; (*reducir*) to reduce, cut down ♦ *vi*: ~ **con** to border on; ~**se** *vr*: ~**se a** to limit o.s. to

límite ['limite] *nm* (*gen*) limit; (*fin*) end; (*frontera*) border; ~ **de velocidad** speed limit

limítrofe [li'mitrofe] *adj* neighbouring

limón [li'mon] *nm* lemon ♦ *adj*: **amarillo** ~ lemon-yellow; **limonada** *nf* lemonade

limosna [li'mosna] *nf* alms *pl*; **vivir de** ~ to live on charity

limpiaparabrisas [limpjapara'ßrisas] *nm inv* windscreen (*BRIT*) *o* windshield (*US*) wiper

limpiar [lim'pjar] *vt* to clean; (*con trapo*) to wipe; (*quitar*) to wipe away; (*zapatos*) to shine, polish; (*fig*) to clean up

limpieza [lim'pjeθa] *nf* (*estado*) cleanliness; (*acto*) cleaning; (: *de las calles*) cleansing; (: *de zapatos*) polishing; (*habilidad*) skill; (*fig: POLICÍA*) clean-up; (*pureza*) purity; **operación de** ~ mopping-up operation; ~ **en seco** dry cleaning

limpio, a ['limpjo, a] *adj* clean; (*moralmente*) pure; (*COM*) clear, net; (*fam*) honest ♦ *adv*: **jugar** ~ to play fair; **pasar a** (*ESP*) *o* **en** (*AM*) ~ to make a clean copy

linaje [li'naxe] *nm* lineage, family

lince ['linθe] *nm* lynx

linchar [lin'tʃar] *vt* to lynch

lindar [lin'dar] *vi* to adjoin; ~ **con** to

border on; **linde** *nm o f* boundary; **lindero, a** *adj* adjoining ♦ *nm* boundary

lindo, a ['lindo, a] *adj* pretty, lovely ♦ *adv*: **nos divertimos de lo** ~ we had a marvellous time; **canta muy** ~ (*AM*) he sings beautifully

línea ['linea] *nf* (*gen*) line; **en** ~ (*INFORM*) on line; ~ **aérea** airline; ~ **de meta** goal line; (*de carrera*) finishing line; ~ **recta** straight line

lingote [lin'gote] *nm* ingot

lingüista [lin'gwista] *nm/f* linguist; **lingüística** *nf* linguistics *sg*

lino ['lino] *nm* linen; (*BOT*) flax

linóleo [li'noleo] *nm* lino, linoleum

linterna [lin'terna] *nf* torch (*BRIT*), flashlight (*US*)

lío ['lio] *nm* bundle; (*fam*) fuss; (*desorden*) muddle, mess; **armar un** ~ to make a fuss

liquen ['liken] *nm* lichen

liquidación [likiða'θjon] *nf* liquidation; **venta de** ~ clearance sale

liquidar [liki'ðar] *vt* (*mercancías*) to liquidate; (*deudas*) to pay off; (*empresa*) to wind up

líquido, a ['likiðo, a] *adj* liquid; (*ganancia*) net ♦ *nm* liquid; ~ **imponible** net taxable income

lira ['lira] *nf* (*MUS*) lyre; (*moneda*) lira

lírico, a ['liriko, a] *adj* lyrical

lirio ['lirjo] *nm* (*BOT*) iris

lirón [li'ron] *nm* (*ZOOL*) dormouse; (*fig*) sleepyhead

Lisboa [lis'ßoa] *n* Lisbon

lisiado, a [li'sjaðo, a] *adj* injured ♦ *nm/f* cripple

lisiar [li'sjar] *vt* to maim; ~**se** *vr* to injure o.s.

liso, a ['liso, a] *adj* (*terreno*) flat; (*cabello*) straight; (*superficie*) even; (*tela*) plain

lisonja [li'sonxa] *nf* flattery

lista ['lista] *nf* list; (*de alumnos*) school register; (*de libros*) catalogue; (*de platos*) menu; (*de precios*) price list; **pasar** ~ to call the roll; ~ **de correos** poste restante; ~ **de espera** waiting list; **tela de** ~**s** striped material; **listín** *nm*: ~ (**telefónico**) telephone directory

listo, a ['listo, a] *adj* (*perspicaz*) smart, clever; (*preparado*) ready

listón [lis'ton] *nm* (*de madera, metal*) strip

litera [li'tera] *nf* (*en barco, tren*) berth; (*en dormitorio*) bunk, bunk bed

literal [lite'ral] *adj* literal

literario, a [lite'rarjo, a] *adj* literary

literato, a [lite'rato, a] *adj* literary ♦ *nm/f* writer

literatura [litera'tura] *nf* literature

litigar [liti'ɣar] *vt* to fight ♦ *vi* (*JUR*) to go to law; (*fig*) to dispute, argue

litigio [li'tixjo] *nm* (*JUR*) lawsuit; (*fig*): **en ~ con** in dispute with

litografía [litoɣra'fia] *nf* lithography; (*una ~*) lithograph

litoral [lito'ral] *adj* coastal ♦ *nm* coast, seaboard

litro ['litro] *nm* litre

liviano, a [li'ßjano, a] *adj* (*cosa, objeto*) trivial

lívido, a ['lißiðo, a] *adj* livid

llaga ['ʎaɣa] *nf* wound

llama ['ʎama] *nf* flame; (*ZOOL*) llama

llamada [ʎa'maða] *nf* call; **~ al orden** call to order; **~ a pie de página** reference note

llamamiento [ʎama'mjento] *nm* call

llamar [ʎa'mar] *vt* to call; (*atención*) to attract ♦ *vi* (*por teléfono*) to telephone; (*a la puerta*) to knock (*o* ring); (*por señas*) to beckon; (*MIL*) to call up; **~se** *vr* to be called, be named; **¿cómo se llama usted?** what's your name?

llamarada [ʎama'raða] *nf* (*llamas*) blaze; (*rubor*) flush

llamativo, a [ʎama'tißo, a] *adj* showy; (*color*) loud

llano, a ['ʎano, a] *adj* (*superficie*) flat; (*persona*) straightforward; (*estilo*) clear ♦ *nm* plain, flat ground

llanta ['ʎanta] *nf* (*wheel*) rim; (*AM*): **~ (de goma)** tyre; (*: cámara*) inner (tube)

llanto ['ʎanto] *nm* weeping

llanura [ʎa'nura] *nf* plain

llave ['ʎaße] *nf* key; (*del agua*) tap;

(*MECÁNICA*) spanner; (*de la luz*) switch; (*MUS*) key; **~ inglesa** monkey wrench; **~ maestra** master key; **~ de contacto** (*AUTO*) ignition key; **~ de paso** stopcock; **echar la ~ a** to lock up; **~ro** *nm* keyring

llegada [ʎe'ɣaða] *nf* arrival

llegar [ʎe'ɣar] *vi* to arrive; (*alcanzar*) to reach; (*bastar*) to be enough; **~se** *vr*: **~se a** to approach; **~ a** to manage to, succeed in; **~ a saber** to find out; **~ a ser** to become; **~ a las manos de** to come into the hands of

llenar [ʎe'nar] *vt* to fill; (*espacio*) to cover; (*formulario*) to fill in *o* up; (*fig*) to heap

lleno, a ['ʎeno, a] *adj* full, filled; (*repleto*) full up ♦ *nm* (*TEATRO*) full house; **dar de ~ contra un muro** to hit a wall head-on

llevadero, a [ʎeßa'ðero, a] *adj* bearable, tolerable

llevar [ʎe'ßar] *vt* to take; (*ropa*) to wear; (*cargar*) to carry; (*quitar*) to take away; (*en coche*) to drive; (*transportar*) to transport; (*traer: dinero*) to carry; (*conducir*) to lead; (*MAT*) to carry ♦ *vi* (*suj: camino etc*): **~ a** to lead to; **~se** *vr* to carry off, take away; **llevamos dos días aquí** we have been here for two days; **él me lleva 2 años** he's 2 years older than me; (*COM*): **~ los libros** to keep the books; **~se bien** to get on well (together)

llorar [ʎo'rar] *vt, vi* to cry, weep; **~ de risa** to cry with laughter

lloriquear [ʎorike'ar] *vi* to snivel, whimper

lloro ['ʎoro] *nm* crying, weeping; **llorón, ona** *adj* tearful ♦ *nm/f* cry-baby; **~so, a** *adj* (*gen*) weeping, tearful; (*triste*) sad, sorrowful

llover [ʎo'ßer] *vi* to rain

llovizna [ʎo'ßiθna] *nf* drizzle; **lloviznar** *vi* to drizzle

llueve *etc vb ver* **llover**

lluvia ['ʎußja] *nf* rain; **~ radioactiva** (radioactive) fallout; **lluvioso, a** *adj* rainy

lo [lo] *art def*: **~ bello** the beautiful, what is beautiful, that which is beautiful ♦ *pron* (*persona*) him; (*cosa*) it; *tb ver* **el**

loable [lo'aβle] *adj* praiseworthy; **loar** *vt*
to praise
lobo ['loβo] *nm* wolf; **~ de mar** (*fig*) sea
dog; **~ marino** seal
lóbrego, a ['loβreɣo, a] *adj* dark; (*fig*)
gloomy
lóbulo ['loβulo] *nm* lobe
local [lo'kal] *adj* local ♦ *nm* place, site;
(*oficinas*) premises *pl*; **~idad** *nf* (*barrio*)
locality; (*lugar*) location; (*TEATRO*) seat,
ticket; **~izar** *vt* (*ubicar*) to locate, find;
(*restringir*) to localize; (*situar*) to place
loción [lo'θjon] *nf* lotion
loco, a ['loko, a] *adj* mad ♦ *nm/f* lunatic,
mad person
locomotora [lokomo'tora] *nf* engine,
locomotive
locuaz [lo'kwaθ] *adj* loquacious
locución [loku'θjon] *nf* expression
locura [lo'kura] *nf* madness; (*acto*) crazy
act
locutor, a [loku'tor, a] *nm/f* (*RADIO*)
announcer; (*comentarista*) commentator;
(*TV*) newsreader
locutorio [loku'torjo] *nm* (*en telefónica*)
telephone booth
lodo ['loðo] *nm* mud
lógica ['loxika] *nf* logic
lógico, a ['loxiko, a] *adj* logical
login ['loɡɪn] *nm* login
logística [lo'xistika] *nf* logistics *sg*
logotipo [loɡo'tipo] *nm* logo
logrado, a [lo'ɣraðo, a] *adj* (*interpretación,
reproducción*) polished, excellent
lograr [lo'ɣrar] *vt* to achieve; (*obtener*) to
get, obtain; **~ hacer** to manage to do; **~
que uno venga** to manage to get sb to
come
logro ['loɣro] *nm* achievement, success
loma ['loma] *nf* hillock (*BRIT*), small hill
lombriz [lom'briθ] *nf* worm
lomo ['lomo] *nm* (*de animal*) back; (*CULIN:
de cerdo*) pork loin; (*: de vaca*) rib steak;
(*de libro*) spine
lona ['lona] *nf* canvas
loncha ['lontʃa] *nf* = **lonja**
lonche ['lontʃe] (*AM*) *nm* lunch; **~ría** (*AM*)

nf snack bar, diner (*US*)
Londres ['londres] *n* London
longaniza [loŋɡa'niθa] *nf* pork sausage
longitud [loŋxi'tuð] *nf* length; (*GEO*)
longitude; **tener 3 metros de ~** to be 3
metres long; **~ de onda** wavelength
lonja ['lonxa] *nf* slice; (*de tocino*) rasher; **~
de pescado** fish market
loro ['loro] *nm* parrot
los [los] *art def* the ♦ *pron* them; (*ustedes*)
you; **mis libros y ~ tuyos** my books and
yours; *tb ver* **el**
losa ['losa] *nf* stone; **~ sepulcral**
gravestone
lote ['lote] *nm* portion; (*COM*) lot
lotería [lote'ria] *nf* lottery; (*juego*) lotto

Lotería

i Millions of pounds are spent on
lotteries each year in Spain, two of
which are state-run: the **Lotería
Primitiva** and the **Lotería Nacional**,
with money raised going directly to the
government. One of the most famous
lotteries is run by the wealthy and
influential society for the blind, "la
ONCE".

---

loza ['loθa] *nf* crockery
lubina [lu'βina] *nf* sea bass
lubricante [luβri'kante] *nm* lubricant
lubricar [luβri'kar] *vt* to lubricate
lucha ['lutʃa] *nf* fight, struggle; **~ de
clases** class struggle; **~ libre** wrestling;
luchar *vi* to fight
lucidez [luθi'ðeθ] *nf* lucidity
lúcido, a ['luθiðo, a] *adj* (*persona*) lucid;
(*mente*) logical; (*idea*) crystal-clear
luciérnaga [lu'θjernaxa] *nf* glow-worm
lucir [lu'θir] *vt* to illuminate, light (up);
(*ostentar*) to show off ♦ *vi* (*brillar*) to
shine; **~se** *vr* to make a fool of o.s.
lucro ['lukro] *nm* profit, gain
lúdico, a ['luðiko, a] *adj* (*aspecto,
actividad*) play *cpd*
luego ['lweɣo] *adv* (*después*) next; (*más
tarde*) later, afterwards

lugar [luˈɣar] *nm* place; (*sitio*) spot; **en ~ de** instead of; **hacer ~** to make room; **fuera de ~** out of place; **tener ~** to take place; **~ común** commonplace
lugareño, a [luɣaˈreɲo, a] *adj* village *cpd* ♦ *nm/f* villager
lugarteniente [luɣarteˈnjente] *nm* deputy
lúgubre [ˈluɣußre] *adj* mournful
lujo [ˈluxo] *nm* luxury; (*fig*) profusion, abundance; **~so, a** *adj* luxurious
lujuria [luˈxurja] *nf* lust
lumbre [ˈlumbre] *nf* fire; (*para cigarrillo*) light
lumbrera [lumˈbrera] *nf* luminary
luminoso, a [lumiˈnoso, a] *adj* luminous, shining
luna [ˈluna] *nf* moon; (*de un espejo*) glass; (*de gafas*) lens; (*fig*) crescent; **~ llena/nueva** full/new moon; **estar en la ~** to have one's head in the clouds; **~ de miel** honeymoon
lunar [luˈnar] *adj* lunar ♦ *nm* (*ANAT*) mole; **tela de ~es** spotted material
lunes [ˈlunes] *nm inv* Monday
lupa [ˈlupa] *nf* magnifying glass
lustrar [lusˈtrar] *vt* (*mueble*) to polish; (*zapatos*) to shine; **lustre** *nm* polish; (*fig*) lustre; **dar lustre a** to polish; **lustroso, a** *adj* shining
luto [ˈluto] *nm* mourning; **llevar el** *o* **vestirse de ~** to be in mourning
Luxemburgo [luksemˈburɣo] *nm* Luxembourg
luz [luθ] (*pl* **luces**) *nf* light; **dar a ~ un niño** to give birth to a child; **sacar a la ~** to bring to light; **dar** *o* **encender** (*ESP*) *o* **prender** (*AM*)/**apagar la ~** to switch the light on/off; **a todas luces** by any reckoning; **tener pocas luces** to be dim *o* stupid; **~ roja/verde** red/green light; **~ de freno** brake light; **luces de tráfico** traffic lights; **traje de luces** bullfighter's costume

M, m

m *abr* (= *metro*) m; (= *minuto*) m
macarrones [makaˈrrones] *nmpl* macaroni *sg*
macedonia [maθeˈðonja] *nf*: **~ de frutas** fruit salad
macerar [maθeˈrar] *vt* to macerate
maceta [maˈθeta] *nf* (*de flores*) pot of flowers; (*para plantas*) flowerpot
machacar [matʃaˈkar] *vt* to crush, pound ♦ *vi* (*insistir*) to go on, keep on
machete [maˈtʃete] (*AM*) *nm* machete, (large) knife
machismo [maˈtʃismo] *nm* male chauvinism; **machista** *adj, nm* sexist
macho [ˈmatʃo] *adj* male; (*fig*) virile ♦ *nm* male; (*fig*) he-man
macizo, a [maˈθiθo, a] *adj* (*grande*) massive; (*fuerte, sólido*) solid ♦ *nm* mass, chunk
madeja [maˈðexa] *nf* (*de lana*) skein, hank; (*de pelo*) mass, mop
madera [maˈðera] *nf* wood; (*fig*) nature, character; **una ~** a piece of wood
madero [maˈðero] *nm* beam
madrastra [maˈðrastra] *nf* stepmother
madre [ˈmaðre] *adj* mother *cpd*; (*AM*) tremendous ♦ *nf* mother; (*de vino etc*) dregs *pl*; **~ política/soltera** mother-in-law/unmarried mother
Madrid [maˈðrið] *n* Madrid
madriguera [maðriˈɣera] *nf* burrow
madrileño, a [maðriˈleɲo, a] *adj* of *o* from Madrid ♦ *nm/f* native of Madrid
madrina [maˈðrina] *nf* godmother; (*ARQ*) prop, shore; (*TEC*) brace; (*de boda*) bridesmaid
madrugada [maðruˈɣaða] *nf* early morning; (*alba*) dawn, daybreak
madrugador, a [maðruɣaˈðor, a] *adj* early-rising
madrugar [maðruˈɣar] *vi* to get up early; (*fig*) to get ahead
madurar [maðuˈrar] *vt, vi* (*fruta*) to ripen;

(fig) to mature; **madurez** nf ripeness; maturity; **maduro, a** adj ripe; mature

maestra [ma'estra] nf ver **maestro**

maestría [maes'tria] nf mastery; (habilidad) skill, expertise

maestro, a [ma'estro, a] adj masterly; (principal) main ♦ nm/f master/mistress; (profesor) teacher ♦ nm (autoridad) authority; (MUS) maestro; (AM) skilled workman; ~ **albañil** master mason

magdalena [mavða'lena] nf fairy cake

magia ['maxja] nf magic; **mágico, a** adj magic(al) ♦ nm/f magician

magisterio [maxis'terjo] nm (enseñanza) teaching; (profesión) teaching profession; (maestros) teachers pl

magistrado [maxis'traðo] nm magistrate

magistral [maxis'tral] adj magisterial; (fig) masterly

magnánimo, a [mav'nanimo, a] adj magnanimous

magnate [mav'nate] nm magnate, tycoon

magnético, a [mav'netiko, a] adj magnetic; **magnetizar** vt to magnetize

magnetofón [mavneto'fon] nm tape recorder; **magnetofónico, a** adj: **cinta magnetofónica** recording tape

magnetófono [mavne'tofono] nm = **magnetofón**

magnífico, a [mav'nifiko, a] adj splendid, magnificent

magnitud [mavni'tuð] nf magnitude

mago, a ['mavo, a] nm/f magician; **los Reyes M~s** the Magi, the Three Wise Men

magro, a ['mavro, a] adj (carne) lean

maguey [ma'vei] nm agave

magullar [mavu'ʎar] vt (amoratar) to bruise; (dañar) to damage

mahometano, a [maome'tano, a] adj Mohammedan

mahonesa [mao'nesa] nf mayonnaise

maíz [ma'iθ] nm maize (BRIT), corn (US); sweet corn

majadero, a [maxa'ðero, a] adj silly, stupid

majestad [maxes'tað] nf majesty;

majestuoso, a adj majestic

majo, a ['maxo, a] adj nice; (guapo) attractive, good-looking; (elegante) smart

mal [mal] adv badly; (equivocadamente) wrongly ♦ adj = **malo** ♦ nm evil; (desgracia) misfortune; (daño) harm, damage; (MED) illness; ~ **que bien** rightly or wrongly; **ir de ~ en peor** to get worse and worse

malabarismo [malaβa'rismo] nm juggling; **malabarista** nm/f juggler

malaria [ma'larja] nf malaria

malcriado, a [mal'krjaðo, a] adj spoiled

maldad [mal'daθ] nf evil, wickedness

maldecir [malde'θir] vt to curse ♦ vi: ~ **de** to speak ill of

maldición [maldi'θjon] nf curse

maldito, a [mal'dito, a] adj (condenado) damned; (perverso) wicked; **¡~ sea!** damn it!

maleante [male'ante] nm/f criminal, crook

maledicencia [maleði'θenθja] nf slander, scandal

maleducado, a [maleðu'kaðo, a] adj bad-mannered, rude

malentendido [malenten'diðo] nm misunderstanding

malestar [males'tar] nm (gen) discomfort; (fig: inquietud) uneasiness; (POL) unrest

maleta [ma'leta] nf case, suitcase; (AUTO) boot (BRIT), trunk (US); **hacer las ~s** to pack; **maletera** (AM) nf, **maletero** nm (AUTO) boot (BRIT), trunk (US); **maletín** nm small case, bag

malévolo, a [ma'leβolo, a] adj malicious, spiteful

maleza [ma'leθa] nf (hierbas malas) weeds pl; (arbustos) thicket

malgastar [malvas'tar] vt (tiempo, dinero) to waste; (salud) to ruin

malhechor, a [male'tʃor, a] nm/f delinquent

malhumorado, a [malumo'raðo, a] adj bad-tempered

malicia [ma'liθja] nf (maldad) wickedness; (astucia) slyness, guile; (mala intención) malice, spite; (carácter travieso)

mischievousness; **malicioso, a** *adj*
wicked, evil; (*malévolo*) malicious; (*MED*) malignant

maligno, a [ma'liɣno, a] *adj* evil;
(*malévolo*) malicious; (*MED*) malignant

malla ['maʎa] *nf* mesh; (*de baño*) swimsuit;
(*de ballet, gimnasia*) leotard; **~s** *nfpl*
tights; **~ de alambre** wire mesh

Mallorca [ma'ʎorka] *nf* Majorca

malo, a ['malo, a] *adj* bad; (*falso*) false
♦ *nm/f* villain; **estar ~** to be ill

malograr [malo'ɣrar] *vt* to spoil; (*plan*) to
upset; (*ocasión*) to waste; **~se** *vr* (*plan
etc*) to fail, come to grief; (*persona*) to die
before one's time

malparado, a [malpa'raðo, a] *adj*: **salir ~**
to come off badly

malpensado, a [malpen'saðo, a] *adj*
nasty

malsano, a [mal'sano, a] *adj* unhealthy

malteada [malte'aða] (*AM*) *nf* milk shake

maltratar [maltra'tar] *vt* to ill-treat,
mistreat

maltrecho, a [mal'tretʃo, a] *adj* battered,
damaged

malvado, a [mal'βaðo, a] *adj* evil,
villainous

malversar [malβer'sar] *vt* to embezzle,
misappropriate

Malvinas [mal'βinas]: **Islas ~** *nfpl*
Falkland Islands

malvivir [malβi'βir] *vi* to live poorly

mama ['mama] *nf* (*de animal*) teat; (*de
mujer*) breast

mamá [ma'ma] (*pl* **~s**) (*fam*) *nf* mum,
mummy

mamar [ma'mar] *vt, vi* to suck

mamarracho [mama'rratʃo] *nm* sight,
mess

mamífero [ma'mifero] *nm* mammal

mampara [mam'para] *nf* (*entre
habitaciones*) partition; (*biombo*) screen

mampostería [mamposte'ria] *nf* masonry

manada [ma'naða] *nf* (*ZOOL*) herd; (: *de
leones*) pride; (: *de lobos*) pack

manantial [manan'tjal] *nm* spring

manar [ma'nar] *vi* to run, flow

mancha ['mantʃa] *nf* stain, mark; (*ZOOL*)
patch; **manchar** *vt* (*gen*) to stain, mark;
(*ensuciar*) to soil, dirty

manchego, a [man'tʃeɣo, a] *adj* of o
from La Mancha

manco, a ['manko, a] *adj* (*de un brazo*)
one-armed; (*de una mano*) one-handed;
(*fig*) defective, faulty

mancomunar [mankomu'nar] *vt* to unite,
bring together; (*recursos*) to pool; (*JUR*) to
make jointly responsible;
mancomunidad *nf* union, association;
(*comunidad*) community; (*JUR*) joint
responsibility

mandamiento [manda'mjento] *nm*
(*orden*) order, command; (*REL*)
commandment; **~ judicial** warrant

mandar [man'dar] *vt* (*ordenar*) to order;
(*dirigir*) to lead, command; (*enviar*) to
send; (*pedir*) to order, ask for ♦ *vi* to be
in charge; (*pey*) to be bossy; **¿mande?**
pardon?, excuse me?; **~ hacer un traje** to
have a suit made

mandarina [manda'rina] *nf* tangerine,
mandarin (orange)

mandato [man'dato] *nm* (*orden*) order;
(*POL*: *período*) term of office; (: *territorio*)
mandate; **~ judicial** (*search*) warrant

mandíbula [man'diβula] *nf* jaw

mandil [man'dil] *nm* apron

mando ['mando] *nm* (*MIL*) command; (*de
país*) rule; (*el primer lugar*) lead; (*POL*)
term of office; (*TEC*) control; **~ a la
izquierda** left-hand drive

mandón, ona [man'don, ona] *adj* bossy,
domineering

manejable [mane'xaβle] *adj* manageable

manejar [mane'xar] *vt* to manage;
(*máquina*) to work, operate; (*caballo etc*)
to handle; (*casa*) to run, manage; (*AM*:
AUTO) to drive; **~se** *vr* (*comportarse*) to
act, behave; (*arreglárselas*) to manage;
manejo *nm* management; handling;
running; driving; (*facilidad de trato*) ease,
confidence; **manejos** *nmpl* (*intrigas*)
intrigues

manera [ma'nera] *nf* way, manner,

fashion; **~s** *nfpl* (*modales*) manners; **su ~ de ser** the way he is; (*aire*) his manner; **de ninguna ~** no way, by no means; **de otra ~** otherwise; **de todas ~s** at any rate; **no hay ~ de persuadirle** there's no way of convincing him

manga ['manga] *nf* (*de camisa*) sleeve; (*de riego*) hose

mangar [man'gar] (*fam*) *vt* to pinch, nick

mango ['mango] *nm* handle; (*BOT*) mango

mangonear [mangone'ar] *vi* (*meterse*) to meddle, interfere; (*ser mandón*) to boss people about

manguera [man'gera] *nf* hose

manía [ma'nia] *nf* (*MED*) mania; (*fig: moda*) rage, craze; (*disgusto*) dislike; (*malicia*) spite; **maníaco, a** *adj* maniac(al) ♦ *nm/f* maniac

maniatar [manja'tar] *vt* to tie the hands of

maniático, a [ma'njatiko, a] *adj* maniac(al) ♦ *nm/f* maniac

manicomio [mani'komjo] *nm* mental hospital (*BRIT*), insane asylum (*US*)

manifestación [manifesta'θjon] *nf* (*declaración*) statement, declaration; (*de emoción*) show, display; (*POL: desfile*) demonstration; (: *concentración*) mass meeting

manifestar [manifes'tar] *vt* to show, manifest; (*declarar*) to state, declare; **manifiesto, a** *adj* clear, manifest ♦ *nm* manifesto

manillar [mani'ʎar] *nm* handlebars *pl*

maniobra [ma'njoβra] *nf* manœuvre; **~s** *nfpl* (*MIL*) manœuvres; **maniobrar** *vt* to manœuvre

manipulación [manipula'θjon] *nf* manipulation

manipular [manipu'lar] *vt* to manipulate; (*manejar*) to handle

maniquí [mani'ki] *nm* dummy ♦ *nm/f* model

manirroto, a [mani'rroto, a] *adj* lavish, extravagant ♦ *nm/f* spendthrift

manivela [mani'βela] *nf* crank

manjar [man'xar] *nm* (*tasty*) dish

mano ['mano] *nf* hand; (*ZOOL*) foot, paw;

(*de pintura*) coat; (*serie*) lot, series; **a ~** by hand; **a ~ derecha/izquierda** on the right(-hand side)/left(-hand side); **de primera ~** (at) first hand; **de segunda ~** (at) second hand; **robo a ~ armada** armed robbery; **~ de obra** labour, manpower; **estrechar la ~ a uno** to shake sb's hand

manojo [ma'noxo] *nm* handful, bunch; **~ de llaves** bunch of keys

manopla [ma'nopla] *nf* mitten

manoseado, a [manose'aðo, a] *adj* well-worn

manosear [manose'ar] *vt* (*tocar*) to handle, touch; (*desordenar*) to mess up, rumple; (*insistir en*) to overwork; (*AM*) to caress, fondle

manotazo [mano'taθo] *nm* slap, smack

mansalva [man'salβa]: **a ~** *adv* indiscriminately

mansedumbre [manse'ðumbre] *nf* gentleness, meekness

mansión [man'sjon] *nf* mansion

manso, a ['manso, a] *adj* gentle, mild; (*animal*) tame

manta ['manta] *nf* blanket; (*AM: poncho*) poncho

manteca [man'teka] *nf* fat; (*AM*) butter; **~ de cacahuete/cacao** peanut/cocoa butter; **~ de cerdo** lard

mantecado [mante'kaðo] (*AM*) *nm* ice cream

mantel [man'tel] *nm* tablecloth

mantendré *etc vb ver* **mantener**

mantener [mante'ner] *vt* to support, maintain; (*alimentar*) to sustain; (*conservar*) to keep; (*TEC*) to maintain, service; **~se** *vr* (*seguir de pie*) to be still standing; (*no ceder*) to hold one's ground; (*subsistir*) to sustain o.s., keep going; **mantenimiento** *nm* maintenance; sustenance; (*sustento*) support

mantequilla [mante'kiʎa] *nf* butter

mantilla [man'tiʎa] *nf* mantilla; **~s** *nfpl* (*de bebé*) baby clothes

manto ['manto] *nm* (*capa*) cloak; (*de*

ceremonia) robe, gown

mantuve *etc vb ver* **mantener**

manual [ma'nwal] *adj* manual ♦ *nm* manual, handbook

manufactura [manufak'tura] *nf* manufacture; (*fábrica*) factory; **manufacturado, a** *adj* (*producto*) manufactured

manuscrito, a [manus'krito, a] *adj* handwritten ♦ *nm* manuscript

manutención [manuten'θjon] *nf* maintenance; (*sustento*) support

manzana [man'θana] *nf* apple; (*ARQ*) block (of houses)

manzanilla [manθa'niʎa] *nf* (*planta*) camomile; (*infusión*) camomile tea

manzano [man'θano] *nm* apple tree

maña ['maɲa] *nf* (*gen*) skill, dexterity; (*pey*) guile; (*destreza*) trick, knack

mañana [ma'ɲana] *adv* tomorrow ♦ *nm* future ♦ *nf* morning; **de** *o* **por la ~** in the morning; **¡hasta ~!** see you tomorrow!; **~ por la ~** tomorrow morning

mañoso, a [ma'ɲoso, a] *adj* (*hábil*) skilful; (*astuto*) smart, clever

mapa ['mapa] *nm* map

maqueta [ma'keta] *nf* (scale) model

maquillaje [maki'ʎaxe] *nm* make-up; (*acto*) making up

maquillar [maki'ʎar] *vt* to make up; **~se** *vr* to put on (some) make-up

máquina ['makina] *nf* machine; (*de tren*) locomotive, engine; (*FOTO*) camera; (*AM*: *coche*) car; (*fig*) machinery; **escrito a ~** typewritten; **~ de escribir** typewriter; **~ de coser/lavar** sewing/washing machine

maquinación [makina'θjon] *nf* machination, plot

maquinal [maki'nal] *adj* (*fig*) mechanical, automatic

maquinaria [maki'narja] *nf* (*máquinas*) machinery; (*mecanismo*) mechanism, works *pl*

maquinilla [maki'niʎa] *nf*: **~ de afeitar** razor

maquinista [maki'nista] *nm/f* (*de tren*) engine driver; (*TEC*) operator; (*NAUT*)

engineer

mar [mar] *nm o f* sea; **~ adentro** *o* **afuera** out at sea; **en alta ~** on the high seas; **la ~ de** (*fam*) lots of; **el M~ Negro/Báltico** the Black/Baltic Sea

maraña [ma'raɲa] *nf* (*maleza*) thicket; (*confusión*) tangle

maravilla [mara'ßiʎa] *nf* marvel, wonder; (*BOT*) marigold; **maravillar** *vt* to astonish, amaze; **maravillarse** *vr* to be astonished, be amazed; **maravilloso, a** *adj* wonderful, marvellous

marca ['marka] *nf* (*gen*) mark; (*sello*) stamp; (*COM*) make, brand; **de ~** excellent, outstanding; **~ de fábrica** trademark; **~ registrada** registered trademark

marcado, a [mar'kaðo, a] *adj* marked, strong

marcador [marka'ðor] *nm* (*DEPORTE*) scoreboard; (: *persona*) scorer

marcapasos [marka'pasos] *nm inv* pacemaker

marcar [mar'kar] *vt* (*gen*) to mark; (*número de teléfono*) to dial; (*gol*) to score; (*números*) to record, keep a tally of; (*pelo*) to set ♦ *vi* (*DEPORTE*) to score; (*TEL*) to dial

marcha ['martʃa] *nf* march; (*TEC*) running, working; (*AUTO*) gear; (*velocidad*) speed; (*fig*) progress; (*dirección*) course; **poner en ~** to put into gear; (*fig*) to set in motion, get going; **dar ~ atrás** to reverse, put into reverse; **estar en ~** to be under way, be in motion

marchar [mar'tʃar] *vi* (*ir*) to go; (*funcionar*) to work, go; **~se** *vr* to go (away), leave

marchitar [martʃi'tar] *vt* to wither, dry up; **~se** *vr* (*BOT*) to wither; (*fig*) to fade away; **marchito, a** *adj* withered, faded; (*fig*) in decline

marcial [mar'θjal] *adj* martial, military

marciano, a [mar'θjano, a] *adj*, *nm/f* Martian

marco ['marko] *nm* frame; (*moneda*) mark; (*fig*) framework

marea [ma'rea] *nf* tide

marear [mare'ar] *vt (fig)* to annoy, upset; *(MED):* **~ a uno** to make sb feel sick; **~se** *vr (tener náuseas)* to feel sick; *(desvanecerse)* to feel faint; *(aturdirse)* to feel dizzy; *(fam: emborracharse)* to get tipsy

maremoto [mare'moto] *nm* tidal wave

mareo [ma'reo] *nm (náusea)* sick feeling; *(en viaje)* travel sickness; *(aturdimiento)* dizziness; *(fam: lata)* nuisance

marfil [mar'fil] *nm* ivory

margarina [marva'rina] *nf* margarine

margarita [marva'rita] *nf (BOT)* daisy; **(rueda) ~** daisywheel

margen ['marxen] *nm (borde)* edge, border; *(fig)* margin, space ♦ *nf (de río etc)* bank; **dar ~ para** to give an opportunity for; **mantenerse al ~** to keep out (of things)

marginar [marxi'nar] *vt (socialmente)* to marginalize, ostracize

marica [ma'rika] *(fam) nm* sissy

maricón [mari'kon] *(fam) nm* queer

marido [ma'riðo] *nm* husband

marihuana [mari'wana] *nf* marijuana, cannabis

marina [ma'rina] *nf* navy; **~ mercante** merchant navy

marinero, a [mari'nero, a] *adj* sea *cpd* ♦ *nm* sailor, seaman

marino, a [ma'rino, a] *adj* sea *cpd*, marine ♦ *nm* sailor

marioneta [marjo'neta] *nf* puppet

mariposa [mari'posa] *nf* butterfly

mariquita [mari'kita] *nf* ladybird *(BRIT)*, ladybug *(US)*

mariscos [ma'riskos] *nmpl* shellfish *inv*, seafood(s)

marítimo, a [ma'ritimo, a] *adj* sea *cpd*, maritime

mármol ['marmol] *nm* marble

marqués, esa [mar'kes, esa] *nm/f* marquis/marchioness

marrón [ma'rron] *adj* brown

marroquí [marro'ki] *adj, nm/f* Moroccan ♦ *nm* Morocco (leather)

Marruecos [ma'rrwekos] *nm* Morocco

martes ['martes] *nm inv* Tuesday

Martes y Trece

ⓘ According to Spanish superstition Tuesday is an unlucky day, even more so if it falls on the 13th of the month.
---

martillo [mar'tiʎo] *nm* hammer; **~ neumático** pneumatic drill *(BRIT)*, jackhammer

mártir ['martir] *nm/f* martyr; **martirio** *nm* martyrdom; *(fig)* torture, torment

marxismo [mark'sismo] *nm* Marxism; **marxista** *adj, nm/f* Marxist

marzo ['marθo] *nm* March

PALABRA CLAVE
---

más [mas] *adj, adv* **1**: **~ (que/de)** *(compar)* more (than), ...+er (than); **~ grande/inteligente** bigger/more intelligent; **trabaja ~ (que yo)** he works more (than me); *ver tb* **cada**

2 *(superl)*: **el ~** the most, ...+est; **el ~ grande/inteligente (de)** the biggest/most intelligent (in)

3 *(negativo)*: **no tengo ~ dinero** I haven't got any more money; **no viene ~ por aquí** he doesn't come round here any more

4 *(adicional)*: **no le veo ~ solución que ...** I see no other solution than to ...; **¿quién ~?** anybody else?

5 *(+adj: valor intensivo)*: **¡qué perro ~ sucio!** what a filthy dog!; **¡es ~ tonto!** he's so stupid!

6 *(locuciones)*: **~ o menos** more or less; **los ~** most people; **es ~** furthermore; **~ bien** rather; **¡qué ~ da!** what does it matter!; *ver tb* **no**

7: **por ~**: **por ~ que te esfuerces** no matter how hard you try; **por ~ que quisiera ...** much as I should like to ...

8: **de ~**: **veo que aquí estoy de ~** I can see I'm not needed here; **tenemos uno de ~** we've got one extra

♦ *prep*: **2 ~ 2 son 4** 2 and *o* plus 2 are 4

♦ *nm inv*: **este trabajo tiene sus ~ y**

sus menos this job's got its good points and its bad points

---

mas [mas] *conj* but

masa ['masa] *nf* (*mezcla*) dough; (*volumen*) volume, mass; (*FÍSICA*) mass; **en ~** en masse; **las ~s** (*POL*) the masses

masacre [ma'sakre] *nf* massacre

masaje [ma'saxe] *nm* massage

máscara ['maskara] *nf* mask; **mascarilla** *nf* (*de belleza, MED*) mask

masculino, a [masku'lino, a] *adj* masculine; (*BIO*) male

masía [ma'sia] *nf* farmhouse

masificación [masifika'θjon] *nf* overcrowding

masivo, a [ma'siβo, a] *adj* mass *cpd*

masón [ma'son] *nm* (free)mason

masoquista [maso'kista] *nm/f* masochist

masticar [masti'kar] *vt* to chew

mástil ['mastil] *nm* (*de navío*) mast; (*de guitarra*) neck

mastín [mas'tin] *nm* mastiff

masturbación [masturβa'θjon] *nf* masturbation

masturbarse [mastur'βarse] *vr* to masturbate

mata ['mata] *nf* (*arbusto*) bush, shrub; (*de hierba*) tuft

matadero [mata'ðero] *nm* slaughterhouse, abattoir

matador, a [mata'ðor, a] *adj* killing ♦ *nm/f* killer ♦ *nm* (*TAUR*) matador, bullfighter

matamoscas [mata'moskas] *nm inv* (*palo*) fly swat

matanza [ma'tanθa] *nf* slaughter

matar [ma'tar] *vt, vi* to kill; **~se** *vr* (*suicidarse*) to kill o.s., commit suicide; (*morir*) to be o get killed; **~ el hambre** to stave off hunger

matasellos [mata'seʎos] *nm inv* postmark

mate ['mate] *adj* matt ♦ *nm* (*en ajedrez*) (check)mate; (*AM: hierba*) maté; (: *vasija*) gourd

matemáticas [mate'matikas] *nfpl* mathematics; **matemático, a** *adj*

mathematical ♦ *nm/f* mathematician

materia [ma'terja] *nf* (*gen*) matter; (*TEC*) material; (*ESCOL*) subject; **en ~ de** on the subject of; **~ prima** raw material; **material** *adj* material ♦ *nm* material; (*TEC*) equipment; **materialismo** *nm* materialism; **materialista** *adj* materialist(ic); **materialmente** *adv* materially; (*fig*) absolutely

maternal [mater'nal] *adj* motherly, maternal

maternidad [materni'ðað] *nf* motherhood, maternity; **materno, a** *adj* maternal; (*lengua*) mother *cpd*

matinal [mati'nal] *adj* morning *cpd*

matiz [ma'tiθ] *nm* shade; **~ar** *vt* (*variar*) to vary; (*ARTE*) to blend; **~ar de** to tinge with

matón [ma'ton] *nm* bully

matorral [mato'rral] *nm* thicket

matraca [ma'traka] *nf* rattle

matrícula [ma'trikula] *nf* (*registro*) register; (*AUTO*) registration number; (: *placa*) number plate; **matricular** *vt* to register, enrol

matrimonial [matrimo'njal] *adj* matrimonial

matrimonio [matri'monjo] *nm* (*pareja*) (married) couple; (*unión*) marriage

matriz [ma'triθ] *nf* (*ANAT*) womb; (*TEC*) mould; **casa ~** (*COM*) head office

matrona [ma'trona] *nf* (*persona de edad*) matron; (*comadrona*) midwife

maullar [mau'ʎar] *vi* to mew, miaow

maxilar [maksi'lar] *nm* jaw(bone)

máxima ['maksima] *nf* maxim

máxime ['maksime] *adv* especially

máximo, a ['maksimo, a] *adj* maximum; (*más alto*) highest; (*más grande*) greatest ♦ *nm* maximum

mayo ['majo] *nm* May

mayonesa [majo'nesa] *nf* mayonnaise

mayor [ma'jor] *adj* main, chief; (*adulto*) adult; (*de edad avanzada*) elderly; (*MUS*) major; (*compar: de tamaño*) bigger; (: *de edad*) older; (*superl: de tamaño*) biggest; (: *de edad*) oldest ♦ *nm* (*adulto*) adult; **al**

por ~ wholesale; **~ de edad** adult; **~es** *nmpl* (*antepasados*) ancestors

mayoral [majoˈral] *nm* foreman

mayordomo [majorˈðomo] *nm* butler

mayoría [majoˈria] *nf* majority, greater part

mayorista [majoˈrista] *nm/f* wholesaler

mayoritario, a [majoriˈtarjo, a] *adj* majority *cpd*

mayúscula [maˈjuskula] *nf* capital letter

mayúsculo, a [maˈjuskulo, a] *adj* (*fig*) big, tremendous

mazapán [maθaˈpan] *nm* marzipan

mazo [ˈmaθo] *nm* (*martillo*) mallet; (*de flores*) bunch; (*DEPORTE*) bat

me [me] *pron* (*directo*) me; (*indirecto*) (to) me; (*reflexivo*) (to) myself; **¡dámelo!** give it to me!

mear [meˈar] (*fam*) *vi* to pee, piss (*!*)

mecánica [meˈkanika] *nf* (*ESCOL*) mechanics *sg*; (*mecanismo*) mechanism; *ver tb* **mecánico**

mecánico, a [meˈkaniko, a] *adj* mechanical ♦ *nm/f* mechanic

mecanismo [mekaˈnismo] *nm* mechanism; (*marcha*) gear

mecanografía [mekanoɣraˈfia] *nf* typewriting; **mecanógrafo, a** *nm/f* typist

mecate [meˈkate] (*AM*) *nm* rope

mecedora [meθeˈðora] *nf* rocking chair

mecer [meˈθer] *vt* (*cuna*) to rock; **~se** *vr* to rock; (*ramo*) to sway

mecha [ˈmetʃa] *nf* (*de vela*) wick; (*de bomba*) fuse

mechero [meˈtʃero] *nm* (cigarette) lighter

mechón [meˈtʃon] *nm* (*gen*) tuft; (*de pelo*) lock

medalla [meˈðaʎa] *nf* medal

media [ˈmeðja] *nf* (*ESP*) stocking; (*AM*) sock; (*promedio*) average

mediado, a [meˈðjaðo, a] *adj* half-full; (*trabajo*) half-completed; **a ~s de** in the middle of, halfway through

mediano, a [meˈðjano, a] *adj* (*regular*) medium, average; (*mediocre*) mediocre

medianoche [meðjaˈnotʃe] *nf* midnight

mediante [meˈðjante] *adv* by (means of), through

mediar [meˈðjar] *vi* (*interceder*) to mediate, intervene

medicación [meðikaˈθjon] *nf* medication, treatment

medicamento [meðikaˈmento] *nm* medicine, drug

medicina [meðiˈθina] *nf* medicine

medición [meðiˈθjon] *nf* measurement

médico, a [ˈmeðiko, a] *adj* medical ♦ *nm/f* doctor

medida [meˈðiða] *nf* measure; (*medición*) measurement; (*prudencia*) moderation, prudence; **en cierta/gran ~** up to a point/to a great extent; **un traje a la ~** made-to-measure suit; **~ de cuello** collar size; **a ~ de** in proportion to; (*de acuerdo con*) in keeping with; **a ~ que** (*conforme*) as

medio, a [ˈmeðjo, a] *adj* half (a); (*punto*) mid, middle; (*promedio*) average ♦ *adv* half ♦ *nm* (*centro*) middle, centre; (*promedio*) average; (*método*) means, way; (*ambiente*) environment; **~s** *nmpl* means, resources; **~ litro** half a litre; **las tres y media** half past three; **medio ambiente** environment; **M~ Oriente** Middle East; **a ~ terminar** half finished; **pagar a medias** to share the cost; **~ambiental** *adj* (*política, efectos*) environmental

mediocre [meˈðjokre] *adj* mediocre

mediodía [meðjoˈðia] *nm* midday, noon

medir [meˈðir] *vt, vi* (*gen*) to measure

meditar [meðiˈtar] *vt* to ponder, think over, meditate on; (*planear*) to think out

mediterráneo, a [meðiteˈrraneo, a] *adj* Mediterranean ♦ *nm*: **el M~** the Mediterranean (Sea)

médula [ˈmeðula] *nf* (*ANAT*) marrow; **~ espinal** spinal cord

medusa [meˈðusa] (*ESP*) *nf* jellyfish

megafonía [meɣafoˈnia] *nf* public address system, PA system; **megáfono** *nm* megaphone

megalómano, a [meɣaˈlomano, a] *nm/f* megalomaniac

mejicano, a [mexiˈkano, a] *adj, nm/f* Mexican

Méjico [ˈmexiko] *nm* Mexico

mejilla [meˈxiʎa] *nf* cheek

mejillón [mexiˈʎon] *nm* mussel

mejor [meˈxor] *adj, adv* (*compar*) better; (*superl*) best; **a lo ~** probably; (*quizá*) maybe; **~ dicho** rather; **tanto ~** so much the better

mejora [meˈxora] *nf* improvement; **mejorar** *vt* to improve, make better ♦ *vi* to improve, get better; **mejorarse** *vr* to improve, get better

melancólico, a [melanˈkoliko, a] *adj* (*triste*) sad, melancholy; (*soñador*) dreamy

melena [meˈlena] *nf* (*de persona*) long hair; (*ZOOL*) mane

mellizo, a [meˈʎiθo, a] *adj, nm/f* twin; **~s** *nmpl* (*AM*) cufflinks

melocotón [melokoˈton] (*ESP*) *nm* peach

melodía [meloˈðia] *nf* melody, tune

melodrama [meloˈðrama] *nm* melodrama; **melodramático, a** *adj* melodramatic

melón [meˈlon] *nm* melon

membrillo [memˈbriʎo] *nm* quince; **carne de ~** quince jelly

memorable [memoˈraβle] *adj* memorable

memoria [meˈmorja] *nf* (*gen*) memory; **~s** *nfpl* (*de autor*) memoirs; **memorizar** *vt* to memorize

menaje [meˈnaxe] *nm*: **~ de cocina** kitchenware

mencionar [menθjoˈnar] *vt* to mention

mendigar [mendiˈɣar] *vt* to beg (for)

mendigo, a [menˈdiɣo, a] *nm/f* beggar

mendrugo [menˈdruɣo] *nm* crust

menear [meneˈar] *vt* to move; **~se** *vr* to shake; (*balancearse*) to sway; (*moverse*) to move; (*fig*) to get a move on

menestra [meˈnestra] *nf*: **~ de verduras** vegetable stew

menguante [menˈgwante] *adj* decreasing, diminishing

menguar [menˈgwar] *vt* to lessen, diminish ♦ *vi* to diminish, decrease

menopausia [menoˈpausja] *nf* menopause

menor [meˈnor] *adj* (*más pequeño*: *compar*) smaller; (: *superl*) smallest; (*más joven*: *compar*) younger; (: *superl*) youngest; (*MUS*) minor ♦ *nm/f* (*joven*) young person, juvenile; **no tengo la ~ idea** I haven't the faintest idea; **al por ~** retail; **~ de edad** person under age

Menorca [meˈnorka] *nf* Minorca

PALABRA CLAVE
---

menos [menos] *adj* 1: **~ (que/de)** (*compar*: *cantidad*) less (than); (: *número*) fewer (than); **con ~ entusiasmo** with less enthusiasm; **~ gente** fewer people; *ver tb* **cada**

2 (*superl*): **es el que ~ culpa tiene** he's the least to blame

♦ *adv* 1 (*compar*): **~ (que, de)** less (than); **me gusta ~ que el otro** I like it less than the other one

2 (*superl*): **es el ~ listo (de su clase)** he's the least bright in his class; **de todas ellas es la que ~ me agrada** out of all of them she's the one I like least; **(por) lo ~** at (the very) least

3 (*locuciones*): **no quiero verle y ~ visitarle** I don't want to see him let alone visit him; **tenemos 7 de ~** we're seven short

♦ *prep* except; (*cifras*) minus; **todos ~ él** everyone except (for) him; **5 ~ 2** 5 minus 2

♦ *conj*: **a ~ que**: **a ~ que venga mañana** unless he comes tomorrow

---

menospreciar [menospreˈθjar] *vt* to underrate, undervalue; (*despreciar*) to scorn, despise

mensaje [menˈsaxe] *nm* message; **~ de texto** text message; **~ro, a** *nm/f* messenger

menstruación [menstruaˈθjon] *nf* menstruation

menstruar [mensˈtrwar] *vi* to menstruate

mensual [menˈswal] *adj* monthly; **1000 ptas ~es** 1000 ptas a month; **~idad** *nf* (*salario*) monthly salary; (*COM*) monthly payment, monthly instalment

menta ['menta] *nf* mint

mental [men'tal] *adj* mental; **~idad** *nf* mentality; **~izar** *vt* (*sensibilizar*) to make aware; (*convencer*) to convince; (*padres*) to prepare (mentally); **~izarse** *vr* (*concienciarse*) to become aware; **~izarse (de)** to get used to the idea (of); **~izarse de que ...** (*convencerse*) to get it into one's head that ...

mentar [men'tar] *vt* to mention, name

mente ['mente] *nf* mind

mentir [men'tir] *vi* to lie

mentira [men'tira] *nf* (*una ~*) lie; (*acto*) lying; (*invención*) fiction; **parece ~ que ...** it seems incredible that ..., I can't believe that ...

mentiroso, a [menti'roso, a] *adj* lying
♦ *nm/f* liar

menú [me'nu] (*pl* **~s**) *nm* menu; (*AM*) set meal; **~ del día** set menu

menudo, a [me'nuðo, a] *adj* (*pequeño*) small, tiny; (*sin importancia*) petty, insignificant; **¡~ negocio!** (*fam*) some deal!; **a ~** often, frequently

meñique [me'ɲike] *nm* little finger

meollo [me'oʎo] *nm* (*fig*) core

mercado [mer'kaðo] *nm* market

mercancía [merkan'θia] *nf* commodity; **~s** *nfpl* goods, merchandise *sg*

mercantil [merkan'til] *adj* mercantile, commercial

mercenario, a [merθe'narjo, a] *adj, nm* mercenary

mercería [merθe'ria] *nf* haberdashery (*BRIT*), notions (*US*); (*tienda*) haberdasher's (*BRIT*), notions store (*US*); (*AM*) drapery

mercurio [mer'kurjo] *nm* mercury

merecer [mere'θer] *vt* to deserve, merit
♦ *vi* to be deserving, be worthy; **merece la pena** it's worthwhile; **merecido, a** *adj* (well) deserved; **llevar su merecido** to get one's deserts

merendar [meren'dar] *vt* to have for tea
♦ *vi* to have tea; (*en el campo*) to have a picnic; **merendero** *nm* open-air cafe

merengue [me'renge] *nm* meringue

meridiano [meri'ðjano] *nm* (*GEO*) meridian

merienda [me'rjenda] *nf* (light) tea, afternoon snack; (*de campo*) picnic

mérito ['merito] *nm* merit; (*valor*) worth, value

merluza [mer'luθa] *nf* hake

merma ['merma] *nf* decrease; (*pérdida*) wastage; **mermar** *vt* to reduce, lessen
♦ *vi* to decrease, dwindle

mermelada [merme'laða] *nf* jam

mero, a ['mero, a] *adj* mere; (*AM: fam*) very

merodear [meroðe'ar] *vi*: **~ por** to prowl about

mes [mes] *nm* month

mesa ['mesa] *nf* table; (*de trabajo*) desk; (*GEO*) plateau; **~ directiva** board; **~ redonda** (*reunión*) round table; **poner/ quitar la ~** to lay/clear the table; **mesero, a** (*AM*) *nm/f* waiter/waitress

meseta [me'seta] *nf* (*GEO*) meseta, tableland

mesilla [me'siʎa] *nf*: **~ (de noche)** bedside table

mesón [me'son] *nm* inn

mestizo, a [mes'tiθo, a] *adj* half-caste, of mixed race ♦ *nm/f* half-caste

mesura [me'sura] *nf* moderation, restraint

meta ['meta] *nf* goal; (*de carrera*) finish

metabolismo [metaßo'lismo] *nm* metabolism

metáfora [me'tafora] *nf* metaphor

metal [me'tal] *nm* (*materia*) metal; (*MUS*) brass; **metálico, a** *adj* metallic; (*de metal*) metal ♦ *nm* (*dinero contante*) cash

metalurgia [meta'lurxja] *nf* metallurgy

meteoro [mete'oro] *nm* meteor; **~logía** *nf* meteorology

meter [me'ter] *vt* (*colocar*) to put, place; (*introducir*) to put in, insert; (*involucrar*) to involve; (*causar*) to make, cause; **~se** *vr*: **~se en** to go into, enter; (*fig*) to interfere in, meddle in; **~se a** to start; **~se a escritor** to become a writer; **~se con uno** to provoke sb, pick a quarrel with sb

meticuloso, a [metiku'loso, a] *adj*

meticulous, thorough

metódico, a [me'toðiko, a] *adj* methodical

método ['metoðo] *nm* method

metralleta [metra'ʎeta] *nf* sub-machine-gun

métrico, a ['metriko, a] *adj* metric

metro ['metro] *nm* metre; (*tren*) underground (*BRIT*), subway (*US*)

México ['mexiko] *nm* Mexico; **Ciudad de ~** Mexico City

mezcla ['meθkla] *nf* mixture; **mezclar** *vt* to mix (up); **mezclarse** *vr* to mix, mingle; **mezclarse en** to get mixed up in, get involved in

mezquino, a [meθ'kino, a] *adj* mean

mezquita [meθ'kita] *nf* mosque

mg. *abr* (= *miligramo*) mg

mi [mi] *adj* my ♦ *nm* (*MUS*) E

mí [mi] *pron* me; myself

mía ['mia] *pron ver* **mío**

miaja ['mjaxa] *nf* crumb

michelín [mitʃe'lin] (*fam*) *nm* (*de grasa*) spare tyre

micro ['mikro] (*AM*) *nm* minibus

microbio [mi'kroβjo] *nm* microbe

micrófono [mi'krofono] *nm* microphone

microondas [mikro'ondas] *nm inv* (*tb:* **horno ~**) microwave (oven)

microscopio [mikro'skopjo] *nm* microscope

miedo ['mjeðo] *nm* fear; (*nerviosismo*) apprehension, nervousness; **tener ~** to be afraid; **de ~** wonderful, marvellous; **hace un frío de ~** (*fam*) it's terribly cold; **~so, a** *adj* fearful, timid

miel [mjel] *nf* honey

miembro ['mjembro] *nm* limb; (*socio*) member; **~ viril** penis

mientras ['mjentras] *conj* while; (*duración*) as long as ♦ *adv* meanwhile; **~ tanto** meanwhile; **~ más tiene, más quiere** the more he has, the more he wants

miércoles ['mjerkoles] *nm inv* Wednesday

mierda ['mjerða] (*fam!*) *nf* shit (*!*)

miga ['miɣa] *nf* crumb; (*fig: meollo*) essence; **hacer buenas ~s** (*fam*) to get

on well

mil [mil] *num* thousand; **dos ~ libras** two thousand pounds

milagro [mi'laɣro] *nm* miracle; **~so, a** *adj* miraculous

milésima [mi'lesima] *nf* (*de segundo*) thousandth

mili ['mili] (*fam*) *nf:* **hacer la ~** to do one's military service

milicia [mi'liθja] *nf* militia; (*servicio militar*) military service

milímetro [mi'limetro] *nm* millimetre

militante [mili'tante] *adj* militant

militar [mili'tar] *adj* military ♦ *nm/f* soldier ♦ *vi* (*MIL*) to serve; (*en un partido*) to be a member

milla ['miʎa] *nf* mile

millar [mi'ʎar] *nm* thousand

millón [mi'ʎon] *num* million; **millonario, a** *nm/f* millionaire

mimar [mi'mar] *vt* to spoil, pamper

mimbre ['mimbre] *nm* wicker

mímica ['mimika] *nf* (*para comunicarse*) sign language; (*imitación*) mimicry

mimo ['mimo] *nm* (*caricia*) caress; (*de niño*) spoiling; (*TEATRO*) mime; (*: actor*) mime artist

mina ['mina] *nf* mine; **minar** *vt* to mine; (*fig*) to undermine

mineral [mine'ral] *adj* mineral ♦ *nm* (*GEO*) mineral; (*mena*) ore

minero, a [mi'nero, a] *adj* mining *cpd* ♦ *nm/f* miner

miniatura [minja'tura] *adj inv, nf* miniature

minidisco [mini'disko] *nm* Minidisc ®

minifalda [mini'falda] *nf* miniskirt

mínimo, a ['minimo, a] *adj, nm* minimum

minino, a [mi'nino, a] (*fam*) *nm/f* puss, pussy

ministerio [minis'terjo] *nm* Ministry; **M~ de Hacienda/de Asuntos Exteriores** Treasury (*BRIT*), Treasury Department (*US*)/Foreign Office (*BRIT*), State Department (*US*)

ministro, a [mi'nistro, a] *nm/f* minister

minoría [mino'ria] *nf* minority

minucioso, a [minu'θjoso, a] *adj* thorough, meticulous; *(prolijo)* very detailed

minúscula [mi'nuskula] *nf* small letter

minúsculo, a [mi'nuskulo, a] *adj* tiny, minute

minusválido, a [minus'βaliðo, a] *adj* (physically) handicapped ♦ *nm/f* (physically) handicapped person

minuta [mi'nuta] *nf (de comida)* menu

minutero [minu'tero] *nm* minute hand

minuto [mi'nuto] *nm* minute

mío, a ['mio, a] *pron*: **el ~/la mía** mine; **un amigo ~** a friend of mine; **lo ~** what is mine

miope [mi'ope] *adj* short-sighted

mira ['mira] *nf (de arma)* sight(s) *(pl)*; *(fig)* aim, intention

mirada [mi'raða] *nf* look, glance; *(expresión)* look, expression; **clavar la ~ en** to stare at; **echar una ~ a** to glance at

mirado, a [mi'raðo, a] *adj (sensato)* sensible; *(considerado)* considerate; **bien/mal ~** well/not well thought of; **bien ~** all things considered

mirador [mira'ðor] *nm* viewpoint, vantage point

mirar [mi'rar] *vt* to look at; *(observar)* to watch; *(considerar)* to consider, think over; *(vigilar, cuidar)* to watch, look after ♦ *vi* to look; *(ARQ)* to face; **~se** *vr (dos personas)* to look at each other; **~ bien/mal** to think highly of/have a poor opinion of; **~se al espejo** to look at o.s. in the mirror

mirilla [mi'riʎa] *nf* spyhole, peephole

mirlo ['mirlo] *nm* blackbird

misa ['misa] *nf* mass

miserable [mise'raβle] *adj (avaro)* mean, stingy; *(nimio)* miserable, paltry; *(lugar)* squalid; *(fam)* vile, despicable ♦ *nm/f (malvado)* rogue

miseria [mi'serja] *nf (pobreza)* poverty; *(tacañería)* meanness, stinginess; *(condiciones)* squalor; **una ~** a pittance

misericordia [miseri'korðja] *nf* *(compasión)* compassion, pity; *(piedad)* mercy

misil [mi'sil] *nm* missile

misión [mi'sjon] *nf* mission; **misionero, a** *nm/f* missionary

mismo, a ['mismo, a] *adj (semejante)* same; *(después de pron)* -self; *(para énfasis)* very ♦ *adv*: **aquí/hoy ~** right here/this very day; **ahora ~** right now ♦ *conj*: **lo ~ que** just like, just as; **el ~ traje** the same suit; **en ese ~ momento** at that very moment; **vino el ~ Ministro** the minister himself came; **yo ~ lo vi** I saw it myself; **lo ~** the same (thing); **da lo ~** it's all the same; **quedamos en las mismas** we're no further forward; **por lo ~** for the same reason

misterio [mis'terjo] *nm* mystery; **~so, a** *adj* mysterious

mitad [mi'tað] *nf (medio)* half; *(centro)* middle; **a ~ de precio** (at) half-price; **en** *o* **a ~ del camino** halfway along the road; **cortar por la ~** to cut through the middle

mitigar [miti'var] *vt* to mitigate; *(dolor)* to ease; *(sed)* to quench

mitin ['mitin] *(pl* **mítines***) nm* meeting

mito ['mito] *nm* myth

mixto, a ['miksto, a] *adj* mixed

ml. *abr* (= *mililitro*) ml

mm. *abr* (= *milímetro*) mm

mobiliario [moβi'ljarjo] *nm* furniture

mochila [mo'tʃila] *nf* rucksack *(BRIT)*, back-pack

moción [mo'θjon] *nf* motion

moco ['moko] *nm* mucus; **~s** *nmpl (fam)* snot; **limpiarse los ~s de la nariz** *(fam)* to wipe one's nose

moda ['moða] *nf* fashion; *(estilo)* style; **a la** *o* **de ~** in fashion, fashionable; **pasado de ~** out of fashion

modales [mo'ðales] *nmpl* manners

modalidad [moðali'ðað] *nf* kind, variety

modelar [moðe'lar] *vt* to model

modelo [mo'ðelo] *adj inv, nm/f* model

módem ['moðem] *nm (INFORM)* modem

moderado, a [moðe'raðo, a] *adj*

moderate
moderar [moðe'rar] *vt* to moderate; (*violencia*) to restrain, control; (*velocidad*) to reduce; **~se** *vr* to restrain o.s., control o.s.

modernizar [moðerni'θar] *vt* to modernize

moderno, a [mo'ðerno, a] *adj* modern; (*actual*) present-day

modestia [mo'ðestja] *nf* modesty; **modesto, a** *adj* modest

módico, a ['moðiko, a] *adj* moderate, reasonable

modificar [moðifi'kar] *vt* to modify

modisto, a [mo'ðisto, a] *nm/f* (*diseñador*) couturier, designer; (*que confecciona*) dressmaker

modo ['moðo] *nm* way, manner; (*MUS*) mode; **~s** *nmpl* manners; **de ningún ~** in no way; **de todos ~s** at any rate; **~ de empleo** directions *pl* (for use)

modorra [mo'ðorra] *nf* drowsiness

mofa ['mofa] *nf*: **hacer ~ de** to mock; **mofarse** *vr*: **mofarse de** to mock, scoff at

mogollón [moɣo'ʎon] (*fam*) *adv* a hell of a lot

moho ['moo] *nm* mould, mildew; (*en metal*) rust; **~so, a** *adj* mouldy; rusty

mojar [mo'xar] *vt* to wet; (*humedecer*) to damp(en), moisten; (*calar*) to soak; **~se** *vr* to get wet

mojón [mo'xon] *nm* boundary stone

molde ['molde] *nm* mould; (*COSTURA*) pattern; (*fig*) model; **~ado** *nm* soft perm; **~ar** *vt* to mould

mole ['mole] *nf* mass, bulk; (*edificio*) pile

moler [mo'ler] *vt* to grind, crush

molestar [moles'tar] *vt* to bother; (*fastidiar*) to annoy; (*incomodar*) to inconvenience, put out ♦ *vi* to be a nuisance; **~se** *vr* to bother; (*incomodarse*) to go to trouble; (*ofenderse*) to take offence; **¿(no) te molesta si ...?** do you mind if ...?

molestia [mo'lestja] *nf* bother, trouble; (*incomodidad*) inconvenience; (*MED*)

discomfort; **es una ~** it's a nuisance; **molesto, a** *adj* (*que fastidia*) annoying; (*incómodo*) inconvenient; (*inquieto*) uncomfortable, ill at ease; (*enfadado*) annoyed

molido, a [mo'liðo, a] *adj*: **estar ~** (*fig*) to be exhausted *o* dead beat

molinillo [moli'niʎo] *nm*: **~ de carne/café** mincer/coffee grinder

molino [mo'lino] *nm* (*edificio*) mill; (*máquina*) grinder

momentáneo, a [momen'taneo, a] *adj* momentary

momento [mo'mento] *nm* moment; **de ~** at the moment, for the moment

momia ['momja] *nf* mummy

monarca [mo'narka] *nm/f* monarch, ruler; **monarquía** *nf* monarchy; **monárquico, a** *nm/f* royalist, monarchist

monasterio [monas'terjo] *nm* monastery

mondar [mon'dar] *vt* to peel; **~se** *vr*: **~se de risa** (*fam*) to split one's sides laughing

moneda [mo'neða] *nf* (*tipo de dinero*) currency, money; (*pieza*) coin; **una ~ de 5 pesetas** a 5 peseta piece; **monedero** *nm* purse; **monetario, a** *adj* monetary, financial

monitor, a [moni'tor, a] *nm/f* instructor, coach ♦ *nm* (*TV*) set; (*INFORM*) monitor

monja ['monxa] *nf* nun

monje ['monxe] *nm* monk

mono, a ['mono, a] *adj* (*bonito*) lovely, pretty; (*gracioso*) nice, charming ♦ *nm/f* monkey, ape ♦ *nm* dungarees *pl*; (*overoles*) overalls *pl*

monopatín [monopa'tin] *nm* skateboard

monopolio [mono'poljo] *nm* monopoly; **monopolizar** *vt* to monopolize

monotonía [monoto'nia] *nf* (*sonido*) monotone; (*fig*) monotony

monótono, a [mo'notono, a] *adj* monotonous

monstruo ['monstrwo] *nm* monster ♦ *adj inv* fantastic; **~so, a** *adj* monstrous

montaje [mon'taxe] *nm* assembly; (*TEATRO*) décor; (*CINE*) montage

montaña [mon'taɲa] *nf* (*monte*) mountain; (*sierra*) mountains *pl*, mountainous area; (*AM: selva*) forest; **~ rusa** roller coaster; **montañés, esa** *nm/f* mountaineer; **montañero, a** *nm/f* highlander; **montañismo** *nm* mountaineering

montar [mon'tar] *vt* (*subir a*) to mount, get on; (*TEC*) to assemble, put together; (*negocio*) to set up; (*arma*) to cock; (*colocar*) to lift on to; (*CULIN*) to beat ♦ *vi* to mount, get on; (*sobresalir*) to overlap; **~ en cólera** to get angry; **~ a caballo** to ride, go horseriding

monte ['monte] *nm* (*montaña*) mountain; (*bosque*) woodland; (*área sin cultivar*) wild area, wild country; **M~ de Piedad** pawnshop

montón [mon'ton] *nm* heap, pile; (*fig*): **un ~ de** heaps of, lots of

monumento [monu'mento] *nm* monument

monzón [mon'θon] *nm* monsoon

moño ['moɲo] *nm* bun

moqueta [mo'keta] *nf* fitted carpet

mora ['mora] *nf* blackberry; *ver tb* **moro**

morada [mo'raða] *nf* (*casa*) dwelling, abode

morado, a [mo'raðo, a] *adj* purple, violet ♦ *nm* bruise

moral [mo'ral] *adj* moral ♦ *nf* (*ética*) ethics *pl*; (*moralidad*) morals *pl*, morality; (*ánimo*) morale

moraleja [mora'lexa] *nf* moral

moralidad [morali'ðað] *nf* morals *pl*, morality

morboso, a [mor'ßoso, a] *adj* morbid

morcilla [mor'θiʎa] *nf* blood sausage, ≈ black pudding (*BRIT*)

mordaz [mor'ðaθ] *adj* (*crítica*) biting, scathing

mordaza [mor'ðaθa] *nf* (*para la boca*) gag; (*TEC*) clamp

morder [mor'ðer] *vt* to bite; (*fig: consumir*) to eat away, eat into; **mordisco** *nm* bite

moreno, a [mo'reno, a] *adj* (*color*) (dark) brown; (*de tez*) dark; (*de pelo ~*) dark-haired; (*negro*) black

morfina [mor'fina] *nf* morphine

moribundo, a [mori'ßundo, a] *adj* dying

morir [mo'rir] *vi* to die; (*fuego*) to die down; (*luz*) to go out; **~se** *vr* to die; (*fig*) to be dying; **murió en un accidente** he was killed in an accident; **~se por algo** to be dying for sth

moro, a ['moro, a] *adj* Moorish ♦ *nm/f* Moor

moroso, a [mo'roso, a] *nm/f* bad debtor, defaulter

morral [mo'rral] *nm* haversack

morro ['morro] *nm* (*ZOOL*) snout, nose; (*AUTO, AVIAT*) nose

morsa ['morsa] *nf* walrus

mortadela [morta'ðela] *nf* mortadella

mortaja [mor'taxa] *nf* shroud

mortal [mor'tal] *adj* mortal; (*golpe*) deadly; **~idad** *nf* mortality

mortero [mor'tero] *nm* mortar

mortífero, a [mor'tifero, a] *adj* deadly, lethal

mortificar [mortifi'kar] *vt* to mortify

mosca ['moska] *nf* fly

Moscú [mos'ku] *n* Moscow

mosquearse [moske'arse] (*fam*) *vr* (*enojarse*) to get cross; (*ofenderse*) to take offence

mosquitero [moski'tero] *nm* mosquito net

mosquito [mos'kito] *nm* mosquito

mostaza [mos'taθa] *nf* mustard

mosto ['mosto] *nm* (unfermented) grape juice

mostrador [mostra'ðor] *nm* (*de tienda*) counter; (*de café*) bar

mostrar [mos'trar] *vt* to show; (*exhibir*) to display, exhibit; (*explicar*) to explain; **~se** *vr*: **~se amable** to be kind; to prove to be kind; **no se muestra muy inteligente** he doesn't seem (to be) very intelligent

mota ['mota] *nf* speck, tiny piece; (*en diseño*) dot

mote ['mote] *nm* nickname

motín [mo'tin] *nm* (*del pueblo*) revolt, rising; (*del ejército*) mutiny

motivar [moti'ßar] *vt* (*causar*) to cause, motivate; (*explicar*) to explain, justify; **motivo** *nm* motive, reason

moto ['moto] (*fam*) *nf* = **motocicleta**

motocicleta [motoθi'kleta] *nf* motorbike (*BRIT*), motorcycle

motor [mo'tor] *nm* motor, engine; **~ a chorro** *o* **de reacción/de explosión** jet engine/internal combustion engine

motora [mo'tora] *nf* motorboat

movedizo, a [moße'ðiθo, a] *adj ver* **arena**

mover [mo'ßer] *vt* to move; (*cabeza*) to shake; (*accionar*) to drive; (*fig*) to cause, provoke; **~se** *vr* to move; (*fig*) to get a move on

móvil ['moßil] *adj* mobile; (*pieza de máquina*) moving; (*mueble*) movable ♦ *nm* motive; **movilidad** *nf* mobility; **movilizar** *vt* to mobilize

movimiento [moßi'mjento] *nm* movement; (*TEC*) motion; (*actividad*) activity

mozo, a ['moθo, a] *adj* (*joven*) young ♦ *nm/f* youth, young man/girl

muchacho, a [mu'tʃatʃo, a] *nm/f* (*niño*) boy/girl; (*criado*) servant; (*criada*) maid

muchedumbre [mutʃe'ðumbre] *nf* crowd

PALABRA CLAVE

mucho, a ['mutʃo, a] *adj* **1** (*cantidad*) a lot of, much; (*número*) lots of, a lot of, many; **~ dinero** a lot of money; **hace ~ calor** it's very hot; **muchas amigas** lots *o* a lot of friends

2 (*sg: grande*): **ésta es mucha casa para él** this house is much too big for him
♦ *pron*: **tengo ~ que hacer** I've got a lot to do; **~s dicen que ...** a lot of people say that ...; *ver tb* **tener**
♦ *adv* **1**: **me gusta ~** I like it a lot; **lo siento ~** I'm very sorry; **come ~** he eats a lot; **¿te vas a quedar ~?** are you going to be staying long?

2 (*respuesta*) very; **¿estás cansado? – ¡~!** are you tired? – very!

3 (*locuciones*): **como ~** at (the) most; **con ~: el mejor con ~** by far the best; **ni ~**

menos: no es rico ni ~ menos he's far from being rich

4: **por ~ que: por ~ que le creas** no matter how *o* however much you believe her

---

muda ['muða] *nf* change of clothes

mudanza [mu'ðanθa] *nf* (*de casa*) move

mudar [mu'ðar] *vt* to change; (*ZOOL*) to shed ♦ *vi* to change; **~se** *vr* (*la ropa*) to change; **~se de casa** to move house

mudo, a ['muðo, a] *adj* dumb; (*callado, CINE*) silent

mueble ['mweßle] *nm* piece of furniture; **~s** *nmpl* furniture *sg*

mueca ['mweka] *nf* face, grimace; **hacer ~s a** to make faces at

muela ['mwela] *nf* (*back*) tooth

muelle ['mweʎe] *nm* spring; (*NAUT*) wharf; (*malecón*) pier

muero *etc vb ver* **morir**

muerte ['mwerte] *nf* death; (*homicidio*) murder; **dar ~ a** to kill

muerto, a ['mwerto, a] *pp de* **morir** ♦ *adj* dead ♦ *nm/f* dead man/woman; (*difunto*) deceased; (*cadáver*) corpse; **estar ~ de cansancio** to be dead tired

muestra ['mwestra] *nf* (*señal*) indication, sign; (*demostración*) demonstration; (*prueba*) proof; (*estadística*) sample; (*modelo*) model, pattern; (*testimonio*) token

muestreo [mwes'treo] *nm* sample, sampling

muestro *etc vb ver* **mostrar**

muevo *etc vb ver* **mover**

mugir [mu'xir] *vi* (*vaca*) to moo

mugre ['muxre] *nf* dirt, filth; **mugriento, a** *adj* dirty, filthy

mujer [mu'xer] *nf* woman; (*esposa*) wife; **~iego** *nm* womanizer

mula ['mula] *nf* mule

muleta [mu'leta] *nf* (*para andar*) crutch; (*TAUR*) stick with red cape attached

mullido, a [mu'ʎiðo, a] *adj* (*cama*) soft; (*hierba*) soft, springy

multa ['multa] *nf* fine; **poner una ~ a** to

fine; **multar** *vt* to fine
multicines [multi'θines] *nmpl* multiscreen cinema
multinacional [multinaθjo'nal] *nf* multinational
múltiple ['multiple] *adj* multiple; (*pl*) many, numerous
multiplicar [multipli'kar] *vt* (*MAT*) to multiply; (*fig*) to increase; **~se** *vr* (*BIO*) to multiply; (*fig*) to be everywhere at once
multitud [multi'tuð] *nf* (*muchedumbre*) crowd; **~ de** lots of
mundano, a [mun'dano, a] *adj* worldly
mundial [mun'djal] *adj* world-wide, universal; (*guerra, récord*) world *cpd*
mundo ['mundo] *nm* world; **todo el ~** everybody; **tener ~** to be experienced, know one's way around
munición [muni'θjon] *nf* ammunition
municipal [muniθi'pal] *adj* municipal, local
municipio [muni'θipjo] *nm* (*ayuntamiento*) town council, corporation; (*territorio administrativo*) town, municipality
muñeca [mu'neka] *nf* (*ANAT*) wrist; (*juguete*) doll
muñeco [mu'neko] *nm* (*figura*) figure; (*marioneta*) puppet; (*fig*) puppet, pawn
mural [mu'ral] *adj* mural, wall *cpd* ♦ *nm* mural
muralla [mu'raʎa] *nf* (city) wall(s) (*pl*)
murciélago [mur'θjelaɣo] *nm* bat
murmullo [mur'muʎo] *nm* murmur(ing); (*cuchicheo*) whispering
murmuración [murmura'θjon] *nf* gossip; **murmurar** *vi* to murmur, whisper; (*cotillear*) to gossip
muro ['muro] *nm* wall
muscular [musku'lar] *adj* muscular
músculo ['muskulo] *nm* muscle
museo [mu'seo] *nm* museum; **~ de arte** art gallery
musgo ['musɣo] *nm* moss
música ['musika] *nf* music; *ver tb* **músico**
músico, a ['musiko, a] *adj* musical ♦ *nm/f* musician
muslo ['muslo] *nm* thigh

mustio, a ['mustjo, a] *adj* (*persona*) depressed, gloomy; (*planta*) faded, withered
musulmán, ana [musul'man, ana] *nm/f* Moslem
mutación [muta'θjon] *nf* (*BIO*) mutation; (*cambio*) (sudden) change
mutilar [muti'lar] *vt* to mutilate; (*a una persona*) to maim
mutismo [mu'tismo] *nm* (*de persona*) uncommunicativeness; (*de autoridades*) silence
mutuamente [mutwa'mente] *adv* mutually
mutuo, a ['mutwo, a] *adj* mutual
muy [mwi] *adv* very; (*demasiado*) too; **M~ Señor mío** Dear Sir; **~ de noche** very late at night; **eso es ~ de él** that's just like him

N, n

N *abr* (= *norte*) N
nabo ['naßo] *nm* turnip
nácar ['nakar] *nm* mother-of-pearl
nacer [na'θer] *vi* to be born; (*de huevo*) to hatch; (*vegetal*) to sprout; (*río*) to rise; **nací en Barcelona** I was born in Barcelona; **nació una sospecha en su mente** a suspicion formed in her mind; **nacido, a** *adj* born; **recién nacido** newborn; **naciente** *adj* new, emerging; (*sol*) rising; **nacimiento** *nm* birth; (*de Navidad*) Nativity; (*de río*) source
nación [na'θjon] *nf* nation; **nacional** *adj* national; **nacionalismo** *nm* nationalism; **nacionalista** *nm/f* nationalist; **nacionalizar** *vt* to nationalize; **nacionalizarse** *vr* (*persona*) to become naturalized
nada ['naða] *pron* nothing ♦ *adv* not at all, in no way; **no decir ~** to say nothing, not to say anything; **~ más** nothing else; **de ~** don't mention it
nadador, a [naða'ðor, a] *nm/f* swimmer
nadar [na'ðar] *vi* to swim

nadie ['naðje] *pron* nobody, no-one; ~ **habló** nobody spoke; **no había ~** there was nobody there, there wasn't anybody there

nado ['naðo]: **a ~** *adv*: **pasar a ~** to swim across

nafta ['nafta] (*AM*) *nf* petrol (*BRIT*), gas (*US*)

naipe ['naipe] *nm* (playing) card; **~s** *nmpl* cards

nalgas ['nalɣas] *nfpl* buttocks

nana ['nana] *nf* lullaby

naranja [na'ranxa] *adj inv, nf* orange; **media ~** (*fam*) better half; **naranjada** *nf* orangeade; **naranjo** *nm* orange tree

narciso [nar'θiso] *nm* narcissus

narcótico, a [nar'kotiko, a] *adj, nm* narcotic; **narcotizar** *vt* to drug; **narcotráfico** *nm* drug trafficking *o* running

nardo ['narðo] *nm* lily

narigudo, a [nari'ɣuðo, a] *adj* big-nosed

nariz [na'riθ] *nf* nose

narración [narra'θjon] *nf* narration; **narrador, a** *nm/f* narrator

narrar [na'rrar] *vt* to narrate, recount; **narrativa** *nf* narrative

nata ['nata] *nf* cream

natación [nata'θjon] *nf* swimming

natal [na'tal] *adj*: **ciudad ~** home town; **~idad** *nf* birth rate

natillas [na'tiʎas] *nfpl* custard *sg*

nativo, a [na'tiβo, a] *adj, nm/f* native

nato, a ['nato, a] *adj* born; **un músico ~** a born musician

natural [natu'ral] *adj* natural; (*fruta etc*) fresh ♦ *nm/f* native ♦ *nm* (*disposición*) nature

naturaleza [natura'leθa] *nf* nature; (*género*) nature, kind; **~ muerta** still life

naturalidad [naturali'ðað] *nf* naturalness

naturalmente [natural'mente] *adv* (*de modo natural*) in a natural way; **¡~!** of course!

naufragar [naufra'ɣar] *vi* to sink; **naufragio** *nm* shipwreck; **náufrago, a** *nm/f* castaway, shipwrecked person

nauseabundo, a [nausea'ßundo, a] *adj* nauseating, sickening

náuseas ['nauseas] *nfpl* nausea *sg*; **me da ~** it makes me feel sick

náutico, a ['nautiko, a] *adj* nautical

navaja [na'ßaxa] *nf* knife; (*de barbero, peluquero*) razor

naval [na'ßal] *adj* naval

Navarra [na'ßarra] *n* Navarre

nave ['naße] *nf* (*barco*) ship, vessel; (*ARQ*) nave; **~ espacial** spaceship

navegación [naßeɣa'θjon] *nf* navigation; (*viaje*) sea journey; **~ aérea** air traffic; **~ costera** coastal shipping; **navegador** *nm* (*INFORM*) browser; **navegante** *nm/f* navigator; **navegar** *vi* (*barco*) to sail; (*avión*) to fly

Navidad [naßi'ðað] *nf* Christmas; **~es** *nfpl* Christmas time; **Feliz N~** Merry Christmas; **navideño, a** *adj* Christmas *cpd*

navío [na'ßio] *nm* ship

nazca *etc vb ver* **nacer**

nazi ['naθi] *adj, nm/f* Nazi

NE *abr* (= *nor(d)este*) NE

neblina [ne'ßlina] *nf* mist

nebulosa [neßu'losa] *nf* nebula

necesario, a [neθe'sarjo, a] *adj* necessary

neceser [neθe'ser] *nm* toilet bag; (*bolsa grande*) holdall

necesidad [neθesi'ðað] *nf* need; (*lo inevitable*) necessity; (*miseria*) poverty, need; **en caso de ~** in case of need *o* emergency; **hacer sus ~es** to relieve o.s.

necesitado, a [neθesi'taðo, a] *adj* needy, poor; **~ de** in need of

necesitar [neθesi'tar] *vt* to need, require

necio, a ['neθjo, a] *adj* foolish

necrópolis [ne'kropolis] *nf inv* cemetery

nectarina [nekta'rina] *nf* nectarine

nefasto, a [ne'fasto, a] *adj* ill-fated, unlucky

negación [neɣa'θjon] *nf* negation; (*rechazo*) refusal, denial

negar [ne'ɣar] *vt* (*renegar, rechazar*) to refuse; (*prohibir*) to refuse, deny; (*desmentir*) to deny; **~se** *vr*: **~se a** to refuse to

negativa [neɣa'tißa] *nf* negative; (*rechazo*)

refusal, denial

negativo, a [neɣa'tiβo, a] *adj, nm* negative

negligencia [neɣli'xenθja] *nf* negligence; **negligente** *adj* negligent

negociado [neɣo'θjaðo] *nm* department, section

negociante [neɣo'θjante] *nm/f* businessman/woman

negociar [neɣo'θjar] *vt, vi* to negotiate; ~ **en** to deal in, trade in

negocio [ne'ɣoθjo] *nm* (COM) business; (*asunto*) affair, business; (*operación comercial*) deal, transaction; (*AM*) firm; (*lugar*) place of business; **los ~s** business *sg*; **hacer ~** to do business

negra ['neɣra] *nf* (MUS) crotchet; *ver tb* **negro**

negro, a ['neɣro, a] *adj* black; (*suerte*) awful ♦ *nm* black ♦ *nm/f* black man/woman

nene, a ['nene, a] *nm/f* baby, small child

nenúfar [ne'nufar] *nm* water lily

neologismo [neolo'xismo] *nm* neologism

neón [ne'on] *nm*: **luces/lámpara de ~** neon lights/lamp

neoyorquino, a [neojor'kino, a] *adj* (of) New York

nervio ['nerβjo] *nm* nerve; **nerviosismo** *nm* nervousness, nerves *pl*; ~**so, a** *adj* nervous

neto, a ['neto, a] *adj* net

neumático, a [neu'matiko, a] *adj* pneumatic ♦ *nm* (ESP) tyre (BRIT), tire (US); ~ **de recambio** spare tyre

neurasténico, a [neuras'teniko, a] *adj* (fig) hysterical

neurólogo, a [neu'roloɣo, a] *nm/f* neurologist

neurona [neu'rona] *nf* nerve cell

neutral [neu'tral] *adj* neutral; ~**izar** *vt* to neutralize; (*contrarrestar*) to counteract

neutro, a ['neutro, a] *adj* (BIO, LING) neuter

neutrón [neu'tron] *nm* neutron

nevada [ne'βaða] *nf* snowstorm; (*caída de nieve*) snowfall

nevar [ne'βar] *vi* to snow

nevera [ne'βera] (ESP) *nf* refrigerator (BRIT), icebox (US)

nevería [neβe'ria] (AM) *nf* ice-cream parlour

nexo ['nekso] *nm* link, connection

ni [ni] *conj* nor, neither; (*tb*: ~ **siquiera**) not ... even; ~ **aunque que** not even if; ~ **blanco ~ negro** neither white nor black

Nicaragua [nika'raɣwa] *nf* Nicaragua; **nicaragüense** *adj, nm/f* Nicaraguan

nicho ['nitʃo] *nm* niche

nicotina [niko'tina] *nf* nicotine

nido ['niðo] *nm* nest

niebla ['njeβla] *nf* fog; (*neblina*) mist

niego *etc vb ver* **negar**

nieto, a ['njeto, a] *nm/f* grandson/daughter; ~**s** *nmpl* grandchildren

nieve *etc* ['njeβe] *vb ver* **nevar** ♦ *nf* snow; (AM) icecream

N.I.F. *nm abr* (= *Número de Identificación Fiscal*) *personal identification number used for financial and tax purposes*

nimiedad [nimje'ðað] *nf* triviality

nimio, a ['nimjo, a] *adj* trivial, insignificant

ninfa ['ninfa] *nf* nymph

ningún [nin'ɡun] *adj ver* **ninguno**

ninguno, a [nin'ɡuno, a] (*delante de nm*: **ningún**) *adj* no ♦ *pron* (*nadie*) nobody; (*ni uno*) none, not one; (*ni uno ni otro*) neither; **de ninguna manera** by no means, not at all

niña ['nina] *nf* (ANAT) pupil; *ver tb* **niño**

niñera [ni'nera] *nf* nursemaid, nanny; **niñería** *nf* childish act

niñez [ni'neθ] *nf* childhood; (*infancia*) infancy

niño, a ['nino, a] *adj* (*joven*) young; (*inmaduro*) immature ♦ *nm/f* child, boy/girl

nipón, ona [ni'pon, ona] *adj, nm/f* Japanese

níquel ['nikel] *nm* nickel; **niquelar** *vt* (TEC) to nickel-plate

níspero ['nispero] *nm* medlar

nitidez [niti'ðeθ] *nf* (*claridad*) clarity; (: *de imagen*) sharpness; **nítido, a** *adj* clear;

sharp
nitrato [ni'trato] *nm* nitrate
nitrógeno [ni'troxeno] *nm* nitrogen
nivel [ni'ßel] *nm* (GEO) level; (norma) level,
standard; (altura) height; **~ de aceite** oil
level; **~ de aire** spirit level; **~ de vida**
standard of living; **~ar** *vt* to level out;
(fig) to even up; (COM) to balance
NN. UU. *nfpl abr* (= Naciones Unidas)
UN *sg*
no [no] *adv* no; not; (con verbo) not ♦ *excl*
no!; **~ tengo nada** I don't have anything,
I have nothing; **~ es el mío** it's not mine;
ahora ~ not now; **¿~ lo sabes?** don't
you know?; **~ mucho** not much; **~ bien
termine, lo entregaré** as soon as I finish
I'll hand it over; **~ más: ayer ~ más** just
yesterday; **¡pase ~ más!** come in!; **¡a que
~ lo sabes!** I bet you don't know!;
¡cómo ~! of course!; **los países ~
alineados** the non-aligned countries; **la ~
intervención** non-intervention
noble ['noßle] *adj, nm/f* noble; **~za**
nobility
noche ['notʃe] *nf* night, night-time; (la
tarde) evening; **de ~, por la ~** at night;
es de ~ it's dark

> **Noche de San Juan**

ⓘ The **Noche de San Juan** on the 24th
June is a **fiesta** coinciding with the
summer solstice and which has taken the
place of other ancient pagan festivals.
Traditionally fire plays a major part in
these festivities with celebrations and
dancing taking place around bonfires in
towns and villages across the country.

nochebuena [notʃe'ßwena] *nf* Christmas
Eve

> **Nochebuena**

ⓘ Traditional Christmas celebrations in
Spanish-speaking countries mainly take
place on the night of **Nochebuena**,
Christmas Eve. Families gather together for
a large meal and the more religiously

inclined attend Midnight Mass. While
presents are traditionally given by **los
Reyes Magos** on the 6th January, more
and more people are exchanging gifts on
Christmas Eve.

nochevieja [notʃe'ßjexa] *nf* New Year's
Eve
noción [no'θjon] *nf* notion
nocivo, a [no'θißo, a] *adj* harmful
noctámbulo, a [nok'tambulo, a] *nm/f*
sleepwalker
nocturno, a [nok'turno, a] *adj* (de la
noche) nocturnal, night *cpd*; (de la tarde)
evening *cpd* ♦ *nm* nocturne
nodriza [no'ðriθa] *nf* wet nurse; **buque** o
nave ~ supply ship
nogal [no'ɣal] *nm* walnut tree
nómada ['nomaða] *adj* nomadic ♦ *nm/f*
nomad
nombramiento [nombra'mjento] *nm*
naming; (a un empleo) appointment
nombrar [nom'brar] *vt* (designar) to name;
(mencionar) to mention; (dar puesto a) to
appoint
nombre ['nombre] *nm* name; (sustantivo)
noun; **~ y apellidos** name in full; **~
común/propio** common/proper noun; **~
de pila/de soltera** Christian/maiden
name; **poner ~ a** to call, name
nómina ['nomina] *nf* (lista) payroll; (hoja)
payslip
nominal [nomi'nal] *adj* nominal
nominar [nomi'nar] *vt* to nominate
nominativo, a [nomina'tißo, a] *adj*
(COM): **cheque ~ a X** cheque made out
to X
nono, a ['nono, a] *adj* ninth
nordeste [nor'ðeste] *adj* north-east,
north-eastern, north-easterly ♦ *nm* north-
east
nórdico, a ['norðiko, a] *adj* Nordic
noreste [no'reste] *adj, nm* = **nordeste**
noria ['norja] *nf* (AGR) waterwheel; (de
carnaval) (BRIT) o Ferris (US) wheel
norma ['norma] *nf* rule (of thumb)
normal [nor'mal] *adj* (corriente) normal;

(*habitual*) usual, natural; ~**idad** *nf* normality; **restablecer la ~idad** to restore order; ~**izar** *vt* (*reglamentar*) to normalize; (*TEC*) to standardize; ~**izarse** *vr* to return to normal; ~**mente** *adv* normally

normando, a [nor'mando, a] *adj, nm/f* Norman

normativa [norma'tiβa] *nf* (set of) rules *pl*, regulations *pl*

noroeste [noro'este] *adj* north-west, north-western, north-westerly ♦ *nm* north-west

norte ['norte] *adj* north, northern, northerly ♦ *nm* north; (*fig*) guide

norteamericano, a [norteameri'kano, a] *adj, nm/f* (North) American

Noruega [no'rweɣa] *nf* Norway

noruego, a [no'rweɣo, a] *adj, nm/f* Norwegian

nos [nos] *pron* (*directo*) us; (*indirecto*) us; to us; for us; from us; (*reflexivo*) (to) ourselves; (*recíproco*) (to) each other; ~ **levantamos a las 7** we get up at 7

nosotros, as [no'sotros, as] *pron* (*sujeto*) we; (*después de prep*) us

nostalgia [nos'talxja] *nf* nostalgia

nota ['nota] *nf* note; (*ESCOL*) mark

notable [no'taβle] *adj* notable; (*ESCOL*) outstanding

notar [no'tar] *vt* to notice, note; ~**se** *vr* to be obvious; **se nota que ...** one observes that ...

notarial [nota'rjal] *adj*: **acta** ~ affidavit

notario [no'tarjo] *nm* notary

noticia [no'tiθja] *nf* (*información*) piece of news; **las ~s** the news *sg*; **tener ~s de alguien** to hear from sb

noticiero [noti'θjero] (*AM*) *nm* news bulletin

notificación [notifika'θjon] *nf* notification; **notificar** *vt* to notify, inform

notoriedad [notorje'ðað] *nf* fame, renown; **notorio, a** *adj* (*público*) well-known; (*evidente*) obvious

novato, a [no'βato, a] *adj* inexperienced ♦ *nm/f* beginner, novice

novecientos, as [noβe'θjentos, as] *num* nine hundred

novedad [noβe'ðað] *nf* (*calidad de nuevo*) newness; (*noticia*) piece of news; (*cambio*) change, (new) development

novel [no'βel] *adj* new; (*inexperto*) inexperienced ♦ *nm/f* beginner

novela [no'βela] *nf* novel

noveno, a [no'βeno, a] *adj* ninth

noventa [no'βenta] *num* ninety

novia ['noβja] *nf* ver **novio**

noviazgo [no'βjaθɣo] *nm* engagement

novicio, a [no'βiθjo, a] *nm/f* novice

noviembre [no'βjembre] *nm* November

novillada [noβi'ʎaða] *nf* (*TAUR*) bullfight with young bulls; **novillero** *nm* novice bullfighter; **novillo** *nm* young bull, bullock; **hacer novillos** (*fam*) to play truant

novio, a ['noβjo, a] *nm/f* boyfriend/ girlfriend; (*prometido*) fiancé/fiancée; (*recién casado*) bridegroom/bride; **los ~s** the newly-weds

nubarrón [nuβa'rron] *nm* storm cloud

nube ['nuβe] *nf* cloud

nublado, a [nu'βlaðo, a] *adj* cloudy; **nublarse** *vr* to grow dark

nubosidad [nuβosi'ðað] *nf* cloudiness; **había mucha** ~ it was very cloudy

nuca ['nuka] *nf* nape of the neck

nuclear [nukle'ar] *adj* nuclear

núcleo ['nukleo] *nm* (*centro*) core; (*FÍSICA*) nucleus

nudillo [nu'ðiʎo] *nm* knuckle

nudista [nu'ðista] *adj* nudist

nudo ['nuðo] *nm* knot; ~**so, a** *adj* knotty

nuera ['nwera] *nf* daughter-in-law

nuestro, a ['nwestro, a] *adj* our ♦ *pron* ours; ~ **padre** our father; **un amigo** ~ a friend of ours; **es el** ~ it's ours

nueva ['nweβa] *nf* piece of news

nuevamente [nweβa'mente] *adv* (*otra vez*) again; (*de nuevo*) anew

Nueva York [-jɔrk] *n* New York

Nueva Zelanda [-θe'landa] *nf* New Zealand

nueve ['nweβe] *num* nine

nuevo, a ['nweßo, a] *adj* (*gen*) new; **de ~** again

nuez [nweθ] *nf* walnut; **~ de Adán** Adam's apple; **~ moscada** nutmeg

nulidad [nuli'ðað] *nf* (*incapacidad*) incompetence; (*abolición*) nullity

nulo, a ['nulo, a] *adj* (*inepto, torpe*) useless; (*inválido*) (null and) void; (*DEPORTE*) drawn, tied

núm. *abr* (= *número*) no

numeración [numera'θjon] *nf* (*cifras*) numbers *pl*; (*arábiga, romana etc*) numerals *pl*

numeral [nume'ral] *nm* numeral

numerar [nume'rar] *vt* to number

número ['numero] *nm* (*gen*) number; (*tamaño: de zapato*) size; (*ejemplar: de diario*) number, issue; **sin ~** numberless, unnumbered; **~ de matrícula/de teléfono** registration/telephone number; **~ atrasado** back number

numeroso, a [nume'roso, a] *adj* numerous

nunca ['nunka] *adv* (*jamás*) never; **~ lo pensé** I never thought it; **no viene ~** he never comes; **~ más** never again; **más que ~** more than ever

nupcias ['nupθjas] *nfpl* wedding *sg*, nuptials

nutria ['nutrja] *nf* otter

nutrición [nutri'θjon] *nf* nutrition

nutrido, a [nu'triðo, a] *adj* (*alimentado*) nourished; (*fig: grande*) large; (*abundante*) abundant

nutrir [nu'trir] *vt* (*alimentar*) to nourish; (*dar de comer*) to feed; (*fig*) to strengthen; **nutritivo, a** *adj* nourishing, nutritious

nylon [ni'lon] *nm* nylon

Ñ, ñ

ñato, a ['ɲato, a] (*AM*) *adj* snub-nosed

ñoñería [ɲoɲe'ria] *nf* insipidness

ñoño, a ['ɲoɲo, a] *adj* (*AM: tonto*) silly, stupid; (*soso*) insipid; (*persona*) spineless

O, o

O *abr* (= *oeste*) W

o [o] *conj* or

o/ *abr* (= *orden*) o.

oasis [o'asis] *nm inv* oasis

obcecarse [oßθe'karse] *vr* to get *o* become stubborn

obedecer [oßeðe'θer] *vt* to obey; **obediencia** *nf* obedience; **obediente** *adj* obedient

obertura [oßer'tura] *nf* overture

obesidad [oßesi'ðað] *nf* obesity; **obeso, a** *adj* obese

obispo [o'ßispo] *nm* bishop

objeción [oßxe'θjon] *nf* objection; **poner objeciones** to raise objections

objetar [oßxe'tar] *vt, vi* to object

objetivo, a [oßxe'tißo, a] *adj, nm* objective

objeto [oß'xeto] *nm* (*cosa*) object; (*fin*) aim

objetor, a [oßxe'tor, a] *nm/f* objector

oblicuo, a [o'ßlikwo, a] *adj* oblique; (*mirada*) sidelong

obligación [oßliva'θjon] *nf* obligation; (*COM*) bond

obligar [oßli'var] *vt* to force; **~se** *vr* to bind o.s.; **obligatorio, a** *adj* compulsory, obligatory

oboe [o'ßoe] *nm* oboe

obra ['oßra] *nf* work; (*ARQ*) construction, building; (*TEATRO*) play; **~ maestra** masterpiece; **~s públicas** public works; **por ~ de** thanks to (the efforts of); **obrar** *vt* to work; (*tener efecto*) to have an effect on ♦ *vi* to act, behave; (*tener efecto*) to have an effect; **la carta obra en su poder** the letter is in his/her possession

obrero, a [o'ßrero, a] *adj* (*clase*) working; (*movimiento*) labour *cpd* ♦ *nm/f* (*gen*) worker; (*sin oficio*) labourer

obscenidad [oßsθeni'ðað] *nf* obscenity; **obsceno, a** *adj* obscene

obscu... = **oscu...**

obsequiar [oßse'kjar] vt (*ofrecer*) to present with; (*agasajar*) to make a fuss of, lavish attention on; **obsequio** nm (*regalo*) gift; (*cortesía*) courtesy, attention

observación [oßserßa'θjon] nf observation; (*reflexión*) remark

observador, a [oßserßa'ðor, a] nm/f observer

observar [oßser'ßar] vt to observe; (*anotar*) to notice; **~se** vr to keep to, observe

obsesión [oßse'sjon] nf obsession; **obsesivo, a** adj obsessive

obsoleto, a [oßso'leto, a] adj obsolete

obstáculo [oßs'takulo] nm obstacle; (*impedimento*) hindrance, drawback

obstante [oßs'tante]: **no ~** adv nevertheless

obstinado, a [oßsti'naðo, a] adj obstinate, stubborn

obstinarse [oßsti'narse] vr to be obstinate; **~ en** to persist in

obstrucción [oßstruk'θjon] nf obstruction; **obstruir** vt to obstruct

obtener [oßte'ner] vt (*gen*) to obtain; (*premio*) to win

obturador [oßtura'ðor] nm (*FOTO*) shutter

obvio, a ['oßßjo, a] adj obvious

oca ['oka] nf (*animal*) goose; (*juego*) ≈ snakes and ladders

ocasión [oka'sjon] nf (*oportunidad*) opportunity, chance; (*momento*) occasion, time; (*causa*) cause; **de ~** secondhand; **ocasionar** vt to cause

ocaso [o'kaso] nm (*fig*) decline

occidente [okθi'ðente] nm west

OCDE nf abr (= *Organización de Cooperación y Desarrollo Económico*) OECD

océano [o'θeano] nm ocean; **el ~ Índico** the Indian Ocean

ochenta [o'tʃenta] num eighty

ocho ['otʃo] num eight; **~ días** a week

ocio ['oθjo] nm (*tiempo*) leisure; (*pey*) idleness; **~so, a** adj (*inactivo*) idle; (*inútil*) useless

octavilla [okta'viʎa] nf leaflet, pamphlet

octavo, a [ok'taßo, a] adj eighth

octubre [ok'tußre] nm October

ocular [oku'lar] adj ocular, eye cpd; **testigo ~** eyewitness

oculista [oku'lista] nm/f oculist

ocultar [okul'tar] vt (*esconder*) to hide; (*callar*) to conceal; **oculto, a** adj hidden; (*fig*) secret

ocupación [okupa'θjon] nf occupation

ocupado, a [oku'paðo, a] adj (*persona*) busy; (*plaza*) occupied, taken; (*teléfono*) engaged; **ocupar** vt (*gen*) to occupy; **ocuparse** vr: **ocuparse de** o **en** (*gen*) to concern o.s. with; (*cuidar*) to look after

ocurrencia [oku'rrenθja] nf (*idea*) bright idea

ocurrir [oku'rrir] vi to happen; **~se** vr: **se me ocurrió que ...** it occurred to me that ...

odiar [o'ðjar] vt to hate; **odio** nm hate, hatred; **odioso, a** adj (*gen*) hateful; (*malo*) nasty

odontólogo, a [oðon'tologo, a] nm/f dentist, dental surgeon

OEA nf abr (= *Organización de Estados Americanos*) OAS

oeste [o'este] nm west; **una película del ~** a western

ofender [ofen'der] vt (*agraviar*) to offend; (*insultar*) to insult; **~se** vr to take offence; **ofensa** nf offence; **ofensiva** nf offensive; **ofensivo, a** adj offensive

oferta [o'ferta] nf offer; (*propuesta*) proposal; **la ~ y la demanda** supply and demand; **artículos en ~** goods on offer

oficial [ofi'θjal] adj official ♦ nm (*MIL*) officer

oficina [ofi'θina] nf office; **~ de correos** post office; **~ de turismo** tourist office; **oficinista** nm/f clerk

oficio [o'fiθjo] nm (*profesión*) profession; (*puesto*) post; (*REL*) service; **ser del ~** to be an old hand; **tener mucho ~** to have a lot of experience; **~ de difuntos** funeral service

oficioso, a [ofi'θjoso, a] adj (*pey*) officious; (*no oficial*) unofficial, informal

ofimática [ofi'matika] nf office

automation

ofrecer [ofre'θer] *vt* (*dar*) to offer; (*proponer*) to propose; **~se** *vr* (*persona*) to offer o.s., volunteer; (*situación*) to present itself; **¿qué se le ofrece?, ¿se le ofrece algo?** what can I do for you?, can I get you anything?

ofrecimiento [ofreθi'mjento] *nm* offer

oftalmólogo, a [oftal'molovo, a] *nm/f* ophthalmologist

ofuscar [ofus'kar] *vt* (*por pasión*) to blind; (*por luz*) to dazzle

oída [o'iða] *nf*: **de ~s** by hearsay

oído [o'iðo] *nm* (ANAT) ear; (*sentido*) hearing

oigo *etc vb ver* **oír**

oír [o'ir] *vt* (*gen*) to hear; (*atender a*) to listen to; **¡oiga!** listen!; **~ misa** to attend mass

OIT *nf abr* (= *Organización Internacional del Trabajo*) ILO

ojal [o'xal] *nm* buttonhole

ojalá [oxa'la] *excl* if only (it were so)!, some hope! ♦ *conj* if only ...!, would that ...!; **~ (que) venga hoy** I hope he comes today

ojeada [oxe'aða] *nf* glance

ojera [o'xera] *nf*: **tener ~s** to have bags under one's eyes

ojeriza [oxe'riθa] *nf* ill-will

ojeroso, a [oxe'roso, a] *adj* haggard

ojo ['oxo] *nm* eye; (*de puente*) span; (*de cerradura*) keyhole ♦ *excl* careful!; **tener ~ para** to have an eye for; **~ de buey** porthole

okupa [o'kupa] (*fam*) *nm/f* squatter

ola ['ola] *nf* wave

olé [o'le] *excl* bravo!, olé!

oleada [ole'aða] *nf* big wave, swell; (*fig*) wave

oleaje [ole'axe] *nm* swell

óleo ['oleo] *nm* oil; **oleoducto** *nm* (oil) pipeline

oler [o'ler] *vt* (*gen*) to smell; (*inquirir*) to pry into; (*fig: sospechar*) to sniff out ♦ *vi* to smell; **~ a** to smell of

olfatear [olfate'ar] *vt* to smell; (*inquirir*) to pry into; **olfato** *nm* sense of smell

oligarquía [olivar'kia] *nf* oligarchy

olimpíada [olim'piaða] *nf*: **las O~s** the Olympics; **olímpico, a** [o'limpiko, a] *adj* Olympic

oliva [o'liβa] *nf* (*aceituna*) olive; **aceite de ~** olive oil; **olivo** *nm* olive tree

olla ['oʎa] *nf* pan; (*comida*) stew; **~ a presión** *o* **exprés** pressure cooker; **~ podrida** *type of Spanish stew*

olmo ['olmo] *nm* elm (tree)

olor [o'lor] *nm* smell; **~oso, a** *adj* scented

olvidar [olßi'ðar] *vt* to forget; (*omitir*) to omit; **~se** *vr* (*fig*) to forget o.s.; **se me olvidó** I forgot

olvido [ol'ßiðo] *nm* oblivion; (*despiste*) forgetfulness

ombligo [om'blivo] *nm* navel

omisión [omi'sjon] *nf* (*abstención*) omission; (*descuido*) neglect

omiso, a [o'miso, a] *adj*: **hacer caso ~ de** to ignore, pass over

omitir [omi'tir] *vt* to omit

omnipotente [omnipo'tente] *adj* omnipotent

omóplato [o'moplato] *nm* shoulder blade

OMS *nf abr* (= *Organización Mundial de la Salud*) WHO

once ['onθe] *num* eleven; **~s** (AM) *nfpl* tea break

onda ['onda] *nf* wave; **~ corta/larga/media** short/long/medium wave; **ondear** *vt, vi* to wave; (*tener ondas*) to be wavy; (*agua*) to ripple; **ondearse** *vr* to swing, sway

ondulación [ondula'θjon] *nf* undulation; **ondulado, a** *adj* wavy

ondular [ondu'lar] *vt* (*el pelo*) to wave ♦ *vi* to undulate; **~se** *vr* to undulate

ONG *nf abr* (= *organización no gubernamental*) NGO

ONU ['onu] *nf abr* (= *Organización de las Naciones Unidas*) UNO

opaco, a [o'pako, a] *adj* opaque

opción [op'θjon] *nf* (*gen*) option; (*derecho*) right, option

OPEP ['opep] *nf abr* (= *Organización de*

Países Exportadores de Petróleo) OPEC

ópera ['opera] *nf* opera; **~ bufa** *o* **cómica** comic opera

operación [opera'θjon] *nf* (*gen*) operation; (COM) transaction, deal

operador, a [opera'ðor, a] *nm/f* operator; (CINE: *proyección*) projectionist; (: *rodaje*) cameraman

operar [ope'rar] *vt* (*producir*) to produce, bring about; (MED) to operate on ♦ *vi* (COM) to operate, deal; **~se** *vr* to occur; (MED) to have an operation

opereta [ope'reta] *nf* operetta

opinar [opi'nar] *vt* to think ♦ *vi* to give one's opinion; **opinión** *nf* (*creencia*) belief; (*criterio*) opinion

opio ['opjo] *nm* opium

oponente [opo'nente] *nm/f* opponent

oponer [opo'ner] *vt* (*resistencia*) to put up, offer; **~se** *vr* (*objetar*) to object; (*estar frente a frente*) to be opposed; (*dos personas*) to oppose each other; **~ A a B** to set A against B; **me opongo a pensar que ...** I refuse to believe *o* think that ...

oportunidad [oportuni'ðað] *nf* (*ocasión*) opportunity; (*posibilidad*) chance

oportuno, a [opor'tuno, a] *adj* (*en su tiempo*) opportune, timely; (*respuesta*) suitable; **en el momento ~** at the right moment

oposición [oposi'θjon] *nf* opposition; **oposiciones** *nfpl* (ESCOL) public examinations

opositor, a [oposi'tor, a] *nm/f* (*adversario*) opponent; (*candidato*): **~ (a)** candidate (for)

opresión [opre'sjon] *nf* oppression; **opresivo, a** *adj* oppressive; **opresor, a** *nm/f* oppressor

oprimir [opri'mir] *vt* to squeeze; (*fig*) to oppress

optar [op'tar] *vi* (*elegir*) to choose; **~ por** to opt for; **optativo, a** *adj* optional

óptico, a ['optiko, a] *adj* optic(al) ♦ *nm/f* optician; **óptica** *nf* optician's (shop); **desde esta óptica** from this point of view

optimismo [opti'mismo] *nm* optimism; **optimista** *nm/f* optimist

óptimo, a ['optimo, a] *adj* (*el mejor*) very best

opuesto, a [o'pwesto, a] *adj* (*contrario*) opposite; (*antagónico*) opposing

opulencia [opu'lenθja] *nf* opulence; **opulento, a** *adj* opulent

oración [ora'θjon] *nf* (REL) prayer; (LING) sentence

orador, a [ora'ðor, a] *nm/f* (*conferenciante*) speaker, orator

oral [o'ral] *adj* oral

orangután [orangu'tan] *nm* orangutan

orar [o'rar] *vi* to pray

oratoria [ora'torja] *nf* oratory

órbita ['orßita] *nf* orbit

orden ['orðen] *nm* (*gen*) order ♦ *nf* (*gen*) order; (INFORM) command; **~ del día** agenda; **de primer ~** first-rate; **en ~ de prioridad** in order of priority

ordenado, a [orðe'naðo, a] *adj* (*metódico*) methodical; (*arreglado*) orderly

ordenador [orðena'ðor] *nm* computer; **~ central** mainframe computer

ordenanza [orðe'nanθa] *nf* ordinance

ordenar [orðe'nar] *vt* (*mandar*) to order; (*poner orden*) to put in order, arrange; **~se** *vr* (REL) to be ordained

ordeñar [orðe'nar] *vt* to milk

ordinario, a [orði'narjo, a] *adj* (*común*) ordinary, usual; (*vulgar*) vulgar, common

orégano [o'rexano] *nm* oregano

oreja [o'rexa] *nf* ear; (MECÁNICA) lug, flange

orfanato [orfa'nato] *nm* orphanage

orfandad [orfan'dað] *nf* orphanhood

orfebrería [orfeßre'ria] *nf* gold/silver work

orgánico, a [or'xaniko, a] *adj* organic

organigrama [orxani'xrama] *nm* flow chart

organismo [orxa'nismo] *nm* (BIO) organism; (POL) organization

organización [orxaniθa'θjon] *nf* organization; **organizar** *vt* to organize

órgano ['orxano] *nm* organ

orgasmo [or'xasmo] *nm* orgasm

orgía [or'xia] *nf* orgy

orgullo [or'ɣuʎo] *nm* pride; **orgulloso, a** *adj* (*gen*) proud; (*altanero*) haughty

orientación [orjenta'θjon] *nf* (*posición*) position; (*dirección*) direction

oriental [orjen'tal] *adj* eastern; (*del Lejano Oriente*) oriental

orientar [orjen'tar] *vt* (*situar*) to orientate; (*señalar*) to point; (*dirigir*) to direct; (*guiar*) to guide; **~se** *vr* to get one's bearings

oriente [o'rjente] *nm* east; **Cercano/Medio/Lejano O~** Near/Middle/Far East

origen [o'rixen] *nm* origin

original [orixi'nal] *adj* (*nuevo*) original; (*extraño*) odd, strange; **~idad** *nf* originality

originar [orixi'nar] *vt* to start, cause; **~se** *vr* to originate; **~io, a** *adj* original; **~io de** native of

orilla [o'riʎa] *nf* (*borde*) border; (*de río*) bank; (*de bosque, tela*) edge; (*de mar*) shore

orina [o'rina] *nf* urine; **orinal** *nm* (chamber) pot; **orinar** *vi* to urinate; **orinarse** *vr* to wet o.s.; **orines** *nmpl* urine

oriundo, a [o'rjundo, a] *adj*: **~ de** native of

ornitología [ornitolo'xia] *nf* ornithology, bird-watching

oro [o'ro] *nm* gold; **~s** *nmpl* (NAIPES) hearts

oropel [oro'pel] *nm* tinsel

orquesta [or'kesta] *nf* orchestra; **~ de cámara/sinfónica** chamber/symphony orchestra

orquídea [or'kiðea] *nf* orchid

ortiga [or'tiɣa] *nf* nettle

ortodoxo, a [orto'ðokso, a] *adj* orthodox

ortografía [ortoɣra'fia] *nf* spelling

ortopedia [orto'peðja] *nf* orthopaedics *sg*; **ortopédico, a** *adj* orthopaedic

oruga [o'ruɣa] *nf* caterpillar

orzuelo [or'θwelo] *nm* stye

os [os] *pron* (*gen*) you; (*a vosotros*) to you

osa [o'sa] *nf* (she-)bear; **O~ Mayor/Menor** Great/Little Bear

osadía [osa'ðia] *nf* daring

osar [o'sar] *vi* to dare

oscilación [osθila'θjon] *nf* (*movimiento*) oscillation; (*fluctuación*) fluctuation

oscilar [osθi'lar] *vi* to oscillate; to fluctuate

oscurecer [oskure'θer] *vt* to darken ♦ *vi* to grow dark; **~se** *vr* to grow o get dark

oscuridad [oskuri'ðað] *nf* obscurity; (*tinieblas*) darkness

oscuro, a [os'kuro, a] *adj* dark; (*fig*) obscure; **a oscuras** in the dark

óseo, a ['oseo, a] *adj* bone *cpd*

oso ['oso] *nm* bear; **~ de peluche** teddy bear; **~ hormiguero** anteater

ostentación [ostenta'θjon] *nf* (*gen*) ostentation; (*acto*) display

ostentar [osten'tar] *vt* (*gen*) to show; (*pey*) to flaunt, show off; (*poseer*) to have, possess

ostra ['ostra] *nf* oyster

OTAN ['otan] *nf abr* (= *Organización del Tratado del Atlántico Norte*) NATO

otear [ote'ar] *vt* to observe; (*fig*) to look into

otitis [o'titis] *nf* earache

otoñal [oto'ɲal] *adj* autumnal

otoño [o'toɲo] *nm* autumn

otorgar [otor'ɣar] *vt* (*conceder*) to concede; (*dar*) to grant

otorrino, a [oto'rrino, a], **otorrinola-ringólogo, a** [otorrinolarin'ɣoloɣo, a] *nm/f* ear, nose and throat specialist

---

<t*PALABRA CLAVE*>

otro, a ['otro, a] *adj* **1** (*distinto: sg*) another; (: *pl*) other; **con ~s amigos** with other o different friends
2 (*adicional*): **tráigame ~ café (más), por favor** can I have another coffee please; **~s 10 días más** another ten days
♦ *pron* **1**: **el ~** the other one; **(los) ~s** (the) others; **de ~** somebody else's; **que lo haga ~** let somebody else do it
2 (*recíproco*): **se odian (la) una a (la) otra** they hate one another o each other
3: **~ tanto: comer ~ tanto** to eat the

same *o* as much again; **recibió una decena de telegramas y otras tantas llamadas** he got about ten telegrams and as many calls

---

ovación [oβa'θjon] *nf* ovation
oval [o'βal] *adj* oval; **~ado, a** *adj* oval; **óvalo** *nm* oval
ovario [o'βarjo] *nm* ovary
oveja [o'βexa] *nf* sheep
overol [oβe'rol] (*AM*) *nm* overalls *pl*
ovillo [o'βiʎo] *nm* (*de lana*) ball of wool; **hacerse un ~** to curl up
OVNI ['oβni] *nm abr* (= *objeto volante no identificado*) UFO
ovulación [oβula'θjon] *nf* ovulation; **óvulo** *nm* ovum
oxidación [oksiða'θjon] *nf* rusting
oxidar [oksi'ðar] *vt* to rust; **~se** *vr* to go rusty
óxido ['oksiðo] *nm* oxide
oxigenado, a [oksixe'naðo, a] *adj* (*QUÍM*) oxygenated; (*pelo*) bleached
oxígeno [ok'sixeno] *nm* oxygen
oyente [o'jente] *nm/f* listener, hearer
oyes *etc vb ver* **oír**
ozono [o'θono] *nm* ozone

P, p

P *abr* (= *padre*) Fr.
pabellón [paβe'ʎon] *nm* bell tent; (*ARQ*) pavilion; (*de hospital etc*) block, section; (*bandera*) flag
pacer [pa'θer] *vi* to graze
paciencia [pa'θjenθja] *nf* patience
paciente [pa'θjente] *adj, nm/f* patient
pacificación [paθifika'θjon] *nf* pacification
pacificar [paθifi'kar] *vt* to pacify; (*tranquilizar*) to calm
pacífico, a [pa'θifiko, a] *adj* (*persona*) peaceable; (*existencia*) peaceful; **el (océano) P~** the Pacific (Ocean)
pacifismo [paθi'fismo] *nm* pacifism;

pacifista *nm/f* pacifist
pacotilla [pako'tiʎa] *nf*: **de ~** (*actor, escritor*) third-rate; (*mueble etc*) cheap
pactar [pak'tar] *vt* to agree to *o* on ♦ *vi* to come to an agreement
pacto ['pakto] *nm* (*tratado*) pact; (*acuerdo*) agreement
padecer [paðe'θer] *vt* (*sufrir*) to suffer; (*soportar*) to endure, put up with; **padecimiento** *nm* suffering
padrastro [pa'ðrastro] *nm* stepfather
padre ['paðre] *nm* father ♦ *adj* (*fam*): **un éxito ~** a tremendous success; **~s** *nmpl* parents
padrino [pa'ðrino] *nm* (*REL*) godfather; (*tb*: **~ de boda**) best man; (*fig*) sponsor, patron; **~s** *nmpl* godparents
padrón [pa'ðron] *nm* (*censo*) census, roll
paella [pa'eʎa] *nf* paella, *dish of rice with meat, shellfish etc*
paga ['paɣa] *nf* (*pago*) payment; (*sueldo*) pay, wages *pl*
pagano, a [pa'ɣano, a] *adj, nm/f* pagan, heathen
pagar [pa'ɣar] *vt* to pay; (*las compras, crimen*) to pay for; (*fig: favor*) to repay ♦ *vi* to pay; **~ al contado/a plazos** to pay (in) cash/in instalments
pagaré [paɣa're] *nm* I.O.U.
página ['paxina] *nf* page; **~ de inicio** (*INFORM*) home page
pago ['paɣo] *nm* (*dinero*) payment; **~ anticipado/a cuenta/contra reembolso** advance payment/payment on account/ cash on delivery; **en ~ de** in return for
pág(s). *abr* (= *página(s)*) p(p).
pague *etc vb ver* **pagar**
país [pa'is] *nm* (*gen*) country; (*región*) land; **los P~es Bajos** the Low Countries; **el P~ Vasco** the Basque Country
paisaje [pai'saxe] *nm* landscape, scenery
paisano, a [pai'sano, a] *adj* of the same country ♦ *nm/f* (*compatriota*) fellow countryman/woman; **vestir de ~** (*soldado*) to be in civvies; (*guardia*) to be in plain clothes

paja ['paxa] *nf* straw; (*fig*) rubbish (*BRIT*), trash (*US*)

pajarita [paxa'rita] *nf* (*corbata*) bow tie

pájaro ['paxaro] *nm* bird; **~ carpintero** woodpecker

pajita [pa'xita] *nf* (drinking) straw

pala ['pala] *nf* spade, shovel; (*raqueta etc*) bat; (: *de tenis*) racquet; (*CULIN*) slice; **~ matamoscas** fly swat

palabra [pa'laßra] *nf* word; (*facultad*) (power of) speech; (*derecho de hablar*) right to speak; **tomar la ~** (*en mitin*) to take the floor

palabrota [pala'brota] *nf* swearword

palacio [pa'laθjo] *nm* palace; (*mansión*) mansion, large house; **~ de justicia** courthouse; **~ municipal** town/city hall

paladar [pala'ðar] *nm* palate; **paladear** *vt* to taste

palanca [pa'lanka] *nf* lever; (*fig*) pull, influence

palangana [palan'gana] *nf* washbasin

palco ['palko] *nm* box

Palestina [pales'tina] *nf* Palestine; **palestino, a** *nm/f* Palestinian

paleta [pa'leta] *nf* (*de pintor*) palette; (*de albañil*) trowel; (*de ping-pong*) bat; (*AM*) ice lolly

paleto, a [pa'leto, a] (*fam, pey*) *nm/f* yokel

paliar [pa'ljar] *vt* (*mitigar*) to mitigate, alleviate; **paliativo** *adj* palliative

palidecer [paliðe'θer] *vi* to turn pale; **palidez** *nf* paleness; **pálido, a** *adj* pale

palillo [pa'liλo] *nm* (*mondadientes*) toothpick; (*para comer*) chopstick

paliza [pa'liθa] *nf* beating, thrashing

palma ['palma] *nf* (*ANAT*) palm; (*árbol*) palm tree; **batir** *o* **dar ~s** to clap, applaud; **~da** *nf* slap; **~das** *nfpl* clapping *sg*, applause *sg*

palmar [pal'mar] (*fam*) *vi* (*tb*: **~la**) to die, kick the bucket

palmear [palme'ar] *vi* to clap

palmera [pal'mera] *nf* (*BOT*) palm tree

palmo ['palmo] *nm* (*medida*) span; (*fig*) small amount; **~ a ~** inch by inch

palo ['palo] *nm* stick; (*poste*) post; (*de tienda de campaña*) pole; (*mango*) handle, shaft; (*golpe*) blow, hit; (*de golf*) club; (*de béisbol*) bat; (*NAUT*) mast; (*NAIPES*) suit

paloma [pa'loma] *nf* dove, pigeon

palomitas [palo'mitas] *nfpl* popcorn *sg*

palpar [pal'par] *vt* to touch, feel

palpitación [palpita'θjon] *nf* palpitation

palpitante [palpi'tante] *adj* palpitating; (*fig*) burning

palpitar [palpi'tar] *vi* to palpitate; (*latir*) to beat

palta ['palta] *nf* (*AM*) avocado (pear)

paludismo [palu'ðismo] *nm* malaria

pamela [pa'mela] *nf* picture hat, sun hat

pampa ['pampa] (*AM*) *nf* pampas, prairie

pan [pan] *nm* bread; (*una barra*) loaf; **~ integral** wholemeal (*BRIT*) *o* wholewheat (*US*) bread; **~ rallado** breadcrumbs *pl*

pana ['pana] *nf* corduroy

panadería [panaðe'ria] *nf* baker's (shop); **panadero, a** *nm/f* baker

Panamá [pana'ma] *nm* Panama; **panameño, a** *adj* Panamanian

pancarta [pan'karta] *nf* placard, banner

panda ['panda] *nm* (*ZOOL*) panda

pandereta [pande'reta] *nf* tambourine

pandilla [pan'diλa] *nf* set, group; (*de criminales*) gang; (*pey: camarilla*) clique

panecillo [pane'θiλo] *nm* (bread) roll

panel [pa'nel] *nm* panel; **~ solar** solar panel

panfleto [pan'fleto] *nm* pamphlet

pánico ['paniko] *nm* panic

panorama [pano'rama] *nm* panorama; (*vista*) view

pantalla [pan'taλa] *nf* (*de cine*) screen; (*de lámpara*) lampshade

pantalón [panta'lon] *nm* trousers; **pantalones** *nmpl* trousers

pantano [pan'tano] *nm* (*ciénaga*) marsh, swamp; (*depósito: de agua*) reservoir; (*fig*) jam, difficulty

panteón [pante'on] *nm*: **~ familiar** family tomb

pantera [pan'tera] *nf* panther

panti(e)s ['pantis] *nmpl* tights

pantomima [panto'mima] *nf* pantomime

pantorrilla [panto'rriʎa] *nf* calf (of the leg)

pantufla [pan'tufla] *nf* slipper

panty(s) ['panti(s)] *nm(pl)* tights

panza ['panθa] *nf* belly, paunch

pañal [pa'ɲal] *nm* nappy (*BRIT*), diaper (*US*); **~es** *nmpl* (*fig*) early stages, infancy *sg*

paño ['paɲo] *nm* (*tela*) cloth; (*pedazo de tela*) (piece of) cloth; (*trapo*) duster, rag; **~ higiénico** sanitary towel; **~s menores** underclothes

pañuelo [pa'ɲwelo] *nm* handkerchief, hanky (*fam*); (*para la cabeza*) (head)scarf

papa ['papa] *nm*: **el P~** the Pope ♦ *nf* (*AM*) potato

papá [pa'pa] (*pl* **~s**) (*fam*) *nm* dad(dy), pa (*US*)

papada [pa'paða] *nf* double chin

papagayo [papa'ɣajo] *nm* parrot

papanatas [papa'natas] (*fam*) *nm inv* simpleton

paparrucha [papa'rrutʃa] *nf* piece of nonsense

papaya [pa'paja] *nf* papaya

papear [pape'ar] (*fam*) *vt*, *vi* to scoff

papel [pa'pel] *nm* paper; (*hoja de ~*) sheet of paper; (*TEATRO*, *fig*) role; **~ de calco/ carbón/de cartas** tracing paper/carbon paper/stationery; **~ de envolver/pintado** wrapping paper/wallpaper; **~ de aluminio/higiénico** aluminium (*BRIT*) o aluminum (*US*) foil/toilet paper; **~ de estaño** o **plata** tinfoil; **~ de lija** sandpaper; **~ moneda** paper money; **~ secante** blotting paper

papeleo [pape'leo] *nm* red tape

papelera [pape'lera] *nf* wastepaper basket; (*en la calle*) litter bin

papelería [papele'ria] *nf* stationer's (shop)

papeleta [pape'leta] *nf* (*POL*) ballot paper; (*ESCOL*) report

paperas [pa'peras] *nfpl* mumps *sg*

papilla [pa'piʎa] *nf* (*para niños*) baby food

paquete [pa'kete] *nm* (*de cigarrillos etc*) packet; (*CORREOS etc*) parcel; (*AM*) package tour; (: *fam*) nuisance

par [par] *adj* (*igual*) like, equal; (*MAT*) even ♦ *nm* equal; (*de guantes*) pair; (*de veces*) couple; (*POL*) peer; (*GOLF*, *COM*) par; **abrir de ~ en ~** to open wide

para ['para] *prep* for; **no es ~ comer** it's not for eating; **decir ~ sí** to say to o.s.; **¿~ qué lo quieres?** what do you want it for?; **se casaron ~ separarse otra vez** they married only to separate again; **lo tendré ~ mañana** I'll have it (for) tomorrow; **ir ~ casa** to go home, head for home; **~ profesor es muy estúpido** he's very stupid for a teacher; **¿quién es usted ~ gritar así?** who are you to shout like that?; **tengo bastante ~ vivir** I have enough to live on; *ver tb* **con**

parabién [para'ßjen] *nm* congratulations *pl*

parábola [pa'raßola] *nf* parable; (*MAT*) parabola; **parabólica** *nf* (*tb*: **antena ~**) satellite dish

parabrisas [para'ßrisas] *nm inv* windscreen (*BRIT*), windshield (*US*)

paracaídas [paraka'iðas] *nm inv* parachute; **paracaidista** *nm/f* parachutist; (*MIL*) paratrooper

parachoques [para'tʃokes] *nm inv* (*AUTO*) bumper; (*MECÁNICA etc*) shock absorber

parada [pa'raða] *nf* stop; (*acto*) stopping; (*de industria*) shutdown, stoppage; (*lugar*) stopping place; **~ de autobús** bus stop

paradero [para'ðero] *nm* stopping-place; (*situación*) whereabouts

parado, a [pa'raðo, a] *adj* (*persona*) motionless, standing still; (*fábrica*) closed, at a standstill; (*coche*) stopped; (*AM*) standing (up); (*sin empleo*) unemployed, idle

paradoja [para'ðoxa] *nf* paradox

parador [para'ðor] *nm* parador, state-run hotel

paráfrasis [pa'rafrasis] *nf inv* paraphrase

paraguas [pa'raɣwas] *nm inv* umbrella

Paraguay [para'ɣwai] *nm*: **el ~** Paraguay; **paraguayo, a** *adj*, *nm/f* Paraguayan

paraíso [para'iso] *nm* paradise, heaven

paraje [pa'raxe] *nm* place, spot

paralelo, a [para'lelo, a] *adj* parallel
parálisis [pa'ralisis] *nf inv* paralysis;
   paralítico, a *adj*, *nm/f* paralytic
paralizar [parali'θar] *vt* to paralyse; **~se** *vr*
   to become paralysed; (*fig*) to come to a
   standstill
paramilitar [paramili'tar] *adj* paramilitary
páramo ['paramo] *nm* bleak plateau
parangón [paran'gon] *nm*: **sin ~**
   incomparable
paranoico, a [para'noiko, a] *nm/f*
   paranoiac
parapente [para'pente] *nm* (*deporte*)
   paragliding; (*aparato*) paraglider
parapléjico, a [para'plexiko, a] *adj*, *nm/f*
   paraplegic
parar [pa'rar] *vt* to stop; (*golpe*) to ward
   off ♦ *vi* to stop; **~se** *vr* to stop; (*AM*) to
   stand up; **ha parado de llover** it has
   stopped raining; **van a ir a ~ a comisaría**
   they're going to end up in the police
   station; **~se en** to pay attention to
pararrayos [para'rrajos] *nm inv* lightning
   conductor
parásito, a [pa'rasito, a] *nm/f* parasite
parcela [par'θela] *nf* plot, piece of ground
parche ['partʃe] *nm* patch
parchís [par'tʃis] *nm* ludo
parcial [par'θjal] *adj* (*pago*) part-; (*eclipse*)
   partial; (*JUR*) prejudiced, biased; (*POL*)
   partisan; **~idad** *nf* prejudice, bias
pardillo, a [par'ðiʎo, a] (*pey*) *adj* yokel
parecer [pare'θer] *nm* (*opinión*) opinion,
   view; (*aspecto*) looks *pl* ♦ *vi* (*tener
   apariencia*) to seem, look; (*asemejarse*) to
   look *o* seem like; (*aparecer, llegar*) to
   appear; **~se** *vr* to look alike, resemble
   each other; **~se a** to look like, resemble;
   según parece evidently, apparently; **me
   parece que** I think (that), it seems to me
   that
parecido, a [pare'θiðo, a] *adj* similar
   ♦ *nm* similarity, likeness, resemblance;
   bien ~ good-looking, nice-looking
pared [pa'reð] *nf* wall
pareja [pa'rexa] *nf* (*par*) pair; (*dos
   personas*) couple; (*otro: de un par*) other

   one (of a pair); (*persona*) partner
parentela [paren'tela] *nf* relations *pl*
parentesco [paren'tesko] *nm* relationship
paréntesis [pa'rentesis] *nm inv*
   parenthesis; (*en escrito*) bracket
parezco *etc vb ver* **parecer**
pariente, a [pa'rjente, a] *nm/f* relative,
   relation
parir [pa'rir] *vt* to give birth to ♦ *vi* (*mujer*)
   to give birth, have a baby
París [pa'ris] *n* Paris
parking ['parkin] *nm* car park (*BRIT*),
   parking lot (*US*)
parlamentar [parlamen'tar] *vi* to parley
parlamentario, a [parlamen'tarjo, a] *adj*
   parliamentary ♦ *nm/f* member of
   parliament
parlamento [parla'mento] *nm* parliament
parlanchín, ina [parlan'tʃin, ina] *adj*
   indiscreet ♦ *nm/f* chatterbox
parlar [par'lar] *vi* to chatter (away)
paro ['paro] *nm* (*huelga*) stoppage (of
   work), strike; (*desempleo*) unemployment;
   subsidio de ~ unemployment benefit
parodia [pa'roðja] *nf* parody; **parodiar** *vt*
   to parody
parpadear [parpaðe'ar] *vi* (*ojos*) to blink;
   (*luz*) to flicker
párpado ['parpaðo] *nm* eyelid
parque ['parke] *nm* (*lugar verde*) park; **~
   de atracciones/infantil/zoológico**
   fairground/playground/zoo
parqué [par'ke] *nm* parquet (flooring)
parquímetro [par'kimetro] *nm* parking
   meter
parra ['parra] *nf* (*grape*)vine
párrafo ['parrafo] *nm* paragraph; **echar un
   ~** (*fam*) to have a chat
parranda [pa'rranda] (*fam*) *nf* spree, binge
parrilla [pa'rriʎa] *nf* (*CULIN*) grill; (*de
   coche*) grille; **(carne a la) ~** barbecue;
   ~da *nf* barbecue
párroco ['parroko] *nm* parish priest
parroquia [pa'rrokja] *nf* parish; (*iglesia*)
   parish church; (*COM*) clientele, customers
   pl; **~no, a** *nm/f* parishioner; client,
   customer

parsimonia [parsi'monja] *nf* calmness, level-headedness

parte ['parte] *nm* message; (*informe*) report ♦ *nf* part; (*lado, cara*) side; (*de reparto*) share; (*JUR*) party; **en alguna ~ de Europa** somewhere in Europe; **en/por todas ~s** everywhere; **en gran ~** to a large extent; **la mayor ~ de los españoles** most Spaniards; **de un tiempo a esta ~** for some time past; **de ~ de alguien** on sb's behalf; **¿de ~ de quién?** (*TEL*) who is speaking?; **por ~ de** on the part of; **yo por mi ~** I for my part; **por otra ~** on the other hand; **dar ~** to inform; **tomar ~** to take part

partición [parti'θjon] *nf* division, sharing-out; (*POL*) partition

participación [partiθipa'θjon] *nf* (*acto*) participation, taking part; (*parte, COM*) share; (*de lotería*) shared prize; (*aviso*) notice, notification

participante [partiθi'pante] *nm/f* participant

participar [partiθi'par] *vt* to notify, inform ♦ *vi* to take part, participate

partícipe [par'tiθipe] *nm/f* participant

particular [partiku'lar] *adj* (*especial*) particular, special; (*individual, personal*) private, personal ♦ *nm* (*punto, asunto*) particular, point; (*individuo*) individual; **tiene coche ~** he has a car of his own

partida [par'tiða] *nf* (*salida*) departure; (*COM*) entry, item; (*juego*) game; (*grupo de personas*) band, group; **mala ~** dirty trick; **~ de nacimiento / matrimonio / defunción** birth/marriage/death certificate

partidario, a [parti'ðarjo, a] *adj* partisan ♦ *nm/f* supporter, follower

partido [par'tiðo] *nm* (*POL*) party; (*DEPORTE*) game, match; **sacar ~ de** to profit *o* benefit from; **tomar ~** to take sides

partir [par'tir] *vt* (*dividir*) to split, divide; (*compartir, distribuir*) to share (out), distribute; (*romper*) to break open, split open; (*rebanada*) to cut (off) ♦ *vi* (*ponerse*

en camino) to set off *o* out; (*comenzar*) to start (off *o* out); **~se** *vr* to crack *o* split *o* break (in two *etc*); **a ~ de** (starting) from

partitura [parti'tura] *nf* (*MUS*) score

parto ['parto] *nm* birth; (*fig*) product, creation; **estar de ~** to be in labour

pasa ['pasa] *nf* raisin; **~ de Corinto/de Esmirna** currant/sultana

pasada [pa'saða] *nf* passing, passage; **de ~** in passing, incidentally; **una mala ~** a dirty trick

pasadizo [pasa'ðiθo] *nm* (*pasillo*) passage, corridor; (*callejuela*) alley

pasado, a [pa'saðo, a] *adj* past; (*malo: comida, fruta*) bad; (*muy cocido*) overdone; (*anticuado*) out of date ♦ *nm* past; **~ mañana** the day after tomorrow; **el mes ~** last month

pasador [pasa'ðor] *nm* (*cerrojo*) bolt; (*de pelo*) hair slide; (*horquilla*) grip

pasaje [pa'saxe] *nm* passage; (*pago de viaje*) fare; (*los pasajeros*) passengers *pl*; (*pasillo*) passageway

pasajero, a [pasa'xero, a] *adj* passing; (*situación, estado*) temporary; (*amor, enfermedad*) brief ♦ *nm/f* passenger

pasamontañas [pasamon'taɲas] *nm inv* balaclava helmet

pasaporte [pasa'porte] *nm* passport

pasar [pa'sar] *vt* to pass; (*tiempo*) to spend; (*desgracias*) to suffer, endure; (*noticia*) to give, pass on; (*río*) to cross; (*barrera*) to pass through; (*falta*) to overlook, tolerate; (*contrincante*) to surpass, do better than; (*coche*) to overtake; (*CINE*) to show; (*enfermedad*) to give, infect with ♦ *vi* (*gen*) to pass; (*terminarse*) to be over; (*ocurrir*) to happen; **~se** *vr* (*flores*) to fade; (*comida*) to go bad *o* off; (*fig*) to overdo it, go too far; **~ de** to go beyond, exceed; **~ por** (*AM*) to fetch; **~lo bien/mal** to have a good/bad time; **¡pase!** come in!; **hacer ~** to show in; **~se al enemigo** to go over to the enemy; **se me pasó** I forgot; **no se le pasa nada** he misses nothing; **pase lo que pase** come what may; **¿qué**

pasa? what's going on?, what's up?;
¿qué te pasa? what's wrong?

pasarela [pasa'rela] nf footbridge; (en
barco) gangway

pasatiempo [pasa'tjempo] nm pastime,
hobby

Pascua ['paskwa] nf: ~ **(de Resurrección)**
Easter; ~ **de Navidad** Christmas; ~**s** nfpl
Christmas (time); **¡felices ~s!** Merry
Christmas!

pase ['pase] nm pass; (CINE) performance,
showing

pasear [pase'ar] vt to take for a walk;
(exhibir) to parade, show off ♦ vi to walk,
go for a walk; ~**se** vr to walk, go for a
walk; ~ **en coche** to go for a drive;
paseo nm (avenida) avenue; (distancia
corta) walk, stroll; **dar un** o **ir de paseo**
to go for a walk

pasillo [pa'siʎo] nm passage, corridor

pasión [pa'sjon] nf passion

pasivo, a [pa'siβo, a] adj passive;
(inactivo) inactive ♦ nm (COM) liabilities
pl, debts pl

pasmar [pas'mar] vt (asombrar) to amaze,
astonish; **pasmo** nm amazement,
astonishment; (resfriado) chill; (fig)
wonder, marvel; **pasmoso, a** adj
amazing, astonishing

paso, a ['paso, a] adj dried ♦ nm step;
(modo de andar) walk; (huella) footprint;
(rapidez) speed, pace, rate; (camino
accesible) way through, passage; (cruce)
crossing; (pasaje) passing, passage; (GEO)
pass; (estrecho) strait; ~ **a nivel** (FERRO)
level-crossing; ~ **de peatones** pedestrian
crossing; **a ese** ~ (fig) at that rate; **salir
al** ~ **de** o a to waylay; **estar de** ~ to be
passing through; ~ **elevado** flyover;
prohibido el ~ no entry; **ceda el** ~ give
way

pasota [pa'sota] (fam) adj, nm/f
≈ dropout; **ser un (tipo)** ~ to be a bit of
a dropout; (ser indiferente) not to care
about anything

pasta ['pasta] nf paste; (CULIN: masa)
dough; (: de bizcochos etc) pastry; (fam)

dough; ~**s** nfpl (bizcochos) pastries, small
cakes; (fideos, espaguetis etc) pasta; ~ **de
dientes** o **dentífrica** toothpaste

pastar [pas'tar] vt, vi to graze

pastel [pas'tel] nm (dulce) cake; (ARTE)
pastel; ~ **de carne** meat pie; ~**ería** nf
cake shop

pasteurizado, a [pasteuri'θaðo, a] adj
pasteurized

pastilla [pas'tiʎa] nf (de jabón, chocolate)
bar; (píldora) tablet, pill

pasto ['pasto] nm (hierba) grass; (lugar)
pasture, field

pastor, a [pas'tor, a] nm/f shepherd/ess
♦ nm (REL) clergyman, pastor; ~ **alemán**
Alsatian

pata ['pata] nf (pierna) leg; (pie) foot; (de
muebles) leg; ~**s arriba** upside down;
metedura de ~ (fam) gaffe; **meter la** ~
(fam) to put one's foot in it; (TEC): ~ **de
cabra** crowbar; **tener buena/mala** ~ to
be lucky/unlucky; ~**da** nf kick; (en el
suelo) stamp

patalear [patale'ar] vi (en el suelo) to
stamp one's feet

patata [pa'tata] nf potato; ~**s fritas** chips,
French fries; (de bolsa) crisps

paté [pa'te] nm pâté

patear [pate'ar] vt (pisar) to stamp on,
trample (on); (pegar con el pie) to kick
♦ vi to stamp (with rage), stamp one's
feet

patentar [paten'tar] vt to patent

patente [pa'tente] adj obvious, evident;
(COM) patent ♦ nf patent

paternal [pater'nal] adj fatherly, paternal;
paterno, a adj paternal

patético, a [pa'tetiko, a] adj pathetic,
moving

patilla [pa'tiʎa] nf (de gafas) side(piece);
~**s** nfpl sideburns

patín [pa'tin] nm skate; (de trineo) runner;
patinaje nm skating; **patinar** vi to
skate; (resbalarse) to skid, slip; (fam) to
slip up, blunder

patio ['patjo] nm (de casa) patio,
courtyard; ~ **de recreo** playground

pato ['pato] *nm* duck; **pagar el ~** (*fam*) to take the blame, carry the can

patológico, a [pato'loxiko, a] *adj* pathological

patoso, a [pa'toso, a] (*fam*) *adj* clumsy

patraña [pa'traɲa] *nf* story, fib

patria ['patrja] *nf* native land, mother country

patrimonio [patri'monjo] *nm* inheritance; (*fig*) heritage

patriota [pa'trjota] *nm/f* patriot; **patriotismo** *nm* patriotism

patrocinar [patroθi'nar] *vt* to sponsor; **patrocinio** *nm* sponsorship

patrón, ona [pa'tron, ona] *nm/f* (*jefe*) boss, chief, master/mistress; (*propietario*) landlord/lady; (*REL*) patron saint ♦ *nm* (*TEC, COSTURA*) pattern

patronal [patro'nal] *adj*: **la clase ~** management

patronato [patro'nato] *nm* sponsorship; (*acto*) patronage; (*fundación benéfica*) trust, foundation

patrulla [pa'truʎa] *nf* patrol

pausa ['pausa] *nf* pause, break

pausado, a [pau'saðo, a] *adj* slow, deliberate

pauta ['pauta] *nf* line, guide line

pavimento [paβi'mento] *nm* (*con losas*) pavement, paving

pavo ['paβo] *nm* turkey; **~ real** peacock

pavor [pa'ßor] *nm* dread, terror

payaso, a [pa'jaso, a] *nm/f* clown

payo, a ['pajo, a] *nm/f* non-gipsy

paz [paθ] *nf* peace; (*tranquilidad*) peacefulness, tranquillity; **hacer las paces** to make peace; (*fig*) to make up

pazo ['paθo] *nm* country house

P.D. *abr* (= *posdata*) P.S., p.s.

peaje [pe'axe] *nm* toll

peatón [pea'ton] *nm* pedestrian

peca ['peka] *nf* freckle

pecado [pe'kaðo] *nm* sin; **pecador, a** *adj* sinful ♦ *nm/f* sinner

pecaminoso, a [pekami'noso, a] *adj* sinful

pecar [pe'kar] *vi* (*REL*) to sin; **peca de**

generoso he is generous to a fault

pecera [pe'θera] *nf* fish tank; (*redondo*) goldfish bowl

pecho ['petʃo] *nm* (*ANAT*) chest; (*de mujer*) breast; **dar el ~ a** to breast-feed; **tomar algo a ~** to take sth to heart

pechuga [pe'tʃuʝa] *nf* breast

peculiar [peku'ljar] *adj* special, peculiar; (*característico*) typical, characteristic; **~idad** *nf* peculiarity; special feature, characteristic

pedal [pe'ðal] *nm* pedal; **~ear** *vi* to pedal

pedante [pe'ðante] *adj* pedantic ♦ *nm/f* pedant; **~ría** *nf* pedantry

pedazo [pe'ðaθo] *nm* piece, bit; **hacerse ~s** to smash, shatter

pedernal [peðer'nal] *nm* flint

pediatra [pe'ðjatra] *nm/f* paediatrician

pedido [pe'ðiðo] *nm* (*COM*) order; (*petición*) request

pedir [pe'ðir] *vt* to ask for, request; (*comida, COM: mandar*) to order; (*necesitar*) to need, demand, require ♦ *vi* to ask; **me pidió que cerrara la puerta** he asked me to shut the door; **¿cuánto piden por el coche?** how much are they asking for the car?

pedo ['peðo] (*fam!*) *nm* fart

pega ['peɣa] *nf* snag; **poner ~s (a)** to complain (about)

pegadizo, a [peɣa'ðiθo, a] *adj* (*MUS*) catchy

pegajoso, a [peɣa'xoso, a] *adj* sticky, adhesive

pegamento [peɣa'mento] *nm* gum, glue

pegar [pe'ɣar] *vt* (*papel, sellos*) to stick (on); (*cartel*) to stick up; (*coser*) to sew (on); (*unir: partes*) to join, fix together; (*MED*) to give, infect with; (*dar: golpe*) to give, deal ♦ *vi* (*adherirse*) to stick, adhere; (*ir juntos: colores*) to match, go together; (*golpear*) to hit; (*quemar: el sol*) to strike hot, burn (*fig*); **~se** *vr* (*gen*) to stick; (*dos personas*) to hit each other, fight; (*fam*): **~ un grito** to let out a yell; **~ un salto** to jump (with fright); **~ en** to touch; **~se un tiro** to shoot o.s.

pegatina [peɣa'tina] *nf* sticker
pegote [pe'ɣote] (*fam*) *nm* eyesore, sight
peinado [pei'naðo] *nm* hairstyle
peinar [pei'nar] *vt* to comb; (*hacer estilo*) to style; **~se** *vr* to comb one's hair
peine ['peine] *nm* comb; **~ta** *nf* ornamental comb
p.ej. *abr* (= *por ejemplo*) e.g.
Pekín [pe'kin] *n* Pekin(g)
pelado, a [pe'laðo, a] *adj* (*fruta, patata etc*) peeled; (*cabeza*) shorn; (*campo, fig*) bare; (*fam: sin dinero*) broke
pelaje [pe'laxe] *nm* (*ZOOL*) fur, coat; (*fig*) appearance
pelar [pe'lar] *vt* (*fruta, patatas etc*) to peel; (*cortar el pelo a*) to cut the hair of; (*quitar la piel: animal*) to skin; **~se** *vr* (*la piel*) to peel off; **voy a ~me** I'm going to get my hair cut
peldaño [pel'daɲo] *nm* step
pelea [pe'lea] *nf* (*lucha*) fight; (*discusión*) quarrel, row
peleado, a [pele'aðo, a] *adj*: **estar ~ (con uno)** to have fallen out (with sb)
pelear [pele'ar] *vi* to fight; **~se** *vr* to fight; (*reñirse*) to fall out, quarrel
peletería [pelete'ria] *nf* furrier's, fur shop
pelícano [pe'likano] *nm* pelican
película [pe'likula] *nf* film; (*cobertura ligera*) thin covering; (*FOTO: rollo*) roll o reel of film
peligro [pe'liɣro] *nm* danger; (*riesgo*) risk; **correr ~ de** to run the risk of; **~so, a** *adj* dangerous; risky
pelirrojo, a [peli'rroxo, a] *adj* red-haired, red-headed ♦ *nm/f* redhead
pellejo [pe'ʎexo] *nm* (*de animal*) skin, hide
pellizcar [peʎiθ'kar] *vt* to pinch, nip
pelma ['pelma] (*fam*) *nm/f* pain (in the neck)
pelmazo [pel'maθo] (*fam*) *nm* = **pelma**
pelo ['pelo] *nm* (*cabellos*) hair; (*de barba, bigote*) whisker; (*de animal: pellejo*) hair, fur, coat; **al ~** just right; **venir al ~** to be exactly what one needs; **un hombre de ~ en pecho** a brave man; **por los ~s** by the skin of one's teeth; **no tener ~s en la**

lengua to be outspoken, not mince words; **tomar el ~ a uno** to pull sb's leg
pelota [pe'lota] *nf* ball; **en ~** stark naked; **hacer la ~ (a uno)** (*fam*) to creep (to sb); **~ vasca** pelota
pelotari [pelo'tari] *nm* pelota player
pelotón [pelo'ton] *nm* (*MIL*) squad, detachment
peluca [pe'luka] *nf* wig
peluche [pe'lutʃe] *nm*: **oso/muñeco de ~** teddy bear/soft toy
peludo, a [pe'luðo, a] *adj* hairy, shaggy
peluquería [peluke'ria] *nf* hairdresser's; **peluquero, a** *nm/f* hairdresser
pelusa [pe'lusa] *nf* (*BOT*) down; (*en tela*) fluff
pena ['pena] *nf* (*congoja*) grief, sadness; (*remordimiento*) regret; (*dificultad*) trouble; (*dolor*) pain; (*JUR*) sentence; **merecer** o **valer la ~** to be worthwhile; **a duras ~s** with great difficulty; **~ de muerte** death penalty; **~ pecuniaria** fine; **¡qué ~!** what a shame!
penal [pe'nal] *adj* penal ♦ *nm* (*cárcel*) prison
penalidad [penali'ðað] *nf* (*problema, dificultad*) trouble, hardship; (*JUR*) penalty, punishment; **~es** *nfpl* trouble, hardship
penalti, penalty [pe'nalti] (*pl* **~s** o **~es**) *nm* penalty (kick)
pendiente [pen'djente] *adj* pending, unsettled ♦ *nm* earring ♦ *nf* hill, slope
pene ['pene] *nm* penis
penetración [penetra'θjon] *nf* (*acto*) penetration; (*agudeza*) sharpness, insight
penetrante [pene'trante] *adj* (*herida*) deep; (*persona, arma*) sharp; (*sonido*) penetrating, piercing; (*mirada*) searching; (*viento, ironía*) biting
penetrar [pene'trar] *vt* to penetrate, pierce; (*entender*) to grasp ♦ *vi* to penetrate, go in; (*entrar*) to enter, go in; (*líquido*) to soak in; (*fig*) to pierce
penicilina [peniθi'lina] *nf* penicillin
península [pe'ninsula] *nf* peninsula; **peninsular** *adj* peninsular
penique [pe'nike] *nm* penny

penitencia [peni'tenθja] *nf* penance

penoso, a [pe'noso, a] *adj* (*lamentable*) distressing; (*difícil*) arduous, difficult

pensador, a [pensa'ðor, a] *nm/f* thinker

pensamiento [pensa'mjento] *nm* thought; (*mente*) mind; (*idea*) idea

pensar [pen'sar] *vt* to think; (*considerar*) to think over, think out; (*proponerse*) to intend, plan; (*imaginarse*) to think up, invent ♦ *vi* to think; **~ en** to aim at, aspire to; **pensativo, a** *adj* thoughtful, pensive

pensión [pen'sjon] *nf* (*casa*) boarding o guest house; (*dinero*) pension; (*cama y comida*) board and lodging; **~ completa** full board; **media ~** half-board; **pensionista** *nm/f* (*jubilado*) (old-age) pensioner; (*huésped*) lodger

penúltimo, a [pe'nultimo, a] *adj* penultimate, last but one

penumbra [pe'numbra] *nf* half-light

penuria [pe'nurja] *nf* shortage, want

peña ['peɲa] *nf* (*roca*) rock; (*cuesta*) cliff, crag; (*grupo*) group, circle; (*AM: club*) folk club

peñasco [pe'nasko] *nm* large rock, boulder

peñón [pe'ɲon] *nm* wall of rock; **el P~** the Rock (of Gibraltar)

peón [pe'on] *nm* labourer; (*AM*) farm labourer, farmhand; (*AJEDREZ*) pawn

peonza [pe'onθa] *nf* spinning top

peor [pe'or] *adj* (*comparativo*) worse; (*superlativo*) worst ♦ *adv* worse; worst; **de mal en ~** from bad to worse

pepinillo [pepi'niʎo] *nm* gherkin

pepino [pe'pino] *nm* cucumber; **(no) me importa un ~** I don't care one bit

pepita [pe'pita] *nf* (*BOT*) pip; (*MINERÍA*) nugget

pepito [pe'pito] *nm*: **~ (de ternera)** steak sandwich

pequeñez [peke'ɲeθ] *nf* smallness, littleness; (*trivialidad*) trifle, triviality

pequeño, a [pe'keɲo, a] *adj* small, little

pera ['pera] *nf* pear; **peral** *nm* pear tree

percance [per'kanθe] *nm* setback, misfortune

percatarse [perka'tarse] *vr*: **~ de** to notice, take note of

percebe [per'θeβe] *nm* barnacle

percepción [perθep'θjon] *nf* (*vista*) perception; (*idea*) notion, idea

percha ['pertʃa] *nf* (*coat*)hanger; (*ganchos*) coat hooks *pl*; (*de ave*) perch

percibir [perθi'βir] *vt* to perceive, notice; (*COM*) to earn, get

percusión [perku'sjon] *nf* percussion

perdedor, a [perðe'ðor, a] *adj* losing ♦ *nm/f* loser

perder [per'ðer] *vt* to lose; (*tiempo, palabras*) to waste; (*oportunidad*) to lose, miss; (*tren*) *vi* to lose; **~se** *vr* (*extraviarse*) to get lost; (*desaparecer*) to disappear, be lost to view; (*arruinarse*) to be ruined; **echar a ~** (*comida*) to spoil, ruin; (*oportunidad*) to waste

perdición [perði'θjon] *nf* perdition, ruin

pérdida ['perðiða] *nf* loss; (*de tiempo*) waste; **~s** *nfpl* (*COM*) losses

perdido, a [per'ðiðo, a] *adj* lost

perdiz [per'ðiθ] *nf* partridge

perdón [per'ðon] *nm* (*disculpa*) pardon, forgiveness; (*clemencia*) mercy; **¡~!** sorry!, I beg your pardon!; **perdonar** *vt* to pardon, forgive; (*la vida*) to spare; (*excusar*) to exempt, excuse; **¡perdone (usted)!** sorry!, I beg your pardon!

perdurar [perðu'rar] *vi* (*resistir*) to last, endure; (*seguir existiendo*) to stand, still exist

perecedero, a [pereθe'ðero, a] *adj* perishable

perecer [pere'θer] *vi* to perish, die

peregrinación [perevrina'θjon] *nf* (*REL*) pilgrimage

peregrino, a [pere'xrino, a] *adj* (*idea*) strange, absurd ♦ *nm/f* pilgrim

perejil [pere'xil] *nm* parsley

perenne [pe'renne] *adj* everlasting, perennial

pereza [pe'reθa] *nf* laziness, idleness; **perezoso, a** *adj* lazy, idle

perfección [perfek'θjon] *nf* perfection;

perfeccionar vt to perfect; (*mejorar*) to improve; (*acabar*) to complete, finish
perfectamente [perfekta'mente] adv perfectly
perfecto, a [per'fekto, a] adj perfect; (*total*) complete
perfil [per'fil] nm profile; (*contorno*) silhouette, outline; (ARQ) (cross) section; ~**es** nmpl features; ~**ar** vt (*trazar*) to outline; (*fig*) to shape, give character to
perforación [perfora'θjon] nf perforation; (*con taladro*) drilling; **perforadora** nf punch
perforar [perfo'rar] vt to perforate; (*agujero*) to drill, bore; (*papel*) to punch a hole in ♦ vi to drill, bore
perfume [per'fume] nm perfume, scent
pericia [pe'riθja] nf skill, expertise
periferia [peri'ferja] nf periphery; (*de ciudad*) outskirts pl
periférico [peri'feriko] (AM) nm ring road (BRIT), beltway (US)
perímetro [pe'rimetro] nm perimeter
periódico, a [pe'rjoðiko, a] adj periodic(al) ♦ nm newspaper
periodismo [perjo'ðismo] nm journalism; **periodista** nm/f journalist
periodo [pe'rjoðo] nm period
período [pe'rjoðo] nm = **periodo**
periquito [peri'kito] nm budgerigar, budgie
perito, a [pe'rito, a] adj (*experto*) expert; (*diestro*) skilled, skilful ♦ nm/f expert; skilled worker; (*técnico*) technician
perjudicar [perxuði'kar] vt (*gen*) to damage, harm; **perjudicial** adj damaging, harmful; (*en detrimento*) detrimental; **perjuicio** nm damage, harm
perjurar [perxu'rar] vi to commit perjury
perla ['perla] nf pearl; **me viene de ~s** it suits me fine
permanecer [permane'θer] vi (*quedarse*) to stay, remain; (*seguir*) to continue to be
permanencia [perma'nenθja] nf permanence; (*estancia*) stay
permanente [perma'nente] adj

**permanent, constant ♦ nf perm
permiso [per'miso] nm permission; (*licencia*) permit, licence; **con ~** excuse me; ~ **de** (MIL) to be on leave; ~ **de conducir** driving licence (BRIT), driver's license (US)
permitir [permi'tir] vt to permit, allow
pernera [per'nera] nf trouser leg
pernicioso, a [perni'θjoso, a] adj pernicious
pero ['pero] conj but; (*aún*) yet ♦ nm (*defecto*) flaw, defect; (*reparo*) objection
perpendicular [perpendiku'lar] adj perpendicular
perpetrar [perpe'trar] vt to perpetrate
perpetuar [perpe'twar] vt to perpetuate; **perpetuo, a** adj perpetual
perplejo, a [per'plexo, a] adj perplexed, bewildered
perra ['perra] nf (ZOOL) bitch; **estar sin una ~** to be flat broke
perrera [pe'rrera] nf kennel
perrito [pe'rrito] nm: ~ **caliente** hot dog
perro ['perro] nm dog
persa ['persa] adj, nm/f Persian
persecución [perseku'θjon] nf pursuit, chase; (REL, POL) persecution
perseguir [perse'xir] vt to pursue, hunt; (*cortejar*) to chase after; (*molestar*) to pester, annoy; (REL, POL) to persecute
perseverante [perseße'rante] adj persevering, persistent
perseverar [perseße'rar] vi to persevere, persist
persiana [per'sjana] nf (Venetian) blind
persignarse [persiɣ'narse] vr to cross o.s.
persistente [persis'tente] adj persistent
persistir [persis'tir] vi to persist
persona [per'sona] nf person; ~ **mayor** elderly person
personaje [perso'naxe] nm important person, celebrity; (TEATRO etc) character
personal [perso'nal] adj (*particular*) personal; (*para una persona*) single, for one person ♦ nm personnel, staff; ~**idad** nf personality
personarse [perso'narse] vr to appear in

person

personificar [personifi'kar] *vt* to personify

perspectiva [perspek'tiβa] *nf* perspective; (*vista, panorama*) view, panorama; (*posibilidad futura*) outlook, prospect

perspicacia [perspi'kaθja] *nf* discernment, perspicacity

perspicaz [perspi'kaθ] *adj* shrewd

persuadir [perswa'ðir] *vt* (*gen*) to persuade; (*convencer*) to convince; ~se *vr* to become convinced; **persuasión** *nf* persuasion; **persuasivo, a** *adj* persuasive; convincing

pertenecer [pertene'θer] *vi* to belong; (*fig*) to concern; **perteneciente** *adj*: **perteneciente a** belonging to; **pertenencia** *nf* ownership; **pertenencias** *nfpl* (*bienes*) possessions, property *sg*

pertenezca *etc vb ver* **pertenecer**

pértiga ['pertiva] *nf*: **salto de ~** pole vault

pertinente [perti'nente] *adj* relevant, pertinent; (*apropiado*) appropriate; **~ a** concerning, relevant to

perturbación [perturβa'θjon] *nf* (*POL*) disturbance; (*MED*) upset, disturbance

perturbado, a [pertur'βaðo, a] *adj* mentally unbalanced

perturbar [pertur'βar] *vt* (*el orden*) to disturb; (*MED*) to upset, disturb; (*mentalmente*) to perturb

Perú [pe'ru] *nm*: **el ~** Peru; **peruano, a** *adj, nm/f* Peruvian

perversión [perβer'sjon] *nf* perversion; **perverso, a** *adj* perverse; (*depravado*) depraved

pervertido, a [perβer'tiðo, a] *adj* perverted ♦ *nm/f* pervert

pervertir [perβer'tir] *vt* to pervert, corrupt

pesa ['pesa] *nf* weight; (*DEPORTE*) shot

pesadez [pesa'ðeθ] *nf* (*peso*) heaviness; (*lentitud*) slowness; (*aburrimiento*) tediousness

pesadilla [pesa'ðiʎa] *nf* nightmare, bad dream

pesado, a [pe'saðo, a] *adj* heavy; (*lento*) slow; (*difícil, duro*) tough, hard; (*aburrido*)

boring, tedious; (*tiempo*) sultry

pésame ['pesame] *nm* expression of condolence, message of sympathy; **dar el ~** to express one's condolences

pesar [pe'sar] *vt* to weigh ♦ *vi* to weigh; (*ser pesado*) to weigh a lot, be heavy; (*fig: opinión*) to carry weight; **no pesa mucho** it is not very heavy ♦ *nm* (*arrepentimiento*) regret; (*pena*) grief, sorrow; **a ~ de** *o* **pese a (que)** in spite of, despite

pesca ['peska] *nf* (*acto*) fishing; (*lo pescado*) catch; **ir de ~** to go fishing

pescadería [peskaðe'ria] *nf* fish shop, fishmonger's (*BRIT*)

pescadilla [peska'ðiʎa] *nf* whiting

pescado [pes'kaðo] *nm* fish

pescador, a [peska'ðor, a] *nm/f* fisherman/woman

pescar [pes'kar] *vt* (*tomar*) to catch; (*intentar tomar*) to fish for; (*conseguir: trabajo*) to manage to get ♦ *vi* to fish, go fishing

pescuezo [pes'kweθo] *nm* neck

pesebre [pe'seβre] *nm* manger

peseta [pe'seta] *nf* peseta

pesimista [pesi'mista] *adj* pessimistic ♦ *nm/f* pessimist

pésimo, a ['pesimo, a] *adj* awful, dreadful

peso ['peso] *nm* weight; (*balanza*) scales *pl*; (*moneda*) peso; **~ bruto/neto** gross/ net weight; **vender al ~** to sell by weight

pesquero, a [pes'kero, a] *adj* fishing *cpd*

pesquisa [pes'kisa] *nf* inquiry, investigation

pestaña [pes'taɲa] *nf* (*ANAT*) eyelash; (*borde*) rim; **pestañear** *vi* to blink

peste ['peste] *nf* plague; (*mal olor*) stink, stench

pesticida [pesti'θiða] *nm* pesticide

pestillo [pes'tiʎo] *nm* (*cerrojo*) bolt; (*picaporte*) doorhandle

petaca [pe'taka] *nf* (*de cigarros*) cigarette case; (*de pipa*) tobacco pouch; (*AM: maleta*) suitcase

pétalo ['petalo] *nm* petal

petardo [pe'tardo] *nm* firework, firecracker

petición [peti'θjon] nf (pedido) request, plea; (memorial) petition; (JUR) plea

petrificar [petrifi'kar] vt to petrify

petróleo [pe'troleo] nm oil, petroleum; **petrolero, a** adj petroleum cpd ♦ nm (oil) tanker

peyorativo, a [pejora'tiβo, a] adj pejorative

pez [peθ] nm fish

pezón [pe'θon] nm teat, nipple

pezuña [pe'θuɲa] nf hoof

piadoso, a [pja'ðoso, a] adj (devoto) pious, devout; (misericordioso) kind, merciful

pianista [pja'nista] nm/f pianist

piano ['pjano] nm piano

piar [pjar] vi to cheep

pibe, a ['piβe, a] (AM) nm/f boy/girl

picadero [pika'ðero] nm riding school

picadillo [pika'ðiʎo] nm mince, minced meat

picado, a [pi'kaðo, a] adj pricked, punctured; (CULIN) minced, chopped; (mar) choppy; (diente) bad; (tabaco) cut; (enfadado) cross

picador [pika'ðor] nm (TAUR) picador; (minero) faceworker

picadura [pika'ðura] nf (pinchazo) puncture; (de abeja) sting; (de mosquito) bite; (tabaco picado) cut tobacco

picante [pi'kante] adj hot; (comentario) racy, spicy

picaporte [pika'porte] nm (manija) doorhandle; (pestillo) latch

picar [pi'kar] vt (agujerear, perforar) to prick, puncture; (abeja) to sting; (mosquito, serpiente) to bite; (CULIN) to mince, chop; (incitar) to incite, goad; (dañar, irritar) to annoy, bother; (quemar: lengua) to burn, sting ♦ vi (pez) to bite, take the bait; (sol) to burn, scorch; (abeja, MED) to sting; (mosquito) to bite; **~se** vr (agriarse) to turn sour, go off; (ofenderse) to take offence

picardía [pikar'ðia] nf villainy; (astucia) slyness, craftiness; (una ~) dirty trick; (palabra) rude/bad word o expression

pícaro, a ['pikaro, a] adj (malicioso) villainous; (travieso) mischievous ♦ nm (astuto) crafty sort; (sinvergüenza) rascal, scoundrel

pichón [pi'tʃon] nm young pigeon

pico ['piko] nm (de ave) beak; (punta) sharp point; (TEC) pick, pickaxe; (GEO) peak, summit; **y ~** and a bit

picor [pi'kor] nm itch

picotear [pikote'ar] vt to peck ♦ vi to nibble, pick

picudo, a [pi'kuðo, a] adj pointed, with a point

pidió etc vb ver **pedir**

pido etc vb ver **pedir**

pie [pje] (pl ~s) nm foot; (fig: motivo) motive, basis; (: fundamento) foothold; **ir a ~** to go on foot, walk; **estar de ~** to be standing (up); **ponerse de ~** to stand up; **de ~s a cabeza** from top to bottom; **al ~ de la letra** (citar) literally, verbatim; (copiar) exactly, word for word; **en ~ de guerra** on a war footing; **dar ~ a** to give cause for; **hacer ~** (en el agua) to touch (the) bottom

piedad [pje'ðað] nf (lástima) pity, compassion; (clemencia) mercy; (devoción) piety, devotion

piedra ['pjeðra] nf stone; (roca) rock; (de mechero) flint; (METEOROLOGÍA) hailstone

piel [pjel] nf (ANAT) skin; (ZOOL) skin, hide, fur; (cuero) leather; (BOT) skin, peel

pienso etc vb ver **pensar**

pierdo etc vb ver **perder**

pierna ['pjerna] nf leg

pieza ['pjeθa] nf piece; (habitación) room; **~ de recambio** o **repuesto** spare (part)

pigmeo, a [piɣ'meo, a] adj, nm/f pigmy

pijama [pi'xama] nm pyjamas pl

pila ['pila] nf (ELEC) battery; (montón) heap, pile; (lavabo) sink

píldora ['pildora] nf pill; **la ~ (anticonceptiva)** the (contraceptive) pill

pileta [pi'leta] nf basin, bowl; (AM) swimming pool

pillaje [pi'ʎaxe] nm pillage, plunder

pillar [pi'ʎar] vt (saquear) to pillage,

plunder; (*fam: coger*) to catch; (: *agarrar*) to grasp, seize; (: *entender*) to grasp, catch on to; **~se** *vr:* **~se un dedo con la puerta** to catch one's finger in the door

pillo, a ['piʎo, a] *adj* villainous; (*astuto*) sly, crafty ♦ *nm/f* rascal, rogue, scoundrel

piloto [pi'loto] *nm* pilot; (*de aparato*) (pilot) light; (AUTO: *luz*) tail *o* rear light; (: *conductor*) driver

pimentón [pimen'ton] *nm* paprika

pimienta [pi'mjenta] *nf* pepper

pimiento [pi'mjento] *nm* pepper, pimiento

pin [pin] (*pl* **pins**) *nm* badge

pinacoteca [pinako'teka] *nf* art gallery

pinar [pi'nar] *nm* pine forest (BRIT), pine grove (US)

pincel [pin'θel] *nm* paintbrush

pinchadiscos [pintʃa'ðiskos] *nm/f inv* disc-jockey, DJ

pinchar [pin'tʃar] *vt* (*perforar*) to prick, pierce; (*neumático*) to puncture; (*fig*) to prod

pinchazo [pin'tʃaθo] *nm* (*perforación*) prick; (*de neumático*) puncture; (*fig*) prod

pincho ['pintʃo] *nm* savoury (snack); **~ moruno** shish kebab; **~ de tortilla** small slice of omelette

ping-pong ['pin'pon] *nm* table tennis

pingüino [pin'gwino] *nm* penguin

pino ['pino] *nm* pine (tree)

pinta ['pinta] *nf* spot, drop; (*de líquidos*) spot, drop; (*aspecto*) appearance, look(s) (*pl*); **~do, a** *adj* spotted; (*de colores*) colourful; **~das** *nfpl* graffiti *sg*

pintar [pin'tar] *vt* to paint ♦ *vi* to paint; (*fam*) to count, be important; **~se** *vr* to put on make-up

pintor, a [pin'tor, a] *nm/f* painter

pintoresco, a [pinto'resko, a] *adj* picturesque

pintura [pin'tura] *nf* painting; **~ a la acuarela** watercolour; **~ al óleo** oil painting

pinza ['pinθa] *nf* (ZOOL) claw; (*para colgar ropa*) clothes peg; (TEC) pincers *pl*; **~s** *nfpl* (*para depilar etc*) tweezers *pl*

piña ['piɲa] *nf* (*fruto del pino*) pine cone; (*fruta*) pineapple; (*fig*) group

piñón [pi'ɲon] *nm* (*fruto*) pine nut; (TEC) pinion

pío, a ['pio, a] *adj* (*devoto*) pious, devout; (*misericordioso*) merciful

piojo ['pjoxo] *nm* louse

pionero, a [pjo'nero, a] *adj* pioneering ♦ *nm/f* pioneer

pipa ['pipa] *nf* pipe; **~s** *nfpl* (BOT) (edible) sunflower seeds

pipí [pi'pi] (*fam*) *nm:* **hacer ~** to have a wee(-wee) (BRIT), have to go (wee-wee) (US)

pique ['pike] *nm* (*resentimiento*) pique, resentment; (*rivalidad*) rivalry, competition; **irse a ~** to sink; (*esperanza, familia*) to be ruined

piqueta [pi'keta] *nf* pick(axe)

piquete [pi'kete] *nm* (MIL) squad, party; (*de obreros*) picket

pirado, a [pi'raðo, a] (*fam*) *adj* round the bend ♦ *nm/f* nutter

piragua [pi'raɣwa] *nf* canoe; **piragüismo** *nm* canoeing

pirámide [pi'ramiðe] *nf* pyramid

pirata [pi'rata] *adj*, *nm* pirate ♦ *nm/f:* **~ informático/a** hacker

Pirineo(s) [piri'neo(s)] *nm(pl)* Pyrenees *pl*

pirómano, a [pi'romano, a] *nm/f* (MED, JUR) arsonist

piropo [pi'ropo] *nm* compliment, (piece of) flattery

pirueta [pi'rweta] *nf* pirouette

pis [pis] (*fam*) *nm* pee, piss; **hacer ~** to have a pee; (*para niños*) to wee-wee

pisada [pi'saða] *nf* (*paso*) footstep; (*huella*) footprint

pisar [pi'sar] *vt* (*caminar sobre*) to walk on, tread on; (*apretar con el pie*) to press; (*fig*) to trample on, walk all over ♦ *vi* to tread, step, walk

piscina [pis'θina] *nf* swimming pool

Piscis ['pisθis] *nm* Pisces

piso ['piso] *nm* (*suelo, planta*) floor; (*apartamento*) flat (BRIT), apartment; **primer ~** (ESP) first floor; (AM) ground floor

pisotear [pisote'ar] *vt* to trample (on *o* underfoot)

pista ['pista] *nf* track, trail; (*indicio*) clue; ~ **de aterrizaje** runway; ~ **de baile** dance floor; ~ **de hielo** ice rink; ~ **de tenis** tennis court

pistola [pis'tola] *nf* pistol; (*TEC*) spray-gun; **pistolero, a** *nm/f* gunman/woman, gangster

pistón [pis'ton] *nm* (*TEC*) piston; (*MUS*) key

pitar [pi'tar] *vt* (*silbato*) to blow; (*rechiflar*) to whistle at, boo ♦ *vi* to whistle; (*AUTO*) to sound *o* toot one's horn; (*AM*) to smoke

pitillo [pi'tiʎo] *nm* cigarette

pito ['pito] *nm* whistle; (*de coche*) horn

pitón [pi'ton] *nm* (*ZOOL*) python

pitonisa [pito'nisa] *nf* fortune-teller

pitorreo [pito'rreo] *nm* joke; **estar de** ~ to be joking

pizarra [pi'θarra] *nf* (*piedra*) slate; (*encerado*) blackboard

pizca ['piθka] *nf* pinch, spot; (*fig*) spot, speck; **ni** ~ not a bit

placa ['plaka] *nf* plate; (*distintivo*) badge, insignia; ~ **de matrícula** number plate

placentero, a [plaθen'tero, a] *adj* pleasant, agreeable

placer [pla'θer] *nm* pleasure ♦ *vt* to please

plácido, a ['plaθiðo, a] *adj* placid

plaga ['plaɣa] *nf* pest; (*MED*) plague; (*abundancia*) abundance; **plagar** *vt* to infest, plague; (*llenar*) to fill

plagio ['plaxjo] *nm* plagiarism

plan [plan] *nm* (*esquema, proyecto*) plan; (*idea, intento*) idea, intention; **tener** ~ (*fam*) to have a date; **tener un** ~ (*fam*) to have an affair; **en** ~ **económico** (*fam*) on the cheap; **vamos en** ~ **de turismo** we're going as tourists; **si te pones en ese** ~ ... if that's your attitude ...

plana ['plana] *nf* sheet (of paper), page; (*TEC*) trowel; **en primera** ~ on the front page; ~ **mayor** staff

plancha ['plantʃa] *nf* (*para planchar*) iron; (*rótulo*) plate, sheet; (*NAUT*) gangway; **a la** ~ (*CULIN*) grilled; ~**do** *nm* ironing;

planchar *vt* to iron ♦ *vi* to do the ironing

planeador [planea'ðor] *nm* glider

planear [plane'ar] *vt* to plan ♦ *vi* to glide

planeta [pla'neta] *nm* planet

planicie [pla'niθje] *nf* plain

planificación [planifika'θjon] *nf* planning; ~ **familiar** family planning

plano, a ['plano, a] *adj* flat, level, even ♦ *nm* (*MAT, TEC*) plane; (*FOTO*) shot; (*ARQ*) plan; (*GEO*) map; (*de ciudad*) map, street plan; **primer** ~ close-up; **caer de** ~ to fall flat

planta ['planta] *nf* (*BOT, TEC*) plant; (*ANAT*) sole of the foot, foot; (*piso*) floor; (*AM: personal*) staff; ~ **baja** ground floor

plantación [planta'θjon] *nf* (*AGR*) plantation; (*acto*) planting

plantar [plan'tar] *vt* (*BOT*) to plant; (*levantar*) to erect, set up; ~**se** *vr* to stand firm; ~ **a uno en la calle** to throw sb out; **dejar plantado a uno** (*fam*) to stand sb up

plantear [plante'ar] *vt* (*problema*) to pose; (*dificultad*) to raise

plantilla [plan'tiʎa] *nf* (*de zapato*) insole; (*personal*) personnel; **ser de** ~ to be on the staff

plantón [plan'ton] *nm* (*MIL*) guard, sentry; (*fam*) long wait; **dar (un)** ~ **a uno** to stand sb up

plasmar [plas'mar] *vt* (*dar forma*) to mould, shape; (*representar*) to represent; ~**se** *vr*: ~**se en** to take the form of

plasta ['plasta] (*fam*) *adj inv* boring ♦ *nm/f* bore

plástico, a ['plastiko, a] *adj* plastic ♦ *nm* plastic

Plastilina ® [plasti'lina] *nf* Plasticine ®

plata ['plata] *nf* (*metal*) silver; (*cosas hechas de* ~) silverware; (*AM*) cash, dough; **hablar en** ~ to speak bluntly *o* frankly

plataforma [plata'forma] *nf* platform; ~ **de lanzamiento/perforación** launch(ing) pad/drilling rig

plátano ['platano] *nm* (*fruta*) banana;

(*árbol*) plane tree; banana tree
platea [pla'tea] *nf* (*TEATRO*) pit
plateado, a [plate'aðo, a] *adj* silver; (*TEC*)
silver-plated
plática ['platika] *nf* talk, chat; **platicar** *vi*
to talk, chat
platillo [pla'tiʎo] *nm* saucer; ~s *nmpl*
(*MUS*) cymbals; ~ **volador** *o* **volante**
flying saucer
platino [pla'tino] *nm* platinum; ~s *nmpl*
(*AUTO*) contact points
plato ['plato] *nm* plate, dish; (*parte de
comida*) course; (*comida*) dish; ~
combinado set main course (*served on
one plate*); ~ **fuerte** main course; **primer**
~ first course
playa ['plaja] *nf* beach; (*costa*) seaside; ~
de estacionamiento (*AM*) car park
playera [pla'jera] *nf* (*AM*: *camiseta*) T-shirt;
~s *nfpl* (*zapatos*) canvas shoes
plaza ['plaθa] *nf* square; (*mercado*)
market(place); (*sitio*) room, space; (*en
vehículo*) seat, place; (*colocación*) post,
job; ~ **de toros** bullring
plazo ['plaθo] *nm* (*lapso de tiempo*) time,
period; (*fecha de vencimiento*) expiry date;
(*pago parcial*) instalment; **a corto/largo** ~
short-/long-term; **comprar algo a** ~s to
buy sth on hire purchase (*BRIT*) *o* on time
(*US*)
plazoleta [plaθo'leta] *nf* small square
pleamar [plea'mar] *nf* high tide
plebe ['pleβe] *nf*: **la** ~ the common people
pl, the masses *pl*; (*pey*) the plebs *pl*; ~**yo,
a** *adj* plebeian; (*pey*) coarse, common
plebiscito [pleβis'θito] *nm* plebiscite
plegable [ple'vaβle] *adj* collapsible; (*silla*)
folding
plegar [ple'var] *vt* (*doblar*) to fold, bend;
(*COSTURA*) to pleat; ~**se** *vr* to yield,
submit
pleito ['pleito] *nm* (*JUR*) lawsuit, case; (*fig*)
dispute, feud
plenilunio [pleni'lunjo] *nm* full moon
plenitud [pleni'tuð] *nf* plenitude, fullness;
(*abundancia*) abundance
pleno, a ['pleno, a] *adj* full; (*completo*)

complete ♦ *nm* plenum; **en** ~ **día** in
broad daylight; **en** ~ **verano** at the
height of summer; **en plena cara** full in
the face
pliego *etc* ['pljeχo] *vb ver* **plegar** ♦ *nm*
(*hoja*) sheet (of paper); (*carta*) sealed
letter/document; ~ **de condiciones**
details *pl*, specifications *pl*
pliegue *etc* ['pljeχe] *vb ver* **plegar** ♦ *nm*
fold, crease; (*de vestido*) pleat
plomero [plo'mero] *nm* (*AM*) plumber
plomo ['plomo] *nm* (*metal*) lead; (*ELEC*)
fuse; **sin** ~ unleaded
pluma ['pluma] *nf* feather; (*para escribir*): ~
(**estilográfica**) ink pen; ~ **fuente** (*AM*)
fountain pen
plumero [plu'mero] *nm* (*para el polvo*)
feather duster
plumón [plu'mon] *nm* (*de ave*) down;
(*AM*: *fino*) felt-tip pen; (: *ancho*) marker
plural [plu'ral] *adj* plural; ~**idad** *nf*
plurality
pluriempleo [pluriem'pleo] *nm* having
more than one job
plus [plus] *nm* bonus; ~**valía** *nf* (*COM*)
appreciation
población [poβla'θjon] *nf* population;
(*pueblo, ciudad*) town, city
poblado, a [po'blaðo, a] *adj* inhabited
♦ *nm* (*aldea*) village; (*pueblo*) (small)
town; **densamente** ~ densely populated
poblador, a [poβla'ðor, a] *nm/f* settler,
colonist
poblar [po'βlar] *vt* (*colonizar*) to colonize;
(*fundar*) to found; (*habitar*) to inhabit
pobre ['poβre] *adj* poor ♦ *nm/f* poor
person; ~**za** *nf* poverty
pocilga [po'θilxa] *nf* pigsty
pócima ['poθima] *nf* potion

PALABRA CLAVE

poco, a ['poko, a] *adj* **1** (*sg*) little, not
much; ~ **tiempo** little *o* not much time;
de ~ **interés** of little interest, not very
interesting; **poca cosa** not much
2 (*pl*) few, not many; **unos** ~s a few,
some; ~s **niños comen lo que les**

conviene few children eat what they should

♦ *adv* **1** little, not much; **cuesta ~** it doesn't cost much

2 (+*adj*: = *negativo, antónimo*): **~ amable/inteligente** not very nice/intelligent

3: por ~ me caigo I almost fell

4: a ~: a ~ de haberse casado shortly after getting married

5: ~ a ~ little by little

♦ *nm* a little, a bit; **un ~ triste/de dinero** a little sad/money

podar [po'ðar] *vt* to prune

PALABRA CLAVE

poder [po'ðer] *vi* **1** (*capacidad*) can, be able to; **no puedo hacerlo** I can't do it, I'm unable to do it

2 (*permiso*) can, may, be allowed to; **¿se puede?** may I (*o* we)?; **puedes irte ahora** you may go now; **no se puede fumar en este hospital** smoking is not allowed in this hospital

3 (*posibilidad*) may, might, could; **puede llegar mañana** he may *o* might arrive tomorrow; **pudiste haberte hecho daño** you might *o* could have hurt yourself; **¡podías habérmelo dicho antes!** you might have told me before!

4: puede ser perhaps; **puede ser que lo sepa Tomás** Tomás may *o* might know

5: ¡no puedo más! I've had enough!; **no pude menos que dejarlo** I couldn't help but leave it; **es tonto a más no ~** he's as stupid as they come

6: ~ con: no puedo con este crío this kid's too much for me

♦ *nm* power; **~ adquisitivo** purchasing power; **detentar** *o* **ocupar** *o* **estar en el ~** to be in power

---

poderoso, a [poðe'roso, a] *adj* (*político, país*) powerful

podio ['poðjo] *nm* (*DEPORTE*) podium

podium ['poðjum] = **podio**

podrido, a [po'ðriðo, a] *adj* rotten, bad; (*fig*) rotten, corrupt

podrir [po'ðrir] = **pudrir**

poema [po'ema] *nm* poem

poesía [poe'sia] *nf* poetry

poeta [po'eta] *nm/f* poet; **poético, a** *adj* poetic(al)

poetisa [poe'tisa] *nf* (woman) poet

póker ['poker] *nm* poker

polaco, a [po'lako, a] *adj* Polish ♦ *nm/f* Pole

polar [po'lar] *adj* polar; **~idad** *nf* polarity; **~izarse** *vr* to polarize

polea [po'lea] *nf* pulley

polémica [po'lemika] *nf* polemics *sg*; (*una ~*) controversy, polemic

polen ['polen] *nm* pollen

policía [poli'θia] *nm/f* policeman/woman ♦ *nf* police; **~co, a** *adj* police *cpd*; **novela policíaca** detective story; **policial** *adj* police *cpd*

polideportivo [poliðepor'tiβo] *nm* sports centre *o* complex

poligamia [poli'vamja] *nf* polygamy

polígono [po'livono] *nm* (*MAT*) polygon; **~ industrial** industrial estate

polilla [po'liʎa] *nf* moth

polio ['poljo] *nf* polio

política [po'litika] *nf* politics *sg*; (*económica, agraria etc*) policy; *ver tb* **político**

político, a [po'litiko, a] *adj* political; (*discreto*) tactful; (*de familia*) -in-law ♦ *nm/f* politician; **padre ~** father-in-law

póliza ['poliθa] *nf* certificate, voucher; (*impuesto*) tax stamp; **~ de seguros** insurance policy

polizón [poli'θon] *nm* stowaway

pollera [po'ʎera] (*AM*) *nf* skirt

pollería [poʎe'ria] *nf* poulterer's (shop)

pollo ['poʎo] *nm* chicken

polo ['polo] *nm* (*GEO, ELEC*) pole; (*helado*) ice lolly; (*DEPORTE*) polo; (*suéter*) polo-neck; **~ Norte/Sur** North/South Pole

Polonia [po'lonja] *nf* Poland

poltrona [pol'trona] *nf* easy chair

polución [polu'θjon] nf pollution

polvera [pol'βera] nf powder compact

polvo ['polβo] nm dust; (QUÍM, CULIN, MED) powder; **~s** nmpl (maquillaje) powder sg; **quitar el ~** to dust; **~ de talco** talcum powder; **estar hecho ~** (fam) to be worn out o exhausted

pólvora ['polβora] nf gunpowder; (fuegos artificiales) fireworks pl

polvoriento, a [polβo'rjento, a] adj (superficie) dusty; (sustancia) powdery

pomada [po'maða] nf cream, ointment

pomelo [po'melo] nm grapefruit

pómez ['pomeθ] nf: **piedra ~** pumice stone

pomo ['pomo] nm doorknob

pompa ['pompa] nf (burbuja) bubble; (bomba) pump; (esplendor) pomp, splendour; **pomposo, a** adj splendid, magnificent; (pey) pompous

pómulo ['pomulo] nm cheekbone

pon [pon] vb ver **poner**

ponche ['pontʃe] nm punch

poncho ['pontʃo] nm poncho

ponderar [ponde'rar] vt (considerar) to weigh up, consider; (elogiar) to praise highly, speak in praise of

pondré etc vb ver **poner**

PALABRA CLAVE

poner [po'ner] vt 1 (colocar) to put; (telegrama) to send; (obra de teatro) to put on; (película) to show; **ponlo más fuerte** turn it up; **¿qué ponen en el Excelsior?** what's on at the Excelsior?
2 (tienda) to open; (instalar: gas etc) to put in; (radio, TV) to switch o turn on
3 (suponer): **pongamos que ...** let's suppose that ...
4 (contribuir): **el gobierno ha puesto otro millón** the government has contributed another million
5 (TELEC): **póngame con el Sr. López** can you put me through to Mr. López?
6: **~ de:** le han puesto de director **general** they've appointed him general manager

7 (+adj) to make; **me estás poniendo nerviosa** you're making me nervous
8 (dar nombre): **al hijo le pusieron Diego** they called their son Diego
♦ vi (gallina) to lay
♦ **~se** vr 1 (colocarse): **se puso a mi lado** he came and stood beside me; **tú ponte en esa silla** you go and sit on that chair
2 (vestido, cosméticos) to put on; **¿por qué no te pones el vestido nuevo?** why don't you put on o wear your new dress?
3 (+adj) to turn; to get, become; **se puso muy serio** he got very serious; **después de lavarla la tela se puso azul** after washing it the material turned blue
4: **~se a: se puso a llorar** he started to cry; **tienes que ~te a estudiar** you must get down to studying
5: **~se a bien con uno** to make it up with sb; **~se a mal con uno** to get on the wrong side of sb

---

pongo etc vb ver **poner**

poniente [po'njente] nm (occidente) west; (viento) west wind

pontífice [pon'tifiθe] nm pope, pontiff

popa ['popa] nf stern

popular [popu'lar] adj popular; (cultura) of the people, folk cpd; **~idad** nf popularity; **~izarse** vr to become popular

---

PALABRA CLAVE

por [por] prep 1 (objetivo) for; **luchar ~ la patria** to fight for one's country
2 (+infin): **~ no llegar tarde** so as not to arrive late; **~ citar unos ejemplos** to give a few examples
3 (causa) out of, because of; **~ escasez de fondos** through o for lack of funds
4 (tiempo): **~ la mañana/noche** in the morning/at night; **se queda ~ una semana** she's staying (for) a week
5 (lugar): **pasar ~ Madrid** to pass through Madrid; **ir a Guayaquil ~ Quito** to go to Guayaquil via Quito; **caminar ~ la calle** to walk along the street; ver tb

todo

6 (*cambio, precio*): **te doy uno nuevo ~ el que tienes** I'll give you a new one (in return) for the one you've got

7 (*valor distributivo*): **550 pesetas ~ hora/cabeza** 550 pesetas an *o* per hour/ a *o* per head

8 (*modo, medio*) by; **~ correo/avión** by post/air; **día ~ día** day by day; **entrar ~ la entrada principal** to go in through the main entrance

9: **10 ~ 10 son 100** 10 times 10 is 100

10 (*en lugar de*): **vino él ~ su jefe** he came instead of his boss

11: **~ mí que revienten** as far as I'm concerned they can drop dead

12: **¿~ qué?** why?; **¿~ qué no?** why not?

---

porcelana [porθe'lana] *nf* porcelain; (*china*) china

porcentaje [porθen'taxe] *nm* percentage

porción [por'θjon] *nf* (*parte*) portion, share; (*cantidad*) quantity, amount

pordiosero, a [pordjo'sero, a] *nm/f* beggar

porfiar [por'fjar] *vi* to persist, insist; (*disputar*) to argue stubbornly

pormenor [porme'nor] *nm* detail, particular

pornografía [pornovra'fia] *nf* pornography

poro ['poro] *nm* pore; **~so, a** *adj* porous

porque ['porke] *conj* (*a causa de*) because; (*ya que*) since; (*con el fin de*) so that, in order that

porqué [por'ke] *nm* reason, cause

porquería [porke'ria] *nf* (*suciedad*) filth, dirt; (*acción*) dirty trick; (*objeto*) small thing, trifle; (*fig*) rubbish

porra ['porra] *nf* (*arma*) stick, club

porrazo [po'rraθo] *nm* blow, bump

porro ['porro] (*fam*) *nm* (*droga*) joint (*fam*)

porrón [po'rron] *nm* glass wine jar with a long spout

portaaviones [porta'(a)ßjones] *nm inv* aircraft carrier

portada [por'taða] *nf* (*de revista*) cover

portador, a [porta'ðor, a] *nm/f* carrier, bearer; (*COM*) bearer, payee

portaequipajes [portaeki'paxes] *nm inv* (*AUTO: maletero*) boot; (: *baca*) luggage rack

portal [por'tal] *nm* (*entrada*) vestibule, hall; (*portada*) porch, doorway; (*puerta de entrada*) main door

portamaletas [portama'letas] *nm inv* (*AUTO: maletero*) boot; (: *baca*) roof rack

portarse [por'tarse] *vr* to behave, conduct o.s.

portátil [por'tatil] *adj* portable

portavoz [porta'ßoθ] *nm/f* spokesman/ woman

portazo [por'taθo] *nm*: **dar un ~** to slam the door

porte ['porte] *nm* (*COM*) transport; (*precio*) transport charges *pl*

portento [por'tento] *nm* marvel, wonder; **~so, a** *adj* marvellous, extraordinary

porteño, a [por'teɲo, a] *adj* of *o* from Buenos Aires

portería [porte'ria] *nf* (*oficina*) porter's office; (*DEPORTE*) goal

portero, a [por'tero, a] *nm/f* porter; (*conserje*) caretaker; (*ujier*) doorman; (*DEPORTE*) goalkeeper; **~ automático** intercom

pórtico ['portiko] *nm* (*patio*) portico, porch; (*fig*) gateway; (*arcada*) arcade

portorriqueño, a [portorri'keɲo, a] *adj* Puerto Rican

Portugal [portu'val] *nm* Portugal; **portugués, esa** *adj, nm/f* Portuguese ♦ *nm* (*LING*) Portuguese

porvenir [porße'nir] *nm* future

pos [pos] *prep*: **en ~ de** after, in pursuit of

posada [po'saða] *nf* (*refugio*) shelter, lodging; (*mesón*) guest house; **dar ~ a** to give shelter to, take in

posaderas [posa'ðeras] *nfpl* backside *sg*, buttocks

posar [po'sar] *vt* (*en el suelo*) to lay down, put down; (*la mano*) to place, put gently ♦ *vi* (*modelo*) to sit, pose; **~se** *vr* to settle; (*pájaro*) to perch; (*avión*) to land, come down

posavasos [posa'basos] *nm inv* coaster; (*para cerveza*) beermat

posdata [pos'ðata] *nf* postscript

pose ['pose] *nf* pose

poseedor, a [posee'ðor, a] *nm/f* owner, possessor; (*de récord, puesto*) holder

poseer [pose'er] *vt* to possess, own; (*ventaja*) to enjoy; (*récord, puesto*) to hold

posesión [pose'sjon] *nf* possession; **posesionarse** *vr*: **posesionarse de** to take possession of, take over

posesivo, a [pose'siβo, a] *adj* possessive

posgrado [pos'graðo] *nm*: **curso de ~** postgraduate course

posibilidad [posiβili'ðað] *nf* possibility; (*oportunidad*) chance; **posibilitar** *vt* to make possible; (*hacer realizable*) to make feasible

posible [po'siβle] *adj* possible; (*realizable*) feasible; **de ser ~** if possible; **en lo ~** as far as possible

posición [posi'θjon] *nf* position; (*rango social*) status

positivo, a [posi'tiβo, a] *adj* positive

poso ['poso] *nm* sediment; (*heces*) dregs *pl*

posponer [pospo'ner] *vt* (*relegar*) to put behind/below; (*aplazar*) to postpone

posta ['posta] *nf*: **a ~** deliberately, on purpose

postal [pos'tal] *adj* postal ♦ *nf* postcard

poste ['poste] *nm* (*de telégrafos etc*) post, pole; (*columna*) pillar

póster ['poster] (*pl* **pósteres, pósters**) *nm* poster

postergar [poster'xar] *vt* to postpone, delay

posteridad [posteri'ðað] *nf* posterity

posterior [poste'rjor] *adj* back, rear; (*siguiente*) following, subsequent; (*más tarde*) later; **~idad** *nf*: **con ~idad** later, subsequently

postgrado [post'graðo] *nm* = **posgrado**

postizo, a [pos'tiθo, a] *adj* false, artificial ♦ *nm* hairpiece

postor, a [pos'tor, a] *nm/f* bidder

postre ['postre] *nm* sweet, dessert

postrero, a [pos'trero, a] (*delante de nmsg*: **postrer**) *adj* (*último*) last; (*que viene detrás*) rear

postulado [postu'laðo] *nm* postulate

póstumo, a ['postumo, a] *adj* posthumous

postura [pos'tura] *nf* (*del cuerpo*) posture, position; (*fig*) attitude, position

potable [po'taβle] *adj* drinkable; **agua ~** drinking water

potaje [po'taxe] *nm* thick vegetable soup

pote ['pote] *nm* pot, jar

potencia [po'tenθja] *nf* power; **~l** [poten'θjal] *adj, nm* potential; **~r** *vt* to boost

potente [po'tente] *adj* powerful

potro, a ['potro, a] *nm/f* (*ZOOL*) colt/filly ♦ *nm* (*de gimnasia*) vaulting horse

pozo ['poθo] *nm* well; (*de río*) deep pool; (*de mina*) shaft

P.P. *abr* (= *porte pagado*) CP

práctica ['praktika] *nf* practice; (*método*) method; (*arte, capacidad*) skill; **en la ~** in practice

practicable [prakti'kaβle] *adj* practicable; (*camino*) passable

practicante [prakti'kante] *nm/f* (*MED*: *ayudante de doctor*) medical assistant; (: *enfermero*) nurse; (*quien practica algo*) practitioner ♦ *adj* practising

practicar [prakti'kar] *vt* to practise; (*DEPORTE*) to play; (*realizar*) to carry out, perform

práctico, a ['praktiko, a] *adj* practical; (*instruído*: *persona*) skilled, expert

practique *etc vb ver* **practicar**

pradera [pra'ðera] *nf* meadow; (*US etc*) prairie

prado ['praðo] *nm* (*campo*) meadow, field; (*pastizal*) pasture

Praga ['praxa] *n* Prague

pragmático, a [prax'matiko, a] *adj* pragmatic

preámbulo [pre'ambulo] *nm* preamble, introduction

precario, a [pre'karjo, a] *adj* precarious

precaución [prekau'θjon] *nf* (*medida preventiva*) preventive measure, precaution; (*prudencia*) caution, wariness

precaver [preka'ßer] *vt* to guard against; (*impedir*) to forestall; **~se** *vr*: **~se de** *o* **contra algo** to (be on one's) guard against sth; **precavido, a** *adj* cautious, wary

precedente [preθe'ðente] *adj* preceding; (*anterior*) former ♦ *nm* precedent

preceder [preθe'ðer] *vt, vi* to precede, go before, come before

precepto [pre'θepto] *nm* precept

preciado, a [pre'θjaðo, a] *adj* (*estimado*) esteemed, valuable

preciarse [pre'θjarse] *vr* to boast; **~se de** to pride o.s. on, boast of being

precinto [pre'θinto] *nm* (*tb*: **~ de garantía**) seal

precio ['preθjo] *nm* price; (*costo*) cost; (*valor*) value, worth; (*de viaje*) fare; **~ al contado/de coste/de oportunidad** cash/cost/bargain price; **~ al detalle** *o* **al por menor** retail price; **~ tope** top price

preciosidad [preθjosi'ðað] *nf* (*valor*) (high) value, (great) worth; (*encanto*) charm; (*cosa bonita*) beautiful thing; **es una ~** it's lovely, it's really beautiful

precioso, a [pre'θjoso, a] *adj* precious; (*de mucho valor*) valuable; (*fam*) lovely, beautiful

precipicio [preθi'piθjo] *nm* cliff, precipice; (*fig*) abyss

precipitación [preθipita'θjon] *nf* haste; (*lluvia*) rainfall

precipitado, a [preθipi'taðo, a] *adj* (*conducta*) hasty, rash; (*salida*) hasty, sudden

precipitar [preθipi'tar] *vt* (*arrojar*) to hurl down, throw; (*apresurar*) to hasten; (*acelerar*) to speed up, accelerate; **~se** *vr* to throw o.s.; (*apresurarse*) to rush; (*actuar sin pensar*) to act rashly

precisamente [preθisa'mente] *adv* precisely; (*exactamente*) precisely, exactly

precisar [preθi'sar] *vt* (*necesitar*) to need, require; (*fijar*) to determine exactly, fix;

(*especificar*) to specify

precisión [preθi'sjon] *nf* (*exactitud*) precision

preciso, a [pre'θiso, a] *adj* (*exacto*) precise; (*necesario*) necessary, essential

preconcebido, a [prekonθe'ßiðo, a] *adj* preconceived

precoz [pre'koθ] *adj* (*persona*) precocious; (*calvicie etc*) premature

precursor, a [prekur'sor, a] *nm/f* predecessor, forerunner

predecir [preðe'θir] *vt* to predict, forecast

predestinado, a [preðesti'naðo, a] *adj* predestined

predicar [preði'kar] *vt, vi* to preach

predicción [preðik'θjon] *nf* prediction

predilecto, a [preði'lekto, a] *adj* favourite

predisponer [preðispo'ner] *vt* to predispose; (*pey*) to prejudice; **predisposición** *nf* inclination; prejudice, bias

predominante [preðomi'nante] *adj* predominant

predominar [preðomi'nar] *vt* to dominate ♦ *vi* to predominate; (*prevalecer*) to prevail; **predominio** *nm* predominance; prevalence

preescolar [pre(e)sko'lar] *adj* preschool

prefabricado, a [prefaßri'kaðo, a] *adj* prefabricated

prefacio [pre'faθjo] *nm* preface

preferencia [prefe'renθja] *nf* preference; **de ~** preferably, for preference

preferible [prefe'rißle] *adj* preferable

preferir [prefe'rir] *vt* to prefer

prefiero *etc vb ver* **preferir**

prefijo [pre'fixo] *nm* (*TELEC*) dialling code

pregonar [preɣo'nar] *vt* to proclaim, announce

pregunta [pre'ɣunta] *nf* question; **hacer una ~** to ask a question

preguntar [preɣun'tar] *vt* to ask; (*cuestionar*) to question ♦ *vi* to ask; **~se** *vr* to wonder; **~ por alguien** to ask for sb

preguntón, ona [preɣun'ton, ona] *adj* inquisitive

prehistórico, a [preis'toriko, a] *adj*

prehistoric

prejuicio [pre'xwiθjo] *nm* (*acto*) prejudgement; (*idea preconcebida*) preconception; (*parcialidad*) prejudice, bias

preliminar [prelimi'nar] *adj* preliminary

preludio [pre'luðjo] *nm* prelude

prematuro, a [prema'turo, a] *adj* premature

premeditación [premeðita'θjon] *nf* premeditation

premeditar [premeði'tar] *vt* to premeditate

premiar [pre'mjar] *vt* to reward; (*en un concurso*) to give a prize to

premio ['premjo] *nm* reward; prize; (*COM*) premium

premonición [premoni'θjon] *nf* premonition

prenatal [prena'tal] *adj* antenatal, prenatal

prenda ['prenda] *nf* (*ropa*) garment, article of clothing; (*garantía*) pledge; **~s** *nfpl* (*talentos*) talents, gifts

prendedor [prende'ðor] *nm* brooch

prender [pren'der] *vt* (*captar*) to catch, capture; (*detener*) to arrest; (*COSTURA*) to pin, attach; (*sujetar*) to fasten ♦ *vi* to catch; (*arraigar*) to take root; **~se** *vr* (*encenderse*) to catch fire

prendido, a [pren'diðo, a] (*AM*) *adj* (*luz etc*) on

prensa ['prensa] *nf* press; **la ~** the press; **prensar** *vt* to press

preñado, a [pre'ɲaðo, a] *adj* pregnant; **~ de** pregnant with, full of

preocupación [preokupa'θjon] *nf* worry, concern; (*ansiedad*) anxiety

preocupado, a [preoku'paðo, a] *adj* worried, concerned; (*ansioso*) anxious

preocupar [preoku'par] *vt* to worry; **~se** *vr* to worry; **~se de algo** (*hacerse cargo*) to take care of sth

preparación [prepara'θjon] *nf* (*acto*) preparation; (*estado*) readiness; (*entrenamiento*) training

preparado, a [prepa'raðo, a] *adj* (*dispuesto*) prepared; (*CULIN*) ready (to serve) ♦ *nm* preparation

preparar [prepa'rar] *vt* (*disponer*) to prepare, get ready; (*TEC: tratar*) to prepare, process; (*entrenar*) to teach, train; **~se** *vr*: **~se a** *o* **para** to prepare to *o* for, get ready to *o* for; **preparativo, a** *adj* preparatory, preliminary; **preparativos** *nmpl* preparations; **preparatoria** (*AM*) *nf* sixth-form college (*BRIT*), senior high school (*US*)

prerrogativa [prerrova'tißa] *nf* prerogative, privilege

presa ['presa] *nf* (*cosa apresada*) catch; (*víctima*) victim; (*de animal*) prey; (*de agua*) dam

presagiar [presa'xjar] *vt* to presage, forebode; **presagio** *nm* omen

prescindir [presθin'dir] *vi*: **~ de** (*privarse de*) to do without, go without; (*descartar*) to dispense with

prescribir [preskri'ßir] *vt* to prescribe; **prescripción** *nf* prescription

presencia [pre'senθja] *nf* presence; **presencial** *adj*: **testigo presencial** eyewitness; **presenciar** *vt* to be present at; (*asistir a*) to attend; (*ver*) to see, witness

presentación [presenta'θjon] *nf* presentation; (*introducción*) introduction

presentador, a [presenta'ðor, a] *nm/f* presenter, compère

presentar [presen'tar] *vt* to present; (*ofrecer*) to offer; (*mostrar*) to show, display; (*a una persona*) to introduce; **~se** *vr* (*llegar inesperadamente*) to appear, turn up; (*ofrecerse como candidato*) to run, stand; (*aparecer*) to show, appear; (*solicitar empleo*) to apply

presente [pre'sente] *adj* present ♦ *nm* present; **hacer ~** to state, declare; **tener ~** to remember, bear in mind

presentimiento [presenti'mjento] *nm* premonition, presentiment

presentir [presen'tir] *vt* to have a premonition of

preservación [preserßa'θjon] *nf* protection, preservation

preservar [preser'βar] vt to protect, preserve; **preservativo** nm sheath, condom

presidencia [presi'ðenθja] nf presidency; (de comité) chairmanship

presidente [presi'ðente] nm/f president; (de comité) chairman/woman

presidiario [presi'ðjarjo] nm convict

presidio [pre'sidjo] nm prison, penitentiary

presidir [presi'ðir] vt (dirigir) to preside at, preside over; (: comité) to take the chair at; (dominar) to dominate, rule ♦ vi to preside; to take the chair

presión [pre'sjon] nf pressure; **presionar** vt to press; (fig) to press, put pressure on ♦ vi: **presionar para** to press for

preso, a ['preso, a] nm/f prisoner; **tomar o llevar ~ a uno** to arrest sb, take sb prisoner

prestación [presta'θjon] nf service; (subsidio) benefit; **prestaciones** nfpl (TEC, AUT) performance features

prestado, a [pres'taðo, a] adj on loan; **pedir ~** to borrow

prestamista [presta'mista] nm/f moneylender

préstamo ['prestamo] nm loan; **~ hipotecario** mortgage

prestar [pres'tar] vt to lend, loan; (atención) to pay; (ayuda) to give

presteza [pres'teθa] nf speed, promptness

prestigio [pres'tixjo] nm prestige; **~so, a** adj (honorable) prestigious; (famoso, renombrado) renowned, famous

presto, a ['presto, a] adj (rápido) quick, prompt; (dispuesto) ready ♦ adv at once, right away.

presumido, a [presu'miðo, a] adj (persona) vain

presumir [presu'mir] vt to presume ♦ vi (tener aires) to be conceited; **según cabe ~** as may be presumed, presumably; **presunción** nf presumption; **presunto, a** adj (supuesto) supposed, presumed; (así llamado) so-called; **presuntuoso, a** adj conceited, presumptuous

presuponer [presupo'ner] vt to presuppose

presupuesto [presu'pwesto] pp de **presuponer** ♦ nm (FINANZAS) budget; (estimación: de costo) estimate

pretencioso, a [preten'θjoso, a] adj pretentious

pretender [preten'der] vt (intentar) to try to, seek to; (reivindicar) to claim; (buscar) to seek, try for; (cortejar) to woo, court; **~ que** to expect that; **pretendiente** nm/f (amante) suitor; (al trono) pretender; **pretensión** nf (aspiración) aspiration; (reivindicación) claim; (orgullo) pretension

pretexto [pre'teksto] nm pretext; (excusa) excuse

prevalecer [preβale'θer] vi to prevail

prevención [preβen'θjon] nf prevention; (precaución) precaution

prevenido, a [preβe'niðo, a] adj prepared, ready; (cauteloso) cautious

prevenir [preβe'nir] vt (impedir) to prevent; (predisponer) to prejudice, bias; (avisar) to warn; (preparar) to prepare, get ready; **~se** vr to get ready, prepare; **~se contra** to take precautions against; **preventivo, a** adj preventive, precautionary

prever [pre'βer] vt to foresee

previo, a ['preβjo, a] adj (anterior) previous; (preliminar) preliminary ♦ prep: **~ acuerdo de los otros** subject to the agreement of the others

previsión [preβi'sjon] nf (perspicacia) foresight; (predicción) forecast; **previsto, a** adj anticipated, forecast

prima ['prima] nf (COM) bonus; **~ de seguro** insurance premium; ver tb **primo**

primacía [prima'θia] nf primacy

primario, a [pri'marjo, a] adj primary

primavera [prima'βera] nf spring(-time)

primera [pri'mera] nf (AUTO) first gear; (FERRO: tb: **~ clase**) first class; **de ~** (fam) first-class, first-rate

primero, a [pri'mero, a] (delante de nmsg: **primer**) adj first; (principal) prime ♦ adv first; (*más bien*) sooner, rather; **primera plana** front page

primicia [pri'miθja] *nf* (*tb*: **~ informativa**) scoop

primitivo, a [primi'tiβo, a] *adj* primitive; (*original*) original

primo, a ['primo, a] *adj* prime ♦ *nm/f* cousin; (*fam*) fool, idiot; **~ hermano** first cousin; **materias primas** raw materials

primogénito, a [primo'xenito, a] *adj* first-born

primordial [primor'ðjal] *adj* basic, fundamental

primoroso, a [primo'roso, a] *adj* exquisite, delicate

princesa [prin'θesa] *nf* princess

principal [prinθi'pal] *adj* principal, main ♦ *nm* (*jefe*) chief, principal

príncipe ['prinθipe] *nm* prince

principiante [prinθi'pjante] *nm/f* beginner

principio [prin'θipjo] *nm* (*comienzo*) beginning, start; (*origen*) origin; (*primera etapa*) rudiment, basic idea; (*moral*) principle; **a ~s de** at the beginning of

pringoso, a [prin'yoso, a] *adj* (*grasiento*) greasy; (*pegajoso*) sticky

pringue ['pringe] *nm* (*grasa*) grease, fat, dripping

prioridad [priori'ðað] *nf* priority

prisa ['prisa] *nf* (*apresuramiento*) hurry, haste; (*rapidez*) speed; (*urgencia*) (sense of) urgency; **a** *o* **de ~** quickly; **correr ~** to be urgent; **darse ~** to hurry up; **estar de** *o* **tener ~** to be in a hurry

prisión [pri'sjon] *nf* (*cárcel*) prison; (*período de cárcel*) imprisonment; **prisionero, a** *nm/f* prisoner

prismáticos [pris'matikos] *nmpl* binoculars

privación [priβa'θjon] *nf* deprivation; (*falta*) want, privation

privado, a [pri'βaðo, a] *adj* private

privar [pri'βar] *vt* to deprive; **privativo, a** *adj* exclusive

privilegiado, a [priβile'xjaðo, a] *adj* privileged; (*memoria*) very good

privilegiar [priβile'xjar] *vt* to grant a privilege to; (*favorecer*) to favour

privilegio [priβi'lexjo] *nm* privilege; (*concesión*) concession

pro [pro] *nm* o *f* profit, advantage ♦ *prep*: **asociación ~ ciegos** association for the blind ♦ *prefijo*: **~ soviético/americano** pro-Soviet/American; **en ~ de** on behalf of, for; **los ~s y los contras** the pros and cons

proa ['proa] *nf* bow, prow; **de ~** bow *cpd*, fore

probabilidad [proβaβili'ðað] *nf* probability, likelihood; (*oportunidad, posibilidad*) chance, prospect; **probable** *adj* probable, likely

probador [proβa'ðor] *nm* (*en tienda*) fitting room

probar [pro'βar] *vt* (*demostrar*) to prove; (*someter a prueba*) to test, try out; (*ropa*) to try on; (*comida*) to taste ♦ *vi* to try; **~se un traje** to try on a suit

probeta [pro'βeta] *nf* test tube

problema [pro'βlema] *nm* problem

procedente [proθe'ðente] *adj* (*razonable*) reasonable; (*conforme a derecho*) proper, fitting; **~ de** coming from, originating in

proceder [proθe'ðer] *vi* (*avanzar*) to proceed; (*actuar*) to act; (*ser correcto*) to be right (and proper), be fitting ♦ *nm* (*comportamiento*) behaviour, conduct; **~ de** to come from, originate in; **procedimiento** *nm* procedure; (*proceso*) process; (*método*) means *pl*, method

procesado, a [proθe'saðo, a] *nm/f* accused

procesador [proθesa'ðor] *nm*: **~ de textos** word processor

procesar [proθe'sar] *vt* to try, put on trial

procesión [proθe'sjon] *nf* procession

proceso [pro'θeso] *nm* process; (*JUR*) trial

proclamar [prokla'mar] *vt* to proclaim

procreación [prokrea'θjon] *nf* procreation

procrear [prokre'ar] *vt, vi* to procreate

procurador, a [prokura'ðor, a] *nm/f* attorney

procurar [proku'rar] vt (*intentar*) to try, endeavour; (*conseguir*) to get, obtain; (*asegurar*) to secure; (*producir*) to produce

prodigio [pro'ðixjo] nm prodigy; (*milagro*) wonder, marvel; **~so, a** adj prodigious, marvellous

pródigo, a ['proðiɣo, a] adj: **hijo ~** prodigal son

producción [proðuk'θjon] nf (*gen*) production; (*producto*) output; **~ en serie** mass production

producir [proðu'θir] vt to produce; (*causar*) to cause, bring about; **~se** vr (*cambio*) to come about; (*accidente*) to take place; (*problema etc*) to arise; (*hacerse*) to be produced, be made; (*estallar*) to break out

productividad [proðuktiβi'ðað] nf productivity; **productivo, a** adj productive; (*provechoso*) profitable

producto [pro'ðukto] nm product

productor, a [proðuk'tor, a] adj productive, producing ♦ nm/f producer

proeza [pro'eθa] nf exploit, feat

profanar [profa'nar] vt to desecrate, profane; **profano, a** adj profane ♦ nm/f layman/woman

profecía [profe'θia] nf prophecy

proferir [profe'rir] vt (*palabra, sonido*) to utter; (*injuria*) to hurl, let fly

profesión [profe'sjon] nf profession; **profesional** adj professional

profesor, a [profe'sor, a] nm/f teacher; **~ado** nm teaching profession

profeta [pro'feta] nm/f prophet; **profetizar** vt, vi to prophesy

prófugo, a ['profuɣo, a] nm/f fugitive; (*MIL: desertor*) deserter

profundidad [profundi'ðað] nf depth; **profundizar** vi: **profundizar en** to go deeply into; **profundo, a** adj deep; (*misterio, pensador*) profound

progenitor [proxeni'tor] nm ancestor; **~es** nmpl (*padres*) parents

programa [pro'ɣrama] nm programme (*BRIT*), program (*US*); **~ción** nf programming; **~dor, a** nm/f

programmer; **programar** vt to program

progresar [proɣre'sar] vi to progress, make progress; **progresista** adj, nm/f progressive; **progresivo, a** adj progressive; (*gradual*) gradual; (*continuo*) continuous; **progreso** nm progress

prohibición [proiβi'θjon] nf prohibition, ban

prohibir [proi'βir] vt to prohibit, ban, forbid; **se prohibe fumar, prohibido fumar** no smoking; **"prohibido el paso"** "no entry"

prójimo, a ['proximo, a] nm/f fellow man; (*vecino*) neighbour

proletariado [proleta'rjaðo] nm proletariat

proletario, a [prole'tarjo, a] adj, nm/f proletarian

proliferación [prolifera'θjon] nf proliferation

proliferar [prolife'rar] vi to proliferate; **prolífico, a** adj prolific

prólogo ['proloɣo] nm prologue

prolongación [prolonga'θjon] nf extension; **prolongado, a** adj (*largo*) long; (*alargado*) lengthy

prolongar [prolon'ɣar] vt to extend; (*reunión etc*) to prolong; (*calle, tubo*) to extend

promedio [pro'meðjo] nm average; (*de distancia*) middle, mid-point

promesa [pro'mesa] nf promise

prometer [prome'ter] vt to promise ♦ vi to show promise; **~se** vr (*novios*) to get engaged; **prometido, a** adj promised; engaged ♦ nm/f fiancé/fiancée

prominente [promi'nente] adj prominent

promiscuo, a [pro'miskwo, a] adj promiscuous

promoción [promo'θjon] nf promotion

promotor [promo'tor] nm promoter; (*instigador*) instigator

promover [promo'βer] vt to promote; (*causar*) to cause; (*instigar*) to instigate, stir up

promulgar [promul'ɣar] vt to promulgate; (*anunciar*) to proclaim

pronombre [pro'nombre] nm pronoun

pronosticar [pronosti'kar] *vt* to predict, foretell, forecast; **pronóstico** *nm* prediction, forecast; **pronóstico del tiempo** weather forecast

pronto, a ['pronto, a] *adj* (*rápido*) prompt, quick; (*preparado*) ready ♦ *adv* quickly, promptly; (*en seguida*) at once, right away; (*dentro de poco*) soon; (*temprano*) early ♦ *nm*: **tener ~s de enojo** to be quick-tempered; **de ~** suddenly; **por lo ~** meanwhile, for the present

pronunciación [pronunθja'θjon] *nf* pronunciation

pronunciar [pronun'θjar] *vt* to pronounce; (*discurso*) to make, deliver; **~se** *vr* to revolt, rebel; (*declararse*) to declare o.s.

propagación [propaɣa'θjon] *nf* propagation

propaganda [propa'ɣanda] *nf* (*política*) propaganda; (*comercial*) advertising

propagar [propa'ɣar] *vt* to propagate

propensión [propen'sjon] *nf* inclination, propensity; **propenso, a** *adj* inclined to; **ser propenso a** to be inclined to, have a tendency to

propicio, a [pro'piθjo, a] *adj* favourable, propitious

propiedad [propje'ðað] *nf* property; (*posesión*) possession, ownership; **~ particular** private property

propietario, a [propje'tarjo, a] *nm/f* owner, proprietor

propina [pro'pina] *nf* tip

propio, a ['propjo, a] *adj* own, of one's own; (*característico*) characteristic, typical; (*debido*) proper; (*mismo*) selfsame, very; **el ~ ministro** the minister himself; **¿tienes casa propia?** have you a house of your own?

proponer [propo'ner] *vt* to propose, put forward; (*problema*) to pose; **~se** *vr* to propose, intend

proporción [propor'θjon] *nf* proportion; (*MAT*) ratio; **proporciones** *nfpl* (*dimensiones*) dimensions; (*fig*) size *sg*; **proporcionado, a** *adj* proportionate;

(*regular*) medium, middling; (*justo*) just right; **proporcionar** *vt* (*dar*) to give, supply, provide

proposición [proposi'θjon] *nf* proposition; (*propuesta*) proposal

propósito [pro'posito] *nm* purpose; (*intento*) aim, intention ♦ *adv*: **a ~** by the way, incidentally; (*a posta*) on purpose, deliberately; **a ~ de** about, with regard to

propuesta [pro'pwesta] *vb ver* **proponer** ♦ *nf* proposal

propulsar [propul'sar] *vt* to drive, propel; (*fig*) to promote, encourage; **propulsión** *nf* propulsion; **propulsión a chorro** *o* **por reacción** jet propulsion

prórroga ['prorroɣa] *nf* extension; (*JUR*) stay; (*COM*) deferment; (*DEPORTE*) extra time; **prorrogar** *vt* (*período*) to extend; (*decisión*) to defer, postpone

prorrumpir [prorrum'pir] *vi* to burst forth, break out

prosa ['prosa] *nf* prose

proscrito, a [pro'skrito, a] *adj* banned

proseguir [prose'ɣir] *vt* to continue, carry on ♦ *vi* to continue, go on

prospección [prospek'θjon] *nf* exploration; (*del oro*) prospecting

prospecto [pros'pekto] *nm* prospectus

prosperar [prospe'rar] *vi* to prosper, thrive, flourish; **prosperidad** *nf* prosperity; (*éxito*) success; **próspero, a** *adj* prosperous, flourishing; (*que tiene éxito*) successful

prostíbulo [pros'tiβulo] *nm* brothel (*BRIT*), house of prostitution (*US*)

prostitución [prostitu'θjon] *nf* prostitution

prostituir [prosti'twir] *vt* to prostitute; **~se** *vr* to prostitute o.s., become a prostitute

prostituta [prosti'tuta] *nf* prostitute

protagonista [protaɣo'nista] *nm/f* protagonist

protagonizar [protaɣoni'θar] *vt* to take the chief rôle in

protección [protek'θjon] *nf* protection

protector, a [protek'tor, a] *adj* protective, protecting ♦ *nm/f* protector

proteger [prote'xer] vt to protect; **protegido, a** nm/f protégé/protégée
proteína [prote'ina] nf protein
protesta [pro'testa] nf protest; (declaración) protestation
protestante [protes'tante] adj Protestant
protestar [protes'tar] vt to protest, declare ♦ vi to protest
protocolo [proto'kolo] nm protocol
prototipo [proto'tipo] nm prototype
prov. abr (= provincia) prov
provecho [pro'βetʃo] nm advantage, benefit; (FINANZAS) profit; ¡buen ~! bon appétit!; **en ~ de** to the benefit of; **sacar ~ de** to benefit from, profit by
proveer [proβe'er] vt to provide, supply ♦ vi: **~ a** to provide for
provenir [proβe'nir] vi: **~ de** to come from, stem from
proverbio [pro'βerβjo] nm proverb
providencia [proβi'ðenθja] nf providence
provincia [pro'βinθja] nf province; **~no, a** adj provincial; (del campo) country cpd
provisión [proβi'sjon] nf provision; (abastecimiento) provision, supply; (medida) measure, step
provisional [proβisjo'nal] adj provisional
provocación [proβoka'θjon] nf provocation
provocar [proβo'kar] vt to provoke; (alentar) to tempt, invite; (causar) to bring about, lead to; (promover) to promote; (estimular) to rouse, stimulate; **¿te provoca un café?** (AM) would you like a coffee?; **provocativo, a** adj provocative
próximamente [proksima'mente] adv shortly, soon
proximidad [proksimi'ðað] nf closeness, proximity; **próximo, a** adj near, close; (vecino) neighbouring; (siguiente) next
proyectar [projek'tar] vt (objeto) to hurl, throw; (luz) to cast, shed; (CINE) to screen, show; (planear) to plan
proyectil [projek'til] nm projectile, missile
proyecto [pro'jekto] nm plan; (estimación de costo) detailed estimate

proyector [projek'tor] nm (CINE) projector
prudencia [pru'ðenθja] nf (sabiduría) wisdom; (cuidado) care; **prudente** adj sensible, wise; (conductor) careful
prueba etc ['prweßa] vb ver **probar** ♦ nf proof; (ensayo) test, trial; (degustación) tasting, sampling; (de ropa) fitting; **a ~** on trial; **a ~ de** proof against; **a ~ de agua/fuego** waterproof/fireproof; **someter a ~** to put to the test
prurito [pru'rito] nm itch; (de bebé) nappy (BRIT) o diaper (US) rash
psico... [siko] prefijo psycho...; **~análisis** nm inv psychoanalysis; **~logía** nf psychology; **~lógico, a** adj psychological; **psicólogo, a** nm/f psychologist; **psicópata** nm/f psychopath; **~sis** nf inv psychosis
psiquiatra [si'kjatra] nm/f psychiatrist; **psiquiátrico, a** adj psychiatric
psíquico, a ['sikiko, a] adj psychic(al)
PSOE [pe'soe] nm abr = **Partido Socialista Obrero Español**
pta(s) abr = **peseta(s)**
pts abr = **pesetas**
púa ['pua] nf (BOT, ZOOL) prickle, spine; (para guitarra) plectrum (BRIT), pick (US); **alambre de ~** barbed wire
pubertad [puβer'tað] nf puberty
publicación [puβlika'θjon] nf publication
publicar [puβli'kar] vt (editar) to publish; (hacer público) to publicize; (divulgar) to make public, divulge
publicidad [puβliθi'ðað] nf publicity; (COM: propaganda) advertising; **publicitario, a** adj publicity cpd; advertising cpd
público, a ['puβliko, a] adj public ♦ nm public; (TEATRO etc) audience
puchero [pu'tʃero] nm (CULIN: guiso) stew; (: olla) cooking pot; **hacer ~s** to pout
pude etc vb ver **poder**
púdico, a ['puðiko, a] adj modest
pudiente [pu'ðjente] adj (rico) wealthy, well-to-do
pudiera etc vb ver **poder**
pudor [pu'ðor] nm modesty

pudrir [pu'ðrir] vt to rot; **~se** vr to rot, decay

pueblo ['pweßlo] nm people; (nación) nation; (aldea) village

puedo etc vb ver **poder**

puente ['pwente] nm bridge; **hacer ~** (inf) to take extra days off work between 2 public holidays; to take a long weekend; **~ aéreo** shuttle service; **~ colgante** suspension bridge

---
hacer puente
---

i *When a public holiday in Spain falls on a Tuesday or Thursday it is common practice for employers to make the Monday or Friday a holiday as well and to give everyone a four-day weekend. This is known as* **hacer puente.** *When a named public holiday such as the* **Día de la Constitución** *falls on a Tuesday or Thursday, people refer to the whole holiday period as e.g. the* **puente de la Constitución.**

---

puerco, a ['pwerko, a] nm/f pig/sow ♦ adj (sucio) dirty, filthy; (obsceno) disgusting; **~ de mar** porpoise; **~ marino** dolphin

pueril [pwe'ril] adj childish

puerro ['pwerro] nm leek

puerta ['pwerta] nf door; (de jardín) gate; (portal) doorway; (fig) gateway; (portería) goal; **a la ~** at the door; **a ~ cerrada** behind closed doors; **~ giratoria** revolving door

puerto ['pwerto] nm port; (paso) pass; (fig) haven, refuge

Puerto Rico [pwerto'riko] nm Puerto Rico; **puertorriqueño, a** adj, nm/f Puerto Rican

pues [pwes] adv (entonces) then; (bueno) well, well then; (así que) so ♦ conj (ya que) since; **¡~!** (sí) yes!, certainly!

puesta ['pwesta] nf (apuesta) bet, stake; **~ en marcha** starting; **~ del sol** sunset

puesto, a ['pwesto, a] pp de **poner** ♦ adj: **tener algo ~** to have sth on, be wearing sth ♦ nm (lugar, posición) place; (trabajo) post, job; (COM) stall ♦ conj: **~ que** since, as

púgil ['puxil] nm boxer

pugna ['puɣna] nf battle, conflict; **pugnar** vi (luchar) to struggle, fight; (pelear) to fight

pujar [pu'xar] vi (en subasta) to bid; (esforzarse) to struggle, strain

pulcro, a ['pulkro, a] adj neat, tidy

pulga ['pulɣa] nf flea

pulgada [pul'ɣaða] nf inch

pulgar [pul'ɣar] nm thumb

pulir [pu'lir] vt to polish; (alisar) to smooth; (fig) to polish up, touch up

pulla ['puʎa] nf cutting remark

pulmón [pul'mon] nm lung; **pulmonía** nf pneumonia

pulpa ['pulpa] nf pulp; (de fruta) flesh, soft part

pulpería [pulpe'ria] (AM) nf (tienda) small grocery store

púlpito ['pulpito] nm pulpit

pulpo ['pulpo] nm octopus

pulsación [pulsa'θjon] nf beat; **pulsaciones** pulse rate

pulsar [pul'sar] vt (tecla) to touch, tap; (MUS) to play; (botón) to press, push ♦ vi to pulsate; (latir) to beat, throb; (MED): **~ a uno** to take sb's pulse

pulsera [pul'sera] nf bracelet

pulso ['pulso] nm (ANAT) pulse; (fuerza) strength; (firmeza) steadiness, steady hand

pulverizador [pulßeriθa'ðor] nm spray, spray gun

pulverizar [pulßeri'θar] vt to pulverize; (líquido) to spray

puna ['puna] (AM) nf mountain sickness

punitivo, a [puni'tißo, a] adj punitive

punta ['punta] nf point, tip; (extremidad) end; (fig) touch, trace; **horas ~s** peak hours, rush hours; **sacar ~ a** to sharpen

puntada [pun'taða] nf (COSTURA) stitch

puntal [pun'tal] nm prop, support

puntapié [punta'pje] nm kick

puntear [punte'ar] vt to tick, mark

puntería [punte'ria] nf (de arma) aim,

aiming; (*destreza*) marksmanship
puntero, a [pun'tero, a] *adj* leading ♦ *nm*
(*palo*) pointer
puntiagudo, a [puntja'ɣuðo, a] *adj* sharp,
pointed
puntilla [pun'tiʎa] *nf* (*encaje*) lace edging
o trim; **(andar) de ~s** (to walk) on tiptoe
punto ['punto] *nm* (*gen*) point; (*señal
diminuta*) spot, dot; (*COSTURA, MED*) stitch;
(*lugar*) spot, place; (*momento*) point,
moment; **a ~** ready; **estar a ~ de** to be
on the point of *o* about to; **en ~** on the
dot; **~ muerto** dead centre; (*AUTO*)
neutral (gear); **~ final** full stop (*BRIT*),
period (*US*); **~ y coma** semicolon; **~ de
interrogación** question mark; **~ de vista**
point of view, viewpoint; **hacer ~** (*tejer*)
to knit
puntuación [puntwa'θjon] *nf* punctuation;
(*puntos: en examen*) mark(s) (*pl*);
(: *DEPORTE*) score
puntual [pun'twal] *adj* (*a tiempo*)
punctual; (*exacto*) exact, accurate; **~idad**
nf punctuality; exactness, accuracy; **~izar**
vt to fix, specify
puntuar [pun'twar] *vi* (*DEPORTE*) to score,
count
punzada [pun'θaða] *nf* (*de dolor*) twinge
punzante [pun'θante] *adj* (*dolor*) shooting,
sharp; (*herramienta*) sharp; **punzar** *vt* to
prick, pierce ♦ *vi* to shoot, stab
puñado [pu'ɲaðo] *nm* handful
puñal [pu'ɲal] *nm* dagger; **~ada** *nf* stab
puñetazo [puɲe'taθo] *nm* punch
puño ['puɲo] *nm* (*ANAT*) fist; (*cantidad*)
fistful, handful; (*COSTURA*) cuff; (*de
herramienta*) handle
pupila [pu'pila] *nf* pupil
pupitre [pu'pitre] *nm* desk
puré [pu're] *nm* puree; (*sopa*) (thick) soup;
~ de patatas mashed potatoes
pureza [pu'reθa] *nf* purity
purga ['purɣa] *nf* purge; **purgante** *adj*,
nm purgative; **purgar** *vt* to purge
purgatorio [purɣa'torjo] *nm* purgatory
purificar [purifi'kar] *vt* to purify; (*refinar*)
to refine

puritano, a [puri'tano, a] *adj* (*actitud*)
puritanical; (*iglesia, tradición*) puritan
♦ *nm/f* puritan
puro, a ['puro, a] *adj* pure; (*verdad*)
simple, plain ♦ *adv*: **de ~ cansado** out of
sheer tiredness ♦ *nm* cigar
púrpura ['purpura] *nf* purple; **purpúreo,
a** *adj* purple
pus [pus] *nm* pus
puse *etc vb ver* **poner**
pusiera *etc vb ver* **poner**
pústula ['pustula] *nf* pimple, sore
puta ['puta] (*fam!*) *nf* whore, prostitute
putrefacción [putrefak'θjon] *nf* rotting,
putrefaction
PVP *abr* (*ESP*: = *precio venta al público*)
RRP
pyme, PYME ['pime] *nf abr* (= *Pequeña
y Mediana Empresa*) SME

Q, q

PALABRA CLAVE

que [ke] *conj* **1** (*con oración subordinada*:
muchas veces no se traduce) that; **dijo ~
vendría** he said (that) he would come;
espero ~ lo encuentres I hope (that)
you find it; *ver tb* **el**
2 (*en oración independiente*): **¡~ entre!**
send him in; **¡~ se mejore tu padre!** I
hope your father gets better
3 (*enfático*): **¿me quieres? - ¡~ sí!** do
you love me? – of course!
4 (*consecutivo*: *muchas veces no se
traduce*) that; **es tan grande ~ no lo
puedo levantar** it's so big (that) I can't
lift it
5 (*comparaciones*) than; **yo ~ tú/él** if I
were you/him; *ver tb* **más**; **menos**;
mismo
6 (*valor disyuntivo*): **~ le guste o no**
whether he likes it or not; **~ venga o ~
no venga** whether he comes or not
7 (*porque*): **no puedo, ~ tengo ~
quedarme en casa** I can't, I've got to

stay in
♦ *pron* 1 (*cosa*) that, which; (+*prep*) which; **el sombrero ~ te compraste** the hat (that o which) you bought; **la cama en ~ dormí** the bed (that o which) I slept in
2 (*persona: suj*) that, who; (: *objeto*) that, whom; **el amigo ~ me acompañó al museo** the friend that o who went to the museum with me: **la chica ~ invité** the girl (that o whom) I invited

qué [ke] *adj* what?, which? ♦ *pron* what?; **¡~ divertido!** how funny!; **¿~ edad tienes?** how old are you?; **¿de ~ me hablas?** what are you saying to me?; **¿~ tal?** how are you?, how are things?; **¿~ hay (de nuevo)?** what's new?

quebradizo, a [keβra'δiθo, a] *adj* fragile; (*persona*) frail

quebrado, a [ke'βraδo, a] *adj* (*roto*) broken ♦ *nm/f* bankrupt ♦ *nm* (MAT) fraction

quebrantar [keβran'tar] *vt* (*infringir*) to violate, transgress; **~se** *vr* (*persona*) to fail in health

quebranto [ke'βranto] *nm* damage, harm; (*dolor*) grief, pain

quebrar [ke'βrar] *vt* to break, smash ♦ *vi* to go bankrupt; **~se** *vr* to break, get broken; (MED) to be ruptured

quedar [ke'δar] *vi* to stay, remain; (*encontrarse: sitio*) to be; (*haber aún*) to remain, be left; **~se** *vr* to remain, stay (behind); **~se (con) algo** to keep sth; **~ en** (*acordar*) to agree on/to; **~ en nada** to come to nothing; **~ por hacer** to be still to be done; **~ ciego/mudo** to be left blind/dumb; **no te queda bien ese vestido** that dress doesn't suit you; **eso queda muy lejos** that's a long way (away); **quedamos a las seis** we agreed to meet at six

quedo, a ['keδo, a] *adj* still ♦ *adv* softly, gently

quehacer [kea'θer] *nm* task, job; **~es (domésticos)** *nmpl* household chores

queja ['kexa] *nf* complaint; **quejarse** *vr* (*enfermo*) to moan, groan; (*protestar*) to complain; **quejarse de que** to complain (about the fact) that; **quejido** *nm* moan

quemado, a [ke'maδo, a] *adj* burnt

quemadura [kema'δura] *nf* burn, scald

quemar [ke'mar] *vt* to burn; (*fig: malgastar*) to burn up, squander ♦ *vi* to be burning hot; **~se** *vr* (*consumirse*) to burn (up); (*del sol*) to get sunburnt

quemarropa [kema'rropa]: **a ~** *adv* point-blank

quepo *etc vb ver* **caber**

querella [ke'reʎa] *nf* (JUR) charge; (*disputa*) dispute; **~rse** *vr* (JUR) to file a complaint

PALABRA CLAVE

querer [ke'rer] *vt* 1 (*desear*) to want; **quiero más dinero** I want more money; **quisiera** o **querría un té** I'd like a tea; **sin ~** unintentionally; **quiero ayudar/que vayas** I want to help/you to go
2 (*preguntas: para pedir algo*): **¿quiere abrir la ventana?** could you open the window?; **¿quieres echarme una mano?** can you give me a hand?
3 (*amar*) to love; (*tener cariño a*) to be fond of; **quiere mucho a sus hijos** he's very fond of his children
4 (*requerir*): **esta planta quiere más luz** this plant needs more light
5: **le pedí que me dejara ir pero no quiso** I asked him to let me go but he refused

querido, a [ke'riδo, a] *adj* dear ♦ *nm/f* darling; (*amante*) lover

queso ['keso] *nm* cheese

quicio ['kiθjo] *nm* hinge; **sacar a uno de ~** to get on sb's nerves

quiebra ['kjeβra] *nf* break, split; (COM) bankruptcy; (ECON) slump

quiebro ['kjeβro] *nm* (*del cuerpo*) swerve

quien [kjen] *pron* who; **hay ~ piensa que** there are those who think that; **no hay ~ lo haga** no-one will do it

quién [kjen] *pron* who, whom; **¿~ es?** who's there?

quienquiera [kjen'kjera] (*pl* **quienesquiera**) *pron* whoever

quiero *etc vb ver* **querer**

quieto, a ['kjeto, a] *adj* still; (*carácter*) placid; **quietud** *nf* stillness

quilate [ki'late] *nm* carat

quilla ['kiʎa] *nf* keel

quimera [ki'mera] *nf* chimera; **quimérico, a** *adj* fantastic

químico, a ['kimiko, a] *adj* chemical ♦ *nm/f* chemist ♦ *nf* chemistry

quincalla [kin'kaʎa] *nf* hardware, ironmongery (*BRIT*)

quince ['kinθe] *num* fifteen; **~ días** a fortnight; **~añero, a** *nm/f* teenager; **~na** *nf* fortnight; (*pago*) fortnightly pay; **~nal** *adj* fortnightly

quiniela [ki'njela] *nf* football pools *pl*; **~s** *nfpl* (*impreso*) pools coupon *sg*

quinientos, as [ki'njentos, as] *adj, num* five hundred

quinina [ki'nina] *nf* quinine

quinto, a ['kinto, a] *adj* fifth ♦ *nf* country house; (*MIL*) call-up, draft

quiosco ['kjosko] *nm* (*de música*) bandstand; (*de periódicos*) news stand

quirófano [ki'rofano] *nm* operating theatre

quirúrgico, a [ki'rurxiko, a] *adj* surgical

quise *etc vb ver* **querer**

quisiera *etc vb ver* **querer**

quisquilloso, a [kiski'ʎoso, a] *adj* (*susceptible*) touchy; (*meticuloso*) pernickety

quiste ['kiste] *nm* cyst

quitaesmalte [kitaes'malte] *nm* nail-polish remover

quitamanchas [kita'mantʃas] *nm inv* stain remover

quitanieves [kita'njeβes] *nm inv* snowplough (*BRIT*), snowplow (*US*)

quitar [ki'tar] *vt* to remove, take away; (*ropa*) to take off; (*dolor*) to relieve; **¡quita de ahí!** get away!; **~se** *vr* to withdraw; (*ropa*) to take off; **se quitó el sombrero**

he took off his hat

quite ['kite] *nm* (*esgrima*) parry; (*evasión*) dodge

Quito ['kito] *n* Quito

quizá(s) [ki'θa(s)] *adv* perhaps, maybe

R, r

rábano ['raβano] *nm* radish; **me importa un ~** I don't give a damn

rabia ['raβja] *nf* (*MED*) rabies *sg*; (*ira*) fury, rage; **rabiar** *vi* to have rabies; to rage, be furious; **rabiar por algo** to long for sth

rabieta [ra'βjeta] *nf* tantrum, fit of temper

rabino [ra'βino] *nm* rabbi

rabioso, a [ra'βjoso, a] *adj* rabid; (*fig*) furious

rabo ['raβo] *nm* tail

racha ['ratʃa] *nf* gust of wind: **buena/ mala ~** spell of good/bad luck

racial [ra'θjal] *adj* racial, race *cpd*

racimo [ra'θimo] *nm* bunch

raciocinio [raθjo'θinjo] *nm* reason

ración [ra'θjon] *nf* portion; **raciones** *nfpl* rations

racional [raθjo'nal] *adj* (*razonable*) reasonable; (*lógico*) rational; **~izar** *vt* to rationalize

racionar [raθjo'nar] *vt* to ration (out)

racismo [ra'θismo] *nm* racism; **racista** *adj, nm/f* racist

radar [ra'ðar] *nm* radar

radiactivo, a [raðiak'tiβo, a] *adj* = **radioactivo**

radiador [raðja'ðor] *nm* radiator

radiante [ra'ðjante] *adj* radiant

radical [raði'kal] *adj, nm/f* radical

radicar [raði'kar] *vi*: **~ en** (*dificultad, problema*) to lie in; (*solución*) to consist in; **~se** *vr* to establish o.s., put down (one's) roots

radio ['raðjo] *nf* radio; (*aparato*) radio (set) ♦ *nm* (*MAT*) radius; (*QUÍM*) radium; **~actividad** *nf* radioactivity; **~activo, a** *adj* radioactive; **~difusión** *nf* broadcasting; **~emisora** *nf* transmitter,

radio station; **~escucha** *nm/f* listener;
~grafía *nf* X-ray; **~grafiar** *vt* to X-ray;
~terapia *nf* radiotherapy; **~yente** *nm/f*
listener

ráfaga ['rafaɣa] *nf* (de luz) gust; (de luz) flash; (de
tiros) burst

raído, a [ra'iðo, a] *adj* (ropa) threadbare

raigambre [rai'ɣambre] *nf* (BOT) roots *pl*;
(fig) tradition

raíz [ra'iθ] *nf* root; **~ cuadrada** square
root; **a ~ de** as a result of

raja ['raxa] *nf* (de melón etc) slice; (grieta)
crack; **rajar** *vt* to split; (fam) to slash;
rajarse *vr* to split, crack; **rajarse de** to
back out of

rajatabla [raxa'taβla]: **a ~** *adv*
(estrictamente) strictly, to the letter

rallador [raʎa'ðor] *nm* grater

rallar [ra'ʎar] *vt* to grate

rama ['rama] *nf* branch; **~je** *nm* branches
pl, foliage; **ramal** *nm* (de cuerda) strand;
(FERRO) branch line (BRIT); (AUTO) branch
(road) (BRIT)

rambla ['rambla] *nf* (avenida) avenue

ramificación [ramifika'θjon] *nf*
ramification

ramificarse [ramifi'karse] *vr* to branch
out

ramillete [rami'ʎete] *nm* bouquet

ramo ['ramo] *nm* branch; (sección)
department, section

rampa ['rampa] *nf* ramp

ramplón, ona [ram'plon, ona] *adj*
uncouth, coarse

rana ['rana] *nf* frog; **salto de ~** leapfrog

ranchero [ran'tʃero] *nm* (AM) rancher;
smallholder

rancho ['rantʃo] *nm* (grande) ranch;
(pequeño) small farm

rancio, a ['ranθjo, a] *adj* (comestibles)
rancid; (vino) aged, mellow; (fig) ancient

rango ['rango] *nm* rank, standing

ranura [ra'nura] *nf* groove; (de teléfono
etc) slot

rapar [ra'par] *vt* to shave; (los cabellos) to
crop

rapaz [ra'paθ] (nf: **rapaza**) *nm/f* young

boy/girl ♦ *adj* (ZOOL) predatory

rape ['rape] *nm* (pez) monkfish; **al ~**
cropped

rapé [ra'pe] *nm* snuff

rapidez [rapi'ðeθ] *nf* speed, rapidity;
rápido, a *adj* fast, quick ♦ *adv* quickly
♦ *nm* (FERRO) express; **rápidos** *nmpl*
rapids

rapiña [ra'piɲa] *nm* robbery; **ave de ~**
bird of prey

raptar [rap'tar] *vt* to kidnap; **rapto** *nm*
kidnapping; (impulso) sudden impulse;
(éxtasis) ecstasy, rapture

raqueta [ra'keta] *nf* racquet

raquítico, a [ra'kitiko, a] *adj* stunted; (fig)
poor, inadequate; **raquitismo** *nm*
rickets *sg*

rareza [ra'reθa] *nf* rarity; (fig) eccentricity

raro, a ['raro, a] *adj* (poco común) rare;
(extraño) odd, strange; (excepcional)
remarkable

ras [ras] *nm*: **a ~ de** level with; **a ~ de
tierra** at ground level

rasar [ra'sar] *vt* (igualar) to level

rascacielos [raska'θjelos] *nm inv*
skyscraper

rascar [ras'kar] *vt* (con las uñas etc) to
scratch; (raspar) to scrape; **~se** *vr* to
scratch (o.s.)

rasgar [ras'ɣar] *vt* to tear, rip (up)

rasgo ['rasɣo] *nm* (con pluma) stroke; **~s**
nmpl (facciones) features, characteristics;
a grandes ~s in outline, broadly

rasguñar [rasɣu'ɲar] *vt* to scratch;
rasguño *nm* scratch

raso, a ['raso, a] *adj* (liso) flat, level; (a
baja altura) very low ♦ *nm* satin; **cielo ~**
clear sky

raspadura [raspa'ðura] *nf* (acto) scrape,
scraping; (marca) scratch; **~s** *nfpl* (de
papel etc) scrapings

raspar [ras'par] *vt* to scrape; (arañar) to
scratch; (limar) to file

rastra ['rastra] *nf* (AGR) rake; **a ~s** by
dragging; (fig) unwillingly

rastreador [rastrea'ðor] *nm* tracker; **~ de
minas** minesweeper

rastrear [rastre'ar] *vt* (*seguir*) to track
rastrero, a [ras'trero, a] *adj* (BOT, ZOOL) creeping; (*fig*) despicable, mean
rastrillo [ras'triʎo] *nm* rake
rastro ['rastro] *nm* (AGR) rake; (*pista*) track, trail; (*vestigio*) trace; **el R~** the Madrid fleamarket
rastrojo [ras'troxo] *nm* stubble
rasurador [rasura'ðor] (AM) *nm* electric shaver
rasuradora [rasura'ðora] (AM) *nf* = **rasurador**
rasurarse [rasu'rarse] *vr* to shave
rata ['rata] *nf* rat
ratear [rate'ar] *vt* (*robar*) to steal
ratero, a [ra'tero, a] *adj* light-fingered ♦ *nm/f* (*carterista*) pickpocket; (AM: *de casas*) burglar
ratificar [ratifi'kar] *vt* to ratify
rato ['rato] *nm* while, short time; **a ~s** from time to time; **hay para ~** there's still a long way to go; **al poco ~** soon afterwards; **pasar el ~** to kill time; **pasar un buen/mal ~** to have a good/rough time; **en mis ~s libres** in my spare time
ratón [ra'ton] *nm* mouse; **ratonera** *nf* mousetrap
raudal [rau'ðal] *nm* torrent; **a ~es** in abundance
raya ['raja] *nf* line; (*marca*) scratch; (*en tela*) stripe; (*de pelo*) parting; (*límite*) boundary; (*pez*) ray; (*puntuación*) dash; **a ~s** striped; **pasarse de la ~** to go too far: **tener a ~** to keep in check; **rayar** *vt* to line; to scratch; (*subrayar*) to underline ♦ *vi*: **rayar en** *o* **con** to border on
rayo ['rajo] *nm* (*del sol*) ray, beam; (*de luz*) shaft; (*en una tormenta*) (flash of) lightning; **~s X** X-rays
raza ['raθa] *nf* race; **~ humana** human race
razón [ra'θon] *nf* reason; (*justicia*) right, justice; (*razonamiento*) reasoning; (*motivo*) reason, motive; (MAT) ratio; **a ~ de 10 cada día** at the rate of 10 a day; **"~: ..."** "inquiries to ...": **en ~ de** with regard to; **dar ~ a uno** to agree that sb is right; **tener ~** to be right; **~ directa/inversa** direct/inverse proportion; **~ de ser** raison d'être; **razonable** *adj* reasonable; (*justo, moderado*) fair; **razonamiento** *nm* (*juicio*) judg(e)ment; (*argumento*) reasoning; **razonar** *vt, vi* to reason, argue
reacción [reak'θjon] *nf* reaction; **avión a ~** jet plane; **~ en cadena** chain reaction; **reaccionar** *vi* to react; **reaccionario, a** *adj* reactionary
reacio, a [re'aθjo, a] *adj* stubborn
reactivar [reakti'βar] *vt* to revitalize
reactor [reak'tor] *nm* reactor
readaptación [reaðapta'θjon] *nf*: **~ profesional** industrial retraining
reajuste [rea'xuste] *nm* readjustment
real [re'al] *adj* real; (*del rey, fig*) royal
realce [re'alθe] *nm* (*lustre, fig*) splendour; **poner de ~** to emphasize
realidad [reali'ðað] *nf* reality, fact; (*verdad*) truth
realista [rea'lista] *nm/f* realist
realización [realiθa'θjon] *nf* fulfilment
realizador, a [realiθa'ðor, a] *nm/f* film-maker
realizar [reali'θar] *vt* (*objetivo*) to achieve; (*plan*) to carry out; (*viaje*) to make, undertake; **~se** *vr* to come about, come true
realmente [real'mente] *adv* really, actually
realquilar [realki'lar] *vt* to sublet
realzar [real'θar] *vt* to enhance; (*acentuar*) to highlight
reanimar [reani'mar] *vt* to revive; (*alentar*) to encourage; **~se** *vr* to revive
reanudar [reanu'ðar] *vt* (*renovar*) to renew; (*historia, viaje*) to resume
reaparición [reapari'θjon] *nf* reappearance
rearme [re'arme] *nm* rearmament
rebaja [re'βaxa] *nf* (COM) reduction; (: *descuento*) discount; **~s** *nfpl* (COM) sale; **rebajar** *vt* (*bajar*) to lower; (*reducir*) to reduce; (*disminuir*) to lessen; (*humillar*) to humble
rebanada [reβa'naða] *nf* slice
rebañar [reβa'nar] *vt* (*comida*) to scrape

up; (*plato*) to scrape clean

rebaño [re'βaɲo] *nm* herd; (*de ovejas*) flock

rebasar [reβa'sar] *vt* (*tb:* ~ **de**) to exceed

rebatir [reβa'tir] *vt* to refute

rebeca [re'βeka] *nf* cardigan

rebelarse [reβe'larse] *vr* to rebel, revolt

rebelde [re'βelde] *adj* rebellious; (*niño*) unruly ♦ *nm/f* rebel; **rebeldía** *nf* rebelliousness; (*desobediencia*) disobedience

rebelión [reβe'ljon] *nf* rebellion

reblandecer [reβlande'θer] *vt* to soften

rebobinar [reβoβi'nar] *vt* (*cinta, película de video*) to rewind

rebosante [reβo'sante] *adj* overflowing

rebosar [reβo'sar] *vi* (*líquido, recipiente*) to overflow; (*abundar*) to abound, be plentiful

rebotar [reβo'tar] *vt* to bounce; (*rechazar*) to repel ♦ *vi* (*pelota*) to bounce; (*bala*) to ricochet; **rebote** *nm* rebound; **de rebote** on the rebound

rebozado, a [reβo'θaðo, a] *adj* fried in batter *o* breadcrumbs

rebozar [reβo'θar] *vt* to wrap up; (*CULIN*) to fry in batter *o* breadcrumbs

rebuscado, a [reβus'kaðo, a] *adj* (*amanerado*) affected; (*palabra*) recherché; (*idea*) far-fetched

rebuscar [reβus'kar] *vi*: ~ **(en/por)** to search carefully (in/for)

rebuznar [reβuθ'nar] *vi* to bray

recado [re'kaðo] *nm* (*mensaje*) message; (*encargo*) errand; **tomar un** ~ (*TEL*) to take a message

recaer [reka'er] *vi* to relapse; ~ **en** to fall to *o* on; (*criminal etc*) to fall back into, relapse into; **recaída** *nf* relapse

recalcar [rekal'kar] *vt* (*fig*) to stress, emphasize

recalcitrante [rekalθi'trante] *adj* recalcitrant

recalentar [rekalen'tar] *vt* (*volver a calentar*) to reheat; (*calentar demasiado*) to overheat

recámara [re'kamara] (*AM*) *nf* bedroom

recambio [re'kambjo] *nm* spare; (*de pluma*) refill

recapacitar [rekapaθi'tar] *vi* to reflect

recargado, a [rekar'xaðo, a] *adj* overloaded

recargar [rekar'xar] *vt* to overload; (*batería*) to recharge; **recargo** *nm* surcharge; (*aumento*) increase

recatado, a [reka'taðo, a] *adj* (*modesto*) modest, demure; (*prudente*) cautious

recato [re'kato] *nm* (*modestia*) modesty, demureness; (*cautela*) caution

recaudación [rekauða'θjon] *nf* (*acción*) collection; (*cantidad*) takings *pl*; (*en deporte*) gate; **recaudador, a** *nm/f* tax collector

recelar [reθe'lar] *vt*: ~ **que** (*sospechar*) to suspect that; (*temer*) to fear that ♦ *vi*: ~ **de** to distrust; **recelo** *nm* distrust, suspicion; **receloso, a** *adj* distrustful, suspicious

recepción [reθep'θjon] *nf* reception; **recepcionista** *nm/f* receptionist

receptáculo [reθep'takulo] *nm* receptacle

receptivo, a [reθep'tiβo, a] *adj* receptive

receptor, a [reθep'tor, a] *nm/f* recipient ♦ *nm* (*TEL*) receiver

recesión [reθe'sjon] *nf* (*COM*) recession

receta [re'θeta] *nf* (*CULIN*) recipe; (*MED*) prescription

rechazar [retʃa'θar] *vt* to reject; (*oferta*) to turn down; (*ataque*) to repel

rechazo [re'tʃaθo] *nm* rejection

rechifla [re'tʃifla] *nf* hissing, booing; (*fig*) derision

rechinar [retʃi'nar] *vi* to creak; (*dientes*) to grind

rechistar [retʃis'tar] *vi*: **sin** ~ without a murmur

rechoncho, a [re'tʃontʃo, a] (*fam*) *adj* thickset (*BRIT*), heavy-set (*US*)

rechupete [retʃu'pete]: **de** ~ (*comida*) delicious, scrumptious

recibidor, a [reθiβi'ðor, a] *nm* entrance hall

recibimiento [reθiβi'mjento] *nm* reception, welcome

recibir [reθi'ßir] vt to receive; (dar la bienvenida) to welcome ♦ vi to entertain; **~se** vr: **~se de** to qualify as; **recibo** nm receipt

reciclar [reθi'klar] vt to recycle

recién [re'θjen] adv recently, newly; **los ~ casados** the newly-weds; **el ~ llegado** the newcomer; **el ~ nacido** the newborn child

reciente [re'θjente] adj recent; (fresco) fresh; **~mente** adv recently

recinto [re'θinto] nm enclosure; (área) area, place

recio, a ['reθjo, a] adj strong, tough; (voz) loud ♦ adv hard; loud(ly)

recipiente [reθi'pjente] nm receptacle

reciprocidad [reθiproθi'ðað] nf reciprocity; **recíproco, a** adj reciprocal

recital [reθi'tal] nm (MUS) recital; (LITERATURA) reading

recitar [reθi'tar] vt to recite

reclamación [reklama'θjon] nf claim, demand; (queja) complaint

reclamar [rekla'mar] vt to claim, demand ♦ vi: **~ contra** to complain about; **~ a uno en justicia** to take sb to court; **reclamo** nm (anuncio) advertisement; (tentación) attraction

reclinar [rekli'nar] vt to recline, lean; **~se** vr to lean back

recluir [reklu'ir] vt to intern, confine

reclusión [reklu'sjon] nf (prisión) prison; (refugio) seclusion; **~ perpetua** life imprisonment

recluta [re'kluta] nm/f recruit ♦ nf recruitment; **reclutar** vt (datos) to collect; (dinero) to collect up; **~miento** [rekluta'mjento] nm recruitment

recobrar [reko'ßrar] vt (salud) to recover; (rescatar) to get back; **~se** vr to recover

recodo [re'koðo] nm (de río, camino) bend

recogedor [rekoxe'ðor] nm dustpan

recoger [reko'xer] vt to collect; (AGR) to harvest; (levantar) to pick up; (juntar) to gather; (pasar a buscar) to come for, get; (dar asilo) to give shelter to; (faldas) to gather up; (pelo) to put up; **~se** vr

(retirarse) to retire; **recogido, a** adj (lugar) quiet, secluded; (pequeño) small ♦ nf (CORREOS) collection; (AGR) harvest

recolección [rekolek'θjon] nf (AGR) harvesting; (colecta) collection

recomendación [rekomenda'θjon] nf (sugerencia) suggestion, recommendation; (referencia) reference

recomendar [rekomen'dar] vt to suggest, recommend; (confiar) to entrust

recompensa [rekom'pensa] nf reward, recompense; **recompensar** vt to reward, recompense

recomponer [rekompo'ner] vt to mend

reconciliación [rekonθilja'θjon] nf reconciliation

reconciliar [rekonθi'ljar] vt to reconcile; **~se** vr to become reconciled

recóndito, a [re'kondito, a] adj (lugar) hidden, secret

reconfortar [rekonfor'tar] vt to comfort

reconocer [rekono'θer] vt to recognize; (registrar) to search; (MED) to examine; **reconocido, a** adj recognized; (agradecido) grateful; **reconocimiento** nm recognition; search; examination; gratitude; (confesión) admission

reconquista [rekon'kista] nf reconquest; **la R~** the Reconquest (of Spain)

reconstituyente [rekonstitu'jente] nm tonic

reconstruir [rekonstru'ir] vt to reconstruct

reconversión [rekonßer'sjon] nf: **~ industrial** industrial rationalization

recopilación [rekopila'θjon] nf (resumen) summary; (compilación) compilation; **recopilar** vt to compile

récord ['rekorð] (pl **~s**) adj inv, nm record

recordar [rekor'ðar] vt (acordarse de) to remember; (acordar a otro) to remind ♦ vi to remember

recorrer [reko'rrer] vt (país) to cross, travel through; (distancia) to cover; (registrar) to search; (repasar) to look over; **recorrido** nm run, journey; **tren de largo recorrido** main-line train

recortado, a [rekor'taðo, a] adj uneven,

irregular

recortar [rekor'tar] *vt* to cut out; **recorte** *nm* (*acción, de prensa*) cutting; (*de telas, chapas*) trimming; **recorte presupuestario** budget cut

recostado, a [rekos'taðo, a] *adj* leaning; **estar ~** to be lying down

recostar [rekos'tar] *vt* to lean; **~se** *vr* to lie down

recoveco [reko'βeko] *nm* (*de camino, río etc*) bend; (*en casa*) cubby hole

recreación [rekrea'θjon] *nf* recreation

recrear [rekre'ar] *vt* (*entretener*) to entertain; (*volver a crear*) to recreate; **recreativo, a** *adj* recreational; **recreo** *nm* recreation; (*ESCOL*) break, playtime

recriminar [rekrimi'nar] *vt* to reproach ♦ *vi* to recriminate; **~se** *vr* to reproach each other

recrudecer [rekruðe'θer] *vt, vi* to worsen; **~se** *vr* to worsen

recrudecimiento [rekruðeθi'mjento] *nm* upsurge

recta ['rekta] *nf* straight line

rectángulo, a [rek'tangulo, a] *adj* rectangular ♦ *nm* rectangle

rectificar [rektifi'kar] *vt* to rectify; (*volverse recto*) to straighten ♦ *vi* to correct o.s.

rectitud [rekti'tuð] *nf* straightness; (*fig*) rectitude

recto, a ['rekto, a] *adj* straight; (*persona*) honest, upright ♦ *nm* rectum

rector, a [rek'tor, a] *adj* governing

recuadro [re'kwaðro] *nm* box; (*TIPOGRAFÍA*) inset

recubrir [reku'βrir] *vt*: **~ (con)** (*pintura, crema*) to cover (with)

recuento [re'kwento] *nm* inventory; **hacer el ~ de** to count o reckon up

recuerdo [re'kwerðo] *nm* souvenir; **~s** *nmpl* (*memorias*) memories; **¡~s a tu madre!** give my regards to your mother!

recular [reku'lar] *vi* to back down

recuperable [rekupe'raβle] *adj* recoverable

recuperación [rekupera'θjon] *nf* recovery

recuperar [rekupe'rar] *vt* to recover;

(*tiempo*) to make up; **~se** *vr* to recuperate

recurrir [reku'rrir] *vi* (*JUR*) to appeal; **~ a** to resort to; (*persona*) to turn to; **recurso** *nm* resort; (*medios*) means *pl*, resources *pl*; (*JUR*) appeal

recusar [reku'sar] *vt* to reject, refuse

red [reð] *nf* net, mesh; (*FERRO etc*) network; (*trampa*) trap; **la R~** (*Internet*) the Net

redacción [reðak'θjon] *nf* (*acción*) editing; (*personal*) editorial staff; (*ESCOL*) essay, composition

redactar [reðak'tar] *vt* to draw up, draft; (*periódico*) to edit

redactor, a [reðak'tor, a] *nm/f* editor

redada [re'ðaða] *nf*: **~ policial** police raid, round-up

rededor [reðe'ðor] *nm*: **al o en ~** around, round about

redención [reðen'θjon] *nf* redemption

redicho, a [re'ðitʃo, a] *adj* affected

redil [re'ðil] *nm* sheepfold

redimir [reði'mir] *vt* to redeem

rédito ['reðito] *nm* interest, yield

redoblar [reðo'βlar] *vt* to redouble ♦ *vi* (*tambor*) to roll

redomado, a [reðo'maðo, a] *adj* (*astuto*) sly, crafty; (*perfecto*) utter

redonda [re'ðonda] *nf*: **a la ~** around, round about

redondear [reðonde'ar] *vt* to round, round off

redondel [reðon'del] *nm* (*círculo*) circle; (*TAUR*) bullring, arena

redondo, a [re'ðondo, a] *adj* (*circular*) round; (*completo*) complete

reducción [reðuk'θjon] *nf* reduction

reducido, a [reðu'θiðo, a] *adj* reduced; (*limitado*) limited; (*pequeño*) small

reducir [reðu'θir] *vt* to reduce; to limit; **~se** *vr* to diminish

redundancia [reðun'danθja] *nf* redundancy

reembolsar [re(e)mbol'sar] *vt* (*persona*) to reimburse; (*dinero*) to repay, pay back; (*depósito*) to refund; **reembolso** *nm* reimbursement; refund

reemplazar [re(e)mpla'θar] *vt* to replace;

reemplazo [nm replacement; **de reemplazo** (MIL) reserve

reencuentro [re(e)n'kwentro] nm reunion

referencia [refe'renθja] nf reference; **con ~ a** with reference to

referéndum [refe'rendum] (pl **~s**) nm referéndum

referente [refe'rente] adj: **~ a** concerning, relating to

referir [refe'rir] vt (contar) to tell, recount; (relacionar) to refer, relate; **~se** vr: **~se a** to refer to

refilón [refi'lon]: **de ~** adv obliquely

refinado, a [refi'naðo, a] adj refined

refinamiento [refina'mjento] nm refinement

refinar [refi'nar] vt to refine; **refinería** nf refinery

reflejar [refle'xar] vt to reflect; **reflejo, a** adj reflected; (movimiento) reflex ♦ nm reflection; (ANAT) reflex

reflexión [reflek'sjon] nf reflection; **reflexionar** vt to reflect on ♦ vi to reflect; (detenerse) to pause (to think)

reflexivo, a [reflek'siβo, a] adj thoughtful; (LING) reflexive

reflujo [re'fluxo] nm ebb

reforma [re'forma] nf reform; (ARQ etc) repair; **~ agraria** agrarian reform

reformar [refor'mar] vt to reform; (modificar) to change, alter; (ARQ) to repair; **~se** vr to mend one's ways

reformatorio [reforma'torjo] nm reformatory

reforzar [refor'θar] vt to strengthen; (ARQ) to reinforce; (fig) to encourage

refractario, a [refrak'tarjo, a] adj (TEC) heat-resistant

refrán [re'fran] nm proverb, saying

refregar [refre'ɣar] vt to scrub

refrenar [refre'nar] vt to check, restrain

refrendar [refren'dar] vt to endorse, countersign; (ley) to approve

refrescante [refres'kante] adj refreshing, cooling

refrescar [refres'kar] vt to refresh ♦ vi to cool down; **~se** vr to get cooler; (tomar aire fresco) to go out for a breath of fresh air; (beber) to have a drink

refresco [re'fresko] nm soft drink, cool drink; **"~s"** "refreshments"

refriega [re'frjeɣa] nf scuffle, brawl

refrigeración [refrixera'θjon] nf refrigeration; (de sala) air-conditioning

refrigerador [refrixera'ðor] nm refrigerator (BRIT), icebox (US)

refrigerar [refrixe'rar] vt to refrigerate; (sala) to air-condition

refuerzo [re'fwerθo] nm reinforcement; (TEC) support

refugiado, a [refu'xjaðo, a] nm/f refugee

refugiarse [refu'xjarse] vr to take refuge, shelter

refugio [re'fuxjo] nm refuge; (protección) shelter

refunfuñar [refunfu'nar] vi to grunt, growl; (quejarse) to grumble

refutar [refu'tar] vt to refute

regadera [reɣa'ðera] nf watering can

regadío [reɣa'ðio] nm irrigated land

regalado, a [reɣa'laðo, a] adj comfortable, luxurious; (gratis) free, for nothing

regalar [reɣa'lar] vt (dar) to give (as a present); (entregar) to give away; (mimar) to pamper, make a fuss of

regaliz [reɣa'liθ] nm liquorice

regalo [re'ɣalo] nm (obsequio) gift, present; (gusto) pleasure

regañadientes [reɣaɲa'ðjentes]: **a ~** adv reluctantly

regañar [reɣa'nar] vt to scold ♦ vi to grumble; **regañón, ona** adj nagging

regar [re'ɣar] vt to water, irrigate; (fig) to scatter, sprinkle

regatear [reɣate'ar] vt (COM) to bargain over; (escatimar) to be mean with ♦ vi to bargain, haggle; (DEPORTE) to dribble; **regateo** nm bargaining; dribbling; (del cuerpo) swerve, dodge

regazo [re'ɣaθo] nm lap

regeneración [rexenera'θjon] nf regeneration

regenerar [rexene'rar] vt to regenerate

regentar [rexen'tar] *vt* to direct, manage; **regente** *nm* (*COM*) manager; (*POL*) regent

régimen ['reximen] (*pl* **regímenes**) *nm* regime; (*MED*) diet

regimiento [rexi'mjento] *nm* regiment

regio, a ['rexjo, a] *adj* royal, regal; (*fig: suntuoso*) splendid; (*AM: fam*) great, terrific

región [re'xjon] *nf* region

regir [re'xir] *vt* to govern, rule; (*dirigir*) to manage, run ♦ *vi* to apply, be in force

registrar [rexis'trar] *vt* (*buscar*) to search; (: *en cajón*) to look through; (*inspeccionar*) to inspect; (*anotar*) to register, record; (*INFORM*) to log; **~se** *vr* to register; (*ocurrir*) to happen

registro [re'xistro] *nm* (*acto*) registration; (*MUS, libro*) register; (*inspección*) inspection, search; **~ civil** registry office

regla ['rexla] *nf* (*ley*) rule, regulation; (*de medir*) ruler, rule; (*MED: período*) period

reglamentación [rexlamenta'θjon] *nf* (*acto*) regulation; (*lista*) rules *pl*

reglamentar [rexlamen'tar] *vt* to regulate; **reglamentario, a** *adj* statutory; **reglamento** *nm* rules *pl*, regulations *pl*

regocijarse [revoθi'xarse] *vr*: **~ de** to rejoice, be happy about; **regocijo** *nm* joy, happiness

regodearse [revoðe'arse] *vr* to be glad, be delighted; **regodeo** *nm* delight

regresar [revre'sar] *vi* to come back, go back, return; **regresivo, a** *adj* backward; (*fig*) regressive; **regreso** *nm* return

reguero [re'vero] *nm* (*de sangre etc*) trickle; (*de humo*) trail

regulador [revula'ðor] *nm* regulator; (*de radio etc*) knob, control

regular [revu'lar] *adj* regular; (*normal*) normal, usual; (*común*) ordinary; (*organizado*) regular, orderly; (*mediano*) average; (*fam*) not bad, so-so ♦ *adv* so-so, alright ♦ *vt* (*controlar*) to control, regulate; (*TEC*) to adjust; **por lo ~** as a rule; **~idad** *nf* regularity; **~izar** *vt* to regularize

regusto [re'vusto] *nm* aftertaste

rehabilitación [reaßilita'θjon] *nf* rehabilitation; (*ARQ*) restoration

rehabilitar [reaßili'tar] *vt* to rehabilitate; (*ARQ*) to restore; (*reintegrar*) to reinstate

rehacer [rea'θer] *vt* (*reparar*) to mend, repair; (*volver a hacer*) to redo, repeat; **~se** *vr* (*MED*) to recover

rehén [re'en] *nm* hostage

rehuir [reu'ir] *vt* to avoid, shun

rehusar [reu'sar] *vt, vi* to refuse

reina ['reina] *nf* queen; **~do** *nm* reign

reinante [rei'nante] *adj* (*fig*) prevailing

reinar [rei'nar] *vi* to reign

reincidir [reinθi'ðir] *vi* to relapse

reincorporarse [reinkorpo'rarse] *vr*: **~ a** to rejoin

reino ['reino] *nm* kingdom; **el R~ Unido** the United Kingdom

reintegrar [reinte'vrar] *vt* (*reconstituir*) to reconstruct; (*persona*) to reinstate; (*dinero*) to refund, pay back; **~se** *vr*: **~se a** to return to

reír [re'ir] *vi* to laugh; **~se** *vr* to laugh; **~se de** to laugh at

reiterar [reite'rar] *vt* to reiterate

reivindicación [reißindika'θjon] *nf* (*demanda*) claim, demand; (*justificación*) vindication

reivindicar [reißindi'kar] *vt* to claim

reja ['rexa] *nf* (*de ventana*) grille, bars *pl*; (*en la calle*) grating

rejilla [re'xiʎa] *nf* grating, grille; (*muebles*) wickerwork; (*de ventilación*) vent; (*de coche etc*) luggage rack

rejoneador [rexonea'ðor] *nm* mounted bullfighter

rejuvenecer [rexußene'θer] *vt, vi* to rejuvenate

relación [rela'θjon] *nf* relation, relationship; (*MAT*) ratio; (*narración*) report; **relaciones públicas** public relations; **con ~ a, en ~ con** in relation to; **relacionar** *vt* to relate, connect; **relacionarse** *vr* to be connected, be linked

relajación [relaxa'θjon] *nf* relaxation
relajado, a [rela'xaðo, a] *adj* (*disoluto*)
loose; (*cómodo*) relaxed; (*MED*) ruptured
relajar [rela'xar] *vt* to relax; **~se** *vr* to relax
relamerse [rela'merse] *vr* to lick one's lips
relamido, a [rela'miðo, a] *adj* (*pulcro*)
overdressed; (*afectado*) affected
relámpago [re'lampaɣo] *nm* flash of
lightning; **visita/huelga ~** lightning visit/
strike; **relampaguear** *vi* to flash
relatar [rela'tar] *vt* to tell, relate
relativo, a [rela'tiβo, a] *adj* relative; **en lo
~ a** concerning
relato [re'lato] *nm* (*narración*) story, tale
relegar [rele'ɣar] *vt* to relegate
relevante [rele'βante] *adj* eminent,
outstanding
relevar [rele'βar] *vt* (*sustituir*) to relieve;
~se *vr* to relay; **~ a uno de un cargo** to
relieve sb of his post
relevo [re'leβo] *nm* relief; **carrera de ~s**
relay race
relieve [re'ljeβe] *nm* (*ARTE, TEC*) relief; (*fig*)
prominence, importance; **bajo ~** bas-relief
religión [reli'xjon] *nf* religion; **religioso,
a** *adj* religious ♦ *nm/f* monk/nun
relinchar [relin'tʃar] *vi* to neigh; **relincho**
nm neigh; (*acto*) neighing
reliquia [re'likja] *nf* relic; **~ de familia**
heirloom
rellano [re'ʎano] *nm* (*ARQ*) landing
rellenar [reʎe'nar] *vt* (*llenar*) to fill up;
(*CULIN*) to stuff; (*COSTURA*) to pad;
relleno, a *adj* full up; stuffed ♦ *nm*
stuffing; (*de tapicería*) padding
reloj [re'lo(x)] *nm* clock; **~ (de pulsera)**
wristwatch; **~ despertador** alarm (clock);
poner el ~ to set one's watch (*o* the
clock); **~ero, a** *nm/f* clockmaker;
watchmaker
reluciente [relu'θjente] *adj* brilliant,
shining
relucir [relu'θir] *vi* to shine; (*fig*) to excel
relumbrar [relum'brar] *vi* to dazzle, shine
brilliantly
remachar [rema'tʃar] *vt* to rivet; (*fig*) to
hammer home, drive home; **remache**

nm rivet
remanente [rema'nente] *nm* remainder;
(*COM*) balance; (*de producto*) surplus
remangar [reman'ɡar] *vt* to roll up
remanso [re'manso] *nm* pool
remar [re'mar] *vi* to row
rematado, a [rema'taðo, a] *adj* complete,
utter
rematar [rema'tar] *vt* to finish off; (*COM*)
to sell off cheap ♦ *vi* to end, finish off;
(*DEPORTE*) to shoot
remate [re'mate] *nm* end, finish; (*punta*)
tip; (*DEPORTE*) shot; (*ARQ*) top; **de *o* para
~** to crown it all (*BRIT*), to top it off
remedar [reme'ðar] *vt* to imitate
remediar [reme'ðjar] *vt* to remedy;
(*subsanar*) to make good, repair; (*evitar*)
to avoid
remedio [re'meðjo] *nm* remedy; (*alivio*)
relief, help; (*JUR*) recourse, remedy; **poner
~ a** to correct, stop; **no tener más ~** to
have no alternative; **¡qué ~!** there's no
choice!; **sin ~** hopeless
remedo [re'meðo] *nm* imitation; (*pey*)
parody
remendar [remen'dar] *vt* to repair; (*con
parche*) to patch
remesa [re'mesa] *nf* remittance; (*COM*)
shipment
remiendo [re'mjendo] *nm* mend; (*con
parche*) patch; (*cosido*) darn
remilgado, a [remil'ɣaðo, a] *adj* prim;
(*afectado*) affected
remilgo [re'milɣo] *nm* primness;
(*afectación*) affectation
reminiscencia [reminis'θenθja] *nf*
reminiscence
remiso, a [re'miso, a] *adj* slack, slow
remite [re'mite] *nm* (*en sobre*) name and
address of sender
remitir [remi'tir] *vt* to remit, send ♦ *vi* to
slacken; (*en carta*): **remite: X** sender: X;
remitente *nm/f* sender
remo ['remo] *nm* (*de barco*) oar; (*DEPORTE*)
rowing
remojar [remo'xar] *vt* to steep, soak;
(*galleta etc*) to dip, dunk

remojo [re'moxo] *nm*: **dejar la ropa en ~** to leave clothes to soak

remolacha [remo'latʃa] *nf* beet, beetroot

remolcador [remolka'ðor] *nm* (*NAUT*) tug; (*AUTO*) breakdown lorry

remolcar [remol'kar] *vt* to tow

remolino [remo'lino] *nm* eddy; (*de agua*) whirlpool; (*de viento*) whirlwind; (*de gente*) crowd

remolque [re'molke] *nm* tow, towing; (*cuerda*) towrope; **llevar a ~** to tow

remontar [remon'tar] *vt* to mend; **~se** *vr* to soar; **~se a** (*COM*) to amount to; **~ el vuelo** to soar

remorder [remor'ðer] *vt* to distress, disturb; **~le la conciencia a uno** to have a guilty conscience; **remordimiento** *nm* remorse

remoto, a [re'moto, a] *adj* remote

remover [remo'ßer] *vt* to stir; (*tierra*) to turn over; (*objetos*) to move round

remozar [remo'θar] *vt* (*ARQ*) to refurbish

remuneración [remunera'θjon] *nf* remuneration

remunerar [remune'rar] *vt* to remunerate; (*premiar*) to reward

renacer [rena'θer] *vi* to be reborn; (*fig*) to revive; **renacimiento** *nm* rebirth; **el Renacimiento** the Renaissance

renacuajo [rena'kwaxo] *nm* (*ZOOL*) tadpole

renal [re'nal] *adj* renal, kidney *cpd*

rencilla [ren'θiʎa] *nf* quarrel

rencor [ren'kor] *nm* rancour, bitterness; **~oso, a** *adj* spiteful

rendición [rendi'θjon] *nf* surrender

rendido, a [ren'diðo, a] *adj* (*sumiso*) submissive; (*cansado*) worn-out, exhausted

rendija [ren'dixa] *nf* (*hendedura*) crack, cleft

rendimiento [rendi'mjento] *nm* (*producción*) output; (*TEC, COM*) efficiency

rendir [ren'dir] *vt* (*vencer*) to defeat; (*producir*) to produce; (*dar beneficio*) to yield; (*agotar*) to exhaust ♦ *vi* to pay; **~se** *vr* (*someterse*) to surrender; (*cansarse*) to

wear o.s. out; **~ homenaje** *o* **culto a** to pay homage to

renegar [rene'ßar] *vi* (*renunciar*) to renounce; (*blasfemar*) to blaspheme; (*quejarse*) to complain

RENFE ['renfe] *nf abr* (= *Red Nacional de los Ferrocarriles Españoles*) ≈ BR (*BRIT*)

renglón [ren'glon] *nm* (*línea*) line; (*COM*) item, article; **a ~ seguido** immediately after

renombrado, a [renom'braðo, a] *adj* renowned

renombre [re'nombre] *nm* renown

renovación [renoßa'θjon] *nf* (*de contrato*) renewal; (*ARQ*) renovation

renovar [reno'ßar] *vt* to renew; (*ARQ*) to renovate

renta ['renta] *nf* (*ingresos*) income; (*beneficio*) profit; (*alquiler*) rent; **~ vitalicia** annuity; **rentable** *adj* profitable; **rentar** *vt* to produce, yield

renuncia [re'nunθja] *nf* resignation

renunciar [renun'θjar] *vt* to renounce; (*tabaco, alcohol etc*): **~ a** to give up; (*oferta, oportunidad*) to turn down; (*puesto*) to resign ♦ *vi* to resign

reñido, a [re'niðo, a] *adj* (*batalla*) bitter, hard-fought; **estar ~ con uno** to be on bad terms with sb

reñir [re'nir] *vt* (*regañar*) to scold ♦ *vi* (*estar peleado*) to quarrel, fall out; (*combatir*) to fight

reo ['reo] *nm/f* culprit, offender; **~ de muerte** prisoner condemned to death

reojo [re'oxo] *de* **~** *adv* out of the corner of one's eye

reparación [repara'θjon] *nf* (*acto*) mending, repairing; (*TEC*) repair; (*fig*) amends, reparation

reparar [repa'rar] *vt* to repair; (*fig*) to make amends for; (*observar*) to observe ♦ *vi*: **~ en** (*darse cuenta de*) to notice; (*prestar atención a*) to pay attention to

reparo [re'paro] *nm* (*advertencia*) observation; (*duda*) doubt; (*dificultad*) difficulty; **poner ~s (a)** to raise objections (to)

repartición [reparti'θjon] nf distribution; (división) division; **repartidor, a** nm/f distributor

repartir [repar'tir] vt to distribute, share out; (CORREOS) to deliver; **reparto** nm distribution; delivery; (TEATRO, CINE) cast; (AM: urbanización) housing estate (BRIT), real estate development (US)

repasar [repa'sar] vt (ESCOL) to revise; (MECÁNICA) to check, overhaul; (COSTURA) to mend; **repaso** nm revision; overhaul, checkup; mending

repatriar [repa'trjar] vt to repatriate

repecho [re'petʃo] nm steep incline

repelente [repe'lente] adj repellent, repulsive

repeler [repe'ler] vt to repel

repensar [repen'sar] vt to reconsider

repente [re'pente] nm: **de ~** suddenly; **~ de ira** fit of anger

repentino, a [repen'tino, a] adj sudden

repercusión [reperku'sjon] nf repercussion

repercutir [reperku'tir] vi (objeto) to rebound; (sonido) to echo; **~ en** (fig) to have repercussions on

repertorio [reper'torjo] nm list; (TEATRO) repertoire

repetición [repeti'θjon] nf repetition

repetir [repe'tir] vt to repeat; (plato) to have a second helping of ♦ vi to repeat; (sabor) to come back; **~se** vr (volver sobre un tema) to repeat o.s.

repetitivo, a [repeti'tiβo, a] adj repetitive, repetitious

repicar [repi'kar] vt (campanas) to ring

repique [re'pike] nm pealing, ringing; **~teo** nm pealing; (de tambor) drumming

repisa [re'pisa] nf ledge, shelf; (de ventana) windowsill; **~ de chimenea** mantelpiece

repito etc vb ver **repetir**

replantearse [replante'arse] vr: **~ un problema** to reconsider a problem

replegarse [reple'γarse] vr to fall back, retreat

repleto, a [re'pleto, a] adj replete, full up

réplica ['replika] nf answer; (ARTE) replica

replicar [repli'kar] vi to answer; (objetar) to argue, answer back

repliegue [re'pljeγe] nm (MIL) withdrawal

repoblación [repoβla'θjon] nf repopulation; (de río) restocking; **~ forestal** reafforestation

repoblar [repo'βlar] vt to repopulate; (con árboles) to reafforest

repollo [re'poʎo] nm cabbage

reponer [repo'ner] vt to replace, put back; (TEATRO) to revive; **~se** vr to recover; **~ que** to reply that

reportaje [repor'taxe] nm report, article

reportero, a [repor'tero, a] nm/f reporter

reposacabezas [reposaka'βeθas] nm inv headrest

reposado, a [repo'saðo, a] adj (descansado) restful; (tranquilo) calm

reposar [repo'sar] vi to rest, repose

reposición [reposi'θjon] nf replacement; (CINE) remake

reposo [re'poso] nm rest

repostar [repos'tar] vt to replenish; (AUTO) to fill up (with petrol (BRIT) o gasoline (US))

repostería [reposte'ria] nf confectioner's (shop); **repostero, a** nm/f confectioner

reprender [repren'der] vt to reprimand

represa [re'presa] nf dam; (lago artificial) lake, pool

represalia [repre'salja] nf reprisal

representación [representa'θjon] nf representation; (TEATRO) performance; **representante** nm/f representative; performer

representar [represen'tar] vt to represent; (TEATRO) to perform; (edad) to look; **~se** vr to imagine; **representativo, a** adj representative

represión [repre'sjon] nf repression

reprimenda [repri'menda] nf reprimand, rebuke

reprimir [repri'mir] vt to repress

reprobar [repro'βar] vt to censure, reprove

reprochar [repro'tʃar] vt to reproach; **reproche** nm reproach

reproducción [reproðuk'θjon] *nf* reproduction

reproducir [reproðu'θir] *vt* to reproduce; **~se** *vr* to breed; (*situación*) to recur

reproductor, a [reproðuk'tor, a] *adj* reproductive

reptil [rep'til] *nm* reptile

república [re'puβlika] *nf* republic; **R~ Dominicana** Dominican Republic; **republicano, a** *adj, nm/f* republican

repudiar [repu'ðjar] *vt* to repudiate; (*fe*) to renounce

repuesto [re'pwesto] *nm* (*pieza de recambio*) spare (part); (*abastecimiento*) supply; **rueda de ~** spare wheel

repugnancia [repuɣ'nanθja] *nf* repugnance; **repugnante** *adj* repugnant, repulsive

repugnar [repuɣ'nar] *vt* to disgust

repulsa [re'pulsa] *nf* rebuff

repulsión [repul'sjon] *nf* repulsion, aversion; **repulsivo, a** *adj* repulsive

reputación [reputa'θjon] *nf* reputation

requemado, a [reke'maðo, a] *adj* (*quemado*) scorched; (*bronceado*) tanned

requerimiento [rekeri'mjento] *nm* request; (*JUR*) summons

requerir [reke'rir] *vt* (*pedir*) to ask, request; (*exigir*) to require; (*llamar*) to send for, summon

requesón [reke'son] *nm* cottage cheese

requete... [re'kete] *prefijo* extremely

réquiem ['rekjem] (*pl* **~s**) *nm* requiem

requisito [reki'sito] *nm* requirement, requisite

res [res] *nf* beast, animal

resaca [re'saka] *nf* (*en el mar*) undertow, undercurrent; (*fam*) hangover

resaltar [resal'tar] *vi* to project, stick out; (*fig*) to stand out

resarcir [resar'θir] *vt* to compensate; **~se** *vr* to make up for

resbaladizo, a [resβala'ðiθo, a] *adj* slippery

resbalar [resβa'lar] *vi* to slip, slide; (*fig*) to slip (up); **~se** *vr* to slip, slide; to slip (up); **resbalón** *nm* (*acción*) slip

rescatar [reska'tar] *vt* (*salvar*) to save, rescue; (*objeto*) to get back, recover; (*cautivos*) to ransom

rescate [res'kate] *nm* rescue; (*de objeto*) recovery; **pagar un ~** to pay a ransom

rescindir [resθin'dir] *vt* to rescind

rescisión [resθi'sjon] *nf* cancellation

rescoldo [res'koldo] *nm* embers *pl*

resecar [rese'kar] *vt* to dry thoroughly; (*MED*) to cut out, remove; **~se** *vr* to dry up

reseco, a [re'seko, a] *adj* very dry; (*fig*) skinny

resentido, a [resen'tiðo, a] *adj* resentful

resentimiento [resenti'mjento] *nm* resentment, bitterness

resentirse [resen'tirse] *vr* (*debilitarse: persona*) to suffer; **~ de** (*consecuencias*) to feel the effects of; **~ de** (*o por*) **algo** to resent sth, be bitter about sth

reseña [re'seɲa] *nf* (*cuenta*) account; (*informe*) report; (*LITERATURA*) review

reseñar [rese'ɲar] *vt* to describe; (*LITERATURA*) to review

reserva [re'serβa] *nf* reserve; (*reservación*) reservation; **a ~ de que ...** unless ...; **con toda ~** in strictest confidence

reservado, a [reser'βaðo, a] *adj* reserved; (*retraído*) cold, distant ♦ *nm* private room

reservar [reser'βar] *vt* (*guardar*) to keep; (*habitación, entrada*) to reserve; **~se** *vr* to save o.s.; (*callar*) to keep to o.s.

resfriado [resfri'aðo] *nm* cold; **resfriarse** *vr* to cool; (*MED*) to catch (a) cold

resguardar [resɣwar'ðar] *vt* to protect, shield; **~se** *vr*: **~se de** to guard against; **resguardo** *nm* defence; (*vale*) voucher; (*recibo*) receipt, slip

residencia [resi'ðenθja] *nf* residence; **~l** *nf* (*urbanización*) housing estate

residente [resi'ðente] *adj, nm/f* resident

residir [resi'ðir] *vi* to reside, live; **~ en** to reside in, lie in

residuo [re'siðwo] *nm* residue

resignación [resiɣna'θjon] *nf* resignation; **resignarse** *vr*: **resignarse a** *o* **con** to resign o.s. to, be resigned to

resina [re'sina] *nf* resin
resistencia [resis'tenθja] *nf* (*dureza*) endurance, strength; (*oposición*, ELEC) resistance; **resistente** *adj* strong, hardy; resistant
resistir [resis'tir] *vt* (*soportar*) to bear; (*oponerse a*) to resist, oppose; (*aguantar*) to put up with ♦ *vi* to resist; (*aguantar*) to last, endure; **~se** *vr*: **~se a** to refuse to, resist
resolución [resolu'θjon] *nf* resolution; (*decisión*) decision; **resoluto, a** *adj* resolute
resolver [resol'ßer] *vt* to resolve; (*solucionar*) to solve, resolve; (*decidir*) to decide, settle; **~se** *vr* to make up one's mind
resonancia [reso'nanθja] *nf* (*del sonido*) resonance; (*repercusión*) repercussion
resonar [reso'nar] *vi* to ring, echo
resoplar [reso'plar] *vi* to snort; **resoplido** *nm* heavy breathing
resorte [re'sorte] *nm* spring; (*fig*) lever
respaldar [respal'dar] *vt* to back (up), support; **~se** *vr* to lean back; **~se con** *o* **en** (*fig*) to take one's stand on; **respaldo** *nm* (*de sillón*) back; (*fig*) support, backing
respectivo, a [respek'tißo, a] *adj* respective; **en lo ~ a** with regard to
respecto [res'pekto] *nm*: **al ~** on this matter; **con ~ a, ~ de** with regard to, in relation to
respetable [respe'taßle] *adj* respectable
respetar [respe'tar] *vt* to respect; **respeto** *nm* respect; (*acatamiento*) deference; **respetos** *nmpl* respects; **respetuoso, a** *adj* respectful
respingo [res'pingo] *nm* start, jump
respiración [respira'θjon] *nf* breathing; (MED) respiration; (*ventilación*) ventilation
respirar [respi'rar] *vi* to breathe; **respiratorio, a** *adj* respiratory; **respiro** *nm* breathing; (*fig: descanso*) respite
resplandecer [resplande'θer] *vi* to shine; **resplandeciente** *adj* resplendent, shining; **resplandor** *nm* brilliance,

brightness; (*de luz, fuego*) blaze
responder [respon'der] *vt* to answer ♦ *vi* to answer; (*fig*) to respond; (*pey*) to answer back; **~ de** *o* **por** to answer for; **respondón, ona** *adj* cheeky
responsabilidad [responsaßili'ðað] *nf* responsibility
responsabilizarse [responsaßili'θarse] *vr* to make o.s. responsible, take charge
responsable [respon'saßle] *adj* responsible
respuesta [res'pwesta] *nf* answer, reply
resquebrajar [reskeßra'xar] *vt* to crack, split; **~se** *vr* to crack, split
resquemor [reske'mor] *nm* resentment
resquicio [res'kiθjo] *nm* chink; (*hendedura*) crack
resta ['resta] *nf* (MAT) remainder
restablecer [restaße'θer] *vt* to re-establish, restore; **~se** *vr* to recover
restallar [resta'ʎar] *vi* to crack
restante [res'tante] *adj* remaining; **lo ~** the remainder
restar [res'tar] *vt* (MAT) to subtract; (*fig*) to take away ♦ *vi* to remain, be left
restauración [restaura'θjon] *nf* restoration
restaurante [restau'rante] *nm* restaurant
restaurar [restau'rar] *vt* to restore
restitución [restitu'θjon] *nf* return, restitution
restituir [restitu'ir] *vt* (*devolver*) to return, give back; (*rehabilitar*) to restore
resto ['resto] *nm* (*residuo*) rest, remainder; (*apuesta*) stake; **~s** *nmpl* remains
restregar [restre'var] *vt* to scrub, rub
restricción [restrik'θjon] *nf* restriction
restrictivo, a [restrik'tißo, a] *adj* restrictive
restringir [restrin'xir] *vt* to restrict, limit
resucitar [resuθi'tar] *vt, vi* to resuscitate, revive
resuello [re'sweʎo] *nm* (*aliento*) breath; **estar sin ~** to be breathless
resuelto, a [re'swelto, a] *pp de* **resolver** ♦ *adj* resolute, determined
resultado [resul'taðo] *nm* result; (*conclusión*) outcome; **resultante** *adj*

resulting, resultant

resultar [resul'tar] vi (ser) to be; (llegar a
ser) to turn out to be; (salir bien) to turn
out well; (COM) to amount to; ~ **de** to
stem from; **me resulta difícil hacerlo** it's
difficult for me to do it

resumen [re'sumen] (pl **resúmenes**) nm
summary, résumé; **en ~** in short

resumir [resu'mir] vt to sum up; (cortar)
to abridge, cut down; (condensar) to
summarize

resurgir [resur'xir] vi (reaparecer) to
reappear

resurrección [resurre(k)'θjon] nf
resurrection

retablo [re'taßlo] nm altarpiece

retaguardia [reta'ɣwarðja] nf rearguard

retahíla [reta'ila] nf series, string

retal [re'tal] nm remnant

retar [re'tar] vt to challenge; (desafiar) to
defy, dare

retardar [retar'ðar] vt (demorar) to delay;
(hacer más lento) to slow down; (retener)
to hold back

retazo [re'taθo] nm snippet (BRIT),
fragment

retener [rete'ner] vt (intereses) to withhold

reticente [reti'θente] adj (tono)
insinuating; (postura) reluctant; **ser ~ a
hacer algo** to be reluctant o unwilling to
do sth

retina [re'tina] nf retina

retintín [retin'tin] nm jangle, jingle

retirada [reti'raða] nf (MIL, refugio) retreat;
(de dinero) withdrawal; (de embajador)
recall; **retirado, a** adj (lugar) remote;
(vida) quiet; (jubilado) retired

retirar [reti'rar] vt to withdraw; (quitar) to
remove; (jubilar) to retire, pension off;
~se vr to retreat, withdraw; to retire;
(acostarse) to retire, go to bed; **retiro**
nm retreat; retirement; (pago) pension

reto ['reto] nm dare, challenge

retocar [reto'kar] vt (fotografía) to touch
up, retouch

retoño [re'toɲo] nm sprout, shoot; (fig)
offspring, child

retoque [re'toke] nm retouching

retorcer [retor'θer] vt to twist; (manos,
lavado) to wring; **~se** vr to become
twisted; (mover el cuerpo) to writhe

retorcido, a [retor'θiðo, a] adj (persona)
devious

retórica [re'torika] nf rhetoric; (pey)
affectedness; **retórico, a** adj rhetorical

retornar [retor'nar] vt to return, give back
♦ vi to return, go/come back; **retorno**
nm return

retortijón [retorti'xon] nm twist, twisting

retozar [reto'θar] vi (juguetear) to frolic,
romp; (saltar) to gambol; **retozón, ona**
adj playful

retracción [retrak'θjon] nf retraction

retractarse [retrak'tarse] vr to retract; **me
retracto** I take that back

retraerse [retra'erse] vr to retreat,
withdraw; **retraído, a** adj shy, retiring;
retraimiento nm retirement; (timidez)
shyness

retransmisión [retransmi'sjon] nf repeat
(broadcast)

retransmitir [retransmi'tir] vt (mensaje) to
relay; (TV etc) to repeat, retransmit; (: en
vivo) to broadcast live

retrasado, a [retra'saðo, a] adj late; (MED)
mentally retarded; (país etc) backward,
underdeveloped

retrasar [retra'sar] vt (demorar) to
postpone, put off; (retardar) to slow
down ♦ vi (atrasarse) to be late; (reloj) to
be slow; (producción) to fall (off);
(quedarse atrás) to lag behind; **~se** vr to
be late; to be slow; to fall (off); to lag
behind

retraso [re'traso] nm (demora) delay;
(lentitud) slowness; (tardanza) lateness;
(atraso) backwardness; **~s** (FINANZAS)
nmpl arrears; **llegar con ~** to arrive late;
~ mental mental deficiency

retratar [retra'tar] vt (ARTE) to paint the
portrait of; (fotografiar) to photograph;
(fig) to depict, describe; **~se** vr to have
one's portrait painted; to have one's
photograph taken; **retrato** nm portrait;

(*fig*) likeness; **retrato-robot** *nm* Identikit
® picture
retreta [re'treta] *nf* retreat
retrete [re'trete] *nm* toilet
retribución [retriβu'θjon] *nf* (*recompensa*)
reward; (*pago*) pay, payment
retribuir [retri'βwir] *vt* (*recompensar*) to
reward; (*pagar*) to pay
retro... ['retro] *prefijo* retro...
retroactivo, a [retroak'tiβo, a] *adj*
retroactive, retrospective
retroceder [retroθe'ðer] *vi* (*echarse atrás*)
to move back(wards); (*fig*) to back down
retroceso [retro'θeso] *nm* backward
movement; (*MED*) relapse; (*fig*) backing
down
retrógrado, a [re'troɣraðo, a] *adj*
retrograde, retrogressive; (*POL*) reactionary
retrospectivo, a [retrospek'tiβo, a] *adj*
retrospective
retrovisor [retroβi'sor] *nm* (*tb:* espejo ~)
rear-view mirror
retumbar [retum'bar] *vi* to echo, resound
reúma [re'uma], **reuma** ['reuma] *nm*
rheumatism
reumatismo [reuma'tismo] *nm* = **reúma**
reunificar [reunifi'kar] *vt* to reunify
reunión [reu'njon] *nf* (*asamblea*) meeting;
(*fiesta*) party
reunir [reu'nir] *vt* (*juntar*) to reunite, join
(together); (*recoger*) to gather
(together); (*personas*) to get together; (*cualidades*) to
combine; ~**se** *vr* (*personas: en asamblea*)
to meet, gather
revalidar [reβali'ðar] *vt* (*ratificar*) to
confirm, ratify
revalorizar [reβalori'θar] *vt* to revalue,
reassess
revancha [re'βantʃa] *nf* revenge
revelación [reβela'θjon] *nf* revelation
revelado [reβe'laðo] *nm* developing
revelar [reβe'lar] *vt* to reveal; (*FOTO*) to
develop
reventa [re'βenta] *nf* (*de entradas: para
concierto*) touting
reventar [reβen'tar] *vt* to burst, explode
reventón [reβen'ton] *nm* (*AUTO*) blow-out

(*BRIT*), flat (*US*)
reverencia [reβe'renθja] *nf* reverence;
reverenciar *vt* to revere
reverendo, a [reβe'rendo, a] *adj* reverend
reverente [reβe'rente] *adj* reverent
reversible [reβer'siβle] *adj* (*prenda*)
reversible
reverso [re'βerso] *nm* back, other side; (*de
moneda*) reverse
revertir [reβer'tir] *vi* to revert
revés [re'βes] *nm* back, wrong side; (*fig*)
reverse, setback; (*DEPORTE*) backhand; **al ~**
the wrong way round; (*de arriba abajo*)
upside down; (*ropa*) inside out; **volver
algo del ~** to turn sth round; (*ropa*) to
turn sth inside out
revestir [reβes'tir] *vt* (*cubrir*) to cover, coat
revisar [reβi'sar] *vt* (*examinar*) to check;
(*texto etc*) to revise; **revisión** *nf* revision
revisor, a [reβi'sor, a] *nm/f* inspector;
(*FERRO*) ticket collector
revista [re'βista] *nf* magazine, review;
(*TEATRO*) revue; (*inspección*) inspection;
pasar ~ a to review, inspect
revivir [reβi'βir] *vi* to revive
revocación [reβoka'θjon] *nf* repeal
revocar [reβo'kar] *vt* to revoke
revolcarse [reβol'karse] *vr* to roll about
revolotear [reβolote'ar] *vi* to flutter
revoltijo [reβol'tixo] *nm* mess, jumble
revoltoso, a [reβol'toso, a] *adj* (*travieso*)
naughty, unruly
revolución [reβolu'θjon] *nf* revolution;
revolucionar *vt* to revolutionize;
revolucionario, a *adj, nm/f*
revolutionary
revolver [reβol'βer] *vt* (*desordenar*) to
disturb, mess up; (*mover*) to move about
♦ *vi:* ~ **en** to go through, rummage
(about) in; ~**se** *vr* (*volver contra*) to turn
on *o* against
revólver [re'βolβer] *nm* revolver
revuelo [re'βwelo] *nm* fluttering; (*fig*)
commotion
revuelta [re'βwelta] *nf* (*motín*) revolt;
(*agitación*) commotion
revuelto, a [re'βwelto, a] *pp de* **revolver**

♦ adj (mezclado) mixed-up, in disorder
rey [rei] nm king; **Día de R~es** Twelfth
Night

Reyes Magos

ⓘ On the night before the 6th January
(the Epiphany), children go to bed
expecting **los Reyes Magos** (the Three
Wise Men) to bring them presents. Twelfth
Night processions, known as **cabalgatas**,
take place that evening when 3 people
dressed as **los Reyes Magos** arrive in the
town by land or sea to the delight of the
children.

reyerta [re'jerta] nf quarrel, brawl
rezagado, a [reθa'ɣaðo, a] nm/f straggler
rezagar [reθa'ɣar] vt (dejar atrás) to leave
behind; (retrasar) to delay, postpone
rezar [re'θar] vi to pray; **~ con** (fam) to
concern, have to do with; **rezo** nm
prayer
rezongar [reθon'ɡar] vi to grumble
rezumar [reθu'mar] vt to ooze
ría ['ria] nf estuary
riada [ri'aða] nf flood
ribera [ri'ßera] nf (de río) bank; (: área)
riverside
ribete [ri'ßete] nm (de vestido) border; (fig)
addition; **~ar** vt to edge, border
ricino [ri'θino] nm: **aceite de ~** castor oil
rico, a ['riko, a] adj rich; (adinerado)
wealthy, rich; (lujoso) luxurious; (comida)
delicious; (niño) lovely, cute ♦ nm/f rich
person
rictus ['riktus] nm (mueca) sneer, grin
ridiculez [riðiku'leθ] nf absurdity
ridiculizar [riðikuli'θar] vt to ridicule
ridículo, a [ri'ðikulo, a] adj ridiculous;
hacer el ~ to make a fool of o.s.; **poner
a uno en ~** to make a fool of sb
riego ['rjeɣo] nm (aspersión) watering;
(irrigación) irrigation
riel [rjel] nm rail
rienda ['rjenda] nf rein; **dar ~ suelta a** to
give free rein to
riesgo ['rjesɣo] nm risk; **correr el ~ de** to

run the risk of
rifa ['rifa] nf (lotería) raffle; **rifar** vt to raffle
rifle ['rifle] nm rifle
rigidez [rixi'ðeθ] nf rigidity, stiffness; (fig)
strictness; **rígido, a** adj rigid, stiff; strict,
inflexible
rigor [ri'ɣor] nm strictness, rigour;
(inclemencia) harshness; **de ~** de rigueur,
essential; **riguroso, a** adj rigorous;
harsh; (severo) severe
rimar [ri'mar] vi to rhyme
rimbombante [rimbom'bante] adj
pompous
rímel ['rimel] nm mascara
rímmel ['rimel] nm = **rímel**
rincón [rin'kon] nm corner (inside)
rinoceronte [rinoθe'ronte] nm rhinoceros
riña ['riɲa] nf (disputa) argument; (pelea)
brawl
riñón [ri'ɲon] nm kidney
río etc ['rio] vb ver **reír** ♦ nm river; (fig)
torrent, stream; **~ abajo/arriba**
downstream/upstream; **~ de la Plata**
River Plate
rioja [ri'oxa] nm (vino) rioja (wine)
rioplatense [riopla'tense] adj of o from
the River Plate region
riqueza [ri'keθa] nf wealth, riches pl;
(cualidad) richness
risa ['risa] nf laughter; (una ~) laugh; **¡qué
~!** what a laugh!
risco ['risko] nm crag, cliff
risible [ri'sißle] adj ludicrous, laughable
risotada [riso'taða] nf guffaw, loud laugh
ristra ['ristra] nf string
risueño, a [ri'sweɲo, a] adj (sonriente)
smiling; (contento) cheerful
ritmo ['ritmo] nm rhythm; **a ~ lento**
slowly; **trabajar a ~ lento** to go slow
rito ['rito] nm rite
ritual [ri'twal] adj, nm ritual
rival [ri'ßal] adj, nm/f rival; **~idad** nf
rivalry; **~izar** vi: **~izar con** to rival, vie
with
rizado, a [ri'θaðo, a] adj curly ♦ nm curls
pl
rizar [ri'θar] vt to curl; **~se** vr (pelo) to

curl; (agua) to ripple; **rizo** nm curl; ripple

RNE nf abr = **Radio Nacional de España**

robar [ro'βar] vt to rob; (objeto) to steal; (casa etc) to break into; (NAIPES) to draw

roble ['roβle] nm oak; **~dal** nm oakwood

robo ['roβo] nm robbery, theft

robot [ro'βot] nm robot; **~ (de cocina)** food processor

robustecer [roβuste'θer] vt to strengthen

robusto, a [ro'βusto, a] adj robust, strong

roca ['roka] nf rock

roce ['roθe] nm (caricia) brush; (TEC) friction; (en la piel) graze; **tener ~ con** to be in close contact with

rociar [ro'θjar] vt to spray

rocín [ro'θin] nm nag, hack

rocío [ro'θio] nm dew

rocoso, a [ro'koso, a] adj rocky

rodaballo [roδa'βaλo] nm turbot

rodado, a [ro'δaδo, a] adj (con ruedas) wheeled

rodaja [ro'δaxa] nf slice

rodaje [ro'δaxe] nm (CINE) shooting, filming; (AUTO) **en ~** running in

rodar [ro'δar] vt (vehículo) to wheel (along); (escalera) to roll down; (viajar por) to travel (over) ♦ vi to roll; (coche) to go, run; (CINE) to shoot, film

rodear [roδe'ar] vt to surround ♦ vi to go round; **~se** vr: **~se de amigos** to surround o.s. with friends

rodeo [ro'δeo] nm (ruta indirecta) detour; (evasión) evasion; (AM) rodeo; **hablar sin ~s** to come to the point, speak plainly

rodilla [ro'δiλa] nf knee; **de ~s** kneeling; **ponerse de ~s** to kneel (down)

rodillo [ro'δiλo] nm roller; (CULIN) rolling-pin

roedor, a [roe'δor, a] adj gnawing ♦ nm rodent

roer [ro'er] vt (masticar) to gnaw; (corroer, fig) to corrode

rogar [ro'ɣar] vt, vi (pedir) to ask for; (suplicar) to beg, plead; **se ruega no fumar** please do not smoke

rojizo, a [ro'xiθo, a] adj reddish

rojo, a ['roxo, a] adj, nm red; **al ~ vivo** red-hot

rol [rol] nm list, roll; (papel) role

rollito [ro'λito] nm: **~ de primavera** spring roll

rollizo, a [ro'λiθo, a] adj (objeto) cylindrical; (persona) plump

rollo ['roλo] nm roll; (de cuerda) coil; (madera) log; (fam) bore; **¡qué ~!** what a carry-on!

Roma ['roma] n Rome

romance [ro'manθe] nm (amoroso) romance; (LITERATURA) ballad

romano, a [ro'mano, a] adj, nm/f Roman; **a la romana** in batter

romanticismo [romanti'θismo] nm romanticism

romántico, a [ro'mantiko, a] adj romantic

rombo ['rombo] nm (GEOM) rhombus

romería [rome'ria] nf (REL) pilgrimage; (excursión) trip, outing

---
Romería
---

i Originally a pilgrimage to a shrine or church to express devotion to the Virgin Mary or a local Saint, the **romería** has also become a rural festival which accompanies the pilgrimage. People come from all over to attend, bringing their own food and drink, and spend the day in celebration.

---

romero, a [ro'mero, a] nm/f pilgrim ♦ nm rosemary

romo, a ['romo, a] adj blunt; (fig) dull

rompecabezas [rompeka'βeθas] nm inv riddle, puzzle; (juego) jigsaw (puzzle)

rompeolas [rompe'olas] nm inv breakwater

romper [rom'per] vt to break; (hacer pedazos) to smash; (papel, tela etc) to tear, rip ♦ vi (olas) to break; (sol, diente) to break through; **~ un contrato** to break a contract; **~ a** (empezar a) to start (suddenly) to; **~ a llorar** to burst into tears; **~ con uno** to fall out with sb

ron [ron] nm rum

roncar [ron'kar] vi to snore

ronco, a ['ronko, a] *adj* (*afónico*) hoarse; (*áspero*) raucous

ronda ['ronda] *nf* (*gen*) round; (*patrulla*) patrol; **rondar** *vt* to patrol ♦ *vi* to patrol; (*fig*) to prowl round

ronquido [ron'kiðo] *nm* snore, snoring

ronronear [ronrone'ar] *vi* to purr; **ronroneo** *nm* purr

roña ['roɲa] *nf* (*VETERINARIA*) mange; (*mugre*) dirt, grime; (*óxido*) rust

roñoso, a [ro'ɲoso, a] *adj* (*mugriento*) filthy; (*tacaño*) mean

ropa ['ropa] *nf* clothes, clothing; **~ blanca** linen; **~ de cama** bed linen; **~ interior** underwear; **~ para lavar** washing; **~je** *nm* gown, robes *pl*

ropero [ro'pero] *nm* linen cupboard; (*guardarropa*) wardrobe

rosa ['rosa] *adj* pink ♦ *nf* rose; **~ de los vientos** the compass

rosado, a [ro'saðo, a] *adj* pink ♦ *nm* rosé

rosal [ro'sal] *nm* rosebush

rosario [ro'sarjo] *nm* (*REL*) rosary; **rezar el ~** to say the rosary

rosca ['roska] *nf* (*de tornillo*) thread; (*de humo*) coil, spiral; (*pan, postre*) ring-shaped roll/pastry

rosetón [rose'ton] *nm* rosette; (*ARQ*) rose window

rosquilla [ros'kiʎa] *nf* doughnut-shaped fritter

rostro ['rostro] *nm* (*cara*) face

rotación [rota'θjon] *nf* rotation; **~ de cultivos** crop rotation

rotativo, a [rota'tiβo, a] *adj* rotary

roto, a ['roto, a] *pp de* **romper** ♦ *adj* broken

rotonda [ro'tonda] *nf* roundabout

rótula ['rotula] *nf* kneecap; (*TEC*) ball-and-socket joint

rotulador [rotula'ðor] *nm* felt-tip pen

rotular [rotu'lar] *vt* (*carta, documento*) to head, entitle; (*objeto*) to label; **rótulo** *nm* heading, title; label; (*letrero*) sign

rotundamente [rotunda'mente] *adv* (*negar*) flatly; (*responder, afirmar*) emphatically; **rotundo, a** *adj* round;

(*enfático*) emphatic

rotura [ro'tura] *nf* (*acto*) breaking; (*MED*) fracture

roturar [rotu'rar] *vt* to plough

rozadura [roθa'ðura] *nf* abrasion, graze

rozar [ro'θar] *vt* (*frotar*) to rub; (*arañar*) to scratch; (*tocar ligeramente*) to shave, touch lightly; **~se** *vr* to rub (together); **~se con** (*fam*) to rub shoulders with

rte. *abr* (= *remite, remitente*) sender

RTVE *nf abr* = **Radiotelevisión Española**

rubí [ru'βi] *nm* ruby; (*de reloj*) jewel

rubio, a ['ruβjo, a] *adj* fair-haired, blond(e) ♦ *nm/f* blond/blonde; **tabaco ~** Virginia tobacco

rubor [ru'βor] *nm* (*sonrojo*) blush; (*timidez*) bashfulness; **~izarse** *vr* to blush

rúbrica ['ruβrika] *nf* (*de la firma*) flourish; **rubricar** *vt* (*firmar*) to sign with a flourish; (*concluir*) to sign and seal

rudimentario, a [ruðimen'tarjo, a] *adj* rudimentary; **rudimento** *nm* rudiment

rudo, a ['ruðo, a] *adj* (*sin pulir*) unpolished; (*grosero*) coarse; (*violento*) violent; (*sencillo*) simple

rueda ['rweða] *nf* wheel; (*círculo*) ring, circle; (*rodaja*) slice, round; **~ delantera/trasera/de repuesto** front/back/spare wheel; **~ de prensa** press conference

ruedo ['rweðo] *nm* (*círculo*) circle; (*TAUR*) arena, bullring

ruego *etc* ['rweɣo] *vb ver* **rogar** ♦ *nm* request

rufián [ru'fjan] *nm* scoundrel

rugby ['ruɣβi] *nm* rugby

rugido [ru'xiðo] *nm* roar

rugir [ru'xir] *vi* to roar

rugoso, a [ru'ɣoso, a] *adj* (*arrugado*) wrinkled; (*áspero*) rough; (*desigual*) ridged

ruido ['rwiðo] *nm* noise; (*sonido*) sound; (*alboroto*) racket, row; (*escándalo*) commotion, rumpus; **~so, a** *adj* noisy, loud; (*fig*) sensational

ruin [rwin] *adj* contemptible, mean

ruina ['rwina] *nf* ruin; (*colapso*) collapse; (*de persona*) ruin, downfall

ruindad [rwin'dað] *nf* lowness, meanness;

(acto) low o mean act

ruinoso, a [rwi'noso, a] *adj* ruinous; *(destartalado)* dilapidated, tumbledown; *(COM)* disastrous

ruiseñor [rwise'ɲor] *nm* nightingale

ruleta [ru'leta] *nf* roulette

rulo ['rulo] *nm (para el pelo)* curler

Rumanía [ruma'nia] *nf* Rumania

rumba ['rumba] *nf* rumba

rumbo ['rumbo] *nm (ruta)* route, direction; *(ángulo de dirección)* course, bearing; *(fig)* course of events; **ir con ~ a** to be heading for

rumboso, a [rum'boso, a] *adj* generous

rumiante [ru'mjante] *nm* ruminant

rumiar [ru'mjar] *vt* to chew; *(fig)* to chew over ♦ *vi* to chew the cud

rumor [ru'mor] *nm (ruido sordo)* low sound; *(murmuración)* murmur, buzz

rumorearse [rumore'arse] *vr*: **se rumorea que** it is rumoured that

runrún [run'run] *nm (voces)* murmur, sound of voices; *(fig)* rumour

rupestre [ru'pestre] *adj* rock *cpd*

ruptura [rup'tura] *nf* rupture

rural [ru'ral] *adj* rural

Rusia ['rusja] *nf* Russia; **ruso, a** *adj, nm/f* Russian

rústica ['rustika] *nf*: **libro en ~** paperback (book); *ver tb* **rústico**

rústico, a ['rustiko, a] *adj* rustic; *(ordinario)* coarse, uncouth ♦ *nm/f* yokel

ruta ['ruta] *nf* route

rutina [ru'tina] *nf* routine; **~rio, a** *adj* routine

S, s

S *abr (= santo, a)* St; *(= sur)* S

s. *abr (= siglo)* C.; *(= siguiente)* foll

S.A. *abr (= Sociedad Anónima)* Ltd. *(BRIT)*, Inc. *(US)*

sábado ['saβaðo] *nm* Saturday

sábana ['saβana] *nf* sheet

sabandija [saβan'dixa] *nf* bug, insect

sabañón [saβa'ɲon] *nm* chilblain

saber [sa'βer] *vt* to know; *(llegar a conocer)* to find out, learn; *(tener capacidad de)* to know how to ♦ *vi*: **~ a** to taste of, taste like ♦ *nm* knowledge, learning; **a ~** namely; **¿sabes conducir/ nadar?** can you drive/swim?; **¿sabes francés?** do you speak French?; **~ de memoria** to know by heart; **hacer ~ algo a uno** to inform sb of sth, let sb know sth

sabiduría [saβiðu'ria] *nf (conocimientos)* wisdom; *(instrucción)* learning

sabiendas [sa'βjendas]: **a ~** *adv* knowingly

sabio, a ['saβjo,a] *adj (docto)* learned; *(prudente)* wise, sensible

sabor [sa'βor] *nm* taste, flavour; **~ear** *vt* to taste, savour; *(fig)* to relish

sabotaje [saβo'taxe] *nm* sabotage

saboteador, a [saβotea'ðor, a] *nm/f* saboteur

sabotear [saβote'ar] *vt* to sabotage

sabré *etc vb ver* **saber**

sabroso, a [sa'βroso, a] *adj* tasty; *(fig: fam)* racy, salty

sacacorchos [saka'kortʃos] *nm inv* corkscrew

sacapuntas [saka'puntas] *nm inv* pencil sharpener

sacar [sa'kar] *vt* to take out; *(fig: extraer)* to get (out); *(quitar)* to remove, get out; *(hacer salir)* to bring out; *(conclusión)* to draw; *(novela etc)* to publish, bring out; *(ropa)* to take off; *(obra)* to make; *(premio)* to receive; *(entradas)* to get; *(TENIS)* to serve; **~ adelante** *(niño)* to bring up; *(negocio)* to carry on, go on with; **~ a uno a bailar** to get sb up to dance; **~ una foto** to take a photo; **~ la lengua** to stick out one's tongue; **~ buenas/malas notas** to get good/bad marks

sacarina [saka'rina] *nf* saccharin(e)

sacerdote [saθer'ðote] *nm* priest

saciar [sa'θjar] *vt (hambre, sed)* to satisfy; **~se** *vr (de comida)* to get full up; **comer hasta ~se** to eat one's fill

saco ['sako] *nm* bag; *(grande)* sack; *(su*

contenido) bagful; (*AM*) jacket; **~ de
dormir** sleeping bag
sacramento [sakra'mento] *nm* sacrament
sacrificar [sakrifi'kar] *vt* to sacrifice;
sacrificio *nm* sacrifice
sacrilegio [sakri'lexjo] *nm* sacrilege;
sacrílego, a *adj* sacrilegious
sacristía [sakris'tia] *nf* sacristy
sacro, a ['sakro, a] *adj* sacred
sacudida [saku'ðiða] *nf* (*agitación*) shake,
shaking; (*sacudimiento*) jolt, bump; **~
eléctrica** electric shock
sacudir [saku'ðir] *vt* to shake; (*golpear*) to
hit
sádico, a ['saðiko, a] *adj* sadistic ♦ *nm/f*
sadist; **sadismo** *nm* sadism
saeta [sa'eta] *nf* (*flecha*) arrow
sagacidad [saɣaθi'ðað] *nf* shrewdness,
cleverness; **sagaz** *adj* shrewd, clever
sagitario [saxi'tarjo] *nm* Sagittarius
sagrado, a [sa'ɣraðo, a] *adj* sacred, holy
Sáhara ['saara] *nm*: **el ~** the Sahara
(desert)
sal [sal] *vb ver* **salir** ♦ *nf* salt
sala ['sala] *nf* room; (*~ de estar*) living
room; (*TEATRO*) house, auditorium; (*de
hospital*) ward; **~ de apelación** court; **~
de espera** waiting room; **~ de estar**
living room; **~ de fiestas** dance hall
salado, a [sa'laðo, a] *adj* salty; (*fig*) witty,
amusing; **agua salada** salt water
salar [sa'lar] *vt* to salt, add salt to
salarial [sala'rjal] *adj* (*aumento, revisión*)
wage *cpd*, salary *cpd*
salario [sa'larjo] *nm* wage, pay
salchicha [sal'tʃitʃa] *nf* (*pork*) sausage;
salchichón *nm* (*salami-type*) sausage
saldar [sal'dar] *vt* to pay; (*vender*) to sell
off; (*fig*) to settle, resolve; **saldo** *nm*
(*pago*) settlement; (*de una cuenta*)
balance; (*lo restante*) remnant(s) (*pl*),
remainder; **saldos** *nmpl* (*en tienda*) sale
saldré *etc vb ver* **salir**
salero [sa'lero] *nm* salt cellar
salgo *etc vb ver* **salir**
salida [sa'liða] *nf* (*puerta etc*) exit, way
out; (*acto*) leaving, going out; (*de tren,*

AVIAT) departure; (*TEC*) output, production; (*fig*) way out; (*COM*) opening;
(*GEO, válvula*) outlet; (*de gas*) leak; **calle
sin ~** cul-de-sac; **~ de incendios** fire
escape
saliente [sa'ljente] *adj* (*ARQ*) projecting;
(*sol*) rising; (*fig*) outstanding

┌─────────────────────┐
│ **PALABRA CLAVE** │
└─────────────────────┘

salir [sa'lir] *vi* 1 (*partir: tb:* **~ de**) to leave;
Juan ha salido Juan is out; **salió de la
cocina** he came out of the kitchen
2 (*aparecer*) to appear; (*disco, libro*) to
come out; **anoche salió en la tele** she
appeared *o* was on TV last night; **salió en
todos los periódicos** it was in all the
papers
3 (*resultar*): **la muchacha nos salió muy
trabajadora** the girl turned out to be a
very hard worker; **la comida te ha salido
exquisita** the food was delicious; **sale
muy caro** it's very expensive
4: **~le a uno algo: la entrevista que
hice me salió bien/mal** the interview I
did went *o* turned out well/badly
5: **~ adelante: no sé como haré para ~
adelante** I don't know how I'll get by
♦ **~se** *vr* (*líquido*) to spill; (*animal*) to
escape

saliva [sa'liβa] *nf* saliva
salmo ['salmo] *nm* psalm
salmón [sal'mon] *nm* salmon
salmonete [salmo'nete] *nm* red mullet
salmuera [sal'mwera] *nf* pickle, brine
salón [sa'lon] *nm* (*de casa*) living room,
lounge; (*muebles*) lounge suite; **~ de
belleza** beauty parlour; **~ de baile** dance
hall
salpicadero [salpika'ðero] *nm* (*AUTO*)
dashboard
salpicar [salpi'kar] *vt* (*rociar*) to sprinkle,
spatter; (*esparcir*) to scatter
salpicón [salpi'kon] *nm*: **~ de mariscos**
seafood salad
salsa ['salsa] *nf* sauce; (*con carne asada*)
gravy; (*fig*) spice

saltamontes [salta'montes] *nm inv* grasshopper

saltar [sal'tar] *vt* to jump (over), leap (over); (*dejar de lado*) to skip, miss out ♦ *vi* to jump, leap; (*pelota*) to bounce; (*al aire*) to fly up; (*quebrarse*) to break; (*al agua*) to dive; (*fig*) to explode, blow up

salto ['salto] *nm* jump, leap; (*al agua*) dive; **~ de agua** waterfall; **~ de altura** high jump

saltón, ona [sal'ton, ona] *adj* (*ojos*) bulging, popping; (*dientes*) protruding

salud [sa'luð] *nf* health; **¡(a su) ~!** cheers!, good health!; **~able** *adj* (*de buena ~*) healthy; (*provechoso*) good, beneficial

saludar [salu'ðar] *vt* to greet; (*MIL*) to salute; **saludo** *nm* greeting; **"saludos"** (*en carta*) "best wishes", "regards"

salva ['salβa] *nf*: **~ de aplausos** ovation

salvación [salβa'θjon] *nf* salvation; (*rescate*) rescue

salvado [sal'βaðo] *nm* bran

salvaguardar [salβaɣwar'ðar] *vt* to safeguard

salvajada [salβa'xaða] *nf* atrocity

salvaje [sal'βaxe] *adj* wild; (*tribu*) savage; **salvajismo** *nm* savagery

salvamento [salβa'mento] *nm* rescue

salvapantallas [salβa'pantaʎas] *nm* (*INFORM*) screen saver

salvar [sal'βar] *vt* (*rescatar*) to save, rescue; (*resolver*) to overcome, resolve; (*cubrir distancias*) to cover, travel; (*hacer excepción*) to except, exclude; (*barco*) to salvage

salvavidas [salβa'βiðas] *adj inv*: **bote/chaleco/cinturón ~** lifeboat/life jacket/life belt

salvo, a ['salβo, a] *adj* safe ♦ *adv* except (for), save; **a ~** out of danger; **~ que** unless; **~conducto** *nm* safe-conduct

san [san] *adj* saint; **S~ Juan** St John

sanar [sa'nar] *vt* (*herida*) to heal; (*persona*) to cure ♦ *vi* (*persona*) to get well, recover; (*herida*) to heal

sanción [san'θjon] *nf* sanction; **sancionar** *vt* to sanction

sandalia [san'dalja] *nf* sandal

sandez [san'deθ] *nf* foolishness

sandía [san'dia] *nf* watermelon

sandwich ['sandwitʃ] (*pl* **~s, ~es**) *nm* sandwich

saneamiento [sanea'mjento] *nm* sanitation

sanear [sane'ar] *vt* to clean up; (*terreno*) to drain

Sanfermines

i The **Sanfermines** is a week-long festival in Pamplona made famous by Ernest Hemingway. From the 7th July, the feast of "San Fermín", crowds of mainly young people take to the streets drinking, singing and dancing. Early in the morning bulls are released along the narrow streets leading to the bullring, and young men risk serious injury to show their bravery by running out in front of them, a custom which is also typical of many Spanish villages.

---

sangrar [san'grar] *vt, vi* to bleed; **sangre** *nf* blood

sangría [san'gria] *nf* sangria

sangriento, a [san'grjento, a] *adj* bloody

sanguijuela [sangi'xwela] *nf* (*ZOOL, fig*) leech

sanguinario, a [sangi'narjo, a] *adj* bloodthirsty

sanguíneo, a [san'gineo, a] *adj* blood *cpd*

sanidad [sani'ðað] *nf*: **~ (pública)** public health

San Isidro

i **San Isidro** is the patron saint of Madrid, and gives his name to the week-long festivities which take place around the 15th May. Originally an 18th-century trade fair, the **San Isidro** celebrations now include music, dance, a famous **romería**, theatre and bullfighting.

---

sanitario, a [sani'tarjo, a] *adj* health *cpd*; **~s** *nmpl* toilets (*BRIT*), washroom (*US*)

sano, a ['sano, a] *adj* healthy; (*sin daños*) sound; (*comida*) wholesome; (*entero*) whole, intact; **~ y salvo** safe and sound

Santiago [san'tjaɣo] *nm*: **~ (de Chile)** Santiago

santiamén [santja'men] *nm*: **en un ~** in no time at all

santidad [santi'ðað] *nf* holiness, sanctity

santiguarse [santi'ɣwarse] *vr* to make the sign of the cross

santo, a ['santo, a] *adj* holy; (*fig*) wonderful, miraculous ♦ *nm/f* saint ♦ *nm* saint's day; **~ y seña** password

santuario [san'twarjo] *nm* sanctuary, shrine

saña ['saɲa] *nf* rage, fury

sapo ['sapo] *nm* toad

saque ['sake] *nm* (*TENIS*) service, serve; (*FÚTBOL*) throw-in; **~ de esquina** corner (kick)

saquear [sake'ar] *vt* (*MIL*) to sack; (*robar*) to loot, plunder; (*fig*) to ransack; **saqueo** *nm* sacking; looting, plundering; ransacking

sarampión [saram'pjon] *nm* measles *sg*

sarcasmo [sar'kasmo] *nm* sarcasm; **sarcástico, a** *adj* sarcastic

sardina [sar'ðina] *nf* sardine

sargento [sar'xento] *nm* sergeant

sarmiento [sar'mjento] *nm* (*BOT*) vine shoot

sarna ['sarna] *nf* itch; (*MED*) scabies

sarpullido [sarpu'ʎiðo] *nm* (*MED*) rash

sarro ['sarro] *nm* (*en dientes*) tartar, plaque

sartén [sar'ten] *nf* frying pan

sastre ['sastre] *nm* tailor; **~ría** *nf* (*arte*) tailoring; (*tienda*) tailor's (shop)

Satanás [sata'nas] *nm* Satan

satélite [sa'telite] *nm* satellite

sátira ['satira] *nf* satire

satisfacción [satisfak'θjon] *nf* satisfaction

satisfacer [satisfa'θer] *vt* to satisfy; (*gastos*) to meet; (*pérdida*) to make good; **~se** *vr* to satisfy o.s., be satisfied; (*vengarse*) to take revenge; **satisfecho, a** *adj* satisfied; (*contento*) content(ed), happy; (*tb*: **satisfecho de sí mismo**)

self-satisfied, smug

saturar [satu'rar] *vt* to saturate; **~se** *vr* (*mercado, aeropuerto*) to reach saturation point

sauce ['sauθe] *nm* willow; **~ llorón** weeping willow

sauna ['sauna] *nf* sauna

savia ['saβja] *nf* sap

saxofón [sakso'fon] *nm* saxophone

sazonar [saθo'nar] *vt* to ripen; (*CULIN*) to flavour, season

SE *abr* (= *sudeste*) SE

PALABRA CLAVE

---

se [se] *pron* **1** (*reflexivo: sg: m*) himself; (*: f*) herself; (*: pl*) themselves; (*: cosa*) itself; (*: de Vd*) yourself; (*: de Vds*) yourselves; **~ está preparando** she's preparing herself; *para usos léxicos del pron ver el vb en cuestión, p.ej.* **arrepentirse**

2 (*con complemento indirecto*) to him; to her; to them; to it; to you; **a usted ~ lo dije ayer** I told you yesterday; **~ compró un sombrero** he bought himself a hat; **~ rompió la pierna** he broke his leg

3 (*uso recíproco*) each other, one another; **~ miraron (el uno al otro)** they looked at each other *o* one another

4 (*en oraciones pasivas*): **se han vendido muchos libros** a lot of books have been sold

5 (*impers*): **~ dice que** people say that, it is said that; **allí ~ come muy bien** the food there is very good, you can eat very well there

---

sé *vb ver* **saber**; **ser**

sea *etc vb ver* **ser**

sebo ['seβo] *nm* fat, grease

secador [seka'ðor] *nm*: **~ de pelo** hair-dryer

secadora [seka'ðora] *nf* tumble dryer

secar [se'kar] *vt* to dry; **~se** *vr* to dry (off); (*río, planta*) to dry up

sección [sek'θjon] *nf* section

seco, a ['seko, a] *adj* dry; (*carácter*) cold; (*respuesta*) sharp, curt; **habrá pan a**

secas there will be just bread; **decir algo a secas** to say sth curtly; **parar en ~** to stop dead

secretaría [sekreta'ria] *nf* secretariat

secretario, a [sekre'tarjo, a] *nm/f* secretary

secreto, a [se'kreto, a] *adj* secret; (*persona*) secretive ♦ *nm* secret; (*calidad*) secrecy

secta ['sekta] *nf* sect; **~rio, a** *adj* sectarian

sector [sek'tor] *nm* sector

secuela [se'kwela] *nf* consequence

secuencia [se'kwenθja] *nf* sequence

secuestrar [sekwes'trar] *vt* to kidnap; (*bienes*) to seize, confiscate; **secuestro** *nm* kidnapping; seizure, confiscation

secular [seku'lar] *adj* secular

secundar [sekun'dar] *vt* to second, support

secundario, a [sekun'darjo, a] *adj* secondary

sed [seð] *nf* thirst; **tener ~** to be thirsty

seda ['seða] *nf* silk

sedal [se'ðal] *nm* fishing line

sedante [se'ðante] *nm* sedative

sede ['seðe] *nf* (*de gobierno*) seat; (*de compañía*) headquarters *pl*; **Santa S~** Holy See

sedentario, a [seðen'tarjo, a] *adj* sedentary

sediento, a [se'ðjento, a] *adj* thirsty

sedimento [seði'mento] *nm* sediment

sedoso, a [se'ðoso, a] *adj* silky, silken

seducción [seðuk'θjon] *nf* seduction

seducir [seðu'θir] *vt* to seduce; (*cautivar*) to charm, fascinate; (*atraer*) to attract; **seductor, a** *adj* seductive; charming, fascinating; attractive ♦ *nm/f* seducer

segar [se'ɣar] *vt* (*mies*) to reap, cut; (*hierba*) to mow, cut

seglar [se'ɣlar] *adj* secular, lay

segregación [seɣreɣa'θjon] *nf* segregation. **~ racial** racial segregation

segregar [seɣre'ɣar] *vt* to segregate, separate

seguida [se'ɣiða] *nf*: **en ~** at once, right away

seguido, a [se'ɣiðo, a] *adj* (*continuo*) continuous, unbroken; (*recto*) straight ♦ *adv* (*directo*) straight (on); (*después*) after; (*AM: a menudo*) often; **~s** consecutive, successive; **5 días ~s** 5 days running, 5 days in a row

seguimiento [seɣi'mjento] *nm* chase, pursuit; (*continuación*) continuation

seguir [se'ɣir] *vt* to follow; (*venir después*) to follow on, come after; (*proseguir*) to continue; (*perseguir*) to chase, pursue ♦ *vi* (*gen*) to follow; (*continuar*) to continue, carry *o* go on; **~se** *vr* to follow; **sigo sin comprender** I still don't understand; **sigue lloviendo** it's still raining

según [se'ɣun] *prep* according to ♦ *adv*: **¿irás? – ~** are you going? — it all depends ♦ *conj* as; **~ caminamos** while we walk

segundo, a [se'ɣundo, a] *adj* second ♦ *nm* second ♦ *nf* second meaning; **de segunda mano** second-hand; **segunda (clase)** second class; **segunda enseñanza** secondary education; **segunda (marcha)** (*AUT*) second (gear)

seguramente [seɣura'mente] *adv* surely; (*con certeza*) for sure, with certainty

seguridad [seɣuri'ðað] *nf* safety; (*del estado, de casa etc*) security; (*certidumbre*) certainty; (*confianza*) confidence; (*estabilidad*) stability; **~ social** social security

seguro, a [se'ɣuro, a] *adj* (*cierto*) sure, certain; (*fiel*) trustworthy; (*libre de peligro*) safe; (*bien defendido, firme*) secure ♦ *adv* for sure, certainly ♦ *nm* (*COM*) insurance; **~ contra terceros/a todo riesgo** third party/comprehensive insurance; **~s sociales** social security *sg*

seis [seis] *num* six

seísmo [se'ismo] *nm* tremor, earthquake

selección [selek'θjon] *nf* selection; **seleccionar** *vt* to pick, choose, select

selectividad [selektiβi'ðað] (*ESP*) *nf* university entrance examination

selecto, a [se'lekto, a] *adj* select, choice; (*escogido*) selected

sellar [se'ʎar] *vt* (*documento oficial*) to seal; (*pasaporte, visado*) to stamp

sello ['seʎo] *nm* stamp; (*precinto*) seal

selva ['selβa] *nf* (*bosque*) forest, woods *pl*; (*jungla*) jungle

semáforo [se'maforo] *nm* (*AUTO*) traffic lights *pl*; (*FERRO*) signal

semana [se'mana] *nf* week; **entre ~** during the week; **S~ Santa** Holy Week; **semanal** *adj* weekly; **~rio** *nm* weekly magazine

---
Semana Santa

ⓘ *In Spain celebrations for* **Semana Santa** *(Holy Week) are often spectacular. "Viernes Santo", "Sábado Santo" and "Domingo de Resurrección" (Good Friday, Holy Saturday, Easter Sunday) are all national public holidays, with additional days being given as local holidays. There are fabulous* **procesiones** *all over the country, with members of "cofradías" (brotherhoods) dressing in hooded robes and parading their "pasos" (religious floats and sculptures) through the streets. Seville has the most famous Holy Week processions.*

---

semblante [sem'blante] *nm* face; (*fig*) look

sembrar [sem'brar] *vt* (*objetos*) to sow; (*objetos*) to sprinkle, scatter about; (*noticias etc*) to spread

semejante [seme'xante] *adj* (*parecido*) similar ♦ *nm* fellow man, fellow creature; **~s** alike, similar; **nunca hizo cosa ~** he never did any such thing; **semejanza** *nf* similarity, resemblance

semejar [seme'xar] *vi* to seem like, resemble; **~se** *vr* to look alike, be similar

semen ['semen] *nm* semen

semestral [semes'tral] *adj* half-yearly, bi-annual

semicírculo [semi'θirkulo] *nm* semicircle

semidesnatado, a [semiðesna'taðo, a] *adj* semi-skimmed

semifinal [semifi'nal] *nf* semifinal

semilla [se'miʎa] *nf* seed

seminario [semi'narjo] *nm* (*REL*) seminary; (*ESCOL*) seminar

sémola ['semola] *nf* semolina

Sena ['sena] *nm*: **el ~** the (river) Seine

senado [se'naðo] *nm* senate; **senador, a** *nm/f* senator

sencillez [senθi'ʎeθ] *nf* simplicity; (*de persona*) naturalness; **sencillo, a** *adj* simple; natural, unaffected

senda ['senda] *nf* path, track

senderismo [sende'rismo] *nm* hiking

sendero [sen'dero] *nm* path, track

sendos, as ['sendos, as] *adj pl*: **les dio ~ golpes** he hit both of them

senil [se'nil] *adj* senile

seno ['seno] *nm* (*ANAT*) breast, bust; (*fig*) bosom; **~s** breasts

sensación [sensa'θjon] *nf* sensation; (*sentido*) sense; (*sentimiento*) feeling; **sensacional** *adj* sensational

sensato, a [sen'sato, a] *adj* sensible

sensible [sen'sible] *adj* sensitive; (*apreciable*) perceptible, appreciable; (*pérdida*) considerable; **~ro, a** *adj* sentimental

sensitivo, a [sensi'tiβo, a] *adj* sense *cpd*

sensorial [senso'rjal] *adj* sensory

sensual [sen'swal] *adj* sensual

sentada [sen'taða] *nf* sitting; (*protesta*) sit-in

sentado, a [sen'taðo, a] *adj*: **estar ~** to sit, be sitting (down); **dar por ~** to take for granted, assume

sentar [sen'tar] *vt* to sit, seat; (*fig*) to establish ♦ *vi* (*vestido*) to suit; (*alimento*): **~ bien/mal a** to agree/disagree with; **~se** *vr* (*persona*) to sit, sit down; (*los depósitos*) to settle

sentencia [sen'tenθja] *nf* (*máxima*) maxim, saying; (*JUR*) sentence; **sentenciar** *vt* to sentence

sentido, a [sen'tiðo, a] *adj* (*pérdida*) regrettable; (*carácter*) sensitive ♦ *nm* sense; (*sentimiento*) feeling; (*significado*) sense, meaning; (*dirección*) direction; **mi más ~ pésame** my deepest sympathy; **~**

del humor sense of humour; **~ único** one-way (street); **tener ~** to make sense

sentimental [sentimen'tal] *adj* sentimental; **vida ~** love life

sentimiento [senti'mjento] *nm* feeling

sentir [sen'tir] *vt* to feel; *(percibir)* to perceive, sense; *(lamentar)* to regret, be sorry for ♦ *vi (tener la sensación)* to feel; *(lamentarse)* to feel sorry ♦ *nm* opinion, judgement; **~se bien/mal** to feel well/ill; **lo siento** I'm sorry

seña ['seɲa] *nf* sign; *(MIL)* password; **~s** *nfpl (dirección)* address *sg*; **~s personales** personal description

señal [se'ɲal] *nf* sign; *(síntoma)* symptom; *(FERRO, TELEC)* signal; *(marca)* mark; *(COM)* deposit; **en ~ de** as a token of, as a sign of; **~ar** *vt* to mark; *(indicar)* to point out, indicate

señor [se'ɲor] *nm (hombre)* man; *(caballero)* gentleman; *(dueño)* owner, master; *(trato: antes de nombre propio)* Mr; *(: hablando directamente)* sir; **muy ~ mío** Dear Sir; **el ~ alcalde/presidente** the mayor/president

señora [se'ɲora] *nf (dama)* lady; *(trato: antes de nombre propio)* Mrs; *(: hablando directamente)* madam; *(esposa)* wife; **Nuestra S~** Our Lady

señorita [seɲo'rita] *nf (con nombre y/o apellido)* Miss; *(mujer joven)* young lady

señorito [seɲo'rito] *nm* young gentleman; *(pey)* rich kid

señuelo [se'ɲwelo] *nm* decoy

sepa *etc vb ver* **saber**

separación [separa'θjon] *nf* separation; *(división)* division; *(hueco)* gap

separar [sepa'rar] *vt* to separate; *(dividir)* to divide; **~se** *vr (parte)* to come away; *(partes)* to come apart; *(persona)* to leave, go away; *(matrimonio)* to separate; **separatismo** *nm* separatism

sepia ['sepja] *nf* cuttlefish

septentrional [septentrjo'nal] *adj* northern

septiembre [sep'tjembre] *nm* September

séptimo, a ['septimo, a] *adj, nm* seventh

sepulcral [sepul'kral] *adj (fig: silencio, atmósfera)* deadly; **sepulcro** *nm* tomb, grave

sepultar [sepul'tar] *vt* to bury; **sepultura** *nf (acto)* burial; *(tumba)* grave, tomb

sequedad [seke'ðað] *nf* dryness; *(fig)* brusqueness, curtness

sequía [se'kia] *nf* drought

séquito ['sekito] *nm (de rey etc)* retinue; *(seguidores)* followers *pl*

PALABRA CLAVE
---

ser [ser] *vi* **1** *(descripción)* to be; **es médica/muy alta** she's a doctor/very tall; **la familia es de Cuzco** his (*o* her *etc*) family is from Cuzco; **soy Ana** *(TELEC)* Ana speaking *o* here

2 *(propiedad)*: **es de Joaquín** it's Joaquín's, it belongs to Joaquín

3 *(horas, fechas, números)*: **es la una** it's one o'clock; **son las seis y media** it's half-past six; **es el 1 de junio** it's the first of June; **somos/son seis** there are six of us/them

4 *(en oraciones pasivas)*: **ha sido descubierto ya** it's already been discovered

5: **es de esperar que ...** it is to be hoped *o* I *etc* hope that ...

6 *(locuciones con sub)*: **o sea** that is to say; **sea él sea su hermana** either him or his sister

7: **a no ~ por él ...** but for him ...

8: **a no ~ que: a no ~ que tenga uno ya** unless he's got one already

♦ *nm* being; **~ humano** human being

---

serenarse [sere'narse] *vr* to calm down

sereno, a [se'reno, a] *adj (persona)* calm, unruffled; *(el tiempo)* fine, settled; *(ambiente)* calm, peaceful ♦ *nm* night watchman

serial [ser'jal] *nm* serial

serie ['serje] *nf* series; *(cadena)* sequence, succession; **fuera de ~** out of order; *(fig)* special, out of the ordinary; **fabricación en ~** mass production

seriedad [serje'ðað] *nf* seriousness; *(formalidad)* reliability; **serio, a** *adj* serious; reliable, dependable; grave, serious; **en serio** *adv* seriously

serigrafía [seriɣra'fia] *nf* silk-screen printing

sermón [ser'mon] *nm* (*REL*) sermon

seropositivo, a [seroposi'tißo, a] *adj* HIV positive

serpentear [serpente'ar] *vi* to wriggle; *(camino, río)* to wind, snake

serpentina [serpen'tina] *nf* streamer

serpiente [ser'pjente] *nf* snake; **~ de cascabel** rattlesnake

serranía [serra'nia] *nf* mountainous area

serrar [se'rrar] *vt* = **aserrar**

serrín [se'rrin] *nm* = **aserrín**

serrucho [se'rrutʃo] *nm* saw

servicio [ser'ßiθjo] *nm* service; **~s** *nmpl* toilet(s); **~ incluido** service charge included; **~ militar** military service

servidumbre [serßi'ðumbre] *nf* *(sujeción)* servitude; *(criados)* servants *pl*, staff

servil [ser'ßil] *adj* servile

servilleta [serßi'ʎeta] *nf* serviette, napkin

servir [ser'ßir] *vt* to serve ♦ *vi* to serve; *(tener utilidad)* to be of use, be useful; **~se** *vr* to serve o help o.s.; **~se de algo** to make use of sth, use sth; **sírvase pasar** please come in

sesenta [se'senta] *num* sixty

sesgo ['sesɣo] *nm* slant; *(fig)* slant, twist

sesión [se'sjon] *nf* (*POL*) session, sitting; *(CINE)* showing

seso ['seso] *nm* brain; **sesudo, a** *adj* sensible, wise

seta ['seta] *nf* mushroom; **~ venenosa** toadstool

setecientos, as [sete'θjentos, as] *adj, num* seven hundred

setenta [se'tenta] *num* seventy

seto ['seto] *nm* hedge

seudónimo [seu'ðonimo] *nm* pseudonym

severidad [seßeri'ðað] *nf* severity; **severo, a** *adj* severe

Sevilla [se'ßiʎa] *n* Seville; **sevillano, a** *adj* of o from Seville ♦ *nm/f* native o inhabitant of Seville

sexo ['sekso] *nm* sex

sexto, a ['seksto, a] *adj, nm* sixth

sexual [sek'swal] *adj* sexual; **vida ~** sex life

si [si] *conj* if; **me pregunto ~ ...** I wonder if o whether ...

sí [si] *adv* yes ♦ *nm* consent ♦ *pron* (*uso impersonal*) oneself; *(sg: m)* himself; *(: f)* herself; *(: de cosa)* itself; *(de usted)* yourself; *(pl)* themselves; *(de ustedes)* yourselves; *(recíproco)* each other; **él no quiere pero yo ~** he doesn't want to but I do; **ella ~ vendrá** she will certainly come, she is sure to come; **claro que ~** of course; **creo que ~** I think so

siamés, esa [sja'mes, esa] *adj, nm/f* Siamese

SIDA ['siða] *nm abr* (= *Síndrome de Inmunodeficiencia Adquirida*) AIDS

siderúrgico, a [siðe'rurxico, a] *adj* iron and steel *cpd*

sidra ['siðra] *nf* cider

siembra ['sjembra] *nf* sowing

siempre ['sjempre] *adv* always; *(todo el tiempo)* all the time; **~ que** *(cada vez)* whenever; *(dado que)* provided that; **como ~** as usual; **para ~** for ever

sien [sjen] *nf* temple

siento *etc vb ver* **sentar**; **sentir**

sierra ['sjerra] *nf* (*TEC*) saw; *(cadena de montañas)* mountain range

siervo, a ['sjerßo, a] *nm/f* slave

siesta ['sjesta] *nf* siesta, nap; **echar la ~** to have an afternoon nap o a siesta

siete ['sjete] *num* seven

sífilis ['sifilis] *nf* syphilis

sifón [si'fon] *nm* syphon; **whisky con ~** whisky and soda

sigla ['siɣla] *nf* abbreviation; acronym

siglo ['siɣlo] *nm* century; *(fig)* age

significación [siɣnifika'θjon] *nf* significance

significado [siɣnifi'kaðo] *nm* (*de palabra etc*) meaning

significar [siɣnifi'kar] *vt* to mean, signify; *(notificar)* to make known, express; **significativo, a** *adj* significant

signo ['siɣno] *nm* sign; **~ de admiración** *o* **exclamación** exclamation mark; **~ de interrogación** question mark

sigo *etc vb ver* **seguir**

siguiente [si'ɣjente] *adj* next, following

siguió *etc vb ver* **seguir**

sílaba ['silaβa] *nf* syllable

silbar [sil'βar] *vt, vi* to whistle; **silbato** *nm* whistle; **silbido** *nm* whistle, whistling

silenciador [silenθja'ðor] *nm* silencer

silenciar [silen'θjar] *vt* (*persona*) to silence; (*escándalo*) to hush up; **silencio** *nm* silence, quiet; **silencioso, a** *adj* silent, quiet

silla ['siʎa] *nf* (*asiento*) chair; (*tb:* **~ de montar**) saddle; **~ de ruedas** wheelchair

sillón [si'ʎon] *nm* armchair, easy chair

silueta [si'lweta] *nf* silhouette; (*de edificio*) outline; (*figura*) figure

silvestre [sil'βestre] *adj* wild

simbólico, a [sim'βoliko, a] *adj* symbolic(al)

simbolizar [simboli'θar] *vt* to symbolize

símbolo ['simbolo] *nm* symbol

simetría [sime'tria] *nf* symmetry

simiente [si'mjente] *nf* seed

similar [simi'lar] *adj* similar

simio ['simjo] *nm* ape

simpatía [simpa'tia] *nf* liking; (*afecto*) affection; (*amabilidad*) kindness; **simpático, a** *adj* nice, pleasant; kind

simpatizante [simpati'θante] *nm/f* sympathizer

simpatizar [simpati'θar] *vi*: **~ con** to get on well with

simple ['simple] *adj* simple; (*elemental*) simple, easy; (*mero*) mere; (*puro*) pure, sheer ♦ *nm/f* simpleton; **~za** *nf* simpleness; (*necedad*) silly thing; **simplificar** *vt* to simplify

simposio [sim'posjo] *nm* symposium

simular [simu'lar] *vt* to simulate

simultáneo, a [simul'taneo, a] *adj* simultaneous

sin [sin] *prep* without; **la ropa está ~ lavar** the clothes are unwashed; **~ que** without;

~ embargo however, still

sinagoga [sina'ɣoɣa] *nf* synagogue

sinceridad [sinθeri'ðað] *nf* sincerity; **sincero, a** *adj* sincere

sincronizar [sinkroni'θar] *vt* to synchronize

sindical [sindi'kal] *adj* union *cpd*, trade-union *cpd*; **~ista** *adj, nm/f* trade unionist

sindicato [sindi'kato] *nm* (*de trabajadores*) trade(s) union; (*de negociantes*) syndicate

síndrome ['sindrome] *nm* (*MED*) syndrome; **~ de abstinencia** (*MED*) withdrawal symptoms

sinfín [sin'fin] *nm*: **un ~ de** a great many, no end of

sinfonía [sinfo'nia] *nf* symphony

singular [singu'lar] *adj* singular; (*fig*) outstanding, exceptional; (*raro*) peculiar, odd; **~idad** *nf* singularity, peculiarity; **~izarse** *vr* to distinguish o.s., stand out

siniestro, a [si'njestro, a] *adj* sinister ♦ *nm* (*accidente*) accident

sinnúmero [sin'numero] *nm* = **sinfín**

sino ['sino] *nm* fate, destiny ♦ *conj* (*pero*) but; (*salvo*) except, save

sinónimo, a [si'nonimo, a] *adj* synonymous ♦ *nm* synonym

síntesis ['sintesis] *nf* synthesis; **sintético, a** *adj* synthetic

sintetizar [sinteti'θar] *vt* to synthesize

sintió *vb ver* **sentir**

síntoma ['sintoma] *nm* symptom

sintonía [sinto'nia] *nf* (*RADIO, MUS: de programa*) tuning; **sintonizar** *vt* (*RADIO: emisora*) to tune (in)

sinvergüenza [simber'ɣwenθa] *nm/f* rogue, scoundrel; **¡es un ~!** he's got a nerve!

siquiera [si'kjera] *conj* even if, even though ♦ *adv* at least; **ni ~** not even

sirena [si'rena] *nf* siren

Siria ['sirja] *nf* Syria

sirviente, a [sir'βjente, a] *nm/f* servant

sirvo *etc vb ver* **servir**

sisear [sise'ar] *vt, vi* to hiss

sistema [sis'tema] *nm* system; (*método*) method; **sistemático, a** *adj* systematic

---

sistema educativo

ⓘ The reform of the Spanish **sistema educativo** *(education system) begun in the early 90s has replaced the courses* EGB, BUP *and* COU *with the following:* "Primaria" *a compulsory 6 years;* "Secundaria" *a compulsory 4 years and* "Bachillerato" *an optional 2-year secondary school course, essential for those wishing to go on to higher education.*

---

sitiar [si'tjar] *vt* to besiege, lay siege to
sitio ['sitjo] *nm* (*lugar*) place; (*espacio*) room, space; (*MIL*) siege; ~ **Web** (*INFORM*) website
situación [sitwa'θjon] *nf* situation, position; (*estatus*) position, standing
situado, a [situ'aðo] *adj* situated, placed
situar [si'twar] *vt* to place, put; (*edificio*) to locate, situate
slip [slip] *nm* pants *pl*, briefs *pl*
smoking ['smokin, es'mokin] (*pl* ~**s**) *nm* dinner jacket (*BRIT*), tuxedo (*US*)
snob [es'nob] = **esnob**
SO *abr* (= *suroeste*) SW
sobaco [so'βako] *nm* armpit
sobar [so'βar] *vt* (*ropa*) to rumple; (*comida*) to play around with
soberanía [soβera'nia] *nf* sovereignty; **soberano, a** *adj* sovereign; (*fig*) supreme ♦ *nm/f* sovereign
soberbia [so'βerβja] *nf* pride; haughtiness, arrogance; magnificence
soberbio, a [so'βerβjo, a] *adj* (*orgulloso*) proud; (*altivo*) haughty, arrogant; (*estupendo*) magnificent, superb
sobornar [soβor'nar] *vt* to bribe; **soborno** *nm* bribe
sobra ['soβra] *nf* excess, surplus; ~**s** *nfpl* left-overs, scraps; **de** ~ surplus, extra; **tengo de** ~ I've more than enough; ~**do, a** *adj* (*más que suficiente*) more than enough; (*superfluo*) excessive; **sobrante** *adj* remaining, extra ♦ *nm* surplus
sobrar [so'βrar] *vt* to exceed, surpass ♦ *vi* (*tener de más*) to be more than enough;

(*quedar*) to remain, be left (over)
sobrasada [soβra'saða] *nf* pork sausage spread
sobre ['soβre] *prep* (*gen*) on; (*encima*) on (top of); (*por encima de, arriba de*) over, above; (*más que*) more than; (*además*) in addition to, besides; (*alrededor de*) about ♦ *nm* envelope; ~ **todo** above all
sobrecama [soβre'kama] *nf* bedspread
sobrecargar [soβrekar'var] *vt* (*camión*) to overload; (*COM*) to surcharge
sobredosis [soβre'ðosis] *nf inv* overdose
sobreentender [soβre(e)nten'der] *vt* to deduce, infer; ~**se** *vr*: **se sobreentiende que** ... it is implied that ...
sobrehumano, a [soβreu'mano, a] *adj* superhuman
sobrellevar [soβreʎe'βar] *vt* to bear, endure
sobremesa [soβre'mesa] *nf*: **durante la** ~ after dinner; **ordenador de** ~ desktop computer
sobrenatural [soβrenatu'ral] *adj* supernatural
sobrenombre [soβre'nombre] *nm* nickname
sobrepasar [soβrepa'sar] *vt* to exceed, surpass
sobreponerse [soβrepo'nerse] *vr*: ~ **a** to overcome
sobresaliente [soβresa'ljente] *adj* outstanding, excellent
sobresalir [soβresa'lir] *vi* to project, jut out; (*fig*) to stand out, excel
sobresaltar [soβresal'tar] *vt* (*asustar*) to scare, frighten; (*sobrecoger*) to startle; **sobresalto** *nm* (*movimiento*) start; (*susto*) scare; (*turbación*) sudden shock
sobretodo [soβre'toðo] *nm* overcoat
sobrevenir [soβreβe'nir] *vi* (*ocurrir*) to happen (unexpectedly); (*resultar*) to follow, ensue
sobreviviente [soβreβi'βjente] *adj* surviving ♦ *nm/f* survivor
sobrevivir [soβreβi'βir] *vi* to survive
sobrevolar [soβreβo'lar] *vt* to fly over
sobriedad [soβrje'ðað] *nf* sobriety,

soberness; (*moderación*) moderation, restraint

sobrino, a [so'ßrino, a] *nm/f* nephew/niece

sobrio, a ['soßrjo, a] *adj* sober; (*moderado*) moderate, restrained

socarrón, ona [soka'rron, ona] *adj* (*sarcástico*) sarcastic, ironic(al)

socavar [soka'ßar] *vt* (*hoyo*) to undermine

socavón [soka'ßon] *nm* (*hoyo*) hole

sociable [so'θjaßle] *adj* (*persona*) sociable, friendly; (*animal*) social

social [so'θjal] *adj* social; (*COM*) company cpd

socialdemócrata [soθjalde'mokrata] *nm/f* social democrat

socialista [soθja'lista] *adj, nm/f* socialist

socializar [soθjali'θar] *vt* to socialize

sociedad [soθje'ðað] *nf* society; (*COM*) company; **~ anónima** limited company; **~ de consumo** consumer society

socio, a ['soθjo, a] *nm/f* (*miembro*) member; (*COM*) partner

sociología [soθjolo'xja] *nf* sociology; **sociólogo, a** *nm/f* sociologist

socorrer [soko'rrer] *vt* to help; **socorrista** *nm/f* first aider; (*en piscina, playa*) lifeguard; **socorro** *nm* (*ayuda*) help, aid; (*MIL*) relief; **¡socorro!** help!

soda ['soða] *nf* (*sosa*) soda; (*bebida*) soda (water)

sofá [so'fa] (*pl* **~s**) *nm* sofa, settee; **~-cama** *nm* studio couch; sofa bed

sofisticación [sofistika'θjon] *nf* sophistication

sofocar [sofo'kar] *vt* to suffocate; (*apagar*) to smother, put out; **~se** *vr* to suffocate; (*fig*) to blush, feel embarrassed; **sofoco** *nm* suffocation; embarrassment

sofreír [sofre'ir] *vt* (*CULIN*) to fry lightly

soga ['soya] *nf* rope

sois *vb ver* **ser**

soja ['soxa] *nf* soya

sol [sol] *nm* sun; (*luz*) sunshine, sunlight; **hace ~** it is sunny

solamente [sola'mente] *adv* only, just

solapa [so'lapa] *nf* (*de chaqueta*) lapel; (*de libro*) jacket

solapado, a [sola'paðo, a] *adj* (*intenciones*) underhand; (*gestos, movimiento*) sly

solar [so'lar] *adj* solar, sun cpd

solaz [so'laθ] *nm* recreation, relaxation; **~ar** *vt* (*divertir*) to amuse

soldado [sol'daðo] *nm* soldier; **~ raso** private

soldador [solda'ðor] *nm* soldering iron; (*persona*) welder

soldar [sol'dar] *vt* to solder, weld

soleado, a [sole'aðo, a] *adj* sunny

soledad [sole'ðað] *nf* solitude; (*estado infeliz*) loneliness

solemne [so'lemne] *adj* solemn; **solemnidad** *nf* solemnity

soler [so'ler] *vi* to be in the habit of, be accustomed to; **suele salir a las ocho** she usually goes out at 8 o'clock

solfeo [sol'feo] *nm* solfa

solicitar [soliθi'tar] *vt* (*permiso*) to ask for, seek; (*puesto*) to apply for; (*votos*) to canvass for; (*atención*) to attract

solícito, a [so'liθito, a] *adj* (*diligente*) diligent; (*cuidadoso*) careful; **solicitud** *nf* (*calidad*) great care; (*petición*) request; (*a un puesto*) application

solidaridad [soliðari'ðað] *nf* solidarity; **solidario, a** *adj* (*participación*) joint, common; (*compromiso*) mutually binding

solidez [soli'ðeθ] *nf* solidity; **sólido, a** *adj* solid

soliloquio [soli'lokjo] *nm* soliloquy

solista [so'lista] *nm/f* soloist

solitario, a [soli'tarjo, a] *adj* (*persona*) lonely, solitary; (*lugar*) lonely, desolate ♦ *nm/f* (*reclusa*) recluse; (*en la sociedad*) loner ♦ *nm* solitaire

sollozar [soʎo'θar] *vi* to sob; **sollozo** *nm* sob

solo, a ['solo, a] *adj* (*único*) single, sole; (*sin compañía*) alone; (*solitario*) lonely; **hay una sola dificultad** there is just one difficulty; **a solas** alone, by oneself

sólo ['solo] *adv* only, just

solomillo [solo'miʎo] *nm* sirloin

soltar [sol'tar] vt (*dejar ir*) to let go of; (*desprender*) to unfasten, loosen; (*librar*) to release, set free; (*risa etc*) to let out

soltero, a [sol'tero, a] adj single, unmarried ♦ nm/f bachelor/single woman; **solterón, ona** nm/f old bachelor/spinster

soltura [sol'tura] nf looseness, slackness; (*de los miembros*) agility, ease of movement; (*en el hablar*) fluency, ease

soluble [so'luβle] adj (QUÍM) soluble; (*problema*) solvable; **~ en agua** soluble in water

solución [solu'θjon] nf solution; **solucionar** vt (*problema*) to solve; (*asunto*) to settle, resolve

solventar [solβen'tar] vt (*pagar*) to settle, pay; (*resolver*) to resolve; **solvente** adj (ECON: *empresa, persona*) solvent

sombra ['sombra] nf shadow; (*como protección*) shade; **~s** nfpl (*oscuridad*) darkness sg, shadows; **tener buena/mala ~** to be lucky/unlucky

sombrero [som'brero] nm hat

sombrilla [som'briʎa] nf parasol, sunshade

sombrío, a [som'brio, a] adj (*oscuro*) dark; (*triste*) sombre, sad; (*persona*) gloomy

somero, a [so'mero, a] adj superficial

someter [some'ter] vt (*país*) to conquer; (*persona*) to subject to one's will; (*informe*) to present, submit; **~se** vr to give in, yield, submit; **~ a** to subject to

somier [so'mjer] (pl **somiers**) nm spring mattress

somnífero [som'nifero] nm sleeping pill

somnolencia [somno'lenθja] nf sleepiness, drowsiness

somos vb ver **ser**

son [son] vb ver **ser** ♦ nm sound; **en ~ de broma** as a joke

sonajero [sona'xero] nm (baby's) rattle

sonambulismo [sonambu'lismo] nm sleepwalking; **sonámbulo, a** nm/f sleepwalker

sonar [so'nar] vt to ring ♦ vi to sound; (*hacer ruido*) to make a noise; (*pronunciarse*) to be sounded, be pronounced; (*ser conocido*) to sound familiar; (*campana*) to ring; (*reloj*) to strike, chime; **~se** vr: **~se (las narices)** to blow one's nose; **me suena ese nombre** that name rings a bell

sonda ['sonda] nf (NAUT) sounding; (TEC) bore, drill; (MED) probe

sondear [sonde'ar] vt to sound; to bore (into), drill; to probe, sound; (*fig*) to sound out; **sondeo** nm sounding, boring, drilling; (*fig*) poll, enquiry

sonido [so'niðo] nm sound

sonoro, a [so'noro, a] adj sonorous; (*resonante*) loud, resonant

sonreír [sonre'ir] vi to smile; **~se** vr to smile; **sonriente** adj smiling; **sonrisa** nf smile

sonrojarse [sonro'xarse] vr to blush, go red; **sonrojo** nm blush

soñador, a [soɲa'ðor, a] nm/f dreamer

soñar [so'ɲar] vt, vi to dream; **~ con** to dream about o of

soñoliento, a [soɲo'ljento, a] adj sleepy, drowsy

sopa ['sopa] nf soup

sopesar [sope'sar] vt to consider, weigh up

soplar [so'plar] vt (*polvo*) to blow away, blow off; (*inflar*) to blow up; (*vela*) to blow out ♦ vi to blow; **soplo** nm blow, puff; (*de viento*) puff, gust

soplón, ona [so'plon, ona] (fam), nm/f (*niño*) telltale; (*de policía*) grass (fam)

sopor [so'por] nm drowsiness

soporífero [sopo'rifero] nm sleeping pill

soportable [sopor'taβle] adj bearable

soportar [sopor'tar] vt to bear, carry; (*fig*) to bear, put up with; **soporte** nm support; (*fig*) pillar, support

soprano [so'prano] nf soprano

sorber [sor'βer] vt (*chupar*) to sip; (*absorber*) to soak up, absorb

sorbete [sor'βete] nm iced fruit drink

sorbo ['sorβo] nm (*trago: grande*) gulp, swallow; (: *pequeño*) sip

sordera [sor'ðera] nf deafness

sórdido, a ['sorðiðo, a] adj dirty, squalid

sordo, a ['sorðo, a] *adj* (*persona*) deaf
♦ *nm/f* deaf person; **~mudo, a** *adj* deaf and dumb

sorna ['sorna] *nf* sarcastic tone

soroche [so'rotʃe] (*AM*) *nm* mountain sickness

sorprendente [sorpren'dente] *adj* surprising

sorprender [sorpren'der] *vt* to surprise; **sorpresa** *nf* surprise

sortear [sorte'ar] *vt* to draw lots for; (*rifar*) to raffle; (*dificultad*) to avoid; **sorteo** *nm* (*en lotería*) draw; (*rifa*) raffle

sortija [sor'tixa] *nf* ring; (*rizo*) ringlet, curl

sosegado, a [sose'ɣaðo, a] *adj* quiet, calm

sosegar [sose'ɣar] *vt* to quieten, calm; (*el ánimo*) to reassure ♦ *vi* to rest; **sosiego** *nm* quiet(ness), calm(ness)

soslayo [sos'lajo]: **de ~** *adv* obliquely, sideways

soso, a ['soso, a] *adj* (*CULIN*) tasteless; (*aburrido*) dull, uninteresting

sospecha [sos'petʃa] *nf* suspicion; **sospechar** *vt* to suspect; **sospechoso, a** *adj* suspicious; (*testimonio, opinión*) suspect ♦ *nm/f* suspect

sostén [sos'ten] *nm* (*apoyo*) support; (*sujetador*) bra; (*alimentación*) sustenance, food

sostener [soste'ner] *vt* to support; (*mantener*) to keep up, maintain; (*alimentar*) to sustain, keep going; **~se** *vr* to support o.s.; (*seguir*) to continue, remain; **sostenido, a** *adj* continuous, sustained; (*prolongado*) prolonged

sotana [so'tana] *nf* (*REL*) cassock

sótano ['sotano] *nm* basement

soviético, a [so'ßjetiko, a] *adj* Soviet; **los ~s** the Soviets

soy *vb ver* **ser**

Sr. *abr* (= *Señor*) Mr

Sra. *abr* (= *Señora*) Mrs

S.R.C. *abr* (= *se ruega contestación*) R.S.V.P.

Sres. *abr* (= *Señores*) Messrs

Srta. *abr* (= *Señorita*) Miss

Sta. *abr* (= *Santa*) St

status ['status, e'status] *nm inv* status

Sto. *abr* (= *Santo*) St

su [su] *pron* (*de él*) his; (*de ella*) her; (*de una cosa*) its; (*de ellos, ellas*) their; (*de usted, ustedes*) your

suave ['swaße] *adj* gentle; (*superficie*) smooth; (*trabajo*) easy; (*música, voz*) soft, sweet; **suavidad** *nf* gentleness; smoothness; softness, sweetness; **suavizante** *nm* (*de ropa*) softener; (*del pelo*) conditioner; **suavizar** *vt* to soften; (*quitar la aspereza*) to smooth (out)

subalimentado, a [sußalimen'taðo, a] *adj* undernourished

subasta [su'ßasta] *nf* auction; **subastar** *vt* to auction (off)

subcampeón, ona [sußkampe'on, ona] *nm/f* runner-up

subconsciente [sußkon'sθjente] *adj, nm* subconscious

subdesarrollado, a [sußðesarro'ʎaðo, a] *adj* underdeveloped

subdesarrollo [sußðesa'rroʎo] *nm* underdevelopment

subdirector, a [sußðirek'tor, a] *nm/f* assistant director

súbdito, a ['sußðito, a] *nm/f* subject

subestimar [sußesti'mar] *vt* to underestimate, underrate

subida [su'ßiða] *nf* (*de montaña etc*) ascent, climb; (*de precio*) rise, increase; (*pendiente*) slope, hill

subir [su'ßir] *vt* (*objeto*) to raise, lift up; (*cuesta, calle*) to go up; (*colina, montaña*) to climb; (*precio*) to raise, put up ♦ *vi* to go up, come up; (*a un coche*) to get in; (*a un autobús, tren o avión*) to get on, board; (*precio*) to rise, go up; (*río, marea*) to rise; **~se** *vr* to get up, climb

súbito, a ['sußito, a] *adj* (*repentino*) sudden; (*imprevisto*) unexpected

subjetivo, a [sußxe'tißo, a] *adj* subjective

sublevación [sußleßa'θjon] *nf* revolt, rising

sublevar [sußle'ßar] *vt* to rouse to revolt;

~se *vr* to revolt, rise

sublime [su'ßlime] *adj* sublime

submarinismo [sußmari'nismo] *nm* scuba diving

submarino, a [sußma'rino, a] *adj* underwater ♦ *nm* submarine

subnormal [sußnor'mal] *adj* subnormal ♦ *nm/f* subnormal person

subordinado, a [sußorði'naðo, a] *adj, nm/f* subordinate

subrayar [sußra'jar] *vt* to underline

subsanar [sußsa'nar] *vt* to recitify

subscribir [sußskri'ßir] *vt* = **suscribir**

subsidio [suß'siðjo] *nm (ayuda)* aid, financial help; *(subvención)* subsidy, grant; *(de enfermedad, paro etc)* benefit, allowance

subsistencia [sußsis'tenθja] *nf* subsistence

subsistir [sußsis'tir] *vi* to subsist; *(sobrevivir)* to survive, endure

subterráneo, a [sußte'rraneo, a] *adj* underground, subterranean ♦ *nm* underpass, underground passage

subtítulo [sußti'tulo] *nm (CINE)* subtitle

suburbano, a [sußur'ßano, a] *adj* suburban

suburbio [su'ßurßjo] *nm (barrio)* slum quarter

subvención [sußßen'θjon] *nf (ECON)* subsidy, grant; **subvencionar** *vt* to subsidize

subversión [sußßer'sjon] *nf* subversion; **subversivo, a** *adj* subversive

subyugar [sußju'var] *vt (país)* to subjugate, subdue; *(enemigo)* to overpower; *(voluntad)* to dominate

sucedáneo, a [suθe'ðaneo, a] *adj* substitute ♦ *nm* substitute (food)

suceder [suθe'ðer] *vt, vi* to happen; *(seguir)* to succeed, follow; **lo que sucede es que ...** the fact is that ...; **sucesión** *nf* succession; *(serie)* sequence, series

sucesivamente [suθesißa'mente] *adv*: **y así ~** and so on

sucesivo, a [suθe'sißo, a] *adj* successive, following; **en lo ~** in future, from now on

suceso [su'θeso] *nm (hecho)* event, happening; *(incidente)* incident

suciedad [suθje'ðað] *nf (estado)* dirtiness; *(mugre)* dirt, filth

sucinto, a [su'θinto, a] *adj (conciso)* succinct, concise

sucio, a ['suθjo, a] *adj* dirty

suculento, a [suku'lento, a] *adj* succulent

sucumbir [sukum'bir] *vi* to succumb

sucursal [sukur'sal] *nf* branch (office)

sudadera [suða'ðera] *nf* sweatshirt

Sudáfrica [suð'afrika] *nf* South Africa

Sudamérica [suða'merika] *nf* South America; **sudamericano, a** *adj, nm/f* South American

sudar [su'ðar] *vt, vi* to sweat

sudeste [su'ðeste] *nm* south-east

sudoeste [suðo'este] *nm* south-west

sudor [su'ðor] *nm* sweat; **~oso, a** *adj* sweaty, sweating

Suecia ['sweθja] *nf* Sweden; **sueco, a** *adj* Swedish ♦ *nm/f* Swede

suegro, a ['sweɣro, a] *nm/f* father-/ mother-in-law

suela ['swela] *nf* sole

sueldo ['sweldo] *nm* pay, wage(s) *(pl)*

suele *etc vb ver* **soler**

suelo ['swelo] *nm (tierra)* ground; *(de casa)* floor

suelto, a ['swelto, a] *adj* loose; *(libre)* free; *(separado)* detached; *(ágil)* quick, agile ♦ *nm* (loose) change, small change

sueño *etc* ['sweɲo] *vb ver* **soñar** ♦ *nm* sleep; *(somnolencia)* sleepiness, drowsiness; *(lo soñado, fig)* dream; **tener ~** to be sleepy

suero ['swero] *nm (MED)* serum; *(de leche)* whey

suerte ['swerte] *nf (fortuna)* luck; *(azar)* chance; *(destino)* fate, destiny; *(especie)* sort, kind; **tener ~** to be lucky; **de otra ~** otherwise, if not; **de ~ que** so that, in such a way that

suéter ['sweter] *nm* sweater

suficiente [sufi'θjente] *adj* enough, sufficient ♦ *nm (ESCOL)* pass

sufragio [su'fraxjo] *nm* (*voto*) vote; (*derecho de voto*) suffrage

sufrido, a [su'friðo, a] *adj* (*persona*) tough; (*paciente*) long-suffering, patient

sufrimiento [sufri'mjento] *nm* (*dolor*) suffering

sufrir [su'frir] *vt* (*padecer*) to suffer; (*soportar*) to bear, put up with; (*apoyar*) to hold up, support ♦ *vi* to suffer

sugerencia [suxe'renθja] *nf* suggestion

sugerir [suxe'rir] *vt* to suggest; (*sutilmente*) to hint

sugestión [suxes'tjon] *nf* suggestion; (*sutil*) hint; **sugestionar** *vt* to influence

sugestivo, a [suxes'tiβo, a] *adj* stimulating; (*fascinante*) fascinating

suicida [sui'θiða] *adj* suicidal ♦ *nm/f* suicidal person; (*muerto*) suicide, person who has committed suicide; **suicidarse** *vr* to commit suicide, kill o.s.; **suicidio** *nm* suicide

Suiza ['swiθa] *nf* Switzerland; **suizo, a** *adj, nm/f* Swiss

sujeción [suxe'θjon] *nf* subjection

sujetador [suxeta'ðor] *nm* (*sostén*) bra

sujetar [suxe'tar] *vt* (*fijar*) to fasten; (*detener*) to hold down; **~se** *vr* to subject o.s.; **sujeto, a** *adj* fastened, secure ♦ *nm* subject; (*individuo*) individual; **sujeto a** subject to

suma ['suma] *nf* (*cantidad*) total, sum; (*de dinero*) sum; (*acto*) adding (up), addition; **en ~** in short

sumamente [suma'mente] *adv* extremely, exceedingly

sumar [su'mar] *vt* to add (up) ♦ *vi* to add up

sumario, a [su'marjo, a] *adj* brief, concise ♦ *nm* summary

sumergir [sumer'xir] *vt* to submerge; (*hundir*) to sink

suministrar [sumini'strar] *vt* to supply, provide; **suministro** *nm* supply; (*acto*) supplying, providing

sumir [su'mir] *vt* to sink, submerge; (*fig*) to plunge

sumisión [sumi'sjon] *nf* (*acto*) submission; (*calidad*) submissiveness, docility; **sumiso, a** *adj* submissive, docile

sumo, a ['sumo, a] *adj* great, extreme; (*autoridad*) highest, supreme

suntuoso, a [sun'twoso, a] *adj* sumptuous, magnificent

supe *etc vb ver* **saber**

supeditar [supeði'tar] *vt*: **~ algo a algo** to subordinate sth to sth

super... [super] *prefijo* super..., over...; **~bueno** *adj* great, fantastic

súper ['super] *nf* (*gasolina*) three-star (petrol)

superar [supe'rar] *vt* (*sobreponerse a*) to overcome; (*rebasar*) to surpass, do better than; (*pasar*) to go beyond; **~se** *vr* to excel o.s.

superávit [supe'raβit] *nm inv* surplus

superficial [superfi'θjal] *adj* superficial; (*medida*) surface *cpd*, of the surface

superficie [super'fiθje] *nf* surface; (*área*) area

superfluo, a [su'perflwo, a] *adj* superfluous

superior [supe'rjor] *adj* (*piso, clase*) upper; (*temperatura, número, nivel*) higher; (*mejor: calidad, producto*) superior, better ♦ *nm/f* superior; **~idad** *nf* superiority

supermercado [supermer'kaðo] *nm* supermarket

superponer [superpo'ner] *vt* to superimpose

supersónico, a [super'soniko, a] *adj* supersonic

superstición [supersti'θjon] *nf* superstition; **supersticioso, a** *adj* superstitious

supervisar [superβi'sar] *vt* to supervise

supervivencia [superβi'ßenθja] *nf* survival

superviviente [superβi'ßjente] *adj* surviving

supiera *etc vb ver* **saber**

suplantar [suplan'tar] *vt* to supplant

suplemento [suple'mento] *nm* supplement

suplente [su'plente] *adj, nm/f* substitute

supletorio, a [suple'torjo, a] *adj*

supplementary ♦ *nm* supplement; **teléfono** ~ extension

súplica ['suplika] *nf* request; *(JUR)* petition

suplicar [supli'kar] *vt (cosa)* to beg (for), plead for; *(persona)* to beg, plead with

suplicio [su'pliθjo] *nm* torture

suplir [su'plir] *vt (compensar)* to make good, make up for; *(reemplazar)* to replace, substitute ♦ *vi:* ~ **a** to take the place of, substitute for

supo *etc vb ver* **saber**

suponer [supo'ner] *vt* to suppose; **suposición** *nf* supposition

supremacía [suprema'θia] *nf* supremacy

supremo, a [su'premo, a] *adj* supreme

supresión [supre'sjon] *nf* suppression; *(de derecho)* abolition; *(de palabra etc)* deletion; *(de restricción)* cancellation, lifting

suprimir [supri'mir] *vt* to suppress; *(derecho, costumbre)* to abolish; *(palabra etc)* to delete; *(restricción)* to cancel, lift

supuesto, a [su'pwesto, a] *pp de* **suponer** ♦ *adj (hipotético)* supposed ♦ *nm* assumption, hypothesis; ~ **que** since; **por** ~ of course

sur [sur] *nm* south

surcar [sur'kar] *vt* to plough; **surco** *nm (en metal, disco)* groove; *(AGR)* furrow

surgir [sur'xir] *vi* to arise, emerge; *(dificultad)* to come up, crop up

suroeste [suro'este] *nm* south-west

surtido, a [sur'tiðo, a] *adj* mixed, assorted ♦ *nm (selección)* selection, assortment; *(abastecimiento)* supply, stock; ~**r** *nm (tb:* ~**r de gasolina)* petrol pump *(BRIT)*, gas pump *(US)*

surtir [sur'tir] *vt* to supply, provide ♦ *vi* to spout, spurt

susceptible [susθep'tiβle] *adj* susceptible; *(sensible)* sensitive; ~ **de** capable of

suscitar [susθi'tar] *vt* to cause, provoke; *(interés, sospechas)* to arouse

suscribir [suskri'βir] *vt (firmar)* to sign; *(respaldar)* to subscribe to, endorse; ~**se** *vr* to subscribe; **suscripción** *nf* subscription

susodicho, a [suso'ðitʃo, a] *adj* above-mentioned

suspender [suspen'der] *vt (objeto)* to hang (up), suspend; *(trabajo)* to stop, suspend; *(ESCOL)* to fail; *(interrumpir)* to adjourn; *(atrasar)* to postpone; **suspensión** *nf* suspension; *(fig)* stoppage, suspension

suspenso, a [sus'penso, a] *adj* hanging, suspended; *(ESCOL)* failed ♦ *nm (ESCOL)* fail; **quedar** *o* **estar en** ~ to be pending

suspicacia [suspi'kaθja] *nf* suspicion, mistrust; **suspicaz** *adj* suspicious, distrustful

suspirar [suspi'rar] *vi* to sigh; **suspiro** *nm* sigh

sustancia [sus'tanθja] *nf* substance

sustentar [susten'tar] *vt (alimentar)* to sustain, nourish; *(objeto)* to hold up, support; *(idea, teoría)* to maintain, uphold; *(fig)* to sustain, keep going; **sustento** *nm* support; *(alimento)* sustenance, food

sustituir [sustitu'ir] *vt* to substitute, replace; **sustituto, a** *nm/f* substitute, replacement

susto ['susto] *nm* fright, scare

sustraer [sustra'er] *vt* to remove, take away; *(MAT)* to subtract

susurrar [susu'rrar] *vi* to whisper; **susurro** *nm* whisper

sutil [su'til] *adj (aroma, diferencia)* subtle; *(tenue)* thin; *(inteligencia, persona)* sharp; ~**eza** *nf* subtlety; thinness

suyo, a ['sujo, a] *(con artículo o después del verbo* **ser***) adj (de él)* his; *(de ella)* hers; *(de ellos, ellas)* theirs; *(de Ud, Uds)* yours; **un amigo** ~ a friend of his *(o* hers *o* theirs *o* yours)

T, t

tabacalera [taßaka'lera] *nf*: **T~** *Spanish state tobacco monopoly*

tabaco [ta'ßako] *nm* tobacco; (*fam*) cigarettes *pl*

taberna [ta'ßerna] *nf* bar, pub (*BRIT*)

tabique [ta'ßike] *nm* partition (wall)

tabla ['taßla] *nf* (*de madera*) plank; (*estante*) shelf; (*de vestido*) pleat; (*ARTE*) panel; **~s** *nfpl*: **estar** *o* **quedar en ~s** to draw; **~do** *nm* (*plataforma*) platform; (*TEATRO*) stage

tablao [ta'ßlao] *nm* (*tb*: **~ flamenco**) flamenco show

tablero [ta'ßlero] *nm* (*de madera*) plank, board; (*de ajedrez, damas*) board; **~ de anuncios** notice (*BRIT*) *o* bulletin (*US*) board

tableta [ta'ßleta] *nf* (*MED*) tablet; (*de chocolate*) bar

tablón [ta'ßlon] *nm* (*de suelo*) plank; (*de techo*) beam; **~ de anuncios** notice board (*BRIT*), bulletin board (*US*)

tabú [ta'ßu] *nm* taboo

tabular [taßu'lar] *vt* to tabulate

taburete [taßu'rete] *nm* stool

tacaño, a [ta'kaɲo, a] *adj* mean

tacha ['tatʃa] *nf* flaw; (*TEC*) stud; **tachar** *vt* (*borrar*) to cross out; **tachar de** to accuse of

tácito, a ['taθito, a] *adj* tacit

taciturno, a [taθi'turno, a] *adj* silent

taco ['tako] *nm* (*BILLAR*) cue; (*libro de billetes*) book; (*AM: de zapato*) heel; (*tarugo*) peg; (*palabrota*) swear word

tacón [ta'kon] *nm* heel; **de ~ alto** high-heeled; **taconeo** *nm* (heel) stamping

táctica ['taktika] *nf* tactics *pl*

táctico, a ['taktiko, a] *adj* tactical

tacto ['takto] *nm* touch; (*fig*) tact

taimado, a [tai'maðo, a] *adj* (*astuto*) sly

tajada [ta'xaða] *nf* slice

tajante [ta'xante] *adj* sharp

tajo ['taxo] *nm* (*corte*) cut; (*GEO*) cleft

tal [tal] *adj* such; **~ vez** perhaps ♦ *pron* (*persona*) someone, such a one; (*cosa*) something, such a thing; **~ como** such as; **~ para cual** (*dos iguales*) two of a kind ♦ *adv*: **~ como** (*igual*) just as; **~ cual** (*como es*) just as it is; **¿qué ~?** how are things?; **¿qué ~ te gusta?** how do you like it? ♦ *conj*: **con ~ de que** provided that

taladrar [tala'ðrar] *vt* to drill; **taladro** *nm* drill

talante [ta'lante] *nm* (*humor*) mood; (*voluntad*) will, willingness

talar [ta'lar] *vt* to fell, cut down; (*devastar*) to devastate

talco ['talko] *nm* (*polvos*) talcum powder

talego [ta'leɣo] *nm* sack

talento [ta'lento] *nm* talent; (*capacidad*) ability

TALGO ['talɣo] (*ESP*) *nm abr* (= *tren articulado ligero Goicoechea-Oriol*) ≈ HST (*BRIT*)

talismán [talis'man] *nm* talisman

talla ['taʎa] *nf* (*estatura, fig, MED*) height, stature; (*palo*) measuring rod; (*ARTE*) carving; (*medida*) size

tallado, a [ta'ʎaðo, a] *adj* carved ♦ *nm* carving

tallar [ta'ʎar] *vt* (*madera*) to carve; (*metal etc*) to engrave; (*medir*) to measure

tallarines [taʎa'rines] *nmpl* noodles

talle ['taʎe] *nm* (*ANAT*) waist; (*fig*) appearance

taller [ta'ʎer] *nm* (*TEC*) workshop; (*de artista*) studio

tallo ['taʎo] *nm* (*de planta*) stem; (*de hierba*) blade; (*brote*) shoot

talón [ta'lon] *nm* (*ANAT*) heel; (*COM*) counterfoil; (*cheque*) cheque (*BRIT*), check (*US*)

talonario [talo'narjo] *nm* (*de cheques*) chequebook (*BRIT*), checkbook (*US*); (*de recibos*) receipt book

tamaño, a [ta'maɲo, a] *adj* (*tan grande*) such a big; (*tan pequeño*) such a small ♦ *nm* size; **de ~ natural** full-size

tamarindo [tama'rindo] *nm* tamarind

tambalearse [tambale'arse] *vr* (*persona*) to stagger; (*vehículo*) to sway

también [tam'bjen] *adv* (*igualmente*) also, too, as well; (*además*) besides

tambor [tam'bor] *nm* drum; (*ANAT*) eardrum; ~ **del freno** brake drum

tamiz [ta'miθ] *nm* sieve; ~**ar** *vt* to sieve

tampoco [tam'poko] *adv* nor, neither; **yo ~ lo compré** I didn't buy it either

tampón [tam'pon] *nm* tampon

tan [tan] *adv* so; ~ **es así que ...** so much so that ....

tanda ['tanda] *nf* (*gen*) series; (*turno*) shift

tangente [tan'xente] *nf* tangent

Tánger ['tanxer] *n* Tangier(s)

tangible [tan'xiβle] *adj* tangible

tanque ['tanke] *nm* (*cisterna, MIL*) tank; (*AUTO*) tanker

tantear [tante'ar] *vt* (*calcular*) to reckon (up); (*medir*) to take the measure of; (*probar*) to test, try out; (*tomar la medida: persona*) to take the measurements of; (*situación*) to weigh up; (*persona: opinión*) to sound out ♦ *vi* (*DEPORTE*) to score; **tanteo** *nm* (*cálculo*) (rough) calculation; (*prueba*) test, trial; (*DEPORTE*) scoring

tanto, a ['tanto, a] *adj* (*cantidad*) so much, as much; ~**s** so many, as many; **20 y ~s** 20-odd ♦ *adv* (*cantidad*) so much, as much; (*tiempo*) so long, as long ♦ *conj*: **en ~ que** while; **hasta ~ (que)** until such time as ♦ *nm* (*suma*) certain amount; (*proporción*) so much; (*punto*) point; (*gol*) goal; **un ~ perezoso** somewhat lazy ♦ *pron*: **cado uno paga ~** each one pays so much; ~ **tú como yo** both you and I; ~ **como eso** as much as that; ~ **más ... cuanto que** all the more ... because; ~ **mejor/peor** so much the better/the worse; ~ **si viene como si va** whether he comes or whether he goes; ~ **es así que** so much so that; **por** *o* **por lo ~** therefore; **me he vuelto ronco de** *o* **con ~ hablar** I have become hoarse with so much talking; **a ~s de agosto** on such and such a day in August

tapa ['tapa] *nf* (*de caja, olla*) lid; (*de botella*) top; (*de libro*) cover; (*comida*) snack

tapadera [tapa'ðera] *nf* lid, cover

tapar [ta'par] *vt* (*cubrir*) to cover; (*envolver*) to wrap *o* cover up; (*la vista*) to obstruct; (*persona, falta*) to conceal; (*AM*) to fill; ~**se** *vr* to wrap o.s. up

taparrabo [tapa'rraβo] *nm* loincloth

tapete [ta'pete] *nm* table cover

tapia ['tapja] *nf* (*garden*) wall; **tapiar** *vt* to wall in

tapicería [tapiθe'ria] *nf* tapestry; (*para muebles*) upholstery; (*tienda*) upholsterer's (shop)

tapiz [ta'piθ] *nm* (*alfombra*) carpet; (*tela tejida*) tapestry; ~**ar** *vt* (*muebles*) to upholster

tapón [ta'pon] *nm* (*de botella*) top; (*de lavabo*) plug; ~ **de rosca** screw-top

taquigrafía [takiɣra'fia] *nf* shorthand; **taquígrafo, a** *nm/f* shorthand writer, stenographer

taquilla [ta'kiʎa] *nf* (*donde se compra*) booking office; (*suma recogida*) takings *pl*; **taquillero, a** *adj*: **función taquillera** box office success ♦ *nm/f* ticket clerk

tara ['tara] *nf* (*defecto*) defect; (*COM*) tare

tarántula [ta'rantula] *nf* tarantula

tararear [tarare'ar] *vi* to hum

tardar [tar'ðar] *vi* (*tomar tiempo*) to take a long time; (*llegar tarde*) to be late; (*demorar*) to delay; **¿tarda mucho el tren?** does the train take (very) long?; **a más ~** at the latest; **no tardes en venir** come soon

tarde ['tarðe] *adv* late ♦ *nf* (*de día*) afternoon; (*al anochecer*) evening; **de ~ en ~** from time to time; **¡buenas ~s!** good afternoon!; **a** *o* **por la ~** in the afternoon; in the evening

tardío, a [tar'ðio, a] *adj* (*retrasado*) late; (*lento*) slow (to arrive)

tarea [ta'rea] *nf* task; (*faena*) chore; (*ESCOL*) homework

tarifa [ta'rifa] *nf* (*lista de precios*) price list; (*precio*) tariff

tarima [ta'rima] *nf* (*plataforma*) platform

tarjeta [tar'xeta] *nf* card; **~ postal/de crédito/de Navidad** postcard/credit card/Christmas card

tarro ['tarro] *nm* jar, pot

tarta ['tarta] *nf* (*pastel*) cake; (*de base dura*) tart

tartamudear [tartamuðe'ar] *vi* to stammer; **tartamudo, a** *adj* stammering ♦ *nm/f* stammerer

tártaro, a ['tartaro, a] *adj*: **salsa tártara** tartar(e) sauce

tasa ['tasa] *nf* (*precio*) (fixed) price, rate; (*valoración*) valuation; (*medida, norma*) measure, standard; **~ de cambio/interés** exchange/interest rate; **~s universitarias** university fees; **~s de aeropuerto** airport tax; **~ción** *nf* valuation; **~dor, a** *nm/f* valuer

tasar [ta'sar] *vt* (*arreglar el precio*) to fix a price for; (*valorar*) to value, assess

tasca ['taska] (*fam*) *nf* pub

tatarabuelo, a [tatara'ßwelo, a] *nm/f* great-great-grandfather/mother

tatuaje [ta'twaxe] *nm* (*dibujo*) tattoo; (*acto*) tattooing

tatuar [ta'twar] *vt* to tattoo

taurino, a [tau'rino, a] *adj* bullfighting *cpd*

Tauro ['tauro] *nm* Taurus

tauromaquia [tauro'makja] *nf* tauromachy, (art of) bullfighting

taxi ['taksi] *nm* taxi

taxista [tak'sista] *nm/f* taxi driver

taza ['taθa] *nf* cup; (*de retrete*) bowl; **~ para café** coffee cup; **tazón** *nm* (*taza grande*) mug, large cup; (*de fuente*) basin

te [te] *pron* (*complemento de objeto*) you; (*complemento indirecto*) (to) you; (*reflexivo*) (to) yourself; **¿~ duele mucho el brazo?** does your arm hurt a lot?; **~ equivocas** you're wrong; **¡cálma~!** calm down!

té [te] *nm* tea

tea ['tea] *nf* torch

teatral [tea'tral] *adj* theatre *cpd*; (*fig*) theatrical

teatro [te'atro] *nm* theatre; (*LITERATURA*) plays *pl*, drama

tebeo [te'ßeo] *nm* comic

techo ['tetʃo] *nm* (*externo*) roof; (*interno*) ceiling; **~ corredizo** sunroof

tecla ['tekla] *nf* key; **~do** *nm* keyboard; **teclear** *vi* (*MUS*) to strum; (*con los dedos*) to tap ♦ *vt* (*INFORM*) to key in

técnica ['teknika] *nf* technique; (*tecnología*) technology; *ver tb* **técnico**

técnico, a ['tekniko, a] *adj* technical ♦ *nm/f* technician; (*experto*) expert

tecnología [teknolo'xia] *nf* technology; **tecnológico, a** *adj* technological

tedio ['teðjo] *nm* boredom, tedium; **~so, a** *adj* boring, tedious

teja ['texa] *nf* tile; (*BOT*) lime (tree); **~do** *nm* (tiled) roof

tejemaneje [texema'nexe] *nm* (*lío*) fuss; (*intriga*) intrigue

tejer [te'xer] *vt* to weave; (*hacer punto*) to knit; (*fig*) to fabricate; **tejido** *nm* (*tela*) material, fabric; (*telaraña*) web; (*ANAT*) tissue

tel [tel] *abr* (= **teléfono**) tel

tela ['tela] *nf* (*tejido*) material; (*telaraña*) web; (*en líquido*) skin; **telar** *nm* (*máquina*) loom

telaraña [tela'raɲa] *nf* cobweb

tele ['tele] (*fam*) *nf* telly (*BRIT*), tube (*US*)

tele... ['tele] *prefijo* tele...; **~comunicación** *nf* telecommunication; **~control** *nm* remote control; **~diario** *nm* television news; **~difusión** *nf* (television) broadcast; **~dirigido, a** *adj* remote-controlled

teléf *abr* (= **teléfono**) tel

teleférico [tele'feriko] *nm* (*de esqui*) ski-lift

telefonear [telefone'ar] *vi* to telephone

telefónico, a [tele'foniko, a] *adj* telephone *cpd*

telefonillo [telefo'niʎo] *nm* (*de puerta*) intercom

telefonista [telefo'nista] *nm/f* telephonist

teléfono [te'lefono] *nm* (tele)phone; **estar hablando al ~** to be on the phone; **llamar a uno por ~** to ring sb (up) *o* phone sb (up); **~ móvil** car phone; **~ portátil** mobile phone

telegrafía [televra'fia] *nf* telegraphy
telégrafo [te'levrafo] *nm* telegraph
telegrama [tele'xrama] *nm* telegram
tele: **~impresor** *nm* teleprinter (*BRIT*), teletype (*US*); **~novela** *nf* soap (opera); **~objetivo** *nm* telephoto lens; **~patía** *nf* telepathy; **~pático, a** *adj* telepathic; **~scópico, a** *adj* telescopic; **~scopio** *nm* telescope; **~silla** *nm* chairlift; **~spectador, a** *nm/f* viewer; **~squí** *nm* ski-lift; **~tarjeta** *nf* phonecard; **~tipo** *nm* teletype; **~ventas** *nfpl* telesales
televidente [teleßi'ðente] *nm/f* viewer
televisar [teleßi'sar] *vt* to televise
televisión [teleßi'sjon] *nf* television; **~ digital** digital television
televisor [teleßi'sor] *nm* television set
télex ['teleks] *nm inv* telex
telón [te'lon] *nm* curtain; **~ de acero** (*POL*) iron curtain; **~ de fondo** backcloth, background
tema ['tema] *nm* (*asunto*) subject, topic; (*MUS*) theme; **temática** *nf* (*social, histórica, artística*) range of topics; **temático, a** *adj* thematic
temblar [tem'blar] *vi* to shake, tremble; (*de frío*) to shiver; **temblón, ona** *adj* shaking; **temblor** *nm* trembling; (*de tierra*) earthquake; **tembloroso, a** *adj* trembling
temer [te'mer] *vt* to fear ♦ *vi* to be afraid; **temo que llegue tarde** I am afraid he may be late
temerario, a [teme'rarjo, a] *adj* (*descuidado*) reckless; (*irreflexivo*) hasty; **temeridad** *nf* (*imprudencia*) rashness; (*audacia*) boldness
temeroso, a [teme'roso, a] *adj* (*miedoso*) fearful; (*que inspira temor*) frightful
temible [te'mißle] *adj* fearsome
temor [te'mor] *nm* (*miedo*) fear; (*duda*) suspicion
témpano ['tempano] *nm*: **~ de hielo** ice-floe
temperamento [tempera'mento] *nm* temperament
temperatura [tempera'tura] *nf* temperature

tempestad [tempes'tað] *nf* storm; **tempestuoso, a** *adj* stormy
templado, a [tem'plaðo, a] *adj* (*moderado*) moderate; (*frugal*) frugal; (*agua*) lukewarm; (*clima*) mild; (*MUS*) well-tuned; **templanza** *nf* moderation; mildness
templar [tem'plar] *vt* (*moderar*) to moderate; (*furia*) to restrain; (*calor*) to reduce; (*afinar*) to tune (up); (*acero*) to temper; (*tuerca*) to tighten up; **temple** *nm* (*ajuste*) tempering; (*afinación*) tuning; (*pintura*) tempera
templo ['templo] *nm* (*iglesia*) church; (*pagano etc*) temple
temporada [tempo'raða] *nf* time, period; (*estación*) season
temporal [tempo'ral] *adj* (*no permanente*) temporary; (*REL*) temporal ♦ *nm* storm
tempranero, a [tempra'nero, a] *adj* (*BOT*) early; (*persona*) early-rising
temprano, a [tem'prano, a] *adj* early; (*demasiado pronto*) too soon, too early
ten *vb ver* **tener**
tenaces [te'naθes] *adj pl ver* **tenaz**
tenacidad [tenaθi'ðað] *nf* tenacity; (*dureza*) toughness; (*terquedad*) stubbornness
tenacillas [tena'θiʎas] *nfpl* tongs; (*para el pelo*) curling tongs (*BRIT*) o iron *sg* (*US*); (*MED*) forceps
tenaz [te'naθ] *adj* (*material*) tough; (*persona*) tenacious; (*creencia, resistencia*) stubborn
tenaza(s) [te'naθa(s)] *nf(pl)* (*MED*) forceps; (*TEC*) pliers; (*ZOOL*) pincers
tendedero [tende'ðero] *nm* (*para ropa*) drying place; (*cuerda*) clothes line
tendencia [ten'denθja] *nf* tendency; **tener ~ a** to tend to, have a tendency to; **tendencioso, a** *adj* tendentious
tender [ten'der] *vt* (*extender*) to spread out; (*colgar*) to hang out; (*vía férrea, cable*) to lay; (*estirar*) to stretch ♦ *vi*: **~ a** to tend to, have a tendency towards; **~se** *vr* to lie down; **~ la cama/la mesa** (*AM*)

to make the bed/lay (*BRIT*) *o* set (*US*) the table

tenderete [tende'rete] *nm* (*puesto*) stall; (*exposición*) display of goods

tendero, a [ten'dero, a] *nm/f* shopkeeper

tendido, a [ten'diðo, a] *adj* (*acostado*) lying down, flat; (*colgado*) hanging ♦ *nm* (*TAUR*) front rows of seats; **a galope ~** flat out

tendón [ten'don] *nm* tendon

tendré *etc vb ver* **tener**

tenebroso, a [tene'ßroso, a] *adj* (*oscuro*) dark; (*fig*) gloomy

tenedor [tene'ðor] *nm* (*CULIN*) fork; **~ de libros** book-keeper

tenencia [te'nenθja] *nf* (*de casa*) tenancy; (*de oficio*) tenure; (*de propiedad*) possession

---

PALABRA CLAVE

tener [te'ner] *vt* **1** (*poseer, gen*) to have; (*en la mano*) to hold; **¿tienes un boli?** have you got a pen?; **va a ~ un niño** she's going to have a baby; **¡ten** (*o* **tenga**)!, **¡aquí tienes** (*o* **tiene**)!** here you are!

2 (*edad, medidas*) to be; **tiene 7 años** she's 7 (years old); **tiene 15 cm de largo** it's 15 cm long; *ver* **calor**; **hambre** *etc*

3 (*considerar*): **lo tengo por brillante** I consider him to be brilliant; **~ en mucho a uno** to think very highly of sb

4 (+*pp*: = *pretérito*): **tengo terminada ya la mitad del trabajo** I've done half the work already

5: **~ que hacer algo** to have to do sth; **tengo que acabar este trabajo hoy** I have to finish this job today

6: **¿qué tienes, estás enfermo?** what's the matter with you, are you ill?

♦ **~se** *vr* **1**: **~se en pie** to stand up

2: **~se por** to think o.s.; **se tiene por muy listo** he thinks himself very clever

---

tengo *etc vb ver* **tener**

tenia ['tenja] *nf* tapeworm

teniente [te'njente] *nm* (*rango*) lieutenant; (*ayudante*) deputy

tenis ['tenis] *nm* tennis; **~ de mesa** table tennis; **~ta** *nm/f* tennis player

tenor [te'nor] *nm* (*sentido*) meaning; (*MUS*) tenor; **a ~ de** on the lines of

tensar [ten'sar] *vt* to tighten; (*arco*) to draw

tensión [ten'sjon] *nf* tension; (*TEC*) stress; (*MED*): **~ arterial** blood pressure; **tener la ~ alta** to have high blood pressure

tenso, a ['tenso, a] *adj* tense

tentación [tenta'θjon] *nf* temptation

tentáculo [ten'takulo] *nm* tentacle

tentador, a [tenta'ðor, a] *adj* tempting

tentar [ten'tar] *vt* (*seducir*) to tempt; (*atraer*) to attract; **tentativa** *nf* attempt; **tentativa de asesinato** attempted murder

tentempié [tentem'pje] *nm* snack

tenue ['tenwe] *adj* (*delgado*) thin, slender; (*neblina*) light; (*lazo, vínculo*) slight

teñir [te'ɲir] *vt* to dye; (*fig*) to tinge; **~se** *vr* to dye; **~se el pelo** to dye one's hair

teología [teolo'xia] *nf* theology

teoría [teo'ria] *nf* theory; **en ~** in theory; **teóricamente** *adv* theoretically; **teórico, a** *adj* theoretic(al) ♦ *nm/f* theoretician, theorist; **teorizar** *vi* to theorize

terapéutico, a [tera'peutiko, a] *adj* therapeutic

terapia [te'rapja] *nf* therapy

tercer [ter'θer] *adj ver* **tercero**

tercermundista [terθermun'dista] *adj* Third World *cpd*

tercero, a [ter'θero, a] *adj* (*delante de nmsg*: **tercer**) third ♦ *nm* (*JUR*) third party

terceto [ter'θeto] *nm* trio

terciar [ter'θjar] *vi* (*participar*) to take part; (*hacer de árbitro*) to mediate; **~se** *vr* to come up; **~io, a** *adj* tertiary

tercio ['terθjo] *nm* third

terciopelo [terθjo'pelo] *nm* velvet

terco, a ['terko, a] *adj* obstinate

tergal ® [ter'val] *nm* type of polyester

tergiversar [terxißer'sar] *vt* to distort

termal [ter'mal] *adj* thermal

termas ['termas] nfpl hot springs
térmico, a ['termiko, a] adj thermal
terminación [termina'θjon] nf (final) end; (conclusión) conclusion, ending
terminal [termi'nal] adj, nm, nf terminal
terminante [termi'nante] adj (final) final, definitive; (tajante) categorical; **~mente** adv: **~mente prohibido** strictly forbidden
terminar [termi'nar] vt (completar) to complete, finish; (concluir) to end ♦ vi (llegar a su fin) to end; (parar) to stop; (acabar) to finish; **~se** vr to come to an end; **~ por hacer algo** to end up (by) doing sth
término ['termino] nm end, conclusion; (parada) terminus; (límite) boundary; **~ medio** average; (fig) middle way; **en último ~** (a fin de cuentas) in the last analysis; (como último recurso) as a last resort
terminología [terminolo'xia] nf terminology
termodinámico, a [termoði'namiko, a] adj thermodynamic
termómetro [ter'mometro] nm thermometer
termonuclear [termonukle'ar] adj thermonuclear
termo(s) ® ['termo(s)] nm Thermos ® (flask)
termostato [termo'stato] nm thermostat
ternero, a [ter'nero, a] nm/f (animal) calf ♦ nf (carne) veal
ternura [ter'nura] nf (trato) tenderness; (palabra) endearment; (cariño) fondness
terquedad [terke'ðað] nf obstinacy
terrado [te'rraðo] nm terrace
terraplén [terra'plen] nm embankment
terrateniente [terrate'njente] nm/f landowner
terraza [te'rraθa] nf (balcón) balcony; (tejado) (flat) roof; (AGR) terrace
terremoto [terre'moto] nm earthquake
terrenal [terre'nal] adj earthly
terreno [te'rreno] nm (tierra) land; (parcela) plot; (suelo) soil; (fig) field; **un ~** a piece of land

terrestre [te'rrestre] adj terrestrial; (ruta) land cpd
terrible [te'rriβle] adj terrible, awful
territorio [terri'torjo] nm territory
terrón [te'rron] nm (de azúcar) lump; (de tierra) clod, lump
terror [te'rror] nm terror; **~ífico, a** adj terrifying; **~ista** adj, nm/f terrorist
terso, a ['terso, a] adj (liso) smooth; (pulido) polished; **tersura** nf smoothness
tertulia [ter'tulja] nf (reunión informal) social gathering; (grupo) group, circle
tesis ['tesis] nf inv thesis
tesón [te'son] nm (firmeza) firmness; (tenacidad) tenacity
tesorero, a [teso'rero, a] nm/f treasurer
tesoro [te'soro] nm treasure; (COM, POL) treasury
testaferro [testa'ferro] nm figurehead
testamentario, a [testamen'tarjo, a] adj testamentary ♦ nm/f executor/executrix
testamento [testa'mento] nm will
testar [tes'tar] vi to make a will
testarudo, a [testa'ruðo, a] adj stubborn
testículo [tes'tikulo] nm testicle
testificar [testifi'kar] vt to testify; (fig) to attest ♦ vi to give evidence
testigo [tes'tiɣo] nm/f witness; **~ de cargo/descargo** witness for the prosecution/defence; **~ ocular** eye witness
testimoniar [testimo'njar] vt to testify to; (fig) to show; **testimonio** nm testimony
teta ['teta] nf (de biberón) teat; (ANAT: fam) breast
tétanos ['tetanos] nm tetanus
tetera [te'tera] nf teapot
tétrico, a ['tetriko, a] adj gloomy, dismal
textil [teks'til] adj textile
texto ['teksto] nm text; **textual** adj textual
textura [teks'tura] nf (de tejido) texture
tez [teθ] nf (cutis) complexion
ti [ti] pron you; (reflexivo) yourself
tía ['tia] nf (pariente) aunt; (fam) chick, bird
tibieza [ti'βjeθa] nf (temperatura) tepidness; (actitud) coolness; **tibio, a** adj lukewarm
tiburón [tiβu'ron] nm shark

tic [tik] *nm* (*ruido*) click; (*de reloj*) tick; (*MED*): **~ nervioso** nervous tic

tictac [tik'tak] *nm* (*de reloj*) tick tock

tiempo ['tjempo] *nm* time; (*época, período*) age, period; (*METEOROLOGÍA*) weather; (*LING*) tense; (*DEPORTE*) half; **a ~ in** time; **a un** *o* **al mismo ~** at the same time; **al poco ~** very soon (after); **se quedó poco ~** he didn't stay very long; **hace poco ~** not long ago; **mucho ~** a long time; **de ~ en ~** from time to time; **hace buen/mal ~** the weather is fine/bad; **estar a ~** to be in time; **hace ~** some time ago; **hacer ~** to while away the time; **motor de 2 ~s** two-stroke engine; **primer ~** first half

tienda ['tjenda] *nf* shop, store; **~ (de campaña)** tent; **~ de alimentación** *o* **comestibles** grocer's (*BRIT*), grocery store (*US*)

tienes *etc vb ver* **tener**

tienta *etc* ['tjenta] *vb ver* **tentar** ♦ *nf*: **andar a ~s** to grope one's way along

tiento ['tjento] *vb ver* **tentar** ♦ *nm* (*tacto*) touch; (*precaución*) wariness

tierno, a ['tjerno, a] *adj* (*blando*) tender; (*fresco*) fresh; (*amable*) sweet

tierra ['tjerra] *nf* earth; (*suelo*) soil; (*mundo*) earth, world; (*país*) country, land; **~ adentro** inland

tieso, a ['tjeso, a] *adj* (*rígido*) rigid; (*duro*) stiff; (*fam: orgulloso*) conceited

tiesto ['tjesto] *nm* flowerpot

tifoidea [tifoi'ðea] *nf* typhoid

tifón [ti'fon] *nm* typhoon

tifus ['tifus] *nm* typhus

tigre ['tixre] *nm* tiger

tijera [ti'xera] *nf* scissors *pl*; (*ZOOL*) claw; **~s** *nfpl* scissors; (*para plantas*) shears

tijeretear [tixerete'ar] *vt* to snip

tila ['tila] *nf* lime blossom tea

tildar [til'dar] *vt*: **~ de** to brand as

tilde ['tilde] *nf* (*TIP*) tilde

tilín [ti'lin] *nm* tinkle

tilo ['tilo] *nm* lime tree

timar [ti'mar] *vt* (*estafar*) to swindle

timbal [tim'bal] *nm* small drum

timbrar [tim'brar] *vt* to stamp

timbre ['timbre] *nm* (*sello*) stamp; (*campanilla*) bell; (*tono*) timbre; (*COM*) stamp duty

timidez [timi'ðeθ] *nf* shyness; **tímido, a** *adj* shy

timo ['timo] *nm* swindle

timón [ti'mon] *nm* helm, rudder; **timonel** *nm* helmsman

tímpano ['timpano] *nm* (*ANAT*) eardrum; (*MUS*) small drum

tina ['tina] *nf* tub; (*baño*) bath(tub); **tinaja** *nf* large jar

tinglado [tin'glaðo] *nm* (*cobertizo*) shed; (*fig: truco*) trick; (*intriga*) intrigue

tinieblas [ti'njeßlas] *nfpl* darkness *sg*; (*sombras*) shadows

tino ['tino] *nm* (*habilidad*) skill; (*juicio*) insight

tinta ['tinta] *nf* ink; (*TEC*) dye; (*ARTE*) colour

tinte ['tinte] *nm* dye

tintero [tin'tero] *nm* inkwell

tintinear [tintine'ar] *vt* to tinkle

tinto ['tinto] *nm* red wine

tintorería [tintore'ria] *nf* dry cleaner's

tintura [tin'tura] *nf* (*QUÍM*) dye; (*farmacéutico*) tincture

tío ['tio] *nm* (*pariente*) uncle; (*fam: individuo*) bloke (*BRIT*), guy

tiovivo [tio'ßißo] *nm* merry-go-round

típico, a ['tipiko, a] *adj* typical

tipo ['tipo] *nm* (*clase*) type, kind; (*hombre*) fellow; (*ANAT: de hombre*) build; (: *de mujer*) figure; (*IMPRENTA*) type; **~ bancario/de descuento/de interés/de cambio** bank/discount/interest/exchange rate

tipografía [tipovra'fia] *nf* printing *cpd*; **tipográfico, a** *adj* printing *cpd*

tíquet ['tiket] (*pl* **~s**) *nm* ticket; (*en tienda*) cash slip

tiquismiquis [tikis'mikis] *nm inv* fussy person ♦ *nmpl* (*querellas*) squabbling *sg*; (*escrúpulos*) silly scruples

tira ['tira] *nf* strip; (*fig*) abundance; **~ y afloja** give and take

tirabuzón [tiraßu'θon] *nm* (*rizo*) curl

tirachinas [tira'tʃinas] *nm inv* catapult

tirada [ti'raða] *nf* (*acto*) cast, throw; (*serie*) series; (*TIP*) printing, edition; **de una ~** at one go

tirado, a [ti'raðo, a] *adj* (*barato*) dirt-cheap; (*fam: fácil*) very easy

tirador [tira'ðor] *nm* (*mango*) handle

tiranía [tira'nia] *nf* tyranny; **tirano, a** *adj* tyrannical ♦ *nm/f* tyrant

tirante [ti'rante] *adj* (*cuerda etc*) tight, taut; (*relaciones*) strained ♦ *nm* (*ARQ*) brace; (*TEC*) stay; **~s** *nmpl* (*de pantalón*) braces (*BRIT*), suspenders (*US*); **tirantez** *nf* tightness; (*fig*) tension

tirar [ti'rar] *vt* to throw; (*dejar caer*) to drop; (*volcar*) to upset; (*derribar*) to knock down *o* over; (*desechar*) to throw out *o* away; (*dinero*) to squander; (*imprimir*) to print ♦ *vi* (*disparar*) to shoot; (*de la puerta etc*) to pull; (*fam: andar*) to go; (*tender a, buscar realizar*) to tend to; (*DEPORTE*) to shoot; **~se** *vr* to throw o.s.; **~ abajo** to bring down, destroy; **tira más a su padre** he takes more after his father; **ir tirando** to manage; **a todo ~** at the most

tirita [ti'rita] *nf* (sticking) plaster (*BRIT*), bandaid (*US*)

tiritar [tiri'tar] *vi* to shiver

tiro ['tiro] *nm* (*lanzamiento*) throw; (*disparo*) shot; (*DEPORTE*) shot; (*GOLF, TENIS*) drive; (*alcance*) range; **~ al blanco** target practice; **caballo de ~** cart-horse; **andar de ~s largos** to be all dressed up; **al ~** (*AM*) at once

tirón [ti'ron] *nm* (*sacudida*) pull, tug; **de un ~** in one go, all at once

tiroteo [tiro'teo] *nm* exchange of shots, shooting

tísico, a ['tisiko, a] *adj* consumptive

tisis ['tisis] *nf inv* consumption, tuberculosis

títere ['titere] *nm* puppet

titiritero, a [titiri'tero, a] *nm/f* puppeteer

titubeante [titußе'ante] *adj* (*al andar*) shaky, tottering; (*al hablar*) stammering; (*dudoso*) hesitant

titubear [titußе'ar] *vi* to stagger; to stammer; (*fig*) to hesitate; **titubeo** *nm* staggering; stammering; hesitation

titulado, a [titu'laðo, a] *adj* (*libro*) entitled, (*persona*) titled

titular [titu'lar] *adj* titular ♦ *nm/f* holder ♦ *nm* headline ♦ *vt* to title; **~se** *vr* to be entitled; **título** *nm* title; (*de diario*) headline; (*certificado*) professional qualification; (*universitario*) (university) degree; **a título de** in the capacity of

tiza ['tiθa] *nf* chalk

tiznar [tiθ'nar] *vt* to blacken

tizón [ti'θon] *nm* brand

toalla [to'aʎa] *nf* towel

tobillo [to'ßiʎo] *nm* ankle

tobogán [toßo'yan] *nm* (*montaña rusa*) roller-coaster; (*de niños*) chute, slide

tocadiscos [toka'ðiskos] *nm inv* record player

tocado, a [to'kaðo, a] *adj* (*fam*) touched ♦ *nm* headdress

tocador [toka'ðor] *nm* (*mueble*) dressing table; (*cuarto*) boudoir; (*fam*) ladies' toilet (*BRIT*) *o* room (*US*)

tocante [to'kante]: **~ a** *prep* with regard to

tocar [to'kar] *vt* to touch; (*MUS*) to play; (*referirse a*) to allude to; (*timbre*) to ring ♦ *vi* (*a la puerta*) to knock (on *o* at the door); (*ser de turno*) to fall to, be the turn of; (*ser hora*) to be due; **~se** *vr* (*cubrirse la cabeza*) to cover one's head; (*tener contacto*) to touch (each other); **por lo que a mí me toca** as far as I am concerned; **te toca a tí** it's your turn

tocayo, a [to'kajo, a] *nm/f* namesake

tocino [to'θino] *nm* bacon

todavía [toða'ßia] *adv* (*aun*) even; (*aún*) still, yet; **~ más** yet more; **~ no** not yet

| PALABRA CLAVE |

todo, a ['toðo, a] *adj* **1** (*con artículo sg*) all; **toda la carne** all the meat; **toda la noche** all night, the whole night; **~ el libro** the whole book; **toda una botella** a whole bottle; **~ lo contrario** quite the opposite; **está toda sucia** she's all dirty; **por ~ el país** throughout the whole country

2 (*con artículo pl*) all; every; **~s los libros** all the books; **todas las noches** every night; **~s los que quieran salir** all those who want to leave

♦ *pron* **1** everything, all; **~s** everyone, everybody; **lo sabemos ~** we know everything; **~s querían más tiempo** everybody *o* everyone wanted more time; **nos marchamos ~s** all of us left

2: **con ~**: **con ~ él me sigue gustando** even so I still like him

♦ *adv* all; **vaya ~ seguido** keep straight on *o* ahead

♦ *nm*: **como un ~** as a whole; **del ~**: **no me agrada del ~** I don't entirely like it

todopoderoso, a [toðopoðe'roso, a] *adj* all powerful; (*REL*) almighty

toga ['toxa] *nf* toga; (*ESCOL*) gown

Tokio ['tokjo] *n* Tokyo

toldo ['toldo] *nm* (*para el sol*) sunshade (*BRIT*), parasol; (*tienda*) marquee

tolerancia [tole'ranθja] *nf* tolerance; **tolerante** *adj* (*sociedad*) liberal; (*persona*) open-minded

tolerar [tole'rar] *vt* to tolerate; (*resistir*) to endure

toma ['toma] *nf* (*acto*) taking; (*MED*) dose; **~ (de corriente)** socket

tomar [to'mar] *vt* to take; (*aspecto*) to take on; (*beber*) to drink ♦ *vi* to take; (*AM*) to drink; **~se** *vr* to take; **~se por** to consider o.s. to be; **~ a bien/a mal** to take well/ badly; **~ en serio** to take seriously; **~ el pelo a alguien** to pull sb's leg; **~ la con uno** to pick a quarrel with sb; **¡tome!** here you are!; **~ el sol** to sunbathe

tomate [to'mate] *nm* tomato

tomillo [to'miʎo] *nm* thyme

tomo ['tomo] *nm* (*libro*) volume

ton [ton] *abr* = **tonelada** ♦ *nm*: **sin ~ ni son** without rhyme or reason

tonada [to'naða] *nf* tune

tonalidad [tonali'ðað] *nf* tone

tonel [to'nel] *nm* barrel

tonelada [tone'laða] *nf* ton; **tonelaje** *nm*

tonnage

tónica ['tonika] *nf* (*MUS*) tonic; (*fig*) keynote

tónico, a ['toniko, a] *adj* tonic ♦ *nm* (*MED*) tonic

tonificar [tonifi'kar] *vt* to tone up

tono ['tono] *nm* tone; **fuera de ~** inappropriate; **darse ~** to put on airs

tontería [tonte'ria] *nf* (*estupidez*) foolishness; (*cosa*) stupid thing; (*acto*) foolish act; **~s** *nfpl* (*disparates*) rubbish *sg*, nonsense *sg*

tonto, a ['tonto, a] *adj* stupid, silly ♦ *nm/f* fool

topar [to'par] *vi*: **~ contra** *o* **en** to run into; **~ con** to run up against

tope ['tope] *adj* maximum ♦ *nm* (*fin*) end; (*límite*) limit; (*FERRO*) buffer; (*AUTO*) bumper; **al ~** end to end

tópico, a ['topiko, a] *adj* topical ♦ *nm* platitude

topo ['topo] *nm* (*ZOOL*) mole; (*fig*) blunderer

topografía [topoɣra'fia] *nf* topography; **topógrafo, a** *nm/f* topographer

toque *etc* ['toke] *vb ver* **tocar** ♦ *nm* touch; (*MUS*) beat; (*de campana*) peal; **dar un ~ a** to warn; **~ de queda** curfew

toqué *vb ver* **tocar**

toquetear [tokete'ar] *vt* to finger

toquilla [to'kiʎa] *nf* (*pañuelo*) headscarf; (*chal*) shawl

tórax ['toraks] *nm* thorax

torbellino [torbe'ʎino] *nm* whirlwind; (*fig*) whirl

torcedura [torθe'ðura] *nf* twist; (*MED*) sprain

torcer [tor'θer] *vt* to twist; (*la esquina*) to turn; (*MED*) to sprain ♦ *vi* (*desviar*) to turn off; **~se** *vr* (*ladearse*) to bend; (*desviarse*) to go astray; (*fracasar*) to go wrong; **torcido, a** *adj* twisted; (*fig*) crooked ♦ *nm* curl

tordo, a ['torðo, a] *adj* dappled ♦ *nm* thrush

torear [tore'ar] *vt* (*fig: evadir*) to avoid; (*jugar con*) to tease ♦ *vi* to fight bulls;

toreo *nm* bullfighting; **torero, a** *nm/f* bullfighter

tormenta [tor'menta] *nf* storm; (*fig: confusión*) turmoil

tormento [tor'mento] *nm* torture; (*fig*) anguish

tornar [tor'nar] *vt* (*devolver*) to return, give back; (*transformar*) to transform ♦ *vi* to go back; **~se** *vr* (*ponerse*) to become

tornasolado, a [tornaso'laðo, a] *adj* (*brillante*) iridescent; (*reluciente*) shimmering

torneo [tor'neo] *nm* tournament

tornillo [tor'niλo] *nm* screw

torniquete [torni'kete] *nm* (*MED*) tourniquet

torno ['torno] *nm* (*TEC*) winch; (*tambor*) drum; **en ~ (a)** round, about

toro ['toro] *nm* bull; (*fam*) he-man; **los ~s** bullfighting

toronja [to'ronxa] *nf* grapefruit

torpe ['torpe] *adj* (*poco hábil*) clumsy, awkward; (*necio*) dim; (*lento*) slow

torpedo [tor'peðo] *nm* torpedo

torpeza [tor'peθa] *nf* (*falta de agilidad*) clumsiness; (*lentitud*) slowness; (*error*) mistake

torre ['torre] *nf* tower; (*de petróleo*) derrick

torrefacto, a [torre'facto, a] *adj* roasted

torrente [to'rrente] *nm* torrent

tórrido, a ['torriðo, a] *adj* torrid

torrija [to'rrixa] *nf* French toast

torsión [tor'sjon] *nf* twisting

torso ['torso] *nm* torso

torta ['torta] *nf* cake; (*fam*) slap

tortícolis [tor'tikolis] *nm inv* stiff neck

tortilla [tor'tiλa] *nf* omelette; (*AM*) maize pancake; **~ francesa/española** plain/potato omelette

tórtola ['tortola] *nf* turtledove

tortuga [tor'tuɣa] *nf* tortoise

tortuoso, a [tor'twoso, a] *adj* winding

tortura [tor'tura] *nf* torture; **torturar** *vt* to torture

tos [tos] *nf* cough; **~ ferina** whooping cough

tosco, a ['tosko, a] *adj* coarse

toser [to'ser] *vi* to cough

tostada [tos'taða] *nf* piece of toast; **tostado, a** *adj* toasted; (*por el sol*) dark brown; (*piel*) tanned

tostador [tosta'ðor] *nm* toaster

tostar [tos'tar] *vt* to toast; (*café*) to roast; (*persona*) to tan; **~se** *vr* to get brown

total [to'tal] *adj* total ♦ *adv* in short; (*al fin y al cabo*) when all is said and done ♦ *nm* total; **~ que** to cut (*BRIT*) o make (*US*) a long story short

totalidad [totali'ðað] *nf* whole

totalitario, a [totali'tarjo, a] *adj* totalitarian

tóxico, a ['toksiko, a] *adj* toxic ♦ *nm* poison; **toxicómano, a** *nm/f* drug addict

toxina [to'ksina] *nf* toxin

tozudo, a [to'θuðo, a] *adj* obstinate

traba ['traßa] *nf* bond, tie; (*cadena*) shackle

trabajador, a [traßaxa'ðor, a] *adj* hard-working ♦ *nm/f* worker

trabajar [traßa'xar] *vt* to work; (*AGR*) to till; (*empeñarse en*) to work at; (*convencer*) to persuade ♦ *vi* to work; (*esforzarse*) to strive; **trabajo** *nm* work; (*tarea*) task; (*POL*) labour; (*fig*) effort; **tomarse el trabajo de** to take the trouble to; **trabajo por turno/a destajo** shift work/piecework; **trabajoso, a** *adj* hard

trabalenguas [traßa'lengwas] *nm inv* tongue twister

trabar [tra'ßar] *vt* (*juntar*) to join, unite; (*atar*) to tie down, fetter; (*agarrar*) to seize; (*amistad*) to strike up; **~se** *vr* to become entangled; **trabársele a uno la lengua** to be tongue-tied

tracción [trak'θjon] *nf* traction; **~ delantera/trasera** front-wheel/rear-wheel drive

tractor [trak'tor] *nm* tractor

tradición [traði'θjon] *nf* tradition; **tradicional** *adj* traditional

traducción [traðuk'θjon] *nf* translation

traducir [traðu'θir] *vt* to translate; **traductor, a** *nm/f* translator

traer [tra'er] *vt* to bring; (*llevar*) to carry; (*llevar puesto*) to wear; (*incluir*) to carry; (*causar*) to cause; **~se** *vr*: **~se algo** to be up to sth

traficar [trafi'kar] *vi* to trade

tráfico ['trafiko] *nm* (COM) trade; (AUTO) traffic

tragaluz [traɣa'luθ] *nm* skylight

tragaperras [traɣa'perras] *nm o f inv* slot machine

tragar [tra'ɣar] *vt* to swallow; (*devorar*) to devour, bolt down; **~se** *vr* to swallow

tragedia [tra'xeðja] *nf* tragedy; **trágico, a** *adj* tragic

trago ['traɣo] *nm* (*líquido*) drink; (*bocado*) gulp; (*fam: de bebida*) swig; (*desgracia*) blow

traición [trai'θjon] *nf* treachery; (JUR) treason; (*una ~*) act of treachery; **traicionar** *vt* to betray

traicionero, a [traiθjo'nero, a] *adj* treacherous

traidor, a [trai'ðor, a] *adj* treacherous ♦ *nm/f* traitor

traigo etc *vb ver* **traer**

traje ['traxe] *vb ver* **traer** ♦ *nm* (*de hombre*) suit; (*de mujer*) dress; (*vestido típico*) costume; **~ de baño** swimsuit; **~ de luces** bullfighter's costume

trajera etc *vb ver* **traer**

trajín [tra'xin] *nm* (*fam*) bustle; **trajinar** *vi* (*moverse*) to bustle about

trama ['trama] *nf* (*intriga*) plot; (*de tejido*) weft (BRIT), woof (US); **tramar** *vt* to plot; (TEC) to weave

tramitar [trami'tar] *vt* (*asunto*) to transact; (*negociar*) to negotiate

trámite ['tramite] *nm* (*paso*) step; (JUR) transaction; **~s** *nmpl* (*burocracia*) procedure *sg*; (JUR) proceedings

tramo ['tramo] *nm* (*de tierra*) plot; (*de escalera*) flight; (*de vía*) section

tramoya [tra'moja] *nf* (TEATRO) piece of stage machinery; **tramoyista** *nm/f* scene shifter; (*fig*) trickster

trampa ['trampa] *nf* trap; (*en el suelo*) trapdoor; (*truco*) trick; (*engaño*) fiddle;

trampear *vt, vi* to cheat

trampolín [trampo'lin] *nm* (*de piscina etc*) diving board

tramposo, a [tram'poso, a] *adj* crooked, cheating ♦ *nm/f* crook, cheat

tranca ['tranka] *nf* (*palo*) stick; (*de puerta, ventana*) bar; **trancar** *vt* to bar

trance ['tranθe] *nm* (*momento difícil*) difficult moment *o* juncture; (*estado hipnotizado*) trance

tranquilidad [trankili'ðað] *nf* (*calma*) calmness, stillness; (*paz*) peacefulness

tranquilizar [trankili'θar] *vt* (*calmar*) to calm (down); (*asegurar*) to reassure; **~se** *vr* to calm down; **tranquilo, a** *adj* (*calmado*) calm; (*apacible*) peaceful; (*mar*) calm; (*mente*) untroubled

transacción [transak'θjon] *nf* transaction

transbordador [transßorða'ðor] *nm* ferry

transbordar [transßor'ðar] *vt* to transfer; **transbordo** *nm* transfer; **hacer transbordo** to change (trains *etc*)

transcurrir [transku'rrir] *vi* (*tiempo*) to pass; (*hecho*) to take place

transcurso [trans'kurso] *nm*: **~ del tiempo** lapse (of time)

transeúnte [transe'unte] *nm/f* passer-by

transferencia [transfe'renθja] *nf* transference; (COM) transfer

transferir [transfe'rir] *vt* to transfer

transformador [transforma'ðor] *nm* (ELEC) transformer

transformar [transfor'mar] *vt* to transform; (*convertir*) to convert

tránsfuga ['transfuɣa] *nm/f* (MIL) deserter; (POL) turncoat

transfusión [transfu'sjon] *nf* transfusion

transgenico, a [trans'xeniko, a] *adj* genetically modified, GM

transición [transi'θjon] *nf* transition

transigir [transi'xir] *vi* to compromise, make concessions

transitar [transi'tar] *vi* to go (from place to place); **tránsito** *nm* transit; (AUTO) traffic; **transitorio, a** *adj* transitory

transmisión [transmi'sjon] *nf* (TEC) transmission; (*transferencia*) transfer; **~ en**

directo/exterior live/outside broadcast

transmitir [transmiˈtir] *vt* to transmit;
(*RADIO, TV*) to broadcast

transparencia [transpaˈrenθja] *nf*
transparency; (*claridad*) clearness, clarity;
(*foto*) slide

transparentar [transparenˈtar] *vt* to reveal
♦ *vi* to be transparent; **transparente**
adj transparent; (*claro*) clear

transpirar [transpiˈrar] *vi* to perspire

transportar [transporˈtar] *vt* to transport;
(*llevar*) to carry; **transporte** *nm*
transport; (*COM*) haulage

transversal [transβerˈsal] *adj* transverse,
cross

tranvía [tramˈbia] *nm* tram

trapecio [traˈpeθjo] *nm* trapeze;
trapecista *nm/f* trapeze artist

trapero, a [traˈpero, a] *nm/f* ragman

trapicheo [trapiˈtʃeo] (*fam*) *nm* scheme,
fiddle

trapo [ˈtrapo] *nm* (*tela*) rag; (*de cocina*)
cloth

tráquea [ˈtrakea] *nf* windpipe

traqueteo [trakeˈteo] *nm* rattling

tras [tras] *prep* (*detrás*) behind; (*después*)
after

trasatlántico [trasatˈlantiko] *nm* (*barco*)
(cabin) cruiser

trascendencia [trasθenˈdenθja] *nf*
(*importancia*) importance; (*FILOSOFÍA*)
transcendence

trascendental [trasθendenˈtal] *adj*
important; (*FILOSOFÍA*) transcendental

trascender [trasθenˈder] *vi* (*noticias*) to
come out; (*asunto*) to have a wide effect

trasero, a [traˈsero, a] *adj* back, rear ♦ *nm*
(*ANAT*) bottom

trasfondo [trasˈfondo] *nm* background

trasgredir [trasɣreˈðir] *vt* to contravene

trashumante [trasuˈmante] *adj* (*animales*)
migrating

trasladar [traslaˈðar] *vt* to move; (*persona*)
to transfer; (*postergar*) to postpone;
(*copiar*) to copy; **~se** *vr* (*mudarse*) to
move; **traslado** *nm* move; (*mudanza*)
move, removal

traslucir [trasluˈθir] *vt* to show; **~se** *vr* to
be translucent; (*fig*) to be revealed

trasluz [trasˈluθ] *nm* reflected light; **al ~**
against *o* up to the light

trasnochador, a [trasnotʃaˈðor, a] *nm/f*
night owl

trasnochar [trasnoˈtʃar] *vi* (*acostarse
tarde*) to stay up late

traspapelar [traspapeˈlar] *vt* (*document,
carta*) to mislay, misplace

traspasar [traspaˈsar] *vt* (*suj: bala etc*) to
pierce, go through; (*propiedad*) to sell,
transfer; (*calle*) to cross over; (*límites*) to
go beyond; (*ley*) to break; **traspaso** *nm*
(*venta*) transfer, sale

traspié [trasˈpje] *nm* (*tropezón*) trip; (*error*)
blunder

trasplantar [trasplanˈtar] *vt* to transplant

traste [ˈtraste] *nm* (*MUS*) fret; **dar al ~ con
algo** to ruin sth

trastero [trasˈtero] *nm* storage room

trastienda [trasˈtjenda] *nf* back of shop

trasto [ˈtrasto] (*pey*) *nm* (*cosa*) piece of
junk; (*persona*) dead loss

trastornado, a [trastorˈnaðo, a] *adj* (*loco*)
mad, crazy

trastornar [trastorˈnar] *vt* (*fig: planes*) to
disrupt; (: *nervios*) to shatter; (: *persona*)
to drive crazy; **~se** *vr* (*volverse loco*) to go
mad *o* crazy; **trastorno** *nm* (*acto*)
overturning; (*confusión*) confusion

tratable [traˈtaβle] *adj* friendly

tratado [traˈtaðo] *nm* (*POL*) treaty; (*COM*)
agreement

tratamiento [trataˈmjento] *nm* treatment;
~ de textos (*INFORM*) word processing
cpd

tratar [traˈtar] *vt* (*ocuparse de*) to treat;
(*manejar, TEC*) to handle; (*MED*) to treat;
(*dirigirse a: persona*) to address ♦ *vi:* **~ de**
(*hablar sobre*) to deal with, be about;
(*intentar*) to try to; **~se** *vr* to treat each
other; **~ con** (*COM*) to trade in; (*negociar*)
to negotiate with; (*tener contactos*) to
have dealings with; **¿de qué se trata?**
what's it about?; **trato** *nm* dealings *pl*;
(*relaciones*) relationship; (*comportamiento*)

manner; (COM) agreement

trauma ['trauma] nm trauma

través [tra'ßes] nm (fig) reverse; **al ~** across, crossways; **a ~ de** across; (sobre) over; (por) through

travesaño [traße'saɲo] nm (ARQ) crossbeam; (DEPORTE) crossbar

travesía [traße'sia] nf (calle) cross-street; (NAUT) crossing

travesura [traße'sura] nf (broma) prank; (ingenio) wit

traviesa [tra'ßjesa] nf (ARQ) crossbeam

travieso, a [tra'ßjeso, a] adj (niño) naughty

trayecto [tra'jekto] nm (ruta) road, way; (viaje) journey; (tramo) stretch; **~ria** nf trajectory; (fig) path

traza ['traθa] nf (aspecto) looks pl; (señal) sign; **~do, a** adj: **bien ~do** shapely, well-formed ♦ nm (ARQ) plan, design; (fig) outline

trazar [tra'θar] vt (ARQ) to plan; (ARTE) to sketch; (fig) to trace; (plan) to draw up; **trazo** nm (línea) line; (bosquejo) sketch

trébol ['treßol] nm (BOT) clover

trece ['treθe] num thirteen

trecho ['tretʃo] nm (distancia) distance; (de tiempo) while; **de ~ en ~** at intervals

tregua ['treɣwa] nf (MIL) truce; (fig) respite

treinta ['treinta] num thirty

tremendo, a [tre'mendo, a] adj (terrible) terrible; (imponente: cosa) imposing; (fam: fabuloso) tremendous

trémulo, a ['tremulo, a] adj quivering

tren [tren] nm train; **~ de aterrizaje** undercarriage

trenca ['trenka] nf duffel coat

trenza ['trenθa] nf (de pelo) plait (BRIT), braid (US); **trenzar** vt (pelo) to plait, braid; **trenzarse** vr (AM) to become involved

trepadora [trepa'ðora] nf (BOT) climber

trepar [tre'par] vt, vi to climb

trepidante [trepi'ðante] adj (acción) fast; (ritmo) hectic

tres [tres] num three

tresillo [tre'siʎo] nm three-piece suite;

(MUS) triplet

treta ['treta] nf trick

triángulo ['trjangulo] nm triangle

tribu ['trißu] nf tribe

tribuna [tri'ßuna] nf (plataforma) platform; (DEPORTE) (grand)stand

tribunal [trißu'nal] nm (JUR) court; (comisión, fig) tribunal

tributar [trißu'tar] vt (gen) to pay; **tributo** nm (COM) tax

tricotar [triko'tar] vi to knit

trigal [tri'ɣal] nm wheat field

trigo ['triɣo] nm wheat

trigueño, a [tri'ɣeɲo, a] adj (pelo) corn-coloured

trillado, a [tri'ʎaðo, a] adj threshed; (asunto) trite, hackneyed; **trilladora** nf threshing machine

trillar [tri'ʎar] vt (AGR) to thresh

trimestral [trimes'tral] adj quarterly; (ESCOL) termly

trimestre [tri'mestre] nm (ESCOL) term

trinar [tri'nar] vi (pájaros) to sing; (rabiar) to fume, be angry

trinchar [trin'tʃar] vt to carve

trinchera [trin'tʃera] nf (fosa) trench

trineo [tri'neo] nm sledge

trinidad [trini'ðað] nf trio; (REL): **la T~** the Trinity

trino ['trino] nm trill

tripa ['tripa] nf (ANAT) intestine; (fam: tb: **~s**) insides pl

triple ['triple] adj triple

triplicado, a [tripli'kaðo, a] adj: **por ~** in triplicate

tripulación [tripula'θjon] nf crew

tripulante [tripu'lante] nm/f crewman/woman

tripular [tripu'lar] vt (barco) to man; (AUTO) to drive

triquiñuela [triki'ɲwela] nf trick

tris [tris] nm inv crack; **en un ~** in an instant

triste ['triste] adj sad; (lamentable) sorry, miserable; **~za** nf (aflicción) sadness; (melancolía) melancholy

triturar [tritu'rar] vt (moler) to grind;

(*mascar*) to chew
triunfar [trjun'far] *vi* (*tener éxito*) to triumph; (*ganar*) to win; **triunfo** *nm* triumph
trivial [tri'ßjal] *adj* trivial; **~izar** *vt* to minimize, play down
triza ['triθa] *nf*: **hacer ~s** to smash to bits; (*papel*) to tear to shreds
trocar [tro'kar] *vt* to exchange
trocear [troθe'ar] *vt* (*carne, manzana*) to cut up, cut into pieces
trocha ['trotʃa] *nf* short cut
troche ['trotʃe]: **a ~ y moche** *adv* helter-skelter, pell-mell
trofeo [tro'feo] *nm* (*premio*) trophy; (*éxito*) success
tromba ['tromba] *nf* downpour
trombón [trom'bon] *nm* trombone
trombosis [trom'bosis] *nf inv* thrombosis
trompa ['trompa] *nf* horn; (*trompo*) humming top; (*hocico*) snout; (*fam*): **cogerse una ~** to get tight
trompazo [trom'paθo] *nm* bump, bang
trompeta [trom'peta] *nf* trumpet; (*clarín*) bugle
trompicón [trompi'kon]: **a ~es** *adv* in fits and starts
trompo ['trompo] *nm* spinning top
trompón [trom'pon] *nm* bump
tronar [tro'nar] *vt* (*AM*) to shoot ♦ *vi* to thunder; (*fig*) to rage
tronchar [tron'tʃar] *vt* (*árbol*) to chop down; (*fig: vida*) to cut short; (*: esperanza*) to shatter; (*persona*) to tire out; **~se** *vr* to fall down
tronco ['tronko] *nm* (*de árbol, ANAT*) trunk
trono ['trono] *nm* throne
tropa ['tropa] *nf* (*MIL*) troop; (*soldados*) soldiers *pl*
tropel [tro'pel] *nm* (*muchedumbre*) crowd
tropezar [trope'θar] *vi* to trip, stumble; (*errar*) to slip up; **~ con** to run into; (*topar con*) to bump into; **tropezón** *nm* trip; (*fig*) blunder
tropical [tropi'kal] *adj* tropical
trópico ['tropiko] *nm* tropic
tropiezo [tro'pjeθo] *vb ver* **tropezar** ♦ *nm*

(*error*) slip, blunder; (*desgracia*) misfortune; (*obstáculo*) snag
trotamundos [trota'mundos] *nm inv* globetrotter
trotar [tro'tar] *vi* to trot; **trote** *nm* trot; (*fam*) travelling; **de mucho trote** hard-wearing
trozo ['troθo] *nm* bit, piece
trucha ['trutʃa] *nf* trout
truco ['truko] *nm* (*habilidad*) knack; (*engaño*) trick
trueno ['trweno] *nm* thunder; (*estampido*) bang
trueque *etc* ['trweke] *vb ver* **trocar** ♦ *nm* exchange; (*COM*) barter
trufa ['trufa] *nf* (*BOT*) truffle
truhán, ana [tru'an, ana] *nm/f* rogue
truncar [trun'kar] *vt* (*cortar*) to truncate; (*fig: la vida etc*) to cut short; (*: el desarrollo*) to stunt
tu [tu] *adj* your
tú [tu] *pron* you
tubérculo [tu'ßerkulo] *nm* (*BOT*) tuber
tuberculosis [tußerku'losis] *nf inv* tuberculosis
tubería [tuße'ria] *nf* pipes *pl*; (*conducto*) pipeline
tubo ['tußo] *nm* tube, pipe; **~ de ensayo** test tube; **~ de escape** exhaust (pipe)
tuerca ['twerka] *nf* nut
tuerto, a ['twerto, a] *adj* blind in one eye ♦ *nm/f* one-eyed person
tuerza *etc vb ver* **torcer**
tuétano ['twetano] *nm* marrow; (*BOT*) pith
tufo ['tufo] *nm* (*hedor*) stench
tul [tul] *nm* tulle
tulipán [tuli'pan] *nm* tulip
tullido, a [tu'ʎiðo, a] *adj* crippled
tumba ['tumba] *nf* (*sepultura*) tomb
tumbar [tum'bar] *vt* to knock down; **~se** *vr* (*echarse*) to lie down; (*extenderse*) to stretch out
tumbo ['tumbo] *nm*: **dar ~s** to stagger
tumbona [tum'bona] *nf* (*butaca*) easy chair; (*de playa*) deckchair (*BRIT*), beach chair (*US*)
tumor [tu'mor] *nm* tumour

tumulto [tu'multo] *nm* turmoil
tuna ['tuna] *nf* (*MUS*) student music group;
ver tb **tuno**

---
tuna

i A **tuna** *is a musical group made up of
university students or former students
who dress up in costumes from the "Edad
de Oro", the Spanish Golden Age. These
groups go through the town playing their
guitars, lutes and tambourines and
serenade the young ladies in the halls of
residence or make impromptu appearances
at weddings or parties singing traditional
Spanish songs for a few **pesetas**.*

---

tunante [tu'nante] *nm/f* rascal
tunda ['tunda] *nf* (*golpe*) beating
túnel ['tunel] *nm* tunnel
Túnez ['tuneθ] *nm* Tunisia; (*ciudad*) Tunis
tuno, a ['tuno, a] *nm/f* (*fam*) rogue ♦ *nm*
member of student music group
tupido, a [tu'piðo, a] *adj* (*denso*) dense;
(*tela*) close-woven
turba ['turßa] *nf* crowd
turbante [tur'ßante] *nm* turban
turbar [tur'ßar] *vt* (*molestar*) to disturb;
(*incomodar*) to upset; **~se** *vr* to be
disturbed
turbina [tur'ßina] *nf* turbine
turbio, a ['turßjo, a] *adj* cloudy; (*tema etc*)
confused
turbulencia [turßu'lenθja] *nf* turbulence;
(*fig*) restlessness; **turbulento, a** *adj*
turbulent; (*fig: intranquilo*) restless;
(: *ruidoso*) noisy
turco, a ['turko, a] *adj* Turkish ♦ *nm/f*
Turk
turismo [tu'rismo] *nm* tourism; (*coche*)
car; **turista** *nm/f* tourist; **turístico, a**
adj tourist *cpd*
turnar [tur'nar] *vi* to take (it in) turns; **~se**
vr to take (it in) turns; **turno** *nm* (*de
trabajo*) shift; (*juegos etc*) turn
turquesa [tur'kesa] *nf* turquoise
Turquía [tur'kia] *nf* Turkey
turrón [tu'rron] *nm* (*dulce*) nougat

tutear [tute'ar] *vt* to address as familiar
"tú"; **~se** *vr* to be on familiar terms
tutela [tu'tela] *nf* (*legal*) guardianship;
tutelar *adj* tutelary ♦ *vt* to protect
tutor, a [tu'tor, a] *nm/f* (*legal*) guardian;
(*ESCOL*) tutor
tuve *etc vb ver* **tener**
tuviera *etc vb ver* **tener**
tuyo, a ['tujo, a] *adj* yours, of yours ♦ *pron*
yours; **un amigo ~** a friend of yours; **los
~s** (*fam*) your relations, your family
TV ['te'ße] *nf abr* (= *televisión*) TV
TVE *nf abr* = **Televisión Española**

U, u

u [u] *conj* or
ubicar [ußi'kar] *vt* to place, situate; (*AM:
encontrar*) to find; **~se** *vr* to lie, be
located
ubre ['ußre] *nf* udder
UCI *nf abr* (= *Unidad de Cuidados
Intensivos*) ICU
Ud(s) *abr* = **usted(es)**
UE *nf abr* (= *Unión Europea*) EU
ufanarse [ufa'narse] *vr* to boast; **~ de** to
pride o.s. on; **ufano, a** *adj* (*arrogante*)
arrogant; (*presumido*) conceited
UGT *nf abr* = **Unión General de
Trabajadores**
ujier [u'xjer] *nm* usher; (*portero*)
doorkeeper
úlcera ['ulθera] *nf* ulcer
ulcerar [ulθe'rar] *vt* to make sore; **~se** *vr*
to ulcerate
ulterior [ulte'rjor] *adj* (*más allá*) farther,
further; (*subsecuente, siguiente*)
subsequent
últimamente ['ultimamente] *adv*
(*recientemente*) lately, recently
ultimar [ulti'mar] *vt* to finish; (*finalizar*) to
finalize; (*AM: rematar*) to finish off
ultimátum [ulti'matum] (*pl* **~s**) ultimatum
último, a ['ultimo, a] *adj* last; (*más
reciente*) latest, most recent; (*más bajo*)
bottom; (*más alto*) top; **en las últimas**

on one's last legs; **por ~** finally
ultra ['ultra] _adj_ ultra ♦ _nm/f_ extreme
  right-winger
ultrajar [ultra'xar] _vt_ (_ofender_) to outrage;
  (_insultar_) to insult, abuse; **ultraje** _nm_
  outrage; insult
ultramar [ultra'mar] _nm_: **de** _o_ **en ~**
  abroad, overseas
ultramarinos [ultrama'rinos] _nmpl_
  groceries; **tienda de ~** grocer's (shop)
ultranza [ul'tranθa]: **a ~** _adv_ (_a todo_
  trance) at all costs; (_completo_) outright
ultratumba [ultra'tumba] _nf_: **la vida de ~**
  the next life
umbral [um'bral] _nm_ (_gen_) threshold
umbrío, a [um'brio, a] _adj_ shady

PALABRA CLAVE
---

un, una [un, 'una] _art indef_ a; (_antes de_
vocal) an; **una mujer/naranja** a woman/
an orange
  ♦ _adj_: **unos** (_o_ **unas**): **hay unos regalos**
  para ti there are some presents for you;
  hay unas cervezas en la nevera there
  are some beers in the fridge

---

unánime [u'nanime] _adj_ unanimous;
  unanimidad _nf_ unanimity
undécimo, a [un'deθimo, a] _adj_ eleventh
ungir [un'xir] _vt_ to anoint
ungüento [un'gwento] _nm_ ointment
únicamente ['unikamente] _adv_ solely,
  only
único, a ['uniko, a] _adj_ only, sole; (_sin par_)
  unique
unidad [uni'ðað] _nf_ unity; (_COM, TEC etc_)
  unit
unido, a [u'niðo, a] _adj_ joined, linked; (_fig_)
  united
unificar [unifi'kar] _vt_ to unite, unify
uniformar [unifor'mar] _vt_ to make
  uniform, level up; (_persona_) to put into
  uniform
uniforme [uni'forme] _adj_ uniform, equal;
  (_superficie_) even ♦ _nm_ uniform;
  uniformidad _nf_ uniformity; (_de terreno_)
  levelness, evenness

unilateral [unilate'ral] _adj_ unilateral
unión [u'njon] _nf_ union; (_acto_) uniting,
  joining; (_unidad_) unity; (_TEC_) joint; **la U~**
  Europea the European Union; **la U~**
  Soviética the Soviet Union
unir [u'nir] _vt_ (_juntar_) to join, unite; (_atar_)
  to tie, fasten; (_combinar_) to combine; **~se**
  _vr_ to join together, unite; (_empresas_) to
  merge
unísono [u'nisono] _nm_: **al ~** in unison
universal [unißer'sal] _adj_ universal;
  (_mundial_) world _cpd_
universidad [unißersi'ðað] _nf_ university
universitario, a [unißersi'tarjo, a] _adj_
  university _cpd_ ♦ _nm/f_ (_profesor_) lecturer;
  (_estudiante_) (university) student;
  (_graduado_) graduate
universo [uni'ßerso] _nm_ universe

PALABRA CLAVE
---

uno, a ['uno, a] _adj_ one; **es todo ~** it's all
one and the same; **~s pocos** a few; **~s**
cien about a hundred
  ♦ _pron_ **1** one; **quiero sólo ~** I only want
  one; **~ de ellos** one of them
  2 (_alguien_) somebody, someone; **conozco**
  a ~ que se te parece I know somebody
  _o_ someone who looks like you; **~ mismo**
  oneself; **~s querían quedarse** some
  (people) wanted to stay
  3: **(los) ~s ... (los) otros ...** some ...
  others ...; **una y otra son muy agradables**
  they're both very nice
  ♦ _nf_ one; **es la una** it's one o'clock
  ♦ _nm_ (number) one

---

untar [un'tar] _vt_ (_mantequilla_) to spread;
  (_engrasar_) to grease, oil
uña ['uɲa] _nf_ (_ANAT_) nail; (_garra_) claw;
  (_casco_) hoof; (_arrancaclavos_) claw
uranio [u'ranjo] _nm_ uranium
urbanidad [urßani'ðað] _nf_ courtesy,
  politeness
urbanismo [urßa'nismo] _nm_ town
  planning
urbanización [urßaniθa'θjon] _nf_ (_barrio_,
  colonia) housing estate

urbanizar [urβani'θar] *vt* (*zona*) to develop, urbanize

urbano, a [ur'βano, a] *adj* (*de ciudad*) urban; (*cortés*) courteous, polite

urbe ['urβe] *nf* large city

urdimbre [ur'ðimbre] *nf* (*de tejido*) warp; (*intriga*) intrigue

urdir [ur'ðir] *vt* to warp; (*complot*) to plot, contrive

urgencia [ur'xenθja] *nf* urgency; (*prisa*) haste, rush; (*emergencia*) emergency; **servicios de ~** emergency services; **"Urgencias"** "Casualty"; **urgente** *adj* urgent

urgir [ur'xir] *vi* to be urgent; **me urge** I'm in a hurry for it

urinario, a [uri'narjo, a] *adj* urinary ♦ *nm* urinal

urna ['urna] *nf* urn; (*POL*) ballot box

urraca [u'rraka] *nf* magpie

URSS *nf*: **la ~** the USSR

Uruguay [uru'ɣwai] *nm*: **el ~** Uruguay; **uruguayo, a** *adj, nm/f* Uruguayan

usado, a [u'saðo, a] *adj* used; (*de segunda mano*) secondhand

usar [u'sar] *vt* to use; (*ropa*) to wear; (*tener costumbre*) to be in the habit of; **~se** *vr* to be used; **uso** *nm* use; wear; (*costumbre*) usage, custom; (*moda*) fashion; **al uso** in keeping with custom; **al uso de** in the style of

usted [us'teð] *pron* (*sg*) you *sg*; (*pl*): **~es** you *pl*

usual [u'swal] *adj* usual

usuario, a [usu'arjo, a] *nm/f* user

usura [u'sura] *nf* usury; **usurero, a** *nm/f* usurer

usurpar [usur'par] *vt* to usurp

utensilio [uten'siljo] *nm* tool; (*CULIN*) utensil

útero ['utero] *nm* uterus, womb

útil ['util] *adj* useful ♦ *nm* tool; **utilidad** *nf* usefulness; (*COM*) profit; **utilizar** *vt* to use, utilize

utopía [uto'pia] *nf* Utopia; **utópico, a** *adj* Utopian

uva ['uβa] *nf* grape

---

las uvas

ℹ *In Spain* **las uvas** *play a big part on New Year's Eve* (**Nochevieja**), *when on the stroke of midnight people gather at home, in restaurants or in the* **plaza mayor** *and eat a grape for each stroke of the clock of the* **Puerta del Sol** *in Madrid. It is said to bring luck for the following year.*

V, v

v *abr* (= *voltio*) v

va *vb ver* **ir**

vaca ['baka] *nf* (*animal*) cow; **carne de ~** beef

vacaciones [baka'θjones] *nfpl* holidays

vacante [ba'kante] *adj* vacant, empty ♦ *nf* vacancy

vaciar [ba'θjar] *vt* to empty out; (*ahuecar*) to hollow out; (*moldear*) to cast; **~se** *vr* to empty

vacilante [baθi'lante] *adj* unsteady; (*habla*) faltering; (*dudoso*) hesitant

vacilar [baθi'lar] *vi* to be unsteady; (*al hablar*) to falter; (*dudar*) to hesitate, waver; (*memoria*) to fail

vacío, a [ba'θio, a] *adj* empty; (*puesto*) vacant; (*desocupado*) idle; (*vano*) vain ♦ *nm* emptiness; (*FÍSICA*) vacuum; (*un ~*) (empty) space

vacuna [ba'kuna] *nf* vaccine; **vacunar** *vt* to vaccinate

vacuno, a [ba'kuno, a] *adj* cow *cpd*; **ganado ~** cattle

vacuo, a ['bakwo, a] *adj* empty

vadear [baðe'ar] *vt* (*río*) to ford; **vado** *nm* ford

vagabundo, a [baɣa'βundo, a] *adj* wandering ♦ *nm* tramp

vagamente [baɣa'mente] *adv* vaguely

vagancia [ba'ɣanθja] *nf* (*pereza*) idleness, laziness

vagar [ba'ɣar] *vi* to wander; (*no hacer*

nada) to idle

vagina [ba'xina] *nf* vagina

vago, a ['baɣo, a] *adj* vague; (*perezoso*) lazy ♦ *nm/f* (*vagabundo*) tramp; (*flojo*) lazybones *sg*, idler

vagón [ba'ɣon] *nm* (*FERRO: de pasajeros*) carriage; (*: de mercancías*) wagon

vaguedad [baɣe'ðað] *nf* vagueness

vaho ['bao] *nm* (*vapor*) vapour, steam; (*respiración*) breath

vaina ['baina] *nf* sheath

vainilla [bai'niʎa] *nf* vanilla

vainita [bai'nita] (*AM*) *nf* green *o* French bean

vais *vb ver* **ir**

vaivén [bai'ßen] *nm* to-and-fro movement; (*de tránsito*) coming and going; **vaivenes** *nmpl* (*fig*) ups and downs

vajilla [ba'xiʎa] *nf* crockery, dishes *pl*; **lavar la ~** to do the washing-up (*BRIT*), wash the dishes (*US*)

valdré *etc vb ver* **valer**

vale ['bale] *nm* voucher; (*recibo*) receipt; (*pagaré*) IOU

valedero, a [bale'ðero, a] *adj* valid

valenciano, a [balen'θjano, a] *adj* Valencian

valentía [balen'tia] *nf* courage, bravery

valer [ba'ler] *vt* to be worth; (*MAT*) to equal; (*costar*) to cost ♦ *vi* (*ser útil*) to be useful; (*ser válido*) to be valid; **~se** *vr* to take care of oneself; **~se de** to make use of, take advantage of; **~ la pena** to be worthwhile; **¿vale?** (*ESP*) OK?

valeroso, a [bale'roso, a] *adj* brave, valiant

valgo *etc vb ver* **valer**

valía [ba'lia] *nf* worth, value

validar [bali'ðar] *vt* to validate; **validez** *nf* validity; **válido, a** *adj* valid

valiente [ba'ljente] *adj* brave, valiant ♦ *nm* hero

valioso, a [ba'ljoso, a] *adj* valuable

valla ['baʎa] *nf* fence; (*DEPORTE*) hurdle; **~ publicitaria** hoarding; **vallar** *vt* to fence in

valle ['baʎe] *nm* valley

valor [ba'lor] *nm* value, worth; (*precio*) price; (*valentía*) valour, courage; (*importancia*) importance; **~es** *nmpl* (*COM*) securities; **~ar** *vt* to value

vals [bals] *nm inv* waltz

válvula ['balßula] *nf* valve

vamos *vb ver* **ir**

vampiro, resa [bam'piro, 'resa] *nm/f* vampire

van *vb ver* **ir**

vanagloriarse [banaɣlo'rjarse] *vr* to boast

vandalismo [banda'lismo] *nm* vandalism; **vándalo, a** *nm/f* vandal

vanguardia [ban'gwardja] *nf* vanguard; (*ARTE etc*) avant-garde

vanidad [bani'ðað] *nf* vanity; **vanidoso, a** *adj* vain, conceited

vano, a ['bano, a] *adj* vain

vapor [ba'por] *nm* vapour; (*vaho*) steam; **al ~** (*CULIN*) steamed; **~izar** *vt* to vaporize; **~oso, a** *adj* vaporous

vapulear [bapule'ar] *vt* to beat, thrash

vaquero, a [ba'kero, a] *adj* cattle *cpd* ♦ *nm* cowboy; **~s** *nmpl* (*pantalones*) jeans

vaquilla [ba'kiʎa] *nf* (*ZOOL*) heifer

vara ['bara] *nf* stick; (*TEC*) rod; **~ mágica** magic wand

variable [ba'rjaßle] *adj, nf* variable

variación [baria'θjon] *nf* variation

variar [bar'jar] *vt* to vary; (*modificar*) to modify; (*cambiar de posición*) to switch around ♦ *vi* to vary

varicela [bari'θela] *nf* chickenpox

varices [ba'riθes] *nfpl* varicose veins

variedad [barje'ðað] *nf* variety

varilla [ba'riʎa] *nf* stick; (*BOT*) twig; (*TEC*) rod; (*de rueda*) spoke

vario, a ['barjo, a] *adj* varied; **~s** various, several

varita [ba'rita] *nf*: **~ mágica** magic wand

varón [ba'ron] *nm* male, man; **varonil** *adj* manly, virile

Varsovia [bar'soßja] *n* Warsaw

vas *vb ver* **ir**

vasco, a ['basko, a] *adj, nm/f* Basque

vascongado, a [baskoŋ'gaðo, a] *adj* Basque; **las Vascongadas** the Basque Country

vascuence [bas'kwenθe] *adj* = **vascongado**

vaselina [base'lina] *nf* Vaseline ®

vasija [ba'sixa] *nf* container, vessel

vaso ['baso] *nm* glass, tumbler; (*ANAT*) vessel

vástago ['bastaɣo] *nm* (*BOT*) shoot; (*TEC*) rod; (*fig*) offspring

vasto, a ['basto, a] *adj* vast, huge

Vaticano [bati'kano] *nm*: **el ~** the Vatican

vatio ['batjo] *nm* (*ELEC*) watt

vaya *etc vb ver* **ir**

Vd(s) *abr* = **usted(es)**

ve *vb ver* **ir**; **ver**

vecindad [beθin'dað] *nf* neighbourhood; (*habitantes*) residents *pl*

vecindario [beθin'darjo] *nm* neighbourhood; residents *pl*

vecino, a [be'θino, a] *adj* neighbouring ♦ *nm/f* neighbour; (*residente*) resident

veda ['beða] *nf* prohibition

vedar [be'ðar] *vt* (*prohibir*) to ban, prohibit; (*impedir*) to stop, prevent

vegetación [bexeta'θjon] *nf* vegetation

vegetal [bexe'tal] *adj, nm* vegetable

vegetariano, a [bexeta'rjano, a] *adj, nm/f* vegetarian

vehemencia [be(e)'menθja] *nf* vehemence; **vehemente** *adj* vehement

vehículo [be'ikulo] *nm* vehicle; (*MED*) carrier

veía *etc vb ver* **ver**

veinte ['beinte] *num* twenty

vejación [bexa'θjon] *nf* vexation; (*humillación*) humiliation

vejar [be'xar] *vt* (*irritar*) to annoy, vex; (*humillar*) to humiliate

vejez [be'xeθ] *nf* old age

vejiga [be'xiɣa] *nf* (*ANAT*) bladder

vela ['bela] *nf* (*de cera*) candle; (*NAUT*) sail; (*insomnio*) sleeplessness; (*vigilia*) vigil; (*MIL*) sentry duty; **estar a dos ~s** (*fam: sin dinero*) to be skint

velado, a [be'laðo, a] *adj* veiled; (*sonido*) muffled; (*FOTO*) blurred ♦ *nf* soirée

velar [be'lar] *vt* (*vigilar*) to keep watch over ♦ *vi* to stay awake; **~ por** to watch over, look after

velatorio [bela'torjo] *nm* (*funeral*) wake

veleidad [belei'ðað] *nf* (*ligereza*) fickleness; (*capricho*) whim

velero [be'lero] *nm* (*NAUT*) sailing ship; (*AVIAT*) glider

veleta [be'leta] *nf* weather vane

veliz [be'lis] (*AM*) *nm* suitcase

vello ['beʎo] *nm* down, fuzz

velo ['belo] *nm* veil

velocidad [beloθi'ðað] *nf* speed; (*TEC, AUTO*) gear

velocímetro [belo'θimetro] *nm* speedometer

veloz [be'loθ] *adj* fast

ven *vb ver* **venir**

vena ['bena] *nf* vein

venado [be'naðo] *nm* deer

vencedor, a [benθe'ðor, a] *adj* victorious ♦ *nm/f* victor, winner

vencer [ben'θer] *vt* (*dominar*) to defeat, beat; (*derrotar*) to vanquish; (*superar, controlar*) to overcome, master ♦ *vi* (*triunfar*) to win (through), triumph; (*plazo*) to expire; **vencido, a** *adj* (*derrotado*) defeated, beaten; (*COM*) due ♦ *adv*: **pagar vencido** to pay in arrears; **vencimiento** *nm* (*COM*) maturity

venda ['benda] *nf* bandage; **vendaje** *nm* bandage, dressing; **vendar** *vt* to bandage; **vendar los ojos** to blindfold

vendaval [benda'ßal] *nm* (*viento*) gale

vendedor, a [bende'ðor, a] *nm/f* seller

vender [ben'der] *vt* to sell; **~ al contado/ al por mayor/al por menor** to sell for cash/wholesale/retail

vendimia [ben'dimja] *nf* grape harvest

vendré *etc vb ver* **venir**

veneno [be'neno] *nm* poison; (*de serpiente*) venom; **~so, a** *adj* poisonous; venomous

venerable [bene'raßle] *adj* venerable; **venerar** *vt* (*respetar*) to revere; (*adorar*) to worship

venéreo, a [be'nereo, a] *adj*: **enfermedad venérea** venereal disease

venezolano, a [beneθo'lano, a] *adj* Venezuelan

Venezuela [bene'θwela] *nf* Venezuela

venganza [ben'ganθa] *nf* vengeance, revenge; **vengar** *vt* to avenge; **vengarse** *vr* to take revenge; **vengativo, a** *adj* (*persona*) vindictive

vengo *etc vb ver* **venir**

venia ['benja] *nf* (*perdón*) pardon; (*permiso*) consent

venial [be'njal] *adj* venial

venida [be'niða] *nf* (*llegada*) arrival; (*regreso*) return

venidero, a [beni'ðero, a] *adj* coming, future

venir [be'nir] *vi* to come; (*llegar*) to arrive; (*ocurrir*) to happen; (*fig*): ~ **de** to stem from; ~ **bien/mal** to be suitable/ unsuitable; **el año que viene** next year; **~se abajo** to collapse

venta ['benta] *nf* (*COM*) sale; ~ **a plazos** hire purchase; ~ **al contado/al por mayor/al por menor** *o* **al detalle** cash sale/wholesale/retail; ~ **con derecho a retorno** sale or return; **"en ~"** "for sale"

ventaja [ben'taxa] *nf* advantage; **ventajoso, a** *adj* advantageous

ventana [ben'tana] *nf* window; **ventanilla** *nf* (*de taquilla*) window (*of booking office etc*)

ventilación [bentila'θjon] *nf* ventilation; (*corriente*) draught

ventilador [bentila'ðor] *nm* fan

ventilar [benti'lar] *vt* to ventilate; (*para secar*) to put out to dry; (*asunto*) to air, discuss

ventisca [ben'tiska] *nf* blizzard

ventrílocuo, a [ben'trilokwo, a] *nm/f* ventriloquist

ventura [ben'tura] *nf* (*felicidad*) happiness; (*buena suerte*) luck; (*destino*) fortune; **a la (buena)** ~ at random; **venturoso, a** *adj* happy; (*afortunado*) lucky, fortunate

veo *etc vb ver* **ver**

ver [ber] *vt* to see; (*mirar*) to look at, watch; (*entender*) to understand; (*investigar*) to look into; ♦ *vi* to see; to understand; **~se** *vr* (*encontrarse*) to meet; (*dejarse ~*) to be seen; (*hallarse: en un apuro*) to find o.s., be; **a ~** let's see; **no tener nada que ~ con** to have nothing to do with; **a mi modo de ~** as I see it

vera ['bera] *nf* edge, verge; (*de río*) bank

veracidad [beraθi'ðað] *nf* truthfulness

veranear [berane'ar] *vi* to spend the summer; **veraneo** *nm* summer holiday; **veraniego, a** *adj* summer *cpd*

verano [be'rano] *nm* summer

veras ['beras] *nfpl* truth *sg*; **de ~** really, truly

veraz [be'raθ] *adj* truthful

verbal [ber'ßal] *adj* verbal

verbena [ber'ßena] *nf* (*baile*) open-air dance

verbo ['berßo] *nm* verb; ~**so, a** *adj* verbose

verdad [ber'ðað] *nf* truth; (*fiabilidad*) reliability; **de ~** real, proper; **a decir ~** to tell the truth; ~**ero, a** *adj* (*veraz*) true, truthful; (*fiable*) reliable; (*fig*) real

verde ['berðe] *adj* green; (*chiste*) blue, dirty ♦ *nm* green; **viejo ~** dirty old man; ~**ar** *vi* to turn green; **verdor** *nm* greenness

verdugo [ber'ðuxo] *nm* executioner

verdulero, a [berðu'lero, a] *nm/f* greengrocer

verduras [ber'ðuras] *nfpl* (*CULIN*) greens

vereda [be'reða] *nf* path; (*AM*) pavement (*BRIT*), sidewalk (*US*)

veredicto [bere'ðikto] *nm* verdict

vergonzoso, a [bervon'θoso, a] *adj* shameful; (*tímido*) timid, bashful

vergüenza [ber'xwenθa] *nf* shame, sense of shame; (*timidez*) bashfulness; (*pudor*) modesty; **me da ~** I'm ashamed

verídico, a [be'riðiko, a] *adj* true, truthful

verificar [berifi'kar] *vt* to check; (*corroborar*) to verify; (*llevar a cabo*) to carry out; **~se** *vr* (*predicción*) to prove to be true

verja ['berxa] *nf* (*cancela*) iron gate; (*valla*)

iron railings *pl*; (*de ventana*) grille
vermut [ber'mut] (*pl* **~s**) *nm* vermouth
verosímil [bero'simil] *adj* likely, probable;
(*relato*) credible
verruga [be'rruɣa] *nf* wart
versado, a [ber'saðo, a] *adj*: **~ en** versed
in
versátil [ber'satil] *adj* versatile
versión [ber'sjon] *nf* version
verso ['berso] *nm* verse; **un ~** a line of
poetry
vértebra ['bertebra] *nf* vertebra
verter [ber'ter] *vt* (*líquido: adrede*) to
empty, pour (out); (: *sin querer*) to spill;
(*basura*) to dump ♦ *vi* to flow
vertical [berti'kal] *adj* vertical
vértice ['bertiθe] *nm* vertex, apex
vertidos [ber'tiðos] *nmpl* waste *sg*
vertiente [ber'tjente] *nf* slope; (*fig*) aspect
vertiginoso, a [bertixi'noso, a] *adj* giddy,
dizzy
vértigo ['bertixo] *nm* vertigo; (*mareo*)
dizziness
vesícula [be'sikula] *nf* blister
vespino ® [bes'pino] *nm o nf* moped
vestíbulo [bes'tiβulo] *nm* hall; (*de teatro*)
foyer
vestido [bes'tiðo] *pp de* **vestir**; **~ de
azul/marinero** dressed in blue/as a sailor
♦ *nm* (*ropa*) clothes *pl*, clothing; (*de
mujer*) dress, frock
vestigio [bes'tixjo] *nm* (*huella*) trace; **~s**
nmpl (*restos*) remains
vestimenta [besti'menta] *nf* clothing
vestir [bes'tir] *vt* (*poner: ropa*) to put on;
(*llevar: ropa*) to wear; (*proveer de ropa a*)
to clothe; (*suj: sastre*) to make clothes for
♦ *vi* to dress; (*verse bien*) to look good;
~se *vr* to get dressed, dress o.s.
vestuario [bes'twarjo] *nm* clothes *pl*,
wardrobe; (*TEATRO: cuarto*) dressing room;
(*DEPORTE*) changing room
veta ['beta] *nf* (*vena*) vein, seam; (*en carne*)
streak; (*de madera*) grain
vetar [be'tar] *vt* to veto
veterano, a [bete'rano, a] *adj, nm* veteran
veterinaria [beteri'narja] *nf* veterinary

science; *ver tb* **veterinario**
veterinario, a [beteri'narjo, a] *nm/f*
vet(erinary surgeon)
veto ['beto] *nm* veto
vez [beθ] *nf* time; (*turno*) turn; **a la ~ que**
at the same time as; **a su ~** in its turn;
otra ~ again; **una ~** once; **de una ~** in
one go; **de una ~ para siempre** once
and for all; **en ~ de** instead of; **a** *o*
algunas veces sometimes; **una y otra ~**
repeatedly; **de ~ en cuando** from time to
time; **7 veces 9** 7 times 9; **hacer las
veces de** to stand in for; **tal ~** perhaps
vía ['bia] *nf* track, route; (*FERRO*) line; (*fig*)
way; (*ANAT*) passage, tube ♦ *prep* via, by
way of; **por ~ judicial** by legal means;
por ~ oficial through official channels; **en
~s de** in the process of; **~ aérea** airway;
V~ Láctea Milky Way; **~ pública** public
road *o* thoroughfare
viable ['bjaβle] *adj* (*solución, plan,
alternativa*) feasible
viaducto [bja'ðukto] *nm* viaduct
viajante [bja'xante] *nm* commercial
traveller
viajar [bja'xar] *vi* to travel; **viaje** *nm*
journey; (*gira*) tour; (*NAUT*) voyage; **estar
de viaje** to be on a trip; **viaje de ida y
vuelta** round trip; **viaje de novios**
honeymoon; **viajero, a** *adj* travelling;
(*ZOOL*) migratory ♦ *nm/f* (*quien viaja*)
traveller; (*pasajero*) passenger
vial [bjal] *adj* road *cpd*, traffic *cpd*
víbora ['biβora] *nf* viper; (*AM*) poisonous
snake
vibración [biβra'θjon] *nf* vibration
vibrar [bi'βrar] *vt, vi* to vibrate
vicario [bi'karjo] *nm* curate
vicepresidente [biθepresi'ðente] *nm/f*
vice-president
viceversa [biθe'βersa] *adv* vice versa
viciado, a [bi'θjaðo, a] *adj* (*corrompido*)
corrupt; (*contaminado*) foul,
contaminated; **viciar** *vt* (*pervertir*) to
pervert; (*JUR*) to nullify; (*estropear*) to
spoil; **viciarse** *vr* to become corrupted
vicio ['biθjo] *nm* vice; (*mala costumbre*)

bad habit; **~so, a** adj (muy malo)
vicious; (corrompido) depraved ♦ nm/f
depraved person
vicisitud [biθisi'tuð] nf vicissitude
víctima ['biktima] nf victim
victoria [bik'torja] nf victory; **victorioso,
a** adj victorious
vid [bið] nf vine
vida ['biða] nf (gen) life; (duración) lifetime;
de por ~ for life; **en la/mi ~** never; **estar
con ~** to be still alive; **ganarse la ~** to
earn one's living
vídeo ['bideo] nm video ♦ adj inv:
película ~ video film; **videocámara** nf
camcorder; **videocasete** nm video cassette, videotape; **videoclub** nm video
club; **videojuego** nm video game
vidriero, a [bi'ðrjero, a] nm/f glazier ♦ nf
(ventana) stained-glass window; (AM: de
tienda) shop window; (puerta) glass door
vidrio ['biðrjo] nm glass
vieira ['bjeira] nf scallop
viejo, a ['bjexo, a] adj old ♦ nm/f old
man/woman; **hacerse ~** to get old
Viena ['bjena] n Vienna
vienes etc vb ver **venir**
vienés, esa [bje'nes, esa] adj Viennese
viento ['bjento] nm wind; **hacer ~** to be
windy
vientre ['bjentre] nm belly; (matriz) womb
viernes ['bjernes] nm inv Friday; **V~
Santo** Good Friday
Vietnam [bjet'nam] nm: **el ~** Vietnam;
vietnamita adj Vietnamese
viga ['biɣa] nf beam, rafter; (de metal)
girder
vigencia [bi'xenθja] nf validity; **estar en ~**
to be in force; **vigente** adj valid, in
force; (imperante) prevailing
vigésimo, a [bi'xesimo, a] adj twentieth
vigía [bi'xia] nm look-out
vigilancia [bixi'lanθja] nf: **tener a uno
bajo ~** to keep watch on sb
vigilar [bixi'lar] vt to watch over ♦ vi (gen)
to be vigilant; (hacer guardia) to keep
watch; **~ por** to take care of
vigilia [vi'xilja] nf wakefulness, being

awake; (REL) fast
vigor [bi'ɣor] nm vigour, vitality; **en ~** in
force; **entrar/poner en ~** to come/put
into effect; **~oso, a** adj vigorous
VIH nm abr (= virus de la
inmunodeficiencia humana) HIV; **~
positivo/negativo** HIV-positive/-negative
vil [bil] adj vile, low; **~eza** nf vileness;
(acto) base deed
vilipendiar [bilipen'djar] vt to vilify, revile
villa ['biʎa] nf (casa) villa; (pueblo) small
town; (municipalidad) municipality; **~
miseria** (AM) shantytown
villancico [biʎan'θiko] nm (Christmas)
carol
villorrio [bi'ʎorrjo] nm shantytown
vilo ['bilo]: **en ~** adv in the air, suspended;
(fig) on tenterhooks, in suspense
vinagre [bi'naɣre] nm vinegar
vinagreta [bina'ɣreta] nf vinaigrette,
French dressing
vinculación [binkula'θjon] nf (lazo) link,
bond; (acción) linking
vincular [binku'lar] vt to link, bind;
vínculo nm link, bond
vine etc vb ver **venir**
vinicultura [binikul'tura] nf wine growing
viniera etc vb ver **venir**
vino ['bino] vb ver **venir** ♦ nm wine; **~
blanco/tinto** white/red wine
viña ['biɲa] nf vineyard; **viñedo** nm
vineyard
viola ['bjola] nf viola
violación [bjola'θjon] nf violation; **~
(sexual)** rape
violar [bjo'lar] vt to violate; (sexualmente)
to rape
violencia [bjo'lenθja] nf violence, force;
(incomodidad) embarrassment; (acto
injusto) unjust act; **violentar** vt to force;
(casa) to break into; (agredir) to assault;
(violar) to violate; **violento, a** adj
violent; (furioso) furious; (situación)
embarrassing; (acto) forced, unnatural
violeta [bjo'leta] nf violet
violín [bjo'lin] nm violin
violón [bjo'lon] nm double bass

viraje [bi'raxe] *nm* turn; (*de vehículo*) swerve; (*fig*) change of direction; **virar** *vi* to change direction

virgen ['birxen] *adj, nf* virgin

Virgo ['birxo] *nm* Virgo

viril [bi'ril] *adj* virile; ~**idad** *nf* virility

virtud [bir'tuð] *nf* virtue; **en ~ de** by virtue of; **virtuoso, a** *adj* virtuous ♦ *nm/f* virtuoso

viruela [bi'rwela] *nf* smallpox

virulento, a [biru'lento, a] *adj* virulent

virus ['birus] *nm inv* virus

visa ['bisa] (*AM*) *nf* = **visado**

visado [bi'saðo] *nm* visa

víscera ['bisθera] *nf* (*ANAT, ZOOL*) gut, bowel; ~**s** *nfpl* entrails

visceral [bisθe'ral] *adj* (*odio*) intense; **reacción ~** gut reaction

viscoso, a [bis'koso, a] *adj* viscous

visera [bi'sera] *nf* visor

visibilidad [bisiβili'ðað] *nf* visibility; **visible** *adj* visible; (*fig*) obvious

visillos [bi'siʎos] *nmpl* lace curtains

visión [bi'sjon] *nf* (*ANAT*) vision, (eye)sight; (*fantasía*) vision, fantasy

visita [bi'sita] *nf* call, visit; (*persona*) visitor; **hacer una ~** to pay a visit

visitar [bisi'tar] *vt* to visit, call on

vislumbrar [bislum'brar] *vt* to glimpse, catch a glimpse of

viso [bi'so] *nm* (*del metal*) glint, gleam; (*de tela*) sheen; (*aspecto*) appearance

visón [bi'son] *nm* mink

visor [bi'sor] *nm* (*FOTO*) viewfinder

víspera ['bispera] *nf*: **la ~ de ...** the day before ...

vista ['bista] *nf* sight, vision; (*capacidad de ver*) (eye)sight; (*mirada*) look(s) (*pl*); **a primera ~** at first glance; **hacer la ~ gorda** to turn a blind eye; **volver la ~** to look back; **está a la ~ que** it's obvious that; **en ~ de** in view of; **en ~ de que** in view of the fact that; **¡hasta la ~!** so long!, see you!; **con ~s a** with a view to; ~**zo** *nm* glance; **dar** *o* **echar un ~zo a** to glance at

visto, a ['bisto, a] *pp de* **ver** ♦ *vb ver tb*

vestir ♦ *adj* seen; (*considerado*) considered ♦ *nm*: **~ bueno** approval; **"~ bueno"** "approved"; **por lo ~** apparently; **está ~ que** it's clear that; **está bien/mal ~ que** it's acceptable/unacceptable; **~ que** since, considering that

vistoso, a [bis'toso, a] *adj* colourful

visual [bi'swal] *adj* visual

vital [bi'tal] *adj* life *cpd*; (*fig*) vital; (*persona*) lively, vivacious; ~**icio, a** *adj* for life; ~**idad** *nf* (*de persona, negocio*) energy; (*de ciudad*) liveliness

vitamina [bita'mina] *nf* vitamin

viticultor, a [bitikul'tor, a] *nm/f* wine grower; **viticultura** *nf* wine growing

vitorear [bitore'ar] *vt* to cheer, acclaim

vitrina [bi'trina] *nf* show case; (*AM*) shop window

viudez *nf* widowhood

viudo, a ['bjuðo, a] *nm/f* widower/widow

viva ['biβa] *excl* hurrah!: **¡~ el rey!** long live the king!

vivacidad [biβaθi'ðað] *nf* (*vigor*) vigour; (*vida*) liveliness

vivaracho, a [biβa'ratʃo, a] *adj* jaunty, lively; (*ojos*) bright, twinkling

vivaz [bi'βaθ] *adj* lively

víveres ['biβeres] *nmpl* provisions

vivero [bi'βero] *nm* (*para plantas*) nursery; (*para peces*) fish farm; (*fig*) hotbed

viveza [bi'βeθa] *nf* liveliness; (*agudeza: mental*) sharpness

vivienda [bi'βjenda] *nf* housing; (*una ~*) house; (*piso*) flat (*BRIT*), apartment (*US*)

viviente [bi'βjente] *adj* living

vivir [bi'βir] *vt, vi* to live ♦ *nm* life, living

vivo, a ['biβo, a] *adj* living, alive; (*fig: descripción*) vivid; (*persona: astuto*) smart, clever; **en ~** (*transmisión etc*) live

vocablo [bo'kaβlo] *nm* (*palabra*) word; (*término*) term

vocabulario [bokaβu'larjo] *nm* vocabulary

vocación [boka'θjon] *nf* vocation; **vocacional** (*AM*) *nf* ≈ technical college

vocal [bo'kal] *adj* vocal ♦ *nf* vowel; ~**izar** *vt* to vocalize

vocear [boθe'ar] *vt* (*para vender*) to cry;

(*aclamar*) to acclaim; (*fig*) to proclaim ♦ *vi* to yell; **vocerío** *nm* shouting

vocero [bo'θero] *nm/f* spokesman/woman

voces ['boθes] *pl de* **voz**

vociferar [boθife'rar] *vt* to shout ♦ *vi* to yell

vodka ['boðka] *nm o f* vodka

vol *abr* = **volumen**

volador, a [bola'ðor, a] *adj* flying

volandas [bo'landas]: **en ~** *adv* in the air

volante [bo'lante] *adj* flying ♦ *nm* (*de coche*) steering wheel; (*de reloj*) balance

volar [bo'lar] *vt* (*edificio*) to blow up ♦ *vi* to fly

volátil [bo'latil] *adj* volatile

volcán [bol'kan] *nm* volcano; **~ico, a** *adj* volcanic

volcar [bol'kar] *vt* to upset, overturn; (*tumbar, derribar*) to knock over; (*vaciar*) to empty out ♦ *vi* to overturn; **~se** *vr* to tip over

voleibol [bolei'βol] *nm* volleyball

volqué *etc vb ver* **volcar**

voltaje [bol'taxe] *nm* voltage

voltear [bolte'ar] *vt* to turn over; (*volcar*) to turn upside down

voltereta [bolte'reta] *nf* somersault

voltio ['boltjo] *nm* volt

voluble [bo'luβle] *adj* fickle

volumen [bo'lumen] (*pl* **volúmenes**) *nm* volume; **voluminoso, a** *adj* voluminous; (*enorme*) massive

voluntad [bolun'taθ] *nf* will; (*resolución*) willpower; (*deseo*) desire, wish

voluntario, a [bolun'tarjo, a] *adj* voluntary ♦ *nm/f* volunteer

voluntarioso, a [bolunta'rjoso, a] *adj* headstrong

voluptuoso, a [bolup'twoso, a] *adj* voluptuous

volver [bol'βer] *vt* (*gen*) to turn; (*dar vuelta a*) to turn (over); (*voltear*) to turn round, turn upside down; (*poner al revés*) to turn inside out; (*devolver*) to return ♦ *vi* to return, go back, come back; **~se** *vr* to turn round; **~ la espalda** to turn one's back; **~ triste** *etc* **a uno** to make sb

sad *etc*; **~ a hacer** to do again; **~ en sí** to come to; **~se insoportable/muy caro** to get *o* become unbearable/very expensive; **~se loco** to go mad

vomitar [bomi'tar] *vt, vi* to vomit; **vómito** *nm* vomit

voraz [bo'raθ] *adj* voracious

vos [bos] (*AM*) *pron* you

vosotros, as [bo'sotros, as] *pron* you; (*reflexivo*): **entre/para ~** among/for yourselves

votación [bota'θjon] *nf* (*acto*) voting; (*voto*) vote

votar [bo'tar] *vi* to vote; **voto** *nm* vote; (*promesa*) vow; **votos** (good) wishes

voy *vb ver* **ir**

voz [boθ] *nf* voice; (*grito*) shout; (*rumor*) rumour; (*LING*) word; **dar voces** to shout, yell; **a media ~** in a low voice; **a ~ en cuello** *o* **en grito** at the top of one's voice; **de viva ~** verbally; **en ~ alta** aloud; **~ de mando** command

vuelco ['bwelko] *vb ver* **volcar** ♦ *nm* spill, overturning

vuelo ['bwelo] *vb ver* **volar** ♦ *nm* flight; (*encaje*) lace, frill; **coger al ~** to catch in flight; **~ charter/regular** charter/scheduled flight; **~ libre** (*DEPORTE*) hang-gliding

vuelque *etc vb ver* **volcar**

vuelta ['bwelta] *nf* (*gen*) turn; (*curva*) bend, curve; (*regreso*) return; (*revolución*) revolution; (*de circuito*) lap; (*de papel, tela*) reverse; (*cambio*) change; **a la ~** on one's return; **a ~ de correo** by return of post; **dar ~s** (*suj: cabeza*) to spin; **dar ~s a una idea** to turn over an idea (in one's head); **estar de ~** to be back; **dar una ~** to go for a walk; (*en coche*) to go for a drive; **~ ciclista** (*DEPORTE*) (cycle) tour

vuelto *pp de* **volver**

vuelvo *etc vb ver* **volver**

vuestro, a ['bwestro, a] *adj* your; **un amigo ~** a friend of yours ♦ *pron*: **el ~/la vuestra, los ~s/las vuestras** yours

vulgar [bul'ɣar] *adj* (*ordinario*) vulgar; (*común*) common; **~idad** *nf*

commonness; (*acto*) vulgarity; (*expresión*) coarse expression; ~**izar** *vt* to popularize
vulgo [ˈbulɣo] *nm* common people
vulnerable [bulneˈraβle] *adj* vulnerable
vulnerar [bulneˈrar] *vt* (*ley, acuerdo*) to violate, breach; (*derechos, intimidad*) to violate; (*reputación*) to damage

W, w

Walkman ® [wakˈman] *nm* Walkman ®
wáter [ˈbater] *nm* toilet
whisky [ˈwiski] *nm* whisky, whiskey

X, x

xenofobia [ksenoˈfoβja] *nf* xenophobia
xilófono [ksiˈlofono] *nm* xylophone

Y, y

y [i] *conj* and
ya [ja] *adv* (*gen*) already; (*ahora*) now; (*en seguida*) at once; (*pronto*) soon ♦ *excl* all right! ♦ *conj* (*ahora que*) now that; ~ **lo sé** I know; ~ **que** since
yacer [jaˈθer] *vi* to lie
yacimiento [jaθiˈmjento] *nm* (*de mineral*) deposit; (*arqueológico*) site
yanqui [ˈjanki] *adj, nm/f* Yankee
yate [ˈjate] *nm* yacht
yazco *etc vb ver* **yacer**
yedra [ˈjeðra] *nf* ivy
yegua [ˈjeɣwa] *nf* mare
yema [ˈjema] *nf* (*del huevo*) yolk; (*BOT*) leaf bud; (*fig*) best part; ~ **del dedo** fingertip
yergo *etc vb ver* **erguir**
yermo, a [ˈjermo, a] *adj* (*estéril, fig*) barren ♦ *nm* wasteland
yerno [ˈjerno] *nm* son-in-law
yerro *etc vb ver* **errar**
yeso [ˈjeso] *nm* plaster
yo [jo] *pron* I; **soy** ~ it's me, it is I

yodo [ˈjoðo] *nm* iodine
yoga [ˈjoɣa] *nm* yoga
yogur(t) [joˈɣur(t)] *nm* yoghurt
yugo [ˈjuɣo] *nm* yoke
Yugoslavia [juɣosˈlaβja] *nf* Yugoslavia
yugular [juɣuˈlar] *adj* jugular
yunque [ˈjunke] *nm* anvil
yunta [ˈjunta] *nf* yoke
yuxtaponer [jukstapoˈner] *vt* to juxtapose; **yuxtaposición** *nf* juxtaposition

Z, z

zafar [θaˈfar] *vt* (*soltar*) to untie; (*superficie*) to clear; ~**se** *vr* (*escaparse*) to escape; (*TEC*) to slip off
zafio, a [ˈθafjo, a] *adj* coarse
zafiro [θaˈfiro] *nm* sapphire
zaga [ˈθaɣa] *nf*: **a la** ~ behind, in the rear
zaguán [θaˈɣwan] *nm* hallway
zaherir [θaeˈrir] *vt* (*criticar*) to criticize
zaino, a [ˈθaino, a] *adj* (*caballo*) chestnut
zalamería [θalameˈria] *nf* flattery; **zalamero, a** *adj* flattering; (*cobista*) suave
zamarra [θaˈmarra] *nf* (*chaqueta*) sheepskin jacket
zambullirse [θambuˈʎirse] *vr* to dive
zampar [θamˈpar] *vt* to gobble down
zanahoria [θanaˈorja] *nf* carrot
zancada [θanˈkaða] *nf* stride
zancadilla [θankaˈðiʎa] *nf* trip
zanco [ˈθanko] *nm* stilt
zancudo, a [θanˈkuðo, a] *adj* long-legged ♦ *nm* (*AM*) mosquito
zángano [ˈθangano] *nm* drone
zanja [ˈθanxa] *nf* ditch; **zanjar** *vt* (*resolver*) to resolve
zapata [θaˈpata] *nf* (*MECÁNICA*) shoe
zapatear [θapateˈar] *vi* to tap with one's feet
zapatería [θapateˈria] *nf* (*oficio*) shoemaking; (*tienda*) shoe shop; (*fábrica*) shoe factory; **zapatero, a** *nm/f*

shoemaker

zapatilla [θapa'tiʎa] *nf* slipper; **~ de deporte** training shoe

zapato [θa'pato] *nm* shoe

zapping ['θapin] *nm* channel-hopping; **hacer ~** to flick through the channels

zar [θar] *nm* tsar, czar

zarandear [θarande'ar] *(fam) vt* to shake vigorously

zarpa ['θarpa] *nf (garra)* claw

zarpar [θar'par] *vi* to weigh anchor

zarza ['θarθa] *nf (BOT)* bramble; **zarzal** *nm (matorral)* bramble patch

zarzamora [θarθa'mora] *nf* blackberry

zarzuela [θar'θwela] *nf* Spanish light opera

zigzag [θiɣ'θaɣ] *nm* zigzag; **zigzaguear** *vi* to zigzag

zinc [θink] *nm* zinc

zócalo ['θokalo] *nm (ARQ)* plinth, base

zodíaco [θo'ðiako] *nm (ASTRO)* zodiac

zona ['θona] *nf* zone; **~ fronteriza** border area; **~ (del) euro** Euroland

zoo ['θoo] *nm* zoo

zoología [θoolo'xia] *nf* zoology; **zoológico, a** *adj* zoological ♦ *nm (tb:* **parque ~**) zoo; **zoólogo, a** *nm/f* zoologist

zoom [θum] *nm* zoom lens

zopilote [θopi'lote] *(AM) nm* buzzard

zoquete [θo'kete] *nm (fam)* blockhead

zorro, a ['θorro, a] *adj* crafty ♦ *nm/f* fox/vixen

zozobra [θo'θoβra] *nf (fig)* anxiety; **zozobrar** *vi (hundirse)* to capsize; *(fig)* to fail

zueco ['θweko] *nm* clog

zumbar [θum'bar] *vt (golpear)* to hit ♦ *vi* to buzz; **zumbido** *nm* buzzing

zumo ['θumo] *nm* juice

zurcir [θur'θir] *vt (coser)* to darn

zurdo, a ['θurðo, a] *adj (persona)* left-handed

zurrar [θu'rrar] *(fam) vt* to wallop

USING YOUR COLLINS POCKET DICTIONARY

Supplement by
Roy Simon
reproduced by kind permission of
Tayside Region Education Department

USING YOUR COLLINS POCKET DICTIONARY

Introduction

We are delighted that you have decided to invest in this Collins Pocket Dictionary! Whether you intend to use it in school, at home, on holiday or at work, we are sure that you will find it very useful.

The purpose of this supplement is to help you become aware of the wealth of vocabulary and grammatical information your dictionary contains, to explain how this information is presented and also to point out some of the traps one can fall into when using a Spanish-English English-Spanish dictionary.

In the pages which follow you will find explanations and wordgames (not too difficult!) designed to give you practice in exploring the dictionary's contents and in retrieving information for a variety of purposes. Answers are provided at the end. If you spend a little time on these pages you should be able to use your dictionary more efficiently and effectively. Have fun!

Contents

HOW INFORMATION IS PRESENTED IN YOUR DICTIONARY

A great deal of information is packed into your Collins Pocket Dictionary using colour, various typefaces, sizes of type, symbols, abbreviations and brackets. The purpose of this section is to acquaint you with the conventions used in presenting information.

Headwords

A headword is the word you look up in a dictionary. Headwords are listed in alphabetical order throughout the dictionary. They are printed in colour so that they stand out clearly from all the other words on the dictionary page.

Note that at the top of each page two headwords appear. These tell you which is the first and last word dealt with on the page in question. They are there to help you scan through the dictionary more quickly.

The Spanish alphabet consists of 27 letters: the same 26 letters as the English alphabet, in the same order, plus 'ñ', which comes after letter 'n'. You will need to remember that words containing this letter will be listed slightly differently from what you would expect according to English alphabetical order: thus 'caña' does not come immediately after 'cana', but follows the last word beginning with 'can-' in the list, namely 'canuto'.

Where two Spanish words are distinguished only by an accent, the accented form follows the unaccented, e.g. 'de', 'dé'.

A dictionary entry

An entry is made up of a headword and all the information about that headword. Entries will be short or long depending on how frequently a word is used in either English or Spanish and how many meanings it has. Inevitably, the fuller the dictionary entry the more care is needed in sifting through it to find the information you require.

Meanings

The translations of a headword are given in ordinary type. Where there is more than one meaning or usage, a semi-colon separates one from the other.

completo, a [kom'pleto, a] *adj* complete;
(*perfecto*) perfect; (*lleno*) full ♦ *nm* full
complement
complicado, a [kompli'kaðo, a] *adj*
complicated; **estar ~ en** to be mixed up
in
cómplice ['kompliθe] *nm/f* accomplice
complot [kom'plo(t)] (*pl* ~**s**) *nm* plot

aiming; (*destreza*) marksmanship
puntero, a [pun'tero, a] *adj* leading ♦ *nm*
(*palo*) pointer
puntiagudo, a [puntja'ɣuðo, a] *adj* sharp,
pointed
puntilla [pun'tiʎa] *nf* (*encaje*) lace edging

puritano, a [puri'tano, a] *adj* (*actitud*)
puritanical; (*iglesia, tradición*) puritan
♦ *nm/f* puritan
puro, a ['puro, a] *adj* pure; (*verdad*)
simple, plain ♦ *adv:* **de ~ cansado** out of
sheer tiredness ♦ *nm* cigar

nevar [ne'ßar] *vi* to snow

cuenta *etc* ['kwenta] *vb ver* **contar** ♦ *nf*
(*cálculo*) count, counting; (*en café,
restaurante*) bill (*BRIT*), check (*US*); (*COM*)
account; (*de collar*) bead; **a fin de ~s** in
the end; **caer en la ~** to catch on; **darse
~ de** to realize; **tener en ~** to bear in
mind; **echar ~s** to take stock; **~
corriente / de ahorros** current/savings
account; **~ atrás** countdown;
~kilómetros *nm inv* ≈ milometer; (*de
velocidad*) speedometer

titubear [tituße'ar] *vi* to stagger; to
stammer; (*fig*) to hesitate; **titubeo** *nm*
staggering; stammering; hesitation

iii

In addition, you will often find other words appearing in *italics* in brackets before the translations. These either give some notion of the contexts in which the headword might appear (as with 'lane' opposite – 'lane in the country', 'lane in a race', etc.) or else they provide synonyms (as with 'hit' opposite – 'strike', 'reach', etc.).

Phonetic spellings

The phonetic spelling of each headword – i.e. its pronunciation – is given in square brackets immediately after it. The phonetic transcription of Spanish and English vowels and consonants is given on pages viii to xi at the front of your dictionary.

Additional information about headwords

Information about the usage or form of certain headwords is given in brackets between the phonetics and the translation or translations. Have a look at the entries for 'COU', 'cuenca', 'mast', 'R.S.V.P.' and 'burro' opposite.

This information is usually given in abbreviated form. A helpful list of abbreviations is given on pages vi and vii at the front of your dictionary.

You should be particularly careful with colloquial words or phrases. Words labelled (*fam*) would not normally be used in formal speech, while those labelled (*fam!*) would be considered offensive.

Careful consideration of such style labels will help indicate the degree of formality and appropriateness of a word and could help you avoid many an embarrassing situation when using Spanish!

Expressions in which the headword appears

An entry will often feature certain common expressions in which the headword appears. These expressions are in **bold** type, but in black as opposed to colour. A swung dash (~) is used instead of repeating a headword in an entry. 'Tono' and 'mano' opposite illustrate this point.

Related words

In the Pocket Dictionary words related to certain headwords are sometimes given at the end of an entry, as with 'ambición' and 'accept' opposite. These are easily picked out as they are also in colour. To help you find these words, they are placed in alphabetical order after the headword to which they belong: cf. 'accept', 'general' opposite.

lane [leɪn] *n* (*in country*) camino; (*AUT*) carril *m*; (*in race*) calle *f*

embrollar [embro'ʎar] *vt* (*el asunto*) to confuse, complicate; (*implicar*) to involve, embroil; **~se** *vr* (*confundirse*) to get into a muddle *o* mess

COU [kou] (*ESP*) *nm abr* (= *Curso de Orientación Universitaria*) *1 year course leading to final school-leaving certificate and university entrance examinations*

cuenca ['kwenka] *nf* (*ANAT*) eye socket; (*GEO*) bowl, deep valley

menudo, a [me'nuðo, a] *adj* (*pequeño*) small, tiny; (*sin importancia*) petty, insignificant; **¡~ negocio!** (*fam*) some deal!; **a ~** often, frequently

tono ['tono] *nm* tone; **fuera de ~** inappropriate; **darse ~** to put on airs

ambición [ambi'θjon] *nf* ambition; **ambicionar** *vt* to aspire to; **ambicioso, a** *adj* ambitious

accept [ək'sɛpt] *vt* aceptar; (*responsibility, blame*) admitir; **~able** *adj* aceptable; **~ance** *n* aceptación *f*

hit [hɪt] (*pt, pp* **hit**) *vt* (*strike*) golpear, pegar; (*reach: target*) alcanzar; (*collide with: car*) chocar contra; (*fig: affect*) afectar ♦ *n* golpe *m*; (*success*) éxito; **to ~ it off with sb** llevarse bien con uno; **~-and-run driver** *n conductor(a) que atropella y huye*

repoblación [repoβla'θjon] *nf* repopulation; (*de río*) restocking; **~ forestal** reafforestation

mast [maːst] *n* (*NAUT*) mástil *m*; (*RADIO etc*) torre *f*

R.S.V.P. *abbr* (= *répondez s'il vous plaît*) SRC

burro, a ['burro, a] *nm/f* donkey/she-donkey; (*fig*) ass, idiot

bocazas [bo'kaθas] (*fam*) *nm inv* bigmouth

cabrón [ka'βron] *nm* cuckold; (*fam!*) bastard (!)

mano ['mano] *nf* hand; (*ZOOL*) foot, paw; (*de pintura*) coat; (*serie*) lot, series; **a ~** by hand; **a ~ derecha/izquierda** on the right(-hand side)/left(-hand side); **de primera ~** (at) first hand; **de segunda ~** (at) second hand; **robo a ~ armada** armed robbery; **~ de obra** labour, manpower; **estrechar la ~ a uno** to shake sb's hand

general [xene'ral] *adj* general ♦ *nm* general; **por lo** *o* **en ~** in general; **G~itat** *nf* Catalan parliament; **~izar** *vt* to generalize; **~izarse** *vr* to become generalized, spread; **~mente** *adv* generally

v

'Key' words

Your Collins Pocket Dictionary gives special status to certain Spanish and English words which can be looked on as 'key' words in each language. These are words which have many different usages. 'Poder', 'menos' and 'se' opposite are typical examples in Spanish. You are likely to become familiar with them in your day-to-day language studies.

There will be occasions, however, when you want to check on a particular usage. Your dictionary can be very helpful here. Note how with 'poder', for example, different parts of speech and different usages are clearly indicated by a combination of lozenges - ♦ - and numbers. In addition, further guides to usage are given in the language of the user who needs them. These are bracketed and in italics.

poder [po'ðer] *vi* **1** (*capacidad*) can, be able to; **no puedo hacerlo** I can't do it, I'm unable to do it

2 (*permiso*) can, may, be allowed to; **¿se puede?** may I (*o* we?); **puedes irte ahora** you may go now; **no se puede fumar en este hospital** smoking is not allowed in this hospital

3 (*posibilidad*) may, might, could; **puede llegar mañana** he may *o* might arrive tomorrow; **pudiste haberte hecho daño** you might *o* could have hurt yourself; **¡podías habérmelo dicho antes!** you might have told me before!

4: puede ser: puede ser perhaps; **puede ser que lo sepa Tomás** Tomás may *o* might know

5: ¡no puedo más! I've had enough!; **no pude menos que dejarlo** I couldn't help but leave it; **es tonto a más no ~** he's as stupid as they come

6: ~ con: no puedo con este crío this kid's too much for me

♦ *nm* power; **~ adquisitivo** purchasing power; **detentar** *o* **ocupar** *o* **estar en el ~** to be in power

se [se] *pron* **1** (*reflexivo: sg: m*) himself; (*: f*) herself; (*: pl*) themselves; (*: cosa*) itself; (*: de Vd*) yourself; (*: de Vds*) yourselves; **~ está preparando** she's preparing herself; *para usos léxicos del pron ver el vb en cuestión, p.ej.* **arrepentirse**

2 (*con complemento indirecto*) to him; to her; to them; to it; to you; **a usted ~ lo dije ayer** I told you yesterday; **~ compró un sombrero** he bought himself a hat; **~ rompió la pierna** he broke his leg

3 (*uso recíproco*) each other, one another; **~ miraron (el uno al otro)** they looked at each other *o* one another

4 (*en oraciones pasivas*): **se han vendido muchos libros** a lot of books have been sold

5 (*impers*): **~ dice que** people say that, it is said that; **allí ~ come muy bien** the food there is very good, you can eat very well there

menos [menos] *adj* **1**: **~ (que/de)** (*compar: cantidad*) less (than); (*: número*) fewer (than); **con ~ entusiasmo** with less enthusiasm; **~ gente** fewer people; *ver tb* **cada**

2 (*superl*): **es el que ~ culpa tiene** he is the least to blame

♦ *adv* **1** (*compar*): **~ (que, de)** less (than); **me gusta ~ que el otro** I like it less than the other one

2 (*superl*): **es el ~ listo (de su clase)** he's the least bright in his class; **de todas ellas es la que ~ me agrada** out of all of them she's the one I like least; **(por) lo ~** at (the very) least

3 (*locuciones*): **no quiero verle y ~ visitarle** I don't want to see him let alone visit him; **tenemos 7 de ~** we're seven short

♦ *prep* except; (*cifras*) minus; **todos ~ él** everyone except (for) him; **5 ~ 2** 5 minus 2

♦ *conj*: **a ~ que: a ~ que venga mañana** unless he comes tomorrow

WORDGAME 1

HEADWORDS

Study the following sentences. In each sentence a wrong word spelt very similarly to the correct word has deliberately been put in and the sentence doesn't make sense. This word is shaded each time. Write out each sentence again, putting in the <u>correct</u> word which you will find in your dictionary near the wrong word.

>   Example: Aparcar aquí no es delirio.
>
>   ['Delirio' (= delirium) is the wrong word and
>   should be replaced by 'delito' (= offence)]

1. El mecánico se negó a arrebatarme el coche.

2. El baúl estaba cubierto de pólvora.

3. Es muy caro reventar las fotos en esa tienda.

4. Les gusta mucho dar pasillos a caballo.

5. Para ayunar a su madre pone la mesa todos los días.

6. La ballesta es el animal más grande del mundo.

7. Mientras esquiábamos nos cayó una nevera tremenda.

8. No me gustó el último capota del libro.

9. Tuvimos un pincho y hubo que parar el coche.

10. Hay que cerrar la puerta con candidato.

WORDGAME 2

DICTIONARY ENTRIES

Complete the crossword below by looking up the English words in the list and finding the correct Spanish translations. There is a slight catch, however! All the English words can be translated several ways into Spanish, but only one translation will fit correctly into each part of the crossword. So look carefully through the entries in the English-Spanish section of your dictionary.

1. HORN
2. THROW
3. REMEMBER
4. PERFORMANCE
5. SPEECH
6. WHOLE

7. AMUSE
8. OLD
9. BELL
10. MATERIAL
11. ENDING
12. PART

WORDGAME 3

FINDING MEANINGS

In this list there are eight pairs of words that have some sort of connection with each other. For example, **'curso'** (= 'course') and **'estudiante'** (= 'student') are linked. Find the other pairs by looking up the words in your dictionary.

1. bata
2. nido
3. cuero
4. zapatillas
5. campanario
6. estudiante
7. libro
8. bolso
9. pasarela
10. aleta
11. curso
12. estante
13. urraca
14. barco
15. veleta
16. tiburón

WORDGAME 4

SYNONYMS

Complete the crossword by supplying SYNONYMS of the words below.
You will sometimes find the synonym you are looking for in italics
bracketed at the entries for the words listed below. Sometimes you will
have to turn to the English-Spanish section for help.

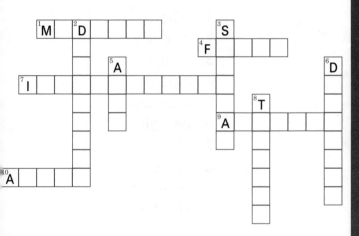

1. maneras
2. desilusión
3. exceder
4. incendio
5. cariño

6. vencer
7. inacabable
8. éxito
9. complacer
10. aeroplano

WORDGAME 5

SPELLING

You will often use your dictionary to check spellings. The person who has compiled this list of ten Spanish words has made <u>three</u> spelling mistakes. Find the three words which have been misspelt and write them out correctly.

1. pájaro
2. acienda
3. oleaje
4. gigante
5. avarrotar
6. peregil
7. ahora
8. velocidad
9. quinientos
10. abridor

WORDGAME 6

ANTONYMS

Complete the crossword by supplying ANTONYMS (i.e. opposites) in Spanish of the words below. Use your dictionary to help.

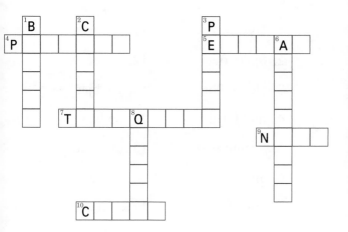

1. feo
2. abrir
3. ligero
4. riqueza
5. salir
6. engordar
7. inquieto
8. poner
9. todo
10. oscuro

WORDGAME 7

PHONETIC SPELLINGS

The phonetic transcriptions of twenty Spanish words are given below. If you study pages viii and ix at the front of your dictionary you should be able to work out what the words are.

1. 'aɣwa
2. θju'ðað
3. alreðe'ðor
4. mu'tʃatʃo
5. 'bjento
6. 'niɲo
7. bol'βer
8. 'kaʎe
9. θiɣ'θaɣ
10. 'xenjo
11. 'gwarða
12. 'tʃoke
13. em'bjar
14. ka'βaʎo
15. aβo'ɣaðo
16. korre'xir
17. ko'mjenθo
18. 'eʎos
19. xer'sei
20. i'ɣwal

WORDGAME 8

EXPRESSIONS IN WHICH THE HEADWORD APPEARS

If you look up the headword 'mismo' in the Spanish-English section of your dictionary you will find that the word can have many meanings. Study the entry carefully and translate the following sentences into English.

1. Ahora mismo se lo llevo.

2. A mí me da lo mismo.

3. Lo mismo que tú estudias francés yo estudio español.

4. En ese mismo momento llegó la policía.

5. Acudió el mismo Presidente.

6. Todos los domingos se ponía el mismo traje.

7. Lo hice yo mismo.

8. Era un hipócrita, y por lo mismo despreciado por todos.

9. Tenemos que empezar hoy mismo.

10. Lo vi aquí mismo.

WORDGAME 9

RELATED WORDS

Fill in the blanks in the pairs of sentences below. The missing words are related to the headwords on the left. Choose the correct 'relative' each time. You will find it in your dictionary near the headword provided.

HEADWORD	RELATED WORDS
estudiante	1. Realiza sus _____ en la Universidad.
	2. Hay que _____ bien el texto.
pertenecer	3. Estos son los terrenos _____ al Ayuntamiento.
	4. Recogió todas sus _____ y se fue.
empleo	5. Es _____ de banco.
	6. Voy a _____ todos los medios a mi alcance.
atractivo	7. Esa perspectiva no me _____ nada.
	8. Aquella mujer ejercía una gran _____ sobre él.
terminante	9. Al _____ de la reunión todos se fueron a tomar café.
	10. No le dejaron _____ lo que estaba diciendo.
falsedad	11. Lo que estás diciendo es completamente _____ .
	12. Se dedicaban a _____ billetes de banco.

WORDGAME 10

'KEY' WORDS

Study carefully the entry **'hacer'** in your dictionary and find translations for the following:

1. it's cold

2. I made them come

3. to study Economics

4. this will make it more difficult

5. to do the cooking

6. they became friends

7. I've been going for a month

8. to turn a deaf ear

9. if it's alright with you

10. to get hold of something

THE DICTIONARY AND GRAMMAR

While it is true that a dictionary can never be a substitute for a detailed grammar reference book, it nevertheless provides a great deal of grammatical information. If you know how to extract this information you will be able to use Spanish more accurately both in speech and in writing.

The Collins Pocket Dictionary presents grammatical information as follows.

Parts of speech

Parts of speech are given in italics immediately after the phonetic spellings of headwords. Abbreviated forms are used. Abbreviations can be checked on pages vi and vii.

Changes in parts of speech within an entry – for example, from adjective to adverb to noun, or from noun to intransitive verb to transitive verb – are indicated by means of lozenges - ♦ - as with the Spanish 'derecho' and the English 'act' opposite.

Genders of Spanish nouns

The gender of each noun in the Spanish-English section of the dictionary is indicated in the following way:

nm = nombre masculino
nf = nombre femenino

You will occasionally see *nm/f* beside an entry. This indicates that a noun – 'habitante', for example – can be either masculine or feminine.

Feminine forms of nouns are shown, as with 'ministro' opposite: the feminine ending is substituted for the masculine, so that 'ministro' becomes 'ministra' in the feminine.

In the English-Spanish section of the dictionary, genders are not shown for masculine nouns ending in '-o' or feminine nouns ending in '-a'. Otherwise, the gender immediately follows the translation. If a noun can be either masculine or feminine, this is shown by *'m/f'* if the form of the noun does not change, or by the feminine ending if it does change, as with 'graduate' and 'dentist' opposite. Note that when an ending is added on to a word rather than substituted for another ending it appears in brackets.

It is most important that you know the correct gender of a Spanish noun, since it is going to determine the form of both adjectives and past participles. If you are in any doubt as to the gender of a noun, it is always best to check it in your dictionary.

estría [es'tria] *nf* groove

tenue ['tenwe] *adj* (*delgado*) thin, slender; (*neblina*) light; (*lazo, vínculo*) slight

derecho, a [de'retʃo, a] *adj* right, right-hand ♦ *nm* (*privilegio*) right; (*lado*) right(-hand) side; (*leyes*) law ♦ *adv* straight, directly; **~s** *nmpl* (*de aduana*) duty *sg*; (*de autor*) royalties; **tener ~ a** to have a right to

act [ækt] *n* acto, acción *f*; (*of play*) acto; (*in music hall etc*) número; (*LAW*) decreto, ley *f* ♦ *vi* (*behave*) comportarse; (*have effect: drug, chemical*) hacer efecto; (*THEATRE*) actuar; (*pretend*) fingir; (*take action*) obrar ♦ *vt* (*part*) hacer el papel de; **in the ~ of: to catch sb in the ~ of ...** pillar a uno en el momento en que ...; **to ~ as** actuar *or* hacer de; **~ing** *adj* suplente ♦ *n* (*activity*) actuación *f*; (*profession*) profesión *f* de actor

criterio [kri'terjo] *nm* criterion; (*juicio*) judgement

manguera [man'gera] *nf* hose

habitante [aβi'tante] *nm/f* inhabitant

ministro, a [mi'nistro, a] *nm/f* minister

graduate [*n* 'grædjuɪt, *vb* 'grædjueɪt] *n* (*US: of high school*) graduado/a; (*of university*) licenciado/a ♦ *vi* graduarse; licenciarse; **graduation** [-'eɪʃən] *n* (*ceremony*) entrega del título

dentist ['dɛntɪst] *n* dentista *m/f*

xix

Adjectives

Adjectives are given in both their masculine and feminine forms, where these are different. The usual rule is to drop the 'o' of the masculine form and add an 'a' to make an adjective feminine, as with 'negro' opposite.

Some adjectives have identical masculine and feminine forms. Where this occurs, there is no 'a' beside the basic masculine form.

Adverbs

The normal 'rule' for forming adverbs in Spanish is to add '-mente' to the feminine form of the adjective. Thus:

seguro > segura > seguramente

The '-mente' ending is often the equivalent of the English '-ly':

seguramente – surely
lentamente – slowly

In your dictionary Spanish adverbs are not generally given, since the English translation can usually be derived from the relevant translation of the adjective headword. Usually the translation can be formed by adding '-ly' to the relevant adjective translation: e.g.

fiel – faithful
fielmente – faithfully

In cases where the basic translation for the adverb cannot be derived from those for the adjective, the adverb is likely to be listed as a headword in alphabetical order. This means it may not be immediately adjacent to the adjective headword: see 'actual' and 'actualmente' opposite.

Information about verbs

A major problem facing language learners is that the form of a verb will change according to the subject and/or the tense being used. A typical Spanish verb can take many different forms – too many to list in a dictionary entry.

negro, a ['neɣro, a] *adj* black; *(suerte)* awful ♦ *nm* black ♦ *nm/f* black man/woman

valiente [ba'ljente] *adj* brave, valiant ♦ *nm* hero

seguramente [seɣura'mente] *adv* surely; *(con certeza)* for sure, with certainty

actual [ak'twal] *adj* present(-day), current; **~idad** *nf* present; **~idades** *nfpl (noticias)* news *sg*; **en la ~idad** at present; *(hoy día)* nowadays
actualizar [aktwali'θar] *vt* to update, modernize
actualmente [aktwal'mente] *adv* at present; *(hoy día)* nowadays

Yet, although verbs are listed in your dictionary in their infinitive forms only, this does not mean that the dictionary is of limited value when it comes to handling the verb system of the Spanish language. On the contrary, it contains much valuable information.

First of all, your dictionary will help you with the meanings of unfamiliar verbs. If you came across the word 'decidió' in a text and looked it up in your dictionary you wouldn't find it. What you must do is assume that it is part of a verb and look for the infinitive form. Thus you will deduce that 'decidió' is a form of the verb 'decidir'. You now have the basic meaning of the word you are concerned with – something to do with English verb 'decide' – and this should be enough to help you understand the text you are reading.

It is usually an easy task to make the connection between the form of a verb and the infinitive. For example, 'decidieran', 'decidirá', 'decidimos' and 'decidido' are all recognisable as parts of the infinitive 'decidir'. However, sometimes it is less obvious – for example, 'pueda', 'podrán' and 'pude' are all parts of 'poder'. The only real solution to this problem is to learn the various forms of the main Spanish regular and irregular verbs.

And this is the second source of help offered by your dictionary as far as verbs are concerned. The verb tables on page xii of the Collins Pocket Dictionary provide a summary of some of the main forms of the main tenses of regular and irregular verbs. Consider the verb 'poder' below where the following information is given:

1	pudiendo	– Present Participle
2	puede	– Imperative
3	puedo, puedes, puede, pueden	– Present Tense forms
4	pude, pudiste, pudo, pudimos, pudisteis, pudieron	– Preterite forms
5	podré *etc*	– 1st Person Singular of the Future Tense
6	pueda, puedas, pueda, puedan	– Present Subjunctive forms
7	pudiera *etc*	– 1st Person Singular of the Imperfect Subjunctive

The regular '-ar', '-er', and '-ir' verbs – 'hablar', 'comer' and 'vivir' – are presented in greater detail. The main tenses and the different endings are given in full. This information can be transferred and applied to all verbs in the list. In addition, the main parts of the most common irregular verbs are listed in the body of the dictionary.

HABLAR

1 hablando
2 habla, hablad
3 hablo, hablas, habla, hablamos, habláis, hablan
4 hablé, hablaste, habló, hablamos, hablasteis, hablaron
5 hablaré, hablarás, hablará, hablaremos, hablaréis, hablarán
6 hable, hables, hable, hablemos, habléis, hablen
7 hablara, hablaras, hablara, habláramos, hablarais, hablaran
8 hablado
9 hablaba, hablabas, hablaba, hablábamos, hablabais, hablaban

In order to make maximum use of the information contained in these pages, a good working knowledge of the various rules affecting Spanish verbs is required. You will acquire this in the course of your Spanish studies and your Collins dictionary will serve as a useful reminder. If you happen to forget how to form the second person singular form of the Future Tense of 'poder' (i.e. how to translate 'you will be able to'), there will be no need to panic – your dictionary contains the information!

WORDGAME 11

PARTS OF SPEECH

In each sentence below a word has been shaded. Put a tick in the appropriate box to indicate the <u>part of speech</u> each time.

SENTENCE	Noun	Adj	Adv	Verb
1. Es estudiante de derecho.				
2. No hables tan alto.				
3. No tiene mucho dinero en su haber.				
4. Es un escrito muy largo.				
5. Vaya todo seguido.				
6. Es un dicho muy frecuente.				
7. Llegamos a casa muy tarde.				
8. Le gusta mucho andar por el campo.				
9. Lo hacemos por tu bien.				
10. A mi parecer es una buena película.				

WORDGAME 12

MEANING CHANGING WITH GENDER

Some Spanish nouns change meaning according to their gender, i.e. according to whether they are masculine or feminine. Look at the pairs of sentences below and fill in the blanks with either 'un', 'una', 'el' or 'la'. Use your dictionary to help.

1. No podía comprender _____ cólera de su padre.

   _____ cólera hace estragos en las regiones tropicales.

2. Perdí _____ pendiente en su casa.

   El coche no podía subir por _____ pendiente.

3. Los niños jugaban con _____ cometa.

   Dicen que en abril caerá _____ cometa.

4. Vimos _____ policía dentro de su coche.

   _____ policía ha descubierto una red de traficantes de droga.

5. Hay que cambiar _____ order de los números.

   En cuanto recibió _____ orden se puso en camino.

6. ¿Ha llegado _____ parte de la policía?

   _____ parte de atrás de la casa es muy sombría.

7. Pasó dos días en _____ coma profundo.

   Tienes que poner _____ coma ahí.

8. Los soldados están todavía en _____ frente.

   El pelo le cubría _____ frente.

ADVERBS

Translate the following Spanish adverbs into English (generally by adding **-ly** to the adjective).

1. recientemente
2. lamentablemente
3. constantemente
4. mensualmente
5. pesadamente
6. inconscientemente
7. inmediatamente
8. ampliamente
9. tenazmente
10. brillantemente

WORDGAME 14

VERB TENSES

Use your dictionary to help you fill in the blanks in the table below.
(Remember the important pages at the front of your dictionary.)

INFINITIVE	PRESENT SUBJUNCTIVE	PRETERITE	FUTURE
tener		yo	
hacer			yo
poder			yo
decir		yo	
agradecer	yo		
saber			yo
reír	yo		
querer		yo	
caber	yo		
ir	yo		
salir			yo
ser		yo	

WORDGAME 15

IRREGULAR VERBS

Use your dictionary to find the <u>first person</u> present indicative of these verbs.

INFINITIVE	PRESENT INDICATIVE
conocer	
saber	
estar	
ofrecer	
poder	
ser	
poner	
divertir	
traer	
decir	
preferir	
negar	
dar	
instruir	

WORDGAME 16

IDENTIFYING INFINITIVES

In the sentences below you will see various Spanish verbs shaded. Use your dictionary to help you find the **infinitive** form of each verb.

1. Cuando era pequeño dormía en la misma habitación que mi hermano.

2. Mis amigos vienen conmigo.

3. No cupieron todos los libros en el estante.

4. ¿Es que no veías lo que pasaba?

5. El sábado saldremos todos juntos.

6. Ya hemos visto la casa.

7. ¿Quieres que lo ponga aquí?

8. Le dije que viniera a las ocho.

9. Nos han escrito tres cartas ya.

10. No sabían qué hacer.

11. Tuvimos que salir temprano.

12. En cuanto supe lo de su padre la llamé por teléfono.

13. ¿Por qué no trajiste el dinero?

14. Prefiero quedarme en casa.

15. Quiero que conozcas a mi padre.

MORE ABOUT MEANING

In this section we will consider some of the problems associated with using a bilingual dictionary.

Overdependence on your dictionary

That the dictionary is an invaluable tool for the language learner is beyond dispute. Nevertheless, it is possible to become overdependent on your dictionary, turning to it in an almost automatic fashion every time you come up against a new word or phrase in a Spanish text. Tackling an unfamiliar text in this way will turn reading in Spanish into an extremely tedious activity. It is possible to argue that if you stop to look up every new word you may actually be *hindering* your ability to read in Spanish – you are so concerned with the individual words that you pay no attention to the text as a whole and to the context which gives them meaning. It is therefore important to develop appropriate reading skills – using clues such as titles, headlines, illustrations, etc., understanding relations within a sentence, etc. to predict or infer what a text is about.

A detailed study of the development of reading skills is not within the scope of this supplement; we are concerned with knowing how to use a dictionary, which is only one of several important skills involved in reading. Nevertheless, it may be instructive to look at one example. You see the following text in a Spanish newspaper and are interested in working out what it is about.

Contextual clues here include the heading in large type, which indicates that this is some sort of announcement, and the names. The verb 'recibir' is very much like the English 'receive' and you will also know 'form' words such as 'una', 'y' and so forth from your general studies in Spanish, as well as essential vocabulary such as 'niña', 'hijos', 'nombre'. Given that this extract appeared in a newspaper,

> ### Natalicios
> La señora de García Rodríguez (don Alfonso), de soltera Laura Montes de la Torre, ha dado a luz una niña, cuarta de sus hijos, que recibirá el nombre de Beatriz y tendrá como padrinos a doña Mercedes Sánchez Serrano y don Felipe Gómez Morales.

you will probably have worked out by now that this is an announcement placed in the 'Personal Column'.

So you have used contextual and word-formation clues to get you to the point where you have understood that this notice has been placed in the personal column because something has happened to señora de García Rodríguez and that somebody is going to be given the name of 'Beatriz'. And you have reached this point *without* opening your dictionary once. Common sense and your knowledge of newspaper contents in this country will suggest that this must be an announcement of someone's birth or death. Thus 'dar a luz' ('to give birth') and 'padrinos' ('godparents') become the only words that you need to look up in order to confirm that this is indeed a birth announcement.

When learning Spanish we are helped considerably by the fact that many Spanish and English words look and sound alike and have exactly the same meaning. Such words are called 'COGNATES'. Many words which look similar in Spanish and English come from a common Latin root. Other words are the same or nearly the same in both languages because the Spanish language has borrowed a word from English or vice versa. The dictionary will often not be necessary where cognates are concerned – provided you know the English word that the Spanish word resembles!

Words with more than one meaning

The need to examine with care *all* the information contained in a dictionary entry must be stressed. This is particularly important with the many Spanish words which have more than one meaning. For example, the Spanish 'destino' can mean 'destiny' as well as 'destination'. How you translated the word would depend on the context in which you found it.

Similarly, if you were trying to translate a phrase such as 'sigo sin saber', you would have to look through the whole entry for 'seguir' to get the right translation. If you restricted your search to the first line of the entry and saw that the first meaning given is 'to follow', you might be tempted to assume that the phrase meant 'I follow without knowing'. But if you examined the entry closely you would see that 'seguir sin . . .' means 'to still do . . . or 'to still be . . . '. So 'sigo sin saber' means 'I still don't know'.

The same need for care applies when you are using the English-Spanish section of your dictionary to translate a word from English into Spanish. Watch out in particular for the lozenges indicating changes in parts of speech.

The noun 'sink' is 'fregadero', while the verb is 'hundir'. If you don't watch what you are doing, you could end up with ridiculous non-Spanish e.g. 'Dejó los platos en el hundir'!

Phrasal verbs

Another potential source of difficulty is English phrasal verbs. These consist of a common verb ('make', 'get', etc.) plus an adverb and/or a preposition to give English expressions such as 'to make out', 'to get on', etc. Entries for such verbs tend to be fairly full, so close examination of the contents is required. Note how these verbs appear in colour within the entry.

sink [sɪŋk] (*pt* **sank**, *pp* **sunk**) *n* fregadero ♦ *vt* (*ship*) hundir, echar a pique; (*foundations*) excavar ♦ *vi* (*gen*) hundirse; **to ~ sth into** hundir algo en; **~ in** *vi* (*fig*) penetrar, calar

make [meɪk] (*pt, pp* **made**) *vt* hacer; (*manufacture*) fabricar; (*mistake*) cometer; (*speech*) pronunciar; (*cause to be*): **to ~ sb sad** poner triste a alguien; (*force*): **to ~ sb do sth** obligar a alguien a hacer algo; (*earn*) ganar; (*equal*): **2 and 2 ~ 4** 2 y 2 son 4 ♦ *n* marca; **to ~ the bed** hacer la cama; **to ~ a fool of sb** poner a alguien en ridículo; **to ~ a profit/loss** obtener ganancias/sufrir pérdidas; **to ~ it** (*arrive*) llegar; (*achieve sth*) tener éxito; **what time do you ~ it?** ¿qué hora tienes?; **to ~ do with** contentarse con; **~ for** *vt fus* (*place*) dirigirse a; **~ out** *vt* (*decipher*) descifrar; (*understand*) entender; (*see*) distinguir; (*cheque*) extender; **~ up** *vt* (*invent*) inventar; (*prepare*) hacer; (*constitute*) constituir ♦ *vi* reconciliarse;

Falsos amigos

We noted above that many Spanish and English words have similar forms *and* meanings. There are, however, many Spanish words which *look* like English words but have a completely *different* meaning. For example, 'la carpeta' means 'the folder'; 'sensible' means 'sensitive'. This can easily lead to serious mistranslations.

Sometimes the meaning of the Spanish word is quite close to the English. For example, 'la moneda' means 'coin' rather than 'money'; 'simpático' means 'nice' rather than 'sympathetic'. But some Spanish words which look similar to English words have two meanings, one the same as the English, the other completely different! 'El plato' can mean 'course' (in a meal) as well as 'plate'; 'la cámara' can mean 'camera', but also 'chamber'.

Such words are often referred to as FALSOS AMIGOS ('false friends'). You will have to look at the context in which they appear to arrive at the correct meaning. If they seem to fit in with the sense of the passage as a whole, you will probably not need to look them up. If they don't make sense, however, you may well be dealing with 'falsos amigos'.

WORDGAME 17

WORDS IN CONTEXT

Study the sentences below. Translations of the shaded words are given at the bottom. Match the number of the sentence and the letter of the translation correctly each time.

1. Tendremos que atarlo con una cuerda.
2. La cuerda del reloj se ha roto.
3. Iremos al cine para entretener a los niños.
4. No me entretengas, que llegaré tarde.
5. Le dieron una patada en la espinilla.
6. Tenía una espinilla enorme en la nariz.
7. Siempre le da mucho sueño después de comer.
8. Anoche me desperté sobresaltada por un mal sueño.
9. El niño tocaba todo lo que veía.
10. Su padre tocaba muy bien la guitarra.
11. Tuvo un acceso de tos.
12. Todas las vías de acceso estaban cerradas.
13. Me gustaría estudiar la carrera de Derecho.
14. Todos querían participar en la carrera.
15. He quebrado el plato sin darme cuenta.
16. No sabían que esa empresa había quebrado.

a. touched
b. shin(bone)
c. entertain
d. spring
e. fit
f. course
g. sleepiness
h. blackhead
i. rope
j. hold up
k. entry
l. race
m. gone bankrupt
n. played
o. dream
p. broken

WORDGAME 18

WORDS WITH MORE THAN ONE MEANING

Look at the advertisements below. The words which are shaded can have more than one meaning. Use your dictionary to help you work out the correct translation in the context.

1

El Pescador
RESTAURANTE

Mariscos de viveros propios
Teléfono 406 12 80 – MADRID 6

P FÁCIL
  APARCAMIENTO

2

Restaurante
LOS CEREZOS

ALTA COCINA REGIONAL
Para amantes de lo tradicional
RESERVAS: 574 34 11/12

3

INTERLANGUE
ANUNCIA CURSO MASTER DE
INGLÉS JURÍDICO PARA
PROFESIONALES DEL DERECHO
Inicio: 20 de octubre

4

¡¡¡BUTACAS PIEL A MEDIDA!!!

APROVECHE GRANDES REBAJAS EN OCTUBRE
¡En fábrica, más calidad y menor precio!
Horario continuado de 9,30 a 20,30 –
incluso sábados

5

GRANDES ALMACENES "EL CONDOR"
IMPORTANTES REBAJAS DE FIN DE TEMPORADA

6

Guía   **TELEVISION**
JUEVES, 19

19.00. – Partido adelantado de la
JORNADA DE LIGA de PRIMERA DIVISION:
Atlético de Madrid – Barcelona (TV-2)

7

Bar-restaurante **"La Ballena"**

platos combinados desde 300 ptas.
helados, postres nuestra especialidad

8

ULTIMAS VIVIENDAS
de 2 y 3 dormitorios con
plaza de garaje opcional
Lunes a Viernes mañanas de 11 a 13,30.
Tardes de 16,30 a 19,30.

9

Calle de
ISABEL LA CATOLICA
N.ᵒˢ 50 - 56
PISOS EXTERIORES
DE 80 m²
FINANCIACION A 11 AÑOS
13 Y 13,5% CON LA CAJA DE BARCELONA

WORDGAME 19

FALSE FRIENDS

Look at the advertisements below. The words which are shaded resemble English words but have different meanings here. Find a correct translation for each word in the context.

1

LA MAYOR COLECCION DE
**ALFOMBRAS
PERSAS Y
ORIENTALES**
*¡¡¡VENTA DE LIQUIDACION
POR CAMBIO DE DOMICILIO!!!*

2

Teatro Nacional:
"El Alcalde de Zalamea"
Localidades en venta a partir de mañana

3

PRODUCTOS BENGOLEA
**¡NO RECURRA A
LA COMPETENCIA!**
Visite nuestro local en Castellana 500

4

OFERTA ESPECIAL
cubiertos de acero inoxidable de
primerísima calidad en planta baja

HAVE FUN WITH YOUR DICTIONARY

Here are some word games for you to try. You will find your dictionary helpful as you attempt the activities.

WORDGAME 20

CODED WORDS

In the boxes below the letters of eight Spanish words have been replaced by numbers. A number represents the same letter each time (though an accent may be required sometimes).

Try to crack the code and find the eight words. If you need help, use your dictionary.

Here is a clue: all the words you are looking for have something to do with TRANSPORT.

1 | C¹ | A² | M³ | 4 | 5 | 6 |

2 | 2 | 7 | 8 | 5 | 9 | 7 | 10 |

3 | 1 | 5 | 1 | 11 | 12 |

4 | 9 | 4 | 1 | 4 | 1 | 13 | 12 | 8 | 2 |

5 | 8 | 14 | 12 | 6 |

6 | 11 | 12 | 13 | 4 | 1 | 5 | 15 | 8 | 12 | 14 | 5 |

7 | 2 | 3 | 9 | 7 | 13 | 2 | 6 | 1 | 4 | 2 |

8 | 3 | 5 | 8 | 5 |

WORDGAME 21

BEHEADED WORDS

If you 'behead' certain Spanish words, i.e. take away their first letter, you are left with another Spanish word. For example, if you behead **'aplomo'** (= 'self-assurance'), you get **'plomo'** (= 'lead'), and **'bala'** (= 'bullet') gives **'ala'** (= 'wing').

The following words have their heads chopped off, i.e. the first letter has been removed. Use your dictionary to help you form a new Spanish word by adding one letter to the start of each word below. You will find that some of them can have more than one answer. Write down the new Spanish word and its meaning.

1. bajo (= low)
2. oler (= to smell)
3. año (= year)
4. oro (= gold)
5. reparar (= to repair)
6. ama (= owner)
7. rendido (= worn-out)
8. cuerdo (= sane)
9. ave (= bird)
10. batir (= to beat)
11. resto (= rest)
12. precio (= price)
13. cera (= wax)
14. hora (= hour)
15. pinar (= pine forest)

WORDGAME 22

PALABRAS CRUZADAS

Complete this crossword by looking up the words listed below in the English-Spanish section of your dictionary. Remember to read through the entry carefully to find the word that will fit.

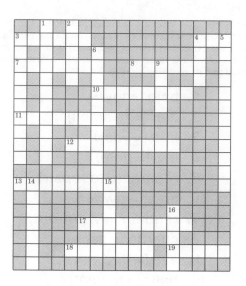

ACROSS

3. to bark
4. wing
7. lie
8. above
10. to work out
11. to lighten
12. to need
13. usual
17. cornet
18. to stink
19. radius

DOWN

1. to identify
2. to go out
3. regrettable
4. to love
5. streamlined
6. heating
9. expensive
14. to oblige
15. tricks
16. now

WORDGAME 23

There are twelve Spanish words hidden in the grid below. Each word is made up of five letters but has been split into two parts.

Find the Spanish words. Each group of letters can only be used once.

Use your dictionary to help you.

bla	lir	bu	ma	que	go
gor	ar	ver	vi	asi	jor
cal	me	ha	jo	lar	so
bo	jía	lo	vol	sa	eno

WORDGAME 24

Here is a list of Spanish words for things you will find in the kitchen. Unfortunately, they have all been jumbled up. Try to work out what each word is and put the word in the boxes on the right. You will see that there are seven shaded boxes below. With the seven letters in the shaded boxes make up <u>another</u> Spanish word for an object you can find in the kitchen.

1. azta   ¿Quieres una_____ de café?

2. eanevr   ¡Mete la mantequilla en la_____!

3. asme   ¡La comida está en la _____!

4. zoac   Su madre está calentando la leche en el_____

5. roegcanldo   ¡No saques el helado del_____todavía!

6. uclclohi   ¿Dónde has puesto el_____del queso?

7. rgoif   ¿Puedes cerrar ya el _____del agua caliente?

The word you are looking for is:

WORDGAME 25

PALABRAS CRUZADAS

Take the four letters given each time and put them in the four empty boxes in the centre of each grid. Arrange them in such a way that you form four six-letter words. Use your dictionary to check the words.

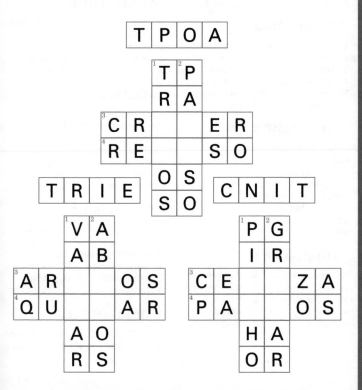

ANSWERS

WORDGAME 1

1	arreglarme	6	ballena
2	polvo	7	nevada
3	revelar	8	capítulo
4	paseos	9	pinchazo
5	ayudar	10	candado

WORDGAME 2

1	cuerno	7	entretener
2	echar	8	antiguo
3	recordar	9	timbre
4	actuación	10	tela
5	habla	11	terminación
6	entero	12	parte

WORDGAME 3

bata + zapatillas
nido + urraca
cuero + bolso
campanario + veleta
estudiante + curso
libro + estante
pasarela + barco
aleta + tiburón

WORDGAME 4

1	modales	6	derrotar
2	decepción	7	interminable
3	superar	8	triunfo
4	fuego	9	agradar
5	amor	10	avión

WORDGAME 5

2	hacienda
5	abalorios
6	perejil

WORDGAME 6

1	bonito	6	adelgazar
2	cerrar	7	tranquilo
3	pesado	8	quitar
4	pobreza	9	nada
5	entrar	10	claro

WORDGAME 7

agua, ciudad, alrededor,
muchacho, viento, niño,
volver, calle, zigzag,
genio, guarda, choque,
enviar, caballo, abogado,
corregir, comienzo, ellos,
jersey, igual

WORDGAME 9

1	estudios	7	atrae
2	estudiar	8	atracción
3	pertenecientes	9	término
4	pertenencias	10	terminar
5	empleado	11	falso
6	emplear	12	falsificar

WORDGAME 11

1 n	2 adv	3 n	4 n	5 adv
6 n	7 adv	8 v	9 n	10 n

WORDGAME 12

1 la; El	5 el; la
2 el; la	6 el; La
3 una; un	7 un; una
4 un; La	8 el; la

WORDGAME 14

tuve	ría
haré	quise
podré	quepa
dije	vaya
agradezca	saldré
sabré	fui

WORDGAME 15

conozco	divierto
sé	traigo
estoy	digo
ofrezco	prefiero
puedo	niego
soy	doy
pongo	instruyo

WORDGAME 16

1	dormir	9	escribir
2	venir	10	saber
3	caber	11	tener
4	ver	12	saber
5	salir	13	traer
6	ver	14	preferir
7	poner	15	conocer
8	venir		

WORDGAME 17

1 i	5 b	9 a	13 f
2 d	6 h	10 n	14 l
3 c	7 g	11 e	15 p
4 j	8 o	12 k	16 m

WORDGAME 18

1 fish farm
2 cuisine
3 law
4 leather
5 significant
6 league
7 set main course
8 space
9 savings bank

WORDGAME 19

1 clearance sale;
  home (Here: address)
2 tickets
3 competition
4 cutlery
5 retirement
6 small hotel; rooms
7 guest house
8 premises
9 address

WORDGAME 20

1	camión	5	tren
2	autobús	6	helicóptero
3	coche	7	ambulancia
4	bicicleta	8	moto

WORDGAME 21

1	abajo	7	prendido
2	doler; moler; soler	8	acuerdo
		9	nave
3	baño; paño; daño; caño	10	abatir
		11	presto
4	coro; loro; moro; poro	12	aprecio
		13	acera
5	preparar	14	ahora
6	cama; dama; fama; gama; mama; rama	15	opinar

WORDGAME 22

ACROSS:
3 ladrar
4 ala
7 mentira
8 encima
10 elaborar
11 aligerar
12 necesitar
13 corriente
17 cucurucho
18 apestar
19 radio

DOWN:
1 identificar
2 salir
3 lamentable
4 amar
5 aerodinámico
6 calefacción
9 caro
14 obligar
15 trucos
16 ahora

WORDGAME 23

enojo	verbo
queso	calma
salir	asilo
volar	largo
vigor	mejor
bujía	habla

WORDGAME 24

1	taza	5	congelador
2	nevera	6	cuchillo
3	mesa	7	grifo
4	cazo		

Missing word – ARMARIO

WORDGAME 25

1)	1	trapos	2	patoso
	3	cráter	4	reposo
2)	1	variar	2	abetos
	3	arreos	4	quitar
3)	1	pincho	2	gritar
	3	ceniza	4	pactos

ENGLISH – SPANISH
INGLÉS – ESPAÑOL

A, a

a [eɪ] n (MUS) la m

[ə] indef art (before vowel or silent h: an)
1 un(a); **~ book** un libro; **an apple** una manzana; **she's ~ doctor** (ella) es médica
2 (instead of the number "one") un(a); **~ year ago** hace un año; **~ hundred/thousand** etc **pounds** cien/mil etc libras
3 (in expressing ratios, prices etc): **3 ~ day/week** 3 al día/a la semana; **10 km an hour** 10 km por hora; **£5 ~ person** £5 por persona; **30p ~ kilo** 30p el kilo

A.A. n abbr (= Automobile Association: BRIT) ≈ RACE m (SP); (= Alcoholics Anonymous) Alcohólicos Anónimos

A.A.A. (US) n abbr (= American Automobile Association) ≈ RACE m (SP)

aback [ə'bæk] adv: **to be taken ~** quedar desconcertado

abandon [ə'bændən] vt abandonar; (give up) renunciar a

abate [ə'beɪt] vi (storm) amainar; (anger) aplacarse; (terror) disminuir

abattoir ['æbətwɑ:*] (BRIT) n matadero

abbey ['æbɪ] n abadía

abbot ['æbət] n abad m

abbreviation [ə'bri:vɪ'eɪʃən] n abreviatura

abdicate ['æbdɪkeɪt] vt renunciar a ♦ vi abdicar

abdomen ['æbdəmən] n abdomen m

abduct [æb'dʌkt] vt raptar, secuestrar

abeyance [ə'beɪəns] n: **in ~** (law) en desuso; (matter) en suspenso

abide [ə'baɪd] vt: **I can't ~ it/him** no lo/le puedo ver; **~ by** vt fus atenerse a

ability [ə'bɪlɪtɪ] n habilidad f, capacidad f; (talent) talento

abject ['æbdʒɛkt] adj (poverty) miserable;

(apology) rastrero

ablaze [ə'bleɪz] adj en llamas, ardiendo

able ['eɪbl] adj capaz; (skilled) hábil; **to be ~ to do sth** poder hacer algo; **~-bodied** adj sano; **ably** adv hábilmente

abnormal [æb'nɔ:məl] adj anormal

aboard [ə'bɔ:d] adv a bordo ♦ prep a bordo de

abode [ə'bəud] n: **of no fixed ~** sin domicilio fijo

abolish [ə'bɒlɪʃ] vt suprimir, abolir

aborigine [æbə'rɪdʒɪnɪ] n aborigen m/f

abort [ə'bɔ:t] vt, vi abortar; **~ion** [ə'bɔ:ʃən] n aborto; **to have an ~ion** abortar, hacerse abortar; **~ive** adj malogrado

about [ə'baut] adv 1 (approximately) más o menos, aproximadamente; **~ a hundred/thousand** etc unos(unas) cien/mil etc; **it takes ~ 10 hours** se tarda unas or más o menos 10 horas; **at ~ 2 o'clock** sobre las dos; **I've just ~ finished** casi he terminado
2 (referring to place) por todas partes; **to leave things lying ~** dejar las cosas (tiradas) por ahí; **to run ~** correr por todas partes; **to walk ~** pasearse, ir y venir
3: **to be ~ to do sth** estar a punto de hacer algo
♦ prep 1 (relating to) de, sobre, acerca de; **a book ~ London** un libro sobre or acerca de Londres; **what is it ~?** ¿de qué se trata?, ¿qué pasa?; **we talked ~ it** hablamos de eso or ello; **what** or **how ~ doing this?** ¿qué tal si hacemos esto?
2 (referring to place) por; **to walk ~ the town** caminar por la ciudad

above [ə'bʌv] *adv* encima, por encima, arriba ♦ *prep* encima de; (*greater than: in number*) más de; (: *in rank*) superior a; **mentioned ~** susodicho; **~ all** sobre todo; **~ board** *adj* legítimo

abrasive [ə'breɪzɪv] *adj* abrasivo; (*manner*) brusco

abreast [ə'brest] *adv* de frente; **to keep ~ of** (*fig*) mantenerse al corriente de

abroad [ə'brɔːd] *adv* (*to be*) en el extranjero; (*to go*) al extranjero

abrupt [ə'brʌpt] *adj* (*sudden*) brusco; (*curt*) áspero

abruptly [ə'brʌptlɪ] *adv* (*leave*) repentinamente; (*speak*) bruscamente

abscess ['æbsɪs] *n* absceso

abscond [əb'skɒnd] *vi* (*thief*): **to ~ with** fugarse con; (*prisoner*): **to ~ (from)** escaparse (de)

absence ['æbsəns] *n* ausencia

absent ['æbsənt] *adj* ausente; **~ee** [-'tiː] *n* ausente *m/f*; **~-minded** *adj* distraído

absolute ['æbsəluːt] *adj* absoluto; **~ly** [-'luːtlɪ] *adv* (*totally*) totalmente; (*certainly!*) ¡por supuesto (que sí)!

absolve [əb'zɒlv] *vt*: **to ~ sb (from)** absolver a alguien (de)

absorb [əb'zɔːb] *vt* absorber; **to be ~ed in a book** estar absorto en un libro; **~ent cotton** (*US*) *n* algodón *m* hidrófilo; **~ing** *adj* absorbente

absorption [əb'zɔːpʃən] *n* absorción *f*

abstain [əb'steɪn] *vi*: **to ~ (from)** abstenerse (de)

abstinence ['æbstɪnəns] *n* abstinencia

abstract ['æbstrækt] *adj* abstracto

absurd [əb'sɔːd] *adj* absurdo

abundance [ə'bʌndəns] *n* abundancia

abuse [*n* ə'bjuːs, *vb* ə'bjuːz] *n* (*insults*) insultos *mpl*, injurias *fpl*; (*ill-treatment*) malos tratos *mpl*; (*misuse*) abuso ♦ *vt* insultar; maltratar; abusar de; **abusive** *adj* ofensivo

abysmal [ə'bɪzməl] *adj* pésimo; (*failure*) garrafal; (*ignorance*) supino

abyss [ə'bɪs] *n* abismo

AC *abbr* (= *alternating current*) corriente *f*

alterna

academic [ækə'dɛmɪk] *adj* académico, universitario; (*pej: issue*) puramente teórico ♦ *n* estudioso/a; profesor(a) *m/f* universitario/a

academy [ə'kædəmɪ] *n* (*learned body*) academia; (*school*) instituto, colegio; **~ of music** conservatorio

accelerate [æk'seləreɪt] *vt, vi* acelerar; **accelerator** (*BRIT*) *n* acelerador *m*

accent ['æksent] *n* acento; (*fig*) énfasis *m*

accept [ək'sept] *vt* aceptar; (*responsibility, blame*) admitir; **~able** *adj* aceptable; **~ance** *n* aceptación *f*

access ['ækses] *n* acceso; **to have ~ to** tener libre acceso a; **~ible** [-'sesəbl] *adj* (*place, person*) accesible; (*knowledge etc*) asequible

accessory [æk'sesərɪ] *n* accesorio; (*LAW*): **to** cómplice de

accident ['æksɪdənt] *n* accidente *m*; (*chance event*) casualidad *f*; **by ~** (*unintentionally*) sin querer; (*by chance*) por casualidad; **~al** [-'dɛntl] *adj* accidental, fortuito; **~ally** [-'dɛntəlɪ] *adv* sin querer; por casualidad; **~ insurance** *n* seguro contra accidentes; **~-prone** *ad*, propenso a los accidentes

acclaim [ə'kleɪm] *vt* aclamar, aplaudir ♦ *n* aclamación *f*, aplausos *mpl*

acclimatize [ə'klaɪmətaɪz] (*US* **acclimate**) *vt*: **to become ~d** aclimatarse

accommodate [ə'kɒmədeɪt] *vt* (*subj: person*) alojar, hospedar; (: *car, hotel etc*) tener cabida para; (*oblige, help*) complacer; **accommodating** *adj* servicial, complaciente

accommodation [əkɒmə'deɪʃən] *n* (*US* **accommodations** *npl*) alojamiento

accompany [ə'kʌmpənɪ] *vt* acompañar

accomplice [ə'kʌmplɪs] *n* cómplice *m/f*

accomplish [ə'kʌmplɪʃ] *vt* (*finish*) concluir; (*achieve*) lograr; **~ed** *adj* experto, hábil; **~ment** *n* (*skill: gen pl*) talento; (*completion*) realización *f*

accord [ə'kɔːd] *n* acuerdo ♦ *vt* conceder;

of his own ~ espontáneamente; ~**ance** *n*: **in ~ance with** de acuerdo con; ~**ing**: ~**ing to** *prep* según; (*in accordance with*) conforme a; ~**ingly** *adv* (*appropriately*) de acuerdo con esto; (*as a result*) en consecuencia

accordion [ə'kɔ:dɪən] *n* acordeón *m*

accost [ə'kɔst] *vt* abordar, dirigirse a

account [ə'kaunt] *n* (*COMM*) cuenta; (*report*) informe *m*; ~**s** *npl* (*COMM*) cuentas *fpl*; **of no** ~ de ninguna importancia; **on** ~ a cuenta; **on no** ~ bajo ningún concepto; **on** ~ **of** a causa de, por motivo de; **to take into** ~, **take** ~ **of** tener en cuenta; ~ **for** *vt fus* (*explain*) explicar; (*represent*) representar; ~**able** *adj*: ~**able (to)** responsable (ante); ~**ancy** *n* contabilidad *f*; ~**ant** *n* contable *m/f*, contador(a) *m/f*; ~ **number** *n* (*at bank etc*) número de cuenta

accrued interest [ə'kru:d-] *n* interés *m* acumulado

accumulate [ə'kju:mjuleɪt] *vt* acumular ♦ *vi* acumularse

accuracy ['ækjurəsɪ] *n* (*of total*) exactitud *f*; (*of description etc*) precisión *f*

accurate ['ækjurɪt] *adj* (*total*) exacto; (*description*) preciso; (*person*) cuidadoso; (*device*) de precisión; ~**ly** *adv* con precisión

accusation [ækju'zeɪʃən] *n* acusación *f*

accuse [ə'kju:z] *vt*: **to ~ sb (of sth)** acusar a uno (de algo); ~**d** *n* (*LAW*) acusado/a

accustom [ə'kʌstəm] *vt* acostumbrar; ~**ed** *adj*: ~**ed to** acostumbrado a

ace [eɪs] *n* as *m*

ache [eɪk] *n* dolor *m* ♦ *vi* doler; **my head** ~**s** me duele la cabeza

achieve [ə'tʃi:v] *vt* (*aim, result*) alcanzar; (*success*) lograr, conseguir; ~**ment** *n* (*completion*) realización *f*; (*success*) éxito

acid ['æsɪd] *adj* ácido; (*taste*) agrio ♦ *n* (*CHEM, inf: LSD*) ácido; ~ **rain** *n* lluvia ácida

acknowledge [ək'nɔlɪdʒ] *vt* (*letter: also*: ~ **receipt of**) acusar recibo de; (*fact, situation, person*) reconocer; ~**ment** *n*

acuse *m* de recibo

acne ['æknɪ] *n* acné *m*

acorn ['eɪkɔ:n] *n* bellota

acoustic [ə'ku:stɪk] *adj* acústico; ~**s** *n, npl* acústica *sg*

acquaint [ə'kweɪnt] *vt*: **to ~ sb with sth** (*inform*) poner a uno al corriente de algo; **to be ~ed with** conocer; ~**ance** *n* (*person*) conocido/a; (*with person, subject*) conocimiento

acquire [ə'kwaɪə*] *vt* adquirir; **acquisition** [ækwɪ'zɪʃən] *n* adquisición *f*

acquit [ə'kwɪt] *vt* absolver, exculpar; **to ~ o.s. well** salir con éxito

acre ['eɪkə*] *n* acre *m*

acrid ['ækrɪd] *adj* acre

acrobat ['ækrəbæt] *n* acróbata *m/f*

across [ə'krɔs] *prep* (*on the other side of*) al otro lado de, del otro lado de; (*crosswise*) a través de ♦ *adv* de un lado a otro, de una parte a otra; a través, al través; (*measurement*): **the road is 10m ~** la carretera tiene 10m de ancho; **to run/swim ~** atravesar corriendo/nadando; ~ **from** enfrente de

acrylic [ə'krɪlɪk] *adj* acrílico ♦ *n* acrílica

act [ækt] *n* acto, acción *f*; (*of play*) acto; (*in music hall etc*) número; (*LAW*) decreto, ley *f* ♦ *vi* (*behave*) comportarse; (*have effect*: *drug, chemical*) hacer efecto; (*THEATRE*) actuar; (*pretend*) fingir; (*take action*) obrar ♦ *vt* (*part*) hacer el papel de; **in the ~ of**: **to catch sb in the ~ of ...** pillar a uno en el momento en que ...; **to ~ as** actuar *or* hacer de; ~**ing** *adj* suplente ♦ *n* (*activity*) actuación *f*; (*profession*) profesión *f* de actor

action ['ækʃən] *n* acción *f*, acto; (*MIL*) acción *f*, batalla; (*LAW*) proceso, demanda; **out of** ~ (*person*) fuera de combate; (*thing*) estropeado; **to take** ~ tomar medidas; ~ **replay** *n* (*TV*) repetición *f*

activate ['æktɪveɪt] *vt* activar

active ['æktɪv] *adj* activo, enérgico; (*volcano*) en actividad; ~**ly** *adv* (*participate*) activamente; (*discourage,*

dislike) enérgicamente; **activity** [-'tɪvɪtɪ] *n*
actividad *f*; **activity holiday** *n*
*vacaciones fpl con actividades
organizadas*
actor ['æktə•] *n* actor *m*
actress ['æktrɪs] *n* actriz *f*
actual ['æktjuəl] *adj* verdadero, real;
(*emphatic use*) propiamente dicho; **~ly**
adv realmente, en realidad; (*even*) incluso
acumen ['ækjumən] *n* perspicacia
acute [ə'kjuːt] *adj* agudo
ad [æd] *n abbr* = **advertisement**
A.D. *adv abbr* (= *anno Domini*) A.C.
adamant ['ædəmənt] *adj* firme, inflexible
adapt [ə'dæpt] *vt* adaptar ♦ *vi*: **to ~ (to)**
adaptarse (a), ajustarse (a); **~able** *adj*
adaptable; **~er, ~or** *n* (*ELEC*) adaptador
m
add [æd] *vt* añadir, agregar; (*figures: also*:
~ up) sumar ♦ *vi*: **to ~ to** (*increase*)
aumentar, acrecentar; **it doesn't ~ up**
(*fig*) no tiene sentido
adder ['ædə•] *n* víbora
addict ['ædɪkt] *n* adicto/a; (*enthusiast*)
entusiasta *m/f*; **~ed** [ə'dɪktɪd] *adj*: **to be**
~ed to ser adicto a; (*football etc*) ser
fanático de; **~ion** [ə'dɪkʃən] *n* (*to drugs
etc*) adicción *f*; **~ive** [ə'dɪktɪv] *adj* que
causa adicción
addition [ə'dɪʃən] *n* (*adding up*) adición *f*;
(*thing added*) añadidura, añadido; **in ~**
además, por añadidura; **in ~ to** además
de; **~al** *adj* adicional
additive ['ædɪtɪv] *n* aditivo
address [ə'drɛs] *n* dirección *f*, señas *fpl*;
(*speech*) discurso ♦ *vt* (*letter*) dirigir;
(*speak to*) dirigirse a, dirigir la palabra a;
(*problem*) tratar
adept ['ædɛpt] *adj*: **~ at** experto *or* hábil
en
adequate ['ædɪkwɪt] *adj* (*satisfactory*)
adecuado; (*enough*) suficiente
adhere [əd'hɪə•] *vi*: **to ~ to** (*stick to*)
pegarse a, adherirse a; (*fig: abide by*) observar; (*: belief
etc*) ser partidario de
adhesive [əd'hiːzɪv] *n* adhesivo; **~ tape** *n*
(*BRIT*) cinta adhesiva; (*US: MED*)

esparadrapo
ad hoc [æd'hɔk] *adj* ad hoc
adjacent [ə'dʒeɪsənt] *adj*: **~ to** contiguo a,
inmediato a
adjective ['ædʒɛktɪv] *n* adjetivo
adjoining [ə'dʒɔɪnɪŋ] *adj* contiguo, vecino
adjourn [ə'dʒəːn] *vt* aplazar ♦ *vi*
suspenderse
adjudicate [ə'dʒuːdɪkeɪt] *vi* sentenciar
adjust [ə'dʒʌst] *vt* (*change*) modificar;
(*clothing*) arreglar; (*machine*) ajustar ♦ *vi*:
to ~ (to) adaptarse (a); **~able** *adj*
ajustable; **~ment** *n* adaptación *f*; (*to
machine, prices*) ajuste *m*
ad-lib [æd'lɪb] *vt, vi* improvisar; **ad lib** *adv*
de forma improvisada
administer [əd'mɪnɪstə•] *vt* administrar;
administration [-'treɪʃən] *n*
(*management*) administración *f*;
(*government*) gobierno; **administrative**
[-trətɪv] *adj* administrativo
admiral ['ædmərəl] *n* almirante *m*; **A~ty**
(*BRIT*) *n* Ministerio de Marina,
Almirantazgo
admiration [ædmə'reɪʃən] *n* admiración *f*
admire [əd'maɪə•] *vt* admirar; **~r** *n* (*fan*)
admirador(a) *m/f*
admission [əd'mɪʃən] *n* (*to university,
club*) ingreso; (*entry fee*) entrada;
(*confession*) confesión *f*
admit [əd'mɪt] *vt* (*confess*) confesar; (*perm.
to enter*) dejar entrar, dar entrada a; (*to
club, organization*) admitir; (*accept: defeat*)
reconocer; **to be ~ted to hospital**
ingresar en el hospital; **~ to** *vt fus*
confesarse culpable de; **~tance** *n*
entrada; **~tedly** *adv* es cierto *or* verdad
que
admonish [əd'mɔnɪʃ] *vt* amonestar
ad nauseam [æd'nɔːsɪæm] *adv* hasta el
cansancio
ado [ə'duː] *n*: **without (any) more ~** sin
más (ni más)
adolescent [ædəu'lɛsnt] *adj, n*
adolescente *m/f*
adopt [ə'dɔpt] *vt* adoptar; **~ed** *adj*
adoptivo; **~ion** [ə'dɔpʃən] *n* adopción *f*

adore [ə'dɔː*] *vt* adorar

Adriatic [eɪdrɪ'ætɪk] *n*: **the ~ (Sea)** el (Mar) Adriático

adrift [ə'drɪft] *adv* a la deriva

adult ['ædʌlt] *n* adulto/a ♦ *adj* (*grown-up*) adulto; (*for adults*) para adultos

adultery [ə'dʌltərɪ] *n* adulterio

advance [əd'vɑːns] *n* (*progress*) adelanto, progreso; (*money*) anticipo, préstamo; (*MIL*) avance *m* ♦ *adj*: **~ booking** venta anticipada; **~ notice**, **~ warning** previo aviso ♦ *vt* (*money*) anticipar; (*theory, idea*) proponer (para la discusión) ♦ *vi* avanzar, adelantarse; **to make ~s (to sb)** hacer proposiciones (a alguien); **in ~** por adelantado; **~d** *adj* avanzado; (*SCOL: studies*) adelantado

advantage [əd'vɑːntɪdʒ] *n* (*also TENNIS*) ventaja; **to take ~ of** (*person*) aprovecharse de; (*opportunity*) aprovechar

Advent ['ædvənt] *n* (*REL*) Adviento

adventure [əd'ventʃə*] *n* aventura; **adventurous** [-tʃərəs] *adj* atrevido; aventurero

adverb ['ædvɜːb] *n* adverbio

adverse ['ædvɜːs] *adj* adverso, contrario

adversity [əd'vɜːsɪtɪ] *n* infortunio

advert ['ædvɜːt] (*BRIT*) *n abbr* = **advertisement**

advertise ['ædvətaɪz] *vi* (*in newspaper etc*) anunciar, hacer publicidad; **to ~ for** (*staff, accommodation etc*) buscar por medio de anuncios ♦ *vt* anunciar; **~ment** [əd'vɜːtɪsmənt] *n* (*COMM*) anuncio; **~r** *n* anunciante *m/f*; **advertising** *n* publicidad *f*, anuncios *mpl*; (*industry*) industria publicitaria

advice [əd'vaɪs] *n* consejo, consejos *mpl*; (*notification*) aviso; **a piece of ~** un consejo; **to take legal ~** consultar con un abogado

advisable [əd'vaɪzəbl] *adj* aconsejable, conveniente

advise [əd'vaɪz] *vt* aconsejar; (*inform*): **to ~ sb of sth** informar a uno de algo; **to ~ sb against sth/doing sth** desaconsejar algo a uno/aconsejar a uno que no haga algo;

~dly [əd'vaɪzɪdlɪ] *adv* (*deliberately*) deliberadamente; **~r** *n* = **advisor**; **advisor** *n* consejero/a; (*consultant*) asesor(a) *m/f*; **advisory** *adj* consultivo

advocate ['ædvəkeɪt] *vt* abogar por ♦ *n* [-kɪt] (*lawyer*) abogado/a; (*supporter*): **~ of** defensor(a) *m/f* de

Aegean [iː'dʒiːən] *n*: **the ~ (Sea)** el (Mar) Egeo

aerial ['ɛərɪəl] *n* antena ♦ *adj* aéreo

aerobics [ɛə'rəubɪks] *n* aerobic *m*

aeroplane ['ɛərəpleɪn] (*BRIT*) *n* avión *m*

aerosol ['ɛərəsɔl] *n* aerosol *m*

aesthetic [iːs'θetɪk] *adj* estético

afar [ə'fɑː*] *adv*: **from ~** desde lejos

affair [ə'fɛə*] *n* asunto; (*also*: **love ~**) aventura (amorosa)

affect [ə'fekt] *vt* (*influence*) afectar, influir en; (*afflict, concern*) afectar; (*move*) conmover; **~ed** *adj* afectado

affection [ə'fekʃən] *n* afecto, cariño; **~ate** *adj* afectuoso, cariñoso

affinity [ə'fɪnɪtɪ] *n* (*bond, rapport*): **to feel an ~ with** sentirse identificado con; (*resemblance*) afinidad *f*

afflict [ə'flɪkt] *vt* afligir

affluence ['æfluəns] *n* opulencia, riqueza

affluent ['æfluənt] *adj* (*wealthy*) acomodado; **the ~ society** la sociedad opulenta

afford [ə'fɔːd] *vt* (*provide*) proporcionar; **can we ~ (to buy) it?** ¿tenemos bastante dinero para comprarlo?

Afghanistan [æf'gænɪstæn] *n* Afganistán *m*

afield [ə'fiːld] *adv*: **far ~** muy lejos

afloat [ə'fləut] *adv* (*floating*) a flote

afoot [ə'fut] *adv*: **there is something ~** algo se está tramando

afraid [ə'freɪd] *adj*: **to be ~ of** (*person*) tener miedo a; (*thing*) tener miedo de; **to be ~ to** tener miedo de, temer; **I am ~ that** me temo que; **I am ~ not/so** lo siento, pero no/es así

afresh [ə'freʃ] *adv* de nuevo, otra vez

Africa ['æfrɪkə] *n* África; **~n** *adj, n* africano/a *m/f*

after ['ɑːftə*] *prep* (*time*) después de; (*place, order*) detrás de, tras ♦ *adv* después ♦ *conj* después (de) que; **what/ who are you ~?** ¿qué/a quién busca usted?; **~ having done/he left** después de haber hecho/después de que se marchó; **to name sb ~ sb** llamar a uno por uno; **it's twenty ~ eight** (*US*) son las ocho y veinte; **to ask ~ sb** preguntar por alguien; **~ all** después de todo, al fin y al cabo; **~ you!** ¡pase usted!; **~-effects** *npl* consecuencias *fpl*, efectos *mpl*; **~math** *n* consecuencias *fpl*, resultados *mpl*; **~noon** *n* tarde *f*; **~s** (*inf*) (*dessert*) postre *m*; **~-sales service** (*BRIT*) *n* servicio de asistencia pos-venta; **~-shave (lotion)** *n* aftershave *m*; **~sun (lotion/cream)** *n* loción *f*/crema para después del sol, aftersun *m*; **~thought** *n* ocurrencia (tardía); **~wards** (*US* **~ward**) *adv* después, más tarde

again [ə'gen] *adv* otra vez, de nuevo; **to do sth ~** volver a hacer algo; **~ and ~** una y otra vez

against [ə'genst] *prep* (*in opposition to*) en contra de; (*leaning on, touching*) contra, junto a

age [eɪdʒ] *n* edad *f*; (*period*) época ♦ *vi* envejecer(se) ♦ *vt* envejecer; **she is 20 years of ~** tiene 20 años; **to come of ~** llegar a la mayoría de edad; **it's been ~s since I saw you** hace siglos que no te veo; **~d 10** de 10 años de edad; **the ~d** ['eɪdʒɪd] *npl* los ancianos; **~ group** *n*: **to be in the same ~ group** tener la misma edad; **~ limit** *n* edad *f* mínima (*or* máxima)

agency ['eɪdʒənsɪ] *n* agencia

agenda [ə'dʒɛndə] *n* orden *m* del día

agent ['eɪdʒənt] *n* agente *m/f*; (*COMM: holding concession*) representante *m/f*, delegado/a; (*CHEM, fig*) agente *m*

aggravate ['ægrəveɪt] *vt* (*situation*) agravar; (*person*) irritar

aggregate ['ægrɪgeɪt] *n* conjunto

aggressive [ə'gresɪv] *adj* (*belligerent*) agresivo; (*assertive*) enérgico

aggrieved [ə'griːvd] *adj* ofendido, agraviado

aghast [ə'gɑːst] *adj* horrorizado

agile ['ædʒaɪl] *adj* ágil

agitate ['ædʒɪteɪt] *vt* (*trouble*) inquietar ♦ *vi*: **to ~ for/against** hacer campaña pro *or* en favor de/en contra de

AGM *n abbr* (= *annual general meeting*) asamblea anual

ago [ə'gəu] *adv*: **2 days ~** hace 2 días; **not long ~** hace poco; **how long ~?** ¿hace cuánto tiempo?

agog [ə'gɒg] *adj* (*eager*) ansioso; (*excited*) emocionado

agonizing ['ægənaɪzɪŋ] *adj* (*pain*) atroz; (*decision, wait*) angustioso

agony ['ægənɪ] *n* (*pain*) dolor *m* agudo; (*distress*) angustia; **to be in ~** retorcerse de dolor

agree [ə'griː] *vt* (*price, date*) acordar, quedar en ♦ *vi* (*have same opinion*): **to ~ (with/that)** estar de acuerdo (con/que); (*correspond*) coincidir, concordar; (*consent*) acceder; **to ~ with** (*subj: person*) estar de acuerdo con, ponerse de acuerdo con; (: *food*) sentar bien a; (*LING*) concordar con; **to ~ to sth/to do sth** consentir en algo/aceptar hacer algo; **to ~ that** (*admit*) estar de acuerdo en que; **~able** *adj* (*sensation*) agradable; (*person*) simpático; (*willing*) de acuerdo, conforme; **~d** *adj* (*time, place*) convenido; **~ment** *n* acuerdo; (*contract*) contrato; **in ~ment** de acuerdo, conforme

agricultural [ægrɪ'kʌltʃərəl] *adj* agrícola

agriculture ['ægrɪkʌltʃə*] *n* agricultura

aground [ə'graund] *adv*: **to run ~** (*NAUT*) encallar, embarrancar

ahead [ə'hed] *adv* (*in front*) delante; (*into the future*): **she had no time to think ~** no tenía tiempo de hacer planes para el futuro; **~ of** delante de; (*in advance of*) antes de; **~ of time** antes de la hora; **go right** *or* **straight ~** (*direction*) siga adelante; (*permission*) hazlo (*or* hágalo)

aid [eɪd] *n* ayuda, auxilio; (*device*) aparato ♦ *vt* ayudar, auxiliar; **in ~ of** a beneficio de

aide [eɪd] n (person, also MIL) ayudante m/f

AIDS [eɪdz] n abbr (= acquired immune deficiency syndrome) SIDA m

ailment ['eɪlmənt] n enfermedad f, achaque m

aim [eɪm] vt (gun, camera) apuntar; (missile, remark) dirigir; (blow) asestar ♦ vi (also: **take ~**) apuntar ♦ n (in shooting: skill) puntería; (objective) propósito, meta; **to ~ at** (with weapon) apuntar a; (objective) aspirar a, pretender; **to ~ to do** tener la intención de hacer; **~less** adj sin propósito, sin objeto

ain't [eɪnt] (inf) = **am not; aren't; isn't**

air [eə*] n aire m; (appearance) aspecto ♦ vt (room) ventilar; (clothes, ideas) airear ♦ cpd aéreo; **to throw sth into the ~** (ball etc) lanzar algo al aire; **by ~** (travel) en avión; **to be on the ~** (RADIO, TV) estar en antena; **~bed** (BRIT) n colchón m neumático; **~-conditioned** adj climatizado; **~ conditioning** n aire acondicionado; **~craft** n inv avión m; **~craft carrier** n porta(a)viones m inv; **~field** n campo de aviación; **A~ Force** n fuerzas fpl aéreas, aviación f; **~ freshener** n ambientador m; **~gun** n escopeta de aire comprimido; **~ hostess** (BRIT) n azafata f; **~ letter** (BRIT) n carta aérea; **~lift** n puente m aéreo; **~line** n línea aérea; **~liner** n avión m de pasajeros; **~mail** n: **by ~mail** por avión; **~plane** (US) n avión m; **~port** n aeropuerto m; **~ raid** n ataque m aéreo; **~sick** adj: **to be ~sick** marearse (en avión); **~space** n espacio aéreo; **~tight** adj hermético; **~-traffic controller** n controlador(a) m/f aéreo/a; **~y** adj (room) bien ventilado; (fig: manner) desenfadado

aisle [aɪl] n (of church) nave f; (of theatre, supermarket) pasillo; **~ seat** n (on plane) asiento de pasillo

ajar [ə'dʒɑː*] adj entreabierto

alarm [ə'lɑːm] n (in shop, bank) alarma; (anxiety) inquietud f ♦ vt asustar,

inquietar; **~ call** n (in hotel etc) alarma; **~ clock** n despertador m

alas [ə'læs] adv desgraciadamente

albeit [ɔːl'biːɪt] conj aunque

album ['ælbəm] n álbum m; (L.P.) elepé m

alcohol ['ælkəhɒl] n alcohol m; **~ic** [-'hɒlɪk] adj, n alcohólico/a m/f

ale [eɪl] n cerveza

alert [ə'lɜːt] adj (attentive) atento; (to danger, opportunity) alerta ♦ n alerta m, alarma ♦ vt poner sobre aviso; **to be on the ~** (also MIL) estar alerta or sobre aviso

algebra ['ældʒɪbrə] n álgebra

Algeria [æl'dʒɪərɪə] n Argelia

alias ['eɪlɪəs] adv alias, conocido por ♦ n (of criminal) apodo; (of writer) seudónimo

alibi ['ælɪbaɪ] n coartada

alien ['eɪlɪən] n (foreigner) extranjero/a; (extraterrestrial) extraterrestre m/f ♦ adj: **~ to** ajeno a; **~ate** vt enajenar, alejar

alight [ə'laɪt] adj ardiendo; (eyes) brillante ♦ vi (person) apearse, bajar; (bird) posarse

align [ə'laɪn] vt alinear

alike [ə'laɪk] adj semejantes, iguales ♦ adv igualmente, del mismo modo; **to look ~** parecerse

alimony ['ælɪmənɪ] n manutención f

alive [ə'laɪv] adj vivo; (lively) alegre

KEYWORD

all [ɔːl] adj (sg) todo/a; (pl) todos/as; **~ day** todo el día; **~ night** toda la noche; **~ men** todos los hombres; **~ five came** vinieron los cinco; **~ the books** todos los libros; **~ his life** toda su vida

♦ pron **1** todo; **I ate it ~, I ate ~ of it** me lo comí todo; **~ of us went** fuimos todos; **~ the boys went** fueron todos los chicos; **is that ~?** ¿eso es todo?, ¿algo más?; (in shop) ¿algo más?, ¿alguna cosa más?

2 (in phrases): **above ~** sobre todo; por encima de todo; **after ~** después de todo; **at ~: not at ~** (in answer to question) en absoluto; (in answer to thanks) ¡de nada!, ¡no hay de qué!; **I'm not at ~ tired** no estoy nada cansado/a; **anything at ~ will do** cualquier cosa viene bien; **~ in ~** a fin

de cuentas
♦ *adv*: ~ **alone** completamente solo/a;
it's not as hard as ~ that no es tan
difícil como lo pintas; ~ **the more/the
better** tanto más/mejor; ~ **but** casi; **the
score is 2 ~** están empatados a 2

all clear *n* (*after attack etc*) fin *m* de la
alerta; (*fig*) luz *f* verde
allege [ə'ledʒ] *vt* pretender; ~**dly**
[ə'ledʒɪdlɪ] *adv* supuestamente, según se
afirma
allegiance [ə'liːdʒəns] *n* lealtad *f*
allergy [ˈælədʒɪ] *n* alergia
alleviate [əˈliːvɪeɪt] *vt* aliviar
alley [ˈælɪ] *n* callejuela
alliance [əˈlaɪəns] *n* alianza
allied [ˈælaɪd] *adj* aliado
alligator [ˈælɪgeɪtə*] *n* (*ZOOL*) caimán *m*
all-in (*BRIT*) *adj, adv* (*charge*) todo incluido
all-night [ɔːl-] (*café, shop*) abierto toda la
noche; (*party*) que dura toda la noche
allocate [ˈæləkeɪt] *vt* (*money etc*) asignar
allot [əˈlɒt] *vt* asignar; ~**ment** *n* ración *f*;
(*garden*) parcela
all-out *adj* (*effort etc*) supremo; **all out**
adv con todas las fuerzas
allow [əˈlaʊ] *vt* permitir, dejar; (*a claim*)
admitir; (*sum, time etc*) dar, conceder;
(*concede*): **to ~ that** reconocer que; **to ~
sb to do** permitir a alguien hacer; **he is
~ed to ...** se le permite ...; ~ **for** *vt fus*
tener en cuenta; ~**ance** *n* subvención *f*;
(*welfare payment*) subsidio, pensión *f*;
(*pocket money*) dinero de bolsillo; (*tax
~ance*) desgravación *f*; **to make ~ances
for** (*person*) disculpar a; (*thing*) tener en
cuenta
alloy [ˈælɔɪ] *n* mezcla
all-: ~ **right** *adv* bien; (*as answer*)
¡conforme!, ¡está bien!; ~~**rounder** *n*:
he's a good ~~rounder se le da bien
todo; ~~**time** *adj* (*record*) de todos los
tiempos
alluring [əˈljuərɪŋ] *adj* atractivo,
tentador(a)
ally [ˈælaɪ] *n* aliado/a ♦ *vt*: **to ~ o.s. with**

aliarse con
almighty [ɔːlˈmaɪtɪ] *adj* todopoderoso;
(*row etc*) imponente
almond [ˈɑːmənd] *n* almendra
almost [ˈɔːlməʊst] *adv* casi
alone [əˈləʊn] *adj* solo; **to leave sb ~**
dejar a uno en paz; **to leave sth ~** no
tocar algo, dejar algo sin tocar; **let ~ ...** y
mucho menos ...
along [əˈlɒŋ] *prep* a lo largo de, por ♦ *adv*:
is he coming ~ with us? ¿viene con
nosotros?; **he was limping ~** iba
cojeando; ~ **with** junto con; **all ~** (*all the
time*) desde el principio; ~**side** *prep* al
lado de ♦ *adv* al lado
aloof [əˈluːf] *adj* reservado ♦ *adv*: **to stand
~** mantenerse apartado
aloud [əˈlaʊd] *adv* en voz alta
alphabet [ˈælfəbet] *n* alfabeto
Alps [ælps] *npl*: **the ~** los Alpes
already [ɔːlˈredɪ] *adv* ya
alright [ˈɔːlˈraɪt] (*BRIT*) *adv* = **all right**
Alsatian [ælˈseɪʃən] *n* (*dog*) pastor *m*
alemán
also [ˈɔːlsəʊ] *adv* también, además
altar [ˈɒltə*] *n* altar *m*
alter [ˈɒltə*] *vt* cambiar, modificar ♦ *vi*
cambiar; ~**ation** [ɒltəˈreɪʃən] *n* cambio; (*to
clothes*) arreglo; (*to building*) arreglos *mpl*
alternate [*adj* ɒlˈtɜːnɪt, *vb* ˈɒltɜːneɪt] *adj*
(*actions etc*) alternativo; (*events*) alterno;
(*US*) = **alternative** ♦ *vi*: **to ~ (with)**
alternar (con); **on ~ days** un día sí y otro
no; **alternating current** [-neɪtɪŋ] *n*
corriente *f* alterna
alternative [ɒlˈtɜːnətɪv] *adj* alternativo ♦ *n*
alternativa; ~ **medicine** medicina
alternativa; ~**ly** *adv*: ~**ly one could ...**
por otra parte se podría ...
although [ɔːlˈðəʊ] *conj* aunque
altitude [ˈæltɪtjuːd] *n* altura
alto [ˈæltəʊ] *n* (*female*) contralto *f*; (*male*)
alto
altogether [ɔːltəˈgeðə*] *adv*
completamente, del todo; (*on the whole*)
en total, en conjunto
aluminium [æljuˈmɪnɪəm] (*BRIT*),

aluminum [ə'luːmɪnəm] (*US*) *n* aluminio

always ['ɔːlweɪz] *adv* siempre

Alzheimer's (disease) ['æltshaɪməz-] *n* enfermedad *f* de Alzheimer

AM *n abbr* (= *Assembly Member*) parlamentario/a *m/f*

am [æm] *vb see* **be**

a.m. *adv abbr* (= *ante meridiem*) de la mañana

amalgamate [ə'mælgəmeɪt] *vi* amalgamarse ♦ *vt* amalgamar, unir

amateur ['æmətə⁎] *n* aficionado/a, amateur *m/f*; **~ish** *adj* inexperto

amaze [ə'meɪz] *vt* asombrar, pasmar; **to be ~d (at)** quedar pasmado (de); **~ment** *n* asombro, sorpresa; **amazing** *adj* extraordinario; (*fantastic*) increíble

Amazon ['æməzən] *n* (*GEO*) Amazonas *m*

ambassador [æm'bæsədə⁎] *n* embajador(a) *m/f*

amber ['æmbə⁎] *n* ámbar *m*; **at ~** (*BRIT: AUT*) en el amarillo

ambiguous [æm'bɪgjuəs] *adj* ambiguo

ambition [æm'bɪʃən] *n* ambición *f*; **ambitious** [-ʃəs] *adj* ambicioso

ambulance ['æmbjuləns] *n* ambulancia

ambush ['æmbuʃ] *n* emboscada ♦ *vt* tender una emboscada a

amenable [ə'miːnəbl] *adj*: **to be ~ to** dejarse influir por

amend [ə'mend] *vt* enmendar; **to make ~s** dar cumplida satisfacción

amenities [ə'miːnɪtɪz] *npl* comodidades *fpl*

America [ə'merɪkə] *n* (*USA*) Estados *mpl* Unidos; **~n** *adj, n* norteamericano/a *m/f*; estadounidense *m/f*

amiable ['eɪmɪəbl] *adj* amable, simpático

amicable ['æmɪkəbl] *adj* amistoso, amigable

amid(st) [ə'mɪd(st)] *prep* entre, en medio de

amiss [ə'mɪs] *adv*: **to take sth ~** tomar algo a mal; **there's something ~** pasa algo

ammonia [ə'məunɪə] *n* amoníaco

ammunition [æmju'nɪʃən] *n* municiones *fpl*

amnesty ['æmnɪstɪ] *n* amnistía

amok [ə'mɔk] *adv*: **to run ~** enloquecerse, desbocarse

among(st) [ə'mʌŋ(st)] *prep* entre, en medio de

amorous ['æmərəs] *adj* amoroso

amount [ə'maunt] *n* (*gen*) cantidad *f*; (*of bill etc*) suma, importe *m* ♦ *vi*: **to ~ to** sumar; (*be same as*) equivaler a, significar

amp(ère) ['æmp(eə⁎)] *n* amperio

ample ['æmpl] *adj* (*large*) grande; (*abundant*) abundante; (*enough*) bastante, suficiente

amplifier ['æmplɪfaɪə⁎] *n* amplificador *m*

amuse [ə'mjuːz] *vt* divertir; (*distract*) distraer, entretener; **~ment** *n* diversión *f*; (*pastime*) pasatiempo; (*laughter*) risa; **~ment arcade** *n* salón *m* de juegos; **~ment park** *n* parque *m* de atracciones

an [æn] *indef art see* **a**

anaemic [ə'niːmɪk] (*US* **anemic**) *adj* anémico; (*fig*) soso, insípido

anaesthetic [ænɪs'θetɪk] *n* (*US* **anesthetic**) anestesia

analog(ue) ['ænəlɔg] *adj* (*computer, watch*) analógico

analyse ['ænəlaɪz] (*US* **analyze**) *vt* analizar; **analysis** [ə'næləsɪs] (*pl* **analyses**) *n* análisis *m inv*; **analyst** [-lɪst] *n* (*political analyst, psychoanalyst*) analista *m/f*

analyze ['ænəlaɪz] (*US*) *vt* = **analyse**

anarchist ['ænəkɪst] *n* anarquista *m/f*

anatomy [ə'nætəmɪ] *n* anatomía

ancestor ['ænsɪstə⁎] *n* antepasado

anchor ['æŋkə⁎] *n* ancla, áncora ♦ *vi* (*also: to drop ~*) anclar ♦ *vt* anclar; **to weigh ~** levar anclas

anchovy ['æntʃəvɪ] *n* anchoa

ancient ['eɪnʃənt] *adj* antiguo

ancillary [æn'sɪlərɪ] *adj* auxiliar

and [ænd] *conj* y; (*before i-, hi- +consonant*) e; **men ~ women** hombres y mujeres; **father ~ son** padre e hijo; **trees ~ grass** árboles y hierba; **~ so on** etcétera, y así sucesivamente; **try ~ come** procura venir; **he talked ~ talked** habló sin parar; **better ~ better** cada vez mejor

Andes ['ændi:z] *npl*: **the ~** los Andes

anemic *etc* [ə'ni:mɪk] (*US*) = **anaemic** *etc*

anesthetic *etc* [ænɪs'θetɪk] (*US*)
  = **anaesthetic** *etc*

anew [ə'nju:] *adv* de nuevo, otra vez

angel ['eɪndʒəl] *n* ángel *m*

anger ['æŋgə*] *n* cólera

angina [æn'dʒaɪnə] *n* angina (del pecho)

angle ['æŋgl] *n* ángulo; **from their ~** desde su punto de vista

angler ['æŋglə*] *n* pescador(a) *m/f* (de caña)

Anglican ['æŋglɪkən] *adj, n* anglicano/a *m/f*

angling ['æŋglɪŋ] *n* pesca con caña

Anglo... [æŋgləu] *prefix* anglo...

angrily ['æŋgrɪlɪ] *adv* coléricamente, airadamente

angry ['æŋgrɪ] *adj* enfadado, airado; (*wound*) inflamado; **to be ~ with sb/at sth** estar enfadado con alguien/por algo; **to get ~** enfadarse, enojarse

anguish ['æŋgwɪʃ] *n* (*physical*) tormentos *mpl*; (*mental*) angustia

animal ['ænɪməl] *n* animal *m*; (*pej: person*) bestia ♦ *adj* animal

animate ['ænɪmɪt] *adj* vivo; **~d** [-meɪtɪd] *adj* animado

aniseed ['ænɪsi:d] *n* anís *m*

ankle ['æŋkl] *n* tobillo *m*; **~ sock** *n* calcetín *m* corto

annex [*n* 'æneks, *vb* æ'neks] *n* (*also: BRIT: annexe*) (*building*) edificio anexo ♦ *vt* (*territory*) anexionar

annihilate [ə'naɪəleɪt] *vt* aniquilar

anniversary [ænɪ'vɜ:sərɪ] *n* aniversario *m*

announce [ə'nauns] *vt* anunciar; **~ment** *n* anuncio; (*official*) declaración *f*; **~r** *n* (*RADIO*) locutor(a) *m/f*; (*TV*) presentador(a) *m/f*

annoy [ə'nɔɪ] *vt* molestar, fastidiar; **don't get ~ed!** ¡no se enfade!; **~ance** *n* enojo; **~ing** *adj* molesto, fastidioso; (*person*) pesado

annual ['ænjuəl] *adj* anual ♦ *n* (*BOT*) anual *m*; (*book*) anuario; **~ly** *adv* anualmente, cada año

annul [ə'nʌl] *vt* anular

annum ['ænəm] *n* see **per**

anonymous [ə'nɒnɪməs] *adj* anónimo

anorak ['ænəræk] *n* anorak *m*

anorexia [ænə'reksɪə] *n* (*MED: also:* **~ nervosa**) anorexia

another [ə'nʌðə*] *adj* (*one more, a different one*) otro ♦ *pron* otro; *see* **one**

answer ['ɑ:nsə*] *n* contestación *f*, respuesta; (*to problem*) solución *f* ♦ *vi* contestar, responder ♦ *vt* (*reply to*) contestar a, responder a; (*problem*) resolver; (*prayer*) escuchar; **in ~ to your letter** contestando or en contestación a su carta; **to ~ the phone** contestar or coger el teléfono; **to ~ the bell** or **the door** acudir a la puerta; **~ back** *vi* replicar, ser respondón/ona; **~ for** *vt fus* responder de or por; **~ to** *vt fus* (*description*) corresponder a; **~able** *adj*: **~able to sb for sth** responsable ante uno de algo; **~ing machine** *n* contestador *m* automático

ant [ænt] *n* hormiga

antagonism [æn'tægənɪzm] *n* antagonismo, hostilidad *f*

antagonize [æn'tægənaɪz] *vt* provocar la enemistad de

Antarctic [ænt'ɑ:ktɪk] *n*: **the ~** el Antártico

antelope ['æntɪləup] *n* antílope *m*

antenatal ['æntɪ'neɪtl] *adj* antenatal, prenatal; **~ clinic** *n* clínica prenatal

anthem ['ænθəm] *n*: **national ~** himno nacional

anthropology [ænθrə'pɒlədʒɪ] *n* antropología

anti... [æntɪ] *prefix* anti...; **~-aircraft** [-'eəkrɑ:ft] *adj* antiaéreo; **~biotic** [-baɪ'ɔtɪk] *n* antibiótico; **~body** ['æntɪbɒdɪ] *n* anticuerpo

anticipate [æn'tɪsɪpeɪt] *vt* prever; (*expect*) esperar, contar con; (*look forward to*) esperar con ilusión; (*do first*) anticiparse a, adelantarse a; **anticipation** [-'peɪʃən] *n* (*expectation*) previsión *f*; (*eagerness*) ilusión *f*, expectación *f*

anticlimax [æntɪ'klaɪmæks] *n* decepción *f*

anticlockwise [æntɪ'klɔkwaɪz] (*BRIT*) *adv* en dirección contraria a la de las agujas del reloj

antics ['æntɪks] *npl* gracias *fpl*

anticyclone [æntɪ'saɪkləun] *n* anticiclón *m*

antidepressant ['æntɪdɪ'presnt] *n* antidepressivo

antidote ['æntɪdəut] *n* antídoto

antifreeze ['æntɪfriːz] *n* anticongelante *m*

antihistamine [æntɪ'hɪstəmiːn] *n* antihistamínico

antiquated ['æntɪkweɪtɪd] *adj* anticuado

antique [æn'tiːk] *n* antigüedad *f* ♦ *adj* antiguo; ~ **dealer** *n* anticuario/a; ~ **shop** *n* tienda de antigüedades

antiquity [æn'tɪkwɪtɪ] *n* antigüedad *f*

antiseptic [æntɪ'septɪk] *adj*, *n* antiséptico

antlers ['æntləz] *npl* cuernas *fpl*, cornamenta *sg*

anus ['eɪnəs] *n* ano

anvil ['ænvɪl] *n* yunque *m*

anxiety [æŋ'zaɪətɪ] *n* inquietud *f*; (*MED*) ansiedad *f*; ~ **to do** deseo de hacer

anxious ['æŋkʃəs] *adj* inquieto, preocupado; (*worrying*) preocupante; (*keen*): **to be ~ to do** tener muchas ganas de hacer

⸻ KEYWORD ⸻

any ['enɪ] *adj* 1 (*in questions etc*) algún/ alguna; **have you ~ butter/children?** ¿tienes mantequilla/hijos?; **if there are ~ tickets left** si quedan billetes, si queda algún billete

2 (*with negative*): **I haven't ~ money/ books** no tengo dinero/libros

3 (*no matter which*) cualquier; ~ **excuse will do** valdrá *or* servirá cualquier excusa; **choose ~ book you like** escoge el libro que quieras; ~ **teacher you ask will tell you** cualquier profesor al que preguntes te lo dirá

4 (*in phrases*): **in ~ case** de todas formas, en cualquier caso; ~ **day now** cualquier día (de estos); **at ~ moment** en cualquier momento, de un momento a otro; **at ~ rate** en todo caso; ~ **time: come (at) ~**

time ven cuando quieras; **he might come (at) ~ time** podría llegar de un momento a otro

♦ *pron* 1 (*in questions etc*): **have you got ~?** ¿tienes alguno(s)/a(s)?; **can ~ of you sing?** ¿sabe cantar alguno de vosotros/ ustedes?

2 (*with negative*): **I haven't ~ (of them)** no tengo ninguno

3 (*no matter which one(s)*): **take ~ of those books (you like)** toma el libro que quieras de ésos

♦ *adv* 1 (*in questions etc*): **do you want ~ more soup/sandwiches?** ¿quieres más sopa/bocadillos?; **are you feeling ~ better?** ¿te sientes algo mejor?

2 (*with negative*): **I can't hear him ~ more** ya no le oigo; **don't wait ~ longer** no esperes más

⸻

anybody ['enɪbɒdɪ] *pron* cualquiera; (*in interrogative sentences*) alguien; (*in negative sentences*): **I don't see ~** no veo a nadie; **if ~ should phone ...** si llama alguien ...

anyhow ['enɪhau] *adv* (*at any rate*) de todos modos, de todas formas; (*haphazard*): **do it ~ you like** hazlo como quieras; **she leaves things just ~** deja las cosas como quiera *or* de cualquier modo; **I shall go ~** de todos modos iré

anyone ['enɪwʌn] *pron* = **anybody**

anything ['enɪθɪŋ] *pron* (*in questions etc*) algo, alguna cosa; (*with negative*) nada; **can you see ~?** ¿ves algo?; **if ~ happens to me ...** si algo me ocurre ...; (*no matter what*): **you can say ~ you like** puedes decir lo que quieras; ~ **will do** vale todo *or* cualquier cosa; **he'll eat ~** come de todo *or* lo que sea

anyway ['enɪweɪ] *adv* (*at any rate*) de todos modos, de todas formas; **I shall go ~** iré de todos modos; (*besides*): **~, I couldn't come even if I wanted to** además, no podría venir aunque quisiera; **why are you phoning, ~?** ¿entonces, por qué llamas?, ¿por qué llamas, pues?

anywhere ['ɛnɪweə*] *adv* (*in questions etc*): **can you see him ~?** ¿le ves por algún lado?; **are you going ~?** ¿vas a algún sitio?; (*with negative*): **I can't see him ~** no le veo por ninguna parte; **~ in the world** (*no matter where*) en cualquier parte (del mundo); **put the books down ~** deja los libros donde quieras

apart [ə'pɑːt] *adv* (*aside*) aparte; (*situation*): **~ (from)** separado (de); (*movement*): **to pull ~** separar; **10 miles ~** separados por 10 millas; **to take ~** desmontar; **~ from** *prep* aparte de

apartheid [ə'pɑːteɪt] *n* apartheid *m*

apartment [ə'pɑːtmənt] *n* (*US*) piso (*SP*), departamento (*AM*), apartamento; (*room*) cuarto; **~ building** (*US*) *n* edificio de apartamentos

apathetic [æpə'θɛtɪk] *adj* apático, indiferente

ape [eɪp] *n* mono ♦ *vt* imitar, remedar

aperitif [ə'pɛrɪtɪf] *n* aperitivo

aperture ['æpətʃjuə*] *n* rendija, resquicio; (*PHOT*) abertura

APEX ['eɪpɛks] *n abbr* (= *Advanced Purchase Excursion Fare*) tarifa APEX *f*

apex *n* ápice *m*; (*fig*) cumbre *f*

apiece [ə'piːs] *adv* cada uno

aplomb [ə'plɔm] *n* aplomo

apologetic [əpɔlə'dʒɛtɪk] *adj* de disculpa; (*person*) arrepentido

apologize [ə'pɔlədʒaɪz] *vi*: **to ~ (for sth to sb)** disculparse (con alguien de algo)

apology [ə'pɔlədʒɪ] *n* disculpa, excusa

apostrophe [ə'pɔstrəfɪ] *n* apóstrofo *m*

appal [ə'pɔːl] *vt* horrorizar, espantar; **~ling** *adj* espantoso; (*awful*) pésimo

apparatus [æpə'reɪtəs] *n* (*equipment*) equipo; (*organization*) aparato; (*in gymnasium*) aparatos *mpl*

apparel [ə'pærl] (*US*) *n* ropa

apparent [ə'pærənt] *adj* aparente; (*obvious*) evidente; **~ly** *adv* por lo visto, al parecer

appeal [ə'piːl] *vi* (*LAW*) apelar ♦ *n* (*LAW*) apelación *f*; (*request*) llamamiento; (*plea*) petición *f*; (*charm*) atractivo; **to ~ for** reclamar; **to ~ to** (*be attractive to*) atraer; **it doesn't ~ to me** no me atrae, no me llama la atención; **~ing** *adj* (*attractive*) atractivo

appear [ə'pɪə*] *vi* aparecer, presentarse; (*LAW*) comparecer; (*publication*) salir (a luz), publicarse; (*seem*) parecer; **to ~ on TV/in "Hamlet"** salir por la tele/hacer un papel en "Hamlet"; **it would ~ that** parecería que; **~ance** *n* aparición *f*; (*look*) apariencia, aspecto

appease [ə'piːz] *vt* (*pacify*) apaciguar; (*satisfy*) satisfacer

appendices [ə'pɛndɪsiːz] *npl of* **appendix**

appendicitis [əpɛndɪ'saɪtɪs] *n* apendicitis *f*

appendix [ə'pɛndɪks] (*pl* **appendices**) *n* apéndice *m*

appetite ['æpɪtaɪt] *n* apetito; (*fig*) deseo, anhelo

appetizer ['æpɪtaɪzə*] *n* (*drink*) aperitivo; (*food*) tapas *fpl* (*SP*)

applaud [ə'plɔːd] *vt*, *vi* aplaudir

applause [ə'plɔːz] *n* aplausos *mpl*

apple ['æpl] *n* manzana; **~ tree** *n* manzano

appliance [ə'plaɪəns] *n* aparato

applicable [ə'plɪkəbl] *adj* (*relevant*): **to be ~ (to)** referirse (a)

applicant ['æplɪkənt] *n* candidato/a; solicitante *m/f*

application [æplɪ'keɪʃən] *n* aplicación *f*; (*for a job etc*) solicitud *f*, petición *f*; **~ form** *n* solicitud *f*

applied [ə'plaɪd] *adj* aplicado

apply [ə'plaɪ] *vt* (*paint etc*) poner; (*law etc: put into practice*) poner en vigor ♦ *vi*: **to ~ to** (*ask*) dirigirse a; (*be applicable*) ser aplicable a; **to ~ for** (*permit, grant, job*) solicitar; **to ~ o.s. to** aplicarse a, dedicarse a

appoint [ə'pɔɪnt] *vt* (*to post*) nombrar; **~ed** *adj*: **at the ~ed time** a la hora señalada; **~ment** *n* (*with client*) cita; (*act*) nombramiento; (*post*) puesto; (*at hairdresser etc*): **to have an ~ment** tener hora; **to make an ~ment (with sb)** citarse (con uno)

appraisal [ə'preɪzl] *n* valoración *f*

appreciate [ə'priːʃieɪt] *vt* apreciar, tener en mucho; (*be grateful for*) agradecer; (*be aware of*) comprender ♦ *vi* (COMM) aumentar(se) en valor; **appreciation** [-'eɪʃən] *n* apreciación *f*; (*gratitude*) reconocimiento, agradecimiento; (COMM) aumento en valor

appreciative [ə'priːʃiətɪv] *adj* apreciativo; (*comment*) agradecido

apprehensive [æprɪ'hensɪv] *adj* aprensivo

apprentice [ə'prentɪs] *n* aprendiz/a *m/f*; **~ship** *n* aprendizaje *m*

approach [ə'prəutʃ] *vi* acercarse ♦ *vt* acercarse a; (*ask, apply to*) dirigirse a; (*situation, problem*) abordar ♦ *n* acercamiento; (*access*) acceso; (*to problem, situation*): **~ (to)** actitud *f* (ante); **~able** *adj* (*person*) abordable; (*place*) accesible

appropriate [*adj* ə'prəuprɪɪt, *vb* ə'prəuprieɪt] *adj* apropiado, conveniente ♦ *vt* (*take*) apropiarse de

approval [ə'pruːvəl] *n* aprobación *f*, visto bueno; (*permission*) consentimiento; **on ~** (COMM) a prueba

approve [ə'pruːv] *vt* aprobar; **~ of** *vt fus* (*thing*) aprobar; (*person*): **they don't ~ of her** (ella) no les parece bien

approximate [ə'prɒksɪmɪt] *adj* aproximado; **~ly** *adv* aproximadamente, más o menos

apricot ['eɪprɪkɒt] *n* albaricoque *m* (SP), damasco (AM)

April ['eɪprəl] *n* abril *m*; **~ Fools' Day** *n* el primero de abril; ≈ día *m* de los Inocentes (*28 December*)

apron ['eɪprən] *n* delantal *m*

apt [æpt] *adj* acertado, apropiado; (*likely*): **~ to do** propenso a hacer

aquarium [ə'kwɛərɪəm] *n* acuario

Aquarius [ə'kwɛərɪəs] *n* Acuario

Arab ['ærəb] *adj*, *n* árabe *m/f*

Arabian [ə'reɪbɪən] *adj* árabe

Arabic ['ærəbɪk] *adj* árabe; (*numerals*) arábigo ♦ *n* árabe *m*

arable ['ærəbl] *adj* cultivable

Aragon ['ærəgən] *n* Aragón *m*

arbitrary ['ɑːbɪtrərɪ] *adj* arbitrario

arbitration [ɑːbɪ'treɪʃən] *n* arbitraje *m*

arcade [ɑː'keɪd] *n* (*round a square*) soportales *mpl*; (*shopping mall*) galería comercial

arch [ɑːtʃ] *n* arco; (*of foot*) arco del pie ♦ *vt* arquear

archaeologist [ɑːkɪ'ɒlədʒɪst] (US **archeologist**) *n* arqueólogo/a

archaeology [ɑːkɪ'ɒlədʒɪ] (US **archeology**) *n* arqueología

archbishop [ɑːtʃ'bɪʃəp] *n* arzobispo

archeology *etc* [ɑːkɪ'ɒlədʒɪ] (US) = **archaeology** *etc*

archery ['ɑːtʃərɪ] *n* tiro al arco

architect ['ɑːkɪtekt] *n* arquitecto/a; **~ure** *n* arquitectura

archives ['ɑːkaɪvz] *npl* archivo

Arctic ['ɑːktɪk] *adj* ártico ♦ *n*: **the ~** el Ártico

ardent ['ɑːdənt] *adj* ardiente, apasionado

arduous ['ɑːdjuəs] *adj* (*task*) arduo; (*journey*) agotador(a)

are [ɑː*] *vb see* **be**

area ['ɛərɪə] *n* área, región *f*; (*part of place*) zona; (MATH *etc*) área, superficie *f*; (*in room: e.g. dining ~*) parte *f*; (*of knowledge, experience*) campo

arena [ə'riːnə] *n* estadio; (*of circus*) pista

aren't [ɑːnt] = **are not**

Argentina [ɑːdʒən'tiːnə] *n* Argentina; **Argentinian** [-'tɪnɪən] *adj*, *n* argentino/a *m/f*

arguably ['ɑːgjuəblɪ] *adv* posiblemente

argue ['ɑːgjuː] *vi* (*quarrel*) discutir, pelearse; (*reason*) razonar, argumentar; **to ~ that** sostener que

argument ['ɑːgjumənt] *n* discusión *f*, pelea; (*reasons*) argumento; **~ative** [-'mentətɪv] *adj* discutidor(a)

Aries ['ɛərɪz] *n* Aries *m*

arise [ə'raɪz] (*pt* **arose**, *pp* **arisen**) *vi* surgir, presentarse

arisen [ə'rɪzn] *pp of* **arise**

aristocrat ['ærɪstəkræt] *n* aristócrata *m/f*

arithmetic [ə'rɪθmətɪk] *n* aritmética

ark [ɑːk] *n*: **Noah's A~** el Arca *f* de Noé
arm [ɑːm] *n* brazo ♦ *vt* armar; **~s** *npl*
armas *fpl*; **~ in ~** cogidos del brazo
armaments ['ɑːməmənts] *npl* armamento
armchair ['ɑːmtʃeə*] *n* sillón *m*, butaca
armed [ɑːmd] *adj* armado; **~ robbery** *n*
robo a mano armada
armour ['ɑːmə*] (*US* **armor**) *n* armadura;
(*MIL: tanks*) blindaje *m*; **~ed car** *n* coche
m (*SP*) *or* carro (*AM*) blindado
armpit ['ɑːmpɪt] *n* sobaco, axila
armrest ['ɑːmrest] *n* apoyabrazos *m inv*
army ['ɑːmɪ] *n* ejército, (*fig*) multitud *f*
aroma [ə'rəumə] *n* aroma *m*, fragancia;
~therapy *n* aromaterapia
arose [ə'rəuz] *pt of* **arise**
around [ə'raund] *adv* alrededor; (*in the
area*) **there is no one else ~** no hay
nadie más por aquí ♦ *prep* alrededor de
arouse [ə'rauz] *vt* despertar; (*anger*)
provocar
arrange [ə'reɪndʒ] *vt* arreglar, ordenar;
(*organize*) organizar; **to ~ to do sth**
quedar en hacer algo; **~ment** *n* arreglo;
(*agreement*) acuerdo; **~ments** *npl*
(*preparations*) preparativos *mpl*
array [ə'reɪ] *n*: **~ of** (*things*) serie *f* de;
(*people*) conjunto de
arrears [ə'rɪəz] *npl* atrasos *mpl*; **to be in ~
with one's rent** estar retrasado en el
pago del alquiler
arrest [ə'rest] *vt* detener; (*sb's attention*)
llamar ♦ *n* detención *f*; **under ~** detenido
arrival [ə'raɪvl] *n* llegada; **new ~** recién
llegado/a; (*baby*) recién nacido
arrive [ə'raɪv] *vi* llegar; (*baby*) nacer
arrogant ['ærəgənt] *adj* arrogante
arrow ['ærəu] *n* flecha
arse [ɑːs] (*BRIT: inf!*) *n* culo, trasero
arson ['ɑːsn] *n* incendio premeditado
art [ɑːt] *n* arte *m*; (*skill*) destreza; **A~s** *npl*
(*SCOL*) Letras *fpl*
artery ['ɑːtərɪ] *n* arteria
art gallery *n* pinacoteca; (*saleroom*)
galería de arte
arthritis [ɑː'θraɪtɪs] *n* artritis *f*
artichoke ['ɑːtɪtʃəuk] *n* alcachofa;

Jerusalem ~ aguaturma
article ['ɑːtɪkl] *n* artículo; (*BRIT: LAW:
training*): **~s** *npl* contrato de aprendizaje;
~ of clothing prenda de vestir
articulate [*adj* ɑː'tɪkjulɪt, *vb* ɑː'tɪkjuleɪt] *adj*
claro, bien expresado ♦ *vt* expresar; **~d
lorry** (*BRIT*) *n* trailer *m*
artificial [ɑːtɪ'fɪʃəl] *adj* artificial; (*affected*)
afectado
artillery [ɑː'tɪlərɪ] *n* artillería
artisan ['ɑːtɪzæn] *n* artesano
artist ['ɑːtɪst] *n* artista *m/f*; (*MUS*) intérprete
m/f; **~ic** [ɑː'tɪstɪk] *adj* artístico; **~ry** *n* arte
m, habilidad *f* (artística)
art school *n* escuela de bellas artes

KEYWORD

as [æz] *conj* **1** (*referring to time*) cuando,
mientras; a medida que; **~ the years
went by** con el paso de los años; **he
came in ~ I was leaving** entró cuando
me marchaba; **~ from tomorrow** desde
or a partir de mañana
2 (*in comparisons*): **~ big ~** tan grande
como; **twice ~ big ~** el doble de grande
que; **~ much money/many books ~**
tanto dinero/tantos libros como; **~ soon
~** en cuanto
3 (*since, because*) como, ya que; **he left
early ~ he had to be home by 10** se fue
temprano ya que tenía que estar en casa
a las 10
4 (*referring to manner, way*): **do ~ you
wish** haz lo que quieras; **~ she said**
como dijo; **he gave it to me ~ a present**
me lo dio de regalo
5 (*in the capacity of*): **he works ~ a
barman** trabaja de barman; **~ chairman
of the company, he ...** como presidente
de la compañía, ...
6 (*concerning*): **~ for** *or* **to that** por *or* en
lo que respecta a eso
7: **~ if** *or* **though** como si; **he looked ~ if
he was ill** parecía como si estuviera
enfermo, tenía aspecto de enfermo; *see
also* **long**; **such**; **well**

a.s.a.p. *abbr* (= *as soon as possible*) cuanto antes

asbestos [æz'bestəs] *n* asbesto, amianto

ascend [ə'send] *vt* subir; (*throne*) ascender or subir a

ascent [ə'sent] *n* subida; (*slope*) cuesta, pendiente *f*

ascertain [æsə'teɪn] *vt* averiguar

ash [æʃ] *n* ceniza; (*tree*) fresno

ashamed [ə'feɪmd] *adj* avergonzado, apenado (*AM*); **to be ~ of** avergonzarse de

ashore [ə'ʃɔ:*] *adv* en tierra; (*swim etc*) a tierra

ashtray ['æʃtreɪ] *n* cenicero

Ash Wednesday *n* miércoles *m* de Ceniza

Asia ['eɪʃə] *n* Asia; **~n** *adj*, *n* asiático/a *m/f*

aside [ə'saɪd] *adv* a un lado ♦ *n* aparte *m*

ask [ɑ:sk] *vt* (*question*) preguntar; (*invite*) invitar; **to ~ sb sth/to do sth** preguntar algo a alguien/pedir a alguien que haga algo; **to ~ sb about sth** preguntar algo a alguien; **to ~ (sb) a question** hacer una pregunta (a alguien); **to ~ sb out to dinner** invitar a cenar a uno; **~ after** *vt fus* preguntar por; **~ for** *vt fus* pedir; (*trouble*) buscar

asking price *n* precio inicial

asleep [ə'sli:p] *adj* dormido; **to fall ~** dormirse, quedarse dormido

asparagus [əs'pærəgəs] *n* (*plant*) espárrago; (*food*) espárragos *mpl*

aspect ['æspekt] *n* aspecto, apariencia; (*direction in which a building etc faces*) orientación *f*

aspersions [əs'pə:ʃənz] *npl*: **to cast ~ on** difamar a, calumniar a

asphyxiation [æsfɪksɪ'eɪʃən] *n* asfixia

aspire [əs'paɪə*] *vi*: **to ~ to** aspirar a, ambicionar

aspirin ['æsprɪn] *n* aspirina

ass [æs] *n* asno, burro; (*inf*: *idiot*) imbécil *m/f*; (*US*: *inf!*) culo, trasero

assailant [ə'seɪlənt] *n* asaltador(a) *m/f*, agresor(a) *m/f*

assassinate [ə'sæsɪneɪt] *vt* asesinar;

assassination [əsæsɪ'neɪʃən] *n* asesinato

assault [ə'sɔ:lt] *n* asalto; (*LAW*) agresión *f* ♦ *vt* asaltar, atacar; (*sexually*) violar

assemble [ə'sembl] *vt* reunir, juntar; (*TECH*) montar ♦ *vi* reunirse, juntarse

assembly [ə'semblɪ] *n* reunión *f*, asamblea; (*parliament*) parlamento; (*construction*) montaje *m*; **~ line** *n* cadena de montaje

assent [ə'sent] *n* asentimiento, aprobación *f*

assert [ə'sə:t] *vt* afirmar; (*authority*) hacer valer; **~ion** [-ʃən] *n* afirmación *f*

assess [ə'ses] *vt* valorar, calcular; (*tax, damages*) fijar; (*for tax*) gravar; **~ment** *n* valoración *f*; (*for tax*) gravamen *m*; **~or** *n* asesor(a) *m/f*

asset ['æset] *n* ventaja; **~s** *npl* (*COMM*) activo; (*property, funds*) fondos *mpl*

assign [ə'saɪn] *vt*: **to ~ (to)** (*date*) fijar (para); (*task*) asignar (a); (*resources*) destinar (a); **~ment** *n* tarea

assist [ə'sɪst] *vt* ayudar; **~ance** *n* ayuda, auxilio; **~ant** *n* ayudante *m/f*; (*BRIT*: *also*: **shop ~ant**) dependiente/a *m/f*

associate [*adj*, *n* ə'səʊʃɪɪt, *vb* ə'səʊʃɪeɪt] *adj* asociado ♦ *n* (*at work*) colega *m/f* ♦ *vt* asociar; (*ideas*) relacionar ♦ *vi*: **to ~ with sb** tratar con alguien

association [əsəʊsɪ'eɪʃən] *n* asociación *f*

assorted [ə'sɔ:tɪd] *adj* surtido, variado

assortment [ə'sɔ:tmənt] *n* (*of shapes, colours*) surtido; (*of books*) colección *f*; (*of people*) mezcla

assume [ə'ʃju:m] *vt* suponer; (*responsibilities*) asumir; (*attitude*) adoptar, tomar

assumption [ə'sʌmpʃən] *n* suposición *f*, presunción *f*; (*of power etc*) toma

assurance [ə'ʃʊərəns] *n* garantía, promesa; (*confidence*) confianza, aplomo; (*insurance*) seguro

assure [ə'ʃʊə*] *vt* asegurar

asthma ['æsmə] *n* asma

astonish [ə'stɒnɪʃ] *vt* asombrar, pasmar; **~ment** *n* asombro, sorpresa

astound [ə'staund] *vt* asombrar, pasmar

astray [ə'streɪ] *adv*: **to go** ~ extraviarse; **to lead** ~ (*morally*) llevar por mal camino

astride [ə'straɪd] *prep* a caballo *or* horcajadas sobre

astrology [æs'trɒlədʒɪ] *n* astrología

astronaut ['æstrənɔːt] *n* astronauta *m/f*

astronomy [æs'trɒnəmɪ] *n* astronomía

asylum [ə'saɪləm] *n* (*refuge*) asilo; (*mental hospital*) manicomio

---

KEYWORD

---

at [æt] *prep* **1** (*referring to position*) en; (*direction*) a; ~ **the top** en lo alto; ~ **home/school** en casa/la escuela; **to look** ~ **sth/sb** mirar algo/a uno
2 (*referring to time*): ~ **4 o'clock** a las 4; ~ **night** por la noche; ~ **Christmas** en Navidad; ~ **times** a veces
3 (*referring to rates, speed etc*): ~ **£1 a kilo** a una libra el kilo; **two** ~ **a time** de dos en dos; ~ **50 km/h** a 50 km/h
4 (*referring to manner*): ~ **a stroke** de un golpe; ~ **peace** en paz
5 (*referring to activity*): **to be** ~ **work** estar trabajando; (*in the office etc*) estar en el trabajo; **to play** ~ **cowboys** jugar a los vaqueros; **to be good** ~ **sth** ser bueno en algo
6 (*referring to cause*): **shocked/surprised/annoyed** ~ **sth** asombrado/sorprendido/fastidiado por algo; **I went** ~ **his suggestion** fui a instancias suyas

---

ate [eɪt] *pt of* **eat**

atheist ['eɪθɪɪst] *n* ateo/a

Athens ['æθɪnz] *n* Atenas

athlete ['æθliːt] *n* atleta *m/f*

athletic [æθ'letɪk] *adj* atlético; ~**s** *n* atletismo

Atlantic [ət'læntɪk] *adj* atlántico ♦ *n*: **the** ~ **(Ocean)** el (Océano) Atlántico

atlas ['ætləs] *n* atlas *m*

A.T.M. *n abbr* (= *automated telling machine*) cajero automático

atmosphere ['ætməsfɪə*] *n* atmósfera; (*of place*) ambiente *m*

atom ['ætəm] *n* átomo; ~**ic** [ə'tɒmɪk] *adj*

atómico; ~**(ic) bomb** *n* bomba atómica; ~**izer** ['ætəmaɪzə*] *n* atomizador *m*

atone [ə'təun] *vi*: **to** ~ **for** expiar

atrocious [ə'trəuʃəs] *adj* atroz

attach [ə'tætʃ] *vt* (*fasten*) atar; (*join*) unir, sujetar; (*document, letter*) adjuntar; (*importance etc*) dar, conceder; **to be** ~**ed to sb/sth** (*to like*) tener cariño a alguien/algo

attaché case [ə'tæʃeɪ-] *n* maletín *m*

attachment [ə'tætʃmənt] *n* (*tool*) accesorio; (*love*): ~ **(to)** apego (a)

attack [ə'tæk] *vt* (*MIL*) atacar; (*subj: criminal*) agredir, asaltar; (*criticize*) criticar; (*task*) emprender ♦ *n* ataque *m*, asalto; (*on sb's life*) atentado; (*fig: criticism*) crítica; (*of illness*) ataque *m*; **heart** ~ infarto (de miocardio); ~**er** *n* agresor(a) *m/f*, asaltante *m/f*

attain [ə'teɪn] *vt* (*also*: ~ **to**) alcanzar; (*achieve*) lograr, conseguir

attempt [ə'tempt] *n* tentativa, intento; (*attack*) atentado ♦ *vt* intentar; ~**ed** *adj*: ~**ed burglary/murder/suicide** tentativa *or* intento de robo/asesinato/suicidio

attend [ə'tend] *vt* asistir a; (*patient*) atender; ~ **to** *vt fus* ocuparse de; (*customer, patient*) atender a; ~**ance** *n* asistencia, presencia; (*people present*) concurrencia; ~**ant** *n* ayudante *m/f*; (*in garage etc*) encargado/a ♦ *adj* (*dangers*) concomitante

attention [ə'tenʃən] *n* atención *f*; (*care*) atenciones *fpl* ♦ *excl* (*MIL*) ¡firme(s)!; **for the** ~ **of ...** (*ADMIN*) atención ...

attentive [ə'tentɪv] *adj* atento

attic ['ætɪk] *n* desván *m*

attitude ['ætɪtjuːd] *n* actitud *f*; (*disposition*) disposición *f*

attorney [ə'tɜːnɪ] *n* (*lawyer*) abogado/a; **A~ General** *n* (*BRIT*) ≈ Presidente *m* del Consejo del Poder Judicial (*SP*); (*US*) ≈ ministro de justicia

attract [ə'trækt] *vt* atraer; (*sb's attention*) llamar; ~**ion** [ə'trækʃən] *n* encanto; (*gen pl: amusements*) diversiones *fpl*; (*PHYSICS*) atracción *f*; (*fig: towards sb, sth*) atractivo;

~ive adj guapo; (interesting) atrayente

attribute [n 'ætrɪbjuːt, vb ə'trɪbjuːt] n atributo ♦ vt: to ~ sth to atribuir algo a

attrition [ə'trɪʃən] n: war of ~ guerra de agotamiento

aubergine ['əubəʒiːn] (BRIT) n berenjena; (colour) morado

auburn ['ɔːbən] adj color castaño rojizo

auction ['ɔːkʃən] n (also: sale by ~) subasta ♦ vt subastar; ~eer [-'nɪə*] n subastador(a) m/f

audible ['ɔːdɪbl] adj audible, que se puede oír

audience ['ɔːdɪəns] n público; (RADIO) radioescuchas mpl; (TV) telespectadores mpl; (interview) audiencia

audio-visual [ɔːdɪəu'vɪzjuəl] adj audiovisual; ~ aid n ayuda audiovisual

audit ['ɔːdɪt] vt revisar, intervenir

audition [ɔː'dɪʃən] n audición f

auditor ['ɔːdɪtə*] n interventor(a) m/f, censor(a) m/f de cuentas

augment [ɔːg'mɛnt] vt aumentar

augur ['ɔːgə*] vi: it ~s well es un buen augurio

August ['ɔːgəst] n agosto

aunt [ɑːnt] n tía; ~ie n diminutive of aunt; ~y n diminutive of aunt

au pair ['əu'pɛə*] n (also: ~ girl) (chica) au pair f

auspicious [ɔːs'pɪʃəs] adj propicio, de buen augurio

Australia [ɔs'treɪlɪə] n Australia; ~n adj, n australiano/a m/f

Austria ['ɔstrɪə] n Austria; ~n adj, n austríaco/a m/f

authentic [ɔː'θɛntɪk] adj auténtico

author ['ɔːθə*] n autor(a) m/f

authoritarian [ɔːθɔrɪ'tɛərɪən] adj autoritario

authoritative [ɔː'θɔrɪtətɪv] adj autorizado; (manner) autoritario

authority [ɔː'θɔrɪtɪ] n autoridad f; (official permission) autorización f; the authorities npl las autoridades

authorize ['ɔːθəraɪz] vt autorizar

auto ['ɔːtəu] (US) n coche m (SP), carro (AM), automóvil m

auto: ~biography [ɔːtəbaɪ'ɔgrəfɪ] n autobiografía; ~graph ['ɔːtəgrɑːf] n autógrafo ♦ vt (photo etc) dedicar; (programme) firmar; ~mated ['ɔːtəmeɪtɪd] adj automatizado; ~matic [ɔːtə'mætɪk] adj automático ♦ n (gun) pistola automática; (car) coche m automático; ~matically adv automáticamente; ~mation [ɔː'tɔməʃən] n reconversión f; ~mobile ['ɔːtəməbiːl] (US) n coche m (SP), carro (AM), automóvil m; ~nomy [ɔː'tɔnəmɪ] n autonomía

autumn ['ɔːtəm] n otoño

auxiliary [ɔːg'zɪlɪərɪ] adj, n auxiliar m/f

avail [ə'veɪl] vt: to ~ o.s. of aprovechar(se) de ♦ n: to no ~ en vano, sin resultado

available [ə'veɪləbl] adj disponible; (unoccupied) libre; (person: unattached) soltero y sin compromiso

avalanche ['ævəlɑːnʃ] n alud m, avalancha

avant-garde ['ævɑ̃'gɑːd] adj de vanguardia

Ave. abbr = avenue

avenge [ə'vɛndʒ] vt vengar

avenue ['ævənjuː] n avenida; (fig) camino

average ['ævərɪdʒ] n promedio, término medio ♦ adj medio, de término medio; (ordinary) regular, corriente ♦ vt sacar un promedio de; on ~ por regla general; ~ out vi: to ~ out at salir en un promedio de

averse [ə'vəːs] adj: to be ~ to sth/doing sentir aversión or antipatía por algo/por hacer

avert [ə'vəːt] vt prevenir; (blow) desviar; (one's eyes) apartar

aviary ['eɪvɪərɪ] n pajarera, avería

avocado [ævə'kɑːdəu] n (also: BRIT: ~ pear) aguacate m (SP), palta (AM)

avoid [ə'vɔɪd] vt evitar, eludir

await [ə'weɪt] vt esperar, aguardar

awake [ə'weɪk] (pt awoke, pp awoken or awaked) adj despierto ♦ vt despertar ♦ vi despertarse; to be ~ estar despierto; ~ning n el despertar

award [ə'wɔ:d] n premio; (LAW: *damages*) indemnización f ♦ vt otorgar, conceder; (LAW: *damages*) adjudicar

aware [ə'wɛə⁎] adj: **~ (of)** consciente (de); **to become ~ of/that** (*realize*) darse cuenta de/de que; (*learn*) enterarse de/de que; **~ness** n conciencia; (*knowledge*) conocimiento

away [ə'weɪ] adv fuera; (*movement*): **she went ~** se marchó; (*far ~*) lejos; **two kilometres ~** a dos kilómetros de distancia; **two hours ~ by car** a dos horas en coche; **the holiday was two weeks ~** faltaban dos semanas para las vacaciones; **he's ~ for a week** estará ausente una semana; **to take ~ (from)** quitar (a); (*subtract*) substraer (de); **to work/pedal ~** seguir trabajando/pedaleando; **to fade ~** (*colour*) desvanecerse; (*sound*) apagarse; **~ game** n (SPORT) partido de fuera

awe [ɔ:] n admiración f respetuosa; **~-inspiring** adj imponente

awful [':fəl] adj horroroso; (*quantity*): **an ~ lot (of)** cantidad de (de); **~ly** adv (*very*) terriblemente

awkward [':kwəd] adj desmañado, torpe; (*shape*) incómodo; (*embarrassing*) delicado, difícil

awning [':nɪŋ] n (*of tent, caravan, shop*) toldo

awoke [ə'wəuk] pt of **awake**

awoken [ə'wəukən] pp of **awake**

awry [ə'raɪ] adv: **to be ~** estar descolocado or mal puesto

axe [æks] (US **ax**) n hacha ♦ vt (*project*) cortar; (*jobs*) reducir

axes ['æksi:z] npl of **axis**

axis ['æksɪs] (pl **axes**) n eje m

axle ['æksl] n eje m, árbol m

ay(e) [aɪ] excl sí

B, b

B [bi:] n (MUS) si m

B.A. abbr = **Bachelor of Arts**

baby ['beɪbɪ] n bebé m/f; (US: *inf*: *darling*) mi amor; **~ carriage** (US) n cochecito; **~-sit** vi hacer de canguro; **~-sitter** n canguro/a; **~ wipe** n toallita húmeda (*para bebés*)

bachelor ['bætʃələ⁎] n soltero; **B~ of Arts/Science** licenciado/a en Filosofía y Letras/Ciencias

back [bæk] n (*of person*) espalda; (*of animal*) lomo; (*of hand*) dorso; (*as opposed to front*) parte f de atrás; (*of chair*) respaldo; (*of page*) reverso; (*of book*) final m; (FOOTBALL) defensa m; (*of crowd*): **the ones at the ~** los del fondo ♦ vt (*candidate: also*: **~ up**) respaldar, apoyar; (*horse: at races*) apostar a; (*car*) dar marcha atrás a or con ♦ vi (*car etc*) ir (or salir or entrar) marcha atrás ♦ adj (*payment, rent*) atrasado; (*seats, wheels*) de atrás ♦ adv (*not forward*) (hacia) atrás; (*returned*): **he's ~** está de vuelta, ha vuelto; **he ran ~** volvió corriendo; (*restitution*): **throw the ball ~** devuelve la pelota; **can I have it ~?** ¿me lo devuelve?; (*again*): **he called ~** llamó de nuevo; **~ down** vi echarse atrás; **~ out** vi (*of promise*) volverse atrás; **~ up** vt (*person*) apoyar, respaldar; (*theory*) defender; (COMPUT) hacer una copia preventiva or de reserva; **~bencher** (BRIT) n miembro del parlamento sin cargo relevante; **~bone** n columna vertebral; **~date** vt (*pay rise*) dar efecto retroactivo a; (*letter*) poner fecha atrasada a; **~drop** n telón m de fondo; **~fire** vi (AUT) petardear; (*plans*) fallar, salir mal; **~ground** n fondo; (*of events*) antecedentes mpl; (*basic knowledge*) bases fpl; (*experience*) conocimientos mpl, educación f; **family ~ground** origen m, antecedentes mpl; **~hand** n (TENNIS:

also: **~hand stroke**) revés *m*; **~hander** (*BRIT*) *n* (*bribe*) soborno; **~ing** *n* (*fig*) apoyo, respaldo; **~lash** *n* reacción *f*; **~log** *n*: **~log of work** trabajo atrasado; **~ number** *n* (*of magazine etc*) número atrasado; **~pack** *n* mochila; **~packer** *n* mochilero/a; **~ pay** *n* pago atrasado; **~side** (*inf*) *n* trasero, culo; **~stage** *adv* entre bastidores; **~stroke** *n* espalda; **~up** *adj* suplementario; (*COMPUT*) de reserva ♦ *n* (*support*) apoyo; (*also:* **~-up file**) copia preventiva *or* de reserva; **~ward** *adj* (*person, country*) atrasado; **~wards** *adv* hacia atrás; (*read a list*) al revés; (*fall*) de espaldas; **~yard** *n* traspatio

bacon ['beɪkən] *n* tocino, beicon *m*

bad [bæd] *adj* malo; (*mistake, accident*) grave; (*food*) podrido, pasado; **his ~ leg** su pierna lisiada; **to go ~** (*food*) pasarse

badge [bædʒ] *n* insignia; (*policeman's*) chapa, placa

badger ['bædʒə*] *n* tejón *m*

badly ['bædlɪ] *adv* mal; **to reflect ~ on sb** influir negativamente en la reputación de uno; **~ wounded** gravemente herido; **he needs it ~** le hace gran falta; **to be ~ off (for money)** andar mal de dinero

badminton ['bædmɪntən] *n* bádminton *m*

bad-tempered *adj* de mal genio *or* carácter; (*temporarily*) de mal humor

bag [bæg] *n* bolsa; (*handbag*) bolso; (*satchel*) mochila; (*case*) maleta; **~s of** (*inf*) un montón de; **~gage** *n* equipaje *m*; **~gage allowance** *n* límite *m* de equipaje; **~gage reclaim** *n* recogida de equipajes; **~gy** *adj* amplio; **~pipes** *npl* gaita

Bahamas [bə'hɑːməz] *npl*: **the ~** las Islas Bahamas

bail [beɪl] *n* fianza ♦ *vt* (*prisoner: gen: grant ~ to*) poner en libertad bajo fianza; (*boat: also:* **~ out**) achicar; **on ~** (*prisoner*) bajo fianza; **to ~ sb out** obtener la libertad de uno bajo fianza; *see also* **bale**

bailiff ['beɪlɪf] *n* alguacil *m*

bait [beɪt] *n* cebo ♦ *vt* poner cebo en; (*tease*) tomar el pelo a

bake [beɪk] *vt* cocer (al horno) ♦ *vi* cocerse; **~d beans** *npl* judías *fpl* en salsa de tomate; **~d potato** *n* patata al horno; **~r** *n* panadero; **~ry** *n* panadería; (*for cakes*) pastelería; **baking** *n* (*act*) amasar *m*; (*batch*) hornada; **baking powder** *n* levadura (en polvo)

balance ['bæləns] *n* equilibrio; (*COMM: sum*) balance *m*; (*remainder*) resto; (*scales*) balanza ♦ *vt* equilibrar; (*budget*) nivelar; (*account*) saldar; (*make equal*) equilibrar; **~ of trade/payments** balanza de comercio/pagos; **~d** *adj* (*personality, diet*) equilibrado; (*report*) objetivo; **~ sheet** *n* balance *m*

balcony ['bælkənɪ] *n* (*open*) balcón *m*; (*closed*) galería; (*in theatre*) anfiteatro

bald [bɔːld] *adj* calvo; (*tyre*) liso

bale [beɪl] *n* (*AGR*) paca, fardo; (*of papers etc*) fajo; **~ out** *vi* lanzarse en paracaídas

Balearics [bælɪ'ærɪks] *npl*: **the ~** las Baleares

ball [bɔːl] *n* pelota; (*football*) balón *m*; (*of wool, string*) ovillo; (*dance*) baile *m*; **to play ~** (*fig*) cooperar

ballast ['bæləst] *n* lastre *m*

ball bearings *npl* cojinetes *mpl* de bolas

ballerina [bælə'riːnə] *n* bailarina

ballet ['bæleɪ] *n* ballet *m*; **~ dancer** *n* bailarín/ina *m/f*

balloon [bə'luːn] *n* globo

ballot ['bælət] *n* votación *f*; **~ paper** *n* papeleta (para votar)

ballpoint (pen) ['bɔːlpɔɪnt-] *n* bolígrafo

ballroom ['bɔːlrum] *n* salón *m* de baile

Baltic ['bɔːltɪk] *n*: **the ~ (Sea)** el (Mar) Báltico

ban [bæn] *n* prohibición *f*, proscripción *f* ♦ *vt* prohibir, proscribir

banal [bə'nɑːl] *adj* banal, vulgar

banana [bə'nɑːnə] *n* plátano (*SP*), banana (*AM*)

band [bænd] *n* grupo; (*strip*) faja, tira; (*stripe*) lista; (*MUS: jazz*) orquesta; (*: rock*) grupo; (*: MIL*) banda; **~ together** *vi* juntarse, asociarse

bandage ['bændɪdʒ] *n* venda, vendaje *m*
♦ *vt* vendar
Bandaid ® ['bændeɪd] (*US*) *n* tirita
bandit ['bændɪt] *n* bandido
bandy-legged ['bændɪ'legd] *adj* estevado
bang [bæŋ] *n* (*of gun, exhaust*) estallido,
detonación *f*; (*of door*) portazo; (*blow*)
golpe *m* ♦ *vt* (*door*) cerrar de golpe;
(*one's head*) golpear ♦ *vi* estallar; (*door*)
cerrar de golpe
Bangladesh [bɑːŋglə'deʃ] *n* Bangladesh *m*
bangs [bæŋz] (*US*) *npl* flequillo
banish ['bænɪʃ] *vt* desterrar
banister(s) ['bænɪstə(z)] *n(pl)* barandilla,
pasamanos *m inv*
bank [bæŋk] *n* (*COMM*) banco; (*of river,
lake*) ribera, orilla; (*of earth*) terraplén *m*
♦ *vi* (*AVIAT*) ladearse; **~ on** *vt fus* contar
con; **~ account** *n* cuenta de banco; **~
card** *n* tarjeta bancaria; **~er** *n* banquero;
~er's card (*BRIT*) *n* = **~ card; B~
holiday** (*BRIT*) *n* día *m* festivo; **~ing** *n*
banca; **~note** *n* billete *m* de banco; **~
rate** *n* tipo de interés bancario

bank holiday

ⓘ El término **bank holiday** se aplica en
el Reino Unido a todo día festivo
oficial en el que cierran bancos y
comercios. Los más importantes son en
Navidad, Semana Santa, finales de mayo
y finales de agosto y, al contrario que en
los países de tradición católica, no
coincide necesariamente con una
celebración religiosa.

bankrupt ['bæŋkrʌpt] *adj* quebrado,
insolvente; **to go ~** hacer bancarrota; **to
be ~** estar en quiebra; **~cy** *n* quiebra
bank statement *n* balance *m or* detalle
m de cuenta
banner ['bænə*] *n* pancarta
bannister(s) ['bænɪstə(z)] *n(pl)*
= **banister(s)**
baptism ['bæptɪzəm] *n* bautismo; (*act*)
bautizo
bar [bɑː*] *n* (*pub*) bar *m*; (*counter*)

mostrador *m*; (*rod*) barra; (*of window,
cage*) reja; (*of soap*) pastilla; (*of chocolate*)
tableta; (*fig: hindrance*) obstáculo;
(*prohibition*) proscripción *f*; (*MUS*) barra
♦ *vt* (*road*) obstruir; (*person*) excluir;
(*activity*) prohibir; **the B~** (*LAW*) la
abogacía; **behind ~s** entre rejas; **~ none**
sin excepción
barbaric [bɑː'bærɪk] *adj* bárbaro
barbecue ['bɑːbɪkjuː] *n* barbacoa
barbed wire ['bɑːbd-] *n* alambre *m* de
púas
barber ['bɑːbə*] *n* peluquero, barbero
bar code *n* código de barras
bare [beə*] *adj* desnudo; (*trees*) sin hojas;
(*necessities etc*) básico ♦ *vt* desnudar;
(*teeth*) enseñar; **~back** *adv* a pelo, sin
silla; **~faced** *adj* descarado; **~foot** *adj,
adv* descalzo; **~ly** *adv* apenas
bargain ['bɑːgɪn] *n* pacto, negocio; (*good
buy*) ganga ♦ *vi* negociar; (*haggle*)
regatear; **into the ~** además, por
añadidura; **~ for** *vt fus*: **he got more
than he ~ed for** le resultó peor de lo que
esperaba
barge [bɑːdʒ] *n* barcaza; **~ in** *vi* irrumpir;
(*interrupt: conversation*) interrumpir
bark [bɑːk] *n* (*of tree*) corteza; (*of dog*)
ladrido ♦ *vi* ladrar
barley ['bɑːlɪ] *n* cebada
barmaid ['bɑːmeɪd] *n* camarera
barman ['bɑːmən] *n* camarero, barman *m*
barn [bɑːn] *n* granero
barometer [bə'rɒmɪtə*] *n* barómetro
baron ['bærən] *n* barón *m*; (*press ~ etc*)
magnate *m*; **~ess** *n* baronesa
barracks ['bærəks] *npl* cuartel *m*
barrage ['bærɑːʒ] *n* (*MIL*) descarga,
bombardeo; (*dam*) presa; (*of criticism*)
lluvia, aluvión *m*
barrel ['bærəl] *n* barril *m*; (*of gun*) cañón
m
barren ['bærən] *adj* estéril
barricade [bærɪ'keɪd] *n* barricada
barrier ['bærɪə*] *n* barrera
barring ['bɑːrɪŋ] *prep* excepto, salvo
barrister ['bærɪstə*] (*BRIT*) *n* abogado/a

barrow ['bærəu] *n* (*cart*) carretilla (de mano)

bartender ['bɑːtendə*] (*US*) *n* camarero, barman *m*

barter ['bɑːtə*] *vt*: **to ~ sth for sth** trocar algo por algo

base [beɪs] *n* base *f* ♦ *vt*: **to ~ sth on** basar *or* fundar algo en ♦ *adj* bajo, infame

baseball ['beɪsbɔːl] *n* béisbol *m*

basement ['beɪsmənt] *n* sótano

bases[1] ['beɪsiːz] *npl of* **basis**

bases[2] ['beɪsiz] *npl of* **base**

bash [bæʃ] (*inf*) *vt* golpear

bashful ['bæʃful] *adj* tímido, vergonzoso

basic ['beɪsɪk] *adj* básico; **~ally** *adv* fundamentalmente, en el fondo; (*simply*) sencillamente; **~s** *npl*: **the ~s** los fundamentos

basil ['bæzl] *n* albahaca

basin ['beɪsn] *n* cuenco, tazón *m*; (*GEO*) cuenca; (*also*: **wash~**) lavabo

basis ['beɪsɪs] (*pl* **bases**) *n* base *f*; **on a part-time/trial ~** a tiempo parcial/a prueba

bask [bɑːsk] *vi*: **to ~ in the sun** tomar el sol

basket ['bɑːskɪt] *n* cesta, cesto; canasta; **~ball** *n* baloncesto

Basque [bæsk] *adj, n* vasco/a *m/f*; **~ Country** *n* Euskadi *m*, País *m* Vasco

bass [beɪs] *n* (*MUS*: *instrument*) bajo; (*double ~*) contrabajo; (*singer*) bajo

bassoon [bə'suːn] *n* fagot *m*

bastard ['bɑːstəd] *n* bastardo; (*inf!*) hijo de puta (*!*)

bat [bæt] *n* (*ZOOL*) murciélago; (*for ball games*) palo; (*BRIT*: *for table tennis*) pala ♦ *vt*: **he didn't ~ an eyelid** ni pestañeó

batch [bætʃ] *n* (*of bread*) hornada; (*of letters etc*) lote *m*

bated ['beɪtɪd] *adj*: **with ~ breath** sin respirar

bath [bɑːθ, *pl* bɑːðz] *n* (*action*) baño; (*~tub*) baño (*SP*), bañera (*SP*), tina (*AM*) ♦ *vt* bañar; **to have a ~** bañarse, tomar un baño; *see also* **baths**

bathe [beɪð] *vi* bañarse ♦ *vt* (*wound*) lavar; **~r** *n* bañista *m/f*

bathing ['beɪðɪŋ] *n* el bañarse; **~ costume** (*US* **~ suit**) *n* traje *m* de baño

bath: **~robe** *n* (*man's*) batín *m*; (*woman's*) bata; **~room** *n* (cuarto de) baño; **~s** [bɑːðz] *npl* (*also*: **swimming ~s**) piscina; **~ towel** *n* toalla de baño

baton ['bætən] *n* (*MUS*) batuta; (*ATHLETICS*) testigo; (*weapon*) porra

batter ['bætə*] *vt* maltratar; (*subj*: *rain etc*) azotar ♦ *n* masa (para rebozar); **~ed** *adj* (*hat, pan*) estropeado

battery ['bætəri] *n* (*AUT*) batería; (*of torch*) pila

battle ['bætl] *n* batalla; (*fig*) lucha ♦ *vi* luchar; **~ship** *n* acorazado

bawl [bɔːl] *vi* chillar, gritar; (*child*) berrear

bay [beɪ] *n* (*GEO*) bahía; **B~ of Biscay** ≈ mar Cantábrico; **to hold sb at ~** mantener a alguien a raya; **~ leaf** *n* hoja de laurel

bay window *n* ventana saslediza

bazaar [bə'zɑː*] *n* bazar *m*; (*fete*) venta con fines benéficos

B. & B. *n abbr* (= **bed and breakfast**) cama y desayuno

BBC *n abbr* (= *British Broadcasting Corporation*) *cadena de radio y televisión estatal británica*

B.C. *adv abbr* (= *before Christ*) a. de C.

KEYWORD

be [biː] (*pt* **was, were**, *pp* **been**) *aux vb* **1** (*with present participle*: *forming continuous tenses*): **what are you doing?** ¿qué estás haciendo?, ¿qué haces?; **they're coming tomorrow** vienen mañana; **I've been waiting for you for hours** llevo horas esperándote

2 (*with pp*: *forming passives*) ser (*but often replaced by active or reflective constructions*); **to ~ murdered** ser asesinado; **the box had been opened** habían abierto la caja; **the thief was nowhere to ~ seen** no se veía al ladrón por ninguna parte

3 (*in tag questions*): **it was fun, wasn't it?** fue divertido, ¿no? *or* ¿verdad?; **he's good-looking, isn't he?** es guapo, ¿no te parece?; **she's back again, is she?** entonces, ¿ha vuelto?

4 (+*to* +*infin*): **the house is to ~ sold** (*necessity*) hay que vender la casa; (*future*) van a vender la casa; **he's not to open it** no tiene que abrirlo

♦ *vb* +*complement* 1 (*with n or num complement, but see also* 3, 4, 5 *and impers vb below*) ser; **he's a doctor** es médico; **2 and 2 are 4** 2 y 2 son 4

2 (*with adj complement: expressing permanent or inherent quality*) ser; (*: expressing state seen as temporary or reversible*) estar; **I'm English** soy inglés/esa; **she's tall/pretty** es alta/bonita; **he's young** es joven; **~ careful/good/quiet** ten cuidado/pórtate bien/cállate; **I'm tired** estoy cansado/a; **it's dirty** está sucio/a

3 (*of health*) estar; **how are you?** ¿cómo estás?; **he's very ill** está muy enfermo; **I'm better now** ya estoy mejor

4 (*of age*) tener; **how old are you?** ¿cuántos años tienes?; **I'm sixteen (years old)** tengo dieciséis años

5 (*cost*) costar; ser; **how much was the meal?** ¿cuánto fue *or* costó la comida?; **that'll ~ £5.75, please** son £5.75, por favor; **this shirt is £17** esta camisa cuesta £17

♦ *vi* 1 (*exist, occur etc*) existir, haber; **the best singer that ever was** el mejor cantante que existió jamás; **is there a God?** ¿hay un Dios?, ¿existe Dios?; **~ that as it may** sea como sea; **so ~ it** así sea

2 (*referring to place*) estar; **I won't ~ here tomorrow** no estaré aquí mañana

3 (*referring to movement*): **where have you been?** ¿dónde has estado?

♦ *impers vb* 1 (*referring to time*): **it's 5 o'clock** son las 5; **it's the 28th of April** estamos a 28 de abril

2 (*referring to distance*): **it's 10 km to the village** el pueblo está a 10 km

3 (*referring to the weather*): **it's too hot/cold** hace demasiado calor/frío; **it's windy today** hace viento hoy

4 (*emphatic*): **it's me** soy yo; **it was Maria who paid the bill** fue María la que pagó la cuenta

beach [biːtʃ] *n* playa ♦ *vt* varar
beacon ['biːkən] *n* (*lighthouse*) faro; (*marker*) guía
bead [biːd] *n* cuenta; (*of sweat etc*) gota
beak [biːk] *n* pico
beaker ['biːkə*] *n* vaso de plástico
beam [biːm] *n* (*ARCH*) viga, travesaño; (*of light*) rayo, haz *m* de luz ♦ *vi* brillar; (*smile*) sonreír
bean [biːn] *n* judía; **runner/broad ~** habichuela/haba; **coffee ~** grano de café; **~sprouts** *npl* brotes *mpl* de soja
bear [bɛə*] (*pt* **bore**, *pp* **borne**) *n* oso ♦ *vt* (*weight etc*) llevar; (*cost*) pagar; (*responsibility*) tener; (*endure*) soportar, aguantar; (*children*) parir, tener; (*fruit*) dar ♦ *vi*: **to ~ right/left** torcer a la derecha/izquierda; **~ out** (*suspicions*) corroborar, confirmar; (*person*) dar la razón a; **~ up** *vi* (*remain cheerful*) mantenerse animado
beard [bɪəd] *n* barba; **~ed** *adj* con barba, barbudo
bearer ['bɛərə*] *n* portador(a) *m/f*
bearing ['bɛərɪŋ] *n* porte *m*, comportamiento; (*connection*) relación *f*; **~s** *npl* (*also*: **ball ~s**) cojinetes *mpl* a bolas; **to take a ~** tomar marcaciones; **to find one's ~s** orientarse
beast [biːst] *n* bestia, (*inf*) bruto, salvaje *m*; **~ly** (*inf*) *adj* horrible
beat [biːt] (*pt* **beat**, *pp* **beaten**) *n* (*of heart*) latido; (*MUS*) ritmo, compás *m*; (*of policeman*) ronda ♦ *vt* pegar, golpear; (*eggs*) batir; (*defeat: opponent*) vencer, derrotar; (*: record*) sobrepasar ♦ *vi* (*heart*) latir; (*drum*) redoblar; (*rain, wind*) azotar; **off the ~en track** aislado; **to ~ it** (*inf*) largarse; **~ off** *vt* rechazar; **~ up** *vt* (*attack*) dar una paliza a; **~ing** *n* paliza

beautiful [ˈbjuːtɪful] *adj* precioso, hermoso, bello; **~ly** *adv* maravillosamente

beauty [ˈbjuːtɪ] *n* belleza; **~ salon** *n* salón *m* de belleza; **~ spot** *n* (*TOURISM*) lugar *m* pintoresco

beaver [ˈbiːvə*] *n* castor *m*

became [bɪˈkeɪm] *pt of* **become**

because [bɪˈkɔz] *conj* porque; **~ of** debido a, a causa de

beckon [ˈbɛkən] *vt* (*also*: **~ to**) llamar con señas

become [bɪˈkʌm] (*irreg*: *like* **come**) *vt* (*suit*) favorecer, sentar bien a ♦ *vi* (+*n*) hacerse, llegar a ser; (+*adj*) ponerse, volverse; **to ~ fat** engordar

becoming [bɪˈkʌmɪŋ] *adj* (*behaviour*) decoroso; (*clothes*) favorecedor(a)

bed [bɛd] *n* cama; (*of flowers*) macizo; (*of coal, clay*) capa; (*of river*) lecho; (*of sea*) fondo; **to go to ~** acostarse; **~ and breakfast** *n* (*place*) pensión *f*; (*terms*) cama y desayuno; **~clothes** *npl* ropa de cama; **~ding** *n* ropa de cama

---

bed and breakfast

i Se llama **bed and breakfast** a una forma de alojamiento, en el campo o la ciudad, que ofrece cama y desayuno a precios inferiores a los de un hotel. El servicio se suele anunciar con carteles en los que a menudo se usa únicamente la abreviatura **B. & B.**

---

bedraggled [bɪˈdrægld] *adj* (*untidy*: *person*) desastrado; (*clothes, hair*) desordenado

bed: **~ridden** *adj* postrado (en cama); **~room** *n* dormitorio; **~side** *n*: **at the ~side of** a la cabecera de; **~sit(ter)** (*BRIT*) *n* estudio (*SP*), suite (*AM*); **~spread** *n* cubrecama *m*, colcha; **~time** *n* hora de acostarse

bee [biː] *n* abeja

beech [biːtʃ] *n* haya

beef [biːf] *n* carne *f* de vaca; **roast ~** rosbif *m*; **~burger** *n* hamburguesa; **B~eater** *n* alabardero de la Torre de Londres

beehive [ˈbiːhaɪv] *n* colmena

beeline [ˈbiːlaɪn] *n*: **to make a ~ for** ir derecho a

been [biːn] *pp of* **be**

beer [bɪə*] *n* cerveza

beet [biːt] (*US*) *n* (*also*: **red ~**) remolacha

beetle [ˈbiːtl] *n* escarabajo

beetroot [ˈbiːtruːt] (*BRIT*) *n* remolacha

before [bɪˈfɔː*] *prep* (*of time*) antes de; (*of space*) delante de ♦ *conj* antes (de) que ♦ *adv* antes, anteriormente; delante, adelante; **~ going** antes de marcharse; **~ she goes** antes de que se vaya; **the week ~** la semana anterior; **I've never seen it ~** no lo he visto nunca; **~hand** *adv* de antemano, con anticipación

beg [bɛg] *vi* pedir limosna ♦ *vt* (*entreat*) suplicar, rogar; **to ~ sb to do sth** rogar a uno que haga algo; *see also* **pardon**

began [bɪˈgæn] *pt of* **begin**

beggar [ˈbɛgə*] *n* mendigo/a

begin [bɪˈgɪn] (*pt* **began**, *pp* **begun**) *vt, vi* empezar, comenzar; **to ~ doing** *or* **to do sth** empezar a hacer algo; **~ner** *n* principiante *m/f*; **~ning** *n* principio, comienzo

begun [bɪˈgʌn] *pp of* **begin**

behalf [bɪˈhɑːf] *n*: **on ~ of** en nombre de, por; (*for benefit of*) en beneficio de; **on my/his ~** por mí/él

behave [bɪˈheɪv] *vi* (*person*) portarse, comportarse; (*well*: *also*: **~ o.s.**) portarse bien; **behaviour** (*US* **behavior**) *n* comportamiento, conducta

behind [bɪˈhaɪnd] *prep* detrás de; (*supporting*): **to be ~ sb** apoyar a alguien ♦ *adv* detrás, por detrás, atrás ♦ *n* trasero; **to be ~ (schedule)** ir retrasado; **~ the scenes** (*fig*) entre bastidores

behold [bɪˈhəʊld] (*irreg*: *like* **hold**) *vt* contemplar

beige [beɪʒ] *adj* color beige

Beijing [ˈbeɪˈdʒɪŋ] *n* Pekín *m*

being [ˈbiːɪŋ] *n* ser *m*; (*existence*): **in ~** existente; **to come into ~** aparecer

Beirut [beɪˈruːt] *n* Beirut *m*

Belarus [belə'rus] *n* Bielorrusia
belated [bi'leitid] *adj* atrasado, tardío
belch [beltʃ] *vi* eructar ♦ *vt* (*gen*: ~ **out**: *smoke etc*) arrojar
Belgian ['beldʒən] *adj*, *n* belga *m/f*
Belgium ['beldʒəm] *n* Bélgica
belief [bi'li:f] *n* opinión *f*; (*faith*) fe *f*
believe [bi'li:v] *vt*, *vi* creer; **to ~ in** creer en; **~r** *n* partidario/a; (*REL*) creyente *m/f*, fiel *m/f*
belittle [bi'litl] *vt* quitar importancia a
bell [bel] *n* campana; (*small*) campanilla; (*on door*) timbre *m*
belligerent [bi'lidʒərənt] *adj* agresivo
bellow ['beləu] *vi* bramar; (*person*) rugir
belly ['beli] *n* barriga, panza
belong [bi'lɔŋ] *vi*: **to ~ to** pertenecer a; (*club etc*) ser socio de; **this book ~s here** este libro va aquí; **~ings** *npl* pertenencias *fpl*
beloved [bi'lʌvid] *adj* querido/a
below [bi'ləu] *prep* bajo, debajo de; (*less than*) inferior a ♦ *adv* abajo, (por) debajo; **see ~** véase más abajo
belt [belt] *n* cinturón *m*; (*TECH*) correa, cinta ♦ *vt* (*thrash*) pegar con correa; **~way** (*US*) *n* (*AUT*) carretera de circunvalación
bench [bentʃ] *n* banco; (*BRIT*: *POL*): **the Government/Opposition ~es** (los asientos de) los miembros del Gobierno/ de la Oposición; **the B~** (*LAW*: *judges*) magistratura
bend [bend] (*pt*, *pp* **bent**) *vt* doblar ♦ *vi* inclinarse ♦ *n* (*BRIT*: *in road*, *river*) curva; (*in pipe*) codo; ~ **down** *vi* inclinarse, doblarse; ~ **over** *vi* inclinarse
beneath [bi'ni:θ] *prep* bajo, debajo de; (*unworthy of*) indigno de ♦ *adv* abajo, (por) debajo
benefactor ['benifæktə*] *n* bienhechor *m*
beneficial [beni'fiʃəl] *adj* beneficioso
benefit ['benifit] *n* beneficio; (*allowance of money*) subsidio ♦ *vt* beneficiar ♦ *vi*: **he'll ~ from it** le sacará provecho
benevolent [bi'nevələnt] *adj* (*person*) benévolo

benign [bi'nain] *adj* benigno; (*smile*) afable
bent [bent] *pt*, *pp of* **bend** ♦ *n* inclinación *f* ♦ *adj*: **to be ~ on** estar empeñado en
bequest [bi'kwest] *n* legado
bereaved [bi'ri:vd] *npl*: **the ~** los íntimos de una persona afligidos por su muerte
beret ['berei] *n* boina
Berlin [bə:'lin] *n* Berlín
berm [bə:m] (*US*) *n* (*AUT*) arcén *m*
Bermuda [bə:'mju:də] *n* las Bermudas
berry ['beri] *n* baya
berserk [bə'sə:k] *adj*: **to go ~** perder los estribos
berth [bə:θ] *n* (*bed*) litera; (*cabin*) camarote *m*; (*for ship*) amarradero ♦ *vi* atracar, amarrar
beseech [bi'si:tʃ] (*pt*, *pp* **besought**) *vt* suplicar
beset [bi'set] (*pt*, *pp* **beset**) *vt* (*person*) acosar
beside [bi'said] *prep* junto a, al lado de; **to be ~ o.s. with anger** estar fuera de sí; **that's ~ the point** eso no tiene nada que ver; **~s** *adv* además ♦ *prep* además de
besiege [bi'si:dʒ] *vt* sitiar; (*fig*) asediar
best [best] *adj* (el/la) mejor ♦ *adv* (lo) mejor; **the ~ part of** (*quantity*) la mayor parte de; **at ~** en el mejor de los casos; **to make the ~ of sth** sacar el mejor partido de algo; **to do one's ~** hacer todo lo posible; **to the ~ of my knowledge** que yo sepa; **to the ~ of my ability** como mejor puedo; **~-before date** *n* fecha de consumo preferente; **~ man** *n* padrino de boda
bestow [bi'stəu] *vt* (*title*) otorgar
bestseller ['best'selə*] *n* éxito de librería, bestseller *m*
bet [bet] (*pt*, *pp* **bet** *or* **betted**) *n* apuesta ♦ *vt*: **to ~ money on** apostar dinero por; **to ~ sb sth** apostar algo a uno ♦ *vi* apostar
betray [bi'trei] *vt* traicionar; (*trust*) faltar a; **~al** *n* traición *f*
better ['betə*] *adj*, *adv* mejor ♦ *vt* superar ♦ *n*: **to get the ~ of sb** quedar por

encima de alguien; **you had ~ do it** más
vale que lo hagas; **he thought ~ of it**
cambió de parecer; **to get ~** (MED)
mejorar(se); **~ off** adj mejor; (wealthier)
más acomodado

betting ['betɪŋ] n juego, el apostar; **~
shop** (BRIT) n agencia de apuestas

between [bɪ'twiːn] prep entre ♦ adv (time)
mientras tanto; (place) en medio

beverage ['bevərɪdʒ] n bebida

beware [bɪ'weə*] vi: **to ~ (of)** tener
cuidado (con); **"~ of the dog"** "perro
peligroso"

bewildered [bɪ'wɪldəd] adj aturdido,
perplejo

beyond [bɪ'jɔnd] prep más allá de; (past:
understanding) fuera de; (after: date)
después de, más allá de; (above) superior
a ♦ adv (in space) más allá; (in time)
posteriormente; **~ doubt** fuera de toda
duda; **~ repair** irreparable

bias ['baɪəs] n (prejudice) prejuicio, pasión
f; (preference) predisposición f; **~(s)ed**
adj parcial

bib [bɪb] n babero

Bible ['baɪbl] n Biblia

bicarbonate of soda [baɪ'kɑːbənɪt-] n
bicarbonato sódico

bicker ['bɪkə*] vi pelearse

bicycle ['baɪsɪkl] n bicicleta

bid [bɪd] (pt **bade** or **bid**, pp **bidden** or
bid) n oferta, postura; (in tender)
licitación f; (attempt) tentativa, conato
♦ vi hacer una oferta ♦ vt (offer) ofrecer;
to ~ sb good day dar a uno los buenos
días; **~der** n: **the highest ~der** el mejor
postor; **~ding** n (at auction) ofertas fpl

bide [baɪd] vt: **to ~ one's time** esperar el
momento adecuado

bifocals [baɪ'fəʊklz] npl gafas fpl (SP) or
anteojos mpl (AM) bifocales

big [bɪg] adj grande; (brother, sister) mayor

bigheaded ['bɪg'hedɪd] adj engreído

bigot ['bɪgət] n fanático/a, intolerante m/f;
~ed adj fanático, intolerante; **~ry** n
fanatismo, intolerancia

big top n (at circus) carpa

bike [baɪk] n bici f

bikini [bɪ'kiːnɪ] n bikini m

bilingual [baɪ'lɪŋgwəl] adj bilingüe

bill [bɪl] n cuenta; (invoice) factura; (POL)
proyecto de ley; (US: banknote) billete m;
(of bird) pico; (of show) programa m;
"post no ~s" "prohibido fijar carteles";
to fit or **fill the ~** (fig) cumplir con los
requisitos; **~board** (US) n cartelera

billet ['bɪlɪt] n alojamiento

billfold ['bɪlfəʊld] (US) n cartera

billiards ['bɪljədz] n billar m

billion ['bɪljən] n (BRIT) billón m (millón de
millones); (US) mil millones mpl

bimbo ['bɪmbəʊ] (inf) n tía buena sin seso

bin [bɪn] n (for rubbish) cubo (SP) or bote
m (AM) de la basura; (container) recipiente
m

bind [baɪnd] (pt, pp **bound**) vt atar; (book)
encuadernar; (oblige) obligar ♦ n (inf:
nuisance) lata; **~ing** adj (contract)
obligatorio

binge [bɪndʒ] (inf) n: **to go on a ~** ir de
juerga

bingo ['bɪŋgəʊ] n bingo m

binoculars [bɪ'nɔkjuləz] npl prismáticos
mpl

bio... [baɪə*] prefix: **~chemistry** n
bioquímica; **~degradable**
[baɪəudɪ'greɪdəbl] adj biodegradable;
~graphy [baɪ'ɔgrəfɪ] n biografía;
~logical adj biológico; **~logy** [baɪ'ɔlədʒɪ]
n biología

birch [bɜːtʃ] n (tree) abedul m

bird [bɜːd] n ave f, pájaro; (BRIT: inf: girl)
chica; **~'s eye view** n (aerial view) vista
de pájaro; (overview) visión f de conjunto;
~ watcher n ornitólogo/a

Biro ® ['baɪrəʊ] n bolígrafo

birth [bɜːθ] n nacimiento; **to give ~ to**
parir, dar a luz; **~ certificate** n partida
de nacimiento; **~ control** n (policy)
control m de natalidad; (methods)
métodos mpl anticonceptivos; **~day** n
cumpleaños m inv ♦ cpd (cake, card etc)
de cumpleaños; **~place** n lugar m de
nacimiento; **~ rate** n (tasa de) natalidad

f

biscuit ['bɪskɪt] (*BRIT*) *n* galleta, bizcocho (*AM*)

bisect [baɪ'sɛkt] *vt* bisecar

bishop ['bɪʃəp] *n* obispo; (*CHESS*) alfil *m*

bit [bɪt] *pt of* **bite** ♦ *n* trozo, pedazo, pedacito; (*COMPUT*) bit *m*, bitio; (*for horse*) freno, bocado; **a ~ of** un poco de; **a ~ mad** un poco loco; **~ by ~** poco a poco

bitch [bɪtʃ] *n* perra; (*inf!: woman*) zorra (!)

bite [baɪt] (*pt* **bit**, *pp* **bitten**) *vt, vi* morder; (*insect etc*) picar ♦ *n* (*insect*) picadura; (*mouthful*) bocado; **to ~ one's nails** comerse las uñas; **let's have a ~ (to eat)** (*inf*) vamos a comer algo

bitter ['bɪtə*] *adj* amargo; (*wind*) cortante, penetrante; (*battle*) encarnizado ♦ *n* (*BRIT: beer*) cerveza típica británica a base de lúpulos; **~ness** *n* lo amargo, amargura; (*anger*) rencor *m*

bizarre [bɪ'zɑ:*] *adj* raro, extraño

black [blæk] *adj* negro; (*tea, coffee*) solo ♦ *n* color *m* negro; (*person*): **B~** negro/a ♦ *vt* (*BRIT: INDUSTRY*) boicotear; **to give sb a ~ eye** ponerle a uno el ojo morado; **~ and blue** (*bruised*) amoratado; **to be in the ~** (*bank account*) estar en números negros; **~berry** *n* zarzamora; **~bird** *n* mirlo; **~board** *n* pizarra; **~ coffee** *n* café *m* solo; **~currant** *n* grosella negra; **~en** *vt* (*fig*) desacreditar; **~ ice** *n* hielo invisible en la carretera; **~leg** (*BRIT*) *n* esquirol *m*, rompehuelgas *m inv*; **~list** *n* lista negra; **~mail** *n* chantaje *m* ♦ *vt* chantajear; **~ market** *n* mercado negro; **~out** *n* (*MIL*) oscurecimiento; (*power cut*) apagón *m*; (*TV, RADIO*) interrupción *f* de programas; (*fainting*) desvanecimiento; **B~ Sea** *n*: **the B~ Sea** el Mar Negro; **~ sheep** *n* (*fig*) oveja negra; **~smith** *n* herrero; **~ spot** *n* (*AUT*) lugar *m* peligroso; (*for unemployment etc*) punto negro

bladder ['blædə*] *n* vejiga

blade [bleɪd] *n* hoja; (*of propeller*) paleta; **a ~ of grass** una brizna de hierba

blame [bleɪm] *n* culpa ♦ *vt*: **to ~ sb for sth** echar a uno la culpa de algo; **to be to ~** tener la culpa de

bland [blænd] *adj* (*music, taste*) soso

blank [blæŋk] *adj* en blanco; (*look*) sin expresión ♦ *n* (*of memory*): **my mind is a ~** no puedo recordar nada; (*on form*) blanco, espacio en blanco; (*cartridge*) cartucho sin bala *or* de fogueo; **~ cheque** *n* cheque *m* en blanco

blanket ['blæŋkɪt] *n* manta (*SP*), cobija (*AM*); (*of snow*) capa; (*of fog*) manto

blare [blɛə*] *vi* sonar estrepitosamente

blasé ['blɑ:zeɪ] *adj* hastiado

blast [blɑ:st] *n* (*of wind*) ráfaga, soplo; (*of explosive*) explosión *f* ♦ *vt* (*blow up*) volar; **~-off** *n* (*SPACE*) lanzamiento

blatant ['bleɪtənt] *adj* descarado

blaze [bleɪz] *n* (*fire*) fuego; (*fig: of colour*) despliegue *m*; (*: of glory*) esplendor *m* ♦ *vi* arder en llamas; (*fig*) brillar ♦ *vt*: **to ~ a trail** (*fig*) abrir (un) camino; **in a ~ of publicity** con gran publicidad

blazer ['bleɪzə*] *n* chaqueta de uniforme de colegial o de socio de club

bleach [bli:tʃ] *n* (*also*: **household ~**) lejía ♦ *vt* blanquear; **~ed** *adj* (*hair*) teñido (de rubio); **~ers** (*US*) *npl* (*SPORT*) gradas *fpl* al sol

bleak [bli:k] *adj* (*countryside*) desierto; (*prospect*) poco prometedor(a); (*weather*) crudo; (*smile*) triste

bleat [bli:t] *vi* balar

bleed [bli:d] (*pt, pp* **bled**) *vt, vi* sangrar; **my nose is ~ing** me está sangrando la nariz

bleeper ['bli:pə*] *n* busca *m*

blemish ['blɛmɪʃ] *n* marca, mancha; (*on reputation*) tacha

blend [blɛnd] *n* mezcla ♦ *vt* mezclar; (*colours etc*) combinar, mezclar ♦ *vi* (*colours etc: also*: **~ in**) combinarse, mezclarse

bless [blɛs] (*pt, pp* **blessed** *or* **blest**) *vt* bendecir; **~ you!** (*after sneeze*) ¡Jesús!; **~ing** *n* (*approval*) aprobación *f*; (*godsend*) don *m* del cielo, bendición *f*; (*advantage*) beneficio, ventaja

blew [blu:] *pt of* **blow**

blind [blaɪnd] *adj* ciego; *(fig):* **(to)** ciego
(a) ♦ *n (for window)* persiana ♦ *vt* cegar;
(dazzle) deslumbrar; *(deceive):* **to ~ sb to
...** cegar a uno a ...; **the ~** *npl* los ciegos;
~ alley *n* callejón *m* sin salida; **~
corner** *(BRIT)* *n* esquina escondida; **~
fold** *n* venda ♦ *adv* con los ojos
vendados ♦ *vt* vendar los ojos a; **~ly** *adv*
a ciegas, ciegamente; **~ness** *n* ceguera;
~ spot *n (AUT)* ángulo ciego

blink [blɪŋk] *vi* parpadear, pestañear;
(light) oscilar; **~ers** *npl* anteojeras *fpl*

bliss [blɪs] *n* felicidad *f*

blister ['blɪstə*] *n* ampolla ♦ *vi (paint)*
ampollarse

blizzard ['blɪzəd] *n* ventisca

bloated ['bləutɪd] *adj* hinchado; *(person:
full)* ahíto

blob [blɔb] *n (drop)* gota; *(indistinct object)*
bulto

bloc [blɔk] *n (POL)* bloque *m*

block [blɔk] *n* bloque *m*; *(in pipes)*
obstáculo; *(of buildings)* manzana *(SP)*,
cuadra *(AM)* ♦ *vt* obstruir, cerrar;
(progress) estorbar; **~ of flats** *(BRIT)*
bloque *m* de pisos; **mental ~** bloqueo
mental; **~ade** [-'keɪd] *n* bloqueo ♦ *vt*
bloquear; **~age** *n* estorbo, obstrucción *f*;
~buster *n (book)* bestseller *m*; *(film)*
éxito de público; **~ letters** *npl* letras *fpl*
de molde

bloke [bləuk] *(BRIT: inf)* *n* tipo, tío

blond(e) [blɔnd] *adj, n* rubio/a *m/f*

blood [blʌd] *n* sangre *f*; **~ donor** *n*
donante *m/f* de sangre; **~ group** *n*
grupo sanguíneo; **~hound** *n* sabueso; **~
poisoning** *n* envenenamiento de la
sangre; **~ pressure** *n* presión *f*
sanguínea; **~shed** *n* derramamiento de
sangre; **~shot** *adj* inyectado en sangre;
~stream *n* corriente *f* sanguínea; **~ test**
n análisis *m inv* de sangre; **~thirsty** *adj*
sanguinario; **~ vessel** *n* vaso sanguíneo;
~y *adj* sangriento; *(nose etc)* lleno de
sangre; *(BRIT: inf!):* **this ~y...** este

condenado *o* puñetero ... (!) ♦ *adv:* **~y
strong/good** *(BRIT: inf!)* terriblemente
fuerte/bueno; **~y-minded** *(BRIT: inf)* *adj*
puñetero (!)

bloom [blu:m] *n* flor *f* ♦ *vi* florecer

blossom ['blɔsəm] *n* flor *f* ♦ *vi (also fig)*
florecer

blot [blɔt] *n* borrón *m*; *(fig)* mancha ♦ *vt*
(stain) manchar; **~ out** *vt (view)* tapar

blotchy ['blɔtʃɪ] *adj (complexion)* lleno de
manchas

blotting paper ['blɔtɪŋ-] *n* papel *m*
secante

blouse [blauz] *n* blusa

blow [bləu] *(pt* **blew***, pp* **blown***)* *n* golpe
m; *(with sword)* espadazo ♦ *vi* soplar;
(dust, sand etc) volar; *(fuse)* fundirse ♦ *vt*
(subj: wind) llevarse; *(fuse)* quemar;
(instrument) tocar; **to ~ one's nose**
sonarse; **~ away** *vt* llevarse, arrancar; **~
down** *vt* derribar; **~ off** *vt* arrebatar; **~
out** *vi* apagarse; **~ over** *vi* amainar; **~
up** *vi* estallar ♦ *vt* volar; *(tyre)* inflar;
(PHOT) ampliar; **~-dry** *n* moldeado (con
secador); **~lamp** *(BRIT)* *n* soplete *m*,
lámpara de soldar; **~-out** *n (of tyre)*
pinchazo; **~torch** *n* = **~lamp**

blue [blu:] *adj* azul; *(depressed)* deprimido;
~ film/joke película/chiste *m* verde; **out
of the ~** *(fig)* de repente; **~bell** *n*
campanilla, campánula azul; **~bottle** *n*
moscarda, mosca azul; **~print** *n (fig)*
anteproyecto

bluff [blʌf] *vi* tirarse un farol, farolear ♦ *n*
farol *m*; **to call sb's ~** coger a uno la
palabra

blunder ['blʌndə*] *n* patinazo, metedura
de pata ♦ *vi* cometer un error, meter la
pata

blunt [blʌnt] *adj (pencil)* despuntado;
(knife) desafilado, romo; *(person)* franco,
directo

blur [blə:*] *n (shape):* **to become a ~**
hacerse borroso ♦ *vt (vision)* enturbiar;
(distinction) borrar

blush [blʌʃ] *vi* ruborizarse, ponerse
colorado ♦ *n* rubor *m*

blustery ['blʌstərɪ] *adj (weather)* tempestuoso, tormentoso

boar [bɔː*] *n* verraco, cerdo

board [bɔːd] *n (card~)* cartón *m*; *(wooden)* tabla, tablero; *(on wall)* tablón *m*; *(for chess etc)* tablero; *(committee)* junta, consejo; *(in firm)* mesa *or* junta directiva; *(NAUT, AVIAT)*: **on ~ a** bordo ♦ *vt (ship)* embarcarse en; *(train)* subir a; **full ~** *(BRIT)* pensión completa; **half ~** *(BRIT)* media pensión; **to go by the ~** *(fig)* ser abandonado *or* olvidado; **~ up** *vt (door)* tapiar; **~ and lodging** *n* casa y comida; **~er** *n (SCOL)* interno/a; **~ing card** *(BRIT) n* tarjeta de embarque; **~ing house** *n* casa de huéspedes; **~ing pass** *(US) n* = **~ing card**; **~ing school** *n* internado; **~ room** *n* sala de juntas

boast [bəʊst] *vi*: **to ~ (about** *or* **of)** alardear (de)

boat [bəʊt] *n* barco, buque *m*; *(small)* barca, bote *m*

bob [bɒb] *vi (also*: **~ up and down)** menearse, balancearse; **~ up** *vi* (re)aparecer de repente

bobby ['bɒbɪ] *(BRIT: inf)* n poli *m*

bobsleigh ['bɒbsleɪ] *n* bob *m*

bode [bəʊd] *vi*: **to ~ well/ill (for)** ser prometedor/poco prometedor (para)

bodily ['bɒdɪlɪ] *adj* corporal ♦ *adv (move: person)* en peso

body ['bɒdɪ] *n* cuerpo *m*; *(corpse)* cadáver *m*; *(of car)* caja, carrocería; *(fig: group)* grupo *m*; *(: organization)* organismo *m*; **~-building** *n* culturismo; **~guard** *n* guardaespaldas *m inv*; **~work** *n* carrocería

bog [bɒg] *n* pantano, ciénaga ♦ *vt*: **to get ~ged down** *(fig)* empantanarse, atascarse

bogus ['bəʊgəs] *adj* falso, fraudulento

boil [bɔɪl] *vt (water)* hervir; *(eggs)* pasar por agua, cocer ♦ *vi* hervir; *(fig: with anger)* estar furioso; *(: with heat)* asfixiarse ♦ *n (MED)* furúnculo, divieso; **to come to the ~, to come to a ~** *(US)* comenzar a hervir; **to ~ down to** *(fig)* reducirse a; **~ over** *vi* salirse, rebosar; *(anger etc)* llegar al colmo; **~ed egg** *n* huevo cocido *(SP)*

or pasado *(AM)*; **~ed potatoes** *npl* patatas *fpl (SP) or* papas *fpl (AM)* hervidas; **~er** *n* caldera; **~er suit** *(BRIT) n* mono; **~ing point** *n* punto de ebullición

boisterous ['bɔɪstərəs] *adj (noisy)* bullicioso; *(excitable)* exuberante; *(crowd)* tumultuoso

bold [bəʊld] *adj* valiente, audaz; *(pej)* descarado; *(colour)* llamativo

Bolivia [bə'lɪvɪə] *n* Bolivia; **~n** *adj, n* boliviano/a *m/f*

bollard ['bɒləd] *(BRIT) n (AUT)* poste *m*

bolt [bəʊlt] *n (lock)* cerrojo; *(with nut)* perno, tornillo ♦ *adv*: **~ upright** rígido, erguido ♦ *vt (door)* echar el cerrojo a; *(also*: **~ together)** sujetar con tornillos; *(food)* engullir ♦ *vi* fugarse; *(horse)* desbocarse

bomb [bɒm] *n* bomba ♦ *vt* bombardear; **~ disposal** *n* desmontaje *m* de explosivos; **~er** *n (AVIAT)* bombardero; **~shell** *n (fig)* bomba

bond [bɒnd] *n (promise)* fianza; *(FINANCE)* bono; *(link)* vínculo, lazo; *(COMM)*: **in ~** en depósito bajo fianza

bondage ['bɒndɪdʒ] *n* esclavitud *f*

bone [bəʊn] *n* hueso; *(of fish)* espina ♦ *vt* deshuesar; quitar las espinas a; **~ idle** *adj* gandul; **~ marrow** *n* médula

bonfire ['bɒnfaɪə*] *n* hoguera, fogata

bonnet ['bɒnɪt] *n* gorra; *(BRIT: of car)* capó *m*

bonus ['bəʊnəs] *n (payment)* paga extraordinaria, plus *m*; *(fig)* bendición *f*

bony ['bəʊnɪ] *adj (arm, face)* huesudo; *(MED: tissue)* óseo; *(meat)* lleno de huesos; *(fish)* lleno de espinas

boo [buː] *excl* ¡uh! ♦ *vt* abuchear, rechiflar

booby trap ['buːbɪ-] *n* trampa explosiva

book [bʊk] *n* libro; *(of tickets)* taco; *(of stamps etc)* librito ♦ *vt (ticket)* sacar; *(seat, room)* reservar; **~s** *npl (COMM)* cuentas *fpl*, contabilidad *f*; **~case** *n* librería, estante *m* para libros; **~ing office** *n (BRIT: RAIL)* despacho de billetes *(SP) or* boletos *(AM)*; *(THEATRE)* taquilla *(SP)*, boletería *(AM)*; **~-keeping** *n* contabilidad *f;* ~**let** *n* folleto; ~**maker** *n* corredor *m* de apuestas; ~**seller** *n* librero; ~**shop**, ~ **store** *n* librería

boom [buːm] *n* (*noise*) trueno, estampido; (*in prices etc*) alza rápida; (*ECON, in population*) boom *m* ♦ *vi* (*cannon*) hacer gran estruendo, retumbar; (*ECON*) estar en alza

boon [buːn] *n* favor *m*, beneficio

boost [buːst] *n* estímulo, empuje *m* ♦ *vt* estimular, empujar; ~**er** *n* (*MED*) reinyección *f*

boot [buːt] *n* bota; (*BRIT: of car*) maleta, maletero ♦ *vt* (*COMPUT*) arrancar; **to** ~ (*in addition*) además, por añadidura

booth [buːð] *n* (*telephone* ~, *voting* ~) cabina

booze [buːz] (*inf*) *n* bebida

border [ˈbɔːdəʳ] *n* borde *m*, margen *m*; (*of a country*) frontera; (*for flowers*) arriate *m* ♦ *vt* bordear; (*another country: also*: ~ **on**) lindar con; **B**~**s** *n*: **the B**~**s** región fronteriza entre Escocia e Inglaterra; ~ **on** *vt fus* (*insanity etc*) rayar en; ~**line** *n*: **on the** ~**line** en el límite; ~**line case** *n* caso dudoso

bore [bɔːʳ] *pt of* **bear** ♦ *vt* (*hole*) hacer un agujero en; (*well*) perforar; (*person*) aburrir ♦ *n* (*person*) pelmazo, pesado; (*of gun*) calibre *m*; **to be** ~**d** estar aburrido; ~**dom** *n* aburrimiento

boring [ˈbɔːrɪŋ] *adj* aburrido

born [bɔːn] *adj*: **to be** ~ nacer; **I was** ~ **in 1960** nací en 1960

borne [bɔːn] *pp of* **bear**

borough [ˈbʌrə] *n* municipio

borrow [ˈbɔrəu] *vt*: **to** ~ **sth (from sb)** tomar algo prestado (a alguien)

Bosnia(-Herzegovina) [ˈbɔsnɪə(hɜːzəˈgəuviːnə)] *n* Bosnia (-Herzegovina)

bosom [ˈbuzəm] *n* pecho

boss [bɔs] *n* jefe *m* ♦ *vt* (*also*: ~ **about** or **around**) mangonear; ~**y** *adj* mandón/ona

bosun [ˈbəusn] *n* contramaestre *m*

botany [ˈbɔtənɪ] *n* botánica

botch [bɔtʃ] *vt* (*also*: ~ **up**) arruinar, estropear

both [bəuθ] *adj, pron* ambos/as, los/las dos; ~ **of us went, we** ~ **went** fuimos los dos, ambos fuimos ♦ *adv*: ~ **A and B** tanto A como B

bother [ˈbɔðəʳ] *vt* (*worry*) preocupar; (*disturb*) molestar, fastidiar ♦ *vi* (*also*: ~ **o.s.**) molestarse ♦ *n* (*trouble*) dificultad *f*; (*nuisance*) molestia, lata; **to** ~ **doing** tomarse la molestia de hacer

bottle [ˈbɔtl] *n* botella; (*small*) frasco; (*baby's*) biberón *m* ♦ *vt* embotellar; ~ **up** *vt* suprimir; ~ **bank** *n* contenedor *m* de vidrio; ~**neck** *n* (*AUT*) embotellamiento; (*in supply*) obstáculo; ~**-opener** *n* abrebotellas *m inv*

bottom [ˈbɔtəm] *n* (*of box, sea*) fondo; (*buttocks*) trasero, culo; (*of page*) pie *m*; (*of list*) final *m*; (*of class*) último/a ♦ *adj* (*lowest*) más bajo; (*last*) último

bough [bau] *n* rama

bought [bɔːt] *pt, pp of* **buy**

boulder [ˈbəuldəʳ] *n* canto rodado

bounce [bauns] *vi* (*ball*) (re)botar; (*cheque*) ser rechazado ♦ *vt* hacer (re)botar ♦ *n* (*rebound*) (re)bote *m*; ~**r** (*inf*) *n* gorila *m* (*que echa a los alborotadores de un bar, club etc*)

bound [baund] *pt, pp of* **bind** ♦ *n* (*leap*) salto; (*gen pl: limit*) límite *m* ♦ *vi* (*leap*) saltar ♦ *vt* (*border*) rodear ♦ *adj*: ~ **by** rodeado de; **to be** ~ **to do sth** (*obliged*) tener el deber de hacer algo; **he's** ~ **to come** es seguro que vendrá; **out of** ~**s** prohibido el paso; ~ **for** con destino a

boundary [ˈbaundrɪ] *n* límite *m*

bouquet [ˈbukei] *n* (*of flowers*) ramo

bourgeois [ˈbuəʒwɑː] *adj* burgués/esa *m/f*

bout [baut] *n* (*of malaria etc*) ataque *m*; (*of activity*) período *m*; (*BOXING etc*) combate *m*, encuentro

bow[1] [bəu] *n* (*knot*) lazo; (*weapon, MUS*) arco

bow[2] [bau] *n* (*of the head*) reverencia; (*NAUT: also*: ~**s**) proa ♦ *vi* inclinarse, hacer una reverencia; (*yield*): **to** ~ **to** or **before** ceder ante, someterse a

bowels [bauəlz] *npl* intestinos *mpl*, vientre *m*; (*fig*) entrañas *fpl*

bowl [baul] *n* tazón *m*, cuenco; (*ball*) bola ♦ *vi* (*CRICKET*) arrojar la pelota; *see also* **bowls**

bow-legged ['bəu'legɪd] *adj* estevado

bowler ['bəulə*] *n* (*CRICKET*) lanzador *m* (de la pelota); (*BRIT: also:* ~ **hat**) hongo, bombín *m*

bowling ['bəulɪŋ] *n* (*game*) bochas *fpl*, bolos *mpl*; ~ **alley** *n* bolera; ~ **green** *n* pista para bochas

bowls [bəulz] *n* juego de las bochas, bolos *mpl*

bow tie ['bəu-] *n* corbata de lazo, pajarita

box [bɔks] *n* (*also:* **cardboard** ~) caja, cajón *m*; (*THEATRE*) palco ♦ *vt* encajonar ♦ *vi* (*SPORT*) boxear; ~**er** ['bɔksə*] *n* (*person*) boxeador *m*; ~**ing** ['bɔksɪŋ] *n* (*SPORT*) boxeo; **B~ing Day** (*BRIT*) *n* día en que se dan los aguinaldos, 26 de diciembre; ~**ing gloves** *npl* guantes *mpl* de boxeo; ~**ing ring** *n* ring *m*, cuadrilátero; ~ **office** *n* taquilla (*SP*), boletería (*AM*); ~**room** *n* trastero

---
Boxing Day

i El día 26 de diciembre se conoce como **Boxing Day** y es día festivo en todo el Reino Unido. En el siglo XIX era tradición entregar "Christmas boxes" (aguinaldos) a empleados, carteros y otros proveedores en este día, y de ahí el nombre.

---

boy [bɔɪ] *n* (*young*) niño; (*older*) muchacho, chico; (*son*) hijo

boycott ['bɔɪkɔt] *n* boicot *m* ♦ *vt* boicotear

boyfriend ['bɔɪfrend] *n* novio

boyish ['bɔɪɪʃ] *adj* juvenil; (*girl*) con aspecto de muchacho

B.R. *n abbr* (*formerly* = *British Rail*) ≈ RENFE *f* (*SP*)

bra [brɑː] *n* sostén *m*, sujetador *m*

brace [breɪs] *n* (*BRIT: also:* ~**s:** *on teeth*) corrector *m*, aparato; (*tool*) berbiquí *m*

♦ *vt* (*knees, shoulders*) tensionar; ~**s** *npl* (*BRIT*) tirantes *mpl*; **to** ~ **o.s.** (*fig*) prepararse

bracelet ['breɪslɪt] *n* pulsera, brazalete *m*

bracing ['breɪsɪŋ] *adj* vigorizante, tónico

bracket ['brækɪt] *n* (*TECH*) soporte *m*, puntal *m*; (*group*) clase *f*, categoría; (*also:* **brace** ~) soporte *m*, abrazadera; (*also:* **round** ~) paréntesis *m inv*; (*also:* **square** ~) corchete *m* ♦ *vt* (*word etc*) poner entre paréntesis

brag [bræg] *vi* jactarse

braid [breɪd] *n* (*trimming*) galón *m*; (*of hair*) trenza

brain [breɪn] *n* cerebro; ~**s** *npl* sesos *mpl*; **she's got** ~**s** es muy lista; ~**wash** *vt* lavar el cerebro; ~**wave** *n* idea luminosa; ~**y** *adj* muy inteligente

braise [breɪz] *vt* cocer a fuego lento

brake [breɪk] *n* (*on vehicle*) freno ♦ *vi* frenar; ~ **light** *n* luz *f* de frenado

bran [bræn] *n* salvado

branch [brɑːntʃ] *n* rama; (*COMM*) sucursal *f*; ~ **out** *vi* (*fig*) extenderse

brand [brænd] *n* marca; (*fig: type*) tipo ♦ *vt* (*cattle*) marcar con hierro candente; ~**-new** *adj* flamante, completamente nuevo

brandy ['brændɪ] *n* coñac *m*

brash [bræʃ] *adj* (*forward*) descarado

brass [brɑːs] *n* latón *m*; **the** ~ (*MUS*) los cobres; ~ **band** *n* banda de metal

brat [bræt] (*pej*) *n* mocoso/a

brave [breɪv] *adj* valiente, valeroso ♦ *vt* (*face up to*) desafiar; ~**ry** *n* valor *m*, valentía

brawl [brɔːl] *n* pelea, reyerta

brazen ['breɪzn] *adj* descarado, cínico ♦ *vt*: **to** ~ **it out** echarle cara

Brazil [brə'zɪl] *n* (el) Brasil; ~**ian** *adj*, *n* brasileño/a *m/f*

breach [briːtʃ] *vt* abrir brecha en ♦ *n* (*gap*) brecha; (*breaking*): ~ **of contract** infracción *f* de contrato; ~ **of the peace** perturbación *f* del orden público

bread [bred] *n* pan *m*; ~ **and butter** *n* pan con mantequilla; (*fig*) pan (de cada día); ~**bin** n panera; ~**crumbs** npl migajas fpl; (CULIN) pan rallado; ~**line** n: **on the ~line** en la miseria

breadth [brɛtθ] n anchura; (fig) amplitud f

breadwinner ['brɛdwɪnə*] n sustento m de la familia

break [breɪk] (pt **broke**, pp **broken**) vt romper; (promise) faltar a; (law) violar, infringir; (record) batir ♦ vi romperse, quebrarse; (storm) estallar; (weather) cambiar; (dawn) despuntar; (news etc) darse a conocer ♦ n (gap) abertura; (fracture) fractura; (time) intervalo; (: at school) (período de) recreo; (chance) oportunidad f; **to ~ the news to sb** comunicar la noticia a uno; ~ **down** vt (figures, data) analizar, descomponer ♦ vi (machine) estropearse; (AUT) averiarse; (person) romper a llorar; (talks) fracasar; ~ **even** vi cubrir los gastos; ~ **free** or **loose** vi escaparse; ~ **in** vt (horse etc) domar ♦ vi (burglar) forzar una entrada; (interrupt) interrumpir; ~ **into** vt fus (house) forzar; ~ **off** vi (speaker) pararse, detenerse; (branch) partir; ~ **open** vt (door etc) abrir por la fuerza, forzar; ~ **out** vi estallar; (prisoner) escaparse; **to ~ out in spots** salirle a uno granos; ~ **up** vi (ship) hacerse pedazos; (crowd, meeting) disolverse; (marriage) deshacerse; (SCOL) terminar (el curso) ♦ vt (rocks etc) partir; (journey) partir; (fight etc) acabar con; ~**age** n rotura; ~**down** n (AUT) avería; (in communications) interrupción f; (MED: also: **nervous ~down**) colapso, crisis f nerviosa; (of marriage, talks) fracaso; (of statistics) análisis m inv; ~**down van** (BRIT) n (camión m) grúa; ~**er** n (ola) rompiente f

breakfast ['brɛkfəst] n desayuno

break: ~**in** n robo con allanamiento de morada; ~**ing and entering** n (LAW) violación f de domicilio, allanamiento de morada; ~**through** n (also fig) avance m; ~**water** n rompeolas m inv

breast [brɛst] n (of woman) pecho, seno; (chest) pecho; (of bird) pechuga; ~~-**feed**

(irreg: like **feed**) vt, vi amamantar, criar a los pechos; ~~-**stroke** n braza (de pecho)

breath [brɛθ] n aliento, respiración f; **to take a deep ~** respirar hondo; **out of ~** sin aliento, sofocado

Breathalyser ® ['brɛθəlaɪzə*] (BRIT) n alcoholímetro m

breathe [briːð] vt, vi respirar; ~ **in** vt, vi aspirar; ~ **out** vt, vi espirar; ~**r** n respiro; **breathing** n respiración f

breath: ~**less** adj sin aliento, jadeante; ~**taking** adj imponente, pasmoso

breed [briːd] (pt, pp **bred**) vt criar ♦ vi reproducirse, procrear ♦ n (ZOOL) raza, casta; (type) tipo; ~**ing** n (of person) educación f

breeze [briːz] n brisa

breezy ['briːzɪ] adj de mucho viento, ventoso; (person) despreocupado

brevity ['brɛvɪtɪ] n brevedad f

brew [bruː] vt (tea) hacer; (beer) elaborar ♦ vi (fig: trouble) prepararse; (storm) amenazar; ~**ery** n fábrica de cerveza, cervecería

bribe [braɪb] n soborno ♦ vt sobornar, cohechar; ~**ry** n soborno, cohecho

bric-a-brac ['brɪkəbræk] n inv baratijas fpl

brick [brɪk] n ladrillo; ~**layer** n albañil m

bridal ['braɪdl] adj nupcial

bride [braɪd] n novia; ~**groom** n novio; ~**smaid** n dama de honor

bridge [brɪdʒ] n puente m; (NAUT) puente m de mando; (of nose) caballete m; (CARDS) bridge m ♦ vt (fig): **to ~ a gap** llenar un vacío

bridle ['braɪdl] n brida, freno; ~ **path** n camino de herradura

brief [briːf] adj breve, corto ♦ n (LAW) escrito; (task) cometido, encargo ♦ vt informar; ~**s** npl (for men) calzoncillos mpl; (for women) bragas fpl; ~**case** n cartera (SP), portafolio (AM); ~**ing** n (PRESS) informe m; ~**ly** adv (glance) fugazmente; (say) en pocas palabras

brigadier [brɪgə'dɪə*] n general m de brigada

bright [braɪt] adj brillante; (room)

luminoso; (*day*) de sol; (*person: clever*) listo, inteligente; (: *lively*) alegre; (*colour*) vivo; (*future*) prometedor(a); ~**en** (*also:* ~**en up**) *vt* (*room*) hacer más alegre; (*event*) alegrar ♦ *vi* (*weather*) despejarse; (*person*) animarse, alegrarse; (*prospects*) mejorar

brilliance [ˈbrɪljəns] *n* brillo, brillantez *f*; (*of talent etc*) brillantez

brilliant [ˈbrɪljənt] *adj* brillante; (*inf*) fenomenal

brim [brɪm] *n* borde *m*; (*of hat*) ala

brine [braɪn] *n* (CULIN) salmuera

bring [brɪŋ] (*pt, pp* **brought**) *vt* (*thing, person: with you*) traer; (: *to sb*) llevar, conducir; (*trouble, satisfaction*) causar; ~ **about** *vt* ocasionar, producir; ~ **back** *vt* volver a traer; (*return*) devolver; ~ **down** *vt* (*government, plane*) derribar; (*price*) rebajar; ~ **forward** *vt* adelantar; ~ **off** *vt* (*task, plan*) lograr, conseguir; ~ **out** *vt* sacar; (*book etc*) publicar; (*meaning*) subrayar; ~ **round** *vt* (*unconscious person*) hacer volver en sí; ~ **up** *vt* subir; (*person*) educar, criar; (*question*) sacar a colación; (*food: vomit*) devolver, vomitar

brink [brɪŋk] *n* borde *m*

brisk [brɪsk] *adj* (*abrupt: tone*) brusco; (*person*) enérgico, vigoroso; (*pace*) rápido; (*trade*) activo

bristle [ˈbrɪsl] *n* cerda ♦ *vi*: **to ~ in anger** temblar de rabia

Britain [ˈbrɪtən] *n* (*also:* **Great ~**) Gran Bretaña

British [ˈbrɪtɪʃ] *adj* británico ♦ *npl*: **the ~** los británicos; ~ **Isles** *npl*: **the ~ Isles** las Islas Británicas; ~ **Rail** *n* ≈ RENFE *f* (SP)

Briton [ˈbrɪtən] *n* británico/a

brittle [ˈbrɪtl] *adj* quebradizo, frágil

broach [brəutʃ] *vt* (*subject*) abordar

broad [brɔːd] *adj* ancho; (*range*) amplio; (*smile*) abierto; (*general: outlines etc*) general; (*accent*) cerrado; **in ~ daylight** en pleno día; ~**cast** (*irreg: like* **cast**) *n* emisión *f* ♦ *vt* (RADIO) emitir; (TV) transmitir ♦ *vi* emitir; transmitir; ~**en** *vt* ampliar ♦ *vi* ensancharse; **to ~en one's**

mind hacer más tolerante a uno; ~**ly** *adv* en general; ~**-minded** *adj* tolerante, liberal

broccoli [ˈbrɒkəlɪ] *n* brécol *m*

brochure [ˈbrəuʃjuə*] *n* folleto

broil [brɔɪl] *vt* (CULIN) asar a la parrilla

broke [brəuk] *pt of* **break** ♦ *adj* (*inf*) pelado, sin blanca

broken [ˈbrəukən] *pp of* **break** ♦ *adj* roto; (*machine: also:* ~ **down**) averiado; ~ **leg** pierna rota; **in ~ English** en un inglés imperfecto; ~**-hearted** *adj* con el corazón partido

broker [ˈbrəukə*] *n* agente *m/f*, bolsista *m/f*; (*insurance* ~) agente de seguros

brolly [ˈbrɒlɪ] (BRIT: *inf*) *n* paraguas *m inv*

bronchitis [brɒŋˈkaɪtɪs] *n* bronquitis *f*

bronze [brɒnz] *n* bronce *m*

brooch [brəutʃ] *n* prendedor *m*, broche *m*

brood [bruːd] *n* camada, cría ♦ *vi* (*person*) dejarse obsesionar

broom [brum] *n* escoba; (BOT) retama

Bros. *abbr* (= *Brothers*) Hnos

broth [brɒθ] *n* caldo

brothel [ˈbrɒθl] *n* burdel *m*

brother [ˈbrʌðə*] *n* hermano; ~**-in-law** *n* cuñado

brought [brɔːt] *pt, pp of* **bring**

brow [brau] *n* (*forehead*) frente *m*; (*eye~*) ceja; (*of hill*) cumbre *f*

brown [braun] *adj* (*colour*) marrón; (*hair*) castaño; (*tanned*) bronceado, moreno ♦ *n* (*colour*) color *m* marrón or pardo ♦ *vt* (CULIN) dorar; ~ **bread** *n* pan integral

Brownie [ˈbraunɪ] *n* niña exploradora; b~ (US: *cake*) pastel de chocolate con nueces

brown paper *n* papel *m* de estraza

brown sugar *n* azúcar *m* terciado

browse [brauz] *vi* (*through book*) hojear; (*in shop*) mirar; ~**r** *n* (COMPUT) navegador *m*

bruise [bruːz] *n* cardenal *m* (SP), moretón *m* (AM) ♦ *vt* magullar

brunch [brʌntʃ] *n* desayuno-almuerzo

brunette [bruːˈnɛt] *n* morena

brunt [brʌnt] *n*: **to bear the ~ of** llevar el peso de

brush [brʌʃ] *n* cepillo; (*for painting,*

shaving etc) brocha; (*artist's*) pincel *m*; (*with police etc*) roce *m* ♦ *vt* (*sweep*) barrer; (*groom*) cepillar; (*also*: ~ **against**) rozar al pasar; ~ **aside** *vt* rechazar, no hacer caso a; ~ **up** *vt* (*knowledge*) repasar, refrescar; ~**wood** *n* (*sticks*) leña

Brussels ['brʌslz] *n* Bruselas; ~ **sprout** *n* col *f* de Bruselas

brute [bruːt] *n* bruto; (*person*) bestia ♦ *adj*: **by** ~ **force** a fuerza bruta

B.Sc. *abbr* (= *Bachelor of Science*) licenciado en Ciencias

BSE *n abbr* (= *bovine spongiform encephalopathy*) encefalopatía espongiforme bovina

BTW *abbr* (= *by the way*) por cierto

bubble ['bʌbl] *n* burbuja ♦ *vi* burbujear, borbotar; ~ **bath** *n* espuma para el baño; ~ **gum** *n* chicle *m* de globo

buck [bʌk] *n* (*rabbit*) conejo macho; (*deer*) gamo; (*US*: *inf*) dólar *m* ♦ *vi* corcovear; **to pass the** ~ **(to sb)** echar (a uno) el muerto; ~ **up** *vi* (*cheer up*) animarse, cobrar ánimo

---

Buckingham Palace

i **Buckingham Palace** *es la residencia oficial del monarca británico en Londres. El palacio se concluyó en 1703 y fue residencia del Duque de Buckingham hasta que, en 1762, pasó a manos de Jorge III. Fue reconstruido en el siglo XIX y posteriormente reformado a principios de este siglo. Una parte del palacio está actualmente abierta al público.*

---

bucket ['bʌkɪt] *n* cubo, balde *m*

buckle ['bʌkl] *n* hebilla ♦ *vt* abrochar con hebilla ♦ *vi* combarse

bud [bʌd] *n* (*of plant*) brote *m*, yema; (*of flower*) capullo ♦ *vi* brotar, echar brotes

Buddhism ['budɪzm] *n* Budismo

budding ['bʌdɪŋ] *adj* en ciernes, en embrión

buddy ['bʌdɪ] (*US*) *n* compañero, compinche *m*

budge [bʌdʒ] *vt* mover; (*fig*) hacer ceder

♦ *vi* moverse, ceder

budgerigar ['bʌdʒərɪgaː*] *n* periquito

budget ['bʌdʒɪt] *n* presupuesto ♦ *vi*: **to** ~ **for sth** presupuestar algo

budgie ['bʌdʒɪ] *n* = **budgerigar**

buff [bʌf] *adj* (*colour*) color de ante ♦ *n* (*inf*: *enthusiast*) entusiasta *m/f*

buffalo ['bʌfələu] (*pl* ~ *or* ~**es**) *n* (*BRIT*) búfalo; (*US*: *bison*) bisonte *m*

buffer ['bʌfə*] *n* (*COMPUT*) memoria intermedia; (*RAIL*) tope *m*

buffet[1] ['bufeɪ] *n* (*BRIT*: *in station*) bar *m*, cafetería; (*food*) buffet *m*; ~ **car** (*BRIT*) *n* (*RAIL*) coche-comedor *m*

buffet[2] ['bʌfɪt] *vt* golpear

bug [bʌg] *n* (*esp US*: *insect*) bicho, sabandija; (*COMPUT*) error *m*; (*germ*) microbio, bacilo; (*spy device*) micrófono oculto ♦ *vt* (*inf*: *annoy*) fastidiar

buggy ['bʌgɪ] *n* cochecito de niño

bugle ['bjuːgl] *n* corneta, clarín *m*

build [bɪld] (*pt*, *pp* **built**) *n* (*of person*) tipo ♦ *vt* construir, edificar; ~ **up** *vt* (*morale, forces, production*) acrecentar; (*stocks*) acumular; ~**er** *n* (*contractor*) contratista *m/f*; ~**ing** *n* construcción *f*; (*structure*) edificio; ~**ing society** (*BRIT*) *n* sociedad *f* inmobiliaria

built [bɪlt] *pt*, *pp* *of* **build** ♦ *adj*: ~-**in** (*wardrobe etc*) empotrado; ~-**up area** *n* zona urbanizada

bulb [bʌlb] *n* (*BOT*) bulbo; (*ELEC*) bombilla (*SP*), foco (*AM*)

Bulgaria [bʌl'geərɪə] *n* Bulgaria; ~**n** *adj*, *n* búlgaro/a *m/f*

bulge [bʌldʒ] *n* bulto, protuberancia ♦ *vi* bombearse, pandearse; (*pocket etc*): **to** ~ **(with)** rebosar (de)

bulk [bʌlk] *n* masa, mole *f*; **in** ~ (*COMM*) a granel; **the** ~ **of** la mayor parte de; ~**y** *adj* voluminoso, abultado

bull [bul] *n* toro; (*male elephant, whale*) macho; ~**dog** *n* dogo

bulldozer ['buldəuzə*] *n* bulldozer *m*

bullet ['bulɪt] *n* bala

bulletin ['bulɪtɪn] *n* anuncio, parte *m*; (*journal*) boletín *m*; ~ **board** *n* (*US*) tablón *m* de anuncias; (*COMPUT*) tablero de noticias

bulletproof ['bulɪtpruːf] *adj* a prueba de balas

bullfight ['bulfaɪt] *n* corrida de toros; **~er** *n* torero; **~ing** *n* los toros, el toreo

bullion ['buljən] *n* oro (*or* plata) en barras

bullock ['bulək] *n* novillo

bullring ['bulrɪŋ] *n* plaza de toros

bull's-eye *n* centro del blanco

bully ['bulɪ] *n* valentón *m*, matón *m* ♦ *vt* intimidar, tiranizar

bum [bʌm] *n* (*inf: backside*) culo; (*esp US: tramp*) vagabundo

bumblebee ['bʌmblbiː] *n* abejorro

bump [bʌmp] *n* (*blow*) tope *m*, choque *m*; (*jolt*) sacudida; (*on road etc*) bache *m*; (*on head etc*) chichón *m* ♦ *vt* (*strike*) chocar contra; **~ into** *vt fus* chocar contra, tropezar con; (*person*) topar con; **~er** *n* (*AUT*) parachoques *m inv* ♦ *adj*: **~er crop/harvest** cosecha abundante; **~er cars** *npl* coches *mpl* de choque; **~y** *adj* (*road*) lleno de baches

bun [bʌn] *n* (*BRIT: cake*) pastel *m*; (*US: bread*) bollo; (*of hair*) moño

bunch [bʌntʃ] *n* (*of flowers*) ramo; (*of keys*) manojo; (*of bananas*) piña; (*of people*) grupo; **~es** *npl* (*in hair*) coletas *fpl*

bundle ['bʌndl] *n* bulto, fardo; (*of sticks*) haz *m*; (*of papers*) legajo ♦ *vt* (*also*: **~ up**) atar, envolver; **to ~ sth/sb into** meter algo/a alguien precipitadamente en

bungalow ['bʌŋɡələu] *n* bungalow *m*, chalé *m*

bungle ['bʌŋɡl] *vt* hacer mal

bunion ['bʌnjən] *n* juanete *m*

bunk [bʌŋk] *n* litera; **~ beds** *npl* literas *fpl*

bunker ['bʌŋkə*] *n* (*coal store*) carbonera; (*MIL*) refugio; (*GOLF*) bunker *m*

bunny ['bʌnɪ] *n* (*also*: **~ rabbit**) conejito

buoy [bɔɪ] *n* boya; **~ant** *adj* (*ship*) capaz de flotar; (*economy*) boyante; (*person*) optimista

burden ['bəːdn] *n* carga ♦ *vt* cargar

bureau [bjuə'rəu] (*pl* **bureaux**) *n* (*BRIT:*

writing desk) escritorio, buró *m*; (*US: chest of drawers*) cómoda; (*office*) oficina, agencia

bureaucracy [bjuə'rɔkrəsɪ] *n* burocracia

burglar ['bəːɡlə*] *n* ladrón/ona *m/f*; **~ alarm** *n* alarma *f* antirrobo; **~y** *n* robo con allanamiento, robo de una casa

burial ['berɪəl] *n* entierro

burly ['bəːlɪ] *adj* fornido, membrudo

Burma ['bəːmə] *n* Birmania

burn [bəːn] (*pt, pp* **burned** *or* **burnt**) *vt* quemar; (*house*) incendiar ♦ *vi* quemarse, arder; incendiarse; (*sting*) escocer ♦ *n* quemadura; **~ down** *vt* incendiar; **~er** *n* (*on cooker etc*) quemador *m*; **~ing** *adj* (*building etc*) en llamas; (*hot: sand etc*) abrasador(a); (*ambition*) ardiente

burrow ['bʌrəu] *n* madriguera ♦ *vi* hacer una madriguera; (*rummage*) hurgar

bursary ['bəːsərɪ] (*BRIT*) *n* beca

burst [bəːst] (*pt, pp* **burst**) *vt* reventar; (*subj: river: banks etc*) romper ♦ *vi* reventarse; (*tyre*) pincharse ♦ *n* (*of gunfire*) ráfaga; (*also*: **~ pipe**) reventón *m*; **a ~ of energy/speed/enthusiasm** una explosión de energía/un ímpetu de velocidad/un arranque de entusiasmo; **to ~ into flames** estallar en llamas; **to ~ into tears** deshacerse en lágrimas; **to ~ out laughing** soltar la carcajada; **to ~ open** abrirse de golpe; **to be ~ing with** (*subj: container*) estar lleno a rebosar de; (*person*) reventar por *or* de; **~ into** *vt fus* (*room etc*) irrumpir en

bury ['berɪ] *vt* enterrar; (*body*) enterrar, sepultar

bus [bʌs] (*pl* **~es**) *n* autobús *m*

bush [buʃ] *n* arbusto; (*scrub land*) monte *m*; **to beat about the ~** andar(se) con rodeos

bushy [buʃɪ] *adj* (*thick*) espeso, poblado

busily ['bɪzɪlɪ] *adv* afanosamente

business ['bɪznɪs] *n* (*matter*) asunto; (*trading*) comercio, negocios *mpl*; (*firm*) empresa, casa; (*occupation*) oficio; **to be away on ~** estar en viaje de negocios; **it's my ~ to ...** me toca *or* corresponde ...;

it's none of my ~ yo no tengo nada que
ver; **he means ~** habla en serio; **~like**
adj eficiente; **~man** *n* hombre *m* de
negocios; **~ trip** *n* viaje *m* de negocios;
~woman *n* mujer *f* de negocios

usker ['bʌskə*] (BRIT) *n* músico/a
ambulante

us: ~ shelter *n* parada cubierta; **~
station** *n* estación *f* de autobuses; **~~
stop** *n* parada de autobús

ust [bʌst] *n* (ANAT) pecho; (*sculpture*)
busto ♦ *adj* (*inf*: *broken*) roto, estropeado;
to go ~ quebrar

ustle ['bʌsl] *n* bullicio, movimiento ♦ *vi*
menearse, apresurarse; **bustling** *adj*
(*town*) animado, bullicioso

usy ['bɪzɪ] *adj* ocupado, atareado; (*shop,
street*) concurrido, animado; (TEL: *line*)
comunicando ♦ *vt*: **to ~ o.s. with**
ocuparse en; **~body** *n* entrometido/a; **~
signal** (US) *n* (TEL) señal *f* de
comunicando

ut [bʌt] *conj* 1 pero; **he's not very
bright, ~ he's hard-working** no es muy
inteligente, pero es trabajador

2 (*in direct contradiction*) sino; **he's not
English ~ French** no es inglés sino
francés; **he didn't sing ~ he shouted** no
cantó sino que gritó

3 (*showing disagreement, surprise etc*): **~
that's far too expensive!** ¡pero eso es
carísimo!; **~ it does work!** ¡(pero) sí que
funciona!

♦ *prep* (*apart from, except*) menos, salvo;
we've had nothing ~ trouble no hemos
tenido más que problemas; **no-one ~ him
can do it** nadie más que él puede
hacerlo; **who ~ a lunatic would do such
a thing?** ¡sólo un loco haría una cosa así!;
~ for you/your help si no fuera por ti/tu
ayuda; **anything ~ that** cualquier cosa
menos eso

♦ *adv* (*just, only*): **she's ~ a child** no es
más que una niña; **had I ~ known** si lo
hubiera sabido; **I can ~ try** al menos lo

puedo intentar; **it's all ~ finished** está
casi acabado

butcher ['butʃə*] *n* carnicero ♦ *vt* hacer
una carnicería con; (*cattle etc*) matar; **~'s
(shop)** *n* carnicería

butler ['bʌtlə*] *n* mayordomo

butt [bʌt] *n* (*barrel*) tonel *m*; (*of gun*)
culata; (*of cigarette*) colilla; (BRIT: *fig*:
target) blanco ♦ *vt* dar cabezadas contra,
top(et)ar; **~ in** *vi* (*interrupt*) interrumpir

butter ['bʌtə*] *n* mantequilla ♦ *vt* untar
con mantequilla; **~cup** *n* botón *m* de
oro

butterfly ['bʌtəflaɪ] *n* mariposa;
(SWIMMING: *also*: **~ stroke**) braza de
mariposa

buttocks ['bʌtəks] *npl* nalgas *fpl*

button ['bʌtn] *n* botón *m*; (US) placa,
chapa ♦ *vt* (*also*: **~ up**) abotonar,
abrochar ♦ *vi* abrocharse

buttress ['bʌtrɪs] *n* contrafuerte *m*

buy [baɪ] (*pt, pp* bought) *vt* comprar ♦ *n*
compra; **to ~ sb sth/sth from sb**
comprarle algo a alguien; **to ~ sb a drink**
invitar a alguien a tomar algo; **~er** *n*
comprador(a) *m/f*

buzz [bʌz] *n* zumbido; (*inf*: *phone call*)
llamada (por teléfono) ♦ *vi* zumbar; **~er**
n timbre *m*; **~ word** *n* palabra que está
de moda

by [baɪ] *prep* 1 (*referring to cause, agent*)
por; de; **killed ~ lightning** muerto por un
relámpago; **a painting ~ Picasso** un
cuadro de Picasso

2 (*referring to method, manner, means*): **~
bus/car/train** en autobús/coche/tren; **to
pay ~ cheque** pagar con un cheque; **~
moonlight/candlelight** a la luz de la
luna/una vela; **~ saving hard, he ...**
ahorrando, ...

3 (*via, through*) por; **we came ~ Dover**
vinimos por Dover

4 (*close to, past*): **the house ~ the river**
la casa junto al río; **she rushed ~ me**

pasó a mi lado como una exhalación; **I go ~ the post office every day** paso por delante de Correos todos los días
5 (*time: not later than*) para; (: *during*): **~ daylight** de día; **~ 4 o'clock** para las cuatro; **~ this time tomorrow** mañana a estas horas; **~ the time I got here it was too late** cuando llegué ya era demasiado tarde
6 (*amount*): **~ the metre/kilo** por metro/kilo; **paid ~ the hour** pagado por hora
7 (*MATH, measure*): **to divide/multiply ~ 3** dividir/multiplicar por 3; **a room 3 metres ~ 4** una habitación de 3 metros por 4; **it's broader ~ a metre** es un metro más ancho
8 (*according to*) según, de acuerdo con; **it's 3 o'clock ~ my watch** según mi reloj, son las tres; **it's all right ~ me** por mí, está bien
9: **(all) ~ oneself** *etc* todo solo; **he did it (all) ~ himself** lo hizo él solo; **he was standing (all) ~ himself in a corner** estaba de pie solo en un rincón
10: **~ the way** a propósito, por cierto; **this wasn't my idea, ~ the way** pues, no fue idea mía
♦ *adv* **1** *see* **go; pass** *etc*
2: **~ and ~** finalmente; **they'll come back ~ and ~** acabarán volviendo; **~ and large** en líneas generales, en general

bye(-bye) ['baɪ('baɪ)] *excl* adiós, hasta luego
by(e)-law *n* ordenanza municipal
by: **~-election** (*BRIT*) *n* elección *f* parcial; **~gone** ['baɪgɔn] *adj* pasado, del pasado ♦ *n*: **let ~gones be ~gones** lo pasado, pasado está; **~pass** ['baɪpɑ:s] *n* carretera de circunvalación; (*MED*) (operación *f* de) by-pass *m* ♦ *vt* evitar; **~-product** *n* subproducto, derivado; (*of situation*) consecuencia; **~stander** ['baɪstændə*] *n* espectador(a) *m/f*
byte [baɪt] *n* (*COMPUT*) byte *m*, octeto
byword ['baɪwə:d] *n*: **to be a ~ for** ser conocidísimo por

C, c

C [si:] *n* (*MUS*) do *m*
C. *abbr* (= *centigrade*) C.
C.A. *abbr* = **chartered accountant**
cab [kæb] *n* taxi *m*; (*of truck*) cabina
cabbage ['kæbɪdʒ] *n* col *f*, berza
cabin ['kæbɪn] *n* cabaña; (*on ship*) camarote *m*; (*on plane*) cabina; **~ crew** tripulación *f* de cabina; **~ cruiser** *n* yate *m* de motor
cabinet ['kæbɪnɪt] *n* (*POL*) consejo de ministros; (*furniture*) armario; (*also:* **display ~**) vitrina
cable ['keɪbl] *n* cable *m* ♦ *vt* cablegrafiar; **~-car** *n* teleférico; **~ television** *n* televisión *f* por cable
cache [kæʃ] *n* (*of arms, drugs etc*) alijo
cackle ['kækl] *vi* lanzar risotadas; (*hen*) cacarear
cactus ['kæktəs] (*pl* **cacti**) *n* cacto
cadge [kædʒ] (*inf*) *vt* gorronear
Caesarean [si:'zɛərɪən] *adj*: **~ (section)** cesárea
café ['kæfeɪ] *n* café *m*
cafeteria [kæfɪ'tɪərɪə] *n* cafetería
cage [keɪdʒ] *n* jaula
cagey ['keɪdʒɪ] (*inf*) *adj* cauteloso, reservado
cagoule [kə'gu:l] *n* chubasquero
cajole [kə'dʒəʊl] *vt* engatusar
cake [keɪk] *n* (*CULIN: large*) tarta; (: *small*) pastel *m*; (*of soap*) pastilla; **~d** *adj*: **~d with** cubierto de
calculate ['kælkjuleɪt] *vt* calcular; **calculation** [-'leɪʃən] *n* cálculo, cómputo; **calculator** *n* calculadora
calendar ['kæləndə*] *n* calendario; **~ month/year** *n* mes *m*/año civil
calf [kɑ:f] (*pl* **calves**) *n* (*of cow*) ternero, becerro; (*of other animals*) cría; (*also:* **~skin**) piel *f* de becerro; (*ANAT*) pantorrilla
calibre ['kælɪbə*] (*US* **caliber**) *n* calibre *m*
call [kɔ:l] *vt* llamar; (*meeting*) convocar

♦ *vi* (*shout*) llamar; (*TEL*) llamar (por teléfono), telefonear (*esp AM*); (*visit: also:* ~ **in**, ~ **round**) hacer una visita ♦ *n* llamada; (*of bird*) canto; **to be ~ed** llamarse; **on ~** (*on duty*) de guardia; ~ **back** *vi* (*return*) volver; (*TEL*) volver a llamar; ~ **for** *vt fus* (*demand*) pedir, exigir; (*fetch*) venir por (*SP*), pasar por (*AM*); ~ **off** *vt* (*cancel: meeting, race*) cancelar; (: *deal*) anular; (: *strike*) desconvocar; ~ **on** *vt fus* (*visit*) visitar; (*turn to*) acudir a; ~ **out** *vi* gritar; ~ **up** *vt* (*MIL*) llamar al servicio militar; (*TEL*) llamar; ~**box** (*BRIT*) *n* cabina telefónica; ~ **centre** *n* (*BRIT*) centro de atención al cliente; ~**er** *n* visita; (*TEL*) usuario/a; ~ **girl** *n* prostituta; ~**in** (*US*) *n* (programa *m*) coloquio (por teléfono); ~**ing** *n* vocación *f*; (*occupation*) profesión *f*; ~**ing card** (*US*) *n* tarjeta de visita

callous ['kæləs] *adj* insensible, cruel

calm [kɑːm] *adj* tranquilo; (*sea*) liso, en calma ♦ *n* calma, tranquilidad *f* ♦ *vt* calmar, tranquilizar; ~ **down** *vi* calmarse, tranquilizarse ♦ *vt* calmar, tranquilizar

Calor gas ® ['kælə*-] *n* butano

calorie ['kæləri] *n* caloría

calves [kɑːvz] *npl of* **calf**

Cambodia [kæm'bəudjə] *n* Camboya

camcorder ['kæmkɔːdə*] *n* videocámara

came [keim] *pt of* **come**

camel ['kæməl] *n* camello

camera ['kæmərə] *n* máquina fotográfica; (*CINEMA, TV*) cámara; **in ~** (*LAW*) a puerta cerrada; ~**man** *n* cámara *m*

camouflage ['kæməflɑːʒ] *n* camuflaje *m* ♦ *vt* camuflar

camp [kæmp] *n* campamento, camping *m*; (*MIL*) campamento; (*for prisoners*) campo; (*fig: faction*) bando ♦ *vi* acampar ♦ *adj* afectado, afeminado

campaign [kæm'pein] *n* (*MIL, POL etc*) campaña ♦ *vi* hacer campaña

camp: ~**bed** (*BRIT*) *n* cama de campaña; ~**er** *n* campista *m/f*; (*vehicle*) caravana; ~**ing** *n* camping *m*; **to go ~ing** hacer camping; ~**site** *n* camping *m*

campus ['kæmpəs] *n* ciudad *f* universitaria

can¹ [kæn] *n* (*of oil, water*) bidón *m*; (*tin*) lata, bote *m* ♦ *vt* enlatar

┌─────────────┐
│ **KEYWORD** │
└─────────────┘

can² [kæn] (*negative* **cannot, can't**; *conditional and pt* **could**) *aux vb* **1** (*be able to*) poder; **you ~ do it if you try** puedes hacerlo si lo intentas; **I ~'t see you** no te veo

2 (*know how to*) saber; **I ~ swim/play tennis/drive** sé nadar/jugar al tenis/conducir; ~ **you speak French?** ¿hablas *or* sabes hablar francés?

3 (*may*) poder; ~ **I use your phone?** ¿me dejas *or* puedo usar tu teléfono?

4 (*expressing disbelief, puzzlement etc*): **it ~'t be true!** ¡no puede ser (verdad)!; **what CAN he want?** ¿qué querrá?

5 (*expressing possibility, suggestion etc*): **he could be in the library** podría estar en la biblioteca; **she could have been delayed** pudo haberse retrasado

Canada ['kænədə] *n* (el) Canadá; **Canadian** [kə'neidiən] *adj, n* canadiense *m/f*

canal [kə'næl] *n* canal *m*

canary [kə'neəri] *n* canario; **the C~ Islands** *npl* las (Islas) Canarias

cancel ['kænsəl] *vt* cancelar; (*train*) suprimir; (*cross out*) tachar, borrar; ~**lation** [-'leifən] *n* cancelación *f*; supresión *f*

cancer ['kænsə*] *n* cáncer *m*; **C~** (*ASTROLOGY*) Cáncer *m*

candid ['kændid] *adj* franco, abierto

candidate ['kændideit] *n* candidato/a

candle ['kændl] *n* vela; (*in church*) cirio; ~**light** *n*: **by ~light** a la luz de una vela; ~**stick** *n* (*single*) candelero; (*low*) palmatoria; (*bigger, ornate*) candelabro

candour ['kændə*] (*US* **candor**) *n* franqueza

candy ['kændi] *n* azúcar *m* cande; (*US*) caramelo; ~**floss** (*BRIT*) *n* algodón *m* (azucarado)

cane [kein] *n* (*BOT*) caña; (*stick*) vara,

palmeta; *(for furniture)* mimbre *f* ♦ *(BRIT)* vt *(SCOL)* castigar (con vara)
canister [ˈkænɪstə*] *n* bote *m*, lata; *(of gas)* bombona
cannabis [ˈkænəbɪs] *n* marijuana
canned [kænd] *adj* en lata, de lata
cannon [ˈkænən] *(pl ~ or ~s) n* cañón *m*
cannot [ˈkænɔt] = **can not**
canoe [kəˈnuː] *n* canoa; *(SPORT)* piragua; **~ing** *n* piragüismo
canon [ˈkænən] *n (clergyman)* canónigo; *(standard)* canon *m*
can-opener *n* abrelatas *m inv*
canopy [ˈkænəpɪ] *n* dosel *m*; toldo
can't [kænt] = **can not**
canteen [kænˈtiːn] *n (eating place)* cantina; *(BRIT: of cutlery)* juego
canter [ˈkæntə*] *vi* ir a medio galope
canvas [ˈkænvəs] *n (material)* lona; *(painting)* lienzo; *(NAUT)* velas *fpl*
canvass [ˈkænvəs] *vi (POL)*: **to ~ for** solicitar votos por ♦ *vt (COMM)* sondear
canyon [ˈkænjən] *n* cañón *m*
cap [kæp] *n (hat)* gorra; *(of pen)* capuchón *m*; *(of bottle)* tapa, tapón *m*; *(contraceptive)* diafragma *m*; *(for toy gun)* cápsula ♦ *vt (outdo)* superar; *(limit)* recortar
capability [keɪpəˈbɪlɪtɪ] *n* capacidad *f*
capable [ˈkeɪpəbl] *adj* capaz
capacity [kəˈpæsɪtɪ] *n* capacidad *f*; *(position)* calidad *f*
cape [keɪp] *n* capa; *(GEO)* cabo
caper [ˈkeɪpə*] *n (CULIN: gen: ~s)* alcaparra; *(prank)* broma
capital [ˈkæpɪtl] *n (also: ~ **city**)* capital *f*; *(money)* capital *m*; *(also: ~ **letter**)* mayúscula; ~ **gains tax** *n* impuesto sobre las ganancias de capital; **~ism** *n* capitalismo; **~ist** *adj, n* capitalista *m/f*; **~ize on** *vt fus* aprovechar; ~ **punishment** *n* pena de muerte

Capitol

🛈 *El Capitolio* (**Capitol**) *es el edificio del Congreso* (**Congress**) *de los Estados Unidos, situado en la ciudad de Washington. Por extensión, también se suele llamar así al edificio en el que tienen lugar las sesiones parlamentarias de la cámara de representantes de muchos de los estados.*

Capricorn [ˈkæprɪkɔːn] *n (ASTROLOGY)* Capricornio
capsize [kæpˈsaɪz] *vt* volcar, hacer zozobrar ♦ *vi* volcarse, zozobrar
capsule [ˈkæpsjuːl] *n* cápsula
captain [ˈkæptɪn] *n* capitán *m*
caption [ˈkæpʃən] *n (heading)* título; *(to picture)* leyenda
captive [ˈkæptɪv] *adj, n* cautivo/a *m/f*
capture [ˈkæptʃə*] *vt* prender, apresar; *(animal, COMPUT)* capturar; *(place)* tomar; *(attention)* captar, llamar ♦ *n* apresamiento; captura; toma; *(data ~)* formulación *f* de datos
car [kɑː*] *n* coche *m*, carro *(AM)*, automóvil *m*; *(US: RAIL)* vagón *m*
carafe [kəˈræf] *n* jarra
carat [ˈkærət] *n* quilate *m*
caravan [ˈkærəvæn] *n (BRIT)* caravana, ruló *f*; *(in desert)* caravana; **~ning** *n*: **to go ~ning** ir de vacaciones en caravana, viajar en caravana; ~ **site** *(BRIT)* n camping *m* para caravanas
carbohydrate [kɑːbəʊˈhaɪdreɪt] *n* hidrato de carbono; *(food)* fécula
carbon [ˈkɑːbən] *n* carbono; ~ **paper** *n* papel *m* carbón
car boot sale *n* mercadillo organizado en un aparcamiento, en el que se exponen las mercancías en el maletero del coche
carburettor [kɑːbjuˈretə*] *(US* **carburetor**) *n* carburador *m*
card [kɑːd] *n (material)* cartulina; *(index ~ etc)* ficha; *(playing ~)* carta, naipe *m*; *(visiting ~, greetings ~ etc)* tarjeta; **~board** *n* cartón *m*
cardiac [ˈkɑːdɪæk] *adj* cardíaco
cardigan [ˈkɑːdɪɡən] *n* rebeca
cardinal [ˈkɑːdɪnl] *adj* cardinal; *(importance, principal)* esencial ♦ *n* cardenal *m*

card index n fichero

care [kɛə*] n (attention) cuidado; (worry) inquietud f; (charge) cargo, custodia ♦ vi: **to ~ about** (person, animal) tener cariño a; (thing, idea) preocuparse por; **~ of** en casa de, al cuidado de; **in sb's ~** a cargo de uno; **to take ~ to** cuidarse de, tener cuidado de; **to take ~ of** cuidar; (problem etc) ocuparse de; **I don't ~** no me importa; **I couldn't ~ less** eso me trae sin cuidado; **~ for** vt fus cuidar a; (like) querer

career [kə'rɪə*] n profesión f; (in work, school) carrera ♦ vi (also: **~ along**) correr a toda velocidad; **~ woman** n mujer f dedicada a su profesión

care: ~free adj despreocupado; **~ful** adj cuidadoso; (cautious) cauteloso; **(be) ~ful!** ¡tenga cuidado!; **~fully** adv con cuidado, cuidadosamente; con cautela; **~less** adj descuidado; (heedless) poco atento; **~lessness** n descuido; falta de atención; **~r** [ˈkɛərə*] n enfermero/a m/f (official); (unpaid) persona que cuida a un pariente o vecino

caress [kə'rɛs] n caricia ♦ vt acariciar

caretaker [ˈkɛəteɪkə*] n portero/a, conserje m/f

car-ferry n transbordador m para coches

cargo [ˈkɑːgəʊ] (pl **~es**) n cargamento, carga

car hire n alquiler m de automóviles

Caribbean [kærɪ'biːən] n: **the ~ (Sea)** el (Mar) Caribe

caring [ˈkɛərɪŋ] adj humanitario; (behaviour) afectuoso

carnation [kɑː'neɪʃən] n clavel m

carnival [ˈkɑːnɪvəl] n carnaval m; (US: funfair) parque m de atracciones

carol [ˈkærəl] n: **(Christmas) ~** villancico

carp [kɑːp] n (fish) carpa

car park (BRIT) n aparcamiento, parking m

carpenter [ˈkɑːpɪntə*] n carpintero/a

carpet [ˈkɑːpɪt] n alfombra; (fitted) moqueta ♦ vt alfombrar

car phone n teléfono movil

car rental (US) n alquiler m de coches

carriage [ˈkærɪdʒ] n (BRIT: RAIL) vagón m; (horse-drawn) coche m; (of goods) transporte m; (: cost) porte m, flete m; **~way** (BRIT) n (part of road) calzada

carrier [ˈkærɪə*] n (transport company) transportista, empresa de transportes; (MED) portador m; **~ bag** (BRIT) n bolsa de papel or plástico

carrot [ˈkærət] n zanahoria

carry [ˈkærɪ] vt (subj: person) llevar; (transport) transportar; (involve: responsibilities etc) entrañar, implicar; (MED) ser portador de ♦ vi (sound) oírse; **to get carried away** (fig) entusiasmarse; **~ on** vi (continue) seguir (adelante), continuar ♦ vt proseguir, continuar; **~ out** (orders) cumplir; (investigation) llevar a cabo, realizar; **~ cot** (BRIT) n cuna portátil; **~-on** (inf) n (fuss) lío

cart [kɑːt] n carro, carreta ♦ vt (inf: transport) acarrear

carton [ˈkɑːtən] n (box) caja (de cartón); (of milk etc) bote m; (of yogurt) tarrina

cartoon [kɑː'tuːn] n (PRESS) caricatura; (comic strip) tira cómica; (film) dibujos mpl animados

cartridge [ˈkɑːtrɪdʒ] n cartucho; (of pen) recambio; (of record player) cápsula

carve [kɑːv] vt (meat) trinchar; (wood, stone) cincelar, esculpir; (initials etc) grabar; **~ up** vt dividir, repartir; **carving** n (object) escultura; (design) talla; (art) tallado; **carving knife** n trinchante m

car wash n lavado de coches

case [keɪs] n (container) caja; (MED) caso; (for jewels etc) estuche m; (LAW) causa, proceso; (BRIT: also: **suit~**) maleta; **in ~ of** en caso de; **in any ~** en todo caso; **just in ~** por si acaso

cash [kæʃ] n dinero en efectivo, dinero contante ♦ vt cobrar, hacer efectivo; **to pay (in) ~** pagar al contado; **~ on delivery** cóbrese al entregar; **~book** n libro de caja; **~ card** n tarjeta f dinero; **~ desk** (BRIT) n caja; **~ dispenser** n cajero automático

cashew [kæ'ʃuː] n (also: **~ nut**) anacardo

cash flow *n* flujo de fondos, cash-flow *m*
cashier [kæ'ʃɪə•] *n* cajero/a
cashmere ['kæʃmɪə•] *n* cachemira
cash register *n* caja
casing ['keɪsɪŋ] *n* revestimiento
casino [kə'siːnəu] *n* casino
casket ['kɑːskɪt] *n* cofre *m*, estuche *m*; (*US: coffin*) ataúd *m*
casserole ['kæsərəul] *n* (*food, pot*) cazuela
cassette [kæ'set] *n* cassette *f*; ~ **player / recorder** *n* tocacassettes *m inv*, cassette *m*
cast [kɑːst] (*pt, pp* **cast**) *vt* (*throw*) echar, arrojar, lanzar; (*glance, eyes*) dirigir; (*THEATRE*): **to ~ sb as Othello** dar a uno el papel de Otelo ♦ *vi* (*FISHING*) lanzar ♦ *n* (*THEATRE*) reparto; (*also*: **plaster ~**) vaciado; **to ~ one's vote** votar; **to ~ doubt on** suscitar dudas acerca de; **~ off** *vi* (*NAUT*) desamarrar; (*KNITTING*) cerrar (los puntos); **~ on** *vi* (*KNITTING*) poner los puntos
castanets [kæstə'nets] *npl* castañuelas *fpl*
castaway ['kɑːstəwaɪ] *n* náufrago/a
caster sugar ['kɑːstə•-] (*BRIT*) *n* azúcar *m* extrafino
Castile [kæs'tiːl] *n* Castilla; **Castilian** *adj*, *n* castellano/a *m/f*
casting vote ['kɑːstɪŋ-] (*BRIT*) *n* voto decisivo
cast iron *n* hierro fundido
castle ['kɑːsl] *n* castillo; (*CHESS*) torre *f*
castor oil ['kɑːstə•-] *n* aceite *m* de ricino
casual ['kæʒjul] *adj* fortuito, (*irregular: work etc*) eventual, temporero; (*unconcerned*) despreocupado; (*clothes*) de sport; **~ly** *adv* de manera despreocupada; (*dress*) de sport
casualty ['kæʒjultɪ] *n* víctima, herido; (*dead*) muerto; (*MED: department*) urgencias *fpl*
cat [kæt] *n* gato; (*big ~*) felino
Catalan ['kætəlæn] *adj*, *n* catalán/ana *m/f*
catalogue ['kætəlɔg] (*US* **catalog**) *n* catálogo ♦ *vt* catalogar
Catalonia [kætə'ləunɪə] *n* Cataluña
catalyst ['kætəlɪst] *n* catalizador *m*
catalytic convertor [kætə'lɪtɪk kən'vɜːtə•]

n catalizador *m*
catapult ['kætəpʌlt] *n* tirachinas *m inv*
catarrh [kə'tɑː•] *n* catarro
catastrophe [kə'tæstrəfɪ] *n* catástrofe *f*
catch [kætʃ] (*pt, pp* **caught**) *vt* coger (*SP*), agarrar (*AM*); (*arrest*) detener; (*grasp*) asir; (*breath*) contener; (*surprise: person*) sorprender; (*attract: attention*) captar; (*hear*) oír; (*MED*) contagiarse de, coger; (*also*: ~ **up**) alcanzar ♦ *vi* (*fire*) encenderse; (*in branches etc*) enredarse ♦ *n* (*fish etc*) pesca; (*act of catching*) cogida; (*hidden problem*) dificultad *f*; (*game*) pilla-pilla; (*of lock*) pestillo, cerradura; **to ~ fire** encenderse; **to ~ sight of** divisar; ~ **on** *vi* (*understand*) caer en la cuenta; (*grow popular*) hacerse popular; ~ **up** *vi* (*fig*) ponerse al día; ~**ing** ['kætʃɪŋ] *adj* (*MED*) contagioso; ~**ment area** ['kætʃmənt-] (*BRIT*) *n* zona de captación; ~**phrase** ['kætʃfreɪz] *n* lema *m*, eslogan *m*; ~**y** ['kætʃɪ] *adj* (*tune*) pegadizo
category ['kætɪgərɪ] *n* categoría, clase *f*
cater ['keɪtə•] *vi*: **to ~ for** (*BRIT*) abastecer a; (*needs*) atender a; (*COMM: parties etc*) proveer comida a; ~**er** *n* abastecedor(a) *m/f*, proveedor(a) *m/f*; ~**ing** *n* (*trade*) hostelería
caterpillar ['kætəpɪlə•] *n* oruga, gusano
cathedral [kə'θiːdrəl] *n* catedral *f*
catholic ['kæθəlɪk] *adj* (*tastes etc*) amplio; **C~** *adj*, *n* (*REL*) católico/a *m/f*
CAT scan [kæt-] *n* TAC *f*, tomografía
Catseye ® ['kæts'aɪ] (*BRIT*) *n* (*AUT*) catafoto
cattle ['kætl] *npl* ganado
catty ['kætɪ] *adj* malicioso, rencoroso
caucus ['kɔːkəs] *n* (*POL*) camarilla política; (: *US: to elect candidates*) comité *m* electoral
caught [kɔːt] *pt, pp of* **catch**
cauliflower ['kɔlɪflauə•] *n* coliflor *f*
cause [kɔːz] *n* causa, motivo, razón *f*; (*principle: also*: *POL*) causa ♦ *vt* causar
caution ['kɔːʃən] *n* cautela, prudencia; (*warning*) advertencia, amonestación *f*

♦ *vt* amonestar; **cautious** *adj* cauteloso, prudente, precavido
cavalry ['kævəlrı] *n* caballería
cave [keɪv] *n* cueva, caverna; **~ in** *vi* (*roof etc*) derrumbarse, hundirse
caviar(e) ['kævɪɑː'] *n* caviar *m*
CB *n abbr* (= *Citizens' Band (Radio)*) banda ciudadana
CBI *n abbr* (= *Confederation of British Industry*) ≈ C.E.O.E. *f* (*SP*)
cc *abbr* = **cubic centimetres**; = **carbon copy**
CCTV *n abbr* (= *closed-circuit television*) circuito cerrado de televisión
CD *n abbr* (= *compact disc*) DC *m*; (*player*) (reproductor *m* de) disco compacto; **~ player** *n* lector *m* de discos compactos, **~-ROM** [siːdiːˈrɔm] *n abbr* CD-ROM *m*
cease [siːs] *vt*, *vi* cesar; **~fire** *n* alto *m* el fuego; **~less** *adj* incesante
cedar ['siːdə'] *n* cedro
ceiling ['siːlɪŋ] *n* techo; (*fig*) límite *m*
celebrate ['selɪbreɪt] *vt* celebrar ♦ *vi* divertirse; **~d** *adj* célebre; **celebration** [-'breɪʃən] *n* fiesta, celebración *f*
celery ['selərɪ] *n* apio
cell [sel] *n* celda; (*BIOL*) célula
cellar ['selə'] *n* sótano; (*for wine*) bodega
cello ['tʃeləʊ] *n* violoncelo
Cellophane ® ['seləfeɪn] *n* celofán *m*
cellphone ['selfəʊn] *n* teléfono celular
Celt [kelt, selt] *adj*, *n* celta *m/f*; **~ic** *adj* celta
cement [sə'ment] *n* cemento; **~ mixer** *n* hormigonera
cemetery ['semɪtrɪ] *n* cementerio
censor ['sensə'] *n* censor *m* ♦ *vt* (*cut*) censurar; **~ship** *n* censura
censure ['senʃə'] *vt* censurar
census ['sensəs] *n* censo
cent [sent] *n* (*unit of dollar*) centavo, céntimo; (*unit of euro*) céntimo; *see also* **per**
centenary [sen'tiːnərɪ] *n* centenario
center ['sentə'] (*US*) = **centre**
centi... [sentɪ] *prefix*: **~grade** *adj* centígrado; **~litre** (*US* **~liter**) *n* centilitro;

~metre (*US* **~meter**) *n* centímetro
centipede ['sentɪpiːd] *n* ciempiés *m inv*
central ['sentrəl] *adj* central; (*of house etc*) céntrico; **C~ America** *n* Centroamérica; **~ heating** *n* calefacción *f* central; **~ize** *vt* centralizar
centre ['sentə'] (*US* **center**) *n* centro; (*fig*) núcleo ♦ *vt* centrar; **~-forward** *n* (*SPORT*) delantero centro; **~-half** *n* (*SPORT*) medio centro
century ['sentjʊrɪ] *n* siglo; **20th ~** siglo veinte
ceramic [sɪ'ræmɪk] *adj* cerámico; **~s** *n* cerámica
cereal ['siːrɪəl] *n* cereal *m*
ceremony ['serɪmənɪ] *n* ceremonia; **to stand on ~** hacer ceremonias, estar de cumplido
certain ['səːtən] *adj* seguro; (*person*): **a ~ Mr Smith** un tal Sr Smith; (*particular, some*) cierto; **for ~** a ciencia cierta; **~ly** *adv* (*undoubtedly*) ciertamente; (*of course*) desde luego, por supuesto; **~ty** *n* certeza, certidumbre *f*, seguridad *f*; (*inevitability*) certeza
certificate [sə'tɪfɪkɪt] *n* certificado
certified ['səːtɪfaɪd]: **~ mail** (*US*) *n* correo certificado; **~ public accountant** (*US*) *n* contable *m/f* diplomado/a
certify ['səːtɪfaɪ] *vt* certificar; (*award diploma to*) conceder un diploma a; (*declare insane*) declarar loco
cervical ['səːvɪkl] *adj* cervical
cervix ['səːvɪks] *n* cuello del útero
cf. *abbr* (= *compare*) cfr
CFC *n abbr* (= *chlorofluorocarbon*) CFC *m*
ch. *abbr* (= *chapter*) cap
chain [tʃeɪn] *n* cadena; (*of mountains*) cordillera; (*of events*) sucesión *f* ♦ *vt* (*also*: **~ up**) encadenar; **~ reaction** *n* reacción *f* en cadena; **~-smoke** *vi* fumar un cigarrillo tras otro; **~ store** *n* tienda de una cadena, ≈ gran almacén
chair [tʃeə'] *n* silla; (*armchair*) sillón *m*, butaca; (*of university*) cátedra; (*of meeting etc*) presidencia ♦ *vt* (*meeting*) presidir; **~lift** *n* telesilla; **~man** *n* presidente *m*

chalk [tʃɔːk] *n* (GEO) creta; (*for writing*) tiza (*SP*), gis *m* (*AM*)

challenge ['tʃælɪndʒ] *n* desafío, reto ♦ *vt* desafiar, retar; (*statement, right*) poner en duda; **to ~ sb to do sth** retar a uno a que haga algo; **challenging** *adj* exigente; (*tone*) de desafío

chamber ['tʃeɪmbə*] *n* cámara, sala; (POL) cámara; (BRIT: LAW: *gen pl*) despacho; **~ of commerce** cámara de comercio; **~maid** *n* camarera

chamois ['ʃæmwɑː] *n* gamuza

champagne [ʃæm'peɪn] *n* champaña *m*, champán *m*

champion ['tʃæmpɪən] *n* campeón/ona *m/f*; (*of cause*) defensor(a) *m/f*; **~ship** *n* campeonato

chance [tʃɑːns] *n* (*opportunity*) ocasión *f*, oportunidad *f*; (*likelihood*) posibilidad *f*; (*risk*) riesgo ♦ *vt* arriesgar, probar ♦ *adj* fortuito, casual; **to ~ it** arriesgarse, intentarlo; **to take a ~** arriesgarse; **by ~** por casualidad

chancellor ['tʃɑːnsələ*] *n* canciller *m*; **C~ of the Exchequer** (BRIT) *n* Ministro de Hacienda

chandelier [ʃændə'lɪə*] *n* araña (de luces)

change [tʃeɪndʒ] *vt* cambiar; (*replace*) cambiar, reemplazar; (*gear, clothes, job*) cambiar de; (*transform*) transformar ♦ *vi* cambiar(se); (*trains*) hacer transbordo; (*traffic lights*) cambiar de color; (*be transformed*): **to ~ into** transformarse en ♦ *n* cambio; (*alteration*) modificación *f*, transformación *f*; (*of clothes*) muda; (*coins*) suelto, sencillo; (*money returned*) vuelta; **to ~ gear** (AUT) cambiar de marcha; **to ~ one's mind** cambiar de opinión o idea; **for a ~** para variar; **~able** *adj* (*weather*) cambiable; **~ machine** *n* máquina de cambio; **~over** *n* (*to new system*) cambio; **changing** *adj* cambiante; **changing room** (BRIT) *n* vestuario

channel ['tʃænl] *n* (TV) canal *m*; (*of river*) cauce *m*; (*groove*) conducto; (*fig: medium*) medio ♦ *vt* (*river etc*) encauzar; **the**

(English) C~ el Canal (de la Mancha); **the C~ Islands** las Islas Normandas; **the C~ Tunnel** el túnel del Canal de la Mancha, el Eurotúnel; **~-hopping** *n* (TV) zapping *m*

chant [tʃɑːnt] *n* (*of crowd*) gritos *mpl*; (REL) canto ♦ *vt* (*slogan, word*) repetir a gritos

chaos ['keɪɔs] *n* caos *m*

chap [tʃæp] (BRIT: *inf*) *n* (*man*) tío, tipo

chapel ['tʃæpəl] *n* capilla

chaperone ['ʃæpərəun] *n* carabina

chaplain ['tʃæplɪn] *n* capellán *m*

chapped [tʃæpt] *adj* agrietado

chapter ['tʃæptə*] *n* capítulo

char [tʃɑː*] *vt* (*burn*) carbonizar, chamuscar

character ['kærɪktə*] *n* carácter *m*, naturaleza, índole *f*; (*moral strength, personality*) carácter *m*; (*in novel, film*) personaje *m*; **~istic** [-'rɪstɪk] *adj* característico ♦ *n* característica

charcoal ['tʃɑːkəul] *n* carbón *m* vegetal; (ART) carboncillo

charge [tʃɑːdʒ] *n* (LAW) cargo, acusación *f*; (*cost*) precio, coste *m*; (*responsibility*) cargo ♦ *vt* (LAW): **to ~ (with)** acusar (de); (*battery*) cargar; (*price*) pedir; (*customer*) cobrar ♦ *vi* precipitarse; (MIL) cargar, atacar; **~s** *npl*: **to reverse the ~s** (BRIT: TEL) revertir el cobro; **to take ~ of** hacerse cargo de, encargarse de; **to be in ~ of** estar encargado de; (*business*) mandar; **how much do you ~?** ¿cuánto cobra usted?; **to ~ an expense (up) to sb's account** cargar algo a cuenta de alguien; **~ card** *n* tarjeta de cuenta

charity ['tʃærɪtɪ] *n* caridad *f*; (*organization*) sociedad *f* benéfica; (*money, gifts*) limosnas *fpl*

charm [tʃɑːm] *n* encanto, atractivo; (*talisman*) hechizo; (*on bracelet*) dije *m* ♦ *vt* encantar; **~ing** *adj* encantador(a)

chart [tʃɑːt] *n* (*diagram*) cuadro; (*graph*) gráfica; (*map*) carta de navegación ♦ *vt* (*course*) trazar; (*progress*) seguir; **~s** *npl* (*Top 40*): **the ~s** ≈ los 40 principales (SP)

charter ['tʃɑːtə*] *vt* (*plane*) alquilar; (*ship*) fletar ♦ *n* (*document*) carta; (*of university,*

company) estatutos *mpl*; **~ed
accountant** (*BRIT*) *n* contable *m/f*
diplomado/a; **~ flight** *n* vuelo chárter
chase [tʃeɪs] *vt* (*pursue*) perseguir; (*also:* **~
away**) ahuyentar ♦ *n* persecución *f*
chasm ['kæzəm] *n* sima
chassis ['ʃæsɪ] *n* chasis *m*
chat [tʃæt] *vi* (*also:* **have a ~**) charlar ♦ *n*
charla; **~ show** (*BRIT*) *n* programa *m* de
entrevistas
chatter ['tʃætə*] *vi* (*person*) charlar; (*teeth*)
castañetear ♦ *n* (*of birds*) parloteo; (*of
people*) charla, cháchara; **~box** (*inf*) *n*
parlanchín/ina *m/f*
chatty ['tʃætɪ] *adj* (*style*) informal; (*person*)
hablador(a)
chauffeur ['ʃəʊfə*] *n* chófer *m*
chauvinist ['ʃəʊvɪnɪst] *n* (*male ~*) machista
m; (*nationalist*) chovinista *m/f*
cheap [tʃiːp] *adj* barato; (*joke*) de mal
gusto; (*poor quality*) de mala calidad
♦ *adv* barato; **~ day return** *n* billete *m*
de ida y vuelta el mismo día; **~er** *adj*
más barato; **~ly** *adv* barato, a bajo
precio
cheat [tʃiːt] *vi* hacer trampa ♦ *vt*: **to ~ sb
(out of sth)** estafar (algo) a uno ♦ *n*
(*person*) tramposo/a
check [tʃek] *vt* (*examine*) controlar; (*facts*)
comprobar; (*halt*) parar, detener;
(*restrain*) refrenar, restringir ♦ *n*
(*inspection*) control *m*, inspección *f*; (*curb*)
freno; (*US: bill*) nota, cuenta, (*US*)
= **cheque**; (*pattern: gen pl*) cuadro ♦ *adj*
(*also:* **~ed**: *pattern, cloth*) a cuadros; **~ in**
vi (*at hotel*) firmar el registro; (*at airport*)
facturar el equipaje ♦ *vt* (*luggage*)
facturar; **~ out** *vi* (*of hotel*) marcharse; **~
up** *vi*: **to ~ up on sth** comprobar algo; **to
~ up on sb** investigar a alguien; **~ered**
(*US*) *adj* = **check; chequered; ~ers** (*US*)
n juego de damas; **~-in** (*desk*) *n*
mostrador *m* de facturación; **~ing
account** (*US*) *n* cuenta corriente; **~mate**
n jaque *m* mate; **~out** *n* caja; **~point** *n*
(*punto de*) control *m*; **~room** (*US*) *n*
consigna; **~up** *n* (*MED*) reconocimiento

general
cheek [tʃiːk] *n* mejilla; (*impudence*)
descaro; **what a ~!** ¡qué cara!; **~bone** *n*
pómulo; **~y** *adj* fresco, descarado
cheep [tʃiːp] *vi* piar
cheer [tʃɪə*] *vt* vitorear, aplaudir; (*gladden*)
alegrar, animar ♦ *vi* dar vivas ♦ *n* viva *m*;
~s *npl* aplausos *mpl*; **~s!** ¡salud!; **~ up** *vi*
animarse ♦ *vt* alegrar, animar; **~ful** *adj*
alegre
cheerio [tʃɪərɪ'əʊ] (*BRIT*) *excl* ¡hasta luego!
cheese [tʃiːz] *n* queso; **~board** *n* tabla
de quesos
cheetah ['tʃiːtə] *n* leopardo cazador
chef [ʃef] *n* jefe/a *m/f* de cocina
chemical ['kemɪkəl] *adj* químico ♦ *n*
producto químico
chemist ['kemɪst] *n* (*BRIT: pharmacist*)
farmacéutico/a; (*scientist*) químico/a; **~ry**
n química; **~'s** (*shop*) (*BRIT*) *n* farmacia
cheque [tʃek] (*US* **check**) *n* cheque *m*;
~book *n* talonario de cheques (*SP*),
chequera (*AM*); **~ card** *n* tarjeta de
cheque
chequered ['tʃekəd] (*US* **checkered**) *adj*
(*fig*) accidentado
cherish ['tʃerɪʃ] *vt* (*love*) querer, apreciar;
(*protect*) cuidar; (*hope etc*) abrigar
cherry ['tʃerɪ] *n* cereza; (*also:* **~ tree**)
cerezo
chess [tʃes] *n* ajedrez *m*; **~board** *n*
tablero (de ajedrez)
chest [tʃest] *n* (*ANAT*) pecho; (*box*) cofre
m, cajón *m*; **~ of drawers** *n* cómoda
chestnut ['tʃesnʌt] *n* castaña; **~ (tree)** *n*
castaño
chew [tʃuː] *vt* mascar, masticar; **~ing
gum** *n* chicle *m*
chic [ʃiːk] *adj* elegante
chick [tʃɪk] *n* pollito, polluelo; (*inf: girl*)
chica
chicken ['tʃɪkɪn] *n* gallina, pollo; (*food*)
pollo; (*inf: coward*) gallina *m/f*; **~ out**
(*inf*) *vi* rajarse; **~pox** *n* varicela
chicory ['tʃɪkərɪ] *n* (*for coffee*) achicoria;
(*salad*) escarola
chief [tʃiːf] *n* jefe/a *m/f* ♦ *adj* principal; **~**

executive *n* director(a) *m/f* general; **~ly** *adv* principalmente

chilblain ['tʃɪlbleɪn] *n* sabañón *m*

child [tʃaɪld] (*pl* **children**) *n* niño/a; (*offspring*) hijo/a; **~birth** *n* parto; **~hood** *n* niñez *f*, infancia; **~ish** *adj* pueril, aniñado; **~like** *adj* de niño; **~ minder** (*BRIT*) *n* madre *f* de día; **~ren** ['tʃɪldrən] *npl of* **child**

Chile ['tʃɪlɪ] *n* Chile *m*; **~an** *adj*, *n* chileno/a *m/f*

chill [tʃɪl] *n* frío; (*MED*) resfriado ♦ *vt* enfriar; (*CULIN*) congelar

chil(l)i ['tʃɪlɪ] (*BRIT*) *n* chile *m* (*SP*), ají *m* (*AM*)

chilly ['tʃɪlɪ] *adj* frío

chime [tʃaɪm] *n* repique *m*; (*of clock*) campanada ♦ *vi* repicar; sonar

chimney ['tʃɪmnɪ] *n* chimenea; **~ sweep** *n* deshollinador *m*

chimpanzee [tʃɪmpæn'ziː] *n* chimpancé *m*

chin [tʃɪn] *n* mentón *m*, barbilla

china ['tʃaɪnə] *n* porcelana; (*crockery*) loza

China ['tʃaɪnə] *n* China; **Chinese** [tʃaɪ'niːz] *adj* chino ♦ *n inv* chino/a; (*LING*) chino

chink [tʃɪŋk] *n* (*opening*) grieta, hendedura; (*noise*) tintineo

chip [tʃɪp] *n* (*gen pl*: *CULIN*: *BRIT*) patata (*SP*) *or* papa (*AM*) frita; (: *US*: *also*: **potato ~**) patata *or* papa frita; (*of wood*) astilla; (*of glass, stone*) lasca; (*at poker*) ficha; (*COMPUT*) chip *m* ♦ *vt* (*cup, plate*) desconchar

---
chip shop

🛈 *Se denomina* **chip shop** *o "fish-and-chip shop" a un establecimiento en el que se sirven algunas especialidades de comida rápida, muy populares entre los británicos, sobre todo pescado rebozado y patatas fritas.*

---

chiropodist [kɪ'rɔpədɪst] (*BRIT*) *n* pedicuro/a, callista *m/f*

chirp [tʃəːp] *vi* (*bird*) gorjear, piar

chisel ['tʃɪzl] *n* (*for wood*) escoplo; (*for stone*) cincel *m*

chit [tʃɪt] *n* nota

chitchat ['tʃɪttʃæt] *n* chismes *mpl*, habladurías *fpl*

chivalry ['ʃɪvəlrɪ] *n* caballerosidad *f*

chives [tʃaɪvz] *npl* cebollinos *mpl*

chlorine ['klɔːriːn] *n* cloro

chock-a-block ['tʃɔkə'blɔk] *adj* atestado

chock-full ['tʃɔk'ful] *adj* atestado

chocolate ['tʃɔklɪt] *n* chocolate *m*; (*sweet*) bombón *m*

choice [tʃɔɪs] *n* elección *f*, selección *f*; (*option*) opción *f*; (*preference*) preferencia ♦ *adj* escogido

choir ['kwaɪə*] *n* coro; **~boy** *n* niño de coro

choke [tʃəuk] *vi* ahogarse; (*on food*) atragantarse ♦ *vt* estrangular, ahogar; (*block*): **to be ~d with** estar atascado de ♦ *n* (*AUT*) estárter *m*

cholesterol [kə'lestərɔl] *n* colesterol *m*

choose [tʃuːz] (*pt* **chose**, *pp* **chosen**) *vt* escoger, elegir; (*team*) seleccionar; **to ~ to do sth** optar por hacer algo

choosy ['tʃuːzɪ] *adj* delicado

chop [tʃɔp] *vt* (*wood*) cortar, tajar; (*CULIN*: *also*: **~ up**) picar ♦ *n* (*CULIN*) chuleta; **~s** *npl* (*jaws*) boca, labios *mpl*

chopper ['tʃɔpə*] *n* (*helicopter*) helicóptero

choppy ['tʃɔpɪ] *adj* (*sea*) picado, agitado

chopsticks ['tʃɔpstɪks] *npl* palillos *mpl*

chord [kɔːd] *n* (*MUS*) acorde *m*

chore [tʃɔː*] *n* faena, tarea; (*routine task*) trabajo rutinario

chorus ['kɔːrəs] *n* coro; (*repeated part of song*) estribillo

chose [tʃəuz] *pt of* **choose**

chosen ['tʃəuzn] *pp of* **choose**

chowder ['tʃaudə*] *n* (*esp US*) sopa de pescado

Christ [kraɪst] *n* Cristo

christen ['krɪsn] *vt* bautizar

Christian ['krɪstɪən] *adj*, *n* cristiano/a *m/f*; **~ity** [-'ænɪtɪ] *n* cristianismo; **~ name** *n* nombre *m* de pila

Christmas ['krɪsməs] *n* Navidad *f*; **Merry ~!** ¡Felices Pascuas!; **~ card** *n* crismas *m inv*, tarjeta de Navidad; **~ Day** *n* día *m*

de Navidad; ~ **Eve** n Nochebuena; ~ **tree** n árbol m de Navidad

chrome [krəum] n cromo

chronic ['krɒnɪk] adj crónico

chronological [krɒnə'lɒdʒɪkəl] adj cronológico

chubby ['tʃʌbɪ] adj regordete

chuck [tʃʌk] (inf) vt lanzar, arrojar; (BRIT: also: ~ **up**) abandonar; ~ **out** vt (person) echar (fuera); (rubbish etc) tirar

chuckle ['tʃʌkl] vi reírse entre dientes

chug [tʃʌg] vi resoplar; (car, boat: also: ~ **along**) avanzar traqueteando

chum [tʃʌm] n compañero/a

chunk [tʃʌŋk] n pedazo, trozo

church [tʃə:tʃ] n iglesia; **~yard** n cementerio

churn [tʃə:n] n (for butter) mantequera; (for milk) lechera; ~ **out** vt producir en serie

chute [ʃu:t] n (also: **rubbish ~**) vertedero; (for coal etc) rampa de caída

chutney ['tʃʌtnɪ] n condimento a base de frutas de la India

CIA (US) n abbr (= Central Intelligence Agency) CIA f

CID (BRIT) n abbr (= Criminal Investigation Department) ≈ B.I.C. f (SP)

cider ['saɪdə*] n sidra

cigar [sɪ'gɑ:*] n puro

cigarette [sɪgə'rɛt] n cigarrillo (SP), cigarro (AM); pitillo; ~ **case** n pitillera; ~ **end** n colilla

Cinderella [sɪndə'rɛlə] n Cenicienta

cinders ['sɪndəz] npl cenizas fpl

cine camera ['sɪnɪ-] (BRIT) n cámara cinematográfica

cinema ['sɪnəmə] n cine m

cinnamon ['sɪnəmən] n canela

circle ['sə:kl] n círculo; (in theatre) anfiteatro ♦ vi dar vueltas ♦ vt (surround) rodear, cercar; (move round) dar la vuelta a

circuit ['sə:kɪt] n circuito; (tour) gira; (track) pista; (lap) vuelta; **~ous** [sə:'kjuɪtəs] adj indirecto

circular ['sə:kjulə*] adj circular ♦ n circular f

circulate ['sə:kjuleɪt] vi circular; (person: at party etc) hablar con los invitados ♦ vt poner en circulación; **circulation** [-'leɪʃən] n circulación f; (of newspaper) tirada

circumstances ['sə:kəmstənsɪz] npl circunstancias fpl; (financial condition) situación f económica

circus ['sə:kəs] n circo

CIS n abbr (= Commonwealth of Independent States) CEI f

cistern ['sɪstən] n tanque m, depósito; (in toilet) cisterna

citizen ['sɪtɪzn] n (POL) ciudadano/a; (of city) vecino/a, habitante m/f; **~ship** n ciudadanía

citrus fruits ['sɪtrəs-] npl agrios mpl

city ['sɪtɪ] n ciudad f; **the C~** centro financiero de Londres

civic ['sɪvɪk] adj cívico: (authorities) municipal; ~ **centre** (BRIT) n centro público

civil ['sɪvɪl] adj civil; (polite) atento, cortés; ~ **engineer** n ingeniero de caminos(, canales y puertos); **~ian** [sɪ'vɪlɪən] adj civil (no militar) ♦ n civil m/f, paisano/a

civilization [sɪvɪlaɪ'zeɪʃən] n civilización f

civilized ['sɪvɪlaɪzd] adj civilizado

civil: ~ **law** n derecho civil; ~ **servant** n funcionario/a del Estado; **C~ Service** n administración f pública; ~ **war** n guerra civil

claim [kleɪm] vt exigir, reclamar; (rights etc) reivindicar; (assert) pretender ♦ vi (for insurance) reclamar ♦ n reclamación f; pretensión f; **~ant** n demandante m/f

clairvoyant [klɛə'vɔɪənt] n clarividente m/f

clam [klæm] n almeja

clamber ['klæmbə*] vi trepar

clammy ['klæmɪ] adj frío y húmedo

clamour ['klæmə*] (US **clamor**) vi: **to ~ for** clamar por, pedir a voces

clamp [klæmp] n abrazadera, grapa ♦ vt (2 things together) cerrar fuertemente; (one thing on another) afianzar (con abrazadera); (AUT: wheel) poner el cepo a;

~ **down on** vt fus (subj: government, police) reforzar la lucha contra

clang [klæŋ] vi sonar, hacer estruendo

clap [klæp] vi aplaudir; ~**ping** n aplausos mpl

claret ['klærət] n burdeos m inv

clarify ['klærɪfaɪ] vt aclarar

clarinet [klærɪ'net] n clarinete m

clash [klæʃ] n enfrentamiento; choque m; desacuerdo; estruendo ♦ vi (fight) enfrentarse; (beliefs) chocar; (disagree) estar en desacuerdo; (colours) desentonar; (two events) coincidir

clasp [klɑːsp] n (hold) apretón m; (fastener) cierre m ♦ vt apretar; abrazar

class [klɑːs] n clase f ♦ vt clasificar

classic ['klæsɪk] adj, n clásico; ~**al** adj clásico

classified ['klæsɪfaɪd] adj (information) reservado; ~ **advertisement** n anuncio por palabras

classmate ['klɑːsmeɪt] n compañero/a de clase

classroom ['klɑːsrum] n aula

clatter ['klætə*] n estrépito ♦ vi hacer ruido or estrépito

clause [klɔːz] n cláusula; (LING) oración f

claw [klɔː] n (of cat) uña; (of bird of prey) garra; (of lobster) pinza

clay [kleɪ] n arcilla

clean [kliːn] adj limpio; (record, reputation) bueno, intachable; (joke) decente ♦ vt limpiar; (hands etc) lavar; ~ **out** vt limpiar; ~ **up** vt limpiar, asear; ~~**cut** adj (person) bien parecido; ~**er** n (person) asistenta; (substance) producto para la limpieza; ~**er's** n tintorería; ~**ing** n limpieza; ~**liness** ['klenlɪnɪs] n limpieza

cleanse [klenz] vt limpiar; ~**r** n (for face) crema limpiadora

clean-shaven adj sin barba, afeitado

cleansing department (BRIT) n departamento de limpieza

clear [klɪə*] adj claro; (road, way) libre; (conscience) limpio, tranquilo; (skin) terso; (sky) despejado ♦ vt (space) despejar, limpiar; (LAW: suspect) absolver; (obstacle) salvar, saltar por encima de; (cheque) aceptar ♦ vi (fog etc) despejarse ♦ adv: ~ **of** a distancia de; **to** ~ **the table** recoger or levantar la mesa; ~ **up** vt limpiar; (mystery) aclarar, resolver; ~**ance** n (removal) despeje m; (permission) acreditación f; ~~**cut** adj bien definido, nítido; ~**ing** n (in wood) claro; ~**ing bank** (BRIT) n cámara de compensación; ~**ly** adv claramente; (evidently) sin duda; ~**way** (BRIT) n carretera donde no se puede parar

clef [klef] n (MUS) clave f

cleft [kleft] n (in rock) grieta, hendedura

clench [klentʃ] vt apretar, cerrar

clergy ['klɜːdʒɪ] n clero; ~**man** n clérigo

clerical ['klerɪkəl] adj de oficina; (REL) clerical

clerk [klɑːk, (US) klɜːrk] n (BRIT) oficinista m/f; (US) dependiente/a m/f

clever ['klevə*] adj (intelligent) inteligente, listo; (skilful) hábil; (device, arrangement) ingenioso

click [klɪk] vt (tongue) chasquear; (heels) taconear ♦ vi (COMPUT) hacer clic; **to** ~ **on an icon** hacer clic en un icono

client ['klaɪənt] n cliente m/f

cliff [klɪf] n acantilado

climate ['klaɪmɪt] n clima m

climax ['klaɪmæks] n (of battle, career) apogeo; (of film, book) punto culminante; (sexual) orgasmo

climb [klaɪm] vi subir; (plant) trepar; (move with effort): **to** ~ **over a wall/into a car** trepar a una tapia/subir a un coche ♦ vt (stairs) subir; (tree) trepar a; (mountain) escalar ♦ n subida; ~~**down** n vuelta atrás; ~**er** n alpinista m/f (SP), andinista m/f (AM); ~**ing** n alpinismo (SP), andinismo (AM)

clinch [klɪntʃ] vt (deal) cerrar; (argument) remachar

cling [klɪŋ] (pt, pp **clung**) vi: **to** ~ **to** agarrarse a; (clothes) pegarse a

clinic ['klɪnɪk] n clínica; ~**al** adj clínico; (fig) frío

clink [klɪŋk] vi tintinar
clip [klɪp] n (for hair) horquilla; (also:
paper ~) sujetapapeles m inv, clip m; (TV,
CINEMA) fragmento ♦ vt (cut) cortar; (also:
~ together) unir; **~pers** npl (for
gardening) tijeras fpl; **~ping** n
(newspaper) recorte m
cloak [kləuk] n capa, manto ♦ vt (fig)
encubrir, disimular; **~room** n
guardarropa; (BRIT: WC) lavabo (SP), aseos
mpl (SP), baño (AM)
clock [klɒk] n reloj m; **~ in** or **on** vi
fichar, picar; **~ off** or **out** vi fichar or
picar la salida; **~wise** adv en el sentido
de las agujas del reloj; **~work** n aparato
de relojería ♦ adj (toy) de cuerda
clog [klɒg] n zueco, chanclo ♦ vt atascar
♦ vi (also: **~ up**) atascarse
cloister ['klɔɪstə*] n claustro
clone [kləun] n clon m ♦ vt clonar
close[1] [kləus] adj (near): **~ (to)** cerca (de);
(friend) íntimo; (connection) estrecho;
(examination) detallado, minucioso;
(weather) bochornoso; **to have a ~ shave**
(fig) escaparse por un pelo ♦ adv cerca; **~
by, ~ at hand** muy cerca; **~ to** prep cerca
de
close[2] [kləuz] vt (shut) cerrar; (end)
concluir, terminar ♦ vi (shop etc) cerrarse;
(end) concluirse, terminarse ♦ n (end) fin
m, final m, conclusión f; **~ down** vi
cerrarse definitivamente; **~d** adj (shop
etc) cerrado; **~d shop** n taller m gremial
close-knit [kləus'nɪt] adj (fig) muy unido
closely ['kləuslɪ] adv (study) con detalle;
(watch) de cerca; (resemble)
estrechamente
closet ['klɒzɪt] n armario
close-up ['kləusʌp] n primer plano
closure ['kləuʒə*] n cierre m
clot [klɒt] n (gen: **blood ~**) coágulo; (inf:
idiot) imbécil m/f ♦ vi (blood) coagularse
cloth [klɒθ] n (material) tela, paño; (rag)
trapo
clothe [kləuð] vt vestir; **~s** npl ropa; **~s
brush** n cepillo (para la ropa); **~s line** n
cuerda (para tender la ropa); **~s peg** (US

~s pin) n pinza
clothing ['kləuðɪŋ] n = **clothes**
cloud [klaud] n nube f; **~burst** n
aguacero; **~y** adj nublado, nuboso;
(liquid) turbio
clout [klaut] vt dar un tortazo a
clove [kləuv] n clavo; **~ of garlic** diente m
de ajo
clover ['kləuvə*] n trébol m
clown [klaun] n payaso ♦ vi (also: **~
about, ~ around**) hacer el payaso
cloying ['klɔɪɪŋ] adj empalagoso
club [klʌb] n (society) club m; (weapon)
porra, cachiporra; (also: **golf ~**) palo ♦ vt
aporrear ♦ vi: **to ~ together** (for gift)
comprar entre todos; **~s** npl (CARDS)
tréboles mpl; **~ class** n (AVIAT) clase f
preferente; **~house** n local social, sobre
todo en clubs deportivos
cluck [klʌk] vi cloquear
clue [klu:] n pista; (in crosswords)
indicación f; **I haven't a ~** no tengo ni
idea
clump [klʌmp] n (of trees) grupo
clumsy ['klʌmzɪ] adj (person) torpe,
desmañado; (tool) difícil de manejar;
(movement) desgarbado
clung [klʌŋ] pt, pp of **cling**
cluster ['klʌstə*] n grupo ♦ vi agruparse,
apiñarse
clutch [klʌtʃ] n (AUT) embrague m; (grasp):
~es garras fpl ♦ vt asir; agarrar
clutter ['klʌtə*] vt atestar
cm abbr (= centimetre) cm
CND n abbr (= Campaign for Nuclear
Disarmament) plataforma pro desarme
nuclear
Co. abbr = **county; company**
c/o abbr (= care of) c/a, a/c
coach [kəutʃ] n autocar m (SP), coche m
de línea; (horse-drawn) coche m; (of train)
vagón m, coche m; (SPORT) entrenador(a)
m/f, instructor(a) m/f; (tutor) profesor(a)
m/f particular ♦ vt (SPORT) entrenar;
(student) preparar, enseñar; **~ trip** n
excursión f en autocar
coal [kəul] n carbón m; **~ face** n frente m

de carbón; ~field *n* yacimiento de carbón

coalition [kəuə'lɪʃən] *n* coalición *f*

coalman ['kəulmən] (*irreg*) *n* carbonero

coalmine ['kəulmaɪn] *n* mina de carbón

coarse [kɔːs] *adj* basto, burdo; (*vulgar*) grosero, ordinario

coast [kəust] *n* costa, litoral *m* ♦ *vi* (*AUT*) ir en punto muerto; ~al *adj* costero, costanero; ~guard *n* guardacostas *m inv*; ~line *n* litoral *m*

coat [kəut] *n* abrigo; (*of animal*) pelaje *m*, lana; (*of paint*) mano *f*, capa ♦ *vt* cubrir, revestir; ~ of arms *n* escudo de armas; ~ hanger *n* percha (*SP*), gancho (*AM*); ~ing *n* capa, baño

coax [kəuks] *vt* engatusar

cobbler ['kɒblə] *n* zapatero (remendón)

cobbles ['kɒblz] *npl*, **cobblestones** ['kɒblstəunz] *npl* adoquines *mpl*

cobweb ['kɒbweb] *n* telaraña

cocaine [kə'keɪn] *n* cocaína

cock [kɒk] *n* (*rooster*) gallo; (*male bird*) macho ♦ *vt* (*gun*) amartillar; ~erel *n* gallito

cockle ['kɒkl] *n* berberecho

cockney ['kɒknɪ] *n* habitante de ciertos barrios de Londres

cockpit ['kɒkpɪt] *n* cabina

cockroach ['kɒkrəutʃ] *n* cucaracha

cocktail ['kɒkteɪl] *n* coctel *m*, cóctel *m*; ~ cabinet *n* mueble-bar *m*; ~ party *n* coctel *m*, cóctel *m*

cocoa ['kəukəu] *n* cacao; (*drink*) chocolate *m*

coconut ['kəukənʌt] *n* coco

cod [kɒd] *n* bacalao

C.O.D. *abbr* (= *cash on delivery*) C.A.E.

code [kəud] *n* código; (*cipher*) clave *f*; (*dialling* ~) prefijo; (*post* ~) código postal

cod-liver oil ['kɒdlɪvər-] *n* aceite *m* de hígado de bacalao

coercion [kəu'ɜːʃən] *n* coacción *f*

coffee ['kɒfɪ] *n* café *m*; ~ bar *n* (*BRIT*) cafetería; ~ bean *n* grano de café; ~ break *n* descanso (para tomar café); ~pot *n* cafetera; ~ table *n* mesita (para servir el café)

coffin ['kɒfɪn] *n* ataúd *m*

cog [kɒg] *n* (*wheel*) rueda dentada; (*tooth*) diente *m*

cogent ['kəudʒənt] *adj* convincente

cognac ['kɒnjæk] *n* coñac *m*

coil [kɔɪl] *n* rollo; (*ELEC*) bobina, carrete *m*; (*contraceptive*) espiral *f* ♦ *vt* enrollar

coin [kɔɪn] *n* moneda ♦ *vt* (*word*) inventar, idear; ~age *n* moneda; ~-box (*BRIT*) *n* cabina telefónica

coincide [kəuɪn'saɪd] *vi* coincidir; (*agree*) estar de acuerdo; **coincidence** [kəu'ɪnsɪdəns] *n* casualidad *f*

Coke ® [kəuk] *n* Coca-Cola ®

coke [kəuk] *n* (*coal*) coque *m*

colander ['kɒləndə] *n* colador *m*, escurridor *m*

cold [kəuld] *adj* frío ♦ *n* frío; (*MED*) resfriado; **it's** ~ hace frío; **to be** ~ (*person*) tener frío; **to catch** ~ enfriarse; **to catch a** ~ resfriarse, acatarrarse; **in** ~ **blood** a sangre fría; ~-**shoulder** *vt* dar o volver la espalda a; ~ **sore** *n* herpes *mpl or fpl*

coleslaw ['kəulslɔː] *n* especie de ensalada de col

colic ['kɒlɪk] *n* cólico

collapse [kə'læps] *vi* hundirse, derrumbarse; (*MED*) sufrir un colapso ♦ *n* hundimiento, derrumbamiento; (*MED*) colapso; **collapsible** *adj* plegable

collar ['kɒlə] *n* (*of coat, shirt*) cuello; (*of dog etc*) collar; ~bone *n* clavícula

collateral [kə'lætərəl] *n* garantía colateral

colleague ['kɒliːg] *n* colega *m/f*; (*at work*) compañero, a

collect [kə'lekt] *vt* (*litter, mail etc*) recoger; (*as a hobby*) coleccionar; (*BRIT: call and pick up*) recoger; (*debts, subscriptions etc*) recaudar ♦ *vi* reunirse; (*dust*) acumularse; **to call** ~ (*US: TEL*) llamar a cobro revertido; ~ion [kə'lekʃən] *n* colección *f*; (*of mail, for charity*) recogida; ~or *n* coleccionista *m/f*

college ['kɒlɪdʒ] *n* colegio mayor; (*of agriculture, technology*) escuela universitaria

collide [kəˈlaɪd] *vi* chocar
colliery [ˈkɒlɪərɪ] (*BRIT*) *n* mina de carbón
collision [kəˈlɪʒən] *n* choque *m*
colloquial [kəˈləʊkwɪəl] *adj* familiar, coloquial
Colombia [kəˈlɒmbɪə] *n* Colombia; **~n** *adj, n* colombiano/a
colon [ˈkəʊlən] *n* (*sign*) dos puntos; (*MED*) colon *m*
colonel [ˈkɜːnl] *n* coronel *m*
colonial [kəˈləʊnɪəl] *adj* colonial
colony [ˈkɒlənɪ] *n* colonia
colour [ˈkʌləʳ] (*US* **color**) *n* color *m* ♦ *vt* color(e)ar; (*dye*) teñir; (*fig: account*) adornar; (: *judgement*) distorsionar ♦ *vi* (*blush*) sonrojarse; **~s** *npl* (*of party, club*) colores *mpl*; **in ~** en color; **~ in** *vt* colorear; **~ bar** *n* segregación *f* racial; **~-blind** *adj* daltónico; **~ed** *adj* de color; (*photo*) en color; **~ film** *n* película en color; **~ful** *adj* lleno de color; (*story*) fantástico; (*person*) excéntrico; **~ing** *n* (*complexion*) tez *f*; (*in food*) colorante *m*; **~ scheme** *n* combinación *f* de colores; **~ television** *n* televisión *f* en color
colt [kəʊlt] *n* potro
column [ˈkɒləm] *n* columna; **~ist** [ˈkɒləmnɪst] *n* columnista *m/f*
coma [ˈkəʊmə] *n* coma *m*
comb [kəʊm] *n* peine *m*; (*ornamental*) peineta ♦ *vt* (*hair*) peinar; (*area*) registrar a fondo
combat [ˈkɒmbæt] *n* combate *m* ♦ *vt* combatir
combination [kɒmbɪˈneɪʃən] *n* combinación *f*
combine [*vb* kəmˈbaɪn, *n* ˈkɒmbaɪn] *vt* combinar; (*qualities*) reunir ♦ *vi* combinarse ♦ *n* (*ECON*) cartel *m*; **~ (harvester)** *n* cosechadora

---

KEYWORD

come [kʌm] (*pt* **came**, *pp* **come**) *vi* **1**
(*movement towards*) venir; **to ~ running** venir corriendo
2 (*arrive*) llegar; **he's ~ here to work** ha venido aquí para trabajar; **to ~ home**

volver a casa
3 (*reach*): **to ~ to** llegar a; **the bill came to £40** la cuenta ascendía a cuarenta libras
4 (*occur*): **an idea came to me** se me ocurrió una idea
5 (*be, become*): **to ~ loose/undone** *etc* aflojarse/desabrocharse, desatarse *etc*; **I've ~ to like him** por fin ha llegado a gustarme

come about *vi* suceder, ocurrir
come across *vt fus* (*person*) topar con; (*thing*) dar con
come away *vi* (*leave*) marcharse; (*become detached*) desprenderse
come back *vi* (*return*) volver
come by *vt fus* (*acquire*) conseguir
come down *vi* (*price*) bajar; (*tree, building*) ser derribado
come forward *vi* presentarse
come from *vt fus* (*place, source*) ser de
come in *vi* (*visitor*) entrar; (*train, report*) llegar; (*fashion*) ponerse de moda; (*on deal etc*) entrar
come in for *vt fus* (*criticism etc*) recibir
come into *vt fus* (*money*) heredar; (*be involved*) tener que ver con; **to ~ into fashion** ponerse de moda
come off *vi* (*button*) soltarse, desprenderse; (*attempt*) salir bien
come on *vi* (*pupil*) progresar; (*work, project*) desarrollarse; (*lights*) encenderse; (*electricity*) volver; **~ on!** ¡vamos!
come out *vi* (*fact*) salir a la luz; (*book, sun*) salir; (*stain*) quitarse
come round *vi* (*after faint, operation*) volver en sí
come to *vi* (*wake*) volver en sí
come up *vi* (*sun*) salir; (*problem*) surgir; (*event*) aproximarse; (*in conversation*) mencionarse
come up against *vt fus* (*resistance etc*) tropezar con
come up with *vt fus* (*idea*) sugerir; (*money*) conseguir
come upon *vt fus* (*find*) dar con

comeback ['kʌmbæk] n: **to make a ~** (THEATRE) volver a las tablas

comedian [kə'mi:dɪən] n cómico; **comedienne** [-'ɛn] n cómica

comedy ['kɔmɪdɪ] n comedia; (humour) comicidad f

comet ['kɔmɪt] n cometa m

comeuppance [kʌm'ʌpəns] n: **to get one's ~** llevar su merecido

comfort ['kʌmfət] n bienestar m; (relief) alivio ♦ vt consolar; **~s** npl (of home etc) comodidades fpl; **~able** adj cómodo; (financially) acomodado; (easy) fácil; **~ably** adv (sit) cómodamente; (live) holgadamente; **~ station** n (US) servicios mpl

comic ['kɔmɪk] adj (also: **~al**) cómico ♦ n (comedian) cómico; (BRIT: for children) tebeo; (BRIT: for adults) comic m; **~ strip** n tira cómica

coming ['kʌmɪŋ] n venida, llegada ♦ adj que viene; **~(s) and going(s)** n(pl) ir y venir m, ajetreo

comma ['kɔmə] n coma

command [kə'mɑ:nd] n orden f, mandato; (MIL: authority) mando; (mastery) dominio ♦ vt (troops) mandar; (give orders to): **to ~ sb to do** mandar or ordenar a uno hacer; **~eer** [kɔmən'dɪə*] vt requisar; **~er** n (MIL) comandante m/f, jefe/a m/f

commemorate [kə'mɛməreɪt] vt conmemorar

commence [kə'mɛns] vt, vi comenzar, empezar

commend [kə'mɛnd] vt elogiar, alabar; (recommend) recomendar

commensurate [kə'mɛnsərɪt] adj: **~ with** en proporción a, que corresponde a

comment ['kɔmɛnt] n comentario ♦ vi: **to ~ on** hacer comentarios sobre; **"no ~"** (written) "sin comentarios"; (spoken) "no tengo nada que decir"; **~ary** ['kɔməntəri] n comentario; **~ator** ['kɔmənteɪtə*] n comentarista m/f

commerce ['kɔmə:s] n comercio

commercial [kə'mə:ʃəl] adj comercial ♦ n (TV, RADIO) anuncio

commiserate [kə'mɪzəreɪt] vi: **to ~ with** compadecerse de, condolerse de

commission [kə'mɪʃən] n (committee, fee) comisión f ♦ vt (work of art) encargar; **out of ~** fuera de servicio; **~aire** [kəmɪʃə'nɛə*] (BRIT) n portero; **~er** n (POLICE) comisario de policía

commit [kə'mɪt] vt (act) cometer; (resources) dedicar; (to sb's care) entregar; **to ~ o.s. (to do)** comprometerse (a hacer); **to ~ suicide** suicidarse; **~ment** n compromiso; (to ideology etc) entrega

committee [kə'mɪtɪ] n comité m

commodity [kə'mɔdɪtɪ] n mercancía

common ['kɔmən] adj común; (pej) ordinario ♦ n campo común; **the C~s** npl (BRIT) (la Cámara de) los Comunes mpl; **in ~** en común; **~er** n plebeyo; **~ law** n ley f consuetudinaria; **~ly** adv comúnmente; **C~ Market** n Mercado Común; **~place** adj de lo más común; **~room** n sala común; **~ sense** n sentido común; **the C~wealth** n la Commonwealth

commotion [kə'məuʃən] n tumulto, confusión f

commune [n 'kɔmju:n, vb kə'mju:n] n (group) comuna ♦ vi: **to ~ with** comulgar or conversar con

communicate [kə'mju:nɪkeɪt] vt comunicar ♦ vi: **to ~ (with)** comunicarse (con); (in writing) estar en contacto (con)

communication [kəmju:nɪ'keɪʃən] n comunicación f; **~ cord** (BRIT) n timbre m de alarma

communion [kə'mju:nɪən] n (also: **Holy C~**) comunión f

communiqué [kə'mju:nɪkeɪ] n comunicado, parte f

communism ['kɔmjunɪzəm] n comunismo; **communist** adj, n comunista m/f

community [kə'mju:nɪtɪ] n comunidad f; (large group) colectividad f; **~ centre** n centro social; **~ chest** n (US) arca comunitaria, fondo común

commutation ticket [kɔmju'teɪʃən-] (*US*) *n* billete *m* de abono

commute [kə'mju:t] *vi viajar a diario de la casa al trabajo* ♦ *vt* conmutar; **~r** *n* persona (que viaja ... *see vi*)

compact [*adj* kəm'pækt, *n* 'kɔmpækt] *adj* compacto ♦ *n* (*also:* **powder ~**) polvera; **~ disc** *n* compact disc *m*; **~ disc player** *n* reproductor *m* de disco compacto, compact disc *m*

companion [kəm'pænɪən] *n* compañero/a; **~ship** *n* compañerismo

company ['kʌmpənɪ] *n* compañía; (*COMM*) sociedad *f*, compañía; **to keep sb ~** acompañar a uno; **~ secretary** (*BRIT*) *n* secretario/a de compañía

comparative [kəm'pærətɪv] *adj* relativo; (*study*) comparativo; **~ly** *adv* (*relatively*) relativamente

compare [kəm'pɛə*] *vt*: **to ~ sth/sb with/to** comparar algo/a uno con ♦ *vi*: **to ~ (with)** compararse (con); **comparison** [-'pærɪsn] *n* comparación *f*

compartment [kəm'pɑ:tmənt] *n* (*also: RAIL*) compartim(i)ento

compass ['kʌmpəs] *n* brújula; **~es** *npl* (*MATH*) compás *m*

compassion [kəm'pæʃən] *n* compasión *f*; **~ate** *adj* compasivo

compatible [kəm'pætɪbl] *adj* compatible

compel [kəm'pɛl] *vt* obligar

compensate ['kɔmpənseɪt] *vt* compensar ♦ *vi*: **to ~ for** compensar; **compensation** [-'seɪʃən] *n* (*for loss*) indemnización *f*

compère ['kɔmpɛə*] *n* presentador *m*

compete [kəm'pi:t] *vi* (*take part*) tomar parte, concurrir; (*vie with*): **to ~ with** competir con, hacer competencia a

competent ['kɔmpɪtənt] *adj* competente, capaz

competition [kɔmpɪ'tɪʃən] *n* (*contest*) concurso; (*rivalry*) competencia

competitive [kəm'petɪtɪv] *adj* (*ECON, SPORT*) competitivo

competitor [kəm'petɪtə*] *n* (*rival*) competidor(a) *m/f*; (*participant*)

concursante *m/f*

complacency [kəm'pleɪsnsɪ] *n* autosatisfacción *f*

complacent [kəm'pleɪsənt] *adj* autocomplaciente

complain [kəm'pleɪn] *vi* quejarse; (*COMM*) reclamar; **~t** *n* queja; reclamación *f*; (*MED*) enfermedad *f*

complement [*n* 'kɔmplɪmənt, *vb* 'kɔmplɪmənt] *n* complemento; (*esp of ship's crew*) dotación *f* ♦ *vt* (*enhance*) complementar; **~ary** [kɔmplɪ'mɛntərɪ] *adj* complementario

complete [kəm'pli:t] *adj* (*full*) completo; (*finished*) acabado ♦ *vt* (*fulfil*) completar; (*finish*) acabar; (*a form*) llenar; **~ly** *adv* completamente; **completion** [-'pli:ʃən] *n* terminación *f*; (*of contract*) realización *f*

complex ['kɔmpleks] *adj, n* complejo

complexion [kəm'plekʃən] *n* (*of face*) tez *f*, cutis *m*

compliance [kəm'plaɪəns] *n* (*submission*) sumisión *f*; (*agreement*) conformidad *f*; **in ~ with** de acuerdo con

complicate ['kɔmplɪkeɪt] *vt* complicar; **~d** *adj* complicado; **complication** [-'keɪʃən] *n* complicación *f*

compliment [*n* 'kɔmplɪmənt] *n* (*formal*) cumplido ♦ *vt* felicitar; **~s** *npl* (*regards*) saludos *mpl*; **to pay sb a ~** hacer cumplidos a uno; **~ary** [-'mɛntərɪ] *adj* lisonjero; (*free*) de favor

comply [kəm'plaɪ] *vi*: **to ~ with** cumplir con

component [kəm'pəunənt] *adj* componente ♦ *n* (*TECH*) pieza

compose [kəm'pəuz] *vt*: **to be ~d of** componerse de; (*music etc*) componer; **to ~ o.s.** tranquilizarse; **~d** *adj* sosegado; **~r** *n* (*MUS*) compositor(a) *m/f*; **composition** [kɔmpə'zɪʃən] *n* composición *f*

compost ['kɔmpɔst] *n* abono (vegetal)

composure [kəm'pəuʒə*] *n* serenidad *f*, calma

compound ['kɔmpaund] *n* (*CHEM*) compuesto; (*LING*) palabra compuesta;

(*enclosure*) recinto ♦ *adj* compuesto;
(*fracture*) complicado
comprehend [kɔmprɪ'hɛnd] *vt*
comprender; **comprehension** [-'hɛnʃən]
n comprensión *f*
comprehensive [kɔmprɪ'hɛnsɪv] *adj*
exhaustivo; (*INSURANCE*) contra todo
riesgo; ~ **(school)** *n* centro estatal de
enseñanza secundaria; ≈ Instituto
Nacional de Bachillerato (*SP*)
compress [*vb* kəm'prɛs, *n* 'kɔmprɛs] *vt*
comprimir; (*information*) condensar ♦ *n*
(*MED*) compresa
comprise [kəm'praɪz] *vt* (*also*: **be ~d of**)
comprender, constar de; (*constitute*)
constituir
compromise ['kɔmprəmaɪz] *n* (*agreement*)
arreglo ♦ *vt* comprometer ♦ *vi* transigir
compulsion [kəm'pʌlʃən] *n* compulsión *f*;
(*force*) obligación *f*
compulsive [kəm'pʌlsɪv] *adj* compulsivo;
(*viewing, reading*) obligado
compulsory [kəm'pʌlsərɪ] *adj* obligatorio
computer [kəm'pju:tə*] *n* ordenador *m*,
computador *m*, computadora; ~ **game** *n*
juego para ordenador; **~-generated** *adj*
realizado por ordenador, creado por
ordenador; **~ize** *vt* (*data*) computerizar;
(*system*) informatizar; ~ **programmer** *n*
programador(a) *m/f*; ~ **programming** *n*
programación *f*; ~ **science** *n*
informática; **computing** [kəm'pju:tɪŋ] *n*
(*activity, science*) informática
comrade ['kɔmrɪd] *n* (*POL, MIL*) camarada;
(*friend*) compañero/a; **~ship** *n*
camaradería, compañerismo
con [kɔn] *vt* (*deceive*) engañar; (*cheat*)
estafar ♦ *n* estafa
conceal [kən'si:l] *vt* ocultar
conceit [kən'si:t] *n* presunción *f*; **~ed** *adj*
presumido
conceive [kən'si:v] *vt, vi* concebir
concentrate ['kɔnsəntreɪt] *vi* concentrarse
♦ *vt* concentrar
concentration [kɔnsən'treɪʃən] *n*
concentración *f*
concept ['kɔnsɛpt] *n* concepto

concern [kən'sə:n] *n* (*matter*) asunto;
(*COMM*) empresa; (*anxiety*) preocupación *f*
♦ *vt* (*worry*) preocupar; (*involve*) afectar;
(*relate to*) tener que ver con; **to be ~ed**
(about) interesarse (por), preocuparse
(por); **~ing** *prep* sobre, acerca de
concert ['kɔnsət] *n* concierto; **~ed**
[kən'sə:təd] *adj* (*efforts etc*) concertado; ~
hall *n* sala de conciertos
concerto [kən'tʃə:təu] *n* concierto
concession [kən'sɛʃən] *n* concesión *f*; **tax**
~ privilegio fiscal
conclude [kən'klu:d] *vt* concluir; (*treaty*
etc) firmar; (*agreement*) llegar a; (*decide*)
llegar a la conclusión de; **conclusion**
[-'klu:ʒən] *n* conclusión *f*; firma;
conclusive [-'klu:sɪv] *adj* decisivo,
concluyente
concoct [kən'kɔkt] *vt* confeccionar; (*plot*)
tramar; **~ion** [-'kɔkʃən] *n* mezcla
concourse ['kɔŋkɔ:s] *n* vestíbulo
concrete ['kɔnkri:t] *n* hormigón *m* ♦ *adj*
de hormigón; (*fig*) concreto
concur [kən'kə:*] *vi* estar de acuerdo,
asentir
concurrently [kən'kʌrntlɪ] *adv* al mismo
tiempo
concussion [kən'kʌʃən] *n* conmoción *f*
cerebral
condemn [kən'dɛm] *vt* condenar;
(*building*) declarar en ruina
condense [kən'dɛns] *vi* condensarse ♦ *vt*
condensar, abreviar; **~d milk** *n* leche *f*
condensada
condition [kən'dɪʃən] *n* condición *f*,
estado; (*requirement*) condición *f* ♦ *vt*
condicionar; **on ~ that** a condición (de)
que; **~er** *n* suavizante
condolences [kən'dəulənsɪz] *npl* pésame
m
condom ['kɔndəm] *n* condón *m*
condone [kən'dəun] *vt* condonar
conducive [kən'dju:sɪv] *adj*: ~ **to**
conducente a
conduct [*n* 'kɔndʌkt, *vb* kən'dʌkt] *n*
conducta, comportamiento ♦ *vt* (*lead*)
conducir; (*manage*) llevar a cabo, dirigir;

(*MUS*) dirigir; **to ~ o.s.** comportarse; **~ed tour** (*BRIT*) *n* visita acompañada; **~or** *n* (*of orchestra*) director *m*; (*US: on train*) revisor(a) *m/f*; (*on bus*) cobrador *m*; (*ELEC*) conductor *m*; **~ress** *n* (*on bus*) cobradora

cone [kəun] *n* cono; (*pine ~*) piña; (*on road*) pivote *m*; (*for ice-cream*) cucurucho

confectioner [kənˈfekʃənə*] *n* repostero/a; **~'s** (**shop**) *n* confitería; **~y** *n* dulces *mpl*

confer [kənˈfə:*] *vt*: **to ~ sth on** otorgar algo a ♦ *vi* conferenciar

conference [ˈkɔnfərns] *n* (*meeting*) reunión *f*; (*convention*) congreso

confess [kənˈfes] *vt* confesar ♦ *vi* admitir; **~ion** [-ˈfeʃən] *n* confesión *f*

confetti [kənˈfeti] *n* confeti *m*

confide [kənˈfaid] *vi*: **to ~ in** confiar en

confidence [ˈkɔnfidns] *n* (*also*: **self-~**) confianza; (*secret*) confidencia; **in ~** (*speak, write*) en confianza; **~ trick** *n* timo; **confident** *adj* seguro de sí mismo; (*certain*) seguro; **confidential** [kɔnfiˈdenʃəl] *adj* confidencial

confine [kənˈfain] *vt* (*limit*) limitar; (*shut up*) encerrar; **~d** *adj* (*space*) reducido; **~ment** *n* (*prison*) prisión *f*; **~s** [ˈkɔnfainz] *npl* confines *mpl*

confirm [kənˈfə:m] *vt* confirmar; **~ation** [kɔnfəˈmeiʃən] *n* confirmación *f*; **~ed** *adj* empedernido

confiscate [ˈkɔnfiskeit] *vt* confiscar

conflict [*n* ˈkɔnflikt, *vb* kənˈflikt] *n* conflicto ♦ *vi* (*opinions*) chocar; **~ing** *adj* contradictorio

conform [kənˈfɔ:m] *vi* conformarse; **to ~ to** ajustarse a

confound [kənˈfaund] *vt* confundir

confront [kənˈfrʌnt] *vt* (*problems*) hacer frente a; (*enemy, danger*) enfrentarse con; **~ation** [kɔnfrənˈteiʃən] *n* enfrentamiento

confuse [kənˈfju:z] *vt* (*perplex*) aturdir, desconcertar; (*mix up*) confundir; (*complicate*) complicar; **~d** *adj* confuso; (*person*) perplejo; **confusing** *adj* confuso; **confusion** [-ˈfju:ʒən] *n* confusión *f*

congeal [kənˈdʒi:l] *vi* (*blood*) coagularse; (*sauce etc*) cuajarse

congested [kənˈdʒestid] *adj* congestionado; **congestion** *n* congestión *f*

congratulate [kənˈgrætjuleit] *vt*: **to ~ sb (on)** felicitar a uno (por); **congratulations** [-ˈleiʃənz] *npl* felicitaciones *fpl*; **congratulations!** ¡enhorabuena!

congregate [ˈkɔngrigeit] *vi* congregarse; **congregation** [-ˈgeiʃən] *n* (*of a church*) feligreses *mpl*

congress [ˈkɔngres] *n* congreso; (*US*): **C~** Congreso; **C~man** (*irreg*) (*US*) *n* miembro del Congreso

conifer [ˈkɔnifə*] *n* conífera

conjunctivitis [kəndʒʌŋktiˈvaitis] *n* conjuntivitis *f*

conjure [ˈkʌndʒə*] *vi* hacer juegos de manos; **~ up** *vt* (*ghost, spirit*) hacer aparecer; (*memories*) evocar; **~r** *n* ilusionista *m/f*

con man [ˈkɔn-] *n* estafador *m*

connect [kəˈnekt] *vt* juntar, unir; (*ELEC*) conectar; (*TEL: subscriber*) poner; (: *caller*) poner al habla; (*fig*) relacionar, asociar ♦ *vi*: **to ~ with** (*train*) enlazar con; **to be ~ed with** (*associated*) estar relacionado con; **~ion** [-ʃən] *n* juntura, unión *f*; (*ELEC*) conexión *f*; (*RAIL*) enlace *m*; (*TEL*) comunicación *f*; (*fig*) relación *f*

connive [kəˈnaiv] *vi*: **to ~ at** hacer la vista gorda a

connoisseur [kɔniˈsə*] *n* experto/a, entendido/a

conquer [ˈkɔŋkə*] *vt* (*territory*) conquistar; (*enemy, feelings*) vencer; **~or** *n* conquistador *m*

conquest [ˈkɔŋkwest] *n* conquista

cons [kɔnz] *npl see* **convenience**; **pro**

conscience [ˈkɔnʃəns] *n* conciencia

conscientious [kɔnʃiˈenʃəs] *adj* concienzudo; (*objection*) de conciencia

conscious [ˈkɔnʃəs] *adj* (*deliberate*) deliberado; (*awake, aware*) consciente; **~ness** *n* conciencia; (*MED*) conocimiento

conscript ['kɔnskrɪpt] n recluta m; **~ion** [kən'skrɪpʃən] n servicio militar (obligatorio)

consensus [kən'sensəs] n consenso

consent [kən'sent] n consentimiento ♦ vi: **to ~ (to)** consentir (en)

consequence ['kɔnsɪkwəns] n consecuencia; (significance) importancia

consequently ['kɔnsɪkwəntlɪ] adv por consiguiente

conservation [kɔnsə'veɪʃən] n conservación f

conservative [kən'sə:vətɪv] adj conservador(a); (estimate etc) cauteloso; **C~** (BRIT) adj, n (POL) conservador(a) m/f

conservatory [kən'sə:vətrɪ] n invernadero; (MUS) conservatorio

conserve [kən'sə:v] vt conservar ♦ n conserva

consider [kən'sɪdə*] vt considerar; (take into account) tener en cuenta; (study) estudiar, examinar; **to ~ doing sth** pensar en (la posibilidad de) hacer algo; **~able** adj considerable; **~ably** adv notablemente; **~ate** adj considerado; **consideration** [-'reɪʃən] n consideración f; (factor) factor m; **to give sth further consideration** estudiar algo más a fondo; **~ing** prep teniendo en cuenta

consign [kən'saɪn] vt: **to ~ to** (sth unwanted) relegar a; (person) destinar a; **~ment** n envío

consist [kən'sɪst] vi: **to ~ of** consistir en

consistency [kən'sɪstənsɪ] n (of argument etc) coherencia; consecuencia; (thickness) consistencia

consistent [kən'sɪstənt] adj (person) consecuente; (argument etc) coherente

consolation [kɔnsə'leɪʃən] n consuelo

console[1] [kən'səul] vt consolar

console[2] ['kɔnsəul] n consola

consonant ['kɔnsənənt] n consonante f

consortium [kən'sɔ:tɪəm] n consorcio

conspicuous [kən'spɪkjuəs] adj (visible) visible

conspiracy [kən'spɪrəsɪ] n conjura, complot m

constable ['kʌnstəbl] (BRIT) n policía m/f; **chief ~** ≈ jefe m de policía

constabulary [kən'stæbjulərɪ] n ≈ policía

constant ['kɔnstənt] adj constante; **~ly** adv constantemente

constipated ['kɔnstɪpeɪtəd] adj estreñido; **constipation** [kɔnstɪ'peɪʃən] n estreñimiento

constituency [kən'stɪtjuənsɪ] n (POL: area) distrito electoral; (: electors) electorado; **constituent** [-ənt] n (POL) elector(a) m/f; (part) componente m

constitution [kɔnstɪ'tju:ʃən] n constitución f; **~al** adj constitucional

constraint [kən'streɪnt] n obligación f; (limit) restricción f

construct [kən'strʌkt] vt construir; **~ion** [-ʃən] n construcción f; **~ive** adj constructivo

consul ['kɔnsl] n cónsul m/f; **~ate** ['kɔnsjulɪt] n consulado

consult [kən'sʌlt] vt consultar; **~ant** n (BRIT: MED) especialista m/f; (other specialist) asesor(a) m/f; **~ation** [kɔnsəl'teɪʃən] n consulta; **~ing room** (BRIT) n consultorio

consume [kən'sju:m] vt (eat) comerse; (drink) beberse; (fire etc, COMM) consumir; **~r** n consumidor(a) m/f; **~r goods** npl bienes mpl de consumo

consummate ['kɔnsʌmeɪt] vt consumar

consumption [kən'sʌmpʃən] n consumo

cont. abbr (= continued) sigue

contact ['kɔntækt] n contacto; (person) contacto; (: pej) enchufe m ♦ vt ponerse en contacto con; **~ lenses** npl lentes fpl de contacto

contagious [kən'teɪdʒəs] adj contagioso

contain [kən'teɪn] vt contener; **to ~ o.s.** contenerse; **~er** n recipiente m; (for shipping etc) contenedor m

contaminate [kən'tæmɪneɪt] vt contaminar

cont'd abbr (= continued) sigue

contemplate ['kɔntəmpleɪt] vt contemplar; (reflect upon) considerar

contemporary [kən'tempərərɪ] adj, n

contemporáneo/a *m/f*

contempt [kən'tempt] *n* desprecio; ~ **of court** (*LAW*) desacato (a los tribunales); ~**ible** *adj* despreciable; ~**uous** *adj* desdeñoso

contend [kən'tend] *vt* (*argue*) afirmar ♦ *vi*: **to ~ with/for** luchar contra/por; ~**er** *n* (*SPORT*) contendiente *m/f*

content [*adj, vb* kən'tent, *n* 'kɔntent] *adj* (*happy*) contento; (*satisfied*) satisfecho ♦ *vt* contentar; satisfacer ♦ *n* contenido; ~**s** *npl* contenido; (**table of**) ~**s** índice *m* de materias; ~**ed** *adj* contento; satisfecho

contention [kən'tenʃən] *n* (*assertion*) aseveración *f*; (*disagreement*) discusión *f*

contest [*n* 'kɔntest, *vb* kən'test] *n* lucha; (*competition*) concurso ♦ *vt* (*dispute*) impugnar; (*POL*) presentarse como candidato/a en; ~**ant** [kən'testənt] *n* concursante *m/f*; (*in fight*) contendiente *m/f*

context ['kɔntekst] *n* contexto

continent ['kɔntinənt] *n* continente *m*; **the C~** (*BRIT*) el continente europeo; ~**al** [-'nentl] *adj* continental; ~**al breakfast** *n* desayuno estilo europeo; ~**al quilt** (*BRIT*) *n* edredón *m*

contingency [kən'tindʒənsi] *n* contingencia

continual [kən'tinjuəl] *adj* continuo; ~**ly** *adv* constantemente

continuation [kəntinju'eiʃən] *n* prolongación *f*; (*after interruption*) reanudación *f*

continue [kən'tinju:] *vi, vt* seguir, continuar

continuous [kən'tinjuəs] *adj* continuo

contort [kən'tɔ:t] *vt* retorcer

contour ['kɔntuə*] *n* contorno; (*also*: ~ **line**) curva de nivel

contraband ['kɔntrəbænd] *n* contrabando

contraceptive [kɔntrə'septiv] *adj, n* anticonceptivo

contract [*n* 'kɔntrækt, *vb* kən'trækt] *n* contrato ♦ *vi* (*COMM*): **to ~ to do sth** comprometerse por contrato a hacer algo; (*become smaller*) contraerse,

encogerse ♦ *vt* contraer; ~**ion** [kən'trækʃən] *n* contracción *f*; ~**or** *n* contratista *m/f*

contradict [kɔntrə'dikt] *vt* contradecir; ~**ion** [-ʃən] *n* contradicción *f*

contraption [kən'træpʃən] (*pej*) *n* artilugio *m*

contrary¹ ['kɔntrəri] *adj* contrario ♦ *n* lo contrario; **on the ~** al contrario; **unless you hear to the ~** a no ser que le digan lo contrario

contrary² [kən'treəri] *adj* (*perverse*) terco

contrast [*n* 'kɔntrɑ:st, *vt* kən'trɑ:st] *n* contraste *m* ♦ *vt* comparar; **in ~ to** en contraste con

contravene [kɔntrə'vi:n] *vt* infringir

contribute [kən'tribju:t] *vi* contribuir ♦ *vt*: **to ~ £10/an article to** contribuir con 10 libras/un artículo a; **to ~ to** (*charity*) donar a; (*newspaper*) escribir para; (*discussion*) intervenir en; **contribution** [kɔntri'bju:ʃən] *n* (*donation*) donativo; (*BRIT: for social security*) cotización *f*; (*to debate*) intervención *f*; (*to journal*) colaboración *f*; **contributor** *n* contribuyente *m/f*; (*to newspaper*) colaborador(a) *m/f*

contrive [kən'traiv] *vt* (*invent*) idear ♦ *vi*: **to ~ to do** lograr hacer

control [kən'trəul] *vt* controlar; (*process etc*) dirigir; (*machinery*) manejar; (*temper*) dominar; (*disease*) contener ♦ *n* control *m*; ~**s** *npl* (*of vehicle*) instrumentos *mpl* de mando; (*of radio*) controles *mpl*; (*governmental*) medidas *fpl* de control; **under ~** bajo control; **to be in ~ of** tener el mando de; **the car went out of ~** se perdió el control del coche; ~**led substance** *n* sustancia controlada; ~ **panel** *n* tablero de instrumentos; ~ **room** *n* sala de mando; ~ **tower** *n* (*AVIAT*) torre *f* de control

controversial [kɔntrə'və:ʃl] *adj* polémico

controversy ['kɔntrəvə:si] *n* polémica

convalesce [kɔnvə'les] *vi* convalecer

convector [kən'vektə*] *n* calentador *m* de aire

convene [kən'viːn] *vt* convocar ♦ *vi* reunirse

convenience [kən'viːnɪəns] *n* (*easiness*) comodidad *f*; (*suitability*) idoneidad *f*; (*advantage*) ventaja *f*; **at your ~** cuando le sea conveniente; **all modern ~s, all mod cons** (*BRIT*) todo confort

convenient [kən'viːnɪənt] *adj* (*useful*) útil; (*place, time*) conveniente

convent ['kɒnvənt] *n* convento

convention [kən'vɛnʃən] *n* convención *f*; (*meeting*) asamblea; (*agreement*) convenio; **~al** *adj* convencional

converge [kən'vəːdʒ] *vi* convergir; (*people*): **to ~ on** dirigirse todos a

conversant [kən'vəːsnt] *adj*: **to be ~ with** estar al tanto de

conversation [kɒnvə'seɪʃən] *n* conversación *f*; **~al** *adj* familiar; **~al skill** facilidad *f* de palabra

converse [*n* 'kɒnvəːs, *vb* kən'vəːs] *n* inversa ♦ *vi* conversar; **~ly** [-'vəːslɪ] *adv* a la inversa

conversion [kən'vəːʃən] *n* conversión *f*

convert [*vb* kən'vəːt, *n* 'kɒnvəːt] *vt* (*REL, COMM*) convertir; (*alter*): **to ~ sth into/to** transformar algo en/convertir algo a ♦ *n* converso/a; **~ible** *adj* convertible ♦ *n* descapotable *m*

convey [kən'veɪ] *vt* llevar; (*thanks*) comunicar; (*idea*) expresar; **~or belt** *n* cinta transportadora

convict [*vb* kən'vɪkt, *n* 'kɒnvɪkt] *vt* (*find guilty*) declarar culpable a ♦ *n* presidiario/a; **~ion** [-ʃən] *n* condena; (*belief, certainty*) convicción *f*

convince [kən'vɪns] *vt* convencer; **~d** *adj*: **~d of/that** convencido de/de que; **convincing** *adj* convincente

convoluted ['kɒnvəluːtɪd] *adj* (*argument etc*) enrevesado

convoy ['kɒnvɔɪ] *n* convoy *m*

convulse [kən'vʌls] *vt*: **to be ~d with laughter** desternillarse de risa; **convulsion** [-'vʌlʃən] *n* convulsión *f*

cook [kuk] *vt* (*stew etc*) guisar; (*meal*) preparar ♦ *vi* cocer; (*person*) cocinar ♦ *n*

cocinero/a; **~ book** *n* libro de cocina; **~er** *n* cocina; **~ery** *n* cocina; **~ery book** (*BRIT*) *n* = **~ book**; **~ie** (*US*) *n* galleta; **~ing** *n* cocina

cool [kuːl] *adj* fresco; (*not afraid*) tranquilo; (*unfriendly*) frío ♦ *vt* enfriar ♦ *vi* enfriarse; **~ness** *n* frescura; tranquilidad *f*; (*indifference*) falta de entusiasmo

coop [kuːp] *n* gallinero ♦ *vt*: **to ~ up** (*fig*) encerrar

cooperate [kəu'ɒpəreɪt] *vi* cooperar, colaborar; **cooperation** [-'reɪʃən] *n* cooperación *f*, colaboración *f*; **cooperative** [-rətɪv] *adj* (*business*) cooperativo; (*person*) servicial ♦ *n* cooperativa

coordinate [*vb* kəu'ɔːdɪneɪt, *n* kəu'ɔːdɪnət] *vt* coordinar ♦ *n* (*MATH*) coordenada; **~s** *npl* (*clothes*) coordinados *mpl*; **coordination** [-'neɪʃən] *n* coordinación *f*

co-ownership [kəu'əunəʃɪp] *n* co-propiedad *f*

cop [kɒp] (*inf*) *n* poli *m* (*SP*), tira *m* (*AM*)

cope [kəup] *vi*: **to ~ with** (*problem*) hacer frente a

copper ['kɒpə*] *n* (*metal*) cobre *m*; (*BRIT: inf*) poli *m*; **~s** *npl* (*money*) calderilla (*SP*), centavos *mpl* (*AM*)

copulate ['kɒpjuleɪt] *vi* copularse

copy ['kɒpɪ] *n* copia; (*of book etc*) ejemplar *m* ♦ *vt* copiar; **~right** *n* derechos *mpl* de autor

coral ['kɒrəl] *n* coral *m*

cord [kɔːd] *n* cuerda; (*ELEC*) cable *m*; (*fabric*) pana

cordial ['kɔːdɪəl] *adj* cordial ♦ *n* cordial *m*

cordon ['kɔːdn] *n* cordón *m*; **~ off** *vt* acordonar

corduroy ['kɔːdərɔɪ] *n* pana

core [kɔː*] *n* centro, núcleo; (*of fruit*) corazón *m*; (*of problem*) meollo ♦ *vt* quitar el corazón de

coriander [kɒrɪ'ændə*] *n* culantro

cork [kɔːk] *n* corcho; (*tree*) alcornoque *m*; **~screw** *n* sacacorchos *m inv*

corn [kɔːn] *n* (*BRIT: cereal crop*) trigo; (*US: maize*) maíz *m*; (*on foot*) callo; **~ on the**

cob (CULIN) maíz en la mazorca (SP), choclo (AM)

corned beef ['kɔ:nd-] n carne f acecinada (en lata)

corner ['kɔ:nə*] n (outside) esquina; (inside) rincón m; (in road) curva; (FOOTBALL) córner m; (BOXING) esquina ♦ vt (trap) arrinconar; (COMM) acaparar ♦ vi (in car) tomar las curvas; **~stone** n (also fig) piedra angular

cornet ['kɔ:nɪt] n (MUS) corneta; (BRIT: of ice-cream) cucurucho

cornflakes ['kɔ:nfleɪks] npl copos mpl de maíz, cornflakes mpl

cornflour ['kɔ:nflauə*] (BRIT), **cornstarch** ['kɔ:nstɑ:tʃ] (US) n harina de maíz

Cornwall ['kɔ:nwəl] n Cornualles m

corny ['kɔ:nɪ] (inf) adj gastado

coronary ['kɔrənərɪ] n (also: **~ thrombosis**) infarto

coronation [kɔrə'neɪʃən] n coronación f

coroner ['kɔrənə*] n juez m (de instrucción)

corporal ['kɔ:pərl] n cabo ♦ adj: **~ punishment** castigo corporal

corporate ['kɔ:pərɪt] adj (action, ownership) colectivo; (finance, image) corporativo

corporation [kɔ:pə'reɪʃən] n (of town) ayuntamiento; (COMM) corporación f

corps [kɔ:*, pl kɔ:z] n inv cuerpo; **diplomatic ~** cuerpo diplomático; **press ~** gabinete m de prensa

corpse [kɔ:ps] n cadáver m

correct [kə'rekt] adj justo, exacto; (proper) correcto ♦ vt corregir; (exam) corregir, calificar; **~ion** [-ʃən] n (act) corrección f; (instance) rectificación f

correspond [kɔrɪs'pɔnd] vi (write): **to ~ (with)** escribirse (con); (be equivalent to): **to ~ (to)** corresponder (a); (be in accordance): **to ~ (with)** corresponder (con); **~ence** n correspondencia; **~ence course** n curso por correspondencia; **~ent** n corresponsal m/f

corridor ['kɔrɪdɔ:*] n pasillo

corrode [kə'rəud] vt corroer ♦ vi corroerse

corrugated ['kɔrəgeɪtɪd] adj ondulado; **~ iron** n chapa ondulada

corrupt [kə'rʌpt] adj (person) corrupto; (COMPUT) corrompido ♦ vt corromper; (COMPUT) degradar

Corsica ['kɔ:sɪkə] n Córcega

cosmetic [kɔz'metɪk] adj, n cosmético

cosmopolitan [kɔzmə'pɔlɪtn] adj cosmopolita

cost [kɔst] (pt, pp cost) n (price) precio; **~s** npl (COMM) costes mpl; (LAW) costas fpl ♦ vi costar, valer ♦ vt preparar el presupuesto de; **how much does it ~?** ¿cuánto cuesta?; **to ~ sb time/effort** costarle a uno tiempo/esfuerzo; **it ~ him his life** le costó la vida; **at all ~s** cueste lo que cueste

co-star ['kəustɑ:*] n coprotagonista m/f

Costa Rica ['kɔstə'ri:kə] n Costa Rica; **~n** adj, n costarriqueño/a m/f

cost-effective [kɔstɪ'fektɪv] adj rentable

costly ['kɔstlɪ] adj costoso

cost-of-living [kɔstəv'lɪvɪŋ] adj: **~ allowance** plus m de carestía de vida; **~ index** índice m del costo de vida

cost price (BRIT) n precio de coste

costume ['kɔstju:m] n traje m; (BRIT: also: **swimming ~**) traje de baño; **~ jewellery** n bisutería

cosy ['kəuzɪ] (US **cozy**) adj (person) cómodo; (room) acogedor(a)

cot [kɔt] n (BRIT: child's) cuna; (US: campbed) cama de campaña

cottage ['kɔtɪdʒ] n casita de campo; (rustic) barraca; **~ cheese** n requesón m

cotton ['kɔtn] n algodón m; (thread) hilo; **~ on to** (inf) vt fus caer en la cuenta de; **~ candy** (US) n algodón m (azucarado); **~ wool** (BRIT) n algodón m (hidrófilo)

couch [kautʃ] n sofá m; (doctor's etc) diván m

couchette [ku:'ʃet] n litera

cough [kɔf] vi toser ♦ n tos f; **~ drop** n pastilla para la tos

could [kud] pt of can[2]; **~n't** = could not

council ['kaunsl] n consejo; **city or town ~** consejo municipal; **~ estate** (BRIT) n urbanización f de viviendas municipales de alquiler; **~ house** (BRIT) n vivienda municipal de alquiler; **~lor** n concejal(a) m/f

counsel ['kaunsl] n (advice) consejo; (lawyer) abogado/a ♦ vt aconsejar; **~lor** n consejero/a; **~or** n (US) n abogado/a

count [kaunt] vt contar; (include) incluir ♦ vi contar ♦ n cuenta; (of votes) escrutinio; (level) nivel m; (nobleman) conde m; **~ on** vt fus contar con; **~down** n cuenta atrás

countenance ['kauntɪnəns] n semblante m, rostro ♦ vt (tolerate) aprobar, tolerar

counter ['kauntə*] n (in shop) mostrador m; (in games) ficha ♦ vt contrarrestar ♦ adv: **to run ~ to** ser contrario a, ir en contra de; **~act** vt contrarrestar

counterfeit ['kauntəfɪt] n falsificación f, simulación f ♦ vt falsificar ♦ adj falso, falsificado

counterfoil ['kauntəfɔɪl] n talón m

counterpart ['kauntəpɑːt] n homólogo/a

counter-productive [kauntəprə'dʌktɪv] adj contraproducente

countersign ['kauntəsaɪn] vt refrendar

countess ['kauntɪs] n condesa

countless ['kauntlɪs] adj innumerable

country ['kʌntrɪ] n país m; (native land) patria; (as opposed to town) campo; (region) región f, tierra; **~ dancing** (BRIT) n baile m regional; **~ house** n casa de campo; **~man** n (irreg) (compatriot) compatriota m; (rural) campesino, paisano; **~side** n campo

county ['kauntɪ] n condado

coup [kuː] (pl **~s**) n (also: **~ d'état**) golpe m (de estado); (achievement) éxito

couple ['kʌpl] n (of things) par m; (of people) pareja; (married **~**) matrimonio; **a ~ of** un par de

coupon ['kuːpɔn] n cupón m; (voucher) valé m

courage ['kʌrɪdʒ] n valor m, valentía; **~ous** [kə'reɪdʒəs] adj valiente

courgette [kuə'ʒɛt] (BRIT) n calabacín m (SP), calabacita (AM)

courier ['kurɪə*] n mensajero/a; (for tourists) guía m/f (de turismo)

course [kɔːs] n (direction) dirección f; (of river, SCOL) curso; (process) transcurso; (MED): **~ of treatment** tratamiento; (of ship) rumbo; (part of meal) plato; (GOLF) campo; **of ~** desde luego, naturalmente; **of ~!** ¡claro!

court [kɔːt] n (royal) corte f; (LAW) tribunal m, juzgado; (TENNIS etc) pista, cancha ♦ vt (woman) cortejar a; **to take to ~** demandar

courteous ['kəːtɪəs] adj cortés

courtesy ['kəːtəsɪ] n cortesía; **(by) ~ of** por cortesía de; **~ bus**, **~ coach** n autobús m gratuito

court-house ['kɔːthaus] (US) n palacio de justicia

courtier ['kɔːtɪə*] n cortesano

court-martial (pl **courts-martial**) n consejo de guerra

courtroom ['kɔːtrum] n sala de justicia

courtyard ['kɔːtjɑːd] n patio

cousin ['kʌzn] n primo/a; **first ~** primo/a carnal, primo/a hermano/a

cove [kəuv] n cala, ensenada

covenant ['kʌvənənt] n pacto

cover ['kʌvə*] vt cubrir; (feelings, mistake) ocultar; (with lid) tapar; (book etc) forrar; (distance) recorrer; (include) abarcar; (protect: also: INSURANCE) cubrir; (PRESS) investigar; (discuss) tratar ♦ n (cubierta; (lid) tapa; (for chair etc) funda; (envelope) sobre m; (for book) forro; (of magazine) portada; (shelter) abrigo; (INSURANCE) cobertura; (of spy) cobertura, m; **to take ~** (shelter) protegerse, resguardarse; **under ~** (indoors) bajo techo; **under ~ of darkness** al amparo de la oscuridad; **under separate ~** (COMM) por separado; **~ up** vi: **to ~ up for sb** encubrir a uno; **~age** n (TV, PRESS) cobertura; **~alls** (US) npl mono; **~ charge** n precio del cubierto; **~ing** n capa; **~ing letter** (US **~ letter**) n carta de explicación; **~ note** n (INSURANCE) póliza provisional

covert ['kʌvət] *adj* secreto, encubierto

cover-up *n* encubrimiento

cow [kau] *n* vaca; (*infl: woman*) bruja ♦ *vt* intimidar

coward ['kauəd] *n* cobarde *m/f*; **~ice** [-ɪs] *n* cobardía; **~ly** *adj* cobarde

cowboy ['kaubɔɪ] *n* vaquero

cower ['kauə*] *vi* encogerse (de miedo)

coy [kɔɪ] *adj* tímido

cozy ['kəuzɪ] (*US*) *adj* = **cosy**

CPA (*US*) *n abbr* = **certified public accountant**

crab [kræb] *n* cangrejo; **~ apple** *n* manzana silvestre

crack [kræk] *n* grieta; (*noise*) crujido; (*drug*) crack *m* ♦ *vt* agrietar, romper; (*nut*) cascar; (*solve: problem*) resolver; (*: code*) descifrar; (*whip etc*) chasquear; (*knuckles*) crujir; (*joke*) contar ♦ *adj* (*expert*) de primera; **~ down on** *vt fus* adoptar fuertes medidas contra; **~ up** *vi* (*MED*) sufrir una crisis nerviosa; **~er** *n* (*biscuit*) cráquer *m*; (*Christmas ~er*) petardo sorpresa

crackle ['krækl] *vi* crepitar

cradle ['kreɪdl] *n* cuna

craft [krɑːft] *n* (*skill*) arte *m*; (*trade*) oficio; (*cunning*) astucia; (*boat: pl inv*) barco; (*plane: pl inv*) avión *m*

craftsman ['krɑːftsmən] *n* artesano; **~ship** *n* (*quality*) destreza

crafty ['krɑːftɪ] *adj* astuto

crag [kræg] *n* peñasco

cram [kræm] *vt* (*fill*): **to ~ sth with** llenar algo (a reventar) de; (*put*): **to ~ sth into** meter algo a la fuerza en ♦ *vi* (*for exams*) empollar

cramp [kræmp] *n* (*MED*) calambre *m*; **~ed** *adj* apretado, estrecho

cranberry ['krænbərɪ] *n* arándano agrio

crane [kreɪn] *n* (*TECH*) grúa; (*bird*) grulla

crank [kræŋk] *n* manivela; (*person*) chiflado

cranny ['krænɪ] *n see* **nook**

crash [kræʃ] *n* (*noise*) estrépito; (*of cars etc*) choque *m*; (*of plane*) accidente *m* de aviación; (*COMM*) quiebra ♦ *vt* (*car, plane*) estrellar ♦ *vi* (*car, plane*) estrellarse; (*two*

cars) chocar; (*COMM*) quebrar; **~ course** *n* curso acelerado; **~ helmet** *n* casco (protector); **~ landing** *n* aterrizaje *m* forzado

crass [kræs] *adj* grosero, maleducado

crate [kreɪt] *n* cajón *m* de embalaje; (*for bottles*) caja

cravat(e) [krə'væt] *n* pañuelo

crave [kreɪv] *vt, vi*: **to ~ (for)** ansiar, anhelar

crawl [krɔːl] *vi* (*drag o.s.*) arrastrarse; (*child*) andar a gatas, gatear; (*vehicle*) avanzar (lentamente) ♦ *n* (*SWIMMING*) crol *m*

crayfish ['kreɪfɪʃ] *n inv* (*freshwater*) cangrejo de río; (*saltwater*) cigala

crayon ['kreɪən] *n* lápiz *m* de color

craze [kreɪz] *n* (*fashion*) moda

crazy ['kreɪzɪ] *adj* (*person*) loco; (*idea*) disparatado; (*inf: keen*): **~ about sb/sth** loco por uno/algo

creak [kriːk] *vi* (*floorboard*) crujir; (*hinge etc*) chirriar, rechinar

cream [kriːm] *n* (*of milk*) nata, crema; (*lotion*) crema; (*fig*) flor *f* y nata ♦ *adj* (*colour*) color crema; **~ cake** *n* pastel *m* de nata; **~ cheese** *n* queso blanco; **~y** *adj* cremoso; (*colour*) color crema

crease [kriːs] *n* (*fold*) pliegue *m*; (*in trousers*) raya; (*wrinkle*) arruga ♦ *vt* (*wrinkle*) arrugar ♦ *vi* (*wrinkle up*) arrugarse

create [kriː'eɪt] *vt* crear; **creation** [-ʃən] *n* creación *f*; **creative** *adj* creativo; **creator** *n* creador(a) *m/f*

creature ['kriːtʃə*] *n* (*animal*) animal *m*, bicho; (*person*) criatura

crèche [krɛʃ] *n* guardería (infantil)

credence ['kriːdəns] *n*: **to lend** *or* **give ~ to** creer en, dar crédito a

credentials [krɪ'dɛnʃlz] *npl* (*references*) referencias *fpl*; (*identity papers*) documentos *mpl* de identidad

credible ['krɛdɪbl] *adj* creíble; (*trustworthy*) digno de confianza

credit ['krɛdɪt] *n* crédito; (*merit*) honor *m*, mérito ♦ *vt* (*COMM*) abonar; (*believe: also:*

give ~ to) creer, prestar fe a ♦ *adj* crediticio; **~s** *npl* (*CINEMA*) fichas *fpl* técnicas; **to be in ~** (*person*) tener saldo a favor; **to ~ sb with** (*fig*) reconocer a uno el mérito de; **~ card** *n* tarjeta de crédito; **~or** *n* acreedor(a) *m/f*

creed [kriːd] *n* credo

creek [kriːk] *n* cala, ensenada; (*US*) riachuelo

creep [kriːp] (*pt, pp* **crept**) *vi* arrastrarse; **~er** *n* enredadera; **~y** *adj* (*frightening*) horripilante

cremate [krɪˈmeɪt] *vt* incinerar

crematorium [kremaˈtɔːrɪəm] (*pl* **crematoria**) *n* crematorio

crêpe [kreɪp] *n* (*fabric*) crespón *m*; (*also:* **~ rubber**) crepé *m*; **~ bandage** (*BRIT*) *n* venda de crepé

crept [krept] *pt, pp of* **creep**

crescent [ˈkresnt] *n* media luna; (*street*) calle *f* (*en forma de semicírculo*)

cress [kres] *n* berro

crest [krest] *n* (*of bird*) cresta; (*of hill*) cima, cumbre *f*; (*of coat of arms*) blasón *m*; **~fallen** *adj* alicaído

crevice [ˈkrevɪs] *n* grieta, hendedura

crew [kruː] *n* (*of ship etc*) tripulación *f*; (*TV, CINEMA*) equipo; **~-cut** *n* corte *m* al rape; **~-neck** *n* cuello a la caja

crib [krɪb] *n* cuna ♦ *vt* (*inf*) plagiar

crick [krɪk] *n* (*in neck*) tortícolis *f*

cricket [ˈkrɪkɪt] *n* (*insect*) grillo; (*game*) críquet *m*

crime [kraɪm] *n* (*no pl: illegal activities*) crimen *m*; (*illegal action*) delito; **criminal** [ˈkrɪmɪnl] *n* criminal *m/f*, delincuente *m/f* ♦ *adj* criminal; (*illegal*) delictivo; (*law*) penal

crimson [ˈkrɪmzn] *adj* carmesí

cringe [krɪndʒ] *vi* agacharse, encogerse

crinkle [ˈkrɪŋkl] *vt* arrugar

cripple [ˈkrɪpl] *n* lisiado/a, cojo/a ♦ *vt* lisiar, mutilar

crisis [ˈkraɪsɪs] (*pl* **crises**) *n* crisis *f inv*

crisp [krɪsp] *adj* fresco; (*vegetables etc*) crujiente; (*manner*) seco; **~s** (*BRIT*) *npl* patatas *fpl* (*SP*) or papas *fpl* (*AM*) fritas

crisscross [ˈkrɪskrɔs] *adj* entrelazado

criterion [kraɪˈtɪərɪən] (*pl* **criteria**) *n* criterio

critic [ˈkrɪtɪk] *n* crítico/a; **~al** *adj* crítico; (*illness*) grave; **~ally** *adv* (*speak etc*) en tono crítico; (*ill*) gravemente; **~ism** [ˈkrɪtɪsɪzm] *n* crítica; **~ize** [ˈkrɪtɪsaɪz] *vt* criticar

croak [krəuk] *vi* (*frog*) croar; (*raven*) graznar; (*person*) gruñir

Croatia [krəuˈeɪʃə] *n* Croacia

crochet [ˈkrəuʃeɪ] *n* ganchillo

crockery [ˈkrɔkərɪ] *n* loza, vajilla

crocodile [ˈkrɔkədaɪl] *n* cocodrilo

crocus [ˈkrəukəs] *n* croco, crocus *m*

croft [krɔft] *n* granja pequeña

crony [ˈkrəunɪ] (*inf: pej*) *n* compinche *m/f*

crook [kruk] *n* ladrón/ona *m/f*; (*of shepherd*) cayado; **~ed** [ˈkrukɪd] *adj* torcido; (*dishonest*) nada honrado

crop [krɔp] *n* (*produce*) cultivo; (*amount produced*) cosecha; (*riding ~*) látigo de montar ♦ *vt* cortar, recortar; **~ up** *vi* surgir, presentarse

cross [krɔs] *n* cruz *f*; (*hybrid*) cruce *m* ♦ *vt* (*street etc*) cruzar, atravesar ♦ *adj* de mal humor, enojado; **~ out** *vt* tachar; **~ over** *vi* cruzar; **~bar** *n* travesaño; **~country (race)** *n* carrera a campo traviesa, cross *m*; **~-examine** *vt* interrogar; **~-eyed** *adj* bizco; **~fire** *n* fuego cruzado; **~ing** *n* (*sea passage*) travesía; (*also:* **pedestrian ~ing**) paso para peatones; **~ing guard** (*US*) *n persona encargada de ayudar a los niños a cruzar la calle;* **~ purposes** *npl*: **to be at ~ purposes** no comprenderse uno a otro; **~-reference** *n* referencia, llamada; **~roads** *n* cruce *m*, encrucijada; **~ section** *n* corte *m* transversal; (*of population*) muestra (*representativa*); **~walk** (*US*) *n* paso de peatones; **~wind** *n* viento de costado; **~word** *n* crucigrama *m*

crotch [krɔtʃ] *n* (*ANAT, of garment*) entrepierna

crotchet [ˈkrɔtʃɪt] *n* (*MUS*) negra

crouch [krautʃ] *vi* agacharse, acurrucarse

crow [krəu] *n* (*bird*) cuervo; (*of cock*) canto, cacareo ♦ *vi* (*cock*) cantar

crowbar ['krəubɑ:•] *n* palanca

crowd [kraud] *n* muchedumbre *f*, multitud *f* ♦ *vt* (*fill*) llenar ♦ *vi* (*gather*): **to ~ round** reunirse en torno a; (*cram*): **to ~ in** entrar en tropel; **~ed** *adj* (*full*) atestado; (*densely populated*) superpoblado

crown [kraun] *n* corona; (*of head*) coronilla; (*for tooth*) funda; (*of hill*) cumbre *f* ♦ *vt* coronar; (*fig*) completar, rematar; **~ jewels** *npl* joyas *fpl* reales; **~ prince** *n* príncipe *m* heredero

crow's feet *npl* patas *fpl* de gallo

crucial ['kru:ʃl] *adj* decisivo

crucifix ['kru:sɪfɪks] *n* crucifijo; **~ion** [-'fɪkʃən] *n* crucifixión *f*

crude [kru:d] *adj* (*materials*) bruto; (*fig: basic*) tosco; (*: vulgar*) ordinario; **~ (oil)** *n* (petróleo) crudo

cruel ['kruəl] *adj* cruel; **~ty** *n* crueldad *f*

cruise [kru:z] *n* crucero ♦ *vi* (*ship*) hacer un crucero; (*car*) ir a velocidad de crucero; **~r** *n* (*motorboat*) yate *m* de motor; (*warship*) crucero

crumb [krʌm] *n* miga, migaja

crumble ['krʌmbl] *vt* desmenuzar ♦ *vi* (*building, also fig*) desmoronarse; **crumbly** *adj* que se desmigaja fácilmente

crumpet ['krʌmpɪt] *n* ≈ bollo para tostar

crumple ['krʌmpl] *vt* (*paper*) estrujar; (*material*) arrugar

crunch [krʌntʃ] *vt* (*with teeth*) mascar; (*underfoot*) hacer crujir ♦ *n* (*fig*) hora or momento de la verdad; **~y** *adj* crujiente

crusade [kru:'seɪd] *n* cruzada

crush [krʌʃ] *n* (*crowd*) aglomeración *f*; (*infatuation*): **to have a ~ on sb** estar loco por uno; (*drink*): **lemon ~** limonada ♦ *vt* aplastar; (*paper*) estrujar; (*cloth*) arrugar; (*fruit*) exprimir; (*opposition*) aplastar; (*hopes*) destruir

crust [krʌst] *n* corteza; (*of snow, ice*) costra

crutch [krʌtʃ] *n* muleta

crux [krʌks] *n*: **the ~ of** lo esencial de, el quid de

cry [kraɪ] *vi* llorar; (*shout: also: ~ out*) gritar ♦ *n* (*shriek*) chillido; (*shout*) grito; **~ off** *vi* echarse atrás

cryptic ['krɪptɪk] *adj* enigmático, secreto

crystal ['krɪstl] *n* cristal *m*; **~-clear** *adj* claro como el agua

cub [kʌb] *n* cachorro; (*also: ~ scout*) niño explorador

Cuba ['kju:bə] *n* Cuba; **~n** *adj*, *n* cubano/a *m/f*

cube [kju:b] *n* cubo ♦ *vt* (MATH) cubicar; **cubic** *adj* cúbico

cubicle ['kju:bɪkl] *n* (*at pool*) caseta; (*for bed*) cubículo

cuckoo ['kuku:] *n* cuco; **~ clock** *n* reloj *m* de cucú

cucumber ['kju:kʌmbə•] *n* pepino

cuddle ['kʌdl] *vt* abrazar ♦ *vi* abrazarse

cue [kju:] *n* (*snooker ~*) taco; (THEATRE *etc*) señal *f*

cuff [kʌf] *n* (*of sleeve*) puño; (US: *of trousers*) vuelta; (*blow*) bofetada; **off the ~** *adv* de improviso; **~links** *npl* gemelos *mpl*

cuisine [kwɪ'zi:n] *n* cocina

cul-de-sac ['kʌldəsæk] *n* callejón *m* sin salida

cull [kʌl] *vt* (*idea*) sacar ♦ *n* (*of animals*) matanza selectiva

culminate ['kʌlmɪneɪt] *vi*: **to ~ in** terminar en; **culmination** [-'neɪʃən] *n* culminación *f*, colmo

culottes [ku:'lɒts] *npl* falda pantalón *f*

culprit ['kʌlprɪt] *n* culpable *m/f*

cult [kʌlt] *n* culto

cultivate ['kʌltɪveɪt] *vt* (*also fig*) cultivar; **~d** *adj* culto; **cultivation** [-'veɪʃən] *n* cultivo

cultural ['kʌltʃərəl] *adj* cultural

culture ['kʌltʃə•] *n* (*also fig*) cultura; (BIO) cultivo; **~d** *adj* culto

cumbersome ['kʌmbəsəm] *adj* de mucho bulto, voluminoso; (*process*) enrevesado

cunning ['kʌnɪŋ] *n* astucia ♦ *adj* astuto

cup [kʌp] *n* taza; (*as prize*) copa

cupboard ['kʌbəd] *n* armario; (*kitchen*) alacena

cup tie (*BRIT*) *n* partido de copa
curate ['kjuərɪt] *n* cura *m*
curator [kjuə'reɪtə*] *n* director(a) *m/f*
curb [kə:b] *vt* refrenar; (*person*) reprimir ♦ *n* freno; (*US*) bordillo
curdle ['kə:dl] *vi* cuajarse
cure [kjuə*] *vt* curar ♦ *n* cura, curación *f*; (*fig: solution*) remedio
curfew ['kə:fju:] *n* toque *m* de queda
curiosity [kjuərɪ'ɒsɪtɪ] *n* curiosidad *f*
curious ['kjuərɪəs] *adj* curioso; (*person: interested*): **to be ~** sentir curiosidad
curl [kə:l] *n* rizo ♦ *vt* (*hair*) rizar ♦ *vi* rizarse; **~ up** *vi* (*person*) hacerse un ovillo; **~er** *n* rulo; **~y** *adj* rizado
currant ['kʌrnt] *n* pasa (de Corinto); (*black~, red~*) grosella
currency ['kʌrnsɪ] *n* moneda; **to gain ~** (*fig*) difundirse
current ['kʌrnt] *n* corriente *f* ♦ *adj* (*accepted*) corriente; (*present*) actual; **~ account** (*BRIT*) *n* cuenta corriente; **~ affairs** *npl* noticias *fpl* de actualidad; **~ly** *adv* actualmente
curriculum [kə'rɪkjuləm] (*pl* **~s** or **curricula**) *n* plan *m* de estudios; **~ vitae** *n* currículum *m*
curry ['kʌrɪ] *n* curry *m* ♦ *vt*: **to ~ favour with** buscar favores con; **~ powder** *n* curry *m* en polvo
curse [kə:s] *vi* soltar tacos ♦ *vt* maldecir ♦ *n* maldición *f*; (*swearword*) palabrota, taco
cursor ['kə:sə*] *n* (*COMPUT*) cursor *m*
cursory ['kə:sərɪ] *adj* rápido, superficial
curt [kə:t] *adj* corto, seco
curtail [kə:'teɪl] *vt* (*visit etc*) acortar; (*freedom*) restringir; (*expenses etc*) reducir
curtain ['kə:tn] *n* cortina; (*THEATRE*) telón *m*
curts(e)y ['kə:tsɪ] *vi* hacer una reverencia
curve [kə:v] *n* curva ♦ *vi* (*road*) hacer una curva; (*line etc*) curvarse
cushion ['kuʃən] *n* cojín *m*; (*of air*) colchón *m* ♦ *vt* (*shock*) amortiguar
custard ['kʌstəd] *n* natillas *fpl*
custody ['kʌstədɪ] *n* custodia; **to take into**

~ detener
custom ['kʌstəm] *n* costumbre *f*; (*COMM*) clientela; **~ary** *adj* acostumbrado
customer ['kʌstəmə*] *n* cliente *m/f*
customized ['kʌstəmaɪzd] *adj* (*car etc*) hecho a encargo
custom-made *adj* hecho a la medida
customs ['kʌstəmz] *npl* aduana; **~ officer** *n* aduanero/a
cut [kʌt] (*pt, pp* **cut**) *vt* cortar; (*price*) rebajar; (*text, programme*) acortar; (*reduce*) reducir ♦ *vi* cortar ♦ *n* (*of garment*) corte *m*; (*in skin*) cortadura; (*in salary etc*) rebaja, recorte *m*; (*slice of meat*) tajada; **to ~ a tooth** echar un diente; **~ down** *vt* (*tree*) derribar; (*reduce*) reducir; **~ off** *vt* cortar; (*person, place*) aislar; (*TEL*) desconectar; **~ out** *vt* (*shape*) recortar; (*stop: activity etc*) dejar; (*remove*) quitar; **~ up** *vt* cortar (en pedazos); **~back** *n* reducción *f*
cute [kju:t] *adj* mono
cuticle ['kju:tɪkl] *n* cutícula
cutlery ['kʌtlərɪ] *n* cubiertos *mpl*
cutlet ['kʌtlɪt] *n* chuleta; (*nut etc ~*) plato vegetariano hecho con nueces y verdura en forma de chuleta
cut: **~out** *n* (*switch*) dispositivo de seguridad, disyuntor *m*; (*cardboard ~out*) recortable *m*; **~~price** (*US* **~~rate**) *adj* a precio reducido; **~throat** *adj* feroz
cutting ['kʌtɪŋ] *adj* (*remark*) mordaz ♦ *n* (*BRIT: from newspaper*) recorte *m*; (*from plant*) esqueje *m*
CV *n abbr* = **curriculum vitae**
cwt *abbr* = **hundredweight(s)**
cyanide ['saɪənaɪd] *n* cianuro
cybercafé ['saɪbəkæfeɪ] *n* cibercafé *m*
cycle ['saɪkl] *n* ciclo; (*bicycle*) bicicleta ♦ *vi* ir en bicicleta; **~ lane** *n* carril-bici *m*; **~ path** *n* carril-bici *m*; **cycling** *n* ciclismo; **cyclist** *n* ciclista *m/f*
cyclone ['saɪkləun] *n* ciclón *m*
cygnet ['sɪgnɪt] *n* pollo de cisne
cylinder ['sɪlɪndə*] *n* cilindro; (*of gas*) bombona; **~~head gasket** *n* junta de culata

cymbals ['sɪmblz] npl platillos mpl
cynic ['sɪnɪk] n cínico/a; ~al adj cínico;
~ism ['sɪnɪsɪzəm] n cinismo
Cyprus ['saɪprəs] n Chipre f
cyst [sɪst] n quiste m; ~itis [-'taɪtɪs] n
cistitis f
czar [zɑ:ˈ] n zar m
Czech [tʃek] adj, n checo/a m/f; ~
Republic n la República Checa

D, d

D [di:] n (MUS) re m
dab [dæb] vt (eyes, wound) tocar
(ligeramente); (paint, cream) poner un
poco de
dabble ['dæbl] vi: to ~ in ser algo
aficionado a
dad [dæd] n = daddy
daddy ['dædɪ] n papá m
daffodil ['dæfədɪl] n narciso
daft [dɑ:ft] adj tonto
dagger ['dægəˈ] n puñal m, daga
daily ['deɪlɪ] adj diario, cotidiano ♦ adv
todos los días, cada día
dainty ['deɪntɪ] adj delicado
dairy ['dɛərɪ] n (shop) lechería; (on farm)
vaquería; ~ farm n granja; ~ products
npl productos mpl lácteos; ~ store (US)
n lechería
daisy ['deɪzɪ] n margarita
dale [deɪl] n valle m
dam [dæm] n presa ♦ vt construir una
presa sobre, represar
damage ['dæmɪdʒ] n lesión f; daño; (dents
etc) desperfectos mpl; (fig) perjuicio ♦ vt
dañar, perjudicar; (spoil, break) estropear;
~s npl (LAW) daños mpl y perjuicios
damn [dæm] vt condenar; (curse) maldecir
♦ n (inf): I don't give a ~ me importa un
pito ♦ adj (inf: also: ~ed) maldito; ~ (it)!
¡maldito sea!; ~ing adj (evidence)
irrecusable
damp [dæmp] adj húmedo, mojado ♦ n
humedad f ♦ vt (also: ~en: cloth, rag)
mojar; (: enthusiasm) enfriar

damson ['dæmzən] n ciruela damascena
dance [dɑ:ns] n baile m ♦ vi bailar; ~ hall
n salón m de baile; ~r n bailador(a) m/f;
(professional) bailarín/ina m/f; dancing n
baile m
dandelion ['dændɪlaɪən] n diente m de
león
dandruff ['dændrəf] n caspa
Dane [deɪn] n danés/esa m/f
danger ['deɪndʒəˈ] n peligro; (risk) riesgo;
~! (on sign) ¡peligro de muerte!; to be in
~ of correr riesgo de; ~ous adj peligroso;
~ously adv peligrosamente
dangle ['dæŋgl] vt colgar ♦ vi pender,
colgar
Danish ['deɪnɪʃ] adj danés/esa ♦ n (LING)
danés m
dare [dɛəˈ] vt: to ~ sb to do desafiar a
uno a hacer ♦ vi: to ~ (to) do sth
atreverse a hacer algo; I ~ say (I suppose)
puede ser (que); daring adj atrevido,
osado ♦ n atrevimiento, osadía
dark [dɑ:k] adj oscuro; (hair, complexion)
moreno ♦ n: in the ~ a oscuras; to be in
the ~ about (fig) no saber nada de; after
~ después del anochecer; ~en vt (colour)
hacer más oscuro ♦ vi oscurecerse; ~
glasses npl gafas fpl negras (SP),
anteojos mpl negros (AM); ~ness n
oscuridad f; ~room n cuarto oscuro
darling ['dɑ:lɪŋ] adj, n querido/a m/f
darn [dɑ:n] vt zurcir
dart [dɑ:t] n dardo; (in sewing) sisa ♦ vi
precipitarse; ~ away/along vi salir/
marchar disparado; ~board n diana; ~s
n dardos mpl
dash [dæʃ] n (small quantity: of liquid)
gota, chorrito; (: of solid) pizca; (sign)
raya ♦ vt (throw) tirar; (hopes) defraudar
♦ vi precipitarse, ir de prisa; ~ away or
off vi marcharse apresuradamente
dashboard ['dæʃbɔ:d] n (AUT) salpicadero
dashing ['dæʃɪŋ] adj gallardo
data ['deɪtə] npl datos mpl; ~base n base
f de datos; ~ processing n proceso de
datos
date [deɪt] n (day) fecha; (with friend) cita;

(*fruit*) dátil *m* ♦ *vt* fechar; (*person*) salir con; ~ **of birth** fecha de nacimiento; **to** ~ *adv* hasta la fecha; ~d *adj* anticuado; ~ **rape** *n* violación ocurrida durante una cita con un conocido

daub [dɔ:b] *vt* embadurnar

daughter ['dɔ:tə*] *n* hija; ~-in-law *n* nuera, hija política

daunting ['dɔ:ntɪŋ] *adj* desalentador(a)

dawdle ['dɔ:dl] *vi* (*go slowly*) andar muy despacio

dawn [dɔ:n] *n* alba, amanecer *m*; (*fig*) nacimiento *m* ♦ *vi* (*day*) amanecer; (*fig*): **it ~ed on him that ...** cayó en la cuenta de que ...

day [deɪ] *n* día *m*; (*working* ~) jornada; (*hey*~) tiempos *mpl*, días *mpl*; **the ~ before/after** el día anterior/siguiente; **the ~ after tomorrow** pasado mañana; **the ~ before yesterday** anteayer; **the following ~** el día siguiente; **by ~** de día; ~**break** *n* amanecer *m*; ~**dream** *vi* soñar despierto; ~**light** *n* luz *f* (del día); ~ **return** (*BRIT*) *n* billete *m* de ida y vuelta (en un día); ~**time** *n* día *m*; ~-**to**~ *adj* cotidiano

daze [deɪz] *vt* (*stun*) aturdir ♦ *n*: **in a ~** aturdido

dazzle ['dæzl] *vt* deslumbrar

DC *abbr* (= *direct current*) corriente *f* continua

dead [dɛd] *adj* muerto; (*limb*) dormido; (*telephone*) cortado; (*battery*) agotado ♦ *adv* (*completely*) totalmente; (*exactly*) exactamente; **to shoot sb ~** matar a uno a tiros; ~ **tired** muerto (de cansancio); **to stop ~** parar en seco; **the ~** *npl* los muertos; **to be a ~ loss** (*inf*: *person*) ser un inútil; ~**en** *vt* (*blow, sound*) amortiguar; (*pain etc*) aliviar; ~ **end** *n* callejón *m* sin salida; ~ **heat** *n* (*SPORT*) empate *m*; ~**line** *n* fecha (or hora) tope; ~**lock** *n*: **to reach ~lock** llegar a un punto muerto; ~**ly** *adj* mortal, fatal; ~**pan** *adj* sin expresión; **the D~ Sea** *n* el Mar Muerto

deaf [dɛf] *adj* sordo; ~**en** *vt* ensordecer; ~**ness** *n* sordera

deal [di:l] (*pt, pp* **dealt**) *n* (*agreement*) pacto, convenio; (*business* ~) trato ♦ *vt* dar; (*card*) repartir; **a great ~ (of)** bastante, mucho; ~ **in** *vt fus* tratar en, comerciar en; ~ **with** *vt fus* (*people*) tratar con; (*problem*) ocuparse de; (*subject*) tratar de; ~**ings** *npl* (*COMM*) transacciones *fpl*; (*relations*) relaciones *fpl*

dealt [dɛlt] *pt, pp of* **deal**

dean [di:n] *n* (*REL*) deán *m*; (*SCOL: BRIT*) decano; (: *US*) decano; rector *m*

dear [dɪə*] *adj* querido; (*expensive*) caro ♦ *n*: **my** ~ mi querido/a ♦ *excl*: ~ **me!** ¡Dios mío!; **D~ Sir/Madam** (*in letter*) Muy Señor Mío, Estimado Señor/Estimada Señora; **D~ Mr/Mrs X** Estimado/a Señor(a) X; ~**ly** *adv* (*love*) mucho; (*pay*) caro

death [dɛθ] *n* muerte *f*; ~ **certificate** *n* partida de defunción; ~**ly** *adj* (*white*) como un muerto; (*silence*) sepulcral; ~ **penalty** *n* pena de muerte; ~ **rate** *n* mortalidad *f*; ~ **toll** *n* número de víctimas

debacle [deɪˈbɑːkl] *n* desastre *m*

debase [dɪˈbeɪs] *vt* degradar

debatable [dɪˈbeɪtəbl] *adj* discutible

debate [dɪˈbeɪt] *n* debate *m* ♦ *vt* discutir

debit ['dɛbɪt] *n* debe *m* ♦ *vt*: **to ~ a sum to sb** *or* **to sb's account** cargar una suma en cuenta a alguien

debris ['dɛbriː] *n* escombros *mpl*

debt [dɛt] *n* deuda; **to be in ~** tener deudas; ~**or** *n* deudor(a) *m/f*

début ['deɪbjuː] *n* presentación *f*

decade ['dɛkeɪd] *n* decenio, década

decadence ['dɛkədəns] *n* decadencia

decaff ['diːkæf] (*inf*) *n* descafeinado

decaffeinated [dɪˈkæfɪneɪtɪd] *adj* descafeinado

decanter [dɪˈkæntə*] *n* garrafa

decay [dɪˈkeɪ] *n* (*of building*) desmoronamiento; (*of tooth*) caries *f inv* ♦ *vi* (*rot*) pudrirse

deceased [dɪˈsiːst] *n*: **the ~** el/la difunto/a

deceit [dɪˈsiːt] *n* engaño; ~**ful** *adj* engañoso; **deceive** [dɪˈsiːv] *vt* engañar

December [dɪ'sɛmbə*] n diciembre m

decent ['di:sənt] adj (proper) decente; (person: kind) amable, bueno

deception [dɪ'sɛpʃən] n engaño

deceptive [dɪ'sɛptɪv] adj engañoso

decibel ['dɛsɪbɛl] n decibel(io) m

decide [dɪ'saɪd] vt (person) decidir; (question, argument) resolver ♦ vi decidir; to ~ to do/that decidir hacer/que; to ~ on sth decidirse por algo; ~d adj (resolute) decidido; (clear, definite) indudable; ~dly [-dɪdlɪ] adv decididamente; (emphatically) con resolución

deciduous [dɪ'sɪdjuəs] adj de hoja caduca

decimal ['dɛsɪməl] adj decimal ♦ n decimal m; ~ point n coma decimal

decipher [dɪ'saɪfə*] vt descifrar

decision [dɪ'sɪʒən] n decisión f

decisive [dɪ'saɪsɪv] adj decisivo; (person) decidido

deck [dɛk] n (NAUT) cubierta f; (of bus) piso; (record ~) platina f; (of cards) baraja; ~chair n tumbona

declaration [dɛklə'reɪʃən] n declaración f

declare [dɪ'klɛə*] vt declarar

decline [dɪ'klaɪn] n disminución f, descenso ♦ vt rehusar ♦ vi (person, business) decaer; (strength) disminuir

decoder [di:'kəudə*] n (TV) decodificador m

décor ['deɪkɔ:*] n decoración f; (THEATRE) decorado

decorate ['dɛkəreɪt] vt (adorn): to ~ (with) adornar (de), decorar (de); (paint) pintar; (paper) empapelar; decoration [-'reɪʃən] n adorno; (act) decoración f; (medal) condecoración f; decorator n (workman) pintor m (decorador)

decorum [dɪ'kɔ:rəm] n decoro

decoy ['di:kɔɪ] n señuelo

decrease [n 'di:kri:s, vb dɪ'kri:s] n: ~ (in) disminución f (de) ♦ vt disminuir, reducir ♦ vi reducirse

decree [dɪ'kri:] n decreto; ~ nisi n sentencia provisional de divorcio

dedicate ['dɛdɪkeɪt] vt dedicar;

dedication [-'keɪʃən] n (devotion) dedicación f; (in book) dedicatoria

deduce [dɪ'dju:s] vt deducir

deduct [dɪ'dʌkt] vt restar; descontar; ~ion [dɪ'dʌkʃən] n (amount deducted) descuento; (conclusion) deducción f, conclusión f

deed [di:d] n hecho, acto; (feat) hazaña; (LAW) escritura

deep [di:p] adj profundo; (expressing measurements) de profundidad; (voice) bajo; (breath) profundo; (colour) intenso ♦ adv: the spectators stood 20 ~ los espectadores se formaron de 20 en fondo; to be 4 metres ~ tener 4 metros de profundidad; ~en vt ahondar, profundizar ♦ vi aumentar, crecer; ~-freeze n congelador m; ~-fry vt freír en aceite abundante; ~ly adv (breathe) a pleno pulmón; (interested, moved, grateful) profundamente, hondamente; ~-sea diving n buceo de altura; ~-seated adj (beliefs) (profundamente) arraigado

deer [dɪə*] n inv ciervo

deface [dɪ'feɪs] vt (wall, surface) estropear, pintarrajear

default [dɪ'fɔ:lt] n: by ~ (win) por incomparecencia ♦ adj (COMPUT) por defecto

defeat [dɪ'fi:t] n derrota ♦ vt derrotar, vencer; ~ist adj, n derrotista m/f

defect [n 'di:fɛkt, vb dɪ'fɛkt] n defecto ♦ vi: to ~ to the enemy pasarse al enemigo; ~ive [dɪ'fɛktɪv] adj defectuoso

defence [dɪ'fɛns] (US defense) n defensa; ~less adj indefenso

defend [dɪ'fɛnd] vt defender; ~ant n acusado/a; (in civil case) demandado/a; ~er n defensor(a) m/f; (SPORT) defensa m/f

defense [dɪ'fɛns] (US) n = defence

defensive [dɪ'fɛnsɪv] adj defensivo ♦ n: on the ~ a la defensiva

defer [dɪ'fɜ:*] vt aplazar

defiance [dɪ'faɪəns] n desafío; in ~ of en contra de; defiant [dɪ'faɪənt] adj (*challenging*) desafiante, retador(a)

deficiency [dɪ'fɪʃənsɪ] *n* (*lack*) falta; (*defect*) defecto *m*; **deficient** [dɪ'fɪʃənt] *adj* deficiente

deficit ['defɪsɪt] *n* déficit *m*

define [dɪ'faɪn] *vt* (*word etc*) definir; (*limits etc*) determinar

definite ['defɪnɪt] *adj* (*fixed*) determinado; (*obvious*) claro; (*certain*) indudable; **he was ~ about it** no dejó lugar a dudas (sobre ello); **~ly** *adv* desde luego, por supuesto

definition [defɪ'nɪʃən] *n* definición *f*; (*clearness*) nitidez *f*

deflate [di:'fleɪt] *vt* desinflar

deflect [dɪ'flekt] *vt* desviar

defraud [dɪ'frɔ:d] *vt*: **to ~ sb of sth** estafar algo a uno

defrost [di:'frɔst] *vt* descongelar; **~er** (*US*) *n* (*demister*) eliminador *m* de vaho

deft [deft] *adj* diestro, hábil

defunct [dɪ'fʌŋkt] *adj* difunto; (*organization etc*) ya que no existe

defuse [di:'fju:z] *vt* desactivar; (*situation*) calmar

defy [dɪ'faɪ] *vt* (*resist*) oponerse a; (*challenge*) desafiar; (*fig*): **it defies description** resulta imposible describirlo

degenerate [*vb* dɪ'dʒenəreɪt, *adj* dɪ'dʒenərɪt] *vi* degenerar ♦ *adj* degenerado

degree [dɪ'gri:] *n* grado; (*SCOL*) título; **to have a ~ in maths** tener una licenciatura en matemáticas; **by ~s** (*gradually*) poco a poco, por etapas; **to some ~** hasta cierto punto

dehydrated [di:haɪ'dreɪtɪd] *adj* deshidratado; (*milk*) en polvo

de-ice [di:'aɪs] *vt* deshelar

deign [deɪn] *vi*: **to ~ to do** dignarse hacer

dejected [dɪ'dʒektɪd] *adj* abatido, desanimado

delay [dɪ'leɪ] *vt* demorar, aplazar; (*person*) entretener; (*train*) retrasar ♦ *vi* tardar ♦ *n* demora, retraso; **to be ~ed** retrasarse; **without ~** en seguida, sin tardar

delectable [dɪ'lektəbl] *adj* (*person*)

encantador(a); (*food*) delicioso

delegate [*n* 'delɪgɪt, *vb* 'delɪgeɪt] *n* delegado/a ♦ *vt* (*person*) delegar en; (*task*) delegar

delete [dɪ'li:t] *vt* suprimir, tachar

deliberate [*adj* dɪ'lɪbərɪt, *vb* dɪ'lɪbəreɪt] *adj* (*intentional*) intencionado; (*slow*) pausado, lento ♦ *vi* deliberar; **~ly** *adv* (*on purpose*) a propósito

delicacy ['delɪkəsɪ] *n* delicadeza; (*choice food*) manjar *m*

delicate ['delɪkɪt] *adj* delicado; (*fragile*) frágil

delicatessen [delɪkə'tesn] *n* ultramarinos *mpl* finos

delicious [dɪ'lɪʃəs] *adj* delicioso

delight [dɪ'laɪt] *n* (*feeling*) placer *m*, deleite *m*; (*person, experience etc*) encanto, delicia ♦ *vt* encantar, deleitar; **to take ~ in** deleitarse en; **~ed** *adj*: **~ed (at** *or* **with/ to do)** encantado (con/de hacer); **~ful** *adj* encantador(a), delicioso

delinquent [dɪ'lɪŋkwənt] *adj, n* delincuente *m/f*

delirious [dɪ'lɪrɪəs] *adj*: **to be ~** delirar, desvariar; **to be ~ with** estar loco de

deliver [dɪ'lɪvə*] *vt* (*distribute*) repartir; (*hand over*) entregar; (*message*) comunicar; (*speech*) pronunciar; (*MED*) asistir al parto de; **~y** *n* reparto; entrega; (*of speaker*) modo de expresarse; (*MED*) parto, alumbramiento; **to take ~y of** recibir

delude [dɪ'lu:d] *vt* engañar

deluge ['delju:dʒ] *n* diluvio

delusion [dɪ'lu:ʒən] *n* ilusión *f*, engaño

de luxe [də'lʌks] *adj* de lujo

demand [dɪ'mɑ:nd] *vt* (*gen*) exigir; (*rights*) reclamar ♦ *n* exigencia; (*claim*) reclamación *f*; (*ECON*) demanda; **to be in ~** ser muy solicitado; **on ~** a solicitud; **~ing** *adj* (*boss*) exigente; (*work*) absorbente

demean [dɪ'mi:n] *vt*: **to ~ o.s.** rebajarse

demeanour [dɪ'mi:nə*] (*US* **demeanor**) *n* porte *m*, conducta

demented [dɪ'mentɪd] *adj* demente

emise [dɪ'maɪz] n (death) fallecimiento

emister [diː'mɪstə*] n (AUT) eliminador m de vaho

emo ['deməu] (inf) n abbr (= demonstration) manifestación f

emocracy [dɪ'mɔkrəsɪ] n democracia; **democrat** ['deməkræt] n demócrata m/f; **democratic** [demə'krætɪk] adj democrático; (US) demócrata

emolish [dɪ'mɔlɪʃ] vt derribar, demoler; (fig: argument) destruir

emon ['diːmən] n (evil spirit) demonio

emonstrate ['demənstreɪt] vt demostrar; (skill, appliance) mostrar ♦ vi manifestarse; **demonstration** [-'streɪʃən] n (POL) manifestación f; (proof, exhibition) demostración f; **demonstrator** n (POL) manifestante m/f; (COMM) demostrador(a) m/f; vendedor(a) m/f

emote [dɪ'məut] vt degradar

emure [dɪ'mjuə*] adj recatado

en [den] n (of animal) guarida; (room) habitación f

enial [dɪ'naɪəl] n (refusal) negativa; (of report etc) negación f

enim ['denɪm] n tela vaquera; **~s** npl vaqueros mpl

Denmark ['denmɑːk] n Dinamarca

enomination [dɪnɔmɪ'neɪʃən] n valor m; (REL) confesión f

enounce [dɪ'nauns] vt denunciar

ense [dens] adj (crowd) denso; (thick) espeso; (: foliage etc) tupido; (inf: stupid) torpe; **~ly** adv: **~ly populated** con una alta densidad de población

ensity ['densɪtɪ] n densidad f; **single/double-~ disk** (COMPUT) disco de densidad sencilla/doble densidad

ent [dent] n abolladura ♦ vt (also: **make a ~ in**) abollar

ental ['dentl] adj dental; **~ surgeon** n odontólogo/a

entist ['dentɪst] n dentista m/f

entures ['dentʃəz] npl dentadura (postiza)

eny [dɪ'naɪ] vt negar; (charge) rechazar

eodorant [diː'əudərənt] n desodorante m

depart [dɪ'pɑːt] vi irse, marcharse; (train) salir; **to ~ from** (fig: differ from) apartarse de

department [dɪ'pɑːtmənt] n (COMM) sección f; (SCOL) departamento; (POL) ministerio; **~ store** n gran almacén m

departure [dɪ'pɑːtʃə*] n partida, ida; (of train) salida; (of employee) marcha; **a new ~** un nuevo rumbo; **~ lounge** n (at airport) sala de embarque

depend [dɪ'pend] vi: **to ~ on** depender de; (rely on) contar con; **it ~s** depende, según; **~ing on the result** según el resultado; **~able** adj (person) formal, serio; (watch) exacto; (car) seguro; **~ant** n dependiente m/f; **~ent** adj: **to be ~ent on** depender de ♦ n = **dependant**

depict [dɪ'pɪkt] vt (in picture) pintar; (describe) representar

depleted [dɪ'pliːtɪd] adj reducido

deploy [dɪ'plɔɪ] vt desplegar

deport [dɪ'pɔːt] vt deportar

deposit [dɪ'pɔzɪt] n depósito; (CHEM) sedimento; (of ore, oil) yacimiento ♦ vt (gen) depositar; **~ account** (BRIT) n cuenta de ahorros

depot ['depəu] n (storehouse) depósito; (for vehicles) parque m; (US) estación f

depreciate [dɪ'priːʃɪeɪt] vi depreciarse, perder valor

depress [dɪ'pres] vt deprimir; (wages etc) hacer bajar; (press down) apretar; **~ed** adj deprimido; **~ing** adj deprimente; **~ion** [dɪ'preʃən] n depresión f

deprivation [deprɪ'veɪʃən] n privación f

deprive [dɪ'praɪv] vt: **to ~ sb of** privar a uno de; **~d** adj necesitado

depth [depθ] n profundidad f; (of cupboard) fondo; **to be in the ~s of despair** sentir la mayor desesperación; **to be out of one's ~** (in water) no hacer pie; (fig) sentirse totalmente perdido

deputize ['depjutaɪz] vi: **to ~ for sb** suplir a uno

deputy ['depjutɪ] adj: **~ head** subdirector(a) m/f ♦ n sustituto/a, suplente m/f; (US: POL) diputado/a; (US:

also: **~ sheriff**) agente *m* (del sheriff)
derail [dɪ'reɪl] *vt*: **to be ~ed** descarrilarse
deranged [dɪ'reɪndʒd] *adj* trastornado
derby ['dɑːbɪ] (*US*) *n* (*hat*) hongo
derelict ['derɪlɪkt] *adj* abandonado
derisory [dɪ'raɪzərɪ] *adj* (*sum*) irrisorio
derive [dɪ'raɪv] *vt* (*benefit etc*) obtener
♦ *vi*: **to ~ from** derivarse de
derogatory [dɪ'rɔgətərɪ] *adj* despectivo
descend [dɪ'send] *vt, vi* descender, bajar;
to ~ from descender de; **to ~ to** rebajarse
a; **~ant** *n* descendiente *m/f*
descent [dɪ'sent] *n* descenso; (*origin*)
descendencia
describe [dɪs'kraɪb] *vt* describir;
description [-'krɪpʃən] *n* descripción *f*;
(*sort*) clase *f*, género
desecrate ['desɪkreɪt] *vt* profanar
desert [*n* 'dezət, *vb* dɪ'zɜːt] *n* desierto ♦ *vt*
abandonar ♦ *vi* (*MIL*) desertar; **~er**
[dɪ'zɜːtə*] *n* desertor(a) *m/f*; **~ion**
[dɪ'zɜːʃən] *n* deserción *f*; (*LAW*) abandono;
~ island *n* isla desierta; **~s** [dɪ'zɜːts] *npl*:
to get one's just ~s llevar su merecido
deserve [dɪ'zɜːv] *vt* merecer, ser digno de;
deserving *adj* (*person*) digno; (*action,
cause*) meritorio
design [dɪ'zaɪn] *n* (*sketch*) bosquejo;
(*layout, shape*) diseño; (*pattern*) dibujo;
(*intention*) intención *f* ♦ *vt* diseñar
designate [*vb* 'dezɪgneɪt, *adj* 'dezɪgnɪt] *vt*
(*appoint*) nombrar; (*destine*) designar
♦ *adj* designado
designer [dɪ'zaɪnə*] *n* diseñador(a) *m/f*;
(*fashion ~*) modisto/a, diseñador(a) *m/f*
de moda
desirable [dɪ'zaɪərəbl] *adj* (*proper*)
deseable; (*attractive*) atractivo
desire [dɪ'zaɪə*] *n* deseo ♦ *vt* desear
desk [desk] *n* (*in office*) escritorio; (*for
pupil*) pupitre *m*; (*in hotel, at airport*)
recepción *f*; (*BRIT: in shop, restaurant*) caja
desk-top publishing ['desktɔp-] *n*
autoedición *f*
desolate ['desəlɪt] *adj* (*place*) desierto;
(*person*) afligido
despair [dɪs'peə*] *n* desesperación *f* ♦ *vi*:

to ~ of perder la esperanza de
despatch [dɪs'pætʃ] *n, vt* = **dispatch**
desperate ['despərɪt] *adj* desesperado;
(*fugitive*) peligroso; **to be ~ for sth/to do**
necesitar urgentemente algo/hacer; **~ly**
adv desesperadamente; (*very*)
terriblemente, gravemente
desperation [despə'reɪʃən] *n*
desesperación *f*; **in** (**sheer**) **~**
(*absolutamente*) desesperado
despicable [dɪs'pɪkəbl] *adj* vil,
despreciable
despise [dɪs'paɪz] *vt* despreciar
despite [dɪs'paɪt] *prep* a pesar de, pese a
despondent [dɪs'pɔndənt] *adj* deprimido,
abatido
dessert [dɪ'zɜːt] *n* postre *m*; **~spoon** *n*
cuchara (de postre)
destination [destɪ'neɪʃən] *n* destino
destiny ['destɪnɪ] *n* destino
destitute ['destɪtjuːt] *adj* desamparado,
indigente
destroy [dɪs'trɔɪ] *vt* destruir; (*animal*)
sacrificar; **~er** *n* (*NAUT*) destructor *m*
destruction [dɪs'trʌkʃən] *n* destrucción *f*
detach [dɪ'tætʃ] *vt* separar; (*unstick*)
despegar; **~ed** *adj* (*attitude*) objetivo,
imparcial; **~ed house** *n* ≈ chalé *m*,
≈ chalet *m*; **~ment** *n* (*aloofness*) frialdad
f; (*MIL*) destacamento
detail ['diːteɪl] *n* detalle *m*; (*no pl: in
picture etc*) detalles *mpl*; (*trifle*) pequeñez
f ♦ *vt* detallar; (*MIL*) destacar; **in ~**
detalladamente; **~ed** *adj* detallado
detain [dɪ'teɪn] *vt* retener; (*in captivity*)
detener
detect [dɪ'tekt] *vt* descubrir; (*MED, POLICE*)
identificar; (*MIL, RADAR, TECH*) detectar;
~ion [dɪ'tekʃən] *n* descubrimiento;
identificación *f*; **~ive** *n* detective *m/f*;
~ive story *n* novela policíaca; **~or** *n*
detector *m*
detention [dɪ'tenʃən] *n* detención *f*,
arresto; (*SCOL*) castigo
deter [dɪ'tɜː*] *vt* (*dissuade*) disuadir
detergent [dɪ'tɜːdʒənt] *n* detergente *m*
deteriorate [dɪ'tɪərɪəreɪt] *vi* deteriorarse;

deterioration [-'rerʃən] n deterioro
determination [dɪtə:mɪ'neɪʃən] n resolución f
determine [dɪ'tə:mɪn] vt determinar; ~d adj (person) resuelto, decidido; ~d to do resuelto a hacer
deterrent [dɪ'terənt] n (MIL) fuerza de disuasión
detest [dɪ'test] vt aborrecer
detonate ['detəneɪt] vi estallar ♦ vt hacer detonar
detour ['di:tuə*] n (gen, US: AUT) desviación f
detract [dɪ'trækt] vt: to ~ from quitar mérito a, desvirtuar
detriment ['detrɪmənt] n: to the ~ of en perjuicio de; ~al [detrɪ'mentl] adj: ~al (to) perjudicial (a)
devaluation [dɪvælju'eɪʃən] n devaluación f
devalue [di:'vælju:] vt (currency) devaluar; (fig) quitar mérito a
devastate ['devəsteɪt] vt devastar; (fig): to be ~d by quedar destrozado por; devastating adj devastador(a); (fig) arrollador(a)
develop [dɪ'veləp] vt desarrollar; (PHOT) revelar; (disease) coger; (habit) adquirir; (fault) empezar a tener ♦ vi desarrollarse; (advance) progresar; (facts, symptoms) aparecer; ~er n promotor m; ~ing country n país m en (vías de) desarrollo; ~ment n desarrollo; (advance) progreso; (of affair, case) desenvolvimiento; (of land) urbanización f
deviation [di:vɪ'eɪʃən] n desviación f
device [dɪ'vaɪs] n (apparatus) aparato, mecanismo
devil ['devl] n diablo, demonio
devious ['di:vɪəs] adj taimado
devise [dɪ'vaɪz] vt idear, inventar
devoid [dɪ'vɔɪd] adj: ~ of desprovisto de
devolution [di:və'lu:ʃən] n (POL) descentralización f
devote [dɪ'vəut] vt: to ~ sth to dedicar algo a; ~d adj (loyal) leal, fiel; to be ~d to sb querer con devoción a alguien; the

book is ~d to politics el libro trata de la política; ~e [devəu'ti:] n entusiasta m/f; (REL) devoto/a; devotion n dedicación f; (REL) devoción f
devour [dɪ'vauə*] vt devorar
devout [dɪ'vaut] adj devoto
dew [dju:] n rocío
diabetes [daɪə'bi:ti:z] n diabetes f; diabetic [-'betɪk] adj, n diabético/a m/f
diabolical [daɪə'bɔlɪkəl] (inf) adj (weather, behaviour) pésimo
diagnosis [daɪəg'nəusɪs] (pl -ses) n diagnóstico
diagonal [daɪ'ægənl] adj, n diagonal f
diagram ['daɪəgræm] n diagrama m, esquema m
dial ['daɪəl] n esfera, cuadrante m, cara (AM); (on radio etc) selector m; (of phone) disco ♦ vt (number) marcar
dialling ['daɪəlɪŋ]: ~ code n prefijo; ~ tone (US dial tone) n (BRIT) señal f or tono de marcar
dialogue ['daɪəlɔg] (US dialog) n diálogo
diameter [daɪ'æmɪtə*] n diámetro
diamond ['daɪəmənd] n diamante m; (shape) rombo; ~s npl (CARDS) diamantes mpl
diaper ['daɪəpə*] (US) n pañal m
diaphragm ['daɪəfræm] n diafragma m
diarrhoea [daɪə'ri:ə] (US diarrhea) n diarrea
diary ['daɪərɪ] n (daily account) diario; (book) agenda
dice [daɪs] n inv dados mpl ♦ vt (CULIN) cortar en cuadritos
Dictaphone ® ['dɪktəfəun] n dictáfono ®
dictate [dɪk'teɪt] vt dictar; (conditions) imponer; dictation [-'teɪʃən] n dictado; (giving of orders) órdenes fpl
dictator [dɪk'teɪtə*] n dictador m; ~ship n dictadura
dictionary ['dɪkʃənrɪ] n diccionario
did [dɪd] pt of do
didn't ['dɪdənt] = did not
die [daɪ] vi morir; (fig: fade) desvanecerse, desaparecer; to be dying for sth/to do sth morirse por algo/de ganas de hacer

algo; ~ **away** vi (sound, light) perderse; ~ **down** vi apagarse; (wind) amainar; ~ **out** vi desaparecer

diesel ['diːzəl] n vehículo con motor Diesel; ~ **engine** n motor m Diesel; ~ **(oil)** n gasoil m

diet ['daɪət] n dieta; (restricted food) régimen m ♦ vi (also: **be on a ~**) estar a dieta, hacer régimen

differ ['dɪfə*] vi: **to ~ (from)** (be different) ser distinto (a), diferenciarse (de); (disagree) discrepar (de); ~**ence** n diferencia; (disagreement) desacuerdo; ~**ent** adj diferente, distinto; ~**entiate** [-'renʃieɪt] vi: **to ~entiate (between)** distinguir (entre); ~**ently** adv de otro modo, en forma distinta

difficult ['dɪfɪkəlt] adj difícil; ~**y** n dificultad f

diffident ['dɪfɪdənt] adj tímido

dig [dɪg] (pt, pp **dug**) vt (hole, ground) cavar ♦ n (prod) empujón m; (archaeological) excavación f; (remark) indirecta; **to ~ one's nails into** clavar las uñas en; ~ **into** vt fus (savings) consumir; ~ **up** vt (information) desenterrar; (plant) desarraigar

digest [vb daɪ'dʒest, n 'daɪdʒest] vt (food) digerir; (facts) asimilar ♦ n resumen m; ~**ion** [dɪ'dʒestʃən] n digestión f

digit ['dɪdʒɪt] n (number) dígito; (finger) dedo; ~**al** adj digital; ~**al camera** n cámara digital; ~**al TV** n televisión f digital

dignified ['dɪgnɪfaɪd] adj grave, solemne

dignity ['dɪgnɪtɪ] n dignidad f

digress [daɪ'gres] vi: **to ~ from** apartarse de

digs [dɪgz] (BRIT: inf) npl pensión f, alojamiento

dilapidated [dɪ'læpɪdeɪtɪd] adj desmoronado, ruinoso

dilemma [daɪ'lemə] n dilema m

diligent ['dɪlɪdʒənt] adj diligente

dilute [daɪ'luːt] vt diluir

dim [dɪm] adj (light) débil; (outline) indistinto; (room) oscuro; (inf: stupid)

lerdo ♦ vt (light) bajar

dime [daɪm] (US) n moneda de diez centavos

dimension [dɪ'menʃən] n dimensión f

diminish [dɪ'mɪnɪʃ] vt, vi disminuir

diminutive [dɪ'mɪnjutɪv] adj diminuto ♦ n (LING) diminutivo

dimmers ['dɪməz] (US) npl (AUT: dipped headlights) luces fpl cortas; (: parking lights) luces fpl de posición

dimple ['dɪmpl] n hoyuelo

din [dɪn] n estruendo, estrépito

dine [daɪn] vi cenar; ~**r** n (person) comensal m/f

dinghy ['dɪŋgɪ] n bote m; (also: **rubber ~**) lancha (neumática)

dingy ['dɪndʒɪ] adj (room) sombrío; (colour) sucio

dining car ['daɪnɪŋ-] (BRIT) n (RAIL) coche-comedor m

dining room n comedor m

dinner ['dɪnə*] n (evening meal) cena; (lunch) comida; (public) cena, banquete m; ~ **jacket** n smoking m; ~ **party** n cena; ~ **time** n (evening) hora de cenar; (midday) hora de comer

dinosaur ['daɪnəsɔː*] n dinosaurio

dip [dɪp] n (slope) pendiente m; (in sea) baño; (CULIN) salsa ♦ vt (in water) mojar; (ladle etc) meter; (BRIT: AUT): **to ~ one's lights** poner luces de cruce ♦ vi (road etc) descender, bajar

diploma [dɪ'pləumə] n diploma m

diplomacy [dɪ'pləuməsɪ] n diplomacia

diplomat ['dɪpləmæt] n diplomático/a; ~**ic** [dɪplə'mætɪk] adj diplomático

diprod ['dɪprɒd] (US) n = **dipstick**

dipstick ['dɪpstɪk] (BRIT) n (AUT) varilla de nivel (del aceite)

dipswitch ['dɪpswɪtʃ] (BRIT) n (AUT) interruptor m

dire [daɪə*] adj calamitoso

direct [daɪ'rekt] adj directo; (challenge) claro; (person) franco ♦ vt dirigir; (order): **to ~ sb to do sth** mandar a uno hacer algo ♦ adv derecho; **can you ~ me to...?** ¿puede indicarme dónde está...?; ~ **debit**

(*BRIT*) *n* domiciliación *f* bancaria de recibos
direction [dɪˈrekʃən] *n* dirección *f*; **sense of ~** sentido de la dirección; **~s** *npl* (*instructions*) instrucciones *fpl*; **~s for use** modo de empleo
directly [dɪˈrektlɪ] *adv* (*in straight line*) directamente; (*at once*) en seguida
director [dɪˈrektə*] *n* director(a) *m/f*
directory [dɪˈrektərɪ] *n* (*TEL*) guía (telefónica); (*COMPUT*) directorio; **~ enquiries**, **~ assistance** (*US*) *n* (servicio de) información *f*
dirt [dɜːt] *n* suciedad *f*; (*earth*) tierra; **~-cheap** *adj* baratísimo; **~y** *adj* sucio; (*joke*) verde (*SP*), colorado (*AM*) ♦ *vt* ensuciar; (*stain*) manchar; **~y trick** *n* juego sucio
disability [dɪsəˈbɪlɪtɪ] *n* incapacidad *f*
disabled [dɪsˈeɪbld] *adj*: **to be physically ~** ser minusválido/a; **to be mentally ~** ser deficiente mental
disadvantage [dɪsədˈvɑːntɪdʒ] *n* desventaja, inconveniente *m*
disagree [dɪsəˈɡriː] *vi* (*differ*) discrepar; **to ~ (with)** no estar de acuerdo (con); **~able** *adj* desagradable; (*person*) antipático; **~ment** *n* desacuerdo
disallow [dɪsəˈlaʊ] *vt* (*goal*) anular; (*claim*) rechazar
disappear [dɪsəˈpɪə*] *vi* desaparecer; **~ance** *n* desaparición *f*
disappoint [dɪsəˈpɔɪnt] *vt* decepcionar, defraudar; **~ed** *adj* decepcionado; **~ing** *adj* decepcionante; **~ment** *n* decepción *f*
disapproval [dɪsəˈpruːvəl] *n* desaprobación *f*
disapprove [dɪsəˈpruːv] *vi*: **to ~ of** ver mal
disarmament [dɪsˈɑːməmənt] *n* desarme *m*
disarray [dɪsəˈreɪ] *n*: **in ~** (*army, organization*) desorganizado; (*hair, clothes*) desarreglado
disaster [dɪˈzɑːstə*] *n* desastre *m*
disband [dɪsˈbænd] *vt* disolver ♦ *vi* desbandarse

disbelief [dɪsbəˈliːf] *n* incredulidad *f*
disc [dɪsk] *n* disco; (*COMPUT*) = **disk**
discard [dɪsˈkɑːd] *vt* (*old things*) tirar; (*fig*) descartar
discern [dɪˈsɜːn] *vt* percibir, discernir; (*understand*) comprender; **~ing** *adj* perspicaz
discharge [*vb* dɪsˈtʃɑːdʒ, *n* ˈdɪstʃɑːdʒ] *vt* (*task, duty*) cumplir; (*waste*) verter; (*patient*) dar de alta; (*employee*) despedir; (*soldier*) licenciar; (*defendant*) poner en libertad ♦ *n* (*ELEC*) descarga; (*MED*) supuración *f*; (*dismissal*) despedida; (*of duty*) desempeño; (*of debt*) pago, descargo
discipline [ˈdɪsɪplɪn] *n* disciplina ♦ *vt* disciplinar; (*punish*) castigar
disc jockey *n* pinchadiscos *m/f inv*
disclaim [dɪsˈkleɪm] *vt* negar
disclose [dɪsˈkləʊz] *vt* revelar; **disclosure** [-ˈkləʊʒə*] *n* revelación *f*
disco [ˈdɪskəʊ] *n abbr* = **discothèque**
discomfort [dɪsˈkʌmfət] *n* incomodidad *f*; (*unease*) inquietud *f*; (*physical*) malestar *m*
disconcert [dɪskənˈsɜːt] *vt* desconcertar
disconnect [dɪskəˈnekt] *vt* separar; (*ELEC etc*) desconectar
discontent [dɪskənˈtent] *n* descontento; **~ed** *adj* descontento
discontinue [dɪskənˈtɪnjuː] *vt* interrumpir; (*payments*) suspender; **"~d"** (*COMM*) "ya no se fabrica"
discord [ˈdɪskɔːd] *n* discordia; (*MUS*) disonancia
discothèque [ˈdɪskəʊtek] *n* discoteca
discount [*n* ˈdɪskaʊnt, *vb* dɪsˈkaʊnt] *n* descuento ♦ *vt* descontar
discourage [dɪsˈkʌrɪdʒ] *vt* desalentar; (*advise against*): **to ~ sb from doing** disuadir a uno de hacer
discover [dɪsˈkʌvə*] *vt* descubrir; (*error*) darse cuenta de; **~y** *n* descubrimiento
discredit [dɪsˈkredɪt] *vt* desacreditar
discreet [dɪˈskriːt] *adj* (*tactful*) discreto; (*careful*) circunspecto, prudente
discrepancy [dɪˈskrepənsɪ] *n* diferencia
discretion [dɪˈskreʃən] *n* (*tact*) discreción *f*

f; **at the ~ of** a criterio de
discriminate [dɪ'skrɪmɪneɪt] *vi*: **to ~ between** distinguir entre; **to ~ against** discriminar contra; **discriminating** *adj* entendido; **discrimination** [-'neɪʃən] *n* (*discernment*) perspicacia; (*bias*) discriminación *f*
discuss [dɪ'skʌs] *vt* discutir; (*a theme*) tratar; [dɪ'skʌʃən] *n* discusión *f*
disdain [dɪs'deɪn] *n* desdén *m*
disease [dɪ'ziːz] *n* enfermedad *f*
disembark [dɪsɪm'bɑːk] *vt, vi* desembarcar
disentangle [dɪsɪn'tæŋgl] *vt* soltar; (*wire, thread*) desenredar
disfigure [dɪs'fɪgə*] *vt* (*person*) desfigurar; (*object*) afear
disgrace [dɪs'greɪs] *n* ignominia; (*shame*) vergüenza, escándalo ♦ *vt* deshonrar; **~ful** *adj* vergonzoso
disgruntled [dɪs'grʌntld] *adj* disgustado, descontento
disguise [dɪs'gaɪz] *n* disfraz *m* ♦ *vt* disfrazar; **in ~** disfrazado
disgust [dɪs'gʌst] *n* repugnancia ♦ *vt* repugnar, dar asco a; **~ing** *adj* repugnante, asqueroso; (*behaviour etc*) vergonzoso
dish [dɪʃ] *n* (*gen*) plato; **to do** *or* **wash the ~es** fregar los platos; **~ out** *vt* repartir; **~ up** *vt* servir; **~cloth** *n* estropajo
dishearten [dɪs'hɑːtn] *vt* desalentar
dishevelled [dɪ'ʃevəld] (*US* **disheveled**) *adj* (*hair*) despeinado; (*appearance*) desarreglado
dishonest [dɪs'ɒnɪst] *adj* (*person*) poco honrado, tramposo; (*means*) fraudulento; **~y** *n* falta de honradez
dishonour [dɪs'ɒnə*] (*US* **dishonor**) *n* deshonra; **~able** *adj* deshonroso
dishtowel [dɪʃtauəl] (*US*) *n* estropajo
dishwasher ['dɪʃwɔʃə*] *n* lavaplatos *m inv*
disillusion [dɪsɪ'luːʒən] *vt* desilusionar
disinfect [dɪsɪn'fekt] *vt* desinfectar; **~ant** *n* desinfectante *m*
disintegrate [dɪs'ɪntɪgreɪt] *vi* disgregarse, desintegrarse
disinterested [dɪs'ɪntrəstɪd] *adj*

desinteresado
disjointed [dɪs'dʒɔɪntɪd] *adj* inconexo
disk [dɪsk] *n* (*esp US*) = **disc**; (*COMPUT*) disco, disquete *m*; **single-/double-sided ~** disco de una cara/dos caras; **~ drive** *n* disc drive *m*; **~ette** *n* = **disk**
dislike [dɪs'laɪk] *n* antipatía, aversión *f* ♦ *vt* tener antipatía a
dislocate ['dɪslǝkeɪt] *vt* dislocar
dislodge [dɪs'lɒdʒ] *vt* sacar
disloyal [dɪs'lɔɪǝl] *adj* desleal
dismal ['dɪzml] *adj* (*gloomy*) deprimente, triste; (*very bad*) malísimo, fatal
dismantle [dɪs'mæntl] *vt* desmontar, desarmar
dismay [dɪs'meɪ] *n* consternación *f* ♦ *vt* consternar
dismiss [dɪs'mɪs] *vt* (*worker*) despedir; (*pupils*) dejar marchar; (*soldiers*) dar permiso para irse; (*idea, LAW*) rechazar; (*possibility*) descartar; **~al** *n* despido
dismount [dɪs'maunt] *vi* apearse
disobedient [dɪsǝ'biːdɪǝnt] *adj* desobediente
disobey [dɪsǝ'beɪ] *vt* desobedecer
disorder [dɪs'ɔːdǝ*] *n* desorden *m*; (*rioting*) disturbios *mpl*; (*MED*) trastorno; **~ly** *adj* desordenado; (*meeting*) alborotado; (*conduct*) escandaloso
disorientated [dɪs'ɔːrɪenterɪtǝd] *adj* desorientado
disown [dɪs'ǝun] *vt* (*action*) renegar de; (*person*) negar cualquier tipo de relación con
disparaging [dɪs'pærɪdʒɪŋ] *adj* despreciativo
dispassionate [dɪs'pæʃǝnɪt] *adj* (*unbiased*) imparcial
dispatch [dɪs'pætʃ] *vt* enviar ♦ *n* (*sending*) envío; (*PRESS*) informe *m*; (*MIL*) parte *m*
dispel [dɪs'pel] *vt* disipar
dispense [dɪs'pens] *vt* (*medicines*) preparar; **~ with** *vt fus* prescindir de; **~r** *n* (*container*) distribuidor *m* automático; **dispensing chemist** (*BRIT*) *n* farmacia
disperse [dɪs'pǝːs] *vt* dispersar ♦ *vi* dispersarse

dispirited [dɪ'spɪrɪtɪd] *adj* desanimado, desalentado

displace [dɪs'pleɪs] *vt* desplazar, reemplazar; **~d person** *n* (*POL*) desplazado/a

display [dɪs'pleɪ] *n* (*in shop window*) escaparate *m*; (*exhibition*) exposición *f*; (*COMPUT*) visualización *f*; (*of feeling*) manifestación *f* ♦ *vt* exponer; manifestar; (*ostentatiously*) lucir

displease [dɪs'pliːz] *vt* (*offend*) ofender; (*annoy*) fastidiar; **~d** *adj*: **~d with** disgustado con; **displeasure** [-'plɛʒə*] *n* disgusto

disposable [dɪs'pəuzəbl] *adj* desechable; (*income*) disponible; **~ nappy** *n* pañal *m* desechable

disposal [dɪs'pəuzl] *n* (*of rubbish*) destrucción *f*; **at one's ~** a su disposición

dispose [dɪs'pəuz] *vi*: **to ~ of** (*unwanted goods*) deshacerse de; (*problem etc*) resolver; **~d** *adj*: **~d to do** dispuesto a hacer; **to be well-~d towards sb** estar bien dispuesto hacia uno; **disposition** [dɪspə'zɪʃən] *n* (*nature*) temperamento; (*inclination*) propensión *f*

disprove [dɪs'pruːv] *vt* refutar

dispute [dɪs'pjuːt] *n* disputa; (*also*: **industrial ~**) conflicto (laboral) ♦ *vt* (*argue*) disputar, discutir; (*question*) cuestionar

disqualify [dɪs'kwɔlɪfaɪ] *vt* (*SPORT*) desclasificar; **to ~ sb for sth/from doing sth** incapacitar a alguien para algo/hacer algo

disquiet [dɪs'kwaɪət] *n* preocupación *f*, inquietud *f*

disregard [dɪsrɪ'gɑːd] *vt* (*ignore*) no hacer caso de

disrepair [dɪsrɪ'pɛə*] *n*: **to fall into ~** (*building*) desmoronarse

disreputable [dɪs'rɛpjutəbl] *adj* (*person*) de mala fama; (*behaviour*) vergonzoso

disrespectful [dɪsrɪ'spɛktful] *adj* irrespetuoso

disrupt [dɪs'rʌpt] *vt* (*plans*) desbaratar, trastornar; (*conversation*) interrumpir

dissatisfaction [dɪssætɪs'fækʃən] *n* disgusto, descontento

dissect [dɪ'sɛkt] *vt* disecar

dissent [dɪ'sɛnt] *n* disensión *f*

dissertation [dɪsə'teɪʃən] *n* tesina

disservice [dɪs'səːvɪs] *n*: **to do sb a ~** perjudicar a alguien

dissimilar [dɪ'sɪmɪlə*] *adj* distinto

dissipate ['dɪsɪpeɪt] *vt* disipar; (*waste*) desperdiciar

dissolve [dɪ'zɔlv] *vt* disolver ♦ *vi* disolverse; **to ~ in(to) tears** deshacerse en lágrimas

dissuade [dɪ'sweɪd] *vt*: **to ~ sb (from)** disuadir a uno (de)

distance ['dɪstəns] *n* distancia; **in the ~** a lo lejos

distant ['dɪstənt] *adj* lejano; (*manner*) reservado, frío

distaste [dɪs'teɪst] *n* repugnancia; **~ful** *adj* repugnante, desagradable

distended [dɪ'stɛndɪd] *adj* (*stomach*) hinchado

distil [dɪs'tɪl] (*US* **distill**) *vt* destilar; **~lery** *n* destilería

distinct [dɪs'tɪŋkt] *adj* (*different*) distinto; (*clear*) claro; (*unmistakeable*) inequívoco; **as ~ from** a diferencia de; **~ion** [dɪs'tɪŋkʃən] *n* distinción *f*; (*honour*) honor *m*; (*in exam*) sobresaliente *m*; **~ive** *adj* distintivo

distinguish [dɪs'tɪŋgwɪʃ] *vt* distinguir; **to ~ o.s.** destacarse; **~ed** *adj* (*eminent*) distinguido; **~ing** *adj* (*feature*) distintivo

distort [dɪs'tɔːt] *vt* distorsionar; (*shape, image*) deformar; **~ion** [dɪs'tɔːʃən] *n* distorsión *f*; deformación *f*

distract [dɪs'trækt] *vt* distraer; **~ed** *adj* distraído; **~ion** [dɪs'trækʃən] *n* distracción *f*; (*confusion*) aturdimiento

distraught [dɪs'trɔːt] *adj* loco de inquietud

distress [dɪs'trɛs] *n* (*anguish*) angustia, aflicción *f* ♦ *vt* afligir; **~ing** *adj* angustioso; doloroso; **~ signal** *n* señal *f* de socorro

distribute [dɪs'trɪbjuːt] *vt* distribuir; (*share out*) repartir; **distribution** [-'bjuːʃən] *n*

distribución f, reparto; **distributor** n (AUT) distribuidor m; (COMM) distribuidora
district ['dɪstrɪkt] n (of country) zona, región f; (of town) barrio; (ADMIN) distrito; ~ **attorney** (US) n fiscal m/f; ~ **nurse** (BRIT) n enfermera que atiende a pacientes a domicilio
distrust [dɪs'trʌst] n desconfianza ♦ vt desconfiar de
disturb [dɪs'tɜːb] vt (person: bother, interrupt) molestar; (: upset) perturbar, inquietar; (disorganize) alterar; ~**ance** n (upheaval) perturbación f; (political etc: gen pl) disturbio; (of mind) trastorno; ~**ed** adj (worried, upset) preocupado, angustiado; **emotionally** ~**ed** trastornado; (childhood) inseguro; ~**ing** adj inquietante, perturbador(a)
disuse [dɪs'juːs] n: **to fall into** ~ caer en desuso
disused [dɪs'juːzd] adj abandonado
ditch [dɪtʃ] n zanja; (irrigation ~) acequia ♦ vt (inf: partner) deshacerse de; (: plan, car etc) abandonar
dither ['dɪðə*] (pej) vi vacilar
ditto ['dɪtəu] adv ídem, lo mismo
divan [dɪ'væn] n (also: ~ bed) cama turca
dive [daɪv] n (from board) salto; (underwater) buceo; (of submarine) sumersión f ♦ vi (swimmer: into water) saltar; (: under water) zambullirse, bucear; (fish, submarine) sumergirse; (bird) lanzarse en picado; **to** ~ **into** (bag etc) meter la mano en; (place) meterse de prisa en; ~**r** n (underwater) buzo
diverse [daɪ'vɜːs] adj diversos/as, varios/as
diversion [daɪ'vɜːʃən] n (BRIT: AUT) desviación f; (distraction, MIL) diversión f; (of funds) distracción f
divert [daɪ'vɜːt] vt (turn aside) desviar
divide [dɪ'vaɪd] vt dividir; (separate) separar ♦ vi dividirse; (road) bifurcarse; ~**d highway** (US) n carretera de doble calzada
dividend ['dɪvɪdɛnd] n dividendo; (fig): **to pay** ~**s** proporcionar beneficios
divine [dɪ'vaɪn] adj (also fig) divino

diving ['daɪvɪŋ] n (SPORT) salto; (underwater) buceo; ~ **board** n trampolín m
divinity [dɪ'vɪnɪtɪ] n divinidad f; (SCOL) teología
division [dɪ'vɪʒən] n división f; (sharing out) reparto; (disagreement) diferencias fpl; (COMM) sección f
divorce [dɪ'vɔːs] n divorcio ♦ vt divorciarse de; ~**d** adj divorciado; ~**e** [-'siː] n divorciado/a
divulge [daɪ'vʌldʒ] vt divulgar, revelar
D.I.Y. (BRIT) adj, n abbr = **do-it-yourself**
dizzy ['dɪzɪ] adj (spell) de mareo; **to feel** ~ marearse
DJ n abbr = **disc jockey**

___KEYWORD___

do [duː] (pt **did**, pp **done**) n (inf: party etc): **we're having a little** ~ **on Saturday** damos una fiestecita el sábado; **it was rather a grand** ~ fue un acontecimiento a lo grande
♦ aux vb 1 (in negative constructions: not translated) **I don't understand** no entiendo
2 (to form questions: not translated) **didn't you know?** ¿no lo sabías?; **what** ~ **you think?** ¿qué opinas?
3 (for emphasis, in polite expressions): **people** ~ **make mistakes sometimes** sí que se cometen errores a veces; **she does seem rather late** a mí también me parece que se ha retrasado; ~ **sit down/ help yourself** siéntate/sírvete por favor; ~ **take care!** ¡ten cuidado(, te pido)!
4 (used to avoid repeating vb): **she sings better than I** ~ canta mejor que yo; ~ **you agree? – yes, I** ~/**no, I don't** ¿estás de acuerdo? – sí (lo estoy)/no (lo estoy); **she lives in Glasgow — so** ~ **I** vive en Glasgow — yo también; **he didn't like it and neither did we** no le gustó y a nosotros tampoco; **who made this mess? – I did** ¿quién hizo esta chapuza? — yo; **he asked me to help him and I did** me pidió que le ayudara y lo hice

5 (*in question tags*): **you like him, don't you?** te gusta, ¿verdad? *or* ¿no?; **I don't know him, ~ I?** creo que no le conozco
♦ *vt* 1 (*gen, carry out, perform etc*): **what are you ~ing tonight?** ¿qué haces esta noche?; **what can I ~ for you?** ¿en qué puedo servirle?; **to ~ the washing-up/cooking** fregar los platos/cocinar; **to ~ one's teeth/hair/nails** lavarse los dientes/arreglarse el pelo/arreglarse las uñas
2 (*AUT etc*): **the car was ~ing 100** el coche iba a 100; **we've done 200 km already** ya hemos hecho 200 km; **he can ~ 100 in that car** puede ir a 100 en ese coche
♦ *vi* 1 (*act, behave*) hacer; **~ as I ~** haz como yo
2 (*get on, fare*): **he's ~ing well/badly at school** va bien/mal en la escuela; **the firm is ~ing well** la empresa anda *or* va bien; **how ~ you ~?** mucho gusto; (*less formal*) ¿qué tal?
3 (*suit*): **will it ~?** ¿sirve?, ¿está *or* va bien?
4 (*be sufficient*) bastar; **will £10 ~?** ¿será bastante con £10?; **that'll ~** así está bien; **that'll ~!** (*in annoyance*) ¡ya está bien!, ¡basta ya!; **to make ~ (with)** arreglárselas (con)
do away with *vt fus* (*kill, disease*) eliminar; (*abolish: law etc*) abolir; (*withdraw*) retirar
do up *vt* (*laces*) atar; (*zip, dress, shirt*) abrochar; (*renovate: room, house*) renovar
do with *vt fus* (*need*): **I could ~ with a drink/some help** no me vendría mal un trago/un poco de ayuda; (*be connected*) tener que ver con; **what has it got to ~ with you?** ¿qué tiene que ver contigo?
do without *vi* pasar sin; **if you're late for tea then you'll ~ without** si llegas tarde tendrás que quedarte sin cenar ♦ *vt fus* pasar sin; **I can ~ without a car** puedo pasar sin coche

dock [dɔk] *n* (*NAUT*) muelle *m*; (*LAW*)

banquillo (de los acusados); **~s** *npl* (*NAUT*) muelles *mpl*, puerto *sg* ♦ *vi* (*enter ~*) atracar (la) muelle; (*SPACE*) acoplarse; **~er** *n* trabajador *m* portuario, estibador *m*; **~yard** *n* astillero
doctor ['dɔktə*] *n* médico/a; (*Ph.D. etc*) doctor(a) *m/f* ♦ *vt* (*drink etc*) adulterar; **D~ of Philosophy** *n* Doctor en Filosofía y Letras
document ['dɔkjumənt] *n* documento; **~ary** [-'mentərı] *adj* documental ♦ *n* documental *m*
dodge [dɔdʒ] *n* (*fig*) truco ♦ *vt* evadir; (*blow*) esquivar
dodgems ['dɔdʒəmz] (*BRIT*) *npl* coches *mpl* de choque
doe [dəu] *n* (*deer*) cierva, gama; (*rabbit*) coneja
does [dʌz] *vb see* **do**; **~n't** = **does not**
dog [dɔg] *n* perro ♦ *vt* seguir los pasos de; (*subj: bad luck*) perseguir; **~ collar** *n* collar *m* de perro; (*of clergyman*) alzacuellos *m inv*; **~-eared** *adj* sobado
dogged ['dɔgid] *adj* tenaz, obstinado
dogsbody ['dɔgzbɔdı] (*BRIT: inf*) *n* burro de carga
doings ['duıŋz] *npl* (*activities*) actividades *fpl*
do-it-yourself *n* bricolaje *m*
doldrums ['dɔldrəmz] *npl*: **to be in the ~** (*person*) estar abatido; (*business*) estar estancado
dole [dəul] (*BRIT*) *n* (*payment*) subsidio de paro; **on the ~** parado; **~ out** *vt* repartir
doll [dɔl] *n* muñeca; (*US: inf: woman*) muñeca, gachí *f*
dollar ['dɔlə*] *n* dólar *m*
dolled up (*inf*) *adj* arreglado
dolphin ['dɔlfın] *n* delfín *m*
domain [də'meın] *n* (*fig*) campo, competencia; (*land*) dominios *mpl*
dome [dəum] *n* (*ARCH*) cúpula
domestic [də'mestık] *adj* (*animal, duty*) doméstico; (*flight, policy*) nacional; **~ated** *adj* domesticado; (*home-loving*) casero, hogareño
dominate ['dɔmıneıt] *vt* dominar

domineering [dɒmɪ'nɪərɪŋ] *adj* dominante

dominion [də'mɪnɪən] *n* dominio

domino ['dɒmɪnəu] (*pl* **~es**) *n* ficha de dominó; **~es** *n* (*game*) dominó

don [dɒn] (*BRIT*) *n* profesor(a) *m/f* universitario/a

donate [də'neɪt] *vt* donar; **donation** [də'neɪʃən] *n* donativo

done [dʌn] *pp* of **do**

donkey ['dɒŋkɪ] *n* burro

donor ['dəunə*] *n* donante *m/f*; **~ card** *n* carnet *m* de donante

don't [dəunt] = **do not**

donut ['dəunʌt] (*US*) *n* = **doughnut**

doodle ['du:dl] *vi* hacer dibujitos *or* garabatos

doom [du:m] *n* (*fate*) suerte *f* ♦ *vt*: **to be ~ed to failure** estar condenado al fracaso

door [dɔ:*] *n* puerta; **~bell** *n* timbre *m*; **~ handle** *n* tirador *m*; (*of car*) manija; **~man** (*irreg*) *n* (*in hotel*) portero; **~mat** *n* felpudo, estera; **~step** *n* peldaño; **~-to-~** *adj* de puerta en puerta; **~way** *n* entrada, puerta

dope [dəup] *n* (*inf: drug*) droga; (: *person*) imbécil *m/f* ♦ *vt* (*horse etc*) drogar

dormant ['dɔ:mənt] *adj* inactivo

dormitory ['dɔ:mɪtrɪ] *n* (*BRIT*) dormitorio; (*US*) colegio mayor

dormouse ['dɔ:maus] (*pl* **-mice**) *n* lirón *m*

DOS *n abbr* (= *disk operating system*) DOS *m*

dosage ['dəusɪdʒ] *n* dosis *f inv*

dose [dəus] *n* dósis *f inv*

doss house ['dɒss-] (*BRIT*) *n* pensión *f* de mala muerte

dossier ['dɒsɪeɪ] *n* expediente *m*, dosier *m*

dot [dɒt] *n* punto ♦ *vi*: **~ted with** salpicado de; **on the ~** en punto

double ['dʌbl] *adj* doble ♦ *adv* (*twice*): **to cost ~** costar el doble ♦ *n* doble *m* ♦ *vt* doblar ♦ *vi* doblarse; **on the ~, at the ~** (*BRIT*) corriendo; **~ bass** *n* contrabajo; **~ bed** *n* cama de matrimonio; **~ bend** (*BRIT*) *n* doble curva; **~-breasted** *adj* cruzado; **~-click** *vi* (*COMPUT*) hacer doble clic; **~cross** *vt* (*trick*) engañar;

(*betray*) traicionar; **~decker** *n* autobús *m* de dos pisos; **~ glazing** (*BRIT*) *n* doble acristalamiento; **~ room** *n* habitación *f* doble; **~s** *n* (*TENNIS*) juego de dobles; **doubly** *adv* doblemente

doubt [daut] *n* duda ♦ *vt* dudar; (*suspect*) dudar de; **to ~ that** dudar que; **~ful** *adj* dudoso; (*person*): **to be ~ful about sth** tener dudas sobre algo; **~less** *adv* sin duda

dough [dəu] *n* masa, pasta; **~nut** (*US* **donut**) *n* ≈ rosquilla

dove [dʌv] *n* paloma

dovetail ['dʌvteɪl] *vi* (*fig*) encajar

dowdy ['daudɪ] *adj* (*person*) mal vestido; (*clothes*) pasado de moda

down [daun] *n* (*feathers*) plumón *m*, flojel *m* ♦ *adv* (*~wards*) abajo, hacia abajo; (*on the ground*) por *or* en tierra ♦ *prep* abajo ♦ *vt* (*inf: drink*) beberse; **~ with X!** ¡abajo X!; **~-and-out** *n* vagabundo/a; **~-at-heel** *adj* venido a menos; (*appearance*) desaliñado; **~cast** *adj* abatido; **~fall** *n* caída, ruina; **~hearted** *adj* desanimado; **~hill** *adv*: **to go ~hill** (*also fig*) ir cuesta abajo; **~load** *vt* (*COMPUT*) bajar; **~ payment** *n* entrada, pago al contado; **~pour** *n* aguacero; **~right** *adj* (*nonsense, lie*) manifiesto; (*refusal*) terminante; **~size** *vi* (*ECON: company*) reducir la plantilla de

---

Downing Street

Downing Street es la calle de Londres en la que están las residencias oficiales del Presidente del Gobierno (*Prime Minister*), tradicionalmente en el No. 10, y del Ministro de Economía (*Chancellor of the Exchequer*). La calle está situada en el céntrico barrio londinense de Westminster y está cerrada al tráfico de peatones y vehículos. En lenguaje periodístico, se usa también **Downing Street** para referirse al primer ministro o al Gobierno.

Down's syndrome ['daunz-] *n* síndrome *m* de Down

down: **~stairs** *adv* (*below*) (en la casa de)

abajo; (**~wards**) escaleras abajo; **~stream** *adv* aguas *or* río abajo; **~-to-earth** *adj* práctico; **~town** *adv* en el centro de la ciudad; ~ **under** *adv* en Australia (*or* Nueva Zelanda); **~ward** [-wəd] *adj, adv* hacia abajo; **~wards** [-wədz] *adv* hacia abajo

dowry ['dauri] *n* dote *f*

doz. *abbr* = **dozen**

doze [dəuz] *vi* dormitar; ~ **off** *vi* quedarse medio dormido

dozen ['dʌzn] *n* docena; **a ~ books** una docena de libros; **~s of** cantidad de

Dr. *abbr* = **doctor**; **drive**

drab [dræb] *adj* gris, monótono

draft [drɑːft] *n* (*first copy*) borrador *m*; (*POL: of bill*) anteproyecto *m*; (*US: call-up*) quinta ♦ *vt* (*plan*) preparar; (*write roughly*) hacer un borrador de; *see also* **draught**

draftsman ['drɑːftsmən] (*US*) *n* = **draughtsman**

drag [dræg] *vt* arrastrar; (*river*) dragar, rastrear ♦ *vi* (*time*) pasar despacio; (*play, film etc*) hacerse pesado ♦ *n* (*inf*) lata; (*women's clothing*): **in ~** vestido de travesti; ~ **on** *vi* ser interminable; ~ **and drop** *vt* (*COMPUT*) arrastrar y soltar

dragon ['drægən] *n* dragón *m*

dragonfly ['drægənflaɪ] *n* libélula

drain [dreɪn] *n* desaguadero; (*in street*) sumidero; (*source of loss*): **to be a ~ on** consumir, agotar ♦ *vt* (*land, marshes*) desaguar; (*reservoir*) desecar; (*vegetables*) escurrir ♦ *vi* escurrirse; **~age** *n* (*act*) desagüe *m*; (*MED, AGR*) drenaje *m*; (*sewage*) alcantarillado; **~ing board** (*US* **~board**) *n* escurridera, escurridor *m*; **~pipe** *n* tubo de desagüe

drama ['drɑːmə] *n* (*art*) teatro; (*play*) drama *m*; (*excitement*) emoción *f*; **~tic** [drə'mætik] *adj* dramático; (*sudden, marked*) espectacular; **~tist** ['dræmətɪst] *n* dramaturgo/a; **~tize** ['dræmətaɪz] *vt* (*events*) dramatizar

drank [dræŋk] *pt of* **drink**

drape [dreɪp] *vt* (*cloth*) colocar; (*flag*) colgar; **~s** (*US*) *npl* cortinas *fpl*

drastic ['dræstɪk] *adj* (*measure*) severo; (*change*) radical, drástico

draught [drɑːft] (*US* **draft**) *n* (*of air*) corriente *f* de aire; (*NAUT*) calado; **on ~** (*beer*) de barril; ~ **beer** *n* cerveza de barril; **~board** (*BRIT*) *n* tablero de damas; **~s** (*BRIT*) *n* (*game*) juego de damas

draughtsman ['drɑːftsmən] (*US* **draftsman**) (*irreg*) *n* delineante *m*

draw [drɔː] (*pt* **drew**, *pp* **drawn**) *vt* (*picture*) dibujar; (*cart*) tirar de; (*curtain*) correr; (*take out*) sacar; (*attract*) atraer; (*money*) retirar; (*wages*) cobrar ♦ *vi* (*SPORT*) empatar ♦ *n* (*SPORT*) empate *m*; (*lottery*) sorteo; ~ **near** *vi* acercarse; ~ **out** *vi* (*lengthen*) alargarse ♦ *vt* sacar; ~ **up** *vi* (*stop*) pararse ♦ *vt* (*chair*) acercar; (*document*) redactar; **~back** *n* inconveniente *m*, desventaja; **~bridge** *n* puente *m* levadizo

drawer [drɔː*] *n* cajón *m*

drawing ['drɔːɪŋ] *n* dibujo; ~ **board** *n* tablero (de dibujante); ~ **pin** (*BRIT*) *n* chincheta; ~ **room** *n* salón *m*

drawl [drɔːl] *n* habla lenta y cansina

drawn [drɔːn] *pp of* **draw**

dread [drɛd] *n* pavor *m*, terror *m* ♦ *vt* temer, tener miedo *or* pavor a; **~ful** *adj* horroroso

dream [driːm] (*pt, pp* **dreamed** *or* **dreamt**) *n* sueño ♦ *vt, vi* soñar; **~y** *adj* (*distracted*) soñador(a), distraído; (*music*) suave

dreary ['drɪərɪ] *adj* monótono

dredge [drɛdʒ] *vt* dragar

dregs [drɛgz] *npl* posos *mpl*; (*of humanity*) hez *f*

drench [drɛntʃ] *vt* empapar

dress [drɛs] *n* vestido; (*clothing*) ropa ♦ *vt* vestir; (*wound*) vendar ♦ *vi* vestirse; **to get ~ed** vestirse; ~ **up** *vi* vestirse de etiqueta; (*in fancy dress*) disfrazarse; ~ **circle** (*BRIT*) *n* principal *m*; **~er** *n* (*furniture*) aparador *m*; (*US*) cómoda (con espejo); **~ing** *n* (*MED*) vendaje *m*; (*CULIN*) aliño; **~ing gown** (*BRIT*) *n* bata; **~ing room** *n* (*THEATRE*) camarín *m*;

(*SPORT*) vestuario; **~ing table** *n* tocador *m*; **~maker** *n* modista, costurera; **~ rehearsal** *n* ensayo general

drew [druː] *pt of* **draw**

dribble ['drɪbl] *vi* (*baby*) babear ♦ *vt* (*ball*) regatear

dried [draɪd] *adj* (*fruit*) seco; (*milk*) en polvo

drier ['draɪə*] *n* = **dryer**

drift [drɪft] *n* (*of current etc*) flujo; (*of snow*) ventisquero; (*meaning*) significado ♦ *vi* (*boat*) ir a la deriva; (*sand, snow*) amontonarse; **~wood** *n* madera de deriva

drill [drɪl] *n* (*~ bit*) broca; (*tool for DIY etc*) taladro; (*of dentist*) fresa; (*for mining etc*) perforadora, barrena; (*MIL*) instrucción *f* ♦ *vt* perforar, taladrar; (*troops*) enseñar la instrucción a ♦ *vi* (*for oil*) perforar

drink [drɪŋk] (*pt* **drank**, *pp* **drunk**) *n* bebida; (*sip*) trago ♦ *vt*, *vi* beber; **to have a ~** tomar algo; tomar una copa *or* un trago; **a ~ of water** un trago de agua; **~er** *n* bebedor(a) *m/f*; **~ing water** *n* agua potable

drip [drɪp] *n* (*act*) goteo; (*one ~*) gota; (*MED*) gota a gota *m* ♦ *vi* gotear; **~-dry** *adj* (*shirt*) inarrugable; **~ping** *n* (*animal fat*) pringue *m*

drive [draɪv] (*pt* **drove**, *pp* **driven**) *n* (*journey*) viaje *m* (en coche); (*also:* **~way**) entrada; (*energy*) energía, vigor *m*; (*COMPUT: also:* **disk ~**) drive *m* ♦ *vt* (*car*) conducir (*SP*), manejar (*AM*); (*nail*) clavar; (*push*) empujar; (*TECH: motor*) impulsar ♦ *vi* (*AUT: at controls*) conducir; (: *travel*) pasearse en coche; **left-/right-hand ~** conducción *f* a la izquierda/derecha; **to ~ sb mad** volverle loco a uno

drivel ['drɪvl] (*inf*) *n* tonterías *fpl*

driven ['drɪvn] *pp of* **drive**

driver ['draɪvə*] *n* conductor(a) *m/f* (*SP*), chofer *m* (*AM*); (*of taxi, bus*) chofer; **~'s license** (*US*) *n* carnet *m* de conducir

driveway ['draɪvweɪ] *n* entrada

driving ['draɪvɪŋ] *n* el conducir (*SP*), el manejar (*AM*); **~ instructor** *n*

instructor(a) *m/f* de conducción *or* manejo; **~ lesson** *n* clase *f* de conducción *or* manejo; **~ licence** (*BRIT*) *n* permiso de conducir; **~ school** *n* autoescuela; **~ test** *n* examen *m* de conducción *or* manejo

drizzle ['drɪzl] *n* llovizna

drool [druːl] *vi* babear

droop [druːp] *vi* (*flower*) marchitarse; (*shoulders*) encorvarse; (*head*) inclinarse

drop [drɒp] *n* (*of water*) gota; (*lessening*) baja; (*fall*) caída ♦ *vt* dejar caer; (*voice, eyes, price*) bajar; (*passenger*) dejar; (*omit*) omitir ♦ *vi* (*object*) caer; (*wind*) amainar; **~s** *npl* (*MED*) gotas *fpl*; **~ off** *vi* (*sleep*) dormirse ♦ *vt* (*passenger*) dejar; **~ out** *vi* (*withdraw*) retirarse; **~-out** *n* marginado/a; (*SCOL*) estudiante que abandona los estudios; **~per** *n* cuentagotas *m inv*; **~pings** *npl* excremento

drought [draut] *n* sequía

drove [drəuv] *pt of* **drive**

drown [draun] *vt* ahogar ♦ *vi* ahogarse

drowsy ['drauzɪ] *adj* soñoliento; **to be ~** tener sueño

drug [drʌg] *n* medicamento; (*narcotic*) droga ♦ *vt* drogar; **to be on ~s** drogarse; **~ addict** *n* drogadicto/a; **~gist** (*US*) *n* farmacéutico; **~store** (*US*) *n* farmacia

drum [drʌm] *n* tambor *m*; (*for oil, petrol*) bidón *m*; **~s** *npl* batería; **~mer** *n* tambor *m*

drunk [drʌŋk] *pp of* **drink** ♦ *adj* borracho ♦ *n* (*also:* **~ard**) borracho/a; **~en** *adj* borracho; (*laughter, party*) de borrachos

dry [draɪ] *adj* seco; (*day*) sin lluvia; (*climate*) árido, seco ♦ *vt* secar; (*tears*) enjugarse ♦ *vi* secarse; **~ up** *vi* (*river*) secarse; **~-cleaner's** *n* tintorería; **~-cleaning** *n* lavado en seco; **~er** *n* (*for hair*) secador *m*; (*US: for clothes*) secadora; **~ rot** *n* putrefacción *f* fungoide

DSS *n abbr* = **Department of Social Security**

DTP *n abbr* (= *desk-top publishing*) autoedición *f*

dual ['djuəl] *adj* doble; **~ carriageway**

(*BRIT*) *n* carretera de doble calzada; ~-
purpose *adj* de doble uso
dubbed [dʌbd] *adj* (*CINEMA*) doblado
dubious ['dju:brəs] *adj* indeciso;
(*reputation, company*) sospechoso
duchess ['dʌtʃɪs] *n* duquesa
duck [dʌk] *n* pato ♦ *vi* agacharse; ~**ling** *n*
patito
duct [dʌkt] *n* conducto, canal *m*
dud [dʌd] *n* (*object, tool*) engaño, engañifa
♦ *adj*: ~ **cheque** (*BRIT*) cheque *m* sin
fondos
due [dju:] *adj* (*owed*): **he is** ~ **£10** se le
deben 10 libras; (*expected: event*): **the
meeting is** ~ **on Wednesday** la reunión
tendrá lugar el miércoles; (: *arrival*) **the
train is** ~ **at 8am** el tren tiene su llegada
para las 8; (*proper*) debido ♦ *n*: **to give
sb his** (*or* **her**) ~ ser justo con alguien
♦ *adv*: ~ **north** derecho al norte; ~**s** *npl*
(*for club, union*) cuota; (*in harbour*)
derechos *mpl*; **in** ~ **course** a su debido
tiempo; ~ **to** debido a; **to be** ~ **to**
deberse a
duet [dju:'ɛt] *n* dúo
duffel bag ['dʌfəl] *n* bolsa de lona
duffel coat *n* trenca, abrigo de tres
cuartos
dug [dʌg] *pt, pp of* **dig**
duke [dju:k] *n* duque *m*
dull [dʌl] *adj* (*light*) débil; (*stupid*) torpe;
(*boring*) pesado; (*sound, pain*) sordo;
(*weather, day*) gris ♦ *vt* (*pain, grief*) aliviar;
(*mind, senses*) entorpecer
duly ['dju:lɪ] *adv* debidamente; (*on time*) a
su debido tiempo
dumb [dʌm] *adj* mudo; (*pej: stupid*)
estúpido; ~**founded** [dʌm'faundɪd] *adj*
pasmado
dummy ['dʌmɪ] *n* (*tailor's* ~) maniquí *m*;
(*mock-up*) maqueta; (*BRIT: for baby*)
chupete *m* ♦ *adj* falso, postizo
dump [dʌmp] *n* (*also*: **rubbish** ~) basurero,
vertedero; (*inf: place*) cuchitril *m* ♦ *vt* (*put
down*) dejar; (*get rid of*) deshacerse de;
(*COMPUT: data*) transferir
dumpling ['dʌmplɪŋ] *n* bola de masa

hervida
dumpy ['dʌmpɪ] *adj* regordete/a
dunce [dʌns] *n* zopenco
dung [dʌŋ] *n* estiércol *m*
dungarees [dʌŋgə'ri:z] *npl* mono
dungeon ['dʌndʒən] *n* calabozo
duplex ['dju:plɛks] *n* dúplex *m*
duplicate [*n* 'dju:plɪkət, *vb* 'dju:plɪkeɪt] *n*
duplicado ♦ *vt* duplicar; (*photocopy*)
fotocopiar; (*repeat*) repetir; **in** ~ por
duplicado
durable ['djuərəbl] *adj* duradero
duration [djuə'reɪʃən] *n* duración *f*
during ['djuərɪŋ] *prep* durante
dusk [dʌsk] *n* crepúsculo, anochecer *m*
dust [dʌst] *n* polvo ♦ *vt* quitar el polvo a,
desempolvar; (*cake etc*): **to** ~ **with**
espolvorear de; ~**bin** (*BRIT*) *n* cubo de la
basura (*SP*), balde *m* (*AM*); ~**er** *n* paño,
trapo; ~**man** (*BRIT irreg*) *n* basurero; ~**y**
adj polvoriento
Dutch [dʌtʃ] *adj* holandés/esa ♦ *n* (*LING*)
holandés *m*; **the** ~ *npl* los holandeses; **to
go** ~ (*inf*) pagar cada uno lo suyo;
~**man** / **woman** (*irreg*) *n* holandés/esa
m/f
duty ['dju:tɪ] *n* deber *m*; (*tax*) derechos
mpl de aduana; **on** ~ de servicio; (*at
night etc*) de guardia; **off** ~ libre (*de
servicio*); ~-**free** *adj* libre de impuestos
duvet ['du:veɪ] (*BRIT*) *n* edredón *m*
DVD *n abbr* (= *digital versatile* (*or*) *video
disc*) DVD *m*
dwarf [dwɔ:f] (*pl* **dwarves**) *n* enano/a ♦ *vt*
empequeñecer
dwell [dwɛl] (*pt, pp* **dwelt**) *vi* morar; ~ **on**
vt fus explayarse en
dwindle ['dwɪndl] *vi* menguar, disminuir
dye [daɪ] *n* tinte *m* ♦ *vt* teñir
dying ['daɪɪŋ] *adj* moribundo, agonizante
dyke [daɪk] (*BRIT*) *n* dique *m*
dynamic [daɪ'næmɪk] *adj* dinámico
dynamite ['daɪnəmaɪt] *n* dinamita
dynamo ['daɪnəməu] *n* dínamo *f*
dynasty ['dɪnəstɪ] *n* dinastía

E, e

E [iː] *n* (MUS) mi *m*

each [iːtʃ] *adj* cada *inv* ♦ *pron* cada uno;
~ other el uno al otro; **they hate ~ other**
se odian (entre ellos *or* mutuamente);
they have 2 books ~ tienen 2 libros por
persona

eager ['iːgə*] *adj* (keen) entusiasmado; **to
be ~ to do sth** tener muchas ganas de
hacer algo, impacientarse por hacer algo;
to be ~ for tener muchas ganas de

eagle ['iːgl] *n* águila

ear [ɪə*] *n* oreja; oído; (of corn) espiga;
~ache *n* dolor *m* de oídos; **~drum** *n*
tímpano

earl [əːl] *n* conde *m*

earlier ['əːlɪə*] *adj* anterior ♦ *adv* antes

early ['əːlɪ] *adv* temprano; (before time) con
tiempo, con anticipación ♦ *adj* temprano;
(settlers etc) primitivo; (death, departure)
prematuro; (reply) pronto; **to have an ~
night** acostarse temprano; **in the ~** *or* **~ in
the spring** a principios de primavera; **~
retirement** *n* jubilación *f* anticipada

earmark ['ɪəmɑːk] *vt*: **to ~ (for)** reservar
(para), destinar (a)

earn [əːn] *vt* (salary) percibir; (interest)
devengar; (praise) merecerse

earnest ['əːnɪst] *adj* (wish) fervoroso;
(person) serio, formal; **in ~** en serio

earnings ['əːnɪŋz] *npl* (personal) sueldo,
ingresos *mpl*; (company) ganancias *fpl*

ear: ~phones *npl* auriculares *mpl*; **~ring**
n pendiente *m*, arete *m*; **~shot** *n*: **within
~shot** al alcance del oído

earth [əːθ] *n* tierra; (BRIT: ELEC) cable *m* de
toma de tierra ♦ *vt* (BRIT: ELEC) conectar a
tierra; **~enware** *n* loza (de barro);
~quake *n* terremoto; **~y** *adj* (fig: vulgar)
grosero

ease [iːz] *n* facilidad *f*; (comfort) comodidad *f*
♦ *vt* (lessen: problem) mitigar; (: pain)
aliviar; (: tension) reducir; **to ~ sth in/out**
meter/sacar algo con cuidado; **at ~!** (MIL)

¡descansen!; **~ off** *or* **up** *vi* (wind, rain)
amainar; (slow down) aflojar la marcha

easel ['iːzl] *n* caballete *m*

easily ['iːzɪlɪ] *adv* fácilmente

east [iːst] *n* este *m* ♦ *adj* del este, oriental;
(wind) este ♦ *adv* al este, hacia el este;
the E~ el Oriente; (POL) los países del Este

Easter ['iːstə*] *n* Pascua (de Resurrección);
~ egg *n* huevo de Pascua

east: ~erly ['iːstəlɪ] *adj* (to the east) al este;
(from the east) del este; **~ern** ['iːstən] *adj*
del este, oriental; (oriental) oriental;
~ward(s) ['iːstwəd(z)] *adv* hacia el este

easy ['iːzɪ] *adj* fácil; (simple) sencillo;
(comfortable) holgado, cómodo; (relaxed)
tranquilo ♦ *adv*: **to take it** *or* **things ~**
(not worry) tomarlo con calma; (rest)
descansar; **~ chair** *n* sillón *m*; **~-going**
adj acomodadizo

eat [iːt] (pt **ate**, pp **eaten**) *vt* comer; **~
away at** *vt fus* corroer; mermar; **~ into**
vt fus corroer; (savings) mermar

eaves [iːvz] *npl* alero

eavesdrop ['iːvzdrɔp] *vi*: **to ~ (on)**
escuchar a escondidas

ebb [eb] *n* reflujo ♦ *vi* bajar; (fig: also: **~
away**) decaer

ebony ['ebənɪ] *n* ébano

EC *n abbr* (= European Community) CE *f*

ECB *n abbr* (= European Central Bank)
BCE *m*

eccentric [ɪk'sentrɪk] *adj, n* excéntrico/a
m/f

echo ['ekəu] (pl **~es**) *n* eco *m* ♦ *vt* (sound)
repetir ♦ *vi* resonar, hacer eco

éclair [ɪ'kleə*] *n* pastelillo relleno de crema
y con chocolate por encima

eclipse [ɪ'klɪps] *n* eclipse *m*

ecology [ɪ'kɔlədʒɪ] *n* ecología

e-commerce *n abbr* (= electronic
commerce) comercio electrónico

economic [iːkə'nɔmɪk] *adj* económico;
(business etc) rentable; **~al** *adj*
económico; **~s** *n* (SCOL) economía ♦ *npl*
(of project etc) rentabilidad *f*

economize [ɪ'kɔnəmaɪz] *vi* economizar,
ahorrar

economy [ɪˈkɔnəmɪ] n economía; **~ class** n (AVIAT) clase f económica; **~ size** n tamaño económico

ecstasy [ˈɛkstəsɪ] n éxtasis m inv; (drug) éxtasis m inv; **ecstatic** [ɛksˈtætɪk] adj extático

ECU [ˈeɪkjuː] n (= European Currency Unit) ECU m

Ecuador [ˈɛkwədɔːr] n Ecuador m; **~ian** adj, n ecuatoriano/a m/f

eczema [ˈɛksɪmə] n eczema m

edge [ɛdʒ] n (of knife etc) filo; (of object) borde m; (of lake etc) orilla ♦ vt (SEWING) ribetear; **on ~** (fig) = **edgy**; **to ~ away from** alejarse poco a poco de; **~ways** adv: **he couldn't get a word in ~ways** no pudo meter ni baza

edgy [ˈɛdʒɪ] adj nervioso, inquieto

edible [ˈɛdɪbl] adj comestible

Edinburgh [ˈɛdɪnbərə] n Edimburgo

edit [ˈɛdɪt] vt (be editor of) dirigir; (text, report) corregir, preparar; **~ion** [ɪˈdɪʃən] n edición f; **~or** n (of newspaper) director(a) m/f; (of column) redactor(a) m/f; **~orial** [-ˈtɔːrɪəl] adj editorial ♦ n editorial m

educate [ˈɛdjukeɪt] vt (gen) educar; (instruct) instruir

education [ɛdjuˈkeɪʃən] n educación f; (schooling) enseñanza; (SCOL) pedagogía; **~al** adj (policy etc) educacional; (experience) docente; (toy) educativo

EEC n abbr (= European Economic Community) CEE f

eel [iːl] n anguila

eerie [ˈɪərɪ] adj misterioso

effect [ɪˈfɛkt] n efecto ♦ vt efectuar, llevar a cabo; **to take ~** (law) entrar en vigor or vigencia; (drug) surtir efecto; **in ~** en realidad; **~ive** adj eficaz; (actual) verdadero; **~ively** adv eficazmente; (in reality) efectivamente; **~iveness** n eficacia

effeminate [ɪˈfɛmɪnɪt] adj afeminado

efficiency [ɪˈfɪʃənsɪ] n eficiencia;

rendimiento

efficient [ɪˈfɪʃənt] adj eficiente; (machine) de buen rendimiento

effort [ˈɛfət] n esfuerzo; **~less** adj sin ningún esfuerzo; (style) natural

effusive [ɪˈfjuːsɪv] adj efusivo

e.g. adv abbr (= exempli gratia) p. ej.

egg [ɛg] n huevo; **hard-boiled / soft-boiled ~** huevo duro/pasado por agua; **~ on** vt incitar; **~cup** n huevera; **~ plant** (esp US) n berenjena; **~shell** n cáscara de huevo

ego [ˈiːgəu] n ego; **~tism** n egoísmo; **~tist** n egoísta m/f

Egypt [ˈiːdʒɪpt] n Egipto; **~ian** [ɪˈdʒɪpʃən] adj, n egipcio/a m/f

eiderdown [ˈaɪdədaun] n edredón m

eight [eɪt] num ocho; **~een** num diez y ocho, dieciocho; **eighth** [eɪtθ] num octavo; **~y** num ochenta

Eire [ˈɛərə] n Eire m

either [ˈaɪðər] adj cualquiera de los dos; (both, each) cada ♦ pron: **~ (of them)** cualquiera de los dos) ♦ adv tampoco; **on ~ side** en ambos lados; **I don't like ~** no me gusta ninguno/a de los/las dos; **no, I don't ~** no, yo tampoco ♦ conj: **~ yes or no** o sí o no

eject [ɪˈdʒɛkt] vt echar, expulsar; (tenant) desahuciar; **~or seat** n asiento proyectable

elaborate [adj ɪˈlæbərɪt, vb ɪˈlæbəreɪt] adj (complex) complejo ♦ vt (expand) ampliar; (refine) refinar ♦ vi explicar con más detalles

elastic [ɪˈlæstɪk] n elástico ♦ adj elástico; (fig) flexible; **~ band** (BRIT) n gomita

elated [ɪˈleɪtɪd] adj: **to be ~** regocijarse

elbow [ˈɛlbəu] n codo

elder [ˈɛldər] adj mayor ♦ n (tree) saúco; (person) mayor; **~ly** adj de edad, mayor ♦ npl: **the ~ly** los mayores

eldest [ˈɛldɪst] adj, n el/la mayor

elect [ɪˈlɛkt] vt elegir ♦ adj: **the president ~** el presidente electo; **to ~ to do** optar por hacer; **~ion** [ɪˈlɛkʃən] n elección f; **~ioneering** [ɪlɛkʃəˈnɪərɪŋ] n campaña

electoral; **~or** *n* elector(a) *m/f;* **~oral** *adj*
electoral; **~orate** *n* electorado

electric [ɪˈlektrɪk] *adj* eléctrico; **~al** *adj*
eléctrico; **~ blanket** *n* manta eléctrica; **~
fire** *n* estufa eléctrica; **~ian** [ɪlekˈtrɪʃən] *n*
electricista *m/f;* **~ity** [ɪlekˈtrɪsɪtɪ] *n*
electricidad *f;* **electrify** [ɪˈlektrɪfaɪ] *vt*
(*RAIL*) electrificar; (*fig: audience*) electrizar

electronic [ɪlekˈtrɒnɪk] *adj* electrónico; **~
mail** *n* correo electrónico; **~s** *n*
electrónica

elegant [ˈelɪɡənt] *adj* elegante

element [ˈelɪmənt] *n* elemento; (*of kettle
etc*) resistencia; **~ary** [-ˈmentərɪ] *adj*
elemental; (*primitive*) rudimentario;
(*school*) primario

elephant [ˈelɪfənt] *n* elefante *m*

elevation [elɪˈveɪʃən] *n* elevación *f;*
(*height*) altura

elevator [ˈelɪveɪtə*] *n* (*US*) ascensor *m;* (*in
warehouse etc*) montacargas *m inv*

eleven [ɪˈlevn] *num* once; **~ses** (*BRIT*) *npl*
café *m* de las once; **~th** *num* undécimo

elicit [ɪˈlɪsɪt] *vt:* **to ~ (from)** sacar (de)

eligible [ˈelɪdʒəbl] *adj:* **an ~ young man/
woman** un buen partido; **to be ~ for sth**
llenar los requisitos para algo

elm [elm] *n* olmo

elongated [ˈiːlɒŋɡeɪtɪd] *adj* alargado

elope [ɪˈləup] *vi* fugarse (para casarse)

eloquent [ˈeləkwənt] *adj* elocuente

else [els] *adv:* **something ~** otra cosa;
somewhere ~ en otra parte; **everywhere
~** en todas partes menos aquí; **where ~?**
¿dónde más?, ¿en qué otra parte?; **there
was little ~ to do** apenas quedaba otra
cosa que hacer; **nobody ~ spoke** no
habló nadie más; **~where** *adv* (*be*) en
otra parte; (*go*) a otra parte

elude [ɪˈluːd] *vt* (*subj: idea etc*) escaparse a;
(*capture*) esquivar

elusive [ɪˈluːsɪv] *adj* esquivo; (*quality*)
difícil de encontrar

emaciated [ɪˈmeɪsɪeɪtɪd] *adj* demacrado

E-mail, e-mail [ˈiːmeɪl] *n abbr*
(= *electronic mail*) correo electrónico, e-
mail *m*

emancipate [ɪˈmænsɪpeɪt] *vt* emancipar

embankment [ɪmˈbæŋkmənt] *n* terraplén
m

embark [ɪmˈbɑːk] *vi* embarcarse ♦ *vt*
embarcar; **to ~ on** (*journey*) emprender;
(*course of action*) lanzarse a; **~ation**
[embɑːˈkeɪʃən] *n* (*people*) embarco; (*goods*)
embarque *m*

embarrass [ɪmˈbærəs] *vt* avergonzar;
(*government etc*) dejar en mal lugar; **~ed**
adj (*laugh, silence*) embarazoso; **~ing** *adj*
(*situation*) violento; (*question*)
embarazoso; **~ment** *n* (*shame*)
vergüenza; (*problem*): **to be an ~ment for
sb** poner en un aprieto a uno

embassy [ˈembəsɪ] *n* embajada

embedded [ɪmˈbedɪd] *adj* (*object*)
empotrado; (*thorn etc*) clavado

embellish [ɪmˈbelɪʃ] *vt* embellecer; (*story*)
adornar

embers [ˈembəz] *npl* rescoldo, ascua

embezzle [ɪmˈbezl] *vt* desfalcar, malversar

embitter [ɪmˈbɪtə*] *vt* (*fig: sour*) amargar

embody [ɪmˈbɒdɪ] *vt* (*spirit*) encarnar;
(*include*) incorporar

embossed [ɪmˈbɒst] *adj* realzado

embrace [ɪmˈbreɪs] *vt* abrazar, dar un
abrazo a; (*include*) abarcar ♦ *vi* abrazarse
♦ *n* abrazo

embroider [ɪmˈbrɔɪdə*] *vt* bordar; **~y** *n*
bordado

embryo [ˈembrɪəu] *n* embrión *m*

emerald [ˈemərəld] *n* esmeralda

emerge [ɪˈmɜːdʒ] *vi* salir; (*arise*) surgir

emergency [ɪˈmɜːdʒənsɪ] *n* crisis *f inv;* **in
an ~** en caso de urgencia; **state of ~**
estado de emergencia; **~ cord** (*US*) *n*
timbre *m* de alarma; **~ exit** *n* salida de
emergencia; **~ landing** *n* aterrizaje *m*
forzoso; **~ services** *npl* (*fire, police,
ambulance*) servicios *mpl* de urgencia *or*
emergencia

emery board [ˈemərɪ-] *n* lima de uñas

emigrate [ˈemɪɡreɪt] *vi* emigrar

emissions [ɪˈmɪʃənz] *npl* emisión *f*

emit [ɪˈmɪt] *vt* emitir; (*smoke*) arrojar;
(*smell*) despedir; (*sound*) producir

emotion [ɪ'məʊʃən] *n* emoción *f*; ~al *adj* (*needs*) emocional; (*person*) sentimental; (*scene*) conmovedor(a), emocionante; (*speech*) emocionado

emperor ['empərə*] *n* emperador *m*

emphasis ['emfəsɪs] (*pl* **-ses**) *n* énfasis *m inv*

emphasize ['emfəsaɪz] *vt* (*word, point*) subrayar, recalcar; (*feature*) hacer resaltar

emphatic [em'fætɪk] *adj* (*reply*) categórico; (*person*) insistente

empire ['empaɪə*] *n* (*also fig*) imperio *m*

employ [ɪm'plɔɪ] *vt* emplear; **~ee** [-'iː] *n* empleado/a; **~er** *n* patrón/ona *m/f*; empresario; **~ment** *n* (*work*) trabajo; **~ment agency** *n* agencia de colocaciones

empower [ɪm'paʊə*] *vt*: **to ~ sb to do sth** autorizar a uno para hacer algo

empress ['emprɪs] *n* emperatriz *f*

emptiness ['emptɪnɪs] *n* vacío *m*; (*of life etc*) vaciedad *f*

empty ['emptɪ] *adj* vacío; (*place*) desierto; (*house*) desocupado; (*threat*) vano ♦ *vt* vaciar; (*place*) dejar vacío ♦ *vi* vaciarse; (*house etc*) quedar desocupado; **~-handed** *adj* con las manos vacías

EMU *n abbr* (= *European Monetary Union*) UME *f*

emulate ['emjʊleɪt] *vt* emular

emulsion [ɪ'mʌlʃən] *n* emulsión *f*; (*also:* **~ paint**) pintura emulsión

enable [ɪ'neɪbl] *vt*: **to ~ sb to do sth** permitir a uno hacer algo

enamel [ɪ'næməl] *n* esmalte *m*; (*also:* **~ paint**) pintura esmaltada

enchant [ɪn'tʃɑːnt] *vt* encantar; **~ing** *adj* encantador(a)

encl. *abbr* (= *enclosed*) adj

enclose [ɪn'kləʊz] *vt* (*land*) cercar; (*letter etc*) adjuntar; **please find ~d** le mandamos adjunto

enclosure [ɪn'kləʊʒə*] *n* cercado, recinto

encompass [ɪn'kʌmpəs] *vt* abarcar

encore [ɔŋ'kɔ:*] *excl* ¡otra!, ¡bis! ♦ *n* bis *m*

encounter [ɪn'kaʊntə*] *n* encuentro ♦ *vt* encontrar, encontrarse con; (*difficulty*) tropezar con

encourage [ɪn'kʌrɪdʒ] *vt* alentar, animar; (*activity*) fomentar; (*growth*) estimular; **~ment** *n* estímulo; (*of industry*) fomento

encroach [ɪn'krəʊtʃ] *vi*: **to ~ (up)on** invadir; (*rights*) usurpar; (*time*) adueñarse de

encyclop(a)edia [ensaɪkləʊ'piːdɪə] *n* enciclopedia

end [end] *n* (*gen, also aim*) fin *m*; (*of table*) extremo; (*of street*) final *m*; (*SPORT*) lado ♦ *vt* terminar, acabar; (*also:* **bring to an ~, put an ~ to**) acabar con ♦ *vi* terminar, acabar; **in the ~** al fin; **on ~** (*object*) de punta, de cabeza; **to stand on ~** (*hair*) erizarse; **for hours on ~** hora tras hora; **~ up** *vi*: **to ~ up in** terminar en; (*place*) ir a parar en

endanger [ɪn'deɪndʒə*] *vt* poner en peligro; **an ~ed species** una especie en peligro de extinción

endearing [ɪn'dɪərɪŋ] *adj* simpático, atractivo

endeavour [ɪn'devə*] (*US* **endeavor**) *n* esfuerzo; (*attempt*) tentativa ♦ *vi*: **to ~ to do** esforzarse por hacer; (*try*) procurar hacer

ending ['endɪŋ] *n* (*of book*) desenlace *m*; (*LING*) terminación *f*

endive ['endaɪv] *n* (*chicory*) endibia; (*curly*) escarola

endless ['endlɪs] *adj* interminable, inacabable

endorse [ɪn'dɔ:s] *vt* (*cheque*) endosar; (*approve*) aprobar; **~ment** *n* (*on driving licence*) nota de inhabilitación

endure [ɪn'djʊə*] *vt* (*bear*) aguantar, soportar ♦ *vi* (*last*) durar

enemy ['enəmɪ] *adj, n* enemigo/a *m/f*

energetic [enə'dʒetɪk] *adj* enérgico

energy ['enədʒɪ] *n* energía

enforce [ɪn'fɔ:s] *vt* (*LAW*) hacer cumplir

engage [ɪn'geɪdʒ] *vt* (*attention*) llamar; (*interest*) ocupar; (*in conversation*) abordar; (*worker*) contratar; (*AUT*): **to ~ the clutch** embragar ♦ *vi* (*TECH*) engranar; **to ~ in** dedicarse a, ocuparse en; ~d adj (BRIT: busy, in use) ocupado; (betrothed) prometido; **to get ~d** prometerse; ~d tone (BRIT) n (TEL) señal f de comunicando; ~ment n (appointment) compromiso, cita; (booking) contratación f; (to marry) compromiso; (period) noviazgo; ~ment ring n anillo de prometida

engaging [ɪnˈɡeɪdʒɪŋ] adj atractivo

engine [ˈendʒɪn] n (AUT) motor m; (RAIL) locomotora; ~ driver n maquinista m/f

engineer [endʒɪˈnɪə*] n ingeniero; (BRIT: for repairs) mecánico; (on ship, US: RAIL) maquinista m; ~ing n ingeniería

England [ˈɪŋɡlənd] n Inglaterra

English [ˈɪŋɡlɪʃ] adj inglés/esa ♦ n (LING) inglés m; **the ~** npl los ingleses mpl; **the ~ Channel** n (el Canal de) la Mancha; ~man/woman (irreg) n inglés/esa m/f

engraving [ɪnˈɡreɪvɪŋ] n grabado

engrossed [ɪnˈɡrəust] adj: ~ in absorto en

engulf [ɪnˈɡʌlf] vt (subj: water) sumergir, hundir; (: fire) prender; (: fear) apoderarse de

enhance [ɪnˈhɑːns] vt (gen) aumentar; (beauty) realzar

enjoy [ɪnˈdʒɔɪ] vt (health, fortune) disfrutar de, gozar de; (like) gustarle a uno; **to ~ o.s.** divertirse; ~able adj agradable; ~ment n (joy) placer m; (activity) diversión f

enlarge [ɪnˈlɑːdʒ] vt aumentar; (broaden) extender; (PHOT) ampliar ♦ vi: **to ~ on** (subject) tratar con más detalles; ~ment n (PHOT) ampliación f

enlighten [ɪnˈlaɪtn] vt (inform) informar; ~ed adj comprensivo; **the E~ment** n (HISTORY) ≈ la Ilustración, ≈ el Siglo de las Luces

enlist [ɪnˈlɪst] vt alistar; (support) conseguir ♦ vi alistarse

enmity [ˈenmɪtɪ] n enemistad f

enormous [ɪˈnɔːməs] adj enorme

enough [ɪˈnʌf] adj: ~ time/books bastante tiempo/bastantes libros ♦ pron bastante(s) ♦ adv: **big ~** bastante grande; **he has not worked ~** no ha trabajado bastante; **have you got ~?** ¿tiene usted bastante(s)?; **~ to eat** (lo) suficiente or (lo) bastante para comer; **~!** ¡basta ya!; **that's ~, thanks** con eso basta, gracias; **I've had ~ of him** estoy harto de él; **... which, funnily or oddly ~** ... lo que, por extraño que parezca ...

enquire [ɪnˈkwaɪə*] vt, vi = inquire

enrage [ɪnˈreɪdʒ] vt enfurecer

enrol [ɪnˈrəul] (US enroll) vt (members) inscribir; (SCOL) matricular ♦ vi inscribirse; matricularse; ~ment (US enrollment) n inscripción f; matriculación f

en route [ɔnˈruːt] adv durante el viaje

en suite [ɔnˈswiːt] adj: **with ~ bathroom** con baño

ensure [ɪnˈʃuə*] vt asegurar

entail [ɪnˈteɪl] vt suponer

entangled [ɪnˈtæŋɡld] adj: **to become ~ (in)** quedarse enredado (en) or enmarañado (en)

enter [ˈentə*] vt (room) entrar en; (club) hacerse socio de; (army) alistarse en; (sb for a competition) inscribir; (write down) anotar, apuntar; (COMPUT) meter ♦ vi entrar; ~ for vt fus presentarse para; ~ into vt fus (discussion etc) entablar; (agreement) llegar a, firmar

enterprise [ˈentəpraɪz] n empresa; (spirit) iniciativa; **free ~** la libre empresa; **private ~** la iniciativa privada; **enterprising** adj emprendedor(a)

entertain [entəˈteɪn] vt (amuse) divertir; (invite: guest) invitar (a casa); (idea) abrigar; ~er n artista m/f; ~ing adj divertido, entretenido; ~ment n (amusement) diversión f; (show) espectáculo

enthralled [ɪnˈθrɔːld] adj encantado

enthusiasm [ɪnˈθuːzɪæzəm] n entusiasmo

enthusiast [ɪnˈθuːzɪæst] n entusiasta m/f; ~ic [-ˈæstɪk] adj entusiasta; **to be ~ic about** entusiasmarse por

entire [ɪnˈtaɪə*] adj entero; ~ly adv totalmente; ~ty [ɪnˈtaɪərətɪ] n: **in its ~ty** en su totalidad

entitle [ɪnˈtaɪtl] vt: **to ~ sb to sth** dar a

uno derecho a algo; **~d** *adj* (*book*)
titulado; **to be ~d to do** tener derecho a
hacer

entrance [n 'entrəns, vb ɪn'trɑːns] *n*
entrada ♦ *vt* encantar, hechizar; **to gain ~
to** (*university etc*) ingresar en; **~
examination** *n* examen *m* de ingreso;
~ fee *n* cuota; **~ ramp** (*US*) *n* (*AUT*)
rampa de acceso

entrant ['entrənt] *n* (*in race, competition*)
participante *m/f*; (*in examination*)
candidato/a

entrenched [en'trentʃd] *adj* inamovible

entrepreneur [ɔntrəprə'nɜː] *n* empresario

entrust [ɪn'trʌst] *vt*: **to ~ sth to sb** confiar
algo a uno

entry ['entrɪ] *n* entrada; (*in competition*)
participación *f*; (*in register*) apunte *m*; (*in
account*) partida; (*in reference book*)
artículo; **"no ~"** "prohibido el paso";
(*AUT*) "dirección prohibida"; **~ form** *n*
hoja de inscripción; **~ phone** *n* portero
automático

envelop [ɪn'veləp] *vt* envolver

envelope ['envələup] *n* sobre *m*

envious ['envɪəs] *adj* envidioso; (*look*) de
envidia

environment [ɪn'vaɪərənmənt] *n*
(*surroundings*) entorno; (*natural world*):
the ~ el medio ambiente; **~al** [-'mentl]
adj ambiental; medioambiental; **~-
friendly** *adj* no perjudicial para el medio
ambiente

envisage [ɪn'vɪzɪdʒ] *vt* prever

envoy ['envɔɪ] *n* enviado

envy ['envɪ] *n* envidia ♦ *vt* tener envidia a;
to ~ sb sth envidiar algo a uno

epic ['epɪk] *n* épica ♦ *adj* épico

epidemic [epɪ'demɪk] *n* epidemia

epilepsy ['epɪlepsɪ] *n* epilepsia

episode ['epɪsəud] *n* episodio

epitomize [ɪ'pɪtəmaɪz] *vt* epitomar,
resumir

equal ['iːkwl] *adj* igual; (*treatment*)
equitativo ♦ *n* igual *m/f* ♦ *vt* ser igual a;
(*fig*) igualar; **to be ~ to** (*task*) estar a la
altura de; **~ity** [iː'kwɔlɪtɪ] *n* igualdad *f*;

~ize *vi* (*SPORT*) empatar; **~ly** *adv*
igualmente; (*share etc*) a partes iguales

equate [ɪ'kweɪt] *vt*: **to ~ sth with**
equiparar algo con; **equation** [ɪ'kweɪʒən]
n (*MATH*) ecuación *f*

equator [ɪ'kweɪtə] *n* ecuador *m*

equilibrium [iːkwɪ'lɪbrɪəm] *n* equilibrio

equip [ɪ'kwɪp] *vt* equipar; (*person*) proveer;
to be well ~ped estar bien equipado;
~ment *n* equipo; (*tools*) avíos *mpl*

equities ['ekwɪtɪz] (*BRIT*) *npl* (*COMM*)
derechos *mpl* sobre *or* en el activo

equivalent [ɪ'kwɪvələnt] *adj*: **~ (to)**
equivalente (a) ♦ *n* equivalente *m*

era ['ɪərə] *n* era, época

eradicate [ɪ'rædɪkeɪt] *vt* erradicar

erase [ɪ'reɪz] *vt* borrar; **~r** *n* goma de
borrar

erect [ɪ'rekt] *adj* erguido ♦ *vt* erigir,
levantar; (*assemble*) montar; **~ion** [-ʃən] *n*
construcción *f*; (*assembly*) montaje *m*;
(*PHYSIOL*) erección *f*

ERM *n abbr* (= *Exchange Rate Mechanism*)
tipo de cambio europeo

erode [ɪ'rəud] *vt* (*GEO*) erosionar; (*metal*)
corroer, desgastar; (*fig*) desgastar

erotic [ɪ'rɔtɪk] *adj* erótico

errand ['ernd] *n* recado (*SP*), mandado
(*AM*)

erratic [ɪ'rætɪk] *adj* desigual, poco
uniforme

error ['erə] *n* error *m*, equivocación *f*

erupt [ɪ'rʌpt] *vi* entrar en erupción; (*fig*)
estallar; **~ion** [ɪ'rʌpʃən] *n* erupción *f*; (*of
war*) estallido

escalate ['eskəleɪt] *vi* extenderse,
intensificarse

escalator ['eskəleɪtə] *n* escalera móvil

escapade [eskə'peɪd] *n* travesura

escape [ɪ'skeɪp] *n* fuga ♦ *vi* escaparse;
(*flee*) huir, evadirse; (*leak*) fugarse ♦ *vt*
(*responsibility etc*) evitar, eludir;
(*consequences*) escapar a; (*elude*): **his
name ~s me** no me sale su nombre; **to ~
from** (*place*) escaparse de; (*person*)
escaparse a

escort [n 'eskɔːt, vb ɪ'skɔːt] *n* acompañante

m/f; (*MIL*) escolta ♦ *vt* acompañar

Eskimo ['eskɪməʊ] *n* esquimal *m/f*

especially [ɪ'speʃlɪ] *adv* (*above all*) sobre todo; (*particularly*) en particular, especialmente

espionage ['espɪɒnɑːʒ] *n* espionaje *m*

esplanade [esplə'neɪd] *n* (*by sea*) paseo marítimo

Esquire [ɪ'skwaɪə] (*abbr* **Esq.**) *n*: **J. Brown, ~** Sr. D. J. Brown

essay ['eseɪ] *n* (*LITERATURE*) ensayo; (*SCOL*: *short*) redacción *f*; (*: long*) trabajo

essence ['esns] *n* esencia

essential [ɪ'senʃl] *adj* (*necessary*) imprescindible; (*basic*) esencial; **~s** *npl* lo imprescindible, lo esencial; **~ly** *adv* esencialmente

establish [ɪ'stæblɪʃ] *vt* establecer; (*prove*) demostrar; (*relations*) entablar; (*reputation*) ganarse; **~ed** *adj* (*business*) conocido; (*practice*) arraigado; **~ment** *n* establecimiento; **the E~ment** la clase dirigente

estate [ɪ'steɪt] *n* (*land*) finca, hacienda; (*inheritance*) herencia; (*BRIT*: *also*: **housing ~**) urbanización *f*; **~ agent** (*BRIT*) *n* agente *m/f* inmobiliario/a; **~ car** (*BRIT*) *n* furgoneta

esteem [ɪ'stiːm] *n*: **to hold sb in high ~** estimar en mucho a uno

esthetic [ɪs'θetɪk] (*US*) *adj* = **aesthetic**

estimate [*n* 'estɪmət, *vb* 'estɪmeɪt] *n* estimación *f*, apreciación *f*; (*assessment*) tasa, cálculo; (*COMM*) presupuesto ♦ *vt* estimar, tasar; calcular; **estimation** [-'meɪʃən] *n* opinión *f*, juicio; cálculo

estranged [ɪ'streɪndʒd] *adj* separado

estuary ['estjuərɪ] *n* estuario, ría

etc *abbr* (= *et cetera*) etc

eternal [ɪ'tɜːnl] *adj* eterno

eternity [ɪ'tɜːnɪtɪ] *n* eternidad *f*

ethical ['eθɪkl] *adj* ético; **ethics** ['eθɪks] *n* ética ♦ *npl* moralidad *f*

Ethiopia [iːθɪ'əʊpɪə] *n* Etiopía

ethnic ['eθnɪk] *adj* étnico; **~ minority** minoría étnica

ethos ['iːθɒs] *n* genio, carácter *m*

etiquette ['etɪket] *n* etiqueta

EU *n abbr* (= *European Union*) UE *f*

euro ['jʊərəʊ] *n* euro

Eurocheque ['jʊərəʊtʃek] *n* Eurocheque *m*

Euroland [jʊərəʊlænd] *n* Eurolandia

Europe ['jʊərəp] *n* Europa; **~an** [-'piːən] *adj*, *n* europeo/a *m/f*; **~an Community** *n* Comunidad *f* Europea; **~an Union** *n* Unión *f* Europea

evacuate [ɪ'vækjʊeɪt] *vt* (*people*) evacuar; (*place*) desocupar

evade [ɪ'veɪd] *vt* evadir, eludir

evaporate [ɪ'væpəreɪt] *vi* evaporarse; (*fig*) desvanecerse; **~d milk** *n* leche *f* evaporada

evasion [ɪ'veɪʒən] *n* evasión *f*

eve [iːv] *n*: **on the ~ of** en vísperas de

even ['iːvn] *adj* (*level*) llano; (*smooth*) liso; (*speed, temperature*) uniforme; (*number*) par ♦ *adv* hasta, incluso; (*introducing a comparison*) aún, todavía; **~ if**, **~ though** aunque +*sub*; **~ more** aun más; **~ so** aun así; **not ~** ni siquiera; **~ he was there** hasta él estuvo allí; **~ on Sundays** incluso los domingos; **to get ~ with sb** ajustar cuentas con uno

evening ['iːvnɪŋ] *n* tarde *f*; (*late*) noche *f*; **in the ~** por la tarde; **~ class** *n* clase *f* nocturna; **~ dress** *n* (*no pl*: *formal clothes*) traje *m* de etiqueta; (*woman's*) traje *m* de noche

event [ɪ'vent] *n* suceso, acontecimiento; (*SPORT*) prueba; **in the ~ of** en caso de; **~ful** *adj* (*life*) activo; (*day*) ajetreado

eventual [ɪ'ventʃuəl] *adj* final; **~ity** [-'ælɪtɪ] *n* eventualidad *f*; **~ly** *adv* (*finally*) finalmente; (*in time*) con el tiempo

ever ['evə*] *adv* (*at any time*) nunca, jamás; (*at all times*) siempre; (*in question*): **why ~ not?** ¿y por qué no?; **the best ~** lo nunca visto; **have you ~ seen it?** ¿lo ha visto usted alguna vez?; **better than ~** mejor que nunca; **~ since** *adv* desde entonces ♦ *conj* después de que; **~green** *n* árbol *m* de hoja perenne; **~lasting** *adj* eterno, perpetuo

---

KEYWORD

---

every ['ɛvrɪ] *adj* 1 (*each*) cada; ~ **one of them** (*persons*) todos ellos/as; (*objects*) cada uno de ellos/as; ~ **shop in the town was closed** todas las tiendas de la ciudad estaban cerradas

2 (*all possible*) todo/a; **I gave you ~ assistance** se di toda la ayuda posible; **I have ~ confidence in him** tiene toda mi confianza; **we wish you ~ success** te deseamos toda suerte de éxitos

3 (*showing recurrence*) todo/a; ~ **day/ week** todos los días/todas las semanas; ~ **other car had been broken into** habían forzado uno de cada dos coches; **she visits me ~ other/third day** me visita cada dos/tres días; ~ **now and then** de vez en cuando

---

every: ~**body** *pron* = **everyone;** ~**day** *adj* (*daily*) cotidiano, de todos los días; (*usual*) acostumbrado; ~**one** *pron* todos/ as, todo el mundo; ~**thing** *pron* todo; **this shop sells ~thing** esta tienda vende de todo; ~**where** *adv*: **I've been looking for you ~where** te he estado buscando por todas partes; ~**where you go you meet ...** en todas partes encuentras ...

evict [ɪ'vɪkt] *vt* desahuciar; ~**ion** [ɪ'vɪkʃən] *n* desahucio

evidence ['ɛvɪdəns] *n* (*proof*) prueba; (*of witness*) testimonio; (*sign*) indicios *mpl*; **to give ~** prestar declaración, dar testimonio

evident ['ɛvɪdənt] *adj* evidente, manifiesto; ~**ly** *adv* por lo visto

evil ['iːvl] *adj* malo; (*influence*) funesto ♦ *n* mal *m*

evoke [ɪ'vəuk] *vt* evocar

evolution [iːvə'luːʃən] *n* evolución *f*

evolve [ɪ'vɔlv] *vt* desarrollar ♦ *vi* evolucionar, desarrollarse

ewe [juː] *n* oveja

ex- [ɛks] *prefix* ex

exact [ɪg'zækt] *adj* exacto; (*person*) meticuloso ♦ *vt*: **to ~ sth (from)** exigir

algo (de); ~**ing** *adj* exigente; (*conditions*) arduo; ~**ly** *adv* exactamente; (*indicating agreement*) exacto

exaggerate [ɪg'zædʒəreɪt] *vt, vi* exagerar; **exaggeration** [-'reɪʃən] *n* exageración *f*

exalted [ɪg'zɔːltɪd] *adj* eminente

exam [ɪg'zæm] *n abbr* (SCOL)
= **examination**

examination [ɪgzæmɪ'neɪʃən] *n* examen *m*; (MED) reconocimiento

examine [ɪg'zæmɪn] *vt* examinar; (*inspect*) inspeccionar, escudriñar; (MED) reconocer; ~**r** *n* examinador(a) *m/f*

example [ɪg'zɑːmpl] *n* ejemplo; **for ~** por ejemplo

exasperate [ɪg'zɑːspəreɪt] *vt* exasperar, irritar; **exasperation** [-ʃən] *n* exasperación *f*, irritación *f*

excavate ['ɛkskəveɪt] *vt* excavar

exceed [ɪk'siːd] *vt* (*amount*) exceder; (*number*) pasar de; (*speed limit*) sobrepasar; (*powers*) excederse en; (*hopes*) superar; ~**ingly** *adv* sumamente, sobremanera

excellent ['ɛksələnt] *adj* excelente

except [ɪk'sɛpt] *prep* (*also:* ~ **for, ~ing**) excepto, salvo ♦ *vt* exceptuar, excluir; ~ **if/when** excepto si/cuando; ~ **that** salvo que; ~**ion** [ɪk'sɛpʃən] *n* excepción *f*; **to take ~ion to** ofenderse por; ~**ional** [ɪk'sɛpʃənl] *adj* excepcional

excerpt ['ɛksəːpt] *n* extracto

excess [ɪk'sɛs] *n* exceso; ~**es** *npl* (*of cruelty etc*) atrocidades *fpl*; ~ **baggage** *n* exceso de equipaje; ~ **fare** *n* suplemento; ~**ive** *adj* excesivo

exchange [ɪks'tʃeɪndʒ] *n* intercambio; (*conversation*) diálogo; (*also:* **telephone ~**) central *f* (telefónica) ♦ *vt*: **to ~ (for)** cambiar (por); ~ **rate** *n* tipo de cambio

exchequer [ɪks'tʃɛkə*] (BRIT) *n*: **the E~** la Hacienda del Fisco

excise ['ɛksaɪz] *n* impuestos *mpl* sobre el alcohol y el tabaco

excite [ɪk'saɪt] *vt* (*stimulate*) estimular; (*arouse*) excitar; ~**d** *adj*: **to get ~d** emocionarse; ~**ment** *n* (*agitation*)

excitación *f*; (*exhilaration*) emoción *f*;
exciting *adj* emocionante
exclaim [ɪkˈskleɪm] *vi* exclamar;
exclamation [ɛkskləˈmeɪʃən] *n*
exclamación *f*; **exclamation mark** *n*
punto de admiración
exclude [ɪkˈskluːd] *vt* excluir; exceptuar
exclusive [ɪkˈskluːsɪv] *adj* exclusivo; (*club,
district*) selecto; **~ of tax** excluyendo
impuestos; **~ly** *adv* únicamente
excruciating [ɪkˈskruːʃɪeɪtɪŋ] *adj* (*pain*)
agudísimo, atroz; (*noise, embarrassment*)
horrible
excursion [ɪkˈskəːʃən] *n* (*tourist ~*)
excursión *f*
excuse [*n* ɪkˈskjuːs, *vb* ɪkˈskjuːz] *n* disculpa,
excusa; (*pretext*) pretexto ♦ *vt* (*justify*)
justificar; (*forgive*) disculpar, perdonar; **to
~ sb from doing sth** dispensar a uno de
hacer algo; **~ me!** (*attracting attention*)
¡por favor!; (*apologizing*) ¡perdón!; **if you
will ~ me** con su permiso
ex-directory [ˈɛksdɪˈrɛktərɪ] (*BRIT*) *adj* que
no consta en la guía
execute [ˈɛksɪkjuːt] *vt* (*plan*) realizar;
(*order*) cumplir; (*person*) ajusticiar,
ejecutar; **execution** [-ˈkjuːʃən] *n*
realización *f*; cumplimiento; ejecución *f*
executive [ɪgˈzɛkjutɪv] *n* (*person,
committee*) ejecutivo; (*POL: committee*)
poder *m* ejecutivo ♦ *adj* ejecutivo
exemplify [ɪgˈzɛmplɪfaɪ] *vt* ejemplificar;
(*illustrate*) ilustrar
exempt [ɪgˈzɛmpt] *adj*: **~ from** exento de
♦ *vt*: **to ~ sb from** eximir a uno de; **~ion**
[-ʃən] *n* exención *f*
exercise [ˈɛksəsaɪz] *n* ejercicio ♦ *vt*
(*patience*) usar de; (*right*) valerse de; (*dog*)
llevar de paseo; (*mind*) preocupar ♦ *vi*
(*also: to take ~*) hacer ejercicio(s); **~ bike**
n ciclostát ® *m*, bicicleta estática; **~
book** *n* cuaderno
exert [ɪgˈzəːt] *vt* ejercer; **to ~ o.s.**
esforzarse; **~ion** [-ʃən] *n* esfuerzo
exhale [ɛksˈheɪl] *vt* despedir ♦ *vi* exhalar
exhaust [ɪgˈzɔːst] *n* (*AUT: also: ~ pipe*)
escape *m*; (: *fumes*) gases *mpl* de escape

♦ *vt* agotar; **~ed** *adj* agotado; **~ion**
[ɪgˈzɔːstʃən] *n* agotamiento; **nervous ~ion**
postración *f* nerviosa; **~ive** *adj*
exhaustivo
exhibit [ɪgˈzɪbɪt] *n* (*ART*) obra expuesta;
(*LAW*) objeto expuesto ♦ *vt* (*show:
emotions*) manifestar; (: *courage, skill*)
demostrar; (*paintings*) exponer; **~ion**
[ɛksɪˈbɪʃən] *n* exposición *f*; (*of talent etc*)
demostración *f*
exhilarating [ɪgˈzɪləreɪtɪŋ] *adj* estimulante,
tónico
exile [ˈɛksaɪl] *n* exilio; (*person*) exiliado/a
♦ *vt* desterrar, exiliar
exist [ɪgˈzɪst] *vi* existir; (*live*) vivir; **~ence** *n*
existencia; **~ing** *adj* existente, actual
exit [ˈɛksɪt] *n* salida ♦ *vi* (*THEATRE*) hacer
mutis; (*COMPUT*) salir (al sistema); **~ poll**
*n encuesta a la salida de los colegios
electorales*; **~ ramp** (*US*) *n* (*AUT*) vía de
acceso
exodus [ˈɛksədəs] *n* éxodo
exonerate [ɪgˈzɔnəreɪt] *vt*: **to ~ from**
exculpar de
exotic [ɪgˈzɔtɪk] *adj* exótico
expand [ɪkˈspænd] *vt* ampliar; (*number*)
aumentar ♦ *vi* (*population*) aumentar;
(*trade etc*) expandirse; (*gas, metal*)
dilatarse
expanse [ɪkˈspæns] *n* extensión *f*
expansion [ɪkˈspænʃən] *n* (*of population*)
aumento; (*of trade*) expansión *f*
expect [ɪkˈspɛkt] *vt* esperar; (*require*)
contar con; (*suppose*) suponer ♦ *vi*: **to be
~ing** (*pregnant woman*) estar embarazada;
~ancy *n* (*anticipation*) esperanza; **life
~ancy** esperanza de vida; **~ant mother**
n futura madre *f*; **~ation** [ɛkspɛkˈteɪʃən] *n*
(*hope*) esperanza; (*belief*) expectativa
expedient [ɪkˈspiːdɪənt] *adj* conveniente,
oportuno ♦ *n* recurso, expediente *m*
expedition [ɛkspəˈdɪʃən] *n* expedición *f*
expel [ɪkˈspɛl] *vt* arrojar; (*from place*)
expulsar
expend [ɪkˈspɛnd] *vt* (*money*) gastar; (*time,
energy*) consumir; **~iture** *n* gastos *mpl*,
desembolso; consumo

expense [ɪk'spɛns] n gasto, gastos mpl; (high cost) costa; **~s** npl (COMM) gastos mpl; **at the ~ of** a costa de; **~ account** n cuenta de gastos

expensive [ɪk'spɛnsɪv] adj caro, costoso

experience [ɪk'spɪərɪəns] n experiencia ♦ vt experimentar; (suffer) sufrir; **~d** adj experimentado

experiment [ɪk'spɛrɪmənt] n experimento ♦ vi hacer experimentos

expert ['ɛkspəːt] adj experto, perito ♦ n experto/a, perito/a; (specialist) especialista m/f; **~ise** [-'tiːz] n pericia

expire [ɪk'spaɪə*] vi caducar, vencer; **expiry** n vencimiento

explain [ɪk'spleɪn] vt explicar; **explanation** [ɛksplə'neɪʃən] n explicación f; **explanatory** [ɪk'splænətrɪ] adj explicativo; aclaratorio

explicit [ɪk'splɪsɪt] adj explícito

explode [ɪk'spləʊd] vi estallar, explotar; (population) crecer rápidamente; (with anger) reventar

exploit [n 'ɛksplɔɪt, vb ɪk'splɔɪt] n hazaña ♦ vt explotar; **~ation** [-'teɪʃən] n explotación f

exploratory [ɪk'splɔrətrɪ] adj de exploración; (fig: talks) exploratorio, preliminar

explore [ɪk'splɔː*] vt explorar; (fig) examinar; investigar; **~r** n explorador(a) m/f

explosion [ɪk'spləʊʒən] n (also fig) explosión f; **explosive** [ɪks'pləʊsɪv] adj, n explosivo

exponent [ɪk'spəʊnənt] n (of theory etc) partidario/a; (of skill etc) exponente m/f

export [vb ɛk'spɔːt, n 'ɛkspɔːt] vt exportar ♦ n (process) exportación f; (product) producto de exportación ♦ cpd de exportación; **~er** n exportador m

expose [ɪk'spəʊz] vt exponer; (unmask) desenmascarar; **~d** adj expuesto

exposure [ɪk'spəʊʒə*] n exposición f; (publicity) publicidad f; (PHOT: speed) velocidad f de obturación; (: shot) fotografía; **to die from ~** (MED) morir de frío; **~ meter** n fotómetro

express [ɪk'sprɛs] adj (definite) expreso, explícito; (BRIT: letter etc) urgente ♦ n (train) rápido ♦ vt expresar; **~ion** [ɪk'sprɛʃən] n expresión f; (of actor etc) sentimiento; **~ly** adv expresamente; **~way** (US) n (urban motorway) autopista

exquisite [ɛk'skwɪzɪt] adj exquisito

extend [ɪk'stɛnd] vt (visit, street) prolongar; (building) ampliar; (invitation) ofrecer ♦ vi (land) extenderse; (period of time) prolongarse

extension [ɪk'stɛnʃən] n extensión f; (building) ampliación f; (of time) prolongación f; (TEL: in private house) línea derivada; (: in office) extensión f

extensive [ɪk'stɛnsɪv] adj extenso; (damage) importante; (knowledge) amplio; **~ly** adv: **he's travelled ~ly** ha viajado por muchos países

extent [ɪk'stɛnt] n (breadth) extensión f; (scope) alcance m; **to some ~** hasta cierto punto; **to the ~ of...** hasta el punto de...; **to such an ~ that...** hasta tal punto que...; **to what ~?** ¿hasta qué punto?

extenuating [ɪk'stɛnjʊeɪtɪŋ] adj: **~ circumstances** circunstancias fpl atenuantes

exterior [ɛk'stɪərɪə*] adj exterior, externo ♦ n exterior m

external [ɛk'stəːnl] adj externo

extinct [ɪk'stɪŋkt] adj (volcano) extinguido; (race) extinto

extinguish [ɪk'stɪŋgwɪʃ] vt extinguir, apagar; **~er** n extintor m

extort [ɪk'stɔːt] vt obtener por fuerza; **~ionate** adj excesivo, exorbitante

extra ['ɛkstrə] adj adicional ♦ adv (in addition) de más ♦ n (luxury, addition) extra m; (CINEMA, THEATRE) extra m/f, comparsa m/f

extra... ['ɛkstrə] prefix extra...

extract [vb ɪk'strækt, n 'ɛkstrækt] vt sacar; (tooth) extraer; (money, promise) obtener ♦ n extracto

extracurricular [ɛkstrəkə'rɪkjulə*] adj extraescolar, extra-académico

extradite ['ɛkstrədaɪt] vt extraditar
extra: **~marital** adj extramatrimonial;
  ~mural [ɛkstrə'mjuərl] adj extraescolar;
  ~ordinary [ɪk'strɔ:dɪnrɪ] adj
  extraordinario; (odd) raro
extravagance [ɪk'strævəgəns] n derroche
  m, despilfarro; (thing bought)
  extravagancia
extravagant [ɪk'strævəgənt] adj (lavish:
  person) pródigo; (: gift) (demasiado) caro;
  (wasteful) despilfarrador(a)
extreme [ɪk'stri:m] adj extremo,
  extremado ♦ n extremo; **~ly** adv
  sumamente, extremadamente
extricate ['ɛkstrɪkeɪt] vt: **to ~ sth/sb from**
  librar algo/a uno de
extrovert ['ɛkstrəvə:t] n extrovertido/a
eye [aɪ] n ojo ♦ vt mirar de soslayo, ojear;
  to keep an ~ on vigilar; **~bath** n ojera;
  ~brow n ceja; **~drops** npl gotas fpl
  para los ojos, colino; **~lash** n pestaña;
  ~lid n párpado; **~liner** n lápiz m de
  ojos; **~-opener** n revelación f, gran
  sorpresa; **~shadow** n sombreador m de
  ojos; **~sight** n vista; **~sore** n
  monstruosidad f; **~ witness** n testigo
  m/f presencial

F, f

F [ɛf] n (MUS) fa m
F. abbr = **Fahrenheit**
fable ['feɪbl] n fábula
fabric ['fæbrɪk] n tejido, tela
fabulous ['fæbjuləs] adj fabuloso
façade [fə'sɑ:d] n fachada
face [feɪs] n (ANAT) cara, rostro; (of clock)
  esfera (SP), cara (AM); (of mountain) cara,
  ladera; (of building) fachada ♦ vt
  (direction) estar de cara a; (situation) hacer
  frente a; (facts) aceptar; **~ down** (person,
  card) boca abajo; **to lose ~**
  desprestigiarse; **to make** or **pull a ~** hacer
  muecas; **in the ~ of** (difficulties etc) ante;
  on the ~ of it a primera vista; **~ to ~** cara
  a cara; **~ up to** vt fus hacer frente a,

arrostrar; **~ cloth** (BRIT) n manopla; **~
cream** n crema (de belleza); **~ lift** n
estirado facial; (of building) renovación f;
~ powder n polvos mpl; **~-saving** adj
para salvar las apariencias; **~ value** n (of
stamp) valor m nominal; **to take sth at ~
value** (fig) tomar algo en sentido literal
facilities [fə'sɪlɪtɪz] npl (buildings)
  instalaciones fpl; (equipment) servicios
  mpl; **credit ~** facilidades fpl de crédito
facing ['feɪsɪŋ] prep frente a
facsimile [fæk'sɪmɪlɪ] n (replica) facsímil(e)
  m; (machine) telefax m; (fax) fax m
fact [fækt] n hecho; **in ~** en realidad
factor ['fæktə*] n factor m
factory ['fæktərɪ] n fábrica
factual ['fæktjuəl] adj basado en los
  hechos
faculty ['fækəltɪ] n facultad f; (US: teaching
  staff) personal m docente
fad [fæd] n novedad f, moda
fade [feɪd] vi desteñirse; (sound, smile)
  desvanecerse; (light) apagarse; (flower)
  marchitarse; (hope, memory) perderse
fag [fæg] (BRIT: inf) n (cigarette) pitillo (SP),
  cigarro
fail [feɪl] vt (candidate) suspender; (exam)
  no aprobar (SP), reprobar (AM); (subj:
  memory etc) fallar a ♦ vi suspender; (be
  unsuccessful) fracasar; (strength, brakes)
  fallar; (light) acabarse; **to ~ to do sth**
  (neglect) dejar de hacer algo; (be unable)
  no poder hacer algo; **without ~** sin falta;
  ~ing n falta, defecto ♦ prep a falta de;
  ~ure ['feɪljə*] n fracaso; (person)
  fracasado/a; (mechanical etc) fallo
faint [feɪnt] adj débil; (recollection) vago;
  (mark) apenas visible ♦ n desmayo ♦ vi
  desmayarse; **to feel ~** estar mareado,
  marearse
fair [feə*] adj justo; (hair, person) rubio;
  (weather) bueno; (good enough) regular;
  (considerable) considerable ♦ adv (play)
  limpio ♦ n feria; (BRIT: funfair) parque m
  de atracciones; **~ly** adv (justly) con
  justicia; (quite) bastante; **~ness** n justicia,
  imparcialidad f; **~ play** n juego limpio

fairy ['feərɪ] *n* hada; ~ **tale** *n* cuento de hadas

faith [feɪθ] *n* fe *f*; (*trust*) confianza; (*sect*) religión *f*; ~**ful** *adj* (*loyal: troops etc*) leal; (*spouse*) fiel; (*account*) exacto; ~**fully** *adv* fielmente; **yours** ~**fully** (*BRIT: in letters*) le saluda atentamente

fake [feɪk] *n* (*painting etc*) falsificación *f*; (*person*) impostor(a) *m/f* ♦ *adj* falso ♦ *vt* fingir; (*painting etc*) falsificar

falcon ['fɔːlkən] *n* halcón *m*

fall [fɔːl] (*pt* **fell**, *pp* **fallen**) *n* caída; (*in price etc*) descenso; (*US*) otoño ♦ *vi* caer(se); (*price*) bajar, descender; ~**s** *npl* (*water~*) cascada, salto de agua; **to** ~ **flat** (*on one's face*) caerse (boca abajo); (*plan*) fracasar; (*joke, story*) no hacer gracia; ~ **back** *vi* retroceder; ~ **back on** *vt fus* (*remedy etc*) recurrir a; ~ **behind** *vi* quedarse atrás; ~ **down** *vi* (*person*) caerse; (*building, hopes*) derrumbarse; ~ **for** *vt fus* (*trick*) dejarse engañar por; (*person*) enamorarse de; ~ **in** *vi* (*roof*) hundirse; (*MIL*) alinearse; ~ **off** *vi* caerse; (*diminish*) disminuir; ~ **out** *vi* (*friends etc*) reñir; (*hair, teeth*) caerse; ~ **through** *vi* (*plan, project*) fracasar

fallacy ['fæləsɪ] *n* error *m*

fallen ['fɔːlən] *pp of* **fall**

fallout ['fɔːlaut] *n* lluvia radioactiva

fallow ['fæləu] *adj* en barbecho

false [fɔːls] *adj* falso; **under** ~ **pretences** con engaños; ~ **alarm** *n* falsa alarma; ~ **teeth** (*BRIT*) *npl* dentadura postiza

falter ['fɔːltə*] *vi* vacilar; (*engine*) fallar

fame [feɪm] *n* fama

familiar [fə'mɪlɪə*] *adj* conocido, familiar; (*tone*) de confianza; **to be** ~ **with** (*subject*) conocer (bien)

family ['fæmɪlɪ] *n* familia; ~ **business** *n* negocio familiar; ~ **doctor** *n* médico/a de cabecera

famine ['fæmɪn] *n* hambre *f*, hambruna

famished ['fæmɪʃt] *adj* hambriento

famous ['feɪməs] *adj* famoso, célebre; ~**ly** *adv* (*get on*) estupendamente

fan [fæn] *n* abanico; (*ELEC*) ventilador *m*; (*of pop star*) fan *m/f*; (*SPORT*) hincha *m/f* ♦ *vt* abanicar; (*fire, quarrel*) atizar

fanatic [fə'nætɪk] *n* fanático/a

fan belt *n* correa del ventilador

fanciful ['fænsɪful] *adj* (*design, name*) fantástico

fancy ['fænsɪ] *n* (*whim*) capricho, antojo; (*imagination*) imaginación *f* ♦ *adj* (*luxury*) lujoso, de lujo ♦ *vt* (*feel like, want*) tener ganas de; (*imagine*) imaginarse; (*think*) creer; **to take a** ~ **to sb** tomar cariño a uno; **he fancies her** (*inf*) le gusta (ella) mucho; ~ **dress** *n* disfraz *m*; ~-**dress ball** *n* baile *m* de disfraces

fanfare ['fænfeə*] *n* fanfarria (de trompeta)

fang [fæŋ] *n* colmillo

fantastic [fæn'tæstɪk] *adj* (*enormous*) enorme; (*strange, wonderful*) fantástico

fantasy ['fæntəzɪ] *n* (*dream*) sueño; (*unreality*) fantasía

far [fɑː*] *adj* (*distant*) lejano ♦ *adv* lejos; (*much, greatly*) mucho; ~ **away**, ~ **off** (a lo) lejos; ~ **better** mucho mejor; ~ **from** lejos de; **by** ~ con mucho; **go as** ~ **as the farm** vaya hasta la granja; **as** ~ **as I know** que yo sepa; **how** ~? ¿hasta dónde?; (*fig*) ¿hasta qué punto?; ~**away** *adj* remoto; (*look*) distraído

farce [fɑːs] *n* farsa

fare [feə*] *n* (*on trains, buses*) precio (del billete); (*in taxi: cost*) tarifa; (*food*) comida; **half** ~ medio pasaje *m*; **full** ~ pasaje completo

Far East *n*: **the** ~ el Extremo Oriente

farewell [feə'wel] *excl, n* adiós *m*

farm [fɑːm] *n* granja (*SP*), finca (*AM*), estancia (*AM*) ♦ *vt* cultivar; ~**er** *n* granjero (*SP*), estanciero (*AM*); ~**hand** *n* peón *m*; ~**house** *n* granja, casa de hacienda (*AM*); ~**ing** *n* agricultura; (*of crops*) cultivo; (*of animals*) cría; ~**land** *n* tierra de cultivo; ~ **worker** *n* = ~**hand**; ~**yard** *n* corral *m*

far-reaching [fɑː'riːtʃɪŋ] *adj* (*reform, effect*) de gran alcance

fart [fɑːt] (*inf!*) *vi* tirarse un pedo (!)

farther ['fɑːðə*] *adv* más lejos, más allá

♦ *adj* más lejano

farthest ['fɑːðɪst] *superlative of* **far**

fascinate ['fæsɪneɪt] *vt* fascinar; **fascination** [-'neɪʃən] *n* fascinación *f*

fascism ['fæʃɪzəm] *n* fascismo

fashion ['fæʃən] *n* moda; (*~ industry*) industria de la moda; (*manner*) manera ♦ *vt* formar; **in ~** a la moda; **out of ~** pasado de moda; **~able** *adj* de moda; **~ show** *n* desfile *m* de modelos

fast [fɑːst] *adj* rápido; (*dye, colour*) resistente; (*clock*): **to be ~** estar adelantado ♦ *adv* rápidamente, de prisa; (*stuck, held*) firmemente ♦ *n* ayuno ♦ *vi* ayunar; **~ asleep** profundamente dormido

fasten ['fɑːsn] *vt* atar, sujetar; (*coat, belt*) abrochar ♦ *vi* atarse; abrocharse; **~er**, **~ing** *n* cierre *m*; (*of door etc*) cerrojo

fast food *n* comida rápida, platos *mpl* preparados

fastidious [fæs'tɪdɪəs] *adj* (*fussy*) quisquilloso

fat [fæt] *adj* gordo; (*book*) grueso; (*profit*) grande, pingüe ♦ *n* grasa; (*on person*) carnes *fpl*; (*lard*) manteca

fatal ['feɪtl] *adj* (*mistake*) fatal; (*injury*) mortal; **~ity** [fə'tælɪtɪ] *n* (*road death etc*) víctima; **~ly** *adv* fatalmente; mortalmente

fate [feɪt] *n* destino; (*of person*) suerte *f*; **~ful** *adj* fatídico

father ['fɑːðə*] *n* padre *m*; **~-in-law** *n* suegro; **~ly** *adj* paternal

fathom ['fæðəm] *n* braza ♦ *vt* (*mystery*) desentrañar; (*understand*) lograr comprender

fatigue [fə'tiːg] *n* fatiga, cansancio

fatten ['fætn] *vt, vi* engordar

fatty ['fætɪ] *adj* (*food*) graso ♦ *n* (*inf*) gordito/a, gordinflón/ona *m/f*

fatuous ['fætjuəs] *adj* fatuo, necio

faucet ['fɔːsɪt] (*US*) *n* grifo (*SP*), llave *f* (*AM*)

fault [fɔːlt] *n* (*blame*) culpa; (*defect: in person, machine*) defecto; (*GEO*) falla ♦ *vt* criticar; **it's my ~** es culpa mía; **to find ~ with** criticar, poner peros a; **at ~** culpable; **~y** *adj* defectuoso

fauna ['fɔːnə] *n* fauna

favour ['feɪvə*] (*US* **favor**) *n* favor *m*; (*approval*) aprobación *f* ♦ *vt* (*proposition*) estar a favor de, aprobar; (*assist*) ser propicio a; **to do sb a ~** hacer un favor a uno; **to find ~ with sb** caer en gracia a uno; **in ~ of** a favor de; **~able** *adj* favorable; **~ite** ['feɪvrɪt] *adj, n* favorito, preferido

fawn [fɔːn] *n* cervato ♦ *adj* (*also*: **~-coloured**) color de cervato, leonado ♦ *vi*: **to ~ (up)on** adular

fax [fæks] *n* (*document*) fax *m*; (*machine*) telefax *m* ♦ *vt* mandar por telefax

FBI (*US*) *n abbr* (= *Federal Bureau of Investigation*) ≈ BIC *f* (*SP*)

fear [fɪə*] *n* miedo, temor *m* ♦ *vt* tener miedo de, temer; **for ~ of** por si; **~ful** *adj* temeroso, miedoso; (*awful*) terrible; **~less** *adj* audaz

feasible ['fiːzəbl] *adj* factible

feast [fiːst] *n* banquete *m*; (*REL: also*: **~ day**) fiesta ♦ *vi* festejar

feat [fiːt] *n* hazaña

feather ['feðə*] *n* pluma

feature ['fiːtʃə*] *n* característica; (*article*) artículo de fondo ♦ *vt* (*subj: film*) presentar ♦ *vi*: **to ~ in** tener un papel destacado en; **~s** *npl* (*of face*) facciones *fpl*; **~ film** *n* largometraje *m*

February ['februərɪ] *n* febrero

fed [fed] *pt, pp of* **feed**

federal ['fedərəl] *adj* federal

fed up [fed'ʌp] *adj*: **to be ~ (with)** estar harto (de)

fee [fiː] *n* pago; (*professional*) derechos *mpl*, honorarios *mpl*; (*of club*) cuota; **school ~s** matrícula

feeble ['fiːbl] *adj* débil; (*joke*) flojo

feed [fiːd] (*pt, pp* **fed**) *n* comida; (*of animal*) pienso; (*on printer*) dispositivo de alimentación ♦ *vt* alimentar; (*BRIT: baby: breast~*) dar el pecho a; (*animal*) dar de comer a; (*data, information*): **to ~ into** meter en; **~ on** *vt fus* alimentarse de; **~back** *n* reacción *f*, feedback *m*

feel [fiːl] (*pt, pp* **felt**) *n* (*sensation*)

sensación f; (*sense of touch*) tacto; (*impression*) **to have the ~ of** parecerse a ♦ *vt* tocar; (*pain etc*) sentir; (*think, believe*) creer; **to ~ hungry/cold** tener hambre/frío; **to ~ lonely/better** sentirse solo/mejor; **I don't ~ well** no me siento bien; **it ~s soft** es suave al tacto; **to ~ like** (*want*) tener ganas de; **~ about** *or* **around** *vi* tantear; **~er** *n* (*of insect*) antena; **~ing** *n* (*physical*) sensación f; (*foreboding*) presentimiento; (*emotion*) sentimiento

feet [fiːt] *npl of* **foot**

feign [feɪn] *vt* fingir

fell [fel] *pt of* **fall** ♦ *vt* (*tree*) talar

fellow ['feləu] *n* tipo, tío (*SP*); (*comrade*) compañero; (*of learned society*) socio/a ♦ *cpd*: **~ citizen** *n* conciudadano/a; **~ countryman** (*irreg*) *n* compatriota *m*; **~ men** *npl* semejantes *mpl*; **~ship** *n* compañerismo; (*grant*) beca

felony ['feiəni] *n* crimen *m*

felt [felt] *pt, pp of* **feel** ♦ *n* fieltro; **~-tip pen** *n* rotulador *m*

female ['fiːmeil] *n* (*pej: woman*) mujer f, tía; (*ZOOL*) hembra ♦ *adj* femenino; hembra

feminine ['feminin] *adj* femenino

feminist ['feminist] *n* feminista

fence [fens] *n* valla, cerca ♦ *vt* (*also*: **~ in**) cercar ♦ *vi* (*SPORT*) hacer esgrima; **fencing** *n* esgrima

fend [fend] *vi*: **to ~ for o.s.** valerse por sí mismo; **~ off** *vt* (*attack*) rechazar; (*questions*) evadir

fender ['fendə*] *n* guardafuego; (*US: AUT*) parachoques *m inv*

ferment [*vb* fə'ment, *n* 'fəːment] *vi* fermentar ♦ *n* (*fig*) agitación f

fern [fəːn] *n* helecho

ferocious [fə'rəuʃəs] *adj* feroz

ferret ['ferit] *n* hurón *m*

ferry ['feri] *n* (*small*) barca (de pasaje), balsa; (*large: also*: **~boat**) transbordador *m* (*SP*), embarcadero (*AM*) ♦ *vt* transportar

fertile ['fəːtail] *adj* fértil; (*BIOL*) fecundo;

fertilize ['fəːtilaiz] *vt* (*BIOL*) fecundar; (*AGR*) abonar; **fertilizer** *n* abono

fester ['festə*] *vi* ulcerarse

festival ['festivəl] *n* (*REL*) fiesta; (*ART, MUS*) festival *m*

festive ['festiv] *adj* festivo; **the ~ season** (*BRIT: Christmas*) las Navidades

festivities [fes'tivitiz] *npl* fiestas *fpl*

festoon [fes'tuːn] *vt*: **to ~ with** engalanar de

fetch [fetʃ] *vt* ir a buscar; (*sell for*) venderse por

fête [feit] *n* fiesta

fetus ['fiːtəs] (*US*) *n* = **foetus**

feud [fjuːd] *n* (*hostility*) enemistad f; (*quarrel*) disputa

fever ['fiːvə*] *n* fiebre f; **~ish** *adj* febril

few [fjuː] *adj* (*not many*) pocos ♦ *pron* pocos; algunos; **a ~** *adj* unos pocos, algunos; **~er** *adj* menos; **~est** *adj* los/las menos

fiancé [fi'ɑːŋsei] *n* novio, prometido; **~e** *n* novia, prometida

fib [fib] *n* mentirilla

fibre ['faibə*] (*US* **fiber**) *n* fibra; **~glass** (**Fiberglass** ® *US*) *n* fibra de vidrio

fickle ['fikl] *adj* inconstante

fiction ['fikʃən] *n* ficción f; **~al** *adj* novelesco; **fictitious** [fik'tiʃəs] *adj* ficticio

fiddle ['fidl] *n* (*MUS*) violín *m*; (*cheating*) trampa ♦ *vt* (*BRIT: accounts*) falsificar; **~ with** *vt fus* juguetear con

fidget ['fidʒit] *vi* enredar; **stop ~ing!** ¡estáte quieto!

field [fiːld] *n* campo; (*fig*) campo, esfera; (*SPORT*) campo, cancha (*AM*); **~ marshal** *n* mariscal *m*; **~work** *n* trabajo de campo

fiend [fiːnd] *n* demonio

fierce [fiəs] *adj* feroz; (*wind, heat*) fuerte; (*fighting, enemy*) encarnizado

fiery ['faiəri] *adj* (*burning*) ardiente; (*temperament*) apasionado

fifteen [fif'tiːn] *num* quince

fifth [fifθ] *num* quinto

fifty ['fifti] *num* cincuenta; **~-~** *adj* (*deal, split*) a medias ♦ *adv* a medias, mitad por mitad

fig [fɪg] n higo

fight [faɪt] (pt, pp **fought**) n (gen) pelea; (MIL) combate m; (struggle) lucha ♦ vt luchar contra; (cancer, alcoholism) combatir; (election) intentar ganar; (emotion) resistir ♦ vi pelear, luchar; ~er n combatiente m/f; (plane) caza m; ~ing n combate m, pelea

figment ['fɪgmənt] n: **a ~ of the imagination** una quimera

figurative ['fɪgjurətɪv] adj (meaning) figurado; (style) figurativo

figure ['fɪgə*] n (DRAWING, GEOM) figura, dibujo; (number, cipher) cifra; (body, outline) tipo; (personality) figura ♦ vt (esp US) imaginar ♦ vi (appear) figurar; ~ **out** vt (work out) resolver; ~**head** n (NAUT) mascarón m de proa; (pej: leader) figura decorativa; ~ **of speech** n figura retórica

file [faɪl] n (tool) lima; (dossier) expediente m; (folder) carpeta; (COMPUT) fichero; (row) fila ♦ vt limar; (LAW: claim) presentar; (store) archivar; ~ **in/out** vi entrar/salir en fila; **filing cabinet** n fichero, archivador m

fill [fɪl] vt (space): **to ~ (with)** llenar (de); (vacancy, need) cubrir ♦ n: **to eat one's ~** llenarse; ~ **in** vt rellenar; ~ **up** vt llenar (hasta el borde) ♦ vi (AUT) poner gasolina

fillet ['fɪlɪt] n filete m; ~ **steak** n filete m de ternera

filling ['fɪlɪŋ] n (CULIN) relleno; (for tooth) empaste m; ~ **station** n estación f de servicio

film [fɪlm] n película ♦ vt (scene) filmar ♦ vi rodar (una película); ~ **star** n astro, estrella de cine

filter ['fɪltə*] n filtro ♦ vt filtrar; ~ **lane** (BRIT) n carril m de selección; ~-**tipped** adj con filtro

filth [fɪlθ] n suciedad f; ~**y** adj sucio; (language) obsceno

fin [fɪn] n (gen) aleta

final ['faɪnl] adj (last) final, último; (definitive) definitivo, terminante ♦ n (BRIT: SPORT) final f; ~**s** npl (SCOL) examen m

final; (US: SPORT) final f

finale [fɪ'nɑ:lɪ] n final m

final: ~**ist** n (SPORT) finalista m/f; ~**ize** vt concluir, completar; ~**ly** adv (lastly) por último, finalmente; (eventually) por fin

finance [faɪ'næns] n (money) fondos mpl; ~**s** npl finanzas fpl; (personal ~s) situación f económica ♦ vt financiar; **financial** [-'nænʃəl] adj financiero

find [faɪnd] (pt, pp **found**) vt encontrar, hallar; (come upon) descubrir ♦ n hallazgo; descubrimiento; **to ~ sb guilty** (LAW) declarar culpable a uno; ~ **out** vt averiguar; (truth, secret) descubrir; **to ~ out about** (subject) informarse sobre; (by chance) enterarse de; ~**ings** npl (LAW) veredicto, fallo; (of report) recomendaciones fpl

fine [faɪn] adj excelente; (thin) fino ♦ adv (well) bien ♦ n (LAW) multa ♦ vt (LAW) multar; **to be ~** (person) estar bien; (weather) hacer buen tiempo; ~ **arts** npl bellas artes fpl

finery ['faɪnərɪ] n adornos mpl

finger ['fɪŋgə*] n dedo ♦ vt (touch) manosear; **little/index ~** (dedo) meñique m/índice m; ~**nail** n uña; ~**print** n huella dactilar; ~**tip** n yema del dedo

finish ['fɪnɪʃ] n (end) fin m; (SPORT) meta; (polish etc) acabado ♦ vt, vi terminar; **to ~ doing sth** acabar de hacer algo; **to ~ third** llegar el tercero; ~ **off** vt acabar, terminar; (kill) acabar con; ~ **up** vt acabar, terminar ♦ vi ir a parar, terminar; ~**ing line** n línea de llegada or meta

finite ['faɪnaɪt] adj finito; (verb) conjugado

Finland ['fɪnlənd] n Finlandia

Finn [fɪn] n finlandés/esa m/f; ~**ish** adj finlandés/esa ♦ n (LING) finlandés m

fir [fə:*] n abeto

fire ['faɪə*] n fuego; (in hearth) lumbre f; (accidental) incendio; (heater) estufa ♦ vt (gun) disparar; (interest) despertar; (inf: dismiss) despedir ♦ vi (shoot) disparar; **on ~** ardiendo, en llamas; ~ **alarm** n alarma de incendios; ~**arm** n arma de fuego; ~ **brigade** (US ~ **department**) n (cuerpo de) bomberos *mpl*; ~ **engine** *n* coche *m* de bomberos; ~ **escape** *n* escalera de incendios; ~ **extinguisher** *n* extintor *m* (de incendios); ~**guard** *n* rejilla de protección; ~**man** (*irreg*) *n* bombero; ~**place** *n* chimenea; ~**side** *n*: **by the ~side** al lado de la chimenea; ~ **station** *n* parque *m* de bomberos; ~**wood** *n* leña; ~**works** *npl* fuegos *mpl* artificiales

firing squad ['faɪrɪŋ-] *n* pelotón *m* de ejecución

firm [fəːm] *adj* firme; (*look, voice*) resuelto ♦ *n* firma, empresa; ~**ly** *adv* firmemente; resueltamente

first [fəːst] *adj* primero ♦ *adv* (*before others*) primero; (*when listing reasons etc*) en primer lugar, primeramente ♦ *n* (*person: in race*) primero/a; (*AUT*) primera; (*BRIT: SCOL*) título de licenciado con calificación de sobresaliente; **at** ~ al principio; ~ **of all** ante todo; ~ **aid** *n* primera ayuda, primeros auxilios *mpl*; ~-**aid kit** *n* botiquín *m*; ~-**class** *adj* (*excellent*) de primera (categoría); (*ticket etc*) de primera clase; ~-**hand** *adj* de primera mano; F~ **Lady** (*esp US*) *n* primera dama; ~**ly** *adv* en primer lugar; ~ **name** *n* nombre *m* (de pila); ~-**rate** *adj* estupendo

fish [fɪʃ] *n inv* pez *m*; (*food*) pescado ♦ *vt*, *vi* pescar; **to go ~ing** ir de pesca; ~**erman** (*irreg*) *n* pescador *m*; ~ **farm** *n* criadero de peces; ~ **fingers** (*BRIT*) *npl* croquetas *fpl* de pescado; ~**ing boat** *n* barca de pesca; ~**ing line** *n* sedal *m*; ~**ing rod** *n* caña (de pescar); ~**monger's (shop)** (*BRIT*) *n* pescadería; ~ **sticks** (*US*) *npl* = ~ **fingers**; ~**y** (*inf*) *adj* sospechoso

fist [fɪst] *n* puño

fit [fɪt] *adj* (*healthy*) en (buena) forma; (*proper*) adecuado, apropiado ♦ *vt* (*subj: clothes*) estar *or* sentar bien a; (*instal*) poner; (*equip*) proveer, dotar; (*facts*) cuadrar *or* corresponder con ♦ *vi* (*clothes*) sentar bien; (*in space, gap*) caber; (*facts*) coincidir ♦ *n* (*MED*) ataque *m*; ~ **to** (*ready*)

a punto de; ~ **for** apropiado para; **a ~ of anger/pride** un arranque de cólera/orgullo; **this dress is a good ~** este vestido me sienta bien; **by ~s and starts** a rachas; ~ **in** *vi* (*fig: person*) llevarse bien (con todos); ~**ful** *adj* espasmódico, intermitente; ~**ment** *n* módulo adosable; ~**ness** *n* (*MED*) salud *f*; ~**ted carpet** *n* moqueta; ~**ted kitchen** *n* cocina amueblada; ~**ter** *n* ajustador *m*; ~**ting** *adj* apropiado ♦ *n* (*of dress*) prueba; (*of piece of equipment*) instalación *f*; ~**ting room** *n* probador *m*; ~**tings** *npl* instalaciones *fpl*

five [faɪv] *num* cinco; ~**r** (*inf*) *n* (*BRIT*) billete *m* de cinco libras; (*US*) billete *m* de cinco dólares

fix [fɪks] *vt* (*secure*) fijar, asegurar; (*mend*) arreglar; (*prepare*) preparar ♦ *n*: **to be in a ~** estar en un aprieto; ~ **up** *vt* (*meeting*) arreglar; **to ~ sb up with sth** proveer a uno de algo; ~**ation** [fɪk'seɪʃən] *n* obsesión *f*; ~**ed** *adj* (*prices etc*) fijo; ~**ture** *n* (*SPORT*) encuentro; ~**tures** *npl* (*cupboards etc*) instalaciones *fpl* fijas

fizzy ['fɪzɪ] *adj* (*drink*) gaseoso

fjord [fjɔːd] *n* fiordo

flabbergasted ['flæbəgɑːstɪd] *adj* pasmado, alucinado

flabby ['flæbɪ] *adj* gordo

flag [flæg] *n* bandera; (*stone*) losa ♦ *vi* decaer; **to ~ sb down** hacer señas a uno para que se pare; ~**pole** *n* asta de bandera; ~**ship** *n* buque *m* insignia; (*fig*) bandera

flair [fleə*] *n* aptitud *f* especial

flak [flæk] *n* (*MIL*) fuego antiaéreo; (*inf: criticism*) lluvia de críticas

flake [fleɪk] *n* (*of rust, paint*) escama; (*of snow, soap powder*) copo ♦ *vi* (*also: ~ off*) desconcharse

flamboyant [flæm'bɔɪənt] *adj* (*dress*) vistoso; (*person*) extravagante

flame [fleɪm] *n* llama

flamingo [flə'mɪŋɡəu] *n* flamenco

flammable ['flæməbl] *adj* inflamable

flan [flæn] (*BRIT*) *n* tarta

flank [flæŋk] n (of animal) ijar m; (of army) flanco ♦ vt flanquear

flannel ['flænl] n (BRIT: also: **face ~**) manopla; (fabric) franela

flap [flæp] n (of pocket, envelope) solapa ♦ vt (wings, arms) agitar ♦ vi (sail, flag) ondear

flare [flɛə*] n llamarada; (MIL) bengala; (in skirt etc) vuelo; **~ up** vi encenderse; (fig: person) encolerizarse; (: revolt) estallar

flash [flæʃ] n relámpago; (also: **news ~**) noticias fpl de última hora; (PHOT) flash m ♦ vt (light, headlights) lanzar un destello con; (news, message) transmitir; (smile) lanzar ♦ vi brillar; (hazard light etc) lanzar destellos; **in a ~** en un instante; **he ~ed by** or **past** pasó como un rayo; **~back** n (CINEMA) flashback m; **~bulb** n bombilla fusible; **~ cube** n cubo de flash; **~light** n linterna

flashy ['flæʃɪ] (pej) adj ostentoso

flask [flɑːsk] n frasco; (also: **vacuum ~**) termo

flat [flæt] adj llano; (smooth) liso; (tyre) desinflado; (battery) descargado; (beer) muerto; (refusal etc) rotundo; (MUS) desafinado; (rate) fijo ♦ n (BRIT: apartment) piso (SP), departamento (AM); (AUT) pinchazo; (MUS) bemol m; **to work ~ out** trabajar a toda mecha; **~ly** adv terminantemente, de plano; **~ten** vt (also: **~ten out**) allanar; (smooth out) alisar; (building, plants) arrasar

flatter ['flætə*] vt adular, halagar; **~ing** adj halagüeño; (dress) que favorece; **~y** n adulación f

flaunt [flɔːnt] vt ostentar, lucir

flavour ['fleɪvə*] (US **flavor**) n sabor m, gusto ♦ vt sazonar, condimentar; **strawberry-~ed** con sabor a fresa; **~ing** n (in product) aromatizante m

flaw [flɔː] n defecto; **~less** adj impecable

flax [flæks] n lino

flea [fliː] n pulga

fleck [flɛk] n (mark) mota

flee [fliː] (pt, pp **fled**) vt huir de ♦ vi huir, fugarse

fleece [fliːs] n vellón m; (wool) lana ♦ vt (inf) desplumar

fleet [fliːt] n flota; (of lorries etc) escuadra

fleeting ['fliːtɪŋ] adj fugaz

Flemish ['flɛmɪʃ] adj flamenco

flesh [flɛʃ] n carne f; (skin) piel f; (of fruit) pulpa; **~ wound** n herida superficial

flew [fluː] pt of **fly**

flex [flɛks] n cordón m ♦ vt (muscles) tensar; **~ible** adj flexible

flick [flɪk] n capirotazo; chasquido ♦ vt (with hand) dar un capirotazo a; (whip etc) chasquear; (switch) accionar; **~ through** vt fus hojear

flicker ['flɪkə*] vi (light) parpadear; (flame) vacilar

flier ['flaɪə*] n aviador(a) m/f

flight [flaɪt] n vuelo; (escape) huida, fuga; (also: **~ of steps**) tramo (de escaleras); **~ attendant** (US) n camarero/azafata; **~ deck** n (AVIAT) cabina de mandos; (NAUT) cubierta de aterrizaje

flimsy ['flɪmzɪ] adj (thin) muy ligero; (building) endeble; (excuse) flojo

flinch [flɪntʃ] vi encogerse; **to ~ from** retroceder ante

fling [flɪŋ] (pt, pp **flung**) vt arrojar

flint [flɪnt] n pedernal m; (in lighter) piedra

flip [flɪp] vt dar la vuelta a; (switch: turn on) encender; (: turn off) apagar; (coin) echar a cara o cruz

flippant ['flɪpənt] adj poco serio

flipper ['flɪpə*] n aleta

flirt [flɜːt] vi coquetear, flirtear ♦ n coqueta

float [fləʊt] n flotador m; (in procession) carroza; (money) reserva ♦ vi flotar; (swimmer) hacer la plancha

flock [flɒk] n (of sheep) rebaño; (of birds) bandada ♦ vi: **to ~ to** acudir en tropel a

flog [flɒg] vt azotar

flood [flʌd] n inundación f; (of letters, imports etc) avalancha ♦ vt inundar ♦ vi (place) inundarse; (people): **to ~ into** inundar; **~ing** n inundaciones fpl; **~light** n foco

floor [flɔː*] n suelo; (storey) piso; (of sea)

fondo ♦ vt (subj: question) dejar sin respuesta; (: blow) derribar; **ground ~, first ~** (US) planta baja; **first ~, second ~** (US) primer piso; ~**board** n tabla; ~ **show** n cabaret m

flop [flɔp] n fracaso ♦ vi (fail) fracasar; (fall) derrumbarse; ~**py** adj flojo ♦ n (COMPUT: also: ~**py disk**) floppy m

flora ['flɔ:rə] n flora

floral ['flɔ:rl] adj (pattern) floreado

florid ['flɔrɪd] adj florido; (complexion) rubicundo

florist ['flɔrɪst] n florista m/f; ~'**s (shop)** n florería

flounder ['flaundə*] vi (swimmer) patalear; (fig: economy) estar en dificultades ♦ n (ZOOL) platija

flour ['flauə*] n harina

flourish ['flʌrɪʃ] vi florecer ♦ n ademán m, movimiento (ostentoso)

flout [flaut] vt burlarse de

flow [fləu] n (movement) flujo; (of traffic) circulación f; (tide) corriente f ♦ vi (river, blood) fluir; (traffic) circular; ~ **chart** n organigrama m

flower ['flauə*] n flor f ♦ vi florecer; ~ **bed** n macizo; ~**pot** n tiesto; ~**y** adj (fragrance) floral; (pattern) floreado; (speech) florido

flown [fləun] pp of fly

flu [flu:] n: **to have** ~ tener la gripe

fluctuate ['flʌktjueɪt] vi fluctuar

fluent ['flu:ənt] adj (linguist) que habla perfectamente; (speech) elocuente; **he speaks ~ French, he's ~ in French** domina el francés; ~**ly** adv con fluidez

fluff [flʌf] n pelusa; ~**y** adj de pelo suave

fluid ['flu:ɪd] adj (movement) fluido, líquido; (situation) inestable ♦ n fluido, líquido

fluke [flu:k] (inf) n chiripa

flung [flʌŋ] pt, pp of fling

fluoride ['fluəraɪd] n fluoruro

flurry ['flʌrɪ] n (of snow) temporal m; ~ **of activity** frenesí m de actividad

flush [flʌʃ] n rubor m; (fig: of youth etc) resplandor m ♦ vt limpiar con agua ♦ vi ruborizarse ♦ adj: ~ **with** a ras de; **to ~ the toilet** hacer funcionar la cisterna; ~**ed** adj ruborizado

flustered ['flʌstəd] adj aturdido

flute [flu:t] n flauta

flutter ['flʌtə*] n (of wings) revoloteo, aleteo; **a ~ of panic/excitement** una oleada de pánico/excitación ♦ vi revolotear

flux [flʌks] n: **to be in a state of ~** estar continuamente cambiando

fly [flaɪ] (pt **flew**, pp **flown**) n mosca; (on trousers: also: **flies**) bragueta ♦ vt (plane) pilot(e)ar; (cargo) transportar (en avión); (distances) recorrer (en avión) ♦ vi volar; (passengers) ir en avión; (escape) evadirse; (flag) ondear; ~ **away or off** vi emprender el vuelo; ~-**drive** n: ~-**drive holiday** vacaciones que incluyen vuelo y alquiler de coche; ~**ing** n (activity) (el) volar; (action) vuelo ♦ adj: ~**ing visit** visita relámpago; **with ~ing colours** con lucimiento; ~**ing saucer** n platillo volante; ~**ing start** n: **to get off to a** ~**ing start** empezar con buen pie; ~**over** (BRIT) n paso a desnivel or superior; ~**sheet** n (for tent) doble techo

foal [fəul] n potro

foam [fəum] n espuma ♦ vi hacer espuma; ~ **rubber** n goma espuma

fob [fɔb] vt: **to ~ sb off with sth** despachar a uno con algo

focal point ['fəukl-] n (fig) centro de atención

focus ['fəukəs] (pl ~**es**) n foco; (centre) centro ♦ vt (field glasses etc) enfocar ♦ vi: **to ~ (on)** enfocar (a); (issue etc) centrarse en; **in/out of ~** enfocado/desenfocado

fodder ['fɔdə*] n pienso

foetus ['fi:təs] (US **fetus**) n feto

fog [fɔg] n niebla; ~**gy** adj: **it's ~gy** hay niebla, está brumoso; ~ **lamp** (US ~ **light**) n (AUT) faro de niebla

foil [fɔɪl] vt frustrar ♦ n hoja; (kitchen ~) papel m (de) aluminio; (complement) complemento; (FENCING) florete m

fold [fəuld] n (bend, crease) pliegue m;

(*AGR*) redil *m* ♦ *vt* doblar; (*arms*) cruzar; ~ **up** *vi* plegarse, doblarse; (*business*) quebrar ♦ *vt* (*map etc*) plegar; ~**er** *n* (*for papers*) carpeta; (*COMPUT*) directorio; ~**ing** *adj* plegable

foliage ['fəulɪdʒ] *n* follaje *m*

folk [fəuk] *npl* gente *f* ♦ *adj* popular, folklórico; ~**s** *npl* (*family*) familia *sg*, parientes *mpl*; ~**lore** ['fəuklɔ:*] *n* folklore *m*; ~ **song** *n* canción *f* popular *or* folklórica

follow ['fɔləu] *vt* seguir ♦ *vi* seguir; (*result*) resultar; **to ~ suit** hacer lo mismo; ~ **up** *vt* (*letter, offer*) responder a; (*case*) investigar; ~**er** *n* (*of person, belief*) partidario/a; ~**ing** *adj* siguiente ♦ *n* afición *f*, partidarios *mpl*

folly ['fɔlɪ] *n* locura

fond [fɔnd] *adj* (*memory, smile etc*) cariñoso; (*hopes*) ilusorio; **to be ~ of** tener cariño a; (*pastime, food*) ser aficionado a

fondle ['fɔndl] *vt* acariciar

font [fɔnt] *n* pila bautismal; (*TYP*) fundición *f*

food [fu:d] *n* comida; ~ **mixer** *n* batidora; ~ **poisoning** *n* intoxicación *f* alimenticia; ~ **processor** *n* robot *m* de cocina; ~**stuffs** *npl* comestibles *mpl*

fool [fu:l] *n* tonto/a; (*CULIN*) puré *m* de frutas con nata ♦ *vt* engañar ♦ *vi* (*gen*: ~ **around**) bromear; ~**hardy** *adj* temerario; ~**ish** *adj* tonto; (*careless*) imprudente; ~**proof** *adj* (*plan etc*) infalible

foot [fut] (*pl* **feet**) *n* pie *m*; (*measure*) pie *m* (= 304 *mm*); (*of animal*) pata ♦ *vt* (*bill*) pagar; **on** ~ a pie; ~**age** *n* (*CINEMA*) imágenes *fpl*; ~**ball** *n* balón *m*; (*game: BRIT*) fútbol *m*; (: *US*) fútbol *m* americano; ~**ball player** *n* (*BRIT*: *also*: ~**baller**) futbolista *m*; (*US*) jugador *m* de fútbol americano; ~**brake** *n* freno de pie; ~**bridge** *n* puente *m* para peatones; ~**hills** *npl* estribaciones *fpl*; ~**hold** *n* pie *m* firme; ~**ing** *n* (*fig*) posición *f*; **to lose one's ~ing** perder el pie; ~**lights** *npl* candilejas *fpl*; ~**note** *n* nota (al pie de la página); ~**path** *n* sendero; ~**print** *n*

huella, pisada; ~**step** *n* paso; ~**wear** *n* calzado

| KEYWORD |

for [fɔ:] *prep* **1** (*indicating destination, intention*) para; **the train ~ London** el tren con destino a *or* de Londres; **he left ~ Rome** marchó para Roma; **he went ~ the paper** fue por el periódico; **is this ~ me?** ¿es esto para mí?; **it's time ~ lunch** es la hora de comer

2 (*indicating purpose*) para; **what('s it) ~?** ¿para qué (es)?; **to pray ~ peace** rezar por la paz

3 (*on behalf of, representing*): **the MP ~ Hove** el diputado por Hove; **he works ~ the government/a local firm** trabaja para el gobierno/en una empresa local; **I'll ask him ~ you** se lo pediré por ti; **G ~ George** G de Gerona

4 (*because of*) por esta razón; ~ **fear of being criticized** por temor a ser criticado

5 (*with regard to*) para; **it's cold ~ July** hace frío para julio; **he has a gift ~ languages** tiene don de lenguas

6 (*in exchange for*) por; **I sold it ~ £5** lo vendí por £5; **to pay 50 pence ~ a ticket** pagar 50 peniques por un billete

7 (*in favour of*): **are you ~ or against us?** ¿estás con nosotros o contra nosotros?; **I'm all ~ it** estoy totalmente a favor; **vote ~ X** vote (a) X

8 (*referring to distance*): **there are roadworks ~ 5 km** hay obras en 5 km; **we walked ~ miles** caminamos kilómetros y kilómetros

9 (*referring to time*): **he was away ~ 2 years** estuvo fuera (durante) dos años; **it hasn't rained ~ 3 weeks** no ha llovido durante *or* en 3 semanas; **I have known her ~ years** la conozco desde hace años; **can you do it ~ tomorrow?** ¿lo podrás hacer para mañana?

10 (*with infinitive clauses*): **it is not ~ me to decide** la decisión no es cosa mía; **it would be best ~ you to leave** sería mejor que te fueras; **there is still time ~**

you to do it todavía te queda tiempo para hacerlo; **~ this to be possible ...** para que esto sea posible ...
11 (*in spite of*) a pesar de; **~ all his complaints** a pesar de sus quejas
♦ *conj* (*since, as: rather formal*) puesto que

orage ['fɔrɪdʒ] *vi* (*animal*) forrajear; (*person*): **to ~ for** hurgar en busca de

oray ['fɔreɪ] *n* incursión *f*

orbid [fə'bɪd] (*pt* **forbad(e)**, *pp* **forbidden**) *vt* prohibir; **to ~ sb to do sth** prohibir a uno hacer algo; **~ding** *adj* amenazador(a)

orce [fɔːs] *n* fuerza ♦ *vt* forzar; (*push*) meter a la fuerza; **to ~ o.s. to do** hacer un esfuerzo por hacer; **the F~s** *npl* (*BRIT*) las Fuerzas Armadas; **in ~** en vigor; **~d** [fɔːst] *adj* forzado; **~-feed** *vt* alimentar a la fuerza; **~ful** *adj* enérgico

orcibly ['fɔːsəblɪ] *adv* a la fuerza; (*speak*) enérgicamente

ord [fɔːd] *n* vado

ore [fɔː'] *n*: **to come to the ~** empezar a destacar

ore: **~arm** *n* antebrazo; **~boding** *n* presentimiento; **~cast** *n* pronóstico ♦ *vt* (*irreg: like* **cast**) pronosticar; **~court** *n* patio; **~finger** *n* (dedo) índice *m*; **~front** *n*: **in the ~front of** en la vanguardia de

orego *vt* = **forgo**

oregone ['fɔːgɔn] *pp of* **forego** ♦ *adj*: **it's a ~ conclusion** es una conclusión evidente

oreground ['fɔːgraund] *n* primer plano

orehead ['fɔrɪd] *n* frente *f*

oreign ['fɔrɪn] *adj* extranjero; (*trade*) exterior; (*object*) extraño; **~er** *n* extranjero/a; **~ exchange** *n* divisas *fpl*; **F~ Office** (*BRIT*) *n* Ministerio de Asuntos Exteriores; **F~ Secretary** (*BRIT*) *n* Ministro de Asuntos Exteriores

ore: **~leg** *n* pata delantera; **~man** (*irreg*) *n* capataz *m*; (*in construction*) maestro de obras; **~most** *adj* principal ♦ *adv*: **first**

and ~most ante todo

forensic [fə'rensɪk] *adj* forense

fore: **~runner** *n* precursor(a) *m/f*; **~see** (*pt* **foresaw**, *pp* **foreseen**) *vt* prever; **~seeable** *adj* previsible; **~shadow** *vt* prefigurar, anunciar; **~sight** *n* previsión *f*

forest ['fɔrɪst] *n* bosque *m*

forestry ['fɔrɪstrɪ] *n* silvicultura

foretaste ['fɔːteɪst] *n* muestra

foretell [fɔː'tel] (*pt, pp* **foretold**) *vt* predecir, pronosticar

forever [fə'revə'] *adv* para siempre; (*endlessly*) constantemente

foreword ['fɔːwəːd] *n* prefacio

forfeit ['fɔːfɪt] *vt* perder

forgave [fə'geɪv] *pt of* **forgive**

forge [fɔːdʒ] *n* herrería ♦ *vt* (*signature, money*) falsificar; (*metal*) forjar; **~ ahead** *vi* avanzar mucho; **~ry** *n* falsificación *f*

forget [fə'get] (*pt* **forgot**, *pp* **forgotten**) *vt* olvidar ♦ *vi* olvidarse; **~ful** *adj* despistado; **~-me-not** *n* nomeolvides *f inv*

forgive [fə'gɪv] (*pt* **forgave**, *pp* **forgiven**) *vt* perdonar; **to ~ sb for sth** perdonar algo a uno; **~ness** *n* perdón *m*

forgo [fɔː'gəu] (*pt* **forwent**, *pp* **forgone**) *vt* (*give up*) renunciar a; (*go without*) privarse de

forgot [fə'gɔt] *pt of* **forget**

forgotten [fə'gɔtn] *pp of* **forget**

fork [fɔːk] *n* (*for eating*) tenedor *m*; (*for gardening*) horca; (*of roads*) bifurcación *f* ♦ *vi* (*road*) bifurcarse; **~ out** (*inf*) *vt* (*pay*) desembolsar; **~-lift truck** *n* máquina elevadora

forlorn [fə'lɔːn] *adj* (*person*) triste, melancólico; (*place*) abandonado; (*attempt, hope*) desesperado

form [fɔːm] *n* forma; (*BRIT: SCOL*) clase *f*; (*document*) formulario ♦ *vt* formar; (*idea*) concebir; (*habit*) adquirir; **in top ~** en plena forma; **to ~ a queue** hacer cola

formal ['fɔːməl] *adj* (*offer, receipt*) por escrito; (*person etc*) correcto; (*occasion, dinner*) de etiqueta; (*dress*) correcto; (*garden*) (de estilo) clásico; **~ity** [-'mælɪtɪ]

n (*procedure*) trámite *m*; corrección *f*;
etiqueta; **~ly** *adv* oficialmente
format ['fɔ:mæt] *n* formato ♦ *vt* (COMPUT)
formatear
formative ['fɔ:mətɪv] *adj* (*years*) de
formación; (*influence*) formativo
former ['fɔ:mə*] *adj* anterior; (*earlier*)
antiguo; (*ex*) ex; **the ~ ... the latter ...**
aquél ... éste ...; **~ly** *adv* antes
formula ['fɔ:mjulə] *n* fórmula
forsake [fə'seɪk] (*pt* **forsook**, *pp* **forsaken**)
vt (*gen*) abandonar; (*plan*) renunciar a
fort [fɔ:t] *n* fuerte *m*
forte ['fɔ:tɪ] *n* fuerte *m*
forth [fɔ:θ] *adv*: **back and ~** de acá para
allá; **and so ~** y así sucesivamente;
~coming *adj* próximo, venidero; (*help,
information*) disponible; (*character*)
comunicativo; **~right** *adj* franco; **~with**
adv en el acto
fortify ['fɔ:tɪfaɪ] *vt* (*city*) fortificar; (*person*)
fortalecer
fortitude ['fɔ:tɪtjuːd] *n* fortaleza
fortnight ['fɔ:tnaɪt] (BRIT) *n* quince días
mpl; quincena; **~ly** *adj* de cada quince
días, quincenal ♦ *adv* cada quince días,
quincenalmente
fortress ['fɔ:trɪs] *n* fortaleza
fortunate ['fɔ:tʃənɪt] *adj* afortunado; **it is
~ that ...** (es una) suerte que ...; **~ly** *adv*
afortunadamente
fortune ['fɔ:tʃən] *n* suerte *f*; (*wealth*)
fortuna; **~-teller** *n* adivino/a
forty ['fɔ:tɪ] *num* cuarenta
forum ['fɔ:rəm] *n* foro
forward ['fɔ:wəd] *adj* (*movement, position*)
avanzado; (*front*) delantero; (*in time*)
adelantado; (*not shy*) atrevido ♦ *n* (SPORT)
delantero ♦ *vt* (*letter*) remitir; (*career*)
promocionar; **to move ~** avanzar; **~(s)**
adv (hacia) adelante
fossil ['fɔsl] *n* fósil *m*
foster ['fɔstə*] *vt* (*child*) acoger en una
familia; fomentar; **~ child** *n* hijo/a
adoptivo/a
fought [fɔ:t] *pt*, *pp of* **fight**
foul [faul] *adj* sucio, puerco; (*weather, smell*

etc) asqueroso; (*language*) grosero;
(*temper*) malísimo ♦ *n* (SPORT) falta ♦ *vt*
(*dirty*) ensuciar; **~ play** *n* (LAW) muerte *f*
violenta
found [faund] *pt*, *pp of* **find** ♦ *vt* fundar;
~ation [-'deɪʃən] *n* (*act*) fundación *f*;
(*basis*) base *f*; (*also*: **~ation cream**) crema
base; **~ations** *npl* (*of building*) cimientos
mpl
founder ['faundə*] *n* fundador(a) *m/f* ♦ *vi*
hundirse
foundry ['faundrɪ] *n* fundición *f*
fountain ['fauntɪn] *n* fuente *f*; **~ pen** *n*
pluma (estilográfica) (SP), pluma-fuente *f*
(AM)
four [fɔ:*] *num* cuatro; **on all ~s** a gatas;
~-poster (bed) *n* cama de dosel;
~teen *num* catorce; **~th** *num* cuarto
fowl [faul] *n* ave *f* (de corral)
fox [fɔks] *n* zorro ♦ *vt* confundir
foyer ['fɔɪeɪ] *n* vestíbulo
fraction ['frækʃən] *n* fracción *f*
fracture ['fræktʃə*] *n* fractura
fragile ['frædʒaɪl] *adj* frágil
fragment ['frægmənt] *n* fragmento
fragrant ['freɪgrənt] *adj* fragante, oloroso
frail [freɪl] *adj* frágil; (*person*) débil
frame [freɪm] *n* (TECH) armazón *m*; (*of
person*) cuerpo; (*of picture, door etc*)
marco; (*of spectacles: also*: **~s**) montura
♦ *vt* enmarcar; **~ of mind** *n* estado de
ánimo; **~work** *n* marco
France [frɑːns] *n* Francia
franchise ['fræntʃaɪz] *n* (POL) derecho de
votar, sufragio; (COMM) licencia,
concesión *f*
frank [fræŋk] *adj* franco ♦ *vt* (*letter*)
franquear; **~ly** *adv* francamente
frantic ['fræntɪk] *adj* (*distraught*)
desesperado; (*hectic*) frenético
fraternity [frə'tɜːnɪtɪ] *n* (*feeling*) fraternidad
f; (*group of people*) círculos *mpl*
fraud [frɔːd] *n* fraude *m*; (*person*)
impostor(a) *m/f*
fraught [frɔːt] *adj*: **~ with** lleno de
fray [freɪ] *vi* deshilacharse
freak [friːk] *n* (*person*) fenómeno; (*event*)

suceso anormal

freckle ['frɛkl] n peca

free [fri:] adj libre; (gratis) gratuito ♦ vt (prisoner etc) poner en libertad; (jammed object) soltar; **~ (of charge), for ~** gratis; **~dom** ['fri:dəm] n libertad f; **F~fone** ® ['fri:fəʊn] n número gratuito; **~-for-all** n riña general; **~ gift** n prima; **~hold** n propiedad f vitalicia; **~ kick** n tiro libre; **~lance** adj independiente ♦ adv por cuenta propia; **~ly** adv libremente; (liberally) generosamente; **F~mason** n francmasón m; **F~post** ® n porte m pagado; **~-range** adj (hen, eggs) de granja; **~ trade** n libre comercio; **~way** (US) n autopista; **~ will** n libre albedrío; **of one's own ~ will** por su propia voluntad

freeze [fri:z] (pt **froze**, pp **frozen**) vi (weather) helar; (liquid, pipe, person) helarse, congelarse ♦ vt helar; (food, prices, salaries) congelar ♦ n helada; (on arms, wages) congelación f; **~-dried** adj liofilizado; **~r** n congelador m (SP), congeladora (AM)

freezing ['fri:zɪŋ] adj helado; **3 degrees below ~** tres grados bajo cero; **~ point** n punto de congelación

freight [freɪt] n (goods) carga; (money charged) flete m; **~ train** n (US) tren m de mercancías

French [frɛntʃ] adj francés/esa ♦ n (LING) francés m; **the ~** npl los franceses; **~ bean** n judía verde; **~ fried potatoes** npl patatas fpl (SP) or papas fpl (AM) fritas; **~ fries** (US) npl = **~ fried potatoes**; **~man/woman** (irreg) n francés/esa m/f; **~ window** n puerta de cristal

frenzy ['frɛnzɪ] n frenesí m

frequent [adj 'fri:kwənt, vb frɪ'kwɛnt] adj frecuente ♦ vt frecuentar; **~ly** [-əntlɪ] adv frecuentemente, a menudo

fresh [frɛʃ] adj fresco; (bread) tierno; (new) nuevo; **~en** vi (wind, air) soplar más recio; **~en up** vi (person) arreglarse, lavarse; **~er** (BRIT: inf) n (UNIV) estudiante

m/f de primer año; **~ly** adv (made, painted etc) recién; **~man** (US irreg) n = **~er**; **~ness** n frescura; **~water** adj (fish) de agua dulce

fret [frɛt] vi inquietarse

friar ['fraɪə*] n fraile m; (before name) fray m

friction ['frɪkʃən] n fricción f

Friday ['fraɪdɪ] n viernes m inv

fridge [frɪdʒ] (BRIT) n nevera (SP), refrigeradora (AM)

fried [fraɪd] adj frito

friend [frɛnd] n amigo/a; **~ly** adj simpático; (government) amigo; (place) acogedor(a); (match) amistoso; **~ly fire** fuego amigo, disparos mpl del propio bando; **~ship** n amistad f

frieze [fri:z] n friso

fright [fraɪt] n (terror) terror m; (scare) susto; **to take ~** asustarse; **~en** vt asustar; **~ened** adj asustado; **~ening** adj espantoso; **~ful** adj espantoso, horrible

frill [frɪl] n volante m

fringe [frɪndʒ] n (BRIT: of hair) flequillo; (on lampshade etc) flecos mpl; (of forest etc) borde m, margen m; **~ benefits** npl beneficios mpl marginales

frisk [frɪsk] vt cachear, registrar

frisky ['frɪskɪ] adj juguetón/ona

fritter ['frɪtə*] n buñuelo; **~ away** vt desperdiciar

frivolous ['frɪvələs] adj frívolo

frizzy ['frɪzɪ] adj rizado

fro [frəʊ] see **to**

frock [frɔk] n vestido

frog [frɔg] n rana; **~man** n hombre-rana m

frolic ['frɔlɪk] vi juguetear

KEYWORD

from [frɔm] prep **1** (indicating starting place) de, desde; **where do you come ~?** ¿de dónde eres?; **~ London to Glasgow** de Londres a Glasgow; **to escape ~ sth/ sb** escaparse de algo/alguien
2 (indicating origin etc) de; **a letter/ telephone call ~ my sister** una carta/

llamada de mi hermana; **tell him ~ me that ...** dígale de mi parte que ...
3 (*indicating time*): **~ one o'clock to** *or* **until** *or* **till two** de(sde) la una a *or* hasta las dos; **~ January (on)** a partir de enero
4 (*indicating distance*) de; **the hotel is 1 km ~ the beach** el hotel está a 1 km de la playa
5 (*indicating price, number etc*) de; **prices range ~ £10 to £50** los precios van desde £10 a *or* hasta £50; **the interest rate was increased ~ 9% to 10%** el tipo de interés fue incrementado de un 9% a un 10%
6 (*indicating difference*) de; **he can't tell red ~ green** no sabe distinguir el rojo del verde; **to be different ~ sb/sth** ser diferente a algo/alguien
7 (*because of, on the basis of*): **~ what he says** por lo que dice; **weak ~ hunger** debilitado por el hambre

front [frʌnt] *n* (*foremost part*) parte *f* delantera; (*of house*) fachada; (*of dress*) delantero; (*of promenade: also:* **sea ~**) paseo marítimo; (*MIL, POL, METEOROLOGY*) frente *m*; (*fig: appearances*) apariencias *fpl* ♦ *adj* (*wheel, leg*) delantero; (*row, line*) primero; **in ~ (of)** delante (de); **~ door** *n* puerta principal; **~ier** ['frʌntɪə*] *n* frontera; **~ page** *n* primera plana; **~ room** (*BRIT*) *n* salón *m*, sala; **~-wheel drive** *n* tracción *f* delantera
frost [frɒst] *n* helada; (*also:* **hoar~**) escarcha; **~bite** *n* congelación *f*; **~ed** *adj* (*glass*) deslustrado; **~y** *adj* (*weather*) de helada; (*welcome etc*) glacial
froth [frɒθ] *n* espuma
frown [fraun] *vi* fruncir el ceño
froze [frəuz] *pt of* **freeze**
frozen ['frəuzn] *pp of* **freeze**
fruit [fruːt] *n inv* fruta; fruto; (*fig*) fruto; resultados *mpl*; **~erer** *n* frutero/a; **~erer's** (*shop*) *n* frutería; **~ful** *adj* provechoso; **~ion** [fruː'ɪʃən] *n*: **to come to ~ion** realizarse; **~ juice** *n* zumo (*SP*) *or* jugo (*AM*) de fruta; **~ machine** (*BRIT*) *n*

máquina *f* tragaperras; **~ salad** *n* macedonia (*SP*) *or* ensalada (*AM*) de frutas
frustrate [frʌs'treɪt] *vt* frustrar
fry [fraɪ] (*pt, pp* **fried**) *vt* freír; **small ~** gente *f* menuda; **~ing pan** *n* sartén *f*
ft. *abbr* = **foot; feet**
fudge [fʌdʒ] *n* (*CULIN*) caramelo blando
fuel [fjuəl] *n* (*for heating*) combustible *m*; (*coal*) carbón *m*; (*wood*) leña; (*for engine*) carburante *m*; **~ oil** *n* fuel oil *m*; **~ tank** *n* depósito (de combustible)
fugitive ['fjuːdʒɪtɪv] *n* fugitivo/a
fulfil [ful'fɪl] *vt* (*function*) cumplir con; (*condition*) satisfacer; (*wish, desire*) realizar; **~ment** (*US* **fulfillment**) *n* satisfacción *f*; (*of promise, desire*) realización *f*
full [ful] *adj* lleno; (*fig*) pleno; (*complete*) completo; (*maximum*) máximo; (*information*) detallado; (*price*) íntegro; (*skirt*) amplio ♦ *adv*: **to know ~ well that** saber perfectamente que; **I'm ~ (up)** no puedo más; **~ employment** pleno empleo; **a ~ two hours** dos horas completas; **at ~ speed** a máxima velocidad; **in ~** (*reproduce, quote*) íntegramente; **~-length** *adj* (*novel etc*) entero; (*coat*) largo; (*portrait*) de cuerpo entero; **~ moon** *n* luna llena; **~-scale** *adj* (*attack, war*) en gran escala; (*model*) de tamaño natural; **~ stop** *n* punto; **~-time** *adj* (*work*) de tiempo completo ♦ *adv*: **to work ~-time** trabajar a tiempo completo; **~y** *adv* completamente; (*at least*) por lo menos; **~y-fledged** *adj* (*teacher, barrister*) diplomado
fumble ['fʌmbl] *vi*: **to ~ with** manejar torpemente
fume [fjuːm] *vi* (*rage*) estar furioso; **~s** *npl* humo, gases *mpl*
fun [fʌn] *n* (*amusement*) diversión *f*; **to have ~** divertirse; **for ~** en broma; **to make ~ of** burlarse de
function ['fʌŋkʃən] *n* función *f* ♦ *vi* funcionar; **~al** *adj* (*operational*) en buen estado; (*practical*) funcional
fund [fʌnd] *n* fondo; (*reserve*) reserva; **~s** *npl* (*money*) fondos *mpl*

fundamental [fʌndə'mentl] *adj* fundamental

funeral ['fjuːnərəl] *n* (*burial*) entierro; (*ceremony*) funerales *mpl*; ~ **parlour** (*BRIT*) *n* funeraria; ~ **service** *n* misa de difuntos, funeral *m*

funfair ['fʌnfeə*] (*BRIT*) *n* parque *m* de atracciones

fungus ['fʌŋgəs] (*pl* **fungi**) *n* hongo; (*mould*) moho

funnel ['fʌnl] *n* embudo; (*of ship*) chimenea

funny ['fʌnɪ] *adj* gracioso, divertido; (*strange*) curioso, raro

fur [fəː*] *n* piel *f*; (*BRIT*: *in kettle etc*) sarro; ~ **coat** *n* abrigo de pieles

furious ['fjuərɪəs] *adj* furioso; (*effort*) violento

furlong ['fəːlɔŋ] *n* octava parte de una milla, = 201.17 m

furnace ['fəːnɪs] *n* horno

furnish ['fəːnɪʃ] *vt* amueblar; (*supply*) suministrar; (*information*) facilitar; ~**ings** *npl* muebles *mpl*

furniture ['fəːnɪtʃə*] *n* muebles *mpl*; **piece of** ~ mueble *m*

furrow ['fʌrəu] *n* surco

furry ['fəːrɪ] *adj* peludo

further ['fəːðə*] *adj* (*new*) nuevo, adicional ♦ *adv* más lejos; (*more*) más; (*moreover*) además ♦ *vt* promover, adelantar; ~ **education** *n* educación *f* superior; ~**more** [fəːðə'mɔː*] *adv* además

furthest ['fəːðɪst] *superlative of* **far**

fury ['fjuərɪ] *n* furia

fuse [fjuːz] (*US* **fuze**) *n* fusible *m*; (*for bomb etc*) mecha ♦ *vt* (*metal*) fundir; (*fig*) fusionar ♦ *vi* fundirse; fusionarse; (*BRIT*: *ELEC*): **to** ~ **the lights** fundir los plomos; ~ **box** *n* caja de fusibles

fuss [fʌs] *n* (*excitement*) conmoción *f*; (*trouble*) jaleo; **to make a** ~ armar un lío *or* jaleo; **to make a** ~ **of sb** mimar a uno; ~**y** *adj* (*person*) exigente; (*too ornate*) recargado

futile ['fjuːtaɪl] *adj* vano

future ['fjuːtʃə*] *adj* futuro; (*coming*)

venidero ♦ *n* futuro; (*prospects*) porvenir; **in** ~ de ahora en adelante

fuze [fjuːz] (*US*) = **fuse**

fuzzy ['fʌzɪ] *adj* (*PHOT*) borroso; (*hair*) muy rizado

G, g

G [dʒiː] *n* (*MUS*) sol *m*

g. *abbr* (= *gram(s)*) gr.

G7 *abbr* (= *Group of Seven*) el grupo de los 7

gabble ['gæbl] *vi* hablar atropelladamente

gable ['geɪbl] *n* aguilón *m*

gadget ['gædʒɪt] *n* aparato

Gaelic ['geɪlɪk] *adj*, *n* (*LING*) gaélico

gag [gæg] *n* (*on mouth*) mordaza; (*joke*) chiste *m* ♦ *vt* amordazar

gaiety ['geɪtɪ] *n* alegría

gaily ['geɪlɪ] *adv* alegremente

gain [geɪn] *n*: ~ **(in)** aumento (de); (*profit*) ganancia ♦ *vt* ganar ♦ *vi* (*watch*) adelantarse; **to** ~ **from/by sth** sacar provecho de algo; **to** ~ **on sb** ganar terreno a uno; **to** ~ **3 lbs** (*in weight*) engordar 3 libras

gal. *abbr* = **gallon**

gala ['gɑːlə] *n* fiesta

gale [geɪl] *n* (*wind*) vendaval *m*

gallant ['gælənt] *adj* valiente; (*towards ladies*) atento

gall bladder ['gɔːl-] *n* vesícula biliar

gallery ['gælərɪ] *n* (*also*: **art** ~: *public*) pinacoteca; (: *private*) galería de arte; (*for spectators*) tribuna

gallon ['gælən] *n* galón *m* (*BRIT* = *4,546 litros*, *US* = *3,785 litros*)

gallop ['gæləp] *n* galope *m* ♦ *vi* galopar

gallows ['gæləuz] *n* horca

gallstone ['gɔːlstəun] *n* cálculo biliar

galore [gə'lɔː*] *adv* en cantidad, en abundancia

gambit ['gæmbɪt] *n* (*fig*): **(opening)** ~ estrategia (inicial)

gamble ['gæmbl] *n* (*risk*) riesgo ♦ *vt* jugar, apostar ♦ *vi* (*take a risk*) jugárselas; (*bet*)

apostar; **to ~ on** apostar a; (*success etc*) contar con; **~r** *n* jugador(a) *m/f*;
gambling *n* juego

game [geɪm] *n* juego; (*match*) partido; (*of cards*) partida; (*HUNTING*) caza ♦ *adj* (*willing*): **to be ~ for anything** atreverse a todo; **big ~** caza mayor; **~keeper** *n* guardabosques *m inv*

gammon ['gæmən] *n* (*bacon*) tocino ahumado; (*ham*) jamón *m* ahumado

gamut ['gæmət] *n* gama

gang [gæŋ] *n* (*of criminals*) pandilla; (*of friends etc*) grupo; (*of workmen*) brigada; **~ up** *vi*: **to ~ up on sb** aliarse contra uno

gangster ['gæŋstə*] *n* gángster *m*

gangway ['gæŋweɪ] *n* (*on ship*) pasarela

gaol [dʒeɪl] (*BRIT*) *n*, *vt* = **jail**

gap [gæp] *n* vacío, hueco (*AM*); (*in trees, traffic*) claro; (*in time*) intervalo; (*difference*): **~ (between)** diferencia (entre)

gap year (*BRIT*: *SCH*) *n* año sabático (*antes de empezar a estudiar en la universidad*)

gape [geɪp] *vi* mirar boquiabierto; (*shirt etc*) abrirse (completamente); **gaping** *adj* (*completamente*) abierto

garage ['gærɑːʒ] *n* garaje *m*; (*for repairs*) taller *m*

garbage ['gɑːbɪdʒ] (*US*) *n* basura; (*inf: nonsense*) tonterías *fpl*; **~ can** *n* cubo (*SP*) *or* bote *m* (*AM*) de la basura

garbled ['gɑːbld] *adj* (*distorted*) falsificado, amañado

garden ['gɑːdn] *n* jardín *m*; **~s** *npl* (*park*) parque *m*; **~er** *n* jardinero/a; **~ing** *n* jardinería

gargle ['gɑːgl] *vi* hacer gárgaras, gargarear (*AM*)

garish ['gɛərɪʃ] *adj* chillón/ona

garland ['gɑːlənd] *n* guirnalda

garlic ['gɑːlɪk] *n* ajo

garment ['gɑːmənt] *n* prenda (de vestir)

garnish ['gɑːnɪʃ] *vt* (*CULIN*) aderezar

garrison ['gærɪsn] *n* guarnición *f*

garter ['gɑːtə*] *n* (*for sock*) liga; (*US*) liguero

gas [gæs] *n* gas *m*; (*fuel*) combustible *m*; (*US: gasoline*) gasolina ♦ *vt* asfixiar con

gas; **~ cooker** (*BRIT*) *n* cocina de gas; **~ cylinder** *n* bombona de gas; **~ fire** *n* estufa de gas

gash [gæʃ] *n* raja; (*wound*) cuchillada ♦ *vt* rajar; acuchillar

gasket ['gæskɪt] *n* (*AUT*) junta de culata

gas mask *n* careta antigás

gas meter *n* contador *m* de gas

gasoline ['gæsəliːn] (*US*) *n* gasolina

gasp [gɑːsp] *n* boqueada; (*of shock etc*) grito sofocado ♦ *vi* (*pant*) jadear

gas station (*US*) *n* gasolinera

gastric ['gæstrɪk] *adj* gástrico

gate [geɪt] *n* puerta; (*iron ~*) verja; **~crash** (*BRIT*) *vt* colarse en; **~way** *n* puerta

gather ['gæðə*] *vt* (*flowers, fruit*) coger (*SP*), recoger; (*assemble*) reunir; (*pick up*) recoger; (*SEWING*) fruncir; (*understand*) entender ♦ *vi* (*assemble*) reunirse; **to ~ speed** ganar velocidad; **~ing** *n* reunión *f*, asamblea

gaudy ['gɔːdɪ] *adj* chillón/ona

gauge [geɪdʒ] *n* (*instrument*) indicador *m* ♦ *vt* medir; (*fig*) juzgar

gaunt [gɔːnt] *adj* (*haggard*) demacrado; (*stark*) desolado

gauntlet ['gɔːntlɪt] *n* (*fig*): **to run the ~ of** exponerse a; **to throw down the ~** arrojar el guante

gauze [gɔːz] *n* gasa

gave [geɪv] *pt of* **give**

gay [geɪ] *adj* (*homosexual*) gay; (*joyful*) alegre; (*colour*) vivo

gaze [geɪz] *n* mirada fija ♦ *vi*: **to ~ at sth** mirar algo fijamente

gazelle [gə'zɛl] *n* gacela

gazumping [gə'zʌmpɪŋ] (*BRIT*) *n la subida del precio de una casa una vez que ya ha sido apalabrado*

GB *abbr* = **Great Britain**

GCE *n abbr* (*BRIT*) = *General Certificate of Education*

GCSE (*BRIT*) *n abbr* (= *General Certificate of Secondary Education*) *examen de reválida que se hace a los 16 años*

gear [gɪə*] *n* equipo, herramientas *fpl*; (*TECH*) engranaje *m*; (*AUT*) velocidad *f*,

marcha ♦ vt (fig: adapt): **to ~ sth to**
adaptar or ajustar algo a; **top** or **high**
(US)/**low ~** cuarta/primera velocidad; **in ~**
en marcha; **~ box** n caja de cambios; **~
lever** n palanca de cambio; **~ shift** (US)
n = **~ lever**

geese [giːs] npl of **goose**
gel [dʒɛl] n gel m
gem [dʒɛm] n piedra preciosa
Gemini ['dʒɛmɪnaɪ] n Géminis m, Gemelos
mpl
gender ['dʒɛndə*] n género
gene [dʒiːn] n gen(e) m
general ['dʒɛnərl] n general m ♦ adj
general; **in ~** en general; **~ delivery** (US)
n lista de correos; **~ election** n
elecciones fpl generales; **~ly** adv
generalmente, en general; **~
practitioner** n médico general
generate ['dʒɛnəreɪt] vt (ELEC) generar;
(jobs, profits) producir
generation [dʒɛnə'reɪʃən] n generación f
generator ['dʒɛnəreɪtə*] n generador m
generosity [dʒɛnə'rɒsɪtɪ] n generosidad f
generous ['dʒɛnərəs] adj generoso
genetic [dʒɪ'nɛtɪk] adj: **~ engineering**
ingeniería genética; **~ fingerprinting**
identificación f genética
Geneva [dʒɪ'niːvə] n Ginebra
genial ['dʒiːnɪəl] adj afable, simpático
genitals ['dʒɛnɪtlz] npl (órganos mpl)
genitales mpl
genius ['dʒiːnɪəs] n genio
genteel [dʒɛn'tiːl] adj fino, elegante
gentle ['dʒɛntl] adj apacible, dulce;
(animal) manso; (breeze, curve etc) suave
gentleman ['dʒɛntlmən] (irreg) n señor m;
(well-bred man) caballero
gently ['dʒɛntlɪ] adv dulcemente;
suavemente
gentry ['dʒɛntrɪ] n alta burguesía
gents [dʒɛnts] n aseos mpl (de caballeros)
genuine ['dʒɛnjuɪn] adj auténtico; (person)
sincero
geography [dʒɪ'ɒgrəfɪ] n geografía
geology [dʒɪ'ɒlədʒɪ] n geología
geometric(al) [dʒɪə'mɛtrɪk(l)] adj

geométrico
geranium [dʒɪ'reɪnjəm] n geranio
geriatric [dʒɛrɪ'ætrɪk] adj, n geriátrico/a
m/f
germ [dʒəːm] n (microbe) microbio,
bacteria; (seed, fig) germen m
German ['dʒəːmən] adj alemán/ana ♦ n
alemán/ana m/f; (LING) alemán m; **~
measles** n rubéola
Germany ['dʒəːmənɪ] n Alemania
gesture ['dʒɛstjə*] n gesto; (symbol)
muestra

┌─────────────┐
│ **KEYWORD** │
└─────────────┘

get [gɛt] (pt, pp **got**, pp **gotten** (US)) vi 1
(become, be) ponerse, volverse; **to ~ old/
tired** envejecer/cansarse; **to ~ drunk**
emborracharse; **to ~ dirty** ensuciarse; **to ~
married** casarse; **when do I ~ paid?**
¿cuándo me pagan or se me paga?; **it's
~ting late** se está haciendo tarde
2 (go): **to ~ to/from** llegar a/de; **to ~
home** llegar a casa
3 (begin) empezar a; **to ~ to know sb**
(llegar a) conocer a uno; **I'm ~ting to like
him** me está empezando a gustar; **let's ~
going** or **started** ¡vamos (a empezar)!
4 (modal aux vb): **you've got to do it**
tienes que hacerlo
♦ vt 1: **to ~ sth done** (finish) terminar
algo; (have done) mandar hacer algo; **to ~
one's hair cut** cortarse el pelo; **to ~ the
car going** or **to go** arrancar el coche; **to
~ sb to do sth** conseguir or hacer que
alguien haga algo; **to ~ sth/sb ready**
preparar algo/a alguien
2 (obtain: money, permission, results)
conseguir; (find: job, flat) encontrar;
(fetch: person, doctor): (object) ir a
buscar, traer; **to ~ sth for sb** conseguir
algo para alguien; **~ me Mr Jones,
please** (TEL) póngame or comuníqueme
(AM) con el Sr. Jones, por favor; **can I ~
you a drink?** ¿quieres algo de beber?
3 (receive: present, letter) recibir; (acquire:
reputation) alcanzar; (: prize) ganar; **what
did you ~ for your birthday?** ¿qué te

regalaron por tu cumpleaños?; **how much did you ~ for the painting?** ¿cuánto sacaste por el cuadro?
4 (*catch*) coger (*SP*), agarrar (*AM*); (*hit: target etc*) dar en; **to ~ sb by the arm/throat** coger or agarrar a uno por el brazo/cuello; **~ him!** ¡cógelo! (*SP*), ¡atrápalo! (*AM*); **the bullet got him in the leg** la bala le dio en la pierna
5 (*take, move*) llevar; **to ~ sth to sb** hacer llegar algo a alguien; **do you think we'll ~ it through the door?** ¿crees que lo podremos meter por la puerta?
6 (*catch, take: plane, bus etc*) coger (*SP*), tomar (*AM*); **where do I ~ the train for Birmingham?** ¿dónde se coge or se toma el tren para Birmingham?
7 (*understand*) entender; (*hear*) oír; **I've got it!** ¡ya lo tengo!, ¡eureka!; **I don't ~ your meaning** no te entiendo; **I'm sorry, I didn't ~ your name** lo siento, no cogí tu nombre
8 (*have, possess*): **to have got** tener
get about *vi* salir mucho; (*news*) divulgarse
get along *vi* (*agree*) llevarse bien; (*depart*) marcharse; (*manage*) = **get by**
get at *vt fus* (*attack*) atacar; (*reach*) alcanzar
get away *vi* marcharse; (*escape*) escaparse
get away with *vt fus* hacer impunemente
get back *vi* (*return*) volver ♦ *vt* recobrar
get by *vi* (*pass*) (lograr) pasar; (*manage*) arreglárselas
get down *vi* bajarse ♦ *vt fus* bajar ♦ *vt* bajar; (*depress*) deprimir
get down to *vt fus* (*work*) ponerse a
get in *vi* entrar; (*train*) llegar; (*arrive home*) volver a casa, regresar
get into *vt fus* entrar en; (*vehicle*) subir a; **to ~ into a rage** enfadarse
get off *vi* (*from train etc*) bajar; (*depart: person, car*) marcharse ♦ *vt* (*remove*) quitar ♦ *vt fus* (*train, bus*) bajar de
get on *vi* (*at exam etc*): **how are you**

~ting on? ¿cómo te va?; (*agree*): **to ~ on (with)** llevarse bien (con) ♦ *vt fus* subir a
get out *vi* salir; (*of vehicle*) bajar ♦ *vt* sacar
get out of *vt fus* salir de; (*duty etc*) escaparse de
get over *vt fus* (*illness*) recobrarse de
get round *vt fus* rodear; (*fig: person*) engatusar a
get through *vi* (*TEL*) (lograr) comunicarse
get through to *vt fus* (*TEL*) comunicar con
get together *vi* reunirse ♦ *vt* reunir, juntar
get up *vi* (*rise*) levantarse ♦ *vt fus* subir
get up to *vt fus* (*reach*) llegar a; (*prank*) hacer

geyser ['giːzə*] *n* (*water heater*) calentador *m* de agua; (*GEO*) géiser *m*
ghastly ['gɑːstlɪ] *adj* horrible
gherkin ['gɜːkɪn] *n* pepinillo
ghetto blaster ['getəʊblɑːstə*] *n* cassette *m* portátil de gran tamaño
ghost [gəʊst] *n* fantasma *m*
giant ['dʒaɪənt] *n* gigante *m/f* ♦ *adj* gigantesco, gigante
gibberish ['dʒɪbərɪʃ] *n* galimatías *m*
giblets ['dʒɪblɪts] *npl* menudillos *mpl*
Gibraltar [dʒɪ'brɔːltə*] *n* Gibraltar *m*
giddy ['gɪdɪ] *adj* mareado
gift [gɪft] *n* regalo; (*ability*) talento; **~ed** *adj* dotado; **~ token** or **voucher** *n* vale *m* canjeable por un regalo
gigantic [dʒaɪ'gæntɪk] *adj* gigantesco
giggle ['gɪgl] *vi* reírse tontamente
gill [dʒɪl] *n* (*measure*) = 0.25 pints (*BRIT* = 0.148l, *US* = 0.118l)
gills [gɪlz] *npl* (*of fish*) branquias *fpl*, agallas *fpl*
gilt [gɪlt] *adj, n* dorado; **~-edged** *adj* (*COMM*) de máxima garantía
gimmick ['gɪmɪk] *n* truco
gin [dʒɪn] *n* ginebra
ginger ['dʒɪndʒə*] *n* jengibre *m*; **~ ale** = **~ beer**; **~ beer** (*BRIT*) *n* gaseosa de

jengibre; ~**bread** *n* pan *m* (*or* galleta) de jengibre

gingerly ['dʒɪndʒəlɪ] *adv* con cautela

gipsy ['dʒɪpsɪ] *n* = **gypsy**

giraffe [dʒɪ'rɑːf] *n* jirafa

girder ['gɜːdə*] *n* viga

girl [gɜːl] *n* (*small*) niña; (*young woman*) chica, joven *f*, muchacha; (*daughter*) hija; **an English** ~ una (chica) inglesa; ~**friend** *n* (*of girl*) amiga; (*of boy*) novia; ~**ish** *adj* de niña

giro ['dʒaɪrəʊ] *n* (*BRIT: bank* ~) giro bancario; (*post office* ~) giro postal; (*state benefit*) cheque quincenal del subsidio de desempleo

gist [dʒɪst] *n* lo esencial

give [gɪv] (*pt* **gave**, *pp* **given**) *vt* dar; (*deliver*) entregar; (*as gift*) regalar ♦ *vi* (*break*) romperse; (*stretch: fabric*) dar de sí; **to** ~ **sb sth**, ~ **sth to sb** dar algo a uno; ~ **away** *vt* (*give free*) regalar; (*betray*) traicionar; (*disclose*) revelar; ~ **back** *vt* devolver; ~ **in** *vi* ceder ♦ *vt* entregar; ~ **off** *vt* despedir; ~ **out** *vt* distribuir; ~ **up** *vi* rendirse, darse por vencido ♦ *vt* renunciar a; **to** ~ **up smoking** dejar de fumar; **to** ~ **o.s. up** entregarse; ~ **way** *vi* ceder; (*BRIT: AUT*) ceder el paso

glacier ['glæsɪə*] *n* glaciar *m*

glad [glæd] *adj* contento

gladly ['glædlɪ] *adv* con mucho gusto

glamorous ['glæmərəs] *adj* encantador(a), atractivo; **glamour** ['glæmə*] *n* encanto, atractivo

glance [glɑːns] *n* ojeada, mirada ♦ *vi*: **to** ~ **at** echar una ojeada a; **glancing** *adj* (*blow*) oblicuo

gland [glænd] *n* glándula

glare [glɛə*] *n* (*of anger*) mirada feroz; (*of light*) deslumbramiento, brillo; **to be in the** ~ **of publicity** ser el foco de la atención pública ♦ *vi* deslumbrar; **to** ~ **at** mirar con odio a; **glaring** *adj* (*mistake*) manifiesto

glass [glɑːs] *n* vidrio, cristal *m*; (*for drinking*) vaso; (*: with stem*) copa; ~**es** *npl*

(*spectacles*) gafas *fpl*; ~**house** *n* invernadero; ~**ware** *n* cristalería

glaze [gleɪz] *vt* (*window*) poner cristales a; (*pottery*) vidriar ♦ *n* vidriado; **glazier** ['gleɪzɪə*] *n* vidriero/a

gleam [gliːm] *vi* brillar

glean [gliːn] *vt* (*information*) recoger

glee [gliː] *n* alegría, regocijo

glen [glɛn] *n* cañada

glib [glɪb] *adj* de mucha labia; (*promise, response*) poco sincero

glide [glaɪd] *vi* deslizarse; (*AVIAT, birds*) planear; ~**r** *n* (*AVIAT*) planeador *m*; **gliding** *n* (*AVIAT*) vuelo sin motor

glimmer ['glɪmə*] *n* luz *f* tenue; (*of interest*) muestra; (*of hope*) rayo

glimpse [glɪmps] *n* vislumbre *m* ♦ *vt* vislumbrar, entrever

glint [glɪnt] *vi* centellear

glisten ['glɪsn] *vi* relucir, brillar

glitter ['glɪtə*] *vi* relucir, brillar

gloat [gləʊt] *vi*: **to** ~ **over** recrearse en

global ['gləʊbl] *adj* mundial; ~ **warming** (re)calentamiento global *or* de la tierra

globe [gləʊb] *n* globo; (*model*) globo terráqueo

gloom [gluːm] *n* tinieblas *fpl*, oscuridad *f*; (*sadness*) tristeza, melancolía; ~**y** *adj* (*dark*) oscuro; (*sad*) triste; (*pessimistic*) pesimista

glorious ['glɔːrɪəs] *adj* glorioso; (*weather etc*) magnífico

glory ['glɔːrɪ] *n* gloria

gloss [glɒs] *n* (*shine*) brillo; (*paint*) pintura de aceite; ~ **over** *vt fus* disimular

glossary ['glɒsərɪ] *n* glosario

glossy ['glɒsɪ] *adj* lustroso; (*magazine*) de lujo

glove [glʌv] *n* guante *m*; ~ **compartment** *n* (*AUT*) guantera

glow [gləʊ] *vi* brillar

glower ['glaʊə*] *vi*: **to** ~ **at** mirar con ceño

glue [gluː] *n* goma (de pegar), cemento ♦ *vt* pegar

glum [glʌm] *adj* (*person, tone*) melancólico

glut [glʌt] *n* superabundancia

glutton ['glʌtn] *n* glotón/ona *m/f*; **a** ~ **for**

work un(a) trabajador(a) incansable
GM *adj abbr* (= *genetically modified*) transgénico
GMO *n abbr* (= *genetically-modified organism*) organismo transgénico
gnat [næt] *n* mosquito
gnaw [nɔː] *vt* roer
gnome [nəum] *n* gnomo
go [gəu] (*pt* **went**, *pp* **gone**; *pl* **~es**) *vi* ir; (*travel*) viajar; (*depart*) irse, marcharse; (*work*) funcionar, marchar; (*be sold*) venderse; (*time*) pasar; (*fit, suit*): **to ~ with** hacer juego con; (*become*) ponerse; (*break etc*) estropearse, romperse ♦ *n*: **to have a ~ (at)** probar suerte (con); **to be on the ~** no parar; **whose ~ is it?** ¿a quién le toca?; **he's going to do it** va a hacerlo; **to ~ for a walk** ir de paseo; **to ~ dancing** ir a bailar; **how did it ~?** ¿qué tal salió *or* resultó?, ¿cómo ha ido?; **to ~ round the back** pasar por detrás; ~ **about** *vi* (*rumour*) propagarse ♦ *vt fus*: **how do I ~ about this?** ¿cómo me las arreglo para hacer esto?; ~ **ahead** *vi* seguir adelante; ~ **along** *vi* ir ♦ *vt fus* bordear; **to ~ along with** (*agree*) estar de acuerdo con; ~ **away** *vi* irse, marcharse; ~ **back** *vi* volver; ~ **back on** *vt fus* (*promise*) faltar a; ~ **by** *vi* (*time*) pasar ♦ *vt fus* guiarse por; ~ **down** *vi* bajar; (*ship*) hundirse; (*sun*) ponerse ♦ *vt fus* bajar; ~ **for** *vt fus* (*fetch*) ir por; (*like*) gustar; (*attack*) atacar; ~ **in** *vi* entrar; ~ **in for** *vt fus* (*competition*) presentarse a; ~ **into** *vt fus* entrar en; (*investigate*) investigar; (*embark on*) dedicarse a; ~ **off** *vi* irse, marcharse; (*food*) pasarse; (*explode*) estallar; (*event*) realizarse ♦ *vt fus* dejar de gustar; **I'm going off him/the idea** ya no me gusta tanto él/la idea; ~ **on** *vi* (*continue*) seguir, continuar; (*happen*) pasar, ocurrir; **to ~ on doing sth** seguir haciendo algo; ~ **out** *vi* salir; (*fire, light*) apagarse; ~ **over** *vi* (*ship*) zozobrar ♦ *vt fus* (*check*) revisar; ~ **through** *vt fus* (*town etc*) atravesar; ~ **up** *vi*, *vt fus* subir; ~ **without** *vt fus* pasarse sin
goad [gəud] *vt* aguijonear

go-ahead *adj* (*person*) dinámico; (*firm*) innovador(a) ♦ *n* luz *f* verde
goal [gəul] *n* meta; (*score*) gol *m*; **~keeper** *n* portero; **~-post** *n* poste *m* (de la portería)
goat [gəut] *n* cabra
gobble ['gɔbl] *vt* (*also*: ~ **down**, ~ **up**) tragarse, engullir
go-between *n* intermediario/a
god [gɔd] *n* dios *m*; **G~** *n* Dios *m*; **~child** *n* ahijado/a; **~daughter** *n* ahijada; **~dess** *n* diosa; **~father** *n* padrino; **~forsaken** *adj* dejado de la mano de Dios; **~mother** *n* madrina; **~send** *n* don *m* del cielo; **~son** *n* ahijado
goggles ['gɔglz] *npl* gafas *fpl*
going ['gəuɪŋ] *n* (*conditions*) estado del terreno ♦ *adj*: **the ~ rate** la tarifa corriente *or* en vigor
gold [gəuld] *n* oro ♦ *adj* de oro; **~en** *adj* (*made of*) de oro; (~ *in colour*) dorado; **~fish** *n* pez *m* de colores; **~mine** *n* (*also fig*) mina de oro; **~-plated** *adj* chapado en oro; **~smith** *n* orfebre *m/f*
golf [gɔlf] *n* golf *m*; ~ **ball** *n* (*for game*) pelota de golf; ~ **club** *n* club *m* de golf; (*stick*) palo (de golf); ~ **course** *n* campo de golf; **~er** *n* golfista *m/f*
gone [gɔn] *pp of* **go**
good [gud] *adj* bueno; (*pleasant*) agradable; (*kind*) bueno, amable; (*well-behaved*) educado ♦ *n* bien *m*, provecho; **~s** *npl* (*COMM*) mercancías *fpl*; **~!** ¡qué bien!; **to be ~ at** tener aptitud para; **to be ~ for** servir para; **it's ~ for you** te hace bien; **would you be ~ enough to ...?** ¿podría hacerme el favor de ...?, ¿sería tan amable de ...?; **a ~ deal (of)** mucho; **a ~ many** muchos; **to make ~** reparar; **it's no ~ complaining** no vale la pena (de) quejarse; **for ~** para siempre, definitivamente; ~ **morning/afternoon!** ¡buenos días/buenas tardes!; ~ **evening!** ¡buenas noches!; ~ **night!** ¡buenas noches!; **~bye!** ¡adiós!; **to say ~bye** despedirse; **G~ Friday** *n* Viernes *m* Santo; **~-looking** *adj* guapo; **~-natured**

adj amable, simpático; **~ness** *n* (*of person*) bondad *f*; **for ~ness sake!** ¡por Dios!; **~ness gracious!** ¡Dios mío!; **~s train** (*BRIT*) *n* tren *m* de mercancías; **~will** *n* buena voluntad *f*

goose [gu:s] (*pl* **geese**) *n* ganso, oca

gooseberry ['guzbərɪ] *n* grosella espinosa; **to play ~** hacer de carabina

gooseflesh ['gu:sfleʃ] *n* = **goose pimples**

goose pimples *npl* carne *f* de gallina

gore [gɔː*] *vt* cornear ♦ *n* sangre *f*

gorge [gɔːdʒ] *n* barranco *f* ♦ *vr*: **to ~ o.s. (on)** atracarse (de)

gorgeous ['gɔːdʒəs] *adj* (*thing*) precioso; (*weather*) espléndido; (*person*) guapísimo

gorilla [gəˈrɪlə] *n* gorila *m*

gorse [gɔːs] *n* tojo

gory ['gɔːrɪ] *adj* sangriento

go-slow (*BRIT*) *n* huelga de manos caídas

gospel ['gɔspl] *n* evangelio

gossip ['gɔsɪp] *n* (*scandal*) cotilleo, chismes *mpl*; (*chat*) charla; (*person*) cotilla *m/f*, chismoso/a ♦ *vi* cotillear

got [gɔt] *pt, pp of* **get**; **~ten** (*US*) *pp of* **get**

gout [gaut] *n* gota

govern ['gʌvən] *vt* gobernar; (*influence*) dominar; **~ess** *n* institutriz *f*; **~ment** *n* gobierno; **~or** *n* gobernador(a) *m/f*; (*of school etc*) miembro del consejo; (*of jail*) director(a) *m/f*

gown [gaun] *n* traje *m*; (*of teacher, BRIT: of judge*) toga

G.P. *n abbr* = **general practitioner**

grab [græb] *vt* coger (*SP*) *or* agarrar (*AM*), arrebatar ♦ *vi*: **to ~ at** intentar agarrar

grace [greɪs] *n* gracia ♦ *vt* honrar; (*adorn*) adornar; **5 days' ~** un plazo de 5 días; **~ful** *adj* grácil; (*style, shape*) elegante, gracioso; **gracious** ['greɪʃəs] *adj* amable

grade [greɪd] *n* (*quality*) clase *f*, calidad *f*; (*in hierarchy*) grado; (*SCOL: mark*) nota; (*US: school class*) curso ♦ *vt* clasificar; **~ crossing** (*US*) *n* paso a nivel; **~ school** (*US*) *n* escuela primaria

gradient ['greɪdɪənt] *n* pendiente *f*

gradual ['grædjuəl] *adj* paulatino; **~ly** *adv*

paulatinamente

graduate [*n* 'grædjuɪt, *vb* 'grædjueɪt] *n* (*US: of high school*) graduado/a; (*of university*) licenciado/a ♦ *vi* graduarse; licenciarse; **graduation** [-'eɪʃən] *n* (*ceremony*) entrega del título

graffiti [grəˈfiːtɪ] *n* pintadas *fpl*

graft [grɑːft] *n* (*AGR, MED*) injerto; (*BRIT: inf*) trabajo duro; (*bribery*) corrupción *f* ♦ *vt* injertar

grain [greɪn] *n* (*single particle*) grano; (*corn*) granos *mpl*, cereales *mpl*; (*of wood*) fibra

gram [græm] *n* gramo

grammar ['græmə*] *n* gramática; **~ school** (*BRIT*) *n* ≈ instituto de segunda enseñanza, liceo (*SP*)

grammatical [grəˈmætɪkl] *adj* gramatical

gramme [græm] *n* = **gram**

gramophone ['græməfəun] (*BRIT*) *n* tocadiscos *m inv*

grand [grænd] *adj* magnífico, imponente; (*wonderful*) estupendo; (*gesture etc*) grandioso; **~children** *npl* nietos *mpl*; **~dad** (*inf*) *n* yayo, abuelito; **~daughter** *n* nieta; **~eur** ['grændjə*] *n* magnificencia, lo grandioso; **~father** *n* abuelo; **~ma** (*inf*) *n* yaya, abuelita; **~mother** *n* abuela; **~pa** (*inf*) *n* = **~dad**; **~parents** *npl* abuelos *mpl*; **~ piano** *n* piano de cola; **~son** *n* nieto; **~stand** *n* (*SPORT*) tribuna

granite ['grænɪt] *n* granito

granny ['grænɪ] (*inf*) *n* abuelita, yaya

grant [grɑːnt] *vt* (*concede*) conceder; (*admit*) reconocer ♦ *n* (*SCOL*) beca; (*ADMIN*) subvención *f*; **to take sth/sb for ~ed** dar algo por sentado/no hacer ningún caso a uno

granulated sugar ['grænju:leɪtɪd-] (*BRIT*) *n* azúcar *m* blanquilla

grape [greɪp] *n* uva

grapefruit ['greɪpfruːt] *n* pomelo (*SP*), toronja (*AM*)

graph [grɑːf] *n* gráfica; **~ic** ['græfɪk] *adj* gráfico; **~ics** *n* artes *fpl* gráficas ♦ *npl* (*drawings*) dibujos *mpl*

grapple ['græpl] *vi*: **to ~ with sth/sb**

agarrar a algo/uno

grasp [grɑːsp] *vt* agarrar, asir; (*understand*) comprender ♦ *n* (*grip*) asimiento; (*understanding*) comprensión *f*; ~**ing** *adj* (*mean*) avaro

grass [grɑːs] *n* hierba; (*lawn*) césped *m*; ~**hopper** *n* saltamontes *m inv*; ~**-roots** *adj* (*fig*) popular

grate [greɪt] *n* parrilla de chimenea ♦ *vi*: **to ~ (on)** chirriar (sobre) ♦ *vt* (*CULIN*) rallar

grateful ['greɪtful] *adj* agradecido

grater ['greɪtə*] *n* rallador *m*

gratifying ['grætɪfaɪɪŋ] *adj* grato

grating ['greɪtɪŋ] *n* (*iron bars*) reja ♦ *adj* (*noise*) áspero

gratitude ['grætɪtjuːd] *n* agradecimiento

gratuity [grə'tjuːɪtɪ] *n* gratificación *f*

grave [greɪv] *n* tumba ♦ *adj* serio, grave

gravel ['grævl] *n* grava

gravestone ['greɪvstəun] *n* lápida

graveyard ['greɪvjɑːd] *n* cementerio

gravity ['grævɪtɪ] *n* gravedad *f*

gravy ['greɪvɪ] *n* salsa de carne

gray [greɪ] *adj* = **grey**

graze [greɪz] *vi* pacer ♦ *vt* (*touch lightly*) rozar; (*scrape*) raspar ♦ *n* (*MED*) abrasión *f*

grease [griːs] *n* (*fat*) grasa; (*lubricant*) lubricante *m* ♦ *vt* engrasar; lubrificar; ~**proof paper** (*BRIT*) *n* papel *m* apergaminado; **greasy** *adj* grasiento

great [greɪt] *adj* grande; (*inf*) magnífico, estupendo; **G~ Britain** *n* Gran Bretaña; ~**-grandfather** *n* bisabuelo; ~**grandmother** *n* bisabuela; ~**ly** *adv* muy; (*with verb*) mucho; ~**ness** *n* grandeza

Greece [griːs] *n* Grecia

greed [griːd] *n* (*also:* ~**iness**) codicia, avaricia; (*for food*) gula; (*for power etc*) avidez *f*; ~**y** *adj* avaro; (*for food*) glotón/ona

Greek [griːk] *adj* griego ♦ *n* griego/a; (*LING*) griego

green [griːn] *adj* (*also POL*) verde; (*inexperienced*) novato ♦ *n* verde *m*; (*stretch of grass*) césped *m*; (*GOLF*) green

m; ~**s** *npl* (*vegetables*) verduras *fpl*; ~ **belt** *n* zona verde; ~ **card** *n* (*AUT*) carta verde; (*US: work permit*) permiso de trabajo para los extranjeros en EE. UU.; ~**ery** *n* verdura; ~**grocer** (*BRIT*) *n* verdulero/a; ~**house** *n* invernadero; ~**house effect** *n* efecto invernadero; ~**house gas** *n* gases *mpl* de invernadero; ~**ish** *adj* verdoso

Greenland ['griːnlənd] *n* Groenlandia

greet [griːt] *vt* (*welcome*) dar la bienvenida a; (*receive: news*) recibir; ~**ing** *n* (*welcome*) bienvenida; ~**ing(s) card** *n* tarjeta de felicitación

grenade [grə'neɪd] *n* granada

grew [gruː] *pt of* **grow**

grey [greɪ] *adj* gris; (*weather*) sombrío; ~**-haired** *adj* canoso; ~**hound** *n* galgo

grid [grɪd] *n* reja; (*ELEC*) red *f*; ~**lock** *n* (*traffic jam*) retención *f*

grief [griːf] *n* dolor *m*, pena

grievance ['griːvəns] *n* motivo de queja, agravio

grieve [griːv] *vi* afligirse, acongojarse ♦ *vt* dar pena a; **to ~ for** llorar por

grievous ['griːvəs] *adj*: ~ **bodily harm** (*LAW*) daños *mpl* corporales graves

grill [grɪl] *n* (*on cooker*) parrilla; (*also:* **mixed ~**) parrillada ♦ *vt* (*BRIT*) asar a la parrilla; (*inf: question*) interrogar

grille [grɪl] *n* reja; (*AUT*) rejilla

grim [grɪm] *adj* (*place*) sombrío; (*situation*) triste; (*person*) ceñudo

grimace [grɪ'meɪs] *n* mueca ♦ *vi* hacer muecas

grime [graɪm] *n* mugre *f*, suciedad *f*

grin [grɪn] *n* sonrisa abierta ♦ *vi* sonreír abiertamente

grind [graɪnd] (*pt, pp* **ground**) *vt* (*coffee, pepper etc*) moler; (*US: meat*) picar; (*make sharp*) afilar ♦ *n* (*work*) rutina

grip [grɪp] *n* (*hold*) asimiento; (*control*) control *m*, dominio; (*of tyre etc*): **to have a good/bad ~** agarrarse bien/mal; (*handle*) asidero; (*holdall*) maletín *m* ♦ *vt* agarrar; (*viewer, reader*) fascinar; **to get to ~s with** enfrentarse con; ~**ping** *adj* absorbente

grisly ['grɪzlɪ] *adj* horripilante, horrible

gristle ['grɪsl] *n* ternilla

grit [grɪt] *n* gravilla; (*courage*) valor *m* ♦ *vt* (*road*) poner gravilla en; **to ~ one's teeth** apretar los dientes

groan [grəʊn] *n* gemido; quejido ♦ *vi* gemir; quejarse

grocer ['grəʊsə*] *n* tendero (de ultramarinos (*SP*)); **~ies** *npl* comestibles *mpl*; **~'s (shop)** *n* tienda de ultramarinos *or* de abarrotes (*AM*)

groin [grɔɪn] *n* ingle *f*

groom [gru:m] *n* mozo de cuadra; (*also:* **bride~**) novio ♦ *vt* (*horse*) almohazar; (*fig*): **to ~ sb for** preparar a uno para; **well-~ed** de buena presencia

groove [gru:v] *n* ranura, surco

grope [grəʊp]: **to ~ for** *vt fus* buscar a tientas

gross [grəʊs] *adj* (*neglect, injustice*) grave; (*vulgar: behaviour*) grosero; (: *appearance*) de mal gusto; (*COMM*) bruto; **~ly** *adv* (*greatly*) enormemente

grotto ['grɔtəʊ] *n* gruta

grotty ['grɔtɪ] (*inf*) *adj* horrible

ground [graʊnd] *pt, pp of* **grind** ♦ *n* suelo, tierra; (*SPORT*) campo, terreno; (*reason: gen pl*) causa, razón *f*; (*US: also:* **~ wire**) tierra ♦ *vt* (*plane*) mantener en tierra; (*US: ELEC*) conectar con tierra; **~s** *npl* (*of coffee etc*) poso; (*gardens etc*) jardines *mpl*, parque *m*; **on the ~** en el suelo; **to the ~** al suelo; **to gain/lose ~** ganar/perder terreno; **~ cloth** (*US*) *n* = **~sheet**; **~ing** *n* (*in education*) conocimientos *mpl* básicos; **~less** *adj* infundado; **~sheet** (*BRIT*) *n* tela impermeable; suelo; **~ staff** *n* personal *m* de tierra; **~work** *n* preparación *f*

group [gru:p] *n* grupo; (*musical*) conjunto ♦ *vt* (*also:* **~ together**) agrupar ♦ *vi* (*also:* **~ together**) agruparse

grouse [graʊs] *n inv* (*bird*) urogallo ♦ *vi* (*complain*) quejarse

grove [grəʊv] *n* arboleda

grovel ['grɔvl] *vi* (*fig*): **to ~ before** humillarse ante

grow [grəʊ] (*pt* **grew**, *pp* **grown**) *vi* crecer; (*increase*) aumentar; (*expand*) desarrollarse; (*become*) volverse; **to ~ rich/weak** enriquecerse/debilitarse ♦ *vt* cultivar; (*hair, beard*) dejar crecer; **~ up** *vi* crecer, hacerse hombre/mujer; **~er** *n* cultivador(a) *m/f*, productor(a) *m/f*; **~ing** *adj* creciente

growl [graʊl] *vi* gruñir

grown [grəʊn] *pp of* **grow**; **~-up** *n* adulto, mayor *m/f*

growth [grəʊθ] *n* crecimiento, desarrollo; (*what has grown*) brote *m*; (*MED*) tumor *m*

grub [grʌb] *n* larva, gusano; (*inf: food*) comida

grubby ['grʌbɪ] *adj* sucio, mugriento

grudge [grʌdʒ] *n* (*motivo de*) rencor *m* ♦ *vt*: **to ~ sb sth** dar algo a uno de mala gana; **to bear sb a ~** guardar rencor a uno

gruelling ['grʊəlɪŋ] (*US* **grueling**) *adj* penoso, duro

gruesome ['gru:səm] *adj* horrible

gruff [grʌf] *adj* (*voice*) ronco; (*manner*) brusco

grumble ['grʌmbl] *vi* refunfuñar, quejarse

grumpy ['grʌmpɪ] *adj* gruñón/ona

grunt [grʌnt] *vi* gruñir

G-string ['dʒi:strɪŋ] *n* taparrabo

guarantee [gærən'ti:] *n* garantía ♦ *vt* garantizar

guard [gɑ:d] *n* (*squad*) guardia; (*one man*) guardia *m*; (*BRIT: RAIL*) jefe *m* de tren; (*on machine*) dispositivo de seguridad; (*also:* **fire~**) rejilla de protección ♦ *vt* guardar; (*prisoner*) vigilar; **to be on one's ~** estar alerta; **~ against** *vt fus* (*prevent*) protegerse de; **~ed** *adj* (*fig*) cauteloso; **~ian** *n* guardián/ana *m/f*; (*of minor*) tutor(a) *m/f*; **~'s van** *n* (*BRIT: RAIL*) furgón *m*

Guatemala [gwætɪ'mɑ:lə] *n* Guatemala; **~n** *adj, n* guatemalteco/a *m/f*

guerrilla [gə'rɪlə] *n* guerrillero/a

guess [gɛs] *vi* adivinar; (*US*) suponer ♦ *vt*

adivinar; suponer ♦ *n* suposición *f*, conjetura, **to take** *or* **have a ~** tratar de adivinar; **~work** *n* conjeturas *fpl*
guest [gɛst] *n* invitado/a; (*in hotel*) huésped(a) *m/f*; **~ house** *n* casa de huéspedes, pensión *f*; **~ room** *n* cuarto de huéspedes
guffaw [gʌˈfɔː] *vi* reírse a carcajadas
guidance [ˈgaɪdəns] *n* (*advice*) consejos *mpl*
guide [gaɪd] *n* (*person*) guía *m/f*; (*book, fig*) guía ♦ *vt* (*round museum etc*) guiar; (*lead*) conducir; (*direct*) orientar; (*girl*) ~ *n* exploradora; **~book** *n* guía; **~ dog** *n* perro *m* guía; **~lines** *npl* (*advice*) directrices *fpl*
guild [gɪld] *n* gremio
guilt [gɪlt] *n* culpabilidad *f*; **~y** *adj* culpable
guinea pig [ˈgɪnɪ-] *n* cobaya; (*fig*) conejillo de Indias
guise [gaɪz] *n*: **in** *or* **under the ~ of** bajo apariencia de
guitar [gɪˈtɑː*] *n* guitarra
gulf [gʌlf] *n* golfo; (*abyss*) abismo
gull [gʌl] *n* gaviota
gullible [ˈgʌlɪbl] *adj* crédulo
gully [ˈgʌlɪ] *n* barranco
gulp [gʌlp] *vi* tragar saliva ♦ *vt* (*also: ~ down*) tragarse
gum [gʌm] *n* (*ANAT*) encía; (*glue*) goma, cemento; (*sweet*) caramelo de goma; (*also: chewing-~*) chicle *m* ♦ *vt* pegar con goma; **~boots** (*BRIT*) *npl* botas *fpl* de goma
gun [gʌn] *n* (*small*) pistola, revólver *m*; (*shotgun*) escopeta; (*rifle*) fusil *m*; (*cannon*) cañón *m*; **~boat** *n* cañonero; **~fire** *n* disparos *mpl*; **~man** *n* pistolero; **~point** *n*: **at ~point** a mano armada; **~powder** *n* pólvora; **~shot** *n* escopetazo
gurgle [ˈgəːgl] *vi* (*baby*) gorgotear; (*water*) borbotear
gush [gʌʃ] *vi* salir a raudales; (*person*) deshacerse en efusiones
gust [gʌst] *n* (*of wind*) ráfaga

gusto [ˈgʌstəu] *n* entusiasmo
gut [gʌt] *n* intestino; **~s** *npl* (*ANAT*) tripas *fpl*; (*courage*) valor *m*
gutter [ˈgʌtə*] *n* (*of roof*) canalón *m*; (*in street*) cuneta
guy [gaɪ] *n* (*also: ~rope*) cuerda; (*inf: man*) tío (*SP*), tipo; (*figure*) monigote *m*

Guy Fawkes' Night

🛈 La noche del cinco de noviembre, **Guy Fawkes' Night**, *se celebra en el Reino Unido el fracaso de la conspiración de la pólvora ("Gunpowder Plot"), un intento fallido de volar el parlamento de Jaime I en 1605. Esa noche se lanzan fuegos artificiales y se hacen hogueras en las que se queman unos muñecos de trapo que representan a* **Guy Fawkes**, *uno de los cabecillas de la revuelta. Días antes, los niños tienen por costumbre pedir a los transeúntes* "a penny for the guy", *dinero que emplean en comprar cohetes y petardos.*

---

guzzle [ˈgʌzl] *vi* tragar ♦ *vt* engullir
gym [dʒɪm] *n* (*also: gymnasium*) gimnasio; (*also: gymnastics*) gimnasia; **~nast** *n* gimnasta *m/f*; **~ shoes** *npl* zapatillas *fpl* (de deporte); **~ slip** (*BRIT*) *n* túnica de colegiala
gynaecologist [gaɪnɪˈkɔlədʒɪst] (*US* **gynecologist**) *n* ginecólogo/a
gypsy [ˈdʒɪpsɪ] *n* gitano/a

H, h

haberdashery [hæbəˈdæʃərɪ] (*BRIT*) *n* mercería
habit [ˈhæbɪt] *n* hábito, costumbre *f*; (*drug ~*) adicción *f*; (*costume*) hábito
habitual [həˈbɪtjuəl] *adj* acostumbrado, habitual; (*drinker, liar*) empedernido
hack [hæk] *vt* (*cut*) cortar; (*slice*) tajar ♦ *n* (*pej: writer*) escritor(a) *m/f* a sueldo; **~er** *n* (*COMPUT*) pirata *m/f* informático/a
hackneyed [ˈhæknɪd] *adj* trillado

had [hæd] pt, pp of **have**
haddock ['hædək] (pl ~ or ~s) n especie de merluza
hadn't ['hædnt] = **had not**
haemorrhage ['hemərɪdʒ] (US **hemorrhage**) n hemorragia
haemorrhoids ['hemərɔɪdz] (US **hemorrhoids**) npl hemorroides fpl
haggle ['hægl] vi regatear
Hague [heɪg] n: **The ~** La Haya
hail [heɪl] n granizo; (fig) lluvia ♦ vt saludar; (taxi) llamar a; (acclaim) aclamar ♦ vi granizar; ~**stone** n (piedra de) granizo
hair [heə*] n pelo, cabellos mpl; (one ~) pelo, cabello; (on legs etc) vello; **to do one's ~** arreglarse el pelo; **to have grey ~** tener canas fpl; ~**brush** n cepillo (para el pelo); ~**cut** n corte m (de pelo); ~**do** n peinado; ~**dresser** n peluquero/a; ~**dresser's** n peluquería; ~ **dryer** n secador m de pelo; ~**grip** n horquilla; ~**net** n redecilla; ~**piece** n postizo; ~**pin** n horquilla; ~**pin bend** (US ~**pin curve**) n curva de horquilla; ~**raising** adj espeluznante; ~ **removing cream** n crema depilatoria; ~ **spray** n laca; ~**style** n peinado; ~**y** adj peludo, velludo; (inf: frightening) espeluznante
hake [heɪk] (pl inv or ~s) n merluza
half [hɑːf] (pl **halves**) n mitad f; (of beer) ≈ caña (SP), media pinta; (RAIL, BUS) billete m de niño ♦ adj medio ♦ adv medio, a medias; **two and a ~** dos y media; ~ **a dozen** media docena; ~ **a pound** media libra; **to cut sth in ~** cortar algo por la mitad; ~**-caste** ['hɑːfkɑːst] n mestizo/a; ~**-hearted** adj indiferente, poco entusiasta; ~**-hour** n media hora; ~**-mast** n: **at ~-mast** (flag) a media asta; ~**-price** adj, adv a mitad de precio; ~ **term** (BRIT) n (SCOL) vacaciones de mediados del trimestre; ~**-time** n descanso; ~**way** adv a medio camino; (in period of time) a mitad de
hall [hɔːl] n (for concerts) sala; (entrance way) hall m; vestíbulo; ~ **of residence**

(BRIT) n residencia
hallmark ['hɔːlmɑːk] n sello
hallo [hə'ləu] excl = **hello**
Hallowe'en [hæləu'iːn] n víspera de Todos los Santos

Hallowe'en

i La tradición anglosajona dice que en la noche del 31 de octubre, **Hallowe'en**, víspera de Todos los Santos, es posible ver a brujas y fantasmas. En este día los niños se disfrazan y van de puerta en puerta llevando un farol hecho con una calabaza en forma de cabeza humana. Cuando se les abre la puerta gritan "trick or treat", amenazando con gastar una broma a quien no les dé golosinas o algo de calderilla.

---
hallucination [həluːsɪ'neɪʃən] n alucinación f
hallway ['hɔːlweɪ] n vestíbulo
halo ['heɪləu] n (of saint) halo, aureola
halt [hɔːlt] n (stop) alto, parada ♦ vt interrumpir ♦ vi pararse
halve [hɑːv] vt partir por la mitad
halves [hɑːvz] npl of **half**
ham [hæm] n jamón m (cocido)
hamburger ['hæmbəːgə*] n hamburguesa
hamlet ['hæmlɪt] n aldea
hammer ['hæmə*] n martillo ♦ vt (nail) clavar; (force): **to ~ an idea into sb/a message across** meter una idea en la cabeza a uno/machacar una idea ♦ vi dar golpes
hammock ['hæmək] n hamaca
hamper ['hæmpə*] vt estorbar ♦ n cesto
hand [hænd] n mano f; (of clock) aguja; (writing) letra; (worker) obrero ♦ vt dar, pasar; **to give or lend sb a ~** echar una mano a uno, ayudar a uno; **at ~** a mano; **in ~** (time) libre; (job etc) entre manos; **on ~** (person, services) a mano, al alcance; **to ~** (information etc) a mano; **on the one ~ ..., on the other ~ ...** por una parte ... por otra (parte) ...; ~ **in** vt entregar; ~ **out** vt distribuir; ~ **over** vt (deliver)

entregar; **~bag** n bolso (SP), cartera (AM); **~book** n manual m; **~brake** n freno de mano; **~cuffs** npl esposas fpl; **~ful** n puñado

handicap ['hændɪkæp] n minusvalía; (disadvantage) desventaja; (SPORT) handicap m ♦ vt estorbar; **mentally/ physically ~ped** deficiente m/f (mental/ minusválido/a (físico/a)

handicraft ['hændɪkrɑːft] n artesanía; (object) objeto de artesanía

handiwork ['hændɪwɜːk] n obra

handkerchief ['hæŋkətʃɪf] n pañuelo

handle ['hændl] n (of door etc) tirador m; (of cup etc) asa; (of knife etc) mango; (for winding) manivela ♦ vt (touch) tocar; (deal with) encargarse de; (treat: people) manejar; **"~ with care"** "(manéjese) con cuidado"; **to fly off the ~** perder los estribos; **~bar(s)** n(pl) manillar m

hand: **~ luggage** n equipaje m de mano; **~made** adj hecho a mano; **~out** n (money etc) limosna; (leaflet) folleto; **~rail** n pasamanos m inv; **~shake** n apretón m de manos

handsome ['hænsəm] adj guapo; (building) bello; (fig: profit) considerable

handwriting ['hændraɪtɪŋ] n letra

handy ['hændɪ] adj (close at hand) a la mano; (tool etc) práctico; (skilful) hábil, diestro

hang [hæŋ] (pt, pp **hung**) vt colgar; (criminal: pt, pp **hanged**) ahorcar ♦ vi (painting, coat etc) colgar; (hair, drapery) caer; **to get the ~ of sth** (inf) lograr dominar algo; **~ about** or **around** vi haraganear; **~ on** vi (wait) esperar; **~ up** vi (TEL) colgar ♦ vt colgar

hanger ['hæŋə*] n percha; **~-on** n parásito

hang: **~-gliding** ['-glaɪdɪŋ] n vuelo libre; **~over** n (after drinking) resaca; **~-up** n complejo

hanker ['hæŋkə*] vi: **to ~ after** añorar

hankie, **hanky** ['hæŋkɪ] n abbr = **handkerchief**

haphazard [hæp'hæzəd] adj fortuito

happen ['hæpən] vi suceder, ocurrir; (chance): **he ~ed to hear/see** dió la casualidad de que oyó/vió; **as it ~s** da la casualidad de que; **~ing** n suceso, acontecimiento

happily ['hæpɪlɪ] adv (luckily) afortunadamente; (cheerfully) alegremente

happiness ['hæpɪnɪs] n felicidad f; (cheerfulness) alegría

happy ['hæpɪ] adj feliz; (cheerful) alegre; **to be ~ (with)** estar contento (con); **to be ~ to do** estar encantado de hacer; **~ birthday!** ¡feliz cumpleaños!; **~-go-lucky** adj despreocupado; **~ hour** n horas en las que la bebida es más barata, happy hour f

harass ['hærəs] vt acosar, hostigar; **~ment** n persecución f

harbour ['hɑːbə*] (US **harbor**) n puerto ♦ vt (fugitive) dar abrigo a; (hope etc) abrigar

hard [hɑːd] adj duro; (difficult) difícil; (work) arduo; (person) severo; (fact) innegable ♦ adv (work) mucho, duro; (think) profundamente; **to look ~ at** clavar los ojos en; **to try ~** esforzarse; **no ~ feelings!** ¡sin rencor(es)!; **to be ~ of hearing** ser duro de oído; **to be ~ done by** ser tratado injustamente; **~back** n libro en cartoné; **~ cash** n dinero contante; **~ disk** n (COMPUT) disco duro or rígido; **~en** vt endurecer; (fig) curtir ♦ vi endurecerse; curtirse; **~-headed** adj realista; **~ labour** n trabajos mpl forzados

hardly ['hɑːdlɪ] adv apenas; **~ ever** casi nunca

hard: **~ship** n privación f; **~ shoulder** (BRIT) n (AUT) arcén m; **~-up** (inf) adj sin un duro (SP), sin plata (AM); **~ware** n ferretería; (COMPUT) hardware m; (MIL) armamento; **~ware shop** n ferretería; **~-wearing** adj resistente, duradero; **~- working** adj trabajador(a)

hardy ['hɑːdɪ] adj fuerte; (plant) resistente

hare [hɛə*] n liebre f; **~-brained** adj descabellado

harm [hɑːm] n daño, mal m ♦ vt (person) hacer daño a; (health, interests) perjudicar; (thing) dañar; **out of ~'s way** a salvo; **~ful** adj dañino; **~less** adj (person) inofensivo; (joke etc) inocente

harmony ['hɑːmənɪ] n armonía

harness ['hɑːnɪs] n arreos mpl; (for child) arnés m; (safety ~) arneses mpl ♦ vt (horse) enjaezar; (resources) aprovechar

harp [hɑːp] n arpa ♦ vi: **to ~ on (about)** machacar (con)

harrowing ['hærəʊɪŋ] adj angustioso

harsh [hɑːʃ] adj (cruel) duro, cruel; (severe) severo; (sound) áspero; (light) deslumbrador(a)

harvest ['hɑːvɪst] n (~ time) siega; (of cereals etc) cosecha; (of grapes) vendimia ♦ vt cosechar

has [hæz] vb see **have**

hash [hæʃ] n (CULIN) picadillo; (fig: mess) lío

hashish ['hæʃɪʃ] n hachís m

hasn't ['hæznt] = **has not**

hassle ['hæsl] (inf) n lata

haste [heɪst] n prisa; **~n** ['heɪsn] vt acelerar ♦ vi darse prisa; **hastily** adv de prisa; precipitadamente; **hasty** adj apresurado; (rash) precipitado

hat [hæt] n sombrero

hatch [hætʃ] n (NAUT: also: **~way**) escotilla; (also: **service ~**) ventanilla ♦ vi (bird) salir del cascarón ♦ vt incubar; (plot) tramar; **5 eggs have ~ed** han salido 5 pollos

hatchback ['hætʃbæk] n (AUT) tres or cinco puertas m

hatchet ['hætʃɪt] n hacha

hate [heɪt] vt odiar, aborrecer ♦ n odio; **~ful** adj odioso; **hatred** ['heɪtrɪd] n odio

haughty ['hɔːtɪ] adj altanero

haul [hɔːl] vt tirar ♦ n (of fish) redada; (of stolen goods etc) botín m; **~age** (BRIT) n transporte m; (costs) gastos mpl de transporte; **~ier** (US **~er**) n transportista m/f

haunch [hɔːntʃ] n anca; (of meat) pierna

haunt [hɔːnt] vt (subj: ghost) aparecerse en; (obsess) obsesionar ♦ n guarida

---

KEYWORD

have [hæv] (pt, pp **had**) aux vb **1** (gen) haber; **to ~ arrived/eaten** haber llegado/comido; **having finished** or **when he had finished, he left** cuando hubo acabado, se fue

2 (in tag questions): **you've done it, ~n't you?** lo has hecho, ¿verdad? or ¿no?

3 (in short answers and questions): **I ~n't** no; **so I ~** pues, es verdad; **we ~n't paid – yes we ~!** no hemos pagado — ¡sí que hemos pagado!; **I've been there before, ~ you?** he estado allí antes, ¿y tú?

♦ modal aux vb (be obliged): **to ~ (got) to do sth** tener que hacer algo; **you ~n't to tell her** no hay que or no debes decírselo

♦ vt **1** (possess): **he has (got) blue eyes/dark hair** tiene los ojos azules/el pelo negro

2 (referring to meals etc): **to ~ breakfast/lunch/dinner** desayunar/comer/cenar; **to ~ a drink/a cigarette** tomar algo/fumar un cigarrillo

3 (receive) recibir; (obtain) obtener; **may I ~ your address?** ¿puedes darme tu dirección?; **you can ~ it for £5** te lo puedes quedar por £5; **I must ~ it by tomorrow** lo necesito para mañana; **to ~ a baby** tener un niño or bebé

4 (maintain, allow): **I won't ~ it/this nonsense!** ¡no lo permitiré!/¡no permitiré estas tonterías!; **we can't ~ that** no podemos permitir eso

5: **to ~ sth done** hacer or mandar hacer algo; **to ~ one's hair cut** cortarse el pelo; **to ~ sb do sth** hacer que alguien haga algo

6 (experience, suffer): **to ~ a cold/flu** tener un resfriado/la gripe; **she had her bag stolen/her arm broken** le robaron el bolso/se rompió un brazo; **to ~ an operation** operarse

7 (+noun): **to ~ a swim/walk/bath/rest** nadar/dar un paseo/darse un baño/descansar; **let's ~ a look** vamos a ver; **to**

~ **a meeting/party** celebrar una
reunión/una fiesta; **let me ~ a try** déjame
intentarlo
have out *vt*: **to ~ it out with sb** (*settle a
problem etc*) dejar las cosas en claro con
alguien

haven ['heɪvn] *n* puerto; (*fig*) refugio
haven't ['hævnt] = **have not**
havoc ['hævək] *n* estragos *mpl*
hawk [hɔ:k] *n* halcón *m*
hay [heɪ] *n* heno; ~ **fever** *n* fiebre *f* del
heno; ~**stack** *n* almiar *m*
haywire ['heɪwaɪə*] (*inf*) *adj*: **to go ~**
(*plan*) embrollarse
hazard ['hæzəd] *n* peligro ♦ *vt* aventurar;
~**ous** *adj* peligroso; ~ **warning lights**
npl (*AUT*) señales *fpl* de emergencia
haze [heɪz] *n* neblina
hazelnut ['heɪzlnʌt] *n* avellana
hazy ['heɪzɪ] *adj* brumoso; (*idea*) vago
he [hi:] *pron* él; ~ **who ...** él que ...,
quien ...
head [hɛd] *n* cabeza; (*leader*) jefe/a *m/f*;
(*of school*) director(a) *m/f* ♦ *vt* (*list*)
encabezar; (*group*) capitanear; (*company*)
dirigir; ~**s (or tails)** cara (o cruz); ~ **first**
de cabeza; ~ **over heels** (*in love*)
perdidamente; **to ~ the ball** cabecear (la
pelota); ~ **for** *vt fus* dirigirse a; (*disaster*)
ir camino de; ~**ache** *n* dolor *m* de
cabeza; ~**dress** *n* tocado; ~**ing** *n* título;
~**lamp** (*BRIT*) *n* = ~**light**; ~**land** *n*
promontorio; ~**light** *n* faro; ~**line** *n*
titular *m*; ~**long** *adv* (*fall*) de cabeza;
(*rush*) precipitadamente; ~**master/
mistress** *n* director(a) *m/f* (de escuela);
~ **office** *n* oficina central, central *f*; ~~
on *adj* (*collision*) de frente; ~**phones** *npl*
auriculares *mpl*; ~**quarters** *npl* sede *f*
central; (*MIL*) cuartel *m* general; ~**rest** *n*
reposa-cabezas *m inv*; ~**room** *n* (*in car*)
altura interior; (*under bridge*) (límite *m* de)
altura; ~**scarf** *n* pañuelo; ~**strong** *adj*
testarudo; ~ **waiter** *n* maître *m*; ~**way**
n: **to make ~way** (*fig*) hacer progresos;
~**wind** *n* viento contrario; ~**y** *adj*

(*experience, period*) apasionante; (*wine*)
cabezón; (*atmosphere*) embriagador(a)
heal [hi:l] *vt* curar ♦ *vi* cicatrizarse
health [hɛlθ] *n* salud *f*; ~ **food** *n*
alimentos *mpl* orgánicos; **the H~
Service** (*BRIT*) *n* el servicio de salud
pública; ≈ el Insalud (*SP*); ~**y** *adj* sano,
saludable
heap [hi:p] *n* montón *m* ♦ *vt*: **to ~ (up)**
amontonar; **to ~ sth with** llenar algo
hasta arriba de; ~**s of** un montón de
hear [hɪə*] (*pt, pp* **heard**) *vt* (*also LAW*) oír;
(*news*) saber ♦ *vi* oír; **to ~ about** oír
hablar de; **to ~ from sb** tener noticias de
uno; ~**ing** *n* (*sense*) oído; (*LAW*) vista;
~**ing aid** *n* audífono; ~**say** *n* rumores
mpl, hablillas *fpl*
hearse [hə:s] *n* coche *m* fúnebre
heart [hɑ:t] *n* corazón *m*; (*fig*) valor *m*; (*of
lettuce*) cogollo; ~**s** *npl* (*CARDS*) corazones
mpl; **to lose/take** ~ descorazonarse/
cobrar ánimo; **at** ~ en el fondo; **by** ~
(*learn, know*) de memoria; ~ **attack** *n*
infarto (de miocardio); ~**beat** *n* latido
(del corazón); ~**breaking** *adj*
desgarrador(a); ~**broken** *adj*: **she was
~broken about it** esto le partió el
corazón; ~**burn** *n* acedía; ~ **failure** *n*
fallo cardíaco; ~**felt** *adj* (*deeply felt*) más
sentido
hearth [hɑ:θ] *n* (*fireplace*) chimenea
hearty ['hɑ:tɪ] *adj* (*person*) campechano;
(*laugh*) sano; (*dislike, support*) absoluto
heat [hi:t] *n* calor *m*; (*SPORT: also*:
qualifying ~) prueba eliminatoria ♦ *vt*
calentar; ~ **up** *vi* calentarse ♦ *vt* calentar;
~**ed** *adj* caliente; (*fig*) acalorado; ~**er** *n*
estufa; (*in car*) calefacción *f*
heath [hi:θ] (*BRIT*) *n* brezal *m*
heather ['hɛðə*] *n* brezo
heating ['hi:tɪŋ] *n* calefacción *f*
heatstroke ['hi:tstrəuk] *n* insolación *f*
heatwave ['hi:tweɪv] *n* ola de calor
heave [hi:v] *vt* (*pull*) tirar; (*push*) empujar
con esfuerzo; (*lift*) levantar (con esfuerzo)
♦ *vi* (*chest*) palpitar; (*retch*) tener náuseas
♦ *n* tirón *m*; empujón *m*; **to ~ a sigh**

suspirar

heaven ['hɛvn] *n* cielo; (*fig*) una maravilla; **~ly** *adj* celestial; (*fig*) maravilloso

heavily ['hɛvɪlɪ] *adv* pesadamente; (*drink, smoke*) con exceso; (*sleep, sigh*) profundamente; (*depend*) mucho

heavy ['hɛvɪ] *adj* pesado; (*work, blow*) duro; (*sea, rain, meal*) fuerte; (*drinker, smoker*) grande; (*responsibility*) grave; (*schedule*) ocupado; (*weather*) bochornoso; **~ goods vehicle** *n* vehículo pesado; **~weight** *n* (*SPORT*) peso pesado

Hebrew ['hi:bru:] *adj, n* (*LING*) hebreo

heckle ['hɛkl] *vt* interrumpir

hectic ['hɛktɪk] *adj* agitado

he'd [hi:d] = **he would**; **he had**

hedge [hɛdʒ] *n* seto ♦ *vi* contestar con evasivas; **to ~ one's bets** (*fig*) cubrirse

hedgehog ['hɛdʒhɔg] *n* erizo

heed [hi:d] *vt* (*also:* **take ~ of**) (*pay attention to*) hacer caso de; **~less** *adj:* **to be ~less (of)** no hacer caso (de)

heel [hi:l] *n* talón *m*; (*of shoe*) tacón *m* ♦ *vt* (*shoe*) poner tacón a

hefty ['hɛftɪ] *adj* (*person*) fornido; (*parcel, profit*) gordo

heifer ['hɛfə*] *n* novilla, ternera

height [haɪt] *n* (*of person*) estatura; (*of building*) altura; (*high ground*) cerro; (*altitude*) altitud *f*; (*fig: of season*): **at the ~ of summer** en los días más calurosos del verano; (: *of power etc*) cúspide *f*; (: *of stupidity etc*) colmo; **~en** *vt* elevar; (*fig*) aumentar

heir [ɛə*] *n* heredero; **~ess** *n* heredera; **~loom** *n* reliquia de familia

held [hɛld] *pt, pp of* **hold**

helicopter ['hɛlɪkɔptə*] *n* helicóptero

hell [hɛl] *n* infierno; **~!** (*inf*) ¡demonios!

he'll [hi:l] = **he will**; **he shall**

hello [hə'ləu] *excl* ¡hola!; (*to attract attention*) ¡oiga!; (*surprise*) ¡caramba!

helm [hɛlm] *n* (*NAUT*) timón *m*

helmet ['hɛlmɪt] *n* casco

help [hɛlp] *n* ayuda; (*cleaner etc*) criada, asistenta ♦ *vt* ayudar; **~!** ¡socorro!; **~**

yourself sírvete; **he can't ~ it** no es culpa suya; **~er** *n* ayudante *m/f*; **~ful** *adj* útil; (*person*) servicial; (*advice*) útil; **~ing** *n* ración *f*; **~less** *adj* (*incapable*) incapaz; (*defenceless*) indefenso

hem [hɛm] *n* dobladillo ♦ *vt* poner *or* coser el dobladillo; **~ in** *vt* cercar

hemorrhage ['hɛmərɪdʒ] (*US*) *n* = **haemorrhage**

hemorrhoids ['hɛmərɔɪdz] (*US*) *npl* = **haemorrhoids**

hen [hɛn] *n* gallina; (*female bird*) hembra

hence [hɛns] *adv* (*therefore*) por lo tanto; **2 years ~** de aquí a 2 años; **~forth** *adv* de hoy en adelante

hepatitis [hɛpə'taɪtɪs] *n* hepatitis *f*

her [hə:*] *pron* (*direct*) la; (*indirect*) le; (*stressed, after prep*) ella ♦ *adj* su; *see also* **me; my**

herald ['hɛrəld] *n* heraldo ♦ *vt* anunciar; **~ry** *n* heráldica

herb [hə:b] *n* hierba

herd [hə:d] *n* rebaño

here [hɪə*] *adv* aquí; (*at this point*) en este punto; **~ is/are** aquí está/están; **~ she is** aquí está; **~after** *adv* en el futuro; **~by** *adv* (*in letter*) por la presente

heritage ['hɛrɪtɪdʒ] *n* patrimonio

hermit ['hə:mɪt] *n* ermitaño/a

hernia ['hə:nɪə] *n* hernia

hero ['hɪərəu] (*pl* **~es**) *n* héroe *m*; (*in book, film*) protagonista *m*

heroin ['hɛrəun] *n* heroína

heroine ['hɛrəuɪn] *n* heroína; (*in book, film*) protagonista

heron ['hɛrən] *n* garza

herring ['hɛrɪŋ] *n* arenque *m*

hers [hə:z] *pron* (el) suyo/(la) suya *etc; see also* **mine**[1]

herself [hə:'sɛlf] *pron* (*reflexive*) se; (*emphatic*) ella misma; (*after prep*) sí (misma); *see also* **oneself**

he's [hi:z] = **he is**; **he has**

hesitant ['hɛzɪtənt] *adj* vacilante

hesitate ['hɛzɪteɪt] *vi* vacilar; (*in speech*) titubear; (*be unwilling*) resistirse a;

hesitation ['-teɪʃən] n indecisión f; titubeo; dudas fpl
heterosexual [hetərəu'seksjuəl] adj heterosexual
heyday ['heɪdeɪ] n: **the ~ of** el apogeo de
HGV n abbr = **heavy goods vehicle**
hi [haɪ] excl ¡hola!; (to attract attention) ¡oiga!
hiatus [haɪ'eɪtəs] n vacío
hibernate ['haɪbəneɪt] vi invernar
hiccough ['hɪkʌp] = **hiccup**
hiccup ['hɪkʌp] vi hipar; **~s** npl hipo
hide [haɪd] (pt **hid**, pp **hidden**) n (skin) piel f ♦ vt esconder, ocultar ♦ vi: **to ~ (from sb)** esconderse or ocultarse (de uno); **~-and-seek** n escondite m
hideous ['hɪdɪəs] adj horrible
hiding ['haɪdɪŋ] n (beating) paliza; **to be in ~** (concealed) estar escondido
hierarchy ['haɪərɑːkɪ] n jerarquía
hi-fi ['haɪfaɪ] n estéreo, hifi m ♦ adj de alta fidelidad
high [haɪ] adj alto; (speed, number) grande; (price) elevado; (wind) fuerte; (voice) agudo ♦ adv alto, a gran altura; **it is 20 m ~** tiene 20 m de altura; **~ in the air** en las alturas; **~brow** adj intelectual; **~chair** n silla alta; **~er education** n educación f or enseñanza superior; **~handed** adj despótico; **~heeled** adj de tacón alto; **~ jump** n (SPORT) salto de altura; **the H~lands** npl las tierras altas de Escocia; **~light** n (fig: of event) punto culminante; (in hair) reflejo ♦ vt subrayar; **~ly** adv (paid) muy bien; (critical, confidential) sumamente; (a lot): **to speak/think ~ly of** hablar muy bien de/ tener en mucho a; **~ly strung** adj hipertenso; **~ness** n altura; **Her** or **His H~ness** Su Alteza; **~-pitched** adj agudo; **~-rise block** n torre f de pisos; **~ school** n ≈ Instituto Nacional de Bachillerato (SP); **~ season** (BRIT) n temporada alta; **~ street** (BRIT) n calle f mayor; **~way** n carretera; (US) carretera nacional; autopista; **H~way Code** (BRIT) n código de la circulación

hijack ['haɪdʒæk] vt secuestrar; **~er** n secuestrador(a) m/f
hike [haɪk] vi (go walking) ir de excursión (a pie) ♦ n caminata; **~r** n excursionista m/f; **hiking** n senderismo
hilarious [hɪ'leərɪəs] adj divertidísimo
hill [hɪl] n colina; (high) montaña; (slope) cuesta; **~side** n ladera; **~ walking** n senderismo (de montaña); **~y** adj montañoso
hilt [hɪlt] n (of sword) empuñadura; **to the ~** (fig: support) incondicionalmente
him [hɪm] pron (direct) lo, le; (indirect) le; (stressed, after prep) él; see also **me**; **~self** pron (reflexive) se; (emphatic) él mismo; (after prep) sí (mismo); see also **oneself**
hinder ['hɪndə*] vt estorbar, impedir; **hindrance** ['hɪndrəns] n estorbo
hindsight ['haɪndsaɪt] n: **with ~** en retrospectiva
Hindu ['hɪnduː] n hindú m/f
hinge [hɪndʒ] n bisagra, gozne m ♦ vi (fig): **to ~ on** depender de
hint [hɪnt] n (advice) consejo; (sign) dejo ♦ vt: **to ~ that** insinuar que ♦ vi: **to ~ at** hacer alusión a
hip [hɪp] n cadera
hippopotamus [hɪpə'pɒtəməs] (pl **~es** or **hippopotami**) n hipopótamo
hire ['haɪə*] vt (BRIT: car, equipment) alquilar; (worker) contratar ♦ n alquiler m; **for ~** se alquila; (taxi) libre; **~(d) car** (BRIT) n coche m de alquiler; **~ purchase** (BRIT) n compra a plazos
his [hɪz] pron (el) suyo/(la) suya etc ♦ adj su; see also **mine**[1]; **my**
Hispanic [hɪs'pænɪk] adj hispánico
hiss [hɪs] vi silbar
historian [hɪ'stɔːrɪən] n historiador(a) m/f
historic(al) [hɪ'stɒrɪk(l)] adj histórico
history ['hɪstərɪ] n historia
hit [hɪt] (pt, pp **hit**) vt (strike) golpear, pegar; (reach: target) alcanzar; (collide with: car) chocar contra; (fig: affect) afectar ♦ n golpe m; (success) éxito; **to ~ it off with sb** llevarse bien con uno; **~-**

and-run driver n conductor(a) que atropella y huye

hitch [hɪtʃ] vt (fasten) atar, amarrar; (also: ~ **up**) remangar ♦ n (difficulty) dificultad f; **to ~ a lift** hacer autostop

hitch-hike vi hacer autostop; ~**hiking** n autostop m

hi-tech [haɪˈtɛk] adj de alta tecnología

hitherto [ˈhɪðəˈtuː] adv hasta ahora

HIV n abbr (= human immunodeficiency virus) VIH m; ~-**negative/positive** adj VIH negativo/positivo

hive [haɪv] n colmena

HMS abbr = **His (Her) Majesty's Ship**

hoard [hɔːd] n (treasure) tesoro; (stockpile) provisión f ♦ vt acumular; (goods) acaparar; ~**ing** n (for posters) cartelera

hoarse [hɔːs] adj ronco

hoax [həʊks] n trampa

hob [hɔb] n quemador m

hobble [ˈhɔbl] vi cojear

hobby [ˈhɔbɪ] n pasatiempo, afición f

hobo [ˈhəʊbəʊ] (US) n vagabundo

hockey [ˈhɔkɪ] n hockey m

hog [hɔg] n cerdo, puerco ♦ vt (fig) acaparar; **to go the whole ~** poner toda la carne en el asador

hoist [hɔɪst] n (crane) grúa ♦ vt levantar, alzar; (flag, sail) izar

hold [həʊld] (pt, pp **held**) vt sostener; (contain) contener; (have: power, qualification) tener; (keep back) retener; (believe) sostener; (consider) considerar; (keep in position): **to ~ one's head up** mantener la cabeza alta; (meeting) celebrar ♦ vi (withstand pressure) resistir; (be valid) valer ♦ n (grasp) asimiento; (fig) dominio; **~ the line!** (TEL) ¡no cuelgue!; **to ~ one's own** (fig) defenderse; **to catch or get (a) ~ of** agarrarse or asirse de; ~ **back** vt retener; (secret) ocultar; ~ **down** vt (person) sujetar; (job) mantener; ~ **off** vt (enemy) rechazar; ~ **on** vi agarrarse bien; (wait) esperar; ~ **on!** (TEL) ¡(espere) un momento!; ~ **on to** vt fus agarrarse a; (keep) guardar; ~ **out** vt ofrecer ♦ vi (resist) resistir; ~ **up** vt (raise)

levantar; (support) apoyar; (delay) retrasar; (rob) asaltar; ~**all** (BRIT) n bolsa; ~**er** n (container) receptáculo; (of ticket, record) poseedor(a) m/f; (of office, title etc) titular m/f; ~**ing** n (share) interés m; (farmland) parcela; ~**up** n (robbery) atraco; (delay) retraso; (BRIT: in traffic) embotellamiento

hole [həʊl] n agujero

holiday [ˈhɔlədɪ] n vacaciones fpl; (public ~) (día m de) fiesta, día m feriado; **on ~** de vacaciones; ~ **camp** n (BRIT: also: ~ **centre**) centro de vacaciones; ~-**maker** (BRIT) n turista m/f; ~ **resort** n centro turístico

holiness [ˈhəʊlɪnɪs] n santidad f

Holland [ˈhɔlənd] n Holanda

hollow [ˈhɔləʊ] adj hueco; (claim) vacío; (eyes) hundido; (sound) sordo ♦ n hueco; (in ground) hoyo ♦ vt: **to ~ out** excavar

holly [ˈhɔlɪ] n acebo

holocaust [ˈhɔləkɔːst] n holocausto

holy [ˈhəʊlɪ] adj santo, sagrado; (water) bendito

homage [ˈhɔmɪdʒ] n homenaje m

home [həʊm] n casa; (country) patria; (institution) asilo ♦ cpd (domestic) casero, de casa; (ECON, POL) nacional ♦ adv (direction) a casa; (right in: nail etc) a fondo; **at ~** en casa; (in country) en el país; (fig) como pez en el agua; **to go/ come ~** ir/volver a casa; **make yourself at ~** ¡estás en tu casa!; ~ **address** n domicilio; ~**land** n tierra natal; ~**less** adj sin hogar, sin casa; ~**ly** adj (simple) sencillo; ~-**made** adj casero; H~ **Office** (BRIT) n Ministerio del Interior; H~ **page** n página de inicio; ~ **rule** n autonomía; H~ **Secretary** (BRIT) n Ministro del Interior; ~**sick** adj: **to be ~sick** tener morriña, sentir nostalgia; ~ **town** n ciudad f natal; ~**ward** [ˈhəʊmwəd] adj (journey) hacia casa; ~**work** n deberes mpl

homoeopathic [həʊmɪəˈpæθɪk] (US **homeopathic**) adj homeopático

homosexual [həməʊˈsɛksjuəl] adj, n homosexual m/f

Honduran [hɔn'dʒuərən] *adj, n* hondureño/a *m/f*

Honduras [hɔn'dʒuərəs] *n* Honduras *f*

honest ['ɔnɪst] *adj* honrado; (*sincere*) franco, sincero; ~**ly** *adv* honradamente; francamente; ~**y** *n* honradez *f*

honey ['hʌnɪ] *n* miel *f*; ~**comb** *n* panal *m*; ~**moon** *n* luna de miel; ~**suckle** *n* madreselva

honk [hɔŋk] *vi* (*AUT*) tocar el pito, pitar

honorary ['ɔnərərɪ] *adj* (*member, president*) de honor; (*title*) honorífico; ~ **degree** doctorado honoris causa

honour ['ɔnə*] (*US* **honor**) *vt* honrar; (*commitment, promise*) cumplir con ♦ *n* honor *m*, honra; ~**able** *adj* honorable; ~**s degree** *n* (*SCOL*) título de licenciado con calificación alta

hood [hud] *n* capucha; (*BRIT: AUT*) capota; (*US: AUT*) capó *m*; (*of cooker*) campana de humos

hoof [hu:f] (*pl* **hooves**) *n* pezuña

hook [huk] *n* gancho; (*on dress*) corchete *m*, broche *m*; (*for fishing*) anzuelo ♦ *vt* enganchar; (*fish*) pescar

hooligan ['hu:lɪgən] *n* gamberro

hoop [hu:p] *n* aro

hooray [hu:'reɪ] *excl* = **hurray**

hoot [hu:t] (*BRIT*) *vi* (*AUT*) tocar el pito, pitar; (*siren*) sonar la sirena; (*owl*) ulular; ~**er** (*BRIT*) *n* (*AUT*) pito, claxon *m*; (*NAUT*) sirena

Hoover ® ['hu:və*] (*BRIT*) *n* aspiradora ♦ *vt*: **h~** pasar la aspiradora por

hooves [hu:vz] *npl of* **hoof**

hop [hɔp] *vi* saltar, brincar; (*on one foot*) saltar con un pie

hope [həup] *vt, vi* esperar ♦ *n* esperanza; **I ~ so/not** espero que sí/no; ~**ful** *adj* (*person*) optimista; (*situation*) prometedor(a); (*one hopes*): ~**fully he will recover** esperamos que se recupere; ~**less** *adj* desesperado; (*person*): **to be ~less** ser un desastre

hops [hɔps] *npl* lúpulo

horizon [hə'raɪzn] *n* horizonte *m*; ~**tal**

[hɔrɪ'zɔntl] *adj* horizontal

hormone ['hɔ:məun] *n* hormona

horn [hɔ:n] *n* cuerno; (*MUS: also:* **French ~**) trompa; (*AUT*) pito, claxon *m*

hornet ['hɔ:nɪt] *n* avispón *m*

horoscope ['hɔrəskəup] *n* horóscopo

horrible ['hɔrɪbl] *adj* horrible

horrid ['hɔrɪd] *adj* horrible, horroroso

horrify ['hɔrɪfaɪ] *vt* horrorizar

horror ['hɔrə*] *n* horror *m*; ~ **film** *n* película de horror

hors d'oeuvre [ɔ:'də:vrə] *n* entremeses *mpl*

horse [hɔ:s] *n* caballo; ~**back** *n*: **on ~back** a caballo; ~ **chestnut** *n* (*tree*) castaño de Indias; (*nut*) castaña de Indias; ~**man/woman** (*irreg*) *n* jinete/a *m/f*; ~**power** *n* caballo (de fuerza); ~**racing** *n* carreras *fpl* de caballos; ~**radish** *n* rábano picante; ~**shoe** *n* herradura

hose [həuz] *n* (*also:* ~**pipe**) manguera

hospitable [hɔs'pɪtəbl] *adj* hospitalario

hospital ['hɔspɪtl] *n* hospital *m*

hospitality [hɔspɪ'tælɪtɪ] *n* hospitalidad *f*

host [həust] *n* anfitrión *m*; (*TV, RADIO*) presentador *m*; (*REL*) hostia; (*large number*): **a ~ of** multitud de

hostage ['hɔstɪdʒ] *n* rehén *m*

hostel ['hɔstl] *n* hostal *m*; (**youth**) ~ albergue *m* juvenil

hostess ['həustɪs] *n* anfitriona; (*BRIT:* **air ~**) azafata; (*TV, RADIO*) presentadora

hostile ['hɔstaɪl] *adj* hostil

hot [hɔt] *adj* caliente; (*weather*) caluroso, de calor; (*as opposed to warm*) muy caliente; (*spicy*) picante; **to be ~** (*person*) tener calor; (*object*) estar caliente; (*weather*) hacer calor; ~**bed** *n* (*fig*) semillero; ~ **dog** *n* perro caliente

hotel [həu'tel] *n* hotel *m*

hot: ~**house** *n* invernadero; ~ **line** *n* (*POL*) teléfono rojo; ~**ly** *adv* con pasión, apasionadamente; ~**-water bottle** *n* bolsa de agua caliente

hound [haund] *vt* acosar ♦ *n* perro (de caza)

hour ['auə*] *n* hora; ~**ly** *adj* (de) cada hora

house [n haus, pl 'hauzız, vb hauz] n (gen, firm) casa; (POL) cámara; (THEATRE) sala ♦ vt (person) alojar; (collection) albergar; **on the ~** (fig) la casa invita; **~ arrest** n arresto domiciliario; **~boat** n casa flotante; **~bound** adj confinado en casa; **~breaking** n allanamiento de morada; **~hold** n familia; (home) casa; **~keeper** n ama de llaves; **~keeping** n (work) trabajos mpl domésticos; **~keeping (money)** n dinero para gastos domésticos; **~-warming party** n fiesta de estreno de una casa; **~wife** (irreg) n ama de casa; **~work** n faenas fpl (de la casa)

housing ['hauzıŋ] n (act) alojamiento; (houses) viviendas fpl; **~ development, ~ estate** (BRIT) n urbanización f

hovel ['hɔvl] n casucha

hover ['hɔvə*] vi flotar (en el aire); **~craft** n aerodeslizador m

how [hau] adv (in what way) cómo; **~ are you?** ¿cómo estás?; **~ much milk/many people?** ¿cuánta leche/gente?; **~ much does it cost?** ¿cuánto cuesta?; **~ long have you been here?** ¿cuánto hace que estás aquí?; **~ old are you?** ¿cuántos años tienes?; **~ tall is he?** ¿cómo es de alto?; **~ is school?** ¿cómo (te) va (en) la escuela?; **~ was the film?** ¿qué tal la película?; **~ lovely/awful!** ¡qué bonito/horror!

however [hau'ɛvə*] adv: **~ I do it** lo haga como lo haga; **~ cold it is** por mucho frío que haga; **~ fast he runs** por muy rápido que corra; **~ did you do it?** ¿cómo lo hiciste? ♦ conj sin embargo, no obstante

howl [haul] n aullido ♦ vi aullar; (person) dar alaridos; (wind) ulular

H.P. n abbr = **hire purchase**

h.p. abbr = **horse power**

HQ n abbr = **headquarters**

HTML n abbr (= hypertext markup language) lenguaje m de hipertexto

hub [hʌb] n (of wheel) cubo; (fig) centro

hubcap ['hʌbkæp] n tapacubos m inv

huddle ['hʌdl] vi: **to ~ together** acurrucarse

hue [hju:] n color m, matiz m

huff [hʌf] n: **in a ~** enojado

hug [hʌg] vt abrazar; (thing) apretar con los brazos

huge [hju:dʒ] adj enorme

hull [hʌl] n (of ship) casco

hullo [hə'ləu] excl = **hello**

hum [hʌm] vt tararear, canturrear ♦ vi tararear, canturrear; (insect) zumbar

human ['hju:mən] adj, n humano; **~e** [hju:'meın] adj humano, humanitario; **~itarian** [hju:mænı'tɛərıən] adj humanitario; **~ity** [hju:'mænıtı] n humanidad f

humble ['hʌmbl] adj humilde

humdrum ['hʌmdrʌm] adj (boring) monótono, aburrido

humid ['hju:mıd] adj húmedo

humiliate [hju:'mılıeıt] vt humillar

humorous ['hju:mərəs] adj gracioso, divertido

humour ['hju:mə*] (US **humor**) n humorismo, sentido del humor; (mood) humor m ♦ vt (person) complacer

hump [hʌmp] n (in ground) montículo; (camel's) giba

hunch [hʌntʃ] n (premonition) presentimiento; **~back** n joroba m/f; **~ed** adj jorobado

hundred ['hʌndrəd] num ciento; (before n) cien; **~s of** centenares de; **~weight** n (BRIT) = 50.8 kg; 112 lb; (US) = 45.3 kg; 100 lb

hung [hʌŋ] pt, pp of **hang**

Hungarian [hʌŋ'gɛərıən] adj, n húngaro/a m/f

Hungary ['hʌŋgərı] n Hungría

hunger ['hʌŋgə*] n hambre f ♦ vi: **to ~ for** (fig) tener hambre de, anhelar; **~ strike** n huelga de hambre

hungry ['hʌŋgrı] adj: **~ (for)** hambriento (de); **to be ~** tener hambre

hunk [hʌŋk] n (of bread etc) trozo, pedazo

hunt [hʌnt] vt (seek) buscar; (SPORT) cazar ♦ vi (search): **to ~ (for)** buscar; (SPORT) cazar ♦ n búsqueda; caza, cacería; **~er** n cazador(a) m/f; **~ing** n caza

hurdle ['hɜːdl] n (SPORT) valla; (fig) obstáculo

hurl [hɜːl] vt lanzar, arrojar

hurrah [huˈrɑː] excl = **hurray**

hurray [huˈreɪ] excl ¡viva!

hurricane ['hʌrɪkən] n huracán m

hurried ['hʌrɪd] adj (rushed) hecho de prisa; ~ly adv con prisa, apresuradamente

hurry ['hʌrɪ] n prisa ♦ vi (also: ~ **up**) apresurarse, darse prisa ♦ vt (also: ~ **up**: person) dar prisa a; (: work) apresurar, hacer de prisa; **to be in a ~** tener prisa

hurt [hɜːt] (pt, pp **hurt**) vt hacer daño a ♦ vi doler ♦ adj lastimado; ~**ful** adj (remark etc) hiriente

hurtle ['hɜːtl] vi: **to ~ past** pasar como un rayo; **to ~ down** ir a toda velocidad

husband ['hʌzbənd] n marido

hush [hʌʃ] n silencio ♦ vt hacer callar; ~! ¡chitón!, ¡cállate!; ~ **up** vt encubrir

husk [hʌsk] n (of wheat) cáscara

husky ['hʌskɪ] adj ronco ♦ n perro esquimal

hustle ['hʌsl] vt (hurry) dar prisa a ♦ n: ~ **and bustle** ajetreo

hut [hʌt] n cabaña; (shed) cobertizo

hutch [hʌtʃ] n conejera

hyacinth ['haɪəsɪnθ] n jacinto

hydrant ['haɪdrənt] n (also: **fire ~**) boca de incendios

hydraulic [haɪˈdrɔːlɪk] adj hidráulico

hydroelectric [haɪdrəʊˈlektrɪk] adj hidroeléctrico

hydrofoil ['haɪdrəfɔɪl] n aerodeslizador m

hydrogen ['haɪdrədʒən] n hidrógeno

hygiene ['haɪdʒiːn] n higiene f; **hygienic** [-'dʒiːnɪk] adj higiénico

hymn [hɪm] n himno

hype [haɪp] n (inf) bombardeo publicitario

hypermarket ['haɪpəmɑːkɪt] n hipermercado

hyphen ['haɪfn] n guión m

hypnotize ['hɪpnətaɪz] vt hipnotizar

hypocrisy [hɪˈpɒkrɪsɪ] n hipocresía; **hypocrite** ['hɪpəkrɪt] n hipócrita m/f; **hypocritical** [hɪpəˈkrɪtɪkl] adj hipócrita

hypothesis [haɪˈpɒθɪsɪs] (pl **hypotheses**)

n hipótesis f inv

hysteria [hɪˈstɪərɪə] n histeria; **hysterical** [-'sterɪkl] adj histérico; (funny) para morirse de risa; **hysterics** [-'sterɪks] npl histeria; **to be in hysterics** (fig) morirse de risa

I, i

I [aɪ] pron yo

ice [aɪs] n hielo; (~ **cream**) helado ♦ vt (cake) alcorzar ♦ vi (also: ~ **over**, ~ **up**) helarse; ~**berg** n iceberg m; ~**box** n (BRIT) congelador m; (US) nevera (SP), refrigeradora (AM); ~ **cream** n helado; ~ **cube** n cubito de hielo; ~**d** adj (cake) escarchado; (drink) helado; ~ **hockey** n hockey m sobre hielo

Iceland ['aɪslənd] n Islandia

ice: ~ **lolly** (BRIT) n polo; ~ **rink** n pista de hielo; ~ **skating** n patinaje m sobre hielo

icicle ['aɪsɪkl] n carámbano

icing ['aɪsɪŋ] n (CULIN) alcorza; ~ **sugar** (BRIT) n azúcar m glas(eado)

icon ['aɪkɒn] n icono

icy ['aɪsɪ] adj helado

I'd [aɪd] = **I would; I had**

idea [aɪˈdɪə] n idea

ideal [aɪˈdɪəl] n ideal m ♦ adj ideal

identical [aɪˈdentɪkl] adj idéntico

identification [aɪdentɪfɪˈkeɪʃən] n identificación f; (means of) ~ documentos mpl personales

identify [aɪˈdentɪfaɪ] vt identificar

Identikit ® [aɪˈdentɪkɪt] n: ~ **(picture)** retrato-robot m

identity [aɪˈdentɪtɪ] n identidad f; ~ **card** n carnet m de identidad

ideology [aɪdɪˈɒlədʒɪ] n ideología

idiom ['ɪdɪəm] n modismo; (style of speaking) lenguaje m

idiosyncrasy [ɪdɪəʊˈsɪŋkrəsɪ] n idiosincrasia

idiot ['ɪdɪət] n idiota m/f; ~**ic** [-'ɒtɪk] adj tonto

idle ['aɪdl] adj (inactive) ocioso; (lazy)

holgazán/ana; (*unemployed*) parado, desocupado; (*machinery etc*) parado; (*talk etc*) frívolo ♦ *vi* (*machine*) marchar en vacío

idol ['aɪdl] *n* ídolo; **~ize** *vt* idolatrar

i.e. *abbr* (= *that is*) esto es

if [ɪf] *conj* si; **~ necessary** si fuera necesario, si hiciese falta; **~ I were you** yo en tu lugar; **~ so/not** de ser así/si no; **~ only I could!** ¡ojalá pudiera!; *see also* **as**; **even**

igloo ['ɪgluː] *n* iglú *m*

ignite [ɪg'naɪt] *vt* (*set fire to*) encender ♦ *vi* encenderse

ignition [ɪg'nɪʃən] *n* (AUT: *process*) ignición *f*; (: *mechanism*) encendido; **to switch on/off the ~** arrancar/apagar el motor; **~ key** *n* (AUT) llave *f* de contacto

ignorant ['ɪgnərənt] *adj* ignorante; **to be ~ of** ignorar

ignore [ɪg'nɔː*] *vt* (*person, advice*) no hacer caso de; (*fact*) pasar por alto

I'll [aɪl] = **I will; I shall**

ill [ɪl] *adj* enfermo, malo ♦ *n* mal *m* ♦ *adv* mal; **to be taken ~** ponerse enfermo; **~-advised** *adj* (*decision*) imprudente; **~-at-ease** *adj* incómodo

illegal [ɪ'liːgl] *adj* ilegal

illegible [ɪ'ledʒɪbl] *adj* ilegible

illegitimate [ɪlɪ'dʒɪtɪmət] *adj* ilegítimo

ill-fated *adj* malogrado

ill feeling *n* rencor *m*

illiterate [ɪ'lɪtərət] *adj* analfabeto

ill: ~-mannered *adj* mal educado; **~ness** *n* enfermedad *f*; **~-treat** *vt* maltratar

illuminate [ɪ'luːmɪneɪt] *vt* (*room, street*) iluminar, alumbrar; **illumination** [-'neɪʃən] *n* alumbrado; **illuminations** *npl* (*decorative lights*) iluminaciones *fpl*, luces *fpl*

illusion [ɪ'luːʒən] *n* ilusión *f*; (*trick*) truco

illustrate ['ɪləstreɪt] *vt* ilustrar

illustration [ɪlə'streɪʃən] *n* (*act of illustrating*) ilustración *f*; (*example*) ejemplo, ilustración *f*; (*in book*) lámina *f*

illustrious [ɪ'lʌstrɪəs] *adj* ilustre

I'm [aɪm] = **I am**

image ['ɪmɪdʒ] *n* imagen *f*; **~ry** [-ərɪ] *n* imágenes *fpl*

imaginary [ɪ'mædʒɪnərɪ] *adj* imaginario

imagination [ɪmædʒɪ'neɪʃən] *n* imaginación *f*; (*inventiveness*) inventiva

imaginative [ɪ'mædʒɪnətɪv] *adj* imaginativo

imagine [ɪ'mædʒɪn] *vt* imaginarse

imbalance [ɪm'bæləns] *n* desequilibrio

imitate ['ɪmɪteɪt] *vt* imitar; **imitation** [ɪmɪ'teɪʃən] *n* imitación *f*; (*copy*) copia

immaculate [ɪ'mækjulət] *adj* inmaculado

immaterial [ɪmə'tɪərɪəl] *adj* (*unimportant*) sin importancia

immature [ɪmə'tjuə*] *adj* (*person*) inmaduro

immediate [ɪ'miːdɪət] *adj* inmediato; (*pressing*) urgente, apremiante; (*nearest: family*) próximo; (: *neighbourhood*) inmediato; **~ly** *adv* (*at once*) en seguida; (*directly*) inmediatamente; **~ly next to** muy junto a

immense [ɪ'mens] *adj* inmenso, enorme; (*importance*) enorme

immerse [ɪ'məːs] *vt* (*submerge*) sumergir; **to be ~d in** (*fig*) estar absorto en

immersion heater [ɪ'məːʃən-] (BRIT) *n* calentador *m* de inmersión

immigrant ['ɪmɪgrənt] *n* inmigrante *m/f*; **immigration** [ɪmɪ'greɪʃən] *n* inmigración *f*

imminent ['ɪmɪnənt] *adj* inminente

immobile [ɪ'məubaɪl] *adj* inmóvil

immoral [ɪ'mɔrl] *adj* inmoral

immortal [ɪ'mɔːtl] *adj* inmortal

immune [ɪ'mjuːn] *adj*: **~ (to)** inmune (a); **immunity** *n* (MED, *of diplomat*) inmunidad *f*

immunize ['ɪmjunaɪz] *vt* inmunizar

impact ['ɪmpækt] *n* impacto

impair [ɪm'peə*] *vt* perjudicar

impart [ɪm'pɑːt] *vt* comunicar; (*flavour*) proporcionar

impartial [ɪm'pɑːʃl] *adj* imparcial

impassable [ɪm'pɑːsəbl] *adj* (*barrier*) infranqueable; (*river, road*) intransitable

impassive [ɪmˈpæsɪv] *adj* impasible

impatience [ɪmˈpeɪʃəns] *n* impaciencia

impatient [ɪmˈpeɪʃənt] *adj* impaciente; **to get** *or* **grow ~** impacientarse

impeccable [ɪmˈpekəbl] *adj* impecable

impede [ɪmˈpiːd] *vt* estorbar

impediment [ɪmˈpedɪmənt] *n* obstáculo, estorbo; (*also:* **speech ~**) defecto (del habla)

impending [ɪmˈpendɪŋ] *adj* inminente

imperative [ɪmˈperətɪv] *adj* (*tone*) imperioso; (*need*) imprescindible

imperfect [ɪmˈpɜːfɪkt] *adj* (*goods etc*) defectuoso ♦ *n* (LING: *also:* **~ tense**) imperfecto

imperial [ɪmˈpɪərɪəl] *adj* imperial

impersonal [ɪmˈpɜːsənl] *adj* impersonal

impersonate [ɪmˈpɜːsəneɪt] *vt* hacerse pasar por; (THEATRE) imitar

impertinent [ɪmˈpɜːtɪnənt] *adj* impertinente, insolente

impervious [ɪmˈpɜːvɪəs] *adj* impermeable; (*fig*): **~ to** insensible a

impetuous [ɪmˈpetjuəs] *adj* impetuoso

impetus [ˈɪmpətəs] *n* ímpetu *m*; (*fig*) impulso

impinge [ɪmˈpɪndʒ]: **to ~ on** *vt fus* (*affect*) afectar a

implement [*n* ˈɪmplɪmənt, *vb* ˈɪmplɪment] *n* herramienta; (*for cooking*) utensilio ♦ *vt* (*regulation*) hacer efectivo; (*plan*) realizar

implicit [ɪmˈplɪsɪt] *adj* implícito; (*belief, trust*) absoluto

imply [ɪmˈplaɪ] *vt* (*involve*) suponer; (*hint*) dar a entender que

impolite [ɪmpəˈlaɪt] *adj* mal educado

import [*vb* ɪmˈpɔːt, *n* ˈɪmpɔːt] *vt* importar ♦ *n* (COMM) importación *f*; (: *article*) producto importado; (*meaning*) significado, sentido

importance [ɪmˈpɔːtəns] *n* importancia

important [ɪmˈpɔːtənt] *adj* importante; **it's not ~** no importa, no tiene importancia

importer [ɪmˈpɔːtə*] *n* importador(a) *m/f*

impose [ɪmˈpəuz] *vt* imponer ♦ *vi*: **to ~ on sb** abusar de uno; **imposing** *adj* imponente, impresionante

imposition [ɪmpəˈzɪʃn] *n* (*of tax etc*) imposición *f*; **to be an ~ on** (*person*) molestar a

impossible [ɪmˈpɔsɪbl] *adj* imposible; (*person*) insoportable

impotent [ˈɪmpətənt] *adj* impotente

impound [ɪmˈpaund] *vt* embargar

impoverished [ɪmˈpɔvərɪʃt] *adj* necesitado

impractical [ɪmˈpræktɪkl] *adj* (*person, plan*) poco práctico

imprecise [ɪmprɪˈsaɪs] *adj* impreciso

impregnable [ɪmˈpregnəbl] *adj* (*castle*) inexpugnable

impress [ɪmˈpres] *vt* impresionar; (*mark*) estampar; **to ~ sth on sb** hacer entender algo a uno

impression [ɪmˈpreʃən] *n* impresión *f*; (*imitation*) imitación *f*; **to be under the ~ that** tener la impresión de que; **~ist** *n* impresionista *m/f*

impressive [ɪmˈpresɪv] *adj* impresionante

imprint [ˈɪmprɪnt] *n* (*outline*) huella; (PUBLISHING) pie *m* de imprenta

imprison [ɪmˈprɪzn] *vt* encarcelar; **~ment** *n* encarcelamiento; (*term of ~ment*) cárcel *f*

improbable [ɪmˈprɔbəbl] *adj* improbable, inverosímil

improper [ɪmˈprɔpə*] *adj* (*unsuitable: conduct etc*) incorrecto; (: *activities*) deshonesto

improve [ɪmˈpruːv] *vt* mejorar; (*foreign language*) perfeccionar ♦ *vi* mejorarse; **~ment** *n* mejoramiento; perfección *f*; progreso

improvise [ˈɪmprəvaɪz] *vt*, *vi* improvisar

impulse [ˈɪmpʌls] *n* impulso; **to act on ~** obrar sin reflexión; **impulsive** [-ˈpʌlsɪv] *adj* irreflexivo

impure [ɪmˈpjuə*] *adj* (*adulterated*) adulterado; (*morally*) impuro; **impurity** *n* impureza

---

KEYWORD

---

in [ɪn] *prep* **1** (*indicating place, position, with place names*) en; **~ the house/garden** en (la) casa/el jardín; ~ **here/there** aquí/ahí or allí dentro; ~ **London/England** en Londres/Inglaterra

2 (*indicating time*) en; ~ **spring** en (la) primavera; ~ **the afternoon** por la tarde; **at 4 o'clock** ~ **the afternoon** a las 4 de la tarde; **I did it** ~ **3 hours/days** lo hice en 3 horas/días; **I'll see you** ~ **2 weeks** *or* ~ **2 weeks' time** te veré dentro de 2 semanas

3 (*indicating manner etc*) en; ~ **a loud/ soft voice** en voz alta/baja; ~ **pencil/ink** a lápiz/bolígrafo; **the boy** ~ **the blue shirt** el chico de la camisa azul

4 (*indicating circumstances*): ~ **the sun/ shade/rain** al sol/a la sombra/bajo la lluvia; **a change** ~ **policy** un cambio de política

5 (*indicating mood, state*): ~ **tears** en lágrimas, llorando; ~ **anger/despair** enfadado/desesperado; **to live** ~ **luxury** vivir lujosamente

6 (*with ratios, numbers*): **1** ~ **10 households, 1 household** ~ **10** una de cada 10 familias; **20 pence** ~ **the pound** 20 peniques por libra; **they lined up** ~ **twos** se alinearon de dos en dos

7 (*referring to people, works*) en; entre; **the disease is common** ~ **children** la enfermedad es común entre los niños; ~ **(the works of) Dickens** en (las obras de) Dickens

8 (*indicating profession etc*): **to be** ~ **teaching** estar en la enseñanza

9 (*after superlative*) de; **the best pupil** ~ **the class** el/la mejor alumno/a de la clase

10 (*with present participle*): ~ **saying this** al decir esto

♦ *adv*: **to be** ~ (*person: at home*) estar en casa; (*work*) estar; (*train, ship, plane*) haber llegado; (*in fashion*) estar de moda; **she'll be** ~ **later today** llegará más tarde hoy; **to ask sb** ~ hacer pasar a uno; **to run/limp** *etc* ~ entrar corriendo/cojeando *etc*

♦ *n*: **the ~s and outs** (*of proposal,*

situation etc) los detalles

in. *abbr* = **inch**

inability [ɪnə'bɪlɪtɪ] *n*: ~ **(to do)** incapacidad *f* (de hacer)

inaccurate [ɪn'ækjurət] *adj* inexacto, incorrecto

inadequate [ɪn'ædɪkwət] *adj* (*income, reply etc*) insuficiente; (*person*) incapaz

inadvertently [ɪnəd'vɜːtntlɪ] *adv* por descuido

inadvisable [ɪnəd'vaɪzəbl] *adj* poco aconsejable

inane [ɪ'neɪn] *adj* necio, fatuo

inanimate [ɪn'ænɪmət] *adj* inanimado

inappropriate [ɪnə'prəʊprɪət] *adj* inadecuado; (*improper*) poco oportuno

inarticulate [ɪnɑː'tɪkjulət] *adj* (*person*) incapaz de expresarse; (*speech*) mal pronunciado

inasmuch as [ɪnəz'mʌtʃ-] *conj* puesto que, ya que

inauguration [ɪnɔːgju'reɪʃən] *n* ceremonia de apertura

inborn [ɪn'bɔːn] *adj* (*quality*) innato

inbred [ɪn'bred] *adj* innato; (*family*) engendrado por endogamia

Inc. *abbr* (*US*: = *incorporated*) S.A.

incapable [ɪn'keɪpəbl] *adj* incapaz

incapacitate [ɪnkə'pæsɪteɪt] *vt*: **to** ~ **sb** incapacitar a uno

incense [*n* 'ɪnsɛns, *vb* ɪn'sɛns] *n* incienso
♦ *vt* (*anger*) indignar, encolerizar

incentive [ɪn'sɛntɪv] *n* incentivo, estímulo

incessant [ɪn'sɛsnt] *adj* incesante, continuo; **~ly** *adv* constantemente

incest ['ɪnsɛst] *n* incesto

inch [ɪntʃ] *n* pulgada; **to be within an** ~ **of** estar a dos dedos de; **he didn't give an** ~ no dio concesión alguna

incident ['ɪnsɪdnt] *n* incidente *m*

incidental [ɪnsɪ'dentl] *adj* accesorio; ~ **to** relacionado con; **~ly** [-'dentəlɪ] *adv* (*by the way*) a propósito

incite [ɪn'saɪt] *vt* provocar

inclination [ɪnklɪ'neɪʃən] *n* (*tendency*) tendencia, inclinación *f*; (*desire*) deseo;

(*disposition*) propensión *f*
incline [*n* 'ɪnklaɪn, *vb* ɪn'klaɪn] *n* pendiente *m*, cuesta ♦ *vt* (*head*) poner de lado ♦ *vi* inclinarse; **to be ~d to** (*tend*) ser propenso a
include [ɪn'kluːd] *vt* (*incorporate*) incluir; (*in letter*) adjuntar; **including** *prep* incluso, inclusive
inclusion [ɪn'kluːʒən] *n* inclusión *f*
inclusive [ɪn'kluːsɪv] *adj* inclusivo; **~ of tax** incluidos los impuestos
income ['ɪŋkʌm] *n* (*earned*) ingresos *mpl*; (*from property etc*) renta; (*from investment etc*) rédito; **~ tax** *n* impuesto sobre la renta
incoming ['ɪnkʌmɪŋ] *adj* (*flight, government etc*) entrante
incomparable [ɪn'kɒmpərəbl] *adj* incomparable, sin par
incompatible [ɪnkəm'pætɪbl] *adj* incompatible
incompetent [ɪn'kɒmpɪtənt] *adj* incompetente
incomplete [ɪnkəm'pliːt] *adj* (*partial: achievement etc*) incompleto; (*unfinished: painting etc*) inacabado
incongruous [ɪn'kɒŋgruəs] *adj* (*strange*) discordante; (*inappropriate*) incongruente
inconsiderate [ɪnkən'sɪdərət] *adj* desconsiderado
inconsistent [ɪnkən'sɪstənt] *adj* inconsecuente; (*contradictory*) incongruente; **~ with** (que) no concuerda con
inconspicuous [ɪnkən'spɪkjuəs] *adj* (*colour, building etc*) discreto; (*person*) que llama poco la atención
inconvenience [ɪnkən'viːnjəns] *n* inconveniences *mpl*; (*trouble*) molestia, incomodidad *f* ♦ *vt* incomodar
inconvenient [ɪnkən'viːnjənt] *adj* incómodo, poco práctico; (*time, place, visitor*) inoportuno
incorporate [ɪn'kɔːpəreɪt] *vt* incorporar; (*contain*) comprender; (*add*) agregar; **~d** *adj*: **~d company** (*US*) ≈ sociedad *f* anónima

incorrect [ɪnkə'rekt] *adj* incorrecto
increase [*n* 'ɪnkriːs, *vb* ɪn'kriːs] *n* aumento ♦ *vi* aumentar; (*grow*) crecer; (*price*) subir ♦ *vt* aumentar; (*price*) subir; **increasing** *adj* creciente; **increasingly** *adv* cada vez más, más y más
incredible [ɪn'kredɪbl] *adj* increíble
incubator ['ɪnkjubeɪtə*] *n* incubadora
incumbent [ɪn'kʌmbənt] *adj*: **it is ~ on him to ...** le incumbe ...
incur [ɪn'kɜː*] *vt* (*expenditure*) incurrir; (*loss*) sufrir; (*anger, disapproval*) provocar
indebted [ɪn'detɪd] *adj*: **to be ~ to sb** estar agradecido a uno
indecent [ɪn'diːsnt] *adj* indecente; **~ assault** (*BRIT*) *n* atentado contra el pudor; **~ exposure** *n* exhibicionismo
indecisive [ɪndɪ'saɪsɪv] *adj* indeciso
indeed [ɪn'diːd] *adv* efectivamente, en realidad; (*in fact*) en efecto; (*furthermore*) es más; **yes ~!** ¡claro que sí!
indefinitely [ɪn'defɪnɪtlɪ] *adv* (*wait*) indefinidamente
indemnity [ɪn'demnɪtɪ] *n* (*insurance*) indemnidad *f*; (*compensation*) indemnización *f*
independence [ɪndɪ'pendns] *n* independencia

Independence Day
---

*El cuatro de julio es **Independence
Day**, la fiesta nacional de Estados
Unidos, que se celebra en conmemoración
de la Declaración de Independencia, escrita
por Thomas Jefferson y aprobada en 1776.
En ella se proclamaba la independencia
total de Gran Bretaña de las trece colonias
americanas que serían el origen de los
Estados Unidos de América.*

---

independent [ɪndɪ'pendənt] *adj* independiente
index ['ɪndeks] (*pl* **~es**) *n* (*in book*) índice *m*; (: *in library etc*) catálogo; (*pl* **indices**: *ratio, sign*) exponente *m*; **~ card** *n* ficha; **~ed** (*US*) *adj* = **~-linked**; **~ finger** *n* índice *m*; **~-linked** (*BRIT*) *adj* vinculado al

índice del coste de la vida

India ['ɪndɪə] *n* la India; ~**n** *adj, n* indio/a *m/f*; **Red ~n** piel roja *m/f*; ~**n Ocean** *n*: **the ~n Ocean** el Océano Índico

indicate ['ɪndɪkeɪt] *vt* indicar; **indication** [-'keɪʃən] *n* indicio, señal *f*; **indicative** [ɪn'dɪkətɪv] *adj*: **to be indicative of** indicar; **indicator** *n* indicador *m*; (AUT) intermitente *m*

indices ['ɪndɪsiːz] *npl of* **index**

indictment [ɪn'daɪtmənt] *n* acusación *f*

indifferent [ɪn'dɪfrənt] *adj* indiferente; (*mediocre*) regular

indigenous [ɪn'dɪdʒɪnəs] *adj* indígena

indigestion [ɪndɪ'dʒestʃən] *n* indigestión *f*

indignant [ɪn'dɪgnənt] *adj*: **to be ~ at sth/with sb** indignarse por algo/con uno

indigo ['ɪndɪgəʊ] *adj* de color añil ♦ *n* añil *m*

indirect [ɪndɪ'rekt] *adj* indirecto

indiscreet [ɪndɪ'skriːt] *adj* indiscreto, imprudente

indiscriminate [ɪndɪ'skrɪmɪnət] *adj* indiscriminado

indisputable [ɪndɪ'spjuːtəbl] *adj* incontestable

indistinct [ɪndɪ'stɪŋkt] *adj* (*noise, memory etc*) confuso

individual [ɪndɪ'vɪdjuəl] *n* individuo ♦ *adj* individual; (*personal*) personal; (*particular*) particular; ~**ly** *adv* (*singly*) individualmente

indoctrinate [ɪn'dɒktrɪneɪt] *vt* adoctrinar

indoor ['ɪndɔː] *adj* (*swimming pool*) cubierto; (*plant*) de interior; (*sport*) bajo cubierta; ~**s** [ɪn'dɔːz] *adv* dentro

induce [ɪn'djuːs] *vt* inducir, persuadir; (*bring about*) producir; (*birth*) provocar; ~**ment** *n* (*incentive*) incentivo; (*pej: bribe*) soborno

indulge [ɪn'dʌldʒ] *vt* (*whim*) satisfacer; (*person*) complacer; (*child*) mimar ♦ *vi*: **to ~ in** darse el gusto de; ~**nce** *n* vicio; (*leniency*) indulgencia; ~**nt** *adj* indulgente

industrial [ɪn'dʌstrɪəl] *adj* industrial; ~ **action** *n* huelga; ~ **estate** (BRIT) *n* polígono (SP) *or* zona (AM) industrial; ~**ist** *n* industrial *m/f*; ~**ize** *vt* industrializar; ~ **park** (US) *n* = ~ **estate**

industrious [ɪn'dʌstrɪəs] *adj* trabajador(a); (*student*) aplicado

industry ['ɪndəstrɪ] *n* industria; (*diligence*) aplicación *f*

inebriated [ɪ'niːbrɪeɪtɪd] *adj* borracho

inedible [ɪn'edɪbl] *adj* incomible; (*poisonous*) no comestible

ineffective [ɪnɪ'fektɪv] *adj* ineficaz, inútil

ineffectual [ɪnɪ'fektjuəl] *adj* = **ineffective**

inefficient [ɪnɪ'fɪʃənt] *adj* ineficaz, ineficiente

inept [ɪ'nept] *adj* incompetente

inequality [ɪnɪ'kwɒlɪtɪ] *n* desigualdad *f*

inert [ɪ'nɜːt] *adj* inerte, inactivo; (*immobile*) inmóvil

inescapable [ɪnɪ'skeɪpəbl] *adj* ineludible

inevitable [ɪn'evɪtəbl] *adj* inevitable; **inevitably** *adv* inevitablemente

inexcusable [ɪnɪks'kjuːzəbl] *adj* imperdonable

inexpensive [ɪnɪk'spensɪv] *adj* económico

inexperienced [ɪnɪk'spɪərɪənst] *adj* inexperto

infallible [ɪn'fælɪbl] *adj* infalible

infamous ['ɪnfəməs] *adj* infame

infancy ['ɪnfənsɪ] *n* infancia

infant ['ɪnfənt] *n* niño/a; (*baby*) niño pequeño, bebé *m*; (*pej*) aniñado

infantry ['ɪnfəntrɪ] *n* infantería

infant school (BRIT) *n* parvulario

infatuated [ɪn'fætjueɪtɪd] *adj*: ~ **with** (*in love*) loco por

infatuation [ɪnfætu'eɪʃən] *n* enamoramiento, pasión *f*

infect [ɪn'fekt] *vt* (*wound*) infectar; (*food*) contaminar; (*person, animal*) contagiar; ~**ion** [ɪn'fekʃən] *n* infección *f*; (*fig*) contagio; ~**ious** [ɪn'fekʃəs] *adj* (*also fig*) contagioso

infer [ɪn'fɜː] *vt* deducir, inferir

inferior [ɪn'fɪərɪə] *adj, n* inferior *m/f*; ~**ity** [-'ɒrətɪ] *n* inferioridad *f*

infertile [ɪn'fɜːtaɪl] *adj* estéril; (*person*) infecundo

infested [ɪn'festɪd] *adj*: ~ **with** plagado de

in-fighting *n* (*fig*) lucha(s) *f(pl)* interna(s)
infinite ['ɪnfɪnɪt] *adj* infinito
infinitive [ɪn'fɪnɪtɪv] *n* infinitivo
infinity [ɪn'fɪnɪtɪ] *n* infinito; (*an* ~)
infinidad *f*
infirmary [ɪn'fəːmərɪ] *n* hospital *m*
inflamed [ɪn'fleɪmd] *adj*: **to become** ~
inflamarse
inflammable [ɪn'flæməbl] *adj* inflamable
inflammation [ɪnflə'meɪʃən] *n* inflamación
f
inflatable [ɪn'fleɪtəbl] *adj* (*ball, boat*)
inflable
inflate [ɪn'fleɪt] *vt* (*tyre, price etc*) inflar;
(*fig*) hinchar; **inflation** [ɪn'fleɪʃən] *n*
(*ECON*) inflación *f*
inflexible [ɪn'fleksəbl] *adj* (*rule*) rígido,
(*person*) inflexible
inflict [ɪn'flɪkt] *vt*: **to ~ sth on sb** infligir
algo en uno
influence ['ɪnfluəns] *n* influencia ♦ *vt*
influir en, influenciar; **under the ~ of
alcohol** en estado de embriaguez;
influential [-'ɛnʃl] *adj* influyente
influenza [ɪnflu'enzə] *n* gripe *f*
influx ['ɪnflʌks] *n* afluencia
inform [ɪn'fɔːm] *vt*: **to ~ sb of sth** informar
a uno sobre *or* de algo ♦ *vi*: **to ~ on sb**
delatar a uno
informal [ɪn'fɔːməl] *adj* (*manner, tone*)
familiar; (*dress, interview, occasion*)
informal; (*visit, meeting*) extraoficial; **~ity**
[-'mælɪtɪ] *n* informalidad *f*; sencillez *f*
informant [ɪn'fɔːmənt] *n* informante *m/f*
information [ɪnfə'meɪʃən] *n* información *f*;
(*knowledge*) conocimientos *mpl*; **a piece
of ~** un dato; **~ desk** *n* (mostrador *m*
de) información *f*; **~ office** *n*
información *f*
informative [ɪn'fɔːmətɪv] *adj* informativo
informer [ɪn'fɔːmə*] *n* (*also*: **police ~**)
soplón/ona *m/f*
infra-red [ɪnfrə'red] *adj* infrarrojo
infrastructure ['ɪnfrəstrʌktʃə*] *n* (*of
system etc*) infraestructura
infringe [ɪn'frɪndʒ] *vt* infringir, violar ♦ *vi*:
to ~ on abusar de; **~ment** *n* infracción *f*;

(*of rights*) usurpación *f*
infuriating [ɪn'fjuərɪeɪtɪŋ] *adj* (*habit, noise*)
enloquecedor(a)
ingenious [ɪn'dʒiːnjəs] *adj* ingenioso;
ingenuity [-dʒɪ'njuːɪtɪ] *n* ingeniosidad *f*
ingenuous [ɪn'dʒenjuəs] *adj* ingenuo
ingot ['ɪŋɡət] *n* lingote *m*, barra
ingrained [ɪn'ɡreɪnd] *adj* arraigado
ingratiate [ɪn'ɡreɪʃɪeɪt] *vt*: **to ~ o.s. with**
congraciarse con
ingredient [ɪn'ɡriːdɪənt] *n* ingrediente *m*
inhabit [ɪn'hæbɪt] *vt* vivir en; **~ant** *n*
habitante *m/f*
inhale [ɪn'heɪl] *vt* inhalar ♦ *vi* (*breathe in*)
aspirar; (*in smoking*) tragar
inherent [ɪn'hɪərənt] *adj*: **~ in** *or* **to**
inherente a
inherit [ɪn'herɪt] *vt* heredar; **~ance** *n*
herencia; (*fig*) patrimonio
inhibit [ɪn'hɪbɪt] *vt* inhibir, impedir; **~ed**
adj (*PSYCH*) cohibido; **~ion** [-'bɪʃən] *n*
cohibición *f*
inhospitable [ɪnhɔs'pɪtəbl] *adj* (*person*)
inhospitalario; (*place*) inhóspito
inhuman [ɪn'hjuːmən] *adj* inhumano
initial [ɪ'nɪʃl] *adj* primero ♦ *n* inicial *f* ♦ *vt*
firmar con las iniciales; **~s** *npl* (*as
signature*) iniciales *fpl*; (*abbreviation*) siglas
fpl; **~ly** *adv* al principio
initiate [ɪ'nɪʃɪeɪt] *vt* iniciar; **to ~
proceedings against sb** (*LAW*) entablar
proceso contra uno
initiative [ɪ'nɪʃətɪv] *n* iniciativa
inject [ɪn'dʒekt] *vt* inyectar; **to ~ sb with
sth** inyectar algo a uno; **~ion** [ɪn'dʒekʃən]
n inyección *f*
injunction [ɪn'dʒʌŋkʃən] *n* interdicto
injure ['ɪndʒə*] *vt* (*hurt*) herir, lastimar; (*fig:
reputation etc*) perjudicar; **~d** *adj* (*person,
arm*) herido, lastimado; **injury** *n* herida,
lesión *f*; (*wrong*) perjuicio, daño; **injury
time** *n* (*SPORT*) (tiempo de) descuento
injustice [ɪn'dʒʌstɪs] *n* injusticia
ink [ɪŋk] *n* tinta
inkling ['ɪŋklɪŋ] *n* sospecha; (*idea*) idea
inlaid ['ɪnleɪd] *adj* (*with wood, gems etc*)
incrustado

inland [adj 'ɪnlənd, adv ɪn'lænd] adj (waterway, port etc) interior ♦ adv tierra adentro; **I~ Revenue** (BRIT) n departamento de impuestos; ≈ Hacienda (SP)

in-laws npl suegros mpl

inlet ['ɪnlɛt] n (GEO) ensenada, cala; (TECH) admisión f, entrada

inmate [ɪn'meɪt] n (in prison) preso/a; presidiario/a; (in asylum) internado/a

inn [ɪn] n posada, mesón m

innate [ɪ'neɪt] adj innato

inner ['ɪnə*] adj (courtyard, calm) interior; (feelings) íntimo; ~ **city** n barrios deprimidos del centro de una ciudad; ~ **tube** n (of tyre) cámara (SP), llanta (AM)

innings ['ɪnɪŋz] n (CRICKET) entrada, turno

innocent ['ɪnəsnt] adj inocente

innocuous [ɪ'nɔkjuəs] adj inocuo

innovation [ɪnəu'veɪʃən] n novedad f

innuendo [ɪnjuː'ɛndəu] (pl ~**es**) n indirecta

inoculation [ɪnɔkju'leɪʃən] n inoculación f

in-patient n paciente m/f interno/a

input ['ɪnput] n entrada; (of resources) inversión f; (COMPUT) entrada de datos

inquest ['ɪnkwɛst] n (coroner's) encuesta judicial

inquire [ɪn'kwaɪə*] vi preguntar ♦ vt: **to ~ whether** preguntar si; **to ~ about** (person) preguntar por; (fact) informarse de; ~ **into** vt fus investigar, indagar; **inquiry** n pregunta; (investigation) investigación f, pesquisa; **"Inquiries"** "Información"; **inquiry office** (BRIT) n oficina de información

inquisitive [ɪn'kwɪzɪtɪv] adj (curious) curioso

ins. abbr = **inches**

insane [ɪn'seɪn] adj loco; (MED) demente

insanity [ɪn'sænɪtɪ] n demencia, locura

inscription [ɪn'skrɪpʃən] n inscripción f; (in book) dedicatoria

inscrutable [ɪn'skruːtəbl] adj inescrutable, insondable

insect ['ɪnsɛkt] n insecto; ~**icide** [ɪn'sɛktɪsaɪd] n insecticida m; ~ **repellent** n loción f contra insectos

insecure [ɪnsɪ'kjuə*] adj inseguro

insemination [ɪnsɛmɪ'neɪʃn] n: **artificial ~** inseminación f artificial

insensitive [ɪn'sɛnsɪtɪv] adj insensible

insert [vb ɪn'sɜːt, n 'ɪnsɜːt] vt (into sth) introducir ♦ n encarte m; ~**ion** [ɪn'sɜːʃən] n inserción f

in-service ['ɪnsɜːvɪs] adj (training, course) a cargo de la empresa

inshore [ɪn'ʃɔː*] adj de bajura ♦ adv (be) cerca de la orilla; (move) hacia la orilla

inside ['ɪnsaɪd] n interior m ♦ adj interior, interno ♦ adv (be) (por) dentro; (go) hacia dentro ♦ prep dentro de; (of time): ~ **10 minutes** en menos de 10 minutos; ~**s** npl (inf: stomach) tripas fpl; ~ **information** n información f confidencial; ~ **lane** n (AUT: in Britain) carril m izquierdo; (: in US, Europe etc) carril m derecho; ~ **out** adv (turn) al revés; (know) a fondo

insider dealing, insider trading n (STOCK EXCHANGE) abuso de información privilegiada

insight ['ɪnsaɪt] n perspicacia

insignificant [ɪnsɪg'nɪfɪknt] adj insignificante

insincere [ɪnsɪn'sɪə*] adj poco sincero

insinuate [ɪn'sɪnjueɪt] vt insinuar

insipid [ɪn'sɪpɪd] adj soso, insulso

insist [ɪn'sɪst] vi insistir; **to ~ on** insistir en; **to ~ that** insistir en que; (claim) exigir que; ~**ent** adj insistente; (noise, action) persistente

insole ['ɪnsəul] n plantilla

insolent ['ɪnsələnt] adj insolente, descarado

insomnia [ɪn'sɔmnɪə] n insomnio

inspect [ɪn'spɛkt] vt inspeccionar, examinar; (troops) pasar revista a; ~**ion** [ɪn'spɛkʃən] n inspección f, examen m; (of troops) revista; ~**or** n inspector(a) m/f; (BRIT: on buses, trains) revisor(a) m/f

inspiration [ɪnspə'reɪʃən] n inspiración f; **inspire** [ɪn'spaɪə*] vt inspirar

instability [ɪnstə'bɪlɪtɪ] n inestabilidad f

install [ɪn'stɔːl] vt instalar; (official)

nombrar; **~ation** [ɪnstəˈleɪʃən] *n*
instalación *f*
instalment [ɪnˈstɔːlmənt] (*US* **installment**)
n plazo; (*of story*) entrega; (*of TV serial
etc*) capítulo; **in ~s** (*pay, receive*) a plazos
instance [ˈɪnstəns] *n* ejemplo, caso; **for ~**
por ejemplo; **in the first ~** en primer
lugar
instant [ˈɪnstənt] *n* instante *m*, momento
♦ *adj* inmediato; (*coffee etc*) instantáneo;
~ly *adv* en seguida
instead [ɪnˈsted] *adv* en cambio; **~ of** en
lugar de, en vez de
instep [ˈɪnstep] *n* empeine *m*
instil [ɪnˈstɪl] *vt*: **to ~ sth into** inculcar algo
a
instinct [ˈɪnstɪŋkt] *n* instinto
institute [ˈɪnstɪtjuːt] *n* instituto;
(*professional body*) colegio ♦ *vt* (*begin*)
iniciar, empezar; (*proceedings*) entablar;
(*system, rule*) establecer
institution [ɪnstɪˈtjuːʃən] *n* institución *f*;
(*MED: home*) asilo; (: *asylum*) manicomio;
(*of system etc*) establecimiento; (*of
custom*) iniciación *f*
instruct [ɪnˈstrʌkt] *vt*: **to ~ sb in sth**
instruir a uno en *or* sobre algo; **to ~ sb to
do sth** dar instrucciones a uno de hacer
algo; **~ion** [ɪnˈstrʌkʃən] *n* (*teaching*)
instrucción *f*; **~ions** *npl* (*orders*) órdenes
fpl; **~ions (for use)** modo de empleo;
~or *n* instructor(a) *m/f*
instrument [ˈɪnstrəmənt] *n* instrumento;
~al [-ˈmentl] *adj* (*MUS*) instrumental; **to
be ~al in** ser (el) artífice de; **~ panel** *n*
tablero (de instrumentos)
insufficient [ɪnsəˈfɪʃənt] *adj* insuficiente
insular [ˈɪnsjulə*] *adj* insular; (*person*)
estrecho de miras
insulate [ˈɪnsjuleɪt] *vt* aislar; **insulation**
[-ˈleɪʃən] *n* aislamiento
insulin [ˈɪnsjulɪn] *n* insulina
insult [*n* ˈɪnsʌlt, *vb* ɪnˈsʌlt] *n* insulto ♦ *vt*
insultar; **~ing** *adj* insultante
insurance [ɪnˈʃuərəns] *n* seguro; **fire/life
~** seguro contra incendios/sobre la vida; **~
agent** *n* agente *m/f* de seguros; **~**

policy *n* póliza (de seguros)
insure [ɪnˈʃuə*] *vt* asegurar
intact [ɪnˈtækt] *adj* íntegro; (*unharmed*)
intacto
intake [ˈɪnteɪk] *n* (*of food*) ingestión *f*; (*of
air*) consumo; (*BRIT: SCOL*): **an ~ of 200 a
year** 200 matriculados al año
integral [ˈɪntɪɡrəl] *adj* (*whole*) íntegro;
(*part*) integrante
integrate [ˈɪntɪɡreɪt] *vt* integrar ♦ *vi*
integrarse
integrity [ɪnˈtegrɪtɪ] *n* honradez *f*, rectitud
f
intellect [ˈɪntəlekt] *n* intelecto; **~ual**
[-ˈlektjuəl] *adj, n* intelectual *m/f*
intelligence [ɪnˈtelɪdʒəns] *n* inteligencia
intelligent [ɪnˈtelɪdʒənt] *adj* inteligente
intelligible [ɪnˈtelɪdʒɪbl] *adj* inteligible,
comprensible
intend [ɪnˈtend] *vt* (*gift etc*): **to ~ sth for**
destinar algo a; **to ~ to do sth** tener
intención de *or* pensar hacer algo
intense [ɪnˈtens] *adj* intenso; **~ly** *adv*
(*extremely*) sumamente
intensify [ɪnˈtensɪfaɪ] *vt* intensificar;
(*increase*) aumentar
intensive [ɪnˈtensɪv] *adj* intensivo; **~ care
unit** *n* unidad *f* de vigilancia intensiva
intent [ɪnˈtent] *n* propósito; (*LAW*)
premeditación *f* ♦ *adj* (*absorbed*) absorto;
(*attentive*) atento; **to all ~s and purposes**
prácticamente; **to be ~ on doing sth**
estar resuelto a hacer algo
intention [ɪnˈtenʃən] *n* intención *f*,
propósito; **~al** *adj* deliberado; **~ally** *adv*
a propósito
intently [ɪnˈtentlɪ] *adv* atentamente,
fijamente
interact [ɪntərˈækt] *vi* influirse
mutuamente; **~ive** *adj* (*COMPUT*)
interactivo
interchange [ˈɪntətʃeɪndʒ] *n* intercambio;
(*on motorway*) intersección *f*; **~able** *adj*
intercambiable
intercom [ˈɪntəkɔm] *n* interfono
intercourse [ˈɪntəkɔːs] *n* (*sexual*)
relaciones *fpl* sexuales

terest ['ɪntrɪst] n (also COMM) interés m
♦ vt interesar; **to be ~ed in** interesarse
por; **~ing** adj interesante; **~ rate** n tipo
or tasa de interés

terface ['ɪntəfeɪs] n (COMPUT) junción f

terfere [ɪntə'fɪə•] vi: **to ~ in**
entrometerse en; **to ~ with** (hinder)
estorbar; (damage) estropear

terference [ɪntə'fɪərəns] n intromisión f;
(RADIO, TV) interferencia

terim ['ɪntərɪm] n: **in the ~** en el ínterin
♦ adj provisional

terior [ɪn'tɪərɪə•] n interior m ♦ adj
interior; **~ designer** n interiorista m/f

terjection [ɪntə'dʒekʃən] n interposición
f; (LING) interjección f

terlock [ɪntə'lɔk] vi entrelazarse

terlude ['ɪntəluːd] n intervalo; (THEATRE)
intermedio

termediate [ɪntə'miːdɪət] adj
intermedio

termission [ɪntə'mɪʃən] n intermisión f;
(THEATRE) descanso

tern [vb ɪn'təːn, n 'ɪntəːn] vt internar ♦ n
(US) interno/a

ternal [ɪn'təːnl] adj (layout, pipes,
security) interior; (injury, structure, memo)
internal; **~ly** adv: **"not to be taken ~ly"**
"uso externo"; **I~ Revenue Service**
(US) n departamento de impuestos;
≈ Hacienda (SP)

ternational [ɪntə'næʃənl] adj
internacional ♦ n (BRIT: match) partido
internacional

ternet ['ɪntənet] n: **the ~** Internet m or
f; **~ café** n cibercafé m; **~ Service
Provider** n proveedor m de (accesso a)
Internet

terplay ['ɪntəpleɪ] n interacción f

terpret [ɪn'təːprɪt] vt interpretar; (translate) traducir; (understand) entender ♦ vi
hacer de intérprete; **~er** n intérprete m/f

terrogate [ɪn'terəʊgeɪt] vt interrogar;
interrogation [-'geɪʃən] n interrogatorio

terrupt [ɪntə'rʌpt] vt, vi interrumpir;
~ion [-'rʌpʃən] n interrupción f

tersect [ɪntə'sekt] vi (roads) cruzarse;

~ion [-'sekʃən] n (of roads) cruce m

intersperse [ɪntə'spəːs] vt: **to ~ with**
salpicar de

intertwine [ɪntə'twaɪn] vt entrelazarse

interval ['ɪntəvl] n intervalo; (BRIT: THEATRE,
SPORT) descanso; (: SCOL) recreo; **at ~s** a
ratos, de vez en cuando

intervene [ɪntə'viːn] vi intervenir; (event)
interponerse; (time) transcurrir;
intervention n intervención f

interview ['ɪntəvjuː] n entrevista ♦ vt
entrevistarse con; **~er** n entrevistador(a)
m/f

intestine [ɪn'testɪn] n intestino

intimacy ['ɪntɪməsɪ] n intimidad f

intimate [adj 'ɪntɪmət, vb 'ɪntɪmeɪt] adj
íntimo; (friendship) estrecho; (knowledge)
profundo ♦ vt dar a entender

into ['ɪntuː] prep en; (towards) a; (inside)
hacia el interior de; **~ 3 pieces/French**
en 3 pedazos/al francés

intolerable [ɪn'tɔlərəbl] adj intolerable,
insoportable

intolerant [ɪn'tɔlərənt] adj: **~ (of)**
intolerante (con o para)

intoxicated [ɪn'tɔksɪkeɪtɪd] adj
embriagado

intractable [ɪn'træktəbl] adj (person)
intratable; (problem) espinoso

intranet ['ɪntrənet] n intranet f

intransitive [ɪn'trænsɪtɪv] adj intransitivo

intravenous [ɪntrə'viːnəs] adj intravenoso

in-tray n bandeja de entrada

intricate ['ɪntrɪkət] adj (design, pattern)
intrincado

intrigue [ɪn'triːg] n intriga ♦ vt fascinar;
intriguing adj fascinante

intrinsic [ɪn'trɪnsɪk] adj intrínseco

introduce [ɪntrə'djuːs] vt introducir,
meter; (speaker, TV show etc) presentar;
to ~ sb (to sb) presentar uno (a otro); **to
~ sb to** (pastime, technique) introducir a
uno a; **introduction** [-'dʌkʃən] n
introducción f; (of person) presentación f;
introductory [-'dʌktərɪ] adj
introductorio; (lesson, offer) de
introducción

introvert ['ɪntrəvɜːt] n introvertido/a ♦ adj (*also*: **~ed**) introvertido

intrude [ɪn'truːd] vi (*person*) entrometerse; **to ~ on** estorbar; **~r** n intruso/a; **intrusion** [-ʒən] n invasión f

intuition [ɪntjuː'ɪʃən] n intuición f

inundate ['ɪnʌndeɪt] vt: **to ~ with** inundar de

invade [ɪn'veɪd] vt invadir

invalid [n 'ɪnvəlɪd, adj ɪn'vælɪd] n (MED) minusválido/a ♦ adj (*not valid*) inválido, nulo

invaluable [ɪn'væljuəbl] adj inestimable

invariable [ɪn'veərɪəbl] adj invariable

invent [ɪn'vent] vt inventar; **~ion** [ɪn'venʃən] n invento; (*lie*) ficción f, mentira; **~ive** adj inventivo; **~or** n inventor(a) m/f

inventory ['ɪnvəntrɪ] n inventario

invert [ɪn'vɜːt] vt invertir

inverted commas (BRIT) npl comillas fpl

invest [ɪn'vest] vt invertir ♦ vi: **to ~ in** (*company etc*) invertir dinero en; (*fig: sth useful*) comprar

investigate [ɪn'vestɪgeɪt] vt investigar; **investigation** [-'geɪʃən] n investigación f, pesquisa

investment [ɪn'vestmənt] n inversión f

investor [ɪn'vestə*] n inversionista m/f

invigilator [ɪn'vɪdʒɪleɪtə*] n persona que vigila en un examen

invigorating [ɪn'vɪgəreɪtɪŋ] adj vigorizante

invisible [ɪn'vɪzɪbl] adj invisible

invitation [ɪnvɪ'teɪʃən] n invitación f

invite [ɪn'vaɪt] vt invitar; (*opinions etc*) solicitar, pedir; **inviting** adj atractivo; (*food*) apetitoso

invoice ['ɪnvɔɪs] n factura ♦ vt facturar

involuntary [ɪn'vɒləntrɪ] adj involuntario

involve [ɪn'vɒlv] vt suponer, implicar; tener que ver con; (*concern, affect*) corresponder; **to ~ sb (in sth)** comprometer a uno (con algo); **~d** adj complicado; **to be ~d in** (*take part*) tomar parte en; (*be engrossed*) estar muy metido en; **~ment** n participación f; dedicación f

inward ['ɪnwəd] adj (*movement*) interior, interno; (*thought, feeling*) íntimo; **~(s)** adv hacia dentro

I/O abbr (COMPUT = *input/output*) entrada/salida

iodine ['aɪəudiːn] n yodo

ion ['aɪən] n ion m; **ioniser** ['aɪənaɪzə*] n ionizador m

iota [aɪ'əutə] n jota, ápice m

IOU n abbr (= *I owe you*) pagaré m

IQ n abbr (= *intelligence quotient*) cociente m intelectual

IRA n abbr (= *Irish Republican Army*) IRA m

Iran [ɪ'rɑːn] n Irán m; **~ian** [ɪ'reɪnɪən] adj, n iraní m/f

Iraq [ɪ'rɑːk] n Iraq; **~i** adj, n iraquí m/f

irate [aɪ'reɪt] adj enojado, airado

Ireland ['aɪələnd] n Irlanda

iris ['aɪrɪs] (pl **~es**) n (ANAT) iris m; (BOT) lirio

Irish ['aɪrɪʃ] adj irlandés/esa ♦ npl: **the ~** los irlandeses; **~man/woman** (*irreg*) n irlandés/esa m/f; **~ Sea** n: **the ~ Sea** el mar de Irlanda

iron ['aɪən] n hierro; (*for clothes*) plancha ♦ cpd de hierro ♦ vt (*clothes*) planchar; **~ out** vt (*fig*) allanar

ironic(al) [aɪ'rɒnɪk(l)] adj irónico

ironing ['aɪənɪŋ] n (*activity*) planchado; (*clothes: ironed*) ropa planchada; (: *to be ironed*) ropa por planchar; **~ board** n tabla de planchar

ironmonger's (shop) ['aɪənmʌŋgəz] (BRIT) n ferretería, quincallería

irony ['aɪrənɪ] n ironía

irrational [ɪ'ræʃənl] adj irracional

irreconcilable [ɪrekən'saɪləbl] adj (*ideas*) incompatible; (*enemies*) irreconciliable

irregular [ɪ'regjulə*] adj irregular; (*surface*) desigual; (*action, event*) anómalo; (*behaviour*) poco ortodoxo

irrelevant [ɪ'reləvənt] adj fuera de lugar, inoportuno

irresolute [ɪ'rezəluːt] adj indeciso

irrespective [ɪrɪ'spektɪv]: **~ of** prep sin tener en cuenta, no importa

irresponsible [ɪrɪ'spɒnsɪbl] *adj* (*act*) irresponsable; (*person*) poco serio

irrigate ['ɪrɪgeɪt] *vt* regar; **irrigation** [-'geɪʃən] *n* riego

irritable ['ɪrɪtəbl] *adj* (*person*) de mal humor

irritate ['ɪrɪteɪt] *vt* fastidiar; (*MED*) picar; **irritating** *adj* fastidioso; **irritation** [-'teɪʃən] *n* fastidio; enfado; picazón *f*

IRS (*US*) *n abbr* = **Internal Revenue Service**

is [ɪz] *vb see* **be**

Islam ['ɪzlɑːm] *n* Islam *m*; **~ic** [ɪz'læmɪk] *adj* islámico

island ['aɪlənd] *n* isla; **~er** *n* isleño/a

isle [aɪl] *n* isla

isn't ['ɪznt] = **is not**

isolate ['aɪsəleɪt] *vt* aislar; **~d** *adj* aislado; **isolation** [-'leɪʃən] *n* aislamiento

ISP *n abbr* = **Internet Service Provider**

Israel ['ɪzreɪl] *n* Israel *m*; **~i** [ɪz'reɪlɪ] *adj, n* israelí *m/f*

issue ['ɪsjuː] *n* (*problem, subject*) cuestión *f*; (*outcome*) resultado; (*of banknotes etc*) emisión *f*; (*of newspaper etc*) edición *f* ♦ *vt* (*rations, equipment*) distribuir, repartir; (*orders*) dar; (*certificate, passport*) expedir; (*decree*) promulgar; (*magazine*) publicar; (*cheques*) extender; (*banknotes, stamps*) emitir; **at ~** en cuestión; **to take ~ with sb (over)** estar en desacuerdo con uno (sobre); **to make an ~ of sth** hacer una cuestión de algo

Istanbul [ɪstæn'buːl] *n* Estambul *m*

KEYWORD

it [ɪt] *pron* **1** (*specific: subject: not generally translated*) él/ella; (*: direct object*) lo, la; (*: indirect object*) le; (*after prep*) él/ella; (*abstract concept*) ello; **~'s on the table** está en la mesa; **I can't find ~** no lo (*or* la) encuentro; **give ~ to me** dámelo (*or* dámela); **I spoke to him about ~** le hablé del asunto; **what did you learn from ~?** ¿qué aprendiste de él (*or* ella)?; **did you go to ~?** (*party, concert etc*) ¿fuiste?

2 (*impersonal*): **~'s raining** llueve, está lloviendo; **~'s 6 o'clock/the 10th of August** son las 6/es el 10 de agosto; **how far is ~? – ~'s 10 miles/2 hours on the train** ¿a qué distancia está? — a 10 millas/2 horas en tren; **who is ~? – ~'s me** ¿quién es? — soy yo

---

Italian [ɪ'tæljən] *adj* italiano ♦ *n* italiano/a; (*LING*) italiano

italics [ɪ'tælɪks] *npl* cursiva

Italy ['ɪtəlɪ] *n* Italia

itch [ɪtʃ] *n* picazón *f* ♦ *vi* (*part of body*) picar; **to ~ to do sth** rabiar por hacer algo; **~y** *adj*: **my hand is ~y** me pica la mano

it'd ['ɪtd] = **it would; it had**

item ['aɪtəm] *n* artículo; (*on agenda*) asunto (a tratar); (*also: news ~*) noticia; **~ize** *vt* detallar

itinerary [aɪ'tɪnərərɪ] *n* itinerario

it'll ['ɪtl] = **it will; it shall**

its [ɪts] *adj* su; sus *pl*

it's [ɪts] = **it is; it has**

itself [ɪt'self] *pron* (*reflexive*) sí mismo/a; (*emphatic*) él mismo/ella misma

ITV *n abbr* (*BRIT*: = *Independent Television*) cadena de televisión comercial independiente del Estado

I.U.D. *n abbr* (= *intra-uterine device*) DIU *m*

I've [aɪv] = **I have**

ivory ['aɪvərɪ] *n* marfil *m*

ivy ['aɪvɪ] *n* (*BOT*) hiedra

J, j

jab [dʒæb] *vt*: **to ~ sth into sth** clavar algo en algo ♦ *n* (*inf*) (*MED*) pinchazo

jack [dʒæk] *n* (*AUT*) gato; (*CARDS*) sota; **~ up** *vt* (*AUT*) levantar con gato

jackal ['dʒækɔːl] *n* (*ZOOL*) chacal *m*

jacket ['dʒækɪt] *n* chaqueta, americana, saco (*AM*); (*of book*) sobrecubierta

jack: **~-knife** *vi* colear; **~ plug** *n* (*ELEC*) enchufe *m* de clavija; **~pot** *n* premio gordo

jaded ['dʒeɪdɪd] *adj* (*tired*) cansado; (*fed-up*) hastiado

jagged ['dʒægɪd] *adj* dentado

jail [dʒeɪl] *n* cárcel *f* ♦ *vt* encarcelar

jam [dʒæm] *n* mermelada; (*also:* **traffic ~**) embotellamiento; (*inf: difficulty*) apuro ♦ *vt* (*passage etc*) obstruir; (*mechanism, drawer etc*) atascar; (*RADIO*) interferir ♦ *vi* atascarse, trabarse; **to ~ sth into sth** meter algo a la fuerza en algo

Jamaica [dʒə'meɪkə] *n* Jamaica

jangle ['dʒæŋgl] *vi* entrechocar (ruidosamente)

janitor ['dʒænɪtə*] *n* (*caretaker*) portero, conserje *m*

January ['dʒænjuərɪ] *n* enero

Japan [dʒə'pæn] *n* (el) Japón; **~ese** [dʒæpə'niːz] *adj* japonés/esa ♦ *n inv* japonés/esa *m/f*; (*LING*) japonés *m*

jar [dʒɑː*] *n* tarro, bote *m* ♦ *vi* (*sound*) chirriar; (*colours*) desentonar

jargon ['dʒɑːgən] *n* jerga

jasmine ['dʒæzmɪn] *n* jazmín *m*

jaundice ['dʒɔːndɪs] *n* ictericia

jaunt [dʒɔːnt] *n* excursión *f*

javelin ['dʒævlɪn] *n* jabalina

jaw [dʒɔː] *n* mandíbula

jay [dʒeɪ] *n* (*ZOOL*) arrendajo

jaywalker ['dʒeɪwɔːkə*] *n* peatón/ona *m/f* imprudente

jazz [dʒæz] *n* jazz *m*; **~ up** *vt* (*liven up*) animar, avivar

jealous ['dʒeləs] *adj* celoso; (*envious*) envidioso; **~y** *n* celos *mpl*; envidia

jeans [dʒiːnz] *npl* vaqueros *mpl*, tejanos *mpl*

Jeep ® [dʒiːp] *n* jeep *m*

jeer [dʒɪə*] *vi*: **to ~ (at)** (*mock*) mofarse (de)

jelly ['dʒelɪ] *n* (*jam*) jalea; (*dessert etc*) gelatina; **~fish** *n inv* medusa (*SP*), aguaviva (*AM*)

jeopardy ['dʒepədɪ] *n*: **to be in ~** estar en peligro

jerk [dʒɜːk] *n* (*jolt*) sacudida; (*wrench*) tirón *m*; (*inf*) imbécil *m/f* ♦ *vt* tirar

bruscamente de ♦ *vi* (*vehicle*) traquetear

jersey ['dʒɜːzɪ] *n* jersey *m*; (*fabric*) (tejido de) punto

Jesus ['dʒiːzəs] *n* Jesús *m*

jet [dʒet] *n* (*of gas, liquid*) chorro; (*AVIAT*) avión *m* a reacción; (*stone*) negro como el azabache; **~ engine** *n* motor *m* a reacción; **~ lag** *n* desorientación *f* después de un largo vuelo

jettison ['dʒetɪsn] *vt* desechar

jetty ['dʒetɪ] *n* muelle *m*, embarcadero

Jew [dʒuː] *n* judío

jewel ['dʒuːəl] *n* joya; (*in watch*) rubí *m*; **~ler** (*US* **~er**) *n* joyero/a; **~ler's** (*US* **~ry store**) *n* joyería; **~lery** (*US* **~ry**) *n* joyas *fpl*, alhajas *fpl*

Jewess ['dʒuːɪs] *n* judía

Jewish ['dʒuːɪʃ] *adj* judío

jibe [dʒaɪb] *n* mofa

jiffy ['dʒɪfɪ] (*inf*) *n*: **in a ~** en un santiamén

jigsaw ['dʒɪgsɔː] *n* (*also:* **~ puzzle**) rompecabezas *m inv*, puzle *m*

jilt [dʒɪlt] *vt* dejar plantado a

jingle ['dʒɪŋgl] *n* musiquilla ♦ *vi* tintinear

jinx [dʒɪŋks] *n*: **there's a ~ on it** está gafado

jitters ['dʒɪtəz] (*inf*) *npl*: **to get the ~** ponerse nervioso

job [dʒɔb] *n* (*task*) tarea; (*post*) empleo; **it's not my ~** no me incumbe a mí; **it's a good ~ that ...** menos mal que ...; **just the ~!** ¡estupendo!; **~ centre** (*BRIT*) *n* oficina estatal de colocaciones; **~less** *adj* sin trabajo

jockey ['dʒɔkɪ] *n* jockey *m/f* ♦ *vi*: **to ~ for position** maniobrar para conseguir una posición

jog [dʒɔg] *vt* empujar (ligeramente) ♦ *vi* (*run*) hacer footing; **to ~ sb's memory** refrescar la memoria a uno; **~ along** *vi* (*fig*) ir tirando; **~ging** *n* footing *m*

join [dʒɔɪn] *vt* (*things*) juntar, unir; (*club*) hacerse socio de; (*POL: party*) afiliarse a; (*queue*) ponerse en; (*meet: people*) reunirse con ♦ *vi* (*roads*) juntarse; (*rivers*) confluir ♦ *n* juntura; **~ in** *vi* tomar parte, participar ♦ *vt fus* tomar parte *or* participar en; ~ **up** *vi* reunirse; (*MIL*) alistarse

joiner ['dʒɔɪnə*] (*BRIT*) *n* carpintero/a; ~**y** *n* carpintería

joint [dʒɔɪnt] *n* (*TECH*) junta, unión *f*; (*ANAT*) articulación *f*; (*BRIT: CULIN*) pieza de carne (para asar); (*inf: place*) tugurio; (*: of cannabis*) porro ♦ *adj* (*common*) común; (*combined*) combinado; ~ **account** (*with bank etc*) cuenta común

joke [dʒəuk] *n* chiste *m*; (*also:* **practical ~**) broma ♦ *vi* bromear; **to play a ~ on** gastar una broma a; ~**r** *n* (*CARDS*) comodín *m*

jolly ['dʒɔlɪ] *adj* (*merry*) alegre; (*enjoyable*) divertido ♦ *adv* (*BRIT: inf*) muy, terriblemente

jolt [dʒəult] *n* (*jerk*) sacudida; (*shock*) susto ♦ *vt* (*physically*) sacudir; (*emotionally*) asustar

jostle ['dʒɔsl] *vt* dar empellones a, codear

jot [dʒɔt] *n*: **not one ~** ni jota, ni pizca; ~ **down** *vt* apuntar; ~**ter** (*BRIT*) *n* bloc *m*

journal ['dʒə:nl] *n* (*magazine*) revista; (*diary*) periódico, diario; ~**ism** *n* periodismo; ~**ist** *n* periodista *m/f*, reportero/a

journey ['dʒə:nɪ] *n* viaje *m*; (*distance covered*) trayecto

jovial ['dʒəuvɪəl] *adj* risueño, jovial

joy [dʒɔɪ] *n* alegría; ~**ful** *adj* alegre; ~**ous** *adj* alegre; ~ **ride** *n* (*illegal*) paseo en coche robado; ~**rider** *n* gamberro que roba un coche para dar una vuelta y luego abandonarlo; ~ **stick** *n* (*AVIAT*) palanca de mando; (*COMPUT*) palanca de control

JP *n abbr* = **Justice of the Peace**

Jr *abbr* = **junior**

jubilant ['dʒə:bɪlnt] *adj* jubiloso

judge [dʒʌdʒ] *n* juez *m/f*; (*fig: expert*) perito ♦ *vt* juzgar; (*consider*) considerar; **judg(e)ment** *n* juicio

judiciary [dʒu:'dɪʃɪərɪ] *n* poder *m* judicial

judicious [dʒu:'dɪʃəs] *adj* juicioso

judo ['dʒu:dəu] *n* judo

jug [dʒʌg] *n* jarra

juggernaut ['dʒʌgənɔ:t] (*BRIT*) *n* (*huge truck*) trailer *m*

juggle ['dʒʌgl] *vi* hacer juegos malabares; ~**r** *n* malabarista *m/f*

juice [dʒu:s] *n* zumo, jugo (*esp AM*); **juicy** *adj* jugoso

jukebox ['dʒu:kbɔks] *n* máquina de discos

July [dʒu:'laɪ] *n* julio

jumble ['dʒʌmbl] *n* revoltijo ♦ *vt* (*also:* **~ up**) revolver; ~ **sale** (*BRIT*) *n* venta de objetos usados con fines benéficos

---

jumble sale

ℹ️ *Los* **jumble sales** *son unos mercadillos que se organizan con fines benéficos en los locales de un colegio, iglesia u otro centro público. En ellos puede comprarse todo tipo de artículos baratos de segunda mano, sobre todo ropa, juguetes, libros, vajillas o muebles.*

---

jumbo (jet) ['dʒʌmbəu-] *n* jumbo

jump [dʒʌmp] *vi* saltar, dar saltos; (*with fear etc*) pegar un bote; (*increase*) aumentar ♦ *vt* saltar ♦ *n* salto; aumento; **to ~ the queue** (*BRIT*) colarse

jumper ['dʒʌmpə*] *n* (*BRIT: pullover*) suéter *m*, jersey *m*; (*US: dress*) mandil *m*; ~ **cables** (*US*) *npl* = **jump leads**

jump leads (*BRIT*) *npl* cables *mpl* puente de batería

jumpy ['dʒʌmpɪ] (*inf*) *adj* nervioso

Jun. *abbr* = **junior**

junction ['dʒʌŋkʃən] *n* (*BRIT: of roads*) cruce *m*; (*RAIL*) empalme *m*

juncture ['dʒʌŋktʃə*] *n*: **at this ~** en este momento, en esta coyuntura

June [dʒu:n] *n* junio

jungle ['dʒʌŋgl] *n* selva, jungla

junior ['dʒu:nɪə*] *adj* (*in age*) menor, más joven; (*brother/sister etc*): **7 years her ~** siete años menor que ella; (*position*) subalterno ♦ *n* menor *m/f*, joven *m/f*; ~ **school** (*BRIT*) *n* escuela primaria

junk [dʒʌŋk] *n* (*cheap goods*) baratijas *fpl*; (*rubbish*) basura; ~ **food** *n* alimentos preparados y envasados de escaso valor *nutritivo*

junkie ['dʒʌŋkɪ] (*inf*) *n* drogadicto/a, yonqui *m/f*

junk mail *n* propaganda de buzón

junk shop *n* tienda de objetos usados

Junr *abbr* = **junior**

juror ['dʒuərə*] *n* jurado

jury ['dʒuərɪ] *n* jurado

just [dʒʌst] *adj* justo ♦ *adv* (*exactly*) exactamente; (*only*) sólo, solamente; **he's ~ done it/left** acaba de hacerlo/irse; **~ right** perfecto; **~ two o'clock** las dos en punto; **she's ~ as clever as you** (ella) es tan lista como tú; **~ as well that ...** menos mal que ...; **~ as he was leaving** en el momento en que se marchaba; **~ before/enough** justo antes/lo suficiente; **~ here** aquí mismo; **he ~ missed** ha fallado por poco; **~ listen to this** escucha esto un momento

justice ['dʒʌstɪs] *n* justicia; (*US: judge*) juez *m*; **to do ~ to** (*fig*) hacer justicia a; **J~ of the Peace** *n* juez *m* de paz

justify ['dʒʌstɪfaɪ] *vt* justificar; (*text*) alinear

jut [dʒʌt] *vi* (*also*: **~ out**) sobresalir

juvenile ['dʒuːvənaɪl] *adj* (*court*) de menores; (*humour, mentality*) infantil ♦ *n* menor *m* de edad

K, k

K *abbr* (= *one thousand*) mil; (= *kilobyte*) kilobyte *m*, kilocteto

kangaroo [kæŋgə'ruː] *n* canguro

karate [kə'rɑːtɪ] *n* karate *m*

kebab [kə'bæb] *n* pincho moruno

keel [kiːl] *n* quilla; **on an even ~** (*fig*) en equilibrio

keen [kiːn] *adj* (*interest, desire*) grande, vivo; (*eye, intelligence*) agudo; (*competition*) reñido; (*edge*) afilado; (*eager*) entusiasta; **to be ~ to do** *or* **on doing sth** tener muchas ganas de hacer algo; **to be ~ on sth/sb** interesarse por algo/uno

keep [kiːp] (*pt, pp* **kept**) *vt* (*preserve, store*) guardar; (*hold back*) quedarse con; (*maintain*) mantener; (*detain*) detener; (*shop*) ser propietario de; (*feed: family etc*) mantener; (*promise*) cumplir; (*chickens, bees etc*) criar; (*accounts*) llevar; (*diary*) escribir; (*prevent*): **to ~ sb from doing sth** impedir a uno hacer algo ♦ *vi* (*food*) conservarse; (*remain*) seguir, continuar ♦ *n* (*of castle*) torreón *m*; (*food etc*) comida, subsistencia; (*inf*): **for ~s** para siempre; **to ~ doing sth** seguir haciendo algo; **to ~ sb happy** tener a uno contento; **to ~ a place tidy** mantener un lugar limpio; **to ~ sth for o.s.** guardar algo para sí mismo; **to ~ sth (back) from sb** ocultar algo a uno; **to ~ time** (*clock*) mantener la hora exacta; ~ **on** *vi*: **to ~ on doing** seguir *or* continuar haciendo; **to ~ on (about sth)** no parar de hablar (de algo); ~ **out** *vi* (*stay out*) permanecer fuera; **"~ out"** "prohibida la entrada"; ~ **up** *vt* mantener, conservar ♦ *vi* no retrasarse; **to ~ up with** (*pace*) ir al paso de; (*level*) mantenerse a la altura de; ~**er** *n* guardián/ana *m/f*; ~-**fit** *n* gimnasia (para mantenerse en forma); ~**ing** *n* (*care*) cuidado; **in ~ing with** de acuerdo con; ~**sake** *n* recuerdo

kennel ['kɛnl] *n* perrera; ~**s** *npl* residencia canina

Kenya ['kɛnjə] *n* Kenia

kept [kɛpt] *pt, pp of* **keep**

kerb [kə:b] (*BRIT*) *n* bordillo

kernel ['kə:nl] *n* (*nut*) almendra; (*fig*) meollo

ketchup ['kɛtʃəp] *n* salsa de tomate, catsup *m*

kettle ['kɛtl] *n* hervidor *m* de agua; ~ **drum** *n* (*MUS*) timbal *m*

key [kiː] *n* llave *f*; (*MUS*) tono; (*of piano, typewriter*) tecla ♦ *adj* (*issue etc*) clave *inv* ♦ *vt* (*also*: **~ in**) teclear; ~**board** *n* teclado; ~**ed up** *adj* (*person*) nervioso; ~**hole** *n* ojo (de la cerradura); ~**hole surgery** *n* cirugía cerrada, cirugía no invasiva; ~**note** *n* (*MUS*) tónica; (*of speech*) punto principal *or* clave; ~**ring** *n* llavero

khaki ['kɑːkɪ] n caqui

kick [kɪk] vt dar una patada or un puntapié a; (inf: habit) quitarse de ♦ vi (horse) dar coces ♦ n patada; puntapié m; (of animal) coz f; (thrill): **he does it for ~s** lo hace por pura diversión; ~ **off** vi (SPORT) hacer el saque inicial

kid [kɪd] n (inf: child) chiquillo/a; (animal) cabrito; (leather) cabritilla ♦ vi (inf) bromear

kidnap ['kɪdnæp] vt secuestrar; ~per n secuestrador(a) m/f; ~ping n secuestro

kidney ['kɪdnɪ] n riñón m

kill [kɪl] vt matar; (murder) asesinar ♦ n matanza; **to ~ time** matar el tiempo; ~er n asesino/a; ~ing n (one) asesinato; (several) matanza; **to make a ~ing** (fig) hacer su agosto; ~joy (BRIT) n aguafiestas m/f inv

kiln [kɪln] n horno

kilo ['kiːləu] n kilo; ~byte n (COMPUT) kilobyte m, kiloocteto; ~gram(me) ['kɪləugræm] n kilo, kilogramo; ~metre ['kɪləmiːtə*] (US ~meter) n kilómetro; ~watt ['kɪləuwɔt] n kilovatio

kilt [kɪlt] n falda escocesa

kin [kɪn] n see next

kind [kaɪnd] adj amable, atento ♦ n clase f, especie f; (species) género; **in ~** (COMM) en especie; **a ~ of** una especie de; **to be two of a ~** ser tal para cual

kindergarten ['kɪndəgɑːtn] n jardín m de la infancia

kind-hearted adj bondadoso, de buen corazón

kindle ['kɪndl] vt encender; (arouse) despertar

kindly ['kaɪndlɪ] adj bondadoso; cariñoso ♦ adv bondadosamente, amablemente; **will you ~ ...** sea usted tan amable de ...

kindness ['kaɪndnɪs] n (quality) bondad f, amabilidad f; (act) favor m

king [kɪŋ] n rey m; ~dom n reino; ~fisher n martín m pescador; ~-size adj de tamaño extra

kiosk ['kiːɔsk] n quiosco; (BRIT: TEL) cabina

kipper ['kɪpə*] n arenque m ahumado

kiss [kɪs] n beso ♦ vt besar; **to ~ (each other)** besarse; ~ **of life** n respiración f boca a boca

kit [kɪt] n (equipment) equipo; (tools etc) (caja de) herramientas fpl; (assembly ~) juego de armar

kitchen ['kɪtʃɪn] n cocina; ~ **sink** n fregadero

kite [kaɪt] n (toy) cometa

kitten ['kɪtn] n gatito/a

kitty ['kɪtɪ] n (pool of money) fondo común

km abbr (= kilometre) km

knack [næk] n: **to have the ~ of doing sth** tener el don de hacer algo

knapsack ['næpsæk] n mochila

knead [niːd] vt amasar

knee [niː] n rodilla; ~cap n rótula

kneel [niːl] (pt, pp knelt) vi (also: ~ **down**) arrodillarse

knew [njuː] pt of **know**

knickers ['nɪkəz] (BRIT) npl bragas fpl

knife [naɪf] (pl knives) n cuchillo ♦ vt acuchillar

knight [naɪt] n caballero; (CHESS) caballo; ~hood (BRIT) n (title): **to receive a ~hood** recibir el título de Sir

knit [nɪt] vt tejer, tricotar ♦ vi hacer punto, tricotar; (bones) soldarse; **to ~ one's brows** fruncir el ceño; ~ting n labor f de punto; ~ting machine n máquina de tricotar; ~ting needle n aguja de hacer punto; ~wear n prendas fpl de punto

knives [naɪvz] npl of **knife**

knob [nɔb] n (of door) tirador m; (of stick) puño; (on radio, TV) botón m

knock [nɔk] vt (strike) golpear; (bump into) chocar contra; (inf) criticar ♦ vi (at door etc): **to ~ at/on** llamar a ♦ n golpe m; (on door) llamada; ~ **down** vt atropellar; ~ **off** (inf) vi (finish) salir del trabajo ♦ vt (from price) descontar; (inf: steal) birlar; ~ **out** vt dejar sin sentido; (BOXING) poner fuera de combate, dejar K.O.; (in competition) eliminar; ~ **over** vt (object) tirar; (person) atropellar; ~er n (on door) aldabón m; ~out n (BOXING) K.O. m, knockout *m* ♦ *cpd* (*competition etc*) eliminatorio

knot [nɒt] *n* nudo ♦ *vt* anudar

know [nəu] (*pt* knew, *pp* known) *vt* (*facts*) saber; (*be acquainted with*) conocer; (*recognize*) reconocer, conocer; to ~ how to swim saber nadar; to ~ about *or* of sb/sth saber de uno/algo; ~-all *n* sabelotodo *m/f*; ~-how *n* conocimientos *mpl*; ~ing *adj* (*look*) de complicidad; ~ingly *adv* (*purposely*) adrede; (*smile, look*) con complicidad

knowledge [ˈnɒlɪdʒ] *n* conocimiento; (*learning*) saber *m*, conocimientos *mpl*; ~able *adj* entendido

knuckle [ˈnʌkl] *n* nudillo

Koran [kɔˈrɑːn] *n* Corán *m*

Korea [kəˈrɪə] *n* Corea

kosher [ˈkəuʃəʳ] *adj* autorizado por la ley judía

Kosovo [ˈkɒsəvəu] *n* Kosovo *m*

L, l

L (*BRIT*) *abbr* = learner driver

l. *abbr* (= *litre*) l

lab [læb] *n abbr* = laboratory

label [ˈleɪbl] *n* etiqueta ♦ *vt* poner etiqueta a

labor *etc* [ˈleɪbəʳ] (*US*) = labour

laboratory [ləˈbɔrətərɪ] *n* laboratorio

laborious [ləˈbɔːrɪəs] *adj* penoso

labour [ˈleɪbəʳ] (*US* labor) *n* (*hard work*) trabajo; (~ *force*) mano *f* de obra; (*MED*): to be in ~ estar de parto ♦ *vi*: to ~ (at sth) trabajar (en algo) ♦ *vt*: to ~ a point insistir en un punto; L~, the L~ party (*BRIT*) el partido laborista, los laboristas *mpl*; ~ed *adj* (*breathing*) fatigoso; ~er *n* peón *m*; farm ~er peón *m*; (*day ~er*) jornalero

lace [leɪs] *n* encaje *m*; (*of shoe etc*) cordón *m* ♦ *vt* (*shoes: also:* ~ up) atarse (los zapatos)

lack [læk] *n* (*absence*) falta ♦ *vt* faltarle a uno, carecer de; through *or* for ~ of por

falta de; to be ~ing faltar, no haber; to be ~ing in sth faltarle a uno algo

lacquer [ˈlækəʳ] *n* laca

lad [læd] *n* muchacho, chico

ladder [ˈlædəʳ] *n* escalera (de mano); (*BRIT: in tights*) carrera

laden [ˈleɪdn] *adj*: ~ (with) cargado (de)

ladle [ˈleɪdl] *n* cucharón *m*

lady [ˈleɪdɪ] *n* señora; (*dignified*) dama; "ladies and gentlemen ..." "señoras y caballeros ..."; young ~ señorita; the ladies' (room) los servicios de señoras; ~bird (*US* ~bug) *n* mariquita; ~like *adj* fino; L~ship *n*: your L~ship su Señoría

lag [læg] *n* retraso ♦ *vi* (*also:* ~ behind) retrasarse, quedarse atrás ♦ *vt* (*pipes*) revestir

lager [ˈlɑːgəʳ] *n* cerveza (rubia)

lagoon [ləˈguːn] *n* laguna

laid [leɪd] *pt, pp of* lay; ~ back (*inf*) *adj* relajado; ~ up *adj*: to be ~ up (with) tener que guardar cama (a causa de)

lain [leɪn] *pp of* lie

lake [leɪk] *n* lago

lamb [læm] *n* cordero; (*meat*) (carne *f* de) cordero; ~ chop *n* chuleta de cordero; lambswool *n* lana de cordero

lame [leɪm] *adj* cojo; (*excuse*) poco convincente

lament [ləˈment] *n* quejo ♦ *vt* lamentarse de

laminated [ˈlæmɪneɪtɪd] *adj* (*metal*) laminado; (*wood*) contrachapado; (*surface*) plastificado

lamp [læmp] *n* lámpara; ~post (*BRIT*) *n* (poste *m* de) farol *m*; ~shade *n* pantalla

lance [lɑːns] *vt* (*MED*) abrir con lanceta

land [lænd] *n* tierra; (*country*) país *m*; (*piece of* ~) terreno; (*estate*) tierras *fpl*, finca ♦ *vi* (*from ship*) desembarcar; (*AVIAT*) aterrizar; (*fig: fall*) caer, terminar ♦ *vt* (*passengers, goods*) desembarcar; to ~ sb with sth (*inf*) hacer cargar a uno con algo; ~ up *vi*: to ~ up in/at ir a parar a/en; ~fill site [ˈlændfɪl-] *n* vertedero; ~ing *n* aterrizaje *m*; (*of staircase*) rellano; ~ing gear *n* (*AVIAT*) tren *m* de aterrizaje;

~**lady** n (of rented house, pub etc) dueña;
~**lord** n propietario; (of pub etc) patrón
m; ~**mark** n lugar m conocido; **to be a
~mark** (fig) marcar un hito histórico;
~**owner** n terrateniente m/f; ~**scape** n
paisaje m; ~**scape gardener** n
arquitecto de jardines; ~**slide** n (GEO)
corrimiento de tierras; (fig: POL) victoria
arrolladora

lane [leɪn] n (in country) camino m; (AUT)
carril m; (in race) calle f

language ['læŋgwɪdʒ] n lenguaje m;
(national tongue) idioma m, lengua; **bad
~** palabrotas fpl; ~ **laboratory** n
laboratorio de idiomas

lank [læŋk] adj (hair) lacio
lanky ['læŋkɪ] adj larguirucho
lantern ['læntn] n linterna, farol m
lap [læp] n (of track) vuelta; (of body)
regazo; **to sit on sb's ~** sentarse en las
rodillas de uno ♦ vt (also: ~ **up**) beber a
lengüetadas ♦ vi (waves) chapotear; ~ **up**
vt (fig) tragarse

lapel [ləˈpel] n solapa
Lapland ['læplænd] n Laponia
lapse [læps] n fallo; (moral) desliz m; (of
time) intervalo ♦ vi (expire) caducar;
(time) pasar, transcurrir; **to ~ into bad
habits** caer en malos hábitos

laptop (computer) ['læptɔp-] n
(ordenador m) portátil m

larch [lɑːtʃ] n alerce m
lard [lɑːd] n manteca (de cerdo)
larder ['lɑːdə*] n despensa
large [lɑːdʒ] adj grande; **at ~** (free) en
libertad; (generally) en general; ~**ly** adv
(mostly) en su mayor parte; (introducing
reason) en gran parte; ~**scale** adj (map)
en gran escala; (fig) importante

lark [lɑːk] n (bird) alondra; (joke) broma
laryngitis [lærɪnˈdʒaɪtɪs] n laringitis f
laser ['leɪzə*] n láser m; ~ **printer** n
impresora (por) láser

lash [læʃ] n latigazo; (also: **eye~**) pestaña
♦ vt azotar; (tie): **to ~ to/together** atar
a/atar; ~ **out** vi: **to ~ out (at sb)** (hit)
arremeter (contra uno); **to ~ out against**

sb lanzar invectivas contra uno
lass [læs] (BRIT) n chica
lasso [læˈsuː] n lazo
last [lɑːst] adj último; (end: of series etc)
final ♦ adv (most recently) la última vez;
(finally) por último ♦ vi durar; (continue)
continuar, seguir; ~ **night** anoche; ~
week la semana pasada; **at ~** por fin; ~
but one penúltimo; ~**ditch** adj
(attempt) último, desesperado; ~**ing** adj
duradero; ~**ly** adv por último, finalmente;
~**minute** adj de última hora

latch [lætʃ] n pestillo
late [leɪt] adj (far on: in time, process etc) al
final de; (not on time) tarde, atrasado;
(dead) fallecido; (behind time,
schedule) con retraso; **of ~** últimamente; ~
at night a última hora de la noche; **in ~
May** hacia fines de mayo; **the ~ Mr X** el
difunto Sr X; ~**comer** n recién llegado/a;
~**ly** adv últimamente; ~**r** adj (date etc)
posterior; (version etc) más reciente ♦ adv
más tarde, después; ~**st** ['leɪtɪst] adj
último; **at the ~st** a más tardar

lathe [leɪð] n torno
lather ['lɑːðə*] n espuma (de jabón) ♦ vt
enjabonar

Latin ['lætɪn] n latín m ♦ adj latino; ~
America n América latina; ~
American adj, n latinoamericano/a
latitude ['lætɪtjuːd] n latitud f; (fig) libertad
f

latter ['lætə*] adj último; (of two) segundo
♦ n: **the ~** el último, éste; ~**ly** adv
últimamente

laudable ['lɔːdəbl] adj loable
laugh [lɑːf] n risa ♦ vi reír(se); **(to do sth)
for a ~** (hacer algo) en broma; ~ **at** vt
fus reírse de; ~ **off** vt tomar algo a risa;
~**able** adj ridículo; ~**ing stock** n: **the
~ing stock of** el hazmerreír de; ~**ter** n
risa

launch [lɔːntʃ] n lanzamiento; (boat)
lancha ♦ vt (ship) botar; (rocket etc)
lanzar; (fig) comenzar; ~ **into** vt fus
lanzarse a; ~**(ing) pad** n plataforma de
lanzamiento

launder ['lɔːndə*] vt lavar

Launderette ® [lɔːn'drɛt] (BRIT) n lavandería (automática)

Laundromat ® ['lɔːndrəmæt] (US) n = **Launderette**

laundry ['lɔːndrɪ] n (dirty) ropa sucia; (clean) colada; (room) lavadero

lavatory ['lævətərɪ] n wáter m

lavender ['lævəndə*] n lavanda

lavish ['lævɪʃ] adj (amount) abundante; (person): ~ with pródigo en ♦ vt: to ~ sth on sb colmar a uno de algo

law [lɔː] n ley f; (SCOL) derecho; (a rule) regla; (professions connected with ~) jurisprudencia; ~-abiding adj respetuoso de la ley; ~ and order n orden m público; ~ court n tribunal m (de justicia); ~ful adj legítimo, lícito; ~less adj (action) criminal

lawn [lɔːn] n césped m; ~mower n cortacésped m; ~ tennis n tenis m sobre hierba

law school (US) n (SCOL) facultad f de derecho

lawsuit ['lɔːsuːt] n pleito

lawyer ['lɔːjə*] n abogado/a; (for sales, wills etc) notario/a

lax [læks] adj laxo

laxative ['læksətɪv] n laxante m

lay [leɪ] (pt, pp laid) pt of lie ♦ adj laico; (not expert) lego ♦ vt (place) colocar; (eggs, table) poner; (cable) tender; (carpet) extender; ~ aside or by vt dejar a un lado; ~ down vt (pen etc) dejar; (rules etc) establecer; to ~ down the law (pej) imponer las normas; ~ off vt (workers) despedir; ~ on vt (meal, facilities) proveer; ~ out vt (spread out) disponer, exponer; ~about (inf) n vago/ a; ~-by (BRIT: AUT) área de aparcamiento

layer ['leɪə*] n capa

layman ['leɪmən] (irreg) n lego

layout ['leɪaut] n (design) plan m, trazado; (PRESS) composición f

laze [leɪz] vi (also: ~ about) holgazanear

lazy ['leɪzɪ] adj perezoso, vago; (movement)

lento

lb. abbr = **pound** (weight)

lead[1] [liːd] (pt, pp led) n (front position) delantera; (clue) pista; (ELEC) cable m; (for dog) correa; (THEATRE) papel m principal ♦ vt (walk etc in front of) ir a la cabeza de; (guide): to ~ sb somewhere conducir a uno a algún sitio; (be leader of) dirigir; (start, guide: activity) protagonizar ♦ vi (road, pipe etc) conducir a; (SPORT) ir primero; to be in the ~ (SPORT) llevar la delantera; (fig) ir a la cabeza; to ~ the way (also fig) llevar la delantera; ~ away vt llevar; ~ back vt (person, route) llevar de vuelta; ~ on vt (tease) engañar; ~ to vt fus producir, provocar; ~ up to vt fus (events) conducir a; (in conversation) preparar el terreno para

lead[2] [lɛd] n (metal) plomo; (in pencil) mina; ~ed petrol n gasolina con plomo

leader ['liːdə*] n jefe/a m/f, líder m; (SPORT) líder m; ~ship n dirección f; (position) mando; (quality) iniciativa

leading ['liːdɪŋ] adj (main) principal; (first) primero; (front) delantero; ~ lady n (THEATRE) primera actriz f; ~ light n (person) figura principal; ~ man (irreg) n (THEATRE) primer galán m

lead singer [liːd-] n cantante m/f

leaf [liːf] (pl leaves) n hoja ♦ vi: to ~ through hojear; to turn over a new ~ reformarse

leaflet ['liːflɪt] n folleto

league [liːg] n sociedad f; (FOOTBALL) liga; to be in ~ with haberse confabulado con

leak [liːk] n (of liquid, gas) escape m, fuga; (in pipe) agujero; (in roof) gotera; (in security) filtración f ♦ vi (shoes, ship) hacer agua; (pipe) tener (un) escape; (roof) gotear; (liquid, gas) escaparse, fugarse; (fig) divulgarse ♦ vt (fig) filtrar

lean [liːn] (pt, pp leaned or leant) adj (thin) flaco; (meat) magro ♦ vt: to ~ sth on sth apoyar algo en algo ♦ vi (slope) inclinarse; to ~ against apoyarse contra; to ~ on apoyarse en; ~ back/forward vi inclinarse hacia atrás/adelante; ~ out

vi asomarse; ~ **over** *vi* inclinarse; ~**ing**
n: ~**ing (towards)** inclinación *f* (hacia);
leant [lɛnt] *pt, pp of* **lean**

leap [li:p] (*pt, pp* **leaped** *or* **leapt**) *n* salto
♦ *vi* saltar; ~**frog** *n* pídola; ~ **year** *n*
año bisiesto

learn [lə:n] (*pt, pp* **learned** *or* **learnt**) *vt*
aprender ♦ *vi* aprender; **to ~ about sth**
enterarse de algo; **to ~ to do sth**
aprender a hacer algo; ~**ed** ['lə:nɪd] *adj*
erudito; ~**er** *n* (*BRIT: also:* ~**er driver**)
principiante *m/f*; ~**ing** *n* el saber *m*,
conocimientos *mpl*

lease [li:s] *n* arriendo ♦ *vt* arrendar
leash [li:ʃ] *n* correa

least [li:st] *adj*: **the ~** (*slightest*) el menor,
el más pequeño; (*smallest amount of*)
mínimo ♦ *adv* (*+vb*) menos; (*+adj*): **the ~
expensive** el/la menos costoso/a; **the ~
possible effort** el menor esfuerzo posible;
at ~ por lo menos, al menos; **you could
at ~ have written** por lo menos podías
haber escrito; **not in the ~** en absoluto

leather ['lɛðə*] *n* cuero

leave [li:v] (*pt, pp* **left**) *vt* dejar; (*go away
from*) abandonar; (*place etc: permanently*)
salir de ♦ *vi* irse; (*train etc*) salir ♦ *n*
permiso; **to ~ sth to sb** (*money etc*) legar
algo a uno; (*responsibility etc*) encargar a
uno de algo; **to be left** quedar, sobrar;
there's some milk left over sobra *or*
queda algo de leche; **on ~** de permiso; ~
behind *vt* (*on purpose*) dejar;
(*accidentally*) dejarse; ~ **out** *vt* omitir; ~
of absence *n* permiso de ausentarse

leaves [li:vz] *npl of* **leaf**

Lebanon ['lɛbənən] *n*: **the ~** el Líbano

lecherous ['lɛtʃərəs] (*pej*) *adj* lascivo

lecture ['lɛktʃə*] *n* conferencia; (*SCOL*)
clase *f* ♦ *vi* dar una clase ♦ *vt* (*scold*): **to
~ sb on** *or* **about sth** echar una
reprimenda a uno por algo; **to give a ~
on** dar una conferencia sobre; ~**r** *n*
conferenciante *m/f*; (*BRIT: at university*)
profesor(a) *m/f*

led [lɛd] *pt, pp of* **lead**

ledge [lɛdʒ] *n* repisa; (*of window*) alféizar

m; (*of mountain*) saliente *m*

ledger ['lɛdʒə*] *n* libro mayor

leech [li:tʃ] *n* sanguijuela

leek [li:k] *n* puerro

leer [lɪə*] *vi*: **to ~ at sb** mirar de manera
lasciva a uno

leeway ['li:weɪ] *n* (*fig*): **to have some ~**
tener cierta libertad de acción

left [lɛft] *pt, pp of* **leave** ♦ *adj* izquierdo;
(*remaining*): **there are 2 ~** quedan dos
♦ *n* izquierda ♦ *adv* a la izquierda; **on** *or*
to the ~ a la izquierda; **the L~** (*POL*) la
izquierda; ~**-handed** *adj* zurdo; **the ~-
hand side** *n* la izquierda; ~**-luggage
(office)** (*BRIT*) *n* consigna; ~**-overs** *npl*
sobras *fpl*; ~**-wing** *adj* (*POL*) de
izquierdas, izquierdista

leg [lɛg] *n* pierna; (*of animal, chair*) pata;
(*trouser ~*) pernera; (*CULIN: of lamb*)
pierna; (*of chicken*) pata; (*of journey*)
etapa

legacy ['lɛgəsɪ] *n* herencia

legal ['li:gl] *adj* (*permitted by law*) lícito; (*of
law*) legal; ~ **holiday** (*US*) *n* fiesta oficial;
~**ize** *vt* legalizar; ~**ly** *adv* legalmente; ~
tender *n* moneda de curso legal

legend ['lɛdʒənd] *n* (*also fig: person*)
leyenda

legislation [lɛdʒɪs'leɪʃən] *n* legislación *f*

legislature ['lɛdʒɪslətʃə*] *n* cuerpo
legislativo

legitimate [lɪ'dʒɪtɪmət] *adj* legítimo

leg-room *n* espacio para las piernas

leisure ['lɛʒə*] *n* ocio, tiempo libre; **at ~**
con tranquilidad; ~ **centre** *n* centro de
recreo; ~**ly** *adj* sin prisa, lento

lemon ['lɛmən] *n* limón *m*; ~**ade** *n* (*fizzy*)
gaseosa; ~ **tea** *n* té *m* con limón

lend [lɛnd] (*pt, pp* **lent**) *vt*: **to ~ sth to sb**
prestar algo a alguien; ~**ing library** *n*
biblioteca de préstamo

length [lɛŋθ] *n* (*size*) largo, longitud *f*;
(*distance*): **the ~ of** todo lo largo de; (*of
swimming pool, cloth*) largo; (*of wood,
string*) trozo; (*amount of time*) duración *f*;
at ~ (*at last*) por fin, finalmente;
(*lengthily*) largamente; ~**en** *vt* alargar

♦ *vi* alargarse; **~ways** *adv* a lo largo; **~y**
adj largo, extenso
lenient ['li:nɪənt] *adj* indulgente
lens [lenz] *n* (*of spectacles*) lente *f*; (*of
camera*) objetivo
Lent [lent] *n* Cuaresma
lent [lent] *pt, pp of* **lend**
lentil ['lentl] *n* lenteja
Leo ['li:əʊ] *n* Leo
leotard ['li:əta:d] *n* mallas *fpl*
leprosy ['leprəsɪ] *n* lepra
lesbian ['lezbɪən] *n* lesbiana
less [les] *adj* (*in size, degree etc*) menor; (*in
quality*) menos ♦ *pron, adv* menos ♦ *prep*:
~ tax/10% discount menos impuestos/el
10 por ciento de descuento; **~ than half**
menos de la mitad; **~ than ever** menos
que nunca; **~ and ~** cada vez menos; **the
~ he works ...** cuanto menos trabaja ...;
~en *vi* disminuir, reducirse ♦ *vt*
disminuir, reducir; **~er** ['lesə*] *adj* menor;
to a ~er extent en menor grado
lesson ['lesn] *n* clase *f*; (*warning*) lección *f*
let [let] (*pt, pp* **let**) *vt* (*allow*) dejar,
permitir; (*BRIT: lease*) alquilar; **to ~ sb do
sth** dejar que uno haga algo; **to ~ sb
know sth** comunicar algo a uno; **~'s go**
¡vamos!; **~ him come** que venga; **"to ~"**
"se alquila"; **~ down** *vt* (*tyre*) desinflar;
(*disappoint*) defraudar; **~ go** *vi, vt* soltar;
~ in *vt* dejar entrar; (*visitor etc*) hacer
pasar; **~ off** *vt* (*culprit*) dejar escapar;
(*gun*) disparar; (*bomb*) accionar; (*firework*)
hacer estallar; **~ on** (*inf*) *vi* divulgar; **~
out** *vt* dejar salir; (*sound*) soltar; **~ up** *vi*
amainar, disminuir
lethal ['li:θl] *adj* (*weapon*) mortífero;
(*poison, wound*) mortal
letter ['letə*] *n* (*of alphabet*) letra;
(*correspondence*) carta; **~ bomb** *n* carta-
bomba; **~box** (*BRIT*) *n* buzón *m*; **~ing** *n*
letras *fpl*
lettuce ['letɪs] *n* lechuga
let-up *n* disminución *f*
leukaemia [lu:'ki:mɪə] *n* (*US* **leukemia**) *n*
leucemia
level ['levl] *adj* (*flat*) llano ♦ *adv*: **to draw**

~ with llegar a la altura de ♦ *n* nivel *m*;
(*height*) altura ♦ *vt* nivelar; allanar;
(*destroy: building*) derribar; (: *forest*)
arrasar; **to be ~ with** estar a nivel de;
"A" ~s (*BRIT*) *npl* ≈ exámenes *mpl* de
bachillerato superior, B.U.P.; **"O" ~s**
(*BRIT*) *npl* ≈ exámenes *mpl* de octavo de
básica; **on the ~** (*fig: honest*) serio; **~ off**
or **out** *vi* (*prices etc*) estabilizarse; **~
crossing** (*BRIT*) *n* paso a nivel; **~-
headed** *adj* sensato
lever ['li:və*] *n* (*also fig*) palanca ♦ *vt*: **to ~
up** levantar con palanca; **~age** *n* (*using
bar etc*) apalancamiento; (*fig: influence*)
influencia
levy ['levɪ] *n* impuesto ♦ *vt* exigir, recaudar
lewd [lu:d] *adj* lascivo; (*joke*) obsceno,
colorado (*AM*)
liability [laɪə'bɪlətɪ] *n* (*pej: person, thing*)
estorbo, lastre *m*; (*JUR: responsibility*)
responsabilidad *f*; **liabilities** *npl* (*COMM*)
pasivo
liable ['laɪəbl] *adj* (*subject*): **~ to** sujeto a;
(*responsible*): **~ for** responsable de; (*likely*):
~ to do propenso a hacer
liaise [lɪ'eɪz] *vi*: **to ~ with** enlazar con;
liaison [li:'eɪzɒn] *n* (*coordination*) enlace
m; (*affair*) relaciones *fpl* amorosas
liar ['laɪə*] *n* mentiroso/a
libel ['laɪbl] *n* calumnia ♦ *vt* calumniar
liberal ['lɪbərəl] *adj* liberal; (*offer, amount
etc*) generoso
liberate ['lɪbəreɪt] *vt* (*people: from poverty
etc*) librar; (*prisoner*) libertar; (*country*)
liberar
liberty ['lɪbətɪ] *n* libertad *f*; (*criminal*): **to
be at ~** estar en libertad; **to be at ~ to
do** estar libre para hacer; **to take the ~ of
doing sth** tomarse la libertad de hacer
algo
Libra ['li:brə] *n* Libra
librarian [laɪ'breərɪən] *n* bibliotecario/a
library ['laɪbrərɪ] *n* biblioteca
libretto [lɪ'bretəʊ] *n* libreto
Libya ['lɪbɪə] *n* Libia; **~n** *adj, n* libio/a *m/f*
lice [laɪs] *npl of* **louse**
licence ['laɪsəns] (*US* **license**) *n* licencia;

(*permit*) permiso *m*; (*also:* **driving ~**, (*US*) **driver's ~**) carnet *m* de conducir (*SP*), permiso (*AM*)

license ['laɪsəns] *n* (*US*) = **licence ♦** *vt* autorizar, dar permiso a; **~d** *adj* (*for alcohol*) autorizado para vender bebidas alcohólicas; (*car*) matriculado; **~ plate** (*US*) *n* placa (de matrícula)

lick [lɪk] *vt* lamer; (*inf: defeat*) dar una paliza a; **to ~ one's lips** relamerse

licorice ['lɪkərɪs] (*US*) *n* = **liquorice**

lid [lɪd] *n* (*of box, case*) tapa; (*of pan*) tapadera

lido ['laɪdəu] *n* (*BRIT*) piscina

lie [laɪ] (*pt* **lay**, *pp* **lain**) *vi* estar echado, estar acostado; (*of object: be situated*) estar, encontrarse; (*tell lies: pt, pp* **lied**) mentir ♦ *n* mentira; **to ~ low** (*fig*) mantenerse a escondidas; **~ about** *or* **around** *vi* (*things*) estar tirado; (*BRIT: people*) estar tumbado; **~-down** (*BRIT*) *n*: **to have a ~-down** echarse (una siesta); **~-in** (*BRIT*) *n*: **to have a ~-in** quedarse en la cama

lieu [luː]: **in ~ of** *prep* en lugar de

lieutenant [lɛf'tɛnənt, (*US*) luː'tɛnənt] *n* (*MIL*) teniente *m*

life [laɪf] (*pl* **lives**) *n* vida; **to come to ~** animarse; **~ assurance** (*BRIT*) *n* seguro de vida; **~belt** (*BRIT*) *n* salvavidas *m inv*; **~boat** *n* lancha de socorro; **~guard** *n* vigilante *m/f*, socorrista *m/f*; **~ insurance** *n* = **~ assurance**; **~ jacket** *n* chaleco salvavidas; **~less** *adj* sin vida; (*dull*) soso; **~like** *adj* (*model etc*) que parece vivo; (*realistic*) realista; **~long** *adj* de toda la vida; **~ preserver** (*US*) *n* cinturón *m*/chaleco salvavidas; **~ sentence** *n* cadena perpetua; **~-size** *adj* de tamaño natural; **~ span** *n* vida; **~style** *n* estilo de vida; **~ support system** *n* (*MED*) sistema *m* de respiración asistida; **~time** *n* (*of person*) vida; (*of thing*) período de vida

lift [lɪft] *vt* levantar; (*end: ban, rule*) levantar, suprimir ♦ *vi* (*fog*) disiparse ♦ *n* (*BRIT: machine*) ascensor *m*; **to give sb a**

~ (*BRIT*) llevar a uno en el coche; **~-off** *n* despegue *m*

light [laɪt] (*pt, pp* **lighted** *or* **lit**) *n* luz *f*; (*lamp*) luz *f*, lámpara; (*AUT*) faro; (*for cigarette etc*): **have you got a ~?** ¿tienes fuego? ♦ *vt* (*candle, cigarette, fire*) encender (*SP*), prender (*AM*); (*room*) alumbrar ♦ *adj* (*colour*) claro; (*not heavy, also fig*) ligero; (*room*) con mucha luz; (*gentle, graceful*) ágil; **~s** *npl* (*traffic ~s*) semáforos *mpl*; **to come to ~** salir a luz; **in the ~ of** (*new evidence etc*) a la luz de; **~ up** *vi* (*smoke*) encender un cigarrillo; (*face*) iluminarse ♦ *vt* (*illuminate*) iluminar, alumbrar; (*set fire to*) encender; **~ bulb** *n* bombilla (*SP*), foco (*AM*); **~en** *vt* (*make less heavy*) aligerar; **~er** *n* (*also:* **cigarette ~er**) encendedor *m*, mechero; **~-headed** *adj* (*dizzy*) mareado; (*excited*) exaltado; **~-hearted** *adj* (*person*) alegre; (*remark etc*) divertido; **~house** *n* faro; **~ing** *n* (*system*) alumbrado; **~ly** *adv* ligeramente; (*not seriously*) con poca seriedad; **to get off ~ly** ser castigado con poca severidad; **~ness** *n* (*in weight*) ligereza

lightning ['laɪtnɪŋ] *n* relámpago, rayo; **~ conductor** (*US* **~ rod**) *n* pararrayos *m inv*

light: **~ pen** *n* lápiz *m* óptico; **~weight** *adj* (*suit*) ligero ♦ *n* (*BOXING*) peso ligero; **~ year** *n* año luz

like [laɪk] *vt* gustarle a uno ♦ *prep* como ♦ *adj* parecido, semejante ♦ *n*: **and the ~** y otros por el estilo; **his ~s and dislikes** sus gustos y aversiones; **I would ~, I'd ~** me gustaría; (*for purchase*) quisiera; **would you ~ a coffee?** ¿te apetece un café?; **I ~ swimming** me gusta nadar; **she ~s apples** le gustan las manzanas; **to be** *or* **look ~ sb/sth** parecerse a alguien/ algo; **what does it look/taste/sound ~?** ¿cómo es/a qué sabe/cómo suena?; **that's just ~ him** es muy de él, es característico de él; **do it ~ this** hazlo así; **it is nothing ~ ...** no tiene parecido alguno con ...; **~able** *adj* simpático, agradable

likelihood [ˈlaɪklɪhud] n probabilidad f
likely [ˈlaɪklɪ] adj probable; **he's ~ to leave** es probable que se vaya; **not ~!** ¡ni hablar!
likeness [ˈlaɪknɪs] n semejanza, parecido; **that's a good ~** se parece mucho
likewise [ˈlaɪkwaɪz] adv igualmente; **to do ~** hacer lo mismo
liking [ˈlaɪkɪŋ] n: **~ (for)** (person) cariño (a); (thing) afición (a); **to be to sb's ~** ser del gusto de uno
lilac [ˈlaɪlək] n (tree) lilo; (flower) lila
lily [ˈlɪlɪ] n lirio, azucena; **~ of the valley** n lirio de los valles
limb [lɪm] n miembro
limber [ˈlɪmbə*]: **to ~ up** vi (SPORT) hacer ejercicios de calentamiento
limbo [ˈlɪmbəu] n: **to be in ~** (fig) quedar a la expectativa
lime [laɪm] n (tree) limero; (fruit) lima; (GEO) cal f
limelight [ˈlaɪmlaɪt] n: **to be in the ~** (fig) ser el centro de atención
limerick [ˈlɪmərɪk] n especie de poema humorístico
limestone [ˈlaɪmstəun] n piedra caliza
limit [ˈlɪmɪt] n límite m ♦ vt limitar; **~ed** adj limitado; **to be ~ed to** limitarse a; **~ed (liability) company** (BRIT) n sociedad f anónima
limousine [ˈlɪməziːn] n limusina
limp [lɪmp] n: **to have a ~** tener cojera ♦ vi cojear ♦ adj flojo; (material) fláccido
limpet [ˈlɪmpɪt] n lapa
line [laɪn] n línea; (rope) cuerda; (for fishing) sedal m; (wire) hilo; (row, series) fila, hilera; (of writing) renglón m, línea; (of song) verso; (on face) arruga; (RAIL) vía ♦ vt (road etc) llenar; (SEWING) forrar; **to ~ the streets** llenar las aceras; **in ~ with** alineado con; (according to) de acuerdo con; **~ up** vi hacer cola ♦ vt alinear; (prepare) preparar; organizar
lined [laɪnd] adj (face) arrugado; (paper) rayado
linen [ˈlɪnɪn] n ropa blanca; (cloth) lino
liner [ˈlaɪnə*] n vapor m de línea,

transatlántico; (for bin) bolsa (de basura)
linesman [ˈlaɪnzmən] n (SPORT) juez m de línea
line-up n (US: queue) cola; (SPORT) alineación f
linger [ˈlɪŋgə*] vi retrasarse, tardar en marcharse; (smell, tradition) persistir
lingerie [ˈlænʒəriː] n lencería
linguist [ˈlɪŋgwɪst] n lingüista m/f; **~ics** n lingüística
lining [ˈlaɪnɪŋ] n forro; (ANAT) (membrana) mucosa
link [lɪŋk] n (of a chain) eslabón m; (relationship) relación f, vínculo ♦ vt vincular, unir; (associate): **to ~ with** or **to** relacionar con; **~s** npl (GOLF) campo de golf; **~ up** vt acoplar ♦ vi unirse
lino [ˈlaɪnəu] n = **linoleum**
linoleum [lɪˈnəuliəm] n linóleo
lion [ˈlaɪən] n león m; **~ess** n leona
lip [lɪp] n labio
liposuction [ˈlɪpəusʌkʃən] n liposucción f
lip: ~read vi leer los labios; **~ salve** n crema protectora para labios; **~ service** n: **to pay ~ service to sth** (pej) prometer algo de boquilla; **~stick** n lápiz m de labios, carmín m
liqueur [lɪˈkjuə*] n licor m
liquid [ˈlɪkwɪd] adj, n líquido; **~ize** [-aɪz] vt (CULIN) licuar; **~izer** [-aɪzə*] n licuadora
liquor [ˈlɪkə*] n licor m, bebidas fpl alcohólicas
liquorice [ˈlɪkərɪs] (BRIT) n regaliz m
liquor store (US) n bodega, tienda de vinos y bebidas alcohólicas
Lisbon [ˈlɪzbən] n Lisboa
lisp [lɪsp] n ceceo ♦ vi cecear
list [lɪst] n lista ♦ vt (mention) enumerar; (put on a list) poner en una lista; **~ed building** (BRIT) n monumento declarado de interés histórico-artístico
listen [ˈlɪsn] vi escuchar, oír; **to ~ to sb/ sth** escuchar a uno/algo; **~er** n oyente m/f; (RADIO) radioyente m/f
listless [ˈlɪstlɪs] adj apático, indiferente
lit [lɪt] pt, pp of **light**
liter [ˈliːtə*] (US) n = **litre**

literacy ['lɪtərəsɪ] n capacidad f de leer y escribir

literal ['lɪtərl] adj literal

literary ['lɪtərərɪ] adj literario

literate ['lɪtərət] adj que sabe leer y escribir; (educated) culto

literature ['lɪtərɪtʃə*] n literatura; (brochures etc) folletos mpl

lithe [laɪð] adj ágil

litigation [lɪtɪ'geɪʃən] n litigio

litre ['liːtə*] (US liter) n litro

litter ['lɪtə*] n (rubbish) basura; (young animals) camada, cría; ~ bin (BRIT) n papelera; ~ed adj: ~ed with (scattered) lleno de

little ['lɪtl] adj (small) pequeño; (not much) poco ♦ adv poco; a ~ un poco (de); ~ house / bird casita/pajarito; a ~ bit un poquito; ~ by ~ poco a poco; ~ finger n dedo meñique

live¹ [laɪv] adj (animal) vivo; (wire) conectado; (broadcast) en directo; (shell) cargado

live² [lɪv] vi vivir; ~ down vt hacer olvidar; ~ on vt fus (food, salary) vivir de; ~ together vi vivir juntos; ~ up to vt fus (fulfil) cumplir con

livelihood ['laɪvlɪhud] n sustento

lively ['laɪvlɪ] adj vivo; (interesting: place, book etc) animado

liven up ['laɪvn-] vt animar ♦ vi animarse

liver ['lɪvə*] n hígado

lives [laɪvz] npl of life

livestock ['laɪvstɔk] n ganado

livid ['lɪvɪd] adj lívido; (furious) furioso

living ['lɪvɪŋ] adj (alive) vivo ♦ n: to earn or make a ~ ganarse la vida; ~ conditions npl condiciones fpl de vida; ~ room n sala (de estar); ~ standards npl nivel m de vida; ~ wage n jornal m suficiente para vivir

lizard ['lɪzəd] n lagarto; (small) lagartija

load [ləud] n (weight) peso ♦ vt (COMPUT) cargar; (also: ~ up): to ~ (with) cargar (con or de); a ~ of rubbish (inf) tonterías fpl; a ~ of, ~s of (fig) (gran) cantidad de, montones de; ~ed adj

(vehicle): to be ~ed with estar cargado de; (question) intencionado; (inf: rich) forrado (de dinero)

loaf [ləuf] (pl loaves) n (barra de) pan m

loan [ləun] n préstamo ♦ vt prestar; on ~ prestado

loath [ləuθ] adj: to be ~ to do sth estar poco dispuesto a hacer algo

loathe [ləuð] vt aborrecer; (person) odiar; loathing n aversión f; odio

loaves [ləuvz] npl of loaf

lobby ['lɔbɪ] n vestíbulo, sala de espera; (POL: pressure group) grupo de presión ♦ vt presionar

lobster ['lɔbstə*] n langosta

local ['ləukl] adj local ♦ n (pub) bar m; the ~s los vecinos, los del lugar; ~ anaesthetic n (MED) anestesia local; ~ authority n municipio, ayuntamiento (SP); ~ call n (TEL) llamada local; ~ government n gobierno municipal; ~ity [-'kælɪtɪ] n localidad f; ~ly [-kəlɪ] adv en la vecindad; por aquí

locate [ləu'keɪt] vt (find) localizar; (situate): to be ~d in estar situado en

location [ləu'keɪʃən] n situación f; on ~ (CINEMA) en exteriores

loch [lɔx] n lago

lock [lɔk] n (of door, box) cerradura; (of canal) esclusa; (of hair) mechón m ♦ vt (with key) cerrar (con llave) ♦ vi (door etc) cerrarse (con llave); (wheels) trabarse; ~ in vt encerrar; ~ out vt (person) cerrar la puerta a; ~ up vt (criminal) meter en la cárcel; (mental patient) encerrar; (house) cerrar (con llave) ♦ vi echar la llave

locker ['lɔkə*] n casillero

locket ['lɔkɪt] n medallón m

locksmith ['lɔksmɪθ] n cerrajero/a

lockup ['lɔkʌp] n (jail, cell) cárcel f

locum ['ləukəm] n (MED) (médico/a) interino/a

locust ['ləukəst] n langosta

lodge [lɔdʒ] n casita (del guarda) ♦ vi (person): to ~ (with) alojarse (en casa de); (bullet, bone) incrustarse ♦ vt (complaint) presentar; ~r n huésped(a) m/f

lodgings ['lɒdʒɪŋz] *npl* alojamiento
loft [lɒft] *n* desván *m*
lofty ['lɒftɪ] *adj* (*noble*) sublime; (*haughty*) altanero
log [lɒg] *n* (*of wood*) leño, tronco; (*written account*) diario ♦ *vt* anotar; ~ **in** *or* **on** *vi* (*COMPUT*) entrar en el sistema; ~ **off** *or* **out** *vi* (*COMPUT*) salir del sistema
logbook ['lɒgbuk] *n* (*NAUT*) diario de a bordo; (*AVIAT*) libro de vuelo; (*of car*) documentación *f* (del coche (*SP*) *o* carro (*AM*))
loggerheads ['lɒgəhɛdz] *npl*: **to be at ~ (with)** estar en desacuerdo (con)
logic ['lɒdʒɪk] *n* lógica *f*; ~**al** *adj* lógico
logo ['ləugəu] *n* logotipo
loin [lɔɪn] *n* (*CULIN*) lomo, solomillo
loiter ['lɔɪtə*] *vi* (*linger*) entretenerse
loll [lɒl] *vi* (*also*: ~ **about**) repantigarse
lollipop ['lɒlɪpɒp] *n* pirulí *m*; ~ **man/lady** (*BRIT irreg*) *n see box*

---
lollipop man/lollipop lady

ⓘ *En el Reino Unido, se llama* **lollipop man** *o* **lollipop lady** *a la persona que se ocupa de parar el tráfico en los alrededores de los colegios para que los niños crucen sin peligro. Suelen ser personas ya jubiladas, vestidas con una gabardina de color llamativo y llevan una señal de stop portátil, la cual recuerda por su forma a una piruleta, y de ahí su nombre.*

London ['lʌndən] *n* Londres; ~**er** *n* londinense *m/f*
lone [ləun] *adj* solitario
loneliness ['ləunlɪnɪs] *n* soledad *f*; aislamiento
lonely ['ləunlɪ] *adj* (*situation*) solitario; (*person*) solo; (*place*) aislado
long [lɒŋ] *adj* largo ♦ *adv* mucho tiempo, largamente ♦ *vi*: **to ~ for sth** anhelar algo; **so** *or* **as ~ as** mientras, con tal que; **don't be ~!** ¡no tardes!, ¡vuelve pronto!; **how ~ is the street?** ¿cuánto tiene la calle de largo?; **how ~ is the lesson?**

¿cuánto dura la clase?; **6 metres ~** que mide 6 metros, de 6 metros de largo; **6 months ~** que dura 6 meses, de 6 meses de duración; **all night ~** toda la noche; **he no ~er comes** ya no viene; ~ **before** mucho antes; **before ~** (+*future*) dentro de poco; (+*past*) poco tiempo después; **at ~ last** al fin, por fin; ~**-distance** *adj* (*race*) de larga distancia; (*call*) interurbano; ~**-haired** *adj* de pelo largo; ~**ing** *n* anhelo, ansia; (*nostalgia*) nostalgia ♦ *adj* anhelante
longitude ['lɒŋgɪtjuːd] *n* longitud *f*
long: ~ **jump** *n* salto de longitud; ~**-life** *adj* (*batteries*) de larga duración; (*milk*) uperizado; ~**-lost** *adj* desaparecido hace mucho tiempo; ~**-range** *adj* (*plan*) de gran alcance; (*missile*) de largo alcance; ~**-sighted** (*BRIT*) *adj* présbita; ~**-standing** *adj* de mucho tiempo; ~**-suffering** *adj* sufrido; ~**-term** *adj* a largo plazo; ~ **wave** *n* onda larga; ~**-winded** *adj* prolijo
loo [luː] (*BRIT: inf*) *n* váter *m*
look [luk] *vi* mirar; (*seem*) parecer; (*building etc*): **to ~ south/on to the sea** dar al sur/al mar ♦ *n* (*gen*): **to have a ~** mirar; (*glance*) mirada *f*; (*appearance*) aire *m*, aspecto; ~**s** *npl* (*good ~s*) belleza; ~ **(here)!** (*expressing annoyance etc*) ¡oye!; ~! (*expressing surprise*) ¡mira!; ~ **after** *vt fus* (*care for*) cuidar a; (*deal with*) encargarse de; ~ **at** *vt fus* mirar; (*read quickly*) echar un vistazo a; ~ **back** *vi* mirar hacia atrás; ~ **down on** *vt fus* (*fig*) despreciar, mirar con desprecio; ~ **for** *vt fus* buscar; ~ **forward to** *vt fus* esperar con ilusión; (*in letters*): **we ~ forward to hearing from you** quedamos a la espera de sus gratas noticias; ~ **into** *vt* investigar; ~ **on** *vi* mirar (como espectador); ~ **out** *vi* (*beware*): **to ~ out (for)** tener cuidado (de); ~ **out for** *vt fus* (*seek*) buscar; (*await*) esperar; ~ **round** *vi* volver la cabeza; ~ **through** *vt fus* (*examine*) examinar; ~ **to** *vt fus* (*rely on*)

contar con; ~ **up** *vi* mirar hacia arriba; (*improve*) mejorar ♦ *vt* (*word*) buscar; ~ **up to** *vt fus* admirar; **~-out** *n* (*tower etc*) puesto de observación; (*person*) vigía *m/f*; **to be on the ~-out for sth** estar al acecho de algo

loom [luːm] *vi*: ~ **(up)** (*threaten*) surgir, amenazar; (*event: approach*) aproximarse

loony ['luːnɪ] (*inf*) *n, adj* loco/a *m/f*

loop [luːp] *n* lazo ♦ *vt*: **to ~ sth round sth** pasar algo alrededor de algo; **~hole** *n* escapatoria

loose [luːs] *adj* suelto; (*clothes*) ancho; (*morals, discipline*) relajado; **to be on the ~** estar en libertad; **to be at a ~ end** *or* **at ~ ends** (*US*) no saber qué hacer; **~ change** *n* cambio; **~ chippings** *npl* (*on road*) gravilla suelta; **~ly** *adv* libremente, aproximadamente; **~n** *vt* aflojar

loot [luːt] *n* botín *m* ♦ *vt* saquear

lop off [lɔp-] *vt* (*branches*) podar

lop-sided *adj* torcido

lord [lɔːd] *n* señor *m*; **L~ Smith** Lord Smith; **the L~** el Señor; **my ~** (*to bishop*) Ilustrísima; (*to noble etc*) Señor; **good L~!** ¡Dios mío!; **the (House of) L~s** (*BRIT*) la Cámara de los Lores; **~ship** *n*: **your L~ship** su Señoría

lore [lɔː*] *n* tradiciones *fpl*

lorry ['lɔrɪ] (*BRIT*) *n* camión *m*; ~ **driver** *n* camionero/a

lose [luːz] (*pt, pp* **lost**) *vt* perder ♦ *vi* perder, ser vencido; **to ~ (time)** (*clock*) atrasarse; **~r** *n* perdedor(a) *m/f*

loss [lɔs] *n* pérdida; **heavy ~es** (*MIL*) grandes pérdidas; **to be at a ~** no saber qué hacer; **to make a ~** sufrir pérdidas

lost [lɔst] *pt, pp of* **lose** ♦ *adj* perdido; ~ **property** (*US* ~ **and found**) *n* objetos *mpl* perdidos

lot [lɔt] *n* (*group: of things*) grupo; (*at auctions*) lote *m*; **the ~** el todo, todos; **a ~** (*large number: of books etc*) muchos; (*a great deal*) mucho, bastante; **a ~ of, ~s of** mucho(s) (*pl*); **I read a ~** leo bastante; **to draw ~s (for sth)** echar suertes (para

decidir algo)

lotion ['ləʊʃən] *n* loción *f*

lottery ['lɔtərɪ] *n* lotería

loud [laud] *adj* (*voice, sound*) fuerte; (*laugh, shout*) estrepitoso; (*condemnation etc*) enérgico; (*gaudy*) chillón/ona ♦ *adv* (*speak etc*) fuerte; **out** ~ en voz alta; **~hailer** (*BRIT*) *n* megáfono; **~ly** *adv* (*noisily*) fuerte; (*aloud*) en voz alta; **~speaker** *n* altavoz *m*

lounge [laundʒ] *n* salón *m*, sala (de estar); (*at airport etc*) sala; (*BRIT: also:* **~-bar**) salón-bar *m* ♦ *vi* (*also:* ~ **about** *or* **around**) reposar, holgazanear

louse [laus] (*pl* **lice**) *n* piojo

lousy ['lauzɪ] (*inf*) *adj* (*bad quality*) malísimo, asqueroso; (*ill*) fatal

lout [laut] *n* gamberro/a

lovable ['lʌvəbl] *adj* amable, simpático

love [lʌv] *n* (*romantic, sexual*) amor *m*; (*kind, caring*) cariño ♦ *vt* amar, querer; (*thing, activity*) encantarle a uno; **"~ from Anne"** (*on letter*) "un abrazo (de) Anne"; **to ~ to do** encantarle a uno hacer; **to be/fall in ~ with** estar enamorado/ enamorarse de; **to make ~** hacer el amor; **for the ~ of** por amor de; **"15 ~"** (*TENNIS*) "15 a cero"; **I ~ paella** me encanta la paella; ~ **affair** *n* aventura sentimental; ~ **letter** *n* carta de amor; ~ **life** *n* vida sentimental

lovely ['lʌvlɪ] *adj* (*delightful*) encantador(a); (*beautiful*) precioso

lover ['lʌvə*] *n* amante *m/f*; (*person in love*) enamorado; (*amateur*): **a ~ of** un(a) aficionado/a *or* un(a) amante de

loving ['lʌvɪŋ] *adj* amoroso, cariñoso; (*action*) tierno

low [ləʊ] *adj, ad* bajo ♦ *n* (*METEOROLOGY*) área de baja presión; **to be ~ on** (*supplies etc*) andar mal de; **to feel ~** sentirse deprimido; **to turn (down)** ~ bajar; **~-alcohol** *adj* de bajo contenido en alcohol; **~-calorie** *adj* bajo en calorías; **~-cut** *adj* (*dress*) escotado

lower ['ləʊə*] *adj* más bajo; (*less important*) menos importante ♦ *vt* bajar;

(reduce) reducir ♦ vr: **to ~ o.s. to** (fig) rebajarse a

low: **~-fat** adj (milk, yoghurt) desnatado; (diet) bajo en calorías; **~lands** npl (GEO) tierras fpl bajas; **~ly** adj humilde, inferior; **~ season** n la temporada baja

loyal ['lɔɪəl] adj leal; **~ty** n lealtad f; **~ty card** n tarjeta cliente

lozenge ['lɒzɪndʒ] n (MED) pastilla

L.P. n abbr (= long-playing record) elepé m

L-plates ['el-] (BRIT) npl placas fpl de aprendiz de conductor

---
L-plates
---

*En el Reino Unido las personas que están aprendiendo a conducir deben llevar en la parte delantera y trasera de su vehículo unas placas blancas con una L en rojo conocidas como **L-plates** (de learner). No es necesario que asistan a clases teóricas sino que, desde el principio, se les entrega un carnet de conducir provisional ("provisional driving licence") para que realicen sus prácticas, aunque no pueden circular por las autopistas y deben ir siempre acompañadas por un conductor con carnet definitivo ("full driving licence").*

Ltd abbr (= limited company) S.A.

lubricate ['lu:brɪkeɪt] vt lubricar, engrasar

luck [lʌk] n suerte f; **bad ~** mala suerte; **good ~!** ¡que tengas suerte!, ¡suerte!; **bad or hard or tough ~!** ¡qué pena!; **~ily** adv afortunadamente; **~y** adj afortunado; (at cards etc) con suerte; (object) que trae suerte

ludicrous ['lu:dɪkrəs] adj absurdo

lug [lʌg] vt (drag) arrastrar

luggage ['lʌgɪdʒ] n equipaje m; **~ rack** n (on car) baca, portaequipajes m inv

lukewarm ['lu:kwɔ:m] adj tibio

lull [lʌl] n tregua ♦ vt: **to ~ sb to sleep** arrullar a uno; **to ~ sb into a false sense of security** dar a alguien una falsa sensación de seguridad

lullaby ['lʌləbaɪ] n nana

lumbago [lʌm'beɪgəu] n lumbago

lumber ['lʌmbə*] n (junk) trastos mpl viejos; (wood) maderos mpl; **~ with** vt: **to be ~ed with** tener que cargar con algo; **~jack** n maderero

luminous ['lu:mɪnəs] adj luminoso

lump [lʌmp] n terrón m; (fragment) trozo; (swelling) bulto ♦ vt (also: **~ together**) juntar; **~ sum** n suma global; **~y** adj (sauce) lleno de grumos; (mattress) lleno de bultos

lunatic ['lu:nətɪk] adj loco

lunch [lʌntʃ] n almuerzo, comida ♦ vi almorzar

luncheon ['lʌntʃən] n almuerzo; **~ voucher** (BRIT) n vale m de comida

lunch time n hora de comer

lung [lʌŋ] n pulmón m

lunge [lʌndʒ] vi (also: **~ forward**) abalanzarse; **to ~ at** arremeter contra

lurch [lə:tʃ] vi dar sacudidas ♦ n sacudida; **to leave sb in the ~** dejar a uno plantado

lure [luə*] n (attraction) atracción f ♦ vt tentar

lurid ['luərɪd] adj (colour) chillón/ona; (account) espeluznante

lurk [lə:k] vi (person, animal) estar al acecho; (fig) acechar

luscious ['lʌʃəs] adj (attractive: person, thing) precioso; (food) delicioso

lush [lʌʃ] adj exuberante

lust [lʌst] n lujuria; (greed) codicia

lustre ['lʌstə*] (US **luster**) n lustre m, brillo

lusty ['lʌstɪ] adj robusto, fuerte

Luxembourg ['lʌksəmbə:g] n Luxemburgo

luxuriant [lʌg'zjuərɪənt] adj exuberante

luxurious [lʌg'zjuərɪəs] adj lujoso

luxury ['lʌkʃərɪ] n lujo ♦ cpd de lujo

lying ['laɪɪŋ] n mentiras fpl ♦ adj mentiroso

lyrical ['lɪrɪkl] adj lírico

lyrics ['lɪrɪks] npl (of song) letra

M, m

m. *abbr* = **metre; mile; million**

M.A. *abbr* = **Master of Arts**

mac [mæk] (*BRIT*) *n* impermeable *m*

macaroni [mækə'rəʊnɪ] *n* macarrones *mpl*

machine [mə'ʃiːn] *n* máquina ♦ *vt* (*dress etc*) coser a máquina; (*TECH*) hacer a máquina; ~ **gun** *n* ametralladora; ~ **language** *n* (*COMPUT*) lenguaje *m* máquina; ~**ry** *n* maquinaria; (*fig*) mecanismo

macho ['mætʃəʊ] *adj* machista

mackerel ['mækrl] *n inv* caballa

mackintosh ['mækɪntɒʃ] (*BRIT*) *n* impermeable *m*

mad [mæd] *adj* loco; (*idea*) disparatado; (*angry*) furioso; (*keen*): **to be ~ about sth** volverle loco a uno algo

madam ['mædəm] *n* señora

madden ['mædn] *vt* volver loco

made [meɪd] *pt*, *pp of* **make**

Madeira [mə'dɪərə] *n* (*GEO*) Madera; (*wine*) vino de Madera

made-to-measure (*BRIT*) *adj* hecho a la medida

madly ['mædlɪ] *adv* locamente

madman ['mædmən] (*irreg*) *n* loco

madness ['mædnɪs] *n* locura

Madrid [mə'drɪd] *n* Madrid

magazine [mægə'ziːn] *n* revista; (*RADIO*, *TV*) programa *m* magazina

maggot ['mægət] *n* gusano

magic ['mædʒɪk] *n* magia ♦ *adj* mágico; ~**ian** [mə'dʒɪʃən] *n* mago/a; (*conjurer*) prestidigitador(a) *m/f*

magistrate ['mædʒɪstreɪt] *n* juez *m/f* (*municipal*)

magnet ['mægnɪt] *n* imán *m*; ~**ic** [-'netɪk] *adj* magnético; (*personality*) atrayente

magnificent [mæg'nɪfɪsənt] *adj* magnífico

magnify ['mægnɪfaɪ] *vt* (*object*) ampliar; (*sound*) aumentar; ~**ing glass** *n* lupa

magpie ['mægpaɪ] *n* urraca

mahogany [mə'hɒgənɪ] *n* caoba

maid [meɪd] *n* criada; **old ~** (*pej*) solterona

maiden ['meɪdn] *n* doncella ♦ *adj* (*aunt etc*) solterona; (*speech, voyage*) inaugural; ~ **name** *n* nombre *m* de soltera

mail [meɪl] *n* correo; (*letters*) cartas *fpl* ♦ *vt* echar al correo; ~**box** (*US*) *n* buzón *m*; ~**ing list** *n* lista de direcciones; ~**-order** *n* pedido postal

maim [meɪm] *vt* mutilar, lisiar

main [meɪn] *adj* principal, mayor ♦ *n* (*pipe*) cañería maestra; (*US*) red *f* eléctrica; **the ~s** *npl* (*BRIT*: *ELEC*) la red eléctrica; **in the ~** en general; ~**frame** *n* (*COMPUT*) ordenador *m* central; ~**land** *n* tierra firme; ~**ly** *adv* principalmente; ~ **road** *n* carretera; ~**stay** *n* (*fig*) pilar *m*; ~**stream** *n* corriente *f* principal

maintain [meɪn'teɪn] *vt* mantener; **maintenance** ['meɪntənəns] *n* mantenimiento; (*LAW*) manutención *f*

maize [meɪz] (*BRIT*) *n* maíz *m* (*SP*), choclo (*AM*)

majestic [mə'dʒestɪk] *adj* majestuoso

majesty ['mædʒɪstɪ] *n* majestad *f*; (*title*): **Your M~** Su Majestad

major ['meɪdʒə*] *n* (*MIL*) comandante *m* ♦ *adj* principal; (*MUS*) mayor

Majorca [mə'jɔːkə] *n* Mallorca

majority [mə'dʒɒrɪtɪ] *n* mayoría

make [meɪk] (*pt*, *pp* **made**) *vt* hacer; (*manufacture*) fabricar; (*mistake*) cometer; (*speech*) pronunciar; (*cause to*): **to ~ sb sad** hacer triste a alguien; (*force*): **to ~ sb do sth** obligar a alguien a hacer algo; (*earn*) ganar; (*equal*): **2 and 2 ~ 4** 2 y 2 son 4 ♦ *n* marca; **to ~ the bed** hacer la cama; **to ~ a fool of sb** poner a alguien en ridículo; **to ~ a profit/loss** obtener ganancias/sufrir pérdidas; **to ~ it** (*arrive*) llegar; (*achieve sth*) tener éxito; **what time do you ~ it?** ¿qué hora tienes?; **to ~ do with** contentarse con; ~ **for** *vt fus* (*place*) dirigirse a; ~ **out** *vt* (*decipher*) descifrar; (*understand*) entender; (*see*) distinguir; (*cheque*) extender; ~ **up** *vt* (*invent*) inventar; (*prepare*) hacer; (*constitute*) constituir ♦ *vi* reconciliarse;

(with cosmetics) maquillarse; ~ **up for** *vt fus* compensar; ~-**believe** *n* ficción *f*, invención *f*; ~**r** *n* fabricante *m/f*; *(of film, programme)* autor(a) *m/f*; ~**shift** *adj* improvisado; ~-**up** *n* maquillaje *m*; ~-**up remover** *n* desmaquillador *m*

making ['meɪkɪŋ] *n (fig)*: **in the ~** en vías de formación; **to have the ~s of** *(person)* tener madera de

Malaysia [mə'leɪzɪə] *n* Malasia, Malaysia

male [meɪl] *n (BIOL)* macho ♦ *adj (sex, attitude)* masculino; *(child etc)* varón

malfunction [mæl'fʌŋkʃən] *n* mal funcionamiento

malice ['mælɪs] *n* malicia; **malicious** [mə'lɪʃəs] *adj* malicioso; rencoroso

malignant [mə'lɪgnənt] *adj (MED)* maligno

mall [mɔːl] *(US) n (also:* **shopping ~)** centro comercial

mallet ['mælɪt] *n* mazo

malnutrition [mælnju:'trɪʃən] *n* desnutrición *f*

malpractice [mæl'præktɪs] *n* negligencia profesional

malt [mɔːlt] *n* malta; *(whisky)* whisky *m* de malta

Malta ['mɔːltə] *n* Malta; **Maltese** [-'tiːz] *adj, n inv* maltés/esa *m/f*

mammal ['mæml] *n* mamífero

mammoth ['mæməθ] *n* mamut *m* ♦ *adj* gigantesco

man [mæn] *(pl* **men)** *n* hombre *m*; *(~kind)* el hombre ♦ *vt (NAUT)* tripular; *(MIL)* guarnecer; *(operate: machine)* manejar; **an old ~** un viejo; **~ and wife** marido y mujer

manage ['mænɪdʒ] *vi* arreglárselas, ir tirando ♦ *vt (be in charge of)* dirigir; *(control: person)* manejar; *(: ship)* gobernar; ~**able** *adj* manejable; ~**ment** *n* dirección *f*; ~**r** *n* director(a) *m/f*; *(of pop star)* mánayer *m/f*; *(SPORT)* entrenador(a) *m/f*; ~**ress** *n* directora; entrenadora; ~**rial** [-ə'dʒɪərɪəl] *adj* directivo; **managing director** *n* director(a) *m/f* general

mandarin ['mændərɪn] *n (also:* ~ **orange)**

mandarina; *(person)* mandarín *m*

mandatory ['mændətərɪ] *adj* obligatorio

mane [meɪn] *n (of horse)* crin *f*; *(of lion)* melena

maneuver [mə'nuːvə*] *(US)* = **manoeuvre**

manfully ['mænfəlɪ] *adv* valientemente

mangle ['mæŋgl] *vt* mutilar, destrozar

man: ~**handle** *vt* maltratar; ~**hole** *n* agujero de acceso; ~**hood** *n* edad *f* viril; *(state)* virilidad *f*; ~-**hour** *n* hora-hombre *f*; ~**hunt** *n (POLICE)* búsqueda y captura

mania ['meɪnɪə] *n* manía; ~**c** ['meɪnɪæk] *n* maníaco/a; *(fig)* maniático

manic ['mænɪk] *adj* frenético; ~-**depressive** *n* maníaco/a depresivo/a

manicure ['mænɪkjuə*] *n* manicura

manifest ['mænɪfest] *vt* manifestar, mostrar ♦ *adj* manifiesto

manifesto [mænɪ'festəu] *n* manifiesto

manipulate [mə'nɪpjuleɪt] *vt* manipular

man: ~**kind** [mæn'kaɪnd] *n* humanidad *f*, género humano; ~**ly** *adj* varonil; ~-**made** *adj* artificial

manner ['mænə*] *n* manera, modo; *(behaviour)* conducta, manera de ser; *(type)*: **all ~ of things** toda clase de cosas; ~**s** *npl (behaviour)* modales *mpl*; **bad ~s** mala educación; ~**ism** *n* peculiaridad *f* de lenguaje *(or* de comportamiento)

manoeuvre [mə'nuːvə*] *(US* **maneuver)** *vt, vi* maniobrar ♦ *n* maniobra

manor ['mænə*] *n (also:* ~ **house)** casa solariega

manpower ['mænpauə*] *n* mano *f* de obra

mansion ['mænʃən] *n* palacio, casa grande

manslaughter ['mænslɔːtə*] *n* homicidio no premeditado

mantelpiece ['mæntlpiːs] *n* repisa, chimenea

manual ['mænjuəl] *adj* manual ♦ *n* manual *m*

manufacture [mænju'fæktʃə*] *vt* fabricar ♦ *n* fabricación *f*; ~**r** *n* fabricante *m/f*

manure [mə'njuə*] *n* estiércol *m*

manuscript ['mænjuskrɪpt] *n* manuscrito

many ['menɪ] *adj, pron* muchos/as; **a**

great ~ muchísimos, un buen número de; **~ a time** muchas veces

map [mæp] n mapa m; **to ~ out** vt proyectar

maple ['meɪpl] n arce m (SP), maple m (AM)

mar [mɑː*] vt estropear

marathon ['mærəθən] n maratón m

marble ['mɑːbl] n mármol m; (toy) canica

March [mɑːtʃ] n marzo

march [mɑːtʃ] vi (MIL) marchar; (demonstrators) manifestarse ♦ n marcha; (demonstration) manifestación f

mare [mɛə*] n yegua

margarine [mɑːdʒə'riːn] n margarina

margin ['mɑːdʒɪn] n margen m; (COMM: profit ~) margen m de beneficios; **~al** adj marginal; **~al seat** n (POL) escaño electoral difícil de asegurar

marigold ['mærɪɡəʊld] n caléndula

marijuana [mærɪ'wɑːnə] n marijuana

marina [mə'riːnə] n puerto deportivo

marinate ['mærɪneɪt] vt marinar

marine [mə'riːn] adj marino ♦ n soldado de marina

marital ['mærɪtl] adj matrimonial; **~ status** estado civil

marjoram ['mɑːdʒərəm] n mejorana

mark [mɑːk] n marca, señal f; (in snow, mud etc) huella; (stain) mancha; (BRIT: SCOL) nota; (currency) marco ♦ vt marcar; manchar; (damage: furniture) rayar; (indicate: place etc) señalar; (BRIT: SCOL) calificar, corregir; **to ~ time** marcar el paso; (fig) marcar(se) un ritmo; **~ed** adj (obvious) marcado, acusado; **~er** n (sign) marcador m; (bookmark) señal f (de libro)

market ['mɑːkɪt] n mercado ♦ vt (COMM) comercializar; **~ garden** n (BRIT) huerto; **~ing** n márketing m; **~place** n mercado; **~ research** n análisis m inv de mercados

marksman ['mɑːksmən] n tirador m

marmalade ['mɑːməleɪd] n mermelada de naranja

maroon [mə'ruːn] vt: **to be ~ed** quedar aislado; (fig) quedar abandonado

marquee [mɑː'kiː] n entoldado

marriage ['mærɪdʒ] n (relationship, institution) matrimonio; (wedding) boda; (act) casamiento; **~ certificate** n partida de casamiento

married ['mærɪd] adj casado; (life, love) conyugal

marrow ['mærəʊ] n médula; (vegetable) calabacín m

marry ['mærɪ] vt casarse con; (subj: father, priest etc) casar ♦ vi (also: **get married**) casarse

Mars [mɑːz] n Marte m

marsh [mɑːʃ] n pantano; (salt ~) marisma

marshal ['mɑːʃl] n (MIL) mariscal m; (at sports meeting etc) oficial m; (US: of police, fire department) jefe/a m/f ♦ vt (thoughts etc) ordenar; (soldiers) formar

marshy ['mɑːʃɪ] adj pantanoso

martial law ['mɑːʃl-] n ley f marcial

martyr ['mɑːtə*] n mártir m/f; **~dom** n martirio

marvel ['mɑːvl] n maravilla, prodigio ♦ vi: **to ~ (at)** maravillarse (de); **~lous** (US **~ous**) adj maravilloso

Marxist ['mɑːksɪst] adj, n marxista m/f

marzipan ['mɑːzɪpæn] n mazapán m

mascara [mæs'kɑːrə] n rímel m

masculine ['mæskjʊlɪn] adj masculino

mash [mæʃ] vt machacar; **~ed potatoes** npl puré m de patatas (SP) or papas (AM)

mask [mɑːsk] n máscara ♦ vt (cover): **to ~ one's face** ocultarse la cara; (hide: feelings) esconder

mason ['meɪsn] n (also: **stone~**) albañil m; (also: **free~**) masón m; **~ry** n (in building) mampostería

masquerade [mæskə'reɪd] vi: **to ~ as** disfrazarse de, hacerse pasar por

mass [mæs] n (people) muchedumbre f; (of air, liquid etc) masa; (of detail, hair etc) gran cantidad f; (REL) misa ♦ cpd masivo ♦ vi reunirse; concentrarse; **the ~es** npl las masas; **~es of** (inf) montones de

massacre ['mæsəkə*] n masacre f

massage ['mæsɑːʒ] n masaje m ♦ vt dar masaje en

masseur [mæ'sɜː*] *n* masajista *m*

masseuse [mæ'sɜːz] *n* masajista *f*

massive ['mæsɪv] *adj* enorme; (*support, changes*) masivo

mass media *npl* medios *mpl* de comunicación

mass production *n* fabricación *f* en serie

mast [mɑːst] *n* (*NAUT*) mástil *m*; (*RADIO etc*) torre *f*

master ['mɑːstə*] *n* (*of servant*) amo; (*of situation*) dueño, maestro; (*in primary school*) maestro; (*in secondary school*) profesor *m*; (*title for boys*): **M~ X** Señorito X ♦ *vt* dominar; **M~ of Arts/Science** *n* licenciatura superior en Letras/Ciencias; **~ly** *adj* magistral; **~mind** *n* inteligencia superior ♦ *vt* dirigir, planear; **~piece** *n* obra maestra; **~y** *n* maestría

mat [mæt] *n* estera; (*also*: **door~**) felpudo; (*also*: **table ~**) salvamanteles *m inv*, posavasos *m inv* ♦ *adj* = **matt**

match [mætʃ] *n* cerilla, fósforo; (*game*) partido; (*equal*) igual *m/f* ♦ *vt* (*go well with*) hacer juego con; (*equal*) igualar; (*correspond to*) corresponderse con; (*pair: also*: **~ up**) casar con ♦ *vi* hacer juego; **to be a good ~** hacer juego; **~box** *n* caja de cerillas; **~ing** *adj* que hace juego

mate [meɪt] *n* (*work~*) colega *m/f*; (*inf: friend*) amigo/a; (*animal*) macho *m*/hembra *f*; (*in merchant navy*) segundo de a bordo ♦ *vi* acoplarse, aparearse ♦ *vt* aparear

material [mə'tɪərɪəl] *n* (*substance*) materia; (*information*) material *m*; (*cloth*) tela, tejido ♦ *adj* material; (*important*) esencial; **~s** *npl* materiales *mpl*

maternal [mə'tɜːnl] *adj* maternal

maternity [mə'tɜːnɪtɪ] *n* maternidad *f*; **~ dress** *n* vestido premamá

math [mæθ] (*US*) *n* = **mathematics**

mathematical [mæθə'mætɪkl] *adj* matemático

mathematician [mæθəmə'tɪʃən] *n* matemático/a

mathematics [mæθə'mætɪks] *n*

matemáticas *fpl*

maths [mæθs] (*BRIT*) *n* = **mathematics**

matinée ['mætɪneɪ] *n* sesión *f* de tarde

matrices ['meɪtrɪsiːz] *npl of* **matrix**

matriculation [mətrɪkju'leɪʃən] *n* (formalización *f* de) matrícula

matrimony ['mætrɪmənɪ] *n* matrimonio

matrix ['meɪtrɪks] (*pl* **matrices**) *n* matriz *f*

matron ['meɪtrən] *n* enfermera *f* jefe; (*in school*) ama de llaves

mat(t) [mæt] *adj* mate

matted ['mætɪd] *adj* enmarañado

matter ['mætə*] *n* cuestión *f*, asunto; (*PHYSICS*) sustancia, materia; (*reading ~*) material *m*; (*MED: pus*) pus *m* ♦ *vi* importar; **~s** *npl* (*affairs*) asuntos *mpl*, temas *mpl*; **it doesn't ~** no importa; **what's the ~?** ¿qué pasa?; **no ~ what** pase lo que pase; **as a ~ of course** por rutina; **as a ~ of fact** de hecho; **~-of-fact** *adj* prosaico, práctico

mattress ['mætrɪs] *n* colchón *m*

mature [mə'tjuə*] *adj* maduro ♦ *vi* madurar; **maturity** *n* madurez *f*

maul [mɔːl] *vt* magullar

mauve [məuv] *adj* de color malva (*SP*) or guinda (*AM*)

maximum ['mæksɪməm] (*pl* **maxima**) *adj* máximo ♦ *n* máximo

May [meɪ] *n* mayo

may [meɪ] (*conditional*: **might**) *vi* (*indicating possibility*): **he ~ come** puede que venga; (*be allowed to*): **~ I smoke?** ¿puedo fumar?; (*wishes*): **~ God bless you!** ¡que Dios le bendiga!; **you ~ as well go** bien puedes irte

maybe ['meɪbiː] *adv* quizá(s)

May Day *n* el primero de Mayo

mayhem ['meɪhem] *n* caos *m* total

mayonnaise [meɪə'neɪz] *n* mayonesa

mayor [mɛə*] *n* alcalde *m*; **~ess** *n* alcaldesa

maze [meɪz] *n* laberinto

M.D. *abbr* = **Doctor of Medicine**

me [miː] *pron* (*direct*) me; (*stressed, after pron*) mí; **can you hear ~?** ¿me oyes?; **he heard ME!** me oyó a mí; **it's ~** soy yo;

give them to ~ dámelos/las; **with /
without ~** conmigo/sin mí

meadow ['mɛdəu] n prado, pradera

meagre ['mi:gə*] (US **meager**) adj escaso,
pobre

meal [mi:l] n comida; (flour) harina;
~**time** n hora de comer

mean [mi:n] (pt, pp **meant**) adj (with
money) tacaño; (unkind) mezquino, malo;
(shabby) humilde; (average) medio ♦ vt
(signify) querer decir, significar; (refer to)
referirse a; (intend): **to ~ to do sth** pensar
or pretender hacer algo ♦ n medio,
término medio; ~**s** npl (way) medio,
manera; (money) recursos mpl, medios
mpl; **by ~s of** mediante, por medio de;
by all ~s! ¡naturalmente!, ¡claro que sí!;
do you ~ it? ¿lo dices en serio?; **what do
you ~?** ¿qué quiere decir?; **to be meant
for sb/sth** ser para uno/algo

meander [mɪˈændə*] vi (river) serpentear

meaning ['mi:nɪŋ] n significado, sentido;
(purpose) sentido, propósito; ~**ful** adj
significativo; ~**less** adj sin sentido

meanness ['mi:nnɪs] n (with money)
tacañería; (unkindness) maldad f,
mezquindad f; (shabbiness) humildad f

meant [mɛnt] pt, pp of **mean**

meantime ['mi:ntaɪm] adv (also: **in the ~**)
mientras tanto

meanwhile ['mi:nwaɪl] adv = **meantime**

measles ['mi:zlz] n sarampión m

measure ['mɛʒə*] vt, vi medir ♦ n
medida; (ruler) regla; ~**ments** npl
medidas fpl

meat [mi:t] n carne f; **cold ~** fiambre m;
~**ball** n albóndiga; ~ **pie** n pastel m de
carne

Mecca ['mɛkə] n La Meca

mechanic [mɪˈkænɪk] n mecánico/a; ~**s** n
mecánica ♦ npl mecanismo; ~**al** adj
mecánico

mechanism ['mɛkənɪzəm] n mecanismo

medal ['mɛdl] n medalla; ~**lion** [mɪˈdælɪən]
n medallón m; ~**list** (US ~**ist**) n (SPORT)
medallista m/f

meddle ['mɛdl] vi: **to ~ in** entrometerse

en; **to ~ with sth** manosear algo

media ['mi:dɪə] npl medios mpl de
comunicación ♦ npl of **medium**

mediaeval [mɛdrˈiːvl] adj = **medieval**

mediate ['mi:dɪeɪt] vi mediar; **mediator**
n intermediario/a, mediador(a) m/f

Medicaid ® ['mɛdɪkeɪd] (US) n programa
de ayuda médica para los pobres

medical ['mɛdɪkl] adj médico ♦ n
reconocimiento médico

Medicare ® ['mɛdɪkɛə*] (US) n programa
de ayuda médica para los ancianos

medication [mɛdrˈkeɪʃən] n medicación f

medicine ['mɛdsɪn] n medicina; (drug)
medicamento

medieval [mɛdrˈiːvl] adj medieval

mediocre [miːdrˈəukə*] adj mediocre

meditate ['mɛdɪteɪt] vi meditar

Mediterranean [mɛdɪtəˈreɪnɪən] adj
mediterráneo; **the ~ (Sea)** el (Mar)
Mediterráneo

medium ['mi:dɪəm] (pl **media**) adj
mediano, regular ♦ n (means) medio; (pl
mediums: person) médium m/f; ~ **wave** n
onda media

meek [mi:k] adj manso, sumiso

meet [mi:t] (pt, pp **met**) vt encontrar;
(accidentally) encontrar con, tropezar
con; (by arrangement) reunirse con; (for
the first time) conocer; (go and fetch) ir a
buscar; (opponent) enfrentarse con;
(obligations) cumplir; (encounter: problem)
hacer frente a; (need) satisfacer ♦ vi
encontrarse; (in session) reunirse; (join:
objects) unirse; (for the first time)
conocerse; ~ **with** vt fus (difficulty)
tropezar con; **to ~ with success** tener
éxito; ~**ing** n encuentro; (arranged) cita,
compromiso; (business ~ing) reunión f;
(POL) mítin m

megabyte ['mɛgəbaɪt] n (COMPUT)
megabyte m, megaocteto

megaphone ['mɛgəfəun] n megáfono

melancholy ['mɛlənkəlɪ] n melancolía
♦ adj melancólico

mellow ['mɛləu] adj (wine) añejo; (sound,
colour) suave ♦ vi (person) ablandar

melody ['mɛlədɪ] *n* melodía

melon ['mɛlən] *n* melón *m*

melt [mɛlt] *vi* (*metal*) fundirse; (*snow*) derretirse ♦ *vt* fundir; **~down** *n* (*in nuclear reactor*) fusión *f* de un reactor (nuclear); **~ing pot** *n* (*fig*) crisol *m*

member ['mɛmbə*] *n* (*gen, ANAT*) miembro; (*of club*) socio/a; **M~ of Parliament** (*BRIT*) diputado/a; **M~ of the European Parliament** (*BRIT*) eurodiputado/a; **M~ of the Scottish Parliament** (*BRIT*) diputado/a del Parlamento escocés; **~ship** *n* (*members*) número de miembros; (*state*) filiación *f*; **~ship card** *n* carnet *m* de socio

memento [mə'mɛntəu] *n* recuerdo

memo ['mɛməu] *n* apunte *m*, nota

memoirs ['mɛmwɑːz] *npl* memorias *fpl*

memorandum [mɛmə'rændəm] (*pl* **memoranda**) *n* apunte *m*, nota; (*official note*) acta

memorial [mɪ'mɔːrɪəl] *n* monumento conmemorativo ♦ *adj* conmemorativo

memorize ['mɛməraɪz] *vt* aprender de memoria

memory ['mɛmərɪ] *n* (*also: COMPUT*) memoria; (*instance*) recuerdo; (*of dead person*): **in ~ of** a la memoria de

men [mɛn] *npl of* **man**

menace ['mɛnəs] *n* amenaza ♦ *vt* amenazar; **menacing** *adj* amenazador(a)

mend [mɛnd] *vt* reparar, arreglar; (*darn*) zurcir ♦ *vi* reponerse ♦ *n* arreglo, reparación *f*; zurcido ♦ *n*: **to be on the ~** ir mejorando; **to ~ one's ways** enmendarse; **~ing** *n* reparación *f*; (*clothes*) ropa por remendar

meningitis [mɛnɪn'dʒaɪtɪs] *n* meningitis *f*

menopause ['mɛnəupɔːz] *n* menopausia

menstruation [mɛnstruˈeɪʃən] *n* menstruación *f*

mental ['mɛntl] *adj* mental; **~ity** [-'tælɪtɪ] *n* mentalidad *f*

mention ['mɛnʃən] *n* mención *f* ♦ *vt* mencionar; (*speak of*) hablar de; **don't ~ it!** ¡de nada!

menu ['mɛnjuː] *n* (*set ~*) menú *m*; (*printed*) carta; (*COMPUT*) menú *m*

MEP *n abbr* = **Member of the European Parliament**

merchandise ['məːtʃəndaɪz] *n* mercancías *fpl*

merchant ['məːtʃənt] *n* comerciante *m/f*; **~ bank** (*BRIT*) *n* banco comercial; **~ navy** (*US* **~ marine**) *n* marina mercante

merciful ['məːsɪful] *adj* compasivo; (*fortunate*) afortunado

merciless ['məːsɪlɪs] *adj* despiadado

mercury ['məːkjurɪ] *n* mercurio

mercy ['məːsɪ] *n* compasión *f*; (*REL*) misericordia; **at the ~ of** a la merced de

merely ['mɪəlɪ] *adv* simplemente, sólo

merge [məːdʒ] *vt* (*join*) unir ♦ *vi* unirse; (*COMM*) fusionarse; (*colours etc*) fundirse; **~r** *n* (*COMM*) fusión *f*

meringue [mə'ræŋ] *n* merengue *m*

merit ['mɛrɪt] *n* mérito ♦ *vt* merecer

mermaid ['məːmeɪd] *n* sirena

merry ['mɛrɪ] *adj* alegre; **M~ Christmas!** ¡Felices Pascuas!; **~-go-round** *n* tiovivo

mesh [mɛʃ] *n* malla

mesmerize ['mɛzməraɪz] *vt* hipnotizar

mess [mɛs] *n* (*muddle: of situation*) confusión *f*; (: *of room*) revoltijo; (*dirt*) porquería; (*MIL*) comedor *m*; **~ about** *or* **around** (*inf*) *vi* perder el tiempo; (*pass the time*) entretenerse; **~ about** *or* **around with** (*inf*) *vt fus* divertirse con; **~ up** *vt* (*spoil*) estropear; (*dirty*) ensuciar

message ['mɛsɪdʒ] *n* recado, mensaje *m*

messenger ['mɛsɪndʒə*] *n* mensajero/a

Messrs *abbr* (*on letters:* = *Messieurs*) Sres

messy ['mɛsɪ] *adj* (*dirty*) sucio; (*untidy*) desordenado

met [mɛt] *pt, pp of* **meet**

metal ['mɛtl] *n* metal *m*; **~lic** [-'tælɪk] *adj* metálico

metaphor ['mɛtəfə*] *n* metáfora

meteor ['miːtɪə*] *n* meteoro; **~ite** [-aɪt] *n* meteorito

meteorology [miːtɪə'rɔlədʒɪ] *n* meteorología

meter ['miːtə*] *n* (*instrument*) contador *m*; (*US: unit*) = **metre** ♦ *vt* (*US: POST*) franquear

method ['mɛθəd] *n* método

meths [mɛθs] (*BRIT*) *n*, **methylated spirit** ['mɛθɪleɪtɪd-] (*BRIT*) *n* alcohol *m* metilado *or* desnaturalizado

metre ['miːtə*] (*US* **meter**) *n* metro

metric ['mɛtrɪk] *adj* métrico

metropolitan [mɛtrə'pɒlɪtən] *adj* metropolitano; **the M~ Police** (*BRIT*) la policía londinense

mettle ['mɛtl] *n*: **to be on one's ~** estar dispuesto a mostrar todo lo que uno vale

mew [mjuː] *vi* (*cat*) maullar

mews [mjuːz] *n*: **~ flat** (*BRIT*) *piso acondicionado en antiguos establos o cocheras*

Mexican ['mɛksɪkən] *adj, n* mejicano/a *m/f*, mexicano/a *m/f*

Mexico ['mɛksɪkəʊ] *n* Méjico (*SP*), México (*AM*); **~ City** *n* Ciudad *f* de Méjico *or* México

miaow [miːˈaʊ] *vi* maullar

mice [maɪs] *npl of* **mouse**

micro... [maɪkrəʊ] *prefix* micro...; **~chip** *n* microplaqueta; **~(computer)** *n* microordenador *m*; **~phone** *n* micrófono; **~processor** *n* microprocesador *m*; **~scope** *n* microscopio; **~wave** *n* (*also*: **~wave oven**) horno microondas

mid [mɪd] *adj*: **in ~ May** a mediados de mayo; **in ~ afternoon** a media tarde; **in ~ air** en el aire; **~day** *n* mediodía *m*

middle ['mɪdl] *n* centro; (*half-way point*) medio; (*waist*) cintura ♦ *adj* de en medio; (*course, way*) intermedio; **in the ~ of the night** en plena noche; **~-aged** *adj* de mediana edad; **the M~ Ages** *npl* la Edad Media; **~-class** *adj* de clase media; **the ~ class(es)** *n(pl)* la clase media; **M~ East** *n* Oriente *m* Medio; **~man** *n* intermediario; **~ name** *n* segundo nombre; **~-of-the-road** *adj* moderado; **~weight** *n* (*BOXING*) peso medio

middling ['mɪdlɪŋ] *adj* mediano

midge [mɪdʒ] *n* mosquito

midget ['mɪdʒɪt] *n* enano/a

Midlands ['mɪdləndz] *npl*: **the ~** *la región central de Inglaterra*

midnight ['mɪdnaɪt] *n* medianoche *f*

midst [mɪdst] *n*: **in the ~ of** (*crowd*) en medio de; (*situation, action*) en mitad de

midsummer [mɪd'sʌmə*] *n*: **in ~** en pleno verano

midway [mɪd'weɪ] *adj, adv*: **~ (between)** a medio camino (entre); **~ through** a la mitad (de)

midweek [mɪd'wiːk] *adv* entre semana

midwife ['mɪdwaɪf] (*pl* **midwives**) *n* comadrona, partera

might [maɪt] *vb see* **may** ♦ *n* fuerza, poder *m*; **~y** *adj* fuerte, poderoso

migraine ['miːgreɪn] *n* jaqueca

migrant ['maɪgrənt] *n adj* (*bird*) migratorio; (*worker*) emigrante

migrate [maɪ'greɪt] *vi* emigrar

mike [maɪk] *n abbr* (= **microphone**) micro

mild [maɪld] *adj* (*person*) apacible; (*climate*) templado; (*slight*) ligero; (*taste*) suave; (*illness*) leve; **~ly** *adv* ligeramente; suavemente; **to put it ~ly** para no decir más

mile [maɪl] *n* milla; **~age** *n* número de millas, ≈ kilometraje *m*; **~ometer** [maɪ'lɒmɪtə*] *n* ≈ cuentakilómetros *m inv*; **~stone** *n* mojón *m*

militant ['mɪlɪtnt] *adj, n* militante *m/f*

military ['mɪlɪtəri] *adj* militar

militia [mɪ'lɪʃə] *n* milicia

milk [mɪlk] *n* leche *f* ♦ *vt* (*cow*) ordeñar; (*fig*) chupar; **~ chocolate** *n* chocolate *m* con leche; **~man** (*irreg*) *n* lechero; **~ shake** *n* batido, malteada (*AM*); **~y** *adj* lechoso; **M~y Way** *n* Vía Láctea

mill [mɪl] *n* (*windmill etc*) molino; (*coffee ~*) molinillo; (*factory*) fábrica ♦ *vt* moler ♦ *vi* (*also*: **~ about**) arremolinarse

millennium [mɪ'lɛnɪəm] (*pl* **~s** or **millennia**) *n* milenio, milenario

miller ['mɪlə*] *n* molinero

milli... ['mɪlɪ] *prefix*: **~gram(me)** *n* miligramo; **~metre** (*US* **~meter**) *n* milímetro

million ['mɪljən] *n* millón *m*; **a ~ times** un millón de veces; **~aire** [-jə'nɛə*] *n* millonario/a

milometer [mar'lɔmɪtə*] (BRIT) n
= **mileometer**

mime [maɪm] n mímica; (actor) mimo/a
♦ vt remedar ♦ vi actuar de mimo

mimic ['mɪmɪk] n imitador(a) m/f ♦ adj
mímico ♦ vt remedar, imitar

min. abbr = **minimum; minute(s)**

mince [mɪns] vt picar ♦ n (BRIT: CULIN)
carne f picada; ~**meat** n conserva de
fruta picada; (US: meat) carne f picada; ~
pie n empanadilla rellena de fruta
picada; ~**r** n picadora de carne

mind [maɪnd] n mente f; (intellect)
intelecto; (contrasted with matter) espíritu
m ♦ vt (attend to, look after) ocuparse de,
cuidar; (be careful of) tener cuidado con;
(object to): **I don't ~ the noise** no me
molesta el ruido; **it is on my ~** me
preocupa; **to bear sth in ~** tomar or
tener algo en cuenta; **to make up one's
~** decidirse; **I don't ~** me es igual; **~ you,
...** te advierto que ...; **never ~!** ¡es igual!,
¡no importa!; (don't worry) ¡no te
preocupes!; **"~ the step"** "cuidado con
el escalón"; ~**er** n guardaespaldas m inv;
(child ~er) ≈ niñera; ~**ful** adj: ~**ful of**
consciente de; ~**less** adj (crime) sin
motivo; (work) de autómata

mine[1] [maɪn] pron el mío/la mía etc; **a
friend of ~** un(a) amigo/a mío/mía ♦ adj:
this book is ~ este libro es mío

mine[2] [maɪn] n mina ♦ vt (coal) extraer;
(bomb: beach etc) minar; ~**field** n campo
de minas; **miner** n minero/a

mineral ['mɪnərəl] adj mineral ♦ n mineral
m; ~**s** npl (BRIT: soft drinks) refrescos mpl;
~ **water** n agua mineral

mingle ['mɪŋgl] vi: **to ~ with** mezclarse
con

miniature ['mɪnətʃə*] adj (en) miniatura
♦ n miniatura

minibus ['mɪnɪbʌs] n microbús m

Minidisc ® ['mɪnɪdɪsk] n minidisco

minimal ['mɪnɪml] adj mínimo

minimize ['mɪnɪmaɪz] vt minimizar; (play
down) empequeñecer

minimum ['mɪnɪməm] (pl **minima**) n, adj

mínimo

mining ['maɪnɪŋ] n explotación f minera

miniskirt ['mɪnɪskɜːt] n minifalda

minister ['mɪnɪstə*] n (BRIT: POL) ministro/a
(SP), secretario/a (AM); (REL) pastor m
♦ vi: **to ~ to** atender a

ministry ['mɪnɪstrɪ] n (BRIT: POL) ministerio
(SP), secretaría (AM); (REL) sacerdocio

mink [mɪŋk] n visón m

minnow ['mɪnəu] n pececillo (de agua
dulce)

minor ['maɪnə*] adj (repairs, injuries) leve;
(poet, planet) menor; (MUS) menor ♦ n
(LAW) menor m de edad

Minorca [mɪ'nɔːkə] n Menorca

minority [maɪ'nɔrɪtɪ] n minoría

mint [mɪnt] n (plant) menta, hierbabuena;
(sweet) caramelo de menta ♦ vt (coins)
acuñar; **the (Royal) M~, the (US) M~** la
Casa de la Moneda; **in ~ condition** en
perfecto estado

minus ['maɪnəs] n (also: ~ **sign**) signo de
menos ♦ prep menos; **12 ~ 6 equals 6**
12 menos 6 son 6; **~ 24°C** menos 24
grados

minute[1] ['mɪnɪt] n minuto; (fig)
momento; ~**s** npl (of meeting) actas fpl;
at the last ~ a última hora

minute[2] [maɪ'njuːt] adj diminuto; (search)
minucioso

miracle ['mɪrəkl] n milagro

mirage ['mɪrɑːʒ] n espejismo

mirror ['mɪrə*] n espejo; (in car) retrovisor m

mirth [mɜːθ] n alegría

misadventure [mɪsəd'ventʃə*] n desgracia

misapprehension [mɪsæprɪ'henʃən] n
equivocación f

misappropriate [mɪsə'prəuprɪeɪt] vt
malversar

misbehave [mɪsbɪ'heɪv] vi portarse mal

miscalculate [mɪs'kælkjuleɪt] vt calcular
mal

miscarriage ['mɪskærɪdʒ] n (MED) aborto;
~ **of justice** error m judicial

miscellaneous [mɪsɪ'leɪnɪəs] adj varios/
as, diversos/as

mischief ['mɪstʃɪf] n travesuras fpl,

diabluras *fpl*; (*maliciousness*) malicia;
mischievous [-ʃɪvəs] *adj* travieso
misconception [mɪskən'sepʃən] *n* idea
equivocada; equivocación *f*
misconduct [mɪs'kɒndʌkt] *n* mala
conducta; **professional ~** falta profesional
misdemeanour [mɪsdɪ'miːnə*] (*US*
misdemeanor) *n* delito, ofensa
miser ['maɪzə*] *n* avaro/a
miserable ['mɪzərəbl] *adj* (*unhappy*) triste,
desgraciado; (*unpleasant, contemptible*)
miserable
miserly ['maɪzəlɪ] *adj* avariento, tacaño
misery ['mɪzərɪ] *n* tristeza; (*wretchedness*)
miseria, desdicha
misfire [mɪs'faɪə*] *vi* fallar
misfit ['mɪsfɪt] *n* inadaptado/a
misfortune [mɪs'fɔːtʃən] *n* desgracia
misgiving [mɪs'gɪvɪŋ] *n* (*apprehension*)
presentimiento; **to have ~s about sth**
tener dudas acerca de algo
misguided [mɪs'gaɪdɪd] *adj* equivocado
mishandle [mɪs'hændl] *vt* (*mismanage*)
manejar mal
mishap ['mɪshæp] *n* desgracia,
contratiempo
misinform [mɪsɪn'fɔːm] *vt* informar mal
misinterpret [mɪsɪn'tɜːprɪt] *vt* interpretar
mal
misjudge [mɪs'dʒʌdʒ] *vt* juzgar mal
mislay [mɪs'leɪ] (*irreg*) *vt* extraviar, perder
mislead [mɪs'liːd] (*irreg*) *vt* llevar a
conclusiones erróneas; **~ing** *adj*
engañoso
mismanage [mɪs'mænɪdʒ] *vt* administrar
mal
misplace [mɪs'pleɪs] *vt* extraviar
misprint ['mɪsprɪnt] *n* errata, error *m* de
imprenta
Miss [mɪs] *n* Señorita
miss [mɪs] *vt* (*train etc*) perder; (*fail to hit:
target*) errar; (*regret the absence of*): **I ~
him** (yo) le echo de menos *or* a faltar;
(*fail to see*): **you can't ~ it** no tiene
pérdida ♦ *vi* fallar ♦ *n* (*shot*) tiro fallido *or*
perdido; **~ out** (*BRIT*) *vt* omitir
misshapen [mɪs'ʃeɪpən] *adj* deforme

missile ['mɪsaɪl] *n* (*AVIAT*) mísil *m*; (*object
thrown*) proyectil *m*
missing ['mɪsɪŋ] *adj* (*pupil*) ausente;
(*thing*) perdido; (*MIL*): **~ in action**
desaparecido en combate
mission ['mɪʃən] *n* misión *f*; (*official
representation*) delegación *f*; **~ary** *n*
misionero/a
mist [mɪst] *n* (*light*) neblina; (*heavy*) niebla;
(*at sea*) bruma ♦ *vi* (*eyes: also:* **~ over, ~
up**) llenarse de lágrimas; (*BRIT: windows:
also:* **~ over, ~ up**) empañarse
mistake [mɪs'teɪk] (*vt: irreg*) *n* error *m*
♦ *vt* entender mal; **by ~** por
equivocación; **to make a ~** equivocarse;
to ~ A for B confundir A con B;
mistaken *pp* of **mistake** ♦ *adj*
equivocado; **to be mistaken** equivocarse,
engañarse
mister ['mɪstə*] (*inf*) *n* señor *m*; *see* **Mr**
mistletoe ['mɪsltəʊ] *n* muérdago
mistook [mɪs'tʊk] *pt* of **mistake**
mistress ['mɪstrɪs] *n* (*lover*) amante *f*; (*of
house*) señora (de la casa); (*BRIT: in
primary school*) maestra; (*in secondary
school*) profesora; (*of situation*) dueña
mistrust [mɪs'trʌst] *vt* desconfiar de
misty ['mɪstɪ] *adj* (*day*) de niebla; (*glasses
etc*) empañado
misunderstand [mɪsʌndə'stænd] (*irreg*)
vt, vi entender mal; **~ing** *n*
malentendido
misuse [*n* mɪs'juːs, *vb* mɪs'juːz] *n* mal uso;
(*of power*) abuso; (*of funds*) malversación *f*
♦ *vt* abusar de; malversar
mitt(en) ['mɪt(n)] *n* manopla
mix [mɪks] *vt* mezclar; (*combine*) unir ♦ *vi*
mezclarse; (*people*) llevarse bien ♦ *n*
mezcla; **~ up** *vt* mezclar; (*confuse*)
confundir; **~ed** *adj* mixto; (*feelings etc*)
encontrado; **~ed-up** *adj* (*confused*)
confuso, revuelto; **~er** *n* (*for food*)
licuadora; (*for drinks*) coctelera; (*person*):
he's a good ~er tiene don de gentes;
~ture *n* mezcla; (*also:* **cough ~ture**)
jarabe *m*; **~-up** *n* confusión *f*
mm *abbr* (= *millimetre*) mm

moan [məun] *n* gemido ♦ *vi* gemir; (*inf: complain*): **to ~ (about)** quejarse (de)

moat [məut] *n* foso

mob [mɔb] *n* multitud *f* ♦ *vt* acosar

mobile ['məubaɪl] *adj* móvil ♦ *n* móvil *m*; **~ home** *n* caravana; **~ phone** *n* teléfono portátil

mock [mɔk] *vt* (*ridicule*) ridiculizar; (*laugh at*) burlarse de ♦ *adj* fingido; **~ exam** *n* examen preparatorio antes de los exámenes oficiales; **~ery** *n* burla; **~-up** *n* maqueta

mod [mɔd] *adj see* **convenience**

mode [məud] *n* modo

model ['mɔdl] *n* modelo; (*fashion ~, artist's ~*) modelo *m/f* ♦ *adj* modelo ♦ *vt* (*with clay etc*) modelar (*copy*): **to ~ o.s. on** tomar como modelo a ♦ *vi* ser modelo; **to ~ clothes** pasar modelos, ser modelo; **~ railway** *n* ferrocarril *m* de juguete

modem ['məudəm] *n* modem *m*

moderate [*adj* 'mɔdərət, *vb* 'mɔdəreɪt] *adj* moderado/a ♦ *vi* moderarse, calmarse ♦ *vt* moderar

modern ['mɔdən] *adj* moderno; **~ize** *vt* modernizar

modest ['mɔdɪst] *adj* modesto; (*small*) módico; **~y** *n* modestia

modify ['mɔdɪfaɪ] *vt* modificar

mogul ['məugəl] *n* (*fig*) magnate *m*

mohair ['məuhɛə*] *n* mohair *m*

moist [mɔɪst] *adj* húmedo; **~en** ['mɔɪsn] *vt* humedecer; **~ure** ['mɔɪstʃə*] *n* humedad *f*; **~urizer** ['mɔɪstʃəraɪzə*] *n* crema hidratante

molar ['məulə*] *n* muela

mold [məuld] (*US*) *n*, *vt* = **mould**

mole [məul] *n* (*animal, spy*) topo; (*spot*) lunar *m*

molest [məu'lɛst] *vt* importunar; (*assault sexually*) abusar sexualmente de

mollycoddle ['mɔlɪkɔdl] *vt* mimar

molt [məult] (*US*) *vi* = **moult**

molten ['məultən] *adj* fundido; (*lava*) líquido

mom [mɔm] (*US*) *n* = **mum**

moment ['məumənt] *n* momento; **at the ~** de momento, por ahora; **~ary** *adj* momentáneo; **~ous** [-'mɛntəs] *adj* trascendental, importante

momentum [məu'mɛntəm] *n* momento; (*fig*) ímpetu *m*; **to gather ~** cobrar velocidad; (*fig*) ganar fuerza

mommy ['mɔmɪ] (*US*) *n* = **mummy**

Monaco ['mɔnəkəu] *n* Mónaco

monarch ['mɔnək] *n* monarca *m/f*; **~y** *n* monarquía

monastery ['mɔnəstərɪ] *n* monasterio

Monday ['mʌndɪ] *n* lunes *m inv*

monetary ['mʌnɪtərɪ] *adj* monetario

money ['mʌnɪ] *n* dinero; (*currency*) moneda; **to make ~** ganar dinero; **~ order** *n* giro; **~-spinner** (*inf*) *n*: **to be a ~-spinner** dar mucho dinero

mongrel ['mʌŋgrəl] *n* (*dog*) perro mestizo

monitor ['mɔnɪtə*] *n* (*SCOL*) monitor *m*; (*also:* **television~**) receptor *m* de control; (*of computer*) monitor *m* ♦ *vt* controlar

monk [mʌŋk] *n* monje *m*

monkey ['mʌŋkɪ] *n* mono; **~ nut** (*BRIT*) *n* cacahuete *m* (*SP*), maní *m* (*AM*); **~ wrench** *n* llave *f* inglesa

monopoly [mə'nɔpəlɪ] *n* monopolio

monotone ['mɔnətəun] *n* voz *f* (*or* tono) monocorde

monotonous [mə'nɔtənəs] *adj* monótono

monsoon [mɔn'suːn] *n* monzón *m*

monster ['mɔnstə*] *n* monstruo

monstrous ['mɔnstrəs] *adj* (*huge*) enorme; (*atrocious, ugly*) monstruoso

month [mʌnθ] *n* mes *m*; **~ly** *adj* mensual ♦ *adv* mensualmente

monument ['mɔnjumənt] *n* monumento

moo [muː] *vi* mugir

mood [muːd] *n* humor *m*; (*of crowd, group*) clima *m*; **to be in a good/bad ~** estar de buen/mal humor; **~y** *adj* (*changeable*) de humor variable; (*sullen*) malhumorado

moon· [muːn] *n* luna; **~light** *n* luz *f* de la luna; **~lighting** *n* pluriempleo; **~lit** *adj*: **a ~lit night** una noche de luna

Moor [muə*] *n* moro/a

moor [muə*] n páramo ♦ vt (ship) amarrar ♦ vi echar las amarras

Moorish ['muərɪʃ] adj moro; (architecture) árabe, morisco

moorland ['muələnd] n páramo, brezal m

moose [muːs] n inv alce m

mop [mɔp] n fregona; (of hair) greña, melena ♦ vt fregar; ~ up vt limpiar

mope [məup] vi estar or andar deprimido

moped ['məuped] n ciclomotor m

moral ['mɔrl] adj moral ♦ n moraleja; ~s npl moralidad f, moral f

morale [mɔ'rɑːl] n moral f

morality [mə'rælɪtɪ] n moralidad f

morass [mə'ræs] n pantano

KEYWORD

more [mɔː*] adj 1 (greater in number etc) más; ~ people/work than before más gente/trabajo que antes
2 (additional) más; do you want (some) ~ tea? ¿quieres más té?; is there any ~ wine? ¿queda vino?; it'll take a few ~ weeks tardará unas semanas más; it's 2 kms ~ to the house faltan 2 kms para la casa; ~ time/letters than we expected más tiempo del que/más cartas de las que esperábamos
♦ pron (greater amount, additional amount) más; ~ than 10 más de 10; it cost ~ than the other one/than we expected costó más que el otro/más de lo que esperábamos; is there any ~? ¿hay más?; many/much ~ muchos(as)/mucho(a) más
♦ adv más; ~ dangerous/easily (than) más peligroso/fácilmente (que); ~ and ~ expensive cada vez más caro; ~ or less más o menos; ~ than ever más que nunca

moreover [mɔː'rəuvə*] adv además, por otra parte

morning ['mɔːnɪŋ] n mañana; (early ~) madrugada ♦ cpd matutino, de la mañana; **in the ~** por la mañana; **7 o'clock in the ~** las 7 de la mañana; ~

sickness n náuseas fpl matutinas

Morocco [mə'rɔkəu] n Marruecos m

moron ['mɔːrɔn] (inf) n imbécil m/f

morphine ['mɔːfiːn] n morfina

Morse [mɔːs] n (also: ~ code) (código) Morse

morsel ['mɔːsl] n (of food) bocado

mortar ['mɔːtə*] n argamasa

mortgage ['mɔːgɪdʒ] n hipoteca ♦ vt hipotecar; ~ company (US) n ≈ banco hipotecario

mortuary ['mɔːtjuərɪ] n depósito de cadáveres

Moscow ['mɔskəu] n Moscú

Moslem ['mɔzləm] adj, n = **Muslim**

mosque [mɔsk] n mezquita

mosquito [mɔs'kiːtəu] (pl ~es) n mosquito (SP), zancudo (AM)

moss [mɔs] n musgo

most [məust] adj la mayor parte de, la mayoría de ♦ pron la mayor parte, la mayoría ♦ adv el más; (very) muy; **the ~** (also: +adj) el más; ~ **of them** la mayor parte de ellos; **I saw the ~** lo que vi más; **at the (very) ~** a lo sumo, todo lo más; **to make the ~ of** aprovechar (al máximo); **a ~ interesting book** un libro interesantísimo; ~**ly** adv en su mayor parte, principalmente

MOT (BRIT) n abbr (= Ministry of Transport): **the ~ (test)** inspección (anual) obligatoria de coches y camiones

motel [məu'tel] n motel m

moth [mɔθ] n mariposa nocturna; (clothes ~) polilla

mother ['mʌðə*] n madre f ♦ adj materno ♦ vt (care for) cuidar (como una madre); ~**hood** n maternidad f; ~**-in-law** n suegra; ~**ly** adj maternal; ~**-of-pearl** n nácar m; ~**-to-be** n futura madre f; ~ **tongue** n lengua materna

motion ['məuʃən] n movimiento; (gesture) ademán m, señal f; (at meeting) moción f ♦ vt, vi: **to ~ (to) sb to do sth** hacer señas a uno para que haga algo; ~**less** adj inmóvil; ~ **picture** n película

motivated ['məutɪveɪtɪd] adj motivado

motive ['məʊtɪv] *n* motivo

motley ['mɒtlɪ] *adj* variado

motor ['məʊtə*] *n* motor *m*; (*BRIT: inf: vehicle*) coche *m* (*SP*), carro (*AM*), automóvil *m* ♦ *adj* motor (*f: motora or motriz*); **~bike** *n* moto *f*; **~boat** *n* lancha motora; **~car** (*BRIT*) *n* coche *m*, carro, automóvil *m*; **~cycle** *n* motocicleta; **~cycle racing** *n* motociclismo; **~cyclist** *n* motociclista *m/f*; **~ing** (*BRIT*) *n* automovilismo; **~ist** *n* conductor(a) *m/f*, automovilista *m/f*; **~ racing** (*BRIT*) *n* carreras *fpl* de coches, automovilismo; **~ vehicle** *n* automóvil *m*; **~way** (*BRIT*) *n* autopista

mottled ['mɒtld] *adj* abigarrado

motto ['mɒtəʊ] (*pl* **~es**) *n* lema *m*; (*watchword*) consigna

mould [məʊld] (*US* **mold**) *n* molde *m*; (*mildew*) moho ♦ *vt* moldear; (*fig*) formar; **~y** *adj* enmohecido

moult [məʊlt] (*US* **molt**) *vi* mudar la piel (*or las plumas*)

mound [maʊnd] *n* montón *m*, montículo

mount [maʊnt] *n* monte *m* ♦ *vt* montar, subir a; (*jewel*) engarzar; (*picture*) enmarcar; (*exhibition etc*) organizar ♦ *vi* (*increase*) aumentar; **~ up** *vi* aumentar

mountain ['maʊntɪn] *n* montaña ♦ *cpd* de montaña; **~bike** *n* bicicleta de montaña; **~eer** [-'nɪə*] *n* montañero/a (*SP*), andinista *m/f* (*AM*); **~eering** [-'nɪərɪŋ] *n* montañismo, andinismo; **~ous** *adj* montañoso; **~ rescue team** *n* equipo de rescate de montaña; **~side** *n* ladera de la montaña

mourn [mɔ:n] *vt* llorar, lamentar ♦ *vi*: **to ~ for** llorar la muerte de; **~er** *n* doliente *m/f*; dolorido/a; **~ing** *n* luto; **in ~ing** de luto

mouse [maʊs] (*pl* **mice**) *n* (*ZOOL, COMPUT*) ratón *m*; **~ mat** *n* (*COMPUT*) alfombrilla; **~trap** *n* ratonera

mousse [mu:s] *n* (*CULIN*) crema batida; (*for hair*) espuma (moldeadora)

moustache [məs'tɑ:ʃ] (*US* **mustache**) *n* bigote *m*

mousy ['maʊsɪ] *adj* (*hair*) pardusco

mouth [maʊθ, *pl* maʊðz] *n* boca; (*of river*) desembocadura; **~ful** *n* bocado; **~ organ** *n* armónica; **~piece** *n* (*of musical instrument*) boquilla; (*spokesman*) portavoz *m/f*; **~wash** *n* enjuague *m*; **~watering** *adj* apetitoso

movable ['mu:vəbl] *adj* movible

move [mu:v] *n* (*movement*) movimiento; (*in game*) jugada; (: *turn to play*) turno; (*change: of house*) mudanza; (: *of job*) cambio de trabajo ♦ *vt* mover; (*emotionally*) conmover; (*POL: resolution etc*) proponer ♦ *vi* moverse; (*traffic*) circular; (*also*: **~ house**) trasladarse, mudarse; **to ~ sb to do sth** mover a uno a hacer algo; **to get a ~ on** darse prisa; **~ about** *or* **around** *vi* moverse; (*travel*) viajar; **~ along** *vi* avanzar, adelantarse; **~ away** *vi* alejarse; **~ back** *vi* retroceder; **~ forward** *vi* avanzar; **~ in** *vi* (*to a house*) instalarse; (*police, soldiers*) intervenir; **~ on** *vi* ponerse en camino; **~ out** *vi* (*of house*) mudarse; **~ over** *vi* apartarse, hacer sitio; **~ up** *vi* (*employee*) ser ascendido

moveable ['mu:vəbl] *adj* = **movable**

movement ['mu:vmənt] *n* movimiento

movie ['mu:vɪ] *n* película; **to go to the ~s** ir al cine

moving ['mu:vɪŋ] *adj* (*emotional*) conmovedor(a); (*that moves*) móvil

mow [məʊ] (*pt* **mowed**, *pp* **mowed** *or* **mown**) *vt* (*grass, corn*) cortar, segar; **~ down** *vt* (*shoot*) acribillar; **~er** *n* (*also*: **lawn~er**) cortacéspedes *m inv*, segadora

MP *n abbr* = **Member of Parliament**

MP3 *n* MP3 *m*; **~ player** *n* reproductor *m* MP3

m.p.h. *abbr* = **miles per hour** (*60 m.p.h.* = *96 k.p.h.*)

Mr ['mɪstə*] (*US* **Mr.**) *n*: **~ Smith** (el) Sr. Smith

Mrs ['mɪsɪz] (*US* **Mrs.**) *n*: **~ Smith** (la) Sra. Smith

Ms [mɪz] (*US* **Ms.**) *n* (= *Miss or Mrs*): **~ Smith** (la) Sr(t)a. Smith

M.Sc. *abbr* = **Master of Science**

MSP *n abbr* = **Member of the Scottish Parliament**

much [mʌtʃ] *adj* mucho ♦ *adv* mucho;

(*before pp*) muy ♦ *n or pron* mucho; **how ~ is it?** ¿cuánto es?, ¿cuánto cuesta?; **too ~** demasiado; **it's not ~** no es mucho; **as ~ as** tanto como; **however ~ he tries** por mucho que se esfuerce

muck [mʌk] *n* suciedad *f*; **~ about** or **around** (*inf*) *vi* perder el tiempo; (*enjoy o.s.*) entretenerse; **~ up** (*inf*) *vt* arruinar, estropear

mud [mʌd] *n* barro, lodo

muddle ['mʌdl] *n* desorden *m*, confusión *f*; (*mix-up*) embrollo, lío ♦ *vt* (*also:* **~ up**) embrollar, confundir; **~ through** *vi* salir del paso

muddy ['mʌdɪ] *adj* fangoso, cubierto de lodo

mudguard ['mʌdɡɑːd] *n* guardabarros *m inv*

muffin ['mʌfɪn] *n* panecillo dulce

muffle ['mʌfl] *vt* (*sound*) amortiguar; (*against cold*) embozar; **~d** *adj* (*noise etc*) amortiguado, apagado; **~r** (*US*) *n* (*AUT*) silenciador *m*

mug [mʌɡ] *n* taza grande (*sin platillo*); (*for beer*) jarra; (*inf: face*) jeta; (*: fool*) bobo ♦ *vt* (*assault*) asaltar; **~ging** *n* asalto

muggy ['mʌɡɪ] *adj* bochornoso

mule [mjuːl] *n* mula

multi... [mʌltɪ] *prefix* multi...

multi-level [mʌltɪ'levl] (*US*) *adj* = **multistorey**

multiple ['mʌltɪpl] *adj* múltiple ♦ *n* múltiplo; **~ sclerosis** *n* esclerosis *f* múltiple

multiplex cinema ['mʌltɪpleks-] *n* multicines *mpl*

multiplication [mʌltɪplɪ'keɪʃən] *n* multiplicación *f*

multiply ['mʌltɪplaɪ] *vt* multiplicar ♦ *vi* multiplicarse

multistorey [mʌltɪ'stɔːrɪ] (*BRIT*) *adj* de muchos pisos

multitude ['mʌltɪtjuːd] *n* multitud *f*

mum [mʌm] (*BRIT: inf*) *n* mamá ♦ *adj*: **to keep ~** mantener la boca cerrada

mumble ['mʌmbl] *vt, vi* hablar entre dientes, refunfuñar

mummy ['mʌmɪ] *n* (*BRIT: mother*) mamá; (*embalmed*) momia

mumps [mʌmps] *n* paperas *fpl*

munch [mʌntʃ] *vt, vi* mascar

mundane [mʌn'deɪn] *adj* trivial

municipal [mjuː'nɪsɪpl] *adj* municipal

murder ['mɜːdə*] *n* asesinato; (*in law*) homicidio ♦ *vt* asesinar, matar; **~er/ess** *n* asesino/a; **~ous** *adj* homicida

murky ['mɜːkɪ] *adj* (*water*) turbio; (*street, night*) lóbrego

murmur ['mɜːmə*] *n* murmullo ♦ *vt, vi* murmurar

muscle ['mʌsl] *n* músculo; (*fig: strength*) garra, fuerza; **~ in** *vi* entrometerse; **muscular** ['mʌskjulə*] *adj* muscular; (*person*) musculoso

muse [mjuːz] *vi* meditar ♦ *n* musa

museum [mjuː'zɪəm] *n* museo

mushroom ['mʌʃrum] *n* seta, hongo; (*CULIN*) champiñón *m* ♦ *vi* crecer de la noche a la mañana

music ['mjuːzɪk] *n* música; **~al** *adj* musical; (*sound*) melodioso; (*person*) con talento musical ♦ *n* (*show*) comedia musical; **~al instrument** *n* instrumento musical; **~ hall** *n* teatro de variedades; **~ian** [-'zɪʃən] *n* músico/a

Muslim ['mʌzlɪm] *adj, n* musulmán/ana *m/f*

muslin ['mʌzlɪn] *n* muselina

mussel ['mʌsl] *n* mejillón *m*

must [mʌst] *aux vb* (*obligation*): **I ~ do it** debo hacerlo, tengo que hacerlo; (*probability*): **he ~ be there by now** ya debe (de) estar allí ♦ *n*: **it's a ~** es imprescindible

mustache ['mʌstæʃ] (*US*) *n* = **moustache**

mustard ['mʌstəd] *n* mostaza

muster ['mʌstə*] *vt* juntar, reunir

mustn't ['mʌsnt] = **must not**

mute [mjuːt] *adj, n* mudo/a *m/f*

muted ['mjuːtɪd] *adj* callado; (*colour*) apagado

mutiny ['mjuːtɪnɪ] *n* motín *m* ♦ *vi* amotinarse

mutter ['mʌtə*] *vt, vi* murmurar

mutton ['mʌtn] n carne f de cordero
mutual ['mjuːtʃuəl] adj mutuo; (*interest*) común; **~ly** adv mutuamente
muzzle ['mʌzl] n hocico; (*for dog*) bozal m; (*of gun*) boca ♦ vt (*dog*) poner un bozal a
my [maɪ] adj mi(s); **~ house/brother/ sisters** mi casa/mi hermano/mis hermanas; **I've washed ~ hair/cut ~ finger** me he lavado el pelo/cortado un dedo; **is this ~ pen or yours?** ¿es este bolígrafo mío o tuyo?
myself [maɪ'sɛlf] pron (*reflexive*) me; (*emphatic*) yo mismo; (*after prep*) mí (mismo); *see also* **oneself**
mysterious [mɪs'tɪərɪəs] adj misterioso
mystery ['mɪstərɪ] n misterio
mystify ['mɪstɪfaɪ] vt (*perplex*) dejar perplejo
myth [mɪθ] n mito

N, n

n/a abbr (= *not applicable*) no interesa
nag [næg] vt (*scold*) regañar; **~ging** adj (*doubt*) persistente; (*pain*) continuo
nail [neɪl] n (*human*) uña; (*metal*) clavo ♦ vt clavar; **to ~ sth to sth** clavar algo en algo; **to ~ sb down to doing sth** comprometer a uno a que haga algo; **~brush** n cepillo para las uñas; **~file** n lima para las uñas; **~ polish** n esmalte m or laca para las uñas; **~ polish remover** n quitaesmalte m; **~ scissors** npl tijeras fpl para las uñas; **~ varnish** (*BRIT*) n = **~ polish**
naïve [naɪ'iːv] adj ingenuo
naked ['neɪkɪd] adj (*nude*) desnudo; (*flame*) expuesto al aire
name [neɪm] n nombre m; (*surname*) apellido; (*reputation*) fama, renombre m ♦ vt (*child*) poner nombre a; (*criminal*) identificar; (*price, date etc*) fijar; **what's your ~?** ¿cómo se llama?; **by ~** de nombre; **in the ~ of** en nombre de; **to give one's ~ and address** dar sus señas;

~ly adv a saber; **~sake** n tocayo/a
nanny ['nænɪ] n niñera
nap [næp] n (*sleep*) sueñecito, siesta
nape [neɪp] n: **~ of the neck** nuca, cogote m
napkin ['næpkɪn] n (*also*: **table ~**) servilleta
nappy ['næpɪ] (*BRIT*) n pañal m; **~ rash** n prurito
narcotic [nɑː'kɒtɪk] adj, n narcótico
narrow ['nærəu] adj estrecho, angosto; (*fig: majority etc*) corto; (: *ideas etc*) estrecho ♦ vi (*road*) estrecharse; (*diminish*) reducirse; **to have a ~ escape** escaparse por los pelos; **to ~ sth down** reducir algo; **~ly** adv (*miss*) por poco; **~-minded** adj de miras estrechas
nasty ['nɑːstɪ] adj (*remark*) feo; (*person*) antipático; (*revolting: taste, smell*) asqueroso; (*wound, disease etc*) peligroso, grave
nation ['neɪʃən] n nación f
national ['næʃənl] adj, n nacional m/f; **~ dress** n vestido nacional; **N~ Health Service** (*BRIT*) n servicio nacional de salud pública; ≈ Insalud m (*SP*); **N~ Insurance** (*BRIT*) n seguro social nacional; **~ism** n nacionalismo; **~ist** adj, n nacionalista m/f; **~ity** [-'nælɪtɪ] n nacionalidad f; **~ize** vt nacionalizar; **~ly** adv (*nationwide*) en escala nacional; (*as a nation*) nacionalmente, como nación; **~ park** n parque m nacional
nationwide ['neɪʃənwaɪd] adj en escala or a nivel nacional
native ['neɪtɪv] n (*local inhabitant*) natural m/f, nacional m/f ♦ adj (*indigenous*) indígena; (*country*) natal; (*innate*) natural, innato; **a ~ of Russia** un(a) natural m/f de Rusia; **a ~ speaker of French** un hablante nativo de francés; **N~ American** adj, n americano/a indígena, amerindio/a; **~ language** n lengua materna
Nativity [nə'tɪvɪtɪ] n: **the ~** Navidad f
NATO ['neɪtəu] n abbr (= *North Atlantic Treaty Organization*) OTAN f
natural ['nætʃrəl] adj natural; **~ly** adv

(speak etc) naturalmente; (of course)
desde luego, por supuesto
ature ['neɪtʃə*] n (also: **N~**) naturaleza;
(group, sort) género, clase f; (character)
carácter m, genio; **by ~** por or de
naturaleza
aught [nɔːt] = **nought**
aughty ['nɔːtɪ] adj (child) travieso
ausea ['nɔːsɪə] n náuseas fpl
autical ['nɔːtɪkl] adj náutico, marítimo;
(mile) marino
aval ['neɪvl] adj naval, de marina; ~
officer n oficial m/f de marina
ave [neɪv] n nave f
avel ['neɪvl] n ombligo
avigate ['nævɪgeɪt] vt gobernar ♦ vi
navegar; (AUT) ir de copiloto; **navigation**
[-'geɪʃən] n (action) navegación f; (science)
náutica; **navigator** n navegador(a) m/f,
navegante m/f; (AUT) copiloto m/f
avvy ['nævɪ] (BRIT) n peón m caminero
avy ['neɪvɪ] n marina de guerra; (ships)
armada, flota; **~(-blue)** adj azul marino
azi ['nɑːtsɪ] n nazi m/f
IB abbr (= nota bene) nótese
ear [nɪə*] adj (place, relation) cercano;
(time) próximo ♦ adv cerca ♦ prep (also:
~ to: space) cerca de, junto a; (: time)
cerca de ♦ vt acercarse a, aproximarse a;
~by [nɪə'baɪ] adj cercano, próximo ♦ adv
cerca; **~ly** adv casi, por poco; **I ~ly fell**
por poco me caigo; **~ miss** n tiro
cercano; **~side** n (AUT: in Britain) lado
izquierdo; (: in US, Europe etc) lado
derecho; **~-sighted** adj miope, corto de
vista
eat [niːt] adj (place) ordenado, bien
cuidado; (person) pulcro; (plan) ingenioso;
(spirits) solo; **~ly** adv (tidily) con esmero;
(skilfully) ingeniosamente
ecessarily ['nesɪsrɪlɪ] adv
necesariamente
ecessary ['nesɪsrɪ] adj necesario, preciso
ecessitate [nɪ'sesɪteɪt] vt hacer necesario
ecessity [nɪ'sesɪtɪ] n necesidad f;
necessities npl artículos mpl de primera
necesidad

neck [nek] n (of person, garment, bottle)
cuello; (of animal) pescuezo ♦ vi (inf)
besuquearse; **~ and ~** parejos; **~lace**
['neklɪs] n collar m; **~line** n escote m;
~tie ['nektaɪ] n corbata
née [neɪ] adj: **~ Scott** de soltera Scott
need [niːd] n (lack) escasez f, falta;
(necessity) necesidad f ♦ vt (require)
necesitar; **I ~ to do it** tengo que or debo
hacerlo; **you don't ~ to go** no hace falta
que (te) vayas
needle ['niːdl] n aguja ♦ vt (fig: inf) picar,
fastidiar
needless ['niːdlɪs] adj innecesario; **~ to
say** huelga decir que
needlework ['niːdlwɜːk] n (activity)
costura, labor f de aguja
needn't ['niːdnt] = **need not**
needy ['niːdɪ] adj necesitado
negative ['negətɪv] n (PHOT) negativo;
(LING) negación f ♦ adj negativo; **~
equity** n situación que se da cuando el
valor de la vivienda es menor que el de la
hipoteca que pesa sobre ella
neglect [nɪ'glekt] vt (one's duty) faltar a,
no cumplir con; (child) descuidar,
desatender ♦ n (of house, garden etc)
abandono; (of child) desatención f; (of
duty) incumplimiento
negligee ['neglɪʒeɪ] n (nightgown) salto de
cama
negotiate [nɪ'gəʊʃɪeɪt] vt (treaty, loan)
negociar; (obstacle) franquear; (bend in
road) tomar ♦ vi: **to ~ (with)** negociar
(con); **negotiation** [-'eɪʃən] n
negociación f, gestión f
neigh [neɪ] vi relinchar
neighbour ['neɪbə*] (US **neighbor**) n
vecino/a; **~hood** n (place) vecindad f,
barrio; (people) vecindario; **~ing** adj
vecino; **~ly** adj (person) amable; (attitude)
de buen vecino
neither ['naɪðə*] adj ni ♦ conj: **I didn't
move and ~ did John** no me he movido,
ni Juan tampoco ♦ pron ninguno ♦ adv:
~ good nor bad ni bueno ni malo; **~ is
true** ninguno/a de los/las dos es cierto/a

neon ['niːɔn] *n* neón *m*; ~ **light** *n* lámpara de neón

nephew ['nevjuː] *n* sobrino

nerve [nɜːv] *n* (ANAT) nervio; (*courage*) valor *m*; (*impudence*) descaro, frescura; **a fit of ~s** un ataque de nervios; ~-**racking** *adj* desquiciante

nervous ['nɜːvəs] *adj* (*anxious*, ANAT) nervioso; (*timid*) tímido, miedoso; ~ **breakdown** *n* crisis *f* nerviosa

nest [nest] *n* (*of bird*) nido; (*wasps' ~*) avispero ♦ *vi* anidar; ~ **egg** *n* (*fig*) ahorros *mpl*

nestle ['nesl] *vi*: **to ~ down** acurrucarse

net [net] *n* (*gen*) red *f*; (*fabric*) tul *m* ♦ *adj* (COMM) neto, líquido ♦ *vt* coger (SP) *or* agarrar (AM) con red; (SPORT) marcar; **the Net** (*Internet*) la Red; ~**ball** *n* básquet *m*

Netherlands ['neðələndz] *npl*: **the ~** los Países Bajos

nett [net] *adj* = **net**

netting ['netɪŋ] *n* red *f*, redes *fpl*

nettle ['netl] *n* ortiga

network ['netwɜːk] *n* red *f*

neurotic [njuəˈrɔtɪk] *adj*, neurótico/a

neuter ['njuːtə*] *adj* (LING) neutro ♦ *vt* castrar, capar

neutral ['njuːtrəl] *adj* (*person*) neutral; (*colour etc*, ELEC) neutro ♦ *n* (AUT) punto muerto; ~**ize** *vt* neutralizar

never ['nevə*] *adv* nunca, jamás; **I ~ went** no fui nunca; ~ **in my life** jamás en la vida; *see also* **mind**; ~-**ending** *adj* interminable, sin fin; ~**theless** [nevəðə'les] *adv* sin embargo, no obstante

new [njuː] *adj* nuevo; (*brand new*) a estrenar; (*recent*) reciente; **N~ Age** *n* Nueva Era; ~**born** *adj* recién nacido; ~**comer** [ˈnjuːkʌmə*] *n* recién venido/a *or* llegado/a; ~**fangled** (*pej*) *adj* modernísimo; ~-**found** *adj* (*friend*) nuevo; (*enthusiasm*) recién adquirido; ~**ly** *adv* nuevamente, recién; ~**ly-weds** *npl* recién casados *mpl*

news [njuːz] *n* noticias *fpl*; **a piece of ~** una noticia; **the ~** (RADIO, TV) las noticias

fpl; ~ **agency** *n* agencia de noticias; ~**agent** (BRIT) *n* vendedor(a) *m/f* de periódicos; ~**caster** *n* presentador(a) *m*, *f*, locutor(a) *m/f*; ~ **flash** *n* noticia de última hora; ~**letter** *n* hoja informativa, boletín *m*; ~**paper** *n* periódico, diario; ~**print** *n* papel *m* de periódico; ~**reade** *n* = ~**caster**; ~**reel** *n* noticiario; ~**stand** *n* quiosco *or* puesto de periódicos

newt [njuːt] *n* tritón *m*

New Year *n* Año Nuevo; ~'**s Day** *n* Día *m* de Año Nuevo; ~'**s Eve** *n* Nochevieja

New York ['njuː'jɔːk] *n* Nueva York

New Zealand [njuː'ziːlənd] *n* Nueva Zelanda; ~**er** *n* neozelandés/esa *m/f*

next [nekst] *adj* (*house*, *room*) vecino; (*bus stop*, *meeting*) próximo; (*following*: *page etc*) siguiente ♦ *adv* después; **the ~ day** día siguiente; ~ **time** la próxima vez; ~ **year** el año próximo *or* que viene; ~ **to** junto a, al lado de; ~ **to nothing** casi nada; ~ **please!** ¡el siguiente! ~ **door** *adv* en la casa de al lado ♦ *adj* vecino, de al lado; ~-**of-kin** *n* pariente *m* más cercano

NHS *n abbr* = **National Health Service**

nib [nɪb] *n* plumilla

nibble ['nɪbl] *vt* mordisquear, mordiscar

Nicaragua [nɪkəˈrægjuə] *n* Nicaragua; ~**n** *adj*, *n* nicaragüense *m/f*

nice [naɪs] *adj* (*likeable*) simpático; (*kind*) amable; (*pleasant*) agradable; (*attractive*) bonito, mono, lindo (AM); ~**ly** *adv* amablemente; bien

nick [nɪk] *n* (*wound*) rasguño; (*cut*, *indentation*) mella, muesca ♦ *vt* (*inf*) birlar, robar; **in the ~ of time** justo a tiempo

nickel ['nɪkl] *n* níquel *m*; (US) *moneda de 5 centavos*

nickname ['nɪkneɪm] *n* apodo, mote *m* ♦ *vt* apodar

nicotine ['nɪkətiːn] *n* nicotina

niece [niːs] *n* sobrina

Nigeria [naɪ'dʒɪərɪə] *n* Nigeria; ~**n** *adj*, *n* nigeriano/a *m/f*

niggling ['nɪglɪŋ] *adj* (*trifling*) nimio,

insignificante; (*annoying*) molesto

night [naɪt] *n* noche *f*; (*evening*) tarde *f*; **the ~ before last** anteanoche; **at ~, by ~** de noche, por la noche; **~cap** *n* (*drink*) *bebida que se toma antes de acostarse*; **~ club** *n* cabaret *m*; **~dress** (*BRIT*) *n* camisón *m*; **~fall** *n* anochecer *m*; **~gown** *n* = **~dress**; **~ie** ['naɪtɪ] *n* = **~dress**

nightingale ['naɪtɪŋgeɪl] *n* ruiseñor *m*

night: **~life** *n* vida nocturna; **~ly** *adj* de todas las noches ♦ *adv* todas las noches, cada noche; **~mare** *n* pesadilla; **~porter** *n* portero de noche; **~ school** *n* clase(s) *f(pl)* nocturna(s); **~ shift** *n* turno nocturno *or* de noche; **~-time** *n* noche *f*; **~ watchman** *n* vigilante *m* nocturno

nil [nɪl] (*BRIT*) *n* (*SPORT*) cero, nada

Nile [naɪl] *n*: **the ~** el Nilo

nimble ['nɪmbl] *adj* (*agile*) ágil, ligero; (*skilful*) diestro

nine [naɪn] *num* nueve; **~teen** *num* diecinueve, diez y nueve; **~ty** *num* noventa

ninth [naɪnθ] *adj* noveno

nip [nɪp] *vt* (*pinch*) pellizcar; (*bite*) morder

nipple ['nɪpl] *n* (*ANAT*) pezón *m*

nitrogen ['naɪtrədʒən] *n* nitrógeno

KEYWORD

no [nəʊ] (*pl* **~es**) *adv* (*opposite of "yes"*) no; **are you coming? – ~ (I'm not)** no; **would you like some more? – ~ thank you** ¿quieres más? — no gracias

♦ *adj* (*not any*): **I have ~ money/time/ books** no tengo dinero/tiempo/libros; **~ other man would have done it** ningún otro lo hubiera hecho; **"~ entry"** "prohibido el paso"; **"~ smoking"** "prohibido fumar"

♦ *n* no *m*

nobility [nəʊ'bɪlɪtɪ] *n* nobleza

noble ['nəʊbl] *adj* noble

nobody ['nəʊbədɪ] *pron* nadie

nod [nɒd] *vi* saludar con la cabeza; (*in agreement*) decir que sí con la cabeza; (*doze*) dar cabezadas ♦ *vt*: **to ~ one's head** inclinar la cabeza ♦ *n* inclinación *f* de cabeza; **~ off** *vi* dar cabezadas

noise [nɔɪz] *n* ruido; (*din*) escándalo, estrépito; **noisy** *adj* ruidoso; (*child*) escandaloso

nominate ['nɒmɪneɪt] *vt* (*propose*) proponer; (*appoint*) nombrar; **nominee** [-'niː] *n* candidato/a

non... [nɒn] *prefix* no, des..., in...; **~alcoholic** *adj* no alcohólico; **~chalant** *adj* indiferente; **~committal** *adj* evasivo; **~descript** *adj* soso

none [nʌn] *pron* ninguno/a ♦ *adv* de ninguna manera; **~ of you** ninguno de vosotros; **I've ~ left** no me queda ninguno/a; **he's ~ the worse for it** no le ha hecho ningún mal

nonentity [nɒ'nentɪtɪ] *n* cero a la izquierda, nulidad *f*

nonetheless [nʌnðə'les] *adv* sin embargo, no obstante

non-existent *adj* inexistente

non-fiction *n* literatura no novelesca

nonplussed [nɒn'plʌst] *adj* perplejo

nonsense ['nɒnsəns] *n* tonterías *fpl*, disparates *fpl*; **~!** ¡qué tonterías!

non: **~-smoker** *n* no fumador(a) *m/f*; **~-smoking** *adj* (de) no fumador; **~-stick** *adj* (*pan, surface*) antiadherente; **~-stop** *adj* continuo; (*RAIL*) directo ♦ *adv* sin parar

noodles ['nuːdlz] *npl* tallarines *mpl*

nook [nʊk] *n*: **~s and crannies** escondrijos *mpl*

noon [nuːn] *n* mediodía *m*

no-one *pron* = **nobody**

noose [nuːs] *n* (*hangman's*) dogal *m*

nor [nɔː*] *conj* = **neither** ♦ *adv* see **neither**

norm [nɔːm] *n* norma

normal ['nɔːml] *adj* normal; **~ly** *adv* normalmente

north [nɔːθ] *n* norte *m* ♦ *adj* del norte, norteño ♦ *adv* al *or* hacia el norte; **N~ Africa** *n* África del Norte; **N~ America** *n* América del Norte; **~-east** *n* nor(d)este m; **~erly** ['nɔːðəlɪ] *adj* (*point, direction*) norteño; **~ern** ['nɔːðən] *adj* norteño, del norte; **N~ern Ireland** *n* Irlanda del Norte; **N~ Pole** *n* Polo Norte; **N~ Sea** *n* Mar *m* del Norte; **~ward(s)** ['nɔːwəd(z)] *adv* hacia el norte; **~-west** *n* nor(d)oeste *m*

Norway ['nɔːweɪ] *n* Noruega; **Norwegian** [-'wiːdʒən] *adj* noruego/a ♦ *n* noruego/a; (*LING*) noruego

nose [nəuz] *n* (*ANAT*) nariz *f*; (*ZOOL*) hocico; (*sense of smell*) olfato ♦ *vi*: **to ~ about** curiosear; **~bleed** *n* hemorragia nasal; **~-dive** *n* (*of plane: deliberate*) picado vertical; (: *involuntary*) caída en picado; **~y** (*inf*) *adj* curioso, fisgón/ona

nostalgia [nɔs'tældʒɪə] *n* nostalgia

nostril ['nɔstrɪl] *n* ventana de la nariz

nosy ['nəuzɪ] (*inf*) *adj* = **nosey**

not [nɔt] *adv* no; **~ that ...** no es que ...; **it's too late, isn't it?** es demasiado tarde, ¿verdad *or* no?; **~ yet/now** todavía/ahora no; **why ~?** ¿por qué no?; *see also* **all; only**

notably ['nəutəblɪ] *adv* especialmente

notary ['nəutərɪ] *n* notario/a

notch [nɔtʃ] *n* muesca, corte *m*

note [nəut] *n* (*MUS, record, letter*) nota; (*banknote*) billete *m*; (*tone*) tono ♦ *vt* (*observe*) notar, observar; (*write down*) apuntar, anotar; **~book** *n* libreta, cuaderno; **~d** ['nəutɪd] *adj* célebre, conocido; **~pad** *n* bloc *m*; **~paper** *n* papel *m* para cartas

nothing ['nʌθɪŋ] *n* nada; (*zero*) cero; **he does ~** no hace nada; **~ new** nada nuevo; **~ much** no mucho; **for ~** (*free*) gratis, sin pago; (*in vain*) en balde

notice ['nəutɪs] *n* (*announcement*) anuncio; (*warning*) aviso; (*dismissal*) despido; (*resignation*) dimisión *f*; (*period of time*) plazo ♦ *vt* (*observe*) notar, observar; **to bring sth to sb's ~** (*attention*) llamar la atención de uno sobre algo; **to take ~ of** tomar nota de, prestar atención a; **at short ~** con poca anticipación; **until further ~** hasta nuevo aviso; **to hand in**

one's ~ dimitir; **~able** *adj* evidente, obvio; **~ board** (*BRIT*) *n* tablón *m* de anuncios

notify ['nəutɪfaɪ] *vt*: **to ~ sb (of sth)** comunicar (algo) a uno

notion ['nəuʃən] *n* idea; (*opinion*) opinión *f*

notorious [nəu'tɔːrɪəs] *adj* notorio

nougat ['nuːgɑː] *n* turrón *m*

nought [nɔːt] *n* cero

noun [naun] *n* nombre *m*, sustantivo

nourish ['nʌrɪʃ] *vt* nutrir; (*fig*) alimentar; **~ing** *adj* nutritivo; **~ment** *n* alimento, sustento

novel ['nɔvl] *n* novela ♦ *adj* (*new*) nuevo, original; (*unexpected*) insólito; **~ist** *n* novelista *m/f*; **~ty** *n* novedad *f*

November [nəu'vembə*] *n* noviembre *m*

novice ['nɔvɪs] *n* (*REL*) novicio/a

now [nau] *adv* (*at the present time*) ahora; (*these days*) actualmente, hoy día ♦ *conj*: **~ (that)** ya que, ahora que; **right ~** ahora mismo; **by ~** ya; **just ~** ahora mismo; **~ and then, ~ and again** de vez en cuando; **from ~ on** de ahora en adelante; **~adays** ['nauədeɪz] *adv* hoy (en) día, actualmente

nowhere ['nəuwɛə*] *adv* (*direction*) a ninguna parte; (*location*) en ninguna parte

nozzle ['nɔzl] *n* boquilla

nuance ['njuːɑːns] *n* matiz *m*

nuclear ['njuːklɪə*] *adj* nuclear

nucleus ['njuːklɪəs] (*pl* **nuclei**) *n* núcleo

nude [njuːd] *adj, n* desnudo/a *m/f*; **in the ~** desnudo

nudge [nʌdʒ] *vt* dar un codazo a

nudist ['njuːdɪst] *n* nudista *m/f*

nuisance ['njuːsns] *n* molestia, fastidio; (*person*) pesado, latoso; **what a ~!** ¡qué lata!

null [nʌl] *adj*: **~ and void** nulo y sin efecto

numb [nʌm] *adj*: **~ with cold/fear** entumecido por el frío/paralizado de miedo

number ['nʌmbə*] *n* número; (*quantity*) cantidad *f* ♦ *vt* (*pages etc*) numerar, poner número a; (*amount to*) sumar, ascender a; **to be ~ed among** figurar entre; **a ~ of** varios, algunos; **they were ten in ~** eran diez; **~ plate** (BRIT) n matrícula, placa

numeral ['nju:mərəl] n número, cifra

numerate ['nju:mərit] adj competente en la aritmética

numerous ['nju:mərəs] adj numeroso

nun [nʌn] n monja, religiosa

nurse [nəːs] n enfermero/a; (also: **~maid**) niñera ♦ vt (patient) cuidar, atender

nursery ['nəːsəri] n (institution) guardería infantil; (room) cuarto de los niños; (for plants) criadero, semillero; **~ rhyme** n canción f infantil; **~ school** n parvulario, escuela de párvulos; **~ slope** (BRIT) n (SKI) cuesta para principiantes

nursing ['nəːsɪŋ] n (profession) profesión f de enfermera; (care) asistencia, cuidado; **~ home** n clínica de reposo

nut [nʌt] n (TECH) tuerca; (BOT) nuez f; **~crackers** npl cascanueces m inv

nutmeg ['nʌtmeg] n nuez f moscada

nutritious [nju:'trɪʃəs] adj nutritivo, alimenticio

nuts [nʌts] (inf) adj loco

nutshell ['nʌtʃel] n: **in a ~** en resumidas cuentas

nylon ['naɪlɔn] n nilón m ♦ adj de nilón

O, o

oak [əuk] n roble m ♦ adj de roble

O.A.P. (BRIT) n abbr = **old-age pensioner**

oar [ɔː*] n remo

oasis [əu'eɪsɪs] (pl **oases**) n oasis m inv

oath [əuθ] n juramento; (swear word) palabrota; **on** (BRIT) or **under ~** bajo juramento

oatmeal ['əutmiːl] n harina de avena

oats [əuts] n avena

obedience [ə'biːdɪəns] n obediencia

obedient [ə'biːdɪənt] adj obediente

obey [ə'beɪ] vt obedecer; (instructions, regulations) cumplir

obituary [ə'bɪtjuəri] n necrología

object [n 'ɔbdʒɪkt, vb əb'dʒɛkt] n objeto; (purpose) objeto, propósito; (LING) complemento ♦ vi: **to ~ to** estar en contra de; (proposal) oponerse a; **to ~ that** objetar que; **expense is no ~** no importa cuánto cuesta; **I ~!** ¡yo protesto!; **~ion** [əb'dʒɛkʃən] n protesta; **I have no ~ion to ...** no tengo inconveniente en que ...; **~ionable** [əb'dʒɛkʃənəbl] adj desagradable; (conduct) censurable; **~ive** adj, n objetivo

obligation [ɔblɪ'geɪʃən] n obligación f; (debt) deber m; **without ~** sin compromiso

oblige [ə'blaɪdʒ] vt (do a favour for) complacer, hacer un favor a; **to ~ sb to do sth** forzar or obligar a uno a hacer algo; **to be ~d to sb for sth** estarle agradecido a uno por algo; **obliging** adj servicial, atento

oblique [ə'bliːk] adj oblicuo; (allusion) indirecto

obliterate [ə'blɪtəreɪt] vt borrar

oblivion [ə'blɪvɪən] n olvido; **oblivious** [-ɪəs] adj: **oblivious of** inconsciente de

oblong ['ɔblɔŋ] adj rectangular ♦ n rectángulo

obnoxious [əb'nɔkʃəs] adj odioso, detestable; (smell) nauseabundo

oboe ['əubəu] n oboe m

obscene [əb'siːn] adj obsceno

obscure [əb'skjuə*] adj oscuro ♦ vt oscurecer; (hide: sun) esconder

observant [əb'zəːvnt] adj observador(a)

observation [ɔbzə'veɪʃən] n observación f; (MED) examen m

observe [əb'zəːv] vt observar; (rule) cumplir; **~r** n observador(a) m/f

obsess [əb'sɛs] vt obsesionar; **~ive** adj obsesivo; obsesionante

obsolete ['ɔbsəliːt] adj: **to be ~** estar en desuso

obstacle ['ɔbstəkl] n obstáculo; (nuisance) estorbo; **~ race** n carrera de obstáculos

obstinate ['ɔbstɪnɪt] adj terco, porfiado; (determined) obstinado

obstruct [əb'strʌkt] vt obstruir; (*hinder*) estorbar, obstaculizar; **~ion** [əb'strʌkʃən] n (*action*) obstrucción f; (*object*) estorbo, obstáculo

obtain [əb'teɪn] vt obtener; (*achieve*) conseguir

obvious ['ɔbvɪəs] adj obvio, evidente; **~ly** adv evidentemente, naturalmente; **~ly not** por supuesto que no

occasion [ə'keɪʒən] n oportunidad f, ocasión f; (*event*) acontecimiento; **~al** adj poco frecuente, ocasional; **~ally** adv de vez en cuando

occupant ['ɔkjupənt] n (*of house*) inquilino/a; (*of car*) ocupante m/f

occupation [ɔkju'peɪʃən] n ocupación f; (*job*) trabajo; (*pastime*) ocupaciones fpl; **~al hazard** n riesgo profesional

occupier ['ɔkjupaɪə*] n inquilino/a

occupy ['ɔkjupaɪ] vt (*seat, post, time*) ocupar; (*house*) habitar; **to o.s. in doing** pasar el tiempo haciendo

occur [ə'kə:*] vi pasar, suceder; **to ~ to sb** ocurrírsele a uno; **~rence** [ə'kʌrəns] n acontecimiento; (*existence*) existencia

ocean ['əuʃən] n océano

o'clock [ə'klɔk] adv: **it is 5 ~** son las 5

OCR n abbr = **optical character recognition/reader**

October [ɔk'təubə*] n octubre m

octopus ['ɔktəpəs] n pulpo

odd [ɔd] adj extraño, raro; (*number*) impar; (*sock, shoe etc*) suelto; **60~** 60 y pico; **at ~ times** de vez en cuando; **to be the ~ one out** estar de más; **~ity** n rareza; (*person*) excéntrico; **~-job man** n chico para todo; **~ jobs** npl bricolaje m; **~ly** adv curiosamente, extrañamente; *see also* **enough**; **~ments** npl (*COMM*) retales mpl; **~s** npl (*in betting*) puntos mpl de ventaja; **it makes no ~s** da lo mismo; **at ~s** reñidos/as; **~s and ends** minucias fpl

odometer [ɔ'dɔmɪtə*] (*US*) n cuentakilómetros m inv

odour ['əudə*] (*US* **odor**) n olor m; (*unpleasant*) hedor m

of [ɔv, əv] prep 1 (*gen*) de; **a friend ~ ours** un amigo nuestro; **a boy ~ 10** un chico de 10 años; **that was kind ~ you** eso fue muy amable por or de tu parte
2 (*expressing quantity, amount, dates etc*) de; **a kilo ~ flour** un kilo de harina; **there were 3 ~ them** había tres; **3 ~ us went** tres de nosotros fuimos; **the 5th ~ July** el 5 de julio
3 (*from, out of*) de; **made ~ wood** (hecho) de madera

off [ɔf] adj, adv (*engine*) desconectado; (*light*) apagado; (*tap*) cerrado; (*BRIT: food bad*) pasado, malo; (: *milk*) cortado; (*cancelled*) cancelado ♦ prep de; **to be ~** (*to leave*) irse, marcharse; **to be ~ sick** estar enfermo or de baja; **a day ~** un día libre or sin trabajar; **to have an ~ day** tener un día malo; **he had his coat ~** se había quitado el abrigo; **10% ~** (*COMM*) (con el) 10% de descuento; **5 km ~ (the road)** a 5 km (de la carretera); **~ the coast** frente a la costa; **I'm ~ meat** (*no longer eat/like it*) paso de la carne; **on the ~ chance** por si acaso; **~ and on** de vez en cuando

offal ['ɔfl] (*BRIT*) n (*CULIN*) menudencias fpl

off-colour ['ɔf'kʌlə*] (*BRIT*) adj (*ill*) indispuesto

offence [ə'fɛns] (*US* **offense**) n (*crime*) delito; **to take ~ at** ofenderse por

offend [ə'fɛnd] vt (*person*) ofender; **~er** n delincuente m/f

offensive [ə'fɛnsɪv] adj ofensivo; (*smell etc*) repugnante ♦ n (*MIL*) ofensiva

offer ['ɔfə*] n oferta, ofrecimiento; (*proposal*) propuesta ♦ vt ofrecer; (*opportunity*) facilitar; **"on ~"** (*COMM*) "en oferta"; **~ing** n ofrenda

offhand [ɔf'hænd] adj informal ♦ adv de improviso

office ['ɔfɪs] n (*place*) oficina; (*room*) despacho; (*position*) carga, oficio; **doctor's ~** (*US*) consultorio; **to take ~**

entrar en funciones; **~ automation** *n* ofimática, buromática; **~ block** (*US* **~ building**) *n* bloque *m* de oficinas; **~ hours** *npl* horas *fpl* de oficina; (*US: MED*) horas *fpl* de consulta

fficer ['ɔfɪsə•] *n* (*MIL etc*) oficial *m/f*; (*also:* **police ~**) agente *m/f* de policía; (*of organization*) director(a) *m/f*

ffice worker *n* oficinista *m/f*

fficial [ə'fɪʃl] *adj* oficial, autorizado ♦ *n* funcionario, oficial *m*

ffing ['ɔfɪŋ] *n*: **in the ~** (*fig*) en perspectiva

ff: **~-licence** (*BRIT*) *n* (*shop*) bodega, *tienda de vinos y bebidas alcohólicas*; **~-line** *adj, adv* (*COMPUT*) fuera de línea; **~-peak** *adj* (*electricity*) de banda económica; (*ticket*) *billete de precio reducido por viajar fuera de las horas punta*; **~-putting** (*BRIT*) *adj* (*person*) asqueroso; (*remark*) desalentador(a); **~-season** *adj, adv* fuera de temporada

---

off-licence

ℹ️ *En el Reino Unido la venta de bebidas alcohólicas está estrictamente regulada y se necesita una licencia especial, con la que cuentan los bares, restaurantes y los establecimientos de* **off-licence**, *los únicos lugares en donde se pueden adquirir bebidas alcohólicas para su consumo fuera del local, de donde viene su nombre. También venden bebidas no alcohólicas, tabaco, chocolatinas, patatas fritas etc y a menudo forman parte de una cadena nacional.*

---

ffset ['ɔfset] (*irreg*) *vt* contrarrestar, compensar

ffshoot ['ɔfʃuːt] *n* (*fig*) ramificación *f*

ffshore [ɔf'ʃɔː•] *adj* (*breeze, island*) costera; (*fishing*) de bajura

ffside ['ɔf'saɪd] *adj* (*SPORT*) fuera de juego; (*AUT: in UK*) del lado derecho; (: *in US, Europe etc*) del lado izquierdo

ffspring ['ɔfsprɪŋ] *n inv* descendencia *f*

ff: **~stage** *adv* entre bastidores; **~-the-**

peg (*US* **~-the-rack**) *adv* confeccionado; **~-white** *adj* color crudo

often ['ɔfn] *adv* a menudo, con frecuencia; **how ~ do you go?** ¿cada cuánto vas?

oh [əu] *excl* ¡ah!

oil [ɔɪl] *n* aceite *m*; (*petroleum*) petróleo; (*for heating*) aceite *m* combustible ♦ *vt* engrasar; **~can** *n* lata de aceite; **~field** *n* campo petrolífero; **~ filter** *n* (*AUT*) filtro de aceite; **~ painting** *n* pintura al óleo; **~ rig** *n* torre *f* de perforación; **~ tanker** *n* petrolero; (*truck*) camión *m* cisterna; **~ well** *n* pozo (de petróleo); **~y** *adj* aceitoso; (*food*) grasiento

ointment ['ɔɪntmənt] *n* ungüento

O.K., okay ['əu'keɪ] *excl* O.K., ¡está bien!, ¡vale! (*SP*) ♦ *adj* bien ♦ *vt* dar el visto bueno a

old [əuld] *adj* viejo; (*former*) antiguo; **how ~ are you?** ¿cuántos años tienes?; **he's 10 years ~** tiene 10 años; **~er brother** hermano mayor; **~ age** *n* vejez *f*; **~-age pensioner** (*BRIT*) *n* jubilado/a; **~-fashioned** *adj* anticuado, pasado de moda

olive ['ɔlɪv] *n* (*fruit*) aceituna; (*tree*) olivo ♦ *adj* (*also:* **~-green**) verde oliva; **~ oil** *n* aceite *m* de oliva

Olympic [əu'lɪmpɪk] *adj* olímpico; **the ~ Games, the ~s** las Olimpíadas

omelet(te) ['ɔmlɪt] *n* tortilla (*SP*), tortilla de huevo (*AM*)

omen ['əumən] *n* presagio

ominous ['ɔmɪnəs] *adj* de mal agüero, amenazador(a)

omit [əu'mɪt] *vt* omitir

KEYWORD

on [ɔn] *prep* **1** (*indicating position*) en; sobre; **~ the wall** en la pared; **it's ~ the table** está sobre *or* en la mesa; **~ the left** a la izquierda
2 (*indicating means, method, condition etc*): **~ foot** a pie; **~ the train/plane** (*go*) en tren/avión; (*be*) en el tren/el avión; **~ the radio/television/telephone** por *or* en la radio/televisión/al teléfono; **to be ~**

drugs drogarse; (*MED*) estar a tratamiento; **to be ~ holiday/business** estar de vacaciones/en viaje de negocios
3 (*referring to time*): **~ Friday** el viernes; **~ Fridays** los viernes; **~ June 20th** el 20 de junio; **a week ~ Friday** del viernes en una semana; **~ arrival** al llegar; **~ seeing this** al ver esto
4 (*about, concerning*) sobre, acerca de; **a book ~ physics** un libro de *or* sobre física
♦ *adv* 1 (*referring to dress*): **to have one's coat ~** tener *or* llevar el abrigo puesto; **she put her gloves ~** se puso los guantes
2 (*referring to covering*): **"screw the lid ~ tightly"** "cerrar bien la tapa"
3 (*further, continuously*): **to walk** *etc* **~** seguir caminando *etc*
♦ *adj* 1 (*functioning, in operation*: *machine, radio, TV, light*) encendido/a (*SP*), prendido/a (*AM*); (: *tap*) abierto/a; (: *brakes*) echado/a, puesto/a; **is the meeting still ~?** (*in progress*) ¿todavía continúa la reunión?; (*not cancelled*) ¿va a haber reunión al fin?; **there's a good film ~ at the cinema** ponen una buena película en el cine
2: **that's not ~!** (*inf*: *not possible*) ¡eso ni hablar!; (: *not acceptable*) ¡eso no se hace!

once [wʌns] *adv* una vez; (*formerly*) antiguamente ♦ *conj* una vez que; **~ he had left/it was done** una vez que se había marchado/se hizo; **at ~** en seguida, inmediatamente; (*simultaneously*) a la vez; **~ a week** una vez por semana; **~ more** otra vez; **~ and for all** de una vez por todas; **~ upon a time** érase una vez
oncoming [ˈɒnkʌmɪŋ] *adj* (*traffic*) que viene de frente

KEYWORD

one [wʌn] *num* un(o)/una; **~ hundred and fifty** ciento cincuenta; **~ by ~** uno a uno
♦ *adj* 1 (*sole*) único; **the ~ book which** el único libro que; **the ~ man who** el único que

2 (*same*) mismo/a; **they came in the ~ car** vinieron en un solo coche
♦ *pron* 1: **this ~** éste/ésta; **that ~** ése/ésa; (*more remote*) aquél/aquella; **I've already got (a red)** ~ ya tengo uno/a (rojo/a); **~ by ~** uno/a por uno/a
2: **~ another** os (*SP*), se (*+el uno al otro, unos a otros etc*); **do you two ever see ~ another?** ¿vosotros dos os veis alguna vez? (*SP*), ¿se ven ustedes dos alguna vez?; **the boys didn't dare look at ~ another** los chicos no se atrevieron a mirarse (el uno al otro); **they all kissed ~ another** se besaron unos a otros
3 (*impers*): **~ never knows** nunca se sabe; **to cut ~'s finger** cortarse el dedo; **~ needs to eat** hay que comer

one: **~-day excursion** (*US*) *n* billete *m* de ida y vuelta en un día; **~-man** *adj* (*business*) individual; **~-man band** *n* hombre-orquesta *m*; **~-off** (*BRIT*: *inf*) *n* (*event*) acontecimiento único
oneself [wʌnˈself] *pron* (*reflexive*) se; (*after prep*) sí; (*emphatic*) uno/a mismo/a; **to hurt ~** hacerse daño; **to keep sth for ~** guardarse algo; **to talk to ~** hablar solo
one: **~-sided** *adj* (*argument*) parcial; **~-to-~** *adj* (*relationship*) de dos; **~-way** *adj* (*street*) de sentido único
ongoing [ˈɒŋɡəʊɪŋ] *adj* continuo
onion [ˈʌnjən] *n* cebolla
on-line *adj*, *adv* (*COMPUT*) en línea
onlooker [ˈɒnlʊkə•] *n* espectador(a) *m/f*
only [ˈəʊnlɪ] *adv* solamente, sólo ♦ *adj* único, solo ♦ *conj* solamente que, pero; **an ~ child** un hijo único; **not ~ ... but also ...** no sólo ... sino también ...
onset [ˈɒnset] *n* comienzo
onshore [ˈɒnʃɔː•] *adj* (*wind*) que sopla del mar hacia la tierra
onslaught [ˈɒnslɔːt] *n* ataque *m*, embestida
onto [ˈɒntu] *prep* = **on to**
onward(s) [ˈɒnwəd(z)] *adv* (*move*) (hacia) adelante; **from that time ~** desde entonces en adelante

onyx ['ɔnɪks] n ónice m

ooze [u:z] vi rezumar

opaque [əu'peɪk] adj opaco

OPEC ['əupɛk] n abbr (= Organization of Petroleum-Exporting Countries) OPEP f

open ['əupn] adj abierto; (car) descubierto; (road, view) despejado; (meeting) público; (admiration) manifiesto ♦ vt abrir ♦ vi abrirse; (book etc: commence) comenzar; **in the ~ (air)** al aire libre; **~ on to** vt fus (subj: room, door) dar a; **~ up** vt abrir; (blocked road) despejar ♦ vi abrirse, empezar; **~ing** n abertura; (start) comienzo; (opportunity) oportunidad f; **~ing hours** npl horario de apertura; **~ learning** n enseñanza flexible a tiempo parcial; **~ly** adv abiertamente; **~-minded** adj imparcial; **~-necked** adj (shirt) desabrochado; sin corbata; **~-plan** adj: **~-plan office** gran oficina sin particiones

---
Open University

La **Open University,** *fundada en 1969, está especializada en impartir cursos a distancia que no exigen una dedicación exclusiva. Cuenta con sus propios materiales de apoyo, entre ellos programas de radio y televisión emitidos por la BBC y para conseguir los créditos de la licenciatura es necesaria la presentación de unos trabajos y la asistencia a los cursos de verano.*

---

opera ['ɔpərə] n ópera; **~ house** n teatro de la ópera

operate ['ɔpəreɪt] vt (machine) hacer funcionar; (company) dirigir ♦ vi funcionar; **to ~ on sb** (MED) operar a uno

operatic [ɔpə'rætɪk] adj de ópera

operating table ['ɔpəreɪtɪŋ-] n mesa de operaciones

operating theatre n sala de operaciones

operation [ɔpə'reɪʃən] n operación f; (of machine) funcionamiento; **to be in ~** estar funcionando or en funcionamiento; **to**

have an ~ (MED) ser operado; **~al** adj operacional, en buen estado

operative ['ɔpərətɪv] adj en vigor

operator ['ɔpəreɪtə*] n (of machine) maquinista m/f, operario/a; (TEL) operador(a) m/f, telefonista m/f

opinion [ə'pɪnɪən] n opinión f; **in my ~** en mi opinión, a mi juicio; **~ated** adj testarudo; **~ poll** n encuesta, sondeo

opponent [ə'pəunənt] n adversario/a, contrincante m/f

opportunity [ɔpə'tju:nɪtɪ] n oportunidad f; **to take the ~ of doing** aprovechar la ocasión para hacer

oppose [ə'pəuz] vt oponerse a; **to be ~d to sth** oponerse a algo; **as ~d to** a diferencia de; **opposing** adj opuesto, contrario

opposite ['ɔpəzɪt] adj opuesto, contrario a; (house etc) de enfrente ♦ adv en frente ♦ prep en frente de, frente a ♦ n lo contrario

opposition [ɔpə'zɪʃən] n oposición f

oppressive [ə'presɪv] adj opresivo; (weather) agobiante

opt [ɔpt] vi: **to ~ for** optar por; **to ~ to do** optar por hacer; **~ out** vi: **to ~ out of** optar por no hacer

optical ['ɔptɪkl] adj óptico

optician [ɔp'tɪʃən] n óptico m/f

optimist ['ɔptɪmɪst] n optimista m/f; **~ic** [-'mɪstɪk] adj optimista

option ['ɔpʃən] n opción f; **~al** adj facultativo, discrecional

or [ɔ:*] conj o; (before o, ho) u; (with negative): **he hasn't seen ~ heard anything** no ha visto ni oído nada; **~ else** si no

oral ['ɔ:rəl] adj oral ♦ n examen m oral

orange ['ɔrɪndʒ] n (fruit) naranja ♦ adj color naranja

orbit ['ɔ:bɪt] n órbita ♦ vt, vi orbitar

orchard ['ɔ:tʃəd] n huerto

orchestra ['ɔ:kɪstrə] n orquesta; (US: seating) platea

orchid ['ɔ:kɪd] n orquídea

ordain [ɔ:'deɪn] vt (REL) ordenar, decretar

ordeal [ɔ:'di:l] *n* experiencia horrorosa
order ['ɔ:dǝ*] *n* orden *m*; (*command*)
orden *f*; (*good ~*) buen estado; (*COMM*)
pedido ♦ *vt* (*also:* **put in ~**) arreglar,
poner en orden; (*COMM*) pedir;
(*command*) mandar, ordenar; **in ~** en
orden; (*of document*) en regla; **in
(working) ~** en funcionamiento; **in ~ to
do/that** para hacer/que; **on ~** (*COMM*)
pedido; **to be out of ~** estar
desordenado; (*not working*) no funcionar;
to ~ sb to do sth mandar a uno hacer
algo; **~ form** *n* hoja de pedido; **~ly** *n*
(*MIL*) ordenanza *m*; (*MED*) enfermero/a
(auxiliar) ♦ *adj* ordenado
ordinary ['ɔ:dnrɪ] *adj* corriente, normal;
(*pej*) común y corriente; **out of the ~**
fuera de lo común
Ordnance Survey ['ɔ:dnǝns-] (*BRIT*) *n*
servicio oficial de topografía
ore [ɔ:*] *n* mineral *m*
organ ['ɔ:gǝn] *n* órgano *m*; **~ic** [ɔ:'gænɪk] *adj*
orgánico; **~ism** *n* organismo *m*
organization [ɔ:gǝnaɪ'zeɪʃǝn] *n*
organización *f*
organize ['ɔ:gǝnaɪz] *vt* organizar; **~r** *n*
organizador(a) *m/f*
orgasm ['ɔ:gæzǝm] *n* orgasmo *m*
orgy ['ɔ:dʒɪ] *n* orgía
Orient ['ɔ:rɪǝnt] *n* Oriente *m*; **oriental**
[-'ɛntl] *adj* oriental
orientate ['ɔ:rɪǝnteɪt] *vt*: **to ~ o.s.**
orientarse
origin ['ɒrɪdʒɪn] *n* origen *m*
original [ǝ'rɪdʒɪnl] *adj* original; (*first*)
primero; (*earlier*) primitivo ♦ *n* original *m*;
~ly *adv* al principio
originate [ǝ'rɪdʒɪneɪt] *vi*: **to ~ from, to ~
in** surgir de, tener su origen en
Orkney ['ɔ:knɪ] *n* (*also:* **the Orkney
Islands**) las Orcadas
ornament ['ɔ:nǝmǝnt] *n* adorno; (*trinket*)
chuchería; **~al** [-'mentl] *adj* decorativo, de
adorno
ornate [ɔ:'neɪt] *adj* muy ornado, vistoso
orphan ['ɔ:fn] *n* huérfano/a
orthopaedic [ɔ:θǝ'pi:dɪk] (*US* **orthopedic**)

adj ortopédico
ostensibly [ɔs'tensɪblɪ] *adv* aparentemente
ostentatious [ɔsten'teɪʃǝs] *adj* ostentoso
osteopath ['ɔstɪǝpæθ] *n* osteópata *m/f*
ostracize ['ɔstrǝsaɪz] *vt* hacer el vacío a
ostrich ['ɔstrɪtʃ] *n* avestruz *m*
other ['ʌðǝ*] *adj* otro ♦ *pron*: **the ~ (one)**
el/la otro/a ♦ *adv*: **~ than** aparte de; **~s**
(*~ people*) otros; **the ~ day** el otro día;
~wise *adv* de otra manera ♦ *conj* (*if not*)
si no
otter ['ɔtǝ*] *n* nutria
ouch [autʃ] *excl* ¡ay!
ought [ɔ:t] (*pt* **ought**) *aux vb*: **I ~ to do it**
debería hacerlo; **this ~ to have been
corrected** esto debiera haberse corregido;
he ~ to win (*probability*) debe *or* debiera
ganar
ounce [auns] *n* onza (*28.35g*)
our ['auǝ*] *adj* nuestro; *see also* **my**; **~s**
pron (el) nuestro/(la) nuestra *etc*; *see also*
mine[1]; **~selves** *pron pl* (*reflexive, after
prep*) nosotros; (*emphatic*) nosotros
mismos; *see also* **oneself**
oust [aust] *vt* desalojar
out [aut] *adv* fuera, afuera; (*not at home*)
fuera (de casa); (*light, fire*) apagado; **~
there** allí (fuera); **he's ~** (*absent*) no está,
ha salido; **to be ~ in one's calculations**
equivocarse (en sus cálculos); **to run ~**
salir corriendo; **~ loud** en alta voz; **~ of**
(*outside*) fuera de; (*because of: anger etc*)
por; **~ of petrol** sin gasolina; **"~ of order"**
"no funciona"; **~-and-~** *adj* (*liar, thief
etc*) redomado, empedernido; **~back** *n*
interior *m*; **~board** *adj*: **~board motor**
(motor *m*) fuera borda *m*; **~break** *n* (*of
war*) comienzo; (*of disease*) epidemia; (*of
violence etc*) ola; **~burst** *n* explosión *f*,
arranque *m*; **~cast** *n* paria *m/f*; **~come**
n resultado; **~crop** *n* (*of rock*)
afloramiento; **~cry** *n* protestas *fpl*;
~dated *adj* anticuado, fuera de moda;
~do (*irreg*) *vt* superar; **~door** *adj*
exterior, de aire libre; (*clothes*) de calle;
~doors *adv* al aire libre
outer ['autǝ*] *adj* exterior, externo; **~**

space n espacio exterior

outfit ['autfɪt] n (clothes) conjunto

out: ~going adj (character) extrovertido; (retiring: president etc) saliente; ~goings (BRIT) npl gastos mpl; ~grow (irreg) vt: he has ~grown his clothes su ropa le queda pequeña ya; ~house n dependencia; ~ing n ['autɪŋ] n excursión f, paseo

out: ~law n proscrito ♦ vt proscribir; ~lay n inversión f; ~let n salida; (of pipe) desagüe m; (US: ELEC) toma de corriente; (also: retail ~let) punto de venta; ~line n (shape) contorno, perfil m; (sketch, plan) esbozo ♦ vt (plan etc) esbozar; in ~line (fig) a grandes rasgos; ~live vt sobrevivir a; ~look n (fig: prospects) perspectivas fpl; (: for weather) pronóstico; ~lying adj remoto, aislado; ~moded adj anticuado, pasado de moda; ~number vt superar en número; ~-of-date adj (passport) caducado; (clothes) pasado de moda; ~-of-the-way adj apartado; ~patient n paciente m/f externo/a; ~post n puesto avanzado; ~put n (volumen m de) producción f, rendimiento; (COMPUT) salida

outrage ['autreɪdʒ] n escándalo; (atrocity) atrocidad f ♦ vt ultrajar; ~ous [-'reɪdʒəs] adj monstruoso

outright [adv aut'raɪt, adj 'autraɪt] adv (ask, deny) francamente; (refuse) rotundamente; (win) de manera absoluta; (be killed) en el acto ♦ adj franco; rotundo

outset ['autset] n principio

outside [aut'saɪd] n exterior m ♦ adj exterior, externo ♦ adv fuera ♦ prep fuera de; (beyond) más allá de; at the ~ (fig) a lo sumo; ~ lane n (AUT: in Britain) carril m de la derecha; (: in US, Europe etc) carril m de la izquierda; ~ line n (TEL) línea (exterior); ~r n (stranger) extraño, forastero

out: ~size adj (clothes) de talla grande; ~skirts npl alrededores mpl, afueras fpl; ~spoken adj muy franco; ~standing

adj excepcional, destacado; (remaining) pendiente; ~stay vt: to ~stay one's welcome quedarse más de la cuenta; ~stretched adj (hand) extendido; ~strip vt (competitors, demand) dejar atrás, aventajar; ~-tray n bandeja de salida

outward ['autwəd] adj externo; (journey) de ida

outweigh [aut'weɪ] vt pesar más que

outwit [aut'wɪt] vt ser más listo que

oval ['əuvl] adj ovalado ♦ n óvalo

ovary ['əuvəri] n ovario

oven ['ʌvn] n horno; ~proof adj resistente al horno

over ['əuvə*] adv encima, por encima ♦ adj (or adv) (finished) terminado; (surplus) de sobra ♦ prep (por) encima de; (above) sobre; (on the other side of) al otro lado de; (more than) más de; (during) durante; ~ here (por) aquí; ~ there (por) allí or allá; all ~ (everywhere) por todas partes; ~ and ~ (again) una y otra vez; ~ and above además de; to ask sb ~ invitar a uno a casa; to bend ~ inclinarse

overall [adj, n 'əuvərɔːl, adv əuvər'ɔːl] adj (length etc) total; (study) de conjunto ♦ adv en conjunto ♦ n (BRIT) guardapolvo; ~s npl mono (SP), overol m (AM)

over: ~awe vt: to be ~awed (by) quedar impresionado (con); ~balance vi perder el equilibrio; ~board adv (NAUT) por la borda; ~book ['əuvə'buk] vt sobrereservar

overcast ['əuvəkɑːst] adj encapotado

overcharge [əuvə'tʃɑːdʒ] vt: to ~ sb cobrar un precio excesivo a uno

overcoat ['əuvəkəut] n abrigo, sobretodo

overcome [əuvə'kʌm] (irreg) vt vencer; (difficulty) superar

over: ~crowded adj atestado de gente; (city, country) superpoblado; ~do (irreg) vt exagerar; (overcook) cocer demasiado; to ~do it (work etc) pasarse; ~dose n sobredosis f inv; ~draft n saldo deudor; ~drawn adj (account) en descubierto;

~due adj retrasado; **~estimate** [əuvər'estimeit] vt sobreestimar

overflow [vb əuvə'fləu, n 'əuvəfləu] vi desbordarse ♦ n (also: **~ pipe**) (cañería de) desagüe m

overgrown [əuvə'grəun] adj (garden) invadido por la vegetación

overhaul [vb əuvə'hɔ:l, n 'əuvəhɔ:l] vt revisar, repasar ♦ n revisión f

overhead [adv əuvə'hed, adj, n 'əuvəhed] adv por arriba or encima ♦ adj (cable) aéreo ♦ n (US) = **~s**; **~s** npl (expenses) gastos mpl generales

over: ~hear (irreg) vt oír por casualidad; **~heat** vi (engine) recalentarse; **~joyed** adj encantado, lleno de alegría

overland ['əuvəlænd] adj, adv por tierra

overlap [əuvə'læp] vi traslaparse

over: ~leaf adv al dorso; **~load** vt sobrecargar; **~look** vt (have view of) dar a, tener vistas a; (miss: by mistake) pasar por alto; (excuse) perdonar

overnight [əuvə'nait] adv durante la noche; (fig) de la noche a la mañana ♦ adj de noche; **to stay ~** pasar la noche

overpass ['əuvəpa:s] (US) n paso superior

overpower [əuvə'pauə*] vt dominar; (fig) embargar; **~ing** adj (heat) agobiante; (smell) penetrante

over: ~rate vt sobreestimar; **~ride** (irreg) vt no hacer caso de; **~riding** adj predominante; **~rule** vt (decision) anular; (claim) denegar; **~run** (irreg) vt (country) invadir; (time limit) rebasar, exceder

overseas [əuvə'si:z] adv (abroad: live) en el extranjero; (: travel) al extranjero ♦ adj (trade) exterior; (visitor) extranjero

overshadow [əuvə'ʃædəu] vt: **to be ~ed by** estar a la sombra de

overshoot [əuvə'ʃu:t] (irreg) vt excederse

oversight ['əuvəsait] n descuido

oversleep [əuvə'sli:p] (irreg) vi quedarse dormido

overstep [əuvə'step] vt: **to ~ the mark** pasarse de la raya

overt [əu'və:t] adj abierto

overtake [əuvə'teik] (irreg) vt sobrepasar;

(BRIT: AUT) adelantar

over: ~throw (irreg) vt (government) derrocar; **~time** n horas fpl extraordinarias; **~tone** n (fig) tono

overture ['əuvətʃuə*] n (MUS) obertura; (fig) preludio

over: ~turn vt volcar; (fig: plan) desbaratar; (: government) derrocar ♦ vi volcar; **~weight** adj demasiado gordo or pesado; **~whelm** vt aplastar; (subj: emotion) sobrecoger; **~whelming** adj (victory, defeat) arrollador(a); (feeling) irresistible; **~work** vi trabajar demasiado; **~wrought** [əuvə'rɔ:t] adj sobreexcitado

owe [əu] vt: **to ~ sb sth, to ~ sth to sb** deber algo a uno; **owing to** prep debido a, por causa de

owl [aul] n búho, lechuza

own [əun] vt tener, poseer ♦ adj propio; **a room of my ~** una habitación propia; **to get one's ~ back** tomar revancha; **on one's ~** solo, a solas; **~ up** vi confesar; **~er** n dueño/a; **~ership** n posesión f

ox [ɔks] (pl **~en**) n buey m; **~tail** n: **~tail soup** sopa de rabo de buey

oxygen ['ɔksidʒən] n oxígeno

oyster ['ɔistə*] n ostra

oz. abbr = **ounce(s)**

ozone ['əuzəun]: **~ friendly** adj que no daña la capa de ozono; **~ hole** n agujero m de/en la capa de ozono; **~ layer** n capa f de ozono

P, p

p [pi:] abbr = **penny; pence**

P.A. n abbr = **personal assistant; public address system**

p.a. abbr = **per annum**

pa [pa:] (inf) n papá m

pace [peis] n paso ♦ vi: **to ~ up and down** pasearse de un lado a otro; **to keep ~ with** llevar el mismo paso que; **~maker** n (MED) regulador m cardíaco, marcapasos m inv; (SPORT: also: **~setter**) liebre f

Pacific [pə'sɪfɪk] *n*: **the ~ (Ocean)** el (Océano) Pacífico

pack [pæk] *n* (*packet*) paquete *m*; (*of hounds*) jauría; (*of people*) manada, bando; (*of cards*) baraja; (*bundle*) fardo; (*US: of cigarettes*) paquete *m*; (*back ~*) mochila ♦ *vt* (*fill*) llenar; (*in suitcase etc*) meter, poner; (*cram*) llenar, atestar; **to ~ (one's bags)** hacerse la maleta; **to ~ sb off** despachar a uno; **~ it in!** (*inf*) ¡déjalo!

package ['pækɪdʒ] *n* paquete *m*; (*bulky*) bulto; (*also: ~ deal*) acuerdo global; **~ holiday** *n* vacaciones *fpl* organizadas; **~ tour** *n* viaje *m* organizado

packed lunch *n* almuerzo frío

packet ['pækɪt] *n* paquete *m*

packing ['pækɪŋ] *n* embalaje *m*; **~ case** *n* cajón *m* de embalaje

pact [pækt] *n* pacto

pad [pæd] *n* (*of paper*) bloc *m*; (*cushion*) cojinete *m*; (*inf: home*) casa ♦ *vt* rellenar; **~ding** *n* (*material*) relleno

paddle ['pædl] *n* (*oar*) canalete *m*; (*US: for table tennis*) paleta ♦ *vt* impulsar con canalete ♦ *vi* (*with feet*) chapotear; **paddling pool** (*BRIT*) *n* estanque *m* de juegos

paddock ['pædək] *n* corral *m*

padlock ['pædlɒk] *n* candado

paediatrics [piːdɪ'ætrɪks] (*US* **pediatrics**) *n* pediatría

pagan ['peɪgən] *adj, n* pagano/a *m/f*

page [peɪdʒ] *n* (*of book*) página; (*of newspaper*) plana; (*also: ~ boy*) paje *m* ♦ *vt* (*in hotel etc*) llamar por altavoz a

pageant ['pædʒənt] *n* (*procession*) desfile *m*; (*show*) espectáculo; **~ry** *n* pompa

pager ['peɪdʒə*] *n* (*TEL*) busca *m*

paging device ['peɪdʒɪŋ-] *n* = **pager**

paid [peɪd] *pt, pp of* **pay** ♦ *adj* (*work*) remunerado; (*holiday*) pagado; (*official etc*) a sueldo; **to put ~ to** (*BRIT*) acabar con

pail [peɪl] *n* cubo, balde *m*

pain [peɪn] *n* dolor *m*; **to be in ~** sufrir; **to take ~s to do sth** tomarse grandes molestias en hacer algo; **~ed** *adj*

(*expression*) afligido; **~ful** *adj* doloroso; (*difficult*) penoso; (*disagreeable*) desagradable; **~fully** *adv* (*fig: very*) terriblemente; **~killer** *n* analgésico; **~less** *adj* que no causa dolor; **~staking** ['peɪnzteɪkɪŋ] *adj* (*person*) concienzudo, esmerado

paint [peɪnt] *n* pintura ♦ *vt* pintar; **to ~ the door blue** pintar la puerta de azul; **~brush** *n* (*artist's*) pincel *m*; (*decorator's*) brocha; **~er** *n* pintor(a) *m/f*; **~ing** *n* pintura; **~work** *n* pintura

pair [peə*] *n* (*of shoes, gloves etc*) par *m*; (*of people*) pareja; **a ~ of scissors** unas tijeras; **a ~ of trousers** unos pantalones, un pantalón

pajamas [pə'dʒɑːməz] (*US*) *npl* pijama *m*

Pakistan [pɑːkɪ'stɑːn] *n* Paquistán *m*; **~i** *adj, n* paquistaní *m/f*

pal [pæl] (*inf*) *n* compinche *m/f*, compañero/a

palace ['pæləs] *n* palacio

palatable ['pælɪtəbl] *adj* sabroso

palate ['pælɪt] *n* paladar *m*

pale [peɪl] *adj* (*gen*) pálido; (*colour*) claro ♦ *n*: **to be beyond the ~** pasarse de la raya

Palestine ['pælɪstaɪn] *n* Palestina; **Palestinian** [-'tɪnɪən] *adj, n* palestino/a *m/f*

palette ['pælɪt] *n* paleta

pall [pɔːl] *vi* perder el sabor

pallet ['pælɪt] *n* (*for goods*) pallet *m*

pallid ['pælɪd] *adj* pálido

palm [pɑːm] *n* (*ANAT*) palma; (*also: ~ tree*) palmera, palma ♦ *vt*: **to ~ sth off on sb** (*inf*) encajar algo a uno; **P~ Sunday** *n* Domingo de Ramos

paltry ['pɔːltrɪ] *adj* irrisorio

pamper ['pæmpə*] *vt* mimar

pamphlet ['pæmflət] *n* folleto

pan [pæn] *n* (*also: sauce~*) cacerola, cazuela, olla; (*also: frying ~*) sartén *f*

Panama ['pænəmɑː] *n* Panamá *m*; **the ~ Canal** el Canal de Panamá

pancake ['pænkeɪk] *n* crepe *f*

panda ['pændə] *n* panda *m*; **~ car** (*BRIT*) *n*

coche *m* Z (*SP*)
pandemonium [pændɪˈməʊnɪəm] *n* jaleo
pander [ˈpændə*] *vi*: **to ~ to** complacer a
pane [peɪn] *n* cristal *m*
panel [ˈpænl] *n* (*of wood etc*) panel *m*;
(*RADIO, TV*) panel *m* de invitados; **~ling**
(*US* **~ing**) *n* paneles *mpl*
pang [pæŋ] *n*: **a ~ of regret** (una punzada
de) remordimiento; **hunger ~s** dolores
mpl del hambre
panic [ˈpænɪk] *n* (terror *m*) pánico ♦ *vi*
dejarse llevar por el pánico; **~ky** *adj*
(*person*) asustadizo; **~-stricken** *adj* preso
de pánico
pansy [ˈpænzɪ] *n* (*BOT*) pensamiento; (*inf:
pej*) maricón *m*
pant [pænt] *vi* jadear
panther [ˈpænθə*] *n* pantera
panties [ˈpæntɪz] *npl* bragas *fpl*, pantis
mpl
pantihose [ˈpæntɪhəʊz] (*US*) *n* pantimedias
fpl
pantomime [ˈpæntəmaɪm] (*BRIT*) *n* revista
musical representada en Navidad, basada
en cuentos de hadas

---
pantomime

i En época navideña se ponen en escena
en los teatros británicos las llamadas
pantomimes, que son versiones libres de
cuentos tradicionales como Aladino o El
gato con botas. En ella nunca faltan
personajes como la dama ("dame"), papel
que siempre interpreta un actor, el
protagonista joven ("principal boy"),
normalmente interpretado por una actriz, y
el malvado ("villain"). Es un espectáculo
familiar en el que se anima al público a
participar y aunque va dirigido
principalmente a los niños, cuenta con
grandes dosis de humor para adultos.

---

pantry [ˈpæntrɪ] *n* despensa
pants [pænts] *n* (*BRIT: underwear: woman's*)
bragas *fpl*; (: *man's*) calzoncillos *mpl*; (*US:
trousers*) pantalones *mpl*
paper [ˈpeɪpə*] *n* papel *m*; (*also:* **news~**)

periódico, diario; (*academic essay*) ensayo;
(*exam*) examen *m* ♦ *adj* de papel ♦ *vt*
empapelar (*SP*), tapizar (*AM*); **~s** *npl* (*also:*
identity ~s) papeles *mpl*, documentos
mpl; **~back** *n* libro en rústica; **~ bag** *n*
bolsa de papel; **~ clip** *n* clip *m*; **~
hankie** *n* pañuelo de papel; **~weight** *n*
pisapapeles *m inv*; **~work** *n* trabajo
administrativo
paprika [ˈpæprɪkə] *n* pimentón *m*
par [pɑ:*] *n* par *f*; (*GOLF*) par *m*; **to be on
a ~ with** estar a la par con
parachute [ˈpærəʃu:t] *n* paracaídas *m inv*
parade [pəˈreɪd] *n* desfile *m* ♦ *vt* (*show
off*) hacer alarde de ♦ *vi* desfilar; (*MIL*)
pasar revista
paradise [ˈpærədaɪs] *n* paraíso
paradox [ˈpærədɒks] *n* paradoja; **~ically**
[-ˈdɒksɪklɪ] *adv* paradójicamente
paraffin [ˈpærəfɪn] (*BRIT*) *n* (*also:* **~ oil**)
parafina
paragon [ˈpærəgən] *n* modelo
paragraph [ˈpærəgrɑ:f] *n* párrafo
parallel [ˈpærəlel] *adj* en paralelo; (*fig*)
semejante ♦ *n* (*line*) paralela; (*fig, GEO*)
paralelo
paralyse [ˈpærəlaɪz] *vt* paralizar
paralysis [pəˈrælɪsɪs] *n* parálisis *f inv*
paralyze [ˈpærəlaɪz] (*US*) *vt* = **paralyse**
paramount [ˈpærəmaʊnt] *adj*: **of ~
importance** de suma importancia
paranoid [ˈpærənɔɪd] *adj* (*person, feeling*)
paranoico
paraphernalia [pærəfəˈneɪlɪə] *n* (*gear*)
avíos *mpl*
parasite [ˈpærəsaɪt] *n* parásito/a
parasol [ˈpærəsɒl] *n* sombrilla, quitasol *m*
paratrooper [ˈpærətru:pə*] *n* paracaidista
m/f
parcel [ˈpɑ:sl] *n* paquete *m* ♦ *vt* (*also:* **~
up**) empaquetar, embalar
parched [pɑ:tʃt] *adj* (*person*) muerto de
sed
parchment [ˈpɑ:tʃmənt] *n* pergamino
pardon [ˈpɑ:dn] *n* (*LAW*) indulto ♦ *vt*
perdonar; **~ me!, I beg your ~!** (*I'm
sorry!*) ¡perdone usted!; **(I beg your) ~?**, **~**

me? (*US*) (*what did you say?*) ¿cómo?
parent ['peərənt] *n* (*mother*) madre *f*;
(*father*) padre *m*; **~s** *npl* padres *mpl*; **~al**
[pə'rɛntl] *adj* paternal/maternal
parenthesis [pə'rɛnθɪsɪs] (*pl*
parentheses) *n* paréntesis *m inv*
Paris ['pærɪs] *n* París
parish ['pærɪʃ] *n* parroquia
Parisian [pə'rɪzɪən] *adj, n* parisiense *m/f*
park [pɑːk] *n* parque *m* ♦ *vt* aparcar,
estacionar ♦ *vi* aparcar, estacionarse
parking ['pɑːkɪŋ] *n* aparcamiento,
estacionamiento, ''**no ~**'' ''prohibido
estacionarse''; **~ lot** (*US*) *n* parking *m*; **~
meter** *n* parquímetro; **~ ticket** *n* multa
de aparcamiento
parliament ['pɑːləmənt] *n* parlamento;
(*Spanish*) Cortes *fpl*; **~ary** [-'mɛntərɪ] *adj*
parlamentario

> **Parliament**

> **ⓘ** *El Parlamento británico* (**Parliament**)
> *tiene como sede el palacio de*
> *Westminster, también llamado "Houses of*
> *Parliament" y consta de dos cámaras. La*
> *Cámara de los Comunes ("House of*
> *Commons"), compuesta por 650 diputados*
> (**Members of Parliament**) *elegidos por*
> *sufragio universal en su respectiva*
> *circunscripción electoral* (**constituency**),
> *se reúne 175 días al año y sus sesiones*
> *son moderadas por el Presidente de la*
> *Cámara* (**Speaker**). *La cámara alta es la*
> *Cámara de los Lores ("House of Lords") y*
> *está formada por miembros que han sido*
> *nombrados por el monarca o que han*
> *heredado su escaño. Su poder es limitado,*
> *aunque actúa como tribunal supremo de*
> *apelación, excepto en Escocia.*

parlour ['pɑːlə*] (*US* **parlor**) *n* sala de
recibo, salón *m*, living *m* (*AM*)
parochial [pə'rəukɪəl] (*pej*) *adj* de miras
estrechas
parole [pə'rəul] *n*: **on ~** libre bajo palabra
parquet [pɑːkeɪ] *n*: **~ floor(ing)** parquet
m

parrot ['pærət] *n* loro, papagayo
parry ['pærɪ] *vt* parar
parsley ['pɑːslɪ] *n* perejil *m*
parsnip ['pɑːsnɪp] *n* chirivía
parson ['pɑːsn] *n* cura *m*
part [pɑːt] *n* (*gen, MUS*) parte *f*; (*bit*) trozo,
(*of machine*) pieza; (*THEATRE etc*) papel *m*;
(*of serial*) entrega; (*US: in hair*) raya ♦ *adv*
= **partly** ♦ *vt* separar ♦ *vi* (*people*)
separarse; (*crowd*) apartarse; **to take ~ in**
tomar parte *or* participar en; **to take sth
in good ~** tomar algo en buena parte; **to
take sb's ~** defender a uno; **for my ~** por
mi parte; **for the most ~** en su mayor
parte; **to ~ one's hair** hacerse la raya; **~
with** *vt fus* ceder, entregar; (*money*)
pagar; **~ exchange** (*BRIT*) *n*: **in ~
exchange** como parte del pago
partial ['pɑːʃl] *adj* parcial; **to be ~ to** ser
aficionado a
participant [pɑː'tɪsɪpənt] *n* (*in competition*)
concursante *m/f*; (*in campaign etc*)
participante *m/f*
participate [pɑː'tɪsɪpeɪt] *vi*: **to ~ in**
participar en; **participation** [-'peɪʃən] *n*
participación *f*
participle ['pɑːtɪsɪpl] *n* participio
particle ['pɑːtɪkl] *n* partícula; (*of dust*)
grano
particular [pə'tɪkjulə*] *adj* (*special*)
particular; (*concrete*) concreto; (*given*)
determinado; (*fussy*) quisquilloso;
(*demanding*) exigente; **~s** *npl*
(*information*) datos *mpl*; (*details*)
pormenores *mpl*; **in ~** en particular; **~ly**
adv (*in particular*) sobre todo; (*difficult,
good etc*) especialmente
parting ['pɑːtɪŋ] *n* (*act of*) separación *f*;
(*farewell*) despedida; (*BRIT: in hair*) raya
♦ *adj* de despedida
partisan [pɑːtɪ'zæn] *adj* partidista ♦ *n*
partidario/a
partition [pɑː'tɪʃən] *n* (*POL*) división *f*;
(*wall*) tabique *m*
partly ['pɑːtlɪ] *adv* en parte
partner ['pɑːtnə*] *n* (*COMM*) socio/a;
(*SPORT, at dance*) pareja; (*spouse*) cónyuge

m/f; (*lover*) compañero/a; **~ship** *n*
asociación *f*; (*COMM*) sociedad *f*
partridge ['pɑːtrɪdʒ] *n* perdiz *f*
part-time *adj*, *adv* a tiempo parcial
party ['pɑːtɪ] *n* (*POL*) partido; (*celebration*)
fiesta; (*group*) grupo; (*LAW*) parte *f*
interesada ♦ *cpd* (*POL*) de partido; **~
dress** *n* vestido de fiesta
pass [pɑːs] *vt* (*time, object*) pasar; (*place*)
pasar por; (*overtake*) rebasar; (*exam*)
aprobar; (*approve*) aprobar ♦ *vi* pasar;
(*SCOL*) aprobar, ser aprobado ♦ *n* (*permit*)
permiso; (*membership card*) carnet *m*; (*in
mountains*) puerto, desfiladero; (*SPORT*)
pase *m*; (*SCOL*: *also*: **~ mark**): **to get a ~
in** aprobar en; **to ~ sth through sth** pasar
algo por algo; **to make a ~ at sb** (*inf*)
hacer proposiciones a uno; **~ away** *vi*
fallecer; **~ by** *vi* pasar ♦ *vt* (*ignore*) pasar
por alto; **~ for** *vt fus* pasar por; **~ on** *vt*
transmitir; **~ out** *vi* desmayarse; **~ up** *vt*
(*opportunity*) renunciar a; **~able** *adj*
(*road*) transitable; (*tolerable*) pasable
passage ['pæsɪdʒ] *n* (*also*: **~way**) pasillo;
(*act of passing*) tránsito; (*fare, in book*)
pasaje *m*; (*by boat*) travesía; (*ANAT*) tubo
passbook ['pɑːsbʊk] *n* libreta de banco
passenger ['pæsɪndʒə*] *n* pasajero/a,
viajero/a
passer-by [pɑːsə'baɪ] *n* transeúnte *m/f*
passing ['pɑːsɪŋ] *adj* pasajero; **in ~** de
paso; **~ place** *n* (*AUT*) apartadero
passion ['pæʃən] *n* pasión *f*; **~ate** *adj*
apasionado
passive ['pæsɪv] *adj* (*gen, also LING*)
pasivo; **~ smoking** *n* efectos del tabaco
en fumadores pasivos
Passover ['pɑːsəʊvə*] *n* Pascua (de los
judíos)
passport ['pɑːspɔːt] *n* pasaporte *m*; **~
control** *n* control *m* de pasaporte; **~
office** *n* oficina de pasaportes
password ['pɑːswɜːd] *n* contraseña
past [pɑːst] *prep* (*in front of*) por delante
de; (*further than*) más allá de; (*later than*)
después de ♦ *adj* pasado; (*president etc*)
antiguo ♦ *n* (*time*) pasado; (*of person*)

antecedentes *mpl*; **he's ~ forty** tiene más
de cuarenta años; **ten/quarter ~ eight** las
ocho y diez/cuarto; **for the ~ few/3 days**
durante los últimos días/últimos 3 días; **to
run ~ sb** pasar a uno corriendo
pasta ['pæstə] *n* pasta
paste [peɪst] *n* pasta; (*glue*) engrudo ♦ *vt*
pegar
pasteurized ['pæstəraɪzd] *adj* pasteurizado
pastille ['pæstɪl] *n* pastilla
pastime ['pɑːstaɪm] *n* pasatiempo
pastry ['peɪstrɪ] *n* (*dough*) pasta; (*cake*)
pastel *m*
pasture ['pɑːstʃə*] *n* pasto
pasty[1] ['pæstɪ] *n* empanada
pasty[2] ['peɪstɪ] *adj* (*complexion*) pálido
pat [pæt] *vt* dar una palmadita a; (*dog etc*)
acariciar
patch [pætʃ] *n* (*of material, eye ~*) parche
m; (*mended part*) remiendo; (*of land*)
terreno ♦ *vt* remendar; **(to go through) a
bad ~** (pasar por) una mala racha; **~ up**
vt reparar; (*quarrel*) hacer las paces en;
~work *n* labor *m* de retazos; **~y** *adj*
desigual
pâté ['pæteɪ] *n* paté *m*
patent ['peɪtnt] *n* patente *f* ♦ *vt* patentar
♦ *adj* patente, evidente; **~ leather** *n*
charol *m*
paternal [pə'tɜːnl] *adj* paternal; (*relation*)
paterno
path [pɑːθ] *n* camino, sendero; (*trail, track*)
pista; (*of missile*) trayectoria
pathetic [pə'θetɪk] *adj* patético, lastimoso;
(*very bad*) malísimo
pathological [pæθə'lɒdʒɪkəl] *adj*
patológico
pathway ['pɑːθweɪ] *n* sendero, vereda
patience ['peɪʃns] *n* paciencia; (*BRIT*:
CARDS) solitario
patient ['peɪʃnt] *n* paciente *m/f* ♦ *adj*
paciente, sufrido
patio ['pætɪəʊ] *n* patio
patriot ['peɪtrɪət] *n* patriota *m/f*; **~ic**
[pætrɪ'ɒtɪk] *adj* patriótico
patrol [pə'trəʊl] *n* patrulla ♦ *vt* patrullar
por; **~ car** *n* coche *m* patrulla; **~man**

(US irreg) n policía m

patron ['peɪtrən] n (in shop) cliente m/f;
(of charity) patrocinador(a) m/f; **~ of the
arts** mecenas m; **~ize** ['pætrənaɪz] vt
(shop) ser cliente de; (artist etc) proteger;
(look down on) condescender con; **~
saint** n santo/a patrón/ona m/f

patter ['pætə*] n golpeteo; (sales talk) labia
♦ vi (rain) tamborilear

pattern ['pætən] n (SEWING) patrón m;
(design) dibujo

pauper ['pɔːpə*] n pobre m/f

pause [pɔːz] n pausa ♦ vi hacer una pausa

pave [peɪv] vt pavimentar; **to ~ the way
for** preparar el terreno para

pavement ['peɪvmənt] (BRIT) n acera (SP),
vereda (AM)

pavilion [pə'vɪlɪən] n (SPORT) caseta

paving ['peɪvɪŋ] n pavimento, enlosado; **~
stone** n losa

paw [pɔː] n pata

pawn [pɔːn] n (CHESS) peón m; (fig)
instrumento ♦ vt empeñar; **~ broker** n
prestamista m/f; **~shop** n monte m de
piedad

pay [peɪ] (pt, pp **paid**) n (wage etc) sueldo,
salario ♦ vt pagar ♦ vi (be profitable)
rendir; **to ~ attention (to)** prestar
atención (a); **to ~ sb a visit** hacer una
visita a uno; **to ~ one's respects to sb**
presentar sus respetos a uno; **~ back** vt
(money) reembolsar; (person) pagar; **~ for**
vt fus pagar; **~ in** vt ingresar; **~ off** vt
saldar ♦ vi (scheme, decision) dar
resultado; **~ up** vt pagar (de mala gana);
~able adj: **~able to** pagadero a; **~ day**
n día m de paga; **~ee** n portador(a) m/f;
~ envelope (US) n = **~ packet**; **~ment**
n pago; **monthly ~ment** mensualidad f; **~
packet** (BRIT) n sobre m (de paga); **~
phone** n teléfono público; **~roll** n
nómina; **~ slip** n recibo de sueldo; **~
television** n televisión f de pago

PC n abbr = **personal computer**; (BRIT)
= **police constable** ♦ adj abbr
= **politically correct**

p.c. abbr = **per cent**

pea [piː] n guisante m (SP), chícharo (AM),
arveja (AM)

peace [piːs] n paz f; (calm) paz f,
tranquilidad f; **~ful** adj (gentle) pacífico;
(calm) tranquilo, sosegado

peach [piːtʃ] n melocotón m (SP), durazno
(AM)

peacock ['piːkɔk] n pavo real

peak [piːk] n (of mountain) cumbre f,
cima; (of cap) visera; (fig) cumbre f; **~
hours** npl, **~ period** n horas fpl punta

peal [piːl] n (of bells) repique m; **~ of
laughter** carcajada

peanut ['piːnʌt] n cacahuete m (SP), maní
m (AM); **~ butter** manteca de cacahuete
or maní

pear [pεə*] n pera

pearl [pəːl] n perla

peasant ['pεznt] n campesino/a

peat [piːt] n turba

pebble ['pεbl] n guijarro

peck [pεk] vt (also: **~ at**) picotear ♦ n
picotazo; (kiss) besito; **~ing order** n
orden m de jerarquía; **~ish** (BRIT: inf) adj:
I feel ~ish tengo ganas de picar algo

peculiar [pɪ'kjuːlɪə*] adj (odd) extraño,
raro; (typical) propio, característico; **~ to**
propio de

pedal ['pεdl] n pedal m ♦ vi pedalear

pedantic [pɪ'dæntɪk] adj pedante

peddler ['pεdlə*] n: **drug ~** traficante m/f;
camello

pedestrian [pɪ'dεstrɪən] n peatón/ona m/f
♦ adj pedestre; **~ crossing** (BRIT) n paso
de peatones; **~ precinct** (BRIT), **~ zone**
(US) n zona peatonal

pediatrics [piːdɪ'ætrɪks] (US) n
= **paediatrics**

pedigree ['pεdɪgriː] n genealogía; (of
animal) raza, pedigrí m ♦ cpd (animal) de
raza, de casta

pee [piː] (inf) vi mear

peek [piːk] vi mirar a hurtadillas

peel [piːl] n piel f; (of orange, lemon)
cáscara; (: removed) peladuras fpl ♦ vt
pelar ♦ vi (paint etc) desconcharse;
(wallpaper) despegarse, desprenderse;

(skin) pelar

peep [piːp] n: **to ~ at** esudriñar ♦ n *(noble)* par m; *(equal)* igual m; *(contemporary)* contemporáneo/a; **~age** n nobleza

peeved [piːvd] adj enojado

peg [pɛg] n *(for coat etc)* gancho, colgadero; *(BRIT: also:* **clothes ~)** pinza

Pekingese [piːkɪˈniːz] n *(dog)* pequinés/ esa m/f

pelican [ˈpɛlɪkən] n pelícano; **~ crossing** *(BRIT)* n *(AUT)* paso de peatones señalizado

pellet [ˈpɛlɪt] n bolita; *(bullet)* perdigón m

pelt [pɛlt] vt: **to ~ sb with sth** arrojarle algo a uno ♦ vi *(rain)* llover a cántaros; *(inf: run)* correr ♦ n pellejo

pen [pɛn] n *(fountain ~)* pluma; *(ballpoint ~)* bolígrafo; *(for sheep)* redil m

penal [ˈpiːnl] adj penal; **~ize** vt castigar

penalty [ˈpɛnltɪ] n *(gen)* pena; *(fine)* multa; **~ (kick)** n *(FOOTBALL)* penalty m; *(RUGBY)* golpe m de castigo

penance [ˈpɛnəns] n penitencia

pence [pɛns] npl of **penny**

pencil [ˈpɛnsl] n lápiz m, lapicero *(AM)*; **~ case** n estuche m; **~ sharpener** n sacapuntas m inv

pendant [ˈpɛndnt] n pendiente m

pending [ˈpɛndɪŋ] prep antes de ♦ adj pendiente

pendulum [ˈpɛndjuləm] n péndulo

penetrate [ˈpɛnɪtreɪt] vt penetrar

penfriend [ˈpɛnfrɛnd] *(BRIT)* n amigo/a por carta

penguin [ˈpɛŋgwɪn] n pingüino

penicillin [pɛnɪˈsɪlɪn] n penicilina

peninsula [pəˈnɪnsjulə] n península

penis [ˈpiːnɪs] n pene m

penitentiary [pɛnɪˈtɛnʃərɪ] *(US)* n cárcel f, presidio

penknife [ˈpɛnnaɪf] n navaja

pen name n seudónimo

penniless [ˈpɛnɪlɪs] adj sin dinero

penny [ˈpɛnɪ] *(pl* **pennies** *or (BRIT)* **pence)** n penique m; *(US)* centavo

penpal [ˈpɛnpæl] n amigo/a por carta

pension [ˈpɛnʃən] n *(state benefit)* jubilación f; **~er** *(BRIT)* n jubilado/a; **~ fund** n caja or fondo de pensiones

pentagon [ˈpɛntəgən] n: **the P~** *(US: POL)* el Pentágono

Pentagon

> *Se conoce como* **Pentagon** *al edificio de planta pentagonal que acoge las dependencias del Ministerio de Defensa estadounidense ("Department of Defense") en Arlington, Virginia. En lenguaje periodístico se aplica también a la dirección militar del país.*

Pentecost [ˈpɛntɪkɔst] n Pentecostés m

penthouse [ˈpɛnthaus] n ático de lujo

pent-up [ˈpɛntʌp] adj reprimido

people [ˈpiːpl] npl gente f; *(citizens)* pueblo, ciudadanos mpl; *(POL)*: **the ~** el pueblo ♦ n *(nation, race)* pueblo, nación f; **several ~ came** vinieron varias personas; **~ say that ...** dice la gente que ...

pep [pɛp] *(inf)*: **~ up** vt animar

pepper [ˈpɛpə*] n *(spice)* pimienta; *(vegetable)* pimiento ♦ vt: **to ~ with** *(fig)* salpicar de; **~mint** n *(sweet)* pastilla de menta

peptalk [ˈpɛptɔːk] n: **to give sb a ~** darle a uno una inyección de ánimo

per [pəː*] prep por; **~ day/person** por día/persona; **~ annum** al año; **~ capita** adj, adv per cápita

perceive [pəˈsiːv] vt percibir; *(realize)* darse cuenta de

per cent n por ciento

percentage [pəˈsɛntɪdʒ] n porcentaje m

perception [pəˈsɛpʃən] n percepción f; *(insight)* perspicacia; *(opinion etc)* opinión f; **perceptive** [-ˈsɛptɪv] adj perspicaz

perch [pəːtʃ] n *(fish)* perca; *(for bird)* percha ♦ vi: **to ~ (on)** *(bird)* posarse (en); *(person)* encaramarse (en)

percolator ['pɜːkəleɪtə*] n (also: **coffee ~**) cafetera de filtro

perennial [pə'renɪəl] adj perenne

perfect [adj, n 'pɜːfɪkt, vb pə'fekt] adj perfecto ♦ n (also: **~ tense**) perfecto ♦ vt perfeccionar; **~ly** ['pɜːfɪktlɪ] adv perfectamente

perforate ['pɜːfəreɪt] vt perforar

perform [pə'fɔːm] vt (carry out) realizar, llevar a cabo; (THEATRE) representar; (piece of music) interpretar ♦ vi (well, badly) funcionar; **~ance** n (of a play) representación f; (of actor, athlete etc) actuación f; (of car, engine, company) rendimiento; (of economy) resultados mpl; **~er** n (actor) actor m, actriz f

perfume ['pɜːfjuːm] n perfume m

perhaps [pə'hæps] adv quizá(s), tal vez

peril ['perɪl] n peligro, riesgo

perimeter [pə'rɪmɪtə*] n perímetro

period ['pɪərɪəd] n período; (SCOL) clase f; (full stop) punto; (MED) regla ♦ adj (costume, furniture) de época; **~ic(al)** [-'ɔdɪk(l)] adj periódico; **~ical** [-'ɔdɪkl] n periódico; **~ically** [-'ɔdɪklɪ] adv de vez en cuando, cada cierto tiempo

peripheral [pə'rɪfərəl] adj periférico ♦ n (COMPUT) periférico, unidad f periférica

perish ['perɪʃ] vi perecer; (decay) echarse a perder; **~able** adj perecedero

perjury ['pɜːdʒərɪ] n (LAW) perjurio

perk [pɜːk] n extra m; **~ up** vi (cheer up) animarse

perm [pɜːm] n permanente f

permanent ['pɜːmənənt] adj permanente

permeate ['pɜːmɪeɪt] vi penetrar, trascender ♦ vt penetrar, trascender a

permissible [pə'mɪsɪbl] adj permisible, lícito

permission [pə'mɪʃən] n permiso

permissive [pə'mɪsɪv] adj permisivo

permit [n 'pɜːmɪt, vt pə'mɪt] n permiso, licencia ♦ vt permitir

perplex [pə'pleks] vt dejar perplejo

persecute ['pɜːsɪkjuːt] vt perseguir

persevere [pɜːsɪ'vɪə*] vi persistir

Persian ['pɜːʃən] adj, n persa m/f; **the ~**

Gulf el Golfo Pérsico

persist [pə'sɪst] vi: **to ~ (in doing sth)** persistir (en hacer algo); **~ence** n empeño; **~ent** adj persistente; (determined) porfiado

person ['pɜːsn] n persona; **in ~** en persona; **~al** adj personal; individual; (visit) en persona; **~al assistant** n ayudante m/f personal; **~al column** n anuncios mpl personales; **~al computer** n ordenador m personal; **~ality** [-'nælɪtɪ] n personalidad f; **~ally** adv personalmente; (in person) en persona; **to take sth ~ally** tomarse algo a mal; **~al organizer** n agenda; **~al stereo** n Walkman ® m; **~ify** [-'sɔnɪfaɪ] vt encarnar

personnel [pɜːsə'nel] n personal m

perspective [pə'spektɪv] n perspectiva

Perspex ® ['pɜːspeks] n plexiglás ® m

perspiration [pɜːspɪ'reɪʃən] n transpiración f

persuade [pə'sweɪd] vt: **to ~ sb to do sth** persuadir a uno para que haga algo

Peru [pə'ruː] n el Perú; **Peruvian** adj, n peruano/a m/f

perverse [pə'vɜːs] adj perverso; (wayward) travieso

pervert [n 'pɜːvɜːt, vb pə'vɜːt] n pervertido/a ♦ vt pervertir; (truth, sb's words) tergiversar

pessimist ['pesɪmɪst] n pesimista m/f; **~ic** [-'mɪstɪk] adj pesimista

pest [pest] n (insect) insecto nocivo; (fig) lata, molestia

pester ['pestə*] vt molestar, acosar

pesticide ['pestɪsaɪd] n pesticida m

pet [pet] n animal m doméstico ♦ cpd favorito ♦ vt acariciar; **teacher's ~** favorito/a (del profesor); **~ hate** manía

petal ['petl] n pétalo

peter ['piːtə*]: **to ~ out** vi agotarse, acabarse

petite [pə'tiːt] adj chiquita

petition [pə'tɪʃən] n petición f

petrified ['petrɪfaɪd] adj horrorizado

petrol ['petrəl] (BRIT) n gasolina; **two/four-star ~** gasolina normal/súper; **~ can**

n bidón *m* de gasolina
petroleum [pə'trəʊlɪəm] *n* petróleo
petrol: ~ **pump** (BRIT) *n* (in garage)
surtidor *m* de gasolina; ~ **station** (BRIT)
n gasolinera; ~ **tank** (BRIT) *n* depósito
(de gasolina)
petticoat ['petɪkəʊt] *n* enaguas *fpl*
petty ['petɪ] *adj* (mean) mezquino;
(unimportant) insignificante; ~ **cash** *n*
dinero para gastos menores; ~ **officer** *n*
contramaestre *m*
petulant ['petjʊlənt] *adj* malhumorado
pew [pjuː] *n* banco
pewter ['pjuːtə*] *n* peltre *m*
phantom ['fæntəm] *n* fantasma *m*
pharmacist ['fɑːməsɪst] *n* farmacéutico/a
pharmacy ['fɑːməsɪ] *n* farmacia
phase [feɪz] *n* fase *f* ♦ *vt*: **to** ~ **sth in/out**
introducir/retirar algo por etapas
Ph.D. *abbr* = Doctor of Philosophy
pheasant ['feznt] *n* faisán *m*
phenomenon [fə'nɔmɪnən] (pl
phenomena) *n* fenómeno
philanthropist [fɪ'lænθrəpɪst] *n*
filántropo/a
Philippines ['fɪlɪpiːnz] *npl*: **the** ~ las
Filipinas
philosopher [fɪ'lɔsəfə*] *n* filósofo/a
philosophy [fɪ'lɔsəfɪ] *n* filosofía
phobia ['fəʊbjə] *n* fobia
phone [fəʊn] *n* teléfono ♦ *vt* telefonear,
llamar por teléfono; **to be on the** ~ tener
teléfono; (be calling) estar hablando por
teléfono; ~ **back** *vt*, *vi* volver a llamar; ~
up *vt*, *vi* llamar por teléfono; ~ **book** *n*
guía telefónica; ~ **booth** *n* cabina
telefónica; ~ **box** (BRIT) *n* = ~ **booth**; ~
call *n* llamada (telefónica); ~**card** *n*
teletarjeta; ~**in** (BRIT) *n* (RADIO, TV)
programa *m* de participación (telefónica)
phonetics [fə'netɪks] *n* fonética
phoney ['fəʊnɪ] *adj* falso
photo ['fəʊtəʊ] *n* foto *f*; ~**copier** *n*
fotocopiadora; ~**copy** *n* fotocopia ♦ *vt*
fotocopiar
photograph ['fəʊtəɡrɑːf] *n* fotografía ♦ *vt*
fotografiar; ~**er** [fə'tɔɡrəfə*] *n* fotógrafo;

~**y** [fə'tɔɡrəfɪ] *n* fotografía
phrase [freɪz] *n* frase *f* ♦ *vt* expresar; ~
book *n* libro de frases
physical ['fɪzɪkl] *adj* físico; ~ **education**
n educación *f* física; ~**ly** *adv* físicamente
physician [fɪ'zɪʃən] *n* médico/a
physicist ['fɪzɪsɪst] *n* físico/a
physics ['fɪzɪks] *n* física
physiotherapy [fɪzɪəʊ'θerəpɪ] *n*
fisioterapia
physique [fɪ'ziːk] *n* físico
pianist ['piːənɪst] *n* pianista *m/f*
piano [pɪ'ænəʊ] *n* piano
pick [pɪk] *n* (tool: also: ~**-axe**) pico,
piqueta ♦ *vt* (select) elegir, escoger;
(gather) coger (SP), recoger; (remove, take
out) sacar, quitar; (lock) abrir con ganzúa;
take your ~ escoja lo que quiera; **the** ~
of lo mejor de; **to** ~ **one's nose/teeth**
hurgarse las narices/limpiarse los dientes;
to ~ **a quarrel with sb** meterse con
alguien; ~ **at** *vt fus*: **to** ~ **at one's food**
comer con poco apetito; ~ **on** *vt fus*
(person) meterse con; ~ **out** *vt* escoger;
(distinguish) identificar; ~ **up** *vi* (improve:
sales) ir mejor; (: patient) reponerse;
(: FINANCE) recobrarse ♦ *vt* recoger;
(learn) aprender; (POLICE: arrest) detener;
(person: for sex) ligar; (RADIO) captar; **to** ~
up speed acelerarse; **to** ~ **o.s. up**
levantarse
picket ['pɪkɪt] *n* piquete *m* ♦ *vt* piquetear
pickle ['pɪkl] *n* (also: ~**s**: as condiment)
escabeche *m*; (fig: mess) apuro ♦ *vt*
encurtir
pickpocket ['pɪkpɔkɪt] *n* carterista *m/f*
pickup ['pɪkʌp] *n* (small truck) furgoneta
picnic ['pɪknɪk] *n* merienda ♦ *vi* ir de
merienda; ~ **area** *n* zona de picnic;
(AUT) área de descanso
picture ['pɪktʃə*] *n* cuadro; (painting)
pintura; (photograph) fotografía; (TV)
imagen *f*; (film) película; (fig: description)
descripción *f*; (: situation) situación *f* ♦ *vt*
(imagine) imaginar; ~**s** *npl*: **the** ~**s** (BRIT)
el cine; ~ **book** *n* libro de dibujos
picturesque [pɪktʃə'resk] *adj* pintoresco

pie [paɪ] n pastel m; (open) tarta; (small: of meat) empanada

piece [piːs] n pedazo, trozo; (of cake) trozo; (item): **a ~ of clothing/furniture/advice** una prenda (de vestir)/un mueble/un consejo ♦ vt: **to ~ together** juntar; (TECH) armar; **to take to ~s** desmontar; **~meal** adv poco a poco; **~work** n trabajo a destajo

pie chart n gráfico de sectores or tarta

pier [pɪə*] n muelle m, embarcadero

pierce [pɪəs] vt perforar

piercing [ˈpɪəsɪŋ] adj penetrante

pig [pɪg] n cerdo (SP), puerco (SP), chancho (AM); (pej: unkind person) asqueroso; (: greedy person) glotón/ona m/f

pigeon [ˈpɪdʒən] n paloma; (as food) pichón m; **~hole** n casilla

piggy bank [ˈpɪgɪ-] n hucha (en forma de cerdito)

pig: **~headed** [ˈpɪgˈhedɪd] adj terco, testarudo; **~let** [ˈpɪglɪt] n cochinillo; **~skin** n piel f de cerdo; **~sty** [ˈpɪgstaɪ] n pocilga; **~tail** n (girl's) trenza; (Chinese, TAUR) coleta

pike [paɪk] n (fish) lucio

pilchard [ˈpɪltʃəd] n sardina

pile [paɪl] n montón m; (of carpet, cloth) pelo ♦ vt (also: ~ up) amontonar; (fig) acumular ♦ vi (also: ~ up) amontonarse; acumularse; ~ **into** vt fus (car) meterse en; **~s** [paɪlz] npl (MED) almorranas fpl, hemorroides mpl; **~-up** n (AUT) accidente m múltiple

pilfering [ˈpɪlfərɪŋ] n ratería

pilgrim [ˈpɪlgrɪm] n peregrino/a; **~age** n peregrinación f, romería

pill [pɪl] n píldora; **the ~** la píldora

pillage [ˈpɪlɪdʒ] vt pillar, saquear

pillar [ˈpɪlə*] n pilar m; **~ box** (BRIT) n buzón m

pillion [ˈpɪljən] n (of motorcycle) asiento trasero

pillow [ˈpɪləu] n almohada; **~case** n funda

pilot [ˈpaɪlət] n piloto ♦ cpd (scheme etc) piloto ♦ vt pilotar; ~ **light** n piloto

pimp [pɪmp] n chulo (SP), cafiche m (AM)

pimple [ˈpɪmpl] n grano

PIN n abbr (= personal identification number) número personal

pin [pɪn] n alfiler m ♦ vt prender (con alfiler); **~s and needles** hormigueo; **to ~ sb down** (fig) hacer que uno concrete; **to ~ sth on sb** (fig) colgarle a uno el sambenito de algo

pinafore [ˈpɪnəfɔː*] n delantal m; ~ **dress** (BRIT) n mandil m

pinball [ˈpɪnbɔːl] n mesa americana

pincers [ˈpɪnsəz] npl pinzas fpl, tenazas fpl

pinch [pɪntʃ] n (of salt etc) pizca ♦ vt pellizcar; (inf: steal) birlar; **at a ~** en caso de apuro

pincushion [ˈpɪnkuʃən] n acerico

pine [paɪn] n (also: ~ **tree, wood**) pino ♦ vi: **to ~ for** suspirar por; ~ **away** vi morirse de pena

pineapple [ˈpaɪnæpl] n piña, ananás m

ping [pɪŋ] n (noise) sonido agudo; **~-pong** ® n pingpong ® m

pink [pɪŋk] adj rosado, (color de) rosa ♦ n (colour) rosa; (BOT) clavel m, clavellina

pinpoint [ˈpɪnpɔɪnt] vt precisar

pint [paɪnt] n pinta (BRIT = 568cc; US = 473cc); (BRIT: inf: of beer) pinta de cerveza, ≈ jarra (SP)

pin-up n fotografía erótica

pioneer [paɪəˈnɪə*] n pionero/a

pious [ˈpaɪəs] adj piadoso, devoto

pip [pɪp] n (seed) pepita; **the ~s** (BRIT) la señal

pipe [paɪp] n tubo, caño; (for smoking) pipa ♦ vt conducir en cañerías; **~s** npl (gen) cañería; (also: **bag~s**) gaita; ~ **cleaner** n limpiapipas m inv; ~ **dream** n sueño imposible; **~line** n (for oil) oleoducto; (for gas) gasoducto; **~r** n gaitero/a

piping [ˈpaɪpɪŋ] adv: **to be ~ hot** estar que quema

piquant [ˈpiːkənt] adj picante; (fig) agudo

pique [piːk] n pique m, resentimiento

pirate [ˈpaɪərət] n pirata m/f ♦ vt (cassette,

book) piratear; ~ **radio** (*BRIT*) *n* emisora pirata

Pisces ['paɪsiːz] *n* Piscis *m*

piss [pɪs] (*inf!*) *vi* mear; ~**ed** (*inf!*) *adj* (*drunk*) borracho

pistol ['pɪstl] *n* pistola

piston ['pɪstən] *n* pistón *m*, émbolo

pit [pɪt] *n* hoyo; (*also*: **coal** ~) mina; (*in garage*) foso de inspección; (*also*: **orchestra** ~) platea ♦ *vt*: **to ~ one's wits against sb** medir fuerzas con uno; ~**s** *npl* (*AUT*) box *m*

pitch [pɪtʃ] *n* (*MUS*) tono; (*BRIT*: *SPORT*) campo, terreno; (*fig*) punto; (*tar*) brea ♦ *vt* (*throw*) arrojar, lanzar ♦ *vi* (*fall*) caer(se); **to ~ a tent** montar una tienda (de campaña); ~-**black** *adj* negro como boca de lobo; ~**ed battle** *n* batalla campal

pitfall ['pɪtfɔːl] *n* riesgo

pith [pɪθ] *n* (*of orange*) médula

pithy ['pɪθɪ] *adj* (*fig*) jugoso

pitiful ['pɪtɪful] *adj* (*touching*) lastimoso, conmovedor(a)

pitiless ['pɪtɪlɪs] *adj* despiadado

pittance ['pɪtns] *n* miseria

pity ['pɪtɪ] *n* compasión *f*, piedad *f* ♦ *vt* compadecer(se de); **what a ~!** ¡qué pena!

pizza ['piːtsə] *n* pizza

placard ['plækɑːd] *n* letrero; (*in march etc*) pancarta

placate [plə'keɪt] *vt* apaciguar

place [pleɪs] *n* lugar *m*, sitio; (*seat*) plaza, asiento; (*post*) puesto; (*home*): **at/to his ~** en/a su casa; (*role: in society etc*) papel *m* ♦ *vt* (*object*) poner, colocar; (*identify*) reconocer; **to take ~** tener lugar; **to be ~d** (*in race, exam*) colocarse; **out of ~** (*not suitable*) fuera de lugar; **in the first ~** en primer lugar; **to change ~s with sb** cambiarse de sitio con uno; **~ of birth** lugar *m* de nacimiento

placid ['plæsɪd] *adj* apacible

plague [pleɪg] *n* plaga; (*MED*) peste *f* ♦ *vt* (*fig*) acosar, atormentar

plaice [pleɪs] *n inv* platija

plaid [plæd] *n* (*material*) tartán *m*

plain [pleɪn] *adj* (*unpatterned*) liso; (*clear*) claro, evidente; (*simple*) sencillo; (*not handsome*) poco atractivo ♦ *adv* claramente ♦ *n* llano, llanura; ~ **chocolate** *n* chocolate *m* amargo; ~-**clothes** *adj* (*police*) vestido de paisano; ~**ly** *adv* claramente

plaintiff ['pleɪntɪf] *n* demandante *m/f*

plait [plæt] *n* trenza

plan [plæn] *n* (*drawing*) plano; (*scheme*) plan *m*, proyecto ♦ *vt* proyectar, planificar ♦ *vi* hacer proyectos; **to ~ to do** pensar hacer

plane [pleɪn] *n* (*AVIAT*) avión *m*; (*MATH*, *fig*) plano; (*also*: ~ **tree**) plátano; (*tool*) cepillo

planet ['plænɪt] *n* planeta *m*

plank [plæŋk] *n* tabla

planner ['plænə*] *n* planificador(a) *m/f*

planning ['plænɪŋ] *n* planificación *f*; **family ~** planificación familiar; ~ **permission** *n* permiso para realizar obras

plant [plɑːnt] *n* planta; (*machinery*) maquinaria; (*factory*) fábrica ♦ *vt* plantar; (*field*) sembrar; (*bomb*) colocar

plaster ['plɑːstə*] *n* (*for walls*) yeso; (*also*: ~ **of Paris**) yeso mate; (*BRIT*: *also*: **sticking** ~) tirita (*SP*), esparadrapo, curita (*AM*) ♦ *vt* enyesar; (*cover*): **to ~ with** llenar *or* cubrir de; ~**ed** (*inf*) *adj* borracho; ~**er** *n* yesero

plastic ['plæstɪk] *n* plástico ♦ *adj* de plástico; ~ **bag** *n* bolsa de plástico

Plasticine ® ['plæstɪsiːn] (*BRIT*) *n* plastilina ®

plastic surgery *n* cirujía plástica

plate [pleɪt] *n* (*dish*) plato; (*metal, in book*) lámina; (*dental* ~) placa de dentadura postiza

plateau ['plætəu] (*pl* ~**s** *or* ~**x**) *n* meseta, altiplanicie *f*

plateaux ['plætəuz] *npl of* **plateau**

plate glass *n* vidrio cilindrado

platform ['plætfɔːm] *n* (*RAIL*) andén *m*; (*stage*, *BRIT*: *on bus*) plataforma; (*at meeting*) tribuna; (*POL*) programa *m* (electoral)

platinum ['plætɪnəm] *adj, n* platino

platoon [plə'tu:n] n pelotón m

platter ['plætə*] n fuente f

plausible ['plɔ:zɪbl] adj verosímil; (person) convincente

play [pleɪ] n (THEATRE) obra, comedia ♦ vt (game) jugar; (compete against) jugar contra; (instrument) tocar; (part: in play etc) hacer el papel de; (tape, record) poner ♦ vi jugar; (band) tocar; (tape, record) sonar; **to ~ safe** ir a lo seguro; **~ down** vt quitar importancia a; **~ up** vi (cause trouble to) dar guerra; **~boy** n playboy m; **~er** n jugador(a) m/f; (THEATRE) actor/actriz m/f; (MUS) músico/ a; **~ful** adj juguetón/ona; **~ground** n (in school) patio de recreo; (in park) parque m infantil; **~group** n jardín m de niños; **~ing card** n naipe m, carta; **~ing field** n campo de deportes; **~mate** n compañero/a de juego; **~off** n (SPORT) (partido de) desempate m; **~pen** n corral m; **~thing** n juguete m; **~time** n (SCOL) recreo; **~wright** n dramaturgo/a

plc abbr (= public limited company) ≈ S.A.

plea [pli:] n súplica, petición f; (LAW) alegato, defensa; **~ bargaining** n (LAW) acuerdo entre fiscal y defensor para agilizar los trámites judiciales

plead [pli:d] vt (LAW): **to ~ sb's case** defender a uno; (give as excuse) poner como pretexto ♦ vi (LAW) declararse; (beg): **to ~ with sb** suplicar or rogar a uno

pleasant ['plɛznt] adj agradable; **~ries** npl cortesías fpl

please [pli:z] excl ¡por favor! ♦ vt (give pleasure to) dar gusto a, agradar ♦ vi (think fit): **do as you ~** haz lo que quieras; (inf): ¡haz lo que quieras!, ¡como quieras!; **~d** adj (happy) alegre, contento; **~d (with)** satisfecho (de); **~d to meet you** ¡encantado!, ¡tanto gusto!; **pleasing** adj agradable, grato

pleasure ['plɛʒə*] n placer m, gusto; **"it's a ~"** "el gusto es mío"

pleat [pli:t] n pliegue m

pledge [plɛdʒ] n (promise) promesa, voto

♦ vt prometer

plentiful ['plɛntɪful] adj copioso, abundante

plenty ['plɛntɪ] n: **~ of** mucho(s)/a(s)

pliable ['plaɪəbl] adj flexible

pliers ['plaɪəz] npl alicates mpl, tenazas fpl

plight [plaɪt] n situación f difícil

plimsolls ['plɪmsəlz] (BRIT) npl zapatos mpl de tenis

plinth [plɪnθ] n plinto

plod [plɔd] vi caminar con paso pesado; (fig) trabajar laboriosamente

plonk [plɔŋk] (inf) n (BRIT: wine) vino peleón ♦ vt: **to ~ sth down** dejar caer algo

plot [plɔt] n (scheme) complot m, conjura; (of story, play) argumento; (of land) terreno, lote m (AM) ♦ vt (mark out) trazar; (conspire) tramar, urdir ♦ vi conspirar

plough [plau] (US **plow**) n arado ♦ vt (earth) arar; **to ~ money into** invertir dinero en; **~ through** vt fus (crowd) abrirse paso por la fuerza por; **~man's lunch** (BRIT) n almuerzo de pub a base de pan, queso y encurtidos

pluck [plʌk] vt (fruit) coger (SP), recoger (AM); (musical instrument) puntear; (bird) desplumar; (eyebrows) depilar; **to ~ up courage** hacer de tripas corazón

plug [plʌg] n tapón m; (ELEC) enchufe m, clavija; (AUT: also: **spark(ing) ~**) bujía ♦ vt (hole) tapar; (inf: advertise) dar publicidad a; **~ in** vt (ELEC) enchufar

plum [plʌm] n (fruit) ciruela

plumb [plʌm] vt: **to ~ the depths of** alcanzar los mayores extremos de

plumber ['plʌmə*] n fontanero/a (SP), plomero/a (AM)

plumbing ['plʌmɪŋ] n (trade) fontanería, plomería; (piping) cañería

plummet ['plʌmɪt] vi: **to ~ (down)** caer a plomo

plump [plʌmp] adj rechoncho, rollizo ♦ vi: **to ~ for** (inf: choose) optar por; **~ up** vt mullir

plunder ['plʌndə*] vt pillar, saquear

plunge [plʌndʒ] n zambullida ♦ vt sumergir, hundir ♦ vi (fall) caer; (dive) saltar; (person) arrojarse; **to take the ~** lanzarse; **plunging** adj: **plunging neckline** escote m pronunciado

pluperfect [plu:ˈpəːfɪkt] n pluscuamperfecto

plural [ˈpluərl] adj plural ♦ n plural m

plus [plʌs] n (also: **~ sign**) signo más ♦ prep más, y, además de; **ten/twenty ~** más de diez/veinte

plush [plʌʃ] adj lujoso

plutonium [pluːˈtəʊnɪəm] n plutonio

ply [plaɪ] vt (a trade) ejercer ♦ vi (ship) ir y venir ♦ n (of wool, rope) cabo; **to ~ sb with drink** insistir en ofrecer a uno muchas copas; **~wood** n madera contrachapada

P.M. n abbr = **Prime Minister**

p.m. adv abbr (= post meridiem) de la tarde or noche

pneumatic [njuːˈmætɪk] adj neumático; **~ drill** n martillo neumático

pneumonia [njuːˈməʊnɪə] n pulmonía

poach [pəʊtʃ] vt (cook) escalfar; (steal) cazar (or pescar) en vedado ♦ vi cazar (or pescar) en vedado; **~ed** adj escalfado; **~er** n cazador(a) m/f furtivo/a

P.O. Box n abbr = **Post Office Box**

pocket [ˈpɔkɪt] n bolsillo; (fig: small area) bolsa ♦ vt meter en el bolsillo; (steal) embolsar; **to be out of ~** (BRIT) salir perdiendo; **~book** (US) n cartera; **~ calculator** n calculadora de bolsillo; **~ knife** n navaja; **~ money** n asignación f

pod [pɔd] n vaina

podgy [ˈpɔdʒɪ] adj gordinflón/ona

podiatrist [pɔˈdiːətrɪst] (US) n pedicuro/a

poem [ˈpəʊɪm] n poema m

poet [ˈpəʊɪt] n poeta m/f; **~ic** [-ˈetɪk] adj poético; **~ry** n poesía

poignant [ˈpɔɪnjənt] adj conmovedor(a)

point [pɔɪnt] n punto; (tip) punta; (purpose) fin m, propósito; (use) utilidad f; (significant part) lo significativo; (moment) momento; (ELEC) toma (de corriente); (also: **decimal ~**): **2 ~ 3 (2.3)** dos coma

tres (2,3) ♦ vt señalar; (gun etc): **to ~ at sb** apuntar algo a uno ♦ vi: **to ~ at** señalar; **~s** npl (AUT) contactos mpl; (RAIL) agujas fpl; **to be on the ~ of doing sth** estar a punto de hacer algo; **to make a ~ of** poner empeño en; **to get/miss the ~** comprender/no comprender; **to come to the ~** ir al meollo; **there's no ~ (in doing)** no tiene sentido (hacer); **~ out** vt señalar; **~ to** vt fus (fig) indicar, señalar; **~-blank** adv (say, refuse) sin más hablar; (also: **at ~-blank range**) a quemarropa; **~ed** adj (shape) puntiagudo, afilado; (remark) intencionado; **~edly** adv intencionadamente; **~er** n (needle) aguja, indicador m; **~less** adj sin sentido; **~ of view** n punto de vista

poise [pɔɪz] n aplomo, elegancia

poison [ˈpɔɪzn] n veneno ♦ vt envenenar; **~ing** n envenenamiento; **~ous** adj venenoso; (fumes etc) tóxico

poke [pəʊk] vt (jab with finger, stick etc) empujar; (put): **to ~ sth in(to)** introducir algo en; **~ about** vi fisgonear

poker [ˈpəʊkə*] n atizador m; (CARDS) póker m

poky [ˈpəʊkɪ] adj estrecho

Poland [ˈpəʊlənd] n Polonia

polar [ˈpəʊlə*] adj polar; **~ bear** n oso polar

Pole [pəʊl] n polaco/a

pole [pəʊl] n palo; (fixed) poste m; (GEO) polo; **~ bean** (US) n ≈ judía verde; **~ vault** n salto con pértiga

police [pəˈliːs] n policía ♦ vt vigilar; **~ car** n coche-patrulla m; **~man** (irreg) n policía m, guardia m; **~ state** n estado policial; **~ station** n comisaría; **~woman** (irreg) n mujer f policía

policy [ˈpɔlɪsɪ] n política; (also: **insurance ~**) póliza

polio [ˈpəʊlɪəʊ] n polio f

Polish [ˈpəʊlɪʃ] adj polaco ♦ n (LING) polaco

polish [ˈpɔlɪʃ] n (for shoes) betún m; (for floor) cera (de lustrar); (shine) brillo, lustre m; (fig: refinement) educación f ♦ vt (*shoes*) limpiar; (*make shiny*) pulir, sacar brillo a; ~ **off** *vt* (*food*) despachar; ~**ed** *adj* (*fig: person*) elegante

polite [pə'laɪt] *adj* cortés, atento; ~**ness** *n* cortesía

political [pə'lɪtɪkl] *adj* político; ~**ly** *adv* políticamente; ~**ly correct** políticamente correcto

politician [pɔlɪ'tɪʃən] *n* político/a

politics ['pɔlɪtɪks] *n* política

poll [pəul] *n* (*election*) votación *f*; (*also*: **opinion ~**) sondeo, encuesta ♦ *vt* encuestar; (*votes*) obtener

pollen ['pɔlən] *n* polen *m*

polling day ['pəulɪŋ-] *n* día *m* de elecciones

polling station *n* centro electoral

pollute [pə'lu:t] *vt* contaminar

pollution [pə'lu:ʃən] *n* polución *f*, contaminación *f* del medio ambiente

polo ['pəuləu] *n* (*sport*) polo; ~-**necked** *adj* de cuello vuelto; ~ **shirt** *n* polo, niqui *m*

polyester [pɔlɪ'estə*] *n* poliéster *m*

polystyrene [pɔlɪ'staɪri:n] *n* poliestireno

polythene ['pɔlɪθi:n] (*BRIT*) *n* politeno

pomegranate ['pɔmɪgrænɪt] *n* granada

pomp [pɔmp] *n* pompa

pompous ['pɔmpəs] *adj* pomposo

pond [pɔnd] *n* (*natural*) charca; (*artificial*) estanque *m*

ponder ['pɔndə*] *vt* meditar

ponderous ['pɔndərəs] *adj* pesado

pong [pɔŋ] (*BRIT: inf*) *n* hedor *m*

pony ['pəunɪ] *n* poney *m*, jaca, potro (*AM*); ~**tail** *n* cola de caballo; ~ **trekking** (*BRIT*) *n* excursión *f* a caballo

poodle ['pu:dl] *n* caniche *m*

pool [pu:l] *n* (*natural*) charca; (*also*: **swimming ~**) piscina (*SP*), alberca (*AM*); (*fig: of light etc*) charco; (*SPORT*) chapolín *m* ♦ *vt* juntar; ~**s** *npl* (*football ~s*) quinielas *fpl*; **typing ~** servicio de mecanografía

poor [puə*] *adj* pobre; (*bad*) de mala calidad ♦ *npl*: **the ~** los pobres; ~**ly** *adj* mal, enfermo ♦ *adv* mal

pop [pɔp] *n* (*sound*) ruido seco; (*MUS*) (*música*) pop *m*; (*inf: father*) papá *m*; (*drink*) gaseosa ♦ *vt* (*put quickly*) meter (de prisa) ♦ *vi* reventar; (*cork*) saltar; ~ **in/out** *vi* entrar/salir un momento; ~ **up** *vi* aparecer inesperadamente; ~**corn** *n* palomitas *fpl*

pope [pəup] *n* papa *m*

poplar ['pɔplə*] *n* álamo

popper ['pɔpə*] (*BRIT*) *n* automático

poppy ['pɔpɪ] *n* amapola

Popsicle ® ['pɔpsɪkl] (*US*) *n* polo

pop star *n* estrella del pop

populace ['pɔpjuləs] *n* pueblo, plebe *f*

popular ['pɔpjulə*] *adj* popular

population [pɔpju'leɪʃən] *n* población *f*

porcelain ['pɔ:slɪn] *n* porcelana

porch [pɔ:tʃ] *n* pórtico, entrada; (*US*) veranda

porcupine ['pɔ:kjupaɪn] *n* puerco *m* espín

pore [pɔ:*] *n* poro ♦ *vi*: **to ~ over** engolfarse en

pork [pɔ:k] *n* carne *f* de cerdo (*SP*) or chancho (*AM*)

pornography [pɔ:'nɔgrəfɪ] *n* pornografía

porpoise ['pɔ:pəs] *n* marsopa

porridge ['pɔrɪdʒ] *n* gachas *fpl* de avena

port [pɔ:t] *n* puerto; (*NAUT: left side*) babor *m*; (*wine*) vino de Oporto; ~ **of call** puerto de escala

portable ['pɔ:təbl] *adj* portátil

porter ['pɔ:tə*] *n* (*for luggage*) maletero; (*doorkeeper*) portero/a, conserje *m/f*

portfolio [pɔ:t'fəulɪəu] *n* cartera

porthole ['pɔ:thəul] *n* portilla

portion ['pɔ:ʃən] *n* porción *f*; (*of food*) ración *f*

portrait ['pɔ:treɪt] *n* retrato

portray [pɔ:'treɪ] *vt* retratar; (*subj: actor*) representar

Portugal ['pɔ:tjugl] *n* Portugal *m*

Portuguese [pɔ:tju'gi:z] *adj* portugués/esa ♦ *n inv* portugués/esa *m/f*; (*LING*) portugués *m*

pose [pəuz] *n* postura, actitud *f* ♦ *vi* (*pretend*): **to ~ as** hacerse pasar por ♦ *vt* (*question*) plantear; **to ~ for** posar para

posh [pɒʃ] (inf) adj elegante, de lujo
position [pəˈzɪʃən] n posición f; (job) puesto; (situation) situación f ♦ vt colocar
positive [ˈpɒzɪtɪv] adj positivo; (certain) seguro; (definite) definitivo
possess [pəˈzes] vt poseer; **~ion** [pəˈzeʃən] n posesión f; **~ions** npl (belongings) pertenencias fpl
possibility [pɒsɪˈbɪlɪtɪ] n posibilidad f
possible [ˈpɒsɪbl] adj posible; **as big as ~** lo más grande posible; **possibly** adv posiblemente; **I cannot possibly come** me es imposible venir
post [pəust] n (BRIT: system) correos mpl; (BRIT: letters, delivery) correo; (job, situation) puesto; (pole) poste m ♦ vt (BRIT: send by post) echar al correo; (BRIT: appoint): **to ~ to** enviar a; **~age** n porte m, franqueo; **~age stamp** n sello de correos; **~al** adj postal, de correos; **~al order** n giro postal; **~box** (BRIT) n buzón m; **~card** n tarjeta postal; **~code** (BRIT) n código postal
postdate [pəustˈdeɪt] vt (cheque) poner fecha adelantada a
poster [ˈpəustə*] n cartel m
poste restante [pəustˈrestɔnt] (BRIT) n lista de correos
postgraduate [ˈpəustˈɡrædjuət] n posgraduado/a
posthumous [ˈpɒstjuməs] adj póstumo
postman [ˈpəustmən] (irreg) n cartero
postmark [ˈpəustmɑːk] n matasellos m inv
post-mortem [-ˈmɔːtəm] n autopsia
post office n (building) (oficina de) correos m; (organization): **the Post Office** Administración f General de Correos; **Post Office Box** n apartado postal (SP), casilla de correos (AM)
postpone [pəsˈpəun] vt aplazar
postscript [ˈpəustskrɪpt] n posdata
posture [ˈpɒstʃə*] n postura, actitud f
postwar [pəustˈwɔː*] adj de la posguerra
posy [ˈpəuzɪ] n ramillete m (de flores)
pot [pɒt] n (for cooking) olla; (tea~) tetera; (coffee~) cafetera; (for flowers) maceta; (for jam) tarro, pote m; (inf: marijuana) chocolate m ♦ vt (plant) poner en tiesto; **to go to ~** (inf) irse al traste
potato [pəˈteɪtəu] (pl **~es**) n patata (SP), papa (AM); **~ peeler** n pelapatatas m inv
potent [ˈpəutnt] adj potente, poderoso; (drink) fuerte
potential [pəˈtenʃl] adj potencial, posible ♦ n potencial m; **~ly** adv en potencia
pothole [ˈpɒthəul] n (in road) bache m; (BRIT: underground) gruta; **potholing** (BRIT) n: **to go potholing** dedicarse a la espeleología
potluck [pɒtˈlʌk] n: **to take ~** tomar lo que haya
potted [ˈpɒtɪd] adj (food) en conserva; (plant) en tiesto or maceta; (shortened) resumido
potter [ˈpɒtə*] n alfarero/a ♦ vi: **to ~ around, ~ about** (BRIT) hacer trabajitos; **~y** n cerámica; (factory) alfarería
potty [ˈpɒtɪ] n (child's) orinal m de niño
pouch [pautʃ] n (ZOOL) bolsa; (for tobacco) petaca
poultry [ˈpəultrɪ] n aves fpl de corral; (meat) pollo
pounce [pauns] vi: **to ~ on** precipitarse sobre
pound [paund] n libra (weight = 453g or 16oz; money = 100 pence) ♦ vt (beat) golpear; (crush) machacar ♦ vi (heart) latir; **~ sterling** n libra esterlina
pour [pɔː*] vt echar; (tea etc) servir ♦ vi correr, fluir; **to ~ sb a drink** servirle a uno una copa; **~ away** or **off** vt vaciar, verter; **~ in** vi (people) entrar en tropel; **~ out** vi salir en tropel ♦ vt (drink) echar, servir; (fig): **to ~ out one's feelings** desahogarse; **~ing** adj: **~ing rain** lluvia torrencial
pout [paut] vi hacer pucheros
poverty [ˈpɒvətɪ] n pobreza, miseria; **~-stricken** adj necesitado
powder [ˈpaudə*] n polvo; (face ~) polvos mpl ♦ vt polvorear; **to ~ one's face** empolvarse la cara; **~ compact** n polvera; **~ed milk** n leche f en polvo; **~ room** n aseos mpl

power ['pauə*] n poder m; (strength) fuerza; (nation, TECH) potencia; (drive) empuje m; (ELEC) fuerza, energía ♦ vt impulsar; **to be in ~** (POL) estar en el poder; **~ cut** (BRIT) n apagón m; **~ed** adj: **~ed by** impulsado por; **~ failure** n = **~ cut**; **~ful** adj poderoso; (engine) potente; (speech etc) convincente; **~less** adj: **~less (to do)** incapaz (de hacer); **~ point** (BRIT) n enchufe m; **~ station** n central f eléctrica

p.p. abbr (= per procurationem): **~ J. Smith** p.p. (por poder de) J. Smith; (= pages) págs

PR n abbr = **public relations**

practical ['præktɪkl] adj práctico; **~ity** [-'kælɪtɪ] n factibilidad f; **~ joke** n broma pesada; **~ly** adv (almost) casi

practice ['præktɪs] n (habit) costumbre f; (exercise) práctica, ejercicio; (training) adiestramiento; (MED: of profession) práctica, ejercicio; (MED, LAW: business) consulta ♦ vt, vi (US) = **practise**; **in ~** (in reality) en la práctica; **out of ~** desentrenado

practise ['præktɪs] (US **practice**) vt (carry out) practicar; (profession) ejercer; (train at) practicar ♦ vi ejercer; (train) practicar; **practising** adj (Christian etc) practicante; (lawyer) en ejercicio

practitioner [præk'tɪʃənə*] n (MED) médico/a

prairie ['prɛərɪ] n pampa

praise [preɪz] n alabanza(s) f(pl), elogio(s) m(pl) ♦ vt alabar, elogiar; **~worthy** adj loable

pram [præm] (BRIT) n cochecito de niño

prank [præŋk] n travesura

prawn [prɔːn] n gamba; **~ cocktail** n cóctel m de gambas

pray [preɪ] vi rezar

prayer [prɛə*] n oración f, rezo; (entreaty) ruego, súplica

preach [priːtʃ] vi (also fig) predicar; **~er** n predicador(a) m/f

precaution [prɪ'kɔːʃən] n precaución f

precede [prɪ'siːd] vt, vi preceder

precedent ['presɪdənt] n precedente m

preceding [prɪ'siːdɪŋ] adj anterior

precinct ['priːsɪŋkt] n recinto; **~s** npl contornos mpl; **pedestrian ~** (BRIT) zona peatonal; **shopping ~** (BRIT) centro comercial

precious ['preʃəs] adj precioso

precipitate [prɪ'sɪpɪteɪt] vt precipitar

precise [prɪ'saɪs] adj preciso, exacto; **~ly** adv precisamente, exactamente

precocious [prɪ'kəuʃəs] adj precoz

precondition [priːkən'dɪʃən] n condición f previa

predecessor ['priːdɪsesə*] n antecesor(a) m/f

predicament [prɪ'dɪkəmənt] n apuro

predict [prɪ'dɪkt] vt pronosticar; **~able** adj previsible; **~ion** [-'dɪkʃən] n predicción f

predominantly [prɪ'dɔmɪnəntlɪ] adv en su mayoría

pre-empt [priː'emt] vt adelantarse a

preen [priːn] vt: **to ~ itself** (bird) limpiarse (las plumas); **to ~ o.s.** pavonearse

preface ['prefəs] n prefacio

prefect ['priːfekt] (BRIT) n (in school) monitor(a) m/f

prefer [prɪ'fɔː*] vt preferir; **to ~ doing** or **to do** preferir hacer; **~able** ['prefrəbl] adj preferible; **~ably** ['prefrəblɪ] adv de preferencia; **~ence** ['prefrəns] n preferencia; (priority) prioridad f; **~ential** [prefə'renʃəl] adj preferente

prefix ['priːfɪks] n prefijo

pregnancy ['pregnənsɪ] n (of woman) embarazo; (of animal) preñez f

pregnant ['pregnənt] adj (woman) embarazada; (animal) preñada

prehistoric ['priːhɪs'tɔrɪk] adj prehistórico

prejudice ['predʒudɪs] n prejuicio; **~d** adj (person) predispuesto

premarital ['priː'mærɪtl] adj premarital

premature ['prematʃuə*] adj prematuro

premier ['premɪə*] adj primero, principal ♦ n (POL) primer(a) ministro/a

première ['premɪɛə*] n estreno

premise ['premɪs] n premisa; **~s** npl (of business etc) local m; **on the ~s** en el lugar mismo

premium ['pri:mɪəm] *n* premio; (*insurance*) prima; **to be at a ~** ser muy solicitado; **~ bond** (*BRIT*) *n* bono del estado que participa en una lotería nacional

premonition [premə'nɪʃən] *n* presentimiento

preoccupied [pri:'ɔkjupaɪd] *adj* ensimismado

prep [prep] *n* (*SCOL: study*) deberes *mpl*

prepaid [pri:'peɪd] *adj* porte pagado

preparation [prepə'reɪʃən] *n* preparación *f*; **~s** *npl* preparativos *mpl*

preparatory [prɪ'pærətərɪ] *adj* preparatorio, preliminar; **~ school** *n* escuela preparatoria

prepare [prɪ'pɛə*] *vt* preparar, disponer; (*CULIN*) preparar ♦ *vi*: **to ~ for** (*action*) prepararse *or* disponerse para; (*event*) hacer preparativos para; **~d to** dispuesto a; **~d for** listo para

preposition [prepə'zɪʃən] *n* preposición *f*

preposterous [prɪ'pɔstərəs] *adj* absurdo, ridículo

prep school *n* = **preparatory school**

prerequisite [pri:'rekwɪzɪt] *n* requisito

Presbyterian [prezbɪ'tɪərɪən] *adj, n* presbiteriano/a *m/f*

preschool ['pri:'sku:l] *adj* preescolar

prescribe [prɪ'skraɪb] *vt* (*MED*) recetar

prescription [prɪ'skrɪpʃən] *n* (*MED*) receta

presence ['prezns] *n* presencia; **in sb's ~** en presencia de uno; **~ of mind** aplomo

present [*adj, n* preznt, *vb* prɪ'zent] *adj* (*in attendance*) presente; (*current*) actual ♦ *n* (*gift*) regalo; (*actuality*): **the ~** la actualidad, el presente ♦ *vt* (*introduce, describe*) presentar; (*expound*) exponer; (*give*) presentar, dar, ofrecer; (*THEATRE*) representar; **to give sb a ~** regalar algo a uno; **at ~** actualmente; **~able** [prɪ'zentəbl] *adj*: **to make o.s. ~able** arreglarse; **~ation** [-'teɪʃən] *n* presentación *f*; (*of report etc*) exposición *f*; (*formal ceremony*) entrega de un regalo; **~-day** *adj* actual; **~er** [prɪ'zentə*] *n* (*RADIO, TV*) locutor(a) *m/f*; **~ly** *adv* (*soon*) dentro de poco;

(*now*) ahora

preservative [prɪ'zɜ:vətɪv] *n* conservante *m*

preserve [prɪ'zɜ:v] *vt* (*keep safe*) preservar, proteger; (*maintain*) mantener; (*food*) conservar ♦ *n* (*for game*) coto, vedado; (*often pl: jam*) conserva, confitura

president ['prezɪdənt] *n* presidente *m/f*; **~ial** [-'denʃl] *adj* presidencial

press [pres] *n* (*newspapers*): **the P~** la prensa; (*printer's*) imprenta; (*of button*) pulsación *f* ♦ *vt* empujar; (*button etc*) apretar; (*clothes: iron*) planchar; (*put pressure on: person*) presionar; (*insist*): **to ~ sth on sb** insistir en que uno acepte algo ♦ *vi* (*squeeze*) apretar; (*pressurize*): **to ~ for** presionar por; **we are ~ed for time/money** estamos apurados de tiempo/dinero; **~ on** *vi* avanzar; (*hurry*) apretar el paso; **~ agency** *n* agencia de prensa; **~ conference** *n* rueda de prensa; **~ing** *adj* apremiante; **~ stud** (*BRIT*) *n* botón *m* de presión; **~-up** (*BRIT*) *n* plancha

pressure ['preʃə*] *n* presión *f*; **to put ~ on sb** presionar a uno; **~ cooker** *n* olla a presión; **~ gauge** *n* manómetro; **~ group** *n* grupo de presión; **pressurized** *adj* (*container*) a presión

prestige [pres'ti:ʒ] *n* prestigio

presumably [prɪ'zju:məblɪ] *adv* es de suponer que, cabe presumir que

presume [prɪ'zju:m] *vt*: **to ~ (that)** presumir (que), suponer (que)

pretence [prɪ'tens] (*US* **pretense**) *n* fingimiento; **under false ~s** con engaños

pretend [prɪ'tend] *vt, vi* (*feign*) fingir

pretentious [prɪ'tenʃəs] *adj* presumido; (*ostentatious*) ostentoso, aparatoso

pretext ['pri:tekst] *n* pretexto

pretty ['prɪtɪ] *adj* bonito (*SP*), lindo (*AM*) ♦ *adv* bastante

prevail [prɪ'veɪl] *vi* (*gain mastery*) prevalecer; (*be current*) predominar; **~ing** *adj* (*dominant*) predominante

prevalent ['prevələnt] *adj* (*widespread*) extendido

prevent [prɪ'vɛnt] *vt*: **to ~ sb from doing sth** impedir a uno hacer algo; **to ~ sth from happening** evitar que ocurra algo; **~ative** *adj* = **preventive**; **~ive** *adj* preventivo

preview ['pri:vju:] *n* (*of film*) preestreno

previous ['pri:vɪəs] *adj* previo, anterior; **~ly** *adv* antes

prewar [pri:'wɔ:*] *adj* de antes de la guerra

prey [preɪ] *n* presa ♦ *vi*: **to ~ on** (*feed on*) alimentarse de; **it was ~ing on his mind** le preocupaba, le obsesionaba

price [praɪs] *n* precio ♦ *vt* (*goods*) fijar el precio de; **~less** *adj* que no tiene precio; **~ list** *n* tarifa

prick [prɪk] *n* (*sting*) picadura ♦ *vt* pinchar; (*hurt*) picar; **to ~ up one's ears** aguzar el oído

prickle ['prɪkl] *n* (*sensation*) picor *m*; (*BOT*) espina; **prickly** *adj* espinoso; (*fig: person*) enojadizo; **prickly heat** *n* sarpullido causado por exceso de calor

pride [praɪd] *n* orgullo; (*pej*) soberbia ♦ *vt*: **to ~ o.s. on** enorgullecerse de

priest [pri:st] *n* sacerdote *m*; **~hood** *n* sacerdocio

prim [prɪm] *adj* (*demure*) remilgado; (*prudish*) gazmoño

primarily ['praɪmərɪlɪ] *adv* ante todo

primary ['praɪmərɪ] *adj* (*first in importance*) principal ♦ *n* (*US: POL*) (elección *f*) primaria; **~ school** (*BRIT*) *n* escuela primaria

prime [praɪm] *adj* primero, principal; (*excellent*) selecto, de primera clase ♦ *n*: **in the ~ of life** en la flor de la vida ♦ *vt* (*wood, fig*) preparar; **~ example** ejemplo típico; **P~ Minister** *n* primer(a) ministro/a

primeval [praɪ'mi:vəl] *adj* primitivo

primitive ['prɪmɪtɪv] *adj* primitivo; (*crude*) rudimentario

primrose ['prɪmrəuz] *n* primavera, prímula

Primus (stove) ® ['praɪməs-] (*BRIT*) *n* hornillo de camping

prince [prɪns] *n* príncipe *m*

princess [prɪn'sɛs] *n* princesa

principal ['prɪnsɪpl] *adj* principal, mayor ♦ *n* director(a) *m/f*; **~ity** [-'pælɪtɪ] *n* principado

principle ['prɪnsɪpl] *n* principio; **in ~** en principio; **on ~** por principio

print [prɪnt] *n* (*foot~*) huella; (*finger~*) huella dactilar; (*letters*) letra de molde; (*fabric*) estampado; (*ART*) grabado; (*PHOT*) impresión *f* ♦ *vt* imprimir; (*cloth*) estampar; (*write in capitals*) escribir en letras de molde; **out of ~** agotado; **~ed matter** *n* impresos *mpl*; **~er** *n* (*person*) impresor(a) *m/f*; (*machine*) impresora; **~ing** *n* (*art*) imprenta; (*act*) impresión *f*; **~out** *n* (*COMPUT*) impresión *f*

prior ['praɪə*] *adj* anterior, previo; (*more important*) más importante; **~ to** antes de

priority [praɪ'ɔrɪtɪ] *n* prioridad *f*; **to have ~ (over)** tener prioridad (sobre)

prison ['prɪzn] *n* cárcel *f*, prisión *f* ♦ *cpd* carcelario; **~er** *n* (*in prison*) preso/a; (*captured person*) prisionero; **~er-of-war** *n* prisionero de guerra

privacy ['prɪvəsɪ] *n* intimidad *f*

private ['praɪvɪt] *adj* (*personal*) particular; (*property, industry, discussion etc*) privado; (*person*) reservado; (*place*) tranquilo ♦ *n* soldado raso; **"~"** (*on envelope*) "confidencial"; (*on door*) "prohibido el paso"; **in ~** en privado; **~ enterprise** *n* empresa privada; **~ eye** *n* detective *m/f* privado/a; **~ property** *n* propiedad *f* privada; **~ school** *n* colegio particular

privet ['prɪvɪt] *n* alheña

privilege ['prɪvɪlɪdʒ] *n* privilegio; (*prerogative*) prerrogativa

privy ['prɪvɪ] *adj*: **to be ~ to** estar enterado de

prize [praɪz] *n* premio ♦ *adj* de primera clase ♦ *vt* apreciar, estimar; **~-giving** *n* distribución *f* de premios; **~winner** *n* premiado/a

pro [prəu] *n* (*SPORT*) profesional *m/f* ♦ *prep* a favor de; **the ~s and cons** los pros y los contras

probability [prɔbə'bɪlɪtɪ] *n* probabilidad *f*;

in all ~ con toda probabilidad

probable ['prɒbəbl] adj probable

probably ['prɒbəblɪ] adv probablemente

probation [prə'beɪʃən] n: **on ~** (employee) a prueba; (LAW) en libertad condicional

probe [prəub] n (MED, SPACE) sonda; (enquiry) encuesta, investigación f ♦ vt sondar; (investigate) investigar

problem ['prɒbləm] n problema m

procedure [prə'siːdʒə*] n procedimiento; (bureaucratic) trámites mpl

proceed [prə'siːd] vi (do afterwards): **to ~ to do sth** proceder a hacer algo; (continue): **to ~ (with)** continuar or seguir (con); **~ings** npl acto(s) (pl); (LAW) proceso; **~s** ['prəusiːdz] npl (money) ganancias fpl, ingresos mpl

process ['prəuses] n proceso ♦ vt tratar, elaborar; **~ing** n tratamiento, elaboración f; (PHOT) revelado

procession [prə'seʃən] n desfile m; **funeral ~** cortejo fúnebre

pro-choice [prəu'tʃɔɪs] adj en favor del derecho a elegir de la madre

proclaim [prə'kleɪm] vt anunciar

procrastinate [prəu'kræstɪneɪt] vi demorarse

procure [prə'kjuə*] vt conseguir

prod [prɒd] vt empujar ♦ n empujón m

prodigy ['prɒdɪdʒɪ] n prodigio

produce [n 'prɒdjuːs, vt prə'djuːs] n (AGR) productos mpl agrícolas ♦ vt producir; (play, film, programme) presentar; **~r** n productor(a) m/f; (of film, programme) director(a) m/f; (of record) productor(a) m/f

product ['prɒdʌkt] n producto

production [prə'dʌkʃən] n producción f; (THEATRE) presentación f; **~ line** n línea de producción

productivity [prɒdʌk'tɪvɪtɪ] n productividad f

profession [prə'feʃən] n profesión f; **~al** adj profesional ♦ n profesional m/f; (skilled person) perito

professor [prə'fesə*] n (BRIT) catedrático/a; (US, Canada) profesor(a) m/f

proficient [prə'fɪʃənt] adj experto, hábil

profile ['prəufaɪl] n perfil m

profit ['prɒfɪt] n (COMM) ganancia ♦ vi: **to ~ by** or **from** aprovechar or sacar provecho de; **~ability** [-ə'bɪlɪtɪ] n rentabilidad f; **~able** adj (ECON) rentable

profound [prə'faund] adj profundo

profusely [prə'fjuːslɪ] adv profusamente

programme ['prəugræm] (US **program**) n programa m ♦ vt programar; **~r** (US **programer**) n programador(a) m/f; **programming** (US **programing**) n programación f

progress [n 'prəugres, vi prə'gres] n progreso; (development) desarrollo ♦ vi progresar, avanzar; **in ~** en curso; **~ive** [-'gresɪv] adj progresivo; (person) progresista

prohibit [prə'hɪbɪt] vt prohibir; **to ~ sb from doing sth** prohibir a uno hacer algo; **~ion** [-'bɪʃn] n prohibición f; (US): **P~ion** Ley f Seca

project [n 'prɒdʒekt, vb prə'dʒekt] n proyecto ♦ vt proyectar ♦ vi (stick out) salir, sobresalir; **~ion** [prə'dʒekʃən] n proyección f; (overhang) saliente m; **~or** [prə'dʒektə*] n proyector m

pro-life [prəu'laɪf] adj pro-vida

prolong [prə'lɒŋ] vt prolongar, extender

prom [prɒm] n abbr = **promenade**; (US: ball) baile m de gala

---

Prom

ⓘ El ciclo de conciertos de música clásica más conocido de Londres es el llamado the **Proms** (promenade concerts), que se celebra anualmente en el Royal Albert Hall. Su nombre se debe a que originalmente el público paseaba durante las actuaciones, costumbre que en la actualidad se mantiene de forma simbólica, permitiendo que parte de los asistentes permanezcan de pie. En Estados Unidos se llama **prom** a un baile de gala en un centro de educación secundaria o universitaria.

promenade [prɔmə'nɑːd] *n* (*by sea*) paseo marítimo; ~ **concert** (*BRIT*) *n* concierto (en que parte del público permanece de pie)

prominence ['prɔmɪnəns] *n* importancia

prominent ['prɔmɪnənt] *adj* (*standing out*) saliente; (*important*) eminente, importante

promiscuous [prə'mɪskjuəs] *adj* (*sexually*) promiscuo

promise ['prɔmɪs] *n* promesa ♦ *vt, vi* prometer; **promising** *adj* prometedor(a)

promote [prə'məut] *vt* (*employee*) ascender; (*product, pop star*) hacer propaganda por; (*ideas*) fomentar; ~**r** *n* (*of event*) promotor(a) *m/f*; (*of cause etc*) impulsor(a) *m/f*; **promotion** [-'məuʃən] *n* (*advertising campaign*) campaña de promoción *f*; (*in rank*) ascenso

prompt [prɔmpt] *adj* rápido ♦ *adv*: **at 6 o'clock** ~ a las seis en punto ♦ *n* (*COMPUT*) aviso ♦ *vt* (*urge*) mover, incitar; (*when talking*) instar; (*THEATRE*) apuntar; **to ~ sb to do sth** instar a uno a hacer algo; ~**ly** *adv* rápidamente; (*exactly*) puntualmente

prone [prəun] *adj* (*lying*) postrado; ~ **to** propenso a

prong [prɔŋ] *n* diente *m*, punta

pronoun ['prəunaun] *n* pronombre *m*

pronounce [prə'nauns] *vt* pronunciar; ~**d** *adj* (*marked*) marcado

pronunciation [prənʌnsɪ'eɪʃən] *n* pronunciación *f*

proof [pruːf] *n* prueba ♦ *adj*: ~ **against** a prueba de

prop [prɔp] *n* apoyo, (*fig*) sostén *m* ♦ *vt* (*also*: ~ **up**) apoyar; (*lean*): **to ~ sth against** apoyar algo contra

propaganda [prɔpə'gændə] *n* propaganda

propel [prə'pel] *vt* impulsar, propulsar; ~**ler** *n* hélice *f*

propensity [prə'pensɪtɪ] *n* propensión *f*

proper ['prɔpə*] *adj* (*suited, right*) propio; (*exact*) justo; (*seemly*) correcto, decente; (*authentic*) verdadero; (*referring to place*): **the village** ~ el pueblo mismo; ~**ly** *adv*

(*adequately*) correctamente; (*decently*) decentemente; ~ **noun** *n* nombre *m* propio

property ['prɔpətɪ] *n* propiedad *f*; (*personal*) bienes *mpl* muebles; ~ **owner** *n* dueño/a de propiedades

prophecy ['prɔfɪsɪ] *n* profecía

prophesy ['prɔfɪsaɪ] *vt* (*fig*) predecir

prophet ['prɔfɪt] *n* profeta *m*

proportion [prə'pɔːʃən] *n* proporción *f*; (*share*) parte *f*; ~**al** *adj*: ~**al (to)** en proporción (con); ~**al representation** *n* representación *f* proporcional; ~**ate** *adj*: ~**ate (to)** en proporción (con)

proposal [prə'pəuzl] *n* (*offer of marriage*) oferta de matrimonio; (*plan*) proyecto

propose [prə'pəuz] *vt* proponer ♦ *vi* declararse; **to ~ to do** tener intención de hacer

proposition [prɔpə'zɪʃən] *n* propuesta

proprietor [prə'praɪətə*] *n* propietario/a, dueño/a

propriety [prə'praɪətɪ] *n* decoro

pro rata [-'rɑːtə] *adv* a prorrateo

prose [prəuz] *n* prosa

prosecute ['prɔsɪkjuːt] *vt* (*LAW*) procesar; **prosecution** [-'kjuːʃən] *n* proceso, causa; (*accusing side*) acusación *f*; **prosecutor** *n* acusador(a) *m/f*; (*also*: **public prosecutor**) fiscal *m*

prospect [*n* 'prɔspekt, *vb* prə'spekt] *n* (*possibility*) posibilidad *f*; (*outlook*) perspectiva ♦ *vi*: **to ~ for** buscar; ~**s** *npl* (*for work etc*) perspectivas *fpl*; ~**ing** *n* prospección *f*; ~**ive** [prə'spektɪv] *adj* futuro

prospectus [prə'spektəs] *n* prospecto

prosper ['prɔspə*] *vi* prosperar; ~**ity** [-'sperɪtɪ] *n* prosperidad *f*; ~**ous** *adj* próspero

prostitute ['prɔstɪtjuːt] *n* prostituta; (*male*) *hombre que se dedica a la prostitución*

protect [prə'tekt] *vt* proteger; ~**ion** [-'tekʃən] *n* protección *f*; ~**ive** *adj* protector(a)

protein ['prəutiːn] *n* proteína

protest [*n* 'prəutest, *vb* prə'test] *n* protesta

♦ *vi*: **to ~ about** *or* **at/against** protestar de/contra ♦ *vt* (*insist*): **to ~ (that)** insistir en (que)

Protestant ['prɒtɪstənt] *adj, n* protestante *m/f*

protester [prə'testə*] *n* manifestante *m/f*

protracted [prə'træktɪd] *adj* prolongado

protrude [prə'truːd] *vi* salir, sobresalir

proud [praud] *adj* orgulloso; (*pej*) soberbio, altanero

prove [pruːv] *vt* probar; (*show*) demostrar
  ♦ *vi*: **to ~ (to be) correct** resultar correcto; **to ~ o.s.** probar su valía

proverb ['prɒvəːb] *n* refrán *m*

provide [prə'vaɪd] *vt* proporcionar, dar; **to ~ sb with sth** proveer a uno de algo; **~d (that)** *conj* con tal de que, a condición de que; **~ for** *vt fus* (*person*) mantener a; (*problem etc*) tener en cuenta; **providing** [prə'vaɪdɪŋ] *conj*: **providing (that)** a condición de que, con tal de que

province ['prɒvɪns] *n* provincia; (*fig*) esfera; **provincial** [prə'vɪnʃəl] *adj* provincial; (*pej*) provinciano

provision [prə'vɪʒən] *n* (*supplying*) suministro, abastecimiento; (*of contract etc*) disposición *f*; **~s** *npl* (*food*) comestibles *mpl*; **~al** *adj* provisional

proviso [prə'vaɪzəu] *n* condición *f*, estipulación *f*

provocative [prə'vɒkətɪv] *adj* provocativo

provoke [prə'vəuk] *vt* (*cause*) provocar, incitar; (*anger*) enojar

prowess ['prauɪs] *n* destreza

prowl [praul] *vi* (*also*: **~ about, ~ around**) merodear ♦ *n*: **on the ~** de merodeo; **~er** *n* merodeador(a) *m/f*

proxy ['prɒksɪ] *n*: **by ~** por poderes

prudent ['pruːdənt] *adj* prudente

prune [pruːn] *n* ciruela pasa ♦ *vt* podar

pry [praɪ] *vi*: **to ~ (into)** entrometerse (en)

PS *n abbr* (= *postscript*) P.D.

psalm [sɑːm] *n* salmo

pseudonym ['sjuːdənɪm] *n* seudónimo

psyche ['saɪkɪ] *n* psique *f*

psychiatric [saɪkɪ'ætrɪk] *adj* psiquiátrico

psychiatrist [saɪ'kaɪətrɪst] *n* psiquiatra *m/f*

psychic ['saɪkɪk] *adj* (*also*: **~al**) psíquico

psychoanalyse [saɪkəu'ænəlaɪz] *vt* psicoanalizar; **psychoanalysis** [-ə'nælɪsɪs] *n* psicoanálisis *m inv*

psychological [saɪkə'lɒdʒɪkl] *adj* psicológico

psychologist [saɪ'kɒlədʒɪst] *n* psicólogo/a

psychology [saɪ'kɒlədʒɪ] *n* psicología

PTO *abbr* (= *please turn over*) sigue

pub [pʌb] *n abbr* (= *public house*) pub *m*, bar *m*

---
pub

ℹ *Un* **pub** *es un local público donde se pueden consumir bebidas alcohólicas. La estricta regulación sobre la venta de alcohol prohíbe que se sirva a menores de 18 años y controla las horas de apertura, aunque éstas son más flexibles desde hace unos años. El* **pub** *es, además, un lugar de encuentro donde se sirven comidas ligeras o se juega a los dardos o al billar, entre otras actividades.*

---

puberty ['pjuːbətɪ] *n* pubertad *f*

public ['pʌblɪk] *adj* público ♦ *n*: **the ~** el público; **in ~** en público; **to make ~** hace público; **~ address system** *n* megafonía

publican ['pʌblɪkən] *n* tabernero/a

publication [pʌblɪ'keɪʃən] *n* publicación *f*

public: ~ company *n* sociedad *f* anónima; **~ convenience** (*BRIT*) *n* aseos *mpl* públicos (*SP*), sanitarios *mpl* (*AM*); **~ holiday** *n* día de fiesta (*SP*), (día) feriado (*AM*); **~ house** (*BRIT*) *n* bar *m*, pub *m*

publicity [pʌb'lɪsɪtɪ] *n* publicidad *f*

publicize ['pʌblɪsaɪz] *vt* publicitar

publicly ['pʌblɪklɪ] *adv* públicamente, en público

public: ~ opinion *n* opinión *f* pública; **~ relations** *n* relaciones *fpl* públicas; **~ school** *n* (*BRIT*) escuela privada; (*US*) instituto; **~-spirited** *adj* que tiene sentido del deber ciudadano; **~ transport** *n* transporte *m* público

publish ['pʌblɪʃ] *vt* publicar; **~er** *n*

(person) editor(a) *m/f*; *(firm)* editorial *f*; ~**ing** *n (industry)* industria del libro

ub lunch *n almuerzo que se sirve en un pub*; **to go for a ~** almorzar *o* comer en un pub

ucker ['pʌkə*] *vt (pleat)* arrugar; *(brow etc)* fruncir

udding ['pudɪŋ] *n* pudín *m*; *(BRIT: dessert)* postre *m*; **black ~** morcilla

uddle ['pʌdl] *n* charco

uff [pʌf] *n* soplo; *(of smoke, air)* bocanada; *(of breathing)* resoplido ♦ *vt*: **to ~ one's pipe** chupar la pipa ♦ *vi (pant)* jadear; **~ out** *vt* hinchar; ~ **pastry** *n* hojaldre *m*; **~y** *adj* hinchado

ull [pul] *n (tug)*: **to give sth a ~** dar un tirón a algo ♦ *vt* tirar de; *(press: trigger)* apretar; *(haul)* tirar, arrastrar; *(close: curtain)* echar ♦ *vi* tirar; **to ~ to pieces** hacer pedazos; **to not ~ one's punches** no andarse con bromas; **to ~ one's weight** hacer su parte; **to ~ o.s. together** sobreponerse; **to ~ sb's leg** tomar el pelo a uno; ~ **apart** *vt (break)* romper; ~ **down** *vt (building)* derribar; ~ **in** *vi (car etc)* parar (junto a la acera); *(train)* llegar a la estación; ~ **off** *vt (deal etc)* cerrar; ~ **out** *vi (car, train etc)* salir ♦ *vt* sacar, arrancar; ~ **over** *vi (AUT)* hacerse a un lado; ~ **through** *vi (MED)* reponerse; ~ **up** *vi (stop)* parar ♦ *vt (raise)* levantar; *(uproot)* arrancar, desarraigar

ulley ['pulɪ] *n* polea

ullover ['puləuvə*] *n* jersey *m*, suéter *m*

ulp [pʌlp] *n (of fruit)* pulpa

ulpit ['pulpɪt] *n* púlpito

ulsate [pʌl'seɪt] *vi* pulsar, latir

ulse [pʌls] *n (ANAT)* pulso; *(rhythm)* pulsación *f*; *(BOT)* legumbre *f*

ump [pʌmp] *n* bomba; *(shoe)* zapatilla ♦ *vt* sacar con una bomba; ~ **up** *vt* inflar

umpkin ['pʌmpkɪn] *n* calabaza

un [pʌn] *n* juego de palabras

unch [pʌntʃ] *n (blow)* golpe *m*, puñetazo; *(tool)* punzón *m*; *(drink)* ponche *m* ♦ *vt (hit)*: **to ~ sb/sth** dar un puñetazo *or* golpear a uno/algo; **~line** *n palabras que*

rematan un chiste; **~-up** *(BRIT: inf) n* riña

punctual ['pʌŋktjuəl] *adj* puntual

punctuation [pʌŋktju'eɪʃən] *n* puntuación *f*

puncture ['pʌŋktʃə*] *(BRIT) n* pinchazo ♦ *vt* pinchar

pungent ['pʌndʒənt] *adj* acre

punish ['pʌnɪʃ] *vt* castigar; **~ment** *n* castigo

punk [pʌŋk] *n (also: ~ rocker)* punki *m/f*; *(also: ~ rock)* música punk; *(US: inf: hoodlum)* rufián *m*

punt [pʌnt] *n (boat)* batea

punter ['pʌntə*] *(BRIT) n (gambler)* jugador(a) *m/f*; *(inf)* cliente *m/f*

puny ['pju:nɪ] *adj* débil

pup [pʌp] *n* cachorro

pupil ['pju:pl] *n* alumno/a; *(of eye)* pupila

puppet ['pʌpɪt] *n* títere *m*

puppy ['pʌpɪ] *n* cachorro, perrito

purchase ['pɜ:tʃɪs] *n* compra ♦ *vt* comprar; **~r** *n* comprador(a) *m/f*

pure [pjuə*] *adj* puro

purée ['pjuəreɪ] *n* puré *m*

purely ['pjuəlɪ] *adv* puramente

purge [pɜ:dʒ] *n (MED, POL)* purga ♦ *vt* purgar

purify ['pjuərɪfaɪ] *vt* purificar, depurar

purple ['pɜ:pl] *adj* purpúreo; morado

purpose ['pɜ:pəs] *n* propósito; **on ~** a propósito, adrede; **~ful** *adj* resuelto, determinado

purr [pɜ:*] *vi* ronronear

purse [pɜ:s] *n* monedero; *(US)* bolsa *(SP)*, cartera *(AM)* ♦ *vt* fruncir

pursue [pə'sju:] *vt* seguir; **~r** *n* perseguidor(a) *m/f*

pursuit [pə'sju:t] *n (chase)* caza; *(occupation)* actividad *f*

push [puʃ] *n* empuje *m*, empujón *m*; *(of button)* presión *f*; *(drive)* empuje *m* ♦ *vt* empujar; *(button)* apretar; *(promote)* promover ♦ *vi* empujar; *(demand)*: **to ~ for** luchar por; ~ **aside** *vt* apartar con la mano; ~ **off** *(inf) vi* largarse; ~ **on** *vi* seguir adelante; ~ **through** *vi (crowd)* abrirse paso a empujones ♦ *vt (measure)* despachar; ~ **up** *vt* (*total, prices*) hacer subir; ~**chair** (*BRIT*) *n* sillita de ruedas; ~**er** *n* (*drug ~er*) traficante *m/f* de drogas; ~**over** (*inf*) *n*: **it's a ~over** está tirado; ~-**up** (*US*) *n* plancha; ~**y** (*pej*) *adj* agresivo

puss [pus] (*inf*) *n* minino
pussy(-cat) ['pusı-] (*inf*) *n* = **puss**
put [put] (*pt, pp* **put**) *vt* (*place*) poner, colocar; (~ *into*) meter; (*say*) expresar; (*a question*) hacer; (*estimate*) estimar; ~ **about** *or* **around** *vt* (*rumour*) diseminar; ~ **across** *vt* (*ideas etc*) comunicar; ~ **away** *vt* (*store*) guardar; ~ **back** *vt* (*replace*) devolver a su lugar; (*postpone*) aplazar; ~ **by** *vt* (*money*) guardar; ~ **down** *vt* (*on ground*) poner en el suelo; (*animal*) sacrificar; (*in writing*) apuntar; (*revolt etc*) sofocar; (*attribute*): **to ~ sth down to** atribuir algo a; ~ **forward** *vt* (*ideas*) presentar, proponer; ~ **in** *vt* (*complaint*) presentar; (*time*) dedicar; ~ **off** *vt* (*postpone*) aplazar; (*discourage*) desanimar; ~ **on** *vt* ponerse; (*light etc*) encender; (*play etc*) presentar; (*gain*): **to ~ on weight** engordar; (*brake*) echar; (*record, kettle etc*) poner; (*assume*) adoptar; ~ **out** *vt* (*fire, light*) apagar; (*rubbish etc*) sacar; (*cat etc*) echar; (*one's hand*) alargar; (*inf: person*): **to be ~ out** alterarse; ~ **through** *vt* (*TEL*) poner; (*plan etc*) hacer aprobar; ~ **up** *vt* (*raise*) levantar, alzar; (*hang*) colgar; (*build*) construir; (*increase*) aumentar; (*accommodate*) alojar; ~ **up with** *vt fus* aguantar

putt [pʌt] *n* putt *m*, golpe *m* corto; ~**ing green** *n* green *m*; minigolf *m*
putty ['pʌtı] *n* masilla
put-up ['putʌp] *adj*: ~ **job** (*BRIT*) amaño
puzzle ['pʌzl] *n* rompecabezas *m inv*; (*also*: **crossword ~**) crucigrama *m*; (*mystery*) misterio ♦ *vt* dejar perplejo, confundir ♦ *vi*: **to ~ over sth** devanarse los sesos con algo; **puzzling** *adj* misterioso, extraño
pyjamas [pı'dʒɑːməz] (*BRIT*) *npl* pijama *m*

pylon ['paılən] *n* torre *f* de conducción eléctrica
pyramid ['pırəmıd] *n* pirámide *f*
Pyrenees [pırə'niːz] *npl*: **the ~** los Pirineo
python ['paıθən] *n* pitón *m*

Q, q

quack [kwæk] *n* graznido; (*pej: doctor*) curandero/a
quad [kwɔd] *n abbr* = **quadrangle**; **quadruplet**
quadrangle ['kwɔdræŋgl] *n* patio
quadruple [kwɔ'drupl] *vt, vi* cuadruplicar
quadruplets [kwɔ'druːplıts] *npl* cuatrillizos/as
quail [kweıl] *n* codorniz *f* ♦ *vi*: **to ~ at** *or* **before** amedrentarse ante
quaint [kweınt] *adj* extraño; (*picturesque*) pintoresco
quake [kweık] *vi* temblar ♦ *n abbr* = **earthquake**
Quaker ['kweıkə*] *n* cuáquero/a
qualification [kwɔlıfı'keıʃən] *n* (*ability*) capacidad *f*; (*often pl: diploma etc*) título; (*reservation*) salvedad *f*
qualified ['kwɔlıfaıd] *adj* capacitado; (*professionally*) titulado; (*limited*) limitado
qualify ['kwɔlıfaı] *vt* (*make competent*) capacitar; (*modify*) modificar ♦ *vi* (*in competition*): **to ~ (for)** calificarse (para); (*pass examination(s)*): **to ~ (as)** calificarse (de), graduarse (en); (*be eligible*): **to ~ (for)** reunir los requisitos (para)
quality ['kwɔlıtı] *n* calidad *f*; (*of person*) cualidad *f*; ~ **time** *n* tiempo dedicado a la familia y a los amigos

---
quality press

ⓘ *La expresión* **quality press** *se refiere los periódicos que dan un tratamiento serio de las noticias, ofreciendo información detallada sobre un amplio espectro de temas y un análisis en profundidad de la actualidad. Por su tamaño, considerablemente mayor que el* *de los periódicos sensacionalistas, se les conoce también como "broadsheets".*

qualm [kwɑːm] *n* escrúpulo

quandary ['kwɒndrɪ] *n*: **to be in a ~** tener dudas

quantity ['kwɒntɪtɪ] *n* cantidad *f*; **in ~** en grandes cantidades; **~ surveyor** *n* aparejador(a) *m/f*

quarantine ['kwɒrəntiːn] *n* cuarentena

quarrel ['kwɒrl] *n* riña, pelea ♦ *vi* reñir, pelearse

quarry ['kwɒrɪ] *n* cantera

quart [kwɔːt] *n* ≈ litro

quarter ['kwɔːtə*] *n* cuarto, cuarta parte *f*; (*US: coin*) *moneda de 25 centavos*; (*of year*) trimestre *m*; (*district*) barrio ♦ *vt* dividir en cuartos; (*MIL: lodge*) alojar; **~s** *npl* (*barracks*) cuartel *m*; (*living ~s*) alojamiento; **a ~ of an hour** un cuarto de hora; **~ final** *n* cuarto de final; **~ly** *adj* trimestral ♦ *adv* cada 3 meses, trimestralmente

quartet(te) [kwɔːˈtet] *n* cuarteto

quartz [kwɔːts] *n* cuarzo

quash [kwɒʃ] *vt* (*verdict*) anular

quaver ['kweɪvə*] (*BRIT*) *n* (*MUS*) corchea ♦ *vi* temblar

quay [kiː] *n* (*also*: **~side**) muelle *m*

queasy ['kwiːzɪ] *adj*: **to feel ~** tener náuseas

queen [kwiːn] *n* reina; (*CARDS etc*) dama; **~ mother** *n* reina madre

queer [kwɪə*] *adj* raro, extraño ♦ *n* (*inf*: *highly offensive*) maricón *m*

quell [kwel] *vt* (*feeling*) calmar; (*rebellion etc*) sofocar

quench [kwentʃ] *vt*: **to ~ one's thirst** apagar la sed

query ['kwɪərɪ] *n* (*question*) pregunta ♦ *vt* dudar de

quest [kwest] *n* busca, búsqueda

question ['kwestʃən] *n* pregunta; (*doubt*) duda; (*matter*) asunto, cuestión *f* ♦ *vt* (*doubt*) dudar de; (*interrogate*) interrogar, hacer preguntas a; **beyond ~** fuera de toda duda; **out of the ~** imposible; ni

hablar; **~able** *adj* dudoso; **~ mark** *n* punto de interrogación; **~naire** [-ˈnɛə*] *n* cuestionario

queue [kjuː] (*BRIT*) *n* cola ♦ *vi* (*also*: **~ up**) hacer cola

quibble ['kwɪbl] *vi* sutilizar

quick [kwɪk] *adj* rápido; (*agile*) ágil; (*mind*) listo ♦ *n*: **cut to the ~** (*fig*) herido en lo vivo; **be ~!** ¡date prisa!; **~en** *vt* apresurar ♦ *vi* apresurarse, darse prisa; **~ly** *adv* rápidamente, de prisa; **~sand** *n* arenas *fpl* movedizas; **~-witted** *adj* perspicaz

quid [kwɪd] (*BRIT*: *inf*) *n inv* libra

quiet ['kwaɪət] *adj* (*voice, music etc*) bajo; (*person, place*) tranquilo; (*ceremony*) íntimo ♦ *n* silencio; (*calm*) tranquilidad *f* ♦ *vt, vi* (*US*) = **~en**; **~en** (*also*: **~en down**) *vi* calmarse; (*grow silent*) callarse ♦ *vt* calmar; hacer callar; **~ly** *adv* tranquilamente; (*silently*) silenciosamente; **~ness** *n* silencio; tranquilidad *f*

quilt [kwɪlt] *n* edredón *m*

quin [kwɪn] *n abbr* = **quintuplet**

quintet(te) [kwɪnˈtet] *n* quinteto

quintuplets [kwɪnˈtjuːplɪts] *npl* quintillizos/as

quip [kwɪp] *n* pulla

quirk [kwɜːk] *n* peculiaridad *f*; (*accident*) capricho

quit [kwɪt] (*pt, pp* **quit** *or* **quitted**) *vt* dejar, abandonar; (*premises*) desocupar ♦ *vi* (*give up*) renunciar; (*resign*) dimitir

quite [kwaɪt] *adv* (*rather*) bastante; (*entirely*) completamente; **that's not ~ big enough** no acaba de ser lo bastante grande; **~ a few of them** un buen número de ellos; **~ (so)!** ¡así es!, ¡exactamente!

quits [kwɪts] *adj*: **~ (with)** en paz (con); **let's call it ~** dejémoslo en tablas

quiver ['kwɪvə*] *vi* estremecerse

quiz [kwɪz] *n* concurso ♦ *vt* interrogar; **~zical** *adj* burlón(ona)

quota ['kwəutə] *n* cuota

quotation [kwəuˈteɪʃən] *n* cita; (*estimate*) presupuesto; **~ marks** *npl* comillas *fpl*

quote [kwəut] *n* cita; (*estimate*)

presupuesto ♦ *vt* citar; (*price*) cotizar ♦ *vi*:
to ~ from citar de; **~s** *npl* (*inverted commas*) comillas *fpl*

R, r

rabbi ['ræbaɪ] *n* rabino
rabbit ['ræbɪt] *n* conejo; **~ hutch** *n* conejera
rabble ['ræbl] (*pej*) *n* chusma, populacho
rabies ['reɪbiːz] *n* rabia
RAC (*BRIT*) *n abbr* = **Royal Automobile Club**
rac(c)oon [rə'kuːn] *n* mapache *m*
race [reɪs] *n* carrera; (*species*) raza ♦ *vt* (*horse*) hacer correr; (*engine*) acelerar ♦ *vi* (*compete*) competir; (*run*) correr; (*pulse*) latir a ritmo acelerado; **~ car** (*US*) *n* = **racing car**; **~ car driver** (*US*) *n* = **racing driver**; **~course** *n* hipódromo; **~horse** *n* caballo de carreras; **~track** *n* pista; (*for cars*) autódromo
racial ['reɪʃl] *adj* racial
racing ['reɪsɪŋ] *n* carreras *fpl*; **~ car** (*BRIT*) *n* coche *m* de carreras; **~ driver** (*BRIT*) *n* corredor(a) *m/f* de coches
racism ['reɪsɪzəm] *n* racismo; **racist** [-sɪst] *adj*, *n* racista *m/f*
rack [ræk] *n* (*also*: **luggage ~**) rejilla; (*shelf*) estante *m*; (*also*: **roof ~**) baca, portaequipajes *m inv*; (*dish ~*) escurreplatos *m inv*; (*clothes ~*) percha ♦ *vt* atormentar; **to ~ one's brains** devanarse los sesos
racket ['rækɪt] *n* (*for tennis*) raqueta; (*noise*) ruido, estrépito; (*swindle*) estafa, timo
racquet ['rækɪt] *n* raqueta
racy ['reɪsɪ] *adj* picante, salado
radar ['reɪdɑː*] *n* radar *m*
radiant ['reɪdɪənt] *adj* radiante (de felicidad)
radiate ['reɪdɪeɪt] *vt* (*heat*) radiar; (*emotion*) irradiar ♦ *vi* (*lines*) extenderse
radiation [reɪdɪ'eɪʃən] *n* radiación *f*
radiator ['reɪdɪeɪtə*] *n* radiador *m*

radical ['rædɪkl] *adj* radical
radii ['reɪdɪaɪ] *npl of* **radius**
radio ['reɪdɪəʊ] *n* radio *f*; **on the ~** por radio
radio... [reɪdɪəʊ] *prefix*: **~active** *adj* radioactivo; **~graphy** [reɪdɪ'ɔɡrəfɪ] *n* radiografía; **~logy** [reɪdɪ'ɔlədʒɪ] *n* radiología
radio station *n* emisora
radiotherapy [-'θerəpɪ] *n* radioterapia
radish ['rædɪʃ] *n* rábano
radius ['reɪdɪəs] (*pl* **radii**) *n* radio
RAF *n abbr* = **Royal Air Force**
raffle ['ræfl] *n* rifa, sorteo
raft [rɑːft] *n* balsa; (*also*: **life ~**) balsa salvavidas
rafter ['rɑːftə*] *n* viga
rag [ræɡ] *n* (*piece of cloth*) trapo; (*torn cloth*) harapo; (*pej: newspaper*) periodicucho; (*for charity*) *actividades estudiantiles benéficas*; **~s** *npl* (*torn clothes*) harapos *mpl*; **~ doll** *n* muñeca de trapo
rage [reɪdʒ] *n* rabia, furor *m* ♦ *vi* (*person*) rabiar, estar furioso; (*storm*) bramar; **it's all the ~** (*very fashionable*) está muy de moda
ragged ['ræɡɪd] *adj* (*edge*) desigual, mellado; (*appearance*) andrajoso, harapiento
raid [reɪd] *n* (*MIL*) incursión *f*; (*criminal*) asalto; (*by police*) redada ♦ *vt* invadir, atacar; asaltar
rail [reɪl] *n* (*on stair*) barandilla, pasamanos *m inv*; (*on bridge, balcony*) pretil *m*; (*of ship*) barandilla; (*for clothes*) toallero; **~s** *npl* (*RAIL*) vía; **by ~** por ferrocarril; **~ing(s)** *n(pl)* vallado; **~road** (*US*) *n* = **~way**; **~way** (*BRIT*) *n* ferrocarril *m*, vía férrea; **~way line** (*BRIT*) *n* línea (de ferrocarril); **~wayman** (*BRIT irreg*) *n* ferroviario; **~way station** (*BRIT*) *n* estación *f* de ferrocarril
rain [reɪn] *n* lluvia ♦ *vi* llover; **in the ~** bajo la lluvia; **it's ~ing** llueve, está lloviendo; **~bow** *n* arco iris; **~coat** *n* impermeable *m*; **~drop** *n* gota de lluvia; **~fall** *n* lluvia,

~forest n selvas fpl tropicales; **~y** adj lluvioso

aise [reɪz] n aumento ♦ vt levantar; (increase) aumentar; (improve: morale) subir; (: standards) mejorar; (doubts) suscitar; (a question) plantear; (cattle, family) criar; (crop) cultivar; (army) reclutar; (loan) obtener; **to ~ one's voice** alzar la voz

aisin ['reɪzn] n pasa de Corinto

ake [reɪk] n (tool) rastrillo; (person) libertino ♦ vt (garden) rastrillar

ally ['rælɪ] n (POL etc) reunión f, mitin m; (AUT) rallye m; (TENNIS) peloteo ♦ vt reunir ♦ vi recuperarse; **~ round** vt fus (fig) dar apoyo a

RAM [ræm] n abbr (= random access memory) RAM f

am [ræm] n carnero; (also: **battering ~**) ariete m ♦ vt (crash into) dar contra, chocar con; (push: fist etc) empujar con fuerza

amble ['ræmbl] n caminata, excursión f en el campo ♦ vi (pej: also: **~ on**) divagar; **~r** n excursionista m/f; (BOT) trepadora; **rambling** adj (speech) inconexo; (house) laberíntico; (BOT) trepador(a)

amp [ræmp] n rampa; **on / off ~** (US: AUT) vía de acceso/salida

ampage [ræm'peɪdʒ] n: **to be on the ~** desmandarse ♦ vi: **they went rampaging through the town** recorrieron la ciudad armando alboroto

ampant ['ræmpənt] adj (disease etc): **to be ~** estar extendiéndose mucho

am raid vt atracar (rompiendo el escaparate con un coche)

amshackle ['ræmʃækl] adj destartalado

an [ræn] pt of **run**

anch [rɑːntʃ] n hacienda, estancia; **~er** n ganadero

ancid ['rænsɪd] adj rancio

ancour ['ræŋkə*] (US **rancor**) n rencor m

andom ['rændəm] adj fortuito, sin orden; (COMPUT, MATH) aleatorio ♦ n: **at ~** al azar

andy ['rændɪ] (BRIT: inf) adj cachondo

ang [ræŋ] pt of **ring**

range [reɪndʒ] n (of mountains) cadena de montañas, cordillera; (of missile) alcance m; (of voice) registro; (series) serie f; (of products) surtido; (MIL: also: **shooting ~**) campo de tiro; (also: **kitchen ~**) fogón m ♦ vt (place) colocar; (arrange) arreglar ♦ vi: **to ~ over** (extend) extenderse por; **to ~ from ... to ...** oscilar entre ... y ...

ranger [reɪndʒə*] n guardabosques m inv

rank [ræŋk] n (row) fila; (MIL) rango; (status) categoría; (BRIT: also: **taxi ~**) parada de taxis ♦ vi: **to ~ among** figurar entre ♦ adj fétido, rancio; **the ~ and file** (fig) la base

ransack ['rænsæk] vt (search) registrar; (plunder) saquear

ransom ['rænsəm] n rescate m; **to hold to ~** (fig) hacer chantaje a

rant [rænt] vi divagar, desvariar

rap [ræp] vt golpear, dar un golpecito en ♦ n (music) rap m

rape [reɪp] n violación f; (BOT) colza ♦ vt violar; **~ (seed) oil** n aceite m de colza

rapid ['ræpɪd] adj rápido; **~ity** [rə'pɪdɪtɪ] n rapidez f; **~s** npl (GEO) rápidos mpl

rapist ['reɪpɪst] n violador m

rapport [ræ'pɔː*] n simpatía

rapturous ['ræptʃərəs] adj extático

rare [reə*] adj raro, poco común; (CULIN: steak) poco hecho

rarely ['reəlɪ] adv pocas veces

raring ['reərɪŋ] adj: **to be ~ to go** (inf) tener muchas ganas de empezar

rascal ['rɑːskl] n pillo, pícaro

rash [ræʃ] adj imprudente, precipitado ♦ n (MED) sarpullido, erupción f (cutánea); (of events) serie f

rasher ['ræʃə*] n lonja

raspberry ['rɑːzbərɪ] n frambuesa

rasping ['rɑːspɪŋ] adj: **a ~ noise** un ruido áspero

rat [ræt] n rata

rate [reɪt] n (ratio) razón f; (price) precio; (: of hotel etc) tarifa; (of interest) tipo; (speed) velocidad f ♦ vt (value) tasar; (estimate) estimar; **~s** npl (BRIT: property tax) impuesto municipal; (fees) tarifa; **to ~**

sth/sb as considerar algo/a uno como; **~able value** (BRIT) n valor m impuesto; **~payer** (BRIT) n contribuyente m/f

rather ['rɑːðə*] adv: **it's ~ expensive** es algo caro; (too much) es demasiado caro; (to some extent) más bien; **there's ~ a lot** hay bastante; **I would** or **I'd ~ go** preferiría ir; **or ~** mejor dicho

rating ['reɪtɪŋ] n tasación f; (score) índice m; (of ship) clase f; **~s** npl (RADIO, TV) niveles mpl de audiencia

ratio ['reɪʃɪəu] n razón f; **in the ~ of 100 to 1** a razón de 100 a 1

ration ['ræʃən] n ración f ♦ vt racionar; **~s** npl víveres mpl

rational ['ræʃənl] adj (solution, reasoning) lógico, razonable; (person) cuerdo, sensato; **~e** [-'nɑːl] n razón f fundamental; **~ize** vt justificar

rat race n lucha incesante por la supervivencia

rattle ['rætl] n golpeteo; (of train etc) traqueteo; (for baby) sonaja, sonajero ♦ vi castañetear; (car, bus): **to ~ along** traquetear ♦ vt hacer sonar agitando; **~snake** n serpiente f de cascabel

raucous ['rɔːkəs] adj estridente, ronco

ravage ['rævɪdʒ] vt hacer estragos en, destrozar; **~s** npl estragos mpl

rave [reɪv] vi (in anger) encolerizarse; (with enthusiasm) entusiasmarse; (MED) delirar, desvariar ♦ n (inf: party) rave m

raven ['reɪvən] n cuervo

ravenous ['rævənəs] adj hambriento

ravine [rə'viːn] n barranco

raving ['reɪvɪŋ] adj: **~ lunatic** loco/a de atar

ravishing ['rævɪʃɪŋ] adj encantador(a)

raw [rɔː] adj crudo; (not processed) bruto; (sore) vivo; (inexperienced) novato, inexperto; **~ deal** (inf) n injusticia; **~ material** n materia prima

ray [reɪ] n rayo; **~ of hope** (rayo de) esperanza

raze [reɪz] vt arrasar

razor ['reɪzə*] n (open) navaja; (safety ~) máquina de afeitar; (electric ~) máquina

(eléctrica) de afeitar; **~ blade** n hoja de afeitar

Rd abbr = **road**

re [riː] prep con referencia a

reach [riːtʃ] n alcance m; (of river etc) extensión f entre dos recodos ♦ vt alcanzar, llegar a; (achieve) lograr ♦ vi extenderse; **within ~** al alcance (de la mano); **out of ~** fuera del alcance; **~ out** vt (hand) tender ♦ vi: **to ~ out for sth** alargar or tender la mano para tomar algo

react [riː'ækt] vi reaccionar; **~ion** [-'ækʃən] n reacción f

reactor [riː'æktə*] n (also: **nuclear ~**) reactor m (nuclear)

read [riːd, pt, pp red] (pt, pp **read**) vi leer ♦ vt leer; (understand) entender; (study) estudiar; **~ out** vt leer en alta voz; **~able** adj (writing) legible; (book) leíble; **~er** n lector(a) m/f; (BRIT: at university) profesor(a) m/f adjunto/a; **~ership** n (of paper etc) (número de) lectores mpl

readily ['redɪlɪ] adv (willingly) de buena gana; (easily) fácilmente; (quickly) en seguida

readiness ['redɪnɪs] n buena voluntad f; (preparedness) preparación f; **in ~** (prepared) listo, preparado

reading ['riːdɪŋ] n lectura; (on instrument) indicación f

ready ['redɪ] adj listo, preparado; (willing) dispuesto; (available) disponible ♦ adv: **~-cooked** listo para comer ♦ n: **at the ~** (MIL) listo para tirar; **to get ~** vi prepararse ♦ vt preparar; **~-made** adj confeccionado; **~-to-wear** adj confeccionado

real [rɪəl] adj verdadero, auténtico; **in ~ terms** en términos reales; **~ estate** n bienes mpl raíces; **~istic** [-'lɪstɪk] adj realista

reality [riː'ælɪtɪ] n realidad f

realization [rɪəlaɪ'zeɪʃən] n comprensión ♦ (fulfilment, COMM) realización f

realize ['rɪəlaɪz] vt (understand) darse cuenta de

really ['rɪəlɪ] adv realmente; (for emphasis) verdaderamente; (actually): **what ~ happened** lo que pasó en realidad; **~?** ¿de veras?; **~!** (annoyance) ¡vamos!, ¡por favor!

realm [relm] n reino; (fig) esfera

realtor ® ['rɪəltɔː*] (US) n corredor(a) m/f de bienes raíces

reap [riːp] vt segar; (fig) cosechar, recoger

reappear [riːə'pɪə*] vi reaparecer

rear [rɪə*] adj trasero ♦ n parte f trasera ♦ vt (cattle, family) criar ♦ vi (also: ~ up) (animal) encabritarse; **~guard** n retaguardia

rearmament [riː'ɑːməmənt] n rearme m

rearrange [riːə'reɪndʒ] vt ordenar or arreglar de nuevo

rear-view mirror n (AUT) (espejo) retrovisor m

reason ['riːzn] n razón f ♦ vi: **to ~ with sb** tratar de que uno entre en razón; **it stands to ~ that** es lógico que; **~able** adj razonable; (sensible) sensato; **~ably** adv razonablemente; **~ing** n razonamiento, argumentos mpl

reassurance [riːə'ʃʊərəns] n consuelo

reassure [riːə'ʃʊə*] vt tranquilizar, alentar; **to ~ sb that** tranquilizar a uno asegurando que

rebate ['riːbeɪt] n (on tax etc) desgravación f

rebel [n 'rɛbl, vi rɪ'bɛl] n rebelde m/f ♦ vi rebelarse, sublevarse; **~lious** [rɪ'bɛljəs] adj rebelde; (child) revoltoso

rebirth ['riːbəːθ] n renacimiento

rebound [vi rɪ'baund, n 'riːbaund] vi (ball) rebotar ♦ n rebote m; **on the ~** (also fig) de rebote

rebuff [rɪ'bʌf] n desaire m, rechazo

rebuild [riː'bɪld] (irreg) vt reconstruir

rebuke [rɪ'bjuːk] n reprimenda ♦ vt reprender

rebut [rɪ'bʌt] vt rebatir

recall [vb rɪ'kɔːl, n 'riːkɔl] vt (remember) recordar; (ambassador etc) retirar ♦ n recuerdo; retirada

recap ['riːkæp], **recapitulate** [riːkə'pɪtjuleɪt] vt, vi recapitular

rec'd abbr (= received) rbdo

recede [rɪ'siːd] vi (memory) ir borrándose; (hair) retroceder; **receding** adj (forehead, chin) huidizo; **to have a receding hairline** tener entradas

receipt [rɪ'siːt] n (document) recibo; (for parcel etc) acuse m de recibo; (act of receiving) recepción f; **~s** npl (COMM) ingresos mpl

receive [rɪ'siːv] vt recibir; (guest) acoger; (wound) sufrir; **~r** n (TEL) auricular m; (RADIO) receptor m; (of stolen goods) perista m/f; (COMM) administrador m jurídico

recent ['riːsnt] adj reciente; **~ly** adv recientemente; **~ly arrived** recién llegado

receptacle [rɪ'sɛptɪkl] n receptáculo

reception [rɪ'sɛpʃən] n recepción f; (welcome) acogida; **~ desk** n recepción f; **~ist** n recepcionista m/f

recess [rɪ'sɛs] n (in room) hueco; (for bed) nicho; (secret place) escondrijo; (POL etc: holiday) clausura

recession [rɪ'sɛʃən] n recesión f

recipe ['rɛsɪpɪ] n receta; (for disaster, success) fórmula

recipient [rɪ'sɪpɪənt] n recibidor(a) m/f; (of letter) destinatario/a

recital [rɪ'saɪtl] n recital m

recite [rɪ'saɪt] vt (poem) recitar

reckless ['rɛkləs] adj temerario, imprudente; (driving, driver) peligroso; **~ly** adv imprudentemente; de modo peligroso

reckon ['rɛkən] vt calcular; (consider) considerar; (think): **I ~ that ...** me parece que ...; **~ on** vt fus contar con; **~ing** n cálculo

reclaim [rɪ'kleɪm] vt (land, waste) recuperar; (land: from sea) rescatar; (demand back) reclamar

reclamation [rɛklə'meɪʃən] n (of land) acondicionamiento de tierras

recline [rɪ'klaɪn] vi reclinarse; **reclining** adj (seat) reclinable

recluse [rɪ'kluːs] n recluso/a

recognition [rekəg'nɪʃən] n
reconocimiento; **transformed beyond ~**
irreconocible

recognizable ['rekəgnaɪzəbl] adj: **~ (by)**
reconocible (por)

recognize ['rekəgnaɪz] vt: **to ~ (by/as)**
reconocer (por/como)

recoil [vi rɪ'kɔɪl, n 'riːkɔɪl] vi (person): **to ~
from doing sth** retraerse de hacer algo
♦ n (of gun) retroceso

recollect [rekə'lekt] vt recordar, acordarse
de; **~ion** [-'lekʃən] n recuerdo

recommend [rekə'mend] vt recomendar

reconcile ['rekənsaɪl] vt (two people)
reconciliar; (two facts) compaginar; **to ~
o.s. to sth** conformarse a algo

recondition [riːkən'dɪʃən] vt (machine)
reacondicionar

reconnoitre [rekə'nɔɪtə*] (US reconnoiter)
vt, vi (MIL) reconocer

reconsider [riːkən'sɪdə*] vt repensar

reconstruct [riːkən'strʌkt] vt reconstruir

record [n 'rekɔːd, vt rɪ'kɔːd] n (MUS) disco;
(of meeting etc) acta; (register) registro,
partida; (file) archivo; (also: **criminal ~**)
antecedentes mpl; (written) expediente m;
(SPORT, COMPUT) récord m ♦ vt registrar;
(MUS: song etc) grabar; **in ~ time** en un
tiempo récord; **off the ~** adj no oficial
♦ adv confidencialmente; **~ card** n (in
file) ficha; **~ed delivery** (BRIT) n (POST)
entrega con acuse de recibo; **~er** n (MUS)
flauta de pico; **~ holder** n (SPORT) actual
poseedor(a) m/f del récord; **~ing** n (MUS)
grabación f; **~ player** n tocadiscos m
inv

recount [rɪ'kaʊnt] vt contar

re-count ['riːkaʊnt] n (POL: of votes)
segundo escrutinio

recoup [rɪ'kuːp] vt: **to ~ one's losses**
recuperar las pérdidas

recourse [rɪ'kɔːs] n: **to have ~ to** recurrir
a

recover [rɪ'kʌvə*] vt recuperar ♦ vi (from
illness, shock) recuperarse; **~y** n
recuperación f

recreation [rekrɪ'eɪʃən] n recreo; **~al** adj

de recreo; **~al drug** droga recreativa

recruit [rɪ'kruːt] n recluta m/f ♦ vt reclutar;
(staff) contratar

rectangle ['rektæŋgl] n rectángulo;
rectangular [-'tæŋgjulə*] adj rectangular

rectify ['rektɪfaɪ] vt rectificar

rector ['rektə*] n (REL) párroco; **~y** n casa
del párroco

recuperate [rɪ'kuːpəreɪt] vi reponerse,
restablecerse

recur [rɪ'kə:*] vi repetirse; (pain, illness)
producirse de nuevo; **~rence** [rɪ'kʌrens]
repetición f; **~rent** [rɪ'kʌrent] adj repetido

recycle [ri:'saɪkl] vt reciclar

red [red] n rojo ♦ adj rojo; (hair) pelirrojo;
(wine) tinto; **to be in the ~** (account) estar
en números rojos; (business) tener un
saldo negativo; **to give sb the ~ carpet
treatment** recibir a uno con todos los
honores; **R~ Cross** n Cruz f Roja;
~currant n grosella roja; **~den** vt
enrojecer ♦ vi enrojecerse

redeem [rɪ'diːm] vt redimir; (promises)
cumplir; (sth in pawn) desempeñar; (fig,
also REL) rescatar; **~ing** adj: **~ing feature**
rasgo bueno or favorable

redeploy [riːdɪ'plɔɪ] vt (resources)
reorganizar

red: **~-haired** adj pelirrojo; **~-handed**
adj: **to be caught ~-handed** cogerse (SP)
or pillarse (AM) con las manos en la masa;
~head n pelirrojo/a; **~ herring** n (fig)
pista falsa; **~-hot** adj candente

redirect [riːdaɪ'rekt] vt (mail) reexpedir

red light n: **to go through a ~** (AUT)
pasar la luz roja; **red-light district** n
barrio chino

redo [riː'duː] (irreg) vt rehacer

redress [rɪ'dres] vt reparar

Red Sea n: **the ~** el mar Rojo

redskin ['redskɪn] n piel roja m/f

red tape n (fig) trámites mpl

reduce [rɪ'djuːs] vt reducir; **to ~ sb to
tears** hacer llorar a uno; **to be ~d to
begging** no quedarle a uno otro remedio
que pedir limosna; **"~ speed now"** (AUT,
"reduzca la velocidad"; **at a ~d price** (of

goods) (a precio) rebajado; **reduction**
[rɪ'dʌkʃən] n reducción f; (*of price*) rebaja;
(*discount*) descuento; (*smaller-scale copy*)
copia reducida

dundancy [rɪ'dʌndənsɪ] n (*dismissal*)
despido; (*unemployment*) desempleo

dundant [rɪ'dʌndnt] adj (BRIT: *worker*)
parado, sin trabajo; (*detail, object*)
superfluo; **to be made ~** quedar(se) sin
trabajo

ed [ri:d] n (BOT) junco, caña; (MUS)
lengüeta

ef [ri:f] n (*at sea*) arrecife m

ek [ri:k] vi: **to ~ (of)** apestar (a)

el [ri:l] n carrete m, bobina; (*of film*)
rollo; (*dance*) baile m escocés ♦ vt (*also: ~
up*) devanar; (*also: ~ in*) sacar ♦ vi (*sway*)
tambalear(se)

f [ref] (*inf*) n abbr = **referee**

factory [rɪ'fektərɪ] n comedor m

fer [rɪ'fə:*] vt (*send: patient*) referir;
(: *matter*) remitir ♦ vi: **to ~ to** (*allude to*)
referirse a, aludir a; (*apply to*) relacionarse
con; (*consult*) consultar

feree [refə'ri:] n árbitro; (BRIT: *for job
application*): **to be a ~ for sb**
proporcionar referencias a uno ♦ vt
(*match*) arbitrar en

ference ['refrəns] n referencia; (*for job
application: letter*) carta de
recomendación; **with ~ to** (COMM: *in
letter*) me remito a; **~ book** n libro de
consulta; **~ number** n número de
referencia

fill [vt ri:'fɪl, n 'ri:fɪl] vt rellenar ♦ n
repuesto, recambio

fine [rɪ'faɪn] vt refinar; **~d** adj (*person*)
fino; **~ment** n cultura, educación f; (*of
system*) refinamiento

flect [rɪ'flekt] vt reflejar ♦ vi (*think*)
reflexionar, pensar; **it ~s badly/well on
him** le perjudica/le hace honor; **~ion**
[-'flekʃən] n (*act*) reflexión f; (*image*)
reflejo; (*criticism*) crítica; **on ~ion**
pensándolo bien; **~or** n (AUT) captafaros
m inv; (*of light, heat*) reflector m

flex ['ri:fleks] adj, n reflejo; **~ive**

[rɪ'fleksɪv] adj (LING) reflexivo

reform [rɪ'fɔ:m] n reforma ♦ vt reformar;
~atory (US) n reformatorio

refrain [rɪ'freɪn] vi: **to ~ from doing**
abstenerse de hacer ♦ n estribillo

refresh [rɪ'freʃ] vt refrescar; **~er course**
(BRIT) n curso de repaso; **~ing** adj
refrescante; **~ments** npl refrescos mpl

refrigerator [rɪ'frɪdʒəreɪtə*] n nevera (SP),
refrigeradora (AM)

refuel [ri:'fjuəl] vi repostar (combustible)

refuge ['refju:dʒ] n refugio, asilo; **to take ~
in** refugiarse en

refugee [refju'dʒi:] n refugiado/a

refund [n 'ri:fʌnd, vb rɪ'fʌnd] n reembolso
♦ vt devolver, reembolsar

refurbish [ri:'fə:bɪʃ] vt restaurar, renovar

refusal [rɪ'fju:zəl] n negativa; **to have first
~ on** tener la primera opción a

refuse[1] ['refju:s] n basura; **~ collection**
n recolección f de basuras

refuse[2] [rɪ'fju:z] vt rechazar; (*invitation*)
declinar; (*permission*) denegar ♦ vi: **to ~
to do sth** negarse a hacer algo; (*horse*)
rehusar

regain [rɪ'geɪn] vt recobrar, recuperar

regal ['ri:gl] adj regio, real

regard [rɪ'gɑ:d] n (*look*) mirada; (*esteem*)
respeto; (*attention*) consideración f ♦ vt
(*consider*) considerar; **to give one's ~s to**
saludar de su parte a; **"with kindest ~s"**
"con muchos recuerdos"; **~ing, as ~s,
with ~ to** con respecto a, en cuanto a;
~less adv a pesar de todo; **~less of** sin
reparar en

régime [reɪ'ʒi:m] n régimen m

regiment ['redʒɪmənt] n regimiento; **~al**
[-'mentl] adj militar

region ['ri:dʒən] n región f; **in the ~ of**
(*fig*) alrededor de; **~al** adj regional

register ['redʒɪstə*] n registro ♦ vt
registrar; (*birth*) declarar; (*car*) matricular;
(*letter*) certificar; (*subj: instrument*)
marcar, indicar ♦ vi (*at hotel*) registrarse;
(*as student*) matricularse; (*make
impression*) producir impresión; **~ed** adj
(*letter, parcel*) certificado; **~ed**

trademark *n* marca registrada

registrar ['redʒɪstrɑː*] *n* secretario/a (del registro civil)

registration [redʒɪs'treɪʃən] *n* (*act*) declaración *f*; (AUT: *also*: ~ **number**) matrícula

registry ['redʒɪstrɪ] *n* registro; ~ **office** (BRIT) *n* registro civil; **to get married in a ~ office** casarse por lo civil

regret [rɪ'gret] *n* sentimiento, pesar *m* ♦ *vt* sentir, lamentar; ~**fully** *adv* con pesar; ~**table** *adj* lamentable

regular ['regjulə*] *adj* regular; (*soldier*) profesional; (*usual*) habitual; (: *doctor*) de cabecera ♦ *n* (*client etc*) cliente/a *m/f* habitual; ~**ly** *adv* con regularidad; (*often*) repetidas veces

regulate ['regjuleɪt] *vt* controlar; **regulation** [-'leɪʃən] *n* (*rule*) regla, reglamento

rehearsal [rɪ'həːsəl] *n* ensayo

rehearse [rɪ'həːs] *vt* ensayar

reign [reɪn] *n* reinado; (*fig*) predominio ♦ *vi* reinar; (*fig*) imperar

reimburse [riːɪm'bəːs] *vt* reembolsar

rein [reɪn] *n* (*for horse*) rienda

reindeer ['reɪndɪə*] *n inv* reno

reinforce [riːɪn'fɔːs] *vt* reforzar; ~**d concrete** *n* hormigón *m* armado; ~**ments** *npl* (MIL) refuerzos *mpl*

reinstate [riːɪn'steɪt] *vt* reintegrar; (*tax, law*) reinstaurar

reiterate [riː'ɪtəreɪt] *vt* reiterar, repetir

reject [*n* 'riːdʒekt, *vb* rɪ'dʒekt] *n* (*thing*) desecho ♦ *vt* rechazar; (*suggestion*) descartar; (*coin*) expulsar; ~**ion** [rɪ'dʒekʃən] *n* rechazo

rejoice [rɪ'dʒɔɪs] *vi*: **to ~ at** *or* **over** regocijarse *or* alegrarse de

rejuvenate [rɪ'dʒuːvəneɪt] *vt* rejuvenecer

relapse [rɪ'læps] *n* recaída

relate [rɪ'leɪt] *vt* (*tell*) contar, relatar; (*connect*) relacionar ♦ *vi* relacionarse; ~**d** *adj* afín; (*person*) emparentado; ~**d to** (*subject*) relacionado con; **relating to** *prep* referente a

relation [rɪ'leɪʃən] *n* (*person*) familiar *m/f*, pariente/a *m/f*; (*link*) relación *f*; ~**s** *npl* (*relatives*) familiares *mpl*; ~**ship** *n* relación *f*; (*personal*) relaciones *fpl*; (*also*: **family ~ship**) parentesco

relative ['relətɪv] *n* pariente/a *m/f*, familiar *m/f* ♦ *adj* relativo; ~**ly** *adv* (*comparatively*) relativamente

relax [rɪ'læks] *vi* descansar; (*unwind*) relajarse ♦ *vt* (*one's grip*) soltar, aflojar; (*control*) relajar; (*mind, person*) descansar, ~**ation** [riːlæk'seɪʃən] *n* descanso; (*of rule, control*) relajamiento; (*entertainment*) diversión *f*; ~**ed** *adj* relajado; (*tranquil*) tranquilo; ~**ing** *adj* relajante

relay ['riːleɪ] *n* (*race*) carrera de relevos ♦ *vt* (RADIO, TV) retransmitir

release [rɪ'liːs] *n* (*liberation*) liberación *f*; (*from prison*) puesta en libertad; (*of gas etc*) escape *m*; (*of film etc*) estreno; (*of record*) lanzamiento ♦ *vt* (*prisoner*) poner en libertad; (*gas*) despedir, arrojar; (*from wreckage*) soltar; (*catch, spring etc*) desenganchar; (*film*) estrenar; (*book*) publicar; (*news*) difundir

relegate ['relɪɡeɪt] *vt* relegar; (BRIT: SPORT **to be ~d to** bajar a

relent [rɪ'lent] *vi* ablandarse; ~**less** *adj* implacable

relevant ['relɪvənt] *adj* (*fact*) pertinente; **to** relacionado con

reliable [rɪ'laɪəbl] *adj* (*person, firm*) de confianza, de fiar; (*method, machine*) seguro; (*source*) fidedigno; **reliably** *adv* **to be reliably informed that ...** saber de fuente fidedigna que ...

reliance [rɪ'laɪəns] *n*: ~ **(on)** dependencia (de)

relic ['relɪk] *n* (REL) reliquia; (*of the past*) vestigio

relief [rɪ'liːf] *n* (*from pain, anxiety*) alivio; (*help, supplies*) socorro, ayuda; (ART, GEO) relieve *m*

relieve [rɪ'liːv] *vt* (*pain*) aliviar; (*bring help to*) ayudar, socorrer; (*take over from*) sustituir; (: *guard*) relevar; **to ~ sb of sth** quitar algo a uno; **to ~ o.s.** hacer sus necesidades

religion [rɪ'lɪdʒən] n religión f; **religious** adj religioso

relinquish [rɪ'lɪŋkwɪʃ] vt abandonar; (plan, habit) renunciar a

relish ['relɪʃ] n (CULIN) salsa; (enjoyment) entusiasmo m ♦ vt (food etc) saborear; (enjoy): **to ~ sth** hacerle mucha ilusión a uno algo

relocate [ri:ləu'keɪt] vt cambiar de lugar, mudar ♦ vi mudarse

reluctance [rɪ'lʌktəns] n renuencia

reluctant [rɪ'lʌktənt] adj renuente; ~**ly** adv de mala gana

rely on [rɪ'laɪ-] vt fus depender de; (trust) contar con

remain [rɪ'meɪn] vi (survive) quedar; (be left) sobrar; (continue) quedar(se), permanecer; ~**der** n resto; ~**ing** adj que queda(n); (surviving) restante(s); ~**s** npl restos mpl

remand [rɪ'mɑ:nd] n: **on ~** detenido (bajo custodia) ♦ vt: **to be ~ed in custody** quedar detenido bajo custodia; ~ **home** (BRIT) n reformatorio

remark [rɪ'mɑ:k] n comentario ♦ vt comentar; ~**able** adj (outstanding) extraordinario

remarry [ri:'mærɪ] vi volver a casarse

remedial [rɪ'mi:dɪəl] adj de recuperación

remedy ['remədɪ] n remedio ♦ vt remediar, curar

remember [rɪ'membə*] vt recordar, acordarse de; (bear in mind) tener presente; (send greetings to): **~ me to him** dale recuerdos de mi parte; **remembrance** n recuerdo; **R~ Day** n ≈ día en el que se recuerda a los caídos en las dos guerras mundiales

---

Remembrance Day

i En el Reino Unido el domingo más próximo al 11 de noviembre se conoce como **Remembrance Sunday** o **Remembrance Day**, aniversario de la firma del armisticio de 1918 que puso fin a la Primera Guerra Mundial. Ese día, a las once de la mañana (hora en que se

firmó el armisticio), se recuerda a los que murieron en las dos guerras mundiales con dos minutos de silencio ante los monumentos a los caídos. Allí se colocan coronas de amapolas, flor que también se suele llevar prendida en el pecho tras pagar un donativo destinado a los inválidos de guerra.

---

remind [rɪ'maɪnd] vt: **to ~ sb to do sth** recordar a uno que haga algo; **to ~ sb of sth** (of fact) recordar algo a uno; **she ~s me of her mother** me recuerda a su madre; ~**er** n notificación f; (memento) recuerdo

reminisce [remɪ'nɪs] vi recordar (viejas historias); **reminiscent** adj: **to be reminiscent of sth** recordar algo

remiss [rɪ'mɪs] adj descuidado; **it was ~ of him** fue un descuido de su parte

remission [rɪ'mɪʃən] n remisión f; (of prison sentence) disminución f de pena; (REL) perdón m

remit [rɪ'mɪt] vt (send: money) remitir, enviar; ~**tance** n remesa, envío

remnant ['remnənt] n resto; (of cloth) retal m; ~**s** npl (COMM) restos mpl de serie

remorse [rɪ'mɔ:s] n remordimientos mpl; ~**ful** adj arrepentido; ~**less** adj (fig) implacable, inexorable

remote [rɪ'məut] adj (distant) lejano; (person) distante; ~ **control** n telecontrol m; ~**ly** adv remotamente; (slightly) levemente

remould ['ri:məuld] (BRIT) n (tyre) neumático or llanta (AM) recauchutado/a

removable [rɪ'mu:vəbl] adj (detachable) separable

removal [rɪ'mu:vəl] n (taking away) el quitar; (BRIT: from house) mudanza; (from office: dismissal) destitución f; (MED) extirpación f; ~ **van** (BRIT) n camión m de mudanzas

remove [rɪ'mu:v] vt quitar; (employee) destituir; (name: from list) tachar, borrar; (doubt) disipar; (abuse) suprimir, acabar con; (MED) extirpar

Renaissance [rɪ'neɪsãns] n: **the ~** el Renacimiento

render ['rɛndə*] vt (*thanks*) dar; (*aid*) proporcionar, prestar; (*make*): **to ~ sth useless** hacer algo inútil; **~ing** n (*MUS etc*) interpretación f

rendezvous ['rɒndɪvuː] n cita

renew [rɪ'njuː] vt renovar; (*resume*) reanudar; (*loan etc*) prorrogar; **~able** adj renovable; **~al** n reanudación f; prórroga

renounce [rɪ'nauns] vt renunciar a; (*right, inheritance*) renunciar

renovate ['rɛnəveɪt] vt renovar

renown [rɪ'naun] n renombre m; **~ed** adj renombrado

rent [rɛnt] n (*for house*) arriendo, renta ♦ vt alquilar; **~al** n (*for television, car*) alquiler m

rep [rɛp] n abbr = **representative**; **repertory**

repair [rɪ'pɛə*] n reparación f, compostura ♦ vt reparar, componer; (*shoes*) remendar; **in good/bad ~** en buen/mal estado; **~ kit** n caja de herramientas

repatriate [riː'pætrɪeɪt] vt repatriar

repay [riː'peɪ] (*irreg*) vt (*money*) devolver, reembolsar; (*person*) pagar; (*debt*) liquidar; (*sb's efforts*) devolver, corresponder a; **~ment** n reembolso, devolución f; (*sum of money*) recompensa

repeal [rɪ'piːl] n revocación f ♦ vt revocar

repeat [rɪ'piːt] n (*RADIO, TV*) reposición f ♦ vt repetir ♦ vi repetirse; **~edly** adv repetidas veces

repel [rɪ'pɛl] vt (*drive away*) rechazar; (*disgust*) repugnar; **~lent** adj repugnante ♦ n: **insect ~lent** crema (*or* loción f) anti-insectos

repent [rɪ'pɛnt] vi: **to ~ (of)** arrepentirse (de); **~ance** n arrepentimiento

repercussions [riːpə'kʌʃənz] npl consecuencias fpl

repertory ['rɛpətərɪ] n (*also*: **~ theatre**) teatro de repertorio

repetition [rɛpɪ'tɪʃən] n repetición f

repetitive [rɪ'pɛtɪtɪv] adj repetitivo

replace [rɪ'pleɪs] vt (*put back*) devolver a su sitio; (*take the place of*) reemplazar, sustituir; **~ment** n (*act*) reposición f; (*thing*) recambio; (*person*) suplente m/f

replay ['riːpleɪ] n (*SPORT*) desempate m; (*of tape, film*) repetición f

replenish [rɪ'plɛnɪʃ] vt rellenar; (*stock etc*) reponer

replica ['rɛplɪkə] n copia, reproducción f (exacta)

reply [rɪ'plaɪ] n respuesta, contestación f ♦ vi contestar, responder

report [rɪ'pɔːt] n informe m; (*PRESS etc*) reportaje m; (*BRIT: also*: **school ~**) boletín m escolar; (*of gun*) estallido ♦ vt informar de; (*PRESS etc*) hacer un reportaje sobre; (*notify: accident, culprit*) denunciar ♦ vi (*make a report*) presentar un informe; (*present o.s.*): **to ~ (to sb)** presentarse (ante uno); **~ card** n (*US, Scottish*) cartilla escolar; **~edly** adv según se dice; **~er** n periodista m/f

repose [rɪ'pəuz] n: **in ~** (*face, mouth*) en reposo

reprehensible [rɛprɪ'hɛnsɪbl] adj reprensible, censurable

represent [rɛprɪ'zɛnt] vt representar; (*COMM*) ser agente de; (*describe*): **to ~ sth as** describir algo como; **~ation** [-'teɪʃən] n representación f; **~ations** npl (*protest*) quejas fpl; **~ative** n representante m/f; (*US: POL*) diputado/a m/f ♦ adj representativo

repress [rɪ'prɛs] vt reprimir; **~ion** [-'prɛʃən] n represión f

reprieve [rɪ'priːv] n (*LAW*) indulto; (*fig*) alivio

reprisals [rɪ'praɪzlz] npl represalias fpl

reproach [rɪ'prəutʃ] n reproche m ♦ vt: **to ~ sb for sth** reprochar algo a uno; **~ful** adj de reproche, de acusación

reproduce [riːprə'djuːs] vt reproducir ♦ vi reproducirse; **reproduction** [-'dʌkʃən] n reproducción f

reprove [rɪ'pruːv] vt: **to ~ sb for sth** reprochar algo a uno

reptile ['rɛptaɪl] n reptil m

republic [rɪ'pʌblɪk] n república; **~an** adj,

n republicano/a *m/f*

repudiate [rɪ'pjuːdɪeɪt] *vt* rechazar; (*violence etc*) repudiar

repulsive [rɪ'pʌlsɪv] *adj* repulsivo

reputable ['rɛpjʊtəbl] *adj* (*make etc*) de renombre

reputation [rɛpjʊ'teɪʃən] *n* reputación *f*

reputed [rɪ'pjuːtɪd] *adj* supuesto; ~ly *adv* según dicen *or* se dice

request [rɪ'kwɛst] *n* petición *f*; (*formal*) solicitud *f* ♦ *vt*: **to ~ sth of** *or* **from sb** solicitar algo a uno; ~ **stop** (BRIT) *n* parada discrecional

require [rɪ'kwaɪə*] *vt* (*need: subj: person*) necesitar, tener necesidad de; (: *thing, situation*) exigir; (*want*) pedir; **to ~ sb to do sth** pedir a uno que haga algo; ~**ment** *n* requisito; (*need*) necesidad *f*

requisition [rɛkwɪ'zɪʃən] *n*: ~ **(for)** solicitud *f* (de) ♦ *vt* (MIL) requisar

rescue ['rɛskjuː] *n* rescate *m* ♦ *vt* rescatar; ~ **party** *n* expedición *f* de salvamento; ~**r** *n* salvador(a) *m/f*

research [rɪ'səːtʃ] *n* investigaciones *fpl* ♦ *vt* investigar; ~**er** *n* investigador(a) *m/f*

resemblance [rɪ'zɛmbləns] *n* parecido

resemble [rɪ'zɛmbl] *vt* parecerse a

resent [rɪ'zɛnt] *vt* tomar a mal; ~**ful** *adj* resentido; ~**ment** *n* resentimiento

reservation [rɛzə'veɪʃən] *n* reserva

reserve [rɪ'zəːv] *n* reserva; (SPORT) suplente *m/f* ♦ *vt* (*seats etc*) reservar; ~**s** *npl* (MIL) reserva; **in ~** de reserva; ~**d** *adj* reservado

reshuffle [riː'ʃʌfl] *n*: **Cabinet ~** (POL) remodelación *f* del gabinete

residence ['rɛzɪdəns] *n* (*formal: home*) domicilio; (*length of stay*) permanencia; ~ **permit** (BRIT) *n* permiso de permanencia

resident ['rɛzɪdənt] *n* (*of area*) vecino/a; (*in hotel*) huésped(a) *m/f* ♦ *adj* (*population*) permanente; (*doctor*) residente; ~**ial** [-'dɛnʃəl] *adj* residencial

residue ['rɛzɪdjuː] *n* resto

resign [rɪ'zaɪn] *vt* renunciar a ♦ *vi* dimitir; **to ~ o.s. to** (*situation*) resignarse a; ~**ation** [rɛzɪg'neɪʃən] *n* dimisión *f*; (*state of*

mind) resignación *f*; ~**ed** *adj* resignado

resilient [rɪ'zɪlɪənt] *adj* (*material*) elástico; (*person*) resistente

resist [rɪ'zɪst] *vt* resistir, oponerse a; ~**ance** *n* resistencia

resolute ['rɛzəluːt] *adj* resuelto; (*refusal*) tajante

resolution [rɛzə'luːʃən] *n* (*gen*) resolución *f*

resolve [rɪ'zɔlv] *n* resolución *f* ♦ *vt* resolver ♦ *vi*: **to ~ to do** resolver hacer; ~**d** *adj* resuelto

resort [rɪ'zɔːt] *n* (*town*) centro turístico; (*recourse*) recurso ♦ *vi*: **to ~ to** recurrir a; **in the last ~** como último recurso

resounding [rɪ'zaundɪŋ] *adj* sonoro; (*fig*) clamoroso

resource [rɪ'sɔːs] *n* recurso; ~**s** *npl* recursos *mpl*; ~**ful** *adj* despabilado, ingenioso

respect [rɪs'pɛkt] *n* respeto ♦ *vt* respetar; ~**s** *npl* recuerdos *mpl*, saludos *mpl*; **with ~ to** con respecto a; **in this ~** en cuanto a eso; ~**able** *adj* respetable; (*large: amount*) apreciable; (*passable*) tolerable; ~**ful** *adj* respetuoso

respective [rɪs'pɛktɪv] *adj* respectivo; ~**ly** *adv* respectivamente

respite ['rɛspaɪt] *n* respiro

respond [rɪs'pɔnd] *vi* responder; (*react*) reaccionar; **response** [-'pɔns] *n* respuesta; reacción *f*

responsibility [rɪspɔnsɪ'bɪlɪtɪ] *n* responsabilidad *f*

responsible [rɪs'pɔnsɪbl] *adj* (*character*) serio, formal; (*job*) de confianza; (*liable*): ~ **(for)** responsable (de)

responsive [rɪs'pɔnsɪv] *adj* sensible

rest [rɛst] *n* descanso, reposo; (MUS, *pause*) pausa, silencio; (*support*) apoyo; (*remainder*) resto ♦ *vi* descansar; (*be supported*): **to ~ on** descansar sobre ♦ *vt* (*lean*): **to ~ sth on/against** apoyar algo en *or* sobre/contra; **the ~ of them** (*people, objects*) los demás; **it ~s with him to ...** depende de él el que ...

restaurant ['rɛstərɔŋ] *n* restaurante *m*; ~

car (BRIT) n (RAIL) coche-comedor m

restful ['restful] adj descansado, tranquilo

rest home n residencia para jubilados

restive ['restɪv] adj inquieto; (horse) rebelón(ona)

restless ['restlɪs] adj inquieto

restoration [restə'reɪʃən] n restauración f; devolución f

restore [rɪ'stɔː•] vt (building) restaurar; (sth stolen) devolver; (health) restablecer; (to power) volver a poner a

restrain [rɪs'treɪn] vt (feeling) contener, refrenar; (person): **to ~ (from doing)** disuadir (de hacer); **~ed** adj reservado; **~t** n (restriction) restricción f; (moderation) moderación f; (of manner) reserva

restrict [rɪs'trɪkt] vt restringir, limitar; **~ion** [-kʃən] n restricción f, limitación f; **~ive** adj restrictivo

rest room (US) n aseos mpl

result [rɪ'zʌlt] n resultado ♦ vi: **to ~ in** terminar en, tener por resultado; **as a ~ of** a consecuencia de

resume [rɪ'zjuːm] vt reanudar ♦ vi comenzar de nuevo

résumé ['reɪzjuːmeɪ] n resumen m; (US) currículum m

resumption [rɪ'zʌmpʃən] n reanudación f

resurgence [rɪ'səːdʒəns] n resurgimiento m

resurrection [rezə'rekʃən] n resurrección f

resuscitate [rɪ'sʌsɪteɪt] vt (MED) resucitar

retail ['riːteɪl] adj, adv al por menor; **~er** n detallista m/f; **~ price** n precio de venta al público

retain [rɪ'teɪn] vt (keep) retener, conservar; **~er** n (fee) anticipo

retaliate [rɪ'tælɪeɪt] vi: **to ~ (against)** tomar represalias (contra); **retaliation** [-'eɪʃən] n represalias fpl

retarded [rɪ'tɑːdɪd] adj retrasado

retch [retʃ] vi dársele a uno arcadas

retentive [rɪ'tentɪv] adj (memory) retentivo

retire [rɪ'taɪə•] vi (give up work) jubilarse; (withdraw) retirarse; (go to bed) acostarse; **~d** adj (person) jubilado; **~ment** n (giving up work: state) retiro, (: act) jubilación f; **retiring** adj (leaving)

saliente; (shy) retraído

retort [rɪ'tɔːt] vi contestar

retrace [riː'treɪs] vt: **to ~ one's steps** volver sobre sus pasos, desandar lo andado

retract [rɪ'trækt] vt (statement) retirar; (claws) retraer; (undercarriage, aerial) replegar

retrain [riː'treɪn] vt reciclar; **~ing** n readaptación f profesional

retread ['riːtred] n neumático (SP) or llanta (AM) recauchutado/a

retreat [rɪ'triːt] n (place) retiro; (MIL) retirada ♦ vi retirarse

retribution [retrɪ'bjuːʃən] n desquite m

retrieval [rɪ'triːvəl] n recuperación f

retrieve [rɪ'triːv] vt recobrar; (situation, honour) salvar; (COMPUT) recuperar; (error) reparar; **~r** n perro cobrador

retrospect ['retrəspekt] n: **in ~** retrospectivamente; **~ive** [-'spektɪv] adj retrospectivo; (law) retroactivo

return [rɪ'təːn] n (going or coming back) vuelta, regreso; (of sth stolen etc) devolución f; (FINANCE: from land, shares) ganancia, ingresos mpl ♦ cpd (journey) de regreso; (BRIT: ticket) de ida y vuelta; (match) de vuelta ♦ vi (person etc: come or go back) volver, regresar; (symptoms etc) reaparecer; (regain): **to ~ to** recuperar ♦ vt devolver; (favour, love etc) corresponder a; (verdict) pronunciar; (POL: candidate) elegir; **~s** npl (COMM) ingresos mpl; **in ~ (for)** a cambio (de); **by ~ of post** a vuelta de correo; **many happy ~s (of the day)!** ¡feliz cumpleaños!

reunion [riː'juːnɪən] n (of family) reunión f; (of two people, school) reencuentro

reunite [riːjuː'naɪt] vt reunir; (reconcile) reconciliar

rev [rev] (AUT) n abbr (= revolution) revolución f ♦ vt (also: **~ up**) acelerar

reveal [rɪ'viːl] vt revelar; **~ing** adj revelador(a)

revel ['revl] vi: **to ~ in sth/in doing sth** gozar de algo/con hacer algo

revenge [rɪ'vendʒ] n venganza; **to take ~**

on vengarse de

revenue ['revənju:] n ingresos mpl, rentas fpl

reverberate [rɪ'və:bəreɪt] vi (sound) resonar, retumbar; (fig: shock) repercutir

reverence ['revərəns] n reverencia

Reverend ['revərənd] adj (in titles): **the ~ John Smith** (Anglican) el Reverendo John Smith; (Catholic) el Padre John Smith; (Protestant) el Pastor John Smith

reversal [rɪ'və:sl] n (of order) inversión f; (of direction, policy) cambio; (of decision) revocación f

reverse [rɪ'və:s] n (opposite) contrario; (back: of cloth) revés m; (: of coin) reverso; (: of paper) dorso; (AUT: also: **~ gear**) marcha atrás; (setback) revés m ♦ adj (order) inverso; (direction) contrario; (process) opuesto ♦ vt (decision, AUT) dar marcha atrás a; (position, function) invertir ♦ vi (BRIT: AUT) dar marcha atrás; **~-charge call** (BRIT) n llamada a cobro revertido; **reversing lights** (BRIT) npl (AUT) luces fpl de retroceso

revert [rɪ'və:t] vi: **to ~ to** volver a

review [rɪ'vju:] n (magazine, MIL) revista; (of book, film) reseña; (US: examination) repaso, examen m ♦ vt repasar, examinar; (MIL) pasar revista a; (book, film) reseñar; **~er** n crítico/a

revise [rɪ'vaɪz] vt (manuscript) corregir; (opinion) modificar; (price, procedure) revisar ♦ vi (study) repasar; **revision** [rɪ'vɪʒən] n corrección f; modificación f; (for exam) repaso

revival [rɪ'vaɪvl] n (recovery) reanimación f; (of interest) renacimiento; (THEATRE) reestreno; (of faith) despertar m

revive [rɪ'vaɪv] vt resucitar; (custom) restablecer; (hope) despertar; (play) reestrenar ♦ vi (person) volver en sí; (business) reactivarse

revolt [rɪ'vəult] n rebelión f ♦ vi rebelarse, sublevarse ♦ vt dar asco a, repugnar; **~ing** adj asqueroso, repugnante

revolution [revə'lu:ʃən] n revolución f; **~ary** adj, n revolucionario/a m/f; **~ize** vt

revolucionar

revolve [rɪ'vɔlv] vi dar vueltas, girar; (life, discussion): **to ~ (a)round** girar en torno a

revolver [rɪ'vɔlvə*] n revólver m

revolving [rɪ'vɔlvɪŋ] adj (chair, door etc) giratorio

revue [rɪ'vju:] n (THEATRE) revista

revulsion [rɪ'vʌlʃən] n asco, repugnancia

reward [rɪ'wɔ:d] n premio, recompensa ♦ vt: **to ~ (for)** recompensar or premiar (por); **~ing** adj (fig) valioso

rewind [ri:'waɪnd] (irreg) vt rebobinar

rewire [ri:'waɪə*] vt (house) renovar la instalación eléctrica de

rheumatism ['ru:mətɪzəm] n reumatismo, reúma m

Rhine [raɪn] n: **the ~** el (río) Rin

rhinoceros [raɪ'nɔsərəs] n rinoceronte m

rhododendron [rəudə'dendrn] n rododendro

Rhone [rəun] n: **the ~** el (río) Ródano

rhubarb ['ru:ba:b] n ruibarbo

rhyme [raɪm] n rima; (verse) poesía

rhythm ['rɪðm] n ritmo

rib [rɪb] n (ANAT) costilla ♦ vt (mock) tomar el pelo a

ribbon ['rɪbən] n cinta; **in ~s** (torn) hecho trizas

rice [raɪs] n arroz m; **~ pudding** n arroz m con leche

rich [rɪtʃ] adj rico; (soil) fértil; (food) pesado; (: sweet) empalagoso; (abundant): **~ in** (minerals etc) rico en; **the ~** npl los ricos; **~es** npl riqueza; **~ly** adv ricamente; (deserved, earned) bien

rickets ['rɪkɪts] n raquitismo

rid [rɪd] (pt, pp **rid**) vt: **to ~ sb of sth** librar a uno de algo; **to get ~ of** deshacerse or desembarazarse de

ridden ['rɪdn] pp of **ride**

riddle ['rɪdl] n (puzzle) acertijo; (mystery) enigma m, misterio ♦ vt: **to be ~d with** ser lleno or plagado de

ride [raɪd] (pt **rode**, pp **ridden**) n paseo; (distance covered) viaje m, recorrido ♦ vi (as sport) montar; (go somewhere: on horse, bicycle) dar un paseo, pasearse;

(*travel: on bicycle, motorcycle, bus*) viajar ♦ *vt* (*a horse*) montar a; (*a bicycle, motorcycle*) andar en; (*distance*) recorrer; **to take sb for a ~** (*fig*) engañar a uno; **~r** *n* (*on horse*) jinete/a *m/f*; (*on bicycle*) ciclista *m/f*; (*on motorcycle*) motociclista *m/f*

ridge [rɪdʒ] *n* (*of hill*) cresta; (*of roof*) caballete *m*; (*wrinkle*) arruga

ridicule ['rɪdɪkjuːl] *n* irrisión *f*, burla ♦ *vt* poner en ridículo, burlarse de; **ridiculous** [-'dɪkjuləs] *adj* ridículo

riding ['raɪdɪŋ] *n* equitación *f*, **I like ~** me gusta montar a caballo; **~ school** *n* escuela de equitación

rife [raɪf] *adj*: **to be ~** ser muy común; **to be ~ with** abundar en

riffraff ['rɪfræf] *n* gentuza

rifle ['raɪfl] *n* rifle *m*, fusil *m* ♦ *vt* saquear; **~ through** *vt* (*papers*) registrar; **~ range** *n* campo de tiro; (*at fair*) tiro al blanco

rift [rɪft] *n* (*in clouds*) claro; (*fig: disagreement*) desavenencia

rig [rɪg] *n* (*also: oil ~: at sea*) plataforma petrolera ♦ *vt* (*election etc*) amañar; **~ out** (*BRIT*) *vt* disfrazar; **~ up** *vt* improvisar; **~ging** *n* (*NAUT*) aparejo

right [raɪt] *adj* (*correct*) correcto, exacto; (*suitable*) indicado, debido; (*proper*) apropiado; (*just*) justo; (*morally good*) bueno; (*not left*) derecho ♦ *n* bueno; (*title, claim*) derecho; (*not left*) derecha ♦ *adv* bien, correctamente; (*not left*) a la derecha; (*exactly*): **~ now** ahora mismo ♦ *vt* enderezar; (*correct*) corregir ♦ *excl* ¡bueno!, ¡está bien!; **to be ~** (*person*) tener razón; (*answer*) ser correcto; **is that the ~ time?** ¿es esa la hora buena?; **by ~s** en justicia; **on the ~** a la derecha; **to be in the ~** tener razón; **~ away** en seguida; **~ in the middle** exactamente en el centro; **~ angle** *n* ángulo recto; **~eous** ['raɪtʃəs] *adj* justado, honrado; (*anger*) justificado; **~ful** *adj* legítimo; **~-handed** *adj* diestro; **~-hand man** *n* brazo derecho; **~-hand side** *n*

derecha; **~ly** *adv* correctamente, debidamente; (*with reason*) con razón; **~ of way** *n* (*on path etc*) derecho de paso; (*AUT*) prioridad *f*; **~-wing** *adj* (*POL*) derechista

rigid ['rɪdʒɪd] *adj* rígido; (*person, ideas*) inflexible

rigmarole ['rɪgmərəul] *n* galimatías *m inv*

rigorous ['rɪgərəs] *adj* riguroso

rile [raɪl] *vt* irritar

rim [rɪm] *n* borde *m*; (*of spectacles*) aro; (*of wheel*) llanta

rind [raɪnd] *n* (*of bacon*) corteza; (*of lemon etc*) cáscara; (*of cheese*) costra

ring [rɪŋ] (*pt* **rang**, *pp* **rung**) *n* (*of metal*) aro; (*on finger*) anillo; (*of people*) corro; (*of objects*) círculo; (*gang*) banda; (*for boxing*) cuadrilátero; (*of circus*) pista; (*bull ~*) ruedo, plaza; (*sound of bell*) toque *m* ♦ *vi* (*on telephone*) llamar por teléfono; (*bell*) repicar; (*doorbell, phone*) sonar; (*also: ~ out*) sonar; (*ears*) zumbar ♦ *vt* (*BRIT: TEL*) llamar, telefonear; (*bell etc*) hacer sonar; (*doorbell*) tocar; **to give sb a ~** (*BRIT: TEL*) llamar or telefonear a alguien; **~ back** (*BRIT*) *vt, vi* (*TEL*) devolver la llamada; **~ off** (*BRIT*) *vi* (*TEL*) colgar, cortar la comunicación; **~ up** (*BRIT*) *vt* (*TEL*) llamar, telefonear; **~ing** *n* (*of bell*) repique *m*; (*of phone*) el sonar; (*in ears*) zumbido; **~ing tone** *n* (*TEL*) tono de llamada; **~leader** *n* (*of gang*) cabecilla *m*; **~lets** ['rɪŋlɪts] *npl* rizos *mpl*, bucles *mpl*; **~ road** (*BRIT*) *n* carretera periférica *or* de circunvalación

rink [rɪŋk] *n* (*also: ice ~*) pista de hielo

rinse [rɪns] *n* aclarado; (*dye*) tinte *m* ♦ *vt* aclarar; (*mouth*) enjuagar

riot ['raɪət] *n* motín *m*, disturbio ♦ *vi* amotinarse; **to run ~** desmandarse; **~ous** *adj* alborotado; (*party*) bullicioso

rip [rɪp] *n* rasgón *m*, rasgadura ♦ *vt* rasgar, desgarrar ♦ *vi* rasgarse, desgarrarse; **~cord** *n* cabo de desgarre

ripe [raɪp] *adj* maduro; **~n** *vt* madurar; (*cheese*) curar ♦ *vi* madurar

ripple ['rɪpl] *n* onda, rizo; (*sound*)

murmullo ♦ vi rizarse

rise [raɪz] (pt **rose**, pp **risen**) n (slope) cuesta, pendiente f; (hill) altura; (BRIT: in wages) aumento; (in prices, temperature) subida; (fig: to power etc) ascenso ♦ vi subir; (waters) crecer; (sun, moon) salir; (person: from bed etc) levantarse; (also: ~ **up**: rebel) sublevarse; (in rank) ascender; **to give ~ to** dar lugar or origen a; **to ~ to the occasion** ponerse a la altura de las circunstancias; **risen** ['rɪzn] pp of **rise**; **rising** adj (increasing: number) creciente; (: prices) en aumento or alza; (tide) creciente; (sun, moon) naciente

risk [rɪsk] n riesgo, peligro ♦ vt arriesgar; (run the ~ of) exponerse a; **to take** or **run the ~ of doing** correr el riesgo de hacer; **at ~** en peligro; **at one's own ~** bajo su propia responsabilidad; **~y** adj arriesgado, peligroso

rissole ['rɪsəʊl] n croqueta

rite [raɪt] n rito; **last ~s** exequias fpl

ritual ['rɪtjʊəl] adj ritual ♦ n ritual m, rito

rival ['raɪvl] n rival m/f; (in business) competidor(a) m/f ♦ adj rival, opuesto ♦ vt competir con; **~ry** n competencia

river ['rɪvə*] n río ♦ cpd (port) de río; (traffic) fluvial; **up/down ~** río arriba/ abajo; **~bank** n orilla (del río); **~bed** n lecho, cauce m

rivet ['rɪvɪt] n roblón m, remache m ♦ vt (fig) captar

Riviera [rɪvɪ'ɛərə] n: **the (French) ~** la Costa Azul (francesa)

road [rəʊd] n camino; (motorway etc) carretera; (in town) calle f ♦ cpd (accident) de tráfico; **major/minor ~** carretera principal/secundaria; **~ accident** n accidente m de tráfico; **~block** n barricada; **~hog** n loco/a del volante; **~ map** n mapa m de carreteras; **~ rage** n agresividad en la carretera; **~ safety** n seguridad f vial; **~side** n borde m (del camino); **~sign** n señal f de tráfico; **~ user** n usuario/a de la vía pública; **~way** n calzada; **~works** npl obras fpl; **~worthy** adj (car) en buen estado para

circular

roam [rəʊm] vi vagar

roar [rɔ:*] n rugido; (of vehicle, storm) estruendo; (of laughter) carcajada ♦ vi rugir; hacer estruendo; **to ~ with laughter** reírse a carcajadas; **to do a ~ing trade** hacer buen negocio

roast [rəʊst] n carne f asada, asado ♦ vt asar; (coffee) tostar; **~ beef** n rosbif m

rob [rɒb] vt robar; **to ~ sb of sth** robar algo a uno; (fig: deprive) quitar algo a uno; **~ber** n ladrón/ona m/f; **~bery** n robo

robe [rəʊb] n (for ceremony etc) toga; (also: **bath~**, US) albornoz m

robin ['rɒbɪn] n petirrojo

robot ['rəʊbɒt] n robot m

robust [rəʊ'bʌst] adj robusto, fuerte

rock [rɒk] n roca; (boulder) peña, peñasco; (US: small stone) piedrecita; (BRIT: sweet) ≈ pirulí ♦ vt (swing gently: cradle) balancear, mecer; (: child) arrullar; (shake) sacudir ♦ vi mecerse, balancearse; sacudirse; **on the ~s** (drink) con hielo; (marriage etc) en ruinas; **~ and roll** n rocanrol m; **~-bottom** n (fig) punto más bajo; **~ery** n cuadro alpino

rocket ['rɒkɪt] n cohete m

rocking ['rɒkɪŋ]: **~ chair** n mecedora; **~ horse** n caballo de balancín

rocky ['rɒkɪ] adj rocoso

rod [rɒd] n vara, varilla; (also: **fishing ~**) caña

rode [rəʊd] pt of **ride**

rodent ['rəʊdnt] n roedor m

roe [rəʊ] n (species: also: **~ deer**) corzo; (of fish): **hard/soft ~** hueva/lecha

rogue [rəʊg] n pícaro, pillo

role [rəʊl] n papel m

roll [rəʊl] n rollo; (of bank notes) fajo; (also: **bread ~**) panecillo; (register, list) lista, nómina; (sound: of drums etc) redoble m ♦ vt hacer rodar; (also: **~ up**: string) enrollar; (: sleeves) arremangar; (cigarette) liar; (also: **~ out**: pastry) aplanar; (flatten: road, lawn) apisonar ♦ vi rodar; (drum) redoblar; (ship) balancearse; **~ about or**

around vi (*person*) revolcarse; (*object*) rodar (por); ~ **by** vi (*time*) pasar; ~ **over** vi dar una vuelta; ~ **up** vi (*inf: arrive*) aparecer ♦ vt (*carpet*) arrollar; ~ **call** n: **to take a ~ call** pasar lista; ~**er** n rodillo; (*wheel*) rueda; (*for road*) apisonadora; (*for hair*) rulo; ~**erblade** n patín m (en línea); ~**er coaster** n montaña rusa; ~**er skates** npl patines mpl de rueda

rolling ['rəʊlɪŋ] adj (*landscape*) ondulado; ~ **pin** n rodillo (de cocina); ~ **stock** n (*RAIL*) material m rodante

ROM [rɔm] n abbr (*COMPUT*: = *read only memory*) ROM f

Roman ['rəʊmən] adj romano/a; ~ **Catholic** adj, n católico/a m/f (romano/a)

romance [rə'mæns] n (*love affair*) amor m; (*charm*) lo romántico; (*novel*) novela de amor

Romania [ruː'meɪnɪə] n = **Rumania**

Roman numeral n número romano

romantic [rə'mæntɪk] adj romántico

Rome [rəʊm] n Roma

romp [rɔmp] n retozo, juego ♦ vi (*also:* ~ **about**) jugar, brincar

rompers ['rɔmpəz] npl pelele m

roof [ruːf] (pl ~**s**) n (*gen*) techo; (*of house*) techo, tejado ♦ vt techar, poner techo a; **the ~ of the mouth** el paladar; ~**ing** n techumbre f; ~ **rack** n (*AUT*) baca, portaequipajes m inv

rook [rʊk] n (*bird*) graja; (*CHESS*) torre f

room [ruːm] n cuarto, habitación f, pieza (*esp AM*); (*also:* **bed~**) dormitorio; (*in school etc*) sala; (*space, scope*) sitio, cabida; ~**s** npl (*lodging*) alojamiento; "**~s to let**", "**~s for rent**" (*US*) "se alquilan cuartos"; **single/double ~** habitación individual/doble or para dos personas; ~**ing house** (*US*) n pensión f; ~**mate** n compañero/a de cuarto; ~ **service** n servicio de habitaciones; ~**y** adj espacioso; (*garment*) amplio

roost [ruːst] vi pasar la noche

rooster ['ruːstə*] n gallo

root [ruːt] n raíz f ♦ vi arraigarse; ~ **about**

vi (*fig*) buscar y rebuscar; ~ **for** vt fus (*support*) apoyar a; ~ **out** vt desarraigar

rope [rəʊp] n cuerda; (*NAUT*) cable m ♦ vt (*tie*) atar or amarrar con (una) cuerda; (*climbers: also:* ~ **together**) encordarse; (*an area: also:* ~ **off**) acordonar; **to know the ~s** (*fig*) conocer los trucos (del oficio); ~ **in** vt (*fig*): **to ~ sb in** persuadir a uno a tomar parte

rosary ['rəʊzərɪ] n rosario

rose [rəʊz] pt of **rise** ♦ n rosa; (*shrub*) rosal m; (*on watering can*) roseta

rosé ['rəʊzeɪ] n vino rosado

rosebud ['rəʊzbʌd] n capullo de rosa

rosebush ['rəʊzbʊʃ] n rosal m

rosemary ['rəʊzmərɪ] n romero

roster ['rɔstə*] n: **duty ~** lista de deberes

rostrum ['rɔstrəm] n tribuna

rosy ['rəʊzɪ] adj rosado, sonrosado; **a ~ future** un futuro prometedor

rot [rɔt] n podredumbre f; (*fig: pej*) tonterías fpl ♦ vt pudrir ♦ vi pudrirse

rota ['rəʊtə] n (sistema m de) turnos mpl

rotary ['rəʊtərɪ] adj rotativo

rotate [rəʊ'teɪt] vt (*revolve*) hacer girar, dar vueltas a; (*jobs*) alternar ♦ vi girar, dar vueltas; **rotating** adj rotativo; **rotation** [-'teɪʃən] n rotación f

rotten ['rɔtn] adj podrido; (*dishonest*) corrompido; (*inf: bad*) pocho; **to feel ~** (*ill*) sentirse fatal

rotund [rəʊ'tʌnd] adj regordete

rouble ['ruːbl] (*US* **ruble**) n rublo

rough [rʌf] adj (*skin, surface*) áspero; (*terrain*) quebrado; (*road*) desigual; (*voice*) bronco; (*person, manner*) tosco, grosero; (*weather*) borrascoso; (*treatment*) brutal; (*sea*) picado; (*town, area*) peligroso; (*cloth*) basto; (*plan*) preliminar; (*guess*) aproximado ♦ n (*GOLF*): **in the ~** en las hierbas altas; **to ~ it** vivir sin comodidades; **to sleep ~** (*BRIT*) pasar la noche al raso; ~**age** n fibra(s) f(pl); ~**-and-ready** adj improvisado; ~ **copy** n borrador m; ~ **draft** n = ~ **copy**; ~**ly** adv (*handle*) torpemente; (*make*) toscamente; (*speak*) groseramente;

(*approximately*) aproximadamente; ~ness *n* (*of surface*) aspereza; (*of person*) rudeza

roulette [ru:'let] *n* ruleta

Roumania [ru:'meɪnɪə] *n* = **Rumania**

round [raund] *adj* redondo ♦ *n* círculo; (*BRIT: of toast*) rebanada; (*of policeman*) ronda; (*of milkman*) recorrido; (*of doctor*) visitas *fpl*; (*game: of cards, in competition*) partida; (*of ammunition*) cartucho; (*BOXING*) asalto; (*of talks*) ronda ♦ *vt* (*corner*) doblar ♦ *prep* alrededor de; (*surrounding*): ~ **his neck/the table** en su cuello/alrededor de la mesa; (*in a circular movement*): **to move ~ the room/sail ~ the world** dar una vuelta a la habitación/circunnavigar el mundo; (*in various directions*): **to move ~ a room** moverse por toda la habitación/casa; (*approximately*) alrededor de ♦ *adv*: **all ~** por todos lados; **the long way ~** por el camino menos directo; **all the year ~** durante todo el año; **it's just ~ the corner** (*fig*) está a la vuelta de la esquina; **~ the clock** *adv* las 24 horas; **to go ~ to sb's (house)** ir a casa de uno; **to go ~ the back** pasar por atrás; **enough to go ~** bastante (para todos); **a ~ of applause** una salva de aplausos; **a ~ of drinks/sandwiches** ronda de bebidas/bocadillos; ~ **off** *vt* (*speech etc*) acabar, poner término a; ~ **up** *vt* (*cattle*) acorralar; (*people*) reunir; (*price*) redondear; ~**about** (*BRIT*) *n* (*AUT*) isleta; (*at fair*) tiovivo ♦ *adj* (*route, means*) indirecto; ~**ers** *n* (*game*) juego similar al *béisbol*; ~**ly** *adv* (*fig*) rotundamente; ~**trip** *n* viaje *m* de ida y vuelta; ~**up** *n* rodeo; (*of criminals*) redada; (*of news*) resumen *m*

rouse [rauz] *vt* (*wake up*) despertar; (*stir up*) suscitar; **rousing** *adj* (*cheer, welcome*) caluroso

route [ru:t] *n* ruta, camino; (*of bus*) recorrido; (*of shipping*) derrota

routine [ru:'ti:n] *adj* rutinario ♦ *n* rutina; (*THEATRE*) número

rove [rəuv] *vt* vagar *or* errar por

row[1] [rəu] *n* (*line*) fila, hilera; (*KNITTING*) pasada ♦ *vi* (*in boat*) remar ♦ *vt* conducir remando; **4 days in a ~** 4 días seguidos

row[2] [rau] *n* (*racket*) escándalo; (*dispute*) bronca, pelea; (*scolding*) regaño ♦ *vi* pelear(se)

rowboat ['rəubəut] (*US*) *n* bote *m* de remos

rowdy ['raudɪ] *adj* (*person: noisy*) ruidoso; (*occasion*) alborotado

rowing ['rəuɪŋ] *n* remo; ~ **boat** (*BRIT*) *n* bote *m* de remos

royal ['rɔɪəl] *adj* real; **R~ Air Force** *n* Fuerzas *fpl* Aéreas Británicas; ~**ty** *n* (~ *persons*) familia real; (*payment to author*) derechos *mpl* de autor

rpm *abbr* (= *revs per minute*) r.p.m.

R.S.V.P. *abbr* (= *répondez s'il vous plaît*) SRC

Rt. Hon. *abbr* (*BRIT*: = *Right Honourable*) título honorífico de diputado

rub [rʌb] *vt* frotar; (*scrub*) restregar ♦ *n*: **to give sth a ~** frotar algo; **to ~ sb up** *or* ~ **sb** (*US*) **the wrong way** entrarle uno por mal ojo; ~ **off** *vi* borrarse; ~ **off on** *vt fus* influir en; ~ **out** *vt* borrar

rubber ['rʌbə*] *n* caucho, goma; (*BRIT: eraser*) goma de borrar; ~ **band** *n* goma, gomita; ~ **plant** *n* ficus *m*

rubbish ['rʌbɪʃ] *n* basura; (*waste*) desperdicios *mpl*; (*fig: pej*) tonterías *fpl*; (*junk*) pacotilla; ~ **bin** (*BRIT*) *n* cubo (*SP*) *or* bote *m* (*AM*) de la basura; ~ **dump** *n* vertedero, basurero

rubble ['rʌbl] *n* escombros *mpl*

ruble ['ru:bl] (*US*) *n* = **rouble**

ruby ['ru:bɪ] *n* rubí *m*

rucksack ['rʌksæk] *n* mochila

rudder ['rʌdə*] *n* timón *m*

ruddy ['rʌdɪ] *adj* (*face*) rubicundo; (*inf: damned*) condenado

rude [ru:d] *adj* (*impolite: person*) mal educado; (*: word, manners*) grosero; (*crude*) crudo; (*indecent*) indecente; ~**ness** *n* descortesía

ruffle ['rʌfl] *vt* (*hair*) despeinar; (*clothes*) arrugar; **to get ~d** (*fig: person*) alterarse

rug [rʌg] n alfombra; (BRIT: blanket) manta

rugby ['rʌgbɪ] n (also: ~ **football**) rugby m

rugged ['rʌgɪd] adj (landscape) accidentado; (features) robusto

ruin ['ruːɪn] n ruina ♦ vt arruinar; (spoil) estropear; ~s npl ruinas fpl, restos mpl

rule [ruːl] n (norm) norma, costumbre f; (regulation, ruler) regla; (government) dominio ♦ vt (country, person) gobernar ♦ vi gobernar; (LAW) fallar; **as a ~** por regla general; ~ **out** vt excluir; ~**d** adj (paper) rayado; ~**r** n (sovereign) soberano; (for measuring) regla; **ruling** adj (party) gobernante; (class) dirigente ♦ n (LAW) fallo, decisión f

rum [rʌm] n ron m

Rumania [ruːˈmeɪnɪə] n Rumanía; ~**n** adj rumano/a ♦ n rumano/a m/f; (LING) rumano

rumble ['rʌmbl] n (noise) ruido sordo ♦ vi retumbar, hacer un ruido sordo; (stomach, pipe) sonar

rummage ['rʌmɪdʒ] vi (search) hurgar

rumour ['ruːmə*] (US **rumor**) n rumor m ♦ vt: **it is ~ed that ...** se rumorea que ...

rump [rʌmp] n (of animal) ancas fpl, grupa; ~ **steak** n filete m de lomo

rumpus ['rʌmpəs] n lío, jaleo

run [rʌn] (pt **ran**, pp **run**) n (fast pace): **at a ~** corriendo; (SPORT, in tights) carrera; (outing) paseo, excursión f; (distance travelled) trayecto; (series) serie f; (THEATRE) temporada; (SKI) pista ♦ vt correr; (operate: business) dirigir; (: competition, course) organizar; (: hotel, house) administrar, llevar; (COMPUT) ejecutar; (pass: hand) pasar; (PRESS: feature) publicar ♦ vi correr; (work: machine) funcionar, marchar; (bus, train: operate) circular, ir; (: travel) ir; (continue: play) seguir; (: contract) ser válido; (flow: river) fluir; (colours, washing) desteñirse; (in election) ser candidato; **there was a ~ on** (meat, tickets) hubo mucha demanda de; **in the long ~** a la larga; **on the ~** en fuga; **I'll ~ you to the station** te llevaré a la estación (en coche); **to ~ a risk** correr

un riesgo; **to ~ a bath** llenar la bañera; ~ **about** or **around** vi (children) correr por todos lados; ~ **across** vt fus (find) dar or topar con; ~ **away** vi huir; ~ **down** vt (production) ir reduciendo; (factory) ir restringiendo la producción en; (subj: car) atropellar; (criticize) criticar; **to be ~ down** (person: tired) estar debilitado; ~ **in** (BRIT) vt (car) rodar; ~ **into** vt fus (meet: person, trouble) tropezar con; (collide with) chocar con; ~ **off** vt (water) dejar correr; (copies) sacar ♦ vi huir corriendo; ~ **out** vi (person) salir corriendo; (liquid) irse; (lease) caducar, vencer; (money etc) acabarse; ~ **out of** vt fus quedar sin; ~ **over** vt (AUT) atropellar ♦ vt fus (revise) repasar; ~ **through** vt fus (instructions) repasar; ~ **up** vt (debt) contraer; **to ~ up against** (difficulties) tropezar con; ~**away** adj (horse) desbocado; (truck) sin frenos; (child) escapado de casa

rung [rʌŋ] pp of **ring** ♦ n (of ladder) escalón m, peldaño

runner ['rʌnə*] n (in race: person) corredor(a) m/f; (: horse) caballo; (on sledge) patín m; ~ **bean** (BRIT) n ≈ judía verde; ~**-up** n subcampeón/ona m/f

running ['rʌnɪŋ] n (sport) atletismo; (business) administración f ♦ adj (water, costs) corriente; (commentary) continuo; **to be in/out of the ~ for sth** tener/no tener posibilidades de ganar algo; **6 days ~** 6 días seguidos; ~ **commentary** n (TV, RADIO) comentario en directo; (on guided tour etc) comentario detallado; ~ **costs** npl gastos mpl corrientes

runny ['rʌnɪ] adj fluido; (nose, eyes) gastante

run-of-the-mill adj común y corriente

runt [rʌnt] n (also pej) redrojo, enano

run-up n: ~ **to** (election etc) período previo a

runway ['rʌnweɪ] n (AVIAT) pista de aterrizaje

rural ['ruərl] adj rural

rush [rʌʃ] n ímpetu m; (hurry) prisa; (COMM) demanda repentina; (current) corriente f fuerte; (of feeling) torrente; (BOT) junco ♦ vt apresurar; (work) hacer de prisa ♦ vi correr, precipitarse; ~ **hour** n horas fpl punta

rusk [rʌsk] n bizcocho tostado

Russia ['rʌʃə] n Rusia; ~n adj ruso/a ♦ n ruso/a m/f; (LING) ruso

rust [rʌst] n herrumbre f, moho ♦ vi oxidarse

rustic ['rʌstɪk] adj rústico

rustle ['rʌsl] vi susurrar ♦ vt (paper) hacer crujir

rustproof ['rʌstpruːf] adj inoxidable

rusty ['rʌstɪ] adj oxidado

rut [rʌt] n surco; (ZOOL) celo; **to be in a ~** ser esclavo de la rutina

ruthless ['ruːθlɪs] adj despiadado

rye [raɪ] n centeno

S, s

Sabbath ['sæbəθ] n domingo; (Jewish) sábado

sabotage ['sæbətɑːʒ] n sabotaje m ♦ vt sabotear

saccharin(e) ['sækərɪn] n sacarina

sachet ['sæʃeɪ] n sobrecito

sack [sæk] n (bag) saco, costal m ♦ vt (dismiss) despedir; (plunder) saquear; **to get the ~** ser despedido; ~**ing** n despido; (material) arpillera

sacred ['seɪkrɪd] adj sagrado, santo

sacrifice ['sækrɪfaɪs] n sacrificio ♦ vt sacrificar

sad [sæd] adj (unhappy) triste; (deplorable) lamentable

saddle ['sædl] n silla (de montar); (of cycle) sillín m ♦ vt (horse) ensillar; **to be ~d with sth** (inf) quedar cargado con algo; ~**bag** n alforja

sadistic [sə'dɪstɪk] adj sádico

sadly ['sædlɪ] adv lamentablemente; **to be ~ lacking in** estar por desgracia carente de

sadness ['sædnɪs] n tristeza

s.a.e. abbr (= stamped addressed

envelope) sobre con las propias señas de uno y con sello

safari [sə'fɑːrɪ] n safari m

safe [seɪf] adj (out of danger) fuera de peligro; (not dangerous, sure) seguro; (unharmed) ileso ♦ n caja de caudales, caja fuerte; **~ and sound** sano y salvo; **(just) to be on the ~ side** para mayor seguridad; ~-**conduct** n salvoconducto; ~-**deposit** n (vault) cámara acorazada; (box) caja de seguridad; ~**guard** n protección f, garantía ♦ vt proteger, defender; ~**keeping** n custodia; ~**ly** adv seguramente, con seguridad; **to arrive ~ly** llegar bien; ~ **sex** n sexo seguro or sin riesgo

safety ['seɪftɪ] n seguridad f; ~ **belt** n cinturón m (de seguridad); ~ **pin** n imperdible m (SP), seguro (AM); ~ **valve** n válvula de seguridad

saffron ['sæfrən] n azafrán m

sag [sæg] vi aflojarse

sage [seɪdʒ] n (herb) salvia; (man) sabio

Sagittarius [sædʒɪ'tɛərɪəs] n Sagitario

Sahara [sə'hɑːrə] n: **the ~ (Desert)** el (desierto del) Sáhara

said [sed] pt, pp of say

sail [seɪl] n (on boat) vela; (trip): **to go for a ~** dar un paseo en barco ♦ vt (boat) gobernar ♦ vi (travel: ship) navegar; (SPORT) hacer vela; (begin voyage) salir; **they ~ed into Copenhagen** arribaron a Copenhague; ~ **through** vt fus (exam) aprobar sin ningún problema; ~**boat** (US) n velero, barco de vela; ~**ing** n (SPORT) vela; **to go ~ing** hacer vela; ~**ing boat** n barco de vela; ~**ing ship** n velero; ~**or** n marinero, marino

saint [seɪnt] n santo; ~**ly** adj santo

sake [seɪk] n: **for the ~ of** por

salad ['sæləd] n ensalada; ~ **bowl** n ensaladera; ~ **cream** (BRIT) n (especie f de) mayonesa; ~ **dressing** n aliño

salary ['sælərɪ] n sueldo

sale [seɪl] n venta; (at reduced prices) liquidación f, saldo; (auction) subasta; ~**s** npl (total amount sold) ventas fpl, facturación *f*; **"for ~"** "se vende"; **on ~** en venta; **on ~ or return** (*goods*) venta por reposición; **~room** *n* sala de subastas; **~s assistant** (*US* **~s clerk**) *n* dependiente/a *m/f*; **salesman/woman** (*irreg*) *n* (*in shop*) dependiente/a *m/f*; (*representative*) viajante *m/f*

salmon ['sæmən] *n inv* salmón *m*

salon ['sælɔn] *n* (*hairdressing ~*) peluquería; (*beauty ~*) salón *m* de belleza

saloon [sə'luːn] *n* (*US*) bar *m*, taberna; (*BRIT*: *AUT*) (coche *m* de) turismo; (*ship's lounge*) cámara, salón *m*

salt [sɔlt] *n* sal *f* ♦ *vt* salar; (*put ~ on*) poner sal en; **~ cellar** *n* salero; **~water** *adj* de agua salada; **~y** *adj* salado

salute [sə'luːt] *n* saludo; (*of guns*) salva ♦ *vt* saludar

salvage ['sælvɪdʒ] *n* (*saving*) salvamento, recuperación *f*; (*things saved*) objetos *mpl* salvados ♦ *vt* salvar

salvation [sæl'veɪʃən] *n* salvación *f*; **S~ Army** *n* Ejército de Salvación

same [seɪm] *adj* mismo ♦ *pron*: **the ~** el/la mismo/a, los/las mismos/as; **the ~ book as** el mismo libro que; **at the ~ time** (*at the ~ moment*) al mismo tiempo; (*yet*) sin embargo; **all** *or* **just the ~** sin embargo, aun así; **to do the ~ (as sb)** hacer lo mismo (que uno); **the ~ to you!** ¡igualmente!

sample ['sɑːmpl] *n* muestra ♦ *vt* (*food*) probar; (*wine*) catar

sanction ['sæŋkʃən] *n* aprobación *f* ♦ *vt* sancionar; aprobar; **~s** *npl* (*POL*) sanciones *fpl*

sanctity ['sæŋktɪtɪ] *n* santidad *f*; (*inviolability*) inviolabilidad *f*

sanctuary ['sæŋktjuərɪ] *n* santuario; (*refuge*) asilo, refugio; (*for wildlife*) reserva

sand [sænd] *n* arena; (*beach*) playa ♦ *vt* (*also*: **~ down**) lijar

sandal ['sændl] *n* sandalia

sand: **~box** (*US*) *n* = **~pit**; **~castle** *n* castillo de arena; **~ dune** *n* duna; **~paper** *n* papel *m* de lija; **~pit** *n* (*for children*) cajón *m* de arena; **~stone** *n* piedra arenisca

sandwich ['sændwɪtʃ] *n* bocadillo (*SP*), sandwich *m*, emparedado (*AM*) ♦ *vt* intercalar; **~ed between** apretujado entre; **cheese/ham ~** sandwich de queso/jamón; **~ course** (*BRIT*) *n* curso de medio tiempo

sandy ['sændɪ] *adj* arenoso; (*colour*) rojizo

sane [seɪn] *adj* cuerdo; (*sensible*) sensato

sang [sæŋ] *pt of* **sing**

sanitary ['sænɪtərɪ] *adj* sanitario; (*clean*) higiénico; **~ towel** (*US* **~ napkin**) *n* paño higiénico, compresa

sanitation [sænɪ'teɪʃən] *n* (*in house*) servicios *mpl* higiénicos; (*in town*) servicio de desinfección; **~ department** (*US*) *n* departamento de limpieza y recogida de basuras

sanity ['sænɪtɪ] *n* cordura; (*of judgment*) sensatez *f*

sank [sæŋk] *pt of* **sink**

Santa Claus [sæntə'klɔːz] *n* San Nicolás, Papá Noel

sap [sæp] *n* (*of plants*) savia ♦ *vt* (*strength*) minar, agotar

sapling ['sæplɪŋ] *n* árbol nuevo *or* joven

sapphire ['sæfaɪə*] *n* zafiro

sarcasm ['sɑːkæzm] *n* sarcasmo

sardine [sɑː'diːn] *n* sardina

Sardinia [sɑː'dɪnɪə] *n* Cerdeña

sash [sæʃ] *n* faja

sat [sæt] *pt, pp of* **sit**

Satan ['seɪtn] *n* Satanás *m*

satchel ['sætʃl] *n* (*child's*) cartera (*SP*), mochila (*AM*)

satellite ['sætəlaɪt] *n* satélite *m*; **~ dish** *n* antena de televisión por satélite; **~ television** *n* televisión *f* vía satélite

satin ['sætɪn] *n* raso ♦ *adj* de raso

satire ['sætaɪə*] *n* sátira

satisfaction [sætɪs'fækʃən] *n* satisfacción *f*

satisfactory [sætɪs'fæktərɪ] *adj* satisfactorio

satisfy ['sætɪsfaɪ] *vt* satisfacer; (*convince*) convencer; **~ing** *adj* satisfactorio

Saturday ['sætədɪ] *n* sábado

sauce [sɔːs] *n* salsa; (*sweet*) crema; jarabe *m*; **~pan** *n* cacerola, olla

saucer ['sɔːsə*] n platillo

Saudi ['saʊdɪ]: ~ Arabia n Arabia Saudí or Saudita; ~ (Arabian) adj, n saudí m/f, saudita m/f

sauna ['sɔːnə] n sauna

saunter ['sɔːntə*] vi: to ~ in/out entrar/salir sin prisa

sausage ['sɒsɪdʒ] n salchicha; ~ roll n empanadita de salchicha

sauté ['saʊteɪ] adj salteado

savage ['sævɪdʒ] adj (cruel, fierce) feroz, furioso; (primitive) salvaje ♦ n salvaje m/f ♦ vt (attack) embestir

save [seɪv] vt (rescue) salvar, rescatar; (money, time) ahorrar; (put by, keep: seat) guardar; (COMPUT) salvar (y guardar); (avoid: trouble) evitar; (SPORT) parar ♦ vi (also: ~ up) ahorrar ♦ n (SPORT) parada ♦ prep salvo, excepto

saving ['seɪvɪŋ] n (on price etc) economía ♦ adj: the ~ grace of el único mérito de; ~s npl ahorros mpl; ~s account n cuenta de ahorros; ~s bank n caja de ahorros

saviour ['seɪvjə*] (US savior) n salvador(a) m/f

savour ['seɪvə*] (US savor) vt saborear; ~y adj sabroso; (dish: not sweet) salado

saw [sɔː] (pt sawed, pp sawed or sawn) pt of see ♦ n (tool) sierra ♦ vt serrar; ~dust n (a)serrín m; ~mill n aserradero; ~n-off shotgun n escopeta de cañones recortados

saxophone ['sæksəfəʊn] n saxófono

say [seɪ] (pt, pp said) n: to have one's ~ expresar su opinión ♦ vt decir; to have a or some ~ in sth tener voz or tener que ver en algo; to ~ yes/no decir que sí/no; could you ~ that again? ¿podría repetir eso?; that is to ~ es decir; that goes without ~ing ni que decir tiene; ~ing n dicho, refrán m

scab [skæb] n costra; (pej) esquirol m

scaffold ['skæfəʊld] n cadalso; ~ing n andamio, andamiaje m

scald [skɔːld] n escaldadura ♦ vt escaldar

scale [skeɪl] n (gen, MUS) escala; (of fish)

escama; (of salaries, fees etc) escalafón m ♦ vt (mountain) escalar; (tree) trepar; ~s npl (for weighing: small) balanza; (: large) báscula; on a large ~ en gran escala; ~ of charges tarifa, lista de precios; ~ down vt reducir a escala

scallop ['skɒləp] n (ZOOL) venera; (SEWING) festón m

scalp [skælp] n cabellera ♦ vt escalpar

scampi ['skæmpɪ] npl gambas fpl

scan [skæn] vt (examine) escudriñar; (glance at quickly) dar un vistazo a; (TV, RADAR) explorar, registrar ♦ n (MED): to have a ~ pasar por el escáner

scandal ['skændl] n escándalo; (gossip) chismes mpl

Scandinavia [skændɪ'neɪvɪə] n Escandinavia; ~n adj, n escandinavo/a m/f

scant [skænt] adj escaso; ~y adj (meal) insuficiente; (clothes) ligero

scapegoat ['skeɪpgəʊt] n cabeza de turco, chivo expiatorio

scar [skɑː] n cicatriz f; (fig) señal f ♦ vt dejar señales en

scarce [skeəs] adj escaso; to make o.s. ~ (inf) esfumarse; ~ly adv apenas; scarcity n escasez f

scare [skeə*] n susto, sobresalto; (panic) pánico ♦ vt asustar, espantar; to ~ sb stiff dar a uno un susto de muerte; bomb ~ amenaza de bomba; ~ off or away vt ahuyentar; ~crow n espantapájaros m inv; ~d adj: to be ~d estar asustado

scarf [skɑːf] (pl ~s or scarves) n (long) bufanda; (square) pañuelo

scarlet ['skɑːlɪt] adj escarlata; ~ fever n escarlatina

scarves [skɑːvz] npl of scarf

scary ['skeərɪ] (inf) adj espeluznante

scathing ['skeɪðɪŋ] adj mordaz

scatter ['skætə*] vt (spread) esparcir, desparramar; (put to flight) dispersar ♦ vi desparramarse; dispersarse; ~brained adj ligero de cascos

scavenger ['skævəndʒə*] n (person) basurero/a

scenario [sɪˈnɑːrɪəu] n (THEATRE) argumento; (CINEMA) guión m; (fig) escenario

scene [siːn] n (THEATRE, fig etc) escena; (of crime etc) escenario; (view) panorama m; (fuss) escándalo; ~ry n (THEATRE) decorado; (landscape) paisaje m; **scenic** adj pintoresco

scent [sɛnt] n perfume m, olor m; (fig: track) rastro, pista

sceptic [ˈskɛptɪk] (US **skeptic**) n escéptico/a; ~al adj escéptico

sceptre [ˈsɛptə*] (US **scepter**) n cetro

schedule [ˈʃɛdjuːl, (US) ˈskɛdjuːl] n (timetable) horario; (of events) programa m; (list) lista ♦ vt (visit) fijar la hora de; **to arrive on ~** llegar a la hora debida; **to be ahead of/behind ~** estar adelantado/en retraso; ~**d flight** n vuelo regular

scheme [skiːm] n (plan) plan m, proyecto; (plot) intriga; (arrangement) disposición f; (pension ~ etc) sistema m ♦ vi (intrigue) intrigar; **scheming** adj intrigante ♦ n intrigas fpl

schizophrenic [skɪtzəˈfrɛnɪk] adj esquizofrénico

scholar [ˈskɔlə*] n (pupil) alumno/a; (learned person) sabio/a, erudito/a; ~**ship** n erudición f; (grant) beca

school [skuːl] n escuela, colegio; (in university) facultad f ♦ cpd escolar; ~ **age** n edad f escolar; ~**book** n libro de texto; ~**boy** n alumno; ~ **children** npl alumnos mpl; ~**girl** n alumna; ~**ing** n enseñanza; ~**master/mistress** n (primary) maestro/a; (secondary) profesor(a) m/f; ~**teacher** n (primary) maestro/a; (secondary) profesor(a) m/f

schooner [ˈskuːnə*] n (ship) goleta

sciatica [saɪˈætɪkə] n ciática

science [ˈsaɪəns] n ciencia; ~ **fiction** n ciencia-ficción f; **scientific** [-ˈtɪfɪk] adj científico; **scientist** n científico/a

scissors [ˈsɪzəz] npl tijeras fpl; **a pair of ~** unas tijeras

scoff [skɔf] vt (BRIT: inf: eat) engullir ♦ vi: **to ~ (at)** (mock) mofarse (de)

scold [skəuld] vt regañar

scone [skɔn] n pastel de pan

scoop [skuːp] n (for flour etc) pala; (PRESS) exclusiva; ~ **out** vt excavar; ~ **up** vt recoger

scooter [ˈskuːtə*] n moto f; (toy) patinete m

scope [skəup] n (of plan) ámbito; (of person) competencia; (opportunity) libertad f (de acción)

scorch [skɔːtʃ] vt (clothes) chamuscar; (earth, grass) quemar, secar

score [skɔː*] n (points etc) puntuación f; (MUS) partitura; (twenty) veintena ♦ vt (goal, point) ganar; (mark) rayar; ♦ vi marcar un tanto; (FOOTBALL) marcar (un) gol; (keep score) llevar el tanteo; ~**s of** (very many) decenas de; **on that ~** en lo que se refiere a eso; **to ~ 6 out of 10** obtener una puntuación de 6 sobre 10; ~ **out** vt tachar; ~ **over** vt fus obtener una victoria sobre; ~**board** n marcador m

scorn [skɔːn] n desprecio; ~**ful** adj desdeñoso, despreciativo

Scorpio [ˈskɔːpɪəu] n Escorpión m

scorpion [ˈskɔːpɪən] n alacrán m

Scot [skɔt] n escocés/esa m/f

Scotch [skɔtʃ] n whisky m escocés

Scotland [ˈskɔtlənd] n Escocia

Scots [skɔts] adj escocés/esa; ~**man/woman** (irreg) n escocés/esa m/f; **Scottish** [ˈskɔtɪʃ] adj escocés/esa; **Scottish Parliament** n Parlamento escocés

scoundrel [ˈskaundrəl] n canalla m/f, sinvergüenza m/f

scout [skaut] n (MIL, also: **boy ~**) explorador m; **girl ~** (US) niña exploradora; ~ **around** vi reconocer el terreno

scowl [skaul] vi fruncir el ceño; **to ~ at sb** mirar con ceño a uno

scrabble [ˈskræbl] vi (claw): **to ~ (at)** arañar; (also: ~ **around**: search) revolver todo buscando ♦ n: **S~** ® Scrabble ® m

scraggy [ˈskrægɪ] adj descarnado

scram [skræm] (inf) vi largarse

scramble [ˈskræmbl] n (climb) subida

(difícil); (*struggle*) pelea ♦ *vi*: **to ~ through/out** abrirse paso/salir con dificultad; **to ~ for** pelear por; **~d eggs** *npl* huevos *mpl* revueltos

scrap [skræp] *n* (*bit*) pedacito; (*fig*) pizca; (*fight*) riña, bronca; (*also*: **~ iron**) chatarra, hierro viejo ♦ *vt* (*discard*) desechar, descartar ♦ *vi* reñir, armar (una) bronca; **~s** *npl* (*waste*) sobras *fpl*, desperdicios *mpl*; **~book** *n* álbum *m* de recortes; **~ dealer** *n* chatarrero/a

scrape [skreɪp] *n*: **to get into a ~** meterse en un lío ♦ *vt* raspar; (*skin etc*) rasguñar; (*~ against*) rozar ♦ *vi*: **to ~ through** (*exam*) aprobar por los pelos; **~ together** *vt* (*money*) arañar, juntar

scrap: ~ heap *n* (*fig*): **to be on the ~ heap** estar acabado; **~ merchant** (*BRIT*) *n* chatarrero/a; **~ paper** *n* pedazos *mpl* de papel

scratch [skrætʃ] *n* rasguño; (*from claw*) arañazo ♦ *cpd*: **~ team** equipo improvisado ♦ *vt* (*paint, car*) rayar; (*with claw, nail*) rasguñar, arañar; (*rub: nose etc*) rascarse ♦ *vi* rascarse; **to start from ~** partir de cero; **to be up to ~** cumplir con los requisitos

scrawl [skrɔ:l] *n* garabatos *mpl* ♦ *vi* hacer garabatos

scrawny ['skrɔ:nɪ] *adj* flaco

scream [skri:m] *n* chillido ♦ *vi* chillar

screech [skri:tʃ] *vi* chirriar

screen [skri:n] *n* (*CINEMA, TV*) pantalla; (*movable barrier*) biombo ♦ *vt* (*conceal*) tapar; (*from the wind etc*) proteger; (*film*) proyectar; (*candidates etc*) investigar a; **~ing** *n* (*MED*) investigación *f* médica; **~play** *n* guión *m*; **~ saver** *n* (*COMPUT*) protector *m* de pantalla

screw [skru:] *n* tornillo ♦ *vt* (*also*: **~ in**) atornillar; **~ up** *vt* (*paper etc*) arrugar; **to ~ up one's eyes** arrugar el entrecejo; **~driver** *n* destornillador *m*

scribble ['skrɪbl] *n* garabatos *mpl* ♦ *vt, vi* garabatear

script [skrɪpt] *n* (*CINEMA etc*) guión *m*; (*writing*) escritura, letra

Scripture(s) ['skrɪptʃə*(z)] *n(pl)* Sagrada Escritura

scroll [skrəʊl] *n* rollo

scrounge [skraʊndʒ] (*inf*) *vt*: **to ~ sth off** *or* **from sb** obtener algo de uno de gorra ♦ *n*: **on the ~** de gorra; **~r** *n* gorrón/ona *m/f*

scrub [skrʌb] *n* (*land*) maleza ♦ *vt* fregar, restregar; (*inf: reject*) cancelar, anular

scruff [skrʌf] *n*: **by the ~ of the neck** por el pescuezo

scruffy ['skrʌfɪ] *adj* desaliñado, piojoso

scrum(mage) ['skrʌm(mɪdʒ)] *n* (*RUGBY*) melée *f*

scruple ['skru:pl] *n* (*gen pl*) escrúpulo

scrutinize ['skru:tɪnaɪz] *vt* escudriñar; (*votes*) escrutar; **scrutiny** ['skru:tɪnɪ] *n* escrutinio, examen *m*

scuff [skʌf] *vt* (*shoes, floor*) rayar

scuffle ['skʌfl] *n* refriega

sculptor ['skʌlptə*] *n* escultor(a) *m/f*

sculpture ['skʌlptʃə*] *n* escultura

scum [skʌm] *n* (*on liquid*) espuma; (*pej: people*) escoria

scurry ['skʌrɪ] *vi* correr; **to ~ off** escabullirse

scuttle ['skʌtl] *n* (*also*: **coal ~**) cubo, carbonera ♦ *vt* (*ship*) barrenar ♦ *vi* (*scamper*): **to ~ away, ~ off** escabullirse

scythe [saɪð] *n* guadaña

SDP (*BRIT*) *n abbr* = **Social Democratic Party**

sea [si:] *n* mar *m* ♦ *cpd* de mar, marítimo; **by ~** (*travel*) en barco; **on the ~** (*boat*) en el mar; (*town*) junto al mar; **to be all at ~** (*fig*) estar despistado; **out to ~, at ~** en alta mar; **~board** *n* litoral *m*; **~food** *n* mariscos *mpl*; **~ front** *n* paseo marítimo; **~-going** *adj* de altura; **~gull** *n* gaviota

seal [si:l] *n* (*animal*) foca; (*stamp*) sello ♦ *vt* (*close*) cerrar; **~ off** *vt* (*area*) acordonar

sea level *n* nivel *m* del mar

sea lion *n* león *m* marino

seam [si:m] *n* costura; (*of metal*) juntura; (*of coal*) veta, filón *m*

seaman ['si:mən] (*irreg*) *n* marinero

seance ['seɪɒns] *n* sesión *f* de espiritismo

seaplane ['si:pleɪn] n hidroavión m
seaport ['si:pɔ:t] n puerto de mar
search [sə:tʃ] n (for person, thing) busca, búsqueda; (COMPUT) búsqueda; (inspection: of sb's home) registro ♦ vt (look in) buscar en; (examine) examinar; (person, place) registrar ♦ vi: **to ~ for** buscar; **in ~ of** en busca de; **~ through** vt fus registrar; **~ engine** n (COMPUT) buscador m; **~ing** adj penetrante; **~light** n reflector m; **~ party** n pelotón m de salvamento; **~ warrant** n mandamiento (judicial)
sea: **~shore** n playa, orilla del mar; **~sick** adj mareado; **~side** n playa, orilla del mar; **~side resort** n centro turístico costero
season ['si:zn] n (of year) estación f; (sporting etc) temporada; (of films etc) ciclo ♦ vt (food) sazonar; **in/out of ~** en sazón/fuera de temporada; **~al** adj estacional; **~ed** adj (fig) experimentado; **~ing** n condimento, aderezo; **~ ticket** n abono
seat [si:t] n (in bus, train) asiento; (chair) silla; (PARLIAMENT) escaño; (buttocks) culo, trasero; (of trousers) culera ♦ vt sentar; (have room for) tener cabida para; **to be ~ed** sentarse; **~ belt** n cinturón m de seguridad
sea: **~ water** n agua del mar; **~weed** n alga marina; **~worthy** adj en condiciones de navegar
sec. abbr = **second(s)**
secluded [sɪ'klu:dɪd] adj retirado
seclusion [sɪ'klu:ʒən] n reclusión f
second ['sekənd] adj segundo ♦ adv en segundo lugar ♦ n segundo; (AUT: also: **~ gear**) segunda; (COMM) artículo con algún desperfecto; (BRIT: SCOL: degree) título de licenciado con calificación de notable ♦ vt (motion) apoyar; **~ary** adj secundario; **~ary school** n escuela secundaria; **~-class** adj de segunda clase ♦ adv (RAIL) en segunda; **~hand** adj usado; **~ hand** n (on clock) segundero; **~ly** adv en segundo lugar; **~ment**

[sɪ'kɒndmənt] (BRIT) n traslado temporal; **~-rate** adj de segunda categoría; **~ thoughts** npl: **to have ~ thoughts** cambiar de opinión; **on ~ thoughts** or **thought** (US) pensándolo bien
secrecy ['si:krəsɪ] n secreto
secret ['si:krɪt] adj, n secreto; **in ~** en secreto
secretarial [sekrɪ'teərɪəl] adj de secretario; (course, staff) de secretariado
secretary ['sekrətərɪ] n secretario/a; **S~ of State (for)** (BRIT: POL) Ministro (de)
secretive ['si:krətɪv] adj reservado, sigiloso
secretly ['si:krɪtlɪ] adv en secreto
sect [sekt] n secta; **~arian** [-'teərɪən] adj sectario
section ['sekʃən] n sección f; (part) parte f; (of document) artículo; (of opinion) sector m; (cross-~) corte m transversal
sector ['sektə*] n sector m
secular ['sekjulə*] adj secular, seglar
secure [sɪ'kjuə*] adj seguro; (firmly fixed) firme, fijo ♦ vt (fix) asegurar, afianzar; (get) conseguir
security [sɪ'kjuərɪtɪ] n seguridad f; (for loan) fianza; (: object) prenda
sedate [sɪ'deɪt] adj tranquilo ♦ vt tratar con sedantes
sedation [sɪ'deɪʃən] n (MED) sedación f
sedative ['sedɪtɪv] n sedante m, sedativo
seduce [sɪ'dju:s] vt seducir; **seduction** [-'dʌkʃən] n seducción f; **seductive** [-'dʌktɪv] adj seductor(a)
see [si:] (pt saw, pp seen) vt ver; (accompany): **to ~ sb to the door** acompañar a uno a la puerta; (understand) ver, comprender ♦ vi ver ♦ n (arz)obispado; **to ~ that** (ensure) asegurar que; **~ you soon!** ¡hasta pronto!; **~ about** vt fus atender a, encargarse de; **~ off** vt despedir; **~ through** vt fus (fig) calar ♦ vt (plan) llevar a cabo; **~ to** vt fus atender a, encargarse de
seed [si:d] n semilla; (in fruit) pepita; (fig: gen pl) germen m; (TENNIS etc) preseleccionado/a; **to go to ~** (plant) granar; (fig) descuidarse; **~ling** n planta

de semillero; ~y adj (shabby) desaseado, raído

seeing ['si:ɪŋ] conj: ~ **(that)** visto que, en vista de que

seek [si:k] (pt, pp **sought**) vt buscar; (post) solicitar

seem [si:m] vi parecer; **there ~s to be ...** parece que hay ...; ~**ingly** adv aparentemente, según parece

seen [si:n] pp of **see**

seep [si:p] vi filtrarse

seesaw ['si:sɔ:] n subibaja

seethe [si:ð] vi hervir; **to ~ with anger** estar furioso

see-through adj transparente

segment ['segmənt] n (part) sección f; (of orange) gajo

segregate ['segrɪgeɪt] vt segregar

seize [si:z] vt (grasp) agarrar, asir; (take possession of) secuestrar; (: territory) apoderarse de; (opportunity) aprovecharse de; ~ **(up)on** vt fus aprovechar; ~ **up** vi (TECH) agarrotarse

seizure ['si:ʒə*] n (MED) ataque m; (LAW, of power) incautación f

seldom ['seldəm] adv rara vez

select [sɪ'lekt] adj selecto, escogido ♦ vt escoger, elegir; (SPORT) seleccionar; ~**ion** [-'lekʃən] n selección f, elección f; (COMM) surtido

self [self] (pl **selves**) n uno mismo; **the ~** el yo ♦ prefix auto...; ~**-assured** adj seguro de sí mismo; ~**-catering** (BRIT) adj (flat etc) con cocina; ~**-centred** (US ~**-centered**) adj egocéntrico; ~**-confidence** n confianza en sí mismo; ~**-conscious** adj cohibido; ~**-contained** (BRIT) adj (flat) con entrada particular; ~**-control** n autodominio; ~**-defence** (US ~**-defense**) n defensa propia; ~**-discipline** n autodisciplina; ~**-employed** adj que trabaja por cuenta propia; ~**-evident** adj patente; ~**-governing** adj autónomo; ~**-indulgent** adj autocomplaciente; ~**-interest** n egoísmo; ~**ish** adj egoísta; ~**ishness** n egoísmo; ~**less** adj desinteresado; ~**-**

made adj: ~**-made man** hombre m que se ha hecho a sí mismo; ~**-pity** n lástima de sí mismo; ~**-portrait** n autorretrato; ~**-possessed** adj sereno, dueño de sí mismo; ~**-preservation** n propia conservación f; ~**-respect** n amor m propio; ~**-righteous** adj santurrón/ona; ~**-sacrifice** n abnegación f; ~**-satisfied** adj satisfecho de sí mismo; ~**-service** adj de autoservicio; ~**-sufficient** adj autosuficiente; ~**-taught** adj autodidacta

sell [sel] (pt, pp **sold**) vt vender ♦ vi venderse; **to ~ at** or **for £10** venderse a 10 libras; ~ **off** vt liquidar; ~ **out** vi: **to ~ out of tickets/milk** vender todas las entradas/toda la leche; ~**-by date** n fecha de caducidad; ~**er** n vendedor(a) m/f; ~**ing price** n precio de venta

Sellotape ® ['seləuteɪp] (BRIT) n cinta adhesiva, celo (SP), scotch m (AM)

selves [selvz] npl of **self**

semblance ['sembləns] n apariencia

semen ['si:mən] n semen m

semester [sɪ'mestə*] (US) n semestre m

semi... [semi] prefix semi..., medio...; ~**circle** n semicírculo; ~**colon** n punto y coma; ~**conductor** n semiconductor m; ~**detached (house)** n (casa) semiseparada; ~**-final** n semi-final m

seminar ['semɪnɑ:*] n seminario

seminary ['semɪnərɪ] n (REL) seminario

semiskilled ['semɪskɪld] adj (work, worker) semi-cualificado

semi-skimmed (milk) n leche semidesnatada

senate ['senɪt] n senado; **senator** n senador(a) m/f

send [send] (pt, pp **sent**) vt mandar, enviar; (signal) transmitir; ~ **away** vt despachar; ~ **away for** vt fus pedir; ~ **back** vt devolver; ~ **for** vt fus mandar traer; ~ **off** vt (goods) despachar; (BRIT: SPORT: player) expulsar; ~ **out** vt (invitation) mandar; (signal) emitir; ~ **up** vt (person, price) hacer subir; (BRIT: parody) parodiar; ~**er** n remitente m/f;

~**-off** *n*: **a good ~-off** una buena despedida
senior ['siːnɪə*] *adj* (*older*) mayor, más viejo; (: *on staff*) de más antigüedad; (*of higher rank*) superior; ~ **citizen** *n* persona de la tercera edad; ~**ity** [-'ɔrɪtɪ] *n* antigüedad *f*
sensation [sɛn'seɪʃən] *n* sensación *f*; ~**al** *adj* sensacional
sense [sɛns] *n* (*faculty, meaning*) sentido; (*feeling*) sensación *f*; (*good ~*) sentido común, juicio ♦ *vt* sentir, percibir; **it makes ~** tiene sentido; ~**less** *adj* estúpido, insensato; (*unconscious*) sin conocimiento; ~ **of humour** *n* sentido del humor
sensible ['sɛnsɪbl] *adj* sensato; (*reasonable*) razonable, lógico
sensitive ['sɛnsɪtɪv] *adj* sensible; (*touchy*) susceptible
sensual ['sɛnsjuəl] *adj* sensual
sensuous ['sɛnsjuəs] *adj* sensual
sent [sɛnt] *pt, pp of* **send**
sentence ['sɛntns] *n* (*LING*) oración *f*; (*LAW*) sentencia, fallo ♦ *vt*: **to ~ sb to death/to 5 years (in prison)** condenar a uno a muerte/a 5 años de cárcel
sentiment ['sɛntɪmənt] *n* sentimiento; (*opinion*) opinión *f*; ~**al** [-'mɛntl] *adj* sentimental
sentry ['sɛntrɪ] *n* centinela *m*
separate [*adj* 'sɛprɪt, *vb* 'sɛpəreɪt] *adj* separado; (*distinct*) distinto ♦ *vt* separar; (*part*) dividir ♦ *vi* separarse; ~**s** *npl* (*clothes*) coordinados *mpl*; ~**ly** *adv* por separado; **separation** [-'reɪʃən] *n* separación *f*
September [sɛp'tɛmbə*] *n* se(p)tiembre *m*
septic ['sɛptɪk] *adj* séptico; ~ **tank** *n* fosa séptica
sequel ['siːkwl] *n* consecuencia, resultado; (*of story*) continuación *f*
sequence ['siːkwəns] *n* sucesión *f*, serie *f*; (*CINEMA*) secuencia
sequin ['siːkwɪn] *n* lentejuela
serene [sɪ'riːn] *adj* sereno, tranquilo
sergeant ['sɑːdʒənt] *n* sargento

serial ['sɪərɪəl] *n* (*TV*) telenovela, serie *f* televisiva; (*BOOK*) serie *f*; ~**ize** *vt* emitir como serial; ~ **killer** *n* asesino/a múltiple; ~ **number** *n* número de serie
series ['sɪəriːs] *n inv* serie *f*
serious ['sɪərɪəs] *adj* serio; (*grave*) grave; ~**ly** *adv* en serio; (*ill, wounded etc*) gravemente
sermon ['sɜːmən] *n* sermón *m*
serrated [sɪ'reɪtɪd] *adj* serrado, dentellado
serum ['sɪərəm] *n* suero
servant ['sɜːvənt] *n* servidor(a) *m/f*; (*house ~*) criado/a
serve [sɜːv] *vt* servir; (*customer*) atender; (*subj: train*) pasar por; (*apprenticeship*) hacer; (*prison term*) cumplir ♦ *vi* (*at table*) servir; (*TENNIS*) sacar; **to ~ as/for/to do** servir de/para/para hacer ♦ *n* (*TENNIS*) saque *m*; **it ~s him right** se lo tiene merecido; ~ **out** *vt* (*food*) servir; ~ **up** *vt* = ~ **out**
service ['sɜːvɪs] *n* servicio; (*REL*) misa; (*AUT*) mantenimiento; (*dishes etc*) juego ♦ *vt* (*car etc*) revisar; (: *repair*) reparar; **the S~s** *npl* las fuerzas armadas; **to be of ~ to sb** ser útil a uno; ~ **included/not included** servicio incluído/no incluído; ~**able** *adj* servible, utilizable; ~ **area** *n* (*on motorway*) área de servicio; ~ **charge** (*BRIT*) *n* servicio; ~**man** *n* militar *m*; ~ **station** *n* estación *f* de servicio
serviette [sɜːvɪ'ɛt] (*BRIT*) *n* servilleta
session ['sɛʃən] *n* sesión *f*; **to be in ~** estar en sesión
set [sɛt] (*pt, pp* **set**) *n* juego; (*RADIO*) aparato; (*TV*) televisor *m*; (*of utensils*) batería; (*of cutlery*) cubierto; (*of books*) colección *f*; (*TENNIS*) set *m*; (*group of people*) grupo; (*CINEMA*) plató *m*; (*THEATRE*) decorado; (*HAIRDRESSING*) marcado ♦ *adj* (*fixed*) fijo; (*ready*) listo ♦ *vt* (*place*) poner, colocar; (*fix*) fijar; (*adjust*) ajustar, arreglar; (*decide: rules etc*) establecer, decidir ♦ *vi* (*sun*) ponerse; (*jam, jelly*) cuajarse; (*concrete*) fraguar; (*bone*) componerse; **to be ~ on doing sth** estar empeñado en hacer algo; **to ~ to**

music poner música a; **to ~ on fire** incendiar, poner fuego a; **to ~ free** poner en libertad; **to ~ sth going** poner algo en marcha; **to ~ sail** zarpar, hacerse a la vela; **~ about** *vt fus* ponerse a; **~ aside** *vt* poner aparte, dejar de lado; (*money, time*) reservar; **~ back** *vt* (*cost*): **to ~ sb back £5** costar a uno cinco libras; (: *in time*): **to ~ back (by)** retrasar (por); **~ off** *vi* partir ♦ *vt* (*bomb*) hacer estallar; (*events*) poner en marcha; (*show up well*) hacer resaltar; **~ out** *vi* partir ♦ *vt* (*arrange*) disponer; (*state*) exponer; **to ~ out to do sth** proponerse hacer algo; **~ up** *vt* establecer; **~back** *n* revés *m*, contratiempo; **~ menu** *n* menú *m*

settee [se'ti:] *n* sofá *m*

setting ['setɪŋ] *n* (*scenery*) marco; (*position*) disposición *f*; (*of sun*) puesta; (*of jewel*) engaste *m*, montadura

settle ['setl] *vt* (*argument*) resolver; (*accounts*) ajustar, liquidar; (MED: *calm*) calmar, sosegar ♦ *vi* (*dust etc*) depositarse; (*weather*) serenarse; (*also*: **~ down**) instalarse; tranquilizarse; **to ~ for sth** convenir en aceptar algo; **to ~ on sth** decidirse por algo; **~ in** *vi* instalarse; **~ up** *vi*: **to ~ up with sb** ajustar cuentas con uno; **~ment** *n* (*payment*) liquidación *f*; (*agreement*) acuerdo, convenio; (*village etc*) pueblo; **~r** *n* colono/a, colonizador(a) *m/f*

setup ['setʌp] *n* sistema *m*; (*situation*) situación *f*

seven ['sevn] *num* siete; **~teen** *num* diez y siete, diecisiete; **~th** *num* séptimo; **~ty** *num* setenta

sever ['sevə*] *vt* cortar; (*relations*) romper

several ['sevərl] *adj, pron* varios/as *m/fpl*, algunos/as *m/fpl*; **~ of us** varios de nosotros

severance ['sevərəns] *n* (*of relations*) ruptura; **~ pay** *n* indemnización *f* por despido

severe [sɪ'vɪə*] *adj* severo; (*serious*) grave; (*hard*) duro; (*pain*) intenso; **severity** [sɪ'verɪtɪ] *n* severidad *f*; gravedad *f*; intensidad *f*

sew [səu] (*pt* **sewed**, *pp* **sewn**) *vt, vi* coser; **~ up** *vt* coser, zurcir

sewage ['su:ɪdʒ] *n* aguas *fpl* residuales

sewer ['su:ə*] *n* alcantarilla, cloaca

sewing ['səuɪŋ] *n* costura; **~ machine** *n* máquina de coser

sewn [səun] *pp of* **sew**

sex [seks] *n* sexo; (*lovemaking*): **to have ~** hacer el amor; **~ist** *adj, n* sexista *m/f*; **~ual** ['seksjuəl] *adj* sexual; **~y** *adj* sexy

shabby ['ʃæbɪ] *adj* (*person*) desharrapado; (*clothes*) raído, gastado; (*behaviour*) ruin *inv*

shack [ʃæk] *n* choza, chabola

shackles ['ʃæklz] *npl* grillos *mpl*, grilletes *mpl*

shade [ʃeɪd] *n* sombra; (*for lamp*) pantalla; (*for eyes*) visera; (*of colour*) matiz *m*, tonalidad *f*; (*small quantity*): **a ~ (too big/more)** un poquitín (grande/más) ♦ *vt* dar sombra a; (*eyes*) proteger del sol; **in the ~** en la sombra

shadow ['ʃædəu] *n* sombra ♦ *vt* (*follow*) seguir y vigilar; **~ cabinet** (BRIT) *n* (POL) *gabinete paralelo formado por el partido de oposición*; **~y** *adj* oscuro; (*dim*) indistinto

shady ['ʃeɪdɪ] *adj* sombreado; (*fig: dishonest*) sospechoso; (: *deal*) turbio

shaft [ʃɑ:ft] *n* (*of arrow, spear*) astil *m*; (AUT, TECH) eje *m*, árbol *m*; (*of mine*) pozo; (*of lift*) hueco, caja; (*of light*) rayo

shaggy ['ʃægɪ] *adj* peludo

shake [ʃeɪk] (*pt* **shook**, *pp* **shaken**) *vt* sacudir; (*building*) hacer temblar; (*bottle, cocktail*) agitar ♦ *vi* (*tremble*) temblar; **to ~ one's head** (*in refusal*) negar con la cabeza; (*in dismay*) mover *or* menear la cabeza, incrédulo; **to ~ hands with sb** estrechar la mano a uno; **~ off** *vt* sacudirse; (*fig*) deshacerse de; **~ up** *vt* agitar; (*fig*) reorganizar; **shaky** *adj* (*hand, voice*) trémulo; (*building*) inestable

shall [ʃæl] *aux vb*: **~ I help you?** ¿quieres que te ayude?; **I'll buy three, ~ I?** compro tres, ¿no te parece?

shallow ['ʃæləu] *adj* poco profundo; (*fig*) superficial

sham [ʃæm] *n* fraude *m*, engaño ♦ *vt* fingir, simular

shambles ['ʃæmblz] *n* confusión *f*

shame [ʃeɪm] *n* vergüenza ♦ *vt* avergonzar; **it is a ~ that/to do** es una lástima que/hacer; **what a ~!** ¡qué lástima!; **~ful** *adj* vergonzoso; **~less** *adj* desvergonzado

shampoo [ʃæm'puː] *n* champú *m* ♦ *vt* lavar con champú; **~ and set** *n* lavado y marcado

shamrock ['ʃæmrɔk] *n* trébol *m* (*emblema nacional irlandés*)

shandy ['ʃændɪ] *n* mezcla de cerveza con gaseosa

shan't [ʃɑːnt] = **shall not**

shantytown ['ʃæntɪtaun] *n* barrio de chabolas

shape [ʃeɪp] *n* forma ♦ *vt* formar, dar forma a; (*sb's ideas*) formar; (*sb's life*) determinar; **to take ~** tomar forma; **~ up** *vi* (*events*) desarrollarse; (*person*) formarse; **~d** *suffix*: **heart-~d** en forma de corazón; **~less** *adj* informe, sin forma definida; **~ly** *adj* (*body etc*) esbelto

share [ʃɛə*] *n* (*part*) parte *f*, porción *f*; (*contribution*) cuota; (*COMM*) acción *f* ♦ *vt* dividir; (*have in common*) compartir; **to ~ out** (*among or between*) repartir (entre); **~holder** (*BRIT*) *n* accionista *m/f*

shark [ʃɑːk] *n* tiburón *m*

sharp [ʃɑːp] *adj* (*blade, nose*) afilado; (*point*) puntiagudo; (*outline*) definido; (*pain*) intenso; (*MUS*) desafinado; (*contrast*) marcado; (*voice*) agudo; (*person: quick-witted*) astuto; (: *dishonest*) poco escrupuloso ♦ *n* (*MUS*) sostenido ♦ *adv*: **at 2 o'clock ~** a las 2 en punto; **~en** *vt* afilar; (*pencil*) sacar punta a; (*fig*) agudizar; **~ener** *n* (*also*: **pencil ~ener**) sacapuntas *m inv*; **~-eyed** *adj* de vista aguda; **~ly** *adv* (*turn, stop*) bruscamente; (*stand out, contrast*) claramente; (*criticize, retort*) severamente

shatter ['ʃætə*] *vt* hacer añicos *or* pedazos;

(*fig: ruin*) destruir, acabar con ♦ *vi* hacerse añicos

shave [ʃeɪv] *vt* afeitar, rasurar ♦ *vi* afeitarse, rasurarse ♦ *n*: **to have a ~** afeitarse; **~r** *n* (*also*: **electric ~r**) máquina de afeitar (eléctrica)

shaving ['ʃeɪvɪŋ] *n* (*action*) el afeitarse, rasurado; **~s** *npl* (*of wood etc*) virutas *fpl*; **~ brush** *n* brocha (de afeitar); **~ cream** *n* crema de afeitar; **~ foam** *n* espuma de afeitar

shawl [ʃɔːl] *n* chal *m*

she [ʃiː] *pron* ella; **~-cat** *n* gata

sheaf [ʃiːf] (*pl* **sheaves**) *n* (*of corn*) gavilla; (*of papers*) fajo

shear [ʃɪə*] (*pt* **sheared**, *pp* **sheared** *or* **shorn**) *vt* esquilar, trasquilar; **~s** *npl* (*for hedge*) tijeras *fpl* de jardín

sheath [ʃiːθ] *n* vaina; (*contraceptive*) preservativo

sheaves [ʃiːvz] *npl of* **sheaf**

shed [ʃed] (*pt, pp* **shed**) *n* cobertizo ♦ *vt* (*skin*) mudar; (*tears, blood*) derramar; (*load*) derramar; (*workers*) despedir

she'd [ʃiːd] = **she had; she would**

sheen [ʃiːn] *n* brillo, lustre *m*

sheep [ʃiːp] *n inv* oveja; **~dog** *n* perro pastor; **~skin** *n* piel *f* de carnero

sheer [ʃɪə*] *adj* (*utter*) puro, completo; (*steep*) escarpado; (*material*) diáfano ♦ *adv* verticalmente

sheet [ʃiːt] *n* (*on bed*) sábana; (*of paper*) hoja; (*of glass, metal*) lámina; (*of ice*) capa

sheik(h) [ʃeɪk] *n* jeque *m*

shelf [ʃelf] (*pl* **shelves**) *n* estante *m*

shell [ʃel] *n* (*on beach*) concha; (*of egg, nut etc*) cáscara; (*explosive*) proyectil *m*, obús *m*; (*of building*) armazón *f* ♦ *vt* (*peas*) desenvainar; (*MIL*) bombardear

she'll [ʃiːl] = **she will; she shall**

shellfish ['ʃelfɪʃ] *n inv* crustáceo; (*as food*) mariscos *mpl*

shell suit *n* chándal *m* de calle

shelter ['ʃeltə*] *n* abrigo, refugio ♦ *vt* (*aid*) amparar, proteger; (*give lodging to*) abrigar ♦ *vi* abrigarse, refugiarse; **~ed** *adj* (*life*) protegido; (*spot*) abrigado; **~ed**

housing *n* viviendas vigiladas para ancianos y minusválidos

shelve [ʃelv] *vt* (*fig*) aplazar; **~s** *npl of* **shelf**

shepherd [ˈʃepəd] *n* pastor *m* ♦ *vt* (*guide*) guiar, conducir; **~'s pie** (*BRIT*) *n* pastel *de carne y patatas*

sherry [ˈʃeri] *n* jerez *m*

she's [ʃiːz] = **she is; she has**

Shetland [ˈʃetlənd] *n* (*also:* **the ~ Isles**) las Islas de Zetlandia

shield [ʃiːld] *n* escudo; (*protection*) blindaje *m* ♦ *vt*: **to ~ (from)** proteger (de)

shift [ʃift] *n* (*change*) cambio; (*at work*) turno ♦ *vt* trasladar; (*remove*) quitar ♦ *vi* moverse; **~ work** *n* trabajo a turnos; **~y** *adj* tramposo; (*eyes*) furtivo

shimmer [ˈʃimə*] *n* reflejo trémulo

shin [ʃin] *n* espinilla

shine [ʃain] (*pt, pp* **shone**) *n* brillo, lustre *m* ♦ *vi* brillar, relucir ♦ *vt* (*shoes*) lustrar, sacar brillo a; **to ~ a torch on sth** dirigir una linterna hacia algo

shingle [ˈʃiŋgl] *n* (*on beach*) guijarros *mpl*; **~s** *n* (*MED*) herpes *mpl or fpl*

shiny [ˈʃaini] *adj* brillante, lustroso

ship [ʃip] *n* buque *m*, barco ♦ *vt* (*goods*) embarcar; (*send*) transportar *or* enviar por vía marítima; **~building** *n* construcción *f* de buques; **~ment** *n* (*goods*) envío; **~ping** *n* (*act*) embarque *m*; (*traffic*) buques *mpl*; **~wreck** *n* naufragio ♦ *vt*: **to be ~wrecked** naufragar; **~yard** *n* astillero

shire [ˈʃaiə*] (*BRIT*) *n* condado

shirt [ʃəːt] *n* camisa; **in (one's) ~ sleeves** en mangas de camisa

shit [ʃit] (*inf!*) *excl* ¡mierda! (*!*)

shiver [ˈʃivə*] *n* escalofrío ♦ *vi* temblar, estremecerse; (*with cold*) tiritar

shoal [ʃəul] *n* (*of fish*) banco; (*fig: also:* **~s**) tropel *m*

shock [ʃɔk] *n* (*impact*) choque *m*; (*ELEC*) descarga (eléctrica); (*emotional*) conmoción *f*; (*start*) sobresalto, susto; (*MED*) postración *f* nerviosa ♦ *vt* dar un susto a; (*offend*) escandalizar; ~

absorber *n* amortiguador *m*; **~ing** *adj* (*awful*) espantoso; (*outrageous*) escandaloso

shoddy [ˈʃɔdi] *adj* de pacotilla

shoe [ʃuː] (*pt, pp* **shod**) *n* zapato; (*for horse*) herradura ♦ *vt* (*horse*) herrar; **~brush** *n* cepillo para zapatos; **~lace** *n* cordón *m*; ~ **polish** *n* betún *m*; **~shop** *n* zapatería; **~string** *n* (*fig*): **on a ~string** con muy poco dinero

shone [ʃɔn] *pt, pp of* **shine**

shook [ʃuk] *pt of* **shake**

shoot [ʃuːt] (*pt, pp* **shot**) *n* (*on branch, seedling*) retoño, vástago ♦ *vt* disparar; (*kill*) matar a tiros; (*wound*) pegar un tiro; (*execute*) fusilar; (*film*) rodar, filmar ♦ *vi* (*FOOTBALL*) chutar; ~ **down** *vt* (*plane*) derribar; ~ **in/out** *vi* entrar corriendo/ salir disparado; ~ **up** *vi* (*prices*) dispararse; **~ing** *n* (*shots*) tiros *mpl*; (*HUNTING*) caza con escopeta; **~ing star** *n* estrella fugaz

shop [ʃɔp] *n* tienda; (*workshop*) taller *m* ♦ *vi* (*also:* **go ~ping**) ir de compras; ~ **assistant** (*BRIT*) *n* dependiente/a *m/f*; ~ **floor** (*BRIT*) *n* (*fig*) taller *m*, fábrica; **~keeper** *n* tendero/a; **~lifting** *n* mechería; **~per** *n* comprador(a) *m/f*; **~ping** *n* (*goods*) compras *fpl*; **~ping bag** *n* bolsa (de compras); **~ping centre** (*US* **~ping center**) *n* centro comercial; **~-soiled** *adj* deteriorado; ~ **steward** (*BRIT*) *n* (*INDUSTRY*) enlace *m* sindical; ~ **window** *n* escaparate *m* (*SP*), vidriera (*AM*)

shore [ʃɔː*] *n* orilla ♦ *vt*: **to ~ (up)** reforzar; **on ~** en tierra

shorn [ʃɔːn] *pp of* **shear**

short [ʃɔːt] *adj* corto; (*in time*) breve, de corta duración; (*person*) bajo; (*curt*) brusco, seco; (*insufficient*) insuficiente; **(a pair of) ~s** (unos) pantalones *mpl* cortos; **to be ~ of sth** estar falto de algo; **in ~** en pocas palabras; **~ of doing ...** fuera de hacer ...; **it is ~ for** es la forma abreviada de; **to cut ~** (*speech, visit*) interrumpir, terminar inesperadamente; **everything ~**

of ... todo menos ...; **to fall ~ of** no alcanzar; **to run ~ of** quedarle a uno poco; **to stop ~** parar en seco; **to stop ~ of** detenerse antes de; **~age** *n*: **a ~age of** una falta de; **~bread** *n especie de mantecada*; **~-change** *vt* no dar el cambio completo a; **~-circuit** *n* cortocircuito; **~coming** *n* defecto, deficiencia; **~(crust) pastry** (*BRIT*) *n* pasta quebradiza; **~cut** *n* atajo; **~en** *vt* acortar; (*visit*) interrumpir; **~fall** *n* déficit *m*; **~hand** (*BRIT*) *n* taquigrafía; **~hand typist** (*BRIT*) *n* taquimecanógrafo/a; **~ list** (*BRIT*) *n* (*for job*) lista de candidatos escogidos; **~-lived** *adj* efímero; **~ly** *adv* en breve, dentro de poco; **~-sighted** (*BRIT*) *adj* miope; (*fig*) imprudente; **~-staffed** *adj*: **to be ~-staffed** estar falto de personal; **~ story** *n* cuento; **~-tempered** *adj* enojadizo; **~-term** *adj* (*effect*) a corto plazo; **~wave** *n* (*RADIO*) onda corta

shot [ʃɔt] *pt, pp* of **shoot** ♦ *n* (*sound*) tiro, disparo; (*try*) tentativa; (*injection*) inyección *f*; (*PHOT*) toma, fotografía; **to be a good/poor ~** (*person*) tener buena/mala puntería; **like a ~** (*without any delay*) como un rayo; **~gun** *n* escopeta

should [ʃud] *aux vb*: **I ~ go now** debo irme ahora; **he ~ be there now** debe de haber llegado (ya); **I ~ go if I were you** yo en tu lugar me iría; **I ~ like to** me gustaría

shoulder [ˈʃəuldə*] *n* hombro ♦ *vt* (*fig*) cargar con; **~ bag** *n* cartera de bandolera; **~ blade** *n* omóplato

shouldn't [ˈʃudnt] = **should not**

shout [ʃaut] *n* grito ♦ *vt* gritar ♦ *vi* gritar, dar voces; **~ down** *vt* acallar a gritos; **~ing** *n* griterío

shove [ʃʌv] *n* empujón *m* ♦ *vt* empujar; (*inf: put*): **to ~ sth in** meter algo a empellones; **~ off** (*inf*) *vi* largarse

shovel [ˈʃʌvl] *n* pala; (*mechanical*) excavadora ♦ *vt* mover con pala

show [ʃəu] (*pt* **showed**, *pp* **shown**) *n* (*of emotion*) demostración *f*; (*semblance*)

apariencia; (*exhibition*) exposición *f*; (*THEATRE*) función *f*, espectáculo; (*TV*) show *m* ♦ *vt* mostrar, enseñar; (*courage etc*) mostrar, manifestar; (*exhibit*) exponer; (*film*) proyectar ♦ *vi* mostrarse; (*appear*) aparecer; **for ~** para impresionar; **on ~** (*exhibits etc*) expuesto; **~ in** *vt* (*person*) hacer pasar; **~ off** (*pej*) *vi* presumir ♦ *vt* (*display*) lucir; **~ out** *vt*: **to ~ sb out** acompañar a uno a la puerta; **~ up** *vi* (*stand out*) destacar; (*inf: turn up*) aparecer ♦ *vt* (*unmask*) desenmascarar; **~ business** *n* mundo del espectáculo; **~down** *n* enfrentamiento (final)

shower [ˈʃauə*] *n* (*rain*) chaparrón *m*, chubasco; (*of stones etc*) lluvia; (*for bathing*) ducha (*SP*), regadera (*AM*) ♦ *vi* llover ♦ *vt* (*fig*): **to ~ sb with sth** colmar uno de algo; **to have a ~** ducharse; **~proof** *adj* impermeable

showing [ˈʃəuɪŋ] *n* (*of film*) proyección *f*

show jumping *n* hípica

shown [ʃəun] *pp* of **show**

show: ~-off (*inf*) *n* (*person*) presumido/a; **~piece** *n* (*of exhibition etc*) objeto cumbre; **~room** *n* sala de muestras

shrank [ʃræŋk] *pt* of **shrink**

shrapnel [ˈʃræpnl] *n* metralla

shred [ʃred] *n* (*gen pl*) triza, jirón *m* ♦ *vt* hacer trizas; (*CULIN*) desmenuzar; **~der** *n* (*vegetable ~der*) picadora; (*document ~der*) trituradora (de papel)

shrewd [ʃruːd] *adj* astuto

shriek [ʃriːk] *n* chillido ♦ *vi* chillar

shrill [ʃrɪl] *adj* agudo, estridente

shrimp [ʃrɪmp] *n* camarón *m*

shrine [ʃraɪn] *n* santuario, sepulcro

shrink [ʃrɪŋk] (*pt* **shrank**, *pp* **shrunk**) *vi* encogerse; (*be reduced*) reducirse; (*also: ~ away*) retroceder ♦ *vt* encoger ♦ *n* (*inf: pej*) loquero/a; **to ~ from (doing) sth** no atreverse a hacer algo; **~wrap** *vt* embalar con película de plástico

shrivel [ˈʃrɪvl] (*also: ~ up*) *vt* (*dry*) secar ♦ *vi* secarse

shroud [ʃraud] *n* sudario ♦ *vt*: **~ed in mystery** envuelto en el misterio

Shrove Tuesday [ˈʃrəuv-] n martes m de carnaval

shrub [ʃrʌb] n arbusto; **~bery** n arbustos mpl

shrug [ʃrʌg] n encogimiento de hombros ♦ vt, vi: **to ~ (one's shoulders)** encogerse de hombros; **~ off** vt negar importancia a

shrunk [ʃrʌŋk] pp of **shrink**

shudder [ˈʃʌdə*] n estremecimiento, escalofrío ♦ vi estremecerse

shuffle [ˈʃʌfl] vt (cards) barajar ♦ vi: **to ~ (one's feet)** arrastrar los pies

shun [ʃʌn] vt rehuir, esquivar

shunt [ʃʌnt] vt (train) maniobrar; (object) empujar

shut [ʃʌt] (pt, pp **shut**) vt cerrar ♦ vi cerrarse; **~ down** vt, vi cerrar; **~ off** vt (supply etc) cortar; **~ up** vi (inf: keep quiet) callarse ♦ vt (close) cerrar; (silence) hacer callar; **~ter** n contraventana; (PHOT) obturador m

shuttle [ˈʃʌtl] n lanzadera; (also: **~ service**) servicio rápido y continuo entre dos puntos: (: AVIAT) puente m aéreo; **~cock** n volante m; **~ diplomacy** n viajes mpl diplomáticos

shy [ʃaɪ] adj tímido; **~ness** n timidez f

Sicily [ˈsɪsɪlɪ] n Sicilia

sick [sɪk] adj (ill) enfermo; (nauseated) mareado; (humour) negro; (vomiting): **to be ~** (BRIT) vomitar; **to feel ~** tener náuseas; **to be ~ of** (fig) estar harto de; **~ bay** n enfermería; **~en** vt dar asco a; **~ening** adj (fig) asqueroso

sickle [ˈsɪkl] n hoz f

sick: **~ leave** n baja por enfermedad; **~ly** adj enfermizo; (smell) nauseabundo; **~ness** n enfermedad f, mal m; (vomiting) náuseas fpl; **~ pay** n subsidio de enfermedad

side [saɪd] n (gen) lado; (of body) costado; (of lake) orilla; (of hill) ladera; (team) equipo; ♦ adj (door, entrance) lateral ♦ vi: **to ~ with sb** tomar el partido de uno; **by the ~ of** al lado de; **~ by ~** juntos/as; **from ~ to ~** de un lado para otro; **from**

all ~s de todos lados; **to take ~s (with)** tomar partido (con); **~board** n aparador m; **~boards** (BRIT) npl = **~burns**; **~burns** npl patillas fpl; **~ drum** n tambor m; **~ effect** n efecto secundario; **~light** n (AUT) luz f lateral; **~line** n (SPORT) línea de banda; (fig) empleo suplementario; **~long** adj de soslayo; **~ order** n plato de acompañamiento; **~ show** n (stall) caseta; **~step** n (fig) esquivar; **~ street** n calle f lateral; **~track** vt (fig) desviar (de su propósito); **~walk** n (US) acera; **~ways** adv de lado

siding [ˈsaɪdɪŋ] n (RAIL) apartadero, vía muerta

siege [siːdʒ] n cerco, sitio

sieve [sɪv] n colador m ♦ vt cribar

sift [sɪft] vt cribar; (fig: information) escudriñar

sigh [saɪ] n suspiro ♦ vi suspirar

sight [saɪt] n (faculty) vista; (spectacle) espectáculo; (on gun) mira, alza ♦ vt divisar; **in ~** a la vista; **out of ~** fuera de (la) vista; **on ~** (shoot) sin previo aviso; **~seeing** n excursionismo, turismo; **to go ~seeing** hacer turismo

sign [saɪn] n (with hand) señal f, seña; (trace) huella, rastro; (notice) letrero; (written) signo ♦ vt firmar; (SPORT) fichar; **to ~ sth over to sb** firmar el traspaso de algo a uno; **~ on** vi (BRIT: as unemployed) registrarse como desempleado; (for course) inscribirse ♦ vt (MIL) alistar; (employee) contratar; **~ up** vi (MIL) alistarse; (for course) inscribirse ♦ vt (player) fichar

signal [ˈsɪgnl] n señal f ♦ vi señalizar ♦ vt (person) hacer señas a; (message) comunicar por señales; **~man** (irreg) n (RAIL) guardavía m

signature [ˈsɪgnətʃə*] n firma; **~ tune** n sintonía de apertura de un programa

signet ring [ˈsɪgnət-] n anillo de sello

significance [sɪgˈnɪfɪkəns] n (importance) trascendencia

significant [sɪgˈnɪfɪkənt] adj significativo; (important) trascendente

signify ['sɪgnɪfaɪ] vt significar
sign language n lenguaje m para sordomudos
signpost ['saɪnpəʊst] n indicador m
silence ['saɪlns] n silencio ♦ vt acallar; (guns) reducir al silencio; ~r n (on gun, BRIT: AUT) silenciador m
silent ['saɪlnt] adj silencioso; (not speaking) callado; (film) mudo; **to remain ~** guardar silencio; ~ **partner** n (COMM) socio/a comanditario/a
silhouette [sɪluːˈɛt] n silueta
silicon chip ['sɪlɪkən-] n plaqueta de silicio
silk [sɪlk] n seda ♦ adj de seda; ~y adj sedoso
silly ['sɪlɪ] adj (person) tonto; (idea) absurdo
silt [sɪlt] n sedimento
silver ['sɪlvə*] n plata; (money) moneda suelta ♦ adj de plata; (colour) plateado; ~ **paper** (BRIT) n papel m de plata; ~-**plated** adj plateado; ~**smith** n platero/a; ~**ware** n plata; ~y adj argentino
similar ['sɪmɪlə*] adj: ~ **(to)** parecido or semejante (a); ~**ity** [-ˈlærɪtɪ] n semejanza; ~**ly** adv del mismo modo
simmer ['sɪmə*] vi hervir a fuego lento
simple ['sɪmpl] adj (easy) sencillo; (foolish, COMM: interest) simple; **simplicity** [-ˈplɪsɪtɪ] n sencillez f; **simplify** ['sɪmplɪfaɪ] vt simplificar
simply ['sɪmplɪ] adv (live, talk) sencillamente; (just, merely) sólo
simulate ['sɪmjuːleɪt] vt fingir, simular; ~**d** adj simulado; (fur) de imitación
simultaneous [sɪməlˈteɪnɪəs] adj simultáneo; ~**ly** adv simultáneamente
sin [sɪn] n pecado ♦ vi pecar
since [sɪns] adv desde entonces, después ♦ prep desde ♦ conj (time) desde que; (because) ya que, puesto que; ~ **then, ever** ~ desde entonces
sincere [sɪnˈsɪə*] adj sincero; ~**ly** adv: **yours** ~**ly** (in letters) le saluda atentamente; **sincerity** [-ˈsɛrɪtɪ] n sinceridad f

sinew ['sɪnjuː] n tendón m
sing [sɪŋ] (pt **sang**, pp **sung**) vt, vi cantar
Singapore [sɪŋəˈpɔː*] n Singapur m
singe [sɪndʒ] vt chamuscar
singer ['sɪŋə*] n cantante m/f
singing ['sɪŋɪŋ] n canto
single ['sɪŋgl] adj único, solo; (unmarried) soltero; (not double) simple, sencillo ♦ n (BRIT: also: ~ **ticket**) billete m sencillo; (record) sencillo, single m; ~**s** npl (TENNIS) individual m; ~ **out** vt (choose) escoger; ~ **bed** cama individual; ~-**breasted** adj recto; ~ **file** n: **in** ~ **file** en fila de uno; ~-**handed** adv sin ayuda; ~-**minded** adj resuelto, firme; ~ **parent** n padre m soltero, madre f soltera (o divorciado etc); ~ **parent family** familia monoparental; ~ **room** n cuarto individual
singly ['sɪŋglɪ] adv uno por uno
singular ['sɪŋgjulə*] adj (odd) raro, extraño; (outstanding) excepcional ♦ n (LING) singular m
sinister ['sɪnɪstə*] adj siniestro
sink [sɪŋk] (pt **sank**, pp **sunk**) n fregadero ♦ vt (ship) hundir, echar a pique; (foundations) excavar ♦ vi (gen) hundirse; **to ~ sth into** hundir algo en; ~ **in** vi (fig) penetrar, calar
sinner ['sɪnə*] n pecador(a) m/f
sinus ['saɪnəs] n (ANAT) seno
sip [sɪp] n sorbo ♦ vt sorber, beber a sorbitos
siphon ['saɪfən] n sifón m; ~ **off** vt desvia
sir [sə*] n señor m; **S~ John Smith** Sir John Smith; **yes** ~ sí, señor
siren ['saɪərn] n sirena
sirloin ['səːlɔɪn] n (also: ~ **steak**) solomillo
sister ['sɪstə*] n hermana; (BRIT: nurse) enfermera jefe; ~-**in-law** n cuñada
sit [sɪt] (pt, pp **sat**) vi sentarse; (be sitting) estar sentado; (assembly) reunirse; (for painter) posar ♦ vt (exam) presentarse a; ~ **down** vi sentarse; ~ **in on** vt fus asistir a; ~ **up** vi incorporarse; (not go to bed) velar
sitcom ['sɪtkɔm] n abbr (= situation comedy) comedia de situación

ite [saɪt] *n* sitio; (*also*: **building ~**) solar *m*
♦ *vt* situar

it-in *n* (*demonstration*) sentada

itting ['sɪtɪŋ] *n* (*of assembly etc*) sesión *f*;
(*in canteen*) turno; ~ **room** *n* sala de
estar

ituated ['sɪtjuertɪd] *adj* situado

ituation [sɪtju'eɪʃən] *n* situación *f*; **"~s
vacant"** (*BRIT*) "ofrecen trabajo"

ix [sɪks] *num* seis; **~teen** *num* diez y seis,
dieciséis; **~th** *num* sexto; **~ty** *num*
sesenta

ize [saɪz] *n* tamaño; (*extent*) extensión *f*;
(*of clothing*) talla; (*of shoes*) número; ~
up *vt* formarse una idea de; **~able** *adj*
importante, considerable

izzle ['sɪzl] *vi* crepitar

kate [skeɪt] *n* patín *m*; (*fish: pl inv*) raya
♦ *vi* patinar; **~board** *n* monopatín *m*;
~boarding *n* monopatín *m*; **~r** *n*
patinador(a) *m/f*; **skating** *n* patinaje *m*;
skating rink *n* pista de patinaje

keleton ['skelɪtn] *n* esqueleto; (*TECH*)
armazón *f*; (*outline*) esquema *m*; ~ **staff**
n personal *m* reducido

keptic *etc* ['skeptɪk] (*US*) = **sceptic**

ketch [sketʃ] *n* (*drawing*) dibujo; (*outline*)
esbozo, bosquejo; (*THEATRE*) sketch *m* ♦ *vt*
dibujar; (*plan etc: also*: ~ **out**) esbozar; ~
book *n* libro de dibujos; **~y** *adj*
incompleto

kewer ['skjuːə*] *n* broqueta

ki [skiː] *n* esquí *m* ♦ *vi* esquiar; ~ **boot** *n*
bota de esquí

kid [skɪd] *n* patinazo ♦ *vi* patinar

ki: ~**er** *n* esquiador(a) *m/f*; **~ing** *n* esquí
m; ~ **jump** *n* salto con esquís

kilful ['skɪlful] (*BRIT*) *adj* diestro, experto

ki lift *n* telesilla *m*, telesquí *m*

kill [skɪl] *n* destreza, pericia; técnica; **~ed**
adj hábil, diestro; (*worker*) cualificado;
~full (*US*) *adj* = **skilful**

kim [skɪm] *vt* (*milk*) desnatar; (*glide over*)
rozar, rasar ♦ *vi*: **to ~ through** (*book*)
hojear; **~med milk** *n* leche *f* desnatada

kimp [skɪmp] *vt* (*also*: ~ **on**: *work*)
chapucear; (*cloth etc*) escatimar; **~y** *adj*

escaso; (*skirt*) muy corto

skin [skɪn] *n* piel *f*; (*complexion*) cutis *m*
♦ *vt* (*fruit etc*) pelar; (*animal*) despellejar;
~ **cancer** *n* cáncer *m* de piel; **~-deep**
adj superficial; ~ **diving** *n* buceo; **~ny**
adj flaco; **~tight** *adj* (*dress etc*) muy
ajustado

skip [skɪp] *n* brinco, salto; (*BRIT: container*)
contenedor *m* ♦ *vi* brincar; (*with rope*)
saltar a la comba ♦ *vt* saltarse

ski: ~ **pass** *n* forfait *m* (de esquí); ~
pole *n* bastón *m* de esquiar

skipper ['skɪpə*] *n* (*NAUT, SPORT*) capitán
m

skipping rope ['skɪpɪŋ-] (*BRIT*) *n* comba

skirmish ['skɜːmɪʃ] *n* escaramuza

skirt [skɜːt] *n* falda (*SP*), pollera (*AM*) ♦ *vt*
(*go round*) ladear; **~ing board** (*BRIT*) *n*
rodapié *m*

ski slope *n* pista de esquí

ski suit *n* traje *m* de esquiar

ski tow *n* remonte *m*

skittle ['skɪtl] *n* bolo; **~s** *n* (*game*) boliche
m

skive [skaɪv] (*BRIT: inf*) *vi* gandulear

skull [skʌl] *n* calavera; (*ANAT*) cráneo

skunk [skʌŋk] *n* mofeta

sky [skaɪ] *n* cielo; **~light** *n* tragaluz *m*,
claraboya; **~scraper** *n* rascacielos *m inv*

slab [slæb] *n* (*stone*) bloque *m*; (*flat*) losa;
(*of cake*) trozo

slack [slæk] *adj* (*loose*) flojo; (*slow*) de
poca actividad; (*careless*) descuidado; **~s**
npl pantalones *mpl*; **~en** (*also*: **~en off**)
vi aflojarse ♦ *vt* aflojar; (*speed*) disminuir

slag heap ['slæg-] *n* escorial *m*,
escombrera

slag off (*BRIT: inf*) *vt* poner como un
trapo

slam [slæm] *vt* (*throw*) arrojar
(violentamente); (*criticize*) criticar
duramente ♦ *vi* (*door*) cerrarse de golpe;
to ~ the door dar un portazo

slander ['slɑːndə*] *n* calumnia, difamación
f

slang [slæŋ] *n* argot *m*; (*jargon*) jerga

slant [slɑːnt] *n* sesgo, inclinación *f*; (*fig*)

interpretación *f*; ~ed *adj* (*fig*) parcial; ~ing *adj* inclinado; (*eyes*) rasgado

slap [slæp] *n* palmada; (*in face*) bofetada ♦ *vt* dar una palmada *or* bofetada a; (*paint etc*): to ~ sth on sth embadurnar algo con algo ♦ *adv* (*directly*) exactamente, directamente; ~dash *adj* descuidado; ~stick *n* comedia de golpe y porrazo; ~-up *adj*: a ~-up meal (*BRIT*) un banquetazo, una comilona

slash [slæʃ] *vt* acuchillar; (*fig: prices*) fulminar

slat [slæt] *n* tablilla, listón *m*

slate [sleɪt] *n* pizarra ♦ *vt* (*fig: criticize*) criticar duramente

slaughter ['slɔːtə*] *n* (*of animals*) matanza; (*of people*) carnicería ♦ *vt* matar; ~house *n* matadero

Slav [slɑːv] *adj* eslavo

slave [sleɪv] *n* esclavo/a ♦ *vi* (*also*: ~ away) sudar tinta; ~ry *n* esclavitud *f*

slay [sleɪ] (*pt* slew, *pp* slain) *vt* matar

sleazy ['sliːzɪ] *adj* de mala fama

sledge [sledʒ] *n* trineo; ~hammer *n* mazo

sleek [sliːk] *adj* (*shiny*) lustroso; (*car etc*) elegante

sleep [sliːp] (*pt, pp* slept) *n* sueño ♦ *vi* dormir; to go to ~ quedarse dormido; ~ around *vi* acostarse con cualquiera; ~ in *vi* (*oversleep*) quedarse dormido; ~er *n* (*person*) durmiente *m/f*; (*BRIT: RAIL: on track*) traviesa; (: *train*) coche-cama *m*; ~ing bag *n* saco de dormir; ~ing car *n* coche-cama *m*; ~ing partner (*BRIT*) *n* (*COMM*) socio comanditario; ~ing pill *n* somnífero; ~less *adj*: a ~less night una noche en blanco; ~walker *n* sonámbulo/a; ~y *adj* soñoliento; (*place*) soporífero

sleet [sliːt] *n* aguanieve *f*

sleeve [sliːv] *n* manga; (*TECH*) manguito; (*of record*) portada; ~less *adj* sin mangas

sleigh [sleɪ] *n* trineo

sleight [slaɪt] *n*: ~ of hand escamoteo

slender ['slendə*] *adj* delgado; (*means*) escaso

slept [slept] *pt, pp of* sleep

slew [sluː] *pt of* slay ♦ *vi* (*BRIT: veer*) torcerse

slice [slaɪs] *n* (*of meat*) tajada; (*of bread*) rebanada; (*of lemon*) rodaja; (*utensil*) pala ♦ *vt* cortar (en tajos); rebanar

slick [slɪk] *adj* (*skilful*) hábil, diestro; (*clever*) astuto ♦ *n* (*also*: oil ~) marea negra

slide [slaɪd] (*pt, pp* slid) *n* (*movement*) descenso, desprendimiento; (*in playground*) tobogán *m*; (*PHOT*) diapositiva; (*BRIT: also*: hair ~) pasador *m* ♦ *vt* correr, deslizar ♦ *vi* (*slip*) resbalarse; (*glide*) deslizarse; sliding *adj* (*door*) corredizo; sliding scale *n* escala móvil

slight [slaɪt] *adj* (*slim*) delgado; (*frail*) delicado; (*pain etc*) leve; (*trivial*) insignificante; (*small*) pequeño ♦ *n* desaire *m* ♦ *vt* (*insult*) ofender, desairar; not in the ~est en absoluto; ~ly *adv* ligeramente, un poco

slim [slɪm] *adj* delgado, esbelto; (*fig: chance*) remoto ♦ *vi* adelgazar

slime [slaɪm] *n* limo, cieno

slimming ['slɪmɪŋ] *n* adelgazamiento

slimy ['slaɪmɪ] *adj* cenagoso

sling [slɪŋ] (*pt, pp* slung) *n* (*MED*) cabestrillo; (*weapon*) honda ♦ *vt* tirar, arrojar

slip [slɪp] *n* (*slide*) resbalón *m*; (*mistake*) descuido; (*underskirt*) combinación *f*; (*of paper*) papelito ♦ *vt* (*slide*) deslizar ♦ *vi* deslizarse; (*stumble*) resbalar(se); (*decline*) decaer; (*move smoothly*): to ~ into/out of (*room etc*) introducirse en/salirse de; to give sb the ~ eludir a uno; a ~ of the tongue un lapsus; to ~ sth on/off ponerse/quitarse algo; ~ away *vi* escabullirse; ~ in *vt* meter ♦ *vi* meterse; ~ out *vi* (*go out*) salir (un momento); ~ up *vi* (*make mistake*) equivocarse; meter la pata; ~ped disc *n* vértebra dislocada

slipper ['slɪpə*] *n* zapatilla, pantufla

slippery ['slɪpərɪ] *adj* resbaladizo

slip: ~ road (*BRIT*) *n* carretera de acceso; ~-up *n* (*error*) desliz *m*; ~way *n* grada, gradas *fpl*

slit [slɪt] (*pt, pp* **slit**) *n* raja; (*cut*) corte *m* ♦ *vt* rajar; cortar

slither ['slɪðə*] *vi* deslizarse

sliver ['slɪvə*] *n* (*of glass, wood*) astilla; (*of cheese etc*) raja

slob [slɔb] (*inf*) *n* abandonado/a

slog [slɔg] (*BRIT*) *vi* sudar tinta; **it was a ~** costó trabajo (hacerlo)

slogan ['sləʊgən] *n* eslogan *m*, lema *m*

slope [sləʊp] *n* (*up*) cuesta, pendiente *f*; (*down*) declive *m*; (*side of mountain*) falda, vertiente *m* ♦ *vi*: **to ~ down** estar en declive; **to ~ up** inclinarse; **sloping** *adj* en pendiente; en declive; (*writing*) inclinado

sloppy ['slɔpɪ] *adj* (*work*) descuidado; (*appearance*) desaliñado

slot [slɔt] *n* ranura ♦ *vt*: **to ~ into** encajar en

slot machine *n* (*BRIT: vending machine*) distribuidor *m* automático; (*for gambling*) tragaperras *m inv*

slouch [slaʊtʃ] *vi* andar *etc* con los hombros caídos

Slovenia [sləʊ'viːnɪə] *n* Eslovenia

slovenly ['slʌvənlɪ] *adj* desaliñado, desaseado; (*careless*) descuidado

slow [sləʊ] *adj* lento; (*not clever*) lerdo; (*watch*): **to be ~** atrasar ♦ *adv* lentamente, despacio ♦ *vt, vi* (*also: ~ down, ~ up*) retardar; **"~"** (*road sign*) "disminuir velocidad"; **~down** (*US*) *n* huelga de manos caídas; **~ly** *adv* lentamente, despacio; **~ motion** *n*: **in ~ motion** a cámara lenta

sludge [slʌdʒ] *n* lodo, fango

slug [slʌg] *n* babosa; (*bullet*) posta; **~gish** *adj* lento; (*person*) perezoso

sluice [sluːs] *n* (*gate*) esclusa; (*channel*) canal *m*

slum [slʌm] *n* casucha

slump [slʌmp] *n* (*economic*) depresión *f* ♦ *vi* hundirse; (*prices*) caer en picado

slung [slʌŋ] *pt, pp of* **sling**

slur [sləː*] *n*: **to cast a ~ on** insultar ♦ *vt* (*speech*) pronunciar mal

slush [slʌʃ] *n* nieve *f* a medio derretir

slut [slʌt] *n* putona

sly [slaɪ] *adj* astuto; (*smile*) taimado

smack [smæk] *n* bofetada ♦ *vt* dar con la mano a; (*child, on face*) abofetear ♦ *vi*: **to ~ of** saber a, oler a

small [smɔːl] *adj* pequeño; **~ ads** (*BRIT*) *npl* anuncios *mpl* por palabras; **~ change** *n* suelto, cambio; **~holder** (*BRIT*) *n* granjero/a, parcelero/a; **~ hours** *npl*: **in the ~ hours** a las altas horas (de la noche); **~pox** *n* viruela; **~ talk** *n* cháchara

smart [smaːt] *adj* elegante; (*clever*) listo, inteligente; (*quick*) rápido, vivo ♦ *vi* escocer, picar; **~en up** *vi* arreglarse ♦ *vt* arreglar

smash [smæʃ] *n* (*also: ~-up*) choque *m*; (*MUS*) exitazo ♦ *vt* (*break*) hacer pedazos; (*car etc*) estrellar; (*SPORT: record*) batir ♦ *vi* hacerse pedazos; (*against wall etc*) estrellarse; **~ing** (*inf*) *adj* estupendo

smattering ['smætərɪŋ] *n*: **a ~ of** algo de

smear [smɪə*] *n* mancha; (*MED*) frotis *m inv* ♦ *vt* untar; **~ campaign** *n* campaña de desprestigio

smell [smel] (*pt, pp* **smelt** *or* **smelled**) *n* olor *m*; (*sense*) olfato ♦ *vt, vi* oler; **~y** *adj* maloliente

smile [smaɪl] *n* sonrisa ♦ *vi* sonreír

smirk [sməːk] *n* sonrisa falsa *or* afectada

smith [smɪθ] *n* herrero; **~y** ['smɪðɪ] *n* herrería

smog [smɔg] *n* esmog *m*

smoke [sməʊk] *n* humo ♦ *vi* fumar; (*chimney*) echar humo ♦ *vt* (*cigarettes*) fumar; **~d** *adj* (*bacon, glass*) ahumado; **~r** *n* fumador(a) *m/f*; (*RAIL*) coche *m* fumador; **~ screen** *n* cortina de humo; **~ shop** (*US*) *n* estanco (*SP*), tabaquería (*AM*); **smoking** *n*: **"no smoking"** "prohibido fumar"; **smoky** *adj* (*room*) lleno de humo; (*taste*) ahumado

smolder ['sməʊldə*] (*US*) *vi* = **smoulder**

smooth [smuːð] *adj* liso; (*sea*) tranquilo; (*flavour, movement*) suave; (*sauce*) fino; (*person: pej*) meloso ♦ *vt* (*also: ~ out*) alisar; (*creases, difficulties*) allanar

smother ['smʌðə'] vt sofocar; (repress) contener

smoulder ['sməuldə'] (US **smolder**) vi arder sin llama

smudge [smʌdʒ] n mancha ♦ vt manchar

smug [smʌg] adj presumido; oronda

smuggle ['smʌgl] vt pasar de contrabando; ~r n contrabandista m/f; **smuggling** n contrabando

smutty ['smʌtɪ] adj (fig) verde, obsceno

snack [snæk] n bocado; ~ **bar** n cafetería

snag [snæg] n problema m

snail [sneɪl] n caracol m

snake [sneɪk] n serpiente f

snap [snæp] n (sound) chasquido; (photograph) foto f ♦ adj (decision) instantáneo ♦ vt (break) quebrar; (fingers) castañetear ♦ vi quebrarse; (fig: speak sharply) contestar bruscamente; **to ~ shut** cerrarse de golpe; ~ **at** vt fus (subj: dog) intentar morder; ~ **off** vi partirse; ~ **up** vt agarrar; ~ **fastener** (US) n botón m de presión; ~**py** (inf) adj (answer) instantáneo; (slogan) conciso; **make it ~py!** (hurry up) ¡date prisa!; ~**shot** n foto f (instantánea)

snare [sneə'] n trampa

snarl [snɑːl] vi gruñir

snatch [snætʃ] n (small piece) fragmento ♦ vt (~ away) arrebatar; (fig) agarrar; **to ~ some sleep** encontrar tiempo para dormir

sneak [sniːk] (pt (US) **snuck**) vi: **to ~ in/ out** entrar/salir a hurtadillas ♦ n (inf) soplón/ona m/f; **to ~ up on sb** aparecérsele de improviso a uno; ~**ers** npl zapatos mpl de lona; ~**y** adj furtivo

sneer [snɪə'] vi reír con sarcasmo; (mock): **to ~ at** burlarse de

sneeze [sniːz] vi estornudar

sniff [snɪf] vi sollozar ♦ vt husmear, oler; (drugs) aspirar

snigger ['snɪgə'] vi reírse con disimulo

snip [snɪp] n tijeretazo; (BRIT: inf: bargain) ganga ♦ vt tijeretear

sniper ['snaɪpə'] n francotirador(a) m/f

snippet ['snɪpɪt] n retazo

snob [snɔb] n (e)snob m/f; ~**bery** n (e)snobismo; ~**bish** adj (e)snob

snooker ['snuːkə'] n especie de billar

snoop [snuːp] vi: **to ~ about** fisgonear

snooze [snuːz] n siesta ♦ vi echar una siesta

snore [snɔː'] n ronquido ♦ vi roncar

snorkel ['snɔːkl] n (tubo) respirador m

snort [snɔːt] n bufido ♦ vi bufar

snout [snaut] n hocico, morro

snow [snəu] n nieve f ♦ vi nevar; ~**ball** n bola de nieve ♦ vi (fig) agrandirse, ampliarse; ~**bound** adj bloqueado por la nieve; ~**drift** n ventisquero; ~**drop** n campanilla; ~**fall** n nevada; ~**flake** n copo de nieve; ~**man** (irreg) n figura de nieve; ~**plough** (US ~**plow**) n quitanieves m inv; ~**shoe** n raqueta (de nieve); ~**storm** n nevada, nevasca

snub [snʌb] vt desairar ♦ n desaire m, repulsa; ~-**nosed** adj chato

snuff [snʌf] n rapé m

snug [snʌg] adj (cosy) cómodo; (fitted) ajustado

snuggle ['snʌgl] vi: **to ~ up to sb** arrimarse a uno

KEYWORD

so [səu] adv **1** (thus, likewise) así, de este modo; **if ~** de ser así; **I like swimming – ~ do I** a mí me gusta nadar – a mí también; **I've got work to do – – ~ has Paul** tengo trabajo que hacer — Paul también; **it's 5 o'clock – – ~ it is!** son las cinco — ¡pues es verdad!; **I hope/think ~** espero/creo que sí; ~ **far** hasta ahora; (in past) hasta este momento

2 (in comparisons etc: to such a degree) tan; ~ **quickly (that)** tan rápido (que); ~ **big (that)** tan grande (que); **she's not ~ clever as her brother** no es tan lista como su hermano; **we were ~ worried** estábamos preocupadísimos

3: ~ **much** adj, adv tanto; ~ **many** tantos/as

4 (phrases): **10 or ~** unos 10, 10 o así; ~ **long!** (inf: goodbye) ¡hasta luego!

♦ conj 1 (expressing purpose): ~ **as to do**
para hacer; ~ **(that)** para que +sub
2 (expressing result) así que; ~ **you see, I
could have gone** así que ya ves, (yo)
podría haber ido

soak [səuk] vt (drench) empapar; (steep in
water) remojar ♦ vi remojarse, estar a
remojo; ~ **in** vi penetrar; ~ **up** vt
absorber

soap [səup] n jabón m; ~**flakes** npl
escamas fpl de jabón; ~ **opera** n
telenovela; ~ **powder** n jabón m en
polvo; ~**y** adj jabonoso

soar [sɔː*] vi (on wings) remontarse;
(rocket, prices) dispararse; (building etc)
elevarse

sob [sɔb] n sollozo ♦ vi sollozar

sober ['səubə*] adj (serious) serio; (not
drunk) sobrio; (colour, style) discreto; ~
up vt quitar la borrachera

so-called adj así llamado

soccer ['sɔkə*] n fútbol m

social ['səuʃl] adj n velada, fiesta;
~ **club** n club m; ~**ism** n socialismo;
~**ist** adj, n socialista m/f; ~**ize** vi: **to ~ize
(with)** alternar (con); ~**ly** adv
socialmente; ~ **security** n seguridad f
social; ~ **work** n asistencia social; ~
worker n asistente/a m/f social

society [sə'saɪətɪ] n sociedad f; (club)
asociación f; (also: **high ~**) alta sociedad

sociology [səusɪ'ɔlədʒɪ] n sociología f

sock [sɔk] n calcetín m (SP), media (AM)

socket ['sɔkɪt] n cavidad f; (BRIT: ELEC)
enchufe m

sod [sɔd] n (of earth) césped m; (BRIT: inf!)
cabrón/ona m/f (!)

soda ['səudə] n (CHEM) sosa; (also: ~
water) soda; (US: also: ~ **pop**) gaseosa

sofa ['səufə] n sofá m

soft [sɔft] adj (lenient, not hard) blando;
(gentle, not bright) suave; ~ **drink** n
bebida no alcohólica; ~**en** ['sɔfn] vt
ablandar; suavizar; (effect) amortiguar ♦ vi
ablandarse; suavizarse; ~**ly** adv
suavemente; (gently) delicadamente, con

delicadeza; ~**ness** n blandura; suavidad
f; ~**ware** n (COMPUT) software m

soggy ['sɔgɪ] adj empapado

soil [sɔɪl] n (earth) tierra, suelo ♦ vt
ensuciar; ~**ed** adj sucio

solar ['səulə*] adj: ~ **energy** n energía
solar; ~ **panel** n panel m solar

sold [səuld] pt, pp of **sell**; ~ **out** adj
(COMM) agotado

solder ['səuldə*] vt soldar ♦ n soldadura

soldier ['səuldʒə*] n soldado; (army man)
militar m

sole [səul] n (of foot) planta; (of shoe)
suela; (fish: pl inv) lenguado ♦ adj único

solemn ['sɔləm] adj solemne

sole trader n (COMM) comerciante m
exclusivo

solicit [sə'lɪsɪt] vt (request) solicitar ♦ vi
(prostitute) importunar

solicitor [sə'lɪsɪtə*] (BRIT) n (for wills etc) ≈
notario/a; (in court) ≈ abogado/a

solid ['sɔlɪd] adj sólido; (gold etc) macizo
♦ n sólido; ~**s** npl (food) alimentos mpl
sólidos

solidarity [sɔlɪ'dærɪtɪ] n solidaridad f

solitary ['sɔlɪtərɪ] adj solitario, solo; ~
confinement n incomunicación f

solo ['səuləu] n solo ♦ adv (fly) en solitario;
~**ist** n solista m/f

soluble ['sɔljuːbl] adj soluble

solution [sə'luːʃən] n solución f

solve [sɔlv] vt resolver, solucionar

solvent ['sɔlvənt] adj (COMM) solvente ♦ n
(CHEM) solvente m

KEYWORD

some [sʌm] adj 1 (a certain amount or
number of): ~ **tea / water / biscuits** té/
agua/(unas) galletas; **there's ~ milk in
the fridge** hay leche en el frigo; **there
were ~ people outside** había algunas
personas fuera; **I've got ~ money, but
not much** tengo algo de dinero, pero no
mucho
2 (certain: in contrasts) algunos/as; ~
people say that ... hay quien dice que
...; ~ **films were excellent, but most**

were mediocre hubo películas excelentes, pero la mayoría fueron mediocres
3 (*unspecified*): **~ woman was asking for you** una mujer estuvo preguntando por ti; **he was asking for ~ book (or other)** pedía un libro; **~ day** algún día; **~ day next week** un día de la semana que viene
♦ *pron* 1 (*a certain number*): **I've got ~** (*books etc*) tengo algunos/as
2 (*a certain amount*) algo; **I've got ~** (*money, milk*) tengo algo; **could I have ~ of that cheese?** ¿me puede dar un poco de ese queso?; **I've read ~ of the book** he leído parte del libro
♦ *adv*: **~ 10 people** unas 10 personas, una decena de personas

some: ~body ['sʌmbədɪ] *pron* = **someone**; **~how** *adv* de alguna manera; (*for some reason*) por una u otra razón; **~one** *pron* alguien; **~place** (*US*) *adv* = **somewhere**
somersault ['sʌməsɔ:lt] *n* (*deliberate*) salto mortal; (*accidental*) vuelco ♦ *vi* dar un salto mortal; dar vuelcos
some: ~thing *pron* algo; **would you like ~thing to eat/drink?** ¿te gustaría cenar/tomar algo?; **~time** *adv* (*in future*) algún día, en algún momento; (*in past*): **~time last month** durante el mes pasado; **~times** *adv* a veces; **~what** *adv* algo; **~where** *adv* (*be*) en alguna parte; (*go*) a alguna parte; **~where else** (*be*) en otra parte; (*go*) a otra parte
son [sʌn] *n* hijo
song [sɒŋ] *n* canción *f*
son-in-law *n* yerno
soon [su:n] *adv* pronto, dentro de poco; **~ afterwards** poco después; *see also* **as**; **~er** *adv* (*time*) antes, más temprano; (*preference*): **I would ~er do that** preferiría hacer eso; **~er or later** tarde o temprano
soot [sut] *n* hollín *m*
soothe [su:ð] *vt* tranquilizar; (*pain*) aliviar
sophisticated [sə'fɪstɪkeɪtɪd] *adj*

sofisticado
sophomore ['sɒfəmɔ:*] (*US*) *n* estudiante *m/f* de segundo año
sopping ['sɒpɪŋ] *adj*: **~ (wet)** empapado
soppy ['sɒpɪ] (*pej*) *adj* tonto
soprano [sə'prɑ:nəu] *n* soprano *f*
sorcerer ['sɔ:sərə*] *n* hechicero
sore [sɔ:*] *adj* (*painful*) doloroso, que duele
♦ *n* llaga; **~ly** *adv*: **I am ~ly tempted to** estoy muy tentado a
sorrow ['sɒrəu] *n* pena, dolor *m*; **~s** *npl* pesares *mpl*; **~ful** *adj* triste
sorry ['sɒrɪ] *adj* (*regretful*) arrepentido; (*condition, excuse*) lastimoso; **~!** ¡perdón!, ¡perdone!; **~?** ¿cómo?; **to feel ~ for sb** tener lástima a uno; **I feel ~ for him** me da lástima
sort [sɔ:t] *n* clase *f*, género, tipo ♦ *vt* (*also*: **~ out**: *papers*) clasificar; (: *problems*) arreglar, solucionar; **~ing office** *n* sala de batalla
SOS *n* SOS *m*
so-so *adv* regular, así así
soufflé ['su:fleɪ] *n* suflé *m*
sought [sɔ:t] *pt, pp of* **seek**
soul [səul] *n* alma; **~ful** *adj* lleno de sentimiento
sound [saund] *n* (*noise*) sonido, ruido; (*volume: on TV etc*) volumen *m*; (*GEO*) estrecho ♦ *adj* (*healthy*) sano; (*safe, not damaged*) en buen estado; (*reliable: person*) digno de confianza; (*sensible*) sensato, razonable; (*secure: investment*) seguro ♦ *adv*: **~ asleep** profundamente dormido ♦ *vt* (*alarm*) *vi* sonar, resonar; (*fig: seem*) parecer; **to ~ like** sonar a; **~ out** *vt* sondear; **~ barrier** *n* barrera del sonido; **~bite** *n* cita jugosa; **~ effects** *npl* efectos *mpl* sonoros; **~ly** *adv* (*sleep*) profundamente; (*defeated*) completamente; **~proof** *adj* insonorizado; **~track** *n* (*of film*) banda sonora
soup [su:p] *n* (*thick*) sopa; (*thin*) caldo; **~ plate** *n* plato sopero; **~spoon** *n* cuchara sopera
sour ['sauə*] *adj* agrio; (*milk*) cortado; **it's**

~ grapes (*fig*) están verdes

•urce [sɔːs] *n* fuente *f*

•uth [sauθ] *n* sur *m* ♦ *adj* del sur, sureño
♦ *adv* al sur, hacia el sur; **S~ Africa** *n*
África del Sur; **S~ African** *adj*, *n*
sudafricano/a *m/f*; **S~ America** *n*
América del Sur, Sudamérica; **S~
American** *adj*, *n* sudamericano/a *m/f*;
~-east *n* sudeste *m*; **~erly** ['sʌðəlɪ] *adj*
sur; (*from the* ~) del sur; **~ern** ['sʌðən] *adj*
del sur, meridional; **S~ Pole** *n* Polo Sur;
~ward(s) *adv* hacia el sur; **~-west** *n*
suroeste *m*

•uvenir [suːvə'nɪə*] *n* recuerdo

•vereign ['sɔvrɪn] *adj*, *n* soberano/a *m/f*;
~ty *n* soberanía

•viet ['səuvɪət] *adj* soviético; **the S~
Union** la Unión Soviética

•w[1] [səu] (*pt* **sowed**, *pp* **sown**) *vt*
sembrar

•w[2] [sau] *n* cerda (*SP*), puerca (*SP*),
chancha (*AM*)

•y [sɔɪ] (*US*) *n* = **soya**

•ya ['sɔɪə] (*BRIT*) *n* soja; **~ bean** *n* haba
de soja; **~ sauce** *n* salsa de soja

•a [spɑː] *n* balneario

•ace [speɪs] *n* espacio; (*room*) sitio ♦ *cpd*
espacial ♦ *vt*(*also:* **~ out**) espaciar; **~craft**
n nave *f* espacial; **~man/woman** (*irreg*)
n astronauta *m/f*, cosmonauta *m/f*;
~ship *n* = **~craft**; **spacing** *n* espaciado

•acious ['speɪʃəs] *adj* amplio

•ade [speɪd] *n* (*tool*) pala, laya; **~s** *npl*
(*CARDS: British*) picas *fpl*; (: *Spanish*)
espadas *fpl*

•aghetti [spə'getɪ] *n* espaguetis *mpl*,
fideos *mpl*

•ain [speɪn] *n* España

•an [spæn] *n* (*of bird, plane*) envergadura;
(*of arch*) luz *f*; (*in time*) lapso ♦ *vt*
extenderse sobre, cruzar; (*fig*) abarcar

•aniard ['spænjəd] *n* español(a) *m/f*

•aniel ['spænjəl] *n* perro de aguas

•anish ['spænɪʃ] *adj* español(a) ♦ *n*
(*LING*) español *m*, castellano; **the ~** *npl* los
españoles

•ank [spæŋk] *vt* zurrar

spanner ['spænə*] (*BRIT*) *n* llave *f* (inglesa)

spare [speə*] *adj* de reserva; (*surplus*)
sobrante, de más ♦ *n* = **~ part** ♦ *vt* (*do
without*) pasarse sin; (*refrain from hurting*)
perdonar; **to ~** (*surplus*) sobrante, de
sobra; **~ part** *n* pieza de repuesto; **~
time** *n* tiempo libre; **~ wheel** *n* (*AUT*)
rueda de recambio

sparingly ['speərɪŋlɪ] *adv* con moderación

spark [spɑːk] *n* chispa; (*fig*) chispazo;
~(ing) plug *n* bujía

sparkle ['spɑːkl] *n* centelleo, destello ♦ *vi*
(*shine*) relucir, brillar; **sparkling** *adj*
(*eyes, conversation*) brillante; (*wine*)
espumoso; (*mineral water*) con gas

sparrow ['spærəu] *n* gorrión *m*

sparse [spɑːs] *adj* esparcido, escaso

spartan ['spɑːtən] *adj* (*fig*) espartano

spasm ['spæzəm] *n* (*MED*) espasmo

spastic ['spæstɪk] *n* espástico/a

spat [spæt] *pt, pp of* **spit**

spate [speɪt] *n* (*fig*): **a ~ of** un torrente de

spawn [spɔːn] *vi* desovar, frezar ♦ *n*
huevas *fpl*

speak [spiːk] (*pt* **spoke**, *pp* **spoken**) *vt*
(*language*) hablar; (*truth*) decir ♦ *vi*
hablar; (*make a speech*) intervenir; **to ~ to
sb/of** *or* **about sth** hablar con uno/de *or*
sobre algo; **~ up!** ¡habla fuerte!; **~er** *n* (*in
public*) orador(a) *m/f*; (*also:* **loud~er**)
altavoz *m*; (*for stereo etc*) bafle *m*; (*POL*):
the S~er (*BRIT*) el Presidente de la
Cámara de los Comunes; (*US*) el
Presidente del Congreso

spear [spɪə*] *n* lanza ♦ *vt* alancear; **~head**
vt (*attack etc*) encabezar

spec [spek] (*inf*) *n*: **on ~** como
especulación

special ['speʃl] *adj* especial; (*edition etc*)
extraordinario; (*delivery*) urgente; **~ist** *n*
especialista *m/f*; **~ity** [speʃɪ'ælɪtɪ] (*BRIT*) *n*
especialidad *f*; **~ize** *vi*: **to ~ize (in)**
especializarse (en); **~ly** *adv* sobre todo,
en particular; **~ty** (*US*) *n* = **~ity**

species ['spiːʃiːz] *n inv* especie *f*

specific [spə'sɪfɪk] *adj* específico; **~ally**
adv específicamente

specify ['spesɪfaɪ] *vt, vi* especificar, precisar

specimen ['spesɪmən] *n* ejemplar *m*; (*MED: of urine*) espécimen *m* (: *of blood*) muestra

speck [spek] *n* grano, mota

speckled ['spekld] *adj* moteado

specs [speks] (*inf*) *npl* gafas *fpl* (SP), anteojos *mpl*

spectacle ['spektəkl] *n* espectáculo; **~s** *npl* (*BRIT: glasses*) gafas *fpl* (SP), anteojos *mpl*; **spectacular** [-'tækjulə*] *adj* espectacular; (*success*) impresionante

spectator [spek'teɪtə*] *n* espectador(a) *m/f*

spectrum ['spektrəm] (*pl* **spectra**) *n* espectro

speculate ['spekjuleɪt] *vi*: **to ~ (on)** especular (en); **speculation** [spekju'leɪʃən] *n* especulación *f*

speech [spiːtʃ] *n* (*faculty*) habla; (*formal talk*) discurso; (*spoken language*) lenguaje *m*; **~less** *adj* mudo, estupefacto; **~ therapist** *n* especialista que corrige defectos de pronunciación en los niños

speed [spiːd] *n* velocidad *f*; (*haste*) prisa; (*promptness*) rapidez *f*; **at full** *or* **top ~** a máxima velocidad; **~ up** *vi* acelerarse ♦ *vt* acelerar; **~boat** *n* lancha motora; **~ily** *adv* rápido, rápidamente; **~ing** *n* (*AUT*) exceso de velocidad; **~ limit** *n* límite *m* de velocidad, velocidad *f* máxima; **~ometer** [spɪ'dɔmɪtə*] *n* velocímetro; **~way** *n* (*sport*) pista de carrera; **~y** *adj* (*fast*) veloz, rápido; (*prompt*) pronto

spell [spel] (*pt, pp* **spelt** (BRIT) *or* **spelled**) *n* (*also*: **magic ~**) encanto, hechizo; (*period of time*) rato, período ♦ *vt* deletrear; (*fig*) anunciar, presagiar; **to cast a ~ on sb** hechizar a uno; **he can't ~** pone faltas de ortografía; **~bound** *adj* embelesado, hechizado; **~ing** *n* ortografía

spend [spend] (*pt, pp* **spent**) *vt* (*money*) gastar; (*time*) pasar; (*life*) dedicar; **~thrift** *n* derrochador(a) *m/f*, pródigo/a

sperm [spəːm] *n* esperma

sphere [sfɪə*] *n* esfera

sphinx [sfɪŋks] *n* esfinge *f*

spice [spaɪs] *n* especia ♦ *vt* condimentar

spicy ['spaɪsɪ] *adj* picante

spider ['spaɪdə*] *n* araña

spike [spaɪk] *n* (*point*) punta; (*BOT*) espiga

spill [spɪl] (*pt, pp* **spilt** *or* **spilled**) *vt* derramar, verter ♦ *vi* derramarse; **to ~ over** desbordarse

spin [spɪn] (*pt, pp* **spun**) *n* (*AVIAT*) barren (*trip in car*) paseo (en coche); (*on ball*) efecto ♦ *vt* (*wool etc*) hilar; (*ball etc*) hac girar ♦ *vi* girar, dar vueltas

spinach ['spɪnɪtʃ] *n* espinaca; (*as food*) espinacas *fpl*

spinal ['spaɪnl] *adj* espinal; **~ cord** *n* columna vertebral

spin doctor *n* informador(a) parcial al servicio de un partido político etc

spin-dryer (BRIT) *n* secador *m* centrífugo

spine [spaɪn] *n* espinazo, columna vertebral; (*thorn*) espina; **~less** *adj* (*fig*) débil, pusilánime

spinning ['spɪnɪŋ] *n* hilandería; **~ top** *n* peonza

spin-off *n* derivado, producto secundario

spinster ['spɪnstə*] *n* solterona

spiral ['spaɪərl] *n* espiral *f* ♦ *vi* (*fig: prices*) subir desorbitadamente; **~ staircase** *n* escalera de caracol

spire ['spaɪə*] *n* aguja, chapitel *m*

spirit ['spɪrɪt] *n* (*soul*) alma *f*; (*ghost*) fantasma *m*; (*attitude, sense*) espíritu *m*; (*courage*) valor *m*, ánimo; **~s** *npl* (*drink*) licor(es) *m(pl)*; **in good ~s** alegre, de buen ánimo; **~ed** *adj* enérgico, vigoroso

spiritual ['spɪrɪtjuəl] *adj* espiritual ♦ *n* espiritual *m*

spit [spɪt] (*pt, pp* **spat**) *n* (*for roasting*) asador *m*, espetón *m*; (*saliva*) saliva ♦ *vi* escupir; (*sound*) chisporrotear; (*rain*) lloviznar

spite [spaɪt] *n* rencor *m*, ojeriza ♦ *vt* caus pena a, mortificar; **in ~ of** a pesar de, pese a; **~ful** *adj* rencoroso, malévolo

spittle ['spɪtl] *n* saliva, baba

splash [splæʃ] *n* (*sound*) chapoteo; (*of colour*) mancha ♦ *vt* salpicar ♦ *vi* (*also*: **~**

about) chapotear

spleen [spli:n] n (ANAT) bazo

splendid ['splendid] adj espléndido

splint [splint] n tablilla

splinter ['splintə*] n (of wood etc) astilla; (in finger) espigón m ♦ vi astillarse, hacer astillas

split [split] (pt, pp **split**) n hendedura, raja; (fig) división f; (POL) escisión f ♦ vt partir, rajar; (party) dividir; (share) repartir ♦ vi dividirse, escindirse; ~ **up** vi (couple) separarse; (meeting) acabarse

spoil [spɔil] (pt, pp **spoilt** or **spoiled**) vt (damage) dañar; (mar) estropear; (child) mimar, consentir; ~**s** npl despojo, botín m; ~**sport** n aguafiestas m inv

spoke [spəuk] pt of **speak** ♦ n rayo, radio

spoken ['spəukn] pp of **speak**

spokesman ['spəuksmən] (irreg) n portavoz m; **spokeswoman** ['spəukswumən] (irreg) n portavoz f

sponge [spʌndʒ] n esponja; (also: ~ **cake**) bizcocho ♦ vt (wash) lavar con esponja ♦ vi: to ~ **off** or **on sb** vivir a costa de uno; ~ **bag** (BRIT) n esponjera

sponsor ['spɔnsə*] n patrocinador(a) m/f ♦ vt (applicant, proposal etc) proponer; ~**ship** n patrocinio

spontaneous [spɔn'teiniəs] adj espontáneo

spooky ['spu:ki] (inf) adj espeluznante, horripilante

spool [spu:l] n carrete m

spoon [spu:n] n cuchara; ~~**feed** vt dar de comer con cuchara a; (fig) tratar como un niño a; ~**ful** n cucharada

sport [spɔ:t] n deporte m; (person): **to be a good** ~ ser muy majo ♦ vt (wear) lucir, ostentar; ~**ing** adj deportivo; (generous) caballeroso; **to give sb a ~ing chance** darle a uno una (buena) oportunidad; ~ **jacket** (US) n = ~**s jacket**; ~**s car** n coche m deportivo; ~**s jacket** (BRIT) n chaqueta deportiva; ~**sman** (irreg) n deportista m; ~**smanship** n deportividad f; ~**swear** n trajes mpl de deporte or sport; ~**swoman** (irreg) n

deportista; ~**y** adj deportista

spot [spɔt] n sitio, lugar m; (dot: on pattern) punto, mancha; (pimple) grano; (RADIO) cuña publicitaria; (TV) espacio publicitario; (small amount): **a** ~ **of** un poquito de ♦ vt (notice) notar, observar; **on the** ~ allí mismo; ~ **check** n reconocimiento rápido; ~**less** adj perfectamente limpio; ~**light** n foco, reflector m; (AUT) faro auxiliar; ~**ted** adj (pattern) de puntos; ~**ty** adj (face) con granos

spouse [spauz] n cónyuge m/f

spout [spaut] n (of jug) pico; (of pipe) caño ♦ vi salir en chorro

sprain [sprein] n torcedura ♦ vt: **to** ~ **one's ankle/wrist** torcerse el tobillo/la muñeca

sprang [spræŋ] pt of **spring**

sprawl [sprɔ:l] vi tumbarse

spray [sprei] n rociada; (of sea) espuma; (container) atomizador m; (for paint etc) pistola rociadora; (of flowers) ramita ♦ vt rociar; (crops) regar

spread [spred] (pt, pp **spread**) n extensión f; (for bread etc) pasta para untar; (inf: food) comilona ♦ vt extender; (butter) untar; (wings, sails) desplegar; (work, wealth) repartir; (scatter) esparcir ♦ vi (also: ~ **out**: stain) extenderse; (news) diseminarse; ~ **out** vi (move apart) separarse; ~~**eagled** adj a pata tendida; ~**sheet** n hoja electrónica or de cálculo

spree [spri:] n: **to go on a** ~ ir de juerga

sprightly ['spraitli] adj vivo, enérgico

spring [spriŋ] (pt **sprang**, pp **sprung**) n (season) primavera; (leap) salto, brinco; (coiled metal) resorte m; (of water) fuente f, manantial m ♦ vi saltar, brincar; ~ **up** vi (thing: appear) aparecer; (problem) surgir; ~**board** n trampolín m; ~~**clean(ing)** n limpieza general; ~**time** n primavera

sprinkle ['spriŋkl] vt (pour: liquid) rociar; (: salt, sugar) espolvorear; **to** ~ **water etc on**, ~ **with water etc** rociar or salpicar de agua etc; ~**r** n (for lawn) rociadera; (to *put out fire*) aparato de rociadura automática

sprint [sprɪnt] *n* esprint *m* ♦ *vi* esprintar

sprout [spraut] *vi* brotar, retoñar; **(Brussels) ~s** *npl* coles *fpl* de Bruselas

spruce [spru:s] *n inv* (BOT) pícea ♦ *adj* aseado, pulcro

sprung [sprʌŋ] *pp of* **spring**

spun [spʌn] *pt, pp of* **spin**

spur [spə:*] *n* espuela; (*fig*) estímulo, aguijón *m* ♦ *vt* (*also*: **~ on**) estimular, incitar; **on the ~ of the moment** de improviso

spurious ['spjuəriəs] *adj* falso

spurn [spə:n] *vt* desdeñar, rechazar

spurt [spə:t] *n* chorro; (*of energy*) arrebato ♦ *vi* chorrear

spy [spaɪ] *n* espía *m/f* ♦ *vi*: **to ~ on** espiar a ♦ *vt* (*see*) divisar, lograr ver; **~ing** *n* espionaje *m*

sq. *abbr* = **square**

squabble ['skwɔbl] *vi* reñir, pelear

squad [skwɔd] *n* (MIL) pelotón *m*; (POLICE) brigada; (SPORT) equipo

squadron ['skwɔdrn] *n* (MIL) escuadrón *m*; (AVIAT, NAUT) escuadra

squalid ['skwɔlɪd] *adj* vil; (*fig*: *sordid*) sórdido

squall [skwɔ:l] *n* (*storm*) chubasco; (*wind*) ráfaga

squalor ['skwɔlə*] *n* miseria

squander ['skwɔndə*] *vt* (*money*) derrochar, despilfarrar; (*chances*) desperdiciar

square [skweə*] *n* cuadro; (*in town*) plaza; (*inf*: *person*) carca *m/f* ♦ *adj* cuadrado; (*inf*: *ideas*, *tastes*) trasnochado ♦ *vt* (*arrange*) arreglar; (MATH) cuadrar; (*reconcile*) compaginar; **all ~** igual(es); **to have a ~ meal** comer caliente; **2 metres ~** 2 metros en cuadro; **2 ~ metres** 2 metros cuadrados; **~ly** *adv* de lleno

squash [skwɔʃ] *n* (BRIT: *drink*): **lemon/ orange ~** zumo (SP) *or* jugo (AM) de limón/naranja; (US: BOT) calabacín *m*; (SPORT) squash *m*, frontenis *m* ♦ *vt* aplastar

squat [skwɔt] *adj* achaparrado ♦ *vi* (*also*: **~ down**) agacharse, sentarse en cuclillas; **~ter** *n persona que ocupa ilegalmente una casa*

squeak [skwi:k] *vi* (*hinge*) chirriar, rechinar; (*mouse*) chillar

squeal [skwi:l] *vi* chillar, dar gritos agudos

squeamish ['skwi:mɪʃ] *adj* delicado, remilgado

squeeze [skwi:z] *n* presión *f*; (*of hand*) apretón *m*; (COMM) restricción *f* ♦ *vt* (*hand*, *arm*) apretar; **~ out** *vt* exprimir

squelch [skweltʃ] *vi* chapotear

squid [skwɪd] *n inv* calamar *m*; (CULIN) calamares *mpl*

squiggle ['skwɪgl] *n* garabato

squint [skwɪnt] *vi* bizquear, ser bizco ♦ *n* (MED) estrabismo

squirm [skwə:m] *vi* retorcerse, revolverse

squirrel ['skwɪrəl] *n* ardilla

squirt [skwə:t] *vi* salir a chorros ♦ *vt* chiscar

Sr *abbr* = **senior**

St *abbr* = **saint**; **street**

stab [stæb] *n* (*with knife*) puñalada; (*of pain*) pinchazo; (*inf*: *try*): **to have a ~ at (doing) sth** intentar (hacer) algo ♦ *vt* apuñalar

stable ['steɪbl] *adj* estable ♦ *n* cuadra, caballeriza

stack [stæk] *n* montón *m*, pila ♦ *vt* amontonar, apilar

stadium ['steɪdɪəm] *n* estadio

staff [stɑ:f] *n* (*work force*) personal *m*, plantilla; (BRIT: SCOL) cuerpo docente ♦ *vt* proveer de personal

stag [stæg] *n* ciervo, venado

stage [steɪdʒ] *n* escena; (*point*) etapa; (*platform*) plataforma; (*profession*): **the ~** el teatro ♦ *vt* (*play*) poner en escena, representar; (*organize*) montar, organizar; **in ~s** por etapas; **~coach** *n* diligencia; **~ manager** *n* director(a) *m/f* de escena

stagger ['stægə*] *vi* tambalearse ♦ *vt* (*amaze*) asombrar; (*hours*, *holidays*) escalonar; **~ing** *adj* asombroso

stagnant ['stægnənt] *adj* estancado

stag party *n* despedida de soltero

staid [steɪd] *adj* serio, formal

stain [steɪn] *n* mancha; (*colouring*) tintura ♦ *vt* manchar; (*wood*) teñir; **~ed glass window** *n* vidriera de colores; **~less steel** *n* acero inoxidable; **~ remover** *n* quitamanchas *m inv*

stair [steə*] *n* (*step*) peldaño, escalón *m*; **~s** *npl* escaleras *fpl*; **~case** *n* = **~way**; **~way** *n* escalera

stake [steɪk] *n* estaca, poste *m*; (*COMM*) interés *m*; (*BETTING*) apuesta ♦ *vt* (*money*) apostar; (*life*) arriesgar; (*reputation*) poner en juego; (*claim*) presentar una reclamación; **to be at ~** estar en juego

stale [steɪl] *adj* (*bread*) duro; (*food*) pasado; (*smell*) rancio; (*beer*) agrio

stalemate ['steɪlmeɪt] *n* tablas *fpl* (por ahogado); (*fig*) estancamiento

stalk [stɔ:k] *n* tallo, caña ♦ *vt* acechar, cazar al acecho; **~ off** *vi* irse airado

stall [stɔ:l] *n* (*in market*) puesto; (*in stable*) casilla (de establo) ♦ *vt* (*AUT*) calar; (*fig*) dar largas a ♦ *vi* (*AUT*) calarse; (*fig*) andarse con rodeos; **~s** *npl* (*BRIT: in cinema, theatre*) butacas *fpl*

stallion ['stælɪən] *n* semental *m*

stamina ['stæmɪnə] *n* resistencia

stammer ['stæmə*] *n* tartamudeo ♦ *vi* tartamudear

stamp [stæmp] *n* sello (*SP*), estampilla (*AM*); (*mark, also fig*) marca, huella; (*on document*) timbre *m* ♦ *vi* (*also:* **~ one's foot**) patear ♦ *vt* (*mark*) marcar; (*letter*) poner sellos *or* estampillas en; (*with rubber ~*) sellar; **~ album** *n* álbum *m* para sellos *or* estampillas; **~ collecting** *n* filatelia

stampede [stæm'pi:d] *n* estampida

stance [stæns] *n* postura

stand [stænd] (*pt, pp* **stood**) *n* (*position*) posición *f*, postura; (*for taxis*) parada; (*hall ~*) perchero; (*music ~*) atril *m*; (*SPORT*) tribuna; (*at exhibition*) stand *m* ♦ *vi* (*be*) estar, encontrarse; (*be on foot*) estar de pie; (*rise*) levantarse; (*remain*) quedar en pie; (*in election*) presentar

candidatura ♦ *vt* (*place*) poner, colocar; (*withstand*) aguantar, soportar; (*invite to*) invitar; **to make a ~** (*fig*) mantener una postura firme; **to ~ for parliament** (*BRIT*) presentarse (como candidato) a las elecciones; **~ by** *vi* (*be ready*) estar listo ♦ *vt fus* (*opinion*) aferrarse a; (*person*) apoyar; **~ down** *vi* (*withdraw*) ceder el puesto; **~ for** *vt fus* (*signify*) significar; (*tolerate*) aguantar, permitir; **~ in for** *vt fus* suplir a; **~ out** *vi* destacarse; **~ up** *vi* levantarse, ponerse de pie; **~ up for** *vt fus* defender; **~ up to** *vt fus* hacer frente a

standard ['stændəd] *n* patrón *m*, norma; (*level*) nivel *m*; (*flag*) estandarte *m* ♦ *adj* (*size etc*) normal, corriente; (*text*) básico; **~s** *npl* (*morals*) valores *mpl* morales; **~ lamp** (*BRIT*) *n* lámpara de pie; **~ of living** *n* nivel *m* de vida

stand-by ['stændbaɪ] *n* (*reserve*) recurso seguro; **to be on ~** estar sobre aviso; **~ ticket** *n* (*AVIAT*) (billete *m*) standby *m*

stand-in ['stændɪn] *n* suplente *m/f*

standing ['stændɪŋ] *adj* (*on foot*) de pie, en pie; (*permanent*) permanente ♦ *n* reputación *f*; **of many years' ~** que lleva muchos años; **~ joke** *n* broma permanente; **~ order** (*BRIT*) *n* (*at bank*) orden *f* de pago permanente; **~ room** *n* sitio para estar de pie

stand: **~point** *n* punto de vista; **~still** *n*: **at a ~still** (*industry, traffic*) paralizado; (*car*) parado; **to come to a ~still** quedar paralizado; pararse

stank [stæŋk] *pt of* **stink**

staple ['steɪpl] *n* (*for papers*) grapa ♦ *adj* (*food etc*) básico ♦ *vt* grapar; **~r** *n* grapadora

star [stɑ:*] *n* estrella; (*celebrity*) estrella, astro ♦ *vt* (*THEATRE, CINEMA*) ser el/la protagonista de; **the ~s** *npl* (*ASTROLOGY*) el horóscopo

starboard ['stɑ:bəd] *n* estribor *m*

starch [stɑ:tʃ] *n* almidón *m*

stardom ['stɑ:dəm] *n* estrellato

stare [steə*] *n* mirada fija ♦ *vi*: **to ~ at**

mirar fijo
starfish ['stɑːfɪʃ] *n* estrella de mar
stark [stɑːk] *adj* (*bleak*) severo, escueto
♦ *adv*: ~ **naked** en cueros
starling ['stɑːlɪŋ] *n* estornino
starry ['stɑːrɪ] *adj* estrellado; **~-eyed** *adj*
(*innocent*) inocentón/ona, ingenuo
start [stɑːt] *n* principio, comienzo;
(*departure*) salida; (*sudden movement*)
salto, sobresalto; (*advantage*) ventaja ♦ *vt*
empezar, comenzar; (*cause*) causar;
(*found*) fundar; (*engine*) poner en marcha
♦ *vi* comenzar, empezar; (*with fright*)
asustarse, sobresaltarse; (*train etc*) salir; **to**
~ doing *or* **to do sth** empezar a hacer
algo; **~ off** *vi* empezar, comenzar; (*leave*)
salir, ponerse en camino; **~ up** *vi*
comenzar; (*car*) ponerse en marcha ♦ *vt*
comenzar; poner en marcha; **~er** *n* (*AUT*)
botón *m* de arranque; (*SPORT: official*) juez
m/f de salida; (*BRIT: CULIN*) entrada; **~ing**
point *n* punto de partida
startle ['stɑːtl] *vt* asustar, sobrecoger;
startling *adj* alarmante
starvation [stɑːˈveɪʃən] *n* hambre *f*
starve [stɑːv] *vi* tener mucha hambre; (*to*
death) morir de hambre ♦ *vt* hacer pasar
hambre
state [steɪt] *n* estado ♦ *vt* (*say, declare*)
afirmar; **the S~s** los Estados Unidos; **to**
be in a ~ estar agitado; **~ly** *adj*
majestuoso, imponente; **~ly home** *n*
casa señorial, casa solariega; **~ment** *n*
afirmación *f*; **~sman** (*irreg*) *n* estadista *m*
static ['stætɪk] *n* (*RADIO*) parásitos *mpl*
♦ *adj* estático; **~ electricity** *n* estática
station ['steɪʃən] *n* (*gen*) estación *f*; (*RADIO*)
emisora; (*rank*) posición *f* social ♦ *vt*
colocar, situar; (*MIL*) apostar
stationary ['steɪʃnərɪ] *adj* estacionario, fijo
stationer ['steɪʃənə*] *n* papelero/a; **~'s**
(**shop**) (*BRIT*) *n* papelería; **~y** [-nərɪ] *n*
papel *m* de escribir, artículos *mpl* de
escritorio
station master *n* (*RAIL*) jefe *m* de
estación
station wagon (*US*) *n* ranchera

statistic [stəˈtɪstɪk] *n* estadística; **~s** *n*
(*science*) estadística
statue ['stætjuː] *n* estatua
status ['steɪtəs] *n* estado; (*reputation*)
estatus *m*; **~ symbol** *n* símbolo de
prestigio
statute ['stætjuːt] *n* estatuto, ley *f*;
statutory *adj* estatutario
staunch [stɔːntʃ] *adj* leal, incondicional
stay [steɪ] *n* estancia ♦ *vi* quedar(se); (*as*
guest) hospedarse; **to ~ put** seguir en el
mismo sitio; **to ~ the night/5 days** pasar
la noche/estar 5 días; **~ behind** *vi*
quedar atrás; **~ in** *vi* quedarse en casa; **~**
on *vi* quedarse; **~ out** *vi* (*of house*) no
volver a casa; (*on strike*) permanecer en
huelga; **~ up** *vi* (*at night*) velar, no
acostarse; **~ing power** *n* aguante *m*
stead [stɛd] *n*: **in sb's ~** en lugar de uno;
to stand sb in good ~ ser muy útil a uno
steadfast ['stɛdfɑːst] *adj* firme, resuelto
steadily ['stɛdɪlɪ] *adv* constantemente;
(*firmly*) firmemente; (*work, walk*) sin parar;
(*gaze*) fijamente
steady ['stɛdɪ] *adj* (*firm*) firme; (*regular*)
regular; (*person, character*) sensato,
juicioso; (*boyfriend*) formal; (*look, voice*)
tranquilo ♦ *vt* (*stabilize*) estabilizar;
(*nerves*) calmar
steak [steɪk] *n* (*gen*) filete *m*; (*beef*) bistec
m
steal [stiːl] (*pt* **stole,** *pp* **stolen**) *vt* robar
♦ *vi* robar; (*move secretly*) andar a
hurtadillas
stealth [stɛlθ] *n*: **by ~** a escondidas,
sigilosamente; **~y** *adj* cauteloso, sigiloso
steam [stiːm] *n* vapor *m*; (*mist*) vaho,
humo ♦ *vt* (*CULIN*) cocer al vapor ♦ *vi*
echar vapor; **~ engine** *n* máquina de
vapor; **~er** *n* (buque *m* de) vapor *m*;
~roller *n* apisonadora; **~ship** *n* = **~er**;
~y *adj* (*room*) lleno de vapor; (*window*)
empañado; (*heat, atmosphere*)
bochornoso
steel [stiːl] *n* acero ♦ *adj* de acero;
~works *n* acería
steep [stiːp] *adj* escarpado, abrupto; (*stair-*

empinado; (*price*) exorbitante, excesivo
♦ *vt* empapar, remojar

steeple ['sti:pl] *n* aguja; **~chase** *n*
carrera de obstáculos

steer [stɪə*] *vt* (*car*) conducir (*SP*), manejar
(*AM*); (*person*) dirigir ♦ *vi* conducir,
manejar; **~ing** *n* (*AUT*) dirección *f*; **~ing
wheel** *n* volante *m*

stem [stem] *n* (*of plant*) tallo; (*of glass*) pie
m ♦ *vt* detener; (*blood*) restañar; **~ from**
vt fus ser consecuencia de

stench [stentʃ] *n* hedor *m*

stencil ['stensl] *n* (*pattern*) plantilla ♦ *vt*
hacer un cliché de

stenographer [ste'nɔgrəfə*] (*US*) *n*
taquígrafo/a

step [step] *n* paso; (*on stair*) peldaño,
escalón *m* ♦ *vi*: **to ~ forward/back** dar
un paso adelante/hacia atrás; **~s** *npl*
(*BRIT*) = **~ladder**; **in/out of ~ (with)**
acorde/en disonancia (con); **~ down** *vi*
(*fig*) retirarse; **~ on** *vt fus* pisar; **~ up** *vt*
(*increase*) aumentar; **~brother** *n*
hermanastro; **~daughter** *n* hijastra;
~father *n* padrastro; **~ladder** *n* escalera
doble *or* de tijera; **~mother** *n* madrastra;
~ping stone *n* pasadera; **~sister** *n*
hermanastra; **~son** *n* hijastro

stereo ['stɪərɪəu] *n* estéreo ♦ *adj* (*also*:
~phonic) estéreo, estereofónico

sterile ['sterail] *adj* estéril; **sterilize**
['sterilaiz] *vt* esterilizar

sterling ['stə:lɪŋ] *adj* (*silver*) de ley ♦ *n*
(*ECON*) (libras *fpl*) esterlinas *fpl*; **one
pound ~** una libra esterlina

stern [stə:n] *adj* severo, austero ♦ *n* (*NAUT*)
popa

stew [stju:] *n* cocido (*SP*), estofado (*SP*),
guisado (*AM*) ♦ *vt* estofar, guisar; (*fruit*)
cocer

steward ['stju:əd] *n* camarero; **~ess** *n*
(*esp on plane*) azafata

stick [stɪk] *n* palo; (*of
dynamite*) barreno; (*as weapon*) porra;
(*walking ~*) bastón *m* ♦ *vt* (*glue*) pegar;
(*inf: put*) meter; (*: tolerate*) aguantar,
soportar; (*thrust*): **to ~ sth into** clavar *or*

hincar algo en ♦ *vi* pegarse; (*be
unmoveable*) quedarse parado; (*in mind*)
quedarse grabado; **~ out** *vi* sobresalir; **~
up** *vi* sobresalir; **~ up for** *vt fus*
defender; **~er** *n* (*label*) etiqueta
engomada; (*with slogan*) pegatina; **~ing
plaster** *n* esparadrapo

stick-up ['stɪkʌp] (*inf*) *n* asalto, atraco

sticky ['stɪkɪ] *adj* pegajoso; (*label*)
engomado; (*fig*) difícil

stiff [stɪf] *adj* rígido, tieso; (*hard*) duro;
(*manner*) estirado; (*difficult*) difícil;
(*person*) inflexible; (*price*) exorbitante
♦ *adv*: **scared/bored ~** muerto de
miedo/aburrimiento; **~en** *vi* (*muscles etc*)
agarrotarse; **~ neck** *n* tortícolis *m inv*;
~ness *n* rigidez *f*, tiesura

stifle ['staɪfl] *vt* ahogar, sofocar; **stifling**
adj (*heat*) sofocante, bochornoso

stigma ['stɪgmə] *n* (*fig*) estigma *m*

stile [staɪl] *n* portillo, portilla

stiletto [stɪ'letəu] (*BRIT*) *n* (*also*: **~ heel**)
tacón *m* de aguja

still [stɪl] *adj* inmóvil, quieto ♦ *adv* todavía;
(*even*) aun; (*nonetheless*) sin embargo,
aun así; **~born** *adj* nacido muerto; **~ life**
n naturaleza muerta

stilt [stɪlt] *n* zanco; (*pile*) pilar *m*, soporte
m

stilted ['stɪltɪd] *adj* afectado

stimulate ['stɪmjuleɪt] *vt* estimular

stimulus ['stɪmjuləs] (*pl* **stimuli**) *n*
estímulo, incentivo

sting [stɪŋ] (*pt, pp* **stung**) *n* picadura;
(*pain*) escozor *m*, picazón *f*; (*organ*)
aguijón *m* ♦ *vt, vi* picar

stingy ['stɪndʒɪ] *adj* tacaño

stink [stɪŋk] (*pt* **stank**, *pp* **stunk**) *n* hedor
m, tufo ♦ *vi* heder, apestar; **~ing** *adj*
hediondo, fétido; (*fig: inf*) horrible

stint [stɪnt] *n* tarea, trabajo ♦ *vi*: **to ~ on**
escatimar

stir [stə:*] *n* (*fig: agitation*) conmoción *f*
♦ *vt* (*tea etc*) remover; (*fig: emotions*)
provocar ♦ *vi* moverse; **~ up** *vt* (*trouble*)
fomentar

stirrup ['stɪrəp] *n* estribo

stitch [stɪtʃ] n (SEWING) puntada; (KNITTING) punto; (MED) punto (de sutura); (pain) punzada ♦ vt coser; (MED) suturar

stoat [stəut] n armiño

stock [stɔk] n (COMM: reserves) existencias fpl, stock m; (: selection) surtido; (AGR) ganado, ganadería; (CULIN) caldo; (descent) raza, estirpe f; (FINANCE) capital m ♦ adj (fig: reply etc) clásico ♦ vt (have in ~) tener existencias de; ~s and shares acciones y valores; in ~ en existencia or almacén; out of ~ agotado; to take ~ of (fig) asesorar, examinar; ~ up with vt fus abastecerse de; ~broker ['stɔkbrəukə*] n agente m/f or corredor(a) m/f de bolsa; ~ cube (BRIT) n pastilla de caldo; ~ exchange n bolsa

stocking ['stɔkɪŋ] n media

stock: ~ market n bolsa (de valores); ~pile n reserva ♦ vt acumular, almacenar; ~taking (BRIT) n (COMM) inventario

stocky ['stɔki] adj (strong) robusto; (short) achaparrado

stodgy ['stɔdʒi] adj indigesto, pesado

stoke [stəuk] vt atizar

stole [stəul] pt of steal ♦ n estola

stolen ['stəuln] pp of steal

stomach ['stʌmək] n (ANAT) estómago; (belly) vientre m ♦ vt tragar, aguantar; ~ache n dolor m de estómago

stone [stəun] n piedra; (in fruit) hueso; = 6.348 kg; 14 libras ♦ adj de piedra ♦ vt apedrear; (fruit) deshuesar; ~-cold adj helado; ~-deaf adj sordo como una tapia; ~work n (art) cantería; stony adj pedregoso; (fig) frío

stood [stud] pt, pp of stand

stool [stu:l] n taburete m

stoop [stu:p] vi (also: ~ down) doblarse, agacharse; (also: have a ~) ser cargado de espaldas

stop [stɔp] n parada; (in punctuation) punto ♦ vt parar, detener; (break off) suspender; (block: pay) suspender; (: cheque) invalidar; (also: put a ~ to)

poner término a ♦ vi pararse, detenerse; (end) acabarse; to ~ doing sth dejar de hacer algo; ~ dead vi pararse en seco; ~ off vi interrumpir el viaje; ~ up vt (hole) tapar; ~gap n (person) interino/a; (thing) recurso provisional; ~over n parada; (AVIAT) escala

stoppage ['stɔpɪdʒ] n (strike) paro; (blockage) obstrucción f

stopper ['stɔpə*] n tapón m

stop press n noticias fpl de última hora

stopwatch ['stɔpwɔtʃ] n cronómetro

storage ['stɔ:rɪdʒ] n almacenaje m; ~ heater n acumulador m

store [stɔ:*] n (stock) provisión f; (depot: BRIT: large shop) almacén m; (US) tienda; (reserve) reserva, repuesto ♦ vt almacenar ~s npl víveres mpl; in ~ (fig): to be in ~ for sb esperarle a uno; ~ up vt acumular ~room n despensa

storey ['stɔ:ri] (US story) n piso

stork [stɔ:k] n cigüeña

storm [stɔ:m] n tormenta; (fig: of applause) salva; (: of criticism) nube f ♦ vi (fig) rabiar ♦ vt tomar por asalto; ~y adj tempestuoso

story ['stɔ:ri] n historia; (lie) mentira; (US) = storey; ~book n libro de cuentos

stout [staut] adj (strong) sólido; (fat) gordo, corpulento; (resolute) resuelto ♦ n cerveza negra

stove [stəuv] n (for cooking) cocina; (for heating) estufa

stow [stəu] vt (also: ~ away) meter, poner (NAUT) estibar; ~away n polizón/ona m/f

straggle ['stræɡl] vi (houses etc) extenderse; (lag behind) rezagarse

straight [streɪt] adj recto, derecho; (frank) franco, directo; (simple) sencillo ♦ adv derecho, directamente; (drink) sin mezcla; to put or get sth ~ dejar algo en claro; ~ away, ~ off en seguida; ~en vt (also: ~ out) enderezar, poner derecho; ~-faced adj serio; ~forward adj (simple) sencillo; (honest) honrado, franco

strain [streɪn] n tensión f; (TECH) presión f; (MED) torcedura; (breed) tipo, variedad f

♦ vt (back etc) torcerse; (resources) agotar; (stretch) estirar; (food, tea) colar; **~s** npl (MUS) son m; **~ed** adj (muscle) torcido; (laugh) forzado; (relations) tenso; **~er** n colador m

strait [streit] n (GEO) estrecho; **to be in dire ~s** pasar grandes apuros; **~-jacket** n camisa de fuerza; **~-laced** adj mojigato, gazmoño

strand [strænd] n (of thread) hebra; (of hair) trenza; (of rope) ramal m

stranded ['strændɪd] adj (person: without money) desamparado; (: without transport) colgado

strange [streindʒ] adj (not known) desconocido; (odd) extraño, raro; **~ly** adv de un modo raro; see also **enough**; **~r** n desconocido/a; (from another area) forastero/a

strangle ['stræŋgl] vt estrangular; **~hold** n (fig) dominio completo

strap [stræp] n correa; (of slip, dress) tirante m

strategic [strə'ti:dʒɪk] adj estratégico

strategy ['strætɪdʒɪ] n estrategia

straw [strɔ:] n paja; (drinking ~) caña, pajita; **that's the last ~!** ¡eso es el colmo!

strawberry ['strɔ:bərɪ] n fresa (SP), frutilla (AM)

stray [streɪ] adj (animal) extraviado; (bullet) perdido; (scattered) disperso ♦ vi extraviarse, perderse

streak [stri:k] n raya; (in hair) raya ♦ vt rayar ♦ vi: **to ~ past** pasar como un rayo

stream [stri:m] n riachuelo, arroyo; (of people, vehicles) riada, caravana; (of smoke, insults etc) chorro ♦ vt (SCOL) dividir en grupos por habilidad ♦ vi correr, fluir; **to ~ in/out** (people) entrar/salir en tropel

streamer ['stri:mə*] n serpentina

streamlined ['stri:mlaɪnd] adj aerodinámico

street [stri:t] n calle f; **~car** (US) n tranvía m; **~ lamp** n farol m; **~ plan** n plano; **~wise** (inf) adj que tiene mucha calle

strength [strɛŋθ] n fuerza; (of girder, knot etc) resistencia; (fig: power) poder m; **~en** vt fortalecer, reforzar

strenuous ['strɛnjuəs] adj (energetic, determined) enérgico

stress [strɛs] n presión f; (mental strain) estrés m; (accent) acento ♦ vt subrayar, recalcar; (syllable) acentuar

stretch [strɛtʃ] n (of sand etc) trecho ♦ vi estirarse; (extend): **to ~ to** or **as far as** extenderse hasta ♦ vt extender, estirar; (make demands of) exigir el máximo esfuerzo a; **~ out** vi tenderse ♦ vt (arm etc) extender; (spread) estirar

stretcher ['strɛtʃə*] n camilla

strewn [stru:n] adj: **~ with** cubierto or sembrado de

stricken ['strɪkən] adj (person) herido; (city, industry etc) condenado; **~ with** (disease) afectado por

strict [strɪkt] adj severo; (exact) estricto; **~ly** adv severamente; estrictamente

stride [straɪd] (pt **strode**, pp **stridden**) n zancada, tranco ♦ vi dar zancadas, andar a trancos

strife [straɪf] n lucha

strike [straɪk] (pt, pp **struck**) n huelga; (of oil etc) descubrimiento; (attack) ataque m ♦ vt golpear, pegar; (oil etc) descubrir; (bargain, deal) cerrar ♦ vi declarar la huelga; (attack) atacar; (clock) dar la hora; **on ~** (workers) en huelga; **to ~ a match** encender un fósforo; **~ down** vt derribar; **~ up** vt (MUS) empezar a tocar; (conversation) entablar; (friendship) trabar; **~r** n huelguista m/f; (SPORT) delantero; **striking** adj llamativo

string [strɪŋ] (pt, pp **strung**) n (gen) cuerda; (row) hilera ♦ vt: **to ~ together** ensartar; **to ~ out** extenderse; **the ~s** npl (MUS) los instrumentos de cuerda; **to pull ~s** (fig) mover palancas; **~ bean** n judía verde, habichuela; **~(ed) instrument** n (MUS) instrumento de cuerda

stringent ['strɪndʒənt] adj riguroso, severo

strip [strɪp] n tira; (of land) franja; (of metal) cinta, lámina ♦ vt desnudar; (paint) quitar; (also: **~ down**: machine) desmontar ♦ *vi* desnudarse; **~ cartoon** *n* tira cómica (*SP*), historieta (*AM*)

stripe [straɪp] *n* raya; (*MIL*) galón *m*; **~d** *adj* a rayas, rayado

strip lighting *n* alumbrado fluorescente

stripper ['strɪpə*] *n* artista *m/f* de striptease

strive [straɪv] (*pt* **strove**, *pp* **striven**) *vi*: to **~ for sth/to do sth** luchar por conseguir/hacer algo

strode [strəud] *pt of* **stride**

stroke [strəuk] *n* (*blow*) golpe *m*; (*SWIMMING*) brazada; (*MED*) apoplejía; (*of paintbrush*) toque *m* ♦ *vt* acariciar; **at a ~** de un solo golpe

stroll [strəul] *n* paseo, vuelta ♦ *vi* dar un paseo *or* una vuelta; **~er** (*US*) *n* (*for child*) sillita de ruedas

strong [strɒŋ] *adj* fuerte; **they are 50 ~** son 50; **~hold** *n* fortaleza; (*fig*) baluarte *m*; **~ly** *adv* fuertemente, con fuerza; (*believe*) firmemente, con fuerza; **~room** *n* cámara acorazada

strove [strəuv] *pt of* **strive**

struck [strʌk] *pt, pp of* **strike**

structure ['strʌktʃə*] *n* estructura; (*building*) construcción *f*

struggle ['strʌgl] *n* lucha ♦ *vi* luchar

strum [strʌm] *vt* (*guitar*) rasguear

strung [strʌŋ] *pt, pp of* **string**

strut [strʌt] *n* puntal *m* ♦ *vi* pavonearse

stub [stʌb] *n* (*of ticket etc*) talón *m*; (*of cigarette*) colilla; **to ~ one's toe on sth** dar con el dedo (del pie) contra algo; **~ out** *vt* apagar

stubble ['stʌbl] *n* rastrojo; (*on chin*) barba (incipiente)

stubborn ['stʌbən] *adj* terco, testarudo

stuck [stʌk] *pt, pp of* **stick** ♦ *adj* (*jammed*) atascado; **~-up** *adj* engreído, presumido

stud [stʌd] *n* (*shirt ~*) corchete *m*; (*of boot*) taco; (*earring*) pendiente *m* (de bolita); (*also*: **~ farm**) caballeriza; (*also*: **~ horse**) caballo semental ♦ *vt* (*fig*): **~ded with** salpicado de

student ['stju:dənt] *n* estudiante *m/f* ♦ *adj* estudiantil; **~ driver** (*US*) *n* aprendiz(a)

m/f

studio ['stju:dɪəu] *n* estudio; (*artist's*) taller *m*; **~ flat** (*US* **~ apartment**) *n* estudio

studious ['stju:dɪəs] *adj* estudioso; (*studied*) calculado; **~ly** *adv* (*carefully*) con esmero

study ['stʌdɪ] *n* estudio ♦ *vt* estudiar; (*examine*) examinar, investigar ♦ *vi* estudiar

stuff [stʌf] *n* materia; (*substance*) material *m*, sustancia; (*things*) cosas *fpl* ♦ *vt* llenar; (*CULIN*) rellenar; (*animals*) disecar; (*inf: push*) meter; **~ing** *n* relleno; **~y** *adj* (*room*) mal ventilado; (*person*) de miras estrechas

stumble ['stʌmbl] *vi* tropezar, dar un traspié; **to ~ across, ~ on** (*fig*) tropezar con; **stumbling block** *n* tropiezo, obstáculo

stump [stʌmp] *n* (*of tree*) tocón *m*; (*of limb*) muñón *m* ♦ *vt*: **to be ~ed for an answer** no saber qué contestar

stun [stʌn] *vt* dejar sin sentido

stung [stʌŋ] *pt, pp of* **sting**

stunk [stʌŋk] *pp of* **stink**

stunning ['stʌnɪŋ] *adj* (*fig: news*) pasmoso; (: *outfit etc*) sensacional

stunt [stʌnt] *n* (*in film*) escena peligrosa; (*publicity ~*) truco publicitario; **~man** (*irreg*) *n* doble *m*

stupid ['stju:pɪd] *adj* estúpido, tonto; **~ity** [-'pɪdɪtɪ] *n* estupidez *f*

sturdy ['stə:dɪ] *adj* robusto, fuerte

stutter ['stʌtə*] *n* tartamudeo ♦ *vi* tartamudear

sty [staɪ] *n* (*for pigs*) pocilga

stye [staɪ] *n* (*MED*) orzuelo

style [staɪl] *n* estilo; **stylish** *adj* elegante, a la moda

stylus ['staɪləs] *n* aguja

suave [swɑːv] *adj* cortés

sub... [sʌb] *prefix* sub...; **~conscious** *adj* subconsciente; **~contract** *vt* subcontratar; **~divide** *vt* subdividir

subdue [səb'djuː] *vt* sojuzgar; (*passions*) dominar; **~d** *adj* (*light*) tenue; (*person*) sumiso, manso

subject [n 'sʌbdʒɪkt, vb səb'dʒekt] n súbdito; (SCOL) asignatura; (matter) tema m; (GRAMMAR) sujeto ♦ vt: **to ~ sb to sth** someter a uno a algo; **to be ~ to** (law) estar sujeto a; (subj: person) ser propenso a; **~ive** [-'dʒektɪv] adj subjetivo; **~ matter** n (content) contenido

sublet [sʌb'let] vt subarrendar

submarine [sʌbmə'riːn] n submarino

submerge [səb'məːdʒ] vt sumergir ♦ vi sumergirse

submissive [səb'mɪsɪv] adj sumiso

submit [səb'mɪt] vt someter ♦ vi: **to ~ to sth** someterse a algo

subnormal [sʌb'nɔːməl] adj anormal

subordinate [sə'bɔːdɪnət] adj, n subordinado/a m/f

subpoena [səb'piːnə] n (LAW) citación f

subscribe [səb'skraɪb] vi suscribir; **to ~ to** (opinion, fund) suscribir, aprobar; (newspaper) suscribirse a; **~r** n (to periodical) subscriptor(a) m/f; (to telephone) abonado/a

subscription [səb'skrɪpʃən] n abono; (to magazine) subscripción f

subsequent ['sʌbsɪkwənt] adj subsiguiente, posterior; **~ly** adv posteriormente, más tarde

subside [səb'saɪd] vi hundirse; (flood) bajar; (wind) amainar; **subsidence** [-'saɪdns] n hundimiento; (in road) socavón m

subsidiary [səb'sɪdɪərɪ] adj secundario ♦ n sucursal f, filial f

subsidize ['sʌbsɪdaɪz] vt subvencionar

subsidy ['sʌbsɪdɪ] n subvención f

subsistence [səb'sɪstəns] n subsistencia; **~ allowance** n salario mínimo

substance ['sʌbstəns] n sustancia

substantial [səb'stænʃl] adj sustancial, sustancioso; (fig) importante

substantiate [səb'stænʃɪeɪt] vt comprobar

substitute ['sʌbstɪtjuːt] n (person) suplente m/f; (thing) sustituto ♦ vt: **to ~ A for B** sustituir A por B, reemplazar B por A

subtitle ['sʌbtaɪtl] n subtítulo

subtle ['sʌtl] adj sutil; **~ty** n sutileza

subtotal [sʌb'teutl] n total m parcial

subtract [səb'trækt] vt restar, sustraer; **~ion** [-'trækʃən] n resta, sustracción f

suburb ['sʌbəːb] n barrio residencial; **the ~s** las afueras (de la ciudad); **~an** [sə'bəːbən] adj suburbano; (train etc) de cercanías; **~ia** [sə'bəːbɪə] n barrios mpl residenciales

subway ['sʌbweɪ] n (BRIT) paso subterráneo or inferior; (US) metro

succeed [sək'siːd] vi (person) tener éxito; (plan) salir bien ♦ vt suceder a; **to ~ in doing** lograr hacer; **~ing** adj (following) sucesivo

success [sək'ses] n éxito; **~ful** adj exitoso; (business) próspero; **to be ~ful (in doing)** lograr (hacer); **~fully** adv con éxito

succession [sək'seʃən] n sucesión f, serie f

successive [sək'sesɪv] adj sucesivo, consecutivo

succinct [sək'sɪŋkt] adj sucinto

such [sʌtʃ] adj tal, semejante; (of that kind): **~ a book** tal libro; (so much): **~ courage** tanto valor ♦ adv tan; **~ a long trip** un viaje tan largo; **~ a lot of** tanto(s)/a(s); **~ as** (like) tal como; **as ~** como tal; **~-and-~** adj tal o cual

suck [sʌk] vt chupar; (bottle) sorber; (breast) mamar; **~er** n (ZOOL) ventosa; (inf) bobo, primo

suction ['sʌkʃən] n succión f

Sudan [su'dæn] n Sudán m

sudden ['sʌdn] adj (rapid) repentino, súbito; (unexpected) imprevisto; **all of a ~** de repente; **~ly** adv de repente

suds [sʌdz] npl espuma de jabón

sue [suː] vt demandar

suede [sweɪd] n ante m (SP), gamuza (AM)

suet ['suɪt] n sebo

Suez ['suːɪz] n: **the ~ Canal** el Canal de Suez

suffer ['sʌfə*] vt sufrir, padecer; (tolerate) aguantar, soportar ♦ vi sufrir; **to ~ from** (illness etc) padecer; **~er** n víctima; (MED) enfermo/a; **~ing** n sufrimiento

sufficient [sə'fɪʃənt] *adj* suficiente, bastante; **~ly** *ad* suficientemente, bastante

suffocate ['sʌfəkeɪt] *vi* ahogarse, asfixiarse; **suffocation** [-'keɪʃən] *n* asfixia

sugar ['ʃugəʳ] *n* azúcar *m* ♦ *vt* echar azúcar a, azucarar; **~ beet** *n* remolacha; **~ cane** *n* caña de azúcar

suggest [sə'dʒest] *vt* sugerir; **~ion** [-'dʒestʃən] *n* sugerencia; **~ive** (*pej*) *adj* indecente

suicide ['suɪsaɪd] *n* suicidio; (*person*) suicida *m/f*; *see also* **commit**

suit [su:t] *n* (*man's*) traje *m*; (*woman's*) conjunto; (*LAW*) pleito; (*CARDS*) palo ♦ *vt* convenir; (*clothes*) sentar a, ir bien a; (*adapt*): **to ~ sth to** adaptar *or* ajustar algo a; **well ~ed** (*well matched: couple*) hecho el uno para el otro; **~able** *adj* conveniente; (*apt*) indicado; **~ably** *adv* convenientemente; (*impressed*) apropiadamente

suitcase ['su:tkeɪs] *n* maleta (*SP*), valija (*AM*)

suite [swi:t] *n* (*of rooms, MUS*) suite *f*; (*furniture*): **bedroom / dining room ~** (juego de) dormitorio/comedor

suitor ['su:təʳ] *n* pretendiente *m*

sulfur ['sʌlfəʳ] (*US*) *n* = **sulphur**

sulk [sʌlk] *vi* estar de mal humor; **~y** *adj* malhumorado

sullen ['sʌlən] *adj* hosco, malhumorado

sulphur ['sʌlfəʳ] (*US* **sulfur**) *n* azufre *m*

sultana [sʌl'tɑːnə] *n* (*fruit*) pasa de Esmirna

sultry ['sʌltrɪ] *adj* (*weather*) bochornoso

sum [sʌm] *n* suma; (*total*) total *m*; **~ up** *vt* resumir ♦ *vi* hacer un resumen

summarize ['sʌməraɪz] *vt* resumir

summary ['sʌmərɪ] *n* resumen *m* ♦ *adj* (*justice*) sumario

summer ['sʌməʳ] *n* verano ♦ *cpd* de verano; **in ~** en verano; **~ holidays** *npl* vacaciones *fpl* de verano; **~house** *n* (*in garden*) cenador *m*, glorieta; **~time** *n* (*season*) verano; **~ time** *n* (*by clock*) hora de verano

summit ['sʌmɪt] *n* cima, cumbre *f*; (*also*: **~ conference, ~ meeting**) (conferencia) cumbre *f*

summon ['sʌmən] *vt* (*person*) llamar; (*meeting*) convocar; (*LAW*) citar; **~ up** *vt* (*courage*) armarse de; **~s** *n* llamamiento, llamada ♦ *vt* (*LAW*) citar

sump [sʌmp] (*BRIT*) *n* (*AUT*) cárter *m*

sumptuous ['sʌmptjuəs] *adj* suntuoso

sun [sʌn] *n* sol *m*; **~bathe** *vi* tomar el sol; **~block** *n* filtro solar; **~burn** *n* (*painful*) quemadura; (*tan*) bronceado; **~burnt** *adj* quemado por el sol

Sunday ['sʌndɪ] *n* domingo; **~ school** *n* catequesis *f* dominical

sundial ['sʌndaɪəl] *n* reloj *m* de sol

sundown ['sʌndaun] *n* anochecer *m*

sundry ['sʌndrɪ] *adj* varios/as, diversos/as; **all and ~** todos sin excepción; **sundries** *npl* géneros *mpl* diversos

sunflower ['sʌnflauəʳ] *n* girasol *m*

sung [sʌŋ] *pp of* **sing**

sunglasses ['sʌnglɑːsɪz] *npl* gafas *fpl* (*SP*) *or* anteojos *mpl* de sol

sunk [sʌŋk] *pp of* **sink**

sun: ~light *n* luz *f* del sol; **~lit** *adj* iluminado por el sol; **~ny** *adj* soleado; (*day*) de sol; (*fig*) alegre; **~rise** *n* salida del sol; **~ roof** *n* (*AUT*) techo corredizo; **~screen** *n* protector *m* solar; **~set** *n* puesta del sol; **~shade** *n* (*over table*) sombrilla; **~shine** *n* sol *m*; **~stroke** *n* insolación *f*; **~tan** *n* bronceado; **~tan oil** *n* aceite *m* bronceador

super ['su:pəʳ] (*inf*) *adj* genial

superannuation [su:pərænju'eɪʃən] *n* cuota de jubilación

superb [su:'pə:b] *adj* magnífico, espléndido

supercilious [su:pə'sɪlɪəs] *adj* altanero

superfluous [su'pə:fluəs] *adj* superfluo, de sobra

superhuman [su:pə'hju:mən] *adj* sobrehumano

superimpose ['su:pərɪm'pəuz] *vt* sobreponer

superintendent [su:pərɪn'tendənt] *n*

director(a) *m/f*; (*POLICE*) subjefe/a *m/f*
superior [su'pɪərɪə*] *adj* superior; (*smug*)
desdeñoso ♦ *n* superior *m*; **~ity** [-'ɔrɪtɪ] *n*
superioridad *f*
superlative [su'pə:lətɪv] *n* superlativo
superman ['su:pəmæn] (*irreg*) *n*
superhombre *m*
supermarket ['su:pəmɑ:kɪt] *n*
supermercado
supernatural [su:pə'nætʃərəl] *adj*
sobrenatural ♦ *n*: **the ~** lo sobrenatural
superpower ['su:pəpauə*] *n* (*POL*)
superpotencia
supersede [su:pə'si:d] *vt* suplantar
superstar ['su:pəstɑ:*] *n* gran estrella
superstitious [su:pə'stɪʃəs] *adj*
supersticioso
supertanker ['su:pətæŋkə*] *n*
superpetrolero
supervise ['su:pəvaɪz] *vt* supervisar;
supervision [-'vɪʒən] *n* supervisión *f*;
supervisor *n* supervisor(a) *m/f*
supper ['sʌpə*] *n* cena
supple ['sʌpl] *adj* flexible
supplement [*n* 'sʌplɪmənt, *vb* sʌplɪ'ment]
n suplemento ♦ *vt* suplir; **~ary** [-'mentərɪ]
adj suplementario; **~ary benefit** (*BRIT*) *n*
subsidio suplementario de la seguridad
social
supplier [sə'plaɪə*] *n* (*COMM*)
distribuidor(a) *m/f*
supply [sə'plaɪ] *vt* (*provide*) suministrar;
(*equip*): **to ~ (with)** proveer (de) ♦ *n*
provisión *f*; (*gas, water etc*) suministro;
supplies *npl* (*food*) víveres *mpl*; (*MIL*)
pertrechos *mpl*; **~ teacher** *n* profesor(a)
m/f suplente
support [sə'pɔ:t] *n* apoyo; (*TECH*) soporte
m ♦ *vt* apoyar; (*financially*) mantener;
(*uphold, TECH*) sostener; **~er** *n* (*POL etc*)
partidario/a; (*SPORT*) aficionado/a
suppose [sə'pəuz] *vt* suponer; (*imagine*)
imaginarse; (*duty*): **to be ~d to do sth**
deber hacer algo; **~dly** [sə'pəuzɪdlɪ] *adv*
según cabe suponer; **supposing** *conj* en
caso de que
suppress [sə'pres] *vt* suprimir; (*yawn*)

ahogar
supreme [su'pri:m] *adj* supremo
surcharge ['sə:tʃɑ:dʒ] *n* sobretasa, recargo
sure [ʃuə*] *adj* seguro; (*definite, convinced*)
cierto; **to make ~ of sth/that** asegurarse
de algo/asegurar que; **~!** (*of course*)
¡claro!, ¡por supuesto!; **~ enough**
efectivamente; **~ly** *adv* (*certainly*)
seguramente
surf [sə:f] *n* olas *fpl*
surface ['sə:fɪs] *n* superficie *f* ♦ *vt* (*road*)
revestir ♦ *vi* (*also fig*) salir a la superficie;
by ~ mail por vía terrestre
surfboard ['sə:fbɔ:d] *n* tabla (de surf)
surfeit ['sə:fɪt] *n*: **a ~ of** un exceso de
surfing ['sə:fɪŋ] *n* surf *m*
surge [sə:dʒ] *n* oleada, oleaje *m* ♦ *vi*
(*wave*) romper; (*people*) avanzar en tropel
surgeon ['sə:dʒən] *n* cirujano/a
surgery ['sə:dʒərɪ] *n* cirugía; (*BRIT: room*)
consultorio; **~ hours** (*BRIT*) *npl* horas *fpl*
de consulta
surgical ['sə:dʒɪkl] *adj* quirúrgico; **~ spirit**
(*BRIT*) *n* alcohol *m* de 90°
surname ['sə:neɪm] *n* apellido
surpass [sə:'pɑ:s] *vt* superar, exceder
surplus ['sə:pləs] *n* excedente *m*; (*COMM*)
superávit *m* ♦ *adj* excedente, sobrante
surprise [sə'praɪz] *n* sorpresa ♦ *vt*
sorprender; **surprising** *adj*
sorprendente; **surprisingly** *adv*: **it was
surprisingly easy** me *etc* sorprendió lo
fácil que fue
surrender [sə'rendə*] *n* rendición *f*,
entrega ♦ *vi* rendirse, entregarse
surreptitious [sʌrəp'tɪʃəs] *adj* subrepticio
surrogate ['sʌrəgɪt] *n* sucedáneo; **~
mother** *n* madre *f* portadora
surround [sə'raund] *vt* rodear, circundar;
(*MIL etc*) cercar; **~ing** *adj* circundante;
~ings *npl* alrededores *mpl*, cercanías *fpl*
surveillance [sə:'veɪləns] *n* vigilancia
survey [*n* 'sə:veɪ, *vb* sə:'veɪ] *n* inspección *f*,
reconocimiento; (*inquiry*) encuesta ♦ *vt*
examinar, inspeccionar; (*look at*) mirar,
contemplar; **~or** *n* agrimensor(a) *m/f*
survival [sə'vaɪvl] *n* supervivencia

survive [sə'vaɪv] vi sobrevivir; (custom etc) perdurar ♦ vt sobrevivir a; **survivor** n superviviente m/f

susceptible [sə'sɛptəbl] adj: ~ **(to)** (disease) susceptible (a); (flattery) sensible (a)

suspect [adj, n 'sʌspɛkt, vb səs'pɛkt] adj, n sospechoso/a m/f ♦ vt (person) sospechar de; (think) sospechar

suspend [səs'pɛnd] vt suspender; ~**ed sentence** n (LAW) libertad f condicional; ~**er belt** n portaligas m inv; ~**ers** npl (BRIT) ligas fpl; (US) tirantes mpl

suspense [səs'pɛns] n incertidumbre f, duda; (in film etc) suspense m; **to keep sb in ~** mantener a uno en suspense

suspension [səs'pɛnʃən] n (gen, AUT) suspensión f; (of driving licence) privación f; ~ **bridge** n puente m colgante

suspicion [səs'pɪʃən] n sospecha; (distrust) recelo; **suspicious** [-ʃəs] adj receloso; (causing suspicion) sospechoso

sustain [səs'teɪn] vt sostener, apoyar; (suffer) sufrir, padecer; ~**able** adj sostenible; ~**ed** adj (effort) sostenido

sustenance ['sʌstɪnəns] n sustento

swab [swɔb] n (MED) algodón m

swagger ['swægə*] vi pavonearse

swallow ['swɔləu] n (bird) golondrina ♦ vt tragar; (fig, pride) tragarse; ~ **up** vt (savings etc) consumir

swam [swæm] pt of **swim**

swamp [swɔmp] n pantano, ciénaga ♦ vt (with water etc) inundar; (fig) abrumar, agobiar; ~**y** adj pantanoso

swan [swɔn] n cisne m

swap [swɔp] n canje m, intercambio ♦ vt: **to ~ (for)** cambiar (por)

swarm [swɔːm] n (of bees) enjambre m; (fig) multitud f ♦ vi (bees) formar un enjambre; (people) pulular; **to be ~ing with** ser un hervidero de

swastika ['swɔstɪkə] n esvástica

swat [swɔt] vt aplastar

sway [sweɪ] vi mecerse, balancearse ♦ vt (influence) mover, influir en

swear [swɛə*] (pt **swore**, pp **sworn**) vi

(curse) maldecir; (promise) jurar ♦ vt jurar; ~**word** n taco, palabrota

sweat [swɛt] n sudor m ♦ vi sudar

sweater ['swɛtə*] n suéter m

sweatshirt ['swɛtʃəːt] n suéter m

sweaty ['swɛtɪ] adj sudoroso

Swede [swiːd] n sueco/a

swede [swiːd] (BRIT) n nabo

Sweden ['swiːdn] n Suecia; **Swedish** ['swiːdɪʃ] adj sueco ♦ n (LING) sueco

sweep [swiːp] (pt, pp **swept**) n (act) barrido; (also: **chimney ~**) deshollinador(a) m/f ♦ vt barrer; (with arm) empujar; (subj: current) arrastrar ♦ vi barrer; (arm etc) moverse rápidamente; (wind) soplar con violencia; ~ **away** vt barrer; ~ **past** vi pasar majestuosamente; ~ **up** vi barrer; ~**ing** adj (gesture) dramático; (generalized: statement) generalizado

sweet [swiːt] n (candy) dulce m, caramelo; (BRIT: pudding) postre m ♦ adj dulce; (fig: kind) dulce, amable; (: attractive) mono; ~**corn** n maíz m; ~**en** vt (add sugar to) poner azúcar a; (person) endulzar; ~**heart** n novio/a; ~**ness** n dulzura; ~ **pea** n guisante m de olor

swell [swɛl] (pt **swelled**, pp **swollen** or **swelled**) n (of sea) marejada, oleaje m ♦ adj (US: inf: excellent) estupendo, fenomenal ♦ vt hinchar, inflar ♦ vi (also: ~ **up**) hincharse; (numbers) aumentar; (sound, feeling) ir aumentando; ~**ing** n (MED) hinchazón f

sweltering ['swɛltərɪŋ] adj sofocante, de mucho calor

swept [swɛpt] pt, pp of **sweep**

swerve [swəːv] vi desviarse bruscamente

swift [swɪft] n (bird) vencejo ♦ adj rápido, veloz; ~**ly** adv rápidamente

swig [swɪg] (inf) n (drink) trago

swill [swɪl] vt (also: ~ **out**, ~ **down**) lavar, limpiar con agua

swim [swɪm] (pt **swam**, pp **swum**) n: **to go for a ~** ir a nadar or a bañarse ♦ vi nadar; (head, room) dar vueltas ♦ vt nadar; (the Channel etc) cruzar a nado; ~**mer** n nadador(a) m/f; ~**ming** n

natación f; **~ming cap** n gorro de baño;
~ming costume (BRIT) n bañador m,
traje m de baño; **~ming pool** n piscina
(SP), alberca (AM); **~ming trunks** n
bañador m (de hombre); **~suit** n
= **~ming costume**
swindle ['swɪndl] n estafa ♦ vt estafar
swine [swaɪn] (inf!) canalla (!)
swing [swɪŋ] (pt, pp **swung**) n (in
playground) columpio; (movement)
balanceo, vaivén m; (change of direction)
viraje m; (rhythm) ritmo ♦ vt balancear;
(also: **~ round**) voltear, girar ♦ vi
balancearse, columpiarse; (also: **~ round**)
dar media vuelta; **to be in full ~** estar en
plena marcha; **~ bridge** n puente m
giratorio; **~ door** (US **~ing door**) n
puerta giratoria
swingeing ['swɪndʒɪŋ] (BRIT) adj (cuts)
atroz
swipe [swaɪp] vt (hit) golpear fuerte; (inf:
steal) guindar; **~ card** n tarjeta
magnética deslizante, tarjeta swipe
swirl [swɜːl] vi arremolinarse
Swiss [swɪs] adj, n inv suizo/a m/f
switch [swɪtʃ] n (for light etc) interruptor
m; (change) cambio ♦ vt (change)
cambiar de; **~ off** vt apagar; (engine)
parar; **~ on** vt encender (SP), prender
(AM); (engine, machine) arrancar; **~board**
n (TEL) centralita (de teléfonos) (SP),
conmutador m (AM)
Switzerland ['swɪtsələnd] n Suiza
swivel ['swɪvl] vi (also: **~ round**) girar
swollen ['swəʊlən] pp of **swell**
swoon [swuːn] vi desmayarse
swoop [swuːp] n (by police etc) redada
♦ vi (also: **~ down**) calarse
swop [swɒp] = **swap**
sword [sɔːd] n espada; **~fish** n pez m
espada
swore [swɔː*] pt of **swear**
sworn [swɔːn] pp of **swear** ♦ adj
(statement) bajo juramento; (enemy)
implacable
swot [swɒt] (BRIT) vt, vi empollar
swum [swʌm] pp of **swim**

swung [swʌŋ] pt, pp of **swing**
sycamore ['sɪkəmɔː*] n sicomoro
syllable ['sɪləbl] n sílaba
syllabus ['sɪləbəs] n programa m de
estudios
symbol ['sɪmbl] n símbolo
symmetry ['sɪmɪtrɪ] n simetría
sympathetic [sɪmpə'θetɪk] adj
(understanding) comprensivo; (likeable)
simpático; (showing support): **~ to(wards)**
bien dispuesto hacia
sympathize ['sɪmpəθaɪz] vi: **to ~ with**
(person) compadecerse de; (feelings)
comprender; (cause) apoyar; **~r** n (POL)
simpatizante m/f
sympathy ['sɪmpəθɪ] n (pity) compasión f;
sympathies npl (tendencies) tendencias
fpl; **with our deepest ~** nuestro más
sentido pésame; **in ~** en solidaridad
symphony ['sɪmfənɪ] n sinfonía
symptom ['sɪmptəm] n síntoma m, indicio
synagogue ['sɪnəgɒg] n sinagoga
syndicate ['sɪndɪkɪt] n (gen) sindicato; (of
newspapers) agencia (de noticias)
syndrome ['sɪndrəum] n síndrome m
synopsis [sɪ'nɒpsɪs] (pl **synopses**) n
sinopsis f inv
synthesis ['sɪnθəsɪs] (pl **syntheses**) n
síntesis f inv
synthetic [sɪn'θetɪk] adj sintético
syphilis ['sɪfɪlɪs] n sífilis f
syphon ['saɪfən] = **siphon**
Syria ['sɪrɪə] n Siria; **~n** adj, n sirio/a
syringe [sɪ'rɪndʒ] n jeringa
syrup ['sɪrəp] n jarabe m; (also: **golden ~**)
almíbar m
system ['sɪstəm] n sistema m; (ANAT)
organismo; **~atic** [-'mætɪk] adj
sistemático, metódico; **~ disk** n
(COMPUT) disco del sistema; **~s analyst**
n analista m/f de sistemas

T, t

ta [tɑː] (*BRIT: inf*) *excl* ¡gracias!
tab [tæb] *n* lengüeta; (*label*) etiqueta; **to keep ~s on** (*fig*) vigilar
tabby ['tæbɪ] *n* (*also:* **~ cat**) gato atigrado
table ['teɪbl] *n* mesa; (*of statistics etc*) cuadro, tabla ♦ *vt* (*BRIT: motion etc*) presentar; **to lay** *or* **set the ~** poner la mesa; **~cloth** *n* mantel *m*; **~ of contents** *n* índice *m* de materias; **~ d'hôte** [tɑːblˈdəut] *adj* del menú; **~ lamp** *n* lámpara de mesa; **~mat** *n* (*for plate*) posaplatos *m inv*; (*for hot dish*) salvamantel *m*; **~spoon** *n* cuchara de servir; (*also:* **~spoonful**: *as measurement*) cucharada
tablet ['tæblɪt] *n* (*MED*) pastilla, comprimido; (*of stone*) lápida
table tennis *n* ping-pong *m*, tenis *m* de mesa
table wine *n* vino de mesa
tabloid ['tæblɔɪd] *n* periódico popular sensacionalista

---

tabloid press

ⓘ *El término* **tabloid press** *o* **tabloids** *se usa para referirse a la prensa popular británica, por el tamaño más pequeño de los periódicos. A diferencia de los de la llamada* **quality press**, *estas publicaciones se caracterizan por un lenguaje sencillo, una presentación llamativa y un contenido sensacionalista, centrado a veces en los escándalos financieros y sexuales de los famosos, por lo que también reciben el nombre peyorativo de "*gutter press*".*

---

tack [tæk] *n* (*nail*) tachuela; (*fig*) rumbo ♦ *vt* (*nail*) clavar con tachuelas; (*stitch*) hilvanar ♦ *vi* virar
tackle ['tækl] *n* (*fishing* ~) aparejo (de pescar); (*for lifting*) aparejo ♦ *vt* (*difficulty*) enfrentarse con; (*challenge: person*) hacer frente a; (*grapple with*) agarrar; (*FOOTBALL*) cargar; (*RUGBY*) placar
tacky ['tækɪ] *adj* pegajoso; (*pej*) cutre
tact [tækt] *n* tacto, discreción *f*; **~ful** *adj* discreto, diplomático
tactics ['tæktɪks] *n, npl* táctica
tactless ['tæktlɪs] *adj* indiscreto
tadpole ['tædpəul] *n* renacuajo
tag [tæg] *n* (*label*) etiqueta; **~ along** *vi* ir (*or* venir) también
tail [teɪl] *n* cola; (*of shirt, coat*) faldón *m* ♦ *vt* (*follow*) vigilar a; **~s** *npl* (*formal suit*) levita; **~ away** *vi* (*in size, quality etc*) ir disminuyendo; **~ off** *vi* = **~ away**; **~back** (*BRIT*) *n* (*AUT*) cola; **~ end** *n* cola, parte *f* final; **~gate** *n* (*AUT*) puerta trasera
tailor ['teɪlə*] *n* sastre *m*; **~ing** *n* (*cut*) corte *m*; (*craft*) sastrería; **~-made** *adj* (*also fig*) hecho a la medida
tailwind ['teɪlwɪnd] *n* viento de cola
tainted ['teɪntɪd] *adj* (*food*) pasado; (*water, air*) contaminado; (*fig*) manchado
take [teɪk] (*pt* **took**, *pp* **taken**) *vt* tomar; (*grab*) agarrar (*AM*); (*gain: prize*) ganar; (*require: effort, courage*) exigir; (*tolerate: pain etc*) aguantar; (*hold: passengers etc*) tener cabida para; (*accompany, bring, carry*) llevar; (*exam*) presentarse a; **to ~ sth from** (*drawer etc*) sacar algo de; (*person*) quitar algo a; **I ~ it that ...** supongo que ...; **~ after** *vt fus* parecerse a; **~ apart** *vt* desmontar; **~ away** *vt* (*remove*) quitar; (*carry off*) llevar; (*MATH*) restar; **~ back** *vt* (*return*) devolver; (*one's words*) retractarse de; **~ down** *vt* (*building*) derribar; (*letter etc*) apuntar; **~ in** *vt* (*deceive*) engañar; (*understand*) entender; (*include*) abarcar; (*lodger*) acoger, recibir; **~ off** *vi* (*AVIAT*) despegar ♦ *vt* (*remove*) quitar; **~ on** *vt* (*work*) aceptar; (*employee*) contratar; (*opponent*) desafiar; **~ out** *vt* sacar; **~ over** *vt* (*business*) tomar posesión de; (*country*) tomar el poder ♦ *vi*: **to ~ over from sb** reemplazar a uno; **~ to** *vt fus* (*person*) coger cariño a, encariñarse con; (*activity*) aficionarse a; **~ up** *vt* (*a dress*)

acortar; (*occupy: time, space*) ocupar;
(*engage in: hobby etc*) dedicarse a;
(*accept*): **to ~ sb up on** aceptar; **~away**
(*BRIT*) *adj* (*food*) para llevar ♦ *n* tienda (*or*
restaurante m) de comida para llevar;
~off *n* (*AVIAT*) despegue *m*; **~out** (*US*) *n*
= **~away**; **~over** *n* (*COMM*) absorción *f*

akings ['teɪkɪŋz] *npl* (*COMM*) ingresos *mpl*

alc [tælk] *n* (*also*: **~um powder**) (polvos
de) talco

ale [teɪl] *n* (*story*) cuento; (*account*)
relación *f*; **to tell ~s** (*fig*) chivarse

alent ['tælnt] *n* talento; **~ed** *adj* de
talento

alk [tɔːk] *n* charla; (*conversation*)
conversación *f*; (*gossip*) habladurías *fpl*,
chismes *mpl* ♦ *vi* hablar; **~s** *npl* (*POL etc*)
conversaciones *fpl*; **to ~ about** hablar de;
to ~ sb into doing sth convencer a uno
para que haga algo; **to ~ sb out of doing
sth** disuadir a uno de que haga algo; **to ~
shop** hablar del trabajo; **~ over** *vt*
discutir; **~ative** *adj* hablador(a); **~ show**
n programa *m* de entrevistas

all [tɔːl] *adj* alto; (*object*) grande; **to be 6
feet ~** (*person*) ≈ medir 1 metro 80

ally ['tælɪ] *n* cuenta ♦ *vi*: **to ~ (with)**
corresponder (con)

alon ['tælən] *n* garra

ambourine [tæmbə'riːn] *n* pandereta

ame [teɪm] *adj* domesticado; (*fig*)
mediocre

amper ['tæmpə*] *vi*: **to ~ with** tocar,
andar con

ampon ['tæmpən] *n* tampón *m*

an [tæn] *n* (*also*: **sun~**) bronceado ♦ *vi*
ponerse moreno ♦ *adj* (*colour*) marrón

ang [tæŋ] *n* sabor *m* fuerte

angent ['tændʒənt] *n* (*MATH*) tangente *f*;
to go off at a ~ (*fig*) salirse por la
tangente

angerine [tændʒə'riːn] *n* mandarina

angle ['tæŋgl] *n* enredo; **to get in(to) a ~**
enredarse

ank [tæŋk] *n* (*water ~*) depósito, tanque
m; (*for fish*) acuario; (*MIL*) tanque *m*

anker ['tæŋkə*] *n* (*ship*) buque *m* cisterna;

(*truck*) camión *m* cisterna

tanned [tænd] *adj* (*skin*) moreno

tantalizing ['tæntəlaɪzɪŋ] *adj* tentador(a)

tantamount ['tæntəmaunt] *adj*: **~ to**
equivalente a

tantrum ['tæntrəm] *n* rabieta

tap [tæp] *n* (*BRIT: on sink etc*) grifo (*SP*),
canilla (*AM*); (*gas ~*) llave *f*; (*gentle blow*)
golpecito ♦ *vt* (*hit gently*) dar golpecitos
en; (*resources*) utilizar, explotar;
(*telephone*) intervenir; **on ~** (*fig: resources*)
a mano; **~ dancing** *n* claqué *m*

tape [teɪp] *n* (*also*: **magnetic ~**) cinta
magnética; (*cassette*) cassette *f*, cinta;
(*sticky ~*) cinta adhesiva; (*for tying*) cinta
♦ *vt* (*record*) grabar (en cinta); (*stick with
~*) pegar con cinta adhesiva; **~ deck** *n*
grabadora; **~ measure** *n* cinta métrica,
metro

taper ['teɪpə*] *n* cirio ♦ *vi* afilarse

tape recorder *n* grabadora

tapestry ['tæpɪstrɪ] *n* (*object*) tapiz *m*; (*art*)
tapicería

tar [tɑː] *n* alquitrán *m*, brea

target ['tɑːgɪt] *n* (*gen*) blanco

tariff ['tærɪf] *n* (*on goods*) arancel *m*; (*BRIT:
in hotels etc*) tarifa

tarmac ['tɑːmæk] *n* (*BRIT: on road*)
asfaltado; (*AVIAT*) pista (de aterrizaje)

tarnish ['tɑːnɪʃ] *vt* deslustrar

tarpaulin [tɑː'pɔːlɪn] *n* lona
impermeabilizada

tarragon ['tærəgən] *n* estragón *m*

tart [tɑːt] *n* (*CULIN*) tarta; (*BRIT: inf:
prostitute*) puta ♦ *adj* agrio, ácido; **~ up**
(*BRIT: inf*) *vt* (*building*) remozar; **to ~ o.s.
up** acicalarse

tartan ['tɑːtn] *n* tejido escocés *m*

tartar ['tɑːtə*] *n* (*on teeth*) sarro; **~(e)
sauce** *n* salsa tártara

task [tɑːsk] *n* tarea; **to take to ~** reprender;
~ force *n* (*MIL, POLICE*) grupo de
operaciones

taste [teɪst] *n* (*sense*) gusto; (*flavour*) sabor
m; (*also: after~*) sabor *m*, dejo; (*sample*):
have a ~! ¡prueba un poquito!; (*fig*)
muestra, idea ♦ *vt* (*also fig*) probar ♦ *vi*:

to ~ of or **like** (*fish, garlic etc*) saber a; **you can ~ the garlic (in it)** se nota el sabor a ajo; **in good/bad ~** de buen/mal gusto; **~ful** *adj* de buen gusto; **~less** *adj* (*food*) soso; (*remark etc*) de mal gusto; **tasty** *adj* sabroso, rico

tatters ['tætəz] *npl*: **in ~** hecho jirones

tattoo [tə'tu:] *n* tatuaje *m*; (*spectacle*) espectáculo militar ♦ *vt* tatuar

tatty ['tætɪ] (*BRIT: inf*) *adj* cochambroso

taught [tɔ:t] *pt, pp of* **teach**

taunt [tɔ:nt] *n* burla ♦ *vt* burlarse de

Taurus ['tɔ:rəs] *n* Tauro

taut [tɔ:t] *adj* tirante, tenso

tax [tæks] *n* impuesto ♦ *vt* gravar (con un impuesto); (*fig: memory*) poner a prueba (: *patience*) agotar; **~able** *adj* (*income*) gravable; **~ation** [-'seɪʃən] *n* impuestos *mpl*; **~ avoidance** *n* evasión *f* de impuestos; **~ disc** (*BRIT*) *n* (*AUT*) pegatina del impuesto de circulación; **~ evasion** *n* evasión *f* fiscal; **~-free** *adj* libre de impuestos

taxi ['tæksɪ] *n* taxi *m* ♦ *vi* (*AVIAT*) rodar por la pista; **~ driver** *n* taxista *m/f*; **~ rank** (*BRIT*), **~ stand** *n* parada de taxis

tax: ~ payer *n* contribuyente *m/f*; **~ relief** *n* desgravación *f* fiscal; **~ return** *n* declaración *f* de ingresos

TB *n abbr* = **tuberculosis**

tea [ti:] *n* té *m*; (*BRIT: meal*) ≈ merienda (*SP*); cena; **high ~** (*BRIT*) merienda-cena (*SP*); **~ bag** *n* bolsita de té; **~ break** (*BRIT*) *n* descanso para el té

teach [ti:tʃ] (*pt, pp* **taught**) *vt*: **to ~ sb sth, ~ sth to sb** enseñar algo a uno ♦ *vi* (*be a teacher*) ser profesor(a), enseñar ♦ **~er** *n* (*in secondary school*) profesor(a) *m/f*; (*in primary school*) maestro/a, profesor/a de EGB; **~ing** *n* enseñanza

tea cosy *n* cubretetera *m*

teacup ['ti:kʌp] *n* taza para el té

teak [ti:k] *n* (*madera de*) teca

team [ti:m] *n* equipo *m*; (*of horses*) tiro; **~work** *n* trabajo en equipo

teapot ['ti:pɒt] *n* tetera

tear[1] [tɪə*] *n* lágrima; **in ~s** llorando

tear[2] [tɛə*] (*pt* **tore**, *pp* **torn**) *n* rasgón *m*, desgarrón *m* ♦ *vt* romper, rasgar ♦ *vi* rasgarse; **~ along** *vi* (*rush*) precipitarse; **~ up** *vt* (*sheet of paper etc*) romper

tearful ['tɪəfəl] *adj* lloroso

tear gas ['tɪə-] *n* gas *m* lacrimógeno

tearoom ['ti:ru:m] *n* salón *m* de té

tease [ti:z] *vt* tomar el pelo a

tea set *n* servicio de té

teaspoon *n* cucharita; (*also:* **~ful:** *as measurement*) cucharadita

teat [ti:t] *n* (*of bottle*) tetina

teatime ['ti:taɪm] *n* hora del té

tea towel (*BRIT*) *n* paño de cocina

technical ['teknɪkl] *adj* técnico; **~ college** (*BRIT*) *n* ≈ escuela de artes y oficios (*SP*); **~ity** [-'kælɪtɪ] *n* (*point of law*) formalismo; (*detail*) detalle *m* técnico; **~ly** *adv* en teoría; (*regarding technique*) técnicamente

technician [tek'nɪʃn] *n* técnico/a

technique [tek'ni:k] *n* técnica

technological [teknə'lɒdʒɪkl] *adj* tecnológico

technology [tek'nɒlədʒɪ] *n* tecnología

teddy (bear) ['tedɪ-] *n* osito de felpa

tedious ['ti:dɪəs] *adj* pesado, aburrido

teem [ti:m] *vi*: **to ~ with** rebosar de; **it is ~ing (with rain)** llueve a cántaros

teenage ['ti:neɪdʒ] *adj* (*fashions etc*) juvenil; (*children*) quinceañero; **~r** *n* quinceañero/a

teens [ti:nz] *npl*: **to be in one's ~** ser adolescente

tee-shirt ['ti:ʃə:t] *n* = **T-shirt**

teeter ['ti:tə*] *vi* balancearse; (*fig*): **to ~ on the edge of ...** estar al borde de ...

teeth [ti:θ] *npl of* **tooth**

teethe [ti:ð] *vi* echar los dientes

teething ['ti:ðɪŋ]: **~ ring** *n* mordedor *m*; **~ troubles** *npl* (*fig*) dificultades *fpl* iniciales

teetotal ['ti:'təutl] *adj* abstemio

telegram ['telɪgræm] *n* telegrama *m*

telegraph ['telɪgrɑ:f] *n* telégrafo; **~ pole** *n* poste *m* telegráfico

telepathy [tə'lepəθɪ] *n* telepatía

telephone ['tɛlɪfəun] *n* teléfono ♦ *vt* llamar por teléfono, telefonear; *(message)* dar por teléfono; **to be on the ~** *(talking)* hablar por teléfono; *(possessing ~)* tener teléfono; **~ booth** *n* cabina telefónica; **~ box** *(BRIT) n* = **~ booth**; **~ call** *n* llamada (telefónica); **~ directory** *n* guía (telefónica); **~ number** *n* número de teléfono; **telephonist** [təˈlɛfənɪst] *(BRIT) n* telefonista *m/f*

telesales ['tɛlɪseɪlz] *npl* televenta(s) *f(pl)*

telescope ['tɛlɪskəup] *n* telescopio

television ['tɛlɪvɪʒən] *n* televisión *f*; **on ~** en la televisión; **~ set** *n* televisor *m*

teleworking ['tɛlɪˌwəːkɪŋ] *n* teletrabajo

tell [tɛl] *(pt, pp* **told)** *vt* decir; *(relate: story)* contar; *(distinguish):* **to ~ sth from** distinguir algo de ♦ *vi (talk):* **to ~ (of)** contar; *(have effect)* tener efecto; **to ~ sb to do sth** mandar a uno hacer algo; **~ off** *vt:* **to ~ sb off** regañar a uno; **~er** *n (in bank)* cajero/a; **~ing** *adj (remark)* revelador(a); **~tale** *adj (sign)* indicador(a)

telly ['tɛlɪ] *(BRIT: inf) n abbr (= television)* tele *f*

temp [tɛmp] *n abbr (BRIT: = temporary)* temporero/a

temper ['tɛmpə*] *n (nature)* carácter *m*; *(mood)* humor *m*; *(bad ~)* (mal) genio; *(fit of anger)* acceso de ira ♦ *vt (moderate)* moderar; **to be in a ~** estar furioso; **to lose one's ~** enfadarse, enojarse

temperament ['tɛmprəmənt] *n (nature)* temperamento

temperate ['tɛmprət] *adj (climate etc)* templado

temperature ['tɛmprətʃə*] *n* temperatura; **to have** *or* **run a ~** tener fiebre

temple ['tɛmpl] *n (building)* templo; *(ANAT)* sien *f*

tempo ['tɛmpəu] *(pl* **tempos** *or* **tempi)** *n (MUS)* tempo, tiempo; *(fig)* ritmo

temporarily ['tɛmpərərɪlɪ] *adv* temporalmente

temporary ['tɛmpərəri] *adj* provisional; *(passing)* transitorio; *(worker)* temporero; *(job)* temporal

tempt [tɛmpt] *vt* tentar; **to ~ sb into doing sth** tentar *or* inducir a uno a hacer algo; **~ation** [-ˈteɪʃən] *n* tentación *f*; **~ing** *adj* tentador(a); *(food)* apetitoso/a

ten [tɛn] *num* diez

tenacity [təˈnæsɪtɪ] *n* tenacidad *f*

tenancy ['tɛnənsɪ] *n* arrendamiento, alquiler *m*

tenant ['tɛnənt] *n* inquilino/a

tend [tɛnd] *vt* cuidar ♦ *vi:* **to ~ to do sth** tener tendencia a hacer algo

tendency ['tɛndənsɪ] *n* tendencia

tender ['tɛndə*] *adj (person, care)* tierno, cariñoso; *(meat)* tierno; *(sore)* sensible ♦ *n (COMM: offer)* oferta; *(money):* **legal ~** moneda de curso legal ♦ *vt* ofrecer; **~ness** *n* ternura; *(of meat)* blandura

tenement ['tɛnəmənt] *n* casa de pisos *(SP)*

tennis ['tɛnɪs] *n* tenis *m*; **~ ball** *n* pelota de tenis; **~ court** *n* cancha de tenis; **~ player** *n* tenista *m/f*; **~ racket** *n* raqueta de tenis

tenor ['tɛnə*] *n (MUS)* tenor *m*

tenpin bowling ['tɛnpɪn-] *n (juego de los) bolos*

tense [tɛns] *adj (person)* nervioso; *(moment, atmosphere)* tenso; *(muscle)* tenso, en tensión ♦ *n (LING)* tiempo

tension ['tɛnʃən] *n* tensión *f*

tent [tɛnt] *n* tienda (de campaña) *(SP)*, carpa *(AM)*

tentative ['tɛntətɪv] *adj (person, smile)* indeciso; *(conclusion, plans)* provisional

tenterhooks ['tɛntəhuks] *npl:* **on ~** sobre ascuas

tenth [tɛnθ] *num* décimo

tent peg *n* clavija, estaca

tent pole *n* mástil *m*

tenuous ['tɛnjuəs] *adj* tenue

tenure ['tɛnjuə*] *n (of land etc)* tenencia; *(of office)* ejercicio

tepid ['tɛpɪd] *adj* tibio

term [tɜːm] *n (word)* término; *(period)* período; *(SCOL)* trimestre *m* ♦ *vt* llamar; **~s** *npl (conditions, COMM)* condiciones *fpl*; **in the short/long ~** a corto/largo plazo; **to be on good ~s with sb** llevarse bien

con uno; **to come to ~s with** (*problem*)
aceptar
terminal ['tə:mɪnl] *adj* (*disease*) mortal;
(*patient*) terminal ♦ *n* (COMPUT) terminal
m; (*also*: **air ~**) terminal *f*; (BRIT: *also*:
coach ~) (estación *f*) terminal *f*
terminate ['tə:mɪneɪt] *vt* terminar
terminus ['tə:mɪnəs] (*pl* **termini**) *n*
término, (estación *f*) terminal *f*
terrace ['terəs] *n* terraza; (BRIT: *row of
houses*) hilera de casas adosadas; **the ~s**
(BRIT: SPORT) las gradas *fpl*; **~d** *adj*
(*garden*) en terrazas; (*house*) adosado
terrain [te'reɪn] *n* terreno
terrible ['terɪbl] *adj* terrible, horrible; (*inf*)
atroz; **terribly** *adv* terriblemente; (*very
badly*) malísimamente
terrific [tə'rɪfɪk] *adj* (*very great*) tremendo;
(*wonderful*) fantástico, fenomenal
terrify ['terɪfaɪ] *vt* aterrorizar
territory ['terɪtərɪ] *n* (*also fig*) territorio
terror ['terə*] *n* terror *m*; **~ism** *n*
terrorismo; **~ist** *n* terrorista *m/f*
test [test] *n* (*gen*, CHEM) prueba; (MED)
examen *m*; (SCOL) examen *m*, test *m*;
(*also*: **driving ~**) examen *m* de conducir
♦ *vt* probar, poner a prueba; (MED, SCOL)
examinar
testament ['testəmənt] *n* testamento; **the
Old/New T~** el Antiguo/Nuevo
Testamento
testicle ['testɪkl] *n* testículo
testify ['testɪfaɪ] *vi* (LAW) prestar
declaración; **to ~ to sth** atestiguar algo
testimony ['testɪmənɪ] *n* (LAW) testimonio
test: **~ match** *n* (CRICKET, RUGBY) partido
internacional; **~ tube** *n* probeta
tetanus ['tetanəs] *n* tétano
tether ['teðə*] *vt* atar ♦ *n*: **to be at the
end of one's ~** no aguantar más
text [tekst] *n* texto; **~book** *n* libro de
texto; **~ message** *n* mensaje *m* (de
texto); **~ messaging** *n* envío de
mensajes (de texto)
textiles ['tekstaɪlz] *npl* textiles *mpl*; (*textile
industry*) industria textil
texting ['tekstɪŋ] *n* (COMPUT) envío de

mensajes (de texto)
texture ['tekstʃə*] *n* textura
Thailand ['taɪlænd] *n* Tailandia
Thames [temz] *n*: **the ~** el (río) Támesis
than [ðæn] *conj* (*in comparisons*): **more ~
10/once** más de 10/una vez; **I have
more/less ~ you/Paul** tengo más/
menos que tú/Paul; **she is older ~ you
think** es mayor de lo que piensas
thank [θæŋk] *vt* dar las gracias a,
agradecer; **~ you (very much)** muchas
gracias; **~ God!** ¡gracias a Dios!; **~s** *npl*
gracias *fpl* ♦ *excl* ¡gracias!; **many ~s, ~s a
lot** ¡gracias!; **~s to** *prep* gracias a; **~ful**
adj: **~ful (for)** agradecido (por); **~less**
adj ingrato; **T~sgiving (Day)** *see box*

┌─────────────────────────────┐
│ **Thanksgiving (Day)** │

ⓘ *En Estados Unidos el cuarto jueves de
noviembre es* **Thanksgiving Day**,
*fiesta oficial en la que se recuerda la
celebración que hicieron los primeros
colonos norteamericanos ("Pilgrims" o
"Pilgrim Fathers") tras la estupenda
cosecha de 1621, por la que se dan gracias
a Dios. En Canadá se celebra una fiesta
semejante el segundo lunes de octubre,
aunque no está relacionada con dicha
fecha histórica.*

└─────────────────────────────┘

┌─────────────┐
│ *KEYWORD* │
└─────────────┘

that [ðæt] (*pl* **those**) *adj* (*demonstrative*)
ese/a, *pl* esos/as; (*more remote*) aquel/
aquella, *pl* aquellos/as; **leave those
books on the table** deja esos libros sobre
la mesa; **~ one** ése/ésa; (*more remote*)
aquél/aquélla; **~ one over there** ése/ésa
de ahí; aquél/aquélla de allí
♦ *pron* 1 (*demonstrative*) ése/a, *pl* ésos/as;
(*neuter*) eso; (*more remote*) aquél/aquélla,
pl aquéllos/as; (*neuter*) aquello; **what's ~?**
¿qué es eso (*or* aquello)?; **who's ~?**
¿quién es ése/a (*or* aquél/aquélla)?; **is ~
you?** ¿eres tú?; **will you eat all ~?** ¿vas a
comer todo eso?; **~'s my house** ésa es
mi casa; **~'s what he said** eso es lo que

dijo; **~ is (to say)** es decir
2 (*relative: subject, object*) que; (*with preposition*) (el/la) que *etc*, el/la cual *etc*; **the book (~) I read** el libro que leí; **the books ~ are in the library** los libros que están en la biblioteca; **all (~) I have** todo lo que tengo; **the box (~) I put it in** la caja en la que *or* donde lo puse; **the people (~) I spoke to** la gente con la que hablé
3 (*relative: of time*) que; **the day (~) he came** el día (en) que vino
♦ *conj* que; **he thought ~ I was ill** creyó que yo estaba enfermo
♦ *adv* (*demonstrative*): **I can't work ~ much** no puedo trabajar tanto; **I didn't realise it was ~ bad** no creí que fuera tan malo; **~ high** así de alto

hatched [θætʃt] *adj* (*roof*) de paja; (*cottage*) con tejado de paja
haw [θɔ:] *n* deshielo ♦ *vi* (*ice*) derretirse; (*food*) descongelarse ♦ *vt* (*food*) descongelar

he [ði:, ðə] *def art* **1** (*gen*) el, *f* la, *pl* los, *fpl* las (*NB = el immediately before f n beginning with stressed (h)a*; a+el = al; de+el = del); **~ boy/girl** el chico/la chica; **~ books/flowers** los libros/las flores; **to ~ postman/from ~ drawer** al cartero/del cajón; **I haven't ~ time/money** no tengo tiempo/dinero
2 (*+adj to form n*) los; lo; **~ rich and ~ poor** los ricos y los pobres; **to attempt ~ impossible** intentar lo imposible
3 (*in titles*): **Elizabeth ~ First** Isabel primera; **Peter ~ Great** Pedro el Grande
4 (*in comparisons*): **~ more he works ~ more he earns** cuanto más trabaja más gana

heatre ['θɪətə*] (*US* **theater**) *n* teatro; (*also:* **lecture ~**) aula; (*MED: also:* **operating ~**) quirófano; **~-goer** *n* aficionado/a al teatro

theatrical [θɪˈætrɪkl] *adj* teatral
theft [θeft] *n* robo
their [ðeə*] *adj* su; **~s** *pron* (el) suyo/(la) suya *etc*; *see also* **my; mine¹**
them [ðem, ðəm] *pron* (*direct*) los/las; (*indirect*) les; (*stressed, after prep*) ellos/ellas; *see also* **me**
theme [θi:m] *n* tema *m*; **~ park** *n* parque de atracciones (*en torno a un tema central*); **~ song** *n* tema *m* (musical)
themselves [ðəmˈselvz] *pl pron* (*subject*) ellos mismos/ellas mismas; (*complement*) se; (*after prep*) sí (mismos/as); *see also* **oneself**
then [ðen] *adv* (*at that time*) entonces; (*next*) después; (*later*) luego, después; (*and also*) además ♦ *conj* (*therefore*) en ese caso, entonces ♦ *adj*: **the ~ president** el entonces presidente; **by ~** para entonces; **from ~ on** desde entonces
theology [θɪˈɒlədʒɪ] *n* teología
theory ['θɪərɪ] *n* teoría
therapist ['θerəpɪst] *n* terapeuta *m/f*
therapy ['θerəpɪ] *n* terapia

there ['ðeə*] *adv* **1**: **~ is, ~ are** hay; **~ is no-one here/no bread left** no hay nadie aquí/no queda pan; **~ has been an accident** ha habido un accidente
2 (*referring to place*) ahí; (*distant*) allí; **it's ~** está ahí; **put it in/on/up/down ~** ponlo ahí dentro/encima/arriba/abajo; **I want that book ~** quiero ese libro de ahí; **~ he is!** ¡ahí está!
3: **~, ~** (*esp to child*) ea, ea

there: ~abouts *adv* por ahí; **~after** *adv* después; **~by** *adv* así, de ese modo; **~fore** *adv* por lo tanto; **~'s** = **there is; there has**
thermal ['θə:ml] *adj* termal; (*paper*) térmico
thermometer [θəˈmɒmɪtə*] *n* termómetro
Thermos ® ['θə:məs] *n* (*also:* **~ flask**) termo
thermostat ['θə:məustæt] *n* termostato

thesaurus [θɪˈsɔːrəs] n tesoro
these [ðiːz] pl adj estos/as ♦ pl pron
éstos/as
thesis [ˈθiːsɪs] (pl **theses**) n tesis f inv
they [ðeɪ] pl pron ellos/ellas; (stressed) ellos
(mismos)/ellas (mismas); ~ **say that ...** (it
is said that) se dice que ...; ~'**d** = they
had; they would; ~'**ll** = they shall; they
will; ~'**re** = they are; ~'**ve** = they have
thick [θɪk] adj (in consistency) espeso; (in
size) grueso; (stupid) torpe ♦ n: **in the ~
of the battle** en lo más reñido de la
batalla; **it's 20 cm** ~ tiene 20 cm de
espesor; ~**en** vi espesarse ♦ vt (sauce etc)
espesar; ~**ness** n espesor m; grueso;
~**set** adj fornido
thief [θiːf] (pl **thieves**) n ladrón/ona m/f
thigh [θaɪ] n muslo
thimble [ˈθɪmbl] n dedal m
thin [θɪn] adj (person, animal) flaco; (in
size) delgado; (in consistency) poco
espeso; (hair, crowd) escaso ♦ vt: **to ~
(down)** diluir
thing [θɪŋ] n cosa; (object) objeto, artículo;
(matter) asunto; (mania): **to have a ~
about sb/sth** estar obsesionado con
uno/algo; ~**s** npl (belongings) efectos mpl
(personales); **the best ~ would be to ...**
lo mejor sería ...; **how are ~s?** ¿qué tal?
think [θɪŋk] (pt, pp **thought**) vi pensar ♦ vt
pensar, creer; **what did you ~ of them?**
¿qué te parecieron?; **to ~ about sth/sb**
pensar en algo/uno; **I'll ~ about it** lo
pensaré; **to ~ of doing sth** pensar en
hacer algo; **I ~ so/not** creo que sí/no; **to
~ well of sb** tener buen concepto de
uno; ~ **over** vt reflexionar sobre,
meditar; ~ **up** vt (plan etc) idear; ~ **tank**
n gabinete m de estrategia
thinly [ˈθɪnlɪ] adv (cut) fino; (spread)
ligeramente
third [θəːd] adj (before n) tercer(a);
(following n) tercero/a ♦ n tercero/a;
(fraction) tercio; (BRIT: SCOL: degree) título
de licenciado con calificación de
aprobado; ~**ly** adv en tercer lugar; ~
party insurance (BRIT) n seguro contra

terceros; ~-**rate** adj (de calidad)
mediocre; **T~ World** n Tercer Mundo
thirst [θəːst] n sed f; ~**y** adj (person,
animal) sediento; (work) que da sed; **to
be ~y** tener sed
thirteen [ˈθəːˈtiːn] num trece
thirty [ˈθəːtɪ] num treinta

KEYWORD

---

this [ðɪs] (pl **these**) adj (demonstrative)
este/a; pl estos/as; (neuter) esto; ~ **man/
woman** este hombre/esta mujer; **these
children/flowers** estos chicos/estas
flores; ~ **one (here)** éste/a, esto (de aquí)
♦ pron (demonstrative) éste/a; pl éstos/as;
(neuter) esto; **who is ~?** ¿quién es éste/
ésta?; **what is ~?** ¿qué es esto?; ~ **is
where I live** aquí vivo; ~ **is what he said**
esto es lo que dijo; ~ **is Mr Brown** (in
introductions) le presento al Sr. Brown;
(photo) éste es el Sr. Brown; (on
telephone) habla el Sr. Brown
♦ adv (demonstrative): ~ **high/long** etc as
de alto/largo etc; ~ **far** hasta aquí

---

thistle [ˈθɪsl] n cardo
thorn [θɔːn] n espina
thorough [ˈθʌrə] adj (search) minucioso;
(wash) a fondo; (knowledge, research)
profundo; (person) meticuloso; ~**bred** adj
(horse) de pura sangre; ~**fare** n calle f;
"**no ~fare**" "prohibido el paso"; ~**ly** adv
(search) minuciosamente; (study)
profundamente; (wash) a fondo; (utterly:
bad, wet etc) completamente, totalmente
those [ðəuz] pl adj esos/esas; (more
remote) aquellos/as
though [ðəu] conj aunque ♦ adv sin
embargo
thought [θɔːt] pt, pp of **think** ♦ n
pensamiento; (opinion) opinión f; ~**ful**
adj pensativo; (serious) serio; (considerate)
atento; ~**less** adj desconsiderado
thousand [ˈθauzənd] num mil; **two** ~ dos
mil; ~**s of** miles de; ~**th** num milésimo
thrash [θræʃ] vt azotar; (defeat) derrotar; ~
about or **around** vi debatirse; ~ **out** vt

discutir a fondo

read [θrɛd] *n* hilo; (*of screw*) rosca ♦ *vt* (*needle*) enhebrar; **~bare** *adj* raído

reat [θrɛt] *n* amenaza; **~en** *vi* amenazar ♦ *vt*: **to ~en sb with/to do** amenazar a uno con/con hacer

ree [θri:] *num* tres; **~-dimensional** *adj* tridimensional; **~-piece suit** *n* traje *m* de tres piezas; **~-piece suite** *n* tresillo; **~-ply** *adj* (*wool*) de tres cabos

reshold ['θrɛʃhəuld] *n* umbral *m*

rew [θru:] *pt of* **throw**

rifty ['θrɪftɪ] *adj* económico

rill [θrɪl] *n* (*excitement*) emoción *f*; (*shudder*) estremecimiento ♦ *vt* emocionar; **to be ~ed** (*with gift etc*) estar encantado; **~er** *n* novela (*or obra or película*) de suspense; **~ing** *adj* emocionante

rive [θraɪv] (*pt, pp* **thrived**) *vi* (*grow*) crecer; (*do well*): **to ~ on sth** sentarle muy bien a uno algo; **thriving** *adj* próspero

roat [θrəut] *n* garganta; **to have a sore ~** tener dolor de garganta

rob [θrɔb] *vi* latir; dar punzadas; vibrar

roes [θrəuz] *npl*: **in the ~ of** en medio de

rone [θrəun] *n* trono

rong [θrɔŋ] *n* multitud *f*, muchedumbre *f* ♦ *vt* agolparse en

rottle ['θrɔtl] *n* (*AUT*) acelerador *m* ♦ *vt* estrangular

rough [θru:] *prep* por, a través de; (*time*) durante; (*by means of*) por medio de, mediante; (*owing to*) gracias a ♦ *adj* (*ticket, train*) directo ♦ *adv* completamente, de parte a parte; de principio a fin; **to put sb ~ to sb** (*TEL*) poner *or* pasar a uno con uno; **to be ~** (*TEL*) tener comunicación; (*have finished*) haber terminado; **"no ~ road"** (*BRIT*) "calle sin salida"; **~out** *prep* (*place*) por todas partes de, por todo; (*time*) durante todo ♦ *adv* por *or* en todas partes

row [θrəu] (*pt* **threw**, *pp* **thrown**) *n* tiro; (*SPORT*) lanzamiento ♦ *vt* tirar, echar; (*SPORT*) lanzar; (*rider*) derribar; (*fig*)

desconcertar; **to ~ a party** dar una fiesta; **~ away** *vt* tirar; (*money*) derrochar; **~ off** *vt* deshacerse de; **~ out** *vt* tirar; (*person*) echar; expulsar; **~ up** *vi* vomitar; **~away** *adj* para tirar, desechable; (*remark*) hecho de paso; **~-in** *n* (*SPORT*) saque *m*

thru [θru:] (*US*) = **through**

thrush [θrʌʃ] *n* zorzal *m*, tordo

thrust [θrʌst] (*pt, pp* **thrust**) *vt* empujar (con fuerza)

thud [θʌd] *n* golpe *m* sordo

thug [θʌg] *n* gamberro/a

thumb [θʌm] *n* (*ANAT*) pulgar *m*; **to ~ a lift** hacer autostop; **~ through** *vt fus* (*book*) hojear; **~tack** (*US*) *n* chincheta (*SP*)

thump [θʌmp] *n* golpe *m*; (*sound*) ruido seco *or* sordo ♦ *vt* golpear ♦ *vi* (*heart etc*) palpitar

thunder ['θʌndə*] *n* trueno ♦ *vi* tronar; (*train etc*): **to ~ past** pasar como un trueno; **~bolt** *n* rayo; **~clap** *n* trueno; **~storm** *n* tormenta; **~y** *adj* tormentoso

Thursday ['θə:zdɪ] *n* jueves *m inv*

thus [ðʌs] *adv* así, de este modo

thyme [taɪm] *n* tomillo

thyroid ['θaɪrɔɪd] *n* (*also*: **~ gland**) tiroides *m inv*

tic [tɪk] *n* tic *m*

tick [tɪk] *n* (*sound: of clock*) tictac *m*; (*mark*) palomita; (*ZOOL*) garrapata; (*BRIT: inf*): **in a ~** en un instante ♦ *vi* hacer tictac ♦ *vt* marcar; **~ off** *vt* marcar; (*person*) reñir; **~ over** *vi* (*engine*) girar en marcha lenta; (*fig*) ir tirando

ticket ['tɪkɪt] *n* billete *m* (*SP*), tíquet *m*, boleto (*AM*); (*for cinema etc*) entrada (*SP*), boleto (*AM*); (*in shop: on goods*) etiqueta; (*for raffle*) papeleta; (*for library*) tarjeta; (*parking ~*) multa por estacionamiento ilegal; **~ collector** *n* revisor(a) *m/f*; **~ office** *n* (*THEATRE*) taquilla (*SP*), boletería (*AM*); (*RAIL*) despacho de billetes (*SP*) *or* boletos (*AM*)

tickle ['tɪkl] *vt* hacer cosquillas a ♦ *vi* hacer cosquillas; **ticklish** *adj* (*person*) cosquilloso; (*problem*) delicado

tidal ['taɪdl] *adj* de marea; ~ **wave** *n* maremoto

tidbit ['tɪdbɪt] (*US*) *n* = **titbit**

tiddlywinks ['tɪdlɪwɪŋks] *n juego infantil con fichas de plástico*

tide [taɪd] *n* marea; (*fig: of events etc*) curso, marcha; ~ **over** *vt* (*help out*) ayudar a salir del apuro

tidy ['taɪdɪ] *adj* (*room etc*) ordenado; (*dress, work*) limpio; (*person*) arreglado ♦ *vt* (*also:* ~ **up**) poner en orden

tie [taɪ] *n* (*string etc*) atadura; (*BRIT: also:* **neck~**) corbata; (*fig: link*) vínculo, lazo; (*SPORT etc: draw*) empate *m* ♦ *vt* atar ♦ *vi* (*SPORT etc*) empatar; **to ~ in a bow** atar con un lazo; **to ~ a knot in sth** hacer un nudo en algo; ~ **down** *vt* (*fig: person: restrict*) atar; (: *to price, date etc*) obligar a; ~ **up** *vt* (*parcel*) envolver; (*dog, person*) atar; (*arrangements*) concluir; **to be ~d up** (*busy*) estar ocupado

tier [tɪə*] *n* grada; (*of cake*) piso

tiger ['taɪgə*] *n* tigre *m*

tight [taɪt] *adj* (*rope*) tirante; (*money*) escaso; (*clothes*) ajustado; (*bend*) cerrado; (*shoes, schedule*) apretado; (*budget*) ajustado; (*security*) estricto; (*inf: drunk*) borracho ♦ *adv* (*squeeze*) muy fuerte; (*shut*) bien; ~**en** *vt* (*rope*) estirar; (*screw, grip*) apretar; (*security*) reforzar ♦ *vi* estirarse; apretarse; ~**-fisted** *adj* tacaño; ~**ly** *adv* (*grasp*) muy fuerte; ~**rope** *n* cuerda floja; ~**s** (*BRIT*) *npl* panti *mpl*

tile [taɪl] *n* (*on roof*) teja; (*on floor*) baldosa; (*on wall*) azulejo; ~**d** *adj* de tejas; embaldosado; (*wall*) alicatado

till [tɪl] *n* caja (registradora) ♦ *vt* (*land*) cultivar ♦ *prep, conj* = **until**

tilt [tɪlt] *vt* inclinar ♦ *vi* inclinarse

timber ['tɪmbə*] *n* (*material*) madera

time [taɪm] *n* tiempo; (*epoch: often pl*) época; (*by clock*) hora; (*moment*) momento; (*occasion*) vez *f*; (*MUS*) compás *m* ♦ *vt* calcular *or* medir el tiempo de; (*race*) cronometrar; (*remark, visit etc*) elegir el momento para; **a long ~** mucho

tiempo; **4 at a ~** de 4 en 4; **4 a la vez; for the ~ being** de momento, por ahora; **from ~ to ~** de vez en cuando; **at ~s** a veces; **in ~** (*soon enough*) a tiempo; (*after some time*) con el tiempo; (*MUS*) al compás; **in a week's ~** dentro de una semana; **in no ~** en un abrir y cerrar de ojos; **any ~** cuando sea; **on ~** a la hora; **5 ~s 5** 5 por 5; **what ~ is it?** ¿qué hora es?; **to have a good ~** pasarlo bien, divertirse; ~ **bomb** *n* bomba de efecto retardado; ~**less** *adj* eterno; ~ **limit** *n* plazo; ~**ly** *adj* oportuno; ~ **off** *n* tiempo libre; ~**r** *n* (*in kitchen etc*) programador *m* horario; ~ **scale** (*BRIT*) *n* escala de tiempo; ~**-share** *n* apartamento (*or* casa) a tiempo compartido; ~ **switch** (*BRIT*) *n* interruptor *m* (horario); ~**table** *n* horario; ~ **zone** *n* huso horario

timid ['tɪmɪd] *adj* tímido

timing ['taɪmɪŋ] *n* (*SPORT*) cronometraje *n* **the ~ of his resignation** el momento que eligió para dimitir

tin [tɪn] *n* estaño; (*also:* ~ **plate**) hojalata; (*BRIT: can*) lata; ~**foil** *n* papel *m* de estaño

tinge [tɪndʒ] *n* matiz *m* ♦ *vt:* ~**d with** teñido de

tingle ['tɪŋgl] *vi* (*person*): **to ~ (with)** estremecerse (de); (*hands etc*) hormiguea

tinker ['tɪŋkə*]: ~ **with** *vt fus* jugar con, tocar

tinned [tɪnd] (*BRIT*) *adj* (*food*) en lata, en conserva

tin opener [-əupnə*] (*BRIT*) *n* abrelatas *m inv*

tinsel ['tɪnsl] *n* (guirnalda de) espumillón *m*

tint [tɪnt] *n* matiz *m*; (*for hair*) tinte *m*; ~**ed** *adj* (*hair*) teñido; (*glass, spectacles*) ahumado

tiny ['taɪnɪ] *adj* minúsculo, pequeñito

tip [tɪp] *n* (*end*) punta; (*gratuity*) propina; (*BRIT: for rubbish*) vertedero; (*advice*) consejo ♦ *vt* (*waiter*) dar una propina a; (*tilt*) inclinar; (*empty: also:* ~ **out**) vaciar, echar; (*overturn: also:* ~ **over**) volcar; ~~

off n (hint) advertencia; ~ped (BRIT) adj (cigarette) con filtro

Tipp-Ex ® ['tɪpeks] n Tipp-Ex ® m

tipsy ['tɪpsɪ] (inf) adj alegre, mareado

tiptoe ['tɪptəu] n: on ~ de puntillas

tire ['taɪə*] n (US) = tyre ♦ vt cansar ♦ vi (gen) cansarse; (become bored) aburrirse; ~d adj cansado; to be ~d of sth estar harto de algo; ~less adj incansable; ~some adj aburrido; tiring adj cansado

tissue ['tɪʃuː] n tejido; (paper handkerchief) pañuelo de papel, kleenex ® m; ~ paper n papel m de seda

tit [tɪt] n (bird) herrerillo común; to give ~ for tat dar ojo por ojo

titbit ['tɪtbɪt] (US tidbit) n (food) golosina; (news) noticia sabrosa

title ['taɪtl] n título; ~ deed n (LAW) título de propiedad; ~ role n papel m principal

TM abbr = trademark

<hr>

KEYWORD

to [tuː, tə] prep 1 (direction) a; to go ~ France/London/school/the station ir a Francia/Londres/al colegio/a la estación; to go ~ Claude's/the doctor's ir a casa de Claude/al médico; the road ~ Edinburgh la carretera de Edimburgo

2 (as far as) hasta, a; from here ~ London de aquí a or hasta Londres; to count ~ 10 contar hasta 10; from 40 ~ 50 people entre 40 y 50 personas

3 (with expressions of time): a quarter/ twenty ~ 5 las 5 menos cuarto/veinte

4 (for, of): the key ~ the front door la llave de la puerta principal; she is secretary ~ the director es la secretaria del director; a letter ~ his wife una carta a or para su mujer

5 (expressing indirect object) a; to give sth ~ sb darle algo a alguien; to talk ~ sb hablar con alguien; to be a danger ~ sb ser un peligro para alguien; to carry out repairs ~ sth hacer reparaciones en algo

6 (in relation to): 3 goals ~ 2 3 goles a 2; 30 miles ~ the gallon ≈ 9,4 litros a los cien (kms)

7 (purpose, result): to come ~ sb's aid venir en auxilio or ayuda de alguien; to sentence sb ~ death condenar a uno a muerte; ~ my great surprise con gran sorpresa mía

♦ with vb 1 (simple infin): ~ go/eat ir/ comer

2 (following another vb): to want/try/ start ~ do querer/intentar/empezar a hacer; see also relevant vb

3 (with vb omitted): I don't want ~ no quiero

4 (purpose, result) para; I did it ~ help you lo hice para ayudarte; he came ~ see you vino a verte

5 (equivalent to relative clause): I have things ~ do tengo cosas que hacer; the main thing is ~ try lo principal es intentarlo

6 (after adj etc): ready ~ go listo para irse; too old ~ ... demasiado viejo (como) para ...

♦ adv: pull/push the door ~ tirar de/ empujar la puerta

<hr>

toad [təud] n sapo; ~stool n hongo venenoso

toast [təust] n (CULIN) tostada; (drink, speech) brindis m ♦ vt (CULIN) tostar; (drink to) brindar por; ~er n tostador m

tobacco [tə'bækəu] n tabaco; ~nist n estanquero/a (SP), tabaquero/a (AM); ~nist's (shop) (BRIT) n estanco (SP), tabaquería (AM)

toboggan [tə'bɔgən] n tobogán m

today [tə'deɪ] adv, n (also fig) hoy m

toddler ['tɔdlə*] n niño/a (que empieza a andar)

toe [təu] n dedo (del pie); (of shoe) punta; to ~ the line (fig) conformarse; ~nail n uña del pie

toffee ['tɔfɪ] n toffee m; ~ apple (BRIT) n manzana acaramelada

together [tə'geðə*] adv juntos; (at same time) al mismo tiempo, a la vez; ~ with junto con

toil [tɔɪl] n trabajo duro, labor f ♦ vi

trabajar duramente

toilet ['tɔɪlət] *n* retrete *m*; (*BRIT: room*) servicios *mpl* (*SP*), wáter *m* (*SP*), sanitario (*AM*) ♦ *cpd* (*soap etc*) de aseo; **~ paper** *n* papel *m* higiénico; **~ries** *npl* artículos *mpl* de tocador; **~ roll** *n* rollo de papel higiénico

token ['təʊkən] *n* (*sign*) señal *f*, muestra; (*souvenir*) recuerdo; (*disc*) ficha ♦ *adj* (*strike, payment etc*) simbólico; **book/record ~** (*BRIT*) vale *m* para comprar libros/discos; **gift ~** (*BRIT*) vale-regalo

Tokyo ['təʊkjəʊ] *n* Tokio, Tokío

told [təʊld] *pt, pp of* **tell**

tolerable ['tɔlərəbl] *adj* (*bearable*) soportable; (*fairly good*) pasable

tolerant ['tɔlərnt] *adj*: **~ of** tolerante con

tolerate ['tɔləreɪt] *vt* tolerar

toll [təʊl] *n* (*of casualties*) número de víctimas; (*tax, charge*) peaje *m* ♦ *vi* (*bell*) doblar

tomato [tə'mɑːtəʊ] (*pl* **~es**) *n* tomate *m*

tomb [tuːm] *n* tumba

tomboy ['tɔmbɔɪ] *n* marimacho

tombstone ['tuːmstəʊn] *n* lápida

tomcat ['tɔmkæt] *n* gato (macho)

tomorrow [tə'mɔrəʊ] *adv, n* (*also: fig*) mañana; **the day after ~** pasado mañana; **~ morning** mañana por la mañana

ton [tʌn] *n* tonelada (*BRIT* = *1016 kg; US* = *907 kg*); (*metric ~*) tonelada métrica; **~s of** (*inf*) montones de

tone [təʊn] *n* tono ♦ *vi* (*also: ~ in*) armonizar; **~ down** *vt* (*criticism*) suavizar; (*colour*) atenuar; **~ up** *vt* (*muscles*) tonificar; **~-deaf** *adj* con mal oído

tongs [tɔŋz] *npl* (*for coal*) tenazas *fpl*; (*curling ~*) tenacillas *fpl*

tongue [tʌŋ] *n* lengua; **~ in cheek** irónicamente; **~-tied** *adj* (*fig*) mudo; **~-twister** *n* trabalenguas *m inv*

tonic ['tɔnɪk] *n* (*MED, also fig*) tónico; (*also: ~ water*) (agua) tónica

tonight [tə'naɪt] *adv, n* esta noche; esta tarde

tonsil ['tɔnsl] *n* amígdala; **~litis** [-'laɪtɪs] *n* amigdalitis *f*

too [tuː] *adv* (*excessively*) demasiado; (*also*) también; **~ much** demasiado; **~ many** demasiados/as

took [tuk] *pt of* **take**

tool [tuːl] *n* herramienta; **~ box** *n* caja de herramientas

toot [tuːt] *n* pitido ♦ *vi* tocar el pito

tooth [tuːθ] (*pl* **teeth**) *n* (*ANAT, TECH*) diente *m*; (*molar*) muela; **~ache** *n* dolor *m* de muelas; **~brush** *n* cepillo de dientes; **~paste** *n* pasta de dientes; **~pick** *n* palillo

top [tɔp] *n* (*of mountain*) cumbre *f*, cima; (*of tree*) copa; (*of head*) coronilla; (*of ladder, page*) lo alto; (*of table*) superficie *f*; (*of cupboard*) parte *f* de arriba; (*lid: of box*) tapa; (*: of bottle, jar*) tapón *m*; (*of list etc*) cabeza; (*toy*) peonza; (*garment*) blusa; camiseta ♦ *adj* de arriba; (*in rank*) principal, primero; (*best*) mejor ♦ *vt* (*exceed*) exceder; (*be first in*) encabezar; **on ~ of** (*above*) sobre, encima de; (*in addition to*) además de; **from ~ to bottom** de pies a cabeza; **~ off** (*US*) *vt* = **~ up**; **~ up** *vt* llenar; **~ floor** *n* último piso; **~ hat** *n* sombrero de copa; **~-heavy** *adj* (*object*) mal equilibrado

topic ['tɔpɪk] *n* tema *m*; **~al** *adj* actual

top: ~less *adj* (*bather, bikini*) topless *inv*; **~-level** *adj* (*talks*) al más alto nivel; **~most** *adj* más alto

topple ['tɔpl] *vt* derribar ♦ *vi* caerse

top-secret *adj* de alto secreto

topsy-turvy ['tɔpsɪ'tɜːvɪ] *adj* al revés ♦ *adv* patas arriba

torch [tɔːtʃ] *n* antorcha; (*BRIT: electric*) linterna

tore [tɔː*] *pt of* **tear²**

torment [*n* 'tɔːment, *vt* tɔː'ment] *n* tormento ♦ *vt* atormentar; (*fig: annoy*) fastidiar

torn [tɔːn] *pp of* **tear²**

torrent ['tɔrnt] *n* torrente *m*

tortoise ['tɔːtəs] *n* tortuga; **~shell** ['tɔːtəʃel] *adj* de carey

torture ['tɔːtʃə*] *n* tortura ♦ *vt* torturar; (*fig*) atormentar

Tory ['tɔːrɪ] (BRIT) adj, n (POL) conservador(a) m/f

Toss [tɔs] vt tirar, echar; (one's head) sacudir; **to ~ a coin** echar a cara o cruz; **to ~ up for sth** jugar a cara o cruz algo; **to ~ and turn** (in bed) dar vueltas

Tot [tɔt] n (BRIT: drink) copita; (child) nene/a m/f

Total ['təʊtl] adj total, entero; (emphatic: failure etc) completo, total ♦ n total m, suma ♦ vt (add up) sumar; (amount to) ascender a; **~ly** adv totalmente

Touch [tʌtʃ] n tacto; (contact) contacto ♦ vt tocar; (emotionally) conmover; **a ~ of** (fig) un poquito de; **to get in ~ with sb** ponerse en contacto con uno; **to lose ~** (friends) perder contacto; **~ on** vt fus (topic) aludir (brevemente) a; **~ up** vt (paint) retocar; **~-and-go** adj arriesgado; **~down** n aterrizaje m; (on sea) amerizaje m; (US: FOOTBALL) ensayo; **~ed** adj (moved) conmovido; **~ing** adj (moving) conmovedor(a); **~line** n (SPORT) línea de banda; **~y** adj (person) quisquilloso

Tough [tʌf] adj (material) resistente; (meat) duro; (problem etc) difícil; (policy, stance) inflexible; (person) fuerte; **~en** vt endurecer

Toupée ['tuːpeɪ] n peluca

Tour ['tʊə*] n viaje m, vuelta; (also: **package ~**) viaje m todo comprendido; (of town, museum) visita; (by band etc) gira ♦ vt recorrer, visitar; **~ guide** n guía m turístico, guía f turística

Tourism ['tʊərɪzm] n turismo

Tourist ['tʊərɪst] n turista m/f ♦ cpd turístico; **~ office** n oficina de turismo

Tousled ['taʊzld] adj (hair) despeinado

Tout [taʊt] vi: **to ~ for business** solicitar clientes ♦ n (also: **ticket ~**) revendedor(a) m/f

Tow [təʊ] vt remolcar; **"on or in** (US) **~"** (AUT) "a remolque"

Toward(s) [tə'wɔːd(z)] prep hacia; (attitude) respecto a, con; (purpose) para

Towel ['taʊəl] n toalla; **~ling** n (fabric) felpa; **~ rail** (US **~ rack**) n toallero

Tower ['taʊə*] n torre f; **~ block** (BRIT) n torre f (de pisos); **~ing** adj muy alto, imponente

Town [taʊn] n ciudad f; **to go to ~** ir a la ciudad; (fig) echar la casa por la ventana; **~ centre** n centro de la ciudad; **~ council** n ayuntamiento, consejo municipal; **~ hall** n ayuntamiento; **~ plan** n plano de la ciudad; **~ planning** n urbanismo

Towrope ['təʊrəʊp] n cable m de remolque

Tow truck (US) n camión m grúa

Toy [tɔɪ] n juguete m; **~ with** vt fus jugar con; (idea) acariciar; **~shop** n juguetería

Trace [treɪs] n rastro ♦ vt (draw) trazar, delinear; (locate) encontrar; (follow) seguir la pista de; **tracing paper** n papel m de calco

Track [træk] n (mark) huella, pista; (path: gen) camino, senda; (: of bullet etc) trayectoria; (: of suspect, animal) pista, rastro; (RAIL) vía; (SPORT) pista; (on tape, record) canción f ♦ vt seguir la pista de; **to keep ~ of** mantenerse al tanto de, seguir; **~ down** vt (prey) seguir el rastro de; (sth lost) encontrar; **~suit** n chandal m

Tract [trækt] n (GEO) región f

Traction ['trækʃən] n (power) tracción f; **in ~** (MED) en tracción

Tractor ['træktə*] n tractor m

Trade [treɪd] n comercio; (skill, job) oficio ♦ vi negociar, comerciar ♦ vt (exchange): **to ~ sth (for sth)** cambiar algo (por algo); **~ in** vt (old car etc) ofrecer como parte del pago; **~ fair** n feria comercial; **~mark** n marca de fábrica; **~ name** n marca registrada; **~r** n comerciante m/f; **~sman** (irreg) n (shopkeeper) tendero; **~ union** n sindicato; **~ unionist** n sindicalista m/f

Tradition [trə'dɪʃən] n tradición f; **~al** adj tradicional

Traffic ['træfɪk] n (gen, AUT) tráfico, circulación f, tránsito (AM) ♦ vi: **to ~ in** (pej: liquor, drugs) traficar en; **~ circle**

(US) n isleta; ~ **jam** n embotellamiento; ~ **lights** npl semáforo; ~ **warden** n guardia m/f de tráfico

tragedy ['trædʒədɪ] n tragedia

tragic ['trædʒɪk] adj trágico

trail [treɪl] n (tracks) rastro, pista; (path) camino, sendero; (dust, smoke) estela ♦ vt (drag) arrastrar; (follow) seguir la pista de ♦ vi arrastrar; (in contest etc) ir perdiendo; ~ **behind** vi quedar a la zaga; ~**er** n (AUT) remolque m; (caravan) caravana; (CINEMA) trailer m, avance m; ~**er truck** (US) n trailer m

train [treɪn] n tren m; (of dress) cola; (series) serie f ♦ vt (educate, teach skills to) formar; (sportsman) entrenar; (dog) adiestrar; (point: gun etc): **to** ~ **on** apuntar a ♦ vi (SPORT) entrenarse; (learn a skill): **to** ~ **as a teacher** etc estudiar para profesor etc; **one's** ~ **of thought** el razonamiento de uno; ~**ed** adj (worker) cualificado; (animal) amaestrado; ~**ee** [treɪ'niː] n aprendiz(a) m/f; ~**er** n (SPORT: coach) entrenador(a) m/f; (: shoe): ~**ers** zapatillas fpl (de deporte); (of animals) domador(a) m/f; ~**ing** n formación f; entrenamiento; **to be in** ~**ing** (SPORT) estar entrenando; ~**ing college** n (gen) colegio de formación profesional; (for teachers) escuela de formación del profesorado; ~**ing shoes** npl zapatillas fpl (de deporte)

trait [treɪt] n rasgo

traitor ['treɪtə*] n traidor(a) m/f

tram [træm] (BRIT) n (also: ~**car**) tranvía m

tramp [træmp] n (person) vagabundo/a; (inf. pej: woman) puta

trample ['træmpl] vt: **to** ~ **(underfoot)** pisotear

trampoline ['træmpəliːn] n trampolín m

tranquil ['træŋkwɪl] adj tranquilo; ~**lizer** n (MED) tranquilizante m

transact [træn'zækt] vt (business) despachar; ~**ion** [-'zækʃən] n transacción f, operación f

transfer [n 'trænsfə:*, vb træns'fə:*] n (of employees) traslado; (of money, power) transferencia; (SPORT) traspaso; (picture, design) calcomanía ♦ vt trasladar; transferir; **to** ~ **the charges** (BRIT: TEL) llamar a cobro revertido

transform [træns'fɔːm] vt transformar

transfusion [træns'fjuːʒən] n transfusión f

transient ['trænzɪənt] adj transitorio

transistor [træn'zɪstə*] n (ELEC) transistor m; ~ **radio** n transistor m

transit ['trænzɪt] n: **in** ~ en tránsito

transitive ['trænzɪtɪv] adj (LING) transitivo

transit lounge n sala de tránsito

translate [trænz'leɪt] vt traducir; **translation** [-'leɪʃən] n traducción f; **translator** n traductor(a) m/f

transmit [trænz'mɪt] vt transmitir; ~**ter** n transmisor m

transparency [træns'pɛərnsɪ] n transparencia; (BRIT: PHOT) diapositiva

transparent [træns'pærnt] adj transparente

transpire [træns'paɪə*] vi (turn out) resultar; (happen) ocurrir, suceder; **it** ~**d that ...** se supo que ...

transplant ['trænsplɑːnt] n (MED) transplante m

transport [n 'trænspɔːt, vt træns'pɔːt] n transporte m; (car) coche m (SP), carro (AM), automóvil m ♦ vt transportar; ~**ation** [-'teɪʃən] n transporte m; ~ **café** (BRIT) n bar-restaurant m de carretera

transvestite [trænz'vɛstaɪt] n travestí m/f

trap [træp] n (snare, trick) trampa; (carriage) cabriolé m ♦ vt coger (SP) or agarrar (AM) en una trampa; (trick) engañar; (confine) atrapar; ~ **door** n escotilla

trapeze [trə'piːz] n trapecio

trappings ['træpɪŋz] npl adornos mpl

trash [træʃ] n (rubbish) basura; (pej): **the book/film is** ~ el libro/la película no vale nada; (nonsense) tonterías fpl; ~ **can** (US) n cubo (SP) or balde m (AM) de la basura

travel ['trævl] n el viajar ♦ vi viajar ♦ vt (distance) recorrer; ~**s** npl (journeys) viajes mpl; ~ **agent** n agente m/f de viajes; ~**ler** (US ~**er**) n viajero/a; ~**ler's**

cheque (US ~er's check) n cheque m
de viajero; ~ling (US ~ing) n los viajes, el
viajar; ~ sickness n mareo

trawler ['trɔːlə*] n pesquero de arrastre

tray [treɪ] n bandeja; (on desk) cajón m

treacherous ['tretʃərəs] adj traidor,
traicionero; (dangerous) peligroso

treacle ['triːkl] (BRIT) n melaza

tread [tred] (pt **trod**, pp **trodden**) n (step)
paso, pisada; (sound) ruido de pasos; (of
stair) escalón m; (of tyre) banda de
rodadura ♦ vi pisar; ~ **on** vt fus pisar

treason ['triːzn] n traición f

treasure ['treʒə*] n (also fig) tesoro ♦ vt
(value: object, friendship) apreciar;
(: memory) guardar

treasurer ['treʒərə*] n tesorero/a

treasury ['treʒərɪ] n: **the T~** el Ministerio
de Hacienda

treat [triːt] n (present) regalo ♦ vt tratar; **to
~ sb to sth** invitar a uno a algo

treatment ['triːtmənt] n tratamiento

treaty ['triːtɪ] n tratado

treble ['trebl] adj triple ♦ vt triplicar ♦ vi
triplicarse; ~ **clef** n (MUS) clave f de sol

tree [triː] n árbol m; ~ **trunk** tronco (de
árbol)

trek [trek] n (long journey) viaje m largo y
difícil; (tiring walk) caminata

trellis ['trelɪs] n enrejado

tremble ['trembl] vi temblar

tremendous [trɪ'mendəs] adj tremendo,
enorme; (excellent) estupendo

tremor ['tremə*] n temblor m; (also: **earth
~**) temblor m de tierra

trench [trentʃ] n zanja

trend [trend] n (tendency) tendencia; (of
events) curso; (fashion) moda; ~**y** adj de
moda

trespass ['trespəs] vi: **to ~ on** entrar sin
permiso en; **"no ~ing"** "prohibido el
paso"

trestle ['tresl] n caballete m

trial ['traɪəl] n (LAW) juicio, proceso; (test: of
machine etc) prueba; ~**s** npl (hardships)
dificultades fpl; **by ~ and error** a fuerza
de probar

triangle ['traɪæŋgl] n (MATH, MUS) triángulo

tribe [traɪb] n tribu f

tribunal [traɪ'bjuːnl] n tribunal m

tributary ['trɪbjutərɪ] n (river) afluente m

tribute ['trɪbjuːt] n homenaje m, tributo;
to pay ~ to rendir homenaje a

trick [trɪk] n (skill, knack) tino, truco;
(conjuring ~) truco; (joke) broma; (CARDS)
baza ♦ vt engañar; **to play a ~ on sb**
gastar una broma a uno; **that should do
the ~** a ver si funciona así; ~**ery** n
engaño

trickle ['trɪkl] n (of water etc) goteo ♦ vi
gotear

tricky ['trɪkɪ] adj difícil; delicado

tricycle ['traɪsɪkl] n triciclo

trifle ['traɪfl] n bagatela; (CULIN) dulce de
bizcocho borracho, gelatina, fruta y
natillas ♦ adv: **a ~ long** un poquito
largo; **trifling** adj insignificante

trigger ['trɪgə*] n (of gun) gatillo; ~ **off** vt
desencadenar

trim [trɪm] adj (house, garden) en buen
estado; (person, figure) esbelto ♦ n
(haircut etc) recorte m; (on car)
guarnición f ♦ vt (neaten) arreglar; (cut)
recortar; (decorate) adornar; (NAUT: a sail)
orientar; ~**mings** npl (CULIN) guarnición
f

trip [trɪp] n viaje m; (excursion) excursión f;
(stumble) traspié m ♦ vi (stumble)
tropezar; (go lightly) andar a paso ligero;
on a ~ de viaje; ~ **up** vi tropezar, caerse
♦ vt hacer tropezar or caer

tripe [traɪp] n (CULIN) callos mpl

triple ['trɪpl] adj triple; **triplets** ['trɪplɪts]
npl trillizos/as mpl/fpl; **triplicate**
['trɪplɪkət] n: **in triplicate** por triplicado

trite [traɪt] adj trillado

triumph ['traɪʌmf] n triunfo ♦ vi: **to ~
(over)** vencer; ~**ant** [traɪ'ʌmfənt] adj
(team etc) vencedor(a); (wave, return)
triunfal

trivia ['trɪvɪə] npl trivialidades fpl

trivial ['trɪvɪəl] adj insignificante;
(commonplace) banal

trod [trɔd] pt of **tread**

trodden ['trɔdn] *pp of* **tread**

trolley ['trɔlɪ] *n* carrito; (*also:* ~ **bus**) trolebús *m*

trombone [trɔm'bəun] *n* trombón *m*

troop [tru:p] *n* grupo, banda; ~**s** *npl* (MIL) tropas *fpl*; ~ **in/out** *vi* entrar/salir en tropel; ~**ing the colour** *n* (*ceremony*) presentación *f* de la bandera

trophy ['trəufɪ] *n* trofeo

tropical ['trɔpɪkl] *adj* tropical

trot [trɔt] *n* trote *m* ♦ *vi* trotar; **on the** ~ (*BRIT: fig*) seguidos/as

trouble ['trʌbl] *n* problema *m*, dificultad *f*; (*worry*) preocupación *f*; (*bother, effort*) molestia, esfuerzo; (*unrest*) inquietud *f*; (MED): **stomach** *etc* ~ problemas *mpl* gástricos *etc* ♦ *vt* (*disturb*) molestar; (*worry*) preocupar, inquietar ♦ *vi*: **to ~ to do sth** molestarse en hacer algo; ~**s** *npl* (POL *etc*) conflictos *mpl*; (*personal*) problemas *mpl*; **to be in** ~ estar en un apuro; **it's no ~!** ¡no es molestia (ninguna)!; **what's the ~?** (*with broken TV etc*) ¿cuál es el problema?; (*doctor to patient*) ¿qué pasa?; ~**d** *adj* (*person*) preocupado; (*country, epoch, life*) agitado; ~**maker** *n* agitador(a) *m/f*; (*child*) alborotador *m*; ~**shooter** *n* (*in conflict*) conciliador(a) *m/f*; ~**some** *adj* molesto

trough [trɔf] *n* (*also:* **drinking** ~) abrevadero; (*also:* **feeding** ~) comedero; (*depression*) depresión *f*

troupe [tru:p] *n* grupo

trousers ['trauzəz] *npl* pantalones *mpl*; **short** ~ pantalones *mpl* cortos

trousseau ['tru:səu] (*pl* ~**x** *or* ~**s**) *n* ajuar *m*

trout [traut] *n inv* trucha

trowel ['trauəl] *n* (*of gardener*) palita; (*of builder*) paleta

truant ['truənt] *n*: **to play** ~ (*BRIT*) hacer novillos

truce [tru:s] *n* tregua

truck [trʌk] *n* (*lorry*) camión *m*; (RAIL) vagón *m*; ~ **driver** *n* camionero; ~ **farm** (*US*) *n* huerto

true [tru:] *adj* verdadero; (*accurate*) exacto;

(*genuine*) auténtico; (*faithful*) fiel; **to come** ~ realizarse

truffle ['trʌfl] *n* trufa

truly ['tru:lɪ] *adv* (*really*) realmente; (*truthfully*) verdaderamente; (*faithfully*): **yours** ~ (*in letter*) le saluda atentamente

trump [trʌmp] *n* triunfo

trumpet ['trʌmpɪt] *n* trompeta

truncheon ['trʌntʃən] *n* porra

trundle ['trʌndl] *vi*: **to ~ along** ir sin prisas

trunk [trʌŋk] *n* (*of tree, person*) tronco; (*of elephant*) trompa; (*case*) baúl *m*; (*US: AUT*) maletero; ~**s** *npl* (*also:* **swimming ~s**) bañador *m* (de hombre)

truss [trʌs] *vt*: ~ (**up**) atar

trust [trʌst] *n* confianza; (*responsibility*) responsabilidad *f*; (LAW) fideicomiso ♦ *vt* (*rely on*) tener confianza en; (*hope*) esperar; (*entrust*): **to ~ sth to sb** confiar algo a uno; **to take sth on** ~ aceptar algo a ojos cerrados; ~**ed** *adj* de confianza; ~**ee** [trʌs'ti:] *n* (LAW) fideicomisario; (*of school*) administrador *m*; ~**ful** *adj* confiado; ~**ing** *adj* confiado; ~**worthy** *adj* digno de confianza

truth [tru:θ, *pl* tru:ðz] *n* verdad *f*; ~**ful** *adj* veraz

try [traɪ] *n* tentativa, intento; (RUGBY) ensayo ♦ *vt* (*attempt*) intentar; (*test: also:* ~ **out**) probar, someter a prueba; (LAW) juzgar, procesar; (*strain: patience*) hacer perder ♦ *vi* probar; **to have a** ~ probar suerte; **to ~ to do sth** intentar hacer algo; ~ **again!** ¡vuelve a probar!; ~ **harder!** ¡esfuérzate más!; **well, I tried** al menos lo intenté; ~ **on** *vt* (*clothes*) probarse; ~**ing** *adj* (*experience*) cansado; (*person*) pesado

T-shirt ['ti:ʃə:t] *n* camiseta

T-square *n* regla en T

tub [tʌb] *n* cubo (SP), balde *m* (AM); (*bath*) tina, bañera

tube [tju:b] *n* tubo; (*BRIT: underground*) metro; (*for tyre*) cámara de aire

tuberculosis [tjubə:kju'ləusɪs] *n* tuberculosis *f inv*

tube station (*BRIT*) *n* estación *f* de metro

tubular ['tju:bjulə*] *adj* tubular

TUC (*BRIT*) *n abbr* (= *Trades Union Congress*) *federación nacional de sindicatos*

tuck [tʌk] *vt* (*put*) poner; ~ **away** *vt* (*money*) guardar; (*building*): **to be ~ed away** esconderse, ocultarse; ~ **in** *vt* meter dentro; (*child*) arropar ♦ *vi* (*eat*) comer con apetito; ~ **up** *vt* (*child*) arropar; ~ **shop** *n* (*SCOL*) tienda; ≈ bar *m* (del colegio) (*SP*)

Tuesday [ˈtjuːzdɪ] *n* martes *m inv*

tuft [tʌft] *n* mechón *m*; (*of grass etc*) manojo

tug [tʌg] *n* (*ship*) remolcador *m* ♦ *vt* tirar de; ~**-of-war** *n* lucha de tiro de cuerda; (*fig*) tira y afloja *m*

tuition [tjuːˈɪʃən] *n* (*BRIT*) enseñanza; (: *private* ~) clases *fpl* particulares; (*US: school fees*) matrícula

tulip [ˈtjuːlɪp] *n* tulipán *m*

tumble [ˈtʌmbl] *n* (*fall*) caída ♦ *vi* caer; **to ~ to sth** (*inf*) caer en la cuenta de algo; ~**down** *adj* destartalado; ~ **dryer** (*BRIT*) *n* secadora

tumbler [ˈtʌmblə*] *n* (*glass*) vaso

tummy [ˈtʌmɪ] (*inf*) *n* barriga, tripa

tumour [ˈtjuːmə*] (*US* **tumor**) *n* tumor *m*

tuna [ˈtjuːnə] *n inv* (*also*: ~ **fish**) atún *m*

tune [tjuːn] *n* melodía ♦ *vt* (*MUS*) afinar; (*RADIO, TV, AUT*) sintonizar; **to be in/out of** ~ (*instrument*) estar afinado/desafinado; (*singer*) cantar afinadamente/desafinar; **to be in/out of** ~ **with** (*fig*) estar de acuerdo/en desacuerdo con; ~ **in** *vi*: **to ~ in (to)** (*RADIO, TV*) sintonizar (con); ~ **up** *vi* (*musician*) afinar (su instrumento); ~**ful** *adj* melodioso; ~**r** *n*: **piano** ~**r** afinador(a) *m/f* de pianos

tunic [ˈtjuːnɪk] *n* túnica

Tunisia [tjuːˈnɪzɪə] *n* Túnez *m*

tunnel [ˈtʌnl] *n* túnel *m*; (*in mine*) galería ♦ *vi* construir un túnel/una galería

turban [ˈtɜːbən] *n* turbante *m*

turbulent [ˈtɜːbjulənt] *adj* turbulento

tureen [təˈriːn] *n* sopera

turf [tɜːf] *n* césped *m*; (*clod*) tepe *m* ♦ *vt* cubrir con césped; ~ **out** (*inf*) *vt* echar a

la calle

Turk [tɜːk] *n* turco/a

Turkey [ˈtɜːkɪ] *n* Turquía

turkey [ˈtɜːkɪ] *n* pavo

Turkish [ˈtɜːkɪʃ] *adj, n* turco

turmoil [ˈtɜːmɔɪl] *n*: **in** ~ revuelto

turn [tɜːn] *n* turno; (*in road*) curva; (*of mind, events*) rumbo; (*THEATRE*) número; (*MED*) ataque *m* ♦ *vt* girar, volver; (*collar, steak*) dar la vuelta a; (*page*) pasar; (*change*): **to ~ sth into** convertir algo en ♦ *vi* volver; (*person: look back*) volverse; (*reverse direction*) dar la vuelta; (*milk*) cortarse; (*become*): **to ~ nasty/forty** ponerse feo/cumplir los cuarenta; **a good** ~ un favor; **it gave me quite a** ~ me dio un susto; **"no left** ~**"** (*AUT*) "prohibido girar a la izquierda"; **it's your** ~ te toca a ti; **in** ~ por turnos; **to take** ~**s (at)** turnarse (en); ~ **away** *vi* apartar la vista ♦ *vi* rechazar; ~ **back** *vi* volverse atrás ♦ *vt* hacer retroceder; (*clock*) retrasar; ~ **down** *vt* (*refuse*) rechazar; (*reduce*) bajar; (*fold*) doblar; ~ **in** *vi* (*inf: go to bed*) acostarse ♦ *vt* (*fold*) doblar hacia dentro; ~ **off** *vi* (*from road*) desviarse ♦ *vt* (*light, radio etc*) apagar; (*tap*) cerrar; (*engine*) parar; ~ **on** *vt* (*light, radio etc*) encender (*SP*), prender (*AM*); (*tap*) abrir; (*engine*) poner en marcha; ~ **out** *vt* (*light, gas*) apagar; (*produce*) producir ♦ *vi* (*voters*) concurrir; **to ~ out to be ...** resultar ser ...; ~ **over** *vi* (*person*) volverse ♦ *vt* (*object*) dar la vuelta a; (*page*) volver; ~ **round** *vi* volverse; (*rotate*) girar; ~ **up** *vi* (*person*) llegar, presentarse; (*lost object*) aparecer ♦ *vt* (*gen*) subir; ~**ing** *n* (*in road*) vuelta; ~**ing point** *n* (*fig*) momento decisivo

turnip [ˈtɜːnɪp] *n* nabo

turn: ~**out** *n* concurrencia; ~**over** *n* (*COMM: amount of money*) volumen *m* de ventas; (: *of goods*) movimiento; ~**pike** (*US*) *n* autopista de peaje; ~**stile** *n* torniquete *m*; ~**table** *n* plato; ~**-up** (*BRIT*) *n* (*on trousers*) vuelta

turpentine [ˈtɜːpəntaɪn] *n* (*also*: **turps**)

trementina
turquoise ['tɜːkwɔɪz] n (stone) turquesa
♦ adj color turquesa
turret ['tʌrɪt] n torreón m
turtle ['tɜːtl] n galápago; ~**neck**
(sweater) n jersey m de cuello vuelto
tusk [tʌsk] n colmillo
tutor ['tjuːtə*] n profesor(a) m/f; ~**ial**
[-'tɔːrɪəl] n (SCOL) seminario
tuxedo [tʌk'siːdəu] (US) n smóking m,
esmoquin m
TV [tiː'viː] n abbr (= television) tele f
twang [twæŋ] n (of instrument) punteado;
(of voice) timbre m nasal
tweezers ['twiːzəz] npl pinzas fpl (de
depilar)
twelfth [twelfθ] num duodécimo
twelve [twelv] num doce; **at ~ o'clock**
(midday) a mediodía; (midnight) a
medianoche
twentieth ['twentɪɪθ] adj vigésimo
twenty ['twentɪ] num veinte
twice [twaɪs] adv dos veces; **~ as much**
dos veces más
twiddle ['twɪdl] vi: **to ~ (with) sth** dar
vueltas a algo; **to ~ one's thumbs** (fig)
estar mano sobre mano
twig [twɪg] n ramita
twilight ['twaɪlaɪt] n crepúsculo
twin [twɪn] adj, n gemelo/a m/f ♦ vt
hermanar; ~-**bedded room** n
habitación f doble
twine [twaɪn] n bramante m ♦ vi (plant)
enroscarse
twinge [twɪndʒ] n (of pain) punzada; (of
conscience) remordimiento
twinkle ['twɪŋkl] vi centellear; (eyes) brillar
twirl [twɜːl] vt dar vueltas a ♦ vi dar
vueltas
twist [twɪst] n (action) torsión f; (in road,
coil) vuelta; (in wire, flex) doblez f; (in
story) giro ♦ vt torcer; (weave) trenzar;
(roll around) enrollar; (fig) deformar ♦ vi
serpentear
twit [twɪt] (inf) n tonto
twitch [twɪtʃ] n (pull) tirón m; (nervous) tic
m ♦ vi crisparse

two [tuː] num dos; **to put ~ and ~**
together (fig) atar cabos; ~-**door** adj
(AUT) de dos puertas; ~-**faced** adj (pej:
person) falso; ~**fold** adv: **to increase**
~**fold** doblarse; ~-**piece** (suit) n traje m
de dos piezas; ~-**piece (swimsuit)** n
dos piezas m inv, bikini m; ~**some** n
(people) pareja; ~-**way** adj: ~-**way traffic**
circulación f de dos sentidos
tycoon [taɪ'kuːn] n: **(business) ~** magnate
m
type [taɪp] n (category) tipo, género;
(model) tipo; (TYP) tipo, letra f (letter
etc) escribir a máquina; ~-**cast** adj
(actor) encasillado; ~**face** n letra;
~**script** n texto mecanografiado;
~**writer** n máquina de escribir; ~**written**
adj mecanografiado
typhoid ['taɪfɔɪd] n tifoidea
typical ['tɪpɪkl] adj típico
typing ['taɪpɪŋ] n mecanografía
typist ['taɪpɪst] n mecanógrafo/a
tyrant ['taɪərnt] n tirano/a
tyre ['taɪə*] (US **tire**) n neumático (SP),
llanta (AM); ~ **pressure** n presión f de
los neumáticos

U, u

U-bend ['juː'bend] n (AUT, in pipe) recodo
udder ['ʌdə*] n ubre f
UFO ['juːfəu] n abbr = (unidentified flying
object) OVNI m
ugh [əːh] excl ¡uf!
ugly ['ʌglɪ] adj feo; (dangerous) peligroso
UHT abbr: ~ **milk** leche f UHT, leche f
uperizada
UK n abbr = **United Kingdom**
ulcer ['ʌlsə*] n úlcera; (mouth ~) llaga
Ulster ['ʌlstə*] n Ulster m
ulterior [ʌl'tɪərɪə*] adj: ~ **motive** segundas
intenciones fpl
ultimate ['ʌltɪmət] adj último, final;
(greatest) máximo; ~**ly** adv (in the end)
por último, al final; (fundamentally) a or
en fin de cuentas

mbilical cord [ʌmˈbɪlɪkl-] n cordón m umbilical

mbrella [ʌmˈbrelə] n paraguas m inv; (for sun) sombrilla

mpire [ˈʌmpaɪə*] n árbitro

mpteen [ʌmpˈtiːn] adj enésimos/as; ~th adj: for the ~th time por enésima vez

N n abbr (= United Nations) NN. UU.

nable [ʌnˈeɪbl] adj: to be ~ to do sth no poder hacer algo

naccompanied [ʌnəˈkʌmpənɪd] adj no acompañado; (song) sin acompañamiento

naccustomed [ʌnəˈkʌstəmd] adj: to be ~ to no estar acostumbrado a

nanimous [juːˈnænɪməs] adj unánime

narmed [ʌnˈɑːmd] adj (defenceless) inerme; (without weapon) desarmado

nattached [ʌnəˈtætʃt] adj (person) soltero y sin compromiso; (part etc) suelto

nattended [ʌnəˈtendɪd] adj desatendido

nattractive [ʌnəˈtræktɪv] adj poco atractivo

nauthorized [ʌnˈɔːθəraɪzd] adj no autorizado

navoidable [ʌnəˈvɔɪdəbl] adj inevitable

naware [ʌnəˈweə*] adj: to be ~ of ignorar; ~s adv de improviso

nbalanced [ʌnˈbælənst] adj (report) poco objetivo; (mentally) trastornado

nbearable [ʌnˈbeərəbl] adj insoportable

nbeatable [ʌnˈbiːtəbl] adj (team) invencible; (price) inmejorable; (quality) insuperable

nbelievable [ʌnbɪˈliːvəbl] adj increíble

nbend [ʌnˈbend] (irreg) vi (relax) relajarse ♦ vt (wire) enderezar

nbiased [ʌnˈbaɪəst] adj imparcial

nborn [ʌnˈbɔːn] adj que va a nacer

nbroken [ʌnˈbrəʊkən] adj (seal) intacto; (series) continuo; (record) no batido; (spirit) indómito

nbutton [ʌnˈbʌtn] vt desabrochar

ncalled-for [ʌnˈkɔːldfɔː*] adj gratuito, inmerecido

ncanny [ʌnˈkænɪ] adj extraño

nceremonious [ˈʌnserɪˈməʊnɪəs] adj (abrupt, rude) brusco, hosco

uncertain [ʌnˈsəːtn] adj incierto; (indecisive) indeciso

unchanged [ʌnˈtʃeɪndʒd] adj igual, sin cambios

uncivilized [ʌnˈsɪvɪlaɪzd] adj inculto; (fig: behaviour etc) bárbaro; (hour) inoportuno

uncle [ˈʌŋkl] n tío

uncomfortable [ʌnˈkʌmfətəbl] adj incómodo; (uneasy) inquieto

uncommon [ʌnˈkɔmən] adj poco común, raro

uncompromising [ʌnˈkɔmprəmaɪzɪŋ] adj intransigente

unconcerned [ʌnkənˈsəːnd] adj indiferente, despreocupado

unconditional [ʌnkənˈdɪʃənl] adj incondicional

unconscious [ʌnˈkɔnʃəs] adj sin sentido; (unaware): to be ~ of no darse cuenta de ♦ n: the ~ el inconsciente

uncontrollable [ʌnkənˈtrəʊləbl] adj (child etc) incontrolable; (temper) indomable; (laughter) incontenible

unconventional [ʌnkənˈvenʃənl] adj poco convencional

uncouth [ʌnˈkuːθ] adj grosero, inculto

uncover [ʌnˈkʌvə*] vt descubrir; (take lid off) destapar

undecided [ʌndɪˈsaɪdɪd] adj (character) indeciso; (question) no resuelto

under [ˈʌndə*] prep debajo de; (less than) menos de; (according to) según, de acuerdo con; (sb's leadership) bajo ♦ adv debajo, abajo; ~ there allí abajo; ~ repair en reparación

under... [ˈʌndə*] prefix sub; ~age adj menor de edad; (drinking etc) de los menores de edad; ~carriage (BRIT) n (AVIAT) tren m de aterrizaje; ~charge vt cobrar menos de la cuenta; ~clothes npl ropa interior (SP) or íntima (AM); ~coat n (paint) primera mano; ~cover adj clandestino; ~current n (fig) corriente f oculta; ~cut vt irreg vender más barato que; ~developed adj subdesarrollado; ~dog n desvalido/a; ~done adj (CULIN) poco hecho;

~estimate *vt* subestimar; ~exposed *adj* (*PHOT*) subexpuesto; ~fed *adj* subalimentado; ~foot *adv* con los pies; ~go *vt irreg* sufrir; (*treatment*) recibir; ~graduate *n* estudiante *m/f*; ~ground *n* (*BRIT: railway*) metro; (*POL*) movimiento clandestino ♦ *adj* (*car park*) subterráneo ♦ *adv* (*work*) en la clandestinidad; ~growth *n* maleza; ~hand(ed) *adj* (*fig*) socarrón; ~lie *vt irreg* (*fig*) ser la razón fundamental de; ~line *vt* subrayar; ~mine *vt* socavar, minar; ~neath [ʌndə'ni:θ] *adv* debajo ♦ *prep* debajo de, bajo; ~paid *adj* mal pagado; ~pants *npl* calzoncillos *mpl*; ~pass (*BRIT*) *n* paso subterráneo; ~privileged *adj* desposeído; ~rate *vt* menospreciar, subestimar; ~shirt (*US*) *n* camiseta; ~shorts (*US*) *npl* calzoncillos *mpl*; ~side *n* parte *f* inferior; ~skirt (*BRIT*) *n* enaguas *fpl*

understand [ʌndə'stænd] (*irreg*) *vt, vi* entender, comprender; (*assume*) tener entendido; ~able *adj* comprensible; ~ing *adj* comprensivo ♦ *n* comprensión *f*, entendimiento; (*agreement*) acuerdo

understatement ['ʌndəsteitmənt] *n* modestia (excesiva); **that's an ~!** ¡eso es decir poco!

understood [ʌndə'stud] *pt, pp of* **understand** ♦ *adj* (*agreed*) acordado; (*implied*): **it is ~ that** se sobreentiende que

understudy ['ʌndəstʌdɪ] *n* suplente *m/f*

undertake [ʌndə'teik] (*irreg*) *vt* emprender; **to ~ to do sth** comprometerse a hacer algo

undertaker ['ʌndəteikə*] *n* director(a) *m/f* de pompas fúnebres

undertaking ['ʌndəteikɪŋ] *n* empresa; (*promise*) promesa

under: ~tone *n*: **in an ~tone** en voz baja; ~water *adv* bajo el agua ♦ *adj* submarino; ~wear *n* ropa interior (*SP*) or íntima (*AM*); ~world *n* (*of crime*) hampa, inframundo; ~writer *n* (*INSURANCE*) asegurador(a) *m/f*

undesirable [ʌndɪ'zaɪrəbl] *adj* (*person*) indeseable; (*thing*) poco aconsejable

undo [ʌn'du:] (*irreg*) *vt* (*laces*) desatar; (*button etc*) desabrochar; (*spoil*) deshacer; ~ing *n* ruina, perdición *f*

undoubted [ʌn'dautid] *adj* indudable

undress [ʌn'dres] *vi* desnudarse

undulating ['ʌndjuleitɪŋ] *adj* ondulante

unduly [ʌn'dju:lɪ] *adv* excesivamente, demasiado

unearth [ʌn'ə:θ] *vt* desenterrar

unearthly [ʌn'ə:θlɪ] *adj* (*hour*) inverosímil

uneasy [ʌn'i:zɪ] *adj* intranquilo, preocupado; (*feeling*) desagradable; (*peace*) inseguro

uneducated [ʌn'edjukeitid] *adj* ignorante, inculto

unemployed [ʌnɪm'plɔid] *adj* parado, sin trabajo ♦ *npl*: **the ~** los parados

unemployment [ʌnɪm'plɔimənt] *n* paro, desempleo

unending [ʌn'endɪŋ] *adj* interminable

unerring [ʌn'ə:rɪŋ] *adj* infalible

uneven [ʌn'i:vn] *adj* desigual; (*road etc*) lleno de baches

unexpected [ʌnɪk'spektid] *adj* inesperado; ~ly *adv* inesperadamente

unfailing [ʌn'feilɪŋ] *adj* (*support*) indefectible; (*energy*) inagotable

unfair [ʌn'feə*] *adj*: ~ (**to sb**) injusto (con uno)

unfaithful [ʌn'feiθful] *adj* infiel

unfamiliar [ʌnfə'mɪlɪə*] *adj* extraño, desconocido; **to be ~ with** desconocer

unfashionable [ʌn'fæʃnəbl] *adj* pasado o fuera de moda

unfasten [ʌn'fɑ:sn] *vt* (*knot*) desatar; (*dress*) desabrochar; (*open*) abrir

unfavourable [ʌn'feivərəbl] (*US* **unfavorable**) *adj* desfavorable

unfeeling [ʌn'fi:lɪŋ] *adj* insensible

unfinished [ʌn'fɪnɪʃt] *adj* inacabado, sin terminar

unfit [ʌn'fɪt] *adj* bajo de forma; (*incompetent*): ~ (**for**) incapaz (de); ~ **for work** no apto para trabajar

unfold [ʌn'fəuld] *vt* desdoblar ♦ *vi* abrirse

unforeseen ['ʌnfɔː'siːn] *adj* imprevisto
unforgettable [ʌnfə'getəbl] *adj* inolvidable
unfortunate [ʌn'fɔːtʃnət] *adj* desgraciado; (*event, remark*) inoportuno; **~ly** *adv* desgraciadamente
unfounded [ʌn'faundɪd] *adj* infundado
unfriendly [ʌn'frendlɪ] *adj* antipático; (*behaviour, remark*) hostil, poco amigable
ungainly [ʌn'geɪnlɪ] *adj* desgarbado
ungodly [ʌn'gɔdlɪ] *adj*: **at an ~ hour** a una hora inverosímil
ungrateful [ʌn'greɪtful] *adj* ingrato
unhappiness [ʌn'hæpɪnɪs] *n* tristeza, desdicha
unhappy [ʌn'hæpɪ] *adj* (*sad*) triste; (*unfortunate*) desgraciado; (*childhood*) infeliz; **~ about/with** (*arrangements etc*) poco contento con, descontento de
unharmed [ʌn'hɑːmd] *adj* ileso
unhealthy [ʌn'helθɪ] *adj* (*place*) malsano; (*person*) enfermizo; (*fig: interest*) morboso
unheard-of *adj* inaudito, sin precedente
unhurt [ʌn'hɜːt] *adj* ileso
unidentified [ʌnaɪ'dentɪfaɪd] *adj* no identificado, sin identificar; *see also* **UFO**
uniform ['juːnɪfɔːm] *n* uniforme *m* ♦ *adj* uniforme
unify ['juːnɪfaɪ] *vt* unificar, unir
uninhabited [ʌnɪn'hæbɪtɪd] *adj* desierto
unintentional [ʌnɪn'tenʃənəl] *adj* involuntario
union ['juːnjən] *n* unión *f*; (*also*: **trade ~**) sindicato ♦ *cpd* sindical; **U~ Jack** *n* bandera del Reino Unido
unique [juː'niːk] *adj* único
unison ['juːnɪsn] *n*: **in ~** (*speak, reply, sing*) al unísono
unit ['juːnɪt] *n* unidad *f*; (*section: of furniture etc*) elemento; (*team*) grupo; **kitchen ~** módulo de cocina
unite [juː'naɪt] *vt* unir ♦ *vi* unirse; **~d** *adj* unido; (*effort*) conjunto; **U~d Kingdom** *n* Reino Unido; **U~d Nations (Organization)** *n* Naciones *fpl* Unidas; **U~d States (of America)** *n* Estados *mpl* Unidos

unit trust (*BRIT*) *n* bono fiduciario
unity ['juːnɪtɪ] *n* unidad *f*
universe ['juːnɪvəːs] *n* universo
university [juːnɪ'vəːsɪtɪ] *n* universidad *f*
unjust [ʌn'dʒʌst] *adj* injusto
unkempt [ʌn'kempt] *adj* (*appearance*) descuidado; (*hair*) despeinado
unkind [ʌn'kaɪnd] *adj* poco amable; (*behaviour, comment*) cruel
unknown [ʌn'nəun] *adj* desconocido
unlawful [ʌn'lɔːful] *adj* ilegal, ilícito
unleaded [ʌn'ledɪd] *adj* (*petrol, fuel*) sin plombo
unless [ʌn'les] *conj* a menos que; **~ he comes** a menos que venga; **~ otherwise stated** salvo indicación contraria
unlike [ʌn'laɪk] *adj* (*not alike*) distinto de *or* a; (*not like*) poco propio de ♦ *prep* a diferencia de
unlikely [ʌn'laɪklɪ] *adj* improbable; (*unexpected*) inverosímil
unlimited [ʌn'lɪmɪtɪd] *adj* ilimitado
unlisted [ʌn'lɪstɪd] (*US*) *adj* (*TEL*) que no consta en la guía
unload [ʌn'ləud] *vt* descargar
unlock [ʌn'lɔk] *vt* abrir (con llave)
unlucky [ʌn'lʌkɪ] *adj* desgraciado; (*object, number*) que da mala suerte; **to be ~** tener mala suerte
unmarried [ʌn'mærɪd] *adj* soltero
unmistak(e)able [ʌnmɪs'teɪkəbl] *adj* inconfundible
unnatural [ʌn'nætʃrəl] *adj* (*gen*) antinatural; (*manner*) afectado; (*habit*) perverso
unnecessary [ʌn'nesəsərɪ] *adj* innecesario, inútil
unnoticed [ʌn'nəutɪst] *adj*: **to go** *or* **pass ~** pasar desapercibido
UNO ['juːnəu] *n abbr* (= *United Nations Organization*) ONU *f*
unobtainable [ʌnəb'teɪnəbl] *adj* inconseguible; (*TEL*) inexistente
unobtrusive [ʌnəb'truːsɪv] *adj* discreto
unofficial [ʌnə'fɪʃl] *adj* no oficial; (*news*) sin confirmar
unorthodox [ʌn'ɔːθədɔks] *adj* poco

ortodoxo; (*REL*) heterodoxo

unpack [ʌn'pæk] *vi* deshacer las maletas
♦ *vt* deshacer

unpalatable [ʌn'pælətəbl] *adj* incomible;
(*truth*) desagradable

unparalleled [ʌn'pærəleld] *adj*
(*unequalled*) incomparable

unpleasant [ʌn'pleznt] *adj* (*disagreeable*)
desagradable; (*person, manner*) antipático

unplug [ʌn'plʌg] *vt* desenchufar,
desconectar

unpopular [ʌn'pɔpjulə*] *adj* impopular,
poco popular

unprecedented [ʌn'presɪdəntɪd] *adj* sin
precedentes

unpredictable [ʌnprɪ'dɪktəbl] *adj*
imprevisible

unprofessional [ʌnprə'feʃənl] *adj*
(*attitude, conduct*) poco ético

unqualified [ʌn'kwɔlɪfaɪd] *adj* sin título,
no cualificado; (*success*) total

unquestionably [ʌn'kwestʃənəblɪ] *adv*
indiscutiblemente

unreal [ʌn'rɪəl] *adj* irreal; (*extraordinary*)
increíble

unrealistic [ʌnrɪə'lɪstɪk] *adj* poco realista

unreasonable [ʌn'ri:znəbl] *adj*
irrazonable; (*demand*) excesivo

unrelated [ʌnrɪ'leɪtɪd] *adj* sin relación;
(*family*) no emparentado

unreliable [ʌnrɪ'laɪəbl] *adj* (*person*)
informal; (*machine*) poco fiable

unremitting [ʌnrɪ'mɪtɪŋ] *adj* constante

unreservedly [ʌnrɪ'zə:vɪdlɪ] *adv* sin
reserva

unrest [ʌn'rest] *n* inquietud *f*, malestar *m*;
(*POL*) disturbios *mpl*

unroll [ʌn'rəul] *vt* desenrollar

unruly [ʌn'ru:lɪ] *adj* indisciplinado

unsafe [ʌn'seɪf] *adj* peligroso

unsaid [ʌn'sed] *adj*: **to leave sth ~** dejar
algo sin decir

unsatisfactory ['ʌnsætɪs'fæktərɪ] *adj* poco
satisfactorio

unsavoury [ʌn'seɪvərɪ] (*US* **unsavory**) *adj*
(*fig*) repugnante

unscrew [ʌn'skru:] *vt* destornillar

unscrupulous [ʌn'skru:pjuləs] *adj* sin
escrúpulos

unsettled [ʌn'setld] *adj* inquieto,
intranquilo; (*weather*) variable

unshaven [ʌn'feɪvn] *adj* sin afeitar

unsightly [ʌn'saɪtlɪ] *adj* feo

unskilled [ʌn'skɪld] *adj* (*work*) no
especializado; (*worker*) no cualificado

unspeakable [ʌn'spi:kəbl] *adj* indecible;
(*awful*) incalificable

unstable [ʌn'steɪbl] *adj* inestable

unsteady [ʌn'stedɪ] *adj* inestable

unstuck [ʌn'stʌk] *adj*: **to come ~**
despegarse; (*fig*) fracasar

unsuccessful [ʌnsək'sesful] *adj* (*attempt*)
infructuoso; (*writer, proposal*) sin éxito; **to
be ~** (*in attempting sth*) no tener éxito,
fracasar; **~ly** *adv* en vano, sin éxito

unsuitable [ʌn'su:təbl] *adj* inapropiado;
(*time*) inoportuno

unsure [ʌn'ʃuə*] *adj* inseguro, poco
seguro

unsuspecting ['ʌnsəs'pektɪŋ] *adj*
desprevenido

unsympathetic [ʌnsɪmpə'θetɪk] *adj* poco
comprensivo; (*unlikeable*) antipático

unthinkable [ʌn'θɪŋkəbl] *adj*
inconcebible, impensable

untidy [ʌn'taɪdɪ] *adj* (*room*) desordenado;
(*appearance*) desaliñado

untie [ʌn'taɪ] *vt* desatar

until [ən'tɪl] *prep* hasta ♦ *conj* hasta que; **~
he comes** hasta que venga; **~ now** hasta
ahora; **~ then** hasta entonces

untimely [ʌn'taɪmlɪ] *adj* inoportuno;
(*death*) prematuro

untold [ʌn'təuld] *adj* (*story*) nunca
contado; (*suffering*) indecible; (*wealth*)
incalculable

untoward [ʌntə'wɔ:d] *adj* adverso

unused [ʌn'ju:zd] *adj* sin usar

unusual [ʌn'ju:ʒuəl] *adj* insólito, poco
común; (*exceptional*) inusitado

unveil [ʌn'veɪl] *vt* (*statue*) descubrir

unwanted [ʌn'wɔntɪd] *adj* (*clothing*) viejo;
(*pregnancy*) no deseado

unwelcome [ʌn'welkəm] *adj* inoportuno;

(news) desagradable

unwell [ʌn'wel] *adj*: **to be/feel ~** estar indispuesto/sentirse mal

unwieldy [ʌn'wi:ldɪ] *adj* difícil de manejar

unwilling [ʌn'wɪlɪŋ] *adj*: **to be ~ to do sth** estar poco dispuesto a hacer algo; **~ly** *adv* de mala gana

unwind [ʌn'waɪnd] *(irreg: like wind²)* *vt* desenvolver ♦ *vi (relax)* relajarse

unwise [ʌn'waɪz] *adj* imprudente

unwitting [ʌn'wɪtɪŋ] *adj* inconsciente

unworthy [ʌn'wɜːðɪ] *adj* indigno

unwrap [ʌn'ræp] *vt* desenvolver

unwritten [ʌn'rɪtn] *adj (agreement)* tácito; *(rules, law)* no escrito

KEYWORD

up [ʌp] *prep*: **to go/be ~ sth** subir/estar subido en algo; **he went ~ the stairs/the hill** subió las escaleras/la colina; **we walked/climbed ~ the hill** subimos la colina; **they live further ~ the street** viven más arriba en la calle; **go ~ that road and turn left** sigue por esa calle y gira a la izquierda

♦ *adv* **1** *(upwards, higher)* más arriba; **~ in the mountains** en lo alto (de la montaña); **put it a bit higher ~** ponlo un poco más arriba *or* alto; **~ there** ahí *or* allí arriba; **~ above** en lo alto, por encima, arriba

2: **to be ~** *(out of bed)* estar levantado; *(prices, level)* haber subido

3: **~ to** *(as far as)* hasta; **~ to now** hasta ahora *or* la fecha

4: **to be ~ to** *(depending on)*: **it's ~ to you** depende de ti; **he's not ~ to it** *(job, task etc)* no es capaz de hacerlo; **his work is not ~ to the required standard** su trabajo no da la talla; *(inf: be doing)*: **what is he ~ to?** ¿que estará tramando?

♦ *n*: **~s and downs** altibajos *mpl*

upbringing ['ʌpbrɪŋɪŋ] *n* educación *f*

update [ʌp'deɪt] *vt* poner al día

upgrade [ʌp'greɪd] *vt (house)* modernizar; *(employee)* ascender

upheaval [ʌp'hi:vl] *n* trastornos *mpl*; *(POL)* agitación *f*

uphill [ʌp'hɪl] *adj* cuesta arriba; *(fig: task)* penoso, difícil ♦ *adv*: **to go ~** ir cuesta arriba

uphold [ʌp'həʊld] *(irreg)* *vt* defender

upholstery [ʌp'həʊlstərɪ] *n* tapicería

upkeep ['ʌpki:p] *n* mantenimiento

upon [ə'pɒn] *prep* sobre

upper ['ʌpə*] *adj* superior, de arriba ♦ *n (of shoe: also: ~s)* empeine *m*; **~-class** *adj* de clase alta; **~ hand** *n*: **to have the ~ hand** tener la sartén por el mango; **~most** *adj* el más alto; **what was ~most in my mind** lo que me preocupaba más

upright ['ʌpraɪt] *adj* derecho; *(vertical)* vertical; *(fig)* honrado

uprising ['ʌpraɪzɪŋ] *n* sublevación *f*

uproar ['ʌprɔː*] *n* escándalo

uproot [ʌp'ru:t] *vt (also fig)* desarraigar

upset [*n* 'ʌpset, *vb, adj* ʌp'set] *n (to plan etc)* revés *m*, contratiempo; *(MED)* trastorno ♦ *(irreg)* *vt (glass etc)* volcar; *(plan)* alterar; *(person)* molestar, disgustar ♦ *adj* molesto, disgustado; *(stomach)* revuelto

upshot ['ʌpʃɒt] *n* resultado

upside-down *adv* al revés; **to turn a place ~** *(fig)* revolverlo todo

upstairs [ʌp'steəz] *adv* arriba ♦ *adj (room)* de arriba ♦ *n* el piso superior

upstart ['ʌpstɑːt] *n* advenedizo/a

upstream [ʌp'stri:m] *adv* río arriba

uptake ['ʌpteɪk] *n*: **to be quick/slow on the ~** ser muy listo/torpe

uptight [ʌp'taɪt] *adj* tenso, nervioso

up-to-date *adj* al día

upturn ['ʌptɜːn] *n (in luck)* mejora; *(COMM: in market)* resurgimiento económico

upward ['ʌpwəd] *adj* ascendente; **~(s)** *adv* hacia arriba; *(more than)*: **~(s) of** más de

urban ['ɜːbən] *adj* urbano

urchin ['ɜːtʃɪn] *n* pilluelo, golfillo

urge [ɜːdʒ] *n (desire)* deseo ♦ *vt*: **to ~ sb to do sth** animar a uno a hacer algo

urgent ['ɜːdʒənt] *adj* urgente; *(voice)*

perentorio

urinate ['juərɪneɪt] *vi* orinar

urine ['juərɪn] *n* orina, orines *mpl*

urn [ə:n] *n* urna; (*also:* **tea ~**) cacharro metálico grande para hacer té

Uruguay ['juerəgwaɪ] *n* (el) Uruguay; **~an** [-'gwaɪən] *adj, n* uruguayo/a *m/f*

US *n abbr* (= *United States*) EE. UU.

us [ʌs] *pron* nos; (*after prep*) nosotros/as; *see also* **me**

USA *n abbr* (= *United States (of America)*) EE. UU.

usage ['ju:zɪdʒ] *n* (LING) uso

use [*n* ju:s, *vb* ju:z] *n* uso, empleo; (*usefulness*) utilidad *f* ♦ *vt* usar, emplear; **she ~d to do it** (ella) solía *or* acostumbraba hacerlo; **in ~** en uso; **out of ~** en desuso; **to be of ~** servir; **it's no ~** (*pointless*) es inútil; (*not useful*) no sirve; **to be ~d to** estar acostumbrado a, acostumbrar; **~ up** *vt* (*food*) consumir; (*money*) gastar; **~d** *adj* (*car*) usado; **~ful** *adj* útil; **~fulness** *n* utilidad *f*; **~less** *adj* (*unusable*) inservible; (*pointless*) inútil; (*person*) inepto; **~r** *n* usuario/a; **~r-friendly** *adj* (*computer*) amistoso

usher ['ʌʃə*] *n* (*at wedding*) ujier *m*; **~ette** [-'ret] *n* (*in cinema*) acomodadora

USSR *n* (HIST): **the ~** la URSS

usual ['ju:ʒuəl] *adj* normal, corriente; **as ~** como de costumbre; **~ly** *adv* normalmente

utensil [ju:'tensl] *n* utensilio; **kitchen ~s** batería de cocina

uterus ['ju:tərəs] *n* útero

utility [ju:'tɪlɪtɪ] *n* utilidad *f*; (*public ~*) (empresa de) servicio público; **~ room** *n* ofis *m*

utilize ['ju:tɪlaɪz] *vt* utilizar

utmost ['ʌtməust] *adj* mayor ♦ *n*: **to do one's ~** hacer todo lo posible

utter ['ʌtə*] *adj* total, completo ♦ *vt* pronunciar, proferir; **~ly** *adv* completamente, totalmente

U-turn ['ju:'tə:n] *n* viraje *m* en redondo

V, v

v. *abbr* = **verse**; **versus**; (= *volt*) v; (= *vide*) véase

vacancy ['veɪkənsɪ] *n* (BRIT: *job*) vacante *f*; (*room*) habitación *f* libre; **"no vacancies"** "completo"

vacant ['veɪkənt] *adj* desocupado, libre; (*expression*) distraído

vacate [və'keɪt] *vt* (*house, room*) desocupar; (*job*) dejar (vacante)

vacation [və'keɪʃən] *n* vacaciones *fpl*

vaccinate ['væksɪneɪt] *vt* vacunar

vaccine ['væksi:n] *n* vacuna

vacuum ['vækjum] *n* vacío; **~ cleaner** *n* aspiradora; **~flask** (BRIT) *n* termo; **~-packed** *adj* empaquetado al vacío

vagina [və'dʒaɪnə] *n* vagina

vagrant ['veɪgrnt] *n* vagabundo/a

vague [veɪg] *adj* vago; (*memory*) borroso; (*ambiguous*) impreciso; (*person: absent-minded*) distraído; (: *evasive*): **to be ~** no decir las cosas claramente; **~ly** *adv* vagamente; distraídamente; con evasivas

vain [veɪn] *adj* (*conceited*) presumido; (*useless*) vano, inútil; **in ~** en vano

valentine ['væləntaɪn] *n* (*also:* **~ card**) tarjeta del Día de los Enamorados

valet ['væleɪ] *n* ayuda *m* de cámara

valid ['vælɪd] *adj* válido; (*ticket*) valedero; (*law*) vigente

valley ['vælɪ] *n* valle *m*

valuable ['væljuəbl] *adj* (*jewel*) de valor; (*time*) valioso; **~s** *npl* objetos *mpl* de valor

valuation [vælju'eɪʃən] *n* tasación *f*, valuación *f*; (*judgement of quality*) valoración *f*

value ['vælju:] *n* valor *m*; (*importance*) importancia ♦ *vt* (*fix price of*) tasar, valorar; (*esteem*) apreciar; **~s** *npl* (*principles*) principios *mpl*; **~ added tax** (BRIT) *n* impuesto sobre el valor añadido; **~d** *adj* (*appreciated*) apreciado

valve [vælv] *n* válvula

van [væn] n (AUT) furgoneta (SP), camioneta (AM)

vandal ['vændl] n vándalo/a; **~ism** n vandalismo; **~ize** vt dañar, destruir

vanilla [və'nɪlə] n vainilla

vanish ['vænɪʃ] vi desaparecer

vanity ['vænɪtɪ] n vanidad f

vantage point ['vɑːntɪdʒ-] n (for views) punto panorámico

vapour ['veɪpə*] (US **vapor**) n vapor m; (on breath, window) vaho

variable ['veərɪəbl] adj variable

variation [veərɪ'eɪʃən] n variación f

varicose ['værɪkəus] adj: **~ veins** varices fpl

varied ['veərɪd] adj variado

variety [və'raɪətɪ] n (diversity) diversidad f; (type) variedad f; **~ show** n espectáculo de variedades

various ['veərɪəs] adj (several: people) varios/as; (reasons) diversos/as

varnish ['vɑːnɪʃ] n barniz m; (nail ~) esmalte m ♦ vt barnizar; (nails) pintar (con esmalte)

vary ['veərɪ] vt variar; (change) cambiar ♦ vi variar

vase [vɑːz] n florero

Vaseline ® ['væsɪliːn] n vaselina ®

vast [vɑːst] adj enorme

VAT [væt] (BRIT) n abbr (= value added tax) IVA m

vat [væt] n tina, tinaja

Vatican ['vætɪkən] n: **the ~** el Vaticano

vault [vɔːlt] n (of roof) bóveda; (tomb) panteón m; (in bank) cámara acorazada ♦ vt (also: **~ over**) saltar (por encima de)

vaunted ['vɔːntɪd] adj: **much ~** cacareado, alardeado

VCR n abbr = **video cassette recorder**

VD n abbr = **venereal disease**

VDU n abbr (= visual display unit) UPV f

veal [viːl] n ternera

veer [vɪə*] vi (vehicle) virar; (wind) girar

vegan ['viːgən] n vegetariano/a estricto/a, vegetaliano/a

vegeburger ['vedʒɪbəːgə*] n hamburguesa vegetal

vegetable ['vedʒtəbl] n (BOT) vegetal m; (edible plant) legumbre f, hortaliza ♦ adj vegetal; **~s** npl (cooked) verduras fpl

vegetarian [vedʒɪ'teərɪən] adj, n vegetariano/a m/f

vehement ['viːmənt] adj vehemente, apasionado

vehicle ['viːɪkl] n vehículo; (fig) medio

veil [veɪl] n velo ♦ vt velar; **~ed** adj (fig) velado

vein [veɪn] n vena; (of ore etc) veta

velocity [vɪ'lɔsɪtɪ] n velocidad f

velvet ['velvɪt] n terciopelo

vending machine ['vendɪŋ-] n distribuidor m automático

veneer [və'nɪə*] n chapa, enchapado; (fig) barniz m

venereal disease [vɪ'nɪərɪəl-] n enfermedad f venérea

Venetian blind [vɪ'niːʃən-] n persiana

Venezuela [venɪ'zweɪlə] n Venezuela; **~n** adj, n venezolano/a m/f

vengeance ['vendʒəns] n venganza; **with a ~** (fig) con creces

venison ['venɪsn] n carne f de venado

venom ['venəm] n veneno; (bitterness) odio; **~ous** adj venenoso; lleno de odio

vent [vent] n (in jacket) respiradero; (in wall) rejilla (de ventilación) ♦ vt (fig: feelings) desahogar

ventilator ['ventɪleɪtə*] n ventilador m

venture ['ventʃə*] n empresa ♦ vt (opinion) ofrecer ♦ vi arriesgarse, lanzarse; **business ~** empresa comercial

venue ['venjuː] n lugar m

veranda(h) [və'rændə] n terraza

verb [vəːb] n verbo; **~al** adj verbal

verbatim [vəː'beɪtɪm] adj, adv palabra por palabra

verdict ['vəːdɪkt] n veredicto, fallo; (fig) opinión f, juicio

verge [vəːdʒ] (BRIT) n borde m; **"soft ~s"** (AUT) "arcén m no asfaltado"; **to be on the ~ of doing sth** estar a punto de hacer algo; **~ on** vt fus rayar en

verify ['verɪfaɪ] vt comprobar, verificar

vermin ['vəːmɪn] npl (animals) alimañas

fpl; (*insects, fig*) parásitos *mpl*

vermouth ['vɜːməθ] *n* vermut *m*

versatile ['vɜːsətaɪl] *adj* (*person*) polifacético; (*machine, tool etc*) versátil

verse [vɜːs] *n* poesía; (*stanza*) estrofa; (*in bible*) versículo

version ['vɜːʃən] *n* versión *f*

versus ['vɜːsəs] *prep* contra

vertebra ['vɜːtɪbrə] (*pl* **~e**) *n* vértebra

vertical ['vɜːtɪkl] *adj* vertical

verve [vɜːv] *n* brío

very ['verɪ] *adv* muy ♦ *adj*: **the ~ book which** el mismo libro que; **the ~ last** el último de todos; **at the ~ least** al menos; **~ much** muchísimo

vessel ['vesl] *n* (*ship*) barco; (*container*) vasija; *see* **blood**

vest [vest] *n* (*BRIT*) camiseta; (*US: waistcoat*) chaleco; **~ed interests** *npl* (*COMM*) intereses *mpl* creados

vet [vet] *vt* (*candidate*) investigar ♦ *n abbr* (*BRIT*) = **veterinary surgeon**

veteran ['vetərn] *n* veterano

veterinary surgeon ['vetrɪnərɪ] (*US* **veterinarian**) *n* veterinario/a *m/f*

veto ['viːtəu] (*pl* **~es**) *n* veto ♦ *vt* prohibir, poner el veto a

vex [veks] *vt* fastidiar; **~ed** *adj* (*question*) controvertido

VHF *abbr* (= *very high frequency*) muy alta frecuencia

via ['vaɪə] *prep* por, por medio de

vibrant ['vaɪbrənt] *adj* (*lively*) animado; (*bright*) vivo; (*voice*) vibrante

vibrate [vaɪ'breɪt] *vi* vibrar

vicar ['vɪkə*] *n* párroco (de la Iglesia Anglicana); **~age** *n* parroquia

vice [vaɪs] *n* (*evil*) vicio; (*TECH*) torno de banco

vice- [vaɪs] *prefix* vice-; **~-chairman** *n* vicepresidente *m*

vice squad *n* brigada antivicio

vice versa ['vaɪsɪ'vɜːsə] *adv* viceversa

vicinity [vɪ'sɪnɪtɪ] *n*: **in the ~ (of)** cercano (a)

vicious ['vɪʃəs] *adj* (*attack*) violento; (*words*) cruel; (*horse, dog*) resabido; **~**

circle *n* círculo vicioso

victim ['vɪktɪm] *n* víctima

victor ['vɪktə*] *n* vencedor(a) *m/f*

victory ['vɪktərɪ] *n* victoria

video ['vɪdɪəu] *cpd* video ♦ *n* (~ *film*) videofilm *m*; (*also:* ~ **cassette**) videocassette *f*; (*also:* ~ **cassette recorder**) magnetoscopio; ~ **game** *n* videojuego; ~ **tape** *n* cinta de vídeo

vie [vaɪ] *vi*: **to ~ (with sb for sth)** competir (con uno por algo)

Vienna [vɪ'enə] *n* Viena

Vietnam [vjet'næm] *n* Vietnam *m*; **~ese** [-nə'miːz] *n inv, adj* vietnamita *m/f*

view [vjuː] *n* vista; (*outlook*) perspectiva; (*opinion*) opinión *f*, criterio ♦ *vt* (*look at*) mirar; (*fig*) considerar; **on ~** (*in museum etc*) expuesto; **in full ~ (of)** en plena vista (de); **in ~ of the weather/the fact that** en vista del tiempo/del hecho de que; **in my ~** en mi opinión; **~er** *n* espectador(a) *m/f*; (*TV*) telespectador(a) *m/f*; **~finder** *n* visor *m* de imagen; **~point** *n* (*attitude*) punto de vista; (*place*) mirador *m*

vigour ['vɪgə*] (*US* **vigor**) *n* energía, vigor *m*

vile [vaɪl] *adj* vil, infame; (*smell*) asqueroso; (*temper*) endemoniado

villa ['vɪlə] *n* (*country house*) casa de campo; (*suburban house*) chalet *m*

village ['vɪlɪdʒ] *n* aldea; **~r** *n* aldeano/a

villain ['vɪlən] *n* (*scoundrel*) malvado/a; (*in novel*) malo; (*BRIT: criminal*) maleante *m/f*

vindicate ['vɪndɪkeɪt] *vt* vindicar, justificar

vindictive [vɪn'dɪktɪv] *adj* vengativo

vine [vaɪn] *n* vid *f*

vinegar ['vɪnɪgə*] *n* vinagre *m*

vineyard ['vɪnjɑːd] *n* viña, viñedo

vintage ['vɪntɪdʒ] *n* (*year*) vendimia, cosecha ♦ *cpd* de época; ~ **wine** *n* vino añejo

vinyl ['vaɪnl] *n* vinilo

viola [vɪ'əulə] *n* (*MUS*) viola

violate ['vaɪəleɪt] *vt* violar

violence ['vaɪələns] *n* violencia

violent ['vaɪələnt] *adj* violento; (*intense*) intenso

violet ['vaɪələt] adj violado, violeta ♦ n (plant) violeta

violin [vaɪə'lɪn] n violín m; ~ist n violinista m/f

VIP n abbr (= very important person) VIP m

virgin ['vɜːdʒɪn] n virgen f

Virgo ['vɜːgəu] n Virgo

virtually ['vɜːtjuəlɪ] adv prácticamente

virtual reality ['vɜːtjuəl-] n (COMPUT) mundo or realidad f virtual

virtue ['vɜːtjuː] n virtud f; (advantage) ventaja; by ~ of en virtud de

virtuous ['vɜːtjuəs] adj virtuoso

virus ['vaɪərəs] n (also: COMPUT) virus m

visa ['viːzə] n visado (SP), visa (AM)

visible ['vɪzəbl] adj visible

vision ['vɪʒən] n (sight) vista; (foresight, in dream) visión f

visit ['vɪzɪt] n visita ♦ vt (person: US: also: ~ with) visitar, hacer una visita a; (place) ir a, (ira) conocer; ~ing hours npl (in hospital etc) horas fpl de visita; ~or n (in museum) visitante m/f; (invited to house) visita; (tourist) turista m/f

visor ['vaɪzə*] n visera

visual ['vɪzjuəl] adj visual; ~ aid n medio visual; ~ display unit n unidad f de presentación visual; ~ize vt imaginarse

vital ['vaɪtl] adj (essential) esencial, imprescindible; (dynamic) dinámico; (organ) vital; ~ly adv: ~ly important de primera importancia; ~ statistics npl (fig) medidas fpl vitales

vitamin ['vɪtəmɪn] n vitamina

vivacious [vɪ'veɪʃəs] adj vivaz, alegre

vivid ['vɪvɪd] adj (account) gráfico; (light) intenso; (imagination, memory) vivo; ~ly adv gráficamente; (remember) como si fuera hoy

V-neck ['viːnɛk] n cuello de pico

vocabulary [vəu'kæbjulərɪ] n vocabulario

vocal ['vəukl] adj vocal; (articulate) elocuente; ~ cords npl cuerdas fpl vocales

vocation [vəu'keɪʃən] n vocación f; ~al adj profesional

vodka ['vɔdkə] n vodka m

vogue [vəug] n: in ~ en boga, de moda

voice [vɔɪs] n voz f ♦ vt expresar; ~ mail n fonobuzón m

void [vɔɪd] n vacío m; (hole) hueco ♦ adj (invalid) nulo, inválido; (empty): ~ of carente or desprovisto de

volatile ['vɔlətaɪl] adj (situation) inestable; (person) voluble; (liquid) volátil

volcano [vɔl'keɪnəu] (pl ~es) n volcán m

volition [və'lɪʃən] n: of one's own ~ de su propia voluntad

volley ['vɔlɪ] n (of gunfire) descarga; (of stones etc) lluvia; (fig) torrente m; (TENNIS etc) volea; ~ball n vol(e)ibol m

volt [vəult] n voltio m; ~age n voltaje m

volume ['vɔljuːm] n (gen) volumen m; (book) tomo

voluntary ['vɔləntərɪ] adj voluntario

volunteer [vɔlən'tɪə*] n voluntario/a ♦ vt (information) ofrecer ♦ vi ofrecerse (de voluntario); to ~ to do ofrecerse a hacer

vomit ['vɔmɪt] n vómito ♦ vt, vi vomitar

vote [vəut] n voto; (votes cast) votación f; (right to ~) derecho de votar; (franchise) sufragio ♦ vt (chairman) elegir; (propose): to ~ that proponer que ♦ vi votar, ir a votar; ~ of thanks voto de gracias; ~r n votante m/f; voting n votación f

vouch [vautʃ] to ~ for vt fus garantizar, responder de

voucher ['vautʃə*] n (for meal, petrol) vale m

vow [vau] n voto ♦ vt: to ~ to do/that jurar hacer/que

vowel ['vauəl] n vocal f

voyage ['vɔɪdʒ] n viaje m

vulgar ['vʌlgə*] adj (rude) ordinario, grosero; (in bad taste) de mal gusto; ~ity [-'gærɪtɪ] n grosería; mal gusto

vulnerable ['vʌlnərəbl] adj vulnerable

vulture ['vʌltʃə*] n buitre m

W, w

wad [wɔd] *n* bolita; (*of banknotes etc*) fajo

waddle ['wɔdl] *vi* anadear

wade [weɪd] *vi*: **to ~ through** (*water*) vadear; (*fig: book*) leer con dificultad; **wading pool** (*US*) *n* piscina para niños

wafer ['weɪfə*] *n* galleta, barquillo

waffle ['wɔfl] *n* (*CULIN*) gofre *m* ♦ *vi* dar el rollo

waft [wɔft] *vt* llevar por el aire ♦ *vi* flotar

wag [wæg] *vt* menear, agitar ♦ *vi* moverse, menearse

wage [weɪdʒ] *n* (*also*: **~s**) sueldo, salario ♦ *vt*: **to ~ war** hacer la guerra; **~ earner** *n* asalariado/a; **~ packet** *n* sobre *m* de paga

wager ['weɪdʒə*] *n* apuesta

wag(g)on ['wægən] *n* (*horse-drawn*) carro; (*BRIT: RAIL*) vagón *m*

wail [weɪl] *n* gemido ♦ *vi* gemir

waist [weɪst] *n* cintura, talle *m*; **~coat** (*BRIT*) *n* chaleco; **~line** *n* talle *m*

wait [weɪt] *n* (*interval*) pausa ♦ *vi* esperar; **to lie in ~ for** acechar a; **I can't ~ to** (*fig*) estoy deseando; **to ~ for** esperar (a); **~ behind** *vi* quedarse; **~ on** *vt fus* servir a; **~er** *n* camarero; **~ing** *n*: **"no ~ing"** (*BRIT: AUT*) "prohibido estacionarse"; **~ing list** *n* lista de espera; **~ing room** *n* sala de espera; **~ress** *n* camarera

waive [weɪv] *vt* suspender

wake [weɪk] (*pt* **woke** *or* **waked**, *pp* **woken** *or* **waked**) *vt* (*also*: **~ up**) despertar ♦ *vi* (*also*: **~ up**) despertarse ♦ *n* (*for dead person*) vela, velatorio; (*NAUT*) estela; **waken** *vt*, *vi* = **wake**

Wales [weɪlz] *n* País *m* de Gales; **the Prince of ~** el príncipe de Gales

walk [wɔːk] *n* (*stroll*) paseo; (*hike*) excursión *f* a pie, caminata; (*gait*) paso, andar *m*; (*in park etc*) paseo, alameda ♦ *vi* andar, caminar; (*for pleasure, exercise*) pasear ♦ *vt* (*distance*) recorrer a pie, andar; (*dog*) pasear; **10 minutes' ~ from here** a 10 minutos de aquí andando; **people from all ~s of life** gente de todas las esferas; **~ out** *vi* (*workers*) declararse en huelga; **~ out on** (*inf*) *vt fus* abandonar; **~er** *n* (*person*) paseante *m/f*, caminante *m/f*; **~ie-talkie** ['wɔːkɪ'tɔːkɪ] *n* walkie-talkie *m*; **~ing** *n* el andar; **~ing shoes** *npl* zapatos *mpl* para andar; **~ing stick** *n* bastón *m*; **W~man** ® ['wɔːkmən] *n* Walkman ® *m*; **~out** *n* huelga; **~over** (*inf*) *n*: **it was a ~over** fue pan comido; **~way** *n* paseo

wall [wɔːl] *n* pared *f*; (*exterior*) muro; (*city ~ etc*) muralla; **~ed** *adj* amurallado; (*garden*) con tapia

wallet ['wɔlɪt] *n* cartera (*SP*), billetera (*AM*)

wallflower ['wɔːlflauə*] *n* alhelí *m*; **to be a ~** (*fig*) comer pavo

wallow ['wɔləu] *vi* revolcarse

wallpaper ['wɔːlpeɪpə*] *n* papel *m* pintado ♦ *vt* empapelar

walnut ['wɔːlnʌt] *n* nuez *f*; (*tree*) nogal *m*

walrus ['wɔːlrəs] (*pl* **~** *or* **~es**) *n* morsa

waltz [wɔːlts] *n* vals *m* ♦ *vi* bailar el vals

wand [wɔnd] *n* (*also*: **magic ~**) varita (mágica)

wander ['wɔndə*] *vi* (*person*) vagar; deambular; (*thoughts*) divagar ♦ *vt* recorrer, vagar por

wane [weɪn] *vi* menguar

wangle ['wæŋgl] (*BRIT: inf*) *vt* agenciarse

want [wɔnt] *vt* querer, desear; (*need*) necesitar ♦ *n*: **for ~ of** por falta de; **~s** *npl* (*needs*) necesidades *fpl*; **to ~ to do** querer hacer; **to ~ sb to do sth** querer que uno haga algo; **~ed** *adj* (*criminal*) buscado; **"~ed"** (*in advertisements*) "se busca"; **~ing** *adj*: **to be found ~ing** no estar a la altura de las circunstancias

WAP [wæp] *n abbr* (*COMPUT*: = *wireless application protocol*) WAP *f*

war [wɔː*] *n* guerra; **to make ~ (on)** (*also fig*) declarar la guerra (a)

ward [wɔːd] *n* (*in hospital*) sala; (*POL*) distrito electoral; (*LAW: child: also*: **~ of court**) pupilo/a; **~ off** *vt* (*blow*) desviar, parar; (*attack*) rechazar

warden ['wɔːdn] n (BRIT: of institution) director(a) m/f; (of park, game reserve) guardián/ana m/f; (BRIT: also: **traffic ~**) guardia m/f

warder ['wɔːdə*] (BRIT) n guardián/ana m/ f, carcelero/a

wardrobe ['wɔːdrəub] n armario, guardarropa, ropero (esp AM)

warehouse ['weəhaus] n almacén m, depósito

wares [weəz] npl mercancías fpl

warfare ['wɔːfeə*] n guerra

warhead ['wɔːhed] n cabeza armada

warily ['weərɪlɪ] adv con cautela, cautelosamente

warm [wɔːm] adj caliente; (thanks) efusivo; (clothes etc) abrigado; (welcome, day) caluroso; **it's ~** hace calor; **I'm ~** tengo calor; **~ up** vi (room) calentarse; (person) entrar en calor; (athlete) hacer ejercicios de calentamiento ♦ vt calentar; **~-hearted** adj afectuoso; **~ly** adv afectuosamente; **~th** n calor m

warn [wɔːn] vt avisar, advertir; **~ing** n aviso, advertencia; **~ing light** n luz f de advertencia; **~ing triangle** n (AUT) triángulo señalizador

warp [wɔːp] (in wood) combarse ♦ vt combar; (mind) pervertir

warrant ['wɔrnt] n autorización f; (LAW: to arrest) orden f de detención; (: to search) mandamiento de registro

warranty ['wɔrəntɪ] n garantía

warren ['wɔrən] n (of rabbits) madriguera; (fig) laberinto

warrior ['wɔrɪə*] n guerrero/a

Warsaw ['wɔːsɔː] n Varsovia

warship ['wɔːʃɪp] n buque m o barco de guerra

wart [wɔːt] n verruga

wartime ['wɔːtaɪm] n: **in ~** en tiempos de guerra, en la guerra

wary ['weərɪ] adj cauteloso

was [wɔz] pt of **be**

wash [wɔʃ] vt lavar ♦ vi lavarse; (sea etc): **to ~ against/over sth** llegar hasta/cubrir algo ♦ n (clothes etc) lavado; (of ship) estela; **to have a ~** lavarse; **~ away** vt (stain) quitar lavando; (subj: river etc) llevarse; **~ off** vi quitarse (al lavar); **~ up** vi (BRIT) fregar los platos; (US) lavarse; **~able** adj lavable; **~basin** (US **~bowl**) n lavabo; **~ cloth** (US) n manopla; **~er** n (TECH) arandela; **~ing** n (dirty) ropa sucia; (clean) colada; **~ing machine** n lavadora; **~ing powder** (BRIT) n detergente m (en polvo)

Washington ['wɔʃɪŋtən] n Washington m

wash: ~ing-up (BRIT) n fregado, platos mpl (para fregar); **~ing-up liquid** (BRIT) n líquido lavavajillas; **~-out** (inf) n fracaso; **~room** (US) n servicios mpl

wasn't ['wɔznt] = **was not**

wasp [wɔsp] n avispa

wastage ['weɪstɪdʒ] n desgaste m; (loss) pérdida

waste [weɪst] n derroche m, despilfarro; (of time) pérdida; (food) sobras fpl; (rubbish) basura, desperdicios mpl ♦ adj (material) de desecho; (left over) sobrante; (land) baldío, descampado ♦ vt malgastar, derrochar; (time) perder; (opportunity) desperdiciar; **~s** npl (area of land) tierras fpl baldías; **~ away** vi consumirse; **~ disposal unit** (BRIT) n triturador m de basura; **~ful** adj derrochador(a); (process) antieconómico; **~ ground** (BRIT) n terreno baldío; **~paper basket** n papelera; **~ pipe** n tubo de desagüe

watch [wɔtʃ] n (also: **wrist ~**) reloj m; (MIL: group of guards) centinela m; (act) vigilancia; (NAUT: spell of duty) guardia ♦ vt (look at) mirar, observar; (: match, programme) ver; (spy on, guard) vigilar; (be careful of) cuidarse de, tener cuidado de ♦ vi ver, mirar; (keep guard) montar guardia; **~ out** vi cuidarse, tener cuidado; **~dog** n perro guardián; (fig) persona u organismo encargado de asegurarse de que las empresas actúan dentro de la legalidad; **~ful** adj vigilante, sobre aviso; **~maker** n relojero/a; **~man** (irreg) n see **night**; **~ strap** n pulsera (de reloj)

water ['wɔːtə*] n agua ♦ vt (plant) regar ♦ vi (eyes) llorar; (mouth) hacerse la boca agua; ~ **down** vt (milk etc) aguar; (fig: story) dulcificar, diluir; ~ **closet** n wáter m; ~**colour** n acuarela; ~**cress** n berro; ~**fall** n cascada, salto de agua; ~ **heater** n calentador m de agua; ~**ing can** n regadera; ~ **lily** n nenúfar m; ~**line** n (NAUT) línea de flotación; ~**logged** adj (ground) inundado; ~ **main** n cañería del agua; ~**melon** n sandía; ~**proof** adj impermeable; ~**shed** n (GEO) cuenca; (fig) momento crítico; ~**skiing** n esquí m acuático; ~**tight** adj hermético; ~**way** n vía fluvial or navegable; ~**works** n central f depuradora; ~**y** adj (coffee etc) aguado; (eyes) lloroso

watt [wɔt] n vatio

wave [weɪv] n (of hand) señal f con la mano; (on water) ola; (RADIO, in hair) onda; (fig) oleada ♦ vi agitar la mano; (flag etc) ondear ♦ vt (handkerchief, gun) agitar; ~**length** n longitud f de onda

waver ['weɪvə*] vi (voice, love etc) flaquear; (person) vacilar

wavy ['weɪvɪ] adj ondulado

wax [wæks] n cera ♦ vt encerar ♦ vi (moon) crecer; ~ **paper** (US) n papel m apergaminado; ~**works** n museo de cera ♦ npl figuras fpl de cera

way [weɪ] n camino; (distance) trayecto, recorrido; (direction) dirección f, sentido; (manner) modo, manera; (habit) costumbre f; **which ~? – this ~** ¿por dónde?, ¿en qué dirección? — por aquí; **on the ~** (en route) en (el) camino; **to be on one's ~** estar en camino; **to be in the ~** bloquear el camino; (fig) estorbar; **to go out of one's ~ to do sth** desvivirse por hacer algo; **under ~** en marcha; **to lose one's ~** extraviarse; **in a ~** en cierto modo or sentido; **no ~!** (inf) ¡de eso nada!; **by the ~** ... a propósito ...; **"~ in"** (BRIT) "entrada"; **"~ out"** (BRIT) "salida"; **the ~ back** el camino de vuelta; **"give ~"** (BRIT: AUT) "ceda el paso"

waylay [weɪ'leɪ] (irreg) vt salir al paso a

wayward ['weɪwəd] adj díscolo

W.C. n (BRIT) wáter m

we [wiː] pl pron nosotros/as

weak [wiːk] adj débil, flojo; (tea etc) claro; ~**en** vi debilitarse; (give way) ceder ♦ vt debilitar; ~**ling** n debilucho/a; (morally) persona de poco carácter; ~**ness** n debilidad f; (fault) punto débil; **to have a ~ness for** tener debilidad por

wealth [welθ] n riqueza; (of details) abundancia; ~**y** adj rico

wean [wiːn] vt destetar

weapon ['wepən] n arma

wear [wɛə*] (pt **wore**, pp **worn**) n (use) uso; (deterioration through use) desgaste m; (clothing): **sports/baby~** ropa de deportes/de niños ♦ vt (clothes) llevar; (shoes) calzar; (damage: through use) gastar, usar ♦ vi (last) durar; (rub through etc) desgastarse; **evening ~** ropa de etiqueta; ~ **away** vt gastar ♦ vi desgastarse; ~ **down** vt gastar; (strength) agotar; ~ **off** vi (pain etc) pasar, desaparecer; ~ **out** vt desgastar; (person, strength) agotar; ~ **and tear** n desgaste m

weary ['wɪərɪ] adj cansado; (dispirited) abatido ♦ vi: **to ~ of** cansarse de

weasel ['wiːzl] n (ZOOL) comadreja

weather ['weðə*] n tiempo ♦ vt (storm, crisis) hacer frente a; **under the ~** (fig: ill) indispuesto, pachucho; ~-**beaten** adj (skin) curtido; (building) deteriorado por la intemperie; ~**cock** n veleta; ~ **forecast** n boletín m meteorológico; ~**man** (irreg: inf) n hombre m del tiempo; ~ **vane** n = ~**cock**

weave [wiːv] (pt **wove**, pp **woven**) vt (cloth) tejer; (fig) entretejer; ~**r** n tejedor(a) m/f; **weaving** n tejeduría

web [web] n (of spider) telaraña; (on duck's foot) membrana; (network) red f; **the (World Wide) W~** el or la Web

webcam ['webkæm] n webcam f

webcast ['webkɑːst] n (COMPUT) transmisión por Internet

website ['websaɪt] n sitio Web

wed [wed] (pt, pp **wedded**) vt casar ♦ vi casarse

we'd [wi:d] = we had; we would

wedding ['wedɪŋ] n boda, casamiento; **silver ~ (anniversary)** bodas fpl de plata; **~ day** n día m de la boda; **~ dress** n traje m de novia; **~ present** n regalo de boda; **~ ring** n alianza

wedge [wedʒ] n (of wood etc) cuña; (of cake) trozo ♦ vt acuñar; (push) apretar

Wednesday ['wednzdɪ] n miércoles m inv

wee [wi:] (Scottish) adj pequeñito

weed [wi:d] n mala hierba, maleza ♦ vt escardar, desherbar; **~killer** n herbicida m; **~y** adj (person) mequetréfico

week [wi:k] n semana; **a ~ today/on Friday** de hoy/del viernes en ocho días; **~day** n día m laborable; **~end** n fin de semana; **~ly** adv semanalmente, cada semana ♦ adj semanal ♦ n semanario

weep [wi:p] (pt, pp wept) vi, vt llorar; **~ing willow** n sauce m llorón

weigh [weɪ] vt, vi pesar; **to ~ anchor** levar anclas; **~ down** vt sobrecargar; (fig: with worry) agobiar; **~ up** vt sopesar

weight [weɪt] n peso; (metal ~) pesa; **to lose/put on ~** adelgazar/engordar; **~ing** n (allowance): **(London) ~ing** dietas (por residir en Londres); **~lifter** n levantador m de pesas; **~y** adj pesado; (matters) de relevancia o peso

weir [wɪə*] n presa

weird [wɪəd] adj raro, extraño

welcome ['welkəm] adj bienvenido ♦ n bienvenida ♦ vt dar la bienvenida a; (be glad of) alegrarse de; **thank you — you're ~** gracias — de nada

weld [weld] n soldadura ♦ vt soldar

welfare ['welfeə*] n bienestar m; (social aid) asistencia social; **~ state** n estado del bienestar

well [wel] n fuente f, pozo ♦ adv bien ♦ adj: **to be ~** estar bien (de salud) ♦ excl ¡vaya!, ¡bueno!; **as ~** también; **as ~ as** además de; **~ done!** ¡bien hecho!; **get ~ soon!** ¡que te mejores pronto!; **to do ~** (business) ir bien; (person) tener éxito; **~ up** vi (tears) saltar

we'll [wi:l] = we will; we shall

well: ~-behaved adj bueno; **~-being** n bienestar m; **~-built** adj (person) fornido; **~-deserved** adj merecido; **~-dressed** adj bien vestido; **~-groomed** adj de buena presencia; **~-heeled** (inf) adj (wealthy) rico

wellingtons ['welɪŋtənz] npl (also: **wellington boots**) botas fpl de goma

well: ~-known adj (person) conocido; **~-mannered** adj educado; **~-meaning** adj bienintencionado; **~-off** adj acomodado; **~-read** adj leído; **~-to-do** adj acomodado; **~-wisher** n admirador(a) m/f

Welsh [welʃ] adj galés/esa ♦ n (LING) galés m; **the ~** npl los galeses; **the ~ Assembly** el Parlamento galés; **~man** (irreg) n galés m; **~ rarebit** n pan m con queso tostado; **~woman** (irreg) n galesa

went [went] pt of go

wept [wept] pt, pp of weep

were [wə:*] pt of be

we're [wɪə*] = we are

weren't [wə:nt] = were not

west [west] n oeste m ♦ adj occidental, del oeste ♦ adv al or hacia el oeste; **the W~** el Oeste, el Occidente; **W~ Country** (BRIT) n: **the W~ Country** el suroeste de Inglaterra; **~erly** adj occidental; (wind) del oeste; **~ern** adj occidental ♦ n (CINEMA) película del oeste; **W~ Germany** n Alemania Occidental; **W~ Indian** adj, n antillano/a m/f; **W~ Indies** npl Antillas fpl; **~ward(s)** adv hacia el oeste

wet [wet] adj (damp) húmedo; (~ through) mojado; (rainy) lluvioso ♦ (BRIT) n (POL) conservador(a) m/f moderado/a; **to get ~** mojarse; **"~ paint"** "recién pintado"; **~suit** n traje m térmico

we've [wi:v] = we have

whack [wæk] vt dar un buen golpe a

whale [weɪl] n (ZOOL) ballena

wharf [wɔ:f] (pl wharves) n muelle m

──────────── KEYWORD ────────────

what [wɔt] adj 1 (in direct/indirect questions) qué; **~ size is he?** ¿qué talla usa?; **~ colour/shape is it?** ¿de qué

color/forma es?
2 (*in exclamations*): ~ **a mess!** ¡qué
desastre!; ~ **a fool I am!** ¡qué tonto soy!
♦ *pron* 1 (*interrogative*) qué; ~ **are you
doing?** ¿qué haces or estás haciendo?; ~
is happening? ¿qué pasa or está
pasando?; ~ **is it called?** ¿cómo se
llama?; ~ **about me?** ¿y yo qué?; ~ **about
doing ...?** ¿qué tal si hacemos ...?
2 (*relative*) lo que; **I saw ~ you did/was on
the table** vi lo que hiciste/había en la mesa
♦ *excl* (*disbelieving*) ¡cómo!; ~, **no coffee!**
¡que no hay café!

whatever [wɔt'ɛvə*] *adj*: ~ **book you
choose** cualquier libro que elijas ♦ *pron*:
do ~ is necessary haga lo que sea
necesario; ~ **happens** pase lo que pase;
no reason ~ ninguna razón sea la que
sea; **nothing ~** nada en absoluto
whatsoever [wɔtsəu'ɛvə*] *adj* = **whatever**

wheat [wi:t] *n* trigo
wheedle ['wi:dl] *vt*: **to ~ sb into doing
sth** engatusar a uno para que haga algo;
to ~ sth out of sb sonsacar algo a uno
wheel [wi:l] *n* rueda; (*AUT: also*: **steering
~**) volante *m*; (*NAUT*) timón *m* ♦ *vt* (*pram
etc*) empujar ♦ *vi* (*also*: ~ **round**) dar la
vuelta, girar; ~**barrow** *n* carretilla;
~**chair** *n* silla de ruedas; ~ **clamp** *n*
(*AUT*) cepo
wheeze [wi:z] *vi* resollar

KEYWORD

when [wɛn] *adv* cuando; ~ **did it happen?**
¿cuándo ocurrió?; **I know ~ it happened**
sé cuándo ocurrió
♦ *conj* 1 (*at, during, after the time that*)
cuando; **be careful ~ you cross the road**
ten cuidado al cruzar la calle; **that was ~
I needed you** fue entonces que te
necesité
2 (*on, at which*): **on the day ~ I met him**
el día en qué le conocí
3 (*whereas*) cuando

whenever [wɛn'ɛvə*] *conj* cuando; (*every
time that*) cada vez que ♦ *adv* cuando
sea
where [wɛə*] *adv* dónde ♦ *conj* donde;
this is ~ aquí es donde; ~**abouts** *adv*
dónde ♦ *n*: **nobody knows his ~abouts**
nadie conoce su paradero; ~**as** *conj* visto
que, mientras; ~**by** *pron* por lo cual;
wherever [-'ɛvə*] *conj* dondequiera que;
(*interrogative*) dónde; ~**withal** *n* recursos
mpl
whether ['wɛðə*] *conj* si; **I don't know ~
to accept or not** no sé si aceptar o no; ~
you go or not vayas o no vayas

KEYWORD

which [wɪtʃ] *adj* 1 (*interrogative: direct,
indirect*) qué; ~ **picture(s) do you want?**
¿qué cuadro(s) quieres?; ~ **one?** ¿cuál?
2: **in ~ case** en cuyo caso; **we got there
at 8 pm, by ~ time the cinema was full**
llegamos allí a las 8, cuando el cine
estaba lleno
♦ *pron* 1 (*interrogative*) cual; **I don't mind
~** el/la que sea
2 (*relative: replacing noun*) que;
(: *replacing clause*) lo que; (: *after
preposition*) (el/la) que *etc*, el/la cual *etc*;
the apple ~ you ate/~ is on the table la
manzana que comiste/que está en la
mesa; **the chair on ~ you are sitting** la
silla en la que estás sentado; **he said he
knew, ~ is true/I feared** dijo que lo
sabía, lo cual *or* lo que es cierto/me temía

whichever [wɪtʃ'ɛvə*] *adj*: **take ~ book
you prefer** coja (*SP*) el libro que prefiera;
~ **book you take** cualquier libro que coja
while [waɪl] *n* rato, momento ♦ *conj*
mientras; (*although*) aunque; **for a ~**
durante algún tiempo; ~ **away** *vt* pasar
whim [wɪm] *n* capricho
whimper ['wɪmpə*] *n* sollozo ♦ *vi*
lloriquear
whimsical ['wɪmzɪkl] *adj* (*person*)
caprichoso; (*look*) juguetón/ona
whine [waɪn] *n* (*of pain*) gemido; (*of*

engine) zumbido; (*of siren*) aullido ♦ *vi*
gemir; zumbar; (*fig: complain*) gimotear
whip [wɪp] *n* látigo; (*POL: person*)
*encargado de la disciplina partidaria en
el parlamento* ♦ *vt* azotar; (*CULIN*) batir;
(*move quickly*): **to ~ sth out/off** sacar/
quitar algo de un tirón; **~ped cream** *n*
nata *or* crema montada; **~-round** (*BRIT*)
n colecta
whirl [wɜːl] *vt* hacer girar, dar vueltas a
♦ *vi* girar, dar vueltas; (*leaves etc*)
arremolinarse; **~pool** *n* remolino; **~wind**
n torbellino
whirr [wɜː*] *vi* zumbar
whisk [wɪsk] *n* (*CULIN*) batidor *m* ♦ *vt*
(*CULIN*) batir; **to ~ sb away** *or* **off** llevar
volando a uno
whiskers ['wɪskəz] *npl* (*of animal*) bigotes
mpl; (*of man*) patillas *fpl*
whiskey ['wɪskɪ] (*US, Ireland*) *n* = **whisky**
whisky ['wɪskɪ] *n* whisky *m*
whisper ['wɪspə*] *n* susurro ♦ *vi, vt*
susurrar
whistle ['wɪsl] *n* (*sound*) silbido; (*object*)
silbato ♦ *vi* silbar
white [waɪt] *adj* blanco; (*pale*) pálido ♦ *n*
blanco; (*of egg*) clara; **~ coffee** (*BRIT*) *n*
café *m* con leche; **~-collar worker** *n*
oficinista *m/f*; **~ elephant** *n* (*fig*) maula;
~ lie *n* mentirilla; **~ paper** *n* (*POL*) libro
rojo; **~wash** *n* (*paint*) jalbegue *m*, cal *f*
♦ *vt* (*also fig*) blanquear
whiting ['waɪtɪŋ] *n inv* (*fish*) pescadilla
Whitsun ['wɪtsn] *n* pentecostés *m*
whizz [wɪz] *vi*: **to ~ past** *or* **by** pasar a
toda velocidad; **~ kid** (*inf*) *n* prodigio

KEYWORD

who [huː] *pron* **1** (*interrogative*) quién; **~ is
it?, ~'s there?** ¿quién es?; **~ are you
looking for?** ¿a quién buscas?; **I told her
~ I was** le dije quién era yo
2 (*relative*) que; **the man/woman ~
spoke to me** el hombre/la mujer que
habló conmigo; **those ~ can swim** los
que saben *or* sepan nadar

whodun(n)it [huːˈdʌnɪt] (*inf*) *n* novela
policíaca
whoever [huːˈɛvə*] *pron*: **~ finds it**
cualquiera *or* quienquiera que lo
encuentre; **ask ~ you like** pregunta a
quien quieras; **~ he marries** no importa
con quién se case
whole [həʊl] *adj* (*entire*) todo, entero; (*not
broken*) intacto ♦ *n* todo; (*all*): **the ~ of
the town** toda la ciudad, la ciudad entera
♦ *n* (*total*) total *m*; (*sum*) conjunto; **on
the ~, as a ~** en general; **~food(s)** *n(pl)*
alimento(s) *m(pl)* integral(es); **~hearted**
adj sincero, cordial; **~meal** *adj* integral;
~sale *n* venta al por mayor ♦ *adj* al por
mayor; (*fig: destruction*) sistemático;
~saler *n* mayorista *m/f*; **~some** *adj*
sano; **~wheat** *adj* = **~meal**; **wholly** *adv*
totalmente, enteramente

KEYWORD

whom [huːm] *pron* **1** (*interrogative*): **~ did
you see?** ¿a quién viste?; **to ~ did you
give it?** ¿a quién se lo diste?; **tell me
from ~ you received it** dígame de quién
lo recibí
2 (*relative*) que; **to ~** a quien(es); **of ~** de
quien(es), del/de la que *etc*; **the man ~ I
saw/to ~ I wrote** el hombre que vi/a
quien escribí; **the lady about/with ~ I
was talking** la señora de (la) que/con
quien *or* (la) que hablaba

whooping cough ['huːpɪŋ-] *n* tos *f*
ferina
whore [hɔː*] (*inf: pej*) *n* puta

KEYWORD

whose [huːz] *adj* **1** (*possessive:
interrogative*): **~ book is this?, ~ is this
book?** ¿de quién es este libro?; **~ pencil
have you taken?** ¿de quién es el lápiz
que has cogido?; **~ daughter are you?**
¿de quién eres hija?
2 (*possessive: relative*) cuyo/a, *pl* cuyos/as;
the man ~ son you rescued el hombre
cuyo hijo rescataste; **those ~ passports I**

have aquellas personas cuyos pasaportes tengo; **the woman ~ car was stolen** la mujer a quien le robaron el coche
♦ *pron* de quién; **~ is this?** ¿de quién es esto?; **I know ~ it is** sé de quién es

---

why [waɪ] *adv* por qué; **~ not?** ¿por qué no?; **~ not do it now?** ¿por qué no lo haces (*or* hacemos *etc*) ahora?
♦ *conj*: **I wonder ~ he said that** me pregunto por qué dijo eso; **that's not ~ I'm here** no es por eso (por lo) que estoy aquí; **the reason ~** la razón por la que
♦ *excl* (*expressing surprise, shock, annoyance*) ¡hombre!, ¡vaya! (*explaining*): **~, it's you!** ¡hombre, eres tú!; **~, that's impossible!** ¡pero sí eso es imposible!

---

wicked ['wɪkɪd] *adj* malvado, cruel
wicket ['wɪkɪt] *n* (CRICKET: *stumps*) palos *mpl*; (: *grass area*) terreno de juego
wide [waɪd] *adj* ancho; (*area, knowledge*) vasto, grande; (*choice*) amplio ♦ *adv*: **to open ~** abrir de par en par; **to shoot ~** errar el tiro; **~-angle lens** *n* objetivo de gran angular; **~-awake** *adj* bien despierto; **~ly** *adv* (*travelled*) mucho; (*spaced*) muy; **it is ~ly believed/known that ...** mucha gente piensa/sabe que ...; **~n** *vt* ensanchar; (*experience*) ampliar ♦ *vi* ensancharse; **~ open** *adj* abierto de par en par; **~spread** *adj* extendido, general
widow ['wɪdəʊ] *n* viuda; **~ed** *adj* viudo; **~er** *n* viudo
width [wɪdθ] *n* anchura; (*of cloth*) ancho
wield [wiːld] *vt* (*sword*) blandir; (*power*) ejercer
wife [waɪf] (*pl* **wives**) *n* mujer *f*, esposa
wig [wɪg] *n* peluca
wiggle ['wɪgl] *vt* menear
wild [waɪld] *adj* (*animal*) salvaje; (*plant*) silvestre; (*person*) furioso, violento; (*idea*) descabellado; (*rough: sea*) bravo; (: *land*) agreste; (: *weather*) muy revuelto; **~s** *npl*

regiones *fpl* salvajes, tierras *fpl* vírgenes; **~erness** ['wɪldənɪs] *n* desierto; **~life** *n* fauna; **~ly** *adv* (*behave*) locamente; (*lash out*) a diestro y siniestro; (*guess*) a lo loco; (*happy*) a más no poder
wilful ['wɪlfʊl] (*US* **willful**) *adj* (*action*) deliberado; (*obstinate*) testarudo

---

will [wɪl] *aux vb* 1 (*forming future tense*): **I ~ finish it tomorrow** lo terminaré *or* voy a terminar mañana; **I ~ have finished it by tomorrow** lo habré terminado para mañana; **~ you do it? – yes I ~/no I won't** ¿lo harás? — sí/no
2 (*in conjectures, predictions*): **he ~** *or* **he'll be there by now** ya habrá *or* debe (de) haber llegado; **that ~ be the postman** será *or* debe ser el cartero
3 (*in commands, requests, offers*): **~ you be quiet!** ¿quieres callarte?; **~ you help me?** ¿quieres ayudarme?; **~ you have a cup of tea?** ¿te apetece un té?; **I won't put up with it!** ¡no lo soporto!
♦ *vt* (*pt, pp* **willed**): **to ~ sb to do sth** desear que alguien haga algo; **he ~ed himself to go on** con gran fuerza de voluntad, continuó
♦ *n* voluntad *f*; (*testament*) testamento

---

willing ['wɪlɪŋ] *adj* (*with goodwill*) de buena voluntad; (*enthusiastic*) entusiasta; **he's ~ to do it** está dispuesto a hacerlo; **~ly** *adv* con mucho gusto; **~ness** *n* buena voluntad
willow ['wɪləʊ] *n* sauce *m*
willpower ['wɪlpaʊə*] *n* fuerza de voluntad
willy-nilly [wɪlɪ'nɪlɪ] *adv* quiérase o no
wilt [wɪlt] *vi* marchitarse
win [wɪn] (*pt, pp* **won**) *n* victoria, triunfo
♦ *vt* ganar; (*obtain*) conseguir, lograr ♦ *vi* ganar; **~ over** *vt* convencer a; **~ round** (*BRIT*) *vt* = **~ over**
wince [wɪns] *vi* encogerse
winch [wɪntʃ] *n* torno
wind[1] [wɪnd] *n* viento; (*MED*) gases *mpl*

♦ vt (*take breath away from*) dejar sin aliento a

wind² [waɪnd] (*pt, pp* **wound**) vt enrollar; (*wrap*) envolver; (*clock, toy*) dar cuerda a ♦ vi (*road, river*) serpentear; ~ **up** vt (*clock*) dar cuerda a; (*debate, meeting*) concluir, terminar

windfall [ˈwɪndfɔːl] n golpe m de suerte

winding [ˈwaɪndɪŋ] adj (*road*) tortuoso; (*staircase*) de caracol

wind instrument [wɪnd-] n (*MUS*) instrumento de viento

windmill [ˈwɪndmɪl] n molino de viento

window [ˈwɪndəu] n ventana; (*in car, train*) ventanilla; (*in shop etc*) escaparate m (*SP*), vitrina (*AM*); ~ **box** n jardinera de ventana; ~ **cleaner** n (*person*) limpiador m de cristales; ~ **ledge** n alféizar m, repisa; ~ **pane** n cristal m; ~ **seat** n asiento junto a la ventana; ~-**shopping** n: **to go ~-shopping** ir de escaparates; ~**sill** n alféizar m, repisa

windpipe [ˈwɪndpaɪp] n tráquea

wind power n energía eólica

windscreen [ˈwɪndskriːn] (*US* **windshield**) n parabrisas m inv; ~ **washer** n lavaparabrisas m inv; ~ **wiper** n limpiaparabrisas m inv

windswept [ˈwɪndswept] adj azotado por el viento

windy [ˈwɪndɪ] adj de mucho viento; **it's ~** hace viento

wine [waɪn] n vino; ~ **bar** n enoteca; ~ **cellar** n bodega; ~ **glass** n copa (para vino); ~ **list** n lista de vinos; ~ **waiter** n escanciador m

wing [wɪŋ] n ala; (*AUT*) aleta; ~**s** npl (*THEATRE*) bastidores mpl; ~**er** n (*SPORT*) extremo m

wink [wɪŋk] n guiño, pestañeo ♦ vi guiñar, pestañear

winner [ˈwɪnə*] n ganador(a) m/f

winning [ˈwɪnɪŋ] adj (*team*) ganador(a); (*goal*) decisivo; (*smile*) encantador(a); ~**s** npl ganancias fpl

winter [ˈwɪntə*] n invierno ♦ vi invernar; **wintry** [ˈwɪntrɪ] adj invernal

wipe [waɪp] n: **to give sth a ~** pasar un trapo sobre algo ♦ vt limpiar; (*tape*) borrar; ~ **off** vt limpiar con un trapo; (*remove*) quitar; ~ **out** vt (*debt*) liquidar; (*memory*) borrar; (*destroy*) destruir; ~ **up** vt limpiar

wire [ˈwaɪə*] n alambre m; (*ELEC*) cable m (eléctrico); (*TEL*) telegrama m ♦ vt (*house*) poner la instalación eléctrica en; (*also:* ~ **up**) conectar; (*person: telegram*) telegrafiar

wireless [ˈwaɪəlɪs] (*BRIT*) n radio f

wiring [ˈwaɪərɪŋ] n instalación f eléctrica

wiry [ˈwaɪərɪ] adj (*person*) enjuto y fuerte; (*hair*) crespo

wisdom [ˈwɪzdəm] n sabiduría, saber m; (*good sense*) cordura; ~ **tooth** n muela del juicio

wise [waɪz] adj sabio; (*sensible*) juicioso

...wise [waɪz] suffix: **time~** en cuanto a or respecto al tiempo

wish [wɪʃ] n deseo ♦ vt querer; **best ~es** (*on birthday etc*) felicidades fpl; **with best ~es** (*in letter*) saludos mpl, recuerdos mpl; **to ~ sb goodbye** despedirse de uno; **he ~ed me well** me deseó mucha suerte; **to ~ to do/sb to do sth** querer hacer/ que alguien haga algo; **to ~ for** desear; ~**ful** adj: **it's ~ful thinking** eso sería soñar

wisp [wɪsp] n mechón m; (*of smoke*) voluta

wistful [ˈwɪstful] adj pensativo

wit [wɪt] n ingenio, gracia; (*also:* ~**s**) inteligencia; (*person*) chistoso/a

witch [wɪtʃ] n bruja; ~**craft** n brujería; ~-**hunt** n (*fig*) caza de brujas

---

KEYWORD

---

with [wɪð, wɪθ] prep **1** (*accompanying*) con (con+mí, ti, sí = conmigo, contigo, consigo); **I was ~ him** estaba con él; **we stayed ~ friends** nos quedamos en casa de unos amigos; **I'm (not) ~ you** (*understand*) (no) te entiendo; **to be ~ it** (*inf: person: up-to-date*) estar al tanto; (*: alert*) ser despabilado

2 (*descriptive, indicating manner etc*) con; de; **a room ~ a view** una habitación con vistas; **the man ~ the grey hat/blue eyes** el hombre del sombrero gris/de los ojos azules; **red ~ anger** rojo de ira; **to shake ~ fear** temblar de miedo; **to fill sth ~ water** llenar algo de agua

withdraw [wɪθˈdrɔː] (*irreg*) *vt* retirar, sacar ♦ *vi* retirarse; **to ~ money (from the bank)** retirar fondos (del banco); **~al** *n* retirada; (*of money*) reintegro; **~al symptoms** *npl* (*MED*) síndrome *m* de abstinencia; **~n** *adj* (*person*) reservado, introvertido

wither [ˈwɪðəʳ] *vi* marchitarse

withhold [wɪθˈhəʊld] (*irreg*) *vt* (*money*) retener; (*decision*) aplazar; (*permission*) negar; (*information*) ocultar

within [wɪðˈɪn] *prep* dentro de ♦ *adv* dentro; **~ reach (of)** al alcance (de); **~ sight (of)** a la vista (de); **~ the week** antes de acabar la semana; **~ a mile (of)** a menos de una milla (de)

without [wɪðˈaʊt] *prep* sin; **to go ~ sth** pasar sin algo

withstand [wɪθˈstænd] (*irreg*) *vt* resistir a

witness [ˈwɪtnɪs] *n* testigo *m/f* ♦ *vt* (*event*) presenciar; (*document*) atestiguar la veracidad de; **to bear ~ to** (*fig*) ser testimonio de; **~ box** *n* tribuna de los testigos; **~ stand** (*US*) *n* = **~ box**

witty [ˈwɪtɪ] *adj* ingenioso

wives [waɪvz] *npl of* **wife**

wk *abbr* = **week**

wobble [ˈwɔbl] *vi* temblar; (*chair*) cojear

woe [wəʊ] *n* desgracia

woke [wəʊk] *pt of* **wake**

woken [ˈwəʊkən] *pp of* **wake**

wolf [wulf] *n* lobo; **wolves** [wulvz] *npl of* **wolf**

woman [ˈwʊmən] (*pl* **women**) *n* mujer *f*; **~ doctor** *n* médica; **women's lib** (*inf: pej*) *n* liberación *f* de la mujer; **~ly** *adj* femenino

womb [wuːm] *n* matriz *f*, útero

women [ˈwɪmɪn] *npl of* **woman**

won [wʌn] *pt, pp of* **win**

wonder [ˈwʌndəʳ] *n* maravilla, prodigio; (*feeling*) asombro ♦ *vi*: **to ~ whether/why** preguntarse si/por qué; **to ~ at**

asombrarse de; **to ~ about** pensar sobre *or* en; **it's no ~ (that)** no es de extrañarse (que +*subjun*); **~ful** *adj* maravilloso

won't [wəʊnt] = **will not**

wood [wʊd] *n* (*timber*) madera; (*forest*) bosque *m*; **~ carving** *n* (*act*) tallado en madera; (*object*) talla en madera; **~ed** *adj* arbolado; **~en** *adj* de madera; (*fig*) inexpresivo; **~pecker** *n* pájaro carpintero; **~wind** *n* (*MUS*) instrumentos *mpl* de viento de madera; **~work** *n* carpintería; **~worm** *n* carcoma

wool [wʊl] *n* lana; **to pull the ~ over sb's eyes** (*fig*) engatusar a uno; **~en** (*US*) *adj* = **~len**; **~len** *adj* de lana; **~lens** *npl* géneros *mpl* de lana; **~ly** *adj* lanudo, de lana; (*fig: ideas*) confuso; **~y** (*US*) *adj* = **~ly**

word [wəːd] *n* palabra; (*news*) noticia; (*promise*) palabra (de honor) ♦ *vt* redactar; **in other ~s** en otras palabras; **to break/keep one's ~** faltar a la palabra/ cumplir la promesa; **to have ~s with sb** reñir con uno; **~ing** *n* redacción *f*; **~ processing** *n* proceso de textos; **~ processor** *n* procesador *m* de textos

wore [wɔːʳ] *pt of* **wear**

work [wəːk] *n* trabajo; (*job*) empleo, trabajo; (*ART, LITERATURE*) obra ♦ *vi* trabajar; (*mechanism*) funcionar, marchar; (*medicine*) ser eficaz, surtir efecto ♦ *vt* (*shape*) trabajar; (*stone etc*) tallar; (*mine etc*) explotar; (*machine*) manejar, hacer funcionar; **~s** *n* (*BRIT: factory*) fábrica ♦ *npl* (*of clock, machine*) mecanismo; **to be out of ~** estar parado, no tener trabajo; **to ~ loose** (*part*) desprenderse; (*knot*) aflojarse; **~ on** *vt fus* trabajar en, dedicarse a; (*principle*) basarse en; **~ out** *vi* (*plans etc*) salir bien, funcionar ♦ *vt* (*problem*) resolver; (*plan*) elaborar; **it ~s out at £100** suma 100 libras; **~ up** *vt*: **to get ~ed up** excitarse; **~able** *adj* (*solution*) práctico, factible; **~aholic** [wəːkəˈhɔlɪk] *n* trabajador(a) obsesivo/a *m/f*; **~er** *n* trabajador(a) *m/f*, obrero/a; **~force** *n* mano *f* de obra; **~ing class** *n*

clase *f* obrera; **~ing-class** *adj* obrero;
~ing order *n*: **in ~ing order** en
funcionamiento; **~man** (*irreg*) *n* obrero;
~manship *n* habilidad *f*, trabajo;
~sheet *n* hoja de trabajo; **~shop** *n*
taller *m*; **~ station** *n* puesto *or* estación *f*
de trabajo; **~-to-rule** (*BRIT*) *n* huelga de
celo
world [wə:ld] *n* mundo ♦ *cpd* (*champion*)
del mundo; (*power, war*) mundial; **to
think the ~ of sb** (*fig*) tener un concepto
muy alto de uno; **~ly** *adj* mundano; **~-
wide** *adj* mundial, universal; **W~-Wide
Web** *n*: **the W~-Wide Web** el World
Wide Web
worm [wə:m] *n* (*also:* **earth~**) lombriz *f*
worn [wɔ:n] *pp of* **wear** ♦ *adj* usado; **~-
out** *adj* (*object*) gastado; (*person*)
rendido, agotado
worried ['wʌrɪd] *adj* preocupado
worry ['wʌrɪ] *n* preocupación *f* ♦ *vt*
preocupar, inquietar ♦ *vi* preocuparse;
~ing *adj* inquietante
worse [wə:s] *adj, adv* peor ♦ *n* lo peor; **a
change for the ~** un empeoramiento; **~n**
vt, vi empeorar; **~ off** *adj* (*financially*): **to
be ~ off** tener menos dinero; (*fig*): **you'll
be ~ off this way** de esta forma estarás
peor que nunca
worship ['wə:ʃɪp] *n* adoración *f* ♦ *vt*
adorar; **Your W~** (*BRIT: to mayor*) señor
alcalde; (: *to judge*) señor juez
worst [wə:st] *adj, adv* peor ♦ *n* lo peor; **at
~** en lo peor de los casos
worth [wə:θ] *n* valor *m* ♦ *adj*: **to be ~**
valer, tener *or* merece la pena; **to
be ~ one's while (to do)** merecer la pena
(hacer); **~less** *adj* sin valor; (*useless*)
inútil; **~while** *adj* (*activity*) que merece la
pena; (*cause*) loable
worthy ['wə:ðɪ] *adj* respetable; (*motive*)
honesto; **~ of** digno de

KEYWORD

would [wʊd] *aux vb* **1** (*conditional tense*):
if you asked him he ~ do it si se lo
pidieras, lo haría; **if you had asked him**

he ~ have done it si se lo hubieras
pedido, lo habría *or* hubiera hecho
2 (*in offers, invitations, requests*): **~ you
like a biscuit?** ¿quieres una galleta?;
(*formal*) ¿querría una galleta?; **~ you ask
him to come in?** ¿quiere hacerle pasar?;
~ you open the window please? ¿quiere
or podría abrir la ventana, por favor?
3 (*in indirect speech*): **I said I ~ do it** dije
que lo haría
4 (*emphatic*): **it WOULD have to snow
today!** ¡tenía que nevar precisamente
hoy!
5 (*insistence*): **she ~n't behave** no quiso
comportarse bien
6 (*conjecture*): **it ~ have been midnight**
sería medianoche; **it ~ seem so** parece
ser que sí
7 (*indicating habit*): **he ~ go there on
Mondays** iba allí los lunes

would-be (*pej*) *adj* presunto
wouldn't ['wʊdnt] = **would not**
wound¹ [wu:nd] *n* herida ♦ *vt* herir
wound² [waʊnd] *pt, pp of* **wind**
wove [wəʊv] *pt of* **weave**
woven ['wəʊvən] *pp of* **weave**
wrap [ræp] *vt* (*also:* **~ up**) envolver; **~per**
n (*on chocolate*) papel *m*; (*BRIT: of book*)
sobrecubierta; **~ping paper** *n* papel *m*
de envolver; (*fancy*) papel *m* de regalo
wreak [ri:k] *vt*: **to ~ havoc (on)** hacer
estragos (en); **to ~ vengeance (on)**
vengarse (de)
wreath [ri:θ, *pl* ri:ðz] *n* (*funeral ~*) corona
wreck [rɛk] *n* (*ship: destruction*) naufragio;
(: *remains*) restos *mpl* del barco; (*pej:
person*) ruina ♦ *vt* (*car etc*) destrozar;
(*chances*) arruinar; **~age** *n* restos *mpl*; (*of
building*) escombros *mpl*
wren [rɛn] *n* (*ZOOL*) reyezuelo
wrench [rɛntʃ] *n* (*TECH*) llave *f* inglesa;
(*tug*) tirón *m*; (*fig*) dolor *m* ♦ *vt* arrancar;
to ~ sth from sb arrebatar algo
violentamente a uno
wrestle ['rɛsl] *vi*: **to ~ (with sb)** luchar
(con *or* contra uno); **~r** *n* luchador(a) *m/f*

(de lucha libre); **wrestling** *n* lucha libre
wretched ['rɛtʃɪd] *adj* miserable
wriggle ['rɪgl] *vi* (*also*: **~ about**) menearse, retorcerse
wring [rɪŋ] (*pt, pp* **wrung**) *vt* retorcer; (*wet clothes*) escurrir; (*fig*): **to ~ sth out of sb** sacar algo por la fuerza a uno
wrinkle ['rɪŋkl] *n* arruga ♦ *vt* arrugar ♦ *vi* arrugarse
wrist [rɪst] *n* muñeca; **~watch** *n* reloj *m* de pulsera
writ [rɪt] *n* mandato judicial
write [raɪt] (*pt* **wrote**, *pp* **written**) *vt* escribir; (*cheque*) extender ♦ *vi* escribir; **~ down** *vt* escribir; (*note*) apuntar; **~ off** *vt* (*debt*) borrar (como incobrable); (*fig*) desechar por inútil; **~ out** *vt* escribir; **~ up** *vt* redactar; **~-off** *n* siniestro total; **~r** *n* escritor(a) *m/f*
writhe [raɪð] *vi* retorcerse
writing ['raɪtɪŋ] *n* escritura; (*hand-~*) letra; (*of author*) obras *fpl*; **in ~** por escrito; **~ paper** *n* papel *m* de escribir
written ['rɪtn] *pp of* **write**
wrong [rɒŋ] *adj* (*wicked*) malo; (*unfair*) injusto; (*incorrect*) equivocado, incorrecto; (*not suitable*) inoportuno, inconveniente; (*reverse*) del revés ♦ *adv* equivocadamente ♦ *n* injusticia ♦ *vt* ser injusto con; **you are ~ to do it** haces mal en hacerlo; **you are ~ about that, you've got it ~** en eso estás equivocado; **to be in the ~** no tener razón, tener la culpa; **what's ~?** ¿qué pasa?; **to go ~** (*person*) equivocarse; (*plan*) salir mal; (*machine*) estropearse; **~ful** *adj* injusto; **~ly** *adv* mal, incorrectamente; (*by mistake*) por error; **~ number** *n* (*TEL*): **you've got the ~ number** se ha equivocado de número
wrote [raʊt] *pt of* **write**
wrought iron [rɔːt-] *n* hierro forjado
wrung [rʌŋ] *pt, pp of* **wring**
wt. *abbr* = **weight**
WWW *n abbr* (= *World Wide Web*) WWW *m*

X, x

Xmas ['ɛksməs] *n abbr* = **Christmas**
X-ray ['ɛksreɪ] *n* radiografía ♦ *vt* radiografiar, sacar radiografías de
xylophone ['zaɪləfəun] *n* xilófono

Y, y

yacht [jɒt] *n* yate *m*; **~ing** *n* (*sport*) balandrismo; **~sman/woman** (*irreg*) *n* balandrista *m/f*
Yank [jæŋk] (*pej*) *n* yanqui *m/f*
Yankee ['jæŋkɪ] (*pej*) *n* = **Yank**
yap [jæp] *vi* (*dog*) aullar
yard [jɑːd] *n* patio; (*measure*) yarda; **~stick** *n* (*fig*) criterio, norma
yarn [jɑːn] *n* hilo; (*tale*) cuento, historia
yawn [jɔːn] *n* bostezo ♦ *vi* bostezar; **~ing** *adj* (*gap*) muy abierto
yd(s). *abbr* = **yard(s)**
yeah [jɛə] (*inf*) *adv* sí
year [jɪə*] *n* año; **to be 8 ~s old** tener 8 años; **an eight-~-old child** un niño de ocho años (de edad); **~ly** *adj* anual ♦ *adv* anualmente, cada año
yearn [jɜːn] *vi*: **to ~ for sth** añorar algo, suspirar por algo
yeast [jiːst] *n* levadura
yell [jɛl] *n* grito, alarido ♦ *vi* gritar
yellow ['jɛləu] *adj* amarillo
yelp [jɛlp] *n* aullido ♦ *vi* aullar
yes [jɛs] *adv* sí ♦ *n* sí *m*; **to say/answer ~** decir/contestar que sí
yesterday ['jɛstədɪ] *adv* ayer ♦ *n* ayer *m*; **~ morning/evening** ayer por la mañana/ tarde; **all day ~** todo el día de ayer
yet [jɛt] *adv* ya; (*negative*) todavía ♦ *conj* sin embargo, a pesar de todo; **it is not finished ~** todavía no está acabado; **the best ~** el/la mejor hasta ahora; **as ~** hasta ahora, todavía
yew [juː] *n* tejo
yield [jiːld] *n* (*AGR*) cosecha; (*COMM*)

rendimiento ♦ vt ceder; (*results*) producir, dar; (*profit*) rendir ♦ vi rendirse, ceder; (*US: AUT*) ceder el paso

YMCA n abbr (= *Young Men's Christian Association*) Asociación f de Jóvenes Cristianos

yog(h)ourt ['jəugət] n yogur m

yog(h)urt ['jəugət] n = **yog(h)ourt**

yoke [jəuk] n yugo

yolk [jəuk] n yema (de huevo)

KEYWORD
---

you [ju:] pron 1 (*subject: familiar*) tú, pl vosotros/as (*SP*), ustedes (*AM*); (*polite*) usted, pl ustedes; **~ are very kind** eres/es *etc* muy amable; **~ Spanish enjoy your food** a vosotros (*or* ustedes) los españoles os (*or* les) gusta la comida; **~ and I will go** iremos tú y yo

2 (*object: direct: familiar*) te, pl os (*SP*), les (*AM*); (*polite*) le, pl les, f la, pl las; **I know ~** te/le *etc* conozco

3 (*object: indirect: familiar*) te, pl os (*SP*), les (*AM*); (*polite*) le, pl les; **I gave the letter to ~ yesterday** te/os *etc* di la carta ayer

4 (*stressed*): **I told** *YOU* **to do it** te dije a ti que lo hicieras, es a ti a quien dije que lo hicieras; *see also* **3, 5**

5 (*after prep: NB*: con+ti = contigo: *familiar*) ti, pl vosotros/as (*SP*), ustedes (*AM*); (: *polite*) usted, pl ustedes; **it's for ~** es para ti/vosotros *etc*

6 (*comparisons: familiar*) tú, pl vosotros/as (*SP*), ustedes (*AM*); (: *polite*) usted, pl ustedes; **she's younger than ~** es más joven que tú/vosotros *etc*

7 (*impersonal: one*): **fresh air does ~ good** el aire puro (te) hace bien; **~ never know** nunca se sabe; **~ can't do that!** ¡eso no se hace!

---

you'd [ju:d] = **you had; you would**

you'll [ju:l] = **you will; you shall**

young [jʌŋ] adj joven ♦ npl (*of animal*) cría; (*people*): **the ~** los jóvenes, la juventud; **~er** adj (*brother etc*) menor;

~ster n joven m/f

your [jɔ:*] adj tu; (*pl*) vuestro; (*formal*) su; *see also* **my**

you're [juə*] = **you are**

yours [jɔ:z] pron tuyo; (*pl*) vuestro; (*formal*) suyo; *see also* **faithfully; mine**[1]; **sincerely**

yourself [jɔ:'self] pron tú mismo; (*complement*) te; (*after prep*) ti (mismo); (*formal*) usted mismo; (: *complement*) se; (: *after prep*) sí (mismo); **yourselves** pl pron vosotros mismos; (*after prep*) vosotros (mismos); (*formal*) ustedes (mismos); (: *complement*) se; (: *after prep*) sí mismos; *see also* **oneself**

youth [ju:θ, pl ju:ðz] n juventud f; (*young man*) joven m; **~ club** n club m juvenil; **~ful** adj juvenil; **~ hostel** n albergue m de juventud

you've [ju:v] = **you have**

Yugoslav ['ju:gəusla:v] adj, n yugo(e)slavo/a m/f

Yugoslavia [ju:gəu'sla:vɪə] n Yugoslavia

yuppie ['jʌpɪ] (*inf*) adj, n yupi m/f, yupy m/f

YWCA n abbr (= *Young Women's Christian Association*) Asociación f de Jóvenes Cristianas

Z, z

zany ['zeɪnɪ] adj estrafalario

zap [zæp] vt (*COMPUT*) borrar

zeal [zi:l] n celo, entusiasmo; **~ous** ['zɛləs] adj celoso, entusiasta

zebra ['zi:brə] n cebra; **~ crossing** (*BRIT*) n paso de peatones

zero ['zɪərəu] n cero

zest [zest] n ánimo, vivacidad f; (*of orange*) piel f

zigzag ['zɪgzæg] n zigzag m ♦ vi zigzaguear, hacer eses

zinc [zɪŋk] n cinc m, zinc m

zip [zɪp] n (*also*: **~ fastener,** (*US*) **~per**) cremallera (*SP*), cierre m (*AM*) ♦ vt (*also*: **~ up**) cerrar la cremallera de; **~ code** (*US*)

n código postal
zodiac ['zəudɪæk] *n* zodíaco
zone [zəun] *n* zona
zoo [zu:] *n* (jardín *m*) zoo *m*
zoology [zu:'ɔlədʒɪ] *n* zoología

zoom [zu:m] *vi*: **to ~ past** pasar
zumbando; **~ lens** *n* zoom *m*
zucchini [zu:'ki:nɪ] (*US*) *n(pl)*
calabacín(ines) *m(pl)*